CONTENTS

PART 1

Human Resource Management in Perspective

Chapter 1 The Challenge of Human Resources Management 2

Why Study Human Resources Management? 4

Competitive Challenges and Human Resources Management 5

Challenge 1: Competing, Recruiting, and Staffing Globally 5

Challenge 2: Embracing New Technology 7

Highlights in HRM 1: A Guide to HR Internet Sites 8

Highlights in HRM 2: Automation of Talent Management Functions 11

Challenge 3: Managing Change 12

Challenge 4: Managing Talent, or Human Capital 13

Challenge 5: Responding to the Market 15

Challenge 6: Containing Costs 17

Demographic and Employee Concerns 22

Demographic Changes 22

Highlights in HRM 3: Social Issues in HRM 23

Cultural Changes 28

Highlights in HRM 4: Why Diversity? 30

The Partnership of Line Managers and HR Departments 31

Responsibilities of the Human Resources Manager 32

Competencies of the Human Resources Manager 33

Highlights in HRM 5: SHRM Code of Ethical and Professional Standards in Human Resource Management 35

Role of the Line Manager 38

Summary 39

Key Terms 40

Discussion Questions 41

BizFlix Exercises 41

HRM Experience: Balancing Competitive Challenges and Employee Concerns 42

Case Study 1: The Global Management Consulting Firm Accenture Brings Employees Face to Face   43

Case Study 2: Florida Company Fastens Its Sights on Global Growth   44

Notes and References   45

Chapter 2 Strategy and Human Resources Planning   48

Strategic Planning and Human Resources   50

Strategic Planning and HR Planning: Linking the Processes   51

Step One: Mission, Vision, and Values   51

Step Two: Environmental Analysis   53

Competitive Environment   53

Step Three: Internal Analysis   57

The Three Cs: Culture, Capabilities, and Composition   57

Forecasting: A Critical Element of Planning   61

Highlights in HRM 1: HR Planning and Strategy Questions to Ask Business Managers   64

Assessing a Firm's Human Capital Readiness: Gap Analysis   67

Highlights in HRM 2: Succession-Planning Checklist   68

Step Four: Formulating Strategy   70

Corporate Strategy   70

Business Strategy   72

Highlights in HRM 3: Key HR Activities Associated with Merger or Acquisition Phases   73

Functional Strategy: Ensuring Alignment   75

Step Five: Strategy Implementation   76

Taking Action: Reconciling Supply and Demand   77

Step Six: Evaluation and Assessment   79

Evaluation and Assessment Issues   79

Highlights in HRM 4: Ten Measures of Human Capital   80

Measuring a Firm's Strategic Alignment   81

Ensuring Strategic Flexibility for the Future   82

Summary   84

Key Terms   85

Discussion Questions   85

HRM Experience: Customizing HR for Different Types of Human Capital   86

BizFlix Exercises   87

Case Study 1: Staffing, Down to a Science at Capital One   87

Case Study 2: Matching Talent with Tasks: Dole Implements Succession Planning   89

Notes and References   91

Appendix: Calculating Turnover and Absenteeism   93

HRM Experience: Costs Associated with the Turnover of One Computer Programmer 95

Employee Turnover Rates   93

   Computing the Turnover Rate   93

   Determining the Costs of Turnover   94

Employee Absenteeism Rates   94

   Computing Absenteeism Rates   94

Highlights in Hrm 5: Costs Associated with the Turnover of One Computer Programmer   95

   Comparing Absenteeism Data   96

   Costs of Absenteeism   96

   Absenteeism and HR Planning   96

Notes and References   97

PART 2

Meeting Human Resources Requirements

Chapter 3 Equal Employment Opportunity and Human Resources Management   98

Historical Perspective of EEO Legislation   101

   Changing National Values   101

   Economic Disparity   102

   Early Legal Developments   102

Government Regulation of Equal Employment Opportunity   102

   Major Federal Laws   103

Highlights in HRM 2: Test Your Knowledge of Equal Employment Opportunity Law   104

   Other Federal Laws and Executive Orders   114

   Fair Employment Practice Laws   115

Other Equal Employment Opportunity Issues   116

   Sexual Harassment   116

Highlights in HRM 2: Questions Used in Auditing Sexual Harassment   118

Highlights in HRM 3: Basic Components of an Effective Sexual
Harassment Policy   119

   Sexual Orientation   120

   Immigration Reform and Control   120

Uniform Guidelines on Employee Selection Procedures   121

Enforcing Equal Employment Opportunity Legislation   124

   The Equal Employment Opportunity Commission   124

   Record-Keeping and Posting Requirements   125

Highlights in HRM 4: 2007 EEO-1 Survey   127

   Processing Discrimination Charges   128

Highlights in HRM 5: EEOC Poster   129

Highlights in HRM 6: EEOC Guidelines on Retaliation   131

   Preventing Discrimination Charges   132

Diversity Management: Affirmative Action   133

   Establishing Affirmative Action Programs   133

Highlights in HRM 7: Basic Steps in Developing an Effective
Affirmative Action Program   134

   Managing Diversity: Affirmative Action   135

Summary   137

Key Terms   138

Discussion Questions   138

BizFlix Exercises   139

HRM Experience: Sexual Harassment: A Frank Discussion   140

Case Study 1: Can "FIDO" Come to Work?   141

Case Study 2: Misplaced Affections: Discharge for Sexual Harassment   142

Appendix: Determining Adverse Impact   144

Notes and References   145

**Chapter 4 Job Analysis, Employee Involvement, and Flexible
Work Schedules   148**

Relationship of Job Requirements and HRM Functions   150

   Recruitment   150

   Selection   151

   Training and Development   151

   Performance Appraisal   151

   Compensation Management   151

Job Analysis   152

Job Analysis and Essential Job Functions   152

Gathering Job Information   153

Controlling the Accuracy of Job Information   154

Approaches to Job Analysis   155

Job Descriptions   158

Highlights in HRM 1: Job Description for an Employment Assistant   159

Problems with Job Descriptions   161

Writing Clear and Specific Job Descriptions   161

Job Design   162

Behavioral Concerns   162

Highlights in HRM 2: Empowered Employees Achieve Results   165

Industrial Engineering Considerations   166

Ergonomic Considerations   167

Designing Work for Group/Team Contributions   168

Flexible Work Schedules   174

Highlights in HRM 3: How to Request a Flexible Work Schedule   175

Summary   179

Key Terms   180

Discussion Questions   180

BizFlix Exercises   180

HRM Experience: Establishing Ground Rules for Team Success   181

Case Study 1: Virtual Teams in Action: Building the F-35 Fighter   183

Case Study 2: But My Job Has Changed   183

Notes and References   184

PART 3

Developing Effectiveness in Human Resources

Chapter 5 Expanding the Talent Pool: Recruitment and Careers   186

Recruiting Talent Externally   188

Highlights in HRM 1: Marriott's Recruitment Principles   189

Outside Sources for Recruitment   190

The Global Labor Market   198

Improving the Effectiveness of External Recruitment   198

Recruiting Talent Internally   200

Advantages and Limitations of Recruiting from Within   201
Methods for Identifying Qualified Candidates   202

Career Management: Developing Talent over Time   205
The Goal: Matching Individual and Organizational Needs   206
Identifying Career Opportunities and Requirements   207

Highlights in HRM 2: Career Path of Jeffrey Immelt, CEO, General
Electric   210
Career Development Initiatives   214

Developing a Diverse Talent Pool   220
Recruiting and Developing Women   221
Eliminating Women's Barriers to Advancement   221
Glass Ceiling Audits   223
Preparing Women for Management   223
Accommodating Families   224
Recruiting and Developing Minorities   224
Providing Minority Internships   225
Advancing Minorities to Management   225

Highlights in HRM 3: Diversity Recruitment That Works   226

Other Important Talent Concerns   227
Recruiting the Disabled   227
Less Publicized Disadvantages   229

Highlights in HRM 4: Resources and Tips for Hiring and Retaining
Employees with Disabilities   229
Employing the Older Workforce   231
Employing Dual Career Couples   232

Summary   233

Discussion Questions   234

Key Terms   234

BizFlix Exercises   235

HRM Experience: Career Management   236

Case Study 1: Linking Up with Talent at Osram Sylvania   236

Case Study 2: Preparing a Career Development Plan   238

Appendix: Personal Career Development   241

Notes and References   239

Developing Personal Skills and Competencies   241

Choosing a Career   241

Highlights in HRM 5: Career Competencies at Caterpillar   242

Use of Available Resources   242

Accuracy of Self-Evaluation   243

The Significance of Interest Inventories   243

Highlights in HRM 6: Campbell Interest and Skill Survey: Individual Profile   244

Evaluating Long-Term Employment Opportunities   246

Choosing an Employer   246

Questions to Ask Yourself Before You Accept a Job Offer   247

Becoming an Entrepreneur   247

Keeping a Career in Perspective   248

Developing Off-the-Job Interests   248

Balancing Marital and/or Family Life   249

Planning for Retirement   249

Key Term   250

Notes and References   250

Chapter 6 Employee Selection   252

Matching People and Jobs   254

Person-Job Fit: Beginning with Job Analysis   255

Person-Organization Fit   255

The Selection Process   255

Obtaining Reliable and Valid Information   256

Sources of Information about Job Candidates   259

Application Forms   260

Online Applications   262

Biographical Information Blanks   262

Background Checks   263

Highlights in HRM 1: Sample Reference-Checking Questions   265

Polygraph Tests   267

Honesty and Integrity Tests   267

Graphology   268

Medical Examinations   269

Drug Testing   269

Employment Tests   271

Nature of Employment Tests   271

Highlights in HRM 2: Best Practices for Employee Testing and Selection   272

Classification of Employment Tests   272

The Employment Interview   277
Interviewing Methods   277

Highlights in HRM 3: Sample Situational Interview Question   279

Highlights in HRM 4: iring Managers Reveal Top Five Biggest Mistakes Candidates Make During Job Interviews in CareerBuilder.com Survey   280

Guidelines for Employment Interviewers   283
Diversity Management: Are Your Questions Legal?   286

Highlights in HRM 5: Appropriate and Inappropriate Interview Questions   287

Reaching a Selection Decision   288
Summarizing Information about Applicants   288
Decision-Making Strategy   288
Final Decision   291

Summary   292

Key Terms   293

Discussion Questions   293

HRM Experience: Designing Selection Criteria and Methods   294

BizFlix Exercises   295

Case Study 1: Job Candidate Assessment Tests Go Virtual   295

Case Study 2: Cleaning Up the "Resu-mess"   295

Notes and References   300

Chapter 7 Training and Development   304

The Scope of Training   306
Investments in Training   306
A Systems Approach to Training   307

Phase 1: Conducting the Needs Assessment   308
Organization Analysis   309

Highlights in HRM 1: Notes on Rapid Needs Assessment   310

Task Analysis   311

Highlights in HRM 2: A Competency Assessment for a Managerial Position   312

Person Analysis   314

Phase 2: Designing the Training Program   314
Instructional Objectives   315
Trainee Readiness and Motivation   315

Principles of Learning 316

Characteristics of Instructors 319

Phase 3: Implementing the Training Program 320

Training Methods for Nonmanagerial Employees 320

Methods for Management Development 328

Phase 4: Evaluating the Training Program 333

Criterion 1: Reactions 333

Criterion 2: Learning 334

Criterion 3: Behavior 334

Criterion 4: Results, or Return on Investment (ROI) 335

Highlights in HRM 3: Calculating Training ROI: Examples 336

Highlights in HRM 4: Benchmarking HR Training 337

Special Topics in Training and Development 338

Orientation Training 338

Basic Skills Training 339

Highlights in HRM 5: Checklist for Orienting New Employees 340

Team Training and Cross-Training 341

Ethics Training 343

Diversity Training 344

Highlights in HRM 6: Additional Ethics Training Resources 345

Summary 347

Key Terms 348

Discussion Questions 348

BizFlix Exercises 349

HRM Experience: Training and Learning Principles 349

Case Study 1: Loews Hotels: We Train to Please 295

Case Study 2: Texas Instruments: Learning to Walk in the Customer's Shoes 295

Case Study 3: Kodak Gets the Picture in Executive Education 354

Notes and References 356

Chapter 8 Appraising and Improving Performance 360

Performance Appraisal Programs 362

The Purposes of Performance Appraisal 363

Why Appraisal Programs Sometimes Fail 364

Developing an Effective Appraisal Program 366

What Are the Performance Standards? 367

Are You Complying with the Law?   369

Who Should Appraise Performance?   370

Putting It All Together: 360-Degree Appraisal   374

Training Appraisers   376

Highlights in HRM 1: Supervisor's Checklist for the Performance Appraisal   379

Performance Appraisal Methods   379

Trait Methods   380

Highlights in HRM 2: Graphic Rating Scale with Provision for Comments   381

Highlights in HRM 3: Example of a Mixed-Standard Scale   382

Behavioral Methods   383

Highlights in HRM 4: BARS and BOS Examples   385

Results Methods   386

Highlights in HRM 5: Personal Scorecard   389

Which Performance Appraisal Method to Use?   390

Appraisal Interviews   391

Three Types of Appraisal Interviews   391

Conducting the Appraisal Interview   392

Improving Performance   395

Summary   398

Key Terms   399

Discussion Questions   400

BizFlix Exercises   400

HRM Experience: Performance Diagnosis   401

Case Study 1: Appraising Employees at the San Diego Zoo   402

Case Study 2: Bank of Montreal's Balanced Scorecard   405

Notes and References   406

PART 4   Implementing Compensation and Security

Chapter 9 Managing Compensation   410

Strategic Compensation Planning   412

Linking Compensation to Organizational Objectives   413

The Pay-for-Performance Standard   414

The Bases for Compensation   418

Determining Compensation—The Wage Mix   418

Internal Factors   419

Highlights in HRM 1: Comparison of Compensation Strategies   421

   External Factors   422

Job Evaluation Systems   423

   Job Ranking System   424

   Job Classification System   424

   Point System   424

Highlights in HRM 2: Point Values for Job Factors of the American
Association of Industrial Management   426

   Work Valuation   426

Highlights in HRM 3: Description of Education Factor and Degrees of the
American Association of Industrial Management   427

   Job Evaluation for Management Positions   428

The Compensation Structure   428

   Wage and Salary Surveys   428

Highlights in HRM 4: Bureau of Labor Statistics National
Compensation Survey   430

   The Wage Curve   431

   Pay Grades   431

   Rate Ranges   432

   Competence-Based Pay   434

Government Regulation of Compensation   435

Highlights in HRM 5: Minimum Wage Laws in the States   436

   Davis-Bacon Act of 1931   437

   Walsh-Healy Act of 1936   437

   Fair Labor Standards Act of 1938 (as Amended)   437

Highlights in HRM 6: The Federal Wage Poster   439

Significant Compensation Issues   441

   The Issue of Equal Pay for Comparable Worth   442

   The Issue of Low Salary Budgets   442

   The Issue of Wage Rate Compression   442

Summary   444

Key Terms   445

Discussion Questions   445

HRM Experience: Why This Salary?   446

BizFlix Exercises   447

Case Study 1: Pay Decisions at Performance Sports   448

Case Study 2: Bomb's Away: JetPack's New Pay Strategy   448

Notes and References   450

Chapter 10 Pay-for-Performance: Incentive Rewards   452

Strategic Reasons for Incentive Plans   454

Incentive Plans as Links to Organizational Objectives   454

Requirements for a Successful Incentive Plan   456

Setting Performance Measures   457

Administering Incentive Plans   457

Highlights in HRM 1: Setting Performance Measures—The Keys   458

Individual Incentive Plans   459

Piecework   459

Standard Hour Plan   460

Bonuses   460

Merit Pay   461

Lump Sum Merit Pay   462

Incentive Awards and Recognition   462

Sales Incentives   463

Highlights in HRM 2: Customize Your Noncash Incentive Awards   464

Incentives for Professional Employees   465

The Executive Pay Package   466

Executive Compensation: Ethics and Accountability   469

Highlights in HRM 3: The "Sweetness" of Executive Perks   470

Executive Compensation Reform   470

Group Incentive Plans   471

Team Compensation   471

Gainsharing Incentive Plans   472

Highlights in HRM 4: Lessons Learned: Designing Effective Team Incentives   473

Enterprise Incentive Plans   476

Profit Sharing Plans   476

Employee Stock Options Plans   477

Highlights in HRM 5: Employee Stock Option Plans   478

Employee Stock Ownership Plans (ESOPs)   479

Advantages of ESOPs   479

Summary   480

Key Terms   481

Discussion Questions   481

HRM Experience: Awarding Salary Increases   482

BizFlix Exercises   483

Case Study 1: Out but Rich at Home Depot   483

Case Study 2: Team-Based Incentive Rewards: It's Not All Roses   484

Notes and References   485

Chapter 11 Employee Benefits   488

Employee Benefits Programs   490

   HRIS and Employee Benefits   490

   Requirements for a Sound Benefits Program   491

   Communicating Employee Benefits Information   493

   Concerns of Management   495

Highlights in HRM 1: Crafting an Effective Benefits Communication Program   495

Highlights in HRM 2: A Personalized Statement of Benefits Costs   496

Highlights in HRM 3: U.S. Chamber of Commerce Employee Benefits Survey—2007   497

Employee Benefits Required by Law   499

   Social Security Insurance   499

   Unemployment Insurance   500

   Workers' Compensation Insurance   501

   Consolidated Omnibus Budget Reconciliation Act (COBRA)   501

   Family and Medical Leave Act   502

   Older Workers Benefit Protection Act   503

Discretionary Major Employee Benefits   503

   Health Care Benefits   503

Highlights in HRM 4: "Your Rights": Another Federally Required Poster   504

Highlights in HRM 5: Employers Methods for Containing Health Care Costs   506

   Payment for Time Not Worked   508

   Supplemental Unemployment Benefits   509

   Life Insurance   509

   Long-Term Care Insurance   509

   Retirement Programs   510

   Pension Plans   511

Employee Services: Creating a Work/Life Setting   514

   Employee Assistance Programs   515

   Counseling Services   516

   Child and Elder Care   516

   Other Benefits and Services   517

Summary 518

Key Terms 519

HRM Experience: Understanding Employer Benefit Programs 519

Discussion Questions 520

BizFlix Exercises 520

Case Study 1: Adobe's Family-Friendly Benefits: An Unexpected Backlash 521

Case Study 2: Evaluate the Work/Life Climate in Your Company 522

Notes and References 523

Chapter 12 Promoting Safety and Health 526

Safety and Health: It's the Law 528

HIGHLIGHTS IN HRM 1: Test Your Safety Smarts 529

OSHA's Coverage 530

OSHA Standards 530

Enforcing OSHA Standards 530

OSHA Consultation Assistance 532

Responsibilities and Rights under OSHA 533

Highlights in HRM 2: What Are My Responsibilities under the OSH Act? 534

Right-to-Know Laws 535

OSHA's Enforcement Record 536

Promoting a Safe Work Environment 536

Creating a Culture of Safety 537

Enforcing Safety Rules 538

Investigating and Recording Accidents 539

Creating a Healthy Work Environment 539

Health Hazards and Issues 540

Highlights in HRM 3: Job Safety and Health Protection Poster 541

Highlights in HRM 4: Holsum Bakery's Workplace Smoking Policy 543

Workplace Violence 546

Building Better Health 549

Employee Assistance Programs 551

Highlights in HRM 5: Selected Items from Salt River Project's Substance Abuse Policy 554

The Management of Stress 556

What Is Stress? 557

Job-Related Stress   558

Coping with Stress   558

Summary   559

Key Terms   560

Discussion Questions   561

HRM Experience: Reducing Employee Stress   562

BizFlix Exercises   563

Case Study 1: Rambo Goes Violent   563

Case Study 2: Too Much Stress? You Decide   564

Notes and References   565

PART **5**   **Enhancing Employee-Management Relations**

Chapter 13 Employee Rights and Discipline   568

Employee Rights and Privacy   570

Employee Rights vs. Employer Responsibilities   571

Negligent Hiring   571

Job Protection Rights   571

Highlights in HRM 1: Examples of Employment-at-Will Statements   576

Privacy Rights   578

Electronic Surveillance and Monitoring   581

Disciplinary Policies and Procedures   587

The Results of Inaction   588

Setting Organizational Rules   589

Defining Discipline   590

Investigating the Disciplinary Problem   591

Approaches to Disciplinary Action   593

Discharging Employees   594

Highlights in HRM 2: Banner Health System Corrective Action Process   595

Alternative Dispute Resolution Procedures   598

Managerial Ethics in Employee Relations   601

Summary   602

Key Terms   604

Discussion Questions   604

BizFlix Exercises   605

HRM Experience: Learning about Employee Rights   606

Case Study 1: Discharged for Off-Duty Behavior   607

Case Study 2: You Can't Fire Me! Check Your Policy   607

Notes and References   609

Chapter 14 The Dynamics of Labor Relations   612

Highlights in HRM 1: Test Your Labor Relations Know-How   615

Government Regulation of Labor Relations   616

   Railway Labor Act   616

   Norris-LaGuardia Act   616

   Wagner Act   616

   Taft-Hartley Act   618

   Landrum-Griffin Act   619

The Labor Relations Process   619

   Why Employees Unionize   619

   Organizing Campaigns   621

Highlights in HRM 2: United Food and Commercial Workers International Union Authorization Card   623

   Employer Tactics Opposing Unionization   624

Highlights in HRM 3: Employer "Don'ts" during Union Organizing Campaigns   625

   How Employees Become Unionized   625

   NLRB Representation Election   625

   Impact of Unionization on Managers   626

Highlights in HRM 4: NLRB Election Poster   627

Structures, Functions, and Leadership of Labor Unions   628

   Structure and Functions of the AFL-CIO   629

   Structure and Functions of National Unions   629

   Structure and Functions of Local Unions   630

   Union Leadership Commitment and Philosophies   631

Labor Relations in the Public Sector   631

The Bargaining Process   632

   Preparing for Negotiations   633

   Gathering Bargaining Data   634

   Developing Bargaining Strategies and Tactics   634

   Negotiating the Labor Agreement   635

   Good Faith Bargaining   635

   Interest-Based Bargaining   637

Management and Union Power in Collective Bargaining   637

Resolving Bargaining Deadlocks   639

The Labor Agreement   639

The Issue of Management Rights   640

Union Security Agreements   641

Highlights in HRM 5: Items in a Labor Agreement   640

Administration of the Labor Agreement   641

Negotiated Grievance Procedures   641

The Grievance Procedure in Action   642

Grievance Arbitration   643

Contemporary Challenges to Labor Organizations   645

Foreign Competition and Technological Change   645

Decrease in Union Membership   645

Employers' Focus on Maintaining Nonunion Status   646

Summary   647

Key Terms   648

Discussion Questions   648

HRM Experience: Learn about Unions   649

BizFlix Exercises   650

Case Study 1: A New Ball Game in Detroit   651

Case Study 2: The Arbitration Case of Jesse Stansky   651

Notes and References   653

PART 6   Expanding Human Resources Management Horizons

Chapter 15 International Human Resources Management   656

Managing across Borders   658

How Does the Global Environment Influence Management?   660

Domestic versus International HRM   663

International Staffing   664

Recruiting Internationally   665

Selecting Employees Internationally   668

Highlights in HRM 1: Global Laws and Pacts Prohibiting Discrimination   669

Highlights in HRM 2: Skills of Expatriate Managers   671

Training and Development   673

Content of Training Programs   674

Highlights in HRM 3: Nonverbal Communications in Different Cultures   677

Highlights in HRM 4: Repatriation Checklist   682

Compensation   683

Compensation of Host-Country Employees   683

Compensation of Host-Country Managers   685

Compensation of Expatriate Managers   686

Performance Appraisal   688

Who Should Appraise Performance?   688

Home versus Host-Country Evaluations   689

Performance Criteria   689

Providing Feedback   690

The Labor Environment Worldwide   691

Collective Bargaining in Other Countries   691

International Labor Organizations   692

Labor Participation in Management   693

Summary   694

Key Terms   695

Discussion Questions   695

HRM Experience: An American (Expatriate) in Paris   696

BizFlix Exercises   697

Case Study 1: How about a 900 Percent Raise?   699

Case Study 2: A "TurnAround" Repatriate Plan: U.S. Company Moves Indian Workers Back Home   699

Case Study 3: How Deloitte Builds Global Expertise   700

Notes and References   704

Chapter 16 Creating High-Performance Work Systems   708

Fundamental Principles   710

Egalitarianism and Engagement   711

Shared Information   713

Knowledge Development   714

Performance-Reward Linkage   714

Anatomy of High-Performance Work Systems   715

Work-Flow Design and Teamwork   716

Complementary Human Resources Policies and Practices   716

Management Processes and Leadership   718

Supportive Information Technologies   719

Fitting It All Together   719

Ensuring Internal Fit   719

Establishing External Fit   720

Assessing Strategic Alignment: The HR Scorecard   721

Implementing the System   721

Highlights in HRM 1A: Diagnosing Internal Fit   722

Highlights in HRM 1B: Testing the Alignment of the HR System with HR Deliverables   723

Highlights in HRM 1C: Testing the Alignment of HR Deliverables   723

Building a Business Case for Change   724

Establishing a Communications Plan   725

Involving Unions   726

Navigating the Transition to High-Performance Work Systems   728

Evaluating the Success of the System and Sustaining It   730

Outcomes of High-Performance Work Systems   731

Employee Outcomes and Quality of Work Life   731

Organizational Outcomes and Competitive Advantage   732

Highlights in HRM 2: The Impact of High-Performance Work Systems   724

Summary   734

Key Terms   734

Discussion Questions   735

BizFlix Exercises   735

HRM Experience: Assessing the Strategic Fit of High-Performance Work Systems   736

Case Study 1: Engaging Employees "the Eileen Fisher Way"   737

Case Study 2: Whole Foods Motivates Its Employees in Innovative Ways   739

Notes and References   741

Cases   745

Case 1: United Technologies Seeks Intangibles with Education Plan   745

Case 2: Running the Global Recruiting Machine: ClientLogic   749

Case 3: Job Analysis and Hiring Decisions at Ovania Chemical   752

Case 4: Ill-Fated Love at Centrex Electronics   757

Case 5: Returning Ethics to Putnam   758

Case 6: Realigning HR Practices at Egan's Clothiers   759

Case 7: A Performance Appraisal Snafu   765

Case 8: The Last Straw for Aero Engine   769

Case 9: I.B.M.: Take as Much Vacation Time as You Want To?   771

Case 10: Newell's Decision to Downsize: An Ethical Dilemma   774

Case 11: Someone Has to Go: A Tough Layoff Decision   776

Glossary   778

Name Index   789

Organization Index   791

Subjet Index   801

PREFACE

The 15th edition of *Managing Human Resources* will place your students at the forefront in understanding how organizations can gain a sustainable competitive advantage through people. The role of HR managers is no longer limited to service functions such as recruiting and selecting employees. Today, HR managers assume an active role in the strategic planning and decision making within their organizations. Meeting challenges head-on and using human resources effectively are critical to the success of any work organization. In this edition of the book, we've made improvements that make these points even more strongly.

In the first chapter, we begin by explaining the key challenges to HRM in developing the flexible and skilled workforce needed to compete effectively. Side by side with the competitive challenges, HRM must also address important employee concerns such as managing a diverse workforce, recognizing employee rights, and adjusting to new work attitudes. The chapter also discusses the important partnership with line managers and the competencies required of HR management. Then the textbook continues with the introduction, explanation, and discussion of the individual practices and policies that make up HRM. We recognize the manager's changing role, and emphasize current issues and real-world problems and the policies and practices of HRM used to meet them.

Although we focus on the HR role of managers, we do not exclude the impact and importance of the HR department's strategic role in developing, coordinating, and enforcing policies and procedures relating to HR functions. Whether the reader becomes a manager, a supervisor, or an HR specialist, or is employed in other areas of the organization, *Managing Human Resources* provides a functional and practical understanding of HR programs to enable readers to see how HR affects all employees, the organization, the community, and the larger society.

Issues of strategy and talent have become such central concerns of HR today that we have reorganized and reemphasized the topics in this edition of the book. The second chapter of the book specifically addresses the issues of HR strategy and planning. Chapter 5 focuses on expanding and managing the talent pool in organizations. The detailed coverage of these topics solidifies *Managing Human Resources* as perhaps the premier text for thought leadership, especially the global talent pool.

Organizations in today's competitive world are discovering that it is *how* the individual HR topics are combined that makes all the difference. Managers typically don't focus on HR issues such as staffing, training, and compensation in isolation from one another. Each of these HR practices is combined into an overall system to enhance employee involvement and productivity. *Managing Human Resources* ends with a final chapter that focuses on development of high-performance work systems (HPWS). We outline the various components of the systems including work-flow design, HR practices, management processes, and supporting technologies. We also discuss the strategic processes used to implement high-performance work systems and the outcomes that benefit both the employee and the organization as a whole.

What's Dynamic in the 15th Edition

Many new features and much new information are provided in this revision. We introduce overall text improvements that more accurately reflect HRM in today's business world and help the reader understand HRM issues more effectively.

- HRM Experience: We build upon a popular addition to the previous edition of *Managing Human Resources* by continuing the use of experiential exercises to explore significant issues in HRM. These skill-building exercises help students gain practical experience when dealing with employee/management concerns such as pay-for-performance; effective teaming; employee benefits; reducing employee stress; employee rights; balancing competitive challenges and employee concerns; customizing HR for different types of human capital; designing selection criteria and methods; and assessing the strategic fit of HPWS. Students can work through these new exercises on either an individual or a team basis.

- Human Resources Information Systems (HRIS): Throughout the text, we have specifically highlighted the use of HRIS to facilitate the managing of employees and the efficient performance of HR functions. For example, the impact of information technology on HR and the role of HRIS in such areas as compensation, recruitment, screening and selection, training, job analysis, safety, and talent inventorying and succession management are discussed.

- Diversity: Because we believe that diversity issues are an integral part of every HRM activity, updated and expanded coverage is included throughout the text.

- HRM Strategy: The increasingly important role HRM plays in strategic planning is covered specifically in Chapter 2. However, elsewhere we also discuss the role of human capital and Six Sigma; HR benchmarking; balanced scorecard, strategy mapping, and performance diagnosis; global HR strategy; as well as strategic alignment and the implementation of virtual teams and high-performance work systems.

- Contemporary employment issues such as global recruiting, outsourcing, offshoring, alternative work arrangements, temporary workers, contractors, telecommuting, and so forth are covered throughout the book.

- Global and international HR concerns in particular are covered in more detail in this edition. Today these issues are increasingly seen as "front and center" in many organizations. They include the issues surrounding multinationals, joint ventures, and the Today these issues are increasingly seen as "front and center" in many organizations. They include the issues surrounding multinationals, joint ventures, and the World Trade Organization; low-wage, high-growth countries such as China and India, and the talent shortage and work-visa challenges facing U.S. firms since 9/11. Global rights issues such as data protection, intellectual and property rights, and the International Labor Organization's decent work agenda and efforts to promote fairness among countries as they globalize are also highlighted.

- A complete update of all laws, administrative rulings and guidelines, and court decisions governing HRM includes such recent developments as legislation regarding illegal immigration; the U.S. Supreme Court decision on affirmative action and the promotion of diversity; FLSA changes governing exemptions from overtime payments; stock option reporting requirements;

new medical privacy legislation; body art (tattoos and body piercing); and other employee rights issues.

- The latest versions of the posters of all major federal regulations governing HRM are included.

- We have readdressed the important role of compensation in HRM by heightening our discussion of pay-for-performance, the global pay systems multinationals are beginning to implement today, healthcare cost savings, strategic pension planning, and effective employee awards.

- Expanded discussions cover major issues, including:
  - aggressive union organizing
  - balanced scorecard
  - competency assessment for training
  - cumulative trauma disorders
  - EEO reporting requirements
  - employee fitness programs
  - employee leasing
  - executive compensation reform
  - incentive rewards and recognition programs
  - offshoring and recruiting- and business-process outsourcing
  - pension plans and underfunding
  - performance diagnosis
  - person-organization fit
  - role of human capital
  - strategic planning
  - violence and terrorism in the workplace

- Many new Highlights in HRM boxes present the reader with up-to-date, real-world examples from a variety of large and small organizations.

- Internet: The ever-growing role of the Internet in HR activities is evident throughout the text. A few examples are online recruiting, including recruiting via social networking sites in Chapter 5; online employee screening and testing in Chapter 6; learning management systems, "communities in practice" efforts, and virtual training via Web sites such as Second Life in Chapter 7; and web-based goal setting, performance appraisals, and succession planning systems in Chapter 8.

- There are nine new end-of-chapter case studies highlighting chapter content. These cases have been selected to provide students with both current and practical HR problems and issues.

- Five new extended cases are included at the end of the book. These cases have been carefully selected to reflect current issues in managing human resources, and explore the important topics of virtual HR management, global and cultural, diversity, workforce mobility, employment downsizing, wrongful discharge, ethics, performance appraisal, and the arbitration of employee complaints.

- New Ancillaries: There are new online ancillaries for instructors and students. A completely revised test bank plays a strategic role in the Integrated Learning System. A new set of PowerPoint presentation slides and acetates makes teaching and preparation easier and more convenient. And finally, a new Teaching Assistance Manual provides additional teaching suggestions to enhance other instructor teaching materials.

Features of the Book

Use of the Integrated Learning System (which is described on the front inside cover) continues for the new edition. This integrated structure creates a comprehensive teaching and testing system. Designed to facilitate understanding and retention of the material presented, each chapter contains the following pedagogical features:

- **Learning objectives** listed at the beginning of each chapter provide the basis for the Integrated Learning System. Icons that identify the learning objectives appear throughout the text and end-of-chapter material, and all print ancillaries.
- **Highlights in HRM.** This popular boxed feature provides real-world examples of how organizations perform HR functions. The Highlights are introduced in the text discussion and include topics such as small businesses and international issues.
- **Using the Internet.** All chapters include new government, research, and business Internet references and addresses.
- **Key terms** appear in boldface and are defined in margin notes next to the text discussion. The key terms are also listed at the end of the chapter and appear in the glossary at the end of the text.
- **Figures.** An abundance of graphic materials and flowcharts provides a visual, dynamic presentation of concepts and HR activities. All figures are systematically referenced in the text discussion.
- **Summary.** A paragraph or two for each learning objective provides a brief and focused review of the chapter.
- **Discussion questions** following the chapter summary offer an opportunity to focus on each of the learning objectives in the chapter and stimulate critical thinking. Many of these questions allow for group analysis and class discussion.
- **HRM Experience.** An experiential activity (described earlier) is included in each chapter.
- **Two or more case studies** per chapter present current HRM issues in real-life settings that allow for student consideration and critical analysis.
- **Extended cases.** Eleven extended cases are provided at the end of the main text. These cases use material covered in more than one text chapter and provide capstone opportunities.

Ancillary Teaching and Learning Materials

For Students

Study Guide to Accompany *Managing Human Resources* (ISBN: 0-324- 59261-2). Satish P. Deshpande of Western Michigan University has revised the *Study Guide*. His years of teaching experience allow him to bring a special insight to this popular student supplement. It includes review questions that can be used to check understanding and prepare for examinations on each chapter in this textbook. Using the Integrated Learning System, *Study Guide* questions are arranged by chapter learning objective so the student can quickly refer back to the textbook if further review is needed.

Premium Student Website:

New to this edition is student access to the Bohlander/Snell Premium Student Website for Managing Human Resources. Students can access interactive quizzes, flashcards, PowerPoint slides, learning games, AP News feeds, and more to reinforce chapter concepts. Access to the Premium Student Website is pincode protected. If access did not come packaged with your textbook, visit www.ichapters.com to purchase access to these resources.

Managing Human Resources, 15e Support Web Site
www.cengage.com/management/bohlander.

This Web site provides learning and teaching resources and support for both instructors and students.

For Instructors

The following instructor support materials are available to adopters from your South-Western Cengage Representative, from the Academic Resource Center at 800-423-0563, or through http://www.cengage.com. All printed ancillary materials were prepared by or under the direction of the text authors to guarantee full integration with the text. Multimedia supplements were prepared by experts in those fields.

- **Instructor's Resource Guide** (ISBN: 0-324-59257-4). Prepared by the text authors, for each chapter in the textbook, the **Instructor's Resource Guide** contains a chapter synopsis and learning objectives; a very detailed lecture outline; answers to the end-of-chapter discussion questions and case studies; solutions to the extended cases in the textbook; and suggested answers for the chapter video exercises.
- **Teaching Assistance Manual.** (ISBN 0-324-66536-9). New to this edition, and created by Corinne Livesay of Bryan College, the Teaching Assistance Manual provides additional teaching aids such as *Generating Interest* discussion topics, *Dealing With Trouble Spots* features that provide resources to address challenges, and *Involving Students* sections that suggest activities and resources.
- **Test Bank** (ISBN: 0-324-59259-0). The new test bank was prepared by Paul Keaton of the University of Wisconsin, La Crosse. Each test bank chapter provides over 100 questions and includes a matrix table that classifies each question according to type and learning objective. There are true/false, multiple-choice, and essay items for each chapter, arranged by learning objective. Page references from the text are included. Each objective question is coded to indicate whether it covers knowledge of key terms, understanding of concepts and principles, or application of principles.
- **Computerized Test Bank** (ISBN: 0-324-59260-4). ExamView™ testing software contains all the questions from the printed test bank and allows the instructor to edit, add, delete, or randomly mix questions for customized tests. nest bullet point:
- **PowerPoint™ Presentation Slides** (ISBN: 0-324-59258-2). Created specifically for the new edition by Charlie T. Cook of the University of West Alabama, these presentation slides will add color and interest to lectures. The transparencies are also included within the presentation slide package.
- **Instructor's Resource CD** (ISBN: 0-324-59232-5). The *Instructor's Resource Guide*, test bank, ExamView, and PowerPoint slides are provided on a single CD-ROM.

- **Real to Reel Video Package (0-324-59264-7).** The video package consists of two separate sets of videos:
  - **BizFlix Videos.** BizFlix are short film clips taken from popular Hollywood movies that provide real-world examples of the human resource management concepts students are learning. End-of-chapter BizFlix exercises in the text stimulate students to see how the filmed scenarios apply to chapter topics.
  - **Workplace Videos.** This video collection features both small and large companies with innovative HR practices, many of which have been recognized for their excellence in HR practices.
- **JoinIn™ on TurningPoint®.** Transform any lecture into a truly interactive student experience with JoinIn, created by Corinne Livesay of Bryan College. Combined with your choice of several leading keypad systems, JoinIn turns your ordinary PowerPoint® application into powerful audience response software. With just a click on a handheld device, your students can respond to multiple-choice questions, short polls, interactive exercises, and peer review questions. You can take attendance, check student comprehension of difficult concepts, collect student demographics to better assess student needs, and even administer quizzes without collecting papers or grading. In addition, we provide interactive text-specific slide sets that you can modify and merge with any existing PowerPoint lecture slides for a seamless classroom presentation. This interactive tool is available to qualified college and university adopters. For more information, contact your South-Western Cengage representative or visit http://turningpoint.thomsonlearningconnections.com.
- **WebTutor™.** WebTutor is used by an entire class under the direction of the instructor and is particularly convenient for distance learning courses. It provides Web-based learning resources to students as well as powerful communication and other course management tools including course calendar, chat, and e-mail for instructors. WebTutor is available on WebCT (0-324-478797-9) and Blackboard (0-324-78808-8). See http://webtutor.cengage.com for more information.
- **TextChoice Cases and Exercises.** TextChoice is the home of Cengage Learning's digital content. This Management Cases and Exercises database allows you to easily evaluate and select cases, experiential exercises, and activities and to even include your own material to create a tailor-fit course companion. See http://www.textchoice.com for more information.

Acknowledgments

Because preparation of manuscript for a project as large as *Managing Human Resources* is a continuing process, we would like to acknowledge the work of those colleagues who provided thoughtful feedback for this and the previous editions of the text. We were fortunate to have the results of an extensive survey whose participants offered suggestions based on their actual use of this and other texts in their courses, as well as the careful evaluations of our colleagues. Our appreciation and thanks go to:

Steve Ash, University of Akron
Michael Bedell, California State University, Bakersfield

Mary Connerley, Virginia Tech University
Paula S. Daly, James Madison University
Sharon Davis, Central Texas College
Douglas Dierking, University of Texas, Austin
Suzanne Dyer-Gear, Carroll Community College
Joe J. Eassa, Jr., Palm Beach Atlantic University
Robert E. Ettl, SUNY Stony Brook
Diane Fagan, Webster University
Angela L. Farrar, University of Nevada, Las Vegas
Lou Firenze, Northwood University
Olene L. Fuller, San Jacinto College
Judith Gordon, Boston College
Mike Griffith, Cascade College
Daniel Grundmann, Indiana University
Sally Hackman, Central Methodist College
Rich Havranek, SUNY Institute of Technology
Kim Hester, Arkansas State University
Stephen Hiatt, Catawba College
Alyce Hochhalter, St. Mary Woods College
David J. Hudson, Spalding University
Barbara Luck, Jackson Community College
Avan Jassawalla, SUNY at Geneseo
Pravin Kamdar, Cardinal Stritch University
Jordan J. Kaplan, Long Island University
Steve Karau, Southern Illinois University at Carbondale
Joseph Kavanaugh, Sam Houston State University
John Kelley, Villanova University
Dennis Lee Kovach, Community College of Allegheny County
Kenneth Kovach, University of Maryland
Chalmer E. Labig, Jr., Oklahoma State University
Alecia N. Lawrence, Williamsburg Technical College
Scott W. Lester, University of Wisconsin, Eau Claire
J. Jonathan Lewis, Texas Southern University
Beverly Loach, Central Piedmont Community College
L. M. Lockhart, Penn State Greater Allegheny
Gloria Lopez, New Mexico Highlands University
Larry Maes, Davenport University
Michael Matukonis, SUNY Oneonta
Doug McCabe, Georgetown University
Lee McCain, Seminole Community College
Marjorie L. McInerney, Marshall University
Veronica Meyers, San Diego State University
Julia Morrison, Bloomfield College
Harold Nolan, Georgian Court University
David Nye, Kennedy-Western University
Paul Olsen, Saint Michael's College
Donald Otto, Lindenwood University
Dane Partridge, University of Southern Indiana
Bryan J. Pesta, Cleveland State University

David Pitts, Delaware Technical and Community College
Alex Pomnichowski, Ferris State University
Victor Prosper, University of the Incarnate Word
Michael Raphael, Central Connecticut State University
Charles Rarick, Barry University
June Roux, Salem Community College
Robert Rustic, University of Findlay
Kelli Schutte, Calvin College
Tom Sedwick, Indiana University of Pennsylvania
Jim Sethi, University of Montana Western
Patricia Setlik, William Rainey Harper College
William L. Smith, Emporia State University
Emeric Solymossy, Western Illinois University
Howard Stanger, Canisius College
Scott L. Stevens, Detroit College of Business
Nanette Swarthout, Fontbonne College
Michael T. Korns, Indiana University of PA
Karen Ann Tarnoff, East Tennessee State University
Thomas Taveggia, University of Arizona
Donna Testa, Herkimer County Community College
Alan Tillquist, West Virginia State College
Sue Toombs, Weatherford College
Richard Trotter, University of Baltimore
William Turnley, Kansas State University
Catherine L. Tyler, Oakland University
Barbara Warschawski, Schenectady County Community College
Steve Werner, University of Houston
Liesl Wesson, Texas A&M University
JoAnn Wiggins, Walla Walla University
Jim Wilkinson, Stark State College
L. A. Witt, University of New Orleans
Evelyn Zent, University of Washington, Tacoma
Ryan Zimmerman, Texas A&M University

In the manuscript for this edition, we have drawn not only on the current literature but also on the current practices of organizations that furnished information and illustrations relating to their HR programs. We are indebted to the leaders in the field who have developed the available heritage of information and practices of HRM and who have influenced us through their writings and personal associations. We have also been aided by students in our classes, by former students, by the participants in the management development programs with whom we have been associated, by HR managers, and by our colleagues. In particular, we would like to express our appreciation to Dorothy Galvez and Amy Ray for their helpful insights and support for this edition of the text. We appreciate the efforts of everyone at South-Western Cengage who helped to develop and produce this text and its supplements. They include Joe Sabatino, Executive Editor; Susan Smart, Senior Developmental Editor; Clint Kernan, Marketing Manager; Jim Overly, Senior Marketing Communications Manager; Lysa Kosins, Content Project Manager; Tippy McIntosh, Art Director; and Rob Ellington, our Media Editor.

Our greatest indebtedness is to our wives—Ronnie Bohlander and Marybeth Snell—who have contributed in so many ways to this book over the years. They are always sources of invaluable guidance and assistance. Furthermore, by their continued enthusiasm and support, they have made the process a more pleasant and rewarding experience. We are most grateful to them for their many contributions to this publication, to our lives, and to our families.

George W. Bohlander
Arizona State University

Scott A. Snell
University of Virginia

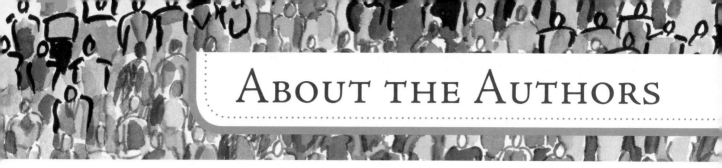

ABOUT THE AUTHORS

George Bohlander

George Bohlander is Professor Emeritus of Management at Arizona State University (ASU). He received his MBA from the University of Southern California and his PhD from the University of California at Los Angeles. His areas of expertise include employment law, Compensation work teams, public policy, and labor relations. He has received the Outstanding Undergraduate Teaching Excellence Award presented by the College of Business at ASU and also received the prestigious ASU Parents Association Professorship for his contributions to students and teaching.

Dr. Bohlander is an active researcher and author. He has published over 50 articles and monographs in professional and practitioner journals such as *National Productivity Review, HR Magazine, Labor Law Journal, The Journal of Collective Bargaining in the Public Sector*, and others. Dr. Bohlander continues to be a consultant to public and private organizations including the U.S. Postal Service, BFGoodrich, McDonnell Douglas, Banner Health Services, and Del Webb. He is also an active labor arbitrator.

Scott Snell

Scott Snell is Professor of Business Administration at the University of Virginia's Darden Graduate School of Business. He teaches in the Leadership and Organization area and specializes in strategic human resource management. In recent years he has worked with companies such as American Express, AstraZeneca, CIGNA, Deutsche Telekom, Heineken, Shell, and the World Bank to address the alignment of human resource issues and strategic management. Professor Snell is the author of over fifty publications in professional journals and edited texts and has co-authored four books: Managing Human Resources, Management: Leading and Collaborating in a Competitive World, M: Management, and Managing People and Knowledge in Professional Service Firms. He has served on the boards of the Society for Human Resource Management Foundation, the Academy of Management's Human Resource Division, the Human Resource Management Journal, the Academy of Management Journal, and the Academy of Management Review.

Prior to joining the Darden faculty in 2007, Dr. Snell was Professor and Director of Executive Education at Cornell University's Center for Advanced Human Resource Studies and Professor of Management in the Smeal College of Business at Pennsylvania State University. He received a BA in Psychology from Miami University, as well as MBA and Ph.D. degrees in Business Administration from Michigan State University. Originally from Lodi, Ohio, he now lives in Charlottesville, Virginia with his wife and three children.

MANAGING
HUMAN RESOURCES

The Challenge of Human Resources Management

After studying this chapter, you should be able to

Objective 1

Identify how firms gain a sustainable competitive advantage through people.

Objective 2

Explain how globalization is influencing human resources management.

Objective 3

Describe the impact of information technology on managing people.

© FRANK FRANKLIN II/AP PHOTOS

CHAPTER 1

Objective 4

Identify the importance of change management.

Objective 5

Describe HR's role in developing intellectual capital.

Objective 6

Explain how TQM, Six Sigma, and reengineering affect HR systems.

Objective 7

Discuss how cost pressures affect HR policies.

Objective 8

Discuss the primary demographic and employee concerns pertaining to HRM.

Objective 9

Provide examples of the roles and competencies of today's HR managers.

There's an old joke that goes . . .

The organization of the future will be so technologically advanced that it will be run by just one person and a dog. The person will be there to feed the dog, and the dog will be there to make sure that the person doesn't touch anything.

In the past, observers feared that machines might one day eliminate the need for people at work. In reality, just the opposite has been occurring. People are more important in today's organizations than ever before. As Ed Gubman, author of *The Talent Solution,* points out, "In many fast-growing economies, it may be easier to access money and technology than good people." Competitive advantage belongs to companies that know how to attract, select, deploy, and develop talent.[1]

We use a lot of words to describe how important people are to organizations. The terms *human resources, human capital, intellectual assets,* and *talent management* imply that it is people who drive the performance of their organizations (along with other resources such as money, materials, and information). Successful organizations are particularly adept at bringing together different kinds of people to achieve a common purpose. This is the essence of human resources management (HRM).

human resources management (HRM)

The process of managing human talent to achieve an organization's objectives

▪▪ WHY STUDY HUMAN RESOURCES MANAGEMENT?

Objective 1

As you embark on this course, you may be wondering how the topic of human resources management relates to your interests and career aspirations. The answer to the question "Why study HRM?" is pretty much the same regardless of whether you plan on working in a HR department or not. Staffing the organization, designing jobs and teams, developing skillful employees, identifying approaches for improving their performance, and rewarding employee successes—all typically labeled HRM issues—are as relevant to line managers as they are to managers in the HR department.

To work with people effectively, we have to understand human behavior, and we have to be knowledgeable about the various systems and practices available to help us build a skilled and motivated workforce. At the same time, we have to be aware of economic, technological, social, legal, and global issues that either facilitate or constrain our efforts to achieve organizational goals.[2] Because employee skills, knowledge, and abilities are among the most distinctive and renewable resources on which a company can draw, their strategic management is more important than ever. As Thomas J. Watson, the founder of IBM, said, "You can get capital and erect buildings, but it takes people to build a business."[3]

While "competing through people" may be a theme for human resources management, the idea remains only a framework for action. On a day-to-day basis, managers focus on specific challenges and issues that pertain to human resources. Figure 1.1 provides an overall framework for human resources management. From this figure, we can see that HR managers have to help blend many aspects of management; at this point, we will simply classify them as either "competitive challenges" or "employee concerns." By balancing sometimes competing demands, HR personnel help firms make the most from their employees by providing a work environment that meets employees' short-term and long-term needs. We will use this framework as a basis for our discussion throughout the rest of this chapter.

FIGURE 1.1 — Overall Framework for Human Resources Management

COMPETITIVE CHALLENGES AND HUMAN RESOURCES MANAGEMENT

Professional organizations such as the Society for Human Resource Management (SHRM) and the Human Resource Planning Society (HRPS) conduct ongoing studies of the most pressing competitive issues facing firms. By seeking the input of chief executives and HR managers, these organizations keep a finger on the pulse of major trends. For the past decade or so, there has been a constant theme around the following issues:

- Competing, recruiting, and staffing globally
- Embracing new technology
- Managing change
- Managing talent, or human capital
- Responding to the market
- Containing costs

These trends extend beyond "people issues" per se, but they all focus on the need to develop a skilled and flexible workforce in order to compete in the twenty-first century.

Challenge 1: Competing, Recruiting, and Staffing Globally

To grow and prosper today, companies are aware that to survive, they will likely to have to seek business opportunities in global markets. Competition—and cooperation—with foreign companies has become an important focal point for business. For example,

Using the Internet

The Society for Human Resource Management's Web site provides membership information, resources, and links to others in the HR field. Go to the Student Resources at:

www.cengage.com/ management/bohlander

2 | Objective

exporting accounts for a large portion of the U.S. economy. In 2007, a record 11.7 percent of what American's produced—or a bit more than one in nine dollars worth of production—went overseas. On the flip side, the United States has imported more than it has exported every year since the early 1970s. In addition, our trade imbalance with the rest of the world is nearly double what it was in 2001. Our biggest trading gap is with China, despite the fact that in 2007, a number of Chinese imports had to be recalled.[4]

The Impact of Globalization

By partnering with firms in other regions of the world and using information technologies to coordinate distant parts of their businesses, companies have shown that they can offer customers "anything, anytime, anywhere" around the world. Even well-known products are losing or have lost their national identities. BMW has traditionally been a German brand, but now the automaker builds cars in Spartanburg, South Carolina. In 2008, In Bev, a Belgian firm, purchased the U.S. beer company Anheuser Busch. Miller Brewing Company, headquartered in Milwaukee, Wisconsin, is owned by a foreign firm as well, having been purchased by South African Breweries in 2002.[5]

But globalization is not of interest only to large firms. While estimates vary widely, approximately 70 to 85 percent of the U.S. economy today is affected by international competition. Even small companies partner with organizations in other countries. For example, SpringHill Greenhouses in Lodi, Ohio, partners with florists through associations such as FTD and Teleflora to work with growers in Holland (tulips and lilies) and Colombia (roses) to serve customers around the world. According to the Small Business Administration, nearly 97 percent of all U.S. exporters are small companies, and these firms employ about half of all the private sector employees in the nation.

Numerous free-trade agreements forged between nations in the last half century have helped quicken the pace of globalization. The first major trade agreement of the twentieth century was made in 1948, following World War II. Called the General Agreement on Tariffs and Trade (GATT), it established rules and guidelines for global commerce between nations and groups of nations. Since GATT began, world trade has increased more than twenty-sevenfold in terms of volume. This is three times faster than the world's overall output has grown during the same period. GATT paved the way for the formation of the European Union in 1986; the North American Free Trade Agreement (NAFTA) in 1994, encompassing the United States, Canada, and Mexico; and the Asia-Pacific Economic Cooperation (APEC) in 1989, which loosened trade restrictions among Pacific Rim countries. The World Trade Organization (WTO), headquartered in Lausanne, Switzerland, now has more than 150 member countries, and new free-trade agreements seem to be forged annually.[6]

Globalization and Corporate Social Responsibility. Even though globalization has led to a great improvement in people's living standards in the last half century, free-trade agreements still stir fierce debate—especially when it comes to jobs. Since 2000, three million U.S. manufacturing jobs have been lost to low-wage nations such as China and India. Other people worry that free trade is creating a "have/have not" world economy, in which the people in developing economies and the world's

globalization
The trend toward opening up foreign markets to international trade and investment

Using the Internet

To learn more about the effects NAFTA has had, go to the Student Resources at:

www.cengage.com/
management/bohlander

environment are being exploited by companies in richer, more developed countries. This has sparked anti-free-trade protests in many nations.

Concerns such as these, coupled with numerous scandals plaguing U.S. corporations in recent years, have led to a new focus on corporate social responsibility, or good citizenship. Companies are discovering that being socially responsible both domestically and abroad helps the bottom line. Moreover, prospective workers are saying corporate responsibility is now more important to their job selection. One of HR's leadership roles is to spearhead the development and implementation of corporate citizenship throughout their organizations.[7] Highlights in HRM 1 lists a number of Internet sites of organizations with different conduct codes which firms internationally are striving to pursue. Also listed are a number of general Web sites useful to HR professionals.

corporate social responsibility
The responsibility of the firm to act in the best interests of the people and communities affected by its activities

How Globalization Affects HRM

For all of the opportunities afforded by international business, when managers talk about "going global," they have to balance a complicated set of issues related to different geographies, including different cultures, employment laws, and business practices. Human resources issues underlie each of these concerns. They include such things as dealing with employees today who, via the Internet, are better informed about global job opportunities and are willing to pursue them, even if it means working for competing companies. Gauging the knowledge and skill base of international workers and figuring out how best to hire and train them, sometimes with materials that must be translated into a number of different languages, is also an issue for firms. Relocating managers and other workers to direct the efforts of an international workforce is a challenge as well. HR personnel are frequently responsible for implementing training programs and enhancing their firms' managers' understanding of other cultures and practices as well as dealing with the culture shock these workers might experience and pay differentials that must be adjusted, depending upon the country. The international arena for HRM has become so crucial and so involved that we have devoted an entire chapter (Chapter 15) to discussing its competitive, cultural, and practical implications.

Challenge 2: Embracing New Technology

Advancements in information technology have enabled organizations to take advantage of the information explosion. With computer networks, unlimited amounts of data can be stored, retrieved, and used in a wide variety of ways, from simple record-keeping to controlling complex equipment. The effect is so dramatic that at a broader level, organizations are changing the way they do business. The use of the Internet to transact business has become so pervasive for both large and small companies that e-commerce has rapidly become the norm for many firms, including traditional brick-and-mortar companies. The Web has also created a new generation of "virtual" workers who work from home, hotels, or wherever their work takes them and who search for jobs via social networking Web sites such as Linked-In, Facebook, and My Space.

3 | Objective

From Touch Labor to Knowledge Workers

Advanced technology tends to reduce the number of jobs that require little skill and to increase the number of jobs that require considerable skill. In general, this transformation has been referred to as a shift from "touch labor" to "knowledge workers,"

knowledge workers
Workers whose responsibilities extend beyond the physical execution of work to include planning, decision-making, and problem-solving

A Guide to HR Internet Sites

HR professionals can access the following Web sites for current information related to human resources.

Codes of Conduct

- Asia-Pacific Economic Cooperation Forum Business Code of Conduct (http://www.cauxroundtable.org/ APECForumBusinessCodeofConduct.html)
- Caux Round Table Principles for Business (http://www.cauxroundtable.org/principles.html)
- Fair Labor Association Workshop Code of Conduct (http://www.fairlabor.org)
- Global Sullivan Principles (http://www.thegsp.org)
- ILO Tripartite Declaration of Principles Concerning Multinational Enterprises and Social Policy (http://www.ilo.org)
- OECD Guidelines for Multinational Enterprises (www.oecd.org/daf/investment/guidelines)
- OECD, Principles of Corporate Governance (http://www.oecd.org)
- Rules of Conduct on Extortion and Bribery in International Business Transactions (International Chamber of Commerce, http://www.iccwbo.org)
- United Nations Universal Declaration of Human Rights (http://www.un.org)

General

- AFL-CIO (http://www.aflcio.org/home.htm)—Union news, issue papers, press releases, links to labor sites.
- American Management Association (http://www.amanet.org/index.htm)—AMA membership, programs, training, and so on.
- FedWorld (http://www.fedworld.gov)—A gateway to many government Web sites.
- HR Professional's Gateway to the Internet (http://www.hrprosgateway.com)—Links to HR-related Web pages.
- Occupational Safety and Health Resources (http://www.osh.net)—OSHA-related sites, government pages, resources, and so on.
- Society for Human Resource Management (http://www.shrm.org)—Current events, information, connections, and articles.
- Telecommuting, Telework, and Alternative Officing (http://www.gilgordon.com)—Telecommuting and flexible hours.
- Training & Development Resource Center (http://www.thetrainingworld.com)—Job mart, training links, and T&D electronic mailing list links.
- U.S. Department of Labor (http://www.dol.gov)—Job bank, labor statistics, press releases, grants, and contract information.

in which employee responsibilities expand to include a richer array of activities such as planning, decision-making, and problem-solving.[8] In many cases, current employees are being retrained to assume new roles and responsibilities. Even when employees are displaced, they also require retraining.

Technology, transportation, communications, and utilities industries tend to spend the most on training. Knowledge-based training has become so important that Manpower Inc., the largest employment agency in the United States, offers free information technology training through its Manpower Training and Development Center (http://www.manpowerglc. com), an online university for its 2.5 million employees worldwide. The Manpower site features more than 6,000 hours of online instruction in technology applications, along with professional development and business skills and telecommunications courses. In fact, Manpower is so focused on developing technical skills in potential employees that it has set up the system so that some training and career planning information is available to those who simply send the company a resume. "Just-in-time" learning delivered via the Internet to employees' desktops when and where they need training has become commonplace. "Virtual" learning has emerged as well. IBM, Cisco, Kelly Services, and Manpower are among the companies that have built training facilities, offices, and meeting rooms inside of the online reality game Second Life. The spaces these companies build online enable them to do certain things more easily and cheaply than they can in the real world—for example, bringing people from several continents into one room for training.[9]

> **Using the Internet**
>
> For more information about Manpower, go to the Student Resources at:
>
> **www.cengage.com/ management/bohlander**

Influence of Technology in HRM

Information technology has, of course, changed the face of HRM in the United States and abroad. Perhaps the most central use of technology in HRM is an organization's **human resources information system (HRIS)**. Organizations determined to improve productivity and lower costs are finding HR a good place to start. Because HR affects the entire workforce—everyone who works for the company must be hired, trained, and paid, usually through HR—the impact of HRIS has been dramatic. It has become a potent weapon for lowering administrative costs, increasing productivity, speeding up response times, and improving decision-making and service to managers and employees.

The most obvious impact has been operational—that is, automating routine activities, alleviating administrative burdens, reducing costs, and improving productivity internal to the HR function itself. The most frequent uses include automating payroll processing, maintaining employee records, and administering benefits programs. One of the big trends in recent years has been toward HRIS "self-service"—setting up systems, usually on an Intranet, to allow managers to access employee records themselves for administrative purposes and to allow employees to access and change their own benefits and other personal information. Merck's HR system was redesigned to enable line managers and employees to enter, retrieve, and edit data in order to make better decisions faster. This has helped alleviate many of the paper burdens Merck's HR group previously faced and offered greater convenience to both managers and their employees.

Today, however, software applications are available to automate far more HR activities than just payroll, records, and benefits information. All sorts of routine HR activities, from front to back, have seen some sort of automation. Companies are now using software to recruit, screen, and pretest applicants online before hiring

human resources information system (HRIS)

A computerized system that provides current and accurate data for purposes of control and decision-making them as well as to train, track, and promote employees once they have been hired. For example, Merck's staffing management system supports the hiring process by tracking applicants' information, scanning resumes, and making the information immediately accessible to line managers so they can search systematically for the people whose skills they want. Managers can search online for internal and external talent by running searches of candidates who have been categorized by skill set.[10]

Corning, Inc. uses HR software, among other things, to set the developmental goals of its employees once they have been hired and gauge how well they are meeting them. Employees can look online to see their own goals and mark their progress as well as see everyone else's goals in the command chain, from the CEO down to their immediate supervisors. This "cascading" of goals has helped Corning's employees align their personal goals with the organization's overall objectives in order to reach higher levels. "Like any large company, we tended to get 'silo-ed' and fragmented the more we grew," said one vice president at a company using a system similar to Corning's. "We needed a better way to pull our global team together and get people focused on what the priorities are for our business." Brown and Williamson Tobacco has used a program called Career Tracker, not only to trace the performance of employees, but also to allow them to create a personalized learning curriculum from materials online. Similarly, Merck worked with a software vendor to develop a system that provides coaching tips and learning tools and resources for employees and managers based on their goals.[11]

Highlights in HRM 2 shows the extent to which various functions are being automated. According to a survey by Cedar Group, a technology consulting firm, prepackaged, or "canned," HR Web-based solutions are as commonly used as custom-designed systems. Generally, companies also have the choice of hosting the applications on their own servers or having "Software as a Service" vendors (or *SaaS* vendors) such as IBM or PeopleSoft do it for them.

So what sort of system should HR professionals choose from among the many options available to them? Experts say the first step in choosing a HRIS is for HR personnel to evaluate the biggest "headaches" they experience, or most time-consuming tasks, and then choose the applications that can have the strongest impact on the firm's financial measures—that is, the ones that get the "biggest bang for the buck." These applications are more likely to get "buy-in" from the firm's top managers. HR managers should then calculate the costs based on average salaries, or HR hours, that could be saved by using a human resources information system, along with the hours of increased productivity that would occur as a result.

Other factors that need to be evaluated include the following:

- *Fit of the application to the firm's employee base.* If many of the firm's employees work on a factory floor, is the system appropriate, or does HR need to install kiosks in employee areas? How will the information be secured? Will employees need to be assigned passwords? Can they access the information from off-site, for example, from their homes?

- *Ability to upgrade or customize the software.* What sorts of costs will be involved to upgrade the software in the coming years?

- *Compatibility with current systems.* Does the HRIS link into existing, or planned, information systems easily and inexpensively?

- *User friendliness.* Does the software provide additional features such as links to learning resources or help for managers who might need it?

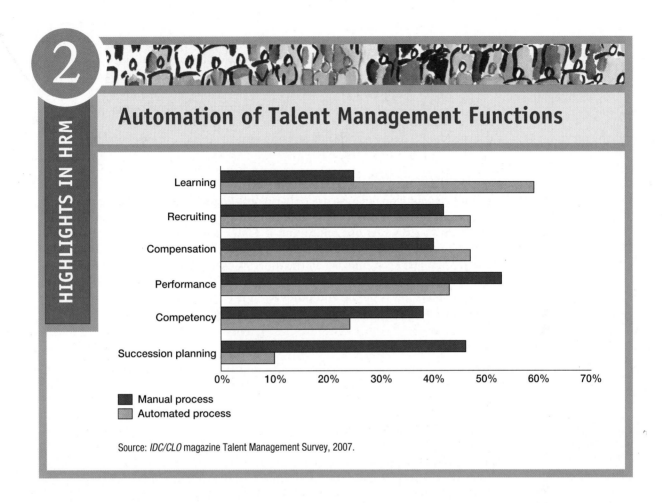

HIGHLIGHTS IN HRM

2

Automation of Talent Management Functions

Legend:
- Manual process
- Automated process

Source: *IDC/CLO* magazine Talent Management Survey, 2007.

- *Availability of technical support.* Should the HRIS system be supported internally, or should the vendor host it? What are the vendor's technical support capabilities?

- *Time required to implement and train staff members to use the HRIS, including HR and payroll personnel, managers, and employees.* Who is responsible for training employees, and how will it be done?

- *Initial costs and annual maintenance costs.* Is a "suite" of applications needed or just a few key applications? Experts advise HR managers to price each application separately and then ask vendors for a "bundled" price.[12]

When an effective HRIS is implemented, perhaps the biggest advantage gained is that HR personnel can concentrate more effectively on the firm's strategic direction instead of on routine tasks. This can include forecasting personnel needs (especially for firms planning to expand, contract, or merge), planning for career and employee promotions, and evaluating the impact of the firm's policies—both those related to HR functions and other functions—to help improve the firm's earnings and strategic direction. "We wanted our HR teams to focus on people issues instead of data problems," explains Sandra Hoffman, CIO of MAPICS, a HR applications provider.

The initial drive to adopt human resources information systems was related to cutting HR costs. But HR managers have since discovered that the systems have allowed them to share information with line managers, who, by having access to it, have been able to come up with better production practices and cost control solutions. As a result, HR managers are now requiring their application providers to provide them with software to meet certain goals, including lowering a company's total spending on employee health care and improving its customer service.[13]

Challenge 3: Managing Change

Technology and globalization are only two of the forces driving change in organizations and HRM. Today, being able to manage change has become paramount to the firm's success. As one pundit put it, "No change means chance." Successful companies, says Harvard Business School professor Rosabeth Moss Kanter, develop a culture that just keeps moving all the time.[14] Given the pace of today's commerce, organizations can rarely stand still for long. In highly competitive environments, where competition is global and innovation is continuous, being able to manage change has become a core competency sought by organizations.

Types of Changes

Programs focused on total quality, continuous improvement, downsizing, reengineering, outsourcing, and the like are all examples of the means organizations are using to modify the way they operate in order to be more successful. Some of these changes are reactive change, resulting when external forces have already affected an organization's performance. For example, Steve Jobs stepped in and saved Apple amid a crisis. Other changes are proactive change, initiated by managers to take advantage of targeted opportunities, particularly in fast-changing industries in which followers are not successful. In 2000, Alan Lafley, the CEO of Procter & Gamble, was looking to change the company by transforming P&G's culture into one that was "curious, collaborative, and courageous, while still retaining its core values." "You need both an external mirror and a rear view of the direction in which you're headed," Lafley wrote in his book *The Game Changer*.[15]

reactive change
Change that occurs after external forces have already affected performance

proactive change
Change initiated to take advantage of targeted opportunities

Managing Change through HR

Two-thirds of firms believe that managing change is their biggest challenge, according to a recent survey by the research institute Roffey Park. Moreover, more than 80 percent of organizations reported some form of *change* initiative currently going on in their companies. Yet many companies lack formal change management programs.[16] This is unfortunate because successful change rarely occurs naturally or easily. Most of the major reasons why change efforts can fail come down to HR issues. Some of the top reasons are as follows:[17]

1. Not establishing a sense of urgency

2. Not creating a powerful coalition to guide the effort

3. Lacking leaders who have a vision

4. Lacking leaders who communicate the vision

5. Not removing obstacles to the new vision or motivating employees

6. Not systematically planning for and creating short-term "wins"

7. Declaring victory too soon

8. Not anchoring changes in the corporate culture, or failing to maintain the momentum of the change

Most employees—regardless of occupation—understand that the way things were done five or ten years ago is very different from how they are done today (or will be done five or ten years from now). Responsibilities change, job assignments change, and work processes change. This change is continuous—a part of the job—rather than temporary. Nevertheless, people often resist change because it requires them to modify or abandon ways of working that have been successful or at least familiar to them. As Dr. Marilyn Buckner, the immediate past president of the Human Resource Planning Society in New York City, put it: "Nontechnical, unattended human factors are, in fact, most often the problem in failed change projects." To manage change, executives and managers, including those in HR, have to envision the future, communicate this vision to employees, set clear expectations for performance, and develop the capability to execute by reorganizing people and reallocating assets. Organizations that have been successful in engineering change typically build into their change management planning these key elements:

- They link the change to the business strategy.

- They create quantifiable benefits.

- They engage key employees, customers, and their suppliers early.

- They integrate required behavior changes.

- They lead clearly, unequivocally, and consistently.

- They invest to implement and sustain change.

- They communicate continuously and personally.

- They sell commitment to the change, not communication about the change.[18]

Challenge 4: Managing Talent, or Human Capital

The idea that organizations "compete through people" highlights the fact that success increasingly depends on an organization's ability to manage talent, or human capital. The term *human capital* describes the economic value of employees' knowledge, skills, and capabilities. Although the value of these assets may not show up directly on a company's balance sheet, it nevertheless has tremendous impact on an organization's performance. The following quotations from notable CEOs illustrate this point:[19]

human capital
The knowledge, skills, and capabilities of individuals that have economic value to an organization

5 | Objective

- "If you look at our semiconductors and melt them down for silicon, that's a tiny fraction of the costs. The rest is intellect and mistakes." (Gordon Moore, Intel)

- "An organization's ability to learn, and translate that learning into action rapidly, is the ultimate competitive business advantage." (Jack Welch, General Electric)

- "Successful companies of the 21st century will be those who do the best jobs of capturing, storing and leveraging what their employees know." (Lew Platt, Hewlett-Packard)

Staffing programs focus on identifying, recruiting, and hiring the best and the brightest talent available. A jobs fair is one resource, and often brings in many applicants for few positions.

© FRANK FRANKLIN II/AP PHOTOS

Human Capital and HRM

Human capital is intangible and cannot be managed the way organizations manage jobs, products, and technologies. One of the reasons for this is that the employees, *not* the organization, own their own human capital. If valued employees leave a company, they take their human capital with them, and any investment the company has made in training and developing those people is lost.

To build human capital in organizations, managers must continue to develop superior knowledge, skills, and experience within their workforce. Staffing programs focus on identifying, recruiting, and hiring the best and the brightest talent available. Training programs complement these staffing practices to provide skill enhancement, particularly in areas that cannot be transferred to another company if an employee leaves.[20] In addition, employees need opportunities for development on the job. The most highly valued intelligence on the part of employees tends to be associated with competencies and capabilities they learn from experience and are not easily taught.[21] Consequently, managers have to do a good job of providing employees with developmental assignments and ensuring their job duties and requirements are flexible enough to allow them to grow and learn.

Beyond the need to invest in employee development, organizations have to find ways of using the knowledge that currently exists within their firms. Too often, employees have skills that go unused. As Robert Buckman, who served as CEO of Buckman Laboratories for twenty-two years, a period of unprecedented growth for the company, noted, "If the greatest database in the company is housed in the individual minds of the associates of the organization, then that is where the power of the organization resides. These individual knowledge bases are continually changing and adapting to the real world in front of them. We have to connect these individual knowledge bases together so that they do whatever they do best in the shortest possible time."[22]

In companies such as Texas Instruments, Procter & Gamble, and HSBC, managers are evaluated on their progress toward meeting developmental goals. These goals focus on skill development and gaining new competencies and capabilities. In a growing number of instances, pay is attached to this knowledge and skill acquisition. Skill-based pay, for example, rewards employees for each new class of jobs they are capable of performing. We will discuss skill-based pay (or pay-for-knowledge) more in Chapter 9.

Developmental assignments, particularly those involving teamwork, can also be a valuable way of facilitating knowledge exchange and mutual learning. Effective communication (whether face-to-face or through information technology) is instrumental in sharing knowledge and making it widely available throughout the organization. As Dave Ulrich, professor of business at the University of Michigan, noted: "Learning capability is *g* times *g*—a business's ability to *generate* new ideas multiplied by its adeptness at *generalizing* them throughout the company."[23]

HR programs and assignments are often the conduit through which knowledge is transferred among employees. A survey by the Human Resource Planning Society revealed that 65 percent of responding companies believed that their HR groups play a key role in developing human capital. Arvinder Dhesi, the new head of talent for the insurance company Aviva, explains that his firm's goal is to treat *everyone* as talent and not just focus on a few. "We talk about the sum of people's experiences as well as their skills," says Dhesi, who notes that Aviva is rolling out new software that will create a "talent profile" of each of the firm's 39,000 employees worldwide. Similarly, Boeing Satellite Systems has created a "lessons learned" site on its Intranet where all areas of the company can store the knowledge they have learned. As information and intellectual capital are posted to the company's electronic newsgroups, they can be analyzed and consolidated by editorial teams. Executives at Boeing estimate that this form of intellectual capital has reduced the cost of developing a satellite by as much as $25 million.[24]

HR managers and line managers each play an important role in creating an organization that understands the value of knowledge, documents the skills and capabilities available to the organization, and identifies ways of utilizing that knowledge to benefit the firm. We will address these issues throughout the text, but particularly in Chapters 5 and 7 on career development and training.

Challenge 5: Responding to the Market

Meeting customer expectations is essential for any organization. In addition to focusing on internal management issues, managers must also meet customer requirements of quality, innovation, variety, and responsiveness. These standards often separate the winners from the losers in today's competitive world. How well does a company understand its customers' needs? How fast can it develop and get a new product to market? How effectively has it responded to special concerns? "Faster, Leaner, Better"—the vision at pharmaceutical company AstraZeneca—requires the organization to constantly align its management processes with customer needs. Management innovations such as total quality management (TQM) and process reengineering are but two of the comprehensive approaches to responding to customers. Each has direct implications for HR.

6 | Objective

Total Quality Management, Six Sigma, and HRM

total quality management (TQM) is a set of principles and practices whose core ideas include understanding customer needs, doing things right the first time, and striving for continuous improvement. Total quality management techniques were developed in the mid-1940s by Dr. W. Edward Deming after studying Japanese companies rebuilding following World War II. The TQM revolution in the United States began in the mid-1980s, led by companies such as Motorola, Xerox, and Ford. But since that time, criteria spelled out in the Malcolm Baldrige National Quality Award have provided the impetus for both large and small companies to rethink their approach to HRM. Currently, the Baldrige Award is given annually in each of six categories: manufacturing, service, small business, education, health care, and nonprofit.[25]

When TQM initiatives work, it is usually because managers have made major changes in their philosophies and HR programs. More recently, companies such as Motorola, GE, Dow Chemical, and Honeywell have adopted a more systematic approach to quality, called **Six Sigma,** which includes major changes in management philosophy and HR programs. Six Sigma is a statistical method of translating a customer's needs into separate tasks and defining the best way to perform each task in concert with the others. By examining the optimal process, Six Sigma can have a powerful effect on the quality of products, the performance of customer service, and the professional development of employees. What makes Six Sigma different from other quality efforts is that it catches mistakes before they happen. In a true Six Sigma environment, variation from standard is reduced to only 3.4 defects per million.[26]

The importance of HR to Six Sigma begins with the formation of teams and extends to training, performance management, communication, culture, and even rewards. As individuals progress through Six Sigma training, they can move up from "green belt" to eventually achieve "black belt" status. Many of Dow's key HR slots require black belt certification, for example. If this all sounds a bit hokey, take note of the successful companies that have made cultural—and performance—transformation as a result: Motorola credits Six Sigma with $16 billion in savings over the course of twelve years; Ford reports that it saved more than $4 billion in one year alone; and Motorola is so committed to Six Sigma that it now conducts Six Sigma training for employees of other firms who attend its Motorola University.[27] The most important quality improvement techniques stress employee motivation, change in corporate culture, and employee education. Organizations known for product and service quality strongly believe that employees are the key to that quality.

One of the reasons that HR programs are so essential to programs such as Six Sigma is that they help balance two opposing forces. According to Laurie Broedling, an organizational psychologist and human resources expert, "One set of forces (the need for order and control) pulls every business toward stagnation, while another set of forces (the need for growth and creativity) drives it toward disintegration." Six Sigma's focus on continuous improvement drives the system toward disequilibrium, while Six Sigma's focus on customers, management systems, and the like provide the restraining forces that keep the system together. HR practices help managers balance these two forces. Like human resources information systems, TQM has helped HR departments progress from a focus on functional activities to strategic planning. Better business thinking builds more strategic HR thinking.[28]

total quality management (TQM)
A set of principles and practices whose core ideas include understanding customer needs, doing things right the first time, and striving for continuous improvement

Six Sigma
A process used to translate customer needs into a set of optimal tasks that are performed in concert with one another

Reengineering and HRM

In addition to TQM and Six Sigma programs, some companies take a more radical approach to process redesign called reengineering. Reengineering has been described as "the fundamental rethinking and radical redesign of business processes to achieve dramatic improvements in cost, quality, service and speed."[29] Reengineering often requires that managers start over from scratch in rethinking how work should be done, how technology and people should interact, and how entire organizations should be structured. HR issues are central to these decisions. First, reengineering requires that managers create an environment for change, and as we mentioned previously, HR issues drive change. Second, reengineering efforts depend on effective leadership and communication processes, two other areas related to HRM. Third, reengineering requires that administrative systems be reviewed and modified. Selection, job descriptions, training, career planning, performance appraisal, compensation, and labor relations are all candidates for change to complement and support reengineering efforts. We will return to these issues and speak more directly to the organizational development tools necessary for reengineering in later chapters.

reengineering
Fundamental rethinking and radical redesign of business processes to achieve dramatic improvements in cost, quality, service, and speed

Challenge 6: Containing Costs

Companies today are facing sharply rising costs, including higher product transportation costs and skyrocketing employee health care costs. As a result, many firms are under extreme pressure to improve their productivity in order to maximize their efficiency and keep their prices competitive. Like other functional department managers, human resources managers are under pressure to show top managers the "bottom line" financial results their departments are achieving. Labor costs are one of the largest expenditures of any organization, particularly in service- and knowledge-intensive companies. Organizations are taking many approaches to lowering labor-related costs. In addition to shifting some of the rising costs of health care back onto employees, firms are also downsizing, outsourcing, offshoring, and engaging in employee leasing in an attempt to enhance productivity. Each of these efforts has a big impact on HR policies and practices.

7 | **Objective**

Downsizing

Downsizing is the planned elimination of jobs. For example, when L. L. Bean saw that sales had fallen, the company undertook a number of efforts to identify what it called "smart cost reductions." Bean's TQM activities helped the company target quality problems and saved an estimated $30 million. But the cuts were not enough, and ultimately Leon Gorman, president of the firm, and Bob Peixotto, vice president of HR and quality, realized the company needed to eliminate some jobs. Instead of simply laying off people, however, the company started early retirement and "sweetened" voluntary separation programs. Then the company offered employee sabbaticals for continuing education.[30]

These efforts, combined with better employee communication, helped soften the blow of layoffs at L. L. Bean. But the pain of downsizing has been widespread throughout the United States. Virtually every major corporation within the country has undergone some cycle of downsizing. Historically, layoffs tended to affect manufacturing firms and line workers in particular, but beginning in the 1990s, the layoffs began to encompass white-collar workers in greater numbers. In fact, in the largest U.S. firms, most of the jobs lost in the last decade have been white-collar jobs

downsizing
Planned elimination of jobs

in knowledge-intensive industries. Engineering, accounting, information technology, and architecture have been among the hardest hit professions.[31]

But downsizing is no longer being regarded as a short-term fix when times are tough. It has now become a tool continually used by companies to adjust to changes in technology, globalization, and the firm's business direction. For example, in a study that surveyed 450 senior HR executives at companies that had downsized, only 21 percent said that financial difficulties had spurred the cutbacks. In fact, 34 percent of the executives said that the downsizing was done to strengthen their companies' future positions; 21 percent said it was done to achieve fundamental staff realignment; and 17 percent said it was due to a merger or acquisition.

Whatever the reason, while some firms improve efficiency (and lower costs) with layoffs, many others do not obtain such benefits. These kinds of trade-offs have led some firms to establish a policy of "no layoffs." For example, in an industry that has seen layoffs in the tens of thousands, Southwest Airlines has not laid off a single employee. In fact, the company has not had layoffs in thirty years. Nucor Steel and the convenience store chain Valero are other companies with no layoff policies. These practices are admittedly an exception, but some firms are taking such an approach because of downsizing's toll on retention and recruitment. A study by Watson Wyatt of 750 companies showed that companies with excellent recruiting and retention policies provide a nearly 8 percent higher return to shareholders compared to those that do not. Those with a strong commitment to job security earned an additional 1.4 percent for shareholders.

Advocates of a no layoff policy often note that layoffs may backfire after taking into account such hidden costs as the following:

- Severance and rehiring costs
- Accrued vacation and sick day payouts
- Pension and benefit payoffs
- Potential lawsuits from aggrieved workers
- Loss of institutional memory and trust in management
- Lack of staffers when the economy rebounds
- Survivors who are risk averse, paranoid, and political

In contrast, companies that avoid downsizing say they get some important benefits from such policies:

- A fiercely loyal, more productive workforce
- Higher customer satisfaction
- Readiness to snap back with the economy
- A recruiting edge
- Workers who are not afraid to innovate, knowing their jobs are safe[32]

More than one executive has concluded that you do not get dedicated and productive employees if at the first sign of trouble you show them that you think they are expendable.

To approach downsizing more intelligently, companies such as Continental Airlines, Dial Corporation, and L. L. Bean have made special efforts to reassign and retrain employees for new positions when their jobs are eliminated. This is consistent with a philosophy of employees as assets, as intellectual capital.

Outsourcing, Offshoring, and Employee Leasing

Over the past twenty-five years, the employment relationship between companies and employees has shifted from relationship-based to transaction-based. Fewer people are working for one employer over the course of their lifetimes, and as we have explained, the Internet has created a workforce that is constantly scanning for new opportunities. In addition, more people are choosing to work on a freelance, or contract, basis or to work part-time, especially women and senior citizens. Outsourcing is evidence of this trend.[33] Outsourcing simply means hiring someone outside the company to perform business processes that could be done within a firm. Companies hire accounting firms to take care of their financial services. They hire advertising firms to handle promotions, software firms to develop data-processing systems, and law firms to handle their legal issues. Maintenance, security, catering, and payroll are often outsourced in order to increase the organization's flexibility and lower its overhead costs.

outsourcing
Contracting outside the organization to have work done that formerly was done by internal employees

The interest in outsourcing has been spurred on by executives who want to focus their organization's activities on what they do best. In fact, some management experts predict companies will one day strip away every function not regarded as crucial. Even now, many firms are outsourcing what would seem to be their core functions. Drug companies such as GlaxoSmithKline are outsourcing their research and development functions to smaller firms that can more cheaply and nimbly create new products for them. Procter & Gamble hopes to outsource half of its product development by the year 2010. Outsourcing is changing the way HR departments

Offshoring involves shifting work to overseas locations. IT People India Ltd. is a global e-recruitment and consulting company that provides human resources focused on the IT industry.

operate as well. The practice has been one of the most prominent HR trends of the last ten years and will continue to be until the last dollar of excess costs has been wrung out.[34]

offshoring

The business practice of sending jobs to other countries

Offshoring, also referred to as "global sourcing," involves shifting work to overseas locations. Almost half of 500 senior finance and HR leaders surveyed said their firms are either offshoring or are considering offshoring in the next three years, according to a study by Hewitt Associates. Spending on offshore services has been rising not just in the United States but worldwide.[35] Figure 1.2 shows the number of jobs estimated to be located offshore in the coming years, along with the fields most likely to be affected. Cost reduction is among the key motivators for these decisions—companies estimate that they can save 40 to 60 percent on labor costs by reallocating work to countries such as India, where highly educated workers can perform the same jobs as U.S. workers at half the price. Other labor markets include the Philippines, Russia, China, Mexico, Brazil, Hungary, and Bosnia. However, a new attitude is emerging. According to Atul Vashistha, the coauthor of the book *Offshore Nation*, CEOs these days are not asking how much offshoring can save them so much as they are asking by how much it can grow their businesses. In some cases, the decisions reflect the allocation of work across the multiple countries in which the company does business. In other cases, managers are finding that if they save money by offshoring, they can rescue failing businesses, make better use of their skilled U.S. labor, and deliver products more cheaply and quickly because they have people across the globe working 24-7 on them.[36]

But hidden costs can sometimes chew up much of the financial gains from offshoring, including those associated with finding foreign vendors, productivity lost during the transition, domestic layoff costs, language difficulties, international regulatory challenges, and political and economic instability that can threaten operations. In Chapter 2, you will learn about the other ways firms can gain a competitive edge besides just cutting labor costs. Nonetheless, offshoring is going to continue to be

FIGURE 1.2

Estimated Number and Types of U.S. Jobs Estimated to Move Offshore between 2010 and 2015

	2010	2015
Management	106,000	259,000
Business	176,000	356,000
Computer	322,000	542,000
Architecture	93,000	191,000
Life sciences	16,000	39,000
Legal	39,000	79,000
Art, design	15,000	30,000
Sales	97,000	218,000
Office	815,000	1,600,000
Total	1,700,000	3,400,000

a key employment strategy as global economies continue to shift. The key is for top managers, finance departments, and the offshoring consulting firms they hire to begin working in conjunction with their companies' HR departments early in the game. "Companies can minimize hidden costs and maximize their returns by enabling HR have a seat at the table early so they can carefully address issues such as skill and language requirements, labor costs by market, alternative talent pools, workforce training, retraining and change management," says Mark Arian, a corporate restructuring and change practice leader for Hewitt. To minimize problems, line and HR managers have to work together with the firm's other functional groups to define and communicate transition plans, minimize the number of unknowns, and help employees identify their employment options.[37]

As an alternative to downsizing, outsourcing, and offshoring, many companies, especially small ones, have decided to sign employee leasing agreements with professional employer organizations (PEOs). A PEO—typically a larger company—takes over the management of a smaller company's HR tasks and becomes a coemployer to its employees. The PEO performs all the HR duties of an employer—hiring, payroll, and performance appraisal. Because PEOs can coemploy a large number of people working at many different companies, they can provide employees with benefits that small companies cannot afford, such as 401k and health care plans, workers' compensation, and even adoption assistance. In addition, many PEOs offer their employees flextime, job sharing, part-time employment, consulting arrangements, seasonal work, and on-call work. The value of employee leasing lies in the fact that an organization can essentially maintain its working relationships with its employees but shift some employment costs to the PEO, in return for a fee. More details on employee leasing will be discussed in Chapter 5.[38]

employee leasing
The process of dismissing employees who are then hired by a leasing company (which handles all HR-related activities) and contracting with that company to lease back the employees

Productivity Enhancements

The results of pure cost-cutting efforts such as downsizing, outsourcing, and employee leasing can be disappointing, however, if managers use them as simple solutions to complex performance problems. Overemphasizing labor costs misses the broader issue of improving a firm's productivity. Employee productivity is the result of a combination of employees' abilities, motivation, and work environment and the technology with which they have to work. Since productivity can be defined as "the output gained from a fixed amount of inputs," organizations can increase their productivity either by reducing their inputs (the cost approach) or by increasing the amount that employees produce, by adding more human and/or physical capital to the process. Companies such as Toyota and Southwest Airlines achieve low costs in their industries not because they scrimp on employees, but because they are the most productive.

In absolute terms, the United States remains the world's most productive nation. U.S. workers produce more output collectively than any other country—more than $63,000 per worker. With that said, the growth in output per worker is now climbing faster in less-developed countries such as China that have lacked expertise and technology in the past but are making strides to close the gap. Even during the 2001–2002 recession, new investments in technology kept the productivity of U.S. workers climbing upward. The problem is that this rapid investment in faster computers and more efficient machine tools is beginning to level off. This will limit how much assistance technology can offer U.S. employees in terms of their productivity in the years to come. Employees are already working more hours than they have at any time since 1973.

FIGURE
1.3

Productivity Enhancements

MOTIVATION
• Job enrichment
• Promotions
• Coaching
• Feedback
• Rewards

ENVIRONMENT
○ Employee empowerment
○ Teams
○ Leader support
○ Culture

ABILITY
• Recruitment
• Selection
• Training
• Development

This means that any additional productivity will have to come from the enhanced ability of employees, their motivation, and their work environment—which makes the job of the HR manager in the coming years all the more crucial.[39] Figure 1.3 shows some of the topics that we cover in this textbook that help managers increase productivity in their organizations.

DEMOGRAPHIC AND EMPLOYEE CONCERNS

Objective 8

In addition to the competitive challenges facing organizations, managers in general—and HR managers in particular—need to be concerned about changes in the makeup and the expectations of their employees. As we noted at the beginning of this chapter, HRM involves being an advocate for employees, being aware of their concerns, and making sure that the exchange between the organization and its employees is *mutually* beneficial. Highlights in HRM 3 shows a summary of social issues in HRM. We will discuss some of these issues here and address all of them in greater detail throughout the book.

Demographic Changes

Among the most significant challenges to managers are the demographic changes occurring in the United States. Because they affect the workforce of an employer, these changes—in employee background, age, gender, and education—are important topics for discussion.

The Diversity/Immigration Challenge

Figure 1.4 shows the current composition of the U.S. population. Minorities in the United States are increasing relative to the total population. In fact, the U.S. Census Bureau estimates whites will no longer make up a majority of Americans by 2042. In four states—Hawaii, New Mexico, California, and Texas—minorities already outnumber non-Hispanic whites. It should come as no surprise to you, then, that U.S. workers are becoming more diverse as well. Much of the growth of the minority workforce has been due to not only to the arrival of immigrants but also high birthrates

HIGHLIGHTS IN HRM

3

Social Issues in HRM

Changing Demographics: The coming decades will bring a more diverse and aging workforce to developed countries such as the United States. This has major implications for all aspects of HRM because it alters traditional experience and expectations regarding the labor pool. Among the issues in this area are:

- Globalization
- Shrinking pool of skilled entry-level workers
- Rising health care costs for employees
- Outsourcing, offshoring, and the use of temporary and part-time employees

- Diversity strategies
- Social Security and retirement issues
- Continual skills development and retraining

Employer/Employee Rights: This area reflects the shift toward organizations and individuals attempting to define rights, obligations, and responsibilities. Among the issues here are:

- Relationship employment versus transactional-based employment
- Concern for the privacy of employees
- Employer-employee ethics

- Comparable worth
- Whistle-blowing
- Legal compliance
- Mandated benefits

Attitudes toward Work and Family: Because of the increase of working women as well as employee mobility and a growing concern about family issues, there is demand for recognizing and supporting family-related concerns. Among the issues are:

- Day care and elder care
- Job sharing
- Job rotation
- Parental leave

- Flextime
- Alternative work schedules
- Telecommuting

among some minority groups, such Hispanics, over the years. But it's not just Hispanics who are increasing. The number of people of Asian descent are expected to double in America by 2050.

Firms have long been criticized for hiring immigrant workers both legal and illegal because people believe they prevent "regular" American from getting jobs. Following 9/11, the backlash increased. The problem is that due tighter immigration restrictions, American employers are currently facing severe labor shortages of both skilled and unskilled workers. In years past, the United States was able to attract the best and brightest of the world's talent, which fueled the country's success. But as you will learn in Chapter 15, that is changing.[40]

Using the Internet

For more information about 7-Eleven's success attracting minority franchisees, go to the Student Resources at:

www.cengage.com/ management/bohlander

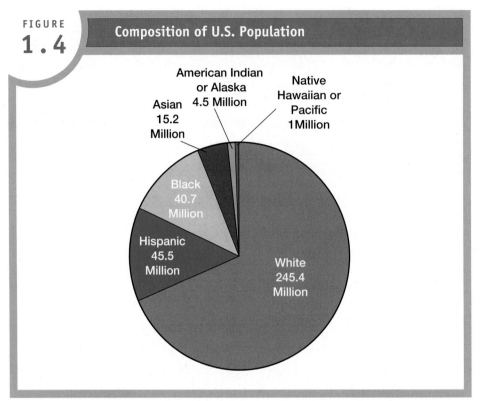

FIGURE 1.4

Composition of U.S. Population

American Indian or Alaska 4.5 Million

Native Hawaiian or Pacific 1 Million

Asian 15.2 Million

Black 40.7 Million

Hispanic 45.5 Million

White 245.4 Million

Source: U.S. Census Bureau.

How a shortage of immigrant labor could undercut competitiveness is not lost on U.S. businesses that need talent on both ends of the spectrum. To accommodate the shift in demographics, demand, and labor trends, these businesses know it's absolutely vital to increased their efforts to recruit and train a more diverse workforce. They realize that immigrants are not only critical to their very survival but add to their strength and allow them to better attract and serve a larger customer base. The hotel chain Marriott and the Big Four Accounting firm Deloitte & Touche are examples. Chapter 15 will discuss in more detail what companies are doing to cope with this difficult situation.[41]

Age Distribution of Employees

Past fluctuations in U.S. birthrates are producing abrupt changes in the makeup of the U.S. labor force. As a result, the U.S. labor force is aging, as are the workforces of more developed countries such as Japan, France, Germany, and the United Kingdom. According to the U.S. Census Bureau, the percentage of people 65 and older in the United States will continue to increase into the year 2025. The age distribution of the nation's workers is already shifting as relatively fewer younger people enter the labor force.[42]

The imbalance in the age distribution of the labor force is having a significant effect on employers. Companies are finding that large portions of their workforces are nearing retirement. Beyond the sheer number of employees they will have to replace, managers are concerned that the expertise of these employees is likely to be drained

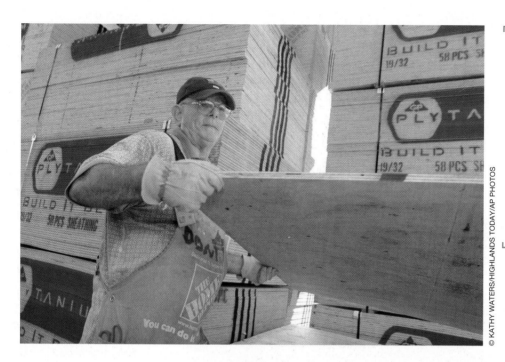

© KATHY WATERS/HIGHLANDS TODAY/AP PHOTOS

Changing demographics throughout the world will bring a more diverse and aging workforce to developed countries. This has major implications for HRM because it alters traditional experience and expectations regarding the labor pool.

too rapidly from the company. As a stopgap measure, employers are making positive efforts to attract older workers, especially those who have taken early retirement. Workers are taking them up on the offer. According to a survey by the AARP, the U.S. advocacy group for people over the age of 50, a solid 80 percent of baby boomers say they expect to work past traditional retirement age. Good health and longer life expectancies play the biggest role in extended work lives. But some retirees have returned to the workforce because of economic needs.

Home Depot, Borders bookstore, AT&T, and Pitney Bowes are among the companies participating in an AARP-sponsored program in an effort to attract older workers. As part of the program, AARP's Web site matches AARP members with corporations looking to hire them. "Whenever our demographics match up with a community, sales are better," says Borders senior vice president of human resources Dan Smith.

Recruiting older workers may sound counterintuitive because they incur higher health care costs. But older workers also have fewer dependents and offer other cost savings. "Our over-50 employee turnover is 10 times less than those under 30," says Smith. "So when you think about the savings you have in training costs, transitions costs, and recruitment costs, you save a lot more on that for the over-50 workers than you do for others."[43]

Like the baby boom, the "echo boom" is also having an effect in the United States. "Echo boomers," or "millennials," are people born roughly between 1977 and 1997. This wave of workers is generally regarded as having a good work ethic and technological know-how. The group is also 80 million people strong, the largest generation ever. (By contrast, there are only 77 million baby boomers in the country.) Similar to the trends with baby boomers, those who constitute this new population bulge are experiencing greater competition for advancement from others of approximately the same age. This situation challenges the ingenuity of managers to develop career patterns for employees to smooth out gaps in the numbers and kinds of workers.[44]

Gender Distribution of the Workforce

Women now constitute over half of the U.S. workforce. Whereas in 1970 only 43 percent of women 16 years and older participated in the labor force, today about 60 percent do. Approximately 71 percent of mothers with school-age children are employed in some capacity. As Figure 1.5 shows, the Bureau of Labor Statistics projects that the number of women joining the U.S. labor force will increase relative to men.[45] The educational attainment of women is also increasing relative to men. Today, three out of every five college graduates are women. Women's wages are increasing comparatively, too. In 1979, on average, women made 62 percent of what men made. Although the gap has not closed, it has narrowed. By 2006, women earned nearly 81 percent of what men made.

FIGURE 1.5

Labor Force and Gender Distributions

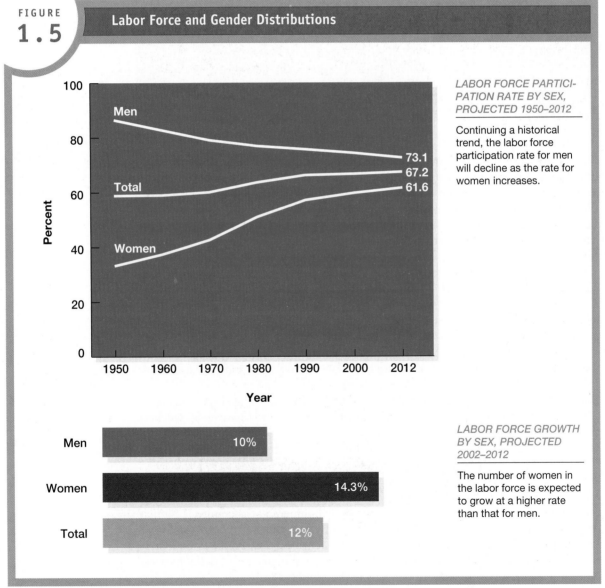

LABOR FORCE PARTICIPATION RATE BY SEX, PROJECTED 1950–2012

Continuing a historical trend, the labor force participation rate for men will decline as the rate for women increases.

LABOR FORCE GROWTH BY SEX, PROJECTED 2002–2012

The number of women in the labor force is expected to grow at a higher rate than that for men.

Source: U.S. Department of Labor.

Employers wanting to attract the talent that women have to offer are taking measures to ensure they are treated equally in the workplace in terms of their advancement opportunities and compensation. In addition, more companies are accommodating working parents by offering them parental leave, part-time employment, flexible work schedules, job sharing, telecommuting, and child and elder care assistance.

Education of the Workforce

Over the years, the educational attainment of the U.S. labor force has risen dramatically.[46] Figure 1.6 shows that it clearly pays to get a college education. Nonetheless, studies by the U.S. Department of Education found that less than half of all high school seniors can handle mathematics problems involving fractions, decimals, percents, elementary geometry, and simple algebra. Between 45 and 50 percent of adults in the United States have only limited reading and writing abilities needed to handle the minimal demands of daily living or job performance. As a result, businesses now spend billions of dollars on basic skills training for their employees. In a speech to the Commonwealth Club of California, David Kearns, the renowned former CEO of Xerox Corporation and ardent education

Using the Internet

The U.S. Department of Labor and U.S. Department of Education Web sites are helpful for providing more information about employment and education. Go to the Student Resources at:

www.cengage.com/
management/bohlander

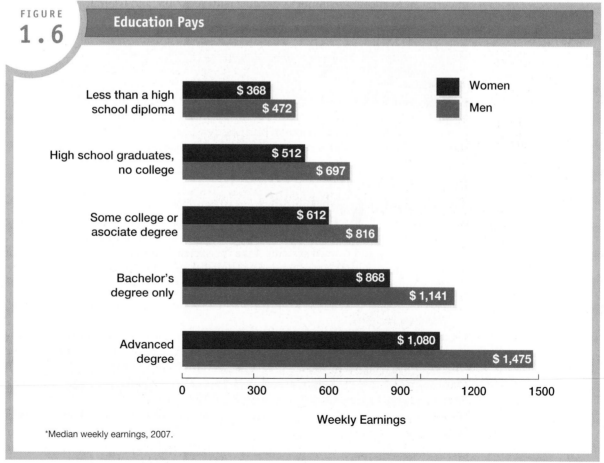

FIGURE 1.6

Education Pays

- Women
- Men

Category	Women	Men
Less than a high school diploma	$368	$472
High school graduates, no college	$512	$697
Some college or asociate degree	$612	$816
Bachelor's degree only	$868	$1,141
Advanced degree	$1,080	$1,475

Weekly Earnings

*Median weekly earnings, 2007.

Source: U.S. Department of Labor.

advocate, said, "The American workforce is in grave jeopardy. We are running out of qualified people. If current demographic and economic trends continue, American business will have to hire a million new workers a year who can't read, write, or count."[47]

It is not just workers with four-year degrees that employers want to hire. Companies are having trouble finding trained and certified workers such as pipe fitters, motorcycle mechanics, and air traffic controllers. As the baby boomer generation retires, the problem will likely worsen. HR departments will have to offer higher compensation packages to attract qualified candidates, and recruiting and selection systems will have to function much more competitively in order to identify talent.

Given the economic downturn and rise in unemployment the United States has experienced recently, this might sound strange. But demographic shifts can, and will, have a huge impact on HR and society. HR managers are interested in these trends because the economy and job market are critical to HR's operations. For example, given that minorities and women have increased their share of the labor force, HR managers frequently analyze how each group is represented in both fast-growing and slow-growing occupations. Women, for example, are fairly well represented in fast-growing occupations such as health services but are also represented in some slow-growth occupations such as secretarial, computer processing, and financial records processing. Blacks and Hispanics have been heavily concentrated in several of the slow-growth and declining groups. Given these data, a number of efforts have been undertaken to encourage minority recruitment, selection, and training.

But these are only the initial efforts to provide an overall environment that values and utilizes a diverse workforce. Managing diversity means being acutely aware of characteristics *common* to employees, while also managing these employees as *individuals*. It means not just tolerating or accommodating all sorts of differences but supporting, nurturing, and utilizing these differences to the organization's advantage.[48] Figure 1.7 summarizes a model for developing a diversity strategy in organizations. While there are important social reasons for including a broader spectrum of workers, there are some essential business reasons as well. Highlights in HRM 4 shows the primary business reasons for diversity management.

managing diversity

Being aware of characteristics common to employees, while also managing employees as individuals

Cultural Changes

The attitudes, beliefs, values, and customs of people in a society are an integral part of their culture. Naturally, their culture affects their behavior on the job and the environment within the organization, influencing their reactions to work assignments, leadership styles, and reward systems. Like the external and internal environments of which it is a part, culture is undergoing continual change. HR policies and procedures therefore must be adjusted to cope with this change.

Employee Rights

Over the past few decades, federal legislation has radically changed the rules for management of employees by granting them many specific rights. Among these are laws granting employees the right to equal employment opportunity (Chapter 3), union representation if they desire it (Chapter 14), a safe and healthful work environment (Chapter 12), pension plans regulated by the government (Chapter 11), equal pay for men and women performing essentially the same job (Chapter 9), and privacy in the workplace. An expanded discussion of the specific areas in which rights and responsibilities are of concern to employers and employees, including the often-cited employment-at-will doctrine, will be presented in Chapter 13.

FIGURE 1.7

Model of Diversity Management Strategy

VALUING DIVERSITY IN THE WORKPLACE

Culture

Organization-wide Image
- Organization fosters mutual respect
- Organization fosters sense of belonging
- Differences are accepted
- Corporate-wide diversity-training program

Concern for Equality
- Equal respect for minority and majority group
- Equal performance expectations for minority and majority group
- Equal rewards for minority and majority group
- Equal pay and income
- Valuing diversity

Opportunity

Career Development
- Promotion of multicultural employees
- Opportunity for development of new skills
- Access to top management positions

Hiring Practices
- Active recruitment and hiring of multicultural employees
- Equal opportunities for minorities
- Affirmative action program

Leadership

Management Practices
- Take all employees seriously
- Recognize the capabilities of all employees
- Support all employees
- Communicate effectively with all employees
- Value a diverse work group
- Respect the cultural beliefs and needs of employees
- Accept non-English-speaking employees

Source: Reprinted by permission of Elsevier from "Managing for Effective Workforce Diversity" by Kathleen Iverson from *The Cornell Hotel and Restaurant Administration Quarterly* 41, no. 2 (April 2000): 31–38.

Concern for Privacy

HR managers and their staffs, as well as line managers in positions of responsibility, generally recognize the importance of discretion in handling all types of information about employees. Since the passage of the federal Privacy Act of 1974, increased attention to privacy has been evident, heightened by the increase in identity theft in recent years. While the Act applies almost exclusively to records maintained by federal agencies, it has drawn attention to the importance of privacy and has led to the passage of additional privacy legislation, including the Health Insurance Portability and Accountability Act of 1996 (HIPAA) and the associated privacy rule issued by the U.S. Department of Health and Human Services, which protects the use and disclosure of personal medical information. Globalization has added another twist to privacy compliance. For example, EU countries prohibit the transfer of personal data to countries with inadequate data protection laws, such as China. In addition to implementing privacy policies, most companies

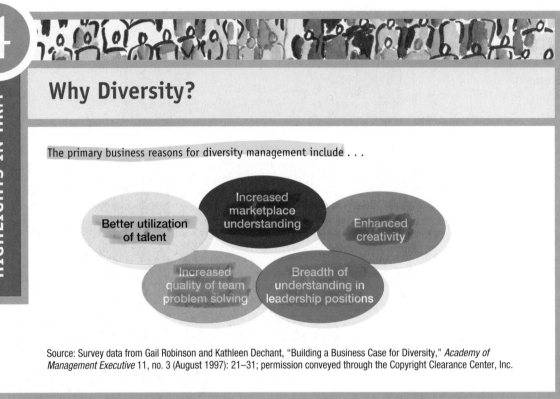

Source: Survey data from Gail Robinson and Kathleen Dechant, "Building a Business Case for Diversity," *Academy of Management Executive* 11, no. 3 (August 1997): 21–31; permission conveyed through the Copyright Clearance Center, Inc.

now try to limit the use of Social Security numbers on time sheets, log-in sheets, and other employment forms. Some companies lock up employee files, conduct background checks on employees who have access to others' files, educate employees in fraud prevention, and contract with outside firms specializing in identity theft.[49]

Although the Electronic Communications Privacy Act of 1986 protects people's electronic communications such as their e-mail, the rules are different when it comes to the privacy that employees can expect with regard to their electronic communications at work. Workers are learning the hard way that their employers have a right to monitor their e-mail and Internet use, for example. The information employees post on the Web—either on social networking sites or on job-hunting sites such as Monster.com—have also become subject to scrutiny by employers. Electronic surveillance in the workplace is also becoming an issue. In Chapter 13, we will discuss the content of privacy programs, along with the privacy employees can expect while on the job, and recommend some privacy guidelines.

Changing Attitudes toward Work

Employees today are less likely to define their personal success only in terms of financial gains. Many employees, especially younger ones, believe satisfaction in life is more likely to result from balancing their work challenges and rewards with those in their personal lives. Though most people still enjoy work and want to excel at it, they tend to be focused on finding interesting work and are more inclined to pursue multiple careers rather than being satisfied with just "having a job." In fact, in a survey of more than 3,000 workers,

86 percent said work fulfillment and work-life balance were their top priorities. Only 35 percent said being successful at work and moving up the ladder were their top priorities. People also appear to be seeking ways of living that are less complicated but more meaningful. These new lifestyles cannot help having an impact on the way employees must be motivated and managed. Consequently, HRM has become more complex than it was when employees were concerned primarily with economic survival.

Balancing Work and Family

Work and the family are connected in many subtle and not-so-subtle social, economic, and psychological ways. Because of the new forms that the family has taken—such as the two-wage-earner and the single-parent family—work organizations are finding it advantageous to provide employees with more family-friendly options. "Family friendly" is a broad term that can include flexible work hours, day care, elder care, part-time work, job sharing, pregnancy leave, parental leave, executive transfers, spousal involvement in career planning, assistance with family problems, and telecommuting. A survey by the HR consulting firm Hewitt Associates found that 31 percent of employers now offer flexible work hours, 46 percent permit job sharing, and 39 percent allow telecommuting. Other companies are exploring the use of four-day workweeks to lessen their employees' commuting costs (particularly with rising gasoline prices).

Companies with programs such as these calculate that accommodating their employees' individual needs and circumstances is a powerful way to attract and retain top-caliber people. Aetna Life and Casualty, for example, cut its turnover by 50 percent after it began offering six-month parental leaves, coupled with an option for part-time work when employees return to the job. Bank of America encourages all its employees to visit their children's schools or volunteer at any school—on company time.[50] With that said, family-friendly companies have to balance the benefits they provide to families versus their single employees. The majority of employees have no children under 18. A Conference Board survey of companies with family-friendly programs found that companies acknowledge that childless employees harbor resentment against employees with children who are able to take advantage of these programs.[51]

THE PARTNERSHIP OF LINE MANAGERS AND HR DEPARTMENTS

We have taken a good deal of time up front in this book to outline today's competitive and social challenges to reinforce the idea that managing people is not something that occurs in a back room called the HR department. Managing people is every manager's business, and successful organizations combine the experience of line managers with the expertise of HR specialists to develop and utilize the talents of employees to their greatest potential. Addressing HR issues is rarely the exclusive responsibility of HR departments acting alone. Instead, HR managers work side by side with line managers to address people-related issues of the organization. While this relationship has not always achieved its ideal, the situation is rapidly improving. HR managers are assuming a greater role in top management planning and decision-making, a trend that reflects the growing awareness among executives that HRM can make important contributions to the success of an organization.

Responsibilities of the Human Resources Manager

Objective 9

Although line managers and HR managers need to work together, their responsibilities are different, as are their competencies and expertise. The major activities for which a HR manager is typically responsible are as follows:

1. *Advice and counsel.* The HR manager often serves as an in-house consultant to supervisors, managers, and executives. Given their knowledge of internal employment issues (policies, labor agreements, past practices, ethics and corporate governance, and the needs of employees) as well as their awareness of external trends (economic and employment data, new legal and regulatory issues, and the like), HR managers can be an invaluable resource for making decisions. For example, larger companies have begun appointing "chief ethics officers" to help their employees wade through gray areas when it comes to right and wrong. The firm's top HR manager is in a good position for this job. In smaller companies, however, this task frequently falls on the shoulders of individual HR managers. These managers need to counsel both employees and executives in this area and areas in which Congress has passed new *corporate governance* laws to prevent, among other things, top executives from abusing their power. (Corporate governance relates to the way rights and responsibilities are shared within corporations, especially between managers and shareholders.) HR managers are also being relied on more heavily to advise compensation committees, which are more closely scrutinizing executives' pay than they have in years past.

2. *Service.* HR managers also perform a host of service activities such as recruiting, selecting, testing, planning and conducting training programs, and hearing employee concerns and complaints. Technical expertise in these areas is essential for HR managers and forms the basis of HR program design and implementation. Moreover, managers must be convinced that the HR staff is there to help them increase their productivity rather than to impose obstacles to their goals. This requires not only the ability on the part of the HR executive to consider problems from the viewpoint of line managers and supervisors, but also skill in communicating with the managers and supervisors.

3. *Policy formulation and implementation.* HR managers generally propose and draft new policies or policy revisions to cover recurring problems or to prevent anticipated problems. Ordinarily, these are proposed to the senior executives of the organization, who actually issue the policies. HR managers may monitor performance of line departments and other staff departments to ensure conformity with established HR policies, procedures, and practices. Perhaps more important, they are a resource to whom managers can turn for policy interpretation.

4. *Employee advocacy.* One of the enduring roles of HR managers is to serve as an employee advocate—listening to employees' concerns and representing their needs to managers—to make certain that the interests of employees and the interests of the organization are aligned with one another. Effective employee relations provides a support structure when disruptive changes interfere with workers' normal daily activities.

In the process of managing human resources, increasing attention is being given to the personal needs of the participants. Thus throughout this book, we will not only emphasize the importance of the contributions that HRM makes to the organization, but also give serious consideration to its effects on the individual and on society. This is important because employees and the public at large are demanding that employers demonstrate greater social responsibility in terms of managing their human resources. Complaints that job stress is devitalizing the lives and injuring the health of employees are not uncommon. Charges of discrimination against women, minorities, the physically and mentally disabled, and the elderly with respect to hiring, training, advancement, and compensation are being leveled against some employers. Issues such as comparable pay for comparable work, living wages, the high cost of health benefits, day care for the children of employees, elder care for their parents, and alternative work schedules are concerns that many employers must address as their workforces grow more diverse. All employers are finding that privacy and confidentiality of information about employees are serious matters and deserve the greatest protection that can be provided.

Formal change management programs help to keep employees focused on the success of the business.

© STOCKBYTE GOLD/GETTY IMAGES

Where employees are organized into unions (covered in Chapter 14), employers can encounter costly collective bargaining proposals, threats of strike, and charges of unfair labor practices. Court litigation, demands for corrective action by governmental agencies, sizable damage awards in response to employee lawsuits, and attempts to erode the employment-at-will doctrine valued by employers are still other hazards that contemporary employers must try to avoid. (We will discuss these issues in detail in Chapter 13.) Good managers recognize the contributions that their HR departments make to their organizations. These managers expect HR personnel to assume a broader role in the overall strategy of their organizations.

Competencies of the Human Resources Manager

As top executives expect HR managers to assume a broader role in overall organizational strategy, many of these managers will need to acquire a complementary set of competencies. These competencies are summarized here and shown graphically in Figure 1.8.

1. *Business mastery.* HR professionals need to know the business of their organization thoroughly. This requires an understanding of its economic and financial capabilities so that they can become a key member of the team of business managers in order to develop the firm's strategic direction. It also requires that HR professionals develop skills at external relations focused on their customers.

2. *HR mastery.* HR professionals are the organization's behavioral science experts. HR professionals should develop expert knowledge in the areas of staffing, development, appraisals, rewards, team building, and communication.

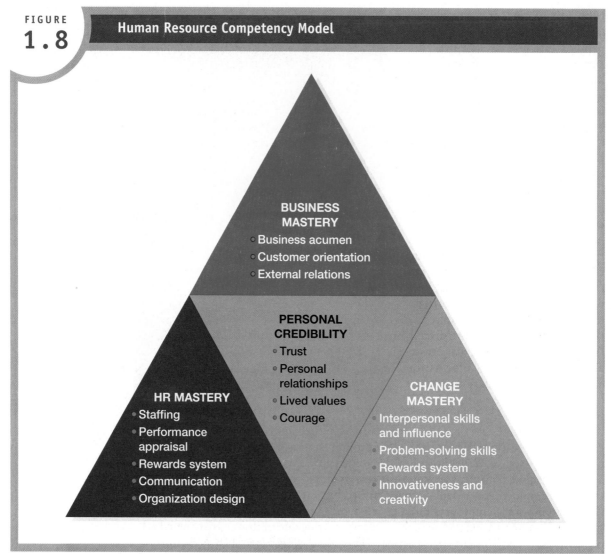

FIGURE
1.8

Human Resource Competency Model

Source: Arthur Yeung, Wayne Brockbank, and Dave Ulrich, "Lower Cost, Higher Value: Human Resource Function in Transformation." Reprinted with permission from *Human Resource Planning*, Vol. 17, No. 3 (1994). Copyright 1994 by The Human Resource Planning Society, 317 Madison Avenue, Suite 1509, New York, NY 10017, Phone: (212) 490-6387, Fax: (212) 682-6851.

3. *Change mastery.* HR professionals have to be able to manage change processes so that their firms' HR activities are effectively merged with the business needs of their organizations. This involves interpersonal and problem-solving skills, as well as innovativeness and creativity.

4. *Personal credibility.* Like other management professionals, HR professionals must establish personal credibility in the eyes of their internal and external customers. Credibility and trust are earned by developing personal relationships with one's customers, demonstrating the values of the firm, standing up for one's own beliefs, and being fair-minded when dealing with others. Highlights in HRM 5 outlines the code of ethics HR professionals should follow, according to the Society for Human Resource Management.

HIGHLIGHTS IN HRM

SHRM Code of Ethical and Professional Standards in Human Resource Management

Society for Human Resource Management
CODE PROVISIONS

Professional Responsibility
Core Principle

As HR professionals, we are responsible for adding value to the organizations we serve and contributing to the ethical success of those organizations. We accept professional responsibility for our individual decisions and actions. We are also advocates for the profession by engaging in activities that enhance its credibility and value.

Intent

- To build respect, credibility and strategic importance for the HR profession within our organizations, the business community, and the communities in which we work.
- To assist the organizations we serve in achieving their objectives and goals.
- To inform and educate current and future practitioners, the organizations we serve, and the general public about principles and practices that help the profession.
- To positively influence workplace and recruitment practices.
- To encourage professional decision-making and responsibility.
- To encourage social responsibility.

Guidelines

1. Adhere to the highest standards of ethical and professional behavior.
2. Measure the effectiveness of HR in contributing to or achieving organizational goals.
3. Comply with the law.
4. Work consistent with the values of the profession.
5. Strive to achieve the highest levels of service, performance and social responsibility.
6. Advocate for the appropriate use and appreciation of human beings as employees.
7. Advocate openly and within the established forums for debate in order to influence decision-making and results.

Professional Development
Core Principle

As professionals we must strive to meet the highest standards of competence and commit to strengthen our competencies on a continuous basis.

(continued)

SHRM Code of Ethical and Professional Standards in Human Resource Management (continued)

Intent

- To expand our knowledge of human resource management to further our understanding of how our organizations function.
- To advance our understanding of how organizations work ("the business of the business").

Guidelines

1. Pursue formal academic opportunities.
2. Commit to continuous learning, skills development and application of new knowledge related to both human resource management and the organizations we serve.
3. Contribute to the body of knowledge, the evolution of the profession and the growth of individuals through teaching, research and dissemination of knowledge.
4. Pursue certification such as CCP, CEBS, PHR, SPHR, etc. where available, or comparable measures of competencies and knowledge.

Ethical Leadership
Core Principle

HR professionals are expected to exhibit individual leadership as a role model for maintaining the highest standards of ethical conduct.

Intent

- To set the standard and be an example for others.
- To earn individual respect and increase our credibility with those we serve.

Guidelines

1. Be ethical; act ethically in every professional interaction.
2. Question pending individual and group actions when necessary to ensure that decisions are ethical and are implemented in an ethical manner.
3. Seek expert guidance if ever in doubt about the ethical propriety of a situation.
4. Through teaching and mentoring, champion the development of others as ethical leaders in the profession and in organizations.

Fairness and Justice
Core Principle

As human resource professionals, we are ethically responsible for promoting and fostering fairness and justice for all employees and their organizations.

SHRM Code of Ethical and Professional Standards in Human Resource Management (continued)

Intent

To create and sustain an environment that encourages all individuals and the organization to reach their fullest potential in a positive and productive manner.

Guidelines

1. Respect the uniqueness and intrinsic worth of every individual.
2. Treat people with dignity, respect and compassion to foster a trusting work environment free of harassment, intimidation, and unlawful discrimination.
3. Ensure that everyone has the opportunity to develop their skills and new competencies.
4. Assure an environment of inclusiveness and a commitment to diversity in the organizations we serve.
5. Develop, administer and advocate policies and procedures that foster fair, consistent and equitable treatment for all.
6. Regardless of personal interests, support decisions made by our organizations that are both ethical and legal.
7. Act in a responsible manner and practice sound management in the country(ies) in which the organizations we serve operate.

Conflicts of Interest
Core Principle

As HR professionals, we must maintain a high level of trust with our stakeholders. We must protect the interests of our stakeholders as well as our professional integrity and should not engage in activities that create actual, apparent or potential conflicts of interest.

Intent

To avoid activities that are in conflict or may appear to be in conflict with any of the provisions of this Code of Ethical and Professional Standards in Human Resource Management or with one's responsibilities and duties as a member of the human resource profession and/or as an employee of any organization.

Guidelines

1. Adhere to and advocate the use of published policies on conflicts of interest within your organization.
2. Refrain from using your position for personal, material or financial gain or the appearance of such.
3. Refrain from giving or seeking preferential treatment in the human resources processes.
4. Prioritize your obligations to identify conflicts of interest or the appearance thereof; when conflicts arise, disclose them to relevant stakeholders.

(continued)

SHRM Code of Ethical and Professional Standards in Human Resource Management (continued)

Use of Information
Core Principle
HR professionals consider and protect the rights of individuals, especially in the acquisition and dissemination of information while ensuring truthful communications and facilitating informed decision-making.

Intent
To build trust among all organization constituents by maximizing the open exchange of information, while eliminating anxieties about inappropriate and/or inaccurate acquisition and sharing of information.

Guidelines
1. Acquire and disseminate information through ethical and responsible means.
2. Ensure only appropriate information is used in decisions affecting the employment relationship.
3. Investigate the accuracy and source of information before allowing it to be used in employment related decisions.
4. Maintain current and accurate HR information.
5. Safeguard restricted or confidential information.
6. Take appropriate steps to ensure the accuracy and completeness of all communicated information about HR policies and practices.
7. Take appropriate steps to ensure the accuracy and completeness of all communicated information used in HR-related training.

Good HR managers help their organizations build a sustained competitive advantage. That is why forward-looking CEOs such as Herb Kelleher, the legendary founder of Southwest Airlines, Howard Schultz at Starbucks, and Jeff Immelt at GE make certain that their top HR executives report directly to them and help them address key issues. At lower levels in the organization, a rapidly growing number of companies, including Ford, Intel, and United Technologies, are assigning HR representatives to their core business teams to make certain that HR issues are addressed on the job and that their HR representatives, in turn, are knowledgeable about core business issues rather than simply focusing on employee-related administrative functions.

Role of the Line Manager

As much as we might say about the role of the HR department, in the final analysis managing people depends on effective supervisors and line managers. As one executive at Merck put it, "Human resources are far too important to be left to the personnel department." Although HR managers have the responsibility for coordinating programs and policies pertaining to people-related issues, managers and employees themselves are ultimately responsible for performing these functions.

We understand that most readers of this book will be line managers and supervisors, rather than HR specialists. The text is, therefore, oriented to *helping people manage people more effectively*, whether they become first-line supervisors or chief executive officers. Students now preparing for careers in organizations will find that the study of HRM provides a background that will be valuable in managerial and supervisory positions. Discussions concerning the role of the HR department can provide a better understanding of the functions performed by this group. Becoming familiar with the role HR managers play should help facilitate closer cooperation between the different departments of firms and enable line and executive-level managers to fully utilize the assistance and services offered by their HR groups.

SUMMARY

Objective 1 People have always been central to organizations, but their strategic importance is growing in today's knowledge-based world. An organization's success increasingly depends on the knowledge, skills, and abilities of its employees.

Objective 2 Globalization influences approximately 70 to 85 percent of the U.S. economy and affects the free flow of trade among countries. This influences the number and kinds of jobs that are available and requires that organizations balance a complicated set of issues related to managing people working under different business conditions in different geographies, cultures, and legal environments. HR functions such as staffing, training, compensation, and the like have to be adjusted to take into account these differences.

Objective 3 Advanced technology has tended to reduce the number of jobs that require little skill and to increase the number of jobs that require considerable skill, a shift we refer to as moving from touch labor to knowledge work. This displaces some employees and requires

that others be retrained. In addition, information technology has influenced HRM through human resources information systems (HRIS) that streamline HR processes, make information more readily available to managers and employees, and enable HR departments to focus on the firm's strategies.

Objective 4 Both proactive and reactive change initiatives require HR managers to work with line managers and executives to create a vision for the future, establish an architecture that enables change, and communicate with employees about the processes of change.

Objective 5 In order to "compete through people," organizations have to do a good job of managing human capital: the knowledge, skills, and capabilities that have value to organizations. Managers must develop strategies for identifying, recruiting, and hiring the best talent available; developing these employees in ways that are firm-specific; helping them to generate new ideas and generalize them through the company; encouraging information sharing; and rewarding collaboration and teamwork.

Objective 6 In order to respond to customer needs better, faster, and more cheaply, organizations have instituted total quality management (TQM) and reengineering programs. Each of these programs requires that HR be involved in changing work processes, training, job design, compensation, and the like. HR issues also arise when communicating with employees about the new work systems, just as with any change initiative. Better business thinking builds more strategic HR thinking.

Objective 7 In order to contain costs, organizations have been downsizing, outsourcing, offshoring, and leasing employees and enhancing productivity. HR's role is to maintain the relationship between a company and its employees while implementing the changes.

Objective 8 The workforce is becoming increasingly diverse, and organizations are doing more to address employee concerns and to maximize the benefit of different kinds of employees. Demographic changes, social and cultural differences, and changing attitudes toward work can provide a rich source of variety for organizations. But to benefit from diversity, managers need to recognize the potential concerns of employees and make certain that the exchange between the organization and employees is mutually beneficial.

Objective 9 In working with line managers to address their organization's challenges, HR managers play a number of important roles; they are called on for advice and ethics counsel, various service activities, policy formulation and implementation, and employee advocacy. To perform these roles effectively, HR managers must contribute business competencies, state-of-the-art HR competencies, and change management competencies. Ultimately, managing people is rarely the exclusive responsibility of the HR function. Every manager's job involves managing people. Consequently, successful companies combine the expertise of HR specialists with the experience of line managers to develop and utilize the talents of employees to their greatest potential.

KEY TERMS

corporate social responsibility
downsizing
employee leasing
globalization
human capital
human resources information system (HRIS)

human resources management (HRM)
knowledge workers
managing diversity
offshoring
outsourcing
proactive change

reactive change
reengineering
Six Sigma
total quality management (TQM)

DISCUSSION QUESTIONS

Objective 1

1. Are people always an organization's most valuable asset? Why or why not?

Objective 2

2. Suppose your boss asked you to summarize the major people-related concerns related to opening an office in China. What issues would be on your list?

Objective 3

3. Will technology eliminate the need for human resources managers?

Objective 4

4. What are the pros and cons of change? Does it help or hurt the performance of organizations? Do you personally like change? Why or why not?

Objective 5

5. Can you think of a situation in which, if a particular person left an organization, the organization's expertise would drop rapidly?

Objective 6

6. Someone once said that TQM "is like paving cow paths." What do you suppose this means in relation to reengineering?

Objective 7

7. Do cost-containment pressures work against the effective management of people? Why or why not?

Objective 8

8. What are the pros and cons of having a more diverse workforce? Is the United States in a better position to compete globally because of its diverse population?

Objective 9

9. In your opinion, what is the most important role HR managers play?

BIZFLIX EXERCISES

Babe: **Herding Sheep, Babe's Way**

This chapter's introduction to human resources management emphasized its role in helping managers bring together different types of people to reach a common purpose. An earlier chapter section, "Demographic and Employee Concerns," highlighted those differences. Watch this scene from *Babe* while recalling those discussions.

Babe is a charming Australian film featuring eccentric, quiet Farmer Hoggett (James Cromwell), who trains a pig he won at the fair to herd his sheep. His eccentricity turns to determination when he enters the pig in the Australian National Sheepdog Championships.

The Academy Award–winning visual effects include a seamless mixture of animatronic doubles, computer images, and live animals.

This scene comes from the "A Pig That Thinks It's a Dog" segment that appears about 40 minutes into the film. Farmer Hoggett's sheepdogs, Rex (voiced by Hugo Weaving) and Fly (voiced by Miriam Margolyes), along with Babe (voiced by Christine Cavanaugh) the pig, accompany him to his sheep herd. Hoggett needs to gather the sheep into a pen so he can shear their wool. Before leaving for the pasture, Farmer Hoggett saw Babe carefully divide some chickens into two groups based on their color. Hoggett suspects that perhaps Babe has some herding skills.

What to Watch for and Ask Yourself

- Are Babe's methods of herding sheep different from those used by the sheepdogs? If yes, what are the differences?

- Does Babe discover that he cannot successfully herd sheep as a sheepdog herds them? What does he do?

- Does Farmer Hoggett accept Babe for what he is—a pig, not a sheepdog?

HRM EXPERIENCE

Balancing Competitive Challenges and Employee Concerns

Human resources management is not just the responsibility of the personnel department. If people are a competitive resource, then line managers play an increasingly important role in managing the workforce. But this is not an either/or situation. Rather than seeing line managers assume the responsibilities of HR managers, we see both groups working together to handle workforce issues. But how exactly do these two groups work together?

Assignment

1. Working in teams of four to six individuals, identify what role the HR department would play in terms of the following activities and what role line managers would play. Where would overlaps occur, and would there be any likely problems?
   a. Recruiting and selection
   b. Training and development
   c. Compensation
   d. Performance evaluation
   e. Labor relations
2. How would potential problems be resolved?
3. Write the groups' findings on flip charts and post for all to see. One member from each team should explain his or her findings to all class members.
4. Point out the similarities and differences across the teams. Save these points and revisit them—possibly revising them—as you study subsequent chapters in this textbook.

CASE STUDY 1

The Global Management Consulting Firm Accenture Brings Employees Face to Face

A team of Filipino IT professionals is responsible for creating Accenture's own social networking tool that allows collaboration among the company's workers worldwide. Aptly called Accenture People, it resembles popular social networking sites, much like Facebook, and allows employees to create their own profiles. But more than a listing of hobbies and other personal interests, these profiles provide a glimpse of each employee's role in Accenture, including technical expertise and the projects in which he or she was involved.

For a global company with numerous business units like Accenture, the idea is to simply make everyone more familiar with each other's background and then encourage knowledge sharing. In the Philippines alone, Accenture has around 15,000 workers doing management consulting, system integration, and BPO (business process outsourcing). In terms of size, the Philippines is behind only to the United States and India in Accenture's global network. "One of the challenges for us is collaboration," said Michael Duff, project manager for Accenture Philippines, who leads a six-person team that developed Accenture People. "Different teams within Accenture have been using tools before that allow people to share knowledge on projects. This time, we put everything into a single system," added Duff, who has been with Accenture for more than eight years.

The idea for a Web-based tool like Accenture People resulted from a leadership development program held in the United States. Since a local team was responsible for some of Accenture's presence on the Internet—including the main Accenture Web page and Accenture Careers—the task of building a social networking tool fell to Duff's team. Accenture People was launched only last December, but Duff estimates about one-third of Accenture's entire global workforce of about 175,000 people have already created profiles. That includes Accenture's chairman and CEO Bill Green.

Duff recalls an instance when someone working for Accenture in London got in touch with him and asked for his help on a particular technology both were using. Like Friendster or MySpace, employees can create blogs and participate in discussion forums—usually best practices and "tips and tricks" on tasks such as programming code, according to Duff—to ask for help on certain projects. For less technical matters, the search button alone makes for a very useful tool for Annbel Tierro, who heads Accenture's system integration unit in the Philippines.

"I get to do a lot of conference calls in a day. It helps to at least have an idea what the person I am talking to looks like or what his or her interests are," said Tierro. "We have speakers who regularly come here, so even before they arrive, at least I am already familiar with their roles and achievements in the company."

Questions

1. How does the Accenture People site help Accenture better serve its customers?
2. How successful do you think Accenture will be at getting its employees to create their profiles?
3. Can you see any drawbacks related to employees creating their own profiles?

Source: Reprinted from Lawrence Casiraya, "Filipino Team Builds Accenture's Internal 'Facebook,'" *Inquirer.net* (February 14, 2008).

CASE STUDY 2

Florida Company Fastens Its Sights on Global Growth

When Robert Kilbey began selling medical supplies out of his twenty-four-foot Airstream trailer in the early 1960s, he came upon a brilliant idea: make the braces and wraps with a new sort of closure—Velcro fasteners—instead of the common laces and hooks-and-eyes. The new hook-and-loop fastener, invented in the early 1940s and now used on everything from automobiles to footwear, caught on with the medical world. Kilbey moved Professional Products, Inc. from his base in Miami to DeFuniak Springs, Florida, where it quietly has become one of Walton County's largest and most stable employers. Forty-two years later his son, Bryan Kilbey, is expanding the company and taking it international. "We will build a new 100,000 square foot building this year," the company's CEO said. "And we are going to open a new sales office for the European market."

"From order to shipping, we can fill an order in 4½ hours," Kilbey said. "These are often specific requests from doctors who like a piece of equipment to work a certain way. So we don't have a lot of inventory." Instead, as general manager Dean Stanton says, the company is vertical in its operations, designing and making most of its own components.

"We make our own elastic," Kilbey said. "We have the thread, the rubber, and we make our own." He said new technology and equipment will be used to streamline production. Some work will be outsourced to other countries, possibly Mexico and Honduras. That decision has not been made. But no jobs will disappear.

"We have never laid off anyone," Kilbey said. "We have worked short weeks, although we haven't done that in 15 years. But we have kept our people." Neither does he go into panic-hiring mode and add employees at crunch time.

"These are highly skilled jobs," Stanton said. "We can't just go out and hire anyone." Stanton said, "We will cross-train people to do other jobs," when some work moves to possibly Mexico, Honduras, and other countries.

Questions

1. How would you describe Professional Products' growth strategy?
2. Why would Professional Products commit to no layoffs in its expansion? Is this a positive move, or could it be detrimental to the company?
3. In addition to training employees for other jobs, what other HR strategies might the firm employ to maintain its relationship with its domestic employees?

Source: Excerpted from Fraser, Morris, "DeFuniak Springs Company Fastens Its Sight on Growth," *Northwest Florida (Fort Walton Beach) Daily News* (via Knight-Ridder/Tribune Business News), March 7, 2005.

NOTES AND REFERENCES

1. Edward L. Gubman, *The Talent Solution: Aligning Strategy and People to Achieve Extraordinary Results* (New York: McGraw-Hill Professional Publishing, 1998).

2. "Retiring Workforce, Widening Skills Gap, Exodus of 'Critical Talent' Threaten Companies: Deloitte Survey," *Canadian Corporate News* (February 15, 2005); "The Importance of HR," *HRFocus* 73, no. 3 (March 1996): 14.

3. T. J. Watson, Jr., *A Business and Its Beliefs: The Ideas That Helped Build IBM* (New York: McGraw-Hill, 1963).

4. "Overall U.S. Trade Deficit Declined in 2007," *Associated Press* (February 14, 2008).

5. "U.S. Firms Extend Global Reach," *Workforce Management* 83, no. 13 (December 1, 2004): 138; Susan Meisinger, "Going Global: A Smart Move for HR Professionals," *HRMagazine* 49, no. 3 (March 2004): 6; "In Bev Flattens SAB Miller," *The New York Times* (June 13, 2003).

6. World Trade Organization, *World Trade Report, 2007* (Geneva: WTO Publications): 34; "One Ninth of All U.S. Production Is for Export," *PPI Trade Fact of the Week* (March 19, 2008).

7. Nancy R. Lockwood, "Corporate Social Responsibility: HR's Leadership Role," *HRMagazine* 49, no. 2 (December 2004): S1–11.

8. "China Engineers Next Great Leap with Wave of 'Knowledge Workers,'" *Milwaukee Journal Sentinel* (via Knight-Ridder/Tribune News Service), December 31, 2003; "Edward Yourdon's New Book Helps 'Knowledge Workers' Put Emotion Aside to Look at the Facts of the New Economic Reality," *PR Newswire* (October 4, 2004); Marshall Goldsmith, "Supervisors of the Smart," *BRW* 30, no. 20 (May 22, 2008): 57–57.

9. Ben Worthen, "Measuring the ROI of Training," *CIO* 14, no. 9 (February 15, 2001): 128–36; Hashi Syedain, "Out of this World," *People Management* 14, no. 8 (April 17, 2008): 20–24.

10. Scott A. Snell, Donna Stueber, and David P. Lepak, "Virtual HR Departments:

Getting Out of the Middle," in R. L. Heneman and D. B. Greenberger (eds.), *Human Resource Management in Virtual Organizations* (Columbus, OH: Information Age Publishing, 2002); Samuel Greengard, "How to Fulfill Technology's Promise," *Workforce* (February 1999): *HR Software Insights* supplement, 10–18.

11. Drew Robb, "Building a Better Workforce: Performance Management Software Can Help You Identify and Develop High-Performing Workers," *HRMagazine* 49, no. 10 (October 2004): 86–92.

12. Robb, "Building a Better Workforce," 86–92; "How to Implement an Effective Process for a New HR Management System," *HRFocus* (January 2005): 3–4; "New Study Finds HRIS Key to Reducing Costs," *Payroll Managers Report* 7, no. 5 (May 2007): 13.

13. Bruce Shutan, "HRMS Flexibility Unlocks Secret to Success," *Employee Benefits* (August 1, 2004); "New Study Finds HRIS Key to Reducing Costs," *Payroll Managers Report* 7, no. 5 (May 2007): 13.

14. John P. Kotter, "Ten Observations," *Executive Excellence* 16, no. 8 (1999): 15–16.

15. "Lessons from Industry about Managing Change," *Seybold Report: Analyzing Publishing Technologies* 8, no. 10 (May 10, 2008): 10.

16. Jennifer J. Laabs, "Change," *Personnel Journal* (July 1996): 54–63; Louisa Peacock, "Change Management Is Biggest Challenge," *Personnel Today* (February 12, 2008): 47–47.

17. Edward E. Lawler III, Alec Levenson, and John W. Boudreau, "HR Metrics and Analytics: Use and Impact," *Human Resource Planning* 27, no. 4 (December 2004): 27–36; Louisa Peacock, "Change Management Is Biggest Challenge," *Personnel Today* (February 12, 2008): 47; Kotter, J.P. 1995. "Leading change: Why transformation efforts fail," *Harvard Business Review* (March/April): 59–67.

18. Lee G. Bolman and Terry E. Deal, "Four Steps to Keeping Change Efforts Heading

in the Right Direction," *Journal of Quality and Participation* 22, no. 3 (May/June 1999): 6–11; "Coaching Employees through the Six Stages of Change," *HRFocus* 79, no. 5 (May 2002): 9; Stefan Stern, "Forever Changing," *Management Today* (February 7, 2005): 40; Dennis Smillie, "Managing Change, Maximizing Technology," *Multi-Housing News* 40, no. 1 (January 2005): 4.

19. Donald C. Busi, "Assignment Reviews (ARs): Moving toward Measuring Your Most Valuable Asset," *Supervision* 66, no. 1 (January 2005): 3–7.

20. David Lepak and Scott Snell. 2003. "Managing the human resource architecture for knowledge-based competition." In S. Jackson, M. Hitt, and A. DeNisi (eds.), *Managing knowledge for sustained competitive advantage: Designing strategies for effective Human Resource Management*. (SIOP Scientific Frontiers Series, 127–154); David Lepak and Scott Snell, "Examining the Human Resource Architecture: The Relationship among Human Capital, Employment, and Human Resource Configurations," *Journal of Management* 28, no. 4 (2002): 517–543; Steve Bates, "Study Links HR Practices with the Bottom Line," *HRMagazine* 46, no. 12 (December 2001): 14; Ann Pomeroy, "Cooking Up Innovation: When It Comes to Helping Employees Create New Products and Services, HR's Efforts Are a Key Ingredient," *HRMagazine* 49, no. 11 (November 2004): 46–54.

21. Gary S. Becker, *Human Capital* (New York: Columbia University Press, 1964); Charles A. O'Reilly III and Jeffrey Pfeffer, "Cisco Systems: Acquiring and Retaining Talent in Hypercompetitive Markets," *Human Resource Planning* 23, no. 3 (2000): 38–52.

22. For more on Buckman Labs and their approach to managing human capital, visit their Web site at http://www.buckman.com. The company is also well known for its knowledge management initiatives, called Knowledge Nurture, as well as its knowledge management system, called K'Netix; see http://www.knowledge-nurture.com.

23. Dave Ulrich, Steve Kerr, and Ron Ashkenas, *The GE Work-Out: How to Implement GE's Revolutionary Method for Busting Bureaucracy & Attacking Organizational Problems* (New York: McGraw-Hill Professional Publishing, 2002).

24. Benoit Guay, "Knowledge Management Is a Team Sport," *Computing Canada* 27, no. 3 (July 13, 2001): 23; Pimm Fox, "Making Support Pay," *Computerworld* 36, no. 11 (March 11, 2002): 28; "Visions of the Future," *Human Resources* (January 2008): 22.

25. C. W. Russ Russo, "Ten Steps to a Baldrige Award Application," *Quality Progress* 34, no. 8 (August 2001): 49–56; "Nonprofits Aim to Apply for Baldrige Award," *Quality* 43, no. 11 (November 2004): 11–13.

26. The term *Six Sigma* is a registered trademark of Motorola. It is based on the Greek letter sigma, used as a symbol of variation in a process (the standard deviation). For more information, see Peter S. Pande, Robert P. Neuman, and Roland R. Cavanagh, *The Six Sigma Way: How GE, Motorola, and Other Top Companies Are Honing Their Performance* (New York: McGraw-Hill, 2000).

27. Joseph A. Defeo, "Six Sigma: Road Map for Survival," *HRFocus* 76, no. 7 (July 1999): 11–12; Michele V. Gee and Paul C. Nystrom, "Strategic Fit between Skills Training and Levels of Quality Management: An Empirical Study of American Manufacturing Plants," *Human Resource Planning* 22, no. 2 (1999): 12–23; Linda Heruing, "Six Sigma in Sight," *HRMagazine* 49, no. 3 (March 2004): 76–81; Paul Teague, "A Take-Charge Approach Worth Imitating," *Purchasing* 136, no. 11 (August, 16 2007): 14.

28. Ed Gubman, "HR Strategy and Planning: From Birth to Business Results," *Human Resource Planning* 27, no. 1 (March 2004): 13–21.

29. M. Hammer and J. Champy, *Reengineering the Corporation* (New York: HarperCollins, 1994). See also Michael Hammer, *Beyond Reengineering: How the Process-Centered Organization Is Changing Our Work and Our Lives* (New York: HarperBusiness, 1996); William M. James, "Best HR Practices for Today's Innovation Management," *Research-Technology Management* 45, no. 1 (January–February 2002): 57–61.

30. "Up to Speed: L. L. Bean Moves Employees as Workloads Shift," *Chief Executive* (July–August 1996): 15; Darrell Rigby, "Look before You Lay Off," *Harvard Business Review* 80, no. 4 (April 2002): 20–21.

31. "WorldatWork Finds One-Third of Companies Downsized after 9/11," *Report on Salary Surveys* (December 2002): 2; Jeanne Whalen, "Glaxo Is Eliminating R&D Jobs as Part of Cost-Cutting Plan," *Wall Street Journal* 251, no. 137 (June 12, 2008).

32. Stephanie Armour, "Some Companies Choose No-Layoff Policy," *USA Today*, December 17, 2001, B-1; Gene Koretz, "Hire Math: Fire 3, Add 5," *Business Week Online* (March 13, 2000); Michelle Conlin, "Where Layoffs Are a Last Resort," *Business Week Online* (October 8, 2001); Lynn Miller, "Downsizing Trend Brings New Change to HR Directors," *HRMagazine* 45, no. 1 (January 2001); Norman E. Amundson, William A. Borgen, Sharalyn Jordan, and Anne C. Erlebach, "Survivors of Downsizing: Helpful and Hindering Experiences," *Career Development Quarterly* 52, no. 3 (March 2004): 256–72.

33. Gubman, "HR Strategy and Planning," 13–21.

34. Gubman, "HR Strategy and Planning," 13–21; Thomas W. Gainey, Brian S. Klaas, and Darla Moore, "Outsourcing the Training Function: Results from the Field," *Human Resource Planning* 25, no. 1 (2002): 16–23, 873, 881; Denise Pelham, "Is It Time to Outsource HR?" *Training* 39, no. 4 (April 2002): 50–52; Tom Anderson, "HR Outsourcing Expected to Surge this Year," *Employee Benefit News* (February 1, 2005); Jessica Marquez, "More Piecemeal Approach to HRO Emerging," *Workforce Management*, 87, no. 8 (May 5, 2008): 10.

35. Karyn Siobhan Robinson, "HR Needs Large Role in Offshoring," *HRMagazine* 590, no. 45 (May 2004): 30–32; Nick Heath, "Global Outsourcing to Grow in 2008," *BusinessWeek* (January 10, 2008).

36. Pete Engardio, Michael Arndt, and Dean Foust, "The Future of Outsourcing," *BusinessWeek* (January 30, 2006).

37. Pam Babcock, "America's Newest Export: White-Collar Jobs," *HRMagazine* 49, no. 4 (April 2004): 50–54.

38. Elliot Spagat, "Procter & Gamble to Outsource about 80% of Back-Office Work," *The Wall Street Journal Online* (June 14, 2002); "Outsourcing HR," *Industry Week* 249, no. 10 (May 15, 2000): 71; Carolyn Hirschman, "For PEOs, Business Is Booming," *HRMagazine* 45, no. 2 (February 2000): 42–47; Brian Klaas, "Trust and the Role of Professional Employer Organizations: Managing HR in Small and Medium Enterprises," *Journal of Managerial Issues* 14, no. 1 (Spring 2002): 31–49; Chris Pentilla, "Got It Covered: If You Can't Afford to Offer Employee Benefits on Your Own, Why Not Join Forces with a PEO?" *Entrepreneur* 32, no. 2 (February 2004): 66–68; Milan Yager, "Outsource to Gain Human Resources Expertise," *Hotel & Motel Management* 223, no. 7 (April 21, 2008): 14.

39. Patrick Barta and Andrew Caffrey, "Productivity Leap Shows Potential of U.S. Economy—Rise at 8.6 Percent Pace, Positive for Profits, Doesn't Bode Very Well for Employment," *The Wall Street Journal*, May 8, 2002, A1; Jon E. Hilsenrath, "The Economy: Big U.S. Service Sectors Boosted Late 1990s Surge in Productivity," *The Wall Street Journal*, April 22, 2002, A2; Karen Lowry Miller, "Economy: Out of Steam—A Dip in U.S. Productivity Provokes Anxious Questions," *Newsweek International* (February 21, 2005): 34; Milan Yager, "Outsource to Gain Human Resources Expertise," *Hotel & Motel Management* 223, no. 7 (April 21, 2008): 14.

40. Mitra Tooss, "Labor Force Projections to 2012: The Graying of the U.S. Workforce," *The U.S. Department of Labor's Bureau of Labor Statistics* 127 (February 2004); Kim L. Hunter, "A Changing Work Force: Why Business—and the PR Profession—Needs More Diversity in Its Ranks," *Public Relations Tactics* 14, no. 7 (July 2007): 13.

41. Irwin Speizer, "Diversity on the Menu: Rachelle Hood, Denny's Chief Diversity Officer, Has Boosted the Company's Image. But That Hasn't Sold More Breakfasts," *Workforce Management* 83, no. 12 (November 1, 2004): 41; Patrick Purcell, "Older Workers: Employment and Retirement Trends," *Journal of Pension*

Planning & Compliance 34, no. 1 (Spring 2008): 32–48.

42. The U.S. Department of Labor's Bureau of Labor Statistics keeps up-to-date projections and percentages in these categories. Interested readers can access this information at http://www.bls.gov.

43. "Work Force Reflects How Much Gray Matters," *The Kansas City Star* (via Knight-Ridder/Tribune Business News), March 6, 2005; Kevin G. Hall, "Age-Old Dilemma," *Fort Worth Star-Telegram* (via Knight-Ridder/Tribune News Service), March 7, 2005, C3–C4; Milan Yager, "A Workforce That Doesn't Retire," *Accounting Today* 22, no. 6 (March 31, 2008): 26–27; Mark L. Alch, "Get Ready for a New Type of Worker in the Workplace: The Net Generation," *Supervision* 69, no. 6 (June 2008): 18–21.

44. Bureau of Labor Statistics, *Women in the Labor Force: A Databook* (2007 Edition).

45. The U.S. Department of Labor's Bureau of Labor Statistics keeps up-to-date projections and percentages in these categories. Interested readers can access this information at http://www.bls.gov.

46. The U.S. Department of Labor's Bureau of Labor Statistics keeps up-to-date projections and percentages on educational requirements for different kinds of jobs. Interested readers can access this information at http://www.bls.gov; Louis Uchitelle, "College Degree Still Pays, but It's Leveling Off," *The New York Times*, January 13, 2005, C1.

47. "Corporate America Can't Write," *Work & Family Newsbrief* (January 2005): 4; J. R. Labbe, "Future of an Illiterate Citizenry Is Dim," *Fort Worth Star-Telegram*, August 26, 2007, C1, C8.

48. Kathleen Iverson, "Managing for Effective Workforce Diversity," *Cornell Hotel and Restaurant Administration Quarterly* 41, no. 2 (April 2000): 31–38; Gail Johnson, "Time to Broaden Diversity Training," *Training* 41, no. 9 (September 2004): 16.

49. "Avoiding Identity Theft," *Aftermarket Business* 114, no. 12 (December 2004): 10.

50. Todd Raphael, "The Drive to Down-shifting," *Workforce* 80, no. 10 (October 2001): 23; Jim Olsztynski, "Flexible Work Schedules May Make More Sense: One in Six Americans Qualifies as a Caregiver Who May Benefit from Flextime," *National Driller* 26, no. 2 (February 2005): 16–19; Karen Springen, "Cutting Back Your Hours," *Newsweek*, 151, no. 19 (May 12, 2008): 60.

51. Leah Carlson, "Flextime Elevated to National Issue," *Employee Benefit News* (September 15, 2004).

STRATEGY AND HUMAN RESOURCES PLANNING

After studying this chapter, you should be able to

Objective | 1 |

Identify the advantages of integrating human resources planning and strategic planning.

Objective | 2 |

Understand how an organization's competitive environment influences its strategic planning.

Objective | 3 |

Understand why it is important for an organization to do an internal resource analysis.

© JOSÉ LUIS PALAEZ, INC./CORBIS

CHAPTER 2

Objective 4

Describe the basic tools used for human resources forecasting.

Objective 5

Explain the linkages between competitive strategies and HR.

Objective 6

Understand what is required for a firm to successfully implement a strategy.

Objective 7

Recognize the methods for assessing and measuring the effectiveness of a firm's strategy.

One of the clichés about the annual reports of companies is that they often claim that "people are our most important asset." Although we might believe this to be true, the fact is that historically managers often have not acted as though they themselves really believed it. In the past, executives often tried to remove human capital from the strategy equation by substituting capital for labor where possible or by creating hierarchical structures that separated those who think from those who actually do the work. But much is changing today.

In a survey by *USA Today* and Deloitte & Touche, nearly 80 percent of corporate executives said the importance of HRM in their firms has grown substantially over the years, and two-thirds said that HR expenditures are now viewed as a strategic investment rather than simply a cost to be minimized. Indeed, research shows that strategically designed and implemented HR systems increase the value of firms, something executives are keenly interested in accomplishing. They are also demanding their human resources groups push past short-term projections and provide detailed forecasts for needs and the associated costs over a two- to three-year horizon.[1]

■ STRATEGIC PLANNING AND HUMAN RESOURCES

Objective 1

As we explained in Chapter 1, "competing through people" is the theme for this book. But the idea remains only a premise for action until we put it into practice. To deliver on this promise, we need to understand some of the systems and processes in organizations that link human resources management and strategic management. A few definitions may be helpful up front.

strategic planning
Procedures for making decisions about the organization's long-term goals and strategies

First of all, strategic planning involves a set of procedures for making decisions about the organization's long-term goals and strategies. In this chapter, we discuss strategic plans as having a strong external orientation that covers major portions of the organization. The plans especially focus on how the organization will position itself relative to its competitors in order to ensure its long-term survival, create value, and grow. Human resources planning (HRP), by comparison, is the process of anticipating and providing for the movement of people into, within, and out of an organization. Overall, its purpose is to help managers deploy their human resources as effectively as possible, where and when they are needed, in order to accomplish the organization's goals. Strategic human resources management (SHRM) combines strategic planning and HR planning. It can be thought of as the pattern of human resources deployments and activities that enable an organization to achieve its strategic goals.

human resources planning (HRP)
The process of anticipating and providing for the movement of people into, within, and out of an organization

strategic human resources management (SHRM)
The pattern of human resources deployments and activities that enable an organization to achieve its strategic goals

HR planning is an essential activity of organizations. Consider CNA Financial Corp., a Chicago-based insurance company, for example. CNA Financial discovered via HR planning that it would run short of underwriters—a key skill pool in the company—in just two years time if their turnover rate continued at its current pace. The global strategies firms are increasingly pursuing, such as mergers, joint ventures, offshoring, the relocation of plants, product innovation plans, and downsizing, are also making HR planning more critical and more complex for managers. The good news, according to Walt Cleaver, the president and CEO of the Human Resource Planning Society, is that the increased global competitiveness, which in many industries has led to the commoditization of products based on price, is making talent the "great differentiator" among firms. After all, it is relatively easy for a competitor to copy your product and make it more cheaply. But duplicating the talents of your employees will prove much more difficult.[2] The dramatic shifts in the composition of the labor force that are occurring also require that HR managers become more involved in planning because these changes affect the full range of a company's HR practices (such as employee recruitment, selection, training, compensation, and motivation).

Strategic Planning and HR Planning: Linking the Processes

As organizations plan for their future, HR managers must be concerned with meshing HRP and strategic planning for the organization as a whole. Via strategic planning, organizations set major objectives for themselves and develop comprehensive plans to achieve those objectives. Human resources planning relates to strategic planning in several ways, but at a fundamental level, we can focus on two issues: strategy formulation and strategy implementation. Human resources planning provides a set of inputs into the strategic *formulation* process in terms of what is possible, that is, whether a firm has the types and numbers of people available to pursue a given strategy. For example, when Barnes & Noble executives contemplated the move into Web-based commerce to compete with Amazon.com, one of the issues they had to address was whether they had the talent needed to succeed in that arena.

In addition to strategy formulation, HRP is important in terms of strategy *implementation.* In other words, once the firm has devised its strategy, the company's executives must make resource allocation decisions to implement that strategy, including decisions related to the firm's structure, processes, and human capital.[3] Companies such as GE, IBM, and CIGNA have taken strides to combine these two aspects of strategic management.[4] All the available evidence suggests that the integration of HRP and strategic planning tends to be most effective when there is a reciprocal relationship between the two processes. When this occurs, a firm's top management team recognizes that strategic planning decisions affect—and are affected by—HR concerns. Figure 2.1 shows how companies align their HRP and strategic planning in this way.

As we look at trends in the best of companies, there is surprisingly little distinction between strategic planning and HRP. The planning cycles are the same, and HRP issues are viewed as being integral to the management of the business. As James Walker, a noted HRP expert, puts it, "Today, virtually *all* business issues have people implications; *all* human resource issues have business implications."[5] HR managers, along with the other top executives of their firms, are therefore important facilitators and strategic partners of the planning process.[6] This is an important point we will return to in the rest of this chapter. Traditionally, authors—and too many HR managers—have treated HR planning and strategic planning as separate activities. That is why in this chapter, we lay out a step-by-step process to show how a firm's HR planning and strategy efforts can be integrated.

▪▪ STEP ONE: MISSION, VISION, AND VALUES

The first step in strategic planning is establishing a mission, vision, and values for the organization. The mission is the basic purpose of the organization, as well as its scope of operations. It is a statement of the organization's reason for existing. The mission often is written in terms of general clients it services. Depending on the scope of the organization, the mission may be broad or narrow. For example, the mission of Google is "to organize the world's information and make it universally accessible

mission

The basic purpose of the organization as well as its scope of operations

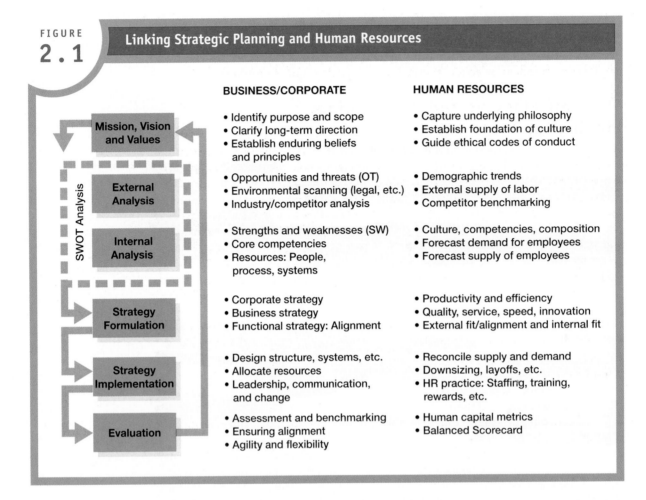

FIGURE 2.1

Linking Strategic Planning and Human Resources

	BUSINESS/CORPORATE	HUMAN RESOURCES
Mission, Vision and Values	• Identify purpose and scope • Clarify long-term direction • Establish enduring beliefs and principles	• Capture underlying philosophy • Establish foundation of culture • Guide ethical codes of conduct
External Analysis	• Opportunities and threats (OT) • Environmental scanning (legal, etc.) • Industry/competitor analysis	• Demographic trends • External supply of labor • Competitor benchmarking
Internal Analysis	• Strengths and weaknesses (SW) • Core competencies • Resources: People, process, systems	• Culture, competencies, composition • Forecast demand for employees • Forecast supply of employees
Strategy Formulation	• Corporate strategy • Business strategy • Functional strategy: Alignment	• Productivity and efficiency • Quality, service, speed, innovation • External fit/alignment and internal fit
Strategy Implementation	• Design structure, systems, etc. • Allocate resources • Leadership, communication, and change	• Reconcile supply and demand • Downsizing, layoffs, etc. • HR practice: Staffing, training, rewards, etc.
Evaluation	• Assessment and benchmarking • Ensuring alignment • Agility and flexibility	• Human capital metrics • Balanced Scorecard

SWOT Analysis

---

strategic vision

A statement about where the company is going and what it can become in the future; clarifies the long-term direction of the company and its strategic intent

core values

The strong and enduring beliefs and principles that the company uses as a foundation for its decisions

and useful."[7] The strategic vision of the organization moves beyond the mission statement to provide a perspective on where the company is headed and what the organization can become in the future. Although the terms *mission* and *vision* often are used interchangeably, the vision statement ideally clarifies the long-term direction of the company and its strategic intent.

Organizational core values are the strong enduring beliefs and principles that the company uses as a foundation for its decisions. Starbucks, for example, lists the following core values:

■ Provide a great work environment and treat each other with respect and dignity.

■ Embrace diversity as an essential component in the way we do business.

■ Apply the highest standards of excellence to the purchasing, roasting, and fresh delivery of our coffee.

■ Develop enthusiastically satisfied customers all of the time.

■ Contribute positively to our communities and our environment.

■ Recognize that profitability is essential to our future success.

These are the underlying parameters for how the company will act toward customers, employees, and the public in general. In many cases, the values capture the underlying philosophy of the company culture and give direction to its employees. The values also place limits on what behavior is seen as ethical and acceptable.

▪▪ STEP TWO: ENVIRONMENTAL ANALYSIS

The mission, vision, and values drive the second component of the strategic management process: analysis of external opportunities and threats. Changes in the external environment have a direct impact on the way organizations are run and people are managed. Some of these changes represent opportunities, and some of them represent real threats to the organization. Because of this, successful strategic management depends on an accurate and thorough evaluation of the environment. Environmental scanning is the systematic monitoring of the major external forces influencing the organization.[8] Managers attend to a variety of external issues; however, the following six are monitored most frequently:

1. Economic factors and development information, including general, regional, and global conditions

2. Industry and competitive trends, including new processes, services, and innovations

3. Technological changes, including information technology, innovations, and automation

4. Government and legislative issues, including laws and administrative rulings

5. Social concerns, including child care, elder care, the environment, and educational priorities

6. Demographic and labor market trends, including the age, composition, and literacy of the labor market, and immigration

By scanning the environment for changes that will likely affect an organization, managers can anticipate their impact and make adjustments early.

Competitive Environment

Many factors in the general environment—factors a firm cannot directly control—can affect its strategic decisions. This is why analyzing the firm's competitive environment is central to strategic planning. The competitive environment includes the specific organizations with which the firm interacts. As Figure 2.2 shows, the competitive environment includes the firm's customers, rival firms, new entrants, substitutes, and suppliers. In strategic planning, firms analyze the competitive environment in order to adapt to or influence the nature of competition. A general rule of thumb about this analysis is: The more power each of these forces has, the less profitable (and therefore attractive) the industry will be. Let us look at each of the five forces.

Customers

One of the most important assessments a firm can make is identifying the needs of its customers. At a fundamental level, a firm's strategy should focus on creating customer value—and different customers often want different things. For example,

2 | **Objective**

environmental scanning
Systematic monitoring of the major external forces influencing the organization

FIGURE 2.2

Five Forces Framework

in the hotel industry, business travelers may want convenient locations with meeting facilities. Vacationers may want resort locations with swimming pools, golf courses, and luxury spas. Other travelers may just want an inexpensive room next to the highway. The point is that increasingly, "one size does not fit all," and organizations need to know how they are going to provide value to customers. That is the foundation for strategy, and it influences the kind of skills and behavior that will be needed from employees. For example, actions and attitudes that lead to excellent customer service can include the following:

- Speed of delivering normal orders
- Willingness to meet extraordinary needs
- Merchandise delivered in good condition
- Readiness to take back defective goods and resupply new goods quickly
- Availability of installation and repair services and parts

Rival Firms

In addition to customer analysis, perhaps the most obvious element of industry analysis is examining the nature of competition. The first question to consider is: Who is the competition? Often the answer is clear to everyone, but sometimes it is not. For example, for many years, Toys "R" Us viewed its main competitors to be other toy stores such as FAO Schwarz or KB Toys. However, other retailers such as Target and Wal-Mart soon moved into this space very successfully. This had a direct effect on human resources planning for Toys "R" Us. While in the past, Toys "R" Us had been successful with a volume-based approach (that is, "stack it high, and let it fly"), bigger retailers soon gained an advantage—who can beat Wal-Mart's volume and cost advantage? As a consequence, Toys "R" Us had to modify its strategy to compete more on customer service and the expertise of its employees. But did Toys "R" Us have the number and kind of employees required to compete in this way? Were its staffing, training, performance management, and compensation practices aligned with this strategy?

New Entrants

As we suggested previously, new companies can sometimes enter an industry and compete well against established firms, and sometimes they cannot. To protect their position, companies often try to establish entry barriers to keep new firms out of the industry. However, when new firms do enter an industry it is often because they have a different—and perhaps better—way to provide value to customers. For example, when JetBlue entered the airline business, it distinguished itself by providing excellent service and low prices in regions where customers did not have many options. The HR implications of this are clear. When we look at the challenges faced by traditional airlines because of the threat of carriers such as JetBlue, Virgin Atlantic Airways, and Southwest Airlines, we can clearly see that new entrants can change the "rules of the game" in an industry. The impact on labor costs, productivity, skills required, and work design are important considerations in both strategic planning and human resources planning.

Substitutes

At times, the biggest opportunity or threat in an industry is not with direct competition, but from substitution. In the telephone industry, for example, cellular technology and VOIP (Voice-Over-the-Internet Protocol) are rapidly substituting for landline phone systems. These substitutes offer the same service or function as traditional firms, but through a different method. That implies that firms may need to adjust their employee skill bases in order to support different technologies, or they may need to think about how they will compete in different ways. As an example, think about how the travel business has changed over the years. Travel agents used to be the key resource for flights, hotels, rental cars, and the like. The focus was almost exclusively on transactions. However, with the advent of online reservation systems, travel agents have had to adapt their approach. Today, they are as likely to compete based on the service they provide and the expertise they have about particular locations.

Suppliers

Organizations rarely create everything on their own, but instead have suppliers that provide them with key inputs. These inputs can include raw materials for production, money (from banks and stockholders), information, and people. This last factor—people, or labor as it is historically called—has direct implications for strategic planning and human resources planning. Because of its central role in both strategic planning and HRP, we explore it next in much more detail.

External Supply of Labor

Many factors influence the labor supply, including demographic changes in the population, national and regional economics, education level of the workforce, demand for specific employee skills, population mobility, and governmental policies.

Consider these U.S. Census Bureau projections about how the U.S. workforce will change between 2006 and 2016:

- The civilian labor force is projected to increase by 12.8 million between 2006 and 2016. This 8.5 percent increase is less than the 13.1 percent increase over the previous decade—1996 to 2006—when the labor force grew by 17.5 million.

- Employment growth will continue to be concentrated in the service-providing sector of the economy. Service-providing industries will generate almost *all* of the employment gain from 2006 to 2016 and will provide more than three-quarters of all jobs in 2016.

- Within the goods-producing sector, construction is the only sector projected to grow. Employment in manufacturing industries will decline by 1.5 million jobs.

- Professional occupations and service occupations—two major occupational groups on opposite ends of the educational and earning ranges—are projected to grow the fastest and add the most jobs, accounting for more than 6 of 10 new jobs created between 2006 and 2016.

- The number of workers in the 55-and-older group is projected to grow by 46.7 percent. This is over five times the growth projected for the labor force overall.

- Youths—people between the ages of 16 and 24—will decline in numbers and will see their share of the labor force fall.

- The Hispanic labor force is expected to grow by nearly 30 percent, reaching 26.9 million by 2016, while the non-Hispanic labor force is projected to grow by only a little over 5 percent.

These labor force trends illustrate the importance of monitoring demographic changes as a part of environmental scanning. Fortunately, labor market analysis is aided by various published documents. Unemployment rates, labor force projection figures, and population characteristics are reported by the U.S. Department of Labor.[9] The *Monthly Labor Review* and *Occupational Outlook Handbook*, both published by the Bureau of Labor Statistics (BLS) of the U.S. Department of Labor, contain information on jobholder characteristics and predicted changes in the workforce. In addition, local chambers of commerce and individual state development and planning agencies can assist both large organizations and new business ventures by providing them with a labor market analysis of their areas. Offshore consulting firms such as IBM and Accenture can be a good source for information about labor trends in other countries.

These sources of information are invaluable. In a rapidly changing environment, it is extremely risky to be caught off guard. Such changes are important for many reasons, some related to operational issues and some to strategic issues. HRP has to focus on both. At an operational level, the change in labor supply directly influences hiring plans that must take into account the demographic composition of the population in the area where the organization is located or plans to locate. Similarly, with a "maturing" workforce, HRP must consider the implications for recruitment and replacement policies.

From a strategic standpoint, changes in the labor supply can limit the strategies available to firms. High-growth companies in particular may find it difficult to find the talent they need to expand their businesses. While unemployment rates vary by sector, the shortage of talent in high-skill jobs continues to create real challenges for firms.

▪▪ Step Three: Internal Analysis

3 | **Objective**

As organizations conduct external analyses of environmental opportunities and threats, they also analyze their internal strengths and weaknesses. Internal analysis provides strategic decisionmakers with an inventory of organizational skills and resources as well as their performance levels.

To be sure, many resources combine to give organizations a competitive advantage. But in contrast to the past, the advantages due to physical assets are being supplanted by intangible assets, including people. As James Brian Quinn noted, "With rare exceptions, the economic and producing power of firms lies more in its intellectual and service capabilities than in its hard assets—land, plant, and equipment."[10]

The Three Cs: Culture, Capabilities, and Composition

In the context of human resource planning, internal analysis focuses especially on "the three Cs": culture, capabilities, and composition.

Culture: Auditing Values, Beliefs, and Attitudes

Think about our initial discussion (in Step One) of mission, vision, and values. Because managers increasingly understand that their employees are critical to their success, they often conduct cultural audits to examine the attitudes and beliefs of their workforces as well as the activities they engage in. At one level, this analysis focuses on whether a firm's critical values are embraced and demonstrated by employees throughout the organization. Employee surveys, for example, can measure how employees feel on a number of critical issues and can be very useful for upward assessment and feedback of (and for) management. However, these audits can go much deeper. Sears, for example, found that positive employee attitudes on ten essential factors—including workload and treatment by bosses—are directly linked to customer satisfaction and revenue increases.[11]

cultural audits
Audits of the culture and quality of work life in an organization

Cultural audits essentially involve discussions among top-level managers of how the organization's culture reveals itself to employees and how it can be influenced or improved. The cultural audit may include such questions as the following:

- How do employees spend their time?
- How do they interact with each other?
- What is their morale level?
- Are employees empowered?
- What is the predominant leadership style of the firm's managers?
- How do employees advance within the organization?

By conducting in-depth interviews and making observations over a period of time, managers are able to learn about the culture of their organization and the attitudes of its employees. With the increased diversity of the U.S. workplace, cultural audits can be used to determine whether there are different groups, or subcultures, within the organization that have distinctly different views about the nature of the work and how it should be done, the quality of the company's managers, and so on. Before any HR planning can take place, managers have to gain a clear idea of how employees view their organization.

Capabilities: People as a Strategic Resource

A growing number of experts now argue that the key to a firm's success is based on establishing a set of core capabilities—bundles of people, processes, and systems that distinguish an organization from its competitors and deliver value to customers. McDonald's, for example, has developed core capabilities in management efficiency and training. Federal Express has core capabilities in package routing, delivery, and employee relations. Royal Dutch Shell has core capabilities in oil exploration and production.[12] Core capabilities tend to be limited in number, but they provide a long-term basis for technology innovation, product development, and service delivery.

core capabilities

Integrated knowledge sets within an organization that distinguish it from its competitors and deliver value to customers

In many cases, people are a key resource that underlies a firm's core capabilities. Particularly in knowledge-based industries such as the software and information services industries, success depends on "people-embodied know-how." This includes the knowledge, skills, and abilities of employees. As a result, a number of companies that previously relied on standard plans for recruiting and managing their employees are designing more tailored plans for them. These personalized plans are designed to address the individual needs of employees so they will be in a better position to help implement their firms' strategies. Microsoft goes so far as to ask certain types of employees to design their own career paths. For example, the company offers software engineers both a management-focused and technical specialist career track and allows them to move back and forth between the two.

Organizations can achieve a sustained competitive advantage through people if they are able to meet the following criteria:[13]

1. *The resources must be valuable.* People are a source of competitive advantage when they improve the efficiency or effectiveness of the company. Value is increased when employees find ways to decrease costs, provide something unique to customers, or some combination of the two. To improve the bottom line, Nordstrom and UPS are among the companies that utilize employee empowerment programs, total quality and continuous improvement efforts, and flexible work arrangements to motivate and spark the creativity of their workers.

2. *The resources must be rare.* People are a source of competitive advantage when their knowledge, skills, and abilities are not equally available to competitors. Companies such as Microsoft, McKinsey, and Four Seasons Hotels therefore invest a great deal to hire and train the best and the brightest employees in order to gain an advantage over their competitors.

3. *The resources must be difficult to imitate.* People are a source of competitive advantage when the capabilities and contributions of a firm's employees cannot be copied by others. Disney, Southwest Airlines, and Starbucks are each known for creating unique cultures that get the most from employees (through teamwork) and are difficult to imitate.

4. *The resources must be organized.* People are a source of competitive advantage when their talents can be combined and deployed to work on new assignments at a moment's notice. Companies such as IBM and GE have invested in information technology to help allocate and track employee assignments to temporary projects. Teamwork and cooperation are two other pervasive methods for ensuring an organized workforce.

These four criteria highlight the importance of people and show the closeness of HRM to strategic management.

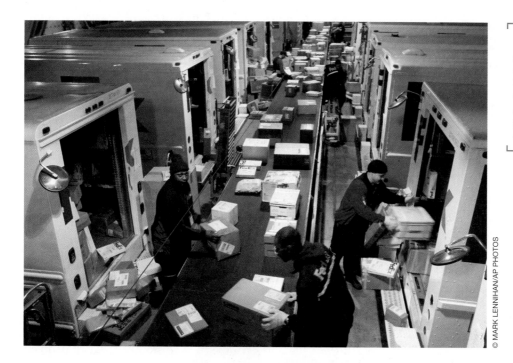

Couriers and package handlers, core employees of the human capital architecture at FedEx, are only a part of the FedEx network.

© MARK LENNIHAN/AP PHOTOS

Composition: The Human Capital Architecture

A related element of internal analysis for organizations that compete on capabilities is determining the composition of the workforce. That is, managers need to determine whether people are available, internally or externally, to execute an organization's strategy. Managers have to make tough decisions about whom to employ internally, whom to contract externally, and how to manage different types of employees with different skills who contribute in different ways to the organization.

Figure 2.3 shows that different skill groups in any given organization can be classified according to the degree to which they create strategic value and are unique to the organization. As a general rule, managers often consider contracting externally (or outsourcing) skill areas that are not central to the firm's core competence. HRP plays an important role in helping managers weigh the costs and benefits of using one approach to employment versus another.

Evidence from research suggests that employment relationships and HR practices for different employees vary according to which segment they occupy in this matrix. Here are some general trends:

Strategic Knowledge Workers. This group of employees tends to have unique skills that are directly linked to the company's strategy and difficult to replace (such as R&D scientists in a pharmaceuticals company or computer scientists in a software development company). These employees typically are engaged in knowledge work that involves considerable autonomy and discretion. Companies tend to make long-term commitments to these employees, investing in their continuous training and development and perhaps giving them an equity stake in the organization.

FIGURE

2.3

Mapping Human Capital

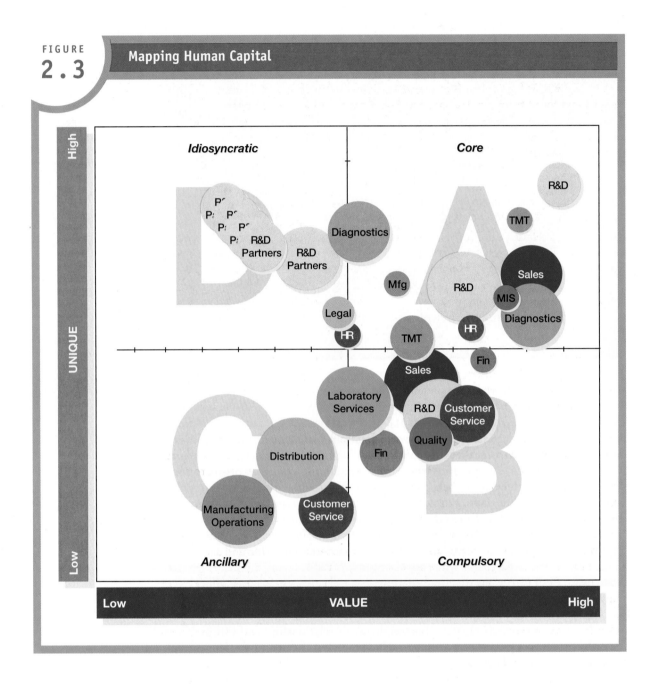

Core Employees. This group of employees has skills that are quite valuable to a company, but not particularly unique or difficult to replace (such as salespeople in a department store or truck drivers for a courier service). These employees tend to be employed in traditional types of jobs. Because their skills are transferable, it is quite possible that they could leave to go to another firm. As a consequence, managers frequently make less investment in training and development and tend to focus more on paying for short-term performance achievements.

Supporting Labor. This group of employees typically has skills that are of less strategic value to the firm and generally available in the labor market (such as clerical workers, maintenance workers, and staff workers in accounting and human resources). Individuals in these jobs are increasingly hired from external agencies on a contract basis to support the strategic knowledge workers and core employees. The scope of their duties tends to be limited, and their employment relationships tend to be transaction-based, focused on rules and procedures, with less investment in development.

Using the Internet

For more information about contract employees, go to the Student Resources at:

www.cengage.com/ management/bohlander

Alliance Partners. This group of individuals has skills that are unique, but frequently not directly related to a company's core strategy (such as attorneys on retainer, consultants, and research lab scientists). Although companies perhaps cannot justify their internal employment, given their indirect link to strategy, these individuals have skills that are specialized and not readily available to all firms. As a consequence, companies tend to establish longer-term alliances and partnerships with them and nurture an ongoing relationship focused on mutual learning. Considerable investment is made in the exchange of information and knowledge.[14]

Forecasting: A Critical Element of Planning

While internal analysis of the three Cs (culture, capabilities, and composition) may reveal a great deal about where the organization is today, things change. In an important sense, strategic planning is about managing that change. Managers must continually forecast both the needs and the capabilities of the firm for the future in order to do an effective job at strategic planning. As shown in Figure 2.4, managers focus on (at least) three key elements: (a) forecasting the demand for labor, (b) forecasting the supply of labor, and (c) balancing supply and demand considerations. Careful attention to each factor helps top managers meet their human resources requirements.

4 Objective

Consider for a moment the high costs of not forecasting—or forecasting poorly. If job vacancies are left unfilled, the resulting loss in efficiency can be very costly, particularly when you consider the amount of time it takes to hire and train replacement employees. As pointless as it may sound, we have seen situations in which employees are laid off in one department while applicants are hired for similar jobs in another department. Poor forecasting that leads to unnecessary layoffs also makes it difficult for employees to accurately assess their own career prospects and development. When this happens, some of a firm's more competent and ambitious workers will be inclined to seek other employment where they feel they will have better career opportunities.[15]

On the plus side, accurate forecasting provides the kind of information managers need to make sound decisions. It can help them ensure that they have the right number and right kinds of people in the right places at the right times, doing things that provide value to both the organization and the employees.

Forecasting a Firm's Demand for Employees

If a key component of forecasting is predicting the number and types of people an organization needs to meet its objectives, the question remains: "How can this be done?" A variety of factors, including a firm's competitive strategy, technology, structure, and productivity, can affect the demand for labor. For example, as we noted in

FIGURE
2.4

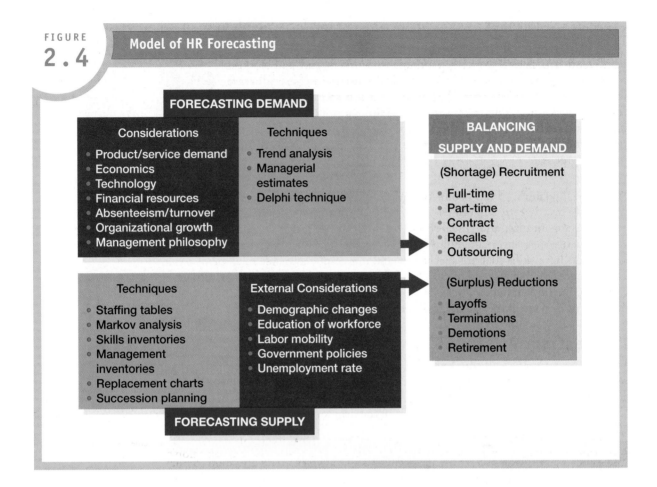

FIGURE 2.4 Model of HR Forecasting

Chapter 1, the use of advanced technology is generally accompanied by less demand for low-skilled workers and more demand for knowledge workers. External factors such as business cycles—economic and seasonal trends—can also play a role. For example, retailers such as The Gap, Bath & Body Works, and Marks & Spencer rely heavily on temporary employees between November and January, during the holiday season. There are two approaches to HR forecasting: quantitative and qualitative, which we discuss next. An organization's demands will ultimately determine which technique is used. Regardless of the method, however, forecasting should not be neglected, even in relatively small organizations.

Quantitative Approaches. Quantitative approaches to forecasting involve the use of statistical or mathematical techniques. One example is trend analysis, whereby a firm's employment requirements are forecasted on the basis of some organizational index. Trend analysis is one of the most commonly used approaches for projecting HR demand and is typically done in several stages:

First, select an appropriate business factor. This should be the best available predictor of human resources needs. Frequently, sales or value added (the selling price of the firm's products minus the costs of the materials and supplies used to make them) is used as a predictor in trend analysis. Second, plot a historical trend of

trend analysis

A quantitative approach to forecasting labor demand based on an organizational index such as sales the business factor in relation to the number of employees. The ratio of employees to the business factor will provide a labor productivity ratio (for example, sales per employee). Third, compute the productivity ratio for at least the past five years. Fourth, calculate human resources demand by multiplying the business factor by the productivity ratio. Finally, project the firm's human resources demand out to the target year. This procedure is illustrated in Figure 2.5 for a hypothetical building contractor.

Other, more sophisticated statistical planning methods include modeling or multiple predictive techniques. Whereas trend analysis relies on a single factor (such as sales) to predict employment needs, the more advanced methods combine several factors, such as interest rates, gross national product, disposable income, and sales, to predict employment levels. Forecasting methods such as these are usually used by larger companies with the help of analysts and statisticians. However, advances in data collection technology and computer software are making it easier and more affordable for smaller businesses to use more sophisticated forecasting techniques.

Qualitative Approaches. Admittedly, forecasting is frequently more an art than a science, providing inexact approximations rather than absolute results. The ever-changing environment in which an organization operates contributes to this situation. For example, estimating changes in the demand for a firm's products or services is a basic forecasting concern, as is anticipating changes in national or regional economics. A firm's internal changes are critical, too. For example, a community hospital anticipating internal changes in its technology or how the facility is organized or managed must consider these factors when it forecasts its staffing needs. Also, the forecasted staffing needs must be in line with the organization's financial resources.

In contrast to quantitative approaches, qualitative approaches to forecasting are less statistical. Management forecasts are the opinions (judgments) of supervisors, department managers, experts, or others knowledgeable about the organization's

management forecasts

The opinions (judgments) of supervisors, department managers, experts, or others knowledgeable about the organization's future employment needs

---

FIGURE

2.5

Example of Trend Analysis of HR Demand

YEAR	BUSINESS FACTOR (SALES IN THOUSANDS) ÷	LABOR PRODUCTIVITY (SALES/EMPLOYEE) =	HUMAN RESOURCES DEMAND (NUMBER OF EMPLOYEES)
2002	$2,351	14.33	164
2003	$2,613	11.12	235
2004	$2,935	8.34	352
2005	$3,306	10.02	330
2006	$3,613	11.12	325
2007	$3,748	11.12	337
2008	$3,880	12.52	310
2009*	$4,095	12.52	327
2010*	$4,283	12.52	342
2011*	$4,446	12.52	355

*Projected figures

future employment needs. For example, at the Ripe Tomato, a growing family dining chain, each restaurant manager is responsible for his or her store's employment forecasts. Another qualitative forecasting method, the Delphi technique, attempts to decrease the subjectivity of forecasts by soliciting and summarizing the judgments of a preselected group of individuals. HR personnel can do this by developing a list of questions to ask the managers in their companies. Highlights in HRM 1 contains a list of good questions to ask. The final forecast thus becomes a collective, or group, judgment.

Ideally, forecasting should include the use of both quantitative and qualitative approaches. Numbers without context—including the context supplied by skilled HR professionals who understand the business and can analyze and interpret the data—are less useful. "The most important software is the one running between your ears," explains Matthew C. Brush, the director of human capital planning at Corning, Inc. Indeed, in small organizations, forecasting may be as informal as having one person who knows the organization and anticipates its future HR requirements.[16]

Forecasting the Supply of Employees

Just as an organization must forecast its future requirements for employees, it must also determine whether sufficient numbers and types of employees are available to staff the openings it anticipates having. As with demand forecasts, the process

HR Planning and Strategy Questions to Ask Business Managers

Workforce planning requires that HR leaders periodically interview their managers to gauge future workforce needs. Here are some sample questions to ask.

- What are your mission, vision, and values?
- What are your current pressing business issues?
- What are our organizational strengths?
- Who are our competitors' organizational strengths? How do we compare?
- What core capabilities do we need to win in our markets?
- What are the required knowledge, skills, and abilities we need to execute the winning strategy?
- What are the barriers to optimally achieving the strategy?
- What types of skills and positions will be required or no longer required?
- Which skills should we have internally versus contract with outside providers?
- What actions need to be taken to align our resources with strategy priorities?
- What recognition and rewards are needed to attract, motivate, and retain the employees we need?
- How will we know if we are effectively executing our workforce plan and staying on track?

Sources: Adapted from Agilent Technologies for The Conference Board and the Society for Human Resource Management.

involves both tracking current employee levels and making future projections about those levels.

Staffing Tables and Markov Analysis. An internal supply analysis can begin with the preparation of staffing tables. Staffing tables are graphic representations of all organizational jobs, along with the numbers of employees currently occupying those jobs (and perhaps also future employment requirements derived from demand forecasts). Another technique, called a Markov analysis, shows the percentage (and actual number) of employees who remain in each of a firm's jobs from one year to the next, as well as the proportions of those who are promoted, demoted, or transferred or exit the organization. As Figure 2.6 shows, a Markov analysis can be used to track the pattern of employee movements through various jobs and to develop a transition matrix for forecasting labor supply.

Forecasting the supply of human resources available to a firm requires that its managers have a good understanding of employee turnover and absenteeism. We have included formulas for computing turnover and absenteeism rates in an Appendix to this chapter. The calculations are easily made and used by managers of both large and small organizations.

Skill Inventories and Management Inventories. Staffing tables, a Markov analysis, turnover rates, and the like tend to focus on the *number* of employees in particular jobs. Other techniques are more oriented toward the *types* of employees and their skills, knowledge, and experiences. Skill inventories can also be prepared that list each

staffing tables

Graphic representations of all organizational jobs, along with the numbers of employees currently occupying those jobs and future (monthly or yearly) employment requirements

Markov analysis

A method for tracking the pattern of employee movements through various jobs

skill inventories

Files of personnel education, experience, interests, skills, and so on that allow managers to quickly match job openings with employee backgrounds

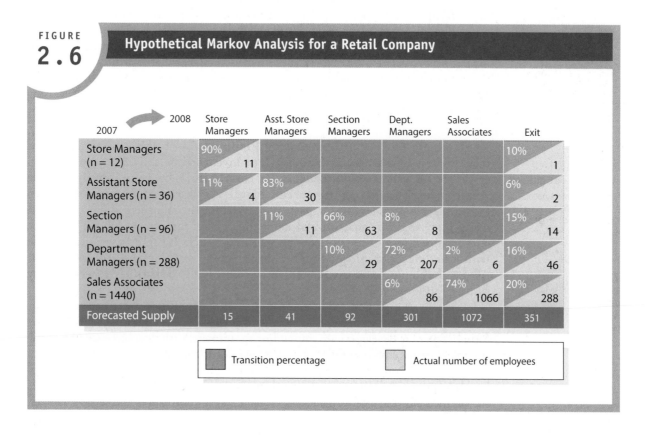

FIGURE 2.6

Hypothetical Markov Analysis for a Retail Company

2007 \ 2008	Store Managers	Asst. Store Managers	Section Managers	Dept. Managers	Sales Associates	Exit
Store Managers (n = 12)	90% / 11					10% / 1
Assistant Store Managers (n = 36)	11% / 4	83% / 30				6% / 2
Section Managers (n = 96)		11% / 11	66% / 63	8% / 8		15% / 14
Department Managers (n = 288)			10% / 29	72% / 207	2% / 6	16% / 46
Sales Associates (n = 1440)				6% / 86	74% / 1066	20% / 288
Forecasted Supply	15	41	92	301	1072	351

■ Transition percentage   □ Actual number of employees

External factors such as business cycles—economic and seasonal trends—can play a role in forecasting the demand for and supply of employees.

© COLORBLIND IMAGES/GETTY IMAGES

employee's education, past work experience, vocational interests, specific abilities and skills, compensation history, and job tenure. Of course, confidentiality is a vital concern in setting up any such inventory. Nevertheless, well-prepared and up-to-date skill inventories allow an organization to quickly match forthcoming job openings with employee backgrounds. When data are gathered on managers, these inventories are called *management inventories*. All of this analysis is made simpler these days through the use of HR information systems and enterprise systems provided by companies such as Oracle-PeopleSoft and SAP. As Chapter 1 explained, the insurance company Aviva is using new, custom software to create talent profiles of its 39,000 employees worldwide.

Replacement Charts and Succession Planning. Both skill and management inventories—broadly referred to as talent inventories—can be used to develop employee replacement charts, which list current jobholders and identify possible replacements should openings occur. Figure 2.7 shows an example of how an organization might develop a replacement chart for the managers in one of its divisions. Note that this chart provides information on the current job performance and promotability of possible replacements. As such, it can be used side by side with other pieces of information for succession planning—the process of identifying, developing, and tracking talented individuals so that they can eventually assume top-level positions.

In a recent study conducted by the Society for Human Resources, three out of four chief executives said succession planning was their most significant challenge for the future. Software developers are responding to this need with new succession planning and talent management software. The software developer Taleo, for example, offers an application based on a firm's organizational chart and baseball-card-like representations of its employees. Clicking on the cards flips them over to show statistics about the employees such as their individual performance review data, career information, and succession data.

replacement charts

Listings of current jobholders and people who are potential replacements if an opening occurs

succession planning

The process of identifying, developing, and tracking key individuals for executive positions

FIGURE
2.7

An Executive Replacement Chart

MANAGER

J. L. Green   A/2

KEY

Names provided are
replacement candidates

A. Promotable now
B. Needing development
C. Not fitted to position
1. Superior performance
2. Above-average
   performance
3. Acceptable
   performance
4. Poor performance

**ASSISTANT TO
MANAGER**

L. B. Martinez   B/1

**ASSISTANT
MANAGER**

R. G. Gorton   A/2
T. M. Brown   B/3

**DIVISION HR
MANAGER**

C. K. Broderick   A/1

**ACCOUNTING
DIVISION MANAGER**

W. Shepard   C/2

**PLANNING DIVISION
MANAGER**

B. Verkozen   A/1
T. Turner   B/1

**TECHNICAL
ADVISOR**

N. T. Lyman   B/3

**NORTHWEST
REGION
MANAGER**

L. C. Green   A/2
A. T. Tupper   C/4

**CENTRAL REGION
MANAGER**

J. Q. Gomez   A/1

**NORTH CENTRAL
REGION MANAGER**

D. K. Lim   B/2

**EASTERN REGION
MANAGER**

O. D. Morris   B/3

This type of automated system is a relatively new development with which managers
are getting acquainted. With or without software, however, more companies are
going to need to engage in succession planning. One study found that only 50 percent
of U.S. companies have succession plans in place, despite the apparent acute need for
it.[17] Highlights in HRM 2 shows a checklist for evaluating the "success" of succession
planning.

Assessing a Firm's Human Capital Readiness:
Gap Analysis

Once a company has assessed both the supply and demand for employee skills, talent,
and know-how, it can begin to understand its human capital readiness. Any

**human capital
readiness**

The process of evaluating the
availability of critical talent in
a company and comparing it
to the firm's supply

HIGHLIGHTS IN HRM

2

Succession-Planning Checklist

RATE THE SUCCESS OF YOUR SUCCESSION PLANNING

For each characteristic of a best-practice succession-planning and management program appearing in the left column below, enter a number to the right to indicate how well you believe your organization manages that characteristic. Ask other decision makers in your organization to complete this form individually. Then compile the scores and compare notes.

Characteristics of a Best-Practice Succession-Planning and Management Program	How Would You Rate Your Organization's Succession Planning and Management Program on the Characteristic?				
Your organization has successfully...	Very Poor (1)	Poor (2)	Neither Poor Nor Good (3)	Good (4)	Very Good (5)
1 Clarified the purpose and desired results of the succession-planning and management program.					
2 Determined what performance is required now for all job categories in the organization by establishing competency models.					
3 Established a means to measure individual performance that is aligned with the competencies currently demonstrated by successful performers.					
4 Determined what performance is needed in the future by establishing future competency models for all job categories.					
5 Created an ongoing means by which to assess individual potential against future competency models.					
6 Established a means by which to narrow gaps through the use of individual development plans (IDPs).					
7 Created a means to follow up and hold people accountable.					
8 Created a means by which to document competence and find organizational talent quickly when needed.					
9 Created and sustained rewards for developing people.					
10 Established a means by which to evaluate the results of the succession planning and management program.					

Total (add up the scores for items 1–10 and place in the box on the right)

SCORES

50–40	Congratulations. The succession-planning and management program in your organization conforms with best practices.
39–30	Pretty good. Your organization is on the way toward establishing a first-rate succession-planning and management program.
9–0	Give yourself a failing grade. You need to take steps immediately to improve the succession-planning and management practices of your organization.

29–20	Okay. While your organization could make improvements, you appear to have some of the major pieces in place for a succession-planning and management program.
19–10	Not good at all. Your organization is probably filling positions on an as-needed basis.

Source: From William J. Rothwell, "Putting Success into Your Succession Planning," *The Journal of Business Strategy* 23, no. 3 (May/June 2002): 32–37. Republished with permission—Thomson Media, One State Street, 26th Floor, New York, NY 10004.

difference between the quantity and quality of employees required versus the quantity and quality of employees available represents a gap that needs to be remedied.

Figure 2.8 shows how Chemico, a specialty chemical manufacturing company, approaches its assessment of human capital readiness. Similar to our discussion in the preceding sections, managers begin by identifying a company's core capabilities and the key people and processes that are critical to those capabilities. Chemico's executive team identified eight key job "families" which comprise about 100 employees of the firm's 1,500 member staff (in other words, less than 10 percent of its workforce). For each of these critical job families, managers identified the critical knowledge, skills, and behaviors necessary to build the core capabilities. They then determined the number of people required for these positions, as well as the number who are currently qualified.

FIGURE 2.8

Assessing a Firm's Human Capital

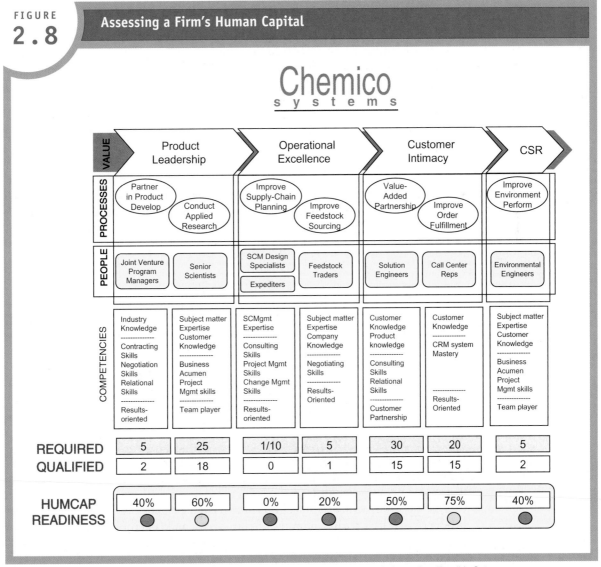

Source: Reprinted from Robert Kaplan and David Norton, *Strategy Maps: Converting Intangible Assets into Tangible Outcomes* (Boston: Harvard Business School Press, 2006), Chapter 8.

As the lower portion of the figure shows, the company's human readiness ranged between 0 percent for supply chain management design specialists and 75 percent for call center representatives.

Once the assessment of the firm's human capital readiness is complete, managers have a much better foundation for establishing their strategy going forward and the specific requirements for developing the talent needed to implement the strategy.[18]

▪▪ STEP FOUR: FORMULATING STRATEGY

Objective 5

The forecasting techniques discussed previously provide critical information for strategic planning. Recall that we noted at the beginning of the chapter that HR analysis is an input to strategy formulation. However, a word of caution is needed here. Because HR forecasting techniques take us deep into the specifics of labor supply and demand, we need to be careful not to lose sight of the larger strategic picture. One of the biggest concerns among executives is that (at times) HR managers cannot "see the forest for the trees" because they become mired in the administrative details of their planning models. SWOT analysis, discussed shortly, helps managers combine various sources of information into a broader framework for analysis.

After managers have analyzed the internal strengths and weaknesses of the firm, as well as external opportunities and threats, they have the information they need to formulate corporate, business, and HR strategies for the organization. A comparison of *strengths, weaknesses, opportunities,* and *threats* normally is referred to as a SWOT analysis. SWOT analysis helps executives summarize the major facts and forecasts derived from external and internal analyses. Strategy formulation builds on SWOT analysis to use the strengths of the organization to capitalize on opportunities, counteract threats, and alleviate internal weaknesses. In short, strategy formulation moves from simple analysis to devising a coherent course of action. Figure 2.9 is an example of a SWOT analysis done on the Valero Energy Corporation. It was conducted by Datamonitor, an online database and analysis service that helps its clients address strategic issues.

SWOT analysis

A comparison of strengths, weaknesses, opportunities, and threats for strategy formulation purposes

Corporate Strategy

In any industry, firms decide where and how they will compete. Corporate strategy focuses on domain selection, that is, the markets in which they will compete. Some firms choose a concentration strategy that focuses on only a limited portion of the industry. For example, Visteon Corporation specializes in electronics, climate, and power train technologies for the automotive industry. In contrast, Henry Ford at one time had fully integrated his company from the ore mines needed to make steel all the way to the showrooms where his cars were sold.

Growth and Diversification

Emerging and growing companies execute their strategies differently than mature companies or those in decline. As companies grow, their strategic choices tend to focus on geographic, volume, and product expansion. HR planning is a vital input to these decisions. Growth hinges on three related elements: (a) increased employee productivity, (b) a greater number of employees, and (c) employees developing or acquiring new skills. Thus, a firm's staffing, training, employee motivation efforts, and the like can either enable the company to grow or limit its potential.

FIGURE 2.9

An Example of a SWOT Analysis

Valero Energy Corporation (Valero) is one of the largest refiners in North America. Its core activities include refining and marketing of petroleum products. With a combined throughput capacity of approximately 3.3 million bpd, Valero is the 15th largest company on the Fortune 500 list. Valero's large refining capacity gives it a significant competitive advantage. However, rising material and labor costs could affect the company's margins.

STRENGTHS	WEAKNESSES
Large refining system	Weak performance in Canada
Leader in conversion capacity and feedstock flexibility	Litigations
Strong revenue growth and capital expenditure	High dependence on the United States

OPPORTUNITIES	THREATS
Growing diesel demand	Material and labor cost
Strategic refocus	Stringent regulations
Rising petrochemical capacity in the Middle East	

Source: Data Monitor.com, June 2007.

As companies diversify into new businesses, managers inevitably are faced with a "make or buy" decision. That is, should they develop the capabilities in-house or contract externally? For example, when IBM entered the personal computer market in the early 1980s, it contracted with (start-up companies) Intel and Microsoft to make the hardware and operating systems for its PC. The decision did not rest solely on human resources issues, but they were an important part of the equation. Interestingly, IBM got out of the PC business altogether in 2005, by selling its PCs product lineup to the Chinese computer manufacturer Lenovo. Instead, IBM is focusing on developing custom technology services for businesses, which it believes will be more profitable in the long run and a harder product for competitors to imitate. To help accomplish this new strategy, the company spent the first part of the decade buying up dozens of business service related companies and their talent.

Some companies diversify far beyond their core businesses. GE, for example, has diversified from its original base in electrical and home appliance products to such wide-ranging industries as health, finance, insurance, truck and air transportation, and even media, with its ownership of NBC. In order to manage such a diverse portfolio, GE has invested heavily in the development of general management skills and leadership ability. CEO Jeffrey Immelt has stated that GE's future depends on pursuing businesses that leverage human capital (in contrast to its traditional focus on manufacturing). This new strategy is strongly linked to human resources. In fact, the strategy is viable only because the company has done such an enviable job developing talent over the years.

Mergers and Acquisitions

In addition to strategies of growth and diversification, corporate America has seen a host of mergers and acquisitions in recent years. These include such firms as Wrigley's and Mars, Delta and Northwest Airlines, Walt Disney and ABC, Exxon and Mobil, and Procter & Gamble and Gillette. While there are some important competitive reasons for mergers such as these, it is unfortunate to note that many of them have not gone well. Not surprisingly, perhaps, the failure rate among firms is very high. Some estimates suggest that only about 15 percent of all mergers achieve their objectives (measured by return on investment, shareholder value, and the like). Often the failure is due to cultural inconsistencies, as well as conflicts among the managers of each firm. Clearly, these concerns point directly to the importance of effective HR planning prior to—and during—the merger process. Highlights in HRM 3 shows key HR activities associated with different phases of a merger or acquisition.

Strategic Alliances and Joint Ventures

Sometimes firms do not acquire or merge with another firm, but instead pursue cooperative strategies such as a strategic alliance or joint venture. Especially when firms enter into international joint ventures, the issues of culture (both company culture and national culture) become paramount. On the front end, HR plays a vital role in assessing the compatibility of cultures and potential problems. As the alliance is formed, HR helps select key executives and develops teamwork across the respective workforces. In addition, HR is typically involved in the design of performance assessment and mutual incentives for the alliance. Of course, one of the controversial issues related to such alliances is the inevitable issue of outsourcing or offshoring work to other locations.

Business Strategy

While we think about corporate strategy as domain selection, business strategy is viewed in terms of domain navigation. It is more focused on how the company will compete against rival firms in order to create value for customers. We can think of value creation in a cost/benefit scenario (that is, value = benefits − costs). Companies can increase the value they offer customers by decreasing the costs of their goods and services or by increasing the benefits their products provide (or some combination of the two). Their business strategies reflect these choices.

Low-Cost Strategy: Compete on Productivity and Efficiency

A low-cost strategy means keeping your costs low enough so that you can offer an attractive price to customers (relative to competitors). Organizations such as Dell, Wal-Mart, and Southwest Airlines have been very successful at using a low-cost strategy. Critical success factors for this strategy focus on efficiency, productivity, and minimizing waste. These types of companies often are large and try to take advantage of economies of scale in production and distribution. In many cases, the large size allows them to sell their products and services at a lower price, which leads to higher market share, volume, and (hopefully) profits. However, even a low-cost leader must offer a product or service that customers find valuable. As Gordon Bethune, the former CEO of Continental Airlines, put it, "You can make a pizza so cheap that no one will buy it."[19] Ultimately organizations need to use a cost strategy to increase value to customers, rather than take it away.

A low-cost strategy has several links to HR planning. The first has to do with productivity. A common misconception about low-cost strategies is that they inevitably

value creation

What the firm adds to a product or service by virtue of making it; the amount of benefits provided by the product or service once the costs of making it are subtracted

3

Key HR Activities Associated with Merger or Acquisition Phases

HR Issues	Key HR Activities

Stage 1—Precombination

- Identifying reasons for the M&A
- Forming M&A team/leader
- Searching for potential partners
- Selecting a partner
- Planning for managing the process
- Planning to learn from the process
- Participate in preselection assessment of target firm

- Assist in conducting thorough due diligence assessment
- Participate in planning for combination
- Assist in developing HR practices that support rapid learning and knowledge transfer

Stage 2—Combination

- Selecting the integration manager(s)
- Designing/implementing transition teams
- Creating the new structure/strategies/leadership
- Retaining key employees
- Managing the change process
- Communicating to and involving stakeholders
- Developing new policies and practices
- Assist in recruiting and selecting integration manager(s)

- Assist with transition team design and staffing
- Develop retention strategies and communicate to top talent
- Assist in deciding who goes
- Facilitate establishment of a new culture
- Provide assistance to ensure implementation of HR policies and practices

Stage 3—Solidification and Assessment

- Solidifying leadership and staffing
- Assessing the new strategies and structures
- Assessing the new culture
- Assessing the concerns of stakeholders
- Revising as needed
- Learning from the process
- Participate in establishing criteria and procedures for assessing staff effectiveness

- Monitor the new culture and recommend approaches to strengthen it
- Participate in stakeholder satisfaction
- Assist in developing and implementing plans for continuous adjustment and learning

Source: Susan E. Jackson and Randall S. Schuler, *Managing Human Resources Through Strategic Partnerships,* 9th ed. (Mason, OH: Thomson/South-Western, 2006), 50.

The merge of Delta and Northwest Airlines was seen as an effective way to improve efficiencies, among other things. The corporations likely went through the key HR activities listed on the previous page.

require cutting labor costs. On the contrary, there are several good examples of companies that pay their employees "top dollar," but gain back cost advantages because of excellent productivity. That is, they get a terrific "bang for the buck." Either they produce more from the workforce they have, or they can produce the same amount with a smaller workforce. Billy Beane, the general manager of the Oakland A's, became famous for making the most of the A's small payroll. Beane did so by developing players and utilizing them more strategically than other major league teams with bigger payroll budgets.

The second way that low-cost strategies are linked to HR pertains to outsourcing. In some cases, companies seeking low cost may consider contracting with an external partner that can perform particular activities or services as well (or better) at a lower cost. This decision directly links strategic planning to human resources planning. Decisions such as these often result in layoffs, transfers, and the like. As noted before, organizations need to have a clear understanding of their core processes and skills in order to make these decisions. Too often, firms approach outsourcing decisions based on costs alone, but this can lead to detrimental effects in the long run if the skills base of its employees suffer and its core capabilities are subsequently eroded.

Differentiation Strategy: Compete on Value Added

While decreasing costs is one important way to enhance customer value, another involves providing something unique and distinctive to customers. A differentiation strategy is often based on high product quality, innovative features, speed to market, or superior service. Ritz-Carlton's commitment to quality and luxury, FedEx's focus on speed and flexible delivery, Neiman Marcus's commitment to fashion and customer service, and Apple's emphasis on innovation and product development are all easily identifiable examples of differentiation strategies.

Each of these strategies is rooted in the management of human resources. Companies that focus on service, for example, need to identify and support ways to empower employees to serve customers better. In contrast to the company that emphasizes low cost and efficiencies, you may find that differentiating companies will bend the rules a bit more, allow more flexibility to let you "have it your way," and customize products and services around the customer's particular needs. In place of rigid rules, service-oriented companies often try to embed their values in the cultural values of the company. For example, one quality Starbucks looks for in prospective employees is the ability to make good decisions on their own. Similarly, Nordstrom's employee handbook consists of just a single 5- × 8-inch card that reads: "Welcome to Nordstrom. Rule #1. Use your good judgment in all situations. There will be no additional rules."

Functional Strategy: Ensuring Alignment

In addition to formulating corporate and business-level strategies, managers also need to "translate" strategic priorities into functional areas of the organization (such as marketing, manufacturing, human resources, and the like). This involves all aspects of the business, but in particular there needs to be a clear alignment between HR and the requirements of an organization's strategy. In this regard, HR policies and practices need to achieve two types of fit: external and internal.[20]

External Fit/Alignment

External fit (or *external alignment*) focuses on the connection between the business objectives and the major initiatives in HR. For example, as we noted earlier, if a company's strategy focuses on achieving low cost, its HR policies and practices need to reinforce this idea by reinforcing efficient and reliable behavior on the part of employees, enhanced productivity, and the like. On the other hand, if the organization competes through innovation and new product development, then its HR policies and practices would be more aligned with the notion of fostering creativity and flexibility.

Internal Fit/Alignment

In addition to external alignment, or fit, managers need to ensure that their HR practices are all aligned with one another internally to establish a configuration that is mutually reinforcing. The entire range of the firm's HR practices—from its job design, staffing, training, performance appraisal, and compensation—need to focus on the same workforce objectives. Unfortunately, often one HR practice, such as training, might be focused on teamwork and sharing, while another HR practice, such as the firm's appraisal and compensation programs, reinforces the ideas of individual achievement. Charles Schwab and Company faced this very situation. The company has a reputation in the financial services industry for developing a culture of teamwork that has been important to its strategy. However, when it changed its compensation strategy to provide more rewards to its high-performing brokers, the firm sent mixed signals to its employees. Which is more important: teamwork or individual high flyers?[21]

◼◼ Step Five: Strategy Implementation

Objective 6

As the old saying goes, "well begun is half done"—but only half. Like any plan, formulating the appropriate strategy is not enough. Managers must also ensure that the new plans are implemented effectively. This is easier said than done. One recent survey revealed that about half of managers say there is a gap between their organization's ability to develop a vision and strategy and actually execute it. Recently organizations have been paying more attention to implementation and execution.[22]

Figure 2.10 shows the now classic 7-S framework and reveals that human resources management is instrumental to almost every aspect of strategy implementation, whether it pertains to structure, systems, style, skills, staff, or shared values. While *strategy* lays out the route that the organization will take in the future, organizational *structure* is the framework in which activities of the organization members are coordinated. If the strategy requires employees to be reorganized or redeployed, HR will be intimately involved. Closely related to structure are *systems* and processes. These include formal and informal procedures that govern the everyday activities of a firm. As organizations consider reengineering and redesign their processes to implement their strategies, HR helps ensure that the best workflow models are in place and— importantly—that employees are involved in sharing their advice, too.

Shared values were discussed earlier in the chapter as a guiding parameter for strategic planning. They arise again as an important issue in implementation as well.

FIGURE
2.10

The 7-S Model

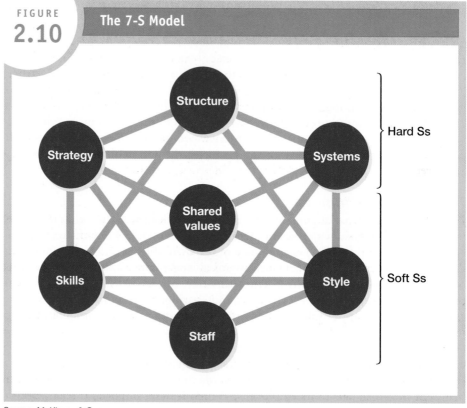

Source: McKinsey & Company.

Strategic change often requires employees and managers to modify, or abandon, their old ways of doing things. HR managers play a central role as guardians of the corporate culture—the principles on which the company is founded and the fundamental ideas around which the business is built. This is tightly connected to the issue of *style*, which refers not only to the leadership approach of top managers, but also the way in which employees present themselves to the outside world (to suppliers, customers, and so on).

Skills and *staff* relate directly to the concerns of human resources management and point to the critical role that HR plays in strategy implementation. At a fundamental level, HR's role in strategy implementation focuses on reconciling (1) human resources demanded and (2) human resources available.

Taking Action: Reconciling Supply and Demand

Through HRP, organizations strive for a proper balance between demand considerations and supply considerations. Demand considerations are based on forecasted trends in business activity. Supply considerations involve determining where and how candidates with the required qualifications can be found to fill a firm's vacancies. Because of the difficulty in locating applicants for the increasing number of jobs that require advanced training, this aspect of planning has been receiving much more attention. Greater planning effort is also needed to recruit members of protected classes for managerial jobs and technical jobs that require advanced levels of education.

In an effort to meet their human resources demands, organizations have many staffing options, including hiring full-time employees, having current employees work overtime, recalling laid-off workers, using temporary or contract employees, and outsourcing or offshoring some of their business processes. However, when forecasts show a surplus of employees, organizations often restrict their hiring, reduce their employees' work hours, and consider layoffs, demotions, and/or terminations. Some organizations try to reduce their workforces by relying on attrition, which is a gradual reduction of employees through resignations, retirements, and deaths. Over the past few decades, early retirements have become a more and more common means for organizations to reduce their excess labor supply. Organizations as diverse as state colleges, health care facilities, and travel companies encourage employees to accept early retirement by offering "sweetened" retirement benefits. The various types of benefits are discussed in Chapter 11.

Organizational Downsizing, Outsourcing, and Offshoring

As we have discussed, organizations have to be constantly prepared to exit and enter new lines of business, restructure, outsource, offshore, and sometimes downsize. Because of either economic or competitive pressures, General Motors, American Airlines, and Motorola are among the many firms that have eliminated thousands of jobs—either because they had too many employees or employees with the wrong skill sets.[23] In many cases, downsizing is part of a longer-term process of restructuring to take advantage of new technology, corporate partnerships, and cost minimization.

Making Layoff Decisions

Decisions about employee layoffs are usually based on seniority and/or performance. In some organizations, especially in Japanese firms and firms with labor agreements, seniority is more likely to be the primary consideration. In other organizations, factors such as ability and productivity take precedence over seniority.

In the case of unionized organizations, the criteria for determining an employee's eligibility for layoff are typically set forth in the union agreement. As a rule, seniority on the job receives significant weight in determining which employees are laid off first. Similar provisions in the union agreement provide for the right of employees to be recalled to jobs that they are still qualified to perform. Organizational policy, as well as provisions in the labor agreement, should therefore establish and define clearly the employment rights of each individual and the basis on which layoff selections will be made and reemployment effected. The rights of employees during layoffs, the conditions concerning their eligibility for recall, and their obligations in accepting recall should also be clarified. It is common for labor agreements to preserve the reemployment rights of employees laid off for periods of up to two years, providing that they do not refuse to return to work if recalled sooner.

It has become customary, however, for employers to give some degree of recognition to seniority even among employees who are not unionized. Unions generally advocate recognizing seniority because they feel that their members should be entitled to certain rights proportionate to the years they have invested in their jobs. Nevertheless, whenever seniority is a basis for determining or even affecting HR decisions, the discretion of managers to make layoff decisions is reduced accordingly. One of the major disadvantages of overemphasizing seniority is that the less competent employees receive the same rewards and security as the more competent ones. Also, the practice of using seniority as the basis for deciding which workers to lay off may well have a disparate impact on women and minority workers, who often have less seniority than other groups.[24]

In cases where economic conditions have brought about layoffs, employees who were let go while in good standing may be recalled to their jobs when the economic outlook brightens and job openings occur. However, in many cases these new jobs require a different set of skills than the jobs they replaced. Identifying individuals for

Organizations have many staffing options, including hiring full-time employees, having current employees work overtime, recalling laid-off workers, or using temporary or contract employees. On the negative side, economic conditions can bring about layoffs.

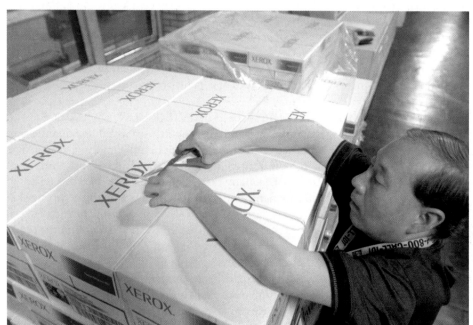

these jobs can be accomplished by searching among previous employees or among current employees who can be reassigned. Frequently, however, the process requires searching externally in the broader labor market.

STEP SIX: EVALUATION AND ASSESSMENT

At one level, it might seem that assessing a firm's effectiveness is the final step in the planning process. That is true. But it is also the first step. Planning is cyclical, of course, and while we have somewhat conveniently placed evaluation at the end of this chapter, it actually provides the inputs to the next cycle in the planning process. Measurement, benchmarking, alignment, fit, and flexibility issues are central to the evaluation process.

7 Objective

Evaluation and Assessment Issues

In order to evaluate their performance, firms need to establish a set of parameters that focus on the "desired outcomes" of their strategic planning, as well as the metrics they will use to monitor how well the organization delivers against those outcomes. Because strategic management is ultimately aimed at creating a competitive advantage, many firms evaluate their performance against other firms. Benchmarking is the process of identifying "best practices" in a given area—for example, productivity, logistics, brand management, training, and so on—and then comparing your practices and performance to those of other companies. To accomplish this, a benchmarking team would collect information on its own company's operations and those of other firms in order to uncover any gaps. The gaps help determine the causes of performance differences, and ultimately the team would map out a set of best practices that lead to world-class performance. Interestingly, the target company for benchmarking does not need to be a competitor. For example, when Xerox wanted to learn about excellent customer service, it benchmarked L. L. Bean. By working with noncompeting companies, Xerox was able to get access to information a competitor would not divulge.

benchmarking
The process of comparing the organization's processes and practices with those of other companies

> ### Using the Internet
>
> For more information on HR benchmarking, go to the Student Resources at:
>
> **www.cengage.com/ management/bohlander**

In the context of HR strategy, the metrics fall into two basic categories: human capital metrics and HR metrics. Human capital metrics assess aspects of the workforce, whereas HR metrics assess the performance of the HR function itself. The Saratoga Institute (now an arm of PriceWaterhouseCoopers) publishes the annual *Human Capital Benchmarking Report*, which includes benchmarking information from almost 900 companies (see Highlights in HRM 4). The Institute's clients can use the information from studies of such areas as pay structure, return on investment per employee, turnover rates, and cost-per-hire and time-to-fill for key employees. This kind of detailed information clarifies potential bases of competitive advantage and reveals a path for developing future HR strategies.

With that said, benchmarking alone will not give a firm a competitive advantage. According author and HRM consultant Mark Huselid, a competitive advantage is based on the unique combination of a company's human capital, strategy, and core capabilities—which differ from firm to firm. This means that HR managers cannot simply rely on the benchmarks and strategies of other firms. Instead, they must develop their own. If they can successfully do so and implement them, they can achieve a sustained competitive advantage.[25]

Ten Measures of Human Capital

The ten areas to measure, as recommended by Jac Fitz-enz, chair of the Saratoga Institute (now part of PricewaterhouseCoopers) will not all apply to your company, but some will:

1. **Your most important issues.** These are the targets of all lower-level measures. Focus on them and ensure that your metrics lead in a direct line to them.

2. **Human capital value added.** How do your workers optimize themselves for the good of the company and for themselves? This is the primary measure of an individual's contribution to profitability.

3. **Human capital ROI.** This is the ratio of dollars spent on pay and benefits to an adjusted profit figure.

4. **Separation cost.** How many people are leaving? From which departments? What does it cost the company? The average cost of separation for an employee is at least six months' equivalent of revenue per employee.

5. **Voluntary separation rate.** Lost personnel equal potential lost opportunity, lost revenue, and the cost of workers having to fill the gaps under greater stress. Cutting the separation rate saves the cost of hiring and keeps customer service quality high.

6. **Total labor-cost/revenue percentage.** This is total benefits and compensation cost as a percentage of organizational revenue and shows how much of what you are taking in through revenue goes to support the company's total labor cost, including temporary, seasonal, and contract or contingent workers. This metric can help you track changes in your workforce. Best approach: Compare it to your revenue factor and compensation, benefits, and contingent off-payroll costs. If the metric is rising, determine whether compensation or benefits costs are up or revenue is down. This will help you decide what actions to take.

7. **Total compensation/revenue percentage.** This is the percentage of the company's revenues allocated to the direct costs of employees. It excludes costs for off-payroll employees who receive a 1099 form (as does the metric in item 6). Before creating strategies to address concerns, compare this metric to your revenue factor, compensation costs, and benefits costs to analyze what is happening with workers.

8. **Training investment factor.** Basic skills are crucial: Workers who cannot read, write, do simple calculations, or talk intelligently with customers need to have these skill deficiencies addressed.

9. **Time to start.** Recruitment will continue to be a challenge. The amount of the time it takes from approval of a job requisition until the person is on the job is a strategic indicator of revenue production.

10. **Revenue factor.** This is the basic measure understood by managers.

Source: "The Top 10 Measures of Human Capital Management," *HRFocus* 78, no. 5 (May 2001): 8. Copyright © 2001. Reprinted by permission of the publisher via Copyright Clearance Center.

Measuring a Firm's Strategic Alignment

Earlier in the chapter, we discussed the importance of strategic alignment and fit as an element of strategy formulation and implementation. As an element of evaluation, some very useful techniques help managers assess the extent to which they have achieved these objectives.

Strategy Mapping and the Balanced Scorecard

One of the tools for mapping a firm's strategy in order to ensure strategic alignment is the Balanced Scorecard (BSC). Developed by Harvard professors Robert Kaplan and David Norton, the BSC is a framework that helps managers translate their firms' strategic goals into operational objectives. The model has four related cells: (1) financial, (2) customer, (3) processes, and (4) learning. The logic of the BSC is firmly rooted in human resources management. People management and learning help organizations improve their internal processes and provide excellent customer service. Internal processes—product development, service, and the like—are critical for creating customer satisfaction and loyalty, and they are also important for ensuring productivity to contain costs for better financial performance. Customer value creation, in turn, drives up revenues, which enhances profitability.

> **Balanced Scorecard (BSC)**
>
> A measurement framework that helps managers translate strategic goals into operational objectives

Figure 2.11 shows how this might work at Starbucks. In each cell, Starbucks would identify the key metrics that help translate strategic goals to operational imperatives. For example, under customer metrics, Starbucks might look at percentage of repeat customers, number of new customers, growth rate, and the like. Under people metrics, managers might measure the numbers of suggestions provided by employees, participation in Starbucks' stock sharing program, employee turnover, training hours spent, and the like. Each of these cells links vertically. People management issues such as rewards, training, and suggestions can be linked to efficient processes (brewing the perfect cup, delivering top-notch customer service, and so forth). These processes then lead to better customer loyalty and growth. Growth and customer loyalty in turn lead to higher profitability and market value.

Measuring Internal Fit

Recall that internal fit means that HR practices are all aligned with one another to establish a configuration that is mutually reinforcing. Figure 2.12 shows an example of how organizations can assess the internal fit of their HR practices. There are essentially three steps. First, managers need to identify the key workforce objectives they hope to achieve. Often this information can come from the people/learning cell of the Balanced Scorecard and might include loyalty, customer service, productivity, and creativity. Second, managers would identify each of the HR practices used to elicit or reinforce those workforce objectives (job design, staffing, training, appraisal, compensation, and so on). Third, managers would evaluate each HR practice on a scale of –5 (not supportive) to 5 (supportive). By tallying up the ratings across managers, organizations can get a very clear idea of which HR practices are working together to achieve the workforce objectives and which are not.

An important caveat to this analysis is that internal fit is a necessary, but insufficient, cause of strategic alignment. A company could have nearly perfect alignment

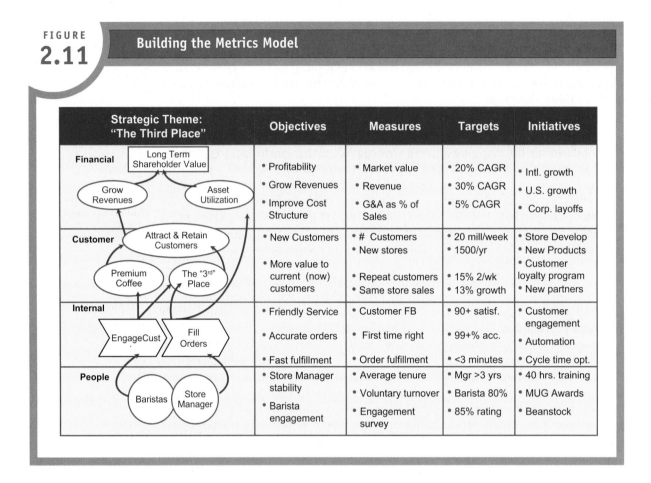

FIGURE 2.11   Building the Metrics Model

among its HR practices, and they still might not be aligned with the competitive strategy. For that reason, it is important for managers to assess both internal fit and external alignment.

Ensuring Strategic Flexibility for the Future

Apart from the need to establish and measure fit between HR and strategy, HR is also focused on ensuring flexibility and agility when the environment changes. Ultimately, successful HRP helps increase organizational capability—the capacity of the organization to continuously act and change in pursuit of sustainable competitive advantage.[26]

Flexibility can be achieved in two primary ways: coordination flexibility and resource flexibility. *Coordination flexibility* occurs through rapid reallocation of resources to new or changing needs. Through HRP, managers can anticipate upcoming events, keep abreast of changes in legal regulations, forecast economic trends, recognize competitor moves, and the like. With advance notice, managers can move people into and out of jobs, retrain them for new skill requirements, and

organizational capability

The capacity of the organization to act and change in pursuit of sustainable competitive advantage

FIGURE 2.12 — Assessing Internal Fit

WORKFORCE OBJECTIVES

ORGANIZATION	SALES PRODUCTIVITY	CUSTOMER SERVICE	MERCHANDISE INFORMATION	STOCK MAINTENANCE	TOTAL
Structure/Workflow					
• Cross-functional teams	3	2	0	−1	4
• Rotation (Depts.)	3	3	−1	−1	4
Staffing					
• Test battery	2	2	1	1	6
• Select for experience	5	3	2	2	12
Training					
• Retail selling skills	4	5	1	1	11
Rewards					
• Results appraisal	5	−4	−2	−5	−6
• Individual incentives	5	−5	−3	−5	−8
Leadership					
• Corporate	3	3	1	0	7
• Store manager	4	2	2	2	10
Technologies					
• Merchandise IS	5	2	5	1	13
• Daily postings	4	−3	4	−1	4
	43/55	10/55	10/55	26/55	57/220

FUNCTIONAL COHESION

SYSTEM COHERENCE — *26%*

5 = Strongly supports the priority
0 = Neutral
−5 = Strongly counterproductive

modify the kinds of incentives they use. Use of a contingency workforce composed of part-timers, temporary employees, and external partners also helps achieve coordination flexibility.[27] *Resource flexibility*, on the other hand, results from having people who can do many different things in different ways. Cross-training, job rotations, team-based work modes, and the like are all focused on establishing a flexible workforce.

We will draw on these ideas throughout the text. But at this point we want to close the chapter by emphasizing that strategic planning is a process designed to ensure superior performance today, as well as establishing the capability and agility to respond tomorrow. As the great hockey player Wayne Gretsky used to say, "I don't skate to where the puck is. I skate to where the puck is going to be."

SUMMARY

Objective 1 Strategic human resources management (SHRM) integrates strategic planning and HR planning. It can be thought of as the pattern of human resources deployments and activities that enable an organization to achieve its strategic goals. HR planning and strategies becomes especially critical when organizations consider global strategies, including mergers, joint ventures, offshoring, the relocation of plants, product innovations, and downsizing, or when dramatic shifts in the composition of the labor force are occurring.

Objective 2 Analyzing the firm's competitive environment is central to strategic planning. The competitive environment includes the specific organizations with which the firm interacts. Firms analyze the competitive environment in order to adapt to or influence the nature of competition.

Objective 3 Conducting an internal analysis to gauge the firm's strengths and weaknesses involves looking at a firm's "three Cs"—its culture, capabilities, and composition. An internal analysis enables strategic decisionmakers to inventory the organization's skills and resources as well as their performance levels.

An organization's success increasingly depends on the knowledge, skills, and abilities of employees, particularly as they help establish a set of core capabilities that distinguish an organization from its competitors. When employees' talents are valuable, rare, difficult to imitate, and organized, a firm can achieve a sustained competitive advantage through its people.

Objective 4 HRP is a systematic process that involves forecasting demand for labor, performing supply analysis, and balancing supply and demand considerations. Forecasting demand requires using either quantitative or qualitative methods to identify the number and type of people needed to meet organizational objectives. Supply analysis involves determining whether sufficient employees are available within the organization to meet demand and also whether potential employees are available on the job market.

Objective 5 As organizations plan for their future, top management and strategic planners must recognize that strategic planning decisions affect—and are affected by—HR functions. On one hand, HRP plays a reactive role in ensuring that the right number and type of employees are available to implement a chosen business plan. On the other hand, HRP can proactively identify and initiate programs needed to develop organizational capabilities on which future strategies can be built. HRP and strategic planning tend to be most effective when there is a reciprocal relationship between the two processes.

Objective 6 Formulating a HR strategy is only half of the HR battle. The strategy must also be implemented. Employment forecasts must be reconciled against the internal and the external supplies of labor the firm faces. This can include having current employees work overtime, hiring full-time, part-time, or contract employees, downsizing, outsourcing, and offshoring. If there is a labor shortage, the firm might have to reformulate its long-term and short-term strategic plans.

Objective 7 Firms need to establish a set of parameters that focus on the "desired outcomes" of strategic planning, as well as the metrics they will use to monitor how well the firm delivers against those outcomes. Issues of measurement, benchmarking, alignment, fit, and flexibility are central to the evaluation process. Firms use benchmarking, strategy mapping, and the Balanced Scorecard (BSC) as tools to gauge their outcomes.

KEY TERMS

Balanced Scorecard (BSC)
benchmarking
core capabilities
core values
cultural audits
environmental scanning
human capital readiness
human resources planning
(HRP)

management forecasts
Markov analysis
mission
organizational capability
replacement charts
skill inventories
staffing tables
strategic human resources
management (SHRM)

strategic planning
strategic vision
succession planning
SWOT analysis
trend analysis
value creation

DISCUSSION QUESTIONS

Objective 1
1. Identify the three key elements of the human resources planning model and discuss the relationships among them.

Objective 2
2. What competitive environmental forces influence a firm's strategy?

Objective 3
3. What criteria must be met if firms are to achieve a competitive advantage through their employees?

Objective 4
4. Which approach do you think should be relied on more heavily for strategy formulation—the quantitative or qualitative approach?

Objective 5
5. Explain the difference between a firm's corporate strategy and business strategy. Why do firms need to look at both aspects?

Objective 6
6. What steps does the firm need to take to reconcile labor supply and labor demand?

Objective 7
7. Why is organizational capability important to a firm and how can HR managers enhance it?

Customizing HR for Different Types of Human Capital

Part of strategic planning in HR is mapping an organization's human capital. When we look at the strategic value of a person's skills as well as their uniqueness, we soon discover that organizations are comprised of different kinds of workers who have very different kinds of skills. Some are core knowledge workers; some are more traditional job-based employees; some are contract workers; and some are external partners. In this context, it is unlikely that we would manage all of these employees the same way (as much as we might want to for fairness). There are differences in HR practices for different groups. That is not bad, but it makes the job of HR managers more difficult.

Assignment

The following are descriptions of three different employees. How would you characterize each worker? What role does each play when it comes to the organization's strategy?

Andrea Bascomb is a highly talented computer programmer for MiniFluff, Inc. She is among the elite set of engineers in the computer industry that is doing leading-edge work on advanced computer modeling. In truth, CEO Bill Ding believes that the future of the company rests on the innovative work that Andrea and her team are doing. He worries that someone might lure Andrea away to work for them. So he wants to give her all the room she needs to grow and stay committed to MiniFluff.

Calvin Duff is a salesperson on the retail side of MiniFluff. He has daily contact with customers and is responsible for making sales and communicating with service personnel. Make no mistake: To many customers, Calvin and his coworkers are the "face" of MiniFluff. Always on the lookout for a better situation, Calvin has thought about working for PeachTree Computing, MiniFluff's main competitor. In truth, other salespeople have found that they can leave MiniFluff and get "up to speed" easily at other firms. Their skills are very transferable, and the transition is not difficult. Bill Ding and other managers at MiniFluff recognize this fact, so they try to keep salespeople loyal and productive, recognizing that many of them do eventually leave.

Evelyn Frank is a part-time secretary for MiniFluff. She handles routine typing and filing work for the company, particularly in peak periods in the summer and around the holidays. She usually works for a few weeks at a time and then takes time off. The executives at MiniFluff have considered either outsourcing the job to an agency or automating it through a new computer system. But for now things are steady.

BIZFLIX EXERCISES

U-571: Setting Strategy

Watch the scene from *U-571.* It shows several aspects of strategic planning described earlier in this chapter.

This action-packed World War II thriller shows a U.S. submarine crew's efforts to retrieve an Enigma encryption device from a disabled German submarine. After the crew gets the device, a German vessel torpedoes and sinks the U.S. submarine. The survivors must now use the disabled German submarine to escape from the enemy with their prize. The film's almost nonstop action and extraordinary special effects look and sound best with a home theater system.

The scene comes from the "160 Meters" segment toward the film's end. Lt. Andrew Tyler (Matthew McConaughey) is now the submarine's commander following the drowning death of Lt. Commander Mike Dahlgren (Bill Paxton), the original commander. Lt. Tyler says, "Chief." Chief Petty Officer Henry Klough (Harvey Keitel) approaches the map table. The film continues to its dramatic end with the execution of the strategy Tyler describes.

What to Watch for and Ask Yourself

- Does Lt. Tyler analyze the submarine's external environment? Does he engage in environmental scanning as described earlier in this chapter?

- What is Lt. Tyler's assessment of the submarine's strengths and weaknesses?

- Does Lt. Tyler consider threats and opportunities in forming his strategic plan? Has he done a SWOT analysis as described earlier in this chapter?

CASE STUDY 1

Staffing, Down to a Science at Capital One

When the financial services industry tumbled into crisis in June 2007, Capital One chairman and CEO Richard Fairbank issued a mandate to strip $700 million out of the company's operating costs by 2009. The cost reduction plan includes consolidating and streamlining functions, reducing layers of management, and eliminating approximately 2,000 jobs. The mandate did not set off a mad scramble in workforce planning, however. Instead, the planning staff simply added new defined variables to their simulations and modified their projections for the company's talent needs.

"The key to workforce planning is to start with the long-term vision of the organization and its future business goals and work back from there," says Matthew Schuyler, chief human resources officer for Capital One and its 27,000 employees. "We anticipate the strategic needs of the business and make sure that we have the workforce required to meet those needs. The $700 million mandate gives us goals and boundaries that we didn't have before. We made the adjustments."

Capital One and other leading companies are now developing a set of best practices for workforce planning that reach into the future for each business unit and evolve with corporate strategic planning. In an increasingly unstable global business environment, the value of a long-term vision is clear, but effective workforce planning requires dedicated resources, heavy analytics, and, perhaps most important, the full engagement of business unit leaders and line managers.

Working Backward

The workforce planning at Capital One stems from a process executed by a metrics and analytics group of 20 people, plus hundreds of executives, managers, and analysts pulled from all the business lines and corporate functions. Leaders and analysts from the business lines work in blended teams with human resources generalists and members of the metrics group to build models for each line and the entire world force. The models flow to Schuyler, who reports directly to the CEO. "You have to garner your long-term vision of the organization from your seat at the table and from the time you spend with business leaders, immersed in places where you can get data," Schuyler says. "You have to probe the business leaders and know the business leaders and know what their endgame looks like." Planning varies by business line. Some lines are stable, while others are restructuring or moving through rapid growth.

Part of Schuyler's job is to ensure that senior business line leaders are engaged in the process. "Their door is open," he notes. "Your ticket through the door is to show business leaders the bundles of money they can save if their workforce is the right size with the right mix and the right skills. Once you're inside, you have to act on the promise." The potential cost savings come from minimizing the inherent costs associated with the size of the workforce, plus savings from lower recruiting and severance costs and avoiding the costs of a disengaged workforce. "The cost of disengagement is difficult to quantify, but business leaders intuitively understand the cost," Schuyler says. "There is a toll paid when a workforce is disempowered, disengaged, and not sufficiently busy."

Workforce planning at Capital One forecasts not only the head count required to meet future business needs, but also the staffing mix—the ratio of internal to external resources—and the skills mix, including any changes in that mix that are required as the business moves forward. Schuyler also looks at any changes in "spans of control," which determine the number of organizational layers, optimal methods for staffing managerial positions, and the related costs. The planners also document both rational and emotional employee engagement, which affect current and future productivity and recruiting, training, and turnover costs.

The responsibility for workforce planning at Capital One resides in human resources, but the hard work takes place inside the business units, where the blended teams operate. This grounding in the business units keeps workforce planning focused on corporate goals. Workforce planning really gets traction when it is linked to the line managers who understand business needs and can project their business growth and productivity changes. The time frames for workforce planning at Capital One vary by unit and function. The legal function, for example, is very stable and can easily plan out two to four years. The credit card division, however, is rapidly evolving, so its forecasts stretch out two to four years but are reviewed every quarter. Likewise, the demand for some jobs follows the business cycle. Collections and recoveries work at Capital One was stable and predictable several years ago, for example. "But because of the current economic conditions, this work is now more important, and we had to ramp up very quickly," Schuyler explains.

Managing Demand and Supply

Schuyler refuses to choose between overshooting and undershooting staffing. "The beauty of workforce planning is that it allows the flexibility to be right on target," he says. "We don't have to wait for the next budget cycle to get it right."

That flexibility derives from a more sophisticated approach to planning that looks at a range of possible scenarios about business conditions and then calculates the labor needed to match them. Capital One's workforce planning models allow business leaders to anticipate the talent requirements for each business option and the human resources and labor cost consequences of the choices they make. Especially for companies that are just beginning to implement a workforce planning process, the best approach is to focus first on the critical roles in the organization and then expand out to cover more positions in greater detail. Avoid the tendency to drown managers in data, by breaking the data down on a critical-jobs basis. At Capital One, the workforce planning process reaches down through the entire executive structure for each business unit—five or six levels of leadership plus groups of managers. Business leaders see the talent management costs and consequences of the business options at hand. Each option carries its own implications for internal and external staffing levels, recruiting, training, promotions, engagement, attrition, and total compensation costs over time. More important, workforce planning allows business leaders and line managers to see how different approaches to talent management can actually expand their business options and boost performance. "If workforce planning is done right, human resources can help business leaders think about what their endgame can be," Schuyler says.

Questions

1. Why do you think it's important for Capital One to calculate the "disengagement" factor of its employees when it comes to workforce planning?
2. What merits do you see to breaking down the planning process by business units through multiple layers of leaders? Do you see any drawbacks of doing so?

Source: Excerpted from Fay Hansen, "The Long View," *Workforce Management* 87, no. 7 (April 21, 2008): 1, 19.

CASE STUDY 2

Matching Talent with Tasks: Dole Implements Succession Planning

With 61,000 workers in more than ninety countries, Dole Food Company has talent all over the world. Only a few hundred of those employees are in top management at the 151-year-old company headquartered in Westlake Village, California. The trouble is, Dole doesn't have comprehensive knowledge of who these managers are or what they can do. If a key job opens up in North America, the business unit leader wouldn't know if the perfect candidate worked in another Dole unit in South America. Dole has no way to match its top managerial talent with its executive needs.

But that is changing. The highly decentralized company is launching a succession planning process, supported by Web-based software, through which Dole executives hope to rectify their inability to promote the best and the brightest across the corporation. The process itself requires a change of culture and could become an agent for further culture change. "The idea of succession planning is contrary to being highly decentralized," says Sue Hagen, vice president of HR for North American operations, who led the effort.

Hagen talked informally to all corporate executives and the leaders and staffs of each business unit to generate consensus for succession planning for corporate positions—corporate officers, business unit presidents, and their direct reports. "The initial group would be about 100," she says. Next year, another few hundred will be included.

"The reaction was mostly positive," Hagen says. Hagen's next step was to hold a series of in-depth interviews with the executives to determine which succession planning processes were needed and how often they should be conducted. The goal was to reflect as much of their thinking as possible. "One division wanted to review succession plans on their people six times a year. Another didn't want to do it at all," she says. Hagen compromised. Succession planning will be conducted twice a year. She also identified four competencies on which everyone would be evaluated: accountability, business acumen, multifunctionality (cross-training), and vision/originality.

Many HRMS software suites have an optional succession planning module, but neither Dole nor its business units have a HRMS. "Since most employees are farm or factory workers, there is not much need for the detailed information a HRMS provides," says Hagen. "It would be overkill. In a way, the succession planning software Dole adopted will become a mini HRMS for top personnel," she adds.

Hagen also wanted an application service provider (ASP) model. Outsourcing, including payroll, is common at Dole. Hagen didn't want to own and support technology, and she didn't want the small corporate information technology staff to have to work on it.

The users of the system—top managers—access the program from the Web with a password. They fill out a resume, including career interests, and note any mobility restrictions. They assess themselves on the four competencies. When they are done, the system automatically notifies their manager, who does an assessment and indicates whether he or she thinks the individual could be promoted. The manager also assesses overall potential and the risk of losing the user. This assessment then goes automatically to the division head, then to the divisional HR director, and then to Hagen. Hagen will use the information to create a career development plan for each individual, including seminars she'll organize. She'll also direct business unit leaders to potential candidates in other units when they have appropriate openings. "The beauty is, for the first time we'll have a database that ties together these talent metrics and can serve as a clearinghouse for people available for opportunities," Hagen says.

"Dole's corporate management hopes all business units will eventually adopt similar succession planning processes and software," Hagen says. "I view this as a pilot, a very visible pilot," she says. "To get the buy-in of individual business units, we'll show them that this was adopted by their senior management and that it works."

Questions

1. Why do you think companies like Dole need succession planning?

2. Do you see any disadvantage of "automating" succession planning?

Source: Excerpted from Bill Roberts, "Matching Talent with Tasks: Dole Implements Succession Planning to Get Ready for Changes at the Top," *HRMagazine* 47, no. 11 (November 2002): 91–95.

NOTES AND REFERENCES

1. "The Importance of HR," *HRFocus* 73, no. 3 (March 1996): 14; "Retiring Workforce, Widening Skills Gap, Exodus of 'Critical Talent' Threaten Companies: Deloitte Survey," *Canadian Corporate News* (February 15, 2005); Brian E. Becker and Mark A. Huselid, "Strategic Human Resources Management: Where Do We Go From Here?" *Journal of Management* 32, no. 6 (January 2006): 898–925.

2. Scott A. Snell, Mark Shadur, and Patrick M. Wright, "Human Resources Strategy: The Era of Our Ways," in M. A. Hitt, R. E. Freeman, and J. S. Harrison (eds.), *Handbook of Strategic Management* (Oxford, Uk: Blackwell, 2002), 627–49; Patrick M. Wright, Benjamin Dunford, and Scott A. Snell, "Human Resources and the Resource-Based View of the Firm," *Journal of Management* 27, no. 6 (2002): 701–21; "What's Affecting HR Operations? Globalization, Sustainability, and Talent," *HR Focus* 84, no. 8 (August 2007): 8; Doris Sims, "Do You Know Where Your Talent Is?" *Training* 45, no. 1 (January 2008): 46–46.

3. "The Importance of HR," 14. For data from a similar survey conducted in Canada, see David Brown, "HR's Role in Business Strategy: Still a Lot of Work to Be Done," *Canadian HR Reporter* 14, no. 19 (November 5, 2001): 1–20; "How Should the HR Dept. of 2004 Be Structured?" *Human Resource Department Management Report*, no. 3 (November 2003): 1.

4. T. J. Watson, Jr., *A Business and Its Beliefs: The Ideas That Helped Build IBM* (New York: McGraw-Hill, 1963), 5; James W. Walker, "Integrating the Human Resource Function with the Business," *Human Resource Planning* 14, no. 2 (1996): 59–77; James W. Walker, "Perspectives," *Human Resource Planning* 25, no. 1 (2002): 12–14.

6. Patrick Wright, Gary McMahan, Scott Snell, and Barry Gerhart, "Comparing Line and HR Executives' Perceptions of HR Effectiveness: Services, Roles, and Contributions," *Human Resource Management* 40, no. 2 (2001): 111–23;

Ryan Langlois, "Fairmont Hotels: Business Strategy Starts with People," *Canadian HR Reporter* 14, no. 19 (November 5, 2001): 19–25.

7. Bala Iyer, "Deconstructing Google," *Computerworld* 42, no. 15 (April 7, 2008): 32–33.

8. Jay J. Jamrog and Miles H. Overholt, "Building a Strategic HR Function: Continuing the Evolution," *Human Resource Planning* 27, no. 1 (March 2004): 51; Gary L. Nielson, Karla L. Martin, and Elizabeth Powers, "The Secrets to Successful Strategy Execution," *Harvard Business Review* 86, no. 6 (June 2008): 60–70.

9. For example, see U.S. Department of Labor, Bureau of Labor Statistics, *Geographic Profiles of Employment and Unemployment*. The data and information are accessible via the Office of Employment Projections home page at http://www.bls.gov/emp.

10. J. B. Quinn, "The Intelligent Enterprise: A New Paradigm," *Academy of Management Executive* 6, no. 4 (2002): 48–63.

11. Jennifer Laabs, "The HR Side of Sears' Comeback," *Workforce* 78, no. 3 (March 1999): 24–29.

12. For more information on methods to identify a firm's core capabilities, see Khalid Hafeez, YanBing Zhang, and Naila Malak, "Core Competence for Sustainable Competitive Advantage: A Structured Methodology for Identifying Core Competence," *IEEE Transactions on Engineering Management* 49, no. 1 (February 2002): 28–35; Quinn, "The Intelligent Enterprise," 48–63; Jane Wollman Rusoff, "Outsourced Solutions: Brokerage Firms Looking to Focus on Their Core Competencies Find the Most Value in a Resource-Rich Clearing Partner," *Research* 27, no. 11 (November 2004): 37–40.

13. Snell, Shadur, and Wright, "Human Resources Strategy," 627–49; Wright, Dunford, and Snell, "Human Resources and the Resource-Based View of the Firm," 701–21; David Collis and Cynthia Montgomery, "Competing on Resources," *Harvard Business Review* 86, no. 7/8 (July–August 2008):

140–150; Susan Cantrell, "The Work Force of One," *Wall Street Journal* 249, no. 140 (June 16, 2007): R10.

14. D. P. Lepak and S. A. Snell, "The Human Resource Architecture: Toward a Theory of Human Capital Development and Allocation," *Academy of Management Review* 24, no. 1 (1999): 31–48; David Lepak and Scott Snell, "Examining the Human Resource Architecture: The Relationship among Human Capital, Employment, and Human Resource Configurations," *Journal of Management* 24, no. 1 (January 1999): 31; Mike Berry, "HR Must Push for Change to Drive Human Capital Strategy," *Personnel Today* (April 6, 2004): 4; Brian E. Becker and Mark A. Huselid, "A Players or A Positions? The Strategic Logic of Workforce Management," *Harvard Business Review* 83, no. 12 (December, 2005): 110–117.

15. Stephenie Overman, "Gearing Up for Tomorrow's Workforce," *HRFocus* 76, no. 2 (February 1999): 1, 15; Kathryn Tyler, "Evaluate Your Next Move," *HRMagazine* 46, no. 11 (November 2001): 66–71; Bill Leonard, "Turnover at the Top," *HRMagazine* 46, no. 5 (May 2001): 46–52.

16. Carolyn Hirschman, "Putting Forecasting in Focus," *HRMagazine* 52, no. 3 (March 2007): 44–49.

17. "Talent Management: Now It's the Top Priority for CEOs & Their Organizations," *HR Focus* 85, no. 2 (February 2008): 8–9; "Finding Top Talent," *Community Banker* 17, no. 4 (April 2008): 15; Paul Bernthal and Richard Wellins, "Trends in Leader Development and Succession," *Human Resource Planning* 29, no. 2 (2006): 31–40; Sarah Needleman, "Demand Rises for Talent-Management Software," *Wall Street Journal* 251, no. 12 (January 15, 2008): B8.

18. Robert Kaplan and David Norton, *Strategy Maps: Converting Intangible Assets into Tangible Outcomes* (Boston: Harvard Business School Press, 2006), Chapter 8.

19. John Huey, "Outlaw Flyboy CEOs," *Fortune* 142, no. 11 (November 13, 2000): 237–50; "Visions of the Future," *Human Resources* (January 2008): special section, 22–22.

20. Brian Becker, Mark Huselid, and Dave Ulrich, *The HR Scorecard: Linking People, Strategy, and Performance* (Cambridge, MA: Harvard Business School Press, 2001). See also Shari Caudron, "How HR Drives Profits," *Workforce* 80, no. 12 (December 2001): 26–31.

21. "A Singular Sensation for Schwab Brokers," *Business Week Online* (January 24, 2002).

22. Larry Bossidy, Ram Charan, and Charles Burck, *Execution: The Art of Getting Things Done* (New York: Crown Business, 2002); Stacey L. Kaplan, "Business Strategy, People Strategy and Total Rewards—Connecting the Dots," *Benefits & Compensation Digest* 44, no. 9 (September 2007): 1–19; Gary L. Neilson, Karla L Martin, and Elizabeth Power, "The Secrets to Successful Strategy, *Harvard Business Review* 86, no. 6 (June 2008): 60–70; Mark Vickers, "HR Growing Pains: Getting from Awkward to Accomplished," *Human Resource Planning* 30, no. 4 (2007): 20–24.

23. Jesse Drucker, "Motorola to Cut 7,000 More Jobs and Take $3.5 Billion in Charges," *The Wall Street Journal* (June 28, 2002): B6; Dennis K. Berman, "Planning to Outsource," *HRFocus* 81, no. 5 (May 2004): 1; David Koenig, "American Airlines Workers Brace for Job Cuts," *Associated Press* (July 3, 2008).

24. Lisa Bransten, "U.S. Examining Sun Microsystems over Complaint," *The Wall Street Journal* (June 25, 2002): B6; Matthew Miklave and A. Jonathan Trafimow, "Expecting Problems from This Dismissal," *Workforce* 80, no. 12 (December 2001): 81–83.

25. Ray Brillinger, "Best Practices: Human Resources Benchmarking," *Canadian HR Reporter* 14, no. 12 (June 18, 2001): 12; Chris Mahoney, "Benchmarking Your Way to Smarter Decisions," *Workforce* 79, no. 10 (October 2000): 100–103; Brian E. Becker and Mark A. Huselid, "Strategic Human Resources Management: Where Do We Go From Here?" *Journal of Management* 32 no. 6 (January 2006): 898–925.

26. P. M. Wright and S. A. Snell, "Toward a Unifying Framework for Exploring Fit and Flexibility in Strategic Human Resource Management," *Academy of Management Review* 22, no. 4 (1998): 756–72; Snell, Shadur, and Wright, "Human Resources Strategy," 627–49; Wright, Dunford, and Snell, "Human Resources and the Resource-Based View of the Firm," 701–21.

27. R. Sanchez, "Strategic Flexibility in Product Competition," *Strategic Management Journal* 16 (1995): 135–59; Wright and Snell, "Toward a Unifying Framework." 756–72.

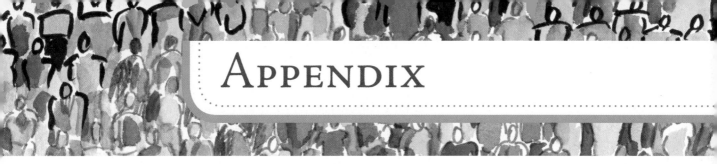

APPENDIX

Calculating Turnover and Absenteeism

Throughout this chapter we have emphasized that HRP depends on having an accurate picture of both the supply of and the demand for employees. Two factors, employee turnover and absenteeism, have a direct impact on HR planning strategy and recruitment processes. In this Appendix, we provide a detailed discussion of turnover and absenteeism, methods for measuring them, and suggestions for managing their impact.

■ EMPLOYEE TURNOVER RATES

Employee turnover refers simply to the movement of employees out of an organization. It is often cited as one of the factors behind the failure of U.S. employee productivity rates to keep pace with those of foreign competitors. It is also one of the chief determinants of labor supply. Even if everything else about an organization stays the same, as employees turn over, its supply of labor goes down. This involves both direct and indirect costs to the organization.

Computing the Turnover Rate

The U.S. Department of Labor suggests the following formula for computing turnover rates:

$$\frac{\text{Number of separations during the month}}{\text{Total number of employees at mid month}} \times 100$$

Thus, if there were 25 separations during a month and the total number of employees at mid month was 500, the turnover rate would be:

$$\frac{25}{100} \times 100 = 5 \text{ percent}$$

Turnover rates are computed on a regular basis to compare specific units such as departments, divisions, and work groups. In many cases, comparisons are made with data provided by other organizations. The *Bureau of National Affairs Quarterly Report on Job Absence and Turnover* is a very good source of comparative turnover data.[1]

Another method of computing the turnover rate is one that reflects only the avoidable separations (S). This rate is computed by subtracting unavoidable separations

(US)—for example, due to pregnancy, return to school, death, or marriage—from all separations. The formula for this method is as follows:

$$\frac{S - US}{M} \times 100 = T \text{ (turnover rate)}$$

where M represents the total number of employees at mid month. For example, if there were 25 separations during a month, 5 of which were US, and the total number of employees at mid month (M) was 500, the turnover rate would be:

$$\frac{25 - 5}{500} \times 100 = 4 \text{ percent}$$

In looking at the impact of turnover on HR planning and recruitment, it is vitally important to recognize that quantitative rates of turnover are not the only factor to be considered. The *quality* of employees who leave an organization is equally important. If poor employees leave, what experts refer to as "functional turnover," this can prove to be beneficial to the organization. The costs of keeping unproductive workers may be far more than the costs to recruit and train a new, more effective performer.

Determining the Costs of Turnover

Replacing an employee is time-consuming and expensive. Costs can generally be broken down into three categories: separation costs for the departing employee, replacement costs, and training costs for the new employee. These costs are conservatively estimated at two to three times the monthly salary of the departing employee, and they do not include indirect costs such as low productivity prior to quitting and lower morale and overtime for other employees because of the vacated job. Consequently, reducing turnover could result in significant savings to an organization. Highlights in HRM 5 details one organization's costs associated with the turnover of a single computer programmer. Note that the major expense is the cost involved in training a replacement.

∎ EMPLOYEE ABSENTEEISM RATES

How frequently employees are absent from their work—the absenteeism rate—is also directly related to HR planning and recruitment. When employees miss work, the organization incurs direct costs of lost wages and decreased productivity. It is not uncommon for organizations to hire extra workers just to make up for the number of absences totaled across all employees. In addition to these direct costs, indirect costs may underlie excessive absenteeism. A certain amount of absenteeism is, of course, unavoidable. There will always be some who must be absent from work because of sickness, accidents, serious family problems, or other legitimate reasons. However, chronic absenteeism may signal deeper problems in the work environment.

Computing Absenteeism Rates

Managers should determine the extent of the absenteeism problem, if any, by maintaining individual and departmental attendance records and by computing absenteeism

Costs Associated with the Turnover of One Computer Programmer

Turnover costs = Separation costs + Replacement costs + Training costs

Separation costs

1. Exit interview = cost for salary and benefits of both interviewer and departing employee during the exit interview = $30 + $30 = $60
2. Administrative and record-keeping action = $30
   Separation costs = $60 + $30 = $90

Replacement costs

1. Advertising for job opening = $2,500
2. Preemployment administrative functions and record-keeping action = $100
3. Selection interview = $250
4. Employment tests = $40
5. Meetings to discuss candidates (salary and benefits of managers while participating in meetings) = $250
   Replacement costs = $2,500 + $100 + $250 + $40 + $250 = $3,140

Training costs

1. Booklets, manuals, and reports = $50
2. Education = $240/day for new employee's salary and benefits × 10 days of workshops, seminars, or courses = $2,400
3. One-to-one coaching = ($240/day per new employee + $240/day per staff coach or job expert) × 20 days of one-to-one coaching = $9,600
4. Salary and benefits of new employee until he or she gets "up to par" = $240/day for salary and benefits × 20 days = $4,800
   Training costs = $50 + $2,400 + $9,600 + $4,800 = $16,850

Total turnover costs = $90 + $3,140 + $16,850 = $20,080

Source: Adapted from the book *Turning Your Human Resources Department into a Profit Center*™ by Michael Mercer, PhD (Barrington, IL: Castlegate Publishers, Inc.). Copyright 2002 Michael Mercer. Reproduced with permission from Michael Mercer, PhD, http://www.DrMercer.com.

rates. Although there is no universally accepted definition of "absence" or a standard formula for computing absenteeism rates, the method most frequently used is that recommended by the U.S. Department of Labor.

$$\frac{\text{Number of worker-days lost through job absence during period}}{\text{Average number of employees} \times \text{number of workdays}} \times 100$$

If 300 worker-days are lost through job absence during a month having 25 scheduled working days at an organization that employs 500 workers, the absenteeism rate for that month is:

$$\frac{300}{300 \times 25} \times 100 = 2.4 \text{ percent}$$

The U.S. Department of Labor defines job absence as the failure of employees to report to work when their schedules require it, whether or not such failure to report is excused. Scheduled vacations, holidays, and prearranged leaves of absence are not counted as job absence.

Comparing Absenteeism Data

The Bureau of Labor Statistics of the U.S. Department of Labor receives data on job absences from the Current Population Survey of Households conducted by the Bureau of the Census, and analyses of these data are published periodically. These analyses permit the identification of problem areas—industries, occupations, or groups of workers with the highest incidence of absence or with rapidly increasing rates of absence. Comparison with other organizations may be made by referring to Bureau of Labor Statistics data reported in the *Monthly Labor Review* or by consulting such reporting services as the Bureau of National Affairs and Commerce Clearing House.[2]

Costs of Absenteeism

Traditional accounting and information systems often do not generate data that reflect the costs of absenteeism. Consequently, their usefulness in HR planning is often limited. To accentuate the impact of absenteeism on organizational performance, managers should translate the data into dollar costs. A system for computing absenteeism costs for an individual organization is available. Organizations with computerized absence reporting systems should find this additional information easy and inexpensive to generate. The cost of each person hour lost to absenteeism is based on the hourly weighted average salary, costs of employee benefits, supervisory costs, and incidental costs.

For example, XYZ Company, with 1,200 employees, has 78,000 person hours lost to absenteeism; the total absence cost is $560,886. When this figure is divided by 1,200 employees, the cost per employee is $467.41. (In this example, we are assuming the absent workers are paid. If absent workers are not paid, their salary figures are omitted from the computation.)

Absenteeism and HR Planning

While an employer may find that the overall absenteeism rate and costs are within an acceptable range, it is still advisable to study the statistics to determine whether there are patterns in the data. Rarely does absenteeism spread itself evenly across an organization. It is very likely that employees in one area (or occupational group) may have nearly perfect attendance records, while others in a different area may be absent frequently. By monitoring these differential attendance records, managers can assess where problems might exist and, more important, begin planning ways to resolve or improve the underlying causes. For example, incentives could be provided for perfect attendance. Alternatively, progressive discipline procedures might be used with employees having a record of recurring absenteeism.

By establishing a comprehensive absenteeism policy, Allen-Bradley cut absenteeism 83.5 percent in a twenty-five-month period. This reduced the strain on labor costs and increased productivity. Part of the company's attendance policy reads:

> It is important to the successful operation of the Motion Control Division that employees be at work each scheduled workday. Each employee is performing an important set of tasks or activities. Excessive and/or avoidable absenteeism places unfair burdens on co-workers and increases the company's cost of doing business by disruption of work schedules, [creating] inefficiency and waste, delays, costly overtime, job pressures and customer complaints.[3]

NOTES AND REFERENCES

1. This quarterly report is part of the *BNA Bulletin to Management*. For an excellent review of the relationship between performance and voluntary turnover, see Charles R. Williams and Linda Parrack Livingstone, "Another Look at the Relationship between Performance and Voluntary Turnover," *Academy of Management Journal* 37, no. 2 (April 1994): 269–98.

2. The loose-leaf publications of these organizations are sources of invaluable information for managers and HR professionals. These publications may be found in most libraries containing business reference books.

3. Allen-Bradley Employee Handbook.

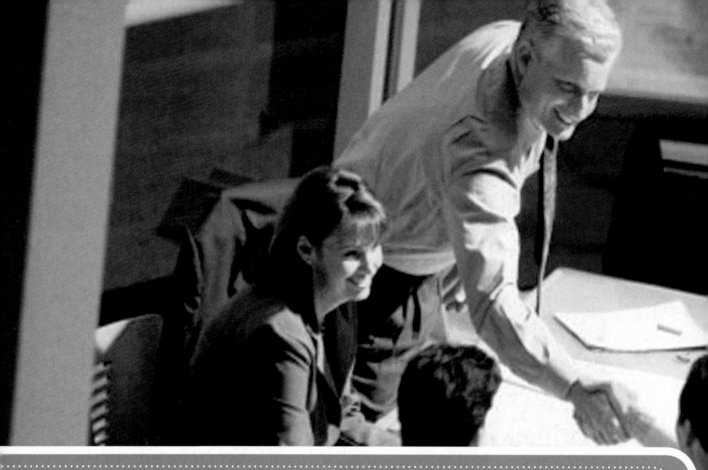

Equal Employment Opportunity and Human Resources Management

After studying this chapter, you should be able to

Objective | 1 |

Explain the reasons behind passage of EEO legislation.

Objective | 2 |

Prepare an outline describing the major laws affecting equal employment opportunity. Describe bona fide occupational qualification and religious preference as EEO issues.

© FISHER/THATCHER/GETTY IMAGES

Objective 3

Discuss sexual harassment and immigration reform and control as EEO concerns.

Objective 4

Explain the use of the *Uniform Guidelines on Employee Selection Procedures*.

Objective 5

Understand the concepts of adverse impact and disparate treatment.

Objective 6

Understand EEOC record-keeping and posting requirements.

Objective 7

Explain how EEO discrimination charges are processed.

Objective 8

Describe affirmative action and the basic steps in developing an affirmative action program.

equal employment opportunity (EEO)

The treatment of individuals in all aspects of employment—hiring, promotion, training, etc.—in a fair and nonbiased manner

Within the field of HRM perhaps no topics continue to receive more attention than equal employment opportunity (EEO) and affirmative action (AA). Equal employment opportunity, or the employment of individuals in a fair and nonbiased manner, has consumed the attention of the media, courts, practitioners, and legislators. Not surprisingly, a more diverse and multicultural workforce has mandated that managers know and comply with a myriad of legal requirements affecting all aspects of the employment relationship. These mandates create legal responsibilities for an organization and each of its managers to comply with various laws and administrative guidelines. Importantly, practitioners agree that when all functions of HRM comply with the law, the organization becomes a fairer and more effective place to work.

However, when managers ignore the legal aspects of HRM, they risk incurring costly and time-consuming litigation, negative public attitudes, and damage to their individual careers.[1] Two highly publicized cases illustrate these points. In a black eye for Walgreens, the nation's largest drugstore chain, in March 2007, the U.S. Equal Employment Opportunity Commission sued the company, alleging it made job assignments and promotions based on race. The government alleged the company assigned Black managers, trainees, and pharmacists to low-performing stores and to stores in Black communities, which denied them favorable jobs and promotions. Robert Johnson, EEOC regional attorney in St. Louis, stated, "Black managers are assigned to stores in Black neighborhoods more often than one would expect, and Black employees are not being promoted to management and within management as often as similar white employees.[2]"

In a case attracting worldwide attention, Sayaka Kobayashi, personal assistant to Hideaki Otaka, chief executive officer for Toyota Motor North America, Inc., sued her boss for alleged romantic and sexual advances she endured over a three-month period. The alleged advances included inappropriate sexual remarks, requests for sexual favors, and groping. The case is noteworthy because of the sloppy manner in which Toyota responded to Kobayashi's initial requests for relief (see section Preventing Discrimination Charges later in the chapter). Since the lawsuit Toyota has reviewed its policies and practices on harassment and discrimination and ordered additional training for executives "to enable them to better recognize, prevent, and handle any instances of inappropriate behavior.[3]" Kobayashi stated that if Toyota had handled her concerns differently the lawsuit would never have happened.

These prominent examples overshadow the hundreds of discrimination lawsuits filed by employees of smaller organizations. For example, in 2007, B&H Photo-Video, a world famous New York City camera store known for the traditional Hasidic dress worn by many of its employees, agreed to pay $4.3 million to Hispanic warehouse employees paid less than other warehouse workers. The company agreed to equalize the wages of its Hispanic employees to those of non-Hispanic and to distribute monies to individuals who were paid less, not promoted, or denied benefits because they are Hispanic.[4]

Equal employment opportunity is not only a legal topic, but it is also an emotional issue. It concerns all individuals, regardless of their sex, race, religion, age, national origin, color, physical condition, or position in an organization. Supervisors should be aware of their personal biases and how these attitudes can influence their dealings with subordinates.[5] It should be emphasized that covert, as well as blatantly intentional, discrimination in employment is illegal.

To comply with the mandates of EEO legislation, employers have been compelled to develop employment policies that incorporate different laws, executive orders (EOs), administrative regulations, and court decisions (case law) designed to end job discrimination.

A basic goal of this chapter is that a good working knowledge of EEO law is required for managers and supervisors involved in making employment decisions. We will also discuss the process of affirmative action which attempts to correct past practices of discrimination by actively recruiting minority group members and the importance of supporting diversity as a proactive business goal.

Historical Perspective of EEO Legislation

1 | Objective

Equal employment opportunity as a national priority has emerged slowly in the United States. Not until the mid-1950s and early 1960s did nondiscriminatory employment become a strong social concern. Three factors seem to have influenced the growth of EEO legislation: (1) changing attitudes toward employment discrimination; (2) published reports highlighting the economic problems of women, minorities, and older workers; and (3) a growing body of disparate laws and government regulations covering discrimination.

Changing National Values

The United States was founded on the principles of individual merit, hard work, and equality. The Constitution grants to all citizens the right to life, liberty, and the pursuit of happiness. A central aim of political action has been to establish justice for all people of the nation.

In spite of these constitutional guarantees, employment discrimination has a long history in the United States. Organizations that claim to offer fair treatment to employees have openly or covertly engaged in discriminatory practices. Well-known organizations such as Dow Chemical, Starbucks, Mitsubishi Motor Manufacturing of America, the U.S. Army, Wal-Mart, Lockheed Martin, Boeing, Home Depot, Morgan Stanley, and American Airlines have violated equal employment laws.

Public attitudes changed dramatically with the beginning of the civil rights movement. During the late 1950s and early 1960s, minorities—especially blacks—publicized their low economic and occupational position through marches, sit-ins, rallies, and clashes with public authorities.[6] The low employment status of women also gained recognition during this period. Supported by concerned individuals and

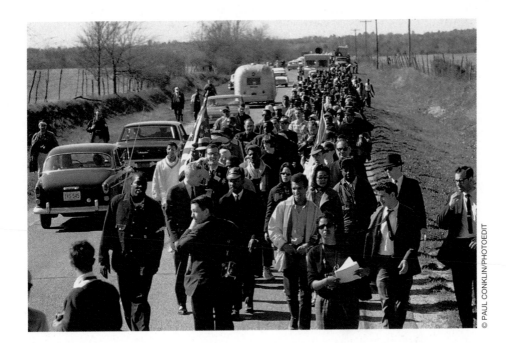

Civil rights marches have long been used to protest discrimination.

© PAUL CONKLIN/PHOTOEDIT

church and civic leaders, the civil rights movement and the women's movement received wide attention through television and print media. These movements had a pronounced influence on changing the attitudes of society at large, the business community, civic leaders, and government officials, resulting in improvements in the civil rights of all individuals. No longer was blatant discrimination to be accepted.

Economic Disparity

The change in government and societal attitudes toward discrimination was further prompted by increasing public awareness of the economic imbalance between nonwhites and whites. Even today, civil rights activists cite government statistics to emphasize this disparity. For example, the June 2008 unemployment rate for black males over age 16 was 9.2 percent, compared with 4.9 percent for white males of the same age.[7] When employed, nonwhites tend to hold unskilled or semiskilled jobs characterized by unstable employment, low status, and low pay. In the fourth quarter of 2007, the median weekly earnings of white males were $788; of black males, $600; and, of Hispanic males, $520.[8] Remarking on the disparity in wages between whites and minorities, Steve Hipple, a Bureau of Labor Statistics economist, notes, "There's still a huge gap, and it hasn't improved over the last 20 years."[9]

Early Legal Developments

Since as early as the nineteenth century, the public has been aware of discriminatory employment practices in the United States. In 1866, Congress passed the Civil Rights Act, which extended to all people the right to enjoy full and equal benefits of all laws, regardless of race. Beginning in the 1930s and 1940s, more specific federal policies covering nondiscrimination began to emerge. In 1933, Congress enacted the Unemployment Relief Act, which prohibited employment discrimination on account of race, color, or creed. In 1941, President Franklin D. Roosevelt issued Executive Order 8802, which was to ensure that every American citizen, "regardless of race, creed, color, or national origin," would be guaranteed equal employment opportunities in World War II defense contracts. Over the next twenty years a variety of other legislative efforts were promoted to resolve inequities in employment practices.

Unfortunately, these early efforts did little to correct employment discrimination. First, at both the state and federal levels, nondiscrimination laws often failed to give any enforcement power to the agency charged with upholding the law. Second, the laws that were passed frequently neglected to list specific discriminatory practices or methods for their correction. Third, employers covered by the acts were required only to comply voluntarily with the equal employment opportunity legislation. Without a compulsory requirement, employers often violated legislation with impunity. Despite these faults, however, early executive orders and laws laid the groundwork for passage of the Civil Rights Act of 1964.

▪▪ GOVERNMENT REGULATION OF EQUAL EMPLOYMENT OPPORTUNITY

Objective 2

Significant laws have been passed barring employment discrimination. These laws influence all of the HRM functions, including recruitment, selection, performance appraisal, training opportunities, promotion, transfers, and compensation. Because today's managers and supervisors are involved in employment activities, knowledge and application of these statutes are critical. It should be understood that managers and supervisors perform their jobs as agents of the employer.[10] Under the business concept of agency, managers and supervisors authorized to deal with employees on the employers' behalf subject themselves and their employers to responsibility for illegal acts taken against employees. Both the manager and the organization can be sued by an employee alleging discrimination. Organizations cannot afford to have managers make HRM decisions without considering the possible legal implications of their actions for the organization and themselves. Highlights in HRM 1 will test your current understanding of EEO laws.

Major Federal Laws

Major federal equal employment opportunity laws have attempted to correct social problems of interest to particular groups of workers, called protected classes.[11] Defined broadly, these include individuals of a minority race, women, older people, and those with physical or mental disabilities. Separate federal laws cover each of these classes. Figure 3.1 lists the major federal laws and their provisions governing equal employment opportunity.

protected classes
Individuals of a minority race, women, older people, and those with disabilities who are covered by federal laws on equal employment opportunity

Equal Pay Act of 1963

The Equal Pay Act outlaws discrimination in pay, employee benefits, and pensions based on the worker's gender.[12] Employers are prohibited from paying employees of one gender at a rate lower than that paid to members of the other gender for doing equal work. Jobs are considered "equal" when they require substantially the same skill, effort, and responsibility under similar working conditions and in the same establishment. For example, male and female plastic molders working for Medical Plastics Laboratory, a company of 125 employees manufacturing medical education products, must not be paid differently because of their gender. However, other employers in this specialized industry may pay their plastic molders wage rates that differ on the basis of different job content or economic conditions from those of Medical Plastics.

Employers do not violate the Equal Pay Act when differences in wages paid to men and women for equal work are based on seniority systems, merit considerations, or quantity or quality of production. However, these exceptions must not be based on the employee's gender or serve to discriminate against one particular gender. Employers may not lower the wages of one gender to comply with the law; rather, they must raise the wages of the gender being underpaid.

The Equal Pay Act was passed as an amendment to the Fair Labor Standards Act (FLSA) and is administered by the Equal Employment Opportunity Commission (EEOC). It covers employers engaged in interstate commerce and most government employees.

> **Using the Internet**
>
> Review the details explaining the responsibilities of the EEOC and complete texts of all the EEO laws. Go to the Student Resources at:
>
> **www.cengage.com/ management/bohlander**

Civil Rights Act of 1964

Title VII of the Civil Rights Act of 1964 is the broadest and most significant of the antidiscrimination statutes. The act bars discrimination in all HR activities, including hiring, training, promotion, transfers, pay, employee benefits, and other conditions

1

HIGHLIGHTS IN HRM

Test Your Knowledge of Equal Employment Opportunity Law

The following questions have been used as "icebreakers" by employers and consultants when training supervisors and managers in EEO legislation. What is your knowledge of EEO laws? Answers are found at the end of this chapter.

1. Two male employees tell a sexually dirty joke. The joke is overheard by a female employee who complains to her supervisor that this is sexual harassment. Is her complaint legitimate?

    _____ Yes   _____ No

2. To be covered by Title VII of the Civil Rights Act, an employer must be engaged in interstate commerce and employ twenty-five or more employees.

    _____ True   _____ False

3. People addicted to illegal drugs are classified as disabled under the Americans with Disabilities Act of 1990.

    _____ Yes   _____ No

4. The Equal Pay Act of 1963 allows employers to pay different wages to men and women who are performing substantially similar work. What are the three defenses for paying a different wage?

    1. _____

    2. _____

    3. _____

5. A person applies with you for a job as a janitor. During the interview, the person mentions that since birth he has sometimes experienced short periods of memory loss. Must you consider this individual a disabled person under the Americans with Disabilities Act of 1990?

    _____ Yes   _____ No

6. On Friday afternoon, you tell Nancy Penley, a computer analyst, that she must work overtime the next day. She refuses, saying that Saturday is her regular religious holiday and she can't work. Do you have the legal right to order her to work on Saturday?

    _____ Yes   _____ No

7. You have just told an applicant that she will not receive the job for which she applied. She claims that you denied her employment because of her age (she's 52). You claim she is not protected under the age discrimination law. Is your reasoning correct?

    _____ Yes   _____ No

8. As an employer, you can select those applicants who are the most qualified in terms of education and experience.

    _____ Yes   _____ No

9. As a manager, you have the legal right to mandate dates for pregnancy leaves.

    _____ True   _____ False

10. State fair employment practice laws cover smaller employers not covered by federal legislation.

    _____ True   _____ False

FIGURE
3.1

Major Laws Affecting Equal Employment Opportunity

LAW	PROVISIONS
Equal Pay Act of 1963	Requires all employers covered by the Fair Labor Standards Act and others to provide equal pay for equal work, regardless of sex.
Title VII of Civil Rights Act of 1964 (amended in 1972, 1991, and 1994)	Prohibits discrimination in employment on the basis of race, color, religion, sex, or national origin; created the Equal Employment Opportunity Commission (EEOC) to enforce the provisions of Title VII.
Age Discrimination in Employment Act of 1967 (amended in 1986 and 1990)	Prohibits private and public employers from discriminating against people age 40 or older in any area of employment because of age; exceptions are permitted when age is a bona fide occupational qualification.
Equal Employment Opportunity Act of 1972	Amended Title VII of Civil Rights Act of 1964; strengthens EEOC's enforcement powers and extends coverage of Title VII to government employees, employees in higher education, and other employers and employees.
Pregnancy Discrimination Act of 1978	Broadens the definition of sex discrimination to include pregnancy, childbirth, or related medical conditions; prohibits employers from discriminating agaist pregnant women in employment benefits if they are capable of performing their job duties.
Americans with Disabilities Act of 1990	Prohibits discrimination in employment against people with physical or mental disabilities or the chronically ill; enjoins employers to make reasonable accommodation to the employment needs of the disabled; covers employers with fifteen or more employees.
Civil Rights Act of 1991	Provides for compensatory and punitive damages and jury trials in cases involving intentional discrimination; requires employers to demonstrate that job practices are job-related and consistent with business necessity; extends coverage to U.S. citizens working for U.S. companies overseas.
Uniformed Services Employment and Reemployment Rights Act of 1994	Protects the employment rights of individuals who enter the military for short periods of service.

of employment. Discrimination is prohibited on the basis of race, color, religion, sex (also referred to as gender), or national origin. Importantly, in response to the growing number of immigrant workers and workplace cultural and ethnic awareness, the EEOC has issued important guidelines on national origin discrimination.[13] A "national origin group" is defined as a group of people sharing a common language, culture, ancestry, and/or similar social characteristics. This definition includes people born in the United States who are not racial or ethnic minorities. Therefore, whether the ancestry of an employee or job applicant is Mexican, Ukrainian, Filipino, Arab, Native American, or any other nationality, he or she is entitled to the same employment opportunities as anyone else.[14] Also prohibited under the act is discrimination based on pregnancy.[15] The law protects hourly employees, supervisors, professional employees, managers, and executives from discriminatory practices. Section 703(a) of Title VII of the Civil Rights Act specifically provides that

> It shall be unlawful employment practice for an employer:
>
> 1. To fail or refuse to hire or to discharge any individual, or otherwise to discriminate against any individual with respect to his [or her] compensation, terms, conditions, or privileges of employment because of such individual's race, color, religion, sex, or national origin. . . .

While the purpose and the coverage of Title VII are extensive, the law does permit various exemptions. For example, as with the Equal Pay Act, managers are permitted to apply employment conditions differently if those differences are based on such objective factors as merit, seniority, or incentive payments. For example, the law would permit the promotion of a male office worker over a female office worker if the promotion was based on the superior skills and abilities of the male. Nowhere does the law require employers to hire, promote, or retain workers who are not qualified to perform their job duties. And managers may still reward employees differently, provided these differences are not predicated on the employees' race, color, sex, religion, or national origin.

The Civil Rights Act of 1964 covers a broad range of organizations. The law includes under its jurisdiction the following:

1. All private employers in interstate commerce who employ fifteen or more employees for twenty or more weeks per year

2. State and local governments

3. Private and public employment agencies, including the U.S. Employment Service

4. Joint labor-management committees that govern apprenticeship or training programs

5. Labor unions having fifteen or more members or employees

6. Public and private educational institutions

7. Foreign subsidiaries of U.S. organizations employing U.S. citizens

Certain employers are excluded from coverage of the Civil Rights Act. Broadly defined, these are (1) U.S. government–owned corporations, (2) bona fide, tax-exempt private clubs, (3) religious organizations employing people of a specific religion, and (4) organizations hiring Native Americans on or near a reservation.

The Civil Rights Act of 1964 established the Equal Employment Opportunity Commission to administer the law and promote equal employment opportunity. The commission's structure and operations will be reviewed later in this chapter.

Bona Fide Occupational Qualification. Under Title VII of the Civil Rights Act, employers are permitted limited exemptions from antidiscrimination regulations if employment preferences are based on a bona fide occupational qualification. A bona fide occupational qualification (BFOQ) permits discrimination when employer hiring preferences are a reasonable necessity for the normal operation of the business. However, a BFOQ is a suitable defense against a discrimination charge only when

---

bona fide occupational qualification (BFOQ)

Suitable defense against a discrimination charge only when age, religion, sex, or national origin is an actual qualification for performing the job age, religion, sex, or national origin is an actual qualification for performing the job. For example, an older person could legitimately be excluded from consideration for employment as a model for teenage designer jeans. It is reasonable to expect the Chicago Bears of the National Football League to hire male locker-room attendants or for Abercrombie and Fitch Clothing Store to employ females as models for women's fashions. Likewise, religion is a BFOQ in organizations that require employees to share a particular religious doctrine.

The EEOC does not favor BFOQs, and both the EEOC and the courts have construed the concept narrowly. The exception does not apply to discrimination based on race or color. When an organization claims a BFOQ, it must be able to prove that hiring on the basis of sex, religion, age, or national origin is a business necessity. **Business necessity** has been interpreted by the courts as a practice that is necessary to the safe and efficient operation of the organization. A commercial driver's license required for over-the-road truck drivers would ensure proper handling of the vehicle and safety to the driver and other motorists. Students often ask, "Why do Asian restaurants hire only Asian American food servers?" While restaurants generally cannot prefer one nationality over another (because the job of serving food can be performed equally well by all nationalities), to ensure the "authenticity" of the dining experience, an Asian restaurant may legitimately use the business-necessity defense to support the preference for hiring Asian American servers.

> **business necessity**
> A work-related practice that is necessary to the safe and efficient operation of an organization

Religious Preference. Freedom to exercise religious choice is guaranteed under the U.S. Constitution. Title VII of the Civil Rights Act also prohibits discrimination based on religion in employment decisions, though it permits employer exemptions. The act defines religion to "include all aspects of religious observance and practice, as well as belief."

Title VII does not require employers to grant complete religious freedom in employment situations. Employers need only make a reasonable accommodation for a current employee's or job applicant's religious observance or practice without incurring undue hardship in the conduct of the business. Managers or supervisors may have to accommodate an employee's religion in the specific areas of (1) holidays and observances (scheduling), (2) personal appearance (wearing beards, veils, or turbans), and (3) religious conduct on the job (missionary work among other employees).

What constitutes "reasonable accommodation" has been difficult to define.[16] In 1977, in the leading case of *TWA v. Hardison*, the Supreme Court attempted to settle this dispute by ruling that employers had only to bear a minimum cost to show accommodation.[17] The Court said that to require otherwise would be discrimination against other employees for whom the expense of permitting time off for religious observance was not incurred. The *Hardison* case is important because it supported union management seniority systems in which the employer had made a reasonable attempt to adjust employee work schedules without undue hardship. While *Hardison* permits reasonable accommodation and undue hardship as a defense against religious discrimination charges, the EEOC investigates complaints on a case-by-case basis; employers are still responsible for supporting their decisions to deny an employee's religious requests.

Using the Internet

To view the EEOC's Facts about Religious Discrimination, go to the Student Resources at:

www.cengage.com/ management/bohlander

Age Discrimination in Employment Act of 1967

U.S. Census Bureau figures show that in 2000, 23 percent of the U.S. population was in the 45–84 age group. By 2010, this portion will rise to 37.2 percent, and by 2020, it will hit 39 percent. Therefore, the chances of age discrimination by employers increase dramatically. Connie Bertram, partner in the law firm Winston and Strawn, notes, "We will see a new wave of age-related claims. Employers need to start thinking about the age spread in various positions and make sure they pay the same attention to age as they do to race and gender in the employment process.[18] Recent figures from the EEOC show that age discrimination complaints compose about 21.8 percent of all discrimination charges. Managers or supervisors may discriminate against older employees by:

- Excluding older workers from important work activities

- Making negative changes in the performance evaluations of older employees

- Denying older employees job-related education, career development, or promotional opportunities

- Selecting younger job applicants over older, better-qualified candidates

- Pressuring older employees into taking early retirement

- Reducing the job duties and responsibilities of older employees

- Terminating older employees through downsizing.[19]

Additionally, since older workers are less likely to agree to relocate or adapt to new job demands, they are prone to employer discrimination.

To make employment decisions based on age illegal, the Age Discrimination in Employment Act (ADEA), as amended, was passed in 1967. The act prohibits specific employers from discriminating against people age 40 or older in any area of employment, including selection, because of age. Employers affected are those with twenty or more employees; unions with twenty-five or more members; employment agencies; and federal, state, and local governments.

Exceptions to the law are permitted when age is a bona fide occupational qualification. A BFOQ may exist when an employer can show that advanced age may affect public safety or organizational efficiency. For example, such conditions might exist for bus or truck drivers or for locomotive engineers. The greater the safety factor, measured by the likelihood of harm thorough accidents, the more stringent may be the job qualification designed to ensure safety. A BFOQ does not exist when an employer argues that younger employees foster a youthful or more energetic organizational image. Employers must also be careful to avoid making offhand remarks (such as "the old man" or our "aging graying sales force") or expressing negative opinions (such as "people over 50 years old have more accidents") about older individuals. These remarks and attitudes can be used as proof of discrimination in age-bias suits.[20]

Using the Internet

AARP offers a number of resources to employers who want to maximize their use of older workers. Go to the Student Resources at:

www.cengage.com/
management/bohlander

Equal Employment Opportunity Act of 1972

In 1972 the Civil Rights Act of 1964 was amended by the Equal Employment Opportunity Act. Two important changes were made. First, the coverage of the act was broadened to include state and local governments and public and private educational institutions. Colleges and universities such as Central Texas College in Killeen; San Diego State University; and Bloomfield College in Bloomfield, New Jersey, are now covered by this statute. Second, the law strengthened the enforcement powers of the EEOC by allowing the agency itself to sue employers in court to enforce the provisions of the act. Regional litigation centers now exist to provide faster and more effective court action.

Pregnancy Discrimination Act of 1978

Before the passage of the Pregnancy Discrimination Act, pregnant women could be forced to resign or take a leave of absence because of their condition. In addition, employers did not have to provide disability or medical coverage for pregnancy. The Pregnancy Discrimination Act amended the Civil Rights Act of 1964 by stating that pregnancy is a disability and that pregnant employees in covered organizations must be treated on an equal basis with employees having other medical conditions. Under the law, it is illegal for employers to deny sick leave for morning sickness or related pregnancy illness if sick leave is permitted for other medical conditions such as flu or surgical operations. Specifically, the Pregnancy Discrimination Act affects employee benefit programs including (1) hospitalization and major medical insurance, (2) temporary disability and salary continuation plans, and (3) sick leave policies.[21]

Furthermore, the law prohibits discrimination in the hiring, promotion, or termination of women because of pregnancy. Women must be evaluated on their ability to perform the job, and employers may not set arbitrary dates for mandatory pregnancy leaves. Leave dates are to be based on the individual pregnant employee's ability to work.

Americans with Disabilities Act of 1990

Discrimination against the disabled was first prohibited in federally funded activities by the Vocational Rehabilitation Act of 1973 (to be discussed later). However, the disabled were not among the protected classes covered by the Civil Rights Act of 1964. To remedy this shortcoming, Congress in 1990 passed the Americans with Disabilities Act (ADA), prohibiting employers from discriminating against individuals with physical and mental disabilities and the chronically ill.[22] The law defines a disability as "(a) a physical or mental impairment that substantially limits one or more of the major activities; (b) a record of such impairment; or (c) being regarded as having such an impairment." Note that the law also protects people "regarded" as having a disability—for example, individuals with disfiguring burns.

Managers and supervisors remark that the ADA is difficult to administer because of the ambiguous definition of a disability, particularly mental impairment. The issue is what is a disability? It sounds like a simple question, yet it is not. Not every mental or physical impairment is considered a disability under the law. For example, significant personality disorders are covered under the EEOC's "Enforcement Guidance on the Americans with Disabilities Act and Psychiatric Disabilities."[23] Covered personality disorders include schizophrenia, bipolar disorders, major affective disorders, personality disorders, and anxiety disorders. These impairments are characterized by aberrant behavior, self-defeating behavior, manipulation of others, and troublesome manners of behavior. However, mental impairments described as "adjustment disorders" or attributed to stress have generally not been subject to ADA coverage. Therefore, employees who claim to be "stressed" over marital problems, financial

© BILLY HUSTACE/STONE/GETTY IMAGES

The ADA prohibits employers from discriminating against individuals regarded as having physical or mental disabilities.

hardships, demands of the work environment, job duties, or harsh, unreasonable treatment from a supervisor would not be classified as disabled under the ADA.

Does the ADA protect individuals who use medication or corrective devices to control the effects of their physical or mental impairments—for example, individuals wearing eyeglasses or those taking medication to ameliorate illnesses such as asthma, diabetes, or epilepsy? In a significant Supreme Court case, *Toyota v. Williams* (2002),[24] the Court ruled that if physical or mental impairments are correctable, then they are not a disability. Specifically, the Court held that (1) to be substantially limited in performing work tasks, an individual must have an impairment that prevents or severely restricts the individual from doing activities that are of central importance to most people's daily lives and (2) it is insufficient for individuals attempting to prove disability status to merely submit evidence of a medical diagnosis of an impairment.

The act does not cover:

1. Homosexuality or bisexuality

2. Gender identity disorders not resulting from physical impairment or other sexual behavior disorders

3. Compulsive gambling, kleptomania, or pyromania

4. Psychoactive substance use disorders resulting from current illegal use of drugs

5. Current illegal use of drugs

6. Infectious or communicable diseases of public health significance (applied to food-handling jobs only and excluding AIDS)

In the cases it does cover, the act requires employers to make a reasonable accommodation for disabled people who are otherwise qualified to work, unless doing so would cause undue hardship to the employer.[25] "Undue hardship" refers to unusual work modifications or excessive expenses that might be incurred by an employer in providing an accommodation. Reasonable accommodation "includes making facilities accessible and usable to disabled persons, restructuring jobs, permitting part-time or modified work schedules, reassigning to a vacant position, changing equipment, and/or expense." "Reasonable" is to be determined according to (1) the nature and cost of the accommodation and (2) the financial resources, size, and profitability of the facility and parent organization. Furthermore, employers cannot use selection procedures that screen out or tend to screen out disabled

reasonable accommodation

An attempt by employers to adjust, without undue hardship, the working conditions or schedules of employees with disabilities or religious preferences people, unless the selection procedure "is shown to be job-related for the position in question and is consistent with business necessity" and acceptable job performance cannot be achieved through reasonable accommodation. ("Essential functions," a pivotal issue for ensuring reasonable accommodation, will be discussed in Chapter 4.)

The act prohibits covered employers from discriminating against a qualified individual regarding application for employment, hiring, advancement, discharge, compensation, training, or other employment conditions. The law incorporates the procedures and remedies found in Title VII of the Civil Rights Act, allowing job applicants or employees initial employment, reinstatement, back pay, and other injunctive relief against employers who violate the statute. The act covers employers with fifteen or more employees. The EEOC enforces the law in the same manner that Title VII of the Civil Rights Act is enforced.

Using the Internet

Retailer Sears has long had a commitment to hiring people with disabilities. Go to the Student Resources at:

www.cengage.com/ management/bohlander

Hiring disabled individuals is not only a legal mandate, but it is also good business. Employers subject to the ADA and those who value the varied skills and abilities of the disabled approach the law as a proactive business requirement. Hiring the disabled emphasizes what these individuals *can* do rather than what they *cannot* do. Jennifer Sheeny of the federal Office of Special Education and Rehabilitative Services advocates hiring disabled students as a way to enhance diversity recruitment and offset labor shortages. Importantly, two of the most comprehensive studies conducted on the ADA show that the law has had a positive effect on both business outcomes and disabled employees. Conducted by the National Council on Disability (NCD), the studies reported positive gains regarding the ADA's four major goals: equal opportunity, full participation, independent living, and economic self-sufficiency for people with disabilities.[26]

It is not suggested that disabled people can be placed in any job without giving careful consideration to their disabilities, nor that employers can always make the workplace "user-friendly," but rather that it is good business to hire qualified disabled people who can work safely and productively. Fortunately, there exist today manual and electronic devices to aid hearing-impaired, visually-impaired, and mobility-impaired employees. In many cases, the simple restructuring of jobs permits disabled persons to qualify for employment. Figure 3.2 identifies specific ways to make the workplace more accessible to the disabled.

Civil Rights Act of 1991

The Civil Rights Act of 1991 amends Title VII of the Civil Rights Act of 1964. One of the major elements of the law is the awarding of damages in cases of intentional discrimination or unlawful harassment. For the first time under federal law, damages are provided to victims of intentional discrimination or unlawful harassment on the basis of sex, religion, national origin, and disability. An employee who claims intentional discrimination can seek compensatory or punitive damages. Compensatory damages include payment for future money losses, emotional pain, suffering, mental anguish, and other nonmonetary losses. Punitive damages are awarded if it can be shown that the employer engaged in discrimination with malice or reckless indifference to the law. Most significantly, the act allows juries rather than federal judges to decide discrimination claims. Compensatory or punitive damages cannot be awarded in cases when an employment practice not intended

FIGURE 3.2

ADA Suggestions for an Accessible Workplace

- Install easy-to-reach switches.
- Provide sloping sidewalks and entrances.
- Install wheelchair ramps.
- Reposition shelves for the easy reach of materials.
- Rearrange tables, chairs, vending machines, dispensers, and other furniture and fixtures.
- Widen doors and hallways.
- Add raised markings on control buttons.
- Provide designated accessible parking spaces.
- Install hand controls or manipulation devices.
- Provide flashing alarm lights.

- Remove turnstiles and revolving doors or provide alternative accessible paths.
- Install holding bars in toilet areas.
- Redesign toilet partitions to increase access space.
- Add paper cup dispensers at water fountains.
- Replace high-pile, low-density carpeting.
- Reposition telephones, water fountains, and other needed equipment.
- Add raised toilet seats.
- Provide a full-length bathroom mirror.

to be discriminatory is shown to have an unlawful adverse impact on members of a protected class. The total damages any one person can receive cannot be more than:

$50,000 for employers having between 15 and 100 employees

$100,000 for employers having between 101 and 200 employees

$200,000 for employers having between 201 and 500 employees

$300,000 for employers having more than 500 employees

In each case, the aggrieved individual must have been employed with the organization for twenty or more calendar weeks.

Under its other provisions, the law:

- Prohibits employers from adjusting employment test scores or using different cutoff test scores on the basis of race, color, religion, sex, or national origin

- Prohibits litigation involving charges of reverse discrimination when employers are under a consent order (court order) to implement an affirmative action program

- Requires that employers defending against a charge of discrimination demonstrate that employment practices are job-related and consistent with *business necessity*

The Civil Rights Act of 1991 states that employees who are sent abroad to work for U.S.-based companies are protected by U.S. antidiscrimination legislation governing age and disability and Title VII of the Civil Rights Act of 1964. Thus employees can sue their U.S. employers for claims of discriminatory treatment while employed in a foreign country. This could occur, for example, in Middle Eastern countries where women are prohibited from holding certain jobs

"Well, how much will it cost to buy Washington DC and take care of all this foolishness about regulations?"

Source: Cartoon by Ted Goff. Reprinted with permission.

or when a foreign country's mandatory retirement law conflicts with the Age Discrimination in Employment Act.

Passed jointly with the Civil Rights Act of 1991 was the Glass Ceiling Act of 1991. The "glass ceiling" represents an invisible barrier that prohibits protected class members from reaching top organizational positions. The Act created the Glass Ceiling Commission to study and report on the status of and obstacles faced by minorities as they strive for top-level management jobs. The Commission's most recent report can be found on the EEO Web site.[27] Additional discussion of the glass ceiling can be found in Chapter 5.

Uniformed Services Employment and Reemployment Rights Act of 1994 (USERRA)

Under this act, individuals who enter the military for a short period of service can return to their private sector jobs without risk of loss of seniority or benefits.[28] For example, military reservists called up to active duty during the Iraq conflict would qualify for reemployment rights under this law. The act protects against discrimination on the basis of military obligation in the areas of hiring, job retention, and advancement. Other provisions under the act require employers to make reasonable efforts to retrain or upgrade skills to qualify employees for reemployment, expand health care and employee pension plan coverage, and extend the length of time an individual may be absent for military duty from four to five years. In 2004, the law was amended by the Veterans Benefits Improvement Act requiring employers to provide a notice of rights, benefits, and obligations of both employees and employers under USERRA.[29] For their part, service members must provide their employers advance notice of their military obligations in order to be protected by the reemployment rights statute. The Labor Department's Veterans Employment and Training Service is responsible for enforcing the law.

Other Federal Laws and Executive Orders

Because the major laws affecting equal employment opportunity do not cover agencies of the federal government and because state laws do not apply to federal employees, it has at times been necessary for the president to issue executive orders to protect federal employees. Executive orders are also used to provide equal employment opportunity to individuals employed by government contractors. Since many large employers—such as General Dynamics, Intel, Dell Computer, and Motorola—and numerous small companies have contracts with the federal government, managers are expected to know and comply with the provisions of executive orders and other laws. The federal laws and executive orders that apply to government agencies and government contractors are summarized in Figure 3.3.

Vocational Rehabilitation Act of 1973

People with disabilities experience discrimination both because of negative attitudes regarding their ability to perform work and because of physical barriers imposed by organizational facilities. The Vocational Rehabilitation Act was passed in 1973 to correct these problems by requiring private employers with federal contracts over $2,500 to take affirmative action to hire individuals with a mental or physical

FIGURE 3.3

EEO Rules Applicable to Federal Contractors and Agencies

LAW	PROVISIONS
Vocational Rehabilitation Act of 1973 (amended in 1974)	Prohibits federal contractors from discriminating against disabled individuals in any program or activity receiving federal financial assistance; requires federal contractors to develop affirmative action plans to hire and promote disabled people.
Executive Order 11246 (1965), as amended by Order 11375 (1966)	Prohibits employment discrimination based on race, color, religion, sex, or national origin by government contractors with contracts exceeding $10,000; requires contractors employing fifty or more workers to develop affirmative action plans when government contracts exceed $50,000 per year.
Executive Order 11478 (1969)	Obligates the federal government to ensure that all personnel actions affecting applicants for employment be free from discrimination based on race, color, religion, sex, or national origin.

disability. Recipients of federal financial assistance, such as public and private colleges and universities, are also covered. Employers must make a reasonable accommodation to hire disabled individuals but are not required to employ unqualified people. In applying the safeguards of this law, the term disabled individual means "any person who (1) has a physical or mental impairment which substantially limits one or more of such person's major life activities, (2) has a record of such an impairment, or (3) is regarded as having such an impairment." This definition closely parallels the definition of disabled individual provided in the Americans with Disabilities Act previously discussed.

A frequently asked question is: "Are employees affected with contagious diseases, such as tuberculosis, subject to the act's coverage?" The answer is yes.[30] In cases when people with contagious diseases are "otherwise qualified" to do their jobs, the law requires employers to make a reasonable accommodation to allow the disabled to perform their jobs.[31] Individuals with AIDS or HIV are also disabled within the meaning of the Rehabilitation Act. Therefore, discrimination on the basis of AIDS/HIV violates the law, and employers must accommodate the employment needs of people with these conditions.

The Rehabilitation Act does not require employers to hire or retain a disabled person if he or she has a contagious disease that poses a direct threat to the health or safety of others and the individual cannot be accommodated. Also, employment is not required when some aspect of the employee's disability prevents that person from carrying out essential parts of the job, nor is it required if the disabled person is not otherwise qualified.

Executive Order 11246

Federal agencies and government contractors with contracts of $10,000 or more must comply with the antidiscrimination provisions of Executive Order 11246. The order prohibits discrimination based on race, color, religion, sex, or national origin in all employment activities. Furthermore, it requires that government contractors or subcontractors having fifty or more employees with contracts in excess of $50,000 develop affirmative action plans; such plans will be discussed later in the chapter.

Executive Order 11246 created the Office of Federal Contract Compliance Programs (OFCCP) to ensure equal employment opportunity in the federal procurement area. The agency issues nondiscriminatory guidelines and regulations similar to those issued by the EEOC. Noncompliance with OFCCP policies can result in the cancellation or suspension of contracts. The OFCCP is further charged with requiring that contractors provide job opportunities to the disabled, disabled veterans, and veterans of the Vietnam War.

Fair Employment Practice Laws

Federal laws and executive orders provide the major regulations governing equal employment opportunity. But, in addition, almost all states and many local governments have passed laws barring employment discrimination. Referred to as fair employment practices (FEPs), these statutes are often more comprehensive than the federal laws. While state and local laws are too numerous to review here, managers should be aware of them and how they affect HRM in their organizations.

disabled individual
Any person who (1) has a physical or mental impairment that substantially limits one or more of the person's major life activities, (2) has a record of such impairment, or (3) is regarded as having such an impairment

fair employment practices (FEPs)
State and local laws governing equal employment opportunity that are often more comprehensive than federal laws and apply to small employers

State and local FEPs also promote the employment of individuals in a fair and unbiased way. They are patterned after federal legislation, although they frequently extend jurisdiction to employers exempt from federal coverage and therefore pertain mainly to smaller employers. While Title VII of the Civil Rights Act exempts employers with fewer than fifteen employees, many states extend antidiscrimination laws to employers with one or more workers. Thus managers and entrepreneurs operating a small business must pay close attention to these laws. Local or state legislation may bar discrimination based on physical appearance, marital status, arrest records, color blindness, or political affiliation. Maryland, California, Vermont, Hawaii, Nevada, New Mexico, and Wisconsin are states protecting employees from discrimination based on sexual orientation.

More than 100 fair employment practices agencies (FEPAs) administer and enforce equal employment opportunity statutes. The Ohio Civil Rights Commission, Massachusetts Commission against Discrimination, Colorado Civil Rights Division, and Pittsburgh Commission on Human Relations are examples. State agencies play an important role in the investigation and resolution of employment discrimination charges. FEPAs and the Equal Employment Opportunity Commission often work together to resolve discrimination complaints.[32]

▪▪ OTHER EQUAL EMPLOYMENT OPPORTUNITY ISSUES

Objective | 3

Federal laws, executive orders, court cases, and state and local statutes provide the broad legal framework for equal employment opportunity. Within these major laws, specific issues are of particular interest to supervisors and managers. The situations discussed here occur in the day-to-day supervision of employees.

Sexual Harassment

Sexual situations in the work environment are not new to organizational life. Sexual feelings are a part of group dynamics, and people who work together may come to develop these kinds of feelings for one another. Unfortunately, however, often these encounters are unpleasant and unwelcome, as witnessed by the many reported instances of sexual harassment.[33] Nationwide, 12,510 sexual harassment complaints were filed in 2007 with the EEOC and state fair employment practice agencies by employees of both small and large employers.[34] About 15 percent of these charges were filed by males. Problems often arise from lack of knowledge of the specific on-the-job behaviors that constitute sexual harassment under the law. Through a questionnaire, it is possible to test employee understanding of what is and what is not sexual harassment. Highlights in HRM 2 is a sampling of questions that could be used during a sexual harassment audit. Such an instrument is a valuable tool for determining what employees know and do not know about sexual harassment.

The EEOC guidelines on sexual harassment are specific, stating that "unwelcome advances, requests for sexual favors, and other verbal or physical conduct of a sexual nature" constitute sexual harassment when submission to the conduct is tied to continuing employment or advancement. The EEOC recognizes two forms of sexual harassment as being illegal under Title VII. The first, *quid pro quo harassment*, occurs when "submission to or rejection of sexual conduct is used as a basis for employment

sexual harassment

Unwelcome advances, requests for sexual favors, and other verbal or physical conduct of a sexual nature in the working environment

Sexual harassment can create a hostile environment, making an employee uncomfortable enough to affect job performance.

decisions."[35] This type of harassment involves a tangible or economic consequence, such as a demotion or loss of pay. If a supervisor promotes a female employee only after she agrees to an after-work date, the conduct is clearly illegal.

The second type of harassment, *hostile environment*, can occur when unwelcome sexual conduct "has the purpose or effect of unreasonably interfering with job performance or creating an intimidating, hostile, or offensive working environment."[36] Thus dirty jokes, vulgar slang, nude pictures, swearing, and personal ridicule and insult constitute sexual harassment when an employee finds them offensive.

For example, the Paradise Valley Unified School District of Phoenix, Arizona, defines sexual harassment as including, but not limited to, suggestive or obscene letters, notes, or invitations; derogatory comments, slurs, jokes, and epithets; assault; blocking movements; leering gestures; and displays of sexually suggestive objects, pictures, or cartoons where such conduct may create a hostile environment for the employee.[37] In today's cyberspace workplace, electronic mail presents a convenient opportunity for sexually harassing activity such as lewd comments, unwanted sexual suggestions and advances, vulgar jokes, and pornographic spam. For example, in one 2007 EEOC case, a female sales manager at a Portales, New Mexico, car dealership was regularly subjected to hostile e-mail messages regarding her anatomy and dress as well as vulgar female comments and sexually offensive names. The EEOC lawsuit claimed that the employee's e-mail messages were "charged with gender bias and sexual animus such that it altered her working conditions."[38] It is strongly recommended that employer sexual harassment policies include strict prohibitions on e-mail harassment.

The EEOC considers an employer guilty of sexual harassment when the employer knew or should have known about the unlawful conduct and failed to remedy it or to take corrective action. Employers are also guilty of sexual harassment when they allow nonemployees (customers or salespeople) to sexually harass employees.[39]

HIGHLIGHTS IN HRM

2

Questions Used in Auditing Sexual Harassment

ACTIVITY	IS THIS SEXUAL HARASSMENT?			ARE YOU AWARE OF THIS BEHAVIOR IN THE ORGANIZATION?	
• Employees post cartoons on bulletin boards containing sexually related material.	Yes	No	Uncertain	Yes	No
• A male employee says to a female employee that she has beautiful eyes and hair.	Yes	No	Uncertain	Yes	No
• A male manager habitually calls all female employees "sweetie" or "darling."	Yes	No	Uncertain	Yes	No
• A manager fails to promote a female (male) employee for not granting sexual favors.	Yes	No	Uncertain	Yes	No
• Male employees use vulgar language and tell sexual jokes that are overheard by, but not directed at, female employees.	Yes	No	Uncertain	Yes	No
• A male employee leans and peers over the back of a female employee when she wears a low-cut dress.	Yes	No	Uncertain	Yes	No
• A supervisor gives a female (male) subordinate a nice gift on her (his) birthday.	Yes	No	Uncertain	Yes	No
• Two male employees share a sexually explicit magazine while observed by a female employee.	Yes	No	Uncertain	Yes	No
• Female office workers are "rated" by male employees as they pass the men's desks.	Yes	No	Uncertain	Yes	No
• Revealing female clothing is given as a gift at an office birthday party.	Yes	No	Uncertain	Yes	No
• A sales representative from a supplier makes "suggestive" sexual remarks to a receptionist.	Yes	No	Uncertain	Yes	No

It is noteworthy that both the Supreme Court and the EEOC hold employers strictly accountable to prevent sexual harassment of both female and male employees. The Supreme Court held in *Oncale v. Sundowner Offshore Services* that same-sex sexual harassment (male-to-male, female-to-female) is covered under Title VII.[40] In the opinion of Justice Antonin Scalia, "What matters is the conduct at issue, not the sex of the people involved and not the presence or absence of sexual desire, whether heterosexual or homosexual." When charges of sexual harassment have been proved, the EEOC has imposed remedies including back pay; reinstatement; and payment of lost benefits, interest charges, and attorney's fees. Sexual harassment involving physical conduct can invite criminal charges, and damages may be assessed against both the employer and the individual offender.[41]

Sexual harassment investigations are one of the most sensitive responsibilities faced by managers. When to investigate, who should handle the investigation, how to interview the complainant and the accused, and the availability of witnesses are a few of the critical elements affecting harassment cases. Additionally, to determine whether the misconduct is hostile or offensive, the manager must look at all the circumstances surrounding the charge of harassment. Important factors include the frequency of the misconduct; the severity of the misconduct; whether it is physically threatening or humiliating, as opposed to merely offensive; and whether it unreasonably interferes with the employee's work performance.[42]

Despite legislation against it, however, sexual harassment is still common in the workplace. Managers and supervisors must take special precautions to try to prevent it.[43] Highlights in HRM 3 presents the Court's suggestions and the EEOC guidelines for an effective policy to minimize sexual harassment in the work environment.

HIGHLIGHTS IN HRM

Basic Components of an Effective Sexual Harassment Policy

1. Develop a comprehensive organization-wide policy on sexual harassment and present it to all current and new employees. Stress that sexual harassment will not be tolerated under any circumstances. Emphasis is best achieved when the policy is publicized and supported by top management.

2. Hold training sessions with supervisors to explain Title VII requirements, their role in providing an environment free of sexual harassment, and proper investigative procedures when charges occur.

3. Establish a formal complaint procedure in which employees can discuss problems without fear of retaliation. The complaint procedure should spell out how charges will be investigated and resolved.

4. Act immediately when employees complain of sexual harassment. Communicate widely that investigations will be conducted objectively and with appreciation for the sensitivity of the issue.

5. When an investigation supports employee charges, discipline the offender at once. For extremely serious offenses, discipline should include penalties up to and including discharge. Discipline should be applied consistently across similar cases and among managers and hourly employees alike.

6. Follow up on all cases to ensure a satisfactory resolution of the problem.

Sexual Orientation

A culture of "changing lifestyles," a growing diversified workforce, and continual employee demands for equal workplace rights has sparked an emotional debate over employment guarantees for homosexuals.[44] The debate intensifies as growing numbers of gays and lesbians openly announce their sexual orientation and legislatures, courts, and company leaders discuss the merits of "gay rights."[45] Presently, what laws protect employees from discrimination based on their sexual orientation?

While Title VII of the Civil Rights Act of 1964 lists "sex" as a protected class, court cases have consistently held that sexual orientation is not a valid defense against discrimination. Currently, no federal law bars discrimination based on one's sexual orientation. For homosexual employees, protection from discrimination largely comes from fair employment practice laws passed at the state or local level. Furthermore, state and local same-sex statutes vary regarding the protection afforded homosexuals and who is covered under the laws. For example, in some states, public—but not private—sector employees are protected from discrimination based on their sexual orientation. Therefore, it becomes important for managers and supervisors to know and follow the legal rights of homosexuals in their geographic area.

Regardless of their legal obligations toward homosexuals, companies—in support of their diversity initiatives—increasingly are fostering "gay-friendly" work places. Organizations such as S. C. Johnson and Sons, Eastman Kodak, Lucent Technologies, Microsoft, and Southern California Edison hold training sessions aimed at overcoming the stereotypes affecting gay and lesbian workers. Defense contractors Raytheon and Lockheed Martin sponsor homosexual support groups, and Wal-Mart has adopted a nondiscrimination policy toward homosexuals. Of the nation's top 500 companies, 70 percent now offer health benefits to same-sex couples (see Chapter 10). A safe prediction is that employment rights for gays and lesbians will intensify, becoming a dynamic area for future legislation.

The EEOC has also ruled that transgender and transsexual individuals are not covered by Title VII of the Civil Rights Act. According to the EEOC, gender only applies to one's sex at the time of birth and not to one's sexual orientation. Therefore, discrimination claims by transsexuals have been rejected on the ground that any such discrimination is not because of sex.[46]

Immigration Reform and Control

Good employment is the magnet that attracts many people to the United States. Currently, however, illegal immigration is an issue of national concern at both the federal and state legislative levels and among employers, unions, civil rights groups, and the general public.[47] The issue of illegal immigration is emotional, economic, and fraught with legal regulations.

To preserve our tradition of legal immigration while closing the door to illegal entry, employers must comply with the requirements of the Immigration Reform and Control Act (IRCA). The law has two employer mandates. First, all employers covered by the law are prohibited from knowingly hiring or retaining unauthorized aliens on the job.[48] Second, employers with four or more employees are prohibited from discriminating in hiring or termination decisions on the basis of national origin or citizenship.[49]

Employers must comply with the law by verifying and maintaining records on the legal rights of applicants to work in the United States. The *Handbook for Employers*, published by the U.S. Department of Justice, lists five actions that employers must take to comply with the law:

1. Have employees fill out their part of Form I-9.

2. Check documents establishing an employee's identity and eligibility to work.

3. Complete the employer's section of Form I-9.

4. Retain Form I-9 for at least three years.

5. Present Form I-9 for inspection to an Immigration and Naturalization Service officer or to a Department of Labor officer upon request.[50]

Employers found to have violated the Act will be ordered to cease the discriminatory practice. They may also be directed to hire, with or without back pay, individuals harmed by the discrimination and pay a fine of up to $1,000 for each person discriminated against. Charges of discrimination based on national origin or citizenship are filed with the Office of Special Counsel in the Department of Justice.

To counter the rise of illegal immigrants, various states have enacted laws making it more difficult for illegal workers to live and work in the United States and for businesses to employ them. State laws may bar benefits and services, such as denying subsidized child care, health care, and public education, for non-U.S. citizens. Employers may face stiffer economic penalties for hiring illegals and encounter stricter documentation procedures. For example, in Colorado, public employers are prohibited from entering into service contracts with contractors who knowingly employ illegal immigrants.[51]

UNIFORM GUIDELINES ON EMPLOYEE SELECTION PROCEDURES

Employers are often uncertain about the appropriateness of specific selection procedures, especially those related to testing and selection. To remedy this concern, the Equal Employment Opportunity Commission, along with three other government agencies, adopted the current Uniform Guidelines on Employee Selection Procedures.[52] The *Uniform Guidelines* is a very important procedural document for managers because it applies to employee selection procedures in the areas of hiring, retention, promotion, transfer, demotion, dismissal, and referral. It is designed to help employers, labor organizations, employment agencies, and licensing and certification boards comply with the requirements of federal laws prohibiting discrimination in employment.[53]

Essentially, the *Uniform Guidelines* recommends that an employer be able to demonstrate that selection procedures are valid in predicting or measuring performance in a particular job. It defines "discrimination" as follows:

> The use of any selection procedure which has an adverse impact on the hiring, promotion, or other employment or membership opportunities of members of any

4 | Objective

Uniform Guidelines on Employee Selection Procedures

A procedural document published in the *Federal Register* to help employers comply with federal regulations against discriminatory actions race, sex, or ethnic group will be considered to be discriminatory and inconsistent with these guidelines, unless the procedure has been validated in accordance with these guidelines (or, certain other provisions are satisfied).[54]

Validity

When using a test or other selection instrument to choose individuals for employment, employers must be able to prove that the selection instrument bears a direct relationship to job success. This proof is established through validation studies that show the job relatedness or lack thereof for the selection instrument under study. The *Uniform Guidelines* provides strict standards for employers to follow as they validate selection procedures. The different methods of testing validity are reviewed in detail in Chapter 6.

Adverse Impact and Disparate Treatment

Objective | 5

adverse impact

A concept that refers to the rejection of a significantly higher percentage of a protected class for employment, placement, or promotion when compared with the successful, nonprotected class

For an applicant or employee to pursue a discrimination case successfully, the individual must establish that the employer's selection procedures resulted in an adverse impact on a protected class. Adverse impact refers to the rejection for employment, placement, or promotion of a significantly higher percentage of a protected class when compared with a nonprotected class.[55] Additionally, when pursuing an adverse impact claim, an individual is alleging that the employer's selection practice has unintentionally discriminated against a protected group.

While the *Uniform Guidelines* does not require an employer to conduct validity studies of selection procedures where no adverse impact exists, it does encourage employers to use selection procedures that are valid. Organizations that validate their selection procedures on a regular basis and use interviews, tests, and other procedures in such a manner as to avoid adverse impact will generally be in compliance with the principles of equal employment legislation.

There are two basic ways to show that adverse impact exists:

four-fifths rule

A rule of thumb followed by the EEOC in determining adverse impact for use in enforcement proceedings

Adverse Rejection Rate, or Four-Fifths Rule. According to the *Uniform Guidelines*, a selection program has an adverse impact when the selection rate for any racial, ethnic, or sex class is less than four-fifths (or 80 percent) of the rate of the class with the highest selection rate. The Equal Employment Opportunity Commission has adopted the four-fifths rule as a rule of thumb to determine adverse impact in enforcement proceedings. The four-fifths rule is not a legal definition of discrimination; rather, it is a method by which the EEOC or any other enforcement agency monitors serious discrepancies in hiring, promotion, or other employment decisions. The Appendix at the end of this chapter explains how adverse impact is determined and gives a realistic example of how the four-fifths rule is computed.

An alternative to the four-fifths rule, and one frequently used in discrimination lawsuits, is to apply standard deviation analysis to the observed applicant flow data. The Supreme Court, in *Hazelwood School District v. United States*, set forth a standard deviation analysis that has been followed by numerous lower courts.[56] This statistical procedure determines whether the difference between the expected selection rates for protected groups and the actual selection rates could be attributed to chance. If chance is eliminated for the lower selection rates of the protected class, it is assumed that the employer's selection technique has an adverse impact on the employment opportunities of that group.

Restricted Policy. Any evidence that an employer has a selection procedure that excludes members of a protected class, whether intentional or not, constitutes adverse impact. For example, hiring individuals who must meet a minimum height or appearance standard (at the expense of protected class members) is evidence of a restricted policy. In one case known to the authors, an organization when downsizing discharged employees primarily age 40 or older. These employees filed a class action suit claiming adverse impact under the Age Discrimination in Employment Act.

The benchmark case in employment selection procedures is *Griggs v. Duke Power Company* (1971). Willie Griggs had applied for the position of coal handler with the Duke Power Company. His request for the position was denied because he was not a high school graduate, a requirement for the position. Griggs claimed the job standard was discriminatory because it did not relate to job success and because the standard had an adverse impact on a protected class.

In the *Griggs* decision, the Supreme Court established two important principles affecting equal employment opportunity.[57] First, the Court ruled that employer discrimination need not be overt or intentional to be present. Rather, employment practices can be illegal even when applied equally to all employees. For example, under this ruling, a new venture pharmaceuticals company requiring all salespeople to be six feet tall would impose an adverse impact on Asians and women, limiting their employment opportunities.

Second, under *Griggs*, employment practices must be job-related. When discrimination charges arise, employers have the burden of proving that employment requirements are job-related or constitute a business necessity. When employers use education, physical, or intelligence standards as a basis for hiring or promotion, these must be absolutely necessary for job success. Under Title VII, good intent, or absence of intent to discriminate, is not a sufficient defense.

In EEO cases, it is important to distinguish between adverse impact and disparate treatment discrimination. Adverse impact cases deal with unintentional discrimination; disparate treatment cases involve instances of purposeful discrimination. For example, disparate treatment would arise when an employer hires men, but no women, with school-age children. Allowing men to apply for craft jobs, such as carpentry or electrical work, but denying this opportunity to women would also show disparate treatment. To win a disparate treatment case, the plaintiff must prove that the employer's actions intended to discriminate, a situation often difficult to substantiate.

disparate treatment
A situation in which protected class members receive unequal treatment or are evaluated by different standards

McDonnell Douglas Test. Individuals who believe they have been unjustly rejected for employment may demonstrate disparate treatment through the McDonnell Douglas test. This test, named for the Supreme Court case *McDonnell Douglas Corp. v. Green* (1973), provides four guidelines for individuals to follow in establishing a case:[58]

1. The person is a member of a protected class.

2. The person applied for a job for which he or she was qualified.

3. The person was rejected, despite being qualified.

4. After rejection, the employer continued to seek other applicants with similar qualifications.

Provided these four guidelines are met, then a prima facie (before further examination) case of discrimination is shown. The burden now shifts to the employer to prove that the action taken against the individual was not discriminatory. For example, in a selection case in which female applicants were denied employment, the supervisor may claim that the male hired was the only applicant qualified to perform the job.

Workforce Utilization Analysis

While employers must be aware of the impact of their selection procedures on protected class members, they must also be concerned with the composition of their internal workforce when compared with their external labor market. The EEOC refers to this comparison as workforce utilization analysis. This concept simply compares an employer's workforce by race and sex for specific job categories against the surrounding labor market. The employer's relevant labor market is that area from which employees are drawn who have the skills needed to successfully perform the job. For example, if the Vision Track Golf Corporation is hiring computer technicians from a labor market composed of 10 percent black workers, 8 percent Hispanic workers, and 2 percent Native American workers, all of whom possess the qualifications for the job, the employer's internal workforce should reflect this racial composition. When this occurs, the employer's workforce is said to be *at parity* with the relevant labor market. If the employer's racial workforce composition is below external figures, then the protected class is said to be *underutilized,* and the employer should take affirmative steps to correct the imbalance.

workforce utilization analysis

A process of classifying protected-class members by number and by the type of job they hold within the organization

ENFORCING EQUAL EMPLOYMENT OPPORTUNITY LEGISLATION

Along with prohibiting employment discrimination, Title VII of the Civil Rights Act created the Equal Employment Opportunity Commission. As the federal government's leading civil rights agency, the EEOC is responsible for ensuring that covered employers comply with the intent of this act. The commission accomplishes this goal primarily by (1) issuing various employment guidelines and monitoring the employment practices of organizations and (2) protecting employee rights through the investigation and prosecution of discrimination charges.[59] Figure 3.4 illustrates the caseload of the EEOC for recent years.

It is important to remember that the EEOC's guidelines are not federal law but administrative rules and regulations published in the *Federal Register.* However, the different guidelines have been given weight by the courts as they interpret the law and therefore should not be taken lightly. In addition to enforcing Title VII, the EEOC has the authority to enforce the Age Discrimination in Employment Act and the Equal Pay Act. Executive Order 12067, which requires the coordination of all federal equal employment opportunity regulations, practices, and policies, is also administered by the EEOC.

The Equal Employment Opportunity Commission

The EEOC consists of five commissioners and a general counsel, all appointed by the president of the United States and confirmed by the Senate. The president

FIGURE
3.4

U.S. Equal Employment Opportunity Commission Case Figures, Fiscal Years 2001–2007

BASIS	FY 2001	FY 2002	FY 2003	FY 2004	FY 2005	FY 2006	FY 2007
Race	28,912	29,910	28,526	27,696	26,740	27,238	30,510
Sex	25,140	25,536	24,362	24,249	23,094	23,247	24,826
Disability	16,470	15,964	15,377	15,346	14,893	15,575	17,734
Age	17,405	19,921	19,124	17,837	16,585	16,548	19,103
Retaliation	22,257	22,768	22,690	22,740	22,278	22,555	26,663
National origin	8,025	9,046	8,450	8,361	8,035	8,327	9,396
Religion	2,217	2,572	2,532	2,466	2,340	2,541	2,880
Equal pay	1,251	1,256	1,167	1,011	970	861	818
Total*	**80,840**	**84,442**	**81,293**	**79,432**	**75,428**	**75,768**	**82,792**

*The number for total charges reflects the number of individual charge filings. Because individuals often file charges under multiple bases, the number of total charges for any given fiscal year will be less than the total of the eight bases listed.

Source: Data compiled by the Office of Research, Information and Planning from EEOC's Charge Data System's national database.

appoints commissioners for staggered five-year terms, and no more than three members of the commission can be of the same political party. One commissioner is appointed to be the EEOC chairperson, who is responsible for the overall administration of the agency. The commission's work consists of formulating EEO policy and approving all litigation involved in maintaining equal employment opportunity.

Appointed for a four-year term, the general counsel is responsible for investigating discrimination charges, conducting agency litigation, and providing legal opinions, in addition to reviewing EEOC regulations, guidelines, and contracts.

The day-to-day operation of the commission is performed through administrative headquarters, districts, and area offices. *District offices* handle discrimination charges and all compliance and litigation enforcement functions. *Area offices* are less than full-service organizations and generally serve as charge-processing and initial investigation units. Much of the EEOC's work is delegated to the district offices and other designated representatives. District directors have authority to receive or consent to the withdrawal of Title VII charges, issue subpoenas, send notices of the filing of charges, dismiss charges, enter into and sign conciliation agreements (voluntary employer settlements), and send out notices of the employee's right to sue. Employees who wish to file discrimination charges and employers responding to complaints work with district or area office personnel.

Record-Keeping and Posting Requirements

Organizations subject to Title VII are required by law to maintain specific employment records and reports. In addition, employers are required to post selected equal employment opportunity notices and to summarize the composition of their

6 | Objective

workforce in order to determine the distribution of protected individuals. These records are for establishing minority group statistical reports. Equal employment opportunity legislation covering federal contractors and subcontractors has special reporting requirements for these employers. Those failing to comply with record-keeping and posting requirements or willfully falsifying records can incur penalties, including fines and imprisonment.

It is important to note that record-keeping requirements are both detailed and comprehensive. For example, managers must generate and retain for specific time periods different employment data under each of the following laws: Title VII, Age Discrimination in Employment Act, and Equal Pay Act. When federal contractors are required to have written affirmative action programs, these must be retained along with supporting documents (such as names of job applicants, rejection ratios, and seniority lists).

EEO-1 report

An employer information report that must be filed annually by employers of 100 or more employees (except state and local government employers) and government contractors and subcontractors to determine an employer's workforce composition

Employers of 100 or more employees (except state and local government employees) and government contractors and subcontractors subject to Executive Order 11286 must file annually an EEO-1 report (Employer Information Report). The report collects data about gender and race/ethnicity by ten different job categories.[60] This comprehensive report is the EEOC's basic document for determining an employer's workforce composition, investigating charges of discrimination, providing information about the employment status of minorities and women, and analyzing employment patterns, such as the representation of female and minority workers within companies, industries, and regions. Employers can now submit the EEO-1 report through the agency's Web-based filing system. Highlights in HRM 4 discusses the Web-based reporting system.

In preparing the EEO-1 report, employee self-identification is the preferred method of identifying gender, race, and ethnic information. If employees decline to self-identify, employment records or observed observation may be used. During the employment process, employers are permitted to collect racial data on job applicants for compiling statistical reports; however, these data must be collected on a separate information sheet, not on the formal job application form. When a charge of discrimination has been filed, the respondent organization must retain all HR records relevant to the case until final disposition of the charge.

To show evidence of its equal employment opportunity and affirmative action efforts, an organization should retain copies of recruitment letters sent to minority agencies, announcements of job openings, and other significant information concerning employee recruitment. Other employment records to keep include data on promotions, demotions, transfers, layoffs or terminations, rates of pay or other terms of compensation, and selections for training or apprenticeship programs. Title VII requires retention of all personnel or employment records, including application forms, for at least six months or until resolution of any HR action, whichever occurs later.

Posters explaining to individuals what their employment rights are and how to file complaints of discrimination have been developed by the EEOC and other administrative agencies. (See Highlights in HRM 5.) The law requires that employers display these posters and other federally

Using the Internet

The poster shown in Highlights in HRM 5 may be downloaded from the EEOC Web site. Go to the Student Resources at:

www.cengage.com/
management/bohlander

2007 EEO-1 Survey

About the EEO-1 Survey

- Who must file
- How to file
- Filing for the first time
- When to file
- Legal basis
- FAQ

Filing Procedures

- EEO-1 Instruction Booklet, with sample form (also available in PDF)

Alternate EEO-1 Reporting Formats

- Data File
- Filing EEO-1 Reports As Computer Printouts:
  - Single-establishment Company Specifications
  - Multi-establishment Company Specifications

Additional Documentation

- EEO-1 Job Classification

The **Employer Information Report EEO-1**, otherwise known as the EEO-1 Report, is required to be filed with the U.S. Equal Employment Opportunity Commission's EEO-1 Joint Reporting Committee. The filing deadline for the 2007 EEO-1 Survey is *September 30, 2007*. Notification letters will be mailed to employers beginning in July 2007.

The **preferred method** for completing the 2007 EEO-1 reports is the web-based filing system. Online filing requires you to log into your company's database with a Login ID and Password. All companies should receive 2007 EEO-1 filing materials by mail no later than mid August 2007. If you cannot locate your Login ID and/or Password, contact the EEO-1 Joint Reporting Committee at **e1.techassistance@eeoc.gov.**

- **No Installation:** The online form is totally web based. There is no Software to download or install.
- **Data Reuse:** As much as possible, information is pre-filled from the previous year to speed up data entry.
- **Secure:** Data is transferred over the internet using encryption, assuring your privacy.
- **Historical Access:** Access up to 10 years worth of EEO-1 data for your establishments.

Login

The EEO-1 online filing application requires you to log in with a Login ID and Password. You may log into your company's 2007 EEO-1 online database and key data immediately upon receipt of the Login ID and Password.

The filing deadline for the 2007 EEO-1 Survey is **September 30, 2007.**

Questions may be addressed to:

EEO-1 Joint Reporting Committee
P.O. Box 19100
Washington, D.C. 20036-9100

Phone: 1-866-286-6440
Fax: 202-663-7i85

Email: e1.techassistance@eeoc.gov

required posters related to HRM in prominent places easily accessible to employees. HR employment offices, cafeterias, centrally located bulletin boards, and time clocks are popular locations. Posting requirements should not be taken lightly. For example, EEO posters show the time limits for filing a charge of discrimination. Failure to post these notices may be used as a basis for excusing the late filing of a discrimination charge.

Processing Discrimination Charges

Employees or job applicants who believe they have been discriminated against may file a discrimination complaint, or charge form, with the EEOC. Filing a charge form initiates an administrative procedure that can be lengthy, time-consuming, and costly for the employer.[61] Both parties, the plaintiff (employee) and the defendant (organization), must be prepared to support their beliefs or actions. If litigation follows, employers will normally take an aggressive approach to defend their position.

Figure 3.5 summarizes the process of filing a discrimination charge with the EEOC.[62] Under the law, charges must be filed within 180 days (300 days in deferral states)[63] of the alleged unlawful practice. The processing of a charge includes notifying the employer that a charge of employment discrimination has been filed. Employers will receive a copy of the charge within ten days of filing.

In states that have FEP laws with appropriate enforcement machinery, the discrimination charge is deferred to the state agency for resolution before action is taken by the EEOC. The EEOC will accept the recommendation of the state agency because deferral states must comply with federal standards. If the state agency fails to resolve the complaint or if the sixty-day deferral period lapses, the case is given back to the EEOC for final investigation.

EEOC investigations are conducted by fully trained equal opportunity specialists (EOSs) who have extensive experience in investigative procedures, theories of discrimination, and relief and remedy techniques. The EOS will gather facts from both sides through telephone calls, letters and questionnaires, field visits, or jointly arranged meetings. While it is generally advisable for them to cooperate in EEOC investigations, employers may resist the commission's efforts by refusing to submit documents or give relevant testimony. However, the EEOC may obtain this information through a court subpoena. Employers who then refuse to supply the information will face contempt-of-court charges.

Once the investigation is under way or completed, several decision points occur. First, the employer may offer a settlement to resolve the case without further investigation. If the offer is accepted, the case is closed. Second, the EEOC may find no violation of law and dismiss the charge. In this case, the charging party is sent a *right-to-sue notice*, which permits the individual to start private litigation, if he or she so desires, in federal court within ninety days. Third, if the EEOC finds "reasonable cause" of discrimination, the commission will attempt to conciliate (settle) the matter between the charging party and the employer. The conciliation process is a voluntary procedure and will not always lead to a settlement.

Employers should keep in mind that when the EEOC negotiates a settlement, it will attempt to obtain full remedial, corrective, and preventive relief. Back pay, reinstatement, transfers, promotions, seniority rights, bonuses, and other "make whole" perquisites of employment are considered appropriate remedies. These settlements can frequently be costly.

HIGHLIGHTS IN HRM

5

EEOC Poster

Equal Employment Opportunity is

THE LAW

Employers Holding Federal Contracts or Subcontracts

Applicants to and employees of companies with a Federal government contract or subcontract are protected under the following Federal authorities:

RACE, COLOR, RELIGION, SEX, NATIONAL ORIGIN

Executive Order 11246, as amended, prohibits job discrimination on the basis of race, color, religion, sex or national origin, and requires affirmative action to ensure equality of opportunity in all aspects of employment.

INDIVIDUALS WITH HANDICAPS

Section 503 of the Rehabilitation Act of 1973, as amended, prohibits job discrimination because of handicap and requires affirmative action to employ and advance in employment qualified individuals with handicaps who, with reasonable accommodation, can perform the essential functions of a job.

VIETNAM ERA AND SPECIAL DISABLED VETERANS

38 U.S.C. 4212 of the Vietnam Era Veterans Readjustment Assistance Act of 1974 prohibits job discrimination and requires affirmative action to employ and advance in employment qualified Vietnam era veterans and qualified special disabled veterans.

Any person who believes a contractor has violated its nondiscrimination or affirmative action obligations under the authorities above should contact immediately:

The Office of Federal Contract Compliance Programs (OFCCP), Employment Standards Administration, U.S. Department of Labor, 200 Constitution Avenue, N.W., Washington, D.C. 20210 or call (202) 523-9368, or an OFCCP regional or district office, listed in most telephone directories under U.S. Government, Department of Labor.

Private Employment, State and Local Governments, Educational Institutions

Applicants to and employees of most private employers, state and local governments, educational institutions, employment agencies and labor organizations are protected under the following Federal laws:

RACE, COLOR, RELIGION, SEX, NATIONAL ORIGIN

Title VII of the Civil Rights Act of 1964, as amended, prohibits discrimination in hiring, promotion, discharge, pay, fringe benefits, job training, classification, referral, and other aspects of employment, on the basis of race, color, religion, sex or national origin.

DISABILITY

The Americans with Disabilities Act of 1990, as amended, protects qualified applicants and employees with disabilities from discrimination in hiring, promotion, discharge, pay, job training, fringe benefits, classification, referral, and other aspects of employment on the basis of disability. The law also requires that covered entities provide qualified applicants and employees with disabilities with reasonable accommodations that do not impose undue hardship.

AGE

The Age Discrimination in Employment Act of 1967, as amended, protects applicants and employees 40 years of age or older from discrimination on the basis of age in hiring, promotion, discharge, compensation, terms, conditions or privileges of employment.

SEX (WAGES)

In addition to sex discrimination prohibited by Title VII of the Civil Rights Act (see above), the Equal Pay Act of 1963, as amended, prohibits sex discrimination in payment of wages to women and men performing substantially equal work in the same establishment.

Retaliation against a person who files a charge of discrimination, participates in an investigation, or opposes an unlawful employment practice is prohibited by all of these Federal laws.

If you believe that you have been discriminated against under any of the above laws, you immediately should contact:

The U.S. Equal Employment Opportunity Commission (EEOC), 1801 L Street, N.W., Washington, D.C. 20507 or an EEOC field office by calling toll free (800) 669-4000. For individuals with hearing impairments, EEOC's toll free TDD number is (800) 800-3302.

Programs or Activities Receiving Federal Financial Assistance

RACE, COLOR, NATIONAL ORIGIN, SEX

In addition to the protection of Title VII of the Civil Rights Act of 1964, Title VI of the Civil Rights Act prohibits discrimination on the basis of race, color or national origin in programs or activities receiving Federal financial assistance. Employment discrimination is covered by Title VI if the primary objective of the financial assistance is provision of employment, or where employment discrimination causes or may cause discrimination in providing services under such programs. Title IX of the Education Amendments of 1972 prohibits employment discrimination on the basis of sex in educational programs or activities which receive Federal assistance.

INDIVIDUALS WITH HANDICAPS

Section 504 of the Rehabilitation Act of 1973, as amended, prohibits employment discrimination on the basis of handicap in any program or activity which receives Federal financial assistance. Discrimination is prohibited in all aspects of employment against handicapped persons who, with reasonable accommodation, can perform the essential functions of a job.

If you believe you have been discriminated against in a program of any institution which receives Federal assistance, you should contact immediately the Federal agency providing such assistance.

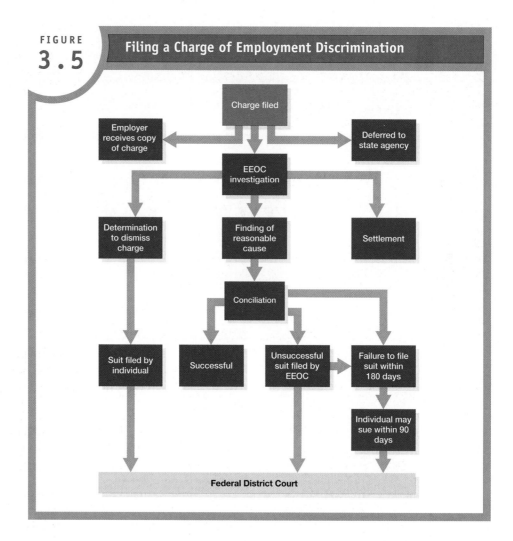

FIGURE 3.5

Filing a Charge of Employment Discrimination

If the employer and the EEOC cannot reach a negotiated settlement, the commission has the power to prosecute the organization in court. However, this decision is made on a case-by-case basis and may depend on the importance of the issue. Failure of the EEOC to take court action or to resolve the charge in 180 days from filing permits employees to pursue litigation within 90 days after receiving a right-to-sue letter issued by the commission.

Retaliation

Importantly, managers and supervisors must not retaliate against individuals who invoke their legal rights to file charges or to support other employees during EEOC proceedings.[64] Title VII of the Civil Rights Act states that an employer may not

> discriminate against any of his employees because the employee has opposed any unlawful employment practice, or because the employee has made a charge, testi-fied, assisted, or participated in any manner in an investigation, proceedings, or hearing under this Act.

In a recent case, a female dispatcher at Pepsi-Cola General Bottlers, Inc., a Chicago soft drink distributor, was awarded $400,000 in damages when she complained about sexual harassment and was retaliated against in violation of Title VII of the Civil Rights Act of 1964.[65] Retaliation can include any punitive action taken against employees who elect to exercise their legal rights before any EEO agency.[66] These actions include discharge, demotion, salary reduction, reduced work responsibilities, and transfer to a less desirable job.[67] Highlights in HRM 6 provide the EEOC Guidelines on Retaliation.

6

HIGHLIGHTS IN HRM

EEOC Guidelines on Retaliation

An employer may not fire, demote, harass, or otherwise "retaliate" against an individual for filing a charge of discrimination, participating in a discrimination proceeding, or otherwise opposing discrimination. The same laws that prohibit discrimination based on race, color, sex, religion, national origin, age, and disability, as well as wage differences between men and women performing substantially equal work, also prohibit retaliation against individuals who oppose unlawful discrimination or participate in an employment discrimination proceeding.

In addition to the protections against retaliation that are included in all of the laws enforced by EEOC, the Americans with Disabilities Act (ADA) also protects individuals from coercion, intimidation, threat, harassment, or interference in their exercise of their own rights or their encouragement of someone else's exercise of rights granted by the ADA.

There are three main terms that are used to describe retaliation. Retaliation occurs when an employer, employment agency, or labor organization takes an **adverse action** against a **covered individual** because he or she engaged in a **protected activity**. These three terms are described below.

Adverse Action

An adverse action is an action taken to try to keep someone from opposing a discriminatory practice, or from participating in an employment discrimination proceeding. Examples of adverse actions include:

- employment actions such as termination, refusal to hire, and denial of promotion,
- other actions affecting employment such as threats, unjustified negative evaluations, unjustified negative references, or increased surveillance.

Adverse actions do not include petty slights and annoyances, such as stray negative comments in an otherwise positive or neutral evaluation, "snubbing" a colleague, or negative comments that are justified by an employee's poor work performance or history.

(continued)

EEOC Guidelines on Retaliation (continued)

Covered Individuals

Covered individuals are people who have opposed unlawful practices, participated in proceedings, or requested accommodations related to employment discrimination based on race, color, sex, religion, national origin, age, or disability. Individuals who have a close association with someone who engaged in such protected activity also are covered individuals. For example, it is illegal to terminate an employee because his spouse participated in employment discrimination litigation.

Opposition to a practice believed to be unlawful discrimination

Opposition is informing an employer that you believe that he/she is engaging in prohibited discrimination. Opposition is protected from retaliation as long as it is based on a reasonable, good-faith belief that the complained of practice violates anti-discrimination law; and the manner of the opposition is reasonable.

Examples of protected opposition include:

- Complaining to anyone about alleged discrimination against oneself or others;
- Threatening to file a charge of discrimination;
- Picketing in opposition to discrimination; or
- Refusing to obey an order reasonably believed to be discriminatory.

Participation in an employment discrimination proceeding.

Participation means taking part in an employment discrimination proceeding. Participation is protected activity even if the proceeding involved claims that ultimately were found to be invalid. Examples of participation include:

- Filing a charge of employment discrimination;
- Cooperating with an internal investigation of alleged discriminatory practices; or
- Serving as a witness in an EEO investigation or litigation.

A protected activity can also include requesting a reasonable accommodation based on religion or disability.

Source: Adapted from U.S. Equal Employment Commission: Retaliation.

http://www.eeoc.gov/types/retaliation.html, November 15, 2007.

Preventing Discrimination Charges

Both large and small employers understand that the foundation to preventing any form of discrimination is a comprehensive EEO policy. The Supreme Court's emphasis on the prevention and correction of discrimination means that the employers that do not have an EEO policy are legally vulnerable. Antidiscrimination policy statements must be inclusive; they must cover all applicable laws and EEOC guidelines and contain practical illustations of specific inappropriate behavior. For the policy to have value, it must be widely disseminated to managers, supervisors, and all non-managerial employess. A complete policy will include specific sanctions for thsoe found guilty of discriminatory behavior.[68]

Since managers and supervisors are key to preventing and correcting discrimination, they, in particular, must be trained to understand employee rights and managerial obligations.[69] A comprehensive training program will include (1) the prohibitions covered in the various EEO statutes, (2) guidance on how to respond to complaints of discrimination, (3) procedures for investigating complaints (see Chapter 13), and (4) suggestions for remedying inappropriate behavior. Perhaps the ultimate key to preventing employment discrimination is for managers and supervisors to create an organizational climate in which the principles of dignity, respect, and the acceptance of a diverse workforce are expected.

DIVERSITY MANAGEMENT: AFFIRMATIVE ACTION

Equal employment opportunity legislation requires managers to provide the same opportunities to all job applicants and employees regardless of race, color, religion, sex, national origin, or age. While EEO law is largely a policy of nondiscrimination, affirmative action requires employers to analyze their workforce and develop a plan of action to correct areas of past discrimination. Affirmative action is achieved by having organizations follow specific guidelines and goals to ensure that they have a balanced and representative workforce. To achieve these goals, employers must make a concerted effort to recruit, select, train, and promote members of protected classes. Employers must locate not only minority candidates who are qualified, but also those who, with a reasonable amount of training or physical accommodation, can be made to qualify for job openings.

> **8 | Objective**
>
> **affirmative action**
> A policy that goes beyond equal employment opportunity by requiring organizations to comply with the law and correct past discriminatory practices by increasing the numbers of minorities and women in specific positions

Establishing Affirmative Action Programs

Employers establish affirmative action programs for several reasons. As noted in Figure 3.3, affirmative action programs are required by the OFCCP for employers with federal contracts greater than $50,000. The OFCCP provides regulations and suggestions for establishing affirmative action plans. Specifically, employers must (1) provide an organizational profile that graphically illustrates their workforce demographics (see workforce utilization analysis previously discussed), (2) establish goals and timetables for employment of underutilized protected classes, (3) develop actions and plans to reduce underutilization, including initiating proactive recruitment and selection methods, and (4) monitor progress of the entire affirmative action program.

Affirmative action programs may also be required by court order when an employer has been found guilty of past discrimination, particularly when discrimination has been pervasive and a long-held organizational practice. For example, an employer practice of denying promotional opportunities to women or persons of color could be corrected through an affirmative action court order. A court-ordered program, often implemented through a *consent degree* between the court and employer, will require the setting of hiring and promotional goals along with stated timetables for compliance. When the requirements of the consent degree are met, the employer is no longer bound by the court order.

Many employers voluntarily develop their own affirmative action programs to ensure that protected class members receive fair treatment in all aspects of employment. Intel, Levi Strauss, the City of Portland, and Hilton Hotels use these programs as a useful way of monitoring the progress of employees while demonstrating good faith employment efforts. Employers with voluntary affirmative action programs will actively encourage employment diversity, post job opportunities with minority agencies, remove unnecessary barriers to employment, and offer comprehensive training and mentoring to protected class members. However, as HR professionals readily note, the success of any voluntary affirmative action program largely depends on the support given it by senior managers and supervisors at all organization levels.[70] The EEOC recommends that organizations developing affirmative action programs follow specific steps, as shown in the Highlights in HRM 7.

In pursuing affirmative action, employers may be accused of reverse discrimination, or giving preference to members of protected classes to the extent that unprotected individuals believe they are suffering discrimination. When these charges occur, organizations are caught between attempting to correct past discriminatory practices and handling present complaints from unprotected members alleging that HR policies are unfair. It is exactly this "catch-22" that has made affirmative action one of the most controversial issues of the past fifty years.

Using the Internet

For information on the Office of Federal Contract Compliance Programs (OFCCP), go to the Student Resources at:

www.cengage.com/management/bohlander

---

reverse discrimination

The act of giving preference to members of protected classes to the extent that unprotected individuals believe they are suffering discrimination

---

HIGHLIGHTS IN HRM

7

Basic Steps in Developing an Effective Affirmative Action Program

1. Issue a written equal employment opportunity policy and affirmative action commitment.
2. Appoint a top official with responsibility and authority to direct and implement the program.
3. Publicize the policy and affirmative action commitment.
4. Survey present minority and female employment by department and job classification.
5. Develop goals and timetables to improve utilization of minorities and women in each area where underutilization has been identified.
6. Develop and implement specific programs to achieve goals.
7. Establish an internal audit and reporting system to monitor and evaluate progress in each aspect of the program.
8. Develop supportive in-house and community programs.

Source: *Affirmative Action and Equal Employment: A Guidebook for Employers,* vol. 1 (Washington, DC: Equal Employment Opportunity Commission, 1974), 16–17.

There exists a long line of Supreme Court cases supporting voluntary affirmative action programs. In two leading cases, *University of California Regents v. Bakke* and *United States Steelworkers of America v. Weber*,[71] the central issue before the Court was equal treatment under the law as guaranteed in the equal protection clause of the Fourteenth Amendment and past employer discriminatory practices. In these cases, the Court ruled that applicants must be evaluated on an individual basis and race can be one factor used in the evaluation process as long as other competitive factors are considered. The Court stated that affirmative action programs were not illegal per se as long as rigid quota systems were not specified for different protected classes. Also, voluntary affirmative action programs are permissible where they attempt to eliminate racial imbalances in traditionally segregated job categories. The Supreme Court did not endorse all voluntary affirmative action programs, but it did give an important push to programs voluntarily implemented and designed to correct past racial or gender imbalances.

Today, employers wishing to implement voluntary affirmative action plans must show justification for the plan and reasonableness of the methods used to implement it. Additionally, voluntary affirmative action programs must be remedial in intent and not punitive.[72] Establishing rigid employment quotas, reserving job positions, hiring unqualified workers, or laying off employees in order to hire or retain protected class members are clearly illegal employer actions.

Managing Diversity: Affirmative Action

Affirmative action is a highly emotional and controversial subject because affirmative action programs affect all employees regardless of gender, race, or ethnicity. At the core of the debate is the concern that affirmative action leads to preferential treatment and quotas for selected individuals and thus results in reverse discrimination against others. Additionally, affirmative action as a national priority has been challenged for the following reasons:

- Affirmative action has not consistently resulted in improvement of the employment status of protected groups.

- Individuals hired under affirmative action programs sometimes feel prejudged and assumed capable only of inferior performance, and in fact, these individuals *are* sometimes viewed by others as "tokens."

- Affirmative action programs of either voluntary or forced compliance have failed to effectively assimilate protected classes into an organization's workforce.

- Preferences shown toward one protected class may create conflicts between other minority groups.

Judicial support for affirmative action as a worthy national goal has changed remarkably over the years. For example, early support for affirmative action was demonstrated through the *Bakke* and *Weber* decisions. However, during the mid-1990s, federal courts increasingly restricted the use of race and ethnicity in awarding scholarships, determining college admissions, making layoff decisions, selecting employees, promoting employees, and awarding government contracts. Several important court cases illustrate this point.

In *Adarand Constructors v. Peña* (1995), the court ruled that federal programs that use race or ethnicity as a basis for decision-making must be strictly scrutinized to ensure that they promote "compelling" governmental interests.[73] In the majority opinion, the Court declared that "strict scrutiny of all governmental racial classifications is essential" to distinguish between legitimate programs that redress past discrimination and programs that "are in fact motivated by illegitimate notions of racial inferiority or simple racial politics."

In a 1996 decision affecting admission standards at the University of Texas law school, the Court ruled in *Hopwood v. State of Texas* that diversity could not constitute a competing state interest justifying racial preference in selection decisions.[74] The Court noted that the school could not discriminate "because there was no compelling justification under the Fourteenth Amendment or Supreme Court precedent for such conduct even if it was designed to correct perceived racial imbalance in the student body."

Then, in a landmark and highly significant affirmative action ruling, the Supreme Court held in *Grutter v. Bollinger* that colleges and universities *can* consider an applicant's race as a factor in admission decisions.[75] The decision upheld an admission policy at the University of Michigan Law School in which officials considered an applicant's race along with other factors when making admission decisions. Writing for the Court, Justice Sandra Day O'Connor noted that colleges and universities have compelling educational reasons for seeking a diverse student body in light of a growing diverse society and a global business environment. Justice O'Connor stated, "Effective participation by members of all racial and ethnic groups in the civil life of our nation is essential if the dream of one nation, indivisible, is to be realized."

Perhaps the greatest current challenge to affirmative action has been laws enacted by states to prohibit preferences in racial or gender hiring. California, Washington, and Michigan have such laws. Five states—Arizona, Missouri, Colorado, Nebraska, and Oklahoma—are targeted for anti-affirmative action initiatives.[76] Opponents argue these laws greatly restrict or prohibit hiring preferences, thereby denying protected class members of important employment opportunities granted under affirmative action programs For example, in California, the law ended long-standing state affirmative action programs in education, public employment, and government contracting.[77] The debate over affirmative action, its alleged benefits and drawbacks, will clearly continue as a legal and societal issue.

The future of affirmative action may rest not in voluntary programs, judicial decisions, or laws but in managerial attitudes that value diversity in the workforce. Managers who embrace a diverse workforce acknowledge individual employee differences and the contributions made by people of varied abilities. Organizations that approach diversity from a practical, business-oriented perspective (rather than a court-ordered affirmative action mandate) will employ and promote protected class members as a means for developing competitive advantage. Viewed in this manner, greater workforce diversity will significantly enhance organizational performance through knowledge of diverse marketplaces and creative problem-solving. For example, Michael Goldstein, chairman of the Toys "R" Us Children's Fund, supports both affirmative action and diversity because "our customers are not one group; they comprise all of America. It's important to be able to serve them." Eastman Kodak maintains that it is committed to diversity because the composition of its customer base and of the workforce is changing. For both of these organizations, commitment to the advantages of diversity automatically achieves the goals of affirmative action.

SUMMARY

Objective 1 Employment discrimination against blacks, Hispanics, women, and other groups has long been practiced by U.S. employers. Prejudice against minority groups is a major cause in their lack of employment gains. Government reports show that the wages and job opportunities of minorities typically lag behind those for whites.

Objective 2 Effective management requires knowing the legal aspects of the employment relationship. Pertinent legislation includes the Equal Pay Act, Title VII of the Civil Rights Act of 1964, Age Discrimination in Employment Act, Equal Employment Opportunity Act of 1972, Pregnancy Discrimination Act, Americans with Disabilities Act, Civil Rights Act of 1991, and various executive orders. Employers are permitted to discriminate against selected protected classes when hiring preferences are a reasonable necessity, constituting a bona fide occupational qualification for normal business operation. The religious preferences of employees must be accommodated as required by law.

Objective 3 Sexual harassment is an area of particular importance to managers and supervisors. Extensive efforts should be made to ensure that both male and female employees are free from all forms of sexually harassing conduct. The Immigration Reform and Control Act was passed to control unauthorized immigration into the United States. The law requires managers to maintain various employment records, and they must not discriminate against job applicants or present employees because of national origin or citizenship status.

Objective 4 The *Uniform Guidelines on Employee Selection Procedures* is designed to help employers comply with federal prohibitions against employment practices that discriminate on the basis of race, color, religion, gender, or national origin. The *Uniform Guidelines* provides employers with a framework for making legally enforceable employment decisions. Employers must be able to show that selection procedures are valid in predicting job performance.

Objective 5 Adverse impact plays an important role in proving employment discrimination. Adverse impact means that an employer's employment practices result in the rejection of a significantly higher percentage of members of minority and other protected groups for some employment activity. A key to an adverse impact discrimination claim is that the employer's employment practice is unintentional in its impact against the protected group. Disparate treatment is intentional discrimination against a protected group. Refusing to hire individuals of a particular religion or denying males, but not females, office clerical jobs are examples of disparate treatment discrimination.

Objective 6 To ensure that organizations comply with antidiscrimination legislation, the EEOC was established to monitor employers' actions. Employers subject to federal laws must maintain required records and report requested employment statistics where mandated. Employers with 100 or more employees must file an EEO-1 report annually. This comprehensive document identifies employees by race/ethnicity and gender for ten job categories. Companies with government contracts of $50,000 or more must file an affirmative action plan with the OFCCP. Employers are required to collect employment data and file reports under various federal and state laws. Employers are also required to post EEO posters and posters for other government programs in prominent locations.

Objective 7 Employees or applicants for employment who believe they have been discriminated against file a discrimination complaint (a charge form) with the EEOC. The employer receives a copy of the charge form which initiates an EEOC investigation of the alleged discrimination. Individuals claiming discrimination must file the complaint within 180 days of the alleged offense, 300 days in deferral states. After the investigation, the Commission may dismiss the charge. The plaintiff will receive a right-to-sue notice which allows the individual to start private litigation. If the EEOC finds reasonable cause for the charge, it will attempt to mediate a settlement between the parties. If an agreement is not reached, the EEOC may elect to sue the employer in federal court. Figure 3.5 illustrates the steps in filing a discrimination charge.

Objective 8 Affirmative action goes beyond providing equal employment opportunity to employees. Affirmative action requires employers to become proactive and correct areas of past discrimination. This is accomplished by employing protected classes for jobs in which they are underrepresented. The employer's goal is to have a balanced internal workforce representative of the employer's relevant labor market.

KEY TERMS

adverse impact
affirmative action
bona fide occupational qualification (BFOQ)
business necessity
charge form
disabled individual

disparate treatment
EEO-1 report
equal employment opportunity
fair employment practices (FEPs)
four-fifths rule
protected classes
reasonable accommodation

reverse discrimination
sexual harassment
Uniform Guidelines on Employee Selection Procedures
workforce utilization analysis

DISCUSSION QUESTIONS

Objective 1 1. EEO legislation was prompted by significant social events. List those events and describe how they influenced the passage of various EEO laws.

Objective 2 2. Cite and describe the major federal laws and court decisions that affect the employment process of both large and small organizations.

Objective 3 3. After receiving several complaints of sexual harassment, the HR department of a city library decided to establish a sexual harassment policy. What should be included in the policy? How should it be implemented?

Objective 4 4. What is the *Uniform Guidelines on Employee Selection Procedures?* To whom do the guidelines apply? What do they cover?

Objective 5 5. Joe Alverez has filed a complaint with the EEO alleging that his employer, Universal Mortgage Company, promotes more whites than Hispanics into managerial positions. Explain the statistical methods used by the EEOC to investigate this adverse impact claim.

Objective 6 6. What is the EEO-1 report? Who does it apply to, and how often must the report be filed? How does the EEOC use the data collected?

Objective 7

7. As a marketing manager, you have recently turned down Nancy Conrad for a position as sales supervisor. Nancy believes the denial was due to her gender, and she has filed a sex discrimination charge with the EEOC. Explain the steps the EEOC will use to process the charge; include Nancy's options during the process.

Objective 8

8. Affirmative action is both a legal and emotional issue affecting employees and employers. Develop as many arguments as you can both supporting and opposing affirmative action as an employer policy. If you were asked to implement such a program, what steps would you follow?

BIZFLIX EXERCISES

Legally Blonde: Sexual Harassment

Review the earlier section "Sexual Harassment" before watching this scene from *Legally Blonde*. Several aspects of that discussion appear in the scene.

Elle Woods' (Reese Witherspoon) boyfriend, Warner Huntington III (Matthew Davis), wants to go to Harvard Law School instead of keeping their relationship alive. Elle pursues him vigorously by applying to and getting accepted to Harvard Law School. This is a charming comedy, dedicated to blonde women everywhere in the world. It is filled with stereotyping, giving many delightful twists to its surprise conclusion.

This scene comes from the "Poor Judgment" segment near the end of the film. It follows the successful use of Elle's hunch about key witness Enrique Salvatore

(Greg Serano) in Brooke Windam's (Ali Larter) trial. The film continues after she leaves Professor Callahan's (Victor Garber) office. Elle sees Emmett (Luke Wilson) in the building lobby and tells him she is quitting the internship.

What to Watch for and Ask Yourself

- Does Professor Callahan sexually harass Elle? If yes, what is the evidence in these scenes?

- If these scenes show sexual harassment, what type of harassment is it? Quid pro quo harassment or hostile environment harassment?

- Did Elle behave appropriately or inappropriately in Professor Callahan's office?

Sexual Harassment: A Frank Discussion

Over the past decade, the problem of sexual harassment has captured the attention of all managers and employees. While it is widely known that sexual harassment is both unethical and illegal, the incidents of sexual harassment continue to plague business. Unfortunately, when these cases arise, they cause morale problems among employees, embarrassment to the organization, and costly legal damages. Consequently, all managers and supervisors play a central role in preventing sexual harassment complaints. It is important that managers understand the definition of sexual harassment, who is covered by sexual harassment guidelines, and how to prevent its occurrence. This skill-building exercise will provide you with knowledge in each of these areas.

Assignment

1. Working in teams of female and male members, develop a list of behaviors that could be classified as quid pro quo harassment or hostile environment. Explore the possibility that some sexual harassing behaviors might be viewed differently by female and male employees. Give examples.
2. Many sexual harassment incidents go unreported. Fully discuss why this can occur and what might be done to reduce this problem.
3. The cornerstone to addressing sexual harassment is achieving organizational awareness through training. Develop a sexual harassment training program for a company of 250 employees that covers, at a minimum, the following: (1) who should attend the training sessions, (2) the content outline for the training program (the list of materials your team wants to teach), (3) specific examples to illustrate the training materials, and (4) how to investigate sexual harassment complaints.
4. This chapter will assist you with this assignment. You can obtain additional materials from EEOC offices and from various HR magazines.
5. Be prepared to present your training outline to other class members.

CASE STUDY 1

Can "FIDO" Come to Work?

The Americans with Disabilities Act permits one reasonable accommodation, the use of "service animals" to assist those with disabilities. For example, seeing-eye dogs are allowed to accompany blind individuals at work. The EEOC guideline is reasonable since guide dogs are necessary to blind individuals, and furthermore, guide dogs are trained not to be a nuisance. However, employees with other ailments, such as depression, anxiety, or stress, now are wanting to bring their animals to work alleging these "companion animals" are a reasonable accommodation to their health or disability needs. The following case illustrates the dilemma employers face when employees with disabilities want to bring their animals to work.

In December 2007, Elizabeth Booth was hired by Case Services Corporation as an accountant in the organization's billing department. Elizabeth is a quadriplegic who uses a wheelchair for mobility. Shortly after her employment, Elizabeth requested that she be allowed to bring her small dog, Mandy, to work. Elizabeth stated that Mandy was a comfort to her and that the dog was specifically trained to pick up small items she might accidentally drop. Elizabeth assured her supervisor that Mandy was a well-mannered dog who would cause no problems for either herself or her coworkers.

Additionally, in support of her request, Elizabeth obtained from her personal physician a letter stating that she sometimes felt stressed at work and that Mandy, as a companion animal, would help relieve Elizabeth's stressful feelings. However, when Elizabeth's request landed on the desk of Howard Upton, HR director for Case Services, the request was quickly denied. After learning of the decision, Elizabeth immediately filed a discrimination charge with the EEOC claiming the company did not provide a reasonable accommodation to her disability or her health needs.

Questions

1. List disadvantages of allowing companion animals to come to work.
2. Does Mandy's ability to pick up dropped items classify her as a service animal? Explain.
3. Does Elizabeth's work stress affect the outcome of this case? Explain.
4. How would you decide this case? Explain.

Source: This case is adapted from James J. McDonald, Jr., "Take Your Dog To Work Everyday," *Employee Relations Law Journal* 32, no. 3 (Winter 2006): 86.

CASE STUDY 2

Misplaced
Affections:
Discharge for
Sexual
Harassment

Peter Lewiston was terminated on July 15, 2008, by the governing board of the Pine Circle Unified School District (PCUSD) for violation of the district's sexual harassment policy. Prior to Lewiston's termination he was a senior maintenance employee with an above-average work record who had worked for the PCUSD for eleven years. He had been a widower since 2003 and was described by his coworkers as a friendly, outgoing, but lonely individual. Beverly Gilbury was a fifth-grade teacher working in the district's Advanced Learning Program. She was 28 years old and married and had worked for PCUSD for six years. At the time of the incidents, Lewiston and Gilbury both worked at the Simpson Elementary School, where their relationship was described as "cooperative." The following sequence of events was reported separately by Lewiston and Gilbury during the district's investigation of this sexual harassment case.

Gilbury reported that her relationship with Lewiston began to change during the last month of the 2007–2008 school year. She believed that Lewiston was paying her more attention and that his behavior was "out of the ordinary" and "sometimes weird." He began spending more time in her classroom talking with the children and with her. At the time she didn't say anything to Lewiston because "I didn't want to hurt his feelings since he is a nice, lonely, older man." However, on May 25, when Lewiston told Gilbury that he was "very fond" of her and that she had "very beautiful eyes," she replied, "Remember, Peter, we're just friends." For the remainder of the school year, there was little contact between them; however, when they did see each other, Lewiston seemed "overly friendly" to her.

June 7, 2008. On the first day of summer school, Gilbury returned to school to find a dozen roses and a card from Lewiston. The card read, "Please forgive me for thinking you could like me. I played the big fool. Yours always, P.L." Later in the day Lewiston asked Gilbury to lunch. She replied, "It's been a long time since anyone sent me roses, but I can't go to lunch. We need to remain just friends." Gilbury told another teacher that she was uncomfortable about receiving the roses and card and that Lewiston wouldn't leave her alone. She expressed concern that Lewiston might get "more romantic" with her.

June 8, 2008. Gilbury arrived at school to find another card from Lewiston. Inside was a handwritten note that read, "I hope you can someday return my affections for you. I need you so much." Later in the day, Lewiston again asked her to lunch, and she declined saying, "I'm a happily married woman." At the close of the school day, when Gilbury went to her car, Lewiston suddenly appeared. He asked to explain himself but Gilbury became agitated and shouted, "I have to leave right now." Lewiston reached inside the car, supposedly to pat her shoulder, but touched her head instead. She believed he meant to stroke her hair. He stated that he was only trying to calm her down. She drove away, very upset.

June 9, 2008. Gilbury received another card and a lengthy letter from Lewiston, stating that he was wrong in trying to develop a relationship with her and he hoped they could still remain friends. He wished her all happiness with her family and job.

June 11, 2008. Gilbury obtained from the Western Justice Court an injunction prohibiting sexual harassment by Lewiston. Shortly thereafter Lewiston appealed the injunction. A notice was mailed to Gilbury giving the dates of the appeal hearing.

The notice stated in part, "If you fail to appear, the injunction may be vacated and the petition dismissed." Gilbury failed to appear at the hearing, and the injunction was set aside. Additionally, on June 11 she had filed with the district's EEOC officer a sexual harassment complaint against Lewiston. After the investigation, the district concluded that Lewiston's actions created an "extremely sexually hostile" environment for Gilbury. The investigative report recommended dismissal based upon the grievous conduct of Lewiston and the initial injunction granted by the Justice Court.

Questions

1. Evaluate the conduct of Peter Lewiston against the EEOC's definition of sexual harassment.
2. Should the intent or motive behind Lewiston's conduct be considered when deciding sexual harassment activities? Explain.
3. If you were the district's EEOC officer, what would you conclude? What disciplinary action, if any, would you take?

Source: This case is adapted from an actual arbitration hearing conducted by George Bohlander. The background information is factual. All names are fictitious.

APPENDIX

Determining Adverse Impact:
The Four-Fifths Rule

Employers can determine adverse impact by using the method outlined in the interpretive manual for the *Uniform Guidelines on Employee Selection Procedures*.

A. Calculate the rate of selection for each group (divide the number of people selected from a group by the number of total applicants from that group).

B. Observe which group has the highest selection.

C. Calculate the impact ratios by comparing the selection rate for each group with that of the highest group (divide the selection rate for a group by the selection rate for the highest group).

D. Observe whether the selection rate for any group is substantially less (usually less than four-fifths, or 80 percent) than the selection rate for the highest group. If it is, adverse impact is indicated in most circumstances.

Example

	JOB APPLICANTS	NUMBER HIRED	SELECTION RATE PERCENT HIRED
Step A	Whites 100	52	52/100 = 52%
	Blacks 50	14	14/50 = 28%
Step B	The group with the highest selection rate is whites, 52 percent.		
Step C	Divide the black selection rate (28 percent) by the white selection rate (52 percent). The black rate is 53.8 percent of the white rate.		
Step D	Since 53.8 percent is less than four-fifths, or 80 percent, adverse impact is indicated.		

Source: Adoption of Questions and Answers to Clarify and Provide a Common Interpretation of the *Uniform Guidelines on Employee Selection Procedures, Federal Register* 44, no. 43 (March 2, 1979): 11998.

ANSWERS TO HIGHLIGHTS IN HRM 1

1. Yes

2. False

3. No

4. Merit, seniority, incentive pay plans

5. Yes

6. Yes, if no reasonable accommodation can be made

7. No

8. Yes, except if under a court order

9. False

10. True

NOTES AND REFERENCES

1. "Morgan Stanley Settles $46 Million Discrimination Suit,", http://www.workforce.com/section/OO/artile/22/17/27.html.

2. Cheryl Wittenauer, "EEOC Files Job Bias Suit vs. Chain," *Arizona Republic*, March 8, 2007, D-1.

3. Michael Orey, "Trouble at Toyota," *Business Week*, May 22, 2006, 46.

4. "B & H Settles Discrimination Suite, Agrees to Pay $4.3 Million," *101 Wins*, October 16, 2007.

5. Michael Orey, "White Men Can't Help It" *Business Week*, May 15, 2006, 54.

6. There are excellent books on the civil rights movement. See for example, Henry Hampton arid Steve Fayer, *Voices of Freedom* (New York, NY: Bantam Dell Publishing Group, 1991)

7. Bureau of Labor Statistics, "Labor Force Statistics from the Current Population Survey," June 2008, http://www.bls.gov/cps.

8. Bureau of Labor Statistics, "Median Usual Weekly Earnings of Full-Time Wage and Salary Workers by Selected Characteristics, Quarterly Average Not Adjusted," *Labor Force Statistics from Current Population Survey*, Fourth Quarter 2007, http://www.bls.gov/cps.

9. Robert J. Grossman, "Race in the Workplace," *HR Magazine* 45, no. 3 (March 2002): 2.

10. Donald J. Peterson and Harvey R. Boiler, "Seeking a Definition of 'Supervisor': A Critical Issue in Sexual Harassment Cases," *Employee Relations Law Journal*, 32, no. 4 (Spring 2007): 87. See also, "Supervisor May Be Broadly Defined in Employer Liability," *HR Focus* 48, no. 9 (September 2003): 149–155.

11. For a practical overview of EEO law, see David J. Walsh, *Employment Law for Human Resource Practice*, 2nd ed. (Mason, OH: South-Western, 2007).

12. Bureau of Labor Statistics for the Fourth Quarter 2007 shows that the average weekly earnings for women were $616 and for men $767. Women "on average" earn about 80 percent of male earnings, a disparity that has not changed in recent years. See, for example, Aaron Bernstein, "Women's Pay: Why the Gap Remains a Chasm," *Business Week*, June 14, 2004, 58. See also, "Reasons for Gender Pay Gap Still Unclear," *HR Focus* 81, no. 2 (February 2004): 12.

13. For information on national origin discrimination, go to http//www.usdoj.gov/crt/legalinfo/natorgin.htm. See also, *Brochure: Federal Protection Against National Origin Discrimination*, U.S. Department of Justice, Civil Rights Division, 950 Pennsylvania Avenue N.W., Washington, DC 20530.

14. Information on national origin guidelines is available on the EEOC's Web site at http://www.eeoc.gov.

15. For an overview of EEO law see, David P. Twomey, *Employment Discrimination Law Manager's Guide*, 6th ed. (Mason, OH: South-Western, 2005). See also David P. Twomey, *Labor and Employment Law*, 13th ed. (Mason, OH: South-Western, 2007).

16. For specific information on religious preference guidelines and employer accommodation, see http://www.eeoc.gov/types/religion.html. See also, Scott M. Wich, "Employee's Vague Request Dooms Accommodation Claim," *HR Magazine* 52, no. 7 (July 2007): 101.

17. TWA v. Hardison, 432 U.S. 63 (1977).

18. Fay Hansen, "Avoiding Age Discrimination Claims in Hiring," *Workforce Magazine* (August 15, 2007) at http://www.workforc.com/section/06/feature/25/05/47/index.html.

19. Lynn D. Lieber, "As Average Age of Workforce Increases, Age Discrimination Verdicts Rise," *Employment Relations Today* 34, no. 1 (Spring 2007): 105.

20. "Age-Based Comments Proof of Discrimination," *Workforce Management* 83, no. 2 (February 2002): 16.

21. Maria Greco Danaher, "Include Pregnancy Leave in Pension Credit," *HR Magazine* 52, no. 11 (November 2007): 98.

22. *The Americans with Disabilities Act: A Primer for Small Business* contains examples, tips, and do's and don'ts. Published by the EEOC, the handbook explains who is protected, how to avoid mistakes during interviews, when employers may ask questions about a medical condition, how to address safety issues, reasonable accommodation obligations, and tax incentives for businesses that hire and retain individuals with disabilities. It's available on the Web or in printed format. Call 202-663-4900 or go to http://www.eeoc.gov.

23. According to the ADA, an employer is not required to retain an employee who presents a "direct threat," implying a significant risk of substantial harm to the health and safety of the individual or others that cannot be eliminated or reduced by reasonable accommodation. Also, some court cases have held that an employee with a psychiatric disability is not a qualified individual because he or she cannot perform the essential functions of the job.

24. *Toyota Motors v. Williams*, 122 S. Ct. 681 (2002).

25. Jonathan R. Mook, "Accommodation Paradigm Shifts," *HR Magazine* 52, no. 1 (January 2007): 115. See also, James J. McDonald, Jr., "Take Your Dog to Work Everyday," *Employee Relations Law Journal* 32, no. 3 (Winter 2006): 86.

26. Bill Leonard, "Studies: ADA Makes Business Better," *HR Magazine* 52, no. 10 (October 2007): 22.

27. http://www.eeoc.gov.

28. Jeffrey Schieberl and Charles P. Leo, "Employers' Legal Obligations to Employees in the Military" *Regent University Law Review* 10, no. 3 (Pepperdine University, 2007). Find additional information on the law at the USERRA Advisor at the Department of Labor Web site (http://www.dol.gov/elaws).

29. Veterans Benefits Improvement Act of 2004, Public Law 108-454 (December 20, 2004).

30. The significant Supreme Court decision in this area is *Nassau Count, Florida v. Arline*, 480 U.S. 273, 43 FEP 81(1987).

31. As currently defined, an "otherwise qualified" employee is one who can perform the "essential functions" of the job under consideration.

32. To learn more about fair employment practice agencies, go to http://www.eeoc.gov. Under the title "Employers & EEOC," click on 'Small Businesses," then click on State and Local Agencies."

33. Chelsea R. Willness, Piers Steel, and Kibeom Lee, "A Meta-Analysis of the Antecedents and Consequences of Workplace Sexual Harassment," *Personal Psychology* 60, no. 1 (Spring 2007): 127. See also, William M. Bulkeley, "Keane Settles Harassment Case with Executive," *The Wall Street Journal*, June 14, 2006, A-13.

34. EEOC charge statistics can be found at http://www.eeoc.gov. EEOC figures do not include the thousands of sexual harassment incidents not reported to governmental agencies or complaints reported to employers and settled internally through in-house complaint procedures.

35. *Guidelines on Discrimination Because of Sex*, 29 C.F.R. Sec. 1604.11(a) (1955).

36. *Guidelines on Discrimination*, Sec. 1605.11(a).

37. Paradise Valley Unified School District No. 69, Phoenix, Arizona.

38. Scott R. Eldridge, "Sexist E-Mail Backfires," *HR Magazine* 52, no. 8 (August 2007): 103.

39. John Hoft and Neal F. Thompson, "Employer Liability for Non-Employee Sexual Harassment," *Journal of the International Academy for Case Studies* 13, no. 6 (2007): 87.

40. *Oncale v. Sundowner Offshore Services, Inc.* 72 PED 45, 175; WL 88039 (U.S. 1998).

41. Margaret Bryant "Harassment Lawsuits and Lessons," *Security Management* 60, no. 4 (April 2006): 50.

42. W. Brian Holladay, "Handling of Unsubstantiated Harassment Charge Upheld," *HR Magazine* 52, no. 6 (June 2007): 142.

43. "Preventing Sexual Harassment and Other Workplace Harassment," *The Bureau of National Affairs*, 2006 edition (Washington, D.C.). Copies can be ordered by calling 1-800-960-1220. See also, Sara Bliss Kiser, Tyne Coley, Marsha Ford, and Erica Moore, "Coffee, Tea, or Me? Romance and Sexual Harassment in the Workplace, *Southern Business Review* 31, no. 2 (Spring 2006): 35.

44. Bruce Elmslie and Edinaldo Tebaldi, "Sexual Orientation and Labor Market Research," *Journal of Labor Research* 28, no. 3 (July 2007): 436. See also, Joy E. Beatty and Susan L. Kirby, "Beyond the Legal Environment: How Stigma Influences Invisible Identity Groups in the Workplace, *Employee Rights and Responsibilities Journal* 18, no. 1 (March 2006): 29.

45. Ed Frauenheim, "Gay Execs Urged to Come Out," *Workforce Management* 86, no. 10 (May 21, 2007): 1.

46. Jon D. Bible, "In a Class by Themselves. The Legal Status of Employee Appearance Policies Under Title VII After Jespersen v. Harrah's Operating Co.," *Employee Relations Law Journal* 32. no. 4 (Spring 2007): 3. See also, "Stan Malos, "Appearance-Based Sex Discrimination and Stereotyping in the Workplace: Whose Conduct Should We Regulate?," *Employee Responsibilities and Rights Journal* 19, no. 2 (June 2007): 95.

47. Mark Schoeff, "DHS Rule Rankles Employer Groups," *Workforce Management* 86, no. 14(August 20, 2007):1.

48. 8 U.S.C.A. § 1324a (a) (1), (2) (2005).

49. 8 U.S.C.A. § 1324B (1) (2005).

50. U.S. Department of Justice, Immigration and Naturalization Service, *Handbook for Employers: Instructions for Completing Form I* (Washington, DC: U.S. Government Printing Office, 2005).

51. "Immigration Reform Now Shifts to the States," *HR Focus* 84, no. 9 (September 2007): 2. See also, Diane Cadrain, "States Enact Own Laws Restricting Immigration," *HR Magazine* 51, no. 8 (August 2006): 27 and J. Smith, "Congress Adopts Piecemeal Take on Immigration Reform," *HR Magazine* 52, no. 9 (September 2007): 23.

52. Equal Employment Opportunity Commission, Civil Service Commission, Department of Labor, and Department of Justice, Adoption by Four Agencies of *Uniform Guidelines on Employee Selection Procedures* (1978), as reproduced in the *Federal Register* 43, no. 166 (August 25, 1978): 38290–315. Discussion relating to the adoption of the *Uniform Guidelines* by four agencies comprises several pages. The guidelines themselves are published on pages 38295–309. Further clarification and expansion on the guidelines may be found in the *Federal Register* 44, no. 43 (March 2, 1979): 11996–12009.

53. For a comprehensive article on the validity of personality tests, see Frederick P. Morgeson, Michael A. Campion, Robert L. Dipboye, and John R. Hollenbeck, "Reconsidering the Use of Personality Tests in Personnel Selection," *Personal Psychology* 60, no. 3 (Autumn 2007): 683.

54. *Uniform Guidelines*, Sec. 3A.

55. *Uniform Guidelines*, Sec. 40. Adverse impact need not be considered for groups that constitute less than 2 percent of the relevant labor force.

56. Hazelwood School District v. United States, 433 U.S. 299, 15 FEP 1 (1977).

57. Griggs v. Duke Power Company, 401 U.S. 424 (1971).

58. McDonnell Douglas Corp. v. Green, 411 U.S. 792, 80 (1973).

59. The primary Web site for the EEOC is http://www.eeogov. This Web site contains a wealth of information about the EEOC including the agency's history and administration, how discrimination charges are filed and processed, training and outreach programs, litigation statistics, and various pamphlets and posters offered free of charge to interested parties.

60. The EEOC's instruction manual for filling out the EEO-1 report can be found at http://www. eeoc.nov/eeol/index.html.

61. David Twomey, *Labor and Employment Law*, 13th ed. (Mason, OH: South-Western, 2007).

62. Howard S. Lavin and Elizabeth E. DiMichele, "The Time for Filing Charges of Discrimination: The Supreme Court's Decision and Its Aftermath," *Employee Relations Law Journal* 33, no. 3 (Winter 2007): 113. See also, Reynolds Holding, "Stumble on the bench," *Time*, June 18, 2007, 56.

63. A *deferral state* is one in which the state EEOC office complies with minimum operating guidelines established by the federal agency. In a deferral state, discrimination charges filed with the federal EEOC office will be deferred to the state agency for investigation and determination. If the state agency is unwilling or unable to resolve the complaint in a specified time period, the complaint is referred back to the federal EEOC office for final disposition.

64. David Sherwyn, Zev Eigen, and Gregg Gilman, "Retaliation: The Fastest Growing Discrimination Claim," *Cornell Hotel and Restaurant Administration Quarterly* 47, no. 4 (November 2006): 350.

65. *EEOC v. Pepsi-Cola General Bottlers, Inc.*, No. 03 C 6576 (N.D., IL, January 18, 2006).

66. Rebecca M. Archer and Stephen T. Lanctot, "Are Your Hands Tied? A Practical Look at Employee Claims of Retaliation," *Employee Relations Law Journal* 33, no. 1 (Summer 2007): 53. See also, Mary Price Birk, "Waking on Eggshells—Avoiding Retaliation Claims When the Employee Does Not Leave," *Employee Relations Law Journal* 32, no. 3 (Winter 2006): 10 and Martin K. LaPointe, "The Supreme Court Sets the Standard for Title VII Retaliation Claims: *Burlington Northern and Santa Fe Railway v. White*," *Labor Law Journal* 57, no. 4 (Winter 2006): 205.

67. Jathan Janove, "Retaliation Nation," *HR Magazine* 51, no. 10 (October 1006): 62.

68. Heather J. Broadwater, "Preventing Workplace Sexual Harassment," *Rural Telecommunications* 25, no. 5 (September/October 2006): 34.

69. Michael W. Johnson, "Harassment and Discrimination Prevention Training," *Labor Law Journal* 55, no. 2 (Summer 2004): 119.

70. "Voluntary Diversity Plans Can Lead to Risk," *HR Focus* 84, no. 6 (June 2007): 2.

71. *University of California Regents v. Bakke*, 438 U.S. 265 (1978) and *United Steelworkers of America v. Weber*, 443, U.S. 193 (1979).

72. *Taxman v. Board of Education of the Township of Piscataway*, 91 F 3d 1547 (3d Cir. (1996). *Cert. dismissed*, 118 S. Ct. 595 (1997).

73. *Adarand Constructors v. Peña*, 515 U.S. 200.67 FEP 1828 (1995).

74. *Hopwood v. State of Texas*, 78 F. 3d 932 (5th Cir. 1996).

75. *Grutter v. Bollinger*, 123 S. Ct. 2325 (2005).

76. Anne Ryman and Matthew Benson, 'Affirmative Action Under Fire," *The Arizona Republic*, November 6, 2007, A-1.

77. Caitlin Knowles Myers. "A Cure for Discrimination? Affirmative Action and the Case of California's Proposition 209," *Industrial and Labor Relations Review* 60, no. 3 (April 2007): 379. See also, Robert K. Robinson, Geralyn McClure, and Karen Epermanis, "The Supreme Court Rulings in *Grutter v. Bollinger* and *Gratz v. Bollinger*: The Brave New World of Affirmative Action in the 21st Century," *Public Personnel Management* 36, no. 1 (Spring 2007): 33.

JOB ANALYSIS, EMPLOYEE INVOLVEMENT, AND FLEXIBLE WORK SCHEDULES

After studying this chapter, you should be able to

Objective | 1

Discuss the relationship between job requirements and the performance of HRM functions.

Objective | 2

Indicate the methods by which job analysis typically is completed.

CHAPTER 4

Objective 3

Identify and explain the various sections of job descriptions.

Objective 4

Provide examples illustrating the various factors that must be taken into account in designing a job.

Objective 5

Discuss the various job characteristics that motivate employees.

Objective 6

Describe the different group techniques used to maximize employee contributions.

Objective 7

Differentiate and explain the different adjustments in work schedules.

A global business environment forces organizations to "reengineer" themselves to gain competitive advantage and profitability.[1] The goal is to become more efficient and effective. To achieve success, companies such as MetLife, AT&T, and Sports Authority are breaking into smaller units and getting leaner and flatter. There is emphasis on smaller scale, less hierarchy, fewer layers, and more decentralized work units.[2] As organizational reshaping takes place, managers want employees to operate more independently and flexibly to meet customer demands. To do this, they require that decisions be made by the people who are closest to the information and who are directly involved in the product or service delivered.[3] The objective is to develop jobs and basic work units that are adaptable enough to thrive in a world of high-velocity change.

In this chapter, we will discuss how jobs can be designed so as to best contribute to the objectives of the organization and at the same time satisfy the needs of the employees who are to perform them. Clearly, the duties and responsibilities present in jobs greatly influence employee productivity, job satisfaction, and employment retention.[4] Therefore, the value of job analysis, which defines clearly and precisely the requirements of each job, will be stressed. Importantly, we will emphasize that these job requirements provide the foundation for making objective and legally defensible decisions in managing human resources. The chapter concludes by reviewing several innovative job design and employee contribution techniques that increase job satisfaction while improving organizational performance. Teamwork and the characteristics of successful teams are highlighted. Stacy Sullivan, director of HR at Google, notes that "the work environment and the sense of team spirit have become a critical job element."

RELATIONSHIP OF JOB REQUIREMENTS AND HRM FUNCTIONS

Objective 1

job
A group of related activities and duties

position
The different duties and responsibilities performed by only one employee

job family
A group of individual jobs with similar characteristics

A job consists of a group of related activities and duties. Ideally, the duties of a job should consist of natural units of work that are similar and related. They should be clear and distinct from those of other jobs to minimize misunderstanding and conflict among employees and to enable employees to recognize what is expected of them. For some jobs, several employees may be required, each of whom will occupy a separate position. A position consists of different duties and responsibilities performed by only one employee. In a city library, for example, four employees (four positions) may be involved in reference work, but all of them have only one job (reference librarian). Where different jobs have similar duties and responsibilities, they may be grouped into a job family for purposes of recruitment, training, compensation, or advancement opportunities.

Recruitment

job specification
A statement of the needed knowledge, skills, and abilities of the person who is to perform the job

Before they can find capable employees for an organization, recruiters need to know the job specifications for the positions they are to fill.[5] A job specification is a statement of the knowledge, skills, and abilities required of the person performing the job. In the HR department for the City of Mesa, Arizona, the job specification for senior HR analyst includes the following:

1. Graduation from a four-year college with major course work (minimum fifteen hours) in human resources management

2. Three to five years experience in employee classification and compensation or selection or recruitment

3. Two years experience in developing/improving job-related compensation and testing instruments and procedures.[6]

Because job specifications establish the qualifications required of applicants for a job opening, they serve an essential role in the recruiting function. These qualifications typically are contained in the notices of job openings. Whether posted on organizational bulletin boards or HRIS Internet sites or included in help wanted advertisements or employment agency listings, job specifications provide a basis for attracting qualified applicants and discouraging unqualified ones.

Selection

In addition to job specifications, managers and supervisors use job descriptions to select employees and orient them to jobs. A job description is a statement of the tasks, duties, and responsibilities of a job. (See "Job Descriptions" later in this chapter.)

In the past, job specifications used as a basis for selection sometimes bore little relation to the duties to be performed under the job description. Examples of such nonjob-related specifications abounded. Applicants for the job of laborer were required to have a high school diploma. Firefighters were required to be at least six feet tall, and applicants for skilled craft positions—plumbers, electricians, machinists— were required to be male. These kinds of job specifications discriminated against members of certain protected classes, many of whom were excluded from these jobs.

Since the landmark *Griggs v. Duke Power* case and the Civil Rights Act of 1991 (see Chapter 3), employers must be able to show that the job specifications used in selecting employees for a particular job relate specifically to the duties of that job. An organization must be careful to ensure that managers with job openings do not hire employees on the basis of "individualized" job requirements that satisfy personal whims but bear little relation to successful job performance. In one case known to the authors, a company desired to hire only tall salespeople—male or female—on the assumption that tall individuals presented a more authoritative stature.

job description

A statement of the tasks, duties, and responsibilities of a job to be performed

Training and Development

Any discrepancies between the knowledge, skill and abilities (often referred to as KSAs) demonstrated by a jobholder and the requirements contained in the description and specification for that job provide clues to training needs. Also, career development as a part of the training function is concerned with preparing employees for advancement to jobs where their capacities can be utilized to the fullest extent possible. The formal qualification requirements set forth in high-level jobs indicate how much more training and development are needed for employees to advance to those jobs.

Performance Appraisal

The requirements contained in the description of a job provide the criteria for evaluating the performance of the holder of that job. The results of performance appraisal may reveal, however, that certain requirements established for a job are not completely valid. As we have already stressed, these criteria must be specific and job-related. If the criteria used to evaluate employee performance are vague and not job-related, employers may find themselves being charged with unfair discrimination.

Compensation Management

In determining the rate to be paid for performing a job, the relative worth of the job is one of the most important factors. This worth is based on what the job demands of an employee in terms of skill, effort, and responsibility, as well as the conditions and hazards under which the work is performed. The systems of job evaluation by which this worth may be measured are discussed in Chapter 9.

▪▪ JOB ANALYSIS

Job analysis is sometimes called the cornerstone of HRM because the information it collects serves so many HRM functions. Job analysis is the process of obtaining information about jobs by determining the duties, tasks, or activities of those jobs.[7] The procedure involves systematically investigating jobs by following a number of predetermined steps specified in advance of the study.[8] When completed, job analysis results in a written report summarizing the information obtained from the analysis of twenty or thirty individual job tasks or activities. HR managers use these data to develop job descriptions and job specifications. These documents, in turn, are used to perform and enhance the different HR functions such as the development of performance appraisal criteria or the content of training classes. The ultimate purpose of job analysis is to improve organizational performance and productivity. Figure 4.1 illustrates how job analysis is performed, including the functions for which it is used.

As contrasted with job design, which reflects subjective opinions about the ideal requirements of a job, job analysis is concerned with objective and verifiable information about the actual requirements of a job. The job descriptions and job specifications developed through job analysis should be as accurate as possible if they are to be of value to those who make HRM decisions. These decisions may involve any of the HR functions—from recruitment to termination of employees.

Job Analysis and Essential Job Functions

It should be emphasized that a major goal of modern job analysis is to help the organization establish the *job-relatedness* of its selection and performance requirements. Job analysis helps both large and small employers meet their legal duty under EEO law. Section 14.C.2 of the *Uniform Guidelines* states: "There shall be a job analysis which—includes an analysis of the important work behaviors required for successful performance. . . . Any job analysis should focus on work behavior(s) and the tasks associated with them." (The *Uniform Guidelines* are discussed more fully in Chapter 3.)

The passage of the Americans with Disabilities Act (ADA) also had a marked impact on the process of job analysis. Specifically, when preparing job descriptions and job specifications, managers and supervisors must adhere to the legal mandates of the ADA. The act requires that job duties and responsibilities be *essential functions* for job success. The purpose of essential functions is to help match and accommodate human capabilities to job requirements. For example, if the job requires the jobholder to read extremely fine print, to climb ladders, or to memorize stock codes, these physical and mental requirements should be stated within the job description. Section 1630.2(n) of the act gives three guidelines for rendering a job function essential: (1) the reason that the position exists is to perform the function, (2) a limited number of employees are available among whom the performance of the function may be distributed, and (3) the function may be highly specialized, requiring needed expertise or abilities to complete the job.[9] Managers who write job descriptions and job specifications in terms of essential functions reduce the risk of discriminating on the basis of a disability. Remember also that once essential functions for a job are defined, the organization is legally required to make a reasonable accommodation to the disability of the individual.

FIGURE
4.1

The Process of Job Analysis

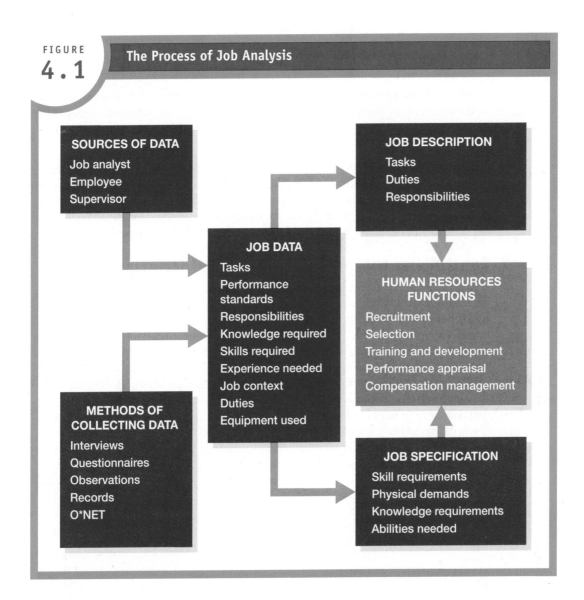

Gathering Job Information

Job data may be obtained in several ways. The more common methods of analyzing jobs are through interviews, questionnaires, observation, and diaries.

■ *Interviews.* The job analyst may question individual employees and managers about the job under review.

■ *Questionnaires.* The job analyst may circulate carefully prepared questionnaires to be filled out individually by jobholders and managers. These forms will be used to obtain data in the areas of job duties and tasks performed, purpose of the job, physical setting, requirements for performing the job (skill, education, experience, physical and mental demands), equipment and materials used, and special health and safety concerns.

- *Observation.* The job analyst may learn about the jobs by observing and recording on a standardized form the activities of jobholders. Videotaping jobs for later study is an approach used by some organizations.

- *Diaries.* Jobholders themselves may be asked to keep a diary of their work activities during an entire work cycle. Diaries are normally filled out at specific times of the work shift (such as every half hour or hour) and maintained for a two- to four-week period.

Although HR specialists, called job analysts, are the personnel primarily responsible for the job analysis program, they usually enlist the cooperation of the employees and managers in the departments where jobs are being analyzed. These managers and employees are the sources of much of the information about the jobs, and they may be asked to prepare rough drafts of the job descriptions and specifications the job analysts need.

Controlling the Accuracy of Job Information

If job analysis is to accomplish its intended purpose, the job data collected must be accurate. Care must be taken to ensure that all important facts are included. A job analyst should be alert for employees who tend to exaggerate the difficulty of their jobs in order to inflate their egos and their paychecks.[10] When interviewing employees or reviewing their questionnaires, the job analyst must look for any responses that do not agree with other facts or impressions the analyst has received. One job analyst noted, "When in doubt about the accuracy of employee responses always double-check the data with others."[11] Furthermore, when job information is collected from employees, a representative group of individuals should be surveyed. For example, the results of one study indicated that the information obtained from job analysis was related to race. In another study, the experience level of job incumbents influenced job analysis outcomes.

A job analyst who doubts the accuracy of information provided by employees should obtain additional information from them, their managers, or other individuals who are familiar with or perform the same job. It is common practice to have the descriptions for each job reviewed by the jobholders and their managers. The job description summaries contained in O*NET, compiled by the U.S. Department of Labor, can also serve as a basis for the job analyst's review.

O*NET and Job Analysis

For many years the U.S. Department of Labor published the *Dictionary of Occupational Titles,* commonly referred to as the *DOT.* This book contained standardized and comprehensive descriptions of about 20,000 jobs. The *DOT* helped bring about a great degree of uniformity in the job titles and descriptions used by employers nationwide.

The Department of Labor has replaced the *DOT* with the O*NET online database.[12] The O*NET database includes all occupations from the *DOT* plus an update of more than 3,500 additional occupations. The database job descriptors include skill abilities, knowledge, tasks, work activities, and experience level requirements. Importantly, in order to remain current with occupational change, the O*NET program collects and publishes data continuously, a feature not available with the old *DOT.* The O*NET database is useful for a variety of HR activities including career counseling and training as well as job analysis.

Using the Internet

To explore the Department of Labor's new O*NET database, including how to convert from the *DOT* to O*NET, go to the Student Resources at:

www.cengage.com/ management/bohlander

Approaches to Job Analysis

The systematic and quantitative definition of job content that job analysis provides is the foundation of many HRM practices. Specifically, the job analysis serves to justify job descriptions and other HRM selection procedures. Several different job analysis approaches are used to gather data, each with specific advantages and disadvantages.[13] Four of the more popular methods are the position analysis system, critical incident method, task inventory analysis, and competency job analysis.

The Position Analysis Questionnaire System

The **position analysis questionnaire (PAQ)** is a quantifiable data collection method covering 194 different worker-oriented tasks. Using a five-point scale, the PAQ seeks to determine the degree, if any, to which the different tasks, or job elements, are involved in performing a particular job.

A sample page from the PAQ covering eleven elements of the Information Input Division is shown in Figure 4.2. The person conducting an analysis with this questionnaire would rate each of the elements using the five-point scale shown in the upper right-hand corner of the sample page. The results obtained with the PAQ are quantitative and can be subjected to statistical analysis. The PAQ also permits dimensions of behavior to be compared across a number of jobs and permits jobs to be grouped on the basis of common characteristics.

position analysis questionnaire (PAQ)

A questionnaire covering 194 different tasks that, by means of a five-point scale, seeks to determine the degree to which different tasks are involved in performing a particular job

The Critical Incident Method

The objective of the **critical incident method** is to identify critical job tasks. Critical job tasks are those important duties and job responsibilities performed by the jobholder that lead to job success. Information about critical job tasks can be collected through interviews with employees or managers or through self-report statements written by employees.

Suppose, for example, that the job analyst is studying the job of reference librarian. The interviewer will ask the employee to describe the job on the basis of what is done, how the job is performed, and what tools and equipment are used. The reference librarian may describe the job as follows:

critical incident method

A job analysis method by which important job tasks are identified for job success

> I assist patrons by answering their questions related to finding books, periodicals, or other library materials. I also give them directions to help them find materials within the building. To perform my job, I may have to look up materials myself or refer patrons to someone who can directly assist them. Some individuals may need training in how to use reference materials or special library facilities. I also give library tours to new patrons. I use computers and a variety of reference books to carry out my job.

After the job data are collected, the analyst then writes separate task statements that represent important job activities. For the reference librarian, one task statement might be: "Listens to patrons and answers their questions related to locating library materials." Typically, the job analyst writes five to ten important task statements for each job under study. The final product is written task statements that are clear, complete, and easily understood by those unfamiliar with the job. The critical incident method is an important job analysis method because it teaches the analyst to focus on employee behaviors critical to job success.

FIGURE

4.2

A Sample Page from the PAQ

INFORMATION INPUT

1 INFORMATION INPUT

1.1   Sources of Job Information

> *Extent of Use (U)*
> NA Does not apply
> 1 Nominal/very infrequent
> 2 Occasional
> 3 Moderate
> 4 Considerable
> 5 Very substantial

Rate each of the following items in terms of the extent to which it is used by the worker as a source of information in performing his job.

1.1.1   Visual Sources of Job Information

01 U Written materials (books, reports, office notes, articles, job instructions, signs, etc.)

02 U Quantitative materials (materials which deal with quantities or amounts, such as graphs, accounts, specifications, tables of numbers, etc.)

03 U Pictorial materials (pictures or picturelike materials used as *sources* of information, for example, drawings, blueprints, diagrams, maps, tracings, photographic films, x-ray films, TV pictures, etc.)

04 U Patterns/related devices (templates, stencils, patterns, etc., used as *sources* of information when *observed* during use; do *not* include here materials described in item 3 above)

05 U Visual displays (dials, gauges, signal lights, radarscopes, speedometers, clocks, etc.)

06 U Measuring devices (rulers, calipers, tire pressure gauges, scales, thickness gauges, pipettes, thermometers, protractors, etc., used to obtain visual information about physical measurements; do *not* include here devices described in item 5 above)

07 U Mechanical devices (tools, equipment, machinery, and other mechanical devices which are *sources* of information when observed during use or operation)

08 U Materials in process (parts, materials, objects, etc., which are *sources* of information when being modified, worked on, or otherwise processed, such as bread dough being mixed, workpiece being turned in a lathe, fabric being cut, shoe being resoled, etc.)

09 U Materials *not* in process (parts, materials, objects, etc., hot in the process of being changed or modified, which are *sources* of information when being inspected, handled, packaged, distributed, or selected, etc., such as items or materials in inventory, storage, or distribution channels, items being inspected, etc.)

10 U Features of nature (landscapes, fields, geological samples, vegetation, cloud formations, and other features of nature which are observed or inspected to provide information)

11 U Man-made features of environment (structures, buildings, dams, highways, bridges, docks, railroads, and other "man-made" or altered aspects of the indoor or outdoor environment which are *observed or inspected* to provide job information; do *not* consider equipment, machines, etc., that an individual uses in his work, as covered by item 7)

Source: *Position Analysis Questionnaire*, copyright 1969, 1989 by Purdue Research Foundation, West Lafayette, IN 47907. Reprinted with permission.

Task Inventory Analysis

The task inventory analysis method can be considered a job-oriented type of job analysis. The technique was pioneered by the U.S. Air Force to analyze jobs held by Air Force specialists. Unlike the PAQ, which uses a standardized form to analyze jobs in different organizations, a task inventory questionnaire can be tailor-made to a specific organization.

The technique is developed by identifying—with the help of employees and managers—a list of tasks and their descriptions that are components of different jobs. The goal is to produce a comprehensive list of task statements that are applicable to all jobs. Task statements then are listed on a task inventory survey form to be completed by the person analyzing the job under review. A task statement might be: "Inventories current supplies to maintain stock levels." The job analysis would also note the importance and frequency of use of the task to the successful completion of the job.

task inventory analysis
An organization-specific list of tasks and their descriptions used as a basis to identify components of jobs

Competency-Based Analysis

The traditional approach to job analysis assumes a static job environment where jobs remain relatively stable apart from incumbents who might hold these jobs. Here, jobs can be meaningfully defined in terms of tasks, duties, processes, and skills necessary for job success. This assumption, unfortunately, discounts technological advances that are often so accelerated that jobs, as they are defined today, may be obsolete tomorrow. The following statement by two HR professionals highlights this concern: "Typically, job analysis looks at how a job is currently done. But the ever-changing business market makes it difficult to keep a job analysis up-to-date. Also, companies are asking

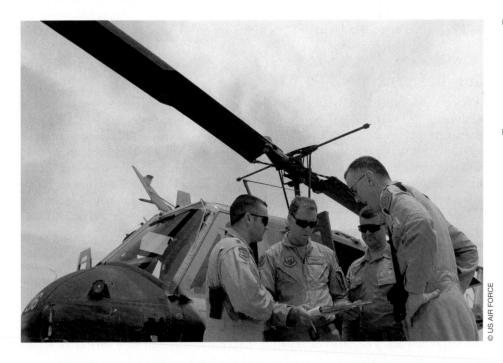

Task inventory analysis uses employees to develop lists of job tasks and descriptions common to all jobs.

© US AIR FORCE

employees to do more, so there is a question of whether 'jobs' as we know them are obsolete." Furthermore, the need to respond to global change can alter the nature of jobs and the requirement of individuals needed to successfully perform them. Therefore, in a dynamic environment where job demands rapidly change, obsolete job analysis information simply hinders an organization's ability to adapt to change.

When organizations operate in a fast-moving environment, managers may adopt a competency-based approach to job analysis.[14] This job analysis method relies on building job profiles that look at the responsibilities and activities of jobs and the worker competencies necessary to accomplish them. The objective is to identify "key" competencies for organizational success. Competencies can be identified through focus groups, surveys, or interviews and might include such things as interpersonal communication skills, decision-making ability, conflict resolution skills, adaptability, or self-motivation. An organization's job descriptions, recruitment requirements, and performance evaluation system will reflect the competencies needed by employees.

HRIS and Job Analysis

Human resource information systems have greatly facilitated the job analysis process. Available today are various software programs designed specifically to analyze jobs and to write job descriptions and job specifications based on those analyses. These programs normally contain generalized task statements that can apply to many different jobs. Managers and employees select those statements that best describe the job under review, indicating the importance of the task to the total job where appropriate. Advanced computer applications of job analysis combine job analysis with job evaluation (see Chapter 9) and the pricing of organizational jobs. Computerized job analysis systems can be expensive to initiate, but where the organization has many jobs to analyze, the cost per job may be low. HR publications such as *HRMagazine* and *Workforce* contain advertisements from numerous software companies offering HRIS job analysis packages.

Job Descriptions

Objective | 3

As previously noted, a job description is a written description of a job and the types of duties it includes. Since there is no standard format for job descriptions, they tend to vary in appearance and content from one organization to another. However, most job descriptions will contain at least three parts: job title, job identification section, and job duties section. If the job specifications are not prepared as a separate document, they are usually stated in the concluding section of the job description. Highlights in HRM 1 shows a job description for a HR employment assistant. This sample job description includes both job duties and job specifications and should satisfy most of the job information needs of managers who must recruit, interview, and orient a new employee.[15]

Job descriptions are of value to both the employees and the employer. From the employees' standpoint, job descriptions can be used to help them learn their job duties and to remind them of the results they are expected to achieve. From the employer's standpoint, written job descriptions can serve as a basis for minimizing the misunderstandings that occur between managers and their subordinates concerning job requirements. They also establish management's right to take corrective action when the duties covered by the job description are not performed as required.

Job Description for an Employment Assistant

Job Identification

JOB TITLE: Employment Assistant

Division:	Southern Area
Department:	Human Resources Management
Job Analyst:	Virginia Sasaki
Date Analyzed:	12/3/08
Wage Category:	Exempt
Report to:	HR Manager
Job Code:	11-17
Date Verified:	12/17/08

Brief Listing of Major Job Duties

JOB STATEMENT

Performs professional human resources work in the areas of *employee recruitment and selection, testing, orientation, transfers, and maintenance of employee human resources files.* May handle special assignments and projects in *EEO/Affirmative Action, employee grievances, training,* or *classification and compensation.* Works under general supervision. Incumbent exercises initiative and independent judgment in the performance of assigned tasks.

Essential Functions and Responsibilities

ESSENTIAL FUNCTIONS

1. Prepares recruitment literature and job advertisements for applicant placement.
2. Schedules and conducts personal interviews to determine applicant suitability for employment. Includes reviewing mailed applications and resumes for qualified personnel.
3. Supervises administration of testing program. Responsible for developing or improving testing instruments and procedures.
4. Presents orientation program to all new employees. Reviews and develops all materials and procedures for orientation program.
5. Coordinates division job posting and transfer program. Establishes job posting procedures. Responsible for reviewing transfer applications, arranging transfer interviews, and determining effective transfer dates.
6. Maintains a daily working relationship with division managers on human resources matters, including recruitment concerns, retention or release of probationary employees, and discipline or discharge of permanent employees.
7. Distributes new or revised human resources policies and procedures to all employees and managers through bulletins, meetings, memorandums, and/or personal contact.
8. Performs related duties as assigned by the human resources manager.

Job Description for an Employment Assistant (continued)

Job Specifications and Requirements

JOB SPECIFICATIONS

1. Four-year college or university degree with major course work in human resources management, business administration, or industrial psychology; OR a combination of experience, education, and training equivalent to a four-year college degree in human resources management.
2. Considerable knowledge of principles of employee selection and assignment of personnel.
3. Ability to express ideas clearly in both written and oral communications.
4. Ability to independently plan and organize one's own activities.
5. Knowledge of human resources computer applications desirable.

Job Title

Selection of a job title is important for several reasons. First, the job title is of psychological importance, providing status to the employee. For instance, "sanitation engineer" is a more appealing title than "garbage collector." Second, if possible, the title should provide some indication of what the duties of the job entail. Titles such as *meat inspector, electronics assembler, salesperson,* and *engineer* obviously hint at the nature of the duties of these jobs. The job title also should indicate the relative level occupied by its holder in the organizational hierarchy. For example, the title *junior engineer* implies that this job occupies a lower level than that of *senior engineer.*

Job Identification Section

The job identification section of a job description usually follows the job title. It includes such items as the departmental location of the job, the person to whom the jobholder reports, and the date the job description was last revised. Sometimes it also contains a payroll or code number, the number of employees performing the job, the number of employees in the department where the job is located, and the O*NET code number. "Statement of the Job" usually appears at the bottom of this section and distinguishes the job from other jobs—something the job title may fail to do.

Job Duties, or Essential Functions, Section

Statements covering job duties are typically arranged in order of importance. These statements should indicate the weight, or value, of each duty. Usually, but not always, the weight of a duty can be gauged by the percentage of time devoted to it. The statements should stress the responsibilities all the duties entail and the results they are to accomplish. It is also general practice to indicate the tools and equipment used by the employee in performing the job. Remember, the job duties section must comply with law by listing only the essential functions of the job to be performed (see "Job Analysis and Essential Job Functions" earlier in this chapter).

Job Specifications Section

As stated earlier, the personal qualifications an individual must possess in order to perform the duties and responsibilities contained in a job description are compiled in the job specification. Typically, the job specification covers two areas: (1) the skill required to perform the job and (2) the physical demands the job places on the employee performing it.

Skills relevant to a job include education or experience, specialized training, personal traits or abilities, and manual dexterities. The physical demands of a job refer to how much walking, standing, reaching, lifting, or talking must be done on the job. The condition of the physical work environment and the hazards employees may encounter are also among the physical demands of a job.

Job specifications should also include interpersonal skills or key competencies necessary for job success. For example, behavioral competencies might include the ability to make decisions on imperfect information, decisiveness, the ability to handle multiple tasks, and conflict resolution skills. Behavioral competencies can be assessed by asking applicants situational interview questions (see Chapter 6). For example, a manager could ask an applicant about a time when he or she had to make a critical decision quickly.

Problems with Job Descriptions

Managers consider job descriptions a valuable tool for performing HRM functions. Nevertheless, several problems are frequently associated with these documents, including the following:

1. If they are poorly written, using vague rather than specific terms, they provide little guidance to the jobholder.

2. They are sometimes not updated as job duties or specifications change.

3. They may violate the law by containing specifications not related to job success.

4. They can limit the scope of activities of the jobholder, reducing organizational flexibility.

Writing Clear and Specific Job Descriptions

When writing a job description, it is essential to use statements that are terse, direct, and simply worded. Unnecessary words or phrases should be eliminated. Typically, the sentences that describe job duties begin with a present-tense verb, with the implied subject of the sentence being the employee performing the job. The term "occasionally" is used to describe duties that are performed once in awhile. The term "may" is used in connection with duties performed only by some workers on the job.

Even when set forth in writing, job descriptions and specifications can still be vague. To the consternation of many employers, however, today's legal environment has created what might be called an "age of specifics." Federal guidelines and court decisions now require that the specific performance requirements of a job be based on *valid* job-related criteria.[16] Personnel decisions that involve either job applicants or employees and are based on criteria that are vague or not job-related are increasingly successfully challenged. Managers of small businesses, in which employees may perform many different job tasks, must be particularly concerned about writing specific job descriptions.

Managers may find that writing job descriptions is a tedious process that distracts from other supervisory responsibilities. Fortunately, software packages are available to simplify this time-consuming yet necessary task. One program provides an initial library of more than 2,500 prewritten job descriptions. Since the program works much like a word processor, text can be easily deleted, inserted, or modified to user demands.

⠶ Job Design

Objective 4

job design

An outgrowth of job analysis that improves jobs through technological and human considerations in order to enhance organization efficiency and employee job satisfaction

It is not uncommon for managers and supervisors to confuse the processes of job analysis and job design. Job analysis is the study of jobs as currently performed by employees. It identifies job duties and the requirements needed to perform the work successfully. Job design, which is an outgrowth of job analysis, is concerned with structuring jobs in order to improve organization efficiency and employee job satisfaction. Job design is concerned with changing, modifying, and enriching jobs in order to capture the talents of employees while improving organization performance.[17] For example, companies such as Harley-Davidson, Banner Health Services, and PageNet, which are engaged in continuous improvement, or process reengineering, may revamp their jobs in order to eliminate unnecessary job tasks or find better ways of performing work. Job design should facilitate the achievement of organizational objectives. At the same time, the design should recognize the capabilities and needs of those who are to perform the job.

As Figure 4.3 illustrates, job design is a combination of four basic considerations: (1) the organizational objectives the job was created to fulfill; (2) industrial engineering considerations, including ways to make the job technologically efficient; (3) ergonomic concerns, including workers' physical and mental capabilities; and (4) behavioral concerns that influence an employee's job satisfaction.[18]

Behavioral Concerns

Two job design methods seek to incorporate the behavioral needs of employees as they perform their individual jobs. Both methods strive to satisfy the intrinsic needs of employees. The job enrichment model and the job characteristics model have long been popular with researchers and practitioners as ways to increase the job satisfaction of employees.

Job Enrichment

job enrichment

Enhancing a job by adding more meaningful tasks and duties to make the work more rewarding or satisfying

Any effort that makes work more rewarding or satisfying by adding more meaningful tasks to an employee's job is called job enrichment. Originally popularized by Frederick Herzberg, job enrichment is touted as fulfilling the high motivational needs of employees, such as self-fulfillment and self-esteem, while achieving long-term job satisfaction and performance goals.[19] Job enrichment, or the *vertical expansion* of jobs, may be accomplished by increasing the autonomy and responsibility of employees. Herzberg discusses five factors for enriching jobs and thereby motivating

FIGURE 4.3 Basis for Job Design

employees: achievement, recognition, growth, responsibility, and performance of the whole job versus only parts of the job. For example, managers can use these five factors to enrich the jobs of employees by:

■ Increasing the level of difficulty and responsibility of the job

■ Allowing employees to retain more authority and control over work outcomes

■ Providing unit or individual job performance reports directly to employees

■ Adding new tasks to the job that require training and growth

■ Assigning individuals specific tasks, enabling them to use their particular competencies or skills

These factors allow employees to assume a greater role in the decision-making process and become more involved in planning, organizing, directing, and controlling their own work. Vertical job enrichment can also be accomplished by organizing workers into teams and giving these teams greater authority for self-management.

In spite of the benefits to be achieved through job enrichment, it must not be considered a panacea for overcoming production problems and employee discontent. Job enrichment programs are more likely to succeed in some jobs and work situations than in others. They are *not* the solution to such problems as dissatisfaction with pay, employee benefits, or employment security. Moreover, not all employees object to the mechanical pacing of an assembly line, nor do all employees seek additional responsibility or challenge. Some prefer routine jobs because these jobs are predictable and concise.

Job Characteristics

job characteristics model

A job design theory that purports that three psychological states (experiencing meaningfulness of the work performed, responsibility for work outcomes, and knowledge of the results of the work performed) of a jobholder result in improved work performance, internal motivation, and lower absenteeism and turnover

Job design studies explored a new field when behavioral scientists focused on identifying various job dimensions that would improve simultaneously the efficiency of organizations and the job satisfaction of employees. Perhaps the theory that best exemplifies this research is the one advanced by Richard Hackman and Greg Oldham.[20] Their job characteristics model proposes that three psychological states of a jobholder result in improved work performance, internal motivation, and lower absenteeism and turnover.[21] A motivated, satisfied, and productive employee (1) experiences *meaningfulness* of the work performed, (2) experiences *responsibility* for work outcomes, and (3) has *knowledge of the results* of the work performed. Hackman and Oldham believe that five core job dimensions produce the three psychological states. The five job characteristics are as follows:

1. *Skill variety:* The degree to which a job entails a variety of different activities, which demand the use of a number of different skills and talents by the jobholder

2. *Task identity:* The degree to which the job requires completion of a whole and identifiable piece of work, that is, doing a job from beginning to end with a visible outcome

3. *Task significance:* The degree to which the job has a substantial impact on the lives or work of other people, whether in the immediate organization or in the external environment

4. *Autonomy:* The degree to which the job provides substantial freedom, independence, and discretion to the individual in scheduling the work and in determining the procedures to be used in carrying it out

5. *Feedback:* The degree to which carrying out the work activities required by the job results in the individual being given direct and clear information about the effectiveness of his or her performance

The job characteristics model appears to work best when certain conditions are met. One of these conditions is that employees must have the psychological desire for the autonomy, variety, responsibility, and challenge of enriched jobs. When this personal characteristic is absent, employees may resist the job redesign effort. In addition, job redesign efforts almost always fail when employees lack the physical or mental skills, abilities, or education needed to perform the job. Forcing enriched jobs on individuals lacking these traits can result in frustrated employees.

Employee Empowerment

employee empowerment

Granting employees power to initiate change, thereby encouraging them to take charge of what they do

Job enrichment and job characteristics are specific programs by which managers or supervisors can formally change the jobs of employees. A less structured method is to allow employees to initiate their own job changes through the concept of empowerment. Employee empowerment is a technique of involving employees in their work through the process of inclusion. Empowerment encourages employees to become innovators and managers of their own work, and it involves them in their jobs in ways that give them more control and autonomous decision-making capabilities (see Highlights in HRM 2). As described by one manager, employee empowerment involves "pushing down decision-making responsibility to those close to internal and external customers."

Empowered Employees Achieve Results

In today's highly competitive and dynamic business environment, employers as diverse as Home Depot, Wal-Mart, Cigna HealthCare, Costco, AutoZone, Disney, and Applebee's have turned to their employees to improve organizational performance. Empowered employees have made improvements in product or service quality, reduced costs, and modified or, in some cases, designed products.

- At Kraft Foods, employees at the company's Sussex, Wisconsin, food plant participated in work redesign changes and team building that increased productivity, reduced overhead, and cut assembly time.
- Avon Products empowered its minority managers to improve sales and service in inner-city markets. Grounded in the belief that minority managers better understand the culture of inner-city residents, Avon turned an unprofitable market into a highly productive sales area.
- Dorothy Galvez, administrative assistant to Robert E. Mittelstaedt, Jr., dean of the W. P. Carey School of Business at Arizona State University, has empowered her position by planning college activities and events, preparing special college reports, learning new educational and business technology, and serving as the dean's representative at college and business events.
- At Ford's factory in Wayne, Michigan, one group of employees made a suggestion saving $115,000 per year on the purchase of gloves used to protect workers who handle sheet metal and glass. The group figured out how to have the gloves washed so they could be used more than once.
- Home Depot's Special Project Support Teams (SPST) work to improve the organization's business and information services. Employees with a wide range of backgrounds and skills collaborate to address a wide range of strategic and tactical business needs.
- American Airlines' "Rainbow Team" of gay employees brought in $192 million in annual revenue by targeting the gay community.

While defining empowerment can become the first step to achieving it, in order for empowerment to grow and thrive, organizations must encourage these conditions:

- *Participation.* Employees must be encouraged to take control of their work tasks. Employees, in turn, must care about improving their work process and interpersonal work relationships.

- *Innovation.* The environment must be receptive to people with innovative ideas and encourage people to explore new paths and to take reasonable risks at reasonable costs. An empowered environment is created when curiosity is as highly regarded as is technical expertise.

- *Access to information.* Employees must have access to a wide range of information. Involved individuals decide what kind of information they need for performing their jobs.

Employee empowerment grows in an organizational culture that promotes satisfaction, support, and recognition.

- *Accountability.* Empowerment does not involve being able to do whatever you want. Empowered employees should be held accountable for their behavior toward others, producing agreed-on results, achieving credibility, and operating with a positive approach.

Additionally, employee empowerment succeeds when the culture of the organization is open and receptive to change.[22] An organization's culture is largely created through the philosophies of senior managers and their leadership traits and behaviors. Effective leadership in an empowered organization is highlighted by managers who are honest, confident, trusting, and receptive to new ideas and who exhibit dignity and respect for employees as partners in organizational success. Conversely, organizations or managers who are autocratic and control-oriented seldom empower their employees or welcome organizational change. Chris Argyris, noted Harvard professor, critically states, "Managers love empowerment in theory, but the command and control model is what they trust and know best."

Industrial Engineering Considerations

industrial engineering

A field of study concerned with analyzing work methods and establishing time standards

The study of work is an important contribution of the scientific management movement. Industrial engineering, which evolved with this movement, is concerned with analyzing work methods and establishing time standards.[23] Specifically, it involves the study of work cycles to determine which, if any, elements can be modified, combined, rearranged, or eliminated to reduce the time needed to complete the cycle. Next, time standards are established by recording the time required to complete each element in the work cycle, using a stopwatch or work-sampling technique. By combining the times for each element, observers can determine the total time required. This time is subsequently adjusted to allow for the skill and effort demonstrated by the observed worker and for interruptions that may occur in performing the work. The adjusted time becomes the time standard for that particular work cycle.

Industrial engineering constitutes a disciplined and objective approach to job design. Unfortunately, the concern of industrial engineering for improving efficiency and simplifying work methods may cause the behavioral considerations in job design to be neglected. What may be improvements in job design and efficiency from an engineering standpoint can sometimes prove psychologically unsound. For example, the assembly line with its simplified and repetitive tasks embodies sound principles of industrial engineering, but these tasks are often not psychologically rewarding for those who must perform them. Thus, to be effective, job design must also provide for the satisfaction of behavioral needs.

Ergonomic Considerations

Consider this statistic. More than 1.8 million workplace injuries occur yearly resulting from motions such as lifting, bending, and typing. These injuries cost employers through lost productivity, medical benefits, and lost time payments. Therefore, ergonomics is an important element of job design.

Ergonomics is the study of people at work and the practice of matching the features of products and jobs to human capabilities, preference, and the limitations of those who are to perform a job. Ergonomics focuses on ensuring that jobs are designed for safe and efficient work while improving the safety, comfort, and performance of users. In short, it seeks to fit the job to the person rather than the person to the job. Additionally, ergonomics attempts to minimize the harmful effects of carelessness, negligence, and other human fallibilities that otherwise may cause product defects, damage to equipment, or even the injury or death of employees.[24] Alan Hedge, professor of ergonomics at Cornell University, notes, "The goal of sound ergonomics is to boost employee performance while reducing injuries and errors."[25]

ergonomics

An interdisciplinary approach to designing equipment and systems that can be easily and efficiently used by human beings

Alan Hedge, a professor of ergonomics at Cornell University, sits in a special chair with a floating arms keyboard designed to be ergonomically correct. In the background are other ergonomic chairs that Hedge and students tested.

© SYRACUSE NEWSPAPER/RANDI ANGLIN/THE IMAGE WORKS

Equipment design must consider the physical abilities of operators to use the equipment and to react through vision, hearing, and touch to the way the equipment operates. For example, there is substantial variation in the way individuals move depending on their physical size, gender, age, and other factors. Designing equipment controls to be compatible with both the physical characteristics and the reaction capabilities of the people who must operate them and the environment in which they work is critically important. Ergonomics also considers the requirements of a diverse workforce, accommodating, for example, women who may lack the strength to operate equipment requiring intense physical force or Asian Americans who may lack the stature to reach equipment controls. Managers must adapt the workplace to the labor force or risk sacrificing quality and productivity.

Ergonomics improves productivity and morale and yields positive return on investment (ROI). Peter Budnick, president of ErgoWeb, Inc., notes, "At our company we look at ergonomics as much more than a musculoskeletal issue. Injuries are one of the natural outcomes of poor workplace design. But so is lost productivity, loss of efficiency, errors and increased waste. We really look at ergonomics as a broad approach to improving human performance."[26] Ergonomics has proven cost-effective at organizations such as Compaq Computer, 3M, Pratt and Whitney, and the U.S. Postal Service. Ergonomics has recently focused on elimination, or at least reduction, of many repetitive motion injuries, particularly those related to the back and wrist. For example, with the increased use of computers, ergonomics has particular application at employee workstations. Figure 4.4 provides a checklist of potential repetitive motion problem areas for employees using computers.

Designing Work for Group/Team Contributions

Although a variety of group techniques have been developed to involve employees more fully in their organizations, all of these techniques have two characteristics in common—enhancing collaboration and increasing synergy. In increasing the degree of collaboration in the work environment, these techniques can improve work processes and organizational decision-making. In increasing group synergy, the techniques underline the adage that the contributions of two or more employees are greater than the sum of their individual efforts. Furthermore, research has shown that working in a group setting strengthens employee commitment to the organization's goals, increases employee acceptance of decisions, and encourages a cooperative approach to workplace tasks.[27] Two collaborative techniques are discussed here: employee involvement groups and employee teams.

Employee Involvement Groups

Groups of five to ten employees doing similar or related work who meet regularly to identify, analyze, and suggest solutions to shared problems are often referred to as employee involvement groups (EIs). Also widely known as *quality circles (QCs)*, EIs are used principally as a means of involving employees in the larger goals of the organization through their suggestions for improving product or service quality and cutting costs.[28] Generally, EIs recommend their solutions to management, which decides whether to implement them.

The employee involvement group process, illustrated in Figure 4.5, begins with EI members brainstorming job-related problems or concerns and gathering data about these issues. The process continues through the generation of solutions and recommendations that are then communicated to management. If the solutions are implemented,

employee involvement groups (EIs)
Groups of employees who meet to resolve problems or offer suggestions for organizational improvement

FIGURE

4.4

Computer Workstation Ergonomics Checklist

Use the following list to identify potential problem areas that should receive further investigation. Any "no" response may point to a problem.

1. Does the workstation ensure proper worker posture, such as

   - Thighs in the horizontal position?
   - Lower legs in the vertical position?
   - Feet flat on the floor or on a footrest?
   - Wrists straight and relaxed?

2. Does the chair

   - Adjust easily?
   - Have a padded seat with a rounded front?
   - Have an adjustable backrest?
   - Provide lumbar support?
   - Have casters?

3. Are the height and tilt of the work surface on which the keyboard is located adjustable?

4. Is the keyboard detachable?

5. Do keying actions require minimal force?

6. Is there an adjustable document holder?

7. Are armrests provided where needed?

8. Are glare and reflections minimized?

9. Does the monitor have brightness and contrast controls?

10. Is there sufficient space for knees and feet?

11. Can the workstation be used for either right- or left-handed activity?

Source: The National Institute for Occupational Safety and Health (NIOSH), *Elements of Ergonomics Programs: A Primer Based on Workplace Evaluations of Musculoskeletal Disorders* (Washington, DC: U.S. Government Printing Office, March 1997).

results are measured, and the EI and its members are usually recognized for the contributions they have made. EIs typically meet four or more hours per month, and the meetings are chaired by a group leader chosen from the group. The leader does not hold an authority position but instead serves as a discussion facilitator.

Although EIs have become an important employee contribution system, they are not without their problems and their critics. First, in order to achieve the results desired, those participating in EIs must receive comprehensive training in problem identification, problem analysis, and various decision-making tools such as statistical analysis and cause-and-effect diagrams. Comprehensive training for EIs is often cited as the most important factor leading to their success. Second, managers should recognize the group when a recommendation is made, regardless of whether the recommendation is adopted. This approach encourages the group to continue coming up with ideas even when they are not all implemented by management. Third, some organizations have found that EIs run out of ideas, and management must feed them

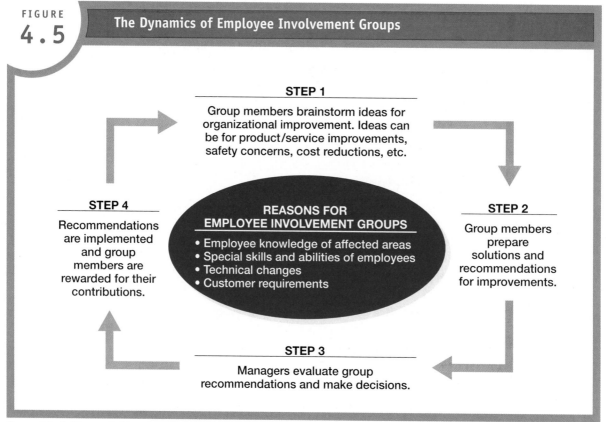

FIGURE 4.5

The Dynamics of Employee Involvement Groups

STEP 1

Group members brainstorm ideas for organizational improvement. Ideas can be for product/service improvements, safety concerns, cost reductions, etc.

STEP 2

Group members prepare solutions and recommendations for improvements.

STEP 3

Managers evaluate group recommendations and make decisions.

STEP 4

Recommendations are implemented and group members are rewarded for their contributions.

REASONS FOR EMPLOYEE INVOLVEMENT GROUPS
- Employee knowledge of affected areas
- Special skills and abilities of employees
- Technical changes
- Customer requirements

Source: Adapted from materials prepared by "The Family and Relationship Center, 7946 Ivahoe Avenue, La Jolla, CA 92037.

ideas to keep the process going. Finally, and most important, managers and supervisors must exhibit a participative/democratic leadership style in which employees are encouraged to work collaboratively with management to improve organizational performance.

Employee Teams

During the past decade perhaps one of the more radical changes to how work is done is the introduction of organizational teams. Jim Barksdale, president and CEO of Netscape Communications, states, "These days it seems as if every time a task needs to be accomplished within an organization, a team is formed to do it." This statement simply emphasizes the increasing importance of teams to organizational success in an ever-dynamic business climate. At such diverse organizations as Federal Express, Hewlett-Packard, Trek Bicycles, Calvin Klein, and LucasFilm, producer of the *Star Wars* and *Indiana Jones* films, the benefits of employee teams have included more integration of individual skills, better performance in terms of quality and quantity, solutions to unique and complex problems, reduced delivery time, reduced turnover and absenteeism, and accomplishments among team members.[29]

Employee teams are a logical outgrowth of employee involvement and the philosophy of empowerment. Although many definitions of teams exist, we define a work team as a group of individuals working together toward a common purpose, in which

employee teams

An employee contributions technique whereby work functions are structured for groups rather than for individuals and team members are given discretion in matters traditionally considered management prerogatives, such as process improvements, product or service development, and individual work assignments

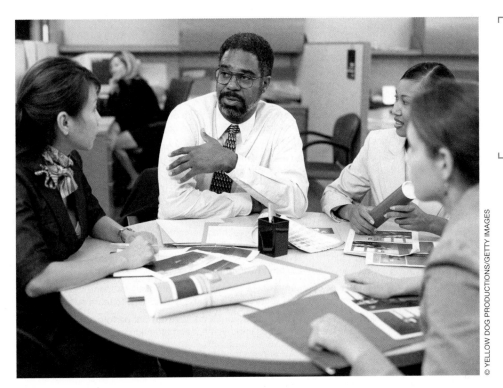

Teams create synergy through the integration of their members' knowledge, skills, and abilities, and the acceptance of individual diversities.

© YELLOW DOG PRODUCTIONS/GETTY IMAGES

members have complementary skills, members' work is mutually dependent, and the group has discretion over tasks performed. Furthermore, teams seek to make members of the work group share responsibility and accountability for their group's performance. Inherent in the concept of employee teams is that employees, not managers, are in the best position to contribute to workplace performance. With work teams, managers accept the notion that the group is the logical work unit for applying resources to resolve organizational problems and concerns.[30]

Teamwork also embraces the concept of *synergy*. Synergy occurs when the interaction and outcome of team members is greater than the sum of their individual efforts.[31] Unfortunately, synergy may not automatically happen, but rather, it must be nurtured within the team environment.[32] Figure 4.6 lists the factors contributing to a synergistic team setting.

Teams can operate in a variety of structures, each with different strategic purposes or functional activities. Figure 4.7 describes common team forms. One form, self-directed teams, is often championed as being the highest form of team structure. Self-directed teams, also called *autonomous work groups*, *self-managed teams*, or *high-performance teams*, are groups of employees who are accountable for a "whole" work process or segment that delivers a product or service to an internal or external customer. For example, in a manufacturing environment, a team might be responsible for a whole product (i.e., a computer screen) or a clearly defined segment of the production process, such as the building of an engine for a passenger car. Similarly, in a service environment, a team is usually responsible for entire groupings of products and services, often serving clients in a designated geographical area. Typical team functions include setting work schedules, dealing directly with external customers,

FIGURE
4.6

Synergistic Team Characteristics

Team synergy is heightened when team members engage in these positive behaviors.

- *Support.* The team exhibits an atmosphere of inclusion. All team members speak up and feel free to offer constructive comments.

- *Listening and Clarification.* Active listening is practiced. Members honestly listen to others and seek clarification on discussion points. Team members summarize discussions held.

- *Disagreement.* Disagreement is seen as natural and is expected. Member comments are nonjudgmental and focus on factual issues rather than personality conflicts.

- *Consensus.* Team members reach agreements through consensus decision-making. Consensus decisions require finding a proposal that is acceptable to all team members, even if not the first choice of individual members. Common ground among ideas is sought.

- *Acceptance.* Team members are valued as individuals, recognizing that each person brings a valuable mix of skills and abilities to team operations.

- *Quality.* Each team member is committed to excellent performance. There is emphasis on continuous improvement and attention to detail.

virtual team

A team with widely dispersed members linked together through computer and telecommunications technology

training team members, setting performance targets, budgeting, inventory management, and purchasing equipment or services. To operate efficiently, team members acquire multiple skills enabling them to perform a variety of job tasks.

To compete in today's national and international markets, managers increasingly form virtual teams. Virtual teams use advanced computer and telecommunications technology to link team members who are geographically dispersed—often worldwide. Management may form a project team (see Figure 4.7) to develop a new pharmaceutical drug and have the team operate in a virtual environment to achieve its goal. For a major U.S. telecommunication client, IBM used a global team to develop a Web-based tool for launching new services. The team included members from Japan, Brazil, and Britain and delivered a finished product in two months, a considerable reduction in product delivery time.[33]

Although virtual teams have many benefits, they are not without their problem.[34] Paulette Tichenor, president of Organizational Renaissance, a team training organization, notes these concerns with virtual teams: language and cultural barriers, unclear objectives, time conflicts due to diverse geographical locations, and selecting people who can work in a collaborative setting.[35]

Navi Radjou, an expert in network innovations, notes, "One problem with distributing work is that you lose the intimacy of talking things through at the local café." To reduce this problem, companies such as Nokia are careful to select people who have a collaborative mindset. At Nokia, team members are encouraged to network online and to share their pictures and personal biographies. In another example, Accenture, a worldwide consulting organization, yearly involves 400 managers in

FIGURE 4.7

Forms of Employee Teams

Cross-Functional Teams. A group staffed with a mix of specialists (e.g., marketing, production, engineering) and formed to accomplish a specific objective. Cross-functional teams are based on assigned rather than voluntary membership.

Project Teams. A group formed specifically to design a new product or service. Members are assigned by management on the basis of their ability to contribute to success. The group normally disbands after task completion.

Self-Directed Teams. Groups of highly trained individuals performing a set of interdependent job tasks within a natural work unit. Team members use consensus decision-making to perform work duties, solve problems, or deal with internal or external customers.

Task Force Teams. A task force is formed by management to immediately resolve a major problem. The group is responsible for developing a long-term plan for problem resolution that may include a charge for implementing the solution proposed.

Process-Improvement Teams. A group made up of experienced people from different departments or functions and charged with improving quality, decreasing waste, or enhancing productivity in processes that affect all departments or functions involved. Team members are normally appointed by management.

virtual team leadership training. The goal is to create team effectiveness and to promote understanding of cross-cultural differences.

Regardless of the structure or purpose of the team, the following characteristics have been identified with successful teams:

- Commitment to shared goals and objectives

- Motivated and energetic team members

- Open and honest communication

- Shared leadership

- Clear role assignments

- Climate of cooperation, collaboration, trust, and accountability

- Recognition of conflict and its positive resolution

Unfortunately, not all teams succeed or operate to their full potential. Therefore, in adopting the work team concept, organizations must address several issues that could present obstacles to effective team function, including overly high expectations, group compensation, specialized team training, career movement, and conflict resolution. For example, new team members must be retrained to work outside their primary functional areas, and compensation systems must be constructed to reward individuals for team accomplishments. Importantly, research shows that teams achieve greater effectiveness when team members initially establish team ground rules, or team norms, for operational and behavioral success. HRM Experience, at the end of the chapter, presents an exercise to set team ground rules.

Another difficulty with work teams is that they alter the traditional manager-employee relationship. Managers often find it hard to adapt to the role of leader rather than supervisor and sometimes feel threatened by the growing power of the team and the reduced power of management. Furthermore, some employees may also have difficulty adapting to a role that includes traditional supervisory responsibilities. Therefore, from our experience in working with teams, extensive attention must be given to training team members as they move through the four stages of team development—forming, storming, norming, and performing.[36] *Complete* training would cover the importance of skills in (1) team leadership, (2) mission/goal setting, (3) conduct of meetings, (4) team decision-making, (5) conflict resolution, (6) effective communication, and (7) diversity awareness.[37]

Flexible Work Schedules

Objective 7

Flexible work schedules are not a true part of job design because job tasks and responsibilities are not changed. Nevertheless, we discuss adjustments in work schedules here because they alter the normal workweek of five eight-hour days in which all employees begin and end their workday at the same time. Employers may depart from the traditional workday or workweek in their attempt to improve organizational productivity and morale by giving employees increased control over the hours they work.[38]

Speaking on the importance of flexible work schedules, Lois Brakon, codirector of the Families and Work Institute, notes, "Flexible schedules are going to be the way good, competitive businesses work." Flexible work schedules may be assigned by the organization or requested by individual employees (see Highlights in HRM 3). The more common flexible work schedules are the compressed workweek, flextime, job sharing, and telecommuting.

Compressed Workweek

Under the compressed workweek, the number of days in the workweek is shortened by lengthening the number of hours worked per day. This schedule is best illustrated by the four-day, forty-hour week, generally referred to as 4/10 or 4/40. Employees working a four-day workweek might work ten hours a day, Monday through Thursday. Although the 4/10 schedule is probably the best known, other compressed arrangements include reducing weekly hours to thirty-eight or thirty-six hours or scheduling eighty hours over nine days (9/80), taking one day off every other week.

Several examples illustrate this popular work arrangement. At AVT Document Exchange Software Group in Tucson, Arizona, all general workers work four ten-hour days, with workers choosing the day they would like off. The organization's information technology employees, working swing and midnight shifts, work four nine-hour days. Working one less hour is comparable to offering a pay differential. In comparison, employees at Nahan Printing Inc., in St. Cloud, Minnesota, work three twelve-hour shifts, while employees at Marcel Dekker in New York City are employed on a Monday-through-Thursday office schedule with employees working a total of thirty-eight hours. At Marcel Dekker, employees are given the option of starting their workday between 7:30 A.M. and 9:30 A.M.

Managers cite the following reasons for implementing compressed workweek schedules:

- Recruitment and retention of employees[39]
- Coordinating employee work schedules with production schedules

HIGHLIGHTS IN HRM

3

How to Request a Flexible Work Schedule

You may be thinking, "My manager would never agree to a flexible work schedule." But that's not necessarily so. When valued employees make reasonable scheduling requests, managers often try to accommodate employee proposals. Here are some proven strategies for securing different types of flexible work hour arrangements.

- *Investigate.* Look into similar arrangements others have made within your company or industry. Research company policy. Be realistic by providing a schedule that will fit the demands of your organization.
- *Be Professional.* Treat your request as a business proposal. Be positive and assume a "can-do" attitude. Be serious and present the proposal as a benefit to both you and your company. Present your idea as a "win-win" arrangement.
- *Write It Out.* Submit your request for a flexible work hour arrangement in a well-organized, detailed written proposal.
- *Promote Yourself.* Explain your value to your organization. Have others speak to your abilities—especially those in authority. Ask to be evaluated based on your quantity and quality of work rather than on the hours you actually spend on the job.
- *Anticipate Questions.* Be prepared for potential problems and have specific answers on how to deal with these issues. For example, how you will communicate or coordinate with other employees.
- *Propose a Review.* Propose review dates to evaluate your new flexible schedule. Continually assess how you work with others and your manager.

Source: Adapted from Julie Shields, "Showing How to Flex It," *Incentive* 178, no. 3 (March 2004): 47.

- Accommodating the leisure time activities of employees while facilitating employee personal appointments—medical, dental, financial
- Improvements in employee job satisfaction and morale[40]

The major disadvantage of the compressed workweek involves federal laws regarding overtime. The Fair Labor Standards Act has stringent rules requiring the payment of overtime to nonsupervisory employees who work more than forty hours a week. (See Chapter 9.) Another disadvantage of the compressed workweek is that it increases the amount of stress on managers and employees, and long workdays can be exhausting.

Flextime

Flextime, or flexible working hours, permits employees the option of choosing daily starting and quitting times, provided that they work a certain number of hours per day or week. With flextime, employees are given considerable latitude in scheduling

flextime

Flexible working hours that permit employees the option of choosing daily starting and quitting times, provided that they work a set number of hours per day or week their work. However, there is a "core period" during the morning and afternoon when *all* employees are required to be on the job. Flexible working hours are most common in service-type organizations—financial institutions, government agencies, and other organizations with large clerical operations. The regional office of Sentry Insurance Company in Scottsdale, Arizona, has found that flextime provides many advantages for employees working in claims, underwriting, and HR areas. At Sentry Insurance, employees work a core period from 9 A.M. to 3 P.M. Flexible time periods are 6 A.M. to 9 A.M. and 3 P.M. to 7 P.M.

Flextime provides both employees and employers with several advantages. By allowing employees greater flexibility in work scheduling, employers can reduce some of the traditional causes of tardiness and absenteeism.[41] Employees can adjust their work to accommodate their particular lifestyles and, in doing so, gain greater job satisfaction. Employees can also schedule their working hours for the time of day when they are most productive. In addition, variations in arrival and departure times can help reduce traffic congestion at the peak commuting hours. In some cases, employees require less time to commute, and the pressures of meeting a rigid schedule are reduced.

From the employer's standpoint, flextime can be most helpful in recruiting and meeting the challenges of age diversity in the workforce.[42] It has proved invaluable to organizations wishing to improve service to customers or clients by extending operating hours. Qwest, a telecommunications company, uses flextime to keep its business offices open for customers who cannot get there during the day. Research demonstrates that flextime can have a positive impact on the performance measures of reliability, quality, and quantity of employee work.

There are, of course, several disadvantages to flextime. First, it is not suited to some jobs. It is not feasible, for example, where specific workstations must be staffed at all times. Second, it can create problems for managers in communicating with and instructing employees. Flextime schedules may also force these managers to extend their workweek if they are to exercise control over their subordinates.

Job Sharing

The arrangement whereby two part-time employees perform a job that otherwise would be held by one full-time employee is called *job sharing*. Job sharers usually work three days a week, "creating an overlap day for extended face-to-face conferencing." Their pay is three-fifths of a regular salary. Employers note that without job sharing two good employees might otherwise be lost. Notable companies with job sharing programs include Sprint, American Express, Lotus Development Company, Carter Howley Hale Stores, and Kaiser Permanente, one of the nation's largest health maintenance organizations.

Job sharing is suited to the needs of families in which one or both spouses desire to work only part-time.[43] It is suited also to the needs of older workers who want to phase into retirement by shortening their workweek. For the employer, the work of part-time employees can be scheduled to conform to peaks in the daily workload. Job sharing can also limit layoffs in hard economic times. A final benefit is that employees engaged in job sharing have time off during the week to accommodate personal needs, so they are less likely to be absent.

Job sharing does have several problems, however. Employers may not want to employ two people to do the work of one because the time required to orient and train a second employee constitutes an added burden. Additionally, managers may find it more difficult to supervise two employees particularly when one job sharer is not dependable, job sharers cannot effectively work together, or they simply distrust one another.[44] The key to making job sharing work is good communications between partners, who can use a number of ways to stay in contact—phone calls, written updates, e-mail, and voice mail.

Telecommuting

Globalization and technology are drastically changing the "Future of Work," that is, how we do our jobs and the offices we do them in. Consider this example, Brian Conchuratt, regional sales manager for Commission Junction, an Internet marketing company, lives in Chandler, Arizona, and telecommutes with his home office in Santa Barbara, California. Furthermore, to communicate with present and future clients, Brian uses "rich" channels of telecommunication technology, including a broadband Internet connection, video conferencing, voice-over-IP phone, VPN (virtual private network), webcam, and mobile e-mail. Charles Grantham, executive producer of Work Design Collaborative, estimates that 15 percent of workers today are "distributed," a figure that could reach 40 percent by 2012.[45]

Telecommuting is the use of personal computers, networks, and other communications technology to do work in the home that is traditionally done in the workplace. A variant of telecommuting is the *virtual office*, where employees are in the field helping customers or are stationed at other remote locations working as if they were in the home office.[46]

Both managers and HR professionals note the following advantages of telecommuting.[47]

- Increased flexibility for employees—better work/life balance
- Reduced absenteeism

telecommuting
Use of personal computers, networks, and other communications technology such as fax machines to do work in the home that is traditionally done in the workplace

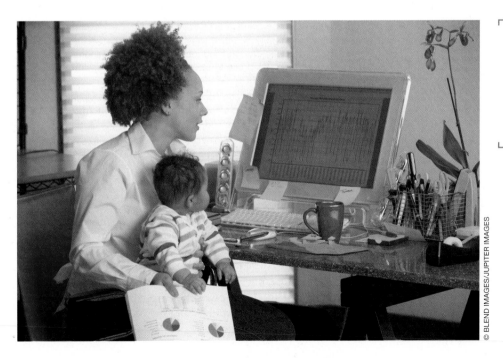

Organizations with telecommuting policies allow employees to better meet their work/life responsibilities while retaining the talents of valued employees.

© BLEND IMAGES/JUPITER IMAGES

- Retention of valued employees who might otherwise quit
- Reduced "carbon footprints" through minimizing daily commuting
- Increased productivity, i.e., reduced wasted office time
- Lower overhead costs and reduced office space

While telecommuting offers significant benefits to employers, it also presents potential drawbacks. These include the loss of creativity as employees are not interacting with one another on a regular basis, the difficulty of developing appropriate performance standards and evaluation systems for telecommuters, and the need to formulate an appropriate technology strategy for allocating the necessary equipment.[48] Traditional line managers accustomed to managing by observation may find supervising distributed employees stressful. Additionally, managers may believe that telecommuting negatively affects employee-supervisor relationships through loss of knowledge or information, training or development, and a sense of connectedness.[49] Employers wishing to have their employees telecommute must comply with wage and hour laws, liability and workers' compensation regulations, equipment purchase or rental agreements with employees, and all federal EEO regulations (see Chapter 3). Employees who are denied the opportunity to work from home may feel discriminated against and resent home telecommuters. Figure 4.8 presents suggestions for establishing a successful telecommuting program.

FIGURE
4.8

Keys for Successful Telecommuting

- *Identify jobs best suited to distance work.* Those involving sales, customer service, and auditing are logical choices.

- *Select responsible employees.* Employees who are self-starters, motivated, and trustworthy and who can work independently are ideal candidates. Establish employee feedback procedures and performance review methods for employee evaluation.

- *Establish formalized telecommuting procedures.* Telecommuting guidelines could cover hours of availability, office reporting periods, performance expectations, and weekly progress reports or e-mail updates.

- *Begin a formal training program.* Training for both telecommuters and managers should include the technical aspects of equipment usage and relationship factors such as how and when to contact the office or availability and location of support facilities.

- *Keep telecommuters informed.* Physical separation can make telecommuters feel isolated and invisible. Department and staff updates, inclusion of telecommuters on project teams, required attendance at meetings, and "chat room" discussions all keep telecommuters "in the loop."

- *Recognize when telecommuting isn't working.* State in telecommunicating policies that the arrangement may be terminated when it no longer serves company needs or if the employee's performance declines.

Source: Adapted from Barbara Hemphill, "Telecommuting Productivity," *Occupational Health and Safety* 73, no. 3 (March 2004): 16.

SUMMARY

Objective 1 Job requirements reflect the different duties, tasks, and responsibilities contained in jobs. Job requirements, in turn, influence HR functions performed by managers, including recruitment, selection, training and development, performance appraisal, compensation, and various labor relations activities.

Objective 2 Job analysis data may be gathered using several collection methods—interviews, questionnaires, observations, and diaries. Other more quantitative approaches include the position analysis questionnaire system, critical incident method, task inventory analysis, and competency-based analysis. It is the prevailing opinion of the courts that HRM decisions on employment, performance appraisal, and promotions must be based on specific criteria that are job-related. These criteria can be determined objectively only by analyzing the requirements of each job.

Objective 3 The format of job descriptions varies widely, often reflecting the needs of the organization and the expertise of the writer. As a minimum, job descriptions should contain a job title, a job identification section, and an essential functions section. A job specification section also may be included. Job descriptions should be written in clear and specific terms with consideration given to their legal implications.

Objective 4 Job design is a combination of four basic considerations: organizational objectives; industrial engineering concerns of analyzing work methods and establishing time standards; ergonomic considerations, which accommodate human capabilities and limitations to job tasks; and employee contributions.

Objective 5 In the job characteristics model, five job factors contribute to increased job performance and satisfaction—skill variety, task identity, task significance, autonomy, and feedback. All factors should be built into jobs, since each factor influences different employee psychological states. When jobs are enriched through the job characteristics model, employees experience more meaningfulness in their jobs, acquire more job responsibility, and receive direct feedback from the tasks they perform.

Objective 6 To improve the internal process of organizations and increase American productivity, greater efforts are being made by organizations to involve groups of employees in work operations. Employee involvement groups are composed of employees in work units charged with offering suggestions for improving product or service quality or fostering workplace effectiveness. Employee teams stress employee collaboration over individual accomplishment. Teams rely on the expertise and different abilities of members to achieve a specific goal or objective. Self-directed teams are characterized by their willingness to perform traditional managerial tasks.

Objective 7 Changes in work schedules—which include the compressed workweek, flextime, job sharing, and telecommuting—permit employees to adjust their work periods to accommodate their particular lifestyles. Employees can select from among these HR techniques to accommodate diverse employee needs while fostering organizational effectiveness.

KEY TERMS

critical incident method	job	job specification
employee empowerment	job analysis	position
employee involvement groups (EIs)	job characteristics model	position analysis questionnaire (PAQ)
employee teams	job description	
ergonomics	job design	task inventory analysis
flextime	job enrichment	telecommuting
industrial engineering	job family	virtual team

DISCUSSION QUESTIONS

Objective 1 1. Place yourself in the position of general manager of a service department. How might formally written job requirements help you manage your work unit?

Objective 2 2. Discuss the various methods by which job analysis can be completed. Compare and contrast these methods, noting the pros or cons of each.

Objective 3 3. Working with a group of three or four students, collect at least five different job descriptions from organizations in your area. Compare the descriptions, highlighting similarities and differences.

Objective 4 4. Explain how industrial engineering and ergonomics can both clash with and complement each other in the design of jobs.

Objective 5 5. The job characteristics model has five components that enhance employee jobs—skill variety, task identity, task significance, autonomy, and feedback. Give an example illustrating how each component can be used to improve the organization and the job of the employee. (Suggestion: Consider your present or a recent job to answer this question.)

Objective 6 6. Figure 4.7 shows the different forms of employee teams. Provide an example of where each type of team can be used. How do teams create synergy?

Objective 7 7. As a small business employer, explain how nontraditional work schedules might make it easier for you to recruit employees.

BIZFLIX EXERCISES

Intolerable Cruelty: Just Doing My Job

This chapter discussed several aspects of job analysis and job design. Try to apply much of that discussion to this scene from the film *Intolerable Cruelty*. Use the following questions below as guides to your viewing.

Ruthless, beautiful Marilyn Rexroth (Catherine Zeta-Jones) matches the brilliance of divorce attorney Miles Massey (George Clooney). Conflict rises and falls as the two try to outwit each other in this charming romantic comedy. The film twists and turns in typical Coen brothers (coscreenwriters; Joel Cohen, director) fashion as it reaches its predictable end.

This scene comes from "The War Room" segment that occurs about 20 minutes into the film. It follows Rex Rexroth's (George Herrmann) escapade with a young woman (Kristen Dattilo). His wife, Marilyn Rexroth, hired private detective Gus Petch (Cedric the Entertainer) to videotape the event. He now needs some legal help. Miles Massey meets his new client and discusses the case. The film continues with a group of women sitting by The Waters swimming pool talking about their ex- and present husbands.

What to Watch for and Ask Yourself

- What knowledge, skills, and abilities (KSAs) are required for the successful performance of Miles Massey's job?

- Recall the earlier chapter section "Job Analysis." Apply some observations from that section to this scene. What duties, tasks, and activities do you infer from the scene for Massey's job?

- Job design views certain job characteristics as important for a person's motivation and satisfaction (see the earlier section "Job Design"). Which of the five core job dimensions appear(s) in Miles Massey's job?

HRM EXPERIENCE

Establishing Ground Rules for Team Success

Professional trainers understand that setting ground rules for teams is a cornerstone for continued team success. Ground rules—or team norms—are agreed-on formal rules that guide group member behavior. Norms established prior to the team's task regulate the behavior of group members. Ground rules simply state how members want to be treated and how members agree to treat others. When team members follow the established norms, then norms help maintain order, promote positive behavior, and can be used to correct undesirable actions. Remember, because teams operate in different settings, different norms may be appropriate in different arrangements.

Assignment

1. Working within your team, select what you believe are the ten most important norms for team behavior.
2. From the following Behavior List, have each team member *silently* select two lists of ten items each of the behaviors they believe most critical for team success. The first list of ten items (your A list) is considered the most important for group conduct. The second list (the B list) is desired items but those not of major importance.
3. In a group discussion, have all team members select a final list of ten items from both lists. These become your team's final norms. Select no more than ten items. During your discussion, items can be modified or combined to meet your team's specific needs.
4. Prepare a written document of chosen behaviors and have all team members sign the form. You have now established a written contract for positive team conduct.

(continued)

Establishing Ground Rules for Team Success (continued)

Behavior List

While working in our team, individuals should...

1. Do their fair share of the work.
2. Check to ensure that everyone clearly understands what is to be done.
3. Encourage planning, including short-range agendas as well as long-range goals.
4. Encourage open and candid opinions about issues.
5. Listen willingly and carefully to other people's ideas, even if those people have a different viewpoint.
6. Prepare thoroughly before meetings.
7. Make team members feel at ease in discussion.
8. Ask questions when they do not clearly understand tasks or procedures.
9. Propose specific analyses of the pros and cons of decisions faced by the team.
10. Follow through on task assignments.
11. Help other members when assistance is requested.
12. Treat all team members as equals.
13. Paraphrase or restate what someone else says in order to check meaning.
14. Openly voice opinions and share ideas.
15. Be flexible in arranging meeting schedules.
16. Compliment others for things they have said or done.
17. Be willing to meet whenever it is necessary to discuss a problem.
18. Deal with conflict directly, bringing it to the attention of the team.
19. Express enthusiasm about what the team is doing.
20. Encourage budgeting of the team's time.
21. At the end of a meeting, restate their own responsibilities to check for agreement.
22. Be serious about the team's work.
23. Arrive on time for regularly scheduled meetings.
24. Be willing to listen to other team members' ideas.
25. Get the team's approval on important matters before proceeding.

CASE STUDY 1

Virtual Teams in Action: Building the F-35 Fighter

The F-35 Lighting II Program, also known as the Joint Fighter Program, is the U.S. Department of Defense's focal point for defining affordable next generation stealth fighter aircraft. As noted by proponents of the program, "The F-35 will bring cutting edge technology to the battle space of the future."

In 2002, the Department of Defense named Lockheed Martin Aeronautics of Fort Worth, Texas, to design and build the fighter with Northrop Grumman and BAE

Systems as major partners. Countries, including Italy, Australia, Canada, Turkey, India, and Israel, have contributed toward development costs of the program. The first flight of the production model occurred at Naval Air Station Fort Worth Joint Reserve Base on December 15, 2006. Jon Beesley, F-35 chief test pilot, stated, "The Lighting II performed beautifully."

Success of the mega project hinged greatly on intricate teamwork and the cooperation of countless individuals. For example, more than 80 suppliers worked at 187 locations worldwide to build components for the fighter. A seventy-five member technology group at Lockheed's aeronautics division linked the suppliers along with the U.S. Air Force, Navy, and Marines to Britain's Defense Ministry to track progress and make midstream design and production changes. Individuals working at more than 40,000 computer stations collaborated to get the first plane airborne in just four years. Speaking of the teamwork involved, Mark Peden, vice president for information systems at Lockheed Aeronautics, said, "It's the true virtual connection."

Teams working both nationally and internationally were connected as if team members were working in the same room. Teams communicated via their computers while looking at shared documents, carried on e-mail chats, and used electronic whiteboards on which geographically separated team members could draw pictures or charts, in real time, as others watched and responded. The Internet was designed to allow people from different companies with incompatible computing systems to interface on Web sites that speak a common language.

Questions

1. What advantages did Lockheed Martin gain by using virtual teams? Explain.
2. Identify and discuss potential problems with using virtual teams—for example, interpersonal, technical, or geographical concerns.
3. Discuss the characteristics that virtual team members should possess.
4. What specific training should virtual teams receive?

CASE STUDY 2

But My Job Has Changed

Job descriptions are a critical tool used for job orientation and training and, importantly, in annual employee performance evaluations. When the duties and responsibilities listed in the job description do not reflect current job content, employee/management disagreements can arise, as this case illustrates.

Both employees and managers agree that Brenda Batten has been an exceptional employee. As a senior technical representative (STR) for Blackhawk Aironics, she is valued for her knowledge in airplane instrumentation. One manager described her as "simply an expert in the complex technology of satellite weather systems."

In May 2007, Blackhawk Aironics implemented a new work reorganization plan. STRs such as Brenda now work largely by telecommuting with managers and engineers at company headquarters in Denton, Texas, and with customers scattered throughout the United States. Additionally, under the new work plan, STRs were given more freedom to deal directly with customers and engineers without supervisory intervention. This freedom greatly facilitated customer service needs and demands in an aviation market everyone considers highly dynamic.

Brenda's current job description reflects the technical dimensions of her position but not the telecommuting requirements now performed. Personal competencies such as decision-making, self-motivation, problem-solving, and communication skills are not covered.

In May 2008, Brenda met with her manager, Martin Eaton, for her annual performance review. Unfortunately, unlike past meetings, which were highly satisfactory, this meeting quickly developed into a disagreement. At the center of the controversy were the factors to be used to measure Brenda's new job demands. Martin wanted to place major emphasis on the tasks and duties listed in her current job description. As he explained to Brenda, "I hardly see you anymore, and I have no objective criteria or performance data by which to measure those behaviors you now use." Brenda, in response, acknowledged that some things in the current job description were still important aspects of her job, but overall the current job description did not capture the full scope of her new duties and responsibilities. Brenda concluded that she was satisfied with Martin's evaluation of the technical aspects of her job, but she was clearly not pleased with the overall evaluation of her performance. As she told Martin, "It's simply not fair; you just don't know what I do now."

Questions

1. Given the facts of this case, is it possible for Brenda and Martin to reach a satisfactory result? Explain.
2. How could an organization go about identifying and measuring the personal competencies of employees?
3. How could the company prevent this problem from occurring in the future? Explain.

Source: Based on an actual case known to the authors. All names and locations are fictitious.

NOTES AND REFERENCES

1. Narasimhaiah Gorla, Ravi Chinta, and Tam Wai Chu, "An Enhanced Business Process Re-engineering Model for Supply Chain Management and a Case Study," *Journal of Information Technology Case and Application Research* 9, no. 2 (2007): 5.
2. Michael Hammer, "The Process Audit," *Harvard Business Review* 85, no. 4 (April 2007): 111.
3. Peter Coy, "COG or Co-worker?; The Organization Man Isn't Extinct or Even Endangered—But the Role Has Been Refined Over the Past 100 Years," *Business Week*, Issue 4047 (August 2007): 58.
4. Arnold B. Bakker, Evangelia Demeroob, and Willem Verbeke, "Using the Job Demands Resources Model to Predict Burnout and Performance," *Human Resources Management* 43, no. 1 (Spring 2004): 83.
5. Valerie L. Myers and Janice L. Dreachslin, "Recruitment and Retention of a Diverse Workforce: Challenges and Opportunities," *Journal of Healthcare Management* 52, no. 5 (September/October 2007): 290.
6. Adapted from job description for "Senior HR Analyst," City of Mesa, Arizona.
7. Paul Lyons, "Charting Skills for Quality Improvement," *The Journal of Quality and Participation* 30, no. 1 (Spring 2007): 30.
8. George T. Milkovich and Jerry M. Newman, *Compensation*, 9th ed. (Boston: McGraw-Hill Companies, 2007).
9. Information on the technical aspects of the Americans with Disabilities Act can be obtained from the Equal Employment Opportunity Commission. See, for example, *The ADA: Questions and Answers, ADA Technical Assistance and Resource Manual*, and *The ADA: Your Responsibility as an Employer*. Publications can be ordered from the EEOC Web site at http://www.eeoc.gov.
10. Frederick P. Morgeson, Kelly Delaney-Klinger, Melinda S. Mayfield, Philip Ferrara, and Michael A. Campion, "Self-Presentation Processes in Job Analysis: A Field Experiment Investigating Inflation in Abilities, Tasks, and Competencies," *Journal of Applied Psychology* 89, no. 4 (August 2004): 674.
11. Interview with job analyst Carol Tucker, Mesa, Arizona, May 10, 2006.

12. The O*NET database Internet site is at http://www.doleta.gov/programs/onet.

13. A detailed description of different job analysis techniques is beyond the scope of this text. For those interested in more comprehensive information or job analysis tools, see Michael T. Bannick, Edward L. Levine, and Frederick P. Morgeson, *Job and Work Analysis: Methods, Research, and Applications for Human Resource Management*, 2nd ed. (Thousand Oaks, CA: Sage, 2007).

14. Jessica Marquez, "A Talent Strategy Overhaul at Pfizer," *Workforce Management* 86, no. 3 (February 12, 2007): 1.

15. Marqie Mader-Clark, *Job Description Handbook*, 1st ed. (Berkeley, CA: Nolo Press, 2006).

16. Chapter 3 discusses the *Uniform Guidelines on Employee Section Procedures* and the necessity for performance standards to be based on valid job-related criteria.

17. Gensheng Liu, Rachna Shah, and Roger G. Schroeder, "Linking Work Design to Mass Customization: A Socio-technical Systems Perspective," *Decision Sciences* 37, no. 4 (November 2006): 519.

18. Pooja Garg and Renu Rastogi, "New Models of Job Design: Motivating Employees' Performance," *The Journal of Management Development* 25, no. 6 (2006): 572.

19. For Herzberg's important article on job enrichment, see Frederick Herzberg, "One More Time: How Do You Motivate Employees?" *Harvard Business Review* 46, no. 2 (January-February 1968): 53–62.

20. For the original article on the job characteristics model, see J. Richard Hackman and Greg R. Oldham, "Motivation through the Design of Work: Test of a Theory," *Organizational Behavior and Human Performance* 16, no. 2 (August 1976): 250–79.

21. Jed DeVaro, Robert Li, and Dana Brookshire, "Analyzing the Job Characteristics Model: New Support from a Cross-Section of Establishments," *The International Journal of Human Resource Management* 18, no. 6 (June 2007): 986.

22. Richard E. Wilmot and Robert Galford, "A Commitment to Trust," *Communication World* 24, no. 2 (March/April 2007): 34.

23. Denise Robitaille, "Invaluable Contributions," *Industrial Engineering* 39, no. 1 (January 2007): 32.

24. Laura Baron, James Vander Spek, and Wendy Young, "The Economics of Ergonomics," *Journal of Accountancy* 222, no. 6 (December 2006): 34.

25. Julian Faraway and Matthew P. Reed, "Statistics for Digital Human Motion Modeling in Ergonomics," *Technometrics* 49, no. 3 (August 2007): 277.

26. Bernie Knill, "Practical Ergonomics for Plant People," *Material Handling Management* 57, no. 2 (September 2002): 53.

27. Andrew J. DuBrin, *Fundamentals of Organizational Behavior*, 4th ed. (Cincinnati, OH: South-Western, 2007), Chapter 10.

28. Keith Ayers, "Get Employees to Help you Increase Productivity and Profitability," *Rural Telecommunications* 26, no. 5 (September/October 2007): 26.

29. Brian Hindo, "The Empire Strikes at Silos," *Business Week*, August 20, 2007, 63.

30. Roy C. Herrenkohl, *Becoming a Team: Achieving a Goal*, 1st ed. (South-Western, 2004).

31. Vojko Potocan and Bostjan Kuralt, "Synergy in Business: Some New Suggestions," *Journal of American Academy of Business* 12, no. 1 (September 2007): 199.

32. Leigh Thompson, "Improving the Creativity of Organizational Work Groups," *The Academy of Management Executive* 17, no. 1 (February 2003): 96.

33. Michael Mandel, "Which Way to the Future," *Business Week*, August 20, 2007, 45.

34. Laura A. Hambley, Thomas A. O'Neil, and Theresa J. B. Klien, "Virtual Team Leadership: The Effects of Leadership Style and Communication Medium on Team Interaction Styles and Outcomes," *Organizational Behavior and Human Decision Processes* 103, no. 1 (May 2007): 1.

35. Interview with Paulette Tichenor, Arizona State University, Tempe, Arizona, January 18, 2007.

36. For a discussion of the stages of team development, see Don Hellriegel and John W. Slocum, Jr., *Organizational Behavior*, 11th ed. (Cincinnati, OH: South-Western, 2007).

37. Stephen B. Knouse, "Building Task Cohesion to Bring Teams Together," *Quality Progress* 40, no. 3 (March 2007): 49.

38. Michelle Conlin, "Smashing the Clock," *Business Week*, December 11, 2006, 60. See also, Susan Meisinger, "Flexible Schedules Make Powerful Perks," *HR Magazine* 52, no. 4 (April 2007): 12.

39. Kathy Gurchiek, "Good News for Moms Reconsidering Work," *HR Magazine* 51, no. 7 (August 2006): 39.

40. James A. Breaugh and N. Kathleen Frye, "An Examination of the Antecedents and Consequences of the Use of Family-friendly Benefits," *Journal of Management Issues* 19, no. 1 (Spring 2007): 35.

41. Rita Zeidner, "Bending with the Times," *HR Magazine* 53, no. 7 (July 2008): 10.

42. Nancy Sutton Bell and Marvin Narz, "Meeting the Challenges of Age Diversity in the Workplace," *The CPA Journal* 77, no. 2 (February 2007): 56.

43. "Have You Considered Job Sharing as a Retention Tool?," *HR Focus* 83, no. 9 (September 2006): 10.

44. Susan Berfield, "Two for the Cubicle," *Business Week*, July 24, 2006, 88.

45. Mandel, 45.

46. Tammy Dewar, "Virtual Teams—Virtually Impossible," *Performance Improvement* 45, no. 5 (May/June 2006): 22.

47. http://www.wikipedip.org/wiki/telecommuting.

48. Wendell Joice, "Implementing Telework: The Technology Issue," *Public Manager* 36, no. 2 (Summer 2007): 64.

49. Marjorie Deruen, "The Remote Connection," *HR Magazine* 52, no. 3 (March 2007): 111.

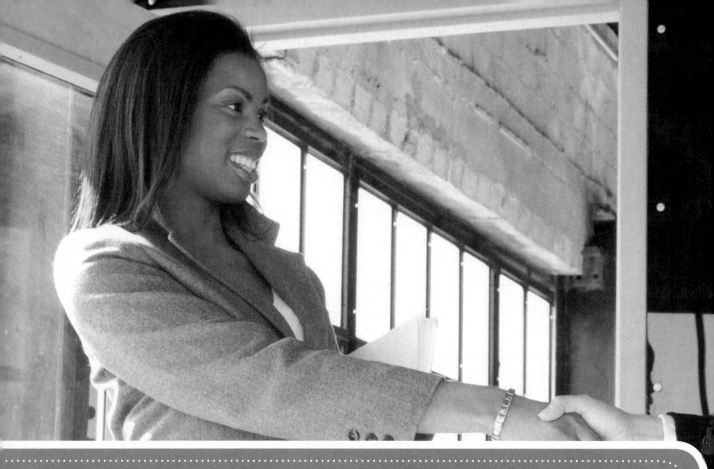

Expanding the Talent Pool: Recruitment and Careers

After studying this chapter, you should be able to

Objective | 1 |

Explain the advantages and disadvantages of external recruitment.

Objective | 2 |

Explain the advantages and disadvantages of recruiting from within the organization.

© SAMOS IMAGES LLC/ALAMY LIMITED

CHAPTER

5

Objective 3

Discuss how job opportunities can be inventoried and employee potential assessed.

Objective 4

Explain how career management programs integrate the needs of individual employees and their organizations.

Objective 5

Describe the conditions that help make a career management program successful.

Objective 6

Explain why diverse recruitment and career development activities are important to companies.

In earlier chapters, we stressed that many HR challenges center on the idea that organizations increasingly compete on the basis of their employees' talents and capabilities. Even though the unemployment rate ticked upward in 2008, employers still face a labor shortage in the coming years. As you have learned, as the baby boomers begin retiring, the demand for labor is expected to far outstrip supply.

The greater competition for talent means that recruiting has become more important for managers. Today, many jobs require higher skill levels. No longer can managers rely on unsolicited applications to fill these positions. To stay apace of their competitors and expand their operations around the world, companies are also looking globally for workers. It is therefore essential that organizations do a good job of broadening their pools of talent—the number and kinds of people able to contribute to the success of the organization and the variety of ways in which they recruit and retain them.

Of course, unlike physical assets, human assets (employees) can decide to leave the firm of their own accord as well as join it. The Internet has helped make workers better informed about opportunities and allowed them telecommute or work off-site. As a result, rival firms are in a better position to lure good employees away. Flatter organizational structures within firms mean that there are fewer positions for promotion. Consequently, individuals often must look for advancement opportunities outside of their companies. At the same time, as economic cycles lead organizations first to hire—and then to lay off—and then to hire again, employment security can be assured only when individuals take control of their own careers. The upshot is that individuals are less likely to work in the same job for extended periods, and in fact, most are unlikely to spend their entire careers with only one firm. In other words, today's labor market—for both employees and employers—has become more "free agent" oriented.[1]

In this chapter, we will discuss various sources and approaches to expanding the talent pool in organizations. Specifically, we will discuss both external sources of recruitment and internal sources (such as promotion, transfers, and the like). But beyond recruiting itself, we will also discuss the approaches that organizations take toward career management over time. As organizations consider the long-term implications for managing their talent, career development is taking on new importance. Finally, at the end of the chapter, we devote special attention to the recruitment and career development of minorities and women.

▪▪ RECRUITING TALENT EXTERNALLY

Objective 1

Recruitment is the process of locating potential individuals who might join an organization and encouraging them to apply for existing or anticipated job openings. During this process, firms make an effort to inform the applicants fully about the qualifications they need for particular jobs and the career opportunities their organizations offer employees. Whether a particular job vacancy will be filled by someone from within the organization or from outside will depend on the availability of personnel, the organization's HR policies, and the requirements of the job to be staffed. Highlights in HRM 1 outlines Marriott's principles for recruiting.

Unless managers intend to reduce the size of the workforce, any job vacancy is a cue that a replacement from outside must be found to replace a departing employee. An old adage goes something like this: "When the president or CEO of the organization retires, a chain reaction of promotions occurs. Everyone moves up a slot, and someone new is hired into a starting position in the mailroom." Of course this almost never occurs, but the story illustrates a philosophy for how some companies

1

HIGHLIGHTS IN HRM

Marriott's Recruitment Principles

#1: Get It Right the First Time. Marriott "hires friendly" and "trains technical." It's better to hire people with "the spirit to serve" and train them to work than hire people who know business and try to teach them to enjoy serving guests. Marriott hires cooks who love to cook and housekeepers who love to clean. They have learned that this approach works both for delivering excellent service and for retaining their employees.

#2: Money Is a Big Thing, But . . . The top concern of Marriott associates is total compensation. But intangible factors taken together, such as work-life balance, leadership quality, opportunity for advancement, work environment, and training, far outweigh money in their decisions to stay or leave. Pay matters less, and the other factors matter more the longer someone works for Marriott. From flexible schedules to tailored benefit packages and development opportunities, Marriott has built systems to address these nonmonetary factors.

#3: A Caring Workplace Is a Bottom-Line Issue. When employees come to work, they feel safe, secure, and welcome. Committed associates are less likely to leave, and associate work commitment is one of the key drivers of guest satisfaction. Managers are accountable for associate satisfaction ratings and for turnover rates. Every day, associates in each of Marriott's full-service hotels participate in a fifteen-minute meeting to review basic values such as respect. Managers also encourage associates to raise their personal concerns. They take the time to celebrate birthdays and anniversaries. Marriott calls this the loyalty program because it builds loyalty among associates and repeat business from customers. The result is that everyone has a stake in making the hotel a success.

#4: Promote from Within. More than 50 percent of Marriott's current managers have been promoted from within. All associates are given the opportunity to advance as far as their abilities will carry them. Elevating veterans to positions of leadership helps Marriott pass on the soul of its business—its corporate culture—from one generation to the next. In addition, promoting from within is a powerful tool for recruitment and retention. Associates cite "opportunity for advancement" as a key factor in their decisions to stay with Marriott. (Accompanying that is a $100-million-a-year commitment to training.)

#5: Build the Employment Brand. Marriott attracts employees the same way it attracts customers. Just as consumers buy experiences, not just products, potential employees are looking for a great work experience when they shop for jobs. Communicating the promise of a great work experience is what employment branding is all about. It's basically a value proposition. According to CEO J. W. Marriott, "For more than 70 years, we've lived by a simple motto: If we take care of our associates they'll take care of our guests. That isn't just a sentiment. It's a strategy—one all businesses must adopt to remain competitive in an environment where our most valuable resource, human capital, drives economic value for our company."

Source: J. W. Marriott, "Competitive Strength," *Executive Excellence* 18, no. 4 (April 2001): 3–4; J. W. Marriott, "Our Competitive Strength: Human Capital," *Executive Speeches* 15, no. 5 (April/May 2001): 18–21.

approach recruiting. More realistically, when there is an opening, managers must make careful decisions about whether to fill the position, and if so, whom to bring into the position, and how best to approach the decision. The question therefore is not whether to bring people into the organization, but rather at which level they are to be brought in. In the past few years, an astonishing number of the nation's largest companies, including McDonald's, Hewlett-Packard, and 3M, have brought in outsiders to be their new CEOs. Stock prices rose and fell based on a CEO's appointment, and hiring someone from the outside was seen as essential for revitalizing the organizations. The problem is that although outside CEOs might be charismatic, they sometimes lack the knowledge and skills they need to be successful in a new industry or are a bad fit with their new companies' culture. Perhaps this why two out of five CEOs fail in their first nineteen months on the job.[2]

Outside Sources for Recruitment

The outside sources from which employers recruit will vary with the type of position to be filled. A computer programmer, for example, is not likely to be recruited from the same source as a machine operator. Trade schools can provide applicants for entry-level positions, though these recruitment sources are not as useful when highly skilled employees are needed. Some firms keep detailed statistics by job type on the sources from which their employees are hired. This helps human resources managers make better decisions about the places to begin recruiting when different job openings arise.

The condition of the labor market may also help determine which recruiting sources an organization will use. During periods of high unemployment, organizations might be able to maintain an adequate supply of qualified applicants from unsolicited resumes alone. A tight labor market, one with low unemployment, might force the employer to advertise heavily and/or seek assistance from local employment agencies. How successful an organization has been in reaching its employee diversity goals can be still another factor in determining the sources from which to recruit. Typically, an employer at any given time will find it necessary to use several recruitment sources.

Several other studies have suggested that an employee's recruitment source can affect that employee's subsequent tenure and job performance in both large and small organizations.[3] In general, applicants who are referred by a current employee, if hired, tend to remain with the organization longer and perform better. Employers are cautioned, however, that relying on only one or two recruitment sources to secure job applicants could have an adverse effect on protected classes.

Advertisements

One of the most common methods of attracting applicants is through advertisements. Although Web sites, newspapers, and trade journals are the media used most often, radio, television, billboards, posters, and e-mail are also used. Advertising has the advantage of reaching a large audience of possible applicants. Some degree of selectivity can be achieved by using newspapers and journals directed toward a particular group of readers. Professional journals, trade journals, and the publications of unions and various fraternal or nonprofit organizations fall into this category.

Preparing recruiting advertisements not only is time-consuming, but also requires creativity in terms of developing their design and message content. Well-written advertisements highlight the major assets of the position while showing the responsiveness of the organization to the job, career, and lifestyle needs of applicants. Also, there appears to be a correlation between the accuracy and completeness of information provided in job advertisements and an organization's recruitment success. The more information disclosed, the better. Among the information typically included in advertisements is that the recruiting organization is an equal opportunity employer.

However, even when a job opening is described thoroughly in an advertisement, many unqualified applicants will still apply. This can create a burden for HR personnel who have to sift through stacks of inquiries and resumes in an effort to locate qualified candidates. In fact, for each vacant position, HR staff and managers typically review 20 to 100 résumés. Fortunately, software developers are designing new tools companies can use to prescreen applicants online, digitize their resumes, distribute the data into company databases, and automate the process of candidate referrals from in-house personnel. Other software developers have created talent search software, which can be customized to search the Web for valuable but "passive" job candidates, based on information they post on industry blogs, mailing lists, association sites, and so forth. AIRS Oxygen 6.0 is one such product. Zoominfo.com is a search engine that can be used to track businesspeople online.[4]

Unsolicited Applications and Resumes

Many employers receive unsolicited applications and resumes from individuals who may or may not be good prospects for employment. Even though the percentage of acceptable applicants from this source generally is not high, it is a source that cannot be ignored. In fact, it is often believed that individuals who contact employers on their own initiative will be better employees than those recruited through college placement services or newspaper advertisements.

Good public relations dictate that any person contacting an organization for a job be treated with courtesy and respect. If there is no present or future possibility of employment in the organization, the applicant should be tactfully and frankly informed as much. Telling an applicant to "fill out an application, and we will keep it on file" when there is no hope for his or her employment is not fair to the applicant. Research has shown that a candidate who has been treated well by a potential employer will, on average, tell one other person. On the other hand, a candidate who has been treated poorly—perhaps receiving a tardy rejection letter or no letter all—will, on average, tell eleven other people.[5]

Internet Recruiting

Looking on the Internet is the most commonly used search tactic by job seekers and recruiters to get the word out about new positions. Both companies and applicants find the approach cheaper, faster, and potentially more effective. There are now more than 40,000 thousand independent job boards on the Web. The top three—Monster, Career-Builder, and Yahoo's Hot Jobs—make up about half of the people recruited from this source. Specialty Internet recruiting sites such as AttorneyJobs.com, Medzilla.com (for the pharmaceutical industry), AMFMJobs.com (for radio personnel), Vets4Hire.com, and 6FigureJobs.com (for executives) are common, too. Staffing experts say it is also a good idea to post your firm's jobs at free association and trade group sites, where your specific talent pool is most likely to congregate.[6] Of course, most large companies post job openings on their own corporate Web sites, usually under a link titled "Careers." Some companies are now posting podcasts that profile the working lives of their different employees, and TMP, a marketing agency, has gone as far as to hold an online career fair inside of the virtual reality Web site Second Life.

Employee Referrals

The recruitment efforts of an organization can be greatly aided by employee referrals, or recommendations from the firm's current employees about potential candidates. In fact, word-of-mouth recommendations are the way most job positions are filled. (Apparently there is truth to the phrase, "It's not what you know, but who you know.") Managers have found that the quality of employee-referred applicants is normally quite high, since employees are generally hesitant to recommend individuals who might not perform well. Companies can also create referral portals on their own Web site with products such as Referred Hire. The software creates a secure domain where employees can log in to recommend friends and professional acquaintances.[7]

There are several suggested ways to increase the effectiveness of employee referral programs be they conveyed online or via word-of-mouth.

- *Up the ante.* Companies pay high commissions to employment agencies and search firms. So why not do the same thing with employees when they provide a good referral? Other recruitment incentives used by organizations include complimentary dinners, discounts on merchandise, all-expenses-paid trips, and free insurance. When employers pay higher bonuses for "hot" skills, employees are more likely to focus on people they know in that area.

- *Pay for performance.* Some firms save part of the referral bonus until the new hire has stayed for six months. This encourages referring employees to help the new hires succeed.

- *Tailor the program.* Companies typically need more of certain types of skills than others, but the referral programs do not always reflect this. Part of a good referral program is educating employees about the kinds of people the organization wants to hire. This includes some communication of the skills required and also a reaffirmation of the values and ethics sought in applicants.

- *Increase visibility.* One of the best ways to publicize a referral program is to celebrate successes. Some companies use novel approaches such as "job of the month" or "celebrity endorsements" from managers. The idea is to keep everyone thinking about bringing in good people.

- *Keep the data.* Even if a referral does not get the job, it might be a good idea to keep the resume on file just in case another vacancy arises.

- *Rethink your taboos.* Some companies are reluctant to take on certain potential hires, such as former employees, relatives, and the like. In a tight labor market, it is a good idea to broaden the search.

- *Widen the program.* Just as it may make sense to consider hiring former employees, it may make sense to ask them for referrals even if they are not candidates for the jobs themselves. A number of companies have mailing lists of "corporate friends" that can be used to seek out potential candidates.

- *Measure results.* No surprise here. After the program is implemented, managers need to take a hard look at the volume of referrals, qualifications of candidates, and success of new hires on the job. These results are then fed back to fine-tune the program.[8]

Some potential negative factors are associated with employee referrals. They include the possibility of corporate "inbreeding" and the violation of EEO regulations. Since employees and their referrals tend to have similar backgrounds, employers who rely heavily on employee referrals to fill job openings may intentionally or unintentionally screen out, and thereby discriminate against, protected classes. Furthermore, organizations may choose not to employ relatives of current employees. The practice of hiring relatives, referred to as nepotism, can invite charges of favoritism, especially in appointments to desirable positions. HR personnel hiring globally, however, need to realize that in other cultures, including Asia and the Middle East, nepotism is the norm. Even in the United States, nepotism gets mixed reviews, in part, because family members are in an ideal position to pass job knowledge and skills on to one another. Many corporate dynasties (Ford Motor Company and the Rockefeller Foundation among them) have been built on nepotism. Labor unions would not have flourished without it. In recent years, a number of law firms and universities have dropped restrictions against hiring spouses on the basis that they are prejudicial.[9]

nepotism

A preference for hiring relatives of current employees

Executive Search Firms

In contrast to public and private employment agencies, which help job seekers find the right job, executive search firms (often called "headhunters") help employers find the right person for a job. Firms such as Korn/Ferry International, Heidrick & Struggles, Mercer & Associates, and the Hunter Group seek out candidates with qualifications that match the requirements of the positions their client firm is seeking to fill. Executive search firms do not advertise in the media for job candidates, nor do they accept a fee from the individual being placed.

The fees charged by search firms can range from anywhere from 25 to 40 percent of the annual salary for the position to be filled. For the recruitment of senior executives, this fee is paid by the client firm, whether or not the recruiting effort results in a hire. It is for this practice that search firms receive the greatest criticism.

Nevertheless, as we noted earlier, hiring new chief executive officers (CEOs) from outside the organization has become commonplace. A large number of these new CEOs are placed in those positions through the services of an executive search firm. However, newer data suggest that CEOs who are promoted from within their organizations actually outperform those hired from the outside. In light of the numerous CEO-related scandals and bankruptcies that have occurred in recent times, human resources personnel are increasingly being called on to demand more from executive search firms and to assist boards of directors in the careful selection of top executives. In some instances, executive search firms have been criticized for selling the "Superman" qualities of outside CEOs—for which firms pay a premium.

THE WALL STREET JOURNAL

"How do you do, sir? My name is John L. Flagman, and I run a successful executive search firm."

Source: From *The Wall Street Journal*—Permission, Cartoon Features Syndicate.

After studying thousands of organizations, Harvard Business School professor Joseph Bower found that CEOs recruited internally know the company and its people but are often blind to the need for radical change. By contrast, CEOs recruited outside the company see the need for change but cannot make it happen because they are unfamiliar with the organization or industry. (Some people believe this is why Bob Nardelli, the former CEO of Home Depot, was unsuccessful when it came to increasing that company's share price.) Bower believes companies need to develop what he calls "inside-outsiders," or internal candidates who have an outside perspective. These employees might have spent much of their time away from the from a company's headquarters or main operations and therefore experienced different opportunities and threats. Bower points out that before A. G. Lafley became the CEO of Procter & Gamble, rather than working in P&G's core detergent business, he worked for years in China building P&G's cosmetics operation there.[10]

Educational Institutions

Educational institutions typically are a source of young applicants with formal training but relatively little full-time work experience. High schools are usually a source of employees for clerical and blue-collar jobs. Community colleges, with their various types of specialized training, can provide candidates for technical jobs. These institutions can also be a source of applicants for a variety of white-collar jobs, including those in the sales and retail fields. Some management trainee jobs are also staffed from this source.

For technical and managerial positions, colleges and universities are generally the primary source. About 30 percent of workers in the United States hold a bachelor's degree—about the same percentage as in 1980. Given these numbers and the strong demand for highly skilled employees, colleges are likely to remain a good recruiting source. In addition, many U.S. universities are setting up campuses overseas. As a result, HR professionals in the coming years will have a new source from which to recruit employees abroad.[11]

Some employers fail to take full advantage of college and university resources because of a poor recruitment program.[12] Consequently, their recruitment efforts fail to attract many potentially good applicants. Another common weakness is the failure to maintain a planned and continuing effort on a long-term basis. Furthermore, some recruiters sent to college campuses are not sufficiently trained or prepared to talk to interested candidates about career opportunities or the requirements of specific openings. This is a grave mistake because research shows that students' perceptions of recruiters have a big impact on the companies for which they choose to work. "It is all about how [students] are treated in the campus recruiting process and the feeling that they get from the people they interact with," says Mary Scott, the founder of a college recruitment consulting firm in West Hartford, Connecticut.

Attempting to visit too many campuses instead of concentrating on selected institutions and the inability to use the campus placement office effectively are other recruiting weaknesses. Mismanaging applicant visits to an organization's headquarters and the failure to follow up with individual candidates or obtain hiring commitments from upper-level managers are among other mistakes that have caused employers to lose well-qualified prospects. To attract high demand graduates, in addition to offering higher pay, firms sometimes employ innovative recruitment techniques such as work-study programs, internships, low-interest loans, and scholarships. Figure 5.1 shows some of the steps firms can take to strengthen their on-campus recruiting relationships.

Using the Internet

All types of media releases, including weekly unemployment figures and special reports, are available at the Department of Labor's Web site. Go to the Student Resources at:

www.cengage.com/
management/bohlander

FIGURE 5.1 Steps for Strengthening a Firm's On-Campus Recruiting Relationships

- Invite professors and advisers to visit your office and take them to lunch.
- Invite them to bring a student group to the office.
- Send press releases and newsletters by mail or e-mail to bring them up to date on the firm's latest news and innovations.
- Provide guest speakers for classes.
- Conduct mock interviews, especially in years when not interviewing for full-time or internship positions.
- Provide scholarships to students.
- Attend the campus career fair, even when the firm is not going to be hiring, so that its name becomes known by the faculty and students.
- Offer job-shadowing programs for students.

Sources: Bruce Busta, D'Arcy Becker, and Jane P. Saly, "Effective Campus Recruiting: The Faculty Perspective," *CPA Journal* 77, no. 7 (July 2007): 62–65; Deborah J. Sessions, "Recruiting Made Easy," *Journal of Accountancy* 201, no. 5 (May 2006): 31–34.

Professional Associations

Many professional associations and societies offer a placement service to members as one of their benefits. Listings of members seeking employment may be advertised in their journals or publicized at their national meetings. A placement center is usually established at national meetings for the mutual benefit of employers and job seekers. The Society for Human Resource Management (SHRM), for example, helps employers and prospective HR employees come together. Mediabistro.com is an association that allows creative people, including editors, writers, television producers, graphic designers, and book publishers, to meet personally and online to showcase their work and hire one another for projects.

Labor Unions

Labor unions have been a principal source of applicants for blue-collar and some professional jobs. Some unions, such as those in the maritime, printing, and construction industries, maintain hiring halls that can provide a supply of applicants, particularly for short-term needs. Employers wishing to use this recruitment source should contact the local union under consideration for employer eligibility requirements and applicant availability.

Public Employment Agencies

Each of the fifty states maintains an employment agency that administers its unemployment insurance program. Many of the state agencies bear such titles as Department of Employment or Department of Human Resources. They are subject to certain regulations and controls administered by the U.S. Employment and Training Administration (ETA).

State agencies maintain local public employment offices in most communities of any size. Individuals who become unemployed must register at one of these offices and be available for "suitable employment" in order to receive their weekly unemployment checks. Consequently, public employment agencies are able to refer to employers with job openings those applicants with the required skills who are available for employment. Most of the local employment offices have a local job bank book published as a daily computer printout. Many of the jobs can also be found on the Web at America's Job Exchange and America's Career InfoNet (ACINet). Employer openings are listed along with other pertinent information, such as number of openings, pay rates, and job specifications. Employment interviewers in an agency can access a list of all job openings in the geographic area for which applicants assigned to them might qualify. Furthermore, applicants looking for a specific job can review the lists and apply directly to organizations with openings.

In addition to matching unemployed applicants with job openings, public employment agencies may assist employers with apprenticeship programs, employment testing, job analysis, evaluation programs, and community wage surveys.

Private Employment and Temporary Agencies

Charging a fee enables private employment agencies to tailor their services to the specific needs of their clients. Snelling Personnel Services, Manpower, Kelly Services, and Olsten Staffing Services are among the largest private employment agencies. However, it is common for agencies to specialize in serving a specific occupational area or professional field. Depending on who is receiving the most service, the fee may be paid by the employer, the job seeker, or both. It is not uncommon for private employment agencies to charge an employer a 25 to 30 percent fee, based on the position's annual salary, if the employer hires an applicant found by the agency.

Private employment agencies differ in the services they offer, their professionalism, and the caliber of their counselors. If counselors are paid on a commission basis, their desire to do a professional job may be offset by their desire to earn a commission. Thus, they may encourage job seekers to accept jobs for which they are not suited. Because of this, job seekers would be wise to take the time to find a recruiter who is knowledgeable, experienced, and professional. When talking with potential recruiters, individuals should discuss openly their philosophies and practices with regard to recruiting strategies, including advertising, in-house recruiting, screening procedures, and costs for these efforts. They should try to find a recruiter who is flexible and who will consider their needs and wants.

In addition to placing permanent workers, many private agencies hire and place workers in temporary positions. An estimated nine out of ten U.S. companies, including both large and small firms, use temporary employees. "Temps" are typically used for short-term assignments or to help when managers cannot justify hiring a full-time employee, such as for vacation fill-ins, for peak work periods, or during an employee's pregnancy leave or sick leave. Increasingly, temps are being employed to fill positions once staffed by permanent employees. This practice adds flexibility because temporaries can be laid off quickly, and with less cost, when work lessens. Some companies use a just-in-time staffing approach in which a core staff of employees is augmented by a trained and highly skilled supplementary workforce. The use of temporaries thus becomes a viable way to maintain proper staffing levels. Also, the employment costs of temporaries are often lower than those of permanent employees because temps are not provided with benefits and can be let go without the need to file unemployment insurance claims.

Because many temporary employees are eventually hired full-time, the practice allows workers and firms to try one another out before a permanent commitment is made. Some companies, however, including Microsoft and FedEx, have encountered legal problems by categorizing permanent workers as "temps" or "independent contractors" in an effort to cut employment costs. To prevent such abuses Congress, the courts, and the U.S. Department of Labor have established criteria that must be followed when it comes to hiring temps. Figure 5.2 shows the largest temporary companies in the United States and the types of temporary employees in which they specialize.

Employee Leasing

Employee leasing by professional employer organizations (PEOs) has grown rapidly since the passage of the Tax Equity and Fiscal Responsibility Act of 1982. As we explained in Chapter 1, today about 700 PEOs oversee two to three million U.S. workers, according to the National Association of Professional Employer Organizations (NAPEO) in Alexandria, Virginia. Basically, a PEO—typically a larger company—takes over the management of a smaller company's HR tasks and becomes a coemployer to its employees. The PEO performs all the HR duties of an employer—recruiting, background checks, hiring, payroll, performance appraisal, benefits administration, and other day-to-day HR activities—and in return is paid a placement fee of normally 4 to 8 percent of payroll cost plus 9 to 20 percent of gross wages. Because PEOs can coemploy a large number of people working at many different companies, they can provide employees with benefits such as 401k and health plans that small companies cannot afford. (The average client of a PEO is a business with nineteen employees.) Unlike temporary agencies, which supply workers only for limited periods, employee leasing companies place their employees with subscribers on a permanent basis. The Society for Human Resource Management reports that companies with fewer than fifty employees can save anywhere from $5,000 to $50,000 in time and labor costs annually by hiring a PEO.[13]

employee leasing
The process of dismissing employees who are then hired by a leasing company (which handles all HR-related activities) and contracting with that company to lease back the employees

---

FIGURE 5.2

Largest Temporary Help Agencies in the United States

ALLEGIS GROUP
www.allegisgroup.com
Technical, industrial, IT, accounting, finance, human resources, sales, legal

EXPRESS PERSONNEL SERVICES
www.expresspersonnel.com
Clerical, accounting, customer service, warehousing, industrial

HUDSON
www.hudson.com
Legal, IT, finance, engineering

KELLY SERVICES
www.kellyservices.com
Office services, accounting, engineering, IT, law, science, marketing, creative services, light industrial, education, health care

MANPOWER
www.manpower.com
Administrative, industrial, IT, engineering, finance, accounting, contact center, skilled trades

RANDSTAD
www.randstad.com
Office, executive office, industrial, technical, call center, finance, accounting

ROBERT HALF INTERNATIONAL
www.rhi.com
Accounting, finance, technical, legal, design/creative, clerical, administrative

TRUEBLUE
www.trueblueinc.com
General labor, light industrial, skilled trades

VEDIOR
www.vedior.com
IT, engineering, accounting, finance, health care, human resources, legal, commercial

VOLT WORKFORCE SOLUTIONS
www.volt.com
Accounting, finance, administrative, call center, creative/design, legal, light industrial, sales, marketing, technical, engineering, IT

The Global Labor Market

As we explained in Chapter 2, companies are no longer simply offshoring work to save labor costs. They are also looking abroad to develop better products around the clock via a global workforce and attract the best talent wherever it may be. Emerging countries such as China and India are also heating up the competition for talent as firms there attempt to staff the burgeoning high-tech industries in these nations. The staffing firm Manpower recently surveyed 36,000 employers in 27 countries around the world and found that 41 percent are having difficulty filling positions due to a lack of suitable talent. It is not just technical positions firms are trying to fill. It is lower-skilled positions, too. Resorts and vacation areas are among the businesses having trouble finding employees to staff their operations. "There aren't enough American teenagers or 20-somethings to fill those service jobs," says Rebecca Wolever of Signature Worldwide, a company that offers employees customer service and sales training.

Recruiting abroad can be very complicated, however. In addition to having to deal with a myriad of local, national, and international laws, employers also have to take into account the different labor costs, preemployment and compensation practices, and cultural differences associated with the countries in which they are recruiting. In volatile areas of the world, security is a concern. Because locals are often unfamiliar with foreign firms and their brands, companies often find the need to develop an employment brand and advertise it to potential recruits. For example, Genpact, a company that helps firms globalize, has set up "storefronts" in eight Indian cities in which it recruits employees. Candidates can walk in and chat with company representatives about what Genpact does and the kinds of opportunities it offers; they can leave their resumes and come back later for voice and accent testing, when necessary.

To help them navigate challenges such as these, many companies utilize firms such as Genpact and Robert Half International, which specialize in global recruiting. These firms help companies address the numerous legal complications associated with obtaining various types of visas and work permits for the foreign workers they are trying to hire. A good starting point for human resources managers looking to hire outside of the United States is *Employees: Handbook on Global Recruiting, Screening, Testing and Interviewing Criteria* by Salvador del Rey and Robert J. Mignin (editors). One chapter is devoted to each of fifty-five nations covered in the reference book and legal guide.

Improving the Effectiveness of External Recruitment

With all of the uncertainties inherent in external recruiting, it is sometimes difficult to determine whether an organization's efforts to locate promising talent are effective and/or cost-efficient. However, managers can do several things to maximize the probability of success. These include calculating yield ratios on recruiting sources, calculating costs of recruitment, training organizational recruiters, and conducting realistic job previews.

Yield Ratios

yield ratio

The percentage of applicants from a recruitment source that make it to the next stage of the selection process

Yield ratios help indicate which recruitment sources are most effective at producing qualified job candidates. Quite simply, a yield ratio is the percentage of applicants from a particular source that make it to the next stage in the selection process. For example, if 100 resumes were obtained from an employment agency and 17 of the applicants submitting those resumes were invited for an on-site interview, the yield ratio for that agency would be 17 percent (17/100). This yield ratio could then be recalculated for each subsequent stage in the selection process (for example, after the interview and again after the final offer), which would result in a cumulative yield ratio. By calculating and comparing yield ratios for each recruitment source, it is possible to find out which sources produce qualified applicants.

Costs of Recruitment

The cost of various recruiting procedures can be computed using a fairly simple set of calculations. For example, the average source cost per hire (SC/H) can be determined by the following formula:

$$\frac{SC}{H} = \frac{AC + AF + RB + NC}{H}$$

where

AC = advertising costs, total monthly expenditure (example: $32,000)
AF = agency fees, total for the month (example: $21,000)
RB = referral bonuses, total paid (example: $2,600)
NC = no-cost hires, walk-ins, nonprofit agencies, etc. (example: $0)
H = total hires (example: 119)

Substituting the example numbers into the formula gives:

$$\frac{SC}{H} = \frac{\$32,000 + \$21,000 + \$2,600 + \$0}{119}$$

$$= \frac{\$55,600}{119}$$

$$= \$467.23 \text{ (source cost of recruits per hire)}$$

When combined with information about yield ratios, these calculations can provide invaluable information to managers about the utility of different approaches to and sources of recruitment. In that way, they can make more informed decisions about both controlling the costs of recruitment and increasing its effectiveness. For example, although advertisements and employee referrals may both yield qualified applicants, managers may find that referral bonuses are a more economical alternative.

Organizational Recruiters

The size of an organization influences who performs the recruitment function. For large employers, professional HR recruiters are typically hired and trained to find new employees. In smaller organizations, recruiting might be done by an HR generalist; if the organization has no HR position, managers and/or supervisors recruit their own employees. At companies such as Macy's and Williams-Sonoma, the members of work teams help select new employees for their groups. Sometimes organizations outsource their recruiting function to a recruiting process outsourcing (RPO) company—especially when it comes to support staff.

Regardless of who does the recruiting, it is imperative that these individuals have a good understanding of the knowledge, skills, abilities, experiences, and other characteristics required for the job. All too often, a new person in the HR department or a line manager is given a recruiting assignment, even before that person has undergone interview training, before he or she fully understands the job being recruiting for, or comprehends the values and goals of the organization. It is important to remember that recruiters significantly influence an applicant's job decision. Because recruiters can often enhance the perceived attractiveness of a job and an organization, they are often a main reason why applicants select one organization over another. On this basis we can conclude that personable, enthusiastic, and competent recruiters have an impact on the success of an organization's recruitment program.

Realistic Job Previews

realistic job preview (RJP)

Informing applicants about all aspects of the job, including both its desirable and undesirable facets

Another way organizations may be able to increase the effectiveness of their recruitment efforts is to provide job applicants with a realistic job preview (RJP). A RJP informs applicants about all aspects of the job, including both its desirable and undesirable facets. In contrast, a typical job preview presents the job in only positive terms. The RJP might also include a tour of the working area, combined with a discussion of any negative health or safety considerations. Proponents of RJPs believe that applicants who are given realistic information regarding a position are more likely to remain on the job and be successful because there will be fewer unpleasant surprises. In fact, a number of research studies on RJPs report these positive results:

- Improved employee job satisfaction
- Reduced voluntary turnover
- Enhanced communication through honesty and openness
- Realistic job expectations

Some companies are taking their realistic job previews online. The bank SunTrust reports cutting its teller recruitment costs in half and upping its retention of tellers by at least 10 percent by doing so. At their own convenience on the Web, SunTrust candidates answer questions and perform various simulated teller tasks, such as looking up account information and entering customer data. Online job previews can help candidates get a better feel for the work than can a written description. They can also help employers screen potentially good candidates.[15]

▪▪ RECRUITING TALENT INTERNALLY

Objective 2

While we typically think about recruiting being focused on attracting potential employees from outside the organization, most managers try to follow a policy of filling job vacancies above the entry-level position through promotions and transfers. By filling vacancies in this way, an organization can capitalize on the investment it has made in recruiting, selecting, training, and developing its current employees, who might look for jobs elsewhere if they lack promotion opportunities. Indeed, experienced employees take with them years of corporate know-how that is hard to replace. Some signs that the firm needs to work harder at grooming internal talent are shown in Figure 5.3. To lessen the chances of losing top performers, some managers actively identify high potential "at risk" employees and take steps to retain these people.[16]

FIGURE
5.3

Warning Signs of a Weak Talent "Bench"

1. It takes a long time to fill key positions.

2. Key positions can be filled only by hiring from the outside.

3. Vacancies in key positions cannot be filled with confidence in the abilities of those chosen for them.

4. Replacements for positions often are unsuccessful in performing their new duties.

5. Promotions are made on the basis of whim, favoritism, or nepotism.

Source: Adapted from William Rothwell, *Effective Succession Planning* (New York: AMACOM, 2000).

Advantages and Limitations of Recruiting from Within

Promotion-from-within policies at Marriott, Nordstrom's, Nucor Steel, and Whole Foods have contributed to the companies' overall growth and success.[17] Promoting employees rewards them for past performance and is intended to encourage them to continue their efforts. It also gives other employees a reason to believe that if they perform similarly, they will be promoted, too. This can improve morale within the organization and support a culture of employee engagement. This may be particularly true for members of protected classes who have encountered difficulties in finding employment and have often faced even greater difficulty in advancing within an organization. The connection is so important that most organizations have integrated promotion policies as an essential part of their EEO/AA programs.

If an organization's promotion policy is to have maximum motivational value, employees must be made aware of that policy. The following is an example of a policy statement that an organization might prepare.

> "Promotion from within" is generally recognized as a foundation of good employment practice, and it is the policy of our organization to promote from within whenever possible when filling a vacancy. The job vacancy will be posted for five calendar days to give all qualified full- and part-time personnel an equal opportunity to apply.

While a transfer lacks the motivational value of a promotion, it sometimes can serve to protect employees from layoffs or broaden their job experiences. Furthermore, the transferred employee's familiarity with the organization and its operations can eliminate the orientation and training costs that recruitment from the outside would entail. Most important, the transferee's performance record is likely to be a more accurate predictor of the candidate's success than the data gained about outside applicants.

Side by side with the potential advantages of internal recruitment, managers need to be aware of potential limitations as well. For example, jobs that require specialized training and experience cannot be easily filled from within the organization and may need to be filled from the outside. This is especially common in small organizations where the existing talent pool is limited. Also, for certain openings it may be necessary or advantageous to hire individuals from the outside who have gained from another employer the knowledge and expertise required for these jobs.

Even though a company's HR policy might encourage job openings to be filled from within the organization, potential candidates from the outside should be considered in order to prevent the "inbreeding" of ideas and attitudes. Indeed, excessive reliance on internal sources can create the risk of "employee cloning." Applicants hired from the outside, particularly for certain technical and managerial positions, can be a source of creativity and innovation, and may bring with them the latest knowledge acquired from their previous employers.

From a different perspective, it is not uncommon for firms to attempt to gain secrets from their competitors by hiring away their employees. Procter & Gamble sued a rival papermaker when it hired former employees who had a great deal of knowledge about the making of Charmin toilet paper and Bounty paper towels—both P&G products. Amazon.com was sued by Wal-Mart, which accused it of hiring away employees who had in-depth knowledge about Wal-Mart's sophisticated inventory systems.[18]

Methods for Identifying Qualified Candidates

Objective 3

The effective use of internal sources requires a system for locating qualified job candidates and for enabling those who consider themselves qualified to apply for the opening. Qualified job candidates within the organization can be located in a number of ways, which we discuss next.

Inventorying Management Talent

As we discussed in Chapter 2, more firms are electronically capturing the qualifications of each of their employees and using this information to identify potential candidates for available jobs. Companies such as PeopleSoft and SAP are leaders in developing automated staffing and skills management software. Similar to the skills inventories mentioned earlier, these information systems allow an organization to rapidly screen its entire workforce to locate suitable candidates to fill an internal opening. These data can also be used to predict the career paths of employees and to anticipate when and where promotion opportunities might arise.[19]

Skill inventories are an important tool for succession planning. They provide an indication of the skills employees have as well as their interests and experiences. In this way, they help managers pay better attention to the developmental needs of employees, both in their present jobs and in managerial jobs to which they may be promoted. An equally important part of this process is identifying high potential employees who may be groomed as replacements for managers who are reassigned, retire, or otherwise vacate a position. At GE, for every position at or above a director level, two or three people are usually identified who can easily step in when the current jobholder moves on.[20]

Job Posting and Bidding

job posting and bidding

Posting vacancy notices and maintaining lists of employees looking for upgraded positions

Organizations communicate information about job openings through a process referred to as job posting and bidding. The jobs are frequently posted on a firm's Intranet or on regular bulletin boards where employees congregate. Job openings can also be announced in employee publications, special handouts, direct mail, and public address messages. Many companies have developed online job posting systems whereby employees looking for upgraded positions can post their names, resumes, and the positions in which they are interested. As a position becomes available, the list of employees seeking that position is retrieved, and the records of these employees are reviewed to select possible candidates for interviews. The employees can be electronically notified about interview schedules and track their progress electronically through the various hiring stages.[21] Job bidding is more effective when it is part of a career development program in which employees are made aware of the opportunities available to them within the organization. For example, HR departments can provide new employees with information on the progression of employees doing their particular jobs, training requirements for each job, and skills and abilities they need to advance within their organizations.

Identifying Talent through Performance Appraisals

Performance appraisals are discussed more fully in Chapter 8. For our purposes here, we want to note that managers measure and evaluate employee performance for several reasons, none of which is more important than making promotion and career decisions. Successful performers are often good candidates for a promotion. In contrast, poorly performing employees may need—and benefit from—a transfer to another area or even a demotion or, in a worst case scenario, termination.

But performance appraisals are not just used for "racking and stacking" the best talent. Identifying and developing all employees is a role that all managers should take seriously. As they conduct formal appraisals, they should be concerned with their subordinates' potential for managerial or advanced technical jobs and encourage their growth in that direction. In addition to immediate managers, others in the organization should have the power to evaluate, nominate, and sponsor employees with promise. A tool called a **9-box grid** is helping firms such as General Mills and others do this by allowing appraisal and assessment data to be compiled into a single visual reference. The grid is a comparative diagram that allows managers to readily see both an employee's actual performance as well as potential performance. This can then help managers determine what the developmental needs of the employee are and what the person's next steps within the organization might be. Figure 5.4 is an example of a 9-box grid.

9-box grid

A comparative diagram that includes appraisal and assessment data to allow managers to easily see an employee's actual and potential performance.

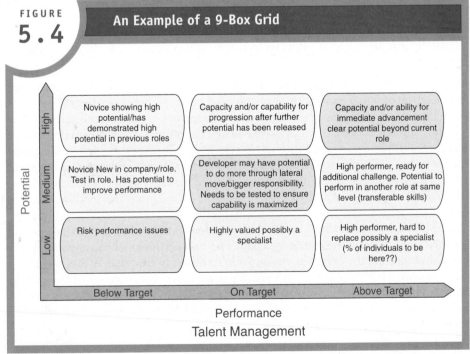

FIGURE 5.4

An Example of a 9-Box Grid

	Below Target	On Target	Above Target
Potential — High	Novice showing high potential/has demonstrated high potential in previous roles	Capacity and/or capability for progression after further potential has been released	Capacity and/or ability for immediate advancement clear potential beyond current role
Potential — Medium	Novice New in company/role. Test in role. Has potential to improve performance	Developer may have potential to do more through lateral move/bigger responsibility. Needs to be tested to ensure capability is maximized	High performer, ready for additional challenge. Potential to perform in another role at same level (transferable skills)
Potential — Low	Risk performance issues	Highly valued possibly a specialist	High performer, hard to replace possibly a specialist (% of individuals to be here??)

Performance

Talent Management

Source: © RapidBI.com 2000–2008

Using Assessment Centers

There are other very effective ways to assess a person's career potential. Pioneered in the mid-1950s by Douglas Bray and his associates at AT&T, assessment centers are considered one of the most valuable and time-honored methods for evaluating personnel. An **assessment center** is a process (not a place) by which individuals are evaluated as they participate in a series of situations that resemble what they might be called on to handle on the job. The popularity of the assessment center can be attributed to its capacity for increasing an organization's ability to select employees who will perform successfully in management positions or to assist and promote the development of skills for their current position. The centers use a variety of methods, including in-basket exercises, leaderless group discussions, and other approaches.

- *In-basket exercises.* This method is used to simulate a problem situation. The participants are given several documents, each describing some problem or situation requiring an immediate response. They are thus forced to make decisions under the pressure of time and also to determine what priority to give each problem.

- *Leaderless group discussions.* With this activity, trainees are gathered in a conference setting to discuss an assigned topic, either with or without designated group roles. The participants are given little or no instruction in how to approach the topic, nor are they told what decision to reach. Leaderless group trainees are evaluated on their initiative, leadership skills, and ability to work effectively in a group setting.

- *Role-playing.* The exercise might involve preparing for and engaging in a customer meeting or a team leader meeting with one's subordinates. A trained assessor then assesses the participant using a structured rating scale.

- *Behavioral interviews.* The interviewer asks the participant a series of question about what he or she would do in particular work circumstances. Sometimes behavioral interviews are combined with videos showing work simulations, and participants are asked at intervals to make choices about what they would do in the situations shown.

At the end of the assessment center period, the assessors' observations are combined to develop an overall picture of the strengths and needs of the participants. A report is normally submitted to senior management, and feedback is given to the participants.

Before an assessment is run, however, the characteristics or dimensions to be studied should be determined through job analyses. The exercises used in the center should reflect the job for which the person is being evaluated.[22] Although assessment centers have proved quite valuable in identifying managerial talent and in helping with the development of individuals, it should be noted that the method tends to favor those who are strong in interpersonal skills and have the ability to influence others. Some individuals find it difficult to perform at their best in a situation that for them is as threatening as taking a test. The manner in which assessment center personnel conduct the exercises and provide feedback to the participants will play a major role in determining how individuals react to the experience. On the upside, after having been assessed, candidates are more likely to have a good idea of the job's requirements and be more willing to accept the firm's decision about who gets promoted.

assessment center

A process by which individuals are evaluated as they participate in a series of situations that resemble what they might be called on to handle on the job

CAREER MANAGEMENT: DEVELOPING TALENT OVER TIME

While we can think of recruitment as a stand-alone activity, limited to a single job at a single point in time, often this is not the case. Inevitably decisions about talent—regardless of whether they pertain to recruiting, transferring, promoting, developing, or deploying people—need to be considered within the context of long-term priorities of the business and the employees. Increasingly, managers are not making these decisions on a "one-off" basis, but rather as part of a comprehensive approach to career management.

Integrating career development with other HR programs creates synergies in which all aspects of HR reinforce one another. Figure 5.5 illustrates how HR structures

4 Objective

FIGURE 5.5

HR's Role in Career Management

THE GOAL: MATCH INDIVIDUAL AND ORGANIZATION NEEDS 1

The Goal: Matching

- Encourage employee ownership of career.
- Create a supportive context.
- Communicate direction of company.
- Establish mutual goal setting and planning.

IDENTIFY CAREER OPPORTUNITIES & REQUIREMENTS 2

Opportunities & Requirements

- Identify future competency needs.
- Establish job progressions/career paths.
- Balance promotions, transfers, exits, etc.
- Establish dual career paths.

INSTITUTE CAREER DEVELOPMENT INITIATIVES 4

Career Development Initiatives

- Provide workbooks and workshops.
- Provide career counseling.
- Provide career self-management training.
- Give developmental feedback.

GAUGE EMPLOYEE POTENTIAL 3

Gauge Employee Potential

- Measure competencies (appraisals).
- Establish talent inventories.
- Establish succession plans.
- Use assessment centers.

relate to some of the essential aspects of the career management process. For example, to plan their careers, employees need organizational information—information that strategic planning, forecasting, succession planning, and skills inventories can provide. Similarly, as they obtain information about themselves and use it in career planning, employees need to know the career paths within the organization and how management views their performance.[23]

The Goal: Matching Individual and Organizational Needs

In the final analysis, a career development program should be viewed as a dynamic process that matches the needs of the organization with the needs of employees. Each party has a distinctive role to play.

The Employee's Role

Although some firms play a role in the planning of their employees' careers, ultimately, employees are responsible for initiating and managing their own career planning. Because having a successful career involves creating your own career path—not just following a path that has been established by the organization—it is up to each individual to identify his or her own knowledge, skills, abilities, interests, and values and seek out information about career options in order to set goals and develop career plans. Managers should encourage employees to take responsibility for their own careers. However, they should also offer them continual feedback about their performance and provide them with self-assessment tools, training, and information about the organization and possible career paths within it. General Motors, for example, has prepared a career development guide that groups jobs by fields of work such as engineering, manufacturing, communications, data processing, financial, HR, and scientific. These categories give employees an understanding of the career possibilities in the various fields.

The Organization's Role: Establishing a Favorable Career Development Climate

If career development is to succeed, it must receive the complete support of top management. Ideally, senior line managers and HR department managers should work together to design and implement a career development system. The system should reflect the goals and culture of the organization, and the HR philosophy should be woven throughout. A HR philosophy can provide employees with a clear set of expectations and directions for their own career development. For a program to be effective, managerial personnel at all levels must be trained in the fundamentals of job design, performance appraisal, career planning, and counseling. One of the most important indicators of managerial support is *mentoring*, either formally as part of an ongoing program or informally as merely a kind gesture to a less experienced employee. Dealing with uncertainty is one of the biggest challenges any individual faces in his or her career, so receiving advice from someone who has gone through similar experiences can be invaluable. We devote an entire section to mentoring later in this chapter.

Blending Individual and Organizational Goals

Of course, a career development program should be based on the organization's needs as well. As Figure 5.6 shows, the organization's needs should be linked with the individual career needs of its employees in a way that improves the effectiveness

FIGURE 5.6 Balancing Individual and Organizational Needs

of workers and their satisfaction as well as achieving the firm's strategic objectives. Before a firm's employees can engage in meaningful career planning, however, not only must they have an awareness of the organization's philosophy, but they must also have a good understanding of the organization's more immediate goals. Otherwise, they might plan for personal change and growth without knowing whether or how their own goals match those of the organization. For example, if the technology of a business is changing and new skills are needed, will the organization retrain its employees to meet this need or hire new talent? Is there growth, stability, or decline in the number of employees needed? How will turnover affect this need? Clearly, an organizational plan that answers these kinds of questions is essential for people's career planning.

At the same time, it would be unrealistic to expect that employees can establish their career goals with *perfect* certainty about where they are going. People change over time, and because of that, their needs and interests change. Similarly, organizations also change their directions and adjust their strategies to cope with change. So while goal setting is critical, building in some flexibility is probably a good idea.

Identifying Career Opportunities and Requirements

While talent management integrates a number of related HR activities, those who direct the process have to keep a steady watch on the needs and requirements of the organization. This involves an analysis of the competencies required for jobs, progression among related jobs, and supply of ready (and potential) talent available to fill those jobs. A variety of approaches can be used to do this, including surveys,

5 | Objective

informal group discussions, and interviews. The process should involve personnel from different groups, such as new employees, managers, longtime employees,
minority employees, and technical and professional employees. Identifying the needs
and problems of these groups provides the starting point for the organization's career
development efforts.

Begin with a Competency Analysis

It is important for an organization to study its jobs carefully in order to identify and
assign weights to the knowledge and skills that each one requires. This can be achieved
with job analysis and evaluation systems such as those used in compensation programs.
The system used at Sears measures three basic competencies for each job: know-how,
problem-solving, and accountability. Know-how is broken down into three types
of job knowledge: technical, managerial, and human relations. Problem-solving and
accountability also have several dimensions. Scores for each of these three major
competencies are assigned to each job, and a total value is computed for each job. For
any planned job transfer, the amount of increase (or decrease) the next job represents
in each of the skill areas, as well as in the total point values, can be computed. This
information is then used to make certain that a transfer to a different job is a move
that requires growth on the part of the employee.

Sears designs career development paths to provide the following experiences:
(1) an increase in at least one skill area on each new assignment, (2) an increase of
at least 10 percent in total points on each new assignment, and (3) assignments in
several different functional areas.[24]

Identify Job Progressions

job progressions

The hierarchy of jobs a new
employee might experience,
ranging from a starting job
to jobs that successively
require more knowledge
and/or skill

career paths

Lines of advancement in an
occupational field within
an organization

Once the skill demands of jobs are identified and weighted according to their importance, it is then possible to plan job progressions. A new employee with no experience is typically assigned to a "starting job." After a period of time in that job, the
employee can be promoted to one that requires more knowledge and/or skill. While
most organizations concentrate on developing job progressions for managerial,
professional, and technical jobs, progressions can be developed for all categories of
jobs. These job progressions then can serve as a basis for developing career paths—the
lines of advancement within an organization—for individuals. Figure 5.7 illustrates
a typical line of advancement in the human resources area of a large multinational
corporation. It is apparent that one must be prepared to move geographically in order
to advance very far in the human resources department of this firm. This would also
be true of other career fields within the organization.

Although these analyses can be quite helpful to employees—and are perhaps
essential for organizations—a word of caution is appropriate here. Many successful
careers are not this methodical, nor do they proceed in a lockstep manner. In today's
working world, career progressions often occur as much through creating and capitalizing on arising opportunities as they do through rational planning. So while it is a
good idea for organizations to map out a career path and individuals would do well to
establish a strategy for advancement, many successful individuals readily admit that
their career paths are quite idiosyncratic to their circumstances. These people often
note that they have been fortunate to be "in the right place at the right time." Other
people's careers progress quite linearly. Highlights in HRM 2 shows an example of
such a career—the career path of Jeffrey Immelt, CEO of General Electric.

FIGURE
5.7

Typical Line of Advancement in HR Management

				Vice president, HR
			Corporate HR director	
		Corporate HR manager	Division HR director	
		Asst. division HR director		
	Regional HR manager	Plant HR manager		
	Asst. plant HR manager			
Regional HR associate	HR supervisor			
HR associate				

Recognize Lots of Possibilities

Career development and planning systems were once primarily focused on promotions and hierarchical advancement. However, in today's flatter organizations and more dynamic work environment, an individual's career advancement can occur along several different paths: transfers, demotions—even exits—and promotions. HR policies have to be flexible enough to adapt as well as helpful enough to support the career change.

A promotion is a change of assignment to a job at a higher level in the organization. The new job normally provides an increase in pay and status and demands more skill or carries more responsibility. Promotions enable an organization to utilize the skills and abilities of its personnel more effectively, and the opportunity to gain a promotion serves as an incentive for good performance. The three principal criteria for determining promotions are merit, seniority, and potential. Often the problem is to determine how much consideration to give to each factor. A common problem in organizations that promote primarily on past performance and seniority is called the Peter Principle. This refers to the situation in which individuals are promoted as long as they have done a good job in their previous job. The trouble is this continues until someone does poorly in his or her new job. Then he or she is no longer promoted. This results in people being promoted to their level of incompetence. There are other intrafirm challenges related to promotions. Sometimes extremely good employees are prevented from being promoted to other departments because their current managers are reluctant to lose them. At other firms, an employee who

promotion
A change of assignment to a job at a higher level in the organization

HIGHLIGHTS IN HRM

2

Career Path of Jeffrey Immelt, CEO, General Electric

1982	Enters GE's Commercial Leadership Program
1983	Manager of Business Development/GTX Product Management, GE Plastics
1984	Manager of Dallas District Sales, GE Plastics
1986	General Manager of Western Region Sales, GE Plastics
1987	General Manager of New Business Development and Marketing Development, GE Plastics
1989	Vice President of Consumer Service, GE Appliances
1991	Vice President of Worldwide Marketing and Product Management, GE Appliances
1992	Vice President of Commercial Division, GE Plastics Americas
1993	Vice President and General Manager, GE Plastics Americas
1997	President and CEO, GE Medical Systems
2000	President, GE
2001	CEO, GE

Source: Christopher A. Bartlett and Andrew McLean, "GE's Talent Machine: The Making of a CEO," *Harvard Business School Press* (May 5, 2004).

tries, but fails, to advance to a position in another department is earmarked for the next round of layoffs.[25]

In flatter organizations, there are fewer promotional opportunities; so many individuals find career advancement through lateral moves. A **transfer** is the placement of an employee in another job for which the duties, responsibilities, status, and remuneration are approximately equal to those of the previous job (although as an incentive, organizations may offer a salary adjustment). Individuals who look forward to change or want a chance to learn more may seek out transfers. In addition, transfers frequently provide a broader foundation for individuals to prepare them for an eventual promotion. A transfer may require the employee to change work group, workplace, work shift, or organizational unit; it may even necessitate moving to another geographic area. Transfers make it possible for an organization to place its employees in jobs where there is a greater need for their services and where they can acquire new knowledge and skills.

A downward transfer, or *demotion*, moves an individual into a lower-level job that can provide developmental opportunities. Although such a move is ordinarily considered unfavorable, some individuals actually may request it in order to return to their "technical roots." It is not uncommon, for example, for organizations to appoint temporary leaders (especially in team environments) with the proviso that they will eventually step down from this position to resume their former position.

transfer

Placement of an individual in another job for which the duties, responsibilities, status, and remuneration are approximately equal to those of the previous job

Transfers, promotions, and demotions require individuals to adjust to new job demands and usually to a different work environment. A transfer that involves moving to a new location within the United States or abroad places greater demands on an employee because it requires that employee to adapt not only to a new work environment, but also to new living conditions. The employee with a family has the added responsibility of helping family members adjust to the new living arrangements. Even though some employers provide all types of relocation services—including covering moving expenses, helping to sell a home, and providing cultural orientation and language training—there is always some loss of productive time. Pretransfer training, whether related to job skills or to lifestyle, has been suggested as one of the most effective ways to reduce lost productivity.

When you consider the numerous changes that may accompany a career move within an organization, it should not surprise you that many individuals are opting to accept career changes that involve *organizational exit*. Given limited career opportunities within firms, coupled with the need for talent in other companies, many individuals are discovering that their best career options may involve switching companies or working for themselves as freelancers, consultants, or entrepreneurs.

While some employees leave voluntarily, other employees are forced to leave. Even so, many organizations now provide outplacement services to help terminated employees find a job elsewhere. These services can be used to enhance a productive employee's career as well as to terminate an employee who is unproductive. If an organization cannot meet its career development responsibilities to its productive workers, HR policy should provide for assistance to be given them in finding more suitable career opportunities elsewhere. Jack Welch, the former chairman of General Electric, was one of the first executives to make a commitment to employees that while the company could no longer guarantee lifetime employment, it would try to ensure *employability*. That is, GE has committed to providing employees with the skills and support they would need to find a job in another organization.[26]

relocation services
Services provided to an employee who is transferred to a new location, which might include help in moving, selling a home, orienting to a new culture, and/or learning a new language

outplacement services
Services provided by organizations to help terminated employees find a new job

Consider Dual Career Paths for Employees

One of the most obvious places where career paths have been changing is in technical and professional areas. One of the ironies of organizations in the past has been that the most successful engineers, scientists, and professionals were often promoted right out of their area of specialization into management. Instead of doing what they were good at, they were promoted into a job they often did not understand and often did not enjoy. It has become apparent that there must be another way to compensate such individuals without elevating them to a management position. The solution has been to develop dual career paths, or tracks, that provide for progression in special areas such as information technology, finance, marketing, and engineering, with compensation that is comparable to that received by managers at different levels. As we explained in Chapter 2, Microsoft offers software engineers both a management-focused and technical-specialist career track and allows them to move back and forth between the two.

Consider the Boundaryless Career

A generation ago, career success was synonymous with ascending a corporate hierarchy over the course of a lifetime spent in a single firm. Today, however, individuals pursuing *boundaryless careers* may prefer to see themselves as self-directed "free agents" who develop a portfolio of employment opportunities by proactively moving from employer to employer, simultaneously developing and utilizing their marketable skills. As shown in Figure 5.8 it is possible to map the different career profiles. Employees pursuing boundaryless careers develop their human capital along dimensions of industry and occupational knowledge. That is, they may be experts in computer programming or have great insights into trends in the banking industry. In contrast, individuals pursuing more traditional careers develop their knowledge in ways specific to a given firm.

Both approaches can be beneficial, but they are not the same. Under the boundaryless career model, success depends on continually learning new skills, developing new relationships, and capitalizing on existing skills and relationships. These individuals place a premium on flexibility and the capacity to do several different types of tasks, learn new jobs, adjust quickly to different group settings and organizational cultures, and move from one firm, occupation, or industry to another. Their employment security depends on their marketable skills rather than their dedication to one organization over time. A number of studies have shown that people with boundaryless careers find them very satisfying. Organizations can also benefit from boundaryless careers because it allows them to attract top talent from all over the world on a project-by-project basis.[27]

Track Career Stages

A person's knowledge, skills, abilities, and attitudes as well as career aspirations change as one matures. While the work that individuals in different occupations perform can vary significantly, the challenges and frustrations that they face at the

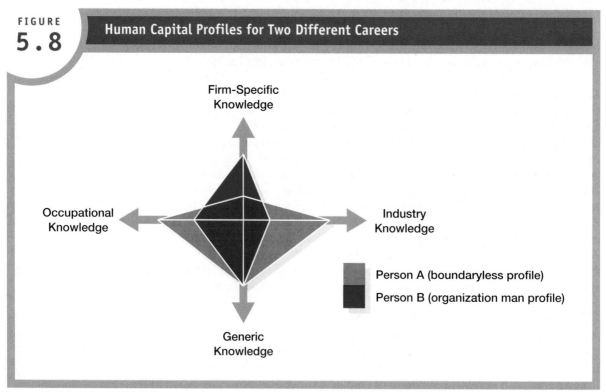

FIGURE 5.8

Human Capital Profiles for Two Different Careers

Source: Scott Snell, Cornell University.

same stage in their careers are remarkably similar. A model describing these stages is shown in Figure 5.9. The stages are: (1) preparation for work, (2) organizational entry, (3) early career, (4) midcareer, and (5) late career. The typical age range and the major tasks of each stage are also presented in the figure.

The first stage—preparation for work—encompasses the period prior to entering an organization, often extending until age 25. It is a period in which individuals must acquire the knowledge, abilities, and skills they will need to compete in the marketplace. It is a time when careful planning, based on sound information, should be the focus. The second stage, typically from ages 18 to 25, is devoted to soliciting job offers and selecting an appropriate job. During this period, one may also be involved in preparing for work. The next three stages entail fitting into a chosen occupation and organization, modifying goals, making choices, remaining productive, and finally, preparing for retirement. In the remainder of the chapter we will examine some of

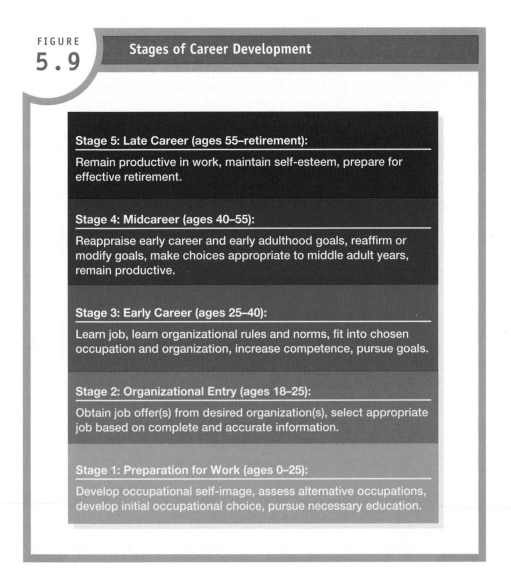

FIGURE 5.9 Stages of Career Development

Stage 5: Late Career (ages 55–retirement):
Remain productive in work, maintain self-esteem, prepare for effective retirement.

Stage 4: Midcareer (ages 40–55):
Reappraise early career and early adulthood goals, reaffirm or modify goals, make choices appropriate to middle adult years, remain productive.

Stage 3: Early Career (ages 25–40):
Learn job, learn organizational rules and norms, fit into chosen occupation and organization, increase competence, pursue goals.

Stage 2: Organizational Entry (ages 18–25):
Obtain job offer(s) from desired organization(s), select appropriate job based on complete and accurate information.

Stage 1: Preparation for Work (ages 0–25):
Develop occupational self-image, assess alternative occupations, develop initial occupational choice, pursue necessary education.

the activities of primary concern to the student, who is likely to be in the early stages. Retirement planning will be discussed in Chapter 11.

Avoid the Plateau Trap

Author Judith Bardwick was the first to label the "plateauing" phenomenon.[28] A career plateau is a situation in which for either organizational or personal reasons the probability of moving up the career ladder is low. According to Bardwick, only 1 percent of the labor force will not plateau in their working lives. There are three types of plateaus: structural, content, and life. A *structural plateau* marks the end of promotions; one will now have to leave the organization to find new opportunities and challenges. A *content plateau* occurs when a person has learned a job too well and is bored with day-to-day activities. A *life plateau* is more profound and may feel like a midlife crisis. People who experience life plateaus often have allowed work or some other major factor to become the most significant aspect of their lives, and they experience a loss of identity and self-esteem when there is no longer success in that area. Figure 5.10 lists some probing questions employees can ask themselves if they find themselves in, or trying to overcome, a career plateau.

Organizations can help individuals cope with plateaus by providing them with opportunities for lateral growth or allowing them to choose their own assignments when opportunities for advancement do not exist. Companies with international divisions can encourage employees to take assignments abroad to expand their horizons. Career enrichment programs can help people learn more about what gives them satisfaction within a company, as well as what kinds of opportunities will make them happiest if they go elsewhere.

Career Development Initiatives

Although career management involves a good deal of analysis and planning, the reality is that it needs to provide a set of tools and techniques that help employees gauge their potential for success in the organization. Informal counseling by HR staff and supervisors is used widely. As we mentioned earlier in the chapter, many

career plateau

A situation in which for either organizational or personal reasons the probability of moving up the career ladder is low

FIGURE 5.10

Career Plateau Questions

1. Do I accept high visibility assignments?
2. Do I continue to advance my education, both formal and vocational?
3. Am I recognized by other leaders in my organization?
4. Am I routinely promoted?
5. Am I known as a versatile employee?
6. Do I continue to get larger-than-normal raises?
7. Do I rate at the high end of the performance ratings?
8. Do I have a plan with measurable objectives, and have I updated it recently?

Source: John Rosche, "Who's Managing Your Career?" *Contract Management* 44, no. 2 (February 2004): 20–22.

organizations give their employees information on educational assistance, EEO/AA programs and policies, salary administration, and job requirements. Career planning workbooks and workshops are also popular means of helping employees identify their potential and the strength of their interests.

In a study undertaken by the human resources consulting firm Drake Beam Morin, the six most successful career management practices used within organizations are as follows:

- Placing clear expectations on employees so that they know what is expected of them throughout their careers with the organization.

- Giving employees the opportunity to transfer to other office locations, both domestically and internationally.

- Providing a clear and thorough succession plan to employees.

- Encouraging performance through rewards and recognition.

- Giving employees the time and resources they need to consider short- and long-term career goals.

- Encouraging employees to continually assess their skills and career direction.

In contrast, organizations also need to be mindful of the internal barriers that inhibit employees' career advancement. Generally, these barriers can include such things as the following:

- Lack of time, budgets, and resources for employees to plan their careers and to undertake training and development.

- Rigid job specifications, lack of leadership support for career management, and a short-term focus.

- Lack of career opportunities and pathways within the organization for employees.[29]

Career Planning Workbooks

Several organizations have prepared workbooks to guide their employees individually through systematic self-assessment of values, interests, abilities, goals, and personal development plans. General Motors' *Career Development Guide* contains a section called "What Do You Want Your Future to Be?" in which the employee makes a personal evaluation. General Electric has developed an extensive set of career development programs, including workbooks to help employees explore life issues that affect career decisions.

Some organizations prefer to use workbooks written for the general public. Popular ones include Richard N. Bolles's *What Color Is Your Parachute?*, *Luck Is No Accident: Making the Most of Happenstance in Your Life and Career* by John D. Krumboltz and Al S. Levin, and *Self-Directed* by John Holland.[30] These same books are recommended to students for help in planning their careers.

Career Planning Workshops

Workshops offer experiences similar to those provided by workbooks. However, they have the advantage of providing a chance to compare and discuss attitudes, concerns, and plans with others in similar situations. Some workshops focus on current job performance and development plans. Others deal with broader life and career plans and values.

As mentioned earlier, employees should be encouraged to assume responsibility for their own careers. A career workshop can help them do that. It can also help them learn how to make career decisions, set career goals, create career options, seek career planning information, and at the same time build confidence and self-esteem.[31]

Career Counseling

career counseling

The process of discussing with employees their current job activities and performance, personal and career interests and goals, personal skills, and suitable career development objectives

Career counseling involves talking with employees about their current job activities and performance, personal and career interests and goals, personal skills, and suitable career development objectives. While some organizations make counseling a part of the annual performance appraisal, career counseling is usually voluntary. Career counseling may be provided by the HR staff, managers and supervisors, specialized staff counselors, or outside consultants. Several techniques for career counseling are outlined at the end of this chapter. (See the chapter Appendix titled Personal Career Development.) As employees approach retirement, they may be encouraged to participate in preretirement programs, which often include counseling along with other helping activities. Preretirement programs will be discussed in Chapter 11.

One interesting development in recent years has been the establishment of the Workforce Investment Act of 1998, which set up "one-stop" service centers in cooperation among businesses and local governments to provide job seekers with a variety of services, including career counseling, skill assessments, training, job search assistance, and referrals to related programs and services. For example, the Northside Workforce Center, based in Fort Worth, Texas, is one of hundreds of nonprofit career centers across the country where unemployed and underemployed workers can apply for unemployment and training benefits, meet with career counselors and veteran's reps, mail and fax resumes to prospective employers free of charge, and gain access to child care. In addition, the American Society for Training and Development (ASTD) publishes a federal training assistance guide that has information on more than 200 federal grants and other assistance programs that can be used for workforce training and development.[32]

Determining Individual Development Needs

Because the requirements of each position and the qualifications of each person are different, no two individuals will have identical developmental needs. For one individual, self-development may consist of developing the ability to write reports, give talks, and lead conferences. For another, it may require developing interpersonal skills in order to communicate and relate more effectively with a diverse workforce. Periodic performance appraisals can provide a basis for determining each employee's progress. Meetings with the employee in which these appraisals are discussed are an essential part of self-improvement efforts.

fast-track program

A program that encourages young managers with high potential to remain with an organization by enabling them to advance more rapidly than those with less potential

In helping individuals plan their careers, it is important for organizations to recognize that younger employees today seek meaningful training assignments that are interesting and involve challenge, responsibility, and a sense of empowerment. They also have a greater concern for the contribution that their work in the organization will make to society. Unfortunately, they are frequently given responsibilities they view as rudimentary, boring, and composed of too many "make-work" activities. Some organizations are attempting to retain young managers with high potential by offering a fast-track program that enables them to advance more rapidly than those with less potential. A fast-track program can provide for a relatively rapid progression—lateral transfers or promotions—through a number of managerial positions designed to expose the employee to different functions within the organization.

Mentoring

It is common to hear people mention individuals at work who influenced them. They frequently refer to their immediate managers who were especially helpful as career developers. But they also mention others at higher levels in the organization who provided them with guidance and support in the development of their careers. Executives and managers who coach, advise, and encourage employees are called mentors.

A mentoring relationship need not be formal. In reality, informal mentoring goes on daily within every type of organization. Generally, the mentor initiates the relationship, but sometimes an employee will approach a potential mentor for advice. Most mentoring relationships develop over time on an informal basis. They frequently end that that way, too. However, proactive organizations emphasize formal mentoring plans that assign a mentor to employees considered for upward movement in the organization. GE, for example, selects the top 20 percent of its performers and allows these people to choose their own mentors from a list of top executives. Under a good mentor, learning focuses on goals, opportunities, expectations, standards, and assistance in fulfilling one's potential. Microsoft, Boeing, Hewlett-Packard, Intel, Southwest Airlines, and State Farm Insurance are among the many companies with mentoring programs.[33]

mentors
Individuals who coach, advise, and encourage individuals of lesser rank

FIGURE
5.11

Top Ten Myths about Mentors

Myth 1: *Mentors exist only for career development.* Sometimes the mentor focuses on formal career development. Sometimes the mentor is teacher, counselor, and friend. Some mentors assume all these roles. This enhances both personal and professional development.

Myth 2: *You need only one mentor.* We can have multiple mentors in our lives. Different mentors provide different things and tap different facets of our lives.

Myth 3: *Mentoring is a one-way process.* Learning flows both ways. The mentor often learns from the protégé, so the growth is reciprocal.

Myth 4: *A mentor has to be older than the protégé.* Age does not matter. Experience and wisdom matter. Do not deprive yourself of learning opportunities from others who have rich experiences.

Myth 5: *A mentor has to be the same gender and race as the protégé.* The purpose of mentoring is to learn. Do not deprive yourself. Seek mentors who are different from you.

Myth 6: *Mentor relationships just happen.* Being in the right place at the right time can help, but the key to selecting a good mentor is what (not whom) you need. Do not be afraid to actively seek a mentor.

Myth 7: *Highly profiled people make the best mentors.* Prestige and success can be good, but good advice, leadership styles, work ethics, and the like vary by individuals. Good mentors are people who challenge you according to your needs, readiness, and aspirations.

Myth 8: *Once a mentor, always a mentor.* Over time, the mentor should pull back and let the protégé go his or her own way. Although the two may maintain contact, the relationship changes over time.

Myth 9: *Mentoring is a complicated process.* The most complicated part is getting out of a bad mentor relationship. If the relationship is not productive, find a tactful way to disengage.

Myth 10: *Mentor-protégé expectations are the same for everyone.* Individuals seek mentors for the same reasons: resources, visibility, enhanced skills, and counsel. But each individual brings different expectations. The key is understanding where the protégé is now, not where he or she should be.

The top ten myths about mentors are shown in Figure 5.11. Figure 5.12 shows a list of the most effective features of mentors as well as partners. In order to form an effective mentoring relationship, an employee seeking a mentor should follow a few general guidelines.

1. *Research the person's background.* Do your homework. The more you know about your potential mentor, the easier it will be to approach him or her and establish a relationship that will work for both of you.

2. *Make contact with the person.* Have a mutual friend or acquaintance introduce you, or get involved with your potential mentor in business settings. That will help the mentor see your skills in action.

3. *Request help on a particular matter.* Let the mentor know that you admire him or her, and ask for help in that arena. For example, you might say, "You're good at dealing with customers. Would it be OK if I came to you for advice on my customers?" Keep your request simple and specific.

4. *Consider what you can offer in exchange.* Mentoring is a two-way street. If you can do something for your potential mentor, then, by all means, tell him or her.

5. *Arrange a meeting.* Once your specific request has been accepted, you are ready to meet with your potential mentor. Never go into this meeting cold. Set goals, identify your desired outcomes, and prepare a list of questions. Listen attentively. Then ask your prepared questions and request specific suggestions.

6. *Follow up.* After the meeting, try some of your potential mentor's suggestions and share the results. Express appreciation by identifying something in particular that was significant to you.

FIGURE 5.12 **Mentoring Functions**

Good Mentors . . .
- Listen and understand
- Challenge and stimulate learning
- Coach
- Build self-confidence
- Provide wise counsel
- Teach by example
- Act as role model
- Share experiences
- Offer encouragement

SUCCESSFUL MENTORING

Good Partners . . .
- Listen
- Act on advice
- Show commitment to learn
- Check ego at the door
- Ask for feedback
- Are open-minded
- Are willing to change
- Are proactive

Source: Matt Starcevich, PhD and Fred Friend, "Effective Mentoring Relationships from the Mentee's Perspective," *Workforce*, supplement (July 1999): 2–3. Used with permission of the Center for Coaching and Mentoring, Inc., http://coachingandmentoring.com.

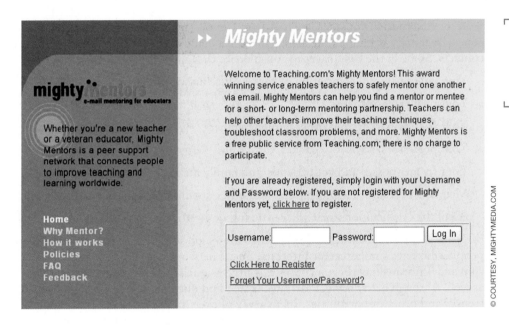

Mighty Mentors, launched by Mighty Media, facilitates online mentoring for teachers.

7. *Ask to meet on an ongoing basis.* After your potential mentor has had a chance not only to meet and interact with you, but also to see the value of what he or she can provide, you are in a good position to request an ongoing relationship. Suggest that you meet with him or her regularly, or ask permission to get help on an ad hoc basis.[34]

When done well, the mentoring process is beneficial for both the pupil and the mentor. One survey found, for example, that 77 percent of companies with successful mentoring programs reported that they effectively increased employee retention.[35]

Not surprisingly, mentoring is also being done over the Internet. *E-mentoring* brings experienced business professionals together with individuals needing counseling. *Women in Technology International (WITI)* is an association that has assembled thousands of women in technology fields in the United States and internationally to act as online mentors to visitors to its Web site. *Mighty Mentors* is a program by Mighty Media (Minneapolis, Minnesota) that provides interactive educational technology. Its mentoring service lets teachers mentor one another via e-mail after they connect online.[36]

Even though participants in e-mentoring typically never meet in person, many form long-lasting e-mail connections that tend to be very beneficial. Still, most participants see these connections as supplements to—rather than substitutes for—in-company mentors.

Networking

As the number of contacts grows, mentoring broadens into a process of **career networking.** As a complement to mentoring, in which relationships are more selective, networking relationships tend to be more varied and temporary. The networks can be internal to a particular organization or connected across many different organizations.

career networking

The process of establishing mutually beneficial relationships with other businesspeople, including potential clients and customers

According to the Monster Career Advice Center (http://career-advice.monster. com/career-networking/home.aspx), there are many ways to identify networking contacts. Some of the best places to consider are the following:

- Your college alumni association or career office networking lists
- Your own extended family
- Your friends' parents and other family members
- Your professors, advisors, coaches, tutors, and clergy
- Your former bosses and your friends' and family members' bosses
- Members of clubs, religious groups, and other organizations to which you belong
- All of the organizations near where you live or go to school

Monster also has a networking feature that allows job seekers to meet up with other people who have similar career interests. Social networking sites such as LinkedIn. com and Tribe.net have begun connecting professionals in formal and informal ways as well. Through networking, individuals often find out about new jobs, professional trends, and other opportunities. In a survey of executives by the human resources firm Drake Beam Morin, 61 percent said that they had found new positions in the previous year through networking. Another study of fifteen high-ranking executive women found that although many of them lacked formal mentors, they had successfully engaged in a kind of "360-degree" networking: The women made it a point to form and maintain relationships with people above, below, and at the same level as themselves, which helped advance their careers.[37]

Career Self-Management Training

Because the employer-employee relationship has become more transactional and employees are being increasingly encouraged to take responsibility for their own career management, many organizations are establishing programs for employees on how they can engage in *career self-management*. The training focuses on two major objectives: (1) helping employees learn to continuously gather feedback and information about their careers and (2) encouraging them to prepare for mobility.

The training is not geared to skills and behaviors associated with a specific job, but rather toward long-term personal effectiveness. Essentially, career self-management is not a process but an event. Employees typically undertake self-assessments to increase their awareness of their own career attitudes and values. In addition, they are encouraged to widen their viewpoint beyond the next company promotion to broader opportunities in the marketplace, attend conferences, and develop good long-term relationships with their bosses or other mentors. Participants might be encouraged to engage in career networking or to identify other means to prepare for job mobility, such as hearing reports from employees who made transitions to new job opportunities both within and outside the organization.[38]

■▪ DEVELOPING A DIVERSE TALENT POOL

Objective 6

In meeting their legal obligation to provide equal employment opportunity, employers often develop formal EEO/affirmative action policies. An essential part of any such policy must be an effort to recruit and promote members of protected classes so that their representation at all levels within the organization approximates their proportionate numbers in the labor market. These efforts include recruiting not only those members who are qualified, but also those who can be made qualified with reasonable training and assistance.

The steps the EEOC recommends for organizations to follow in developing such a program were discussed in Chapter 3. But the reasons to develop a diverse talent pool are not merely legal ones—not by a long shot. Today, ethnic groups represent approximately 30 percent of the total U.S. population. In the next ten years, however, the number is expected to grow to 50 percent. By 2060, the U.S. Census Bureau estimates that ethnic minorities will account for an astounding 90 percent of the population. These groups have a huge amount of buying power, and that power is growing. Some researchers predict that companies failing to diversify their talent pools will have a hard time identifying with their target customers and competing. But perhaps most importantly, as companies face tougher competition in the United States and abroad, they will need all the leadership, productivity, innovation, and creativity the talent pool has to offer. Put simply, a diverse talent pool increases the range of human capital available to the firm.

Recruiting and Developing Women

Women constitute the largest of the protected classes. About 60 percent of women participate in the labor force, and as a group, they represent 47 percent of the total U.S. labor force. The participation rate of working mothers is significantly higher. Approximately 80 percent of mothers with school-age children (ages 6 to 17) are employed in some capacity, and three out of five are the heads of households. In many of the latter cases, these women have the employment disadvantage of having completed, on average, fewer years of school than married women not in the workforce, and they are concentrated in lower-skilled, lower-paying jobs.[39]

A major employment obstacle for women, both skilled and unskilled, is the stereotyped thinking that persists within our society. Still another barrier has been that women in the past had fewer years of experience in the workforce and were not as likely as men to have professional training and preparation for entrance or advancement into management positions. This situation is changing, however. Today, three out of five college graduates are women, and there have been significant increases in the enrollment of women in programs leading to degrees in management and other professional fields. In addition, more women are enrolling in management seminars and certification programs that will further prepare them for higher managerial positions.

As a consequence of these changes, an increasing number of women enter the labor force in managerial positions. Today women account for a greater percentage of all managers than they have in the past. At IBM, for example, 48 different women run $100 million-plus divisions. Relative to their labor force participations, though, women as a whole are underrepresented in the workforce. Some experts suggest that the inequality may be the result of timing. Most people are promoted in their forties. However, because women often leave the workforce temporarily to have children, they might be better prepared when they are in their fifties.[40]

Eliminating Women's Barriers to Advancement

Despite some of the changes taking place, women in management traditionally have been at a disadvantage because they have not been part of the so-called "good old

Artificial barriers or "glass ceilings" are being shattered by successful women executives and entrepreneurs.

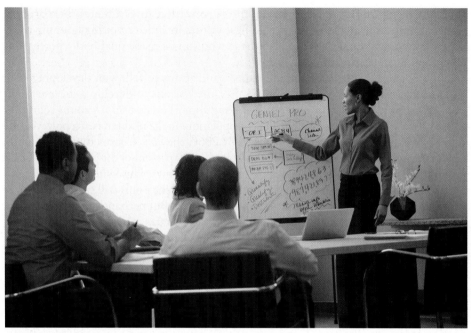

boys" network, an informal network of interpersonal relationships that has traditionally provided a means for senior (male) members of the organization to pass along news of advancement opportunities and other career tips to junior (male) members. Women have typically been outside the network, lacking role models to serve as mentors.

To combat their difficulty in advancing to management positions, women have developed their own women's networks. At Burlington Northern Santa Fe Railway, a women's network serves as a system for encouraging and fostering women's career development and for sharing information, experiences, and insights. Women in lower levels of the company are mentored by women at higher levels. Corporate officers are invited to regularly scheduled network meetings to discuss such matters as planning, development, and company performance. Network members view these sessions as an opportunity to let corporate officers know of women who are interested in and capable of furthering their careers.[41]

An organization devoted to helping employers break down barriers to upward mobility for women is Catalyst, a New York City–based not-for-profit organization. Catalyst (http://www.catalystwomen.org) not only courts corporate officers, but also offers career advice, job placement, continuing education, and related professional development for women of all ages. At its New York headquarters, Catalyst houses an extensive library and audiovisual center that is regarded as the country's leading resource for information on women and work.

There is substantial evidence that stereotyped attitudes toward women are changing. As women pursue career goals assertively and attitudes continue to change, the climate for women in management will become even more favorable. Research has shown that newer male managers tend to be more receptive to the advancement of women managers. With that said and despite the fact that more women hold managerial positions than they have in years past, the proportion of women in top echelons of management, although growing, still remains extremely low. Three women were

CEOs of Fortune 500 companies in 2000. In 2007, thirteen Fortune 500 companies were run by women. Although these data suggest that there has been some progress, there is much left to do to break the "glass ceiling"—the invisible barrier of attitudes, prejudices, and "good old boys" networks that blocks the progress of women who seek important positions in an organization.

Glass Ceiling Audits

The U.S. Department of Labor defines the glass ceiling as "those artificial barriers based on attitudinal or organizational bias that prevent qualified individuals from advancing upward in their organizations into management level positions."[42] "Glass ceiling reviews," also known as "corporate reviews," are conducted by the Department of Labor to identify practices that appear to hinder the upward mobility of both qualified women and minorities. The Department of Labor looks for such things as equal access to the following:

- Upper-level management and executive training
- Rotational assignments
- International assignments
- Opportunities for promotion
- Opportunities for executive development programs at universities
- Desirable compensation packages
- Opportunities to participate on high-profile project teams
- Upper-level special assignments

Organizations are increasingly conducting their own glass ceiling audits prior to government review to avoid fines and externally imposed corrective action. These audits can document any ceilings and the reasons they exist. Self-audits are one step to tapping the potentials of a diversified workforce. Following the largest class action suit ever brought in the United States, Wal-Mart began conducting self-audits. The company now has certain promotion goals for women and minorities. For example, if 40 percent of the qualified people who apply for assistant store manager positions are women, 40 percent of those hired should be women. Minorities and women are also breaking through the glass ceiling by starting their own businesses. As one entrepreneur put it, "It's not hard to break through the glass ceiling when you own it."

Preparing Women for Management

As we noted earlier, opportunities for women to move into management positions are improving. In addition to breaking down the barriers to advancement, the development of women managers demands a better understanding of women's needs and the requirements of the management world.

Many employers now offer special training to women who are on a management career path. They may use their own staff or outside firms to conduct this training. Opportunities are also available for women to participate in seminars and workshops that provide instruction and experiences in a wide variety of management topics.

In addition to formal training opportunities, women today are provided with a wealth of information and guidance in books and magazines. Business sections in

Using the Internet

Many organizations today realize the importance of families to both male and female managers. See how quality of life and family resource programs are included in career planning at DuPont. Go to the Student Resources at:

www.cengage.com/
management/bohlander

bookstores are stocked with numerous books written especially for women who want a better idea of the career opportunities available to them. Many books are devoted to the pursuit of careers in specific fields.[43]

Popular magazines that contain many articles about women and jobs include *Working Woman, Pink, Executive Women's Magazine*, and *Enterprising Women*. These magazines are also recommended reading for men who want a better understanding of the problems that women face in the world of work.

Accommodating Families

One of the major problems women have faced is that of having both a managerial career and a family. Women managers whose children are at an age requiring close parental attention often experience conflict between their responsibility to the children and their duty to the employer. If the conflict becomes too painful, they may decide to forgo their careers, at least temporarily, and leave their jobs. In recent years, many employers, including AFLAC, SunTrust Banks, Quaker Oats Company, Abbott Labs, Bristol-Myers Squibb, IBM, and the accounting firm KPMG, have inaugurated programs that are mutually advantageous to the career-oriented woman and the employer. The programs, which include alternative career paths, extended leave, flextime, job sharing, and telecommuting, provide new ways to balance career and family. AFLAC, for example, offers families hot take-home meals at their on-site cafeterias to ease the burden of employees' having to prepare dinner after leaving the office for the day. The company also subsidizes babysitting for parents on Saturday nights so they can spend some free time together.[44] These efforts are paying off. Both IBM and KPMG, for example, report that their programs have helped them retain and increase their numbers of women workers.

Nonetheless, maintaining a balance between work and family still appears difficult for employees. After reaching a high in 1998, the number of working women with children under age 1 has dropped off slightly. A recent survey by the Pew Research Center of 414 women across the nation found that 60 percent of employed mothers see part-time work as the ideal scenario. That is a 12 percent jump up from a survey taken in 1997. "Women are about to quit their jobs because of this," says Cary Funk with the center. "It's more an expression of the difficulties in combining work and child-raising responsibilities in today's world." It is now not just mothers who are feeling the tug-of-war between work and family. In the last decade, the number of stay-at-home dads has tripled.[45]

Recruiting and Developing Minorities

Since the passage of the Civil Rights Act of 1964, many members of minority groups have been able to realize a substantial improvement in their social and economic well-being. Increasing numbers of blacks and Hispanics are now in the upper income tax brackets by virtue of their entrance into professional, engineering, and managerial positions. However, the proportion of minorities in these areas is still substantially below their proportions in the total population. Moreover, unemployment among minorities, particularly youth, continues to be critically high. The rates climb even higher during economic downturns when employment opportunities become harder to find. For many minorities, employment opportunities still remain exceedingly limited because of educational and societal disadvantages. Also, mainstream, traditional recruitment methods may prove ineffective in reaching them. Community action agencies, civil rights organizations, and church groups within communities can provide a means for recruiters to reach inner-city residents. Special media advertising targeted to this group also may prove effective. Highlights in HRM 3 shows how to design a tailored approach to diversity planning.

Providing Minority Internships

To build ongoing relationships with prospective employees, many companies have increased their sponsorship of internship programs. An internship program offers students an opportunity to learn on the job and gain hands-on experience. For example, in the media industry ABC, NBC, CBS, Fox, and a host of cable companies have made substantial contributions to the Emma L. Bowen Foundation, which provides internships, college scholarships, and postgraduate employment for minorities. *The Chicago Tribune* offers a newsroom training program for aspiring minority journalists who want to work as news reporters. In another effort, Lockheed Martin teamed up with Operation Enterprise, the American Management Association's summer program for high school and college students, to offer ten-week paid internships to students of America's historically black colleges and universities.[46]

Since 1973, Inroads, Inc., an internship organization, has arranged for minority college students to get tutoring, counseling, and summer internships with large corporations. Inroads has 50 offices serving more than 4,500 interns at over 400 companies. The program considers only students who graduate in the top 10 percent of their high school class. In college, the students must maintain a 3.0 grade point average out of a possible 4.0. Participants report that Inroads has raised their aspirations and has taught them how to adjust to the corporate world, and more than three-quarters of them end up taking permanent jobs with companies with whom they have interned. Benefits for the corporation include early access to talented minorities, opportunities to hire college graduates who understand the company's business and its culture, and a greater number of minorities pursuing careers in the traditionally underrepresented fields of engineering and business.[47]

Advancing Minorities to Management

The area of employment that has been the slowest to respond to affirmative action appeals is the advancement of minorities to middle- and top-management positions. That will likely change as the demographics of the United States changes and the percentage of people with minority backgrounds increases. Abbott Laboratories, Sara Lee, and BankBoston are among a growing number of companies that are committed to increasing their ranks of minority managers. These companies believe that increasing the number of the minorities they hire and promote today is critical to their future success.[48] The Society of Human Resources Management offers annual conferences, which offer a training and networking opportunity for HR professionals responsible for recruiting diverse workforces. General Electric provides much-needed access to mentors and actively fosters leadership along the way through minority networks. Its African-American Forum (AAF) began informally but has grown into a major initiative.[49]

In recent years, black women have been rising more rapidly than black men in corporate America. Over the past decade, this group has grown dramatically. The

3

Diversity Recruitment That Works

Workforce diversity will help your organization reach new markets and develop greater intellectual capital. But to leverage diversity, you must first have it—at all levels.

Making It Real

To tap into and retain a diverse pool of top talent, HR professionals must:

- Understand demographic changes in the workforce.
- Ensure that majority groups are not marginalized in the process.
- Educate staff that diversity is not synonymous with minority, and at the same time, try to increase access and opportunities for people of color and other minorities.
- Build long-term relationships with minority organizations, not look for quick fixes.
- Learn how to effectively interview diverse groups.
- Make sure that they are not just "grafting" minorities onto the organization without making appropriate internal culture changes that will enable them to thrive.
- Become the employer of choice for a diverse workforce.
- Ensure retention by developing a diversity-friendly culture.
- Foster a culturally sensitive work environment.
- Network for strategic alliances to enable long-term diversity recruitment.
- Measure the effectiveness of their recruitment efforts.

Putting Theory into Action

To maximize the effectiveness of diversity at all levels of an organization, the diversity has to first exist. Here are some methods an organization may want to try:

- Establish networks with minority colleges.
- Offer corporate internships and scholarships.
- Sponsor job fairs in minority communities. Develop partnerships with minority student professional organizations.
- Develop partnerships with minority organizations, such as the National Black MBA Association.
- Tap all known Web sites where resumes of diverse individuals can be found, such as http://www. HireDiversity.com.

Steps to Take Now

Consider implementing the following initiatives:

- Identify and begin building connections with national minority organizations, not only for access to college-age minority students, but also for access to the organization's members who might be viable candidates for mid- and senior-level positions.

Diversity Recruitment That Works (continued)

- Target recruitment advertising to minority publications such as *The Advocate* and *Hispanic Times*.
- Use your internal employee resource groups. Ask minority employees to provide insight on effective places and ways to recruit diverse candidates. Obviously, this strategy depends on how your existing minority employees view the organization's commitment to diversity.
- Develop training for hiring leaders to ensure that diverse applicants are not discounted in the interviewing process because they are different.
- Understand the "cultural norms" of diverse candidates.
- Partner with your marketing group to ensure that all marketing—not just recruitment advertising—features a diverse mix of individuals.

Source: Condensed from Patricia Digh, "Getting People in the Pool: Diversity Recruitment That Works," *HRMagazine* 44, no. 10 (October 1999): 94–98. Reprinted with the permission of *HRMagazine*, published by the Society for Human Resource Management, Alexandria, VA, via Copyright Clearance Center.

reasons black women are overtaking black men are many and complex. However, in spite of their progress, both black women and black men need continued support in their development and advancement.

While minority managers do play a part in creating a better climate for groups that are discriminated against in advancement opportunities, top managers and the HR department have the primary responsibility for creating conditions within their organizations that are favorable for recognizing and rewarding performance on the basis of objective, nondiscriminatory criteria.

OTHER IMPORTANT TALENT CONCERNS
Recruiting the Disabled

If someone told HR managers where they could find six million working-age people who are proven problem-solvers, provide a tax benefit for their companies, and have higher retention rates than average employees, they likely would ask: "What's the catch?" Not only is there no catch, but such a group of potential employees also currently exists. They are disabled people.[50]

According to the American Association of Disabled People, more than fifty million people—one out of every five Americans—has some sort of disability. Currently, however, only about 30 percent of disabled Americans between ages 21 and 64 are working. The participation rate of those who are severely disabled is lower (about 25 percent). The greatest numbers have impairments that are hearing-, vision-, or back-related.

Of those who do not work, the majority would like to. These individuals have often been rejected for employment because of the mistaken belief that there were no

Many organizations are finding that hiring disabled workers is a good investment.

© INSADCO PHOTOGRAPHY/ALAMY LIMITED

jobs within an organization that they might be able to perform effectively. Fears that the disabled might have more accidents or that they might aggravate existing disabilities have also deterred their employment. The lack of special facilities for physically impaired people, particularly those who use wheelchairs, has been a further employment restriction. However, physical obstructions are being eliminated as employers are making federally legislated improvements to accommodate disabled workers.

Most organizations recognize that the Americans with Disabilities Act of 1990 (see Chapter 3) requires employers to provide "reasonable accommodations" to the known "physical or mental limitations" of their "qualified job candidates or employees with disabilities." For example, an employee in a wheelchair who might not be able to perform duties that involve certain physical activities may be quite capable of working at a bench or a desk. (Recently, Congress has attempted to strengthen the ADA to ensure that people with serious chronic diseases that are treatable are covered, such as those with diabetes, epilepsy, intellectual disabilities, multiple sclerosis, muscular dystrophy, cancer, and many other impairments).

Many managers are unaware of how little these accommodations cost. According to data from the U.S. Department of Labor's Office of Disability Employment, 15 percent of accommodations cost nothing; 51 percent cost between $1 and $500; 12 percent cost between $501 and $1,000; and 22 percent cost more than $1,000. The fact that disabled people are dependable, achieve superior attendance, and experience lower turnover offsets the costs of accommodating them in most cases.

IBM hired its first disabled employee in 1914. This is not surprising, since the company makes software and other products that help eliminate workplace barriers for the disabled. IBM's viewpoint is that no employee should be overlooked because of a disability because he or she might be the person to develop the next generation of hardware or software from which the company will profit. Indeed, several of the company's deaf researchers are doing world-class work with new technologies, including voice recognition technology.

IBM also participates in mentoring and internships for the disabled. The Workforce Recruitment Program for College Students with Disabilities (WRP) is one internship organization. WRP puts together profiles of thousands of college students and recent graduates seeking summer internships or permanent employment nationwide with federal agencies. These profiles are then made available free of charge to business owners. The candidates are skilled in a wide variety of fields, and each has a disability. This effort to help employers find workers and help the disabled find jobs is cosponsored by the U.S. Department of Labor and the Office of Disability Employment Policy. Similarly, the American Association for the Advancement of Science has a program called Entry Point, which has placed more than 400 science and engineering students with disabilities in internships in the public and private sectors. More than 90 percent of these students have gone on to graduate schools or jobs in science and technology. Highlights in HRM 4 lists tips from employers that have been successful in hiring and retaining talented employees with disabilities along with various sources for their recruitment.

Less Publicized Disadvantages

In addition to the widely recognized forms of disability, employees have other physical characteristics that can limit their hiring and advancement opportunities. One

---

4

HIGHLIGHTS IN HRM

Resources and Tips for Hiring and Retaining Employees with Disabilities

Resources

HireDS Career Network

A career resource for employers and disabled job seekers sponsored by Hire Disability Solutions and Monster Worldwide. The joint initiative provides search tools and resume posting, among other resources.

www.hireds.com

Job Accommodation Network

A comprehensive resource for employers, featuring an accommodation toolbox, ADA hotlinks, and other resources. The site also has a section for employees that offers tips on finding and maintaining employment.

www.jan.wvu.edu

(continued)

Resources and Tips for Hiring and Retaining Employees with Disabilities (continued)

Offices of Vocational Rehabilitation

Maintained by all fifty states, the District of Columbia, and all U.S. territories, these offices make it their mission to help disabled workers find and keep jobs. They also are a valuable resource for employers in guiding benefits and legal policies.
www.jan.wvu.edu/SBSES/VOCREHAB.htm

Tips

- *Get the facts and don't make assumptions.* Myths or assumptions are also major barriers to employment. For example, some employers think their workers' compensation insurance will increase if they hire someone with a disability. Not true. Insurance rates are based on the hazards of the operation and the organization's accident experience, not on whether workers have disabilities. Another frequent assumption is that people with disabilities do not have training or education. In fact, many people have college degrees and/or extensive experience making them qualified.
- *Make sure your company is accessible.* This means more than wide doors and ramps. It also means making sure job postings and promotion opportunities are accessible to people with disabilities. Forms and applications should be within reach and interview locations fully accessible. Most important, do not assume accessibility will create a financial hardship. Visit the U.S. Office of Disability Employment Policy (http://www.dol.gov/odep) and JobAccess (http://www.jobaccess.org) for success stories achieved inexpensively.
- *Write job descriptions for all positions.* Written job descriptions identify essential job functions and help applicants identify which jobs he or she would be qualified for and enjoy.
- *Set standards and expectations.* Many people believe that individuals with disabilities receive special treatment and unfair advantages. Be fair and responsible, but do not lower standards or expectations simply because someone has a disability. The purpose of accommodations is to enhance an individual's ability to accomplish work tasks, not to lower expectations.
- *Make a companywide commitment.* The best employment success stories are always found in companies in which the president, CEO, or owner is publicly committed to hiring people with disabilities.
- *Get connected with people who can help.* Several organizations throughout Washington State can help business owners and human resources personnel recruit, interview, hire, train, and retain skilled employees with disabilities. Contact the Washington State Developmental Disabilities Council (http://www.ddc.wa.gov) at (800) 634-4473 or Rehabilitation Enterprises of Washington at (360) 943-7654.

Sources: Ed Holen and Penny Jo Haney, "Consider Employing People with Disabilities," *Wenatchee Business Journal* 17, no. 10 (October 2003): A19; Kelly Butler, "Ten Million Ways to Fill the Talent Gap," *Employee Benefit News* 21, no. 3 (March 2007): 22–24.

such disadvantage is unattractiveness, against which employers can be biased even if unconsciously. "Unattractive" individuals are those whose facial features are considered unpleasant but who do not possess physical disfiguration that would put them in the physically disabled category. For example, in 2005, Abercrombie & Fitch was sued for race and age discrimination based on a hiring practice that allegedly sought college students who fit its brand image: young, attractive, white, male, and preppy. Another disadvantage is obesity. Although the EEOC has said that obesity is not a disability per se (unless it is the result of a physiological condition), in a few cases, courts have held obesity to be a legitimate physical disability.

Employment attorneys say that to some extent, looks-related criteria depend on what you are selling. A Las Vegas club hiring showgirls, for example, is more likely to be in a better position to argue that thinness and good looks are necessary for the job than Delta Air Lines would be. When facing such a situation, attorneys say employers should ask themselves the following question: "Do you think that *not* hiring or terminating the person will do so much good for your company that you are willing to take the risk of being sued?"[51]

Indeed, a number of cities and states, including San Francisco and Washington, D.C., have outlawed discrimination based on body weight or height. In addition, employers are being sued for the new trend of imposing "lifestyle regulations" on their employees. The regulations target smokers, overweight individuals, and even extreme sports enthusiasts because firms know these activities are associated with extra health insurance costs. Employees and attorneys say the regulations are an invasion of privacy.

Finally, there is the illiteracy handicap. Between 45 and 50 percent of adults in the United States have only limited reading and writing abilities needed to handle the minimal demands of daily living or job performance. Employers are encountering increasing numbers of employees, including college graduates, whose deficient reading and writing skills limit their performance on the job. A survey of Fortune 1000 CEOs found that 90 percent recognized the problems of illiteracy—yet just 38 percent acknowledged that it was a problem for their workers.[52]

The U.S. Department of Labor estimates that illiteracy costs U.S. businesses upward of $60 billion a year in lost productivity. To address literacy problems, organizations such as Smith and Wesson, Hewlett-Packard, Motorola, and the City of Phoenix instituted basic skill assessment programs to teach reading, math, and communication skills to employees who show some level of deficiency. America's Literacy Directory (ALD), sponsored by the National Institute for Literacy, connects employers, learners, volunteers, social service providers, and others with literacy programs in all fifty states and U.S. territories. Employees and employers need only go to ALD's online directory and type in their locations to find the literacy help centers nearest them.

Employing the Older Workforce

Today there is a definite trend by organizations to hire older people. Twenty-two percent of employers said they were likely to rehire retirees from other companies in 2008. Another 23 percent were likely to provide incentives for workers at, or approaching retirement age, to keep them on the job longer. Many workers are expressing an interest in postponing their retirements, too.[53] The move has come both as a result of changing workforce demographics and as a change in the attitudes of employers and employees. Organizations realize that older workers have proven employment experience, have job "savvy," and are reliable employees. They are also an excellent recruitment source to staff part-time and full-time positions that are otherwise hard to fill.

As we have indicated, retirees often return or stay in the workforce at the behest of their employers, who cannot afford to lose the knowledge accumulated by longtime employees or their reliable work habits that have a positive effect on the entire work group. To prevent an exodus of talent, employers will need to implement human resources strategies to help retain and attract the talent older workers have to offer. Moreover, as the workforce ages, employers will need to make workplace adaptations to help older workers cope with the physical problems they will experience, such as poorer vision, hearing, and mobility.

For some firms, especially in jobs for which it is difficult to attract and retain skilled, reliable employees, older workers can be the permanent solution to an intractable problem. Many older workers gravitate to non-full-time forms of work, especially independent contracting or consulting, on-call work (such as substitute nursing or teaching), and temporary work in administrative or IT roles. Employers are coming through for them by offering these options as well as flexible hours, job sharing, and telecommuting benefits.

Employing Dual Career Couples

As discussed throughout this book, the employment of both members of a couple has become a way of life in North America. Economic necessity and social forces have encouraged this trend to the point that over 80 percent of all marriages are now dual career partnerships in which both members follow their own careers and actively support each other's career development. As with most lifestyles, the dual career arrangement has its positive and negative sides. A significant number of organizations are concerned with the problems facing dual career couples and offer assistance to them. Flexible working schedules are the most frequent organizational accommodation to these couples. Other arrangements include leave policies under which either parent may stay home with a newborn, policies that allow work to be performed at home, day care on an organization's premises, and job sharing.

The difficulties that dual career couples face include the need for quality child care, time demands, and emotional stress. However, the main problem these couples face is the threat of relocation because gaining the support of a spouse or significant other is crucial for employees. Many large organizations now offer some kind of job-finding assistance for spouses of employees who are relocated, including payment of fees charged by employment agencies, job counseling firms, and executive search firms.

Organizations are also developing networking relationships with other employers to find jobs for the spouses of their relocating employees. These networks can provide a way to "share the wealth and talent" in a community while simultaneously assisting in the recruitment efforts of the participating organizations.[54]

Relocating dual career couples to foreign facilities is a major issue that international employers face. Fewer employees are willing to relocate without assistance for their spouses. Many employers have developed effective approaches for integrating the various allowances typically paid for overseas assignments when husband and wife work for the same employer. Far more complex are the problems that arise when couples work for two different employers. The problems associated with overseas assignments of dual career couples will be examined in greater detail in Chapter 15.

dual career partnerships

Couples in which both members follow their own careers and actively support each other's career development

SUMMARY

Objective 1 In order to expand the talent pool of organizations—the number and kind of people available for employment—organizations must focus on multiple approaches to recruitment and career management. Outside sources for recruitment are especially useful for filling jobs with special qualifications and to acquire individuals with new skills, ideas, and perspectives. Which outside sources and methods are used in recruiting will depend on the recruitment goals of the organization, conditions of the labor market, and specifications of the jobs to be filled.

Objective 2 Employers usually find it advantageous to use internal promotion and transfer to fill as many openings as possible above the entry level. By recruiting from within, an organization can capitalize on the previous investments they have made in recruiting, selecting, training, and developing its current employees. Furthermore, internal promotions reward employees for their past performance and send a signal to other employees that their future efforts will pay off. However, potential candidates from the outside should occasionally be considered in order to prevent the inbreeding of ideas and attitudes.

The legal requirements governing EEO make it mandatory that employers proactively recruit and promote members of protected classes so that their representation at all levels within the organization will approximate their proportionate numbers in the labor market. These efforts include recruiting not only those members who are qualified, but also those who can be made qualified with reasonable training and assistance.

Objective 3 Job opportunities can be identified by studying jobs and determining the knowledge and skills each one requires. Once that is accomplished, key jobs can be identified, and job progressions can be planned. These progressions can then serve as a basis for developing the career paths of employees. Once career paths are developed and employees are identified on the career ladders, it is possible to inventory the jobs and determine where the individuals with the required skills and knowledge are needed or will be needed.

Identifying and developing talent is a responsibility of all managers. In addition to employees' immediate superiors, there should be others in the organization who can nominate and sponsor employees with promise. Many organizations use assessment centers to identify managerial talent and recommend employees engage in developmental activities to reach their full potential. Mentoring has been found to be valuable for providing guidance and support to employees and potential managers.

Objective 4 Beyond recruiting per se, organizations also need to consider the progression of employees through a series of jobs. In this way, firms can manage not only the immediate contribution of individuals to the organization, but also the long-term contribution throughout their careers. A career development program is a dynamic process that should integrate individual employee needs with those of the organization. It is the responsibility of the employee to identify his or her own knowledge, skills, and abilities (KSAs) as well as interests and values and to seek out information about career options. The organization should provide information about its mission, policies, and plans and what it will provide in the way of training and development for the employee.

Objective 5 In order to be successful, a career management program must receive the support of a firm's top managers. The program should reflect the goals and the culture of the organization, and managerial personnel at all levels must be trained in the fundamentals of job design, performance appraisal, career planning, and counseling. Employees should be aware of the organization's philosophy and its goals; otherwise they will not know how their goals match those of the organization. HRM policies, especially those related to the rotation, transfer, and promotion of employees, should be consistent with the firm's goals. The objectives and opportunities of the career development program should be announced widely throughout the organization.

Objective 6   The first step toward facilitating the career development of women is to eliminate barriers to their advancement. Creating women's networks, providing special training for women, accepting women as valued members of the organization, providing mentors for them, and accommodating families have been found to be effective ways to facilitate women's career development.

A diversified workforce is composed of many different groups, an important segment of which is minority groups. In addition to creating conditions that are favorable for recognizing and rewarding the performance of employees, many organizations have special programs such as internships that provide them with hands-on experience as well as special training opportunities. Other groups that require the attention of management are the disabled, older workers, and dual career couples, who often need flexible working options.

KEY TERMS

assessment center
career counseling
career networking
career paths
career plateau
dual career partnerships
employee leasing

fast-track program
job posting and bidding
job progressions
mentors
nepotism
9-box grid
outplacement services

promotion
realistic job preview (RJP)
relocation services
transfer
yield ratio

DISCUSSION QUESTIONS

Objective 1   1. In what ways do executive search firms differ from traditional employment agencies?

Objective 1   2. Explain how realistic job previews (RJPs) operate. Why do they appear to be an effective recruitment technique?

Objective 1   3. More than 50 percent of all MBAs leave their first employer within five years. Although the change may mean career growth for these individuals, it represents a loss to the employers. What are some of the probable reasons a MBA would leave his or her first employer?

Objective 2   4. What are the advantages and disadvantages of filling openings from internal sources?

Objective 3   5. How might retired executives in any organization assist in the career management of current employees?

Objective 4   6. Give some reasons for the trend toward increased emphasis on career management programs.

Objective 5   7. What contributions can a career management program make to an organization that is forced to downsize its operations?

Objective 6   8. What are some of the barriers to advancement opportunities for women in many organizations?

Objective 6   9. How are the career challenges of minorities both similar to and different from those of women?

·········· BIZFLIX EXERCISES ··········

In Good Company: Carter Manages His Career

This chapter described many ways a company can recruit employees. The scenes from the film *In Good Company* show other ways a company can find new employees. Use the following questions as guides while viewing these scenes.

A corporate takeover brings star advertising executive Dan Foreman (Dennis Quaid) a new boss who is half his age. Carter Duryea (Topher Grace)—Dan's new boss—wants to prove his worth as the new marketing chief at *Sports America*, Waterman Publishing's flagship magazine. Carter applies his unique approaches while dating Dan's daughter, Alex (Scarlett Johansson).

These scenes come from the "breaking news" segment that appears in the first five minutes of the film. They follow Carter's presentation of his concepts for marketing cell phones to children under age five. Mark Steckle (Clark Greg) tells his staff that Teddy K. (Malcolm McDowell) asked him to take over marketing at the magazine division of Waterman Publishing, Teddy K.'s recent acquisition. Carter Duryea discusses Mark's move to Waterman Publishing and the prospect of Carter following him to head advertising sales for *Sports America*. The film continues with Dan Foreman soon learning that Carter is his new boss.

What to Watch for and Ask Yourself

- Do these scenes show external or internal recruitment?
- Recall an earlier discussion in this chapter of the employee's role in career planning. What does Carter do to help his career?
- Review the earlier section "Career Development Initiatives." Which of those initiatives appear in these scenes? What is Mark Steckle's role in Carter's career development?

Career Management

We often think that successful people plan their careers out in advance and then work toward their goals in a very logical, sequential manner. Although some successes are designed and implemented this way, others are created through insight, preparedness, and taking advantages of opportunities as they arise.

Assignment

1. Form teams of four to six members. Identify three different people to interview about their careers. One person should be in the early stages of his or her career; one should be in midcareer; and one should be in the final stages of his or her career.

2. Ask each person to identify his or her career goals and how they have changed or are expected to change over time.

3. Ask each person to describe the sequence of events that led to where he or she is. How well does that story align with the traditional model of careers?

4. Ask each person what (if anything) he or she would do differently. Ask what advice he or she has for you about how to approach your career.

CASE STUDY

Linking Up with Talent at Osram Sylvania

To help fill a constant stream of engineering jobs at Osram Sylvania's Towanda plant in Pennsylvania, Maureen Crawford Hentz logs on to LinkedIn. The plant is the largest of the twenty-two manufacturing facilities and twelve R&D laboratories operated by Osram Sylvania. Professional positions for the rural location are staffed through company headquarters in Danvers, Massachusetts, where Crawford Hentz is the manager of talent acquisition.

Osram Sylvania is the North American operation of Munich, Germany-based Osram, one of the world's largest lighting manufacturers and part of global giant Siemens AG. The lighting sector is one of the few types of manufacturing that is still expanding in the United States, so Osram Sylvania maintains an extensive recruiting program and fills hundreds of positions each year. "Because of the constant growth, we must be strategic in recruiting and start filling the pipelines well in advance," Crawford Hentz says. Crawford Hentz says that networking technology is only one part of the company's approach to recruiting. "But it absolutely could become the primary source," she says.

Her enthusiasm for the technology is echoed by recruiters across the United States, who are quickly identifying networking sites as their sourcing tool of choice. The real power of the technology lies in its ability to reach passive candidates for positions that require specialized skills and experience. With U.S. unemployment rates for workers with college degrees now less than 2 percent, recruiters are shifting to networking technology for hard-to-fill positions.

More than 1,000 of Osram Sylvania's 11,200 employees work in the Towanda chemical and metallurgical facility, where open positions include engineering, logistics, and marketing jobs. "The engineering positions are very nuanced and require discrete sets of skills," Crawford Hentz says. "Recruiting for these jobs really hones your skills as a treasure hunter."

Crawford Hentz posts jobs online, searches job boards and sources through industry association sites, and blogs. But LinkedIn is quickly becoming her preferred approach. "LinkedIn can be very strategic," she says. "My profile notes that I am always looking for chemical engineers, and because of the search mechanisms, I receive inquiries from people who I would not normally be able to network with. LinkedIn provides the technological equivalent of an old boys network, but without the old boys."

Crawford Hentz recently sourced six of the seven finalist candidates for a senior level position from LinkedIn. "I expected an arduous recruiting process, and I carefully managed the hiring manager's expectations, but then we filled the position in a matter of weeks," she reports. "Our good brand name recognition brings an instant 'yes' to our networking queries."

One of the benefits of the networking technology is that it can greatly increase the diversity of the talent pool accessible to recruiters. "My hiring manager was on cloud nine when he saw the diversity of the pool created through LinkedIn," Crawford Hentz says. The technology also allows recruiters to source more quickly and leaves more time to meet the needs of valuable candidates. "With the networking technology, people come to the opportunities," Crawford Hentz says. "These are passive candidates, and it's important to take proper care of them. They need time to consider the position. The social networking technology reduces my time to source and allows the candidates extra time for considering the job."

Questions

1. What do you think some of the drawbacks from recruiting from social network sites might be?
2. What other sources of applicants might work just as well or better than social networking sites?
3. Do you think social networking sites could be effectively used to hire talent abroad? Why or why not?

Source: Reprinted from Fay Hansen, "Acquisitions Pipeline," *Workforce Management Online*, December 2006.

CASE STUDY 2

Preparing a Career Development Plan

Sue Ann Scott was a receptionist at the headquarters of a large corporation. A high school graduate, she had no particular skills other than an ability to organize her job duties and a pleasant personality. Unfortunately, she did not have any particular plan for career development; nevertheless, she wanted very much to improve her economic position. Recognizing her educational limitations, she began taking accounting courses on a random basis in an evening adult education program.

Scott also took advantage of the corporation's job bidding system by applying for openings that were posted, even though in many instances she did not meet the specifications listed for them. After being rejected several times, she became discouraged. Her depressed spirits were observed by Elizabeth Burroughs, one of the department managers in the corporation. Burroughs invited Scott to come to her office for a talk about the problems she was having. Scott took full advantage of this opportunity to express her frustrations and disappointments. As she unburdened herself, it became apparent both to her and to Burroughs that during interviews she repeatedly apologized for having "only a high school education," an attitude that had probably made it difficult for the interviewers to select her over other candidates who were more positive about their backgrounds and skills. Burroughs suggested that Scott might try taking a more positive approach during her interviews. For example, she could stress her self-improvement efforts at night school and the fact that she was a dependable and cooperative person who was willing to work hard to succeed in the job for which she was applying.

Following Burroughs's advice, Scott applied for a position as invoice clerk, a job for which she felt she was qualified. She made a very forceful and positive presentation during her interview, stressing the favorable qualities she possessed. As a result of this approach, she got the job. While the pay for an invoice clerk was not much more than that for a receptionist, the position did offer an avenue for possible advancement into the accounting field, in which the accounting courses she was taking would be of value.

Questions

1. What are some of the possible reasons Scott did not seek or receive advice from her immediate supervisor?
2. After reviewing the chapter, suggest all possible ways that Scott can prepare herself for career advancement.

NOTES AND REFERENCES

1. Sherry Sullivan, "The Changing Nature of Careers: A Review and Research Agenda," *Journal of Management* 25, no. 3 (1999): 457–84; Steve Prentice, "A Game Plan for Career Survival," *Canadian HR Reporter* 15, no. 11 (June 3, 2002): 27–28; Mark Tatge, "Prescription for Growth," *Forbes* 171, no. 4 (February 17, 2003): 64–67.

2. Joseph Bower, "Solve the Succession Crisis by Growing Inside-Outside Leaders," *Harvard Business Review* 85, no. 11 (November 2007): 90–96.

3. Douglas P. Shuit, "Monster Board Games," *Workforce Management* 82, no. 2 (November 2003): 37–42; Joe Dysart, "New Directions in Internet Recruiting," *Contractor Magazine*, 53, no. 7 (July 2006): 33–36.

4. Rob Yeung, "Finders Keepers," *Accountancy Magazine* 134, no. 1335 (November 2004): 42–44; Joe Dysart, "New Directions in Internet Recruiting," *Contractor Magazine* 53, no. 7 (July 2006): 33–36.

5. Ibid.

6. Jennifer Taylor Arnold, "Employee Referrals at a Keystroke," *HRMagazine* 51, no. 10 (October 2006): 82–88; Victoria Furnes, "The New Frontier," *Personnel Today* (January 22, 2008): 13–16.

7. Keith Swenson, "Maximizing Employee Referrals," *HRFocus* 76, no. 1 (January 1999): 9–10.

8. "In Praise of Nepotism?" *Business Ethics Quarterly* 15, no. 1 (January 2005): 153–161; Richard Reeve and Gavin Sheridan, "Nepotism: Is It Back?" *New Statesman* 135 (September 29, 2003): 22–25.

9. Roger Kenny, "The Boardroom Role of Human Resources," *Corporate Board* 25, no. 150 (January–February 2005): 12–17; Joseph Bower, "Solve the Succession Crisis by Growing Inside-Outside Leaders," *Harvard Business Review* 85, no. 11 (November 2007): 90–96; Joseph Daniel McCool, "When You Have to Look Outside," *Conference Board Review* 45, no. 3 (May–June 2008): 30–32.

10. Jennifer Schramm, "Globalizing By Degrees," *HRMagazine* 53, no. 4 (April 2008): 144.

11. Leslie Stevens-Huffman, "Commitment, Consistency Are Key to College Recruiting," *Workforce Management* 85, no. 6 (March 27, 2006): 42–43.

12. [no entry shown]

13. Chris Pentilla, "Got It Covered: If You Can't Afford to Offer Employee Benefits on Your Own, Why Not Join Forces with a PEO?" *Entrepreneur* 32, no. 2 (February 2004): 66–68; Bill Leonard, "Small Firms Prepare for Aging Workforce," *HR Magazine* 53, no. 5 (May 2008): 32.

14. Atul Vashistha, "Global Talent Management Part I: Recruiting Globally," *HRO Today* (June 2007).

15. Connie Winkler, "Job Tryouts Go Virtual," *HR Magazine* 51, no. 9 (September 2006): 131–134.

16. Max Messmer, "Recognizing Potential Stars by Promoting from Within," *Strategic Finance* 86, no. 5 (October 2004): 9–11; "Retaining vs. Recruiting?" *T+D* 61 no. 8 (August 2007): 74.

17. J. W. Marriott, "Our Competitive Strength: Human Capital," *Executive Speeches* 15, no. 5 (April–May 2001): 18–21.

18. Debbie Mack, "P&G Fights to Protect Its Bounty," *Corporate Legal Times* 13, no. 135 (February 2003): 64.

19. "How to Implement an Effective Process for a New HR Management System," *HRFocus* 82, no. 1 (January 2005): 3–4.

20. Robert Rodriguez, "Filling the HR Pipeline," *HRMagazine* 49, no. 9 (September 2004): 78–84; James W. Walker, "Perspectives," *Human Resource Planning* 25, no. 1 (2002): 12–14; Stanely Ragalevsky, "CEO Succession: Five Best Practices for Internal Candidates," *Community Banker* 17, no. 2 (February 2008): 24–25.

21. "The Pros and Cons of Online Recruiting," *HR Focus* 81 (April 2004 Supplement): S2.

22. Paul W. B. Atkins and Robert E. Wood, "Self versus Others' Ratings as Predictors of Assessment Center Ratings: Validation Evidence for 360-Degree Feedback Programs," *Personnel Psychology* 55, no. 4 (Winter 2002): 871–905; Michelle A. Dean and Philip L. Roth, "Ethnic and Gender Subgroup Differences in Assessment Center Ratings: A Meta-Analysis," *Journal of Applied Psychology* 93, no. 3 (May 2008): 685–691.

23. Ellen Ernst Kossek, Karen Roberts, Sandra Fisher, and Beverly Demarr, "Career Self-Management: A Quasi-Experimental Assessment of the Effects of a Training Intervention," *Personnel Psychology* 51, no. 4 (Winter 1998): 935–62; Shelly Green, "Attracting Top Talent Despite Business Challenges," *Journal of Career Planning and Employment* 62, no. 4 (Summer 2002): 24–28; Cynthia Jones, "Step by Step: Creating a Strategic Management System for Career Services Delivery," *Journal of Career Planning and Employment* 62, no. 3 (Spring 2002): 21–27.

24. Peg O'Herron and Peggy Simonsen, "Career Development Gets a Charge at Sears Credit," *Personnel Journal* 74, no. 5 (May 1995): 103–106. See also Jules Abend, "Behind the Scenes at: Sears," *Bobbin* 39, no. 11 (June 1998): 22–26; Shari Caudron, "The De-Jobbing of America," *Industry Week* 243, no. 16 (September 5, 1994): 30–36; Edward E. Lawler III, "From Job-Based to Competency-Based Organizations," *Journal of Organizational Behavior* 15, no. 1 (January 1994): 3–15; Douglas T. Hall, "Accelerate Executive Development—At Your Peril!" *Career Development International* 4, no. 4 (1999): 237–39.

25. "How a Talent Management Plan Can Anchor Your Company's Future," *HR Focus* 81, no. 10 (October 2004): 7–10.

26. Elizabeth Craig, John Kimberly, and Hamid Bouchikhhi, "Can Loyalty Be Leased?" *Harvard Business Review* 80, no. 9 (September 2002): 24–34; Edward Potter, "Improving Skills and Employability in the 21st Century," *Industrial and Labor Relations Review* 55, no. 4 (July 2002): 739–45.

27. Suzanne C. de Janasz, Shery E. Sullivan, and Vicki Whiting, "Mentor Networks and Career Success: Lessons for Turbulent Times," *Academy of Management Executive* 17, no. 4 (November 2003): 78–92; Kate Walsh and Judith Gordon, "Creating an Individual Work Identity," *Human Resource Management Review* 18, no. 1 (March 2008): 46–61.

28. Judith Bardwick, *The Plateauing Trap* (New York: AMACOM, 1986). See also Judith Bardwick, *Danger in the Comfort Zone: From Boardroom to Mailroom—How to Break the*

Entitlement Habit That's Killing American Business (New York: AMACOM Book Division, 1995); Max Messmer, "Moving beyond a Career Plateau," *National Public Accountant* 45, no. 7 (September 2000): 20–21; John Rosche, "Who's Managing Your Career?" *Contract Management* 44, no. 2 (February 2004): 20–22; "Attention U.S. Workers," *T+D* 61, no. 10 (October 2007): 12.

29. Larry Cambron, "Career Development Pays," *Far Eastern Economic Review* 164, no. 42 (October 25, 2001): 83.

30. For up-to-date career information and guidance as well as an opportunity for self-analysis, see Richard Bolles, *What Color Is Your Parachute 2008: A Practical Manual for Job-Hunters & Career-Changers* (Berkeley, CA: Ten Speed Press, 2007).

31. Susan Wells, "Smoothing the Way," *HRMagazine* 46, no. 6 (June 2001): 52–58; Heath Row, "Market Yourself," *Fast Company* 58 (May 2002): 24.

32. Bonnie Rothman Morris, "New Skills, and Paying for Them," *The New York Times*, October 29, 2002, G6.

33. de Janasz, Sullivan, and Whiting, "Mentor Networks and Career Success," 78–92; Carole Gaskell, "Reward Coaching Behavior to Encourage Its Use," *People Management* 14, no. 4 (February 21, 2008): 70.

34. Jeff Barbian, "The Road Best Traveled," *Training* 39, no. 5 (May 2002): 38–42; Kathleen Barton, "Will You Mentor Me?" *Training and Development* 56, no. 5 (May 2002): 90–92.

35. Elaine Biech, "Executive Commentary," *Academy of Management Executive* 17, no. 4 (November 2003): 92–94.

36. Anne Field, "No Time to Mentor? Do It Online," *Business Week*, no. 3822 (March 3, 2003): 26; Rhea Borija; "E-Mentors Offer Online Support, Information for Novice Instructors," *Education Week* 21, no. 29 (April 3, 2002): 12. For more information, see the Web sites for these organizations: Mighty Mentors (http://K6educators.about.com/b/a/090852.htm), Nursing Net (http://www.nursingnet.org), and Women in Technology International (http://www.witi.org).

37. de Janasz, Sullivan, and Whiting, "Mentor Networks and Career Success," 78–92; Jill Rachline Marabix, "Job Search 2. Oh!" *U.S. News & World Report* 136, no. 8 (March 8, 2004): 60–63.

38. Thomas A. Stewart, "What's in It for Me?" *Harvard Business Review* 83, no. 1 (January 2005): 8; Marilyn Clarke and Margaret Patrickson, "The New Covenant of Employability," *Employee Relations* 30, no. 2 (2008): 121–141.

39. Julianne Maveaux, "Whose Revolution?" *Working Woman* 26, no. 8 (September 2001): 56–58; Ann Crittendon, "Motherload," *Working Woman* 26, no. 8 (September 2001): 66–68.

40. Louann Brizendine, "One Reason Women Don't Make It to the C-Suite," *Harvard Business Review* 86, no. 6 (June 2008): 36; Christine Larsen, "NAFE Top 30 Companies for Executive Women," *NAFE Magazine* 30, no. 1 (Spring 2007): 8–16; Yoji Cole, "Why Are So Few CEOs People of Color and Women?" *Diversity, Inc.* (November 7, 2007).

41. Anne M. Walsh and Susan C. Borkowski, "Cross-Gender Mentoring and Career Development in the Health Care Industry," *Health Care Management Review* 24, no. 3 (Summer 1999): 7–17.

42. Robert Schwab, "Dancing on the Glass Ceiling," *Colorado Biz* 31, no. 5 (May 2004): 18–23. A host of reports on glass ceiling issues can be found on the U.S. Department of Labor's Web site at http://www.dol.gov.

43. The interested reader should find the following books very informative: Johanna Hunsaker and Phillip Hunsaker, *Strategies and Skills for Managerial Women* (Cincinnati, OH: South-Western, 1991); Marian Ruderman and Patricia Ohlott, *Standing at the Crossroads: Next Steps for High-Achieving Women* (New York: John Wiley and Sons, 2002).

44. Alison Stein Wellner, "Welcoming Back Mom," *HRM Magazine* 49, no. 6 (June 2004): 76–83.

45. "Mothers' Labor Force Participation," *Monthly Labor Review* 137, no. 5 (May 2004): 2; Brian Braiker and Anna Kuchment, "Just Don't Call Me Mr. Mom," *Newsweek* 150, no. 15 (October 8, 2007): 52–55; Melissa Fletcher, "Working Moms Fully in Favor of Going Part-Time," *Fort Worth Star-Telegram* (August 30, 2007): E1, 9.

46. "Recruiting Minorities," *Black Enterprise* 35, no. 6 (January 2005): 53; Debbie Smith, "Building a New Diversity Road Map," *Multichannel News* 25, no. 38 (September 20, 2004): 82.

47. "IFD, INROADS Partner for Summer Enrichment Program Internships," *AHA News* 40, no. 18 (September 6, 2004): 8; Michelle Neal, "Get Real with Diversity," *Oregon Business Magazine*, 29, no. 7 (July 2006): 9–9.

48. Miles White, "Paying More Than Lip Service to Diversity," *Chief Executive* 242, no. 16 (October 2002): 20–22.

49. Yeung, "Finders Keepers," 42–44; Janny Scott, "Nearly Half of Black Men Found Jobless," *The New York Times*, February 28, 2004, B1; Sylvia Ann Hewlett, Carolyn Buck Luce, and Cornel West, "Leadership in Your Midst," *Harvard Business Review* 83, no. 11 (November 2005): 74–82.

50. Joe Mullich, "Hiring without Limits," *Workforce Management* 83, no. 6 (June 1, 2004): 53–60; Julie Hotchkiss, "Growing Part-Time Employment among Workers with Disabilities," *Economic Review* 89, no. 3 (July 2004): 25–42; "Entry Point Interns Top 400 in Seventh Year," *Science* 301, no. 5637 (August 29, 2003): 1195; Kelly Butler, "Ten Million Ways to Fill the Talent Gap, *Employee Benefit News* 21, no. 3 (March 2007): 22–24.

51. Michael Barrier, "Should Looks Count?" *HRM Magazine* 49, no. 9 (September 2004): 64–69; "Be Cautious about Weighing Weight in Your Employment Decisions," *Staff Leader* 17, no. 9 (May 2004): 1–XX; Gregg A. Gilman, "You Can Hire Based on Beauty—within Reason," *Advertising Age* 78, no. 30 (July 30, 2007): 26; "Obese Workers Cost $45 Billion, but What Should Employers Do?" *Hospitals & Health Networks* 82, no. 5 (May 2008): 70.

52. Dannah Baynton, "America's $60 Billion Problem," *Training* 38, no. 5 (May 2001): 50–55.

53. Christopher Reynolds, "Boomers, Act II," *American Demographics* 27, no. 8 (October 2004): 10–12; Theresa Minton-Eversole, "Senate Forum Explores Ways to Keep Aging Workforce Working," *HR Magazine* 48, no. 10 (October 2003): 30; Carly Foster, "Rehiring Retirees among 2008's Top Recruiting Trends," *Employee Benefit News* (January 8, 2008): 5.

54. Janice Rosenberg, "Dual Career Couples Face Expensive Choices," *Bankrate.com* (July 2, 2007); Erin White, "Help Increases for Partners of Relocated Workers," *Wall Street Journal* 251, no. 70 (Marcy 25, 2008): D4.

APPENDIX

Personal Career Development

Because you are likely to spend more time working during your life than doing anything else, it makes sense to plan your career. There are numerous ways for an employer to contribute to an individual employee's career development and at the same time meet the organization's HR needs. Although organizations can certainly be a positive force in the development process, the primary responsibility for personal career growth still rests with the individual. After all, your career is likely to begin before and often continue after a period of employment with a particular organization. To help you, as students and prospective employees, achieve your career objectives, this Appendix is included to provide some background for your personal development and decisions.

◼◼ DEVELOPING PERSONAL SKILLS AND COMPETENCIES

Planning for a career involves more than simply acquiring specific job knowledge and skills. Job know-how is clearly essential, but you must also develop other skills to be successful as an employee. To succeed as a manager, you must achieve still higher-level skills in the areas of communication, time management, self-motivation, interpersonal relationships, and leadership.

Hundreds of self-help books, professional journals, and magazines have been written on these topics or contain articles about them, and myriad opportunities to participate in workshops are available, often sponsored by employers.[1] For example, the pointers on the basic skills of successful career management listed in Highlights in HRM 5 are taken from a competency assessment conducted at Caterpillar.

◼◼ CHOOSING A CAREER

Many years ago, when the management expert Peter Drucker was asked about career choices, he said, "The probability that the first job choice you make is the right one for you is roughly one in a million. If you decide your first choice is the right one, chances are that you are just plain lazy."[2] The implications of this statement are just as true today. You often have to do a lot of searching and changing to find a career path that is psychologically and financially satisfying. According to the U.S. Bureau of Labor Statistics (BLS), education, health services, and professional and business services represent the industry divisions with the strongest projected employment from now until 2016. These industries are projected to grow twice as fast as the

Career Competencies at Caterpillar

During the Caterpillar business unit's career development training process in Joliet, Illinois, the company compiled the following capabilities as necessary for success within the reorganized, changing organization:

- Interpersonal skills: Possesses team-building and leadership skills; can effectively lead groups and facilitate group interaction
- Problem-solving skills: Can analyze and use problem-solving approaches
- Communication skills: Can verbalize articulately, make presentations, and write cogently
- Leadership skills: Is recognized by peers as a natural leader; accomplishes results without formal authority
- Organization and planning skills: Can manage time; sets and achieves goals
- Technical skills: Possesses education specific to assignments and job content; understands and uses appropriate level of technical skills
- Responsibility: Takes initiative; accepts accountability for own work and additional tasks for the good of the group
- Assertiveness: Able and comfortable with communicating openly and directly; demonstrates self-confidence and awareness of others' perceptions
- Flexibility: Can adapt to organizational changes and changing market needs; willingly considers new ideas and implements new ways of doing things
- Judgment: Can determine level of risk and appropriate action; accepts accountability for significant decisions

Source: Peggy Simonsen and Cathy Wells, "African Americans Take Control of Their Careers," *Personnel Journal* 73, no. 4 (April 1994): 99–108. See also David Dubois, "The Seven Stages of One's Career," *Training and Development* 54, no. 12 (December 2000): 45–50.

overall economy. Information technology, leisure and hospitality, and transportation and warehousing are also projected to grow faster than average.

Use of Available Resources

A variety of resources are available to aid in the process of choosing a satisfying career. Counselors at colleges and universities, as well as those in private practice, are equipped to assist individuals in evaluating their aptitudes, abilities, interests, and values as they relate to career selection. Placement offices and continuing education centers offer some type of career planning assistance. In addition to career exploration, most of them offer resume writing help, interview preparation, and job placement assistance. Looking on the Internet is also a great way to jump-start your career planning. For example, About.com's career planning Web site (http://careerplanning.about.com) contains a wealth of information that will help get you started. Most job-posting Web sites, including Monster and CareerBuilder.com, contain free career information as well.

Accuracy of Self-Evaluation

Successful career development depends in part on an individual's ability to conduct an accurate self-evaluation. When you are doing a self-evaluation, you need to consider factors that are personally significant to you. The most important internal factors are your interests, academic aptitude and achievement, occupational aptitudes and skills, social skills, communication skills, and leadership abilities. You also need to consider the salary level, status, opportunities for advancement, and growth for the job you seek. External factors that should be assessed include your family values and expectations, economic conditions, employment trends, and job market information.

The Significance of Interest Inventories

Psychologists who specialize in career counseling typically administer a battery of tests. The *Strong Vocational Interest Bank* (SVIB), developed by E. K. Strong, Jr., was among the first of the interest tests.[3] Somewhat later, G. Frederic Kuder developed inventories to measure degree of interest in mechanical, clerical, scientific, and persuasive activities, among others. Both the Strong and the Kuder interest inventories have been used widely in vocational counseling.

Strong found substantial differences in interests that vary from occupation to occupation and that a person's interest pattern, especially after age 21, tends to become quite stable. By taking his test, now known as the *Strong Interest Inventory*, you can learn the degree to which your interests correspond with those of successful people in a wide range of occupations. Your personality type can also be obtained by using a special scoring key on the *Strong Interest Inventory* answer sheet. This key, developed by John Holland, provides scores on six personality types: (1) realistic, (2) investigative, (3) artistic, (4) social, (5) enterprising, and (6) conventional. These categories characterize not only a type of personality, but also the type of working environment that a person would find most satisfying. In the actual application of Holland's theory, combinations of the six types are examined. For example, a person may be classified as realistic-investigative-enterprising (RIE). Jobs in the RIE category include mechanical engineer, lineperson, and air traffic controller. To facilitate searching for occupations that match your personality type, such as RIE, Holland devised a series of tables that correlate the Holland categories with jobs in the *Dictionary of Occupational Titles* (DOT), described in Chapter 4.[4]

Another inventory that measures both interests and skills is the *Campbell Interest and Skill Survey* (CISS), which can be taken online at a number of sites for a fee, as can the *Strong Interest Inventory*.[5] The CISS can be used not only to help people explore their career path options, but also to help organizations develop their employees or to reassign them because of major organizational changes. In completing the inventory, individuals report their levels of interest and skill using a six-point response scale on 200 interest items and 120 skill items. CISS item responses are translated into seven orientations—influencing, organizing, helping, creating, analyzing, producing, and adventuring—and further categorized into twenty-nine basic scales such as leadership and supervision to identify occupations that reflect today's workplace.

Highlights in HRM 6 shows a sample profile for one individual. Note that at the top of the profile the range of scores is from 30 to 70, with 50 in the midrange. Corresponding verbal descriptions of scores range from very low to very high. Also note that on the profile two types of scores are profiled: interest (a solid diamond ◆) and skill (an open diamond ◇). The interest score ◆ shows how much the individual likes the specified activities; the skill score ◇ shows how confident the individual feels about performing these activities.

There are four noteworthy patterns of combinations of the interest and skill scores as shown in Figure 5.A1: Pursue, Develop, Explore, and Avoid. For the individual whose scores are profiled in Highlights in HRM 6, one would interpret the scores on the seven orientation scales (as shown in the left-hand column of the profile) as follows:

Influencing	Pursue
Organizing	Indeterminate
Helping	Pursue
Creating	Avoid
Analyzing	Avoid
Producing	Indeterminate
Adventuring	Develop

Profiles such as these help individuals see how their interests and skills compare with those of a sample of people happily employed in a wide range of occupations. The About.com Web site includes a number of free self-assessments.

HIGHLIGHTS IN HRM 6

Campbell Interest and Skill Survey: Individual Profile

SAMPLE   ORIENTATIONS AND BASIC SCALES   DATE SCORED 1/3/2009

ORIENTATIONS AND BASIC SCALES	INTEREST	SKILL	VERY LOW	LOW	MID-RANGE	HIGH	VERY HIGH	INTEREST/SKILL PATTERN
	◆	◇	30 35	40 45	50	55 60	65 70	
Influencing	39	47						
Leadership	42	49						
Law/Politics	42	46						
Public Speaking	36	40						Avoid
Sales	44	36						Avoid
Advertising/Marketing	52	42						

Campbell Interest and Skill Survey: Individual Profile (continued)

Organizing	47	58		Explore
Supervision	52	56		Explore
Financial Services	51	52		
Office Practices	58	65		Pursue
Helping	59	63		Pursue
Adult Development	48	56		Explore
Counseling	58	59		Pursue
Child Development	44	59		Explore
Religious Activities	42	49		
Medical Practice	68	61		Pursue
Creating	59	58		Pursue
Art/Design	66	64		Pursue
Performing Arts	54	52		
Writing	36	34		Avoid
International Activities	57	48		Develop
Fashion	69	70		Pursue
Culinary Arts	66	70		Pursue
Analyzing	32	36		Avoid
Mathematics	34	36		Avoid
Science	38	38		Avoid
Producing	57	62		Pursue
Mechanical Crafts	45	51		
Woodworking	63	58		Pursue
Farming/Forestry	54	60		Explore
Plants/Gardens	66	74		Pursue
Animal Care	62	71		Pursue
Adventuring	47	57		Explore
Athletics/Physical Fitness	56	56		Pursue
Military/Law Enforcement	52	54		
Risks/Adventure	59	58		Pursue

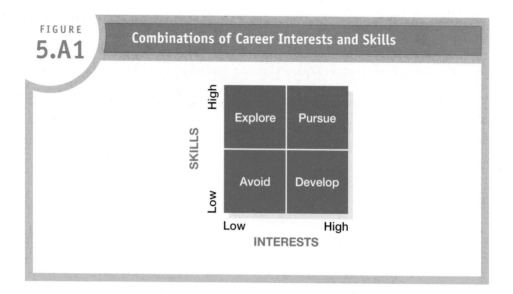

FIGURE
5.A1

Combinations of Career Interests and Skills

Evaluating Long-Term Employment Opportunities

When choosing a career, you should attempt to determine the probable long-term opportunities in the occupational fields you are considering. A source of information that has proved valuable over the years is the *Occupational Outlook Handbook*, published by the U.S. Department of Labor. It is available online and at most libraries. Many libraries also have publications that provide details about jobs and career fields. Other online sources include America's Career InfoNet, sponsored by the U.S. government. The site offers demographic and labor market information at the local, state, and national levels. Most job boards offer similar information.

CHOOSING AN EMPLOYER

Once an individual has made a career choice, even if only tentatively, the next major step is deciding where to work. The choice of employer may be based primarily on location, on the immediate availability of a position, on starting salary, or on other basic considerations. Douglas Hall proposes that people frequently choose an organization on the basis of its climate and how it appears to fit their needs. According to Hall, people with high needs for achievement are more likely to choose aggressive, achievement-oriented organizations. Power-oriented people are more likely to choose influential, prestigious, power-oriented organizations. Affiliative people are more likely to choose warm, friendly, supportive organizations. We know that people whose needs fit with the climate of an organization are rewarded more and are more satisfied than those who fit in less well, so it is natural to reason that fit would also be a factor in a person's choice of an organization.[6]

Knowing something about an employer and industry can give you a competitive edge both in terms of getting an interview, landing a job, and negotiating a good salary. Numerous company directories containing information about privately- and publicly-held companies are available. Hoovers.com is one online source. Corporate Web sites are another source. Often under the "Investors" or "Media" tabs you can find press releases issued by the companies in which you are interested. The releases often highlight the initiatives companies are pursuing and the directions in which they are taking their businesses. Business, industry, and professional publications are a good source, too. Simply "googling" a company can turn up a great deal of information.

Once you have landed an interview, you have the opportunity to learn more about an employer, including the type of people who work there, its corporate culture, benefits, and so forth. If you are offered a job with the firm, a Web site such as salary. com can help you determine whether the firm's offer is appropriate. CNNMoney. com's cost of living calculator titled "How far will my salary go in another city?" can help you figure out whether it is monetarily feasible to relocate for a job. You should ask yourself the following questions before you accept a job offer with a particular company.

Questions to Ask Yourself Before You Accept a Job Offer

- Have I been offered a fair salary? Is it comparable to what other people in the same position are making?
- Have I met my potential boss? Does he or she seem like someone with whom I can have a good working relationship?
- What do I know about my potential coworkers?
- Will I be comfortable in this office environment?
- Is the corporate culture in line with my own values, attitudes, and goals?
- Can I handle the commute to this job?

Source: Excerpted from Dawn Rosenberg McKay, About.com © 2007 About.com, Inc., a part of *The New York Times Company*. All rights reserved.

entrepreneur
One who starts, organizes, manages, and assumes responsibility for a business or other enterprise

▪▪ BECOMING AN ENTREPRENEUR

At the opening of the century, no discussion of careers would be complete if entrepreneurship opportunities were not mentioned. Being an entrepreneur—someone who starts, organizes, manages, and assumes responsibility for a business or other enterprise—offers a personal challenge that many individuals prefer over being an employee. Small businesses are typically run by entrepreneurs who accept the personal financial risks that go with owning a business but who also benefit directly from the success of the business.[7]

Small businesses are actually big employers. They employ half of all private sector employees and account for a little less than half of the total U.S. private payrolls. They also generate 60 to 80 percent of new jobs annually.[8] Someone considering starting a small business can obtain assistance from the Small Business Administration (SBA), which advises and assists millions of small businesses in the United States. It is essential

> **Using the Internet**
>
> Information about starting a business can also be found at the Small Business Administration's Web site. Material concerning SCORE (as a small business resource or a retirement activity) is also available on the Internet. Go to the Student Resources at:
>
> **www.cengage.com/ management/bohlander**

for one considering a small business to obtain as much information as possible from the SBA, libraries, and organizations and individuals who are knowledgeable about the type of business one is considering. For instance, valuable assistance may be obtained from members of the Service Corps of Retired Executives (SCORE), who offer advisory services under the auspices of the SBA.

Since the details of organizing a business are beyond the scope of this book, Figure 5.A2 is presented to provide an overview of the basic steps in starting a new business.[9]

▟ KEEPING A CAREER IN PERSPECTIVE

For most people, work is a primary factor in the overall quality of their lives. It provides a setting for satisfying practically the whole range of human needs and is thus of considerable value to the individual. Nevertheless, it is advisable to keep one's career in perspective so that other important areas of life are not neglected.

Developing Off-the-Job Interests

Satisfaction with one's life is a product of many forces. Unfortunately, when people complain about not having a good work-life balance, often the problem is not too much work, but too little "life," according to Randall Craig of Pinetree Advisors, a human resources strategy consulting firm.[10] Some of the more important ingredients of "life" are physical health, emotional well-being, financial security, harmonious

FIGURE
5.A2

Twelve Steps for Starting a New Business

Source: From *Business in a Changing World*, 3rd edition, by W. Cunningham, R. Aldag, and S. Block: 139 © 1993. Reprinted with permission of South-Western, a division of Cengage Learning: http://www.thomsonrights.com.

interpersonal relationships, freedom from too much stress, and achievement of one's goals. While a career can provide some of the satisfaction that one needs, most people find it necessary to turn to interests and activities outside their career. Off-the-job activities not only provide a respite from daily work responsibilities, but also offer satisfaction in areas unrelated to work. With that said, it is up to you to decide what is important to you and how to spend your work and off-the-job time. Your life is yours to live, and it is shorter than you think.

Balancing Marital and/or Family Life

As we have said, the one event that often poses the greatest threat to family needs is relocation. Families often experience conflicts between the desire to advance the careers of different parents and the desire to stay in one place and put down family roots. Many employers now provide assistance in this area, including relocation counseling, in an effort to reduce the severity of the pain that can accompany relocations.

Although relocation is a serious threat to employees with families, there are also other sources of conflict. Some work-related sources of conflict include the number of hours a person must work per week, frequency of the overtime they work, and frequency and irregularity of shift work. If an employee is experiencing ambiguity and/or conflict with his or her work role, a low level of supervisory support, or disappointment due to unfulfilled work expectations, this can affect his or her family life as well. Other sources of conflict include the need to spend an unusually large amount of time with a person's family members, either to care for children, aging elders, or a spouse. The different employment patterns in a family and dissimilarity in a couple's career orientations are also commonplace and can take a toll on employees.

A number of employers are doing more today to help their employees cope with these problems via alternative work options. Many employees are also actively looking for companies that have family-friendly policies. *Working Mother* magazine annually publishes a survey of the 100 top companies in the United States for working parents. Understand that "to be a success in the business world takes hard work, long hours, persistent effort, and constant attention. To be a success in marriage takes hard work, long hours, persistent effort, and constant attention. . . . The problem is giving each its due and not shortchanging the other."[11]

Planning for Retirement

Although you might be many years from retirement, it is never too early to plan for it. In your twenties, you will want to begin a savings plan and perhaps pay off your student loans. As you get older, your goals will probably change. Perhaps you will want to buy a home, and you will need money for a down payment. Regardless of what stage of your life you are in, you should never neglect saving for your retirement throughout your working years. This is because a small sum of money saved early, compounded with interest over years, can amount to millions of dollars. But if you wait until later, you will have to save a lot of money for it to amount to as much.

Your employer can help you with some aspects of retirement planning by providing you with information about tax-advantaged employer and individual savings plans. Your company might even be able to help you project what your health insurance costs will be in retirement, for example, if you are not covered by company-provided insurance. But although employer-sponsored preretirement programs can be helpful (as we will see in Chapter 11), planning for your own retirement is up to you. Do you want to travel or live in another state or country? What kind of retirement does your spouse envision? How much money will all of this require? Your employer will not be able to answer these questions. However, by reading about the subject of retirement and taking it seriously while you are young, you will be able to answer these questions yourself. Planning early will help you set the stage for a healthy and satisfying retirement as free as possible from worries—especially worries that could have been avoided or minimized had you taken a few easy steps earlier in life.

KEY TERM

entrepreneur

NOTES AND REFERENCES

1. A selection of self-help publications on a variety of topics may be found in any bookstore. College and university bookstores typically have a wide selection in their trade or general books department. Two particularly useful books might be Edward Crip and Richard Mansfield, *The Value-Added Employee: 31 Competencies to Make Yourself Irresistible to Any Company* (London: Butterworth-Heinemann, 2001) and Daniel Goleman, *Emotional Intelligence* (New York: Bantam Books, 1995).

2. Mary Harrington Hall, "A Conversation with Peter Drucker," *Psychology Today* (March 1968): 22.

3. E. K. Strong, Jr., of Stanford University, was active in the measurement of interests from the early 1920s until his death in 1963. Since then his work has been carried on by the staff of the Measurement Research Center, University of Minnesota. The Strong Interest Inventory is distributed by Consulting Psychologists Press, Inc., P.O. Box 60070, Palo Alto, CA 94306, to qualified people under an exclusive license

from the publisher, Stanford University Press.

4. Gary D. Gottfredson and John L. Holland, *Dictionary of Holland Occupational Codes* (Lutz, FL: Psychological Assessment Resources, December 1996); Derek Parker, "The Skills Shortage: Making Headway, But No Easy Answers," *Manufacturers' Monthly* (September 2007).

5. David Lubinski, Camilla P. Benbow, and Jennifer Ryan, "Stability of Vocational Interests among the Intellectually Gifted from Adolescence to Adulthood: A 15-Year Longitudinal Study," *Journal of Applied Psychology* 80, no. 1 (February 1995): 196–200; Hope Samborn, "Left Click, Left Law," *ABA Journal* 92, no. 7 (July 2006): 58.

6. Douglas T. Hall and Jonathan E. Moss, "The New Protean Career Contract: Helping Organizations and Employees Adapt," *Organizational Dynamics* 26, no. 3 (Winter 1998): 22–37. See also Douglas T. Hall, *The Career Is Dead, Long Live the Career: A Relational Approach to Careers* (San Francisco: Jossey-Bass, 1996);

Douglas T. Hall, "Protean Careers of the 21st Century," *Academy of Management Executive* 10, no. 4 (1996): 8–16; Douglas T. Hall and Associates, *Career Development in Organizations* (San Francisco: Jossey-Bass, 1986); Yue-Wah Chay and Samuel Aryee, "The Moderating Influence of Career Growth Opportunities on Careerist Orientation and Work Attitudes: Evidence of the Protean Career Era in Singapore," *Journal of Organizational Behavior* 20, no. 5 (September 1999): 613–23.

7. Julie Rose, "The New Risk Takers," *Fortune Small Business* 12, no. 2 (March 2002): 28–34; Jack Howard, "Balancing Conflicts of Interest When Employing Spouses," *Employee Responsibilities & Rights* 20, no. 1 (March 2008): 29–43.

8. U.S. Bureau of the Census; Advocacy-funded research by Joel Popkin and Company (Research Summary #211); U.S. Department of Labor, Bureau of Labor Statistics, Current Population Survey; U.S. Department of Commerce, International Trade Administration.

9. For information on starting a business, the interested reader might look into Bob Adams, *Adams Streetwise Small Business Startup* (Holbrook, MA: Adams Media Corporation, 1996); Linda Pinson and Jerry Jinnett, *Anatomy of a Business Plan: Starting Smart, Building a Business and Securing Your Company's Future* (Chicago: Upstart, 1996); Kenneth Cook, *AMA Complete Guide to Strategic Planning for Small Business* (Lincolnwood, IL: NTC Business Books, 1995); Priscilla Y. Huff, *101 Best Small Businesses for Women* (Rocklin, CA: Prima, 1996); Constance Jones, *The 220 Best Franchises to Buy: The Sourcebook for Evaluating the Best Franchise Opportunities* (New York: Bantam Doubleday Dell, 1993).

10. Jamie Eckle, "Randall Craig," *Computerworld* 42, no. 26 (June 23, 2008): 36.

11. Christopher Caggiano, "Married . . . with Companies," *Inc.* 17, no. 6 (May 1995): 68–76; Sue Shellenbarger, "Sustaining a Marriage When Job Demands Seem to Be Endless," *The Wall Street Journal*, December 8, 1999, B1; Johan A. Turner, "Work Options for Older Americans: Employee Benefits for the Era of Living Longer," *Benefits Quarterly*, 24, no. 3, (2008): 20–25.

EMPLOYEE SELECTION

After studying this chapter, you should be able to

Objective | 1

Explain the objectives of the personnel selection process.

Objective | 2

Identify the various sources of information used for personnel selection.

© DGA PRODUCTIONS/TAXI/GETTY IMAGES

Objective 3

Compare the value of different types of employment tests.

Objective 4

Illustrate the different approaches to conducting an employment interview.

Objective 5

Describe the various decision strategies for selection.

There is perhaps no more important topic in human resources management than employee selection. If it is true that organizations succeed or fail based on the talents of employees, then managers directly influence that success through the people they hire. Regardless of whether the company is large or small, hiring the best and the brightest employees lays a strong foundation for excellence. Alternatively, it is common to hear managers who do not recognize this point lament the inordinate amount of time they spend trying to fix bad selection decisions. It is a costly activity, too. A recent study by the Society for HR Management found that the cost of hiring someone for a wrong intermediate position is approximately $20,000, and the cost of hiring the wrong person for a senior manager's position is $100,000. In addition, equal employment opportunity legislation, court decisions, and the *Uniform Guidelines* (discussed in Chapter 3) have also provided an impetus for making sure that the selection process is done well. The bottom line is good selection decisions make a difference. So do bad ones.

◼◼ MATCHING PEOPLE AND JOBS

In conjunction with the recruiting process, which is designed to increase the number of applicants whose qualifications meet job requirements and the needs of the organization, selection is the process of reducing that number and choosing from among those individuals who have the relevant qualifications.

Figure 6.1 shows in broad terms that the overall goal of selection is to maximize "hits" and avoid "misses." Hits are accurate predictions, and misses are inaccurate

selection

The process of choosing individuals who have relevant qualifications to fill existing or projected job openings

FIGURE 6.1

The Goal of Selection: Maximize "Hits"

MISS
Inaccurate prediction
(Person would have succeeded on the job)

HIT
Accurate prediction
(Person succeeds on the job)

HIT
Accurate prediction
(Person would not have succeeded on the job)

MISS
Inaccurate prediction
(Person fails on the job)

Job Performance — High / Low

Predicted Success — Low ← → High

ones. The cost of one type of miss would be the direct and indirect expense of hiring an employee who turns out to be unsuccessful. The cost of the other type of miss is an opportunity cost—someone who could have been successful did not get a chance.

While the overall selection program is often the formal responsibility of the HR department, line managers typically make the final decision about hiring people in their unit. It is important therefore that managers understand the objectives, policies, and practices used for selection. In that way, they can be highly involved in the process from the very beginning. Those responsible for making selection decisions should have adequate information upon which to base their decisions. Information about the jobs to be filled, knowledge of the ratio of job openings to the number of applicants, and as much relevant information as possible about the applicants themselves are essential for making sound decisions.

Person-Job Fit: Beginning with Job Analysis

In Chapter 4, we discussed the process of analyzing jobs to develop job descriptions and specifications. Job specifications, in particular, help identify the *individual competencies* employees need for success—the knowledge, skills, abilities, and other factors (KSAOs) that lead to superior performance. By identifying competencies through job analysis, managers can then use selection methods such as interviews, references, psychological tests, and the like to measure applicant KSAOs against the competencies required for the job. This is often referred to as *person-job fit*. Research has demonstrated that complete and unambiguous specification of required competencies (via job analysis) reduces the influence of racial and gender stereotypes and helps the interviewer differentiate between qualified and unqualified applicants. Research also shows that applicants whose KSAOs are well matched to the jobs they are hired for perform better and are more satisfied.[1]

Person-Organization Fit

In addition to the requirements of the job, many organizations also place a priority on finding individuals that meet broader organizational requirements. Companies such as Texas Instruments, Merck, Southwest Airlines, and Starbucks place a high priority on selecting individuals who match the values and culture of their organizations. Although there are at times potential concerns that this may create an overly uniform workforce (and raises diversity concerns), the need for teamwork and flexibility has created a keen interest in this type of person-organization fit. In many instances, managers will pass up potential employees if they do not embrace the values of the organization—even if they have excellent technical skills for the job.[2]

Ordinarily, managers are well acquainted with the requirements pertaining to the skills, physical demands, and other factors for jobs in their organizations. Interviewers and other members of the HR department who participate in selection should maintain a close liaison with the various departments so that they can become thoroughly familiar with the jobs and competencies needed to perform them.

The Selection Process

In most organizations, selection is an ongoing process. Turnover inevitably occurs, leaving vacancies to be filled by applicants from inside or outside the organization or by individuals whose qualifications have been assessed previously. It is common

1 Objective

to have a waiting list of applicants who can be called when permanent or temporary positions become open.

The number of steps in the selection process and their sequence will vary, not only with the organization, but also with the type and level of jobs to be filled. Each step should be evaluated in terms of its contribution to the process. The steps that typically make up the selection process are shown in Figure 6.2. Not all applicants will go through all of these steps. Some may be rejected after the preliminary interview, others after taking tests, and so on.

As Figure 6.2 shows, organizations use several different means to obtain information about applicants. These include application blanks, interviews, tests, medical examinations, and background investigations. Regardless of the method used, it is essential that it conform to accepted ethical standards, including privacy and confidentiality, as well as legal requirements. Above all, it is essential that the information obtained be sufficiently reliable and valid.

reliability
The degree to which interviews, tests, and other selection procedures yield comparable data over time and alternative measures

Obtaining Reliable and Valid Information

The degree to which interviews, tests, and other selection procedures yield comparable data over a period of time is known as reliability. For example, unless interview-

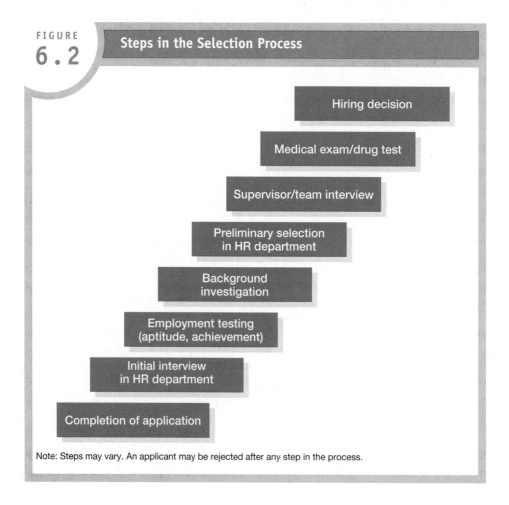

FIGURE
6.2

Steps in the Selection Process

Hiring decision

Medical exam/drug test

Supervisor/team interview

Preliminary selection in HR department

Background investigation

Employment testing (aptitude, achievement)

Initial interview in HR department

Completion of application

Note: Steps may vary. An applicant may be rejected after any step in the process.

ers judge the capabilities of a group of applicants to be the same today as they did yesterday, their judgments are unreliable (that is, unstable). Likewise, a test that gives widely different scores when it is administered to the same individual a few days apart is unreliable.

Reliability also refers to the extent to which two or more methods (interviews and tests, for example) yield similar results or are consistent. Interrater reliability—agreement among two or more raters—is one measure of a method's consistency. Unless the data on which selection decisions are based are reliable, in terms of both stability and consistency, they cannot be used as predictors.

In addition to having reliable information pertaining to a person's suitability for a job, the information must be as valid as possible. Validity refers to what a test or other selection procedure measures and how well it measures it. In the context of personnel selection, validity is essentially an indicator of the extent to which data from a procedure (interview or test, for example) can predict how well a person performs on the job. Like a new medicine, a selection procedure must be validated before it is used. There are two reasons for validating a procedure. First, validity is directly related to increases in employee productivity, as we will demonstrate later. Second, EEO regulations require selection procedures to be valid.[3] Although we commonly refer to "validating" a test or interview procedure, validity in the technical sense refers to the inferences made from the use of a procedure, not the procedure itself.

The *Uniform Guidelines* (see Chapter 3) recognizes and accepts different approaches to validation: criterion-related validity, content validity, and construct validity.

validity
The degree to which a test or selection procedure measures a person's attributes

Criterion-Related Validity

The extent to which a selection tool predicts, or significantly correlates with, important elements of work behavior is known as criterion-related validity. How well a person performs on a test, for example, is compared with his or her actual production records, supervisory ratings, training outcomes, and other measures of success that are appropriate to each type of job. In a sales job, for example, it is common to use sales figures as a basis for comparison. In production jobs, the quantity and quality of output are likely to be the best indicators of job success.

There are two types of criterion-related validity: concurrent and predictive. Concurrent validity involves obtaining criterion data from *current employees* at about the same time that test scores (or other predictor information) are obtained. For example, a supervisor will be asked to rate a group of clerical employees on the quantity and quality of their performance. These employees are then given a clerical aptitude test, and the test scores are compared with the supervisors' ratings to determine the degree of relationship between them. Predictive validity, on the other hand, involves testing *applicants* and obtaining criterion data *after* those applicants have been hired and have been on the job for a certain period of time. For example, applicants are given clerical aptitude tests, which are then filed away for later study. After the individuals have been on the job for several months, supervisors, who should not know the employees' test scores, are asked to rate them on the quality and quantity of their performance. The test scores are then compared with the supervisors' ratings.

Regardless of the method used, cross-validation is essential. Cross-validation is a process in which a test or battery of tests is administered to a different sample of people (drawn from the same population) for the purpose of verifying the results obtained from the original validation study.

criterion-related validity
The extent to which a selection tool predicts, or significantly correlates with, important elements of work behavior

predictive validity
The extent to which applicants' test scores match criterion data obtained from those applicants/employees after they have been on the job for some indefinite period

cross-validation
Verifying the results obtained from a validation study by administering a test or test battery to a different sample (drawn from the same population)

Correlational methods are generally used to determine the relationship between predictor information such as test scores and criterion data. The correlation scatterplots in Figure 6.3 illustrate the difference between a selection test with zero validity (A) and one with high validity (B). Each dot represents a person. Note that in scatterplot A, there is no relationship between test scores and success on the job; in other words, the validity is zero. In scatterplot B, those who score low on the test tend to have low success on the job, whereas those who score high on the test tend to have high success on the job, indicating high validity. In actual practice we would apply a statistical formula to the data to obtain a coefficient of correlation referred to as a *validity coefficient*. Correlation coefficients range from 0.00, denoting a complete absence of relationship, to +1.00 and to −1.00, indicating a perfect positive and perfect negative relationship, respectively.

A thorough survey of the literature shows that the averages of the maximum validity coefficients are 0.45 when the tests are validated against *training* criteria and 0.35 when the tests are validated against *job proficiency* criteria. These figures represent the predictive power of single tests.[4] A higher validity may be obtained by combining two or more tests or other predictors (an interview or biographical data, for instance), using the appropriate statistical formulas. The higher the overall validity is, the greater the chances are of hiring individuals who will be the better performers. The criterion-related method is generally preferred to other validation approaches because it is based on empirical data.

For several decades, personnel psychologists believed that validity coefficients had meaning only for the specific jobs and organizations for which they were being used. However, more recently, as a result of several research studies—many involving clerical jobs—it appears that validity coefficients can often be generalized across

FIGURE 6.3

Correlation Scatterplots

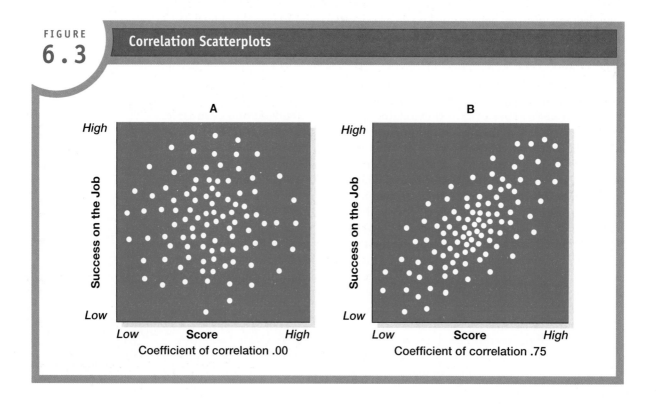

situations, hence the term validity generalization. When there are adequate data to support the existence of validity generalization, developing selection procedures can become less costly and time-consuming. The process involves analyzing jobs and situations and, on the basis of these analyses, consulting tables of generalized validities from previous studies using various predictors in similar circumstances. Because valid, custom tests are more defensible in court if applicants challenge them, it is advisable for organizations to hire an industrial-organizational psychologist experienced in test validation to develop selection procedures based on validity generalization.[5]

validity generalization
The extent to which validity coefficients can be generalized across situations

Content Validity

When it is not feasible to use the criterion-related approach, often because of limited samples of individuals, the content method is used. Content validity is assumed to exist when a selection instrument, such as a test, adequately samples the knowledge and skills a person needs to do a particular job.

The closer the content of the selection instrument is to actual work samples or behaviors, the greater its content validity is. For example, a civil service examination for accountants has high content validity when it requires applicants to solve accounting problems representative of those found on the job. Asking an accountant to lift a sixty-pound box, however, is a selection procedure that has content validity only if the job description indicates that accountants must be able to meet this requirement.

Content validity is the most direct and least complicated type of validity to assess. It is generally used to evaluate job knowledge and skill tests, to be described later. Unlike the criterion-related method, content validity is not expressed in correlational terms. Instead, an index is computed (from evaluations of an expert panel) that indicates the relationship between the content of the test items and a person's performance on the job.[6] While content validity does have its limitations, it has made a positive contribution to job analysis procedures and to the role of expert judgment in sampling and scoring procedures.

content validity
The extent to which a selection instrument, such as a test, adequately samples the knowledge and skills needed to perform a particular job

Construct Validity

The extent to which a selection tool measures a theoretical construct, or trait, is known as construct validity. Typical constructs are intelligence, mechanical comprehension, and anxiety. They are in effect broad, general categories of human functions that are based on the measurement of many discrete behaviors. For example, the Bennett Mechanical Comprehension Test consists of a wide variety of tasks that measure the construct of mechanical comprehension.

Measuring construct validity requires showing that the psychological trait is related to satisfactory job performance and that the test accurately measures the psychological trait. There is a lack of literature covering this concept as it relates to employment practices, probably because it is difficult and expensive to validate a construct and to show how it is job-related.[7]

construct validity
The extent to which a selection tool measures a theoretical construct or trait

▪▪ SOURCES OF INFORMATION ABOUT JOB CANDIDATES

Many sources of information are used to provide as reliable and valid a picture as possible of an applicant's potential for success on the job. In this section, we will study the potential contributions of application forms; biographical information blanks;

2 | Objective

background investigations; polygraph, or lie detector, tests; honesty and integrity tests; graphology; and medical examinations. Because interviewing plays such a major role in selection and because testing presents unique challenges, there will be expanded discussions of these sources of information later in the chapter. Assessment centers, which are often used in managerial selection, were discussed in Chapter 5.

Application Forms

Most organizations require application forms to be completed because they provide a fairly quick and systematic means of obtaining a variety of information about the applicant. As with interviews, the EEOC and the courts have found that many questions asked on application forms disproportionately discriminate against females and minorities and often are not job-related. Application forms should therefore be developed with great care and revised as often as necessary. Because of differences in state laws on fair employment practices (FEPs) (see Chapter 3), organizations operating in more than one state will find it difficult to develop one form that can be used nationally.

Application forms serve several purposes. They provide information for deciding whether an applicant meets the minimum requirements for experience, education, and so on. They provide a basis for questions the interviewer will ask about the applicant's background. They also offer sources for reference checks. For certain jobs, a short application form is appropriate. For example, McDonald's uses a form that is quite brief but asks for information that is highly relevant to job performance. The form also provides information regarding the employer's conformity with various laws and regulations. For scientific, professional, and managerial jobs, a more extended form is likely to be used.

Even when applicants come armed with elaborate resumes, it is important that they complete an application form early in the process. People, even those in high positions, frequently exaggerate their qualifications on their resumes and omit unflattering information. For example, George O'Leary had to resign as head football coach at Notre Dame after admitting to falsely claiming he had played football at New Hampshire and had a master's degree from New York University. Similarly, Radio Shack CEO David Edmondson was forced to resign in 2006, after claiming on his resume that he had earned college degrees in theology and psychology. Not only had he not graduated, but the college he attended did not even offer a psychology degree.[8]

Asking applicants to transcribe specific resume material onto a standardized application form can help alleviate this problem. Far fewer people lie on application forms relative to their resumes, a 2006 survey by CareerBuilder.com found. The applicant is then asked to sign a statement that the information contained on the form is true and that he or she accepts the employer's right to terminate the candidate's employment if any of the information is subsequently found to be false.[9]

Many managers remain unclear about the questions they can ask on an application blank. While most know they should steer clear of issues such as age, race, marital status, and sexual orientation, other issues are less clear. In addition to consulting their state's employment laws, some of which are more restrictive than others, the following are some suggestions for putting together an application form:

- *Application date.* The applicant should date the application. This helps managers know when the form was completed and gives them an idea of the time limit (for example, one year) that the form should be on file.

Using the Internet

You can practice reading and analyzing resumes online. Go to the Student Resources at:

www.cengage.com/management/bohlander

- *Educational background.* The form should contain blanks for grade school, high school, college, and postcollege attendance—but not the dates attended, since that can be connected with age.

- *Experience.* Virtually any questions that focus on work experience related to the job are permissible.

- *Arrests and criminal convictions.* Questions about arrests alone are not permissible. But questions about convictions and guilty pleadings are fine. However, the application must state that answering "yes" will not necessarily disqualify the candidate. Whether it will or not will depend upon whether the conviction is related to the job. For example, someone convicted for illegal drug use could potentially be disqualified for a job working in a pharmaceutical manufacturing plant.

- *National origin.* Such questions are not permitted. However, it is allowable to ask whether the person is legally prevented from working in the United States. This is important because before beginning work, all employees, including U.S. citizens, must complete an I-9 form for their employers to submit to the government verifying that they are eligible to work in the United States. They must also provide supporting documents proving as much.

- *References.* It is advisable to include blanks for the names, addresses, and phone numbers of references provided by applicants. (We will cover this in more detail later.)

- *Disabilities.* This is a potentially tricky area. The Americans with Disabilities Act prohibits discriminating against a person with a disability who, with or without reasonable accommodation, can perform essential job functions. But employers are not allowed to ask applicants questions designed to elicit information about the existence, nature, or severity of a disability. Inquiries about the ability of the person to perform job functions, however, are acceptable. Under the most recent guidelines issued by the EEOC, employers can ask whether an applicant needs reasonable accommodation—*if* the disability is obvious or *if* the applicant has voluntarily disclosed the disability.

- *EEOC and at-will statements.* It is a good idea to state on the application form that the firm does not discriminate and is an EEOC employer. If your state allows it, the form should state that all employees are hired *at-will.* This gives both the employer and employee the right to end the employment relationship at any time without reason. (How the employment-at-will principle works will be discussed in greater detail in Chapter 13.)

Many of these issues will be addressed again, particularly in the section on employment interviews.

Some organizations use what is referred to as a *weighted application blank (WAB).* The WAB involves the use of a common standardized employment application that is designed to distinguish between successful and unsuccessful employees. If managers can identify application items that have predicted employee success in the past, they may use that information to screen other applicants. Some evidence suggests that use of the WAB has been especially helpful for reducing turnover costs in the hospitality industry.

Online Applications

As we explained in Chapter 5, most large companies accept applications online and are also able to mine resumes, spot qualified applicants, and conduct screening tests online. One of the key advantages of accepting applications online is that companies can recruit candidates and fill their job openings much faster. The discount stock broker Charles Schwab claims that using the Internet, it can now fill a job opening in just one week.

Companies report that the downside of posting jobs and accepting online applications is that it can lead to a large volume of them being submitted—many of which fail to meet minimum qualifications. The upside, however, is that generating a larger number of applicants tends to promote greater employee diversity. Home Depot, for example, successfully implemented an online application system called the Job Preference Program to get a broader pool of applicants than it previously had been getting. It ultimately enabled the company to hire more women.[10]

Biographical Information Blanks

One of the oldest methods for predicting job success uses biographical information, or "biodata," about job applicants. As early as 1917, the Life Insurance Agency Management Association constructed and validated a biographical information blank (BIB) for life insurance salespeople. BIBs cover such issues as family life, hobbies, club memberships, sales experience, and investments. Like application

Employers can post a job for 60 days; purchase job inventories for later posting within a year; search resumes to find specific job qualifications; and view, save, and organize resumes online.

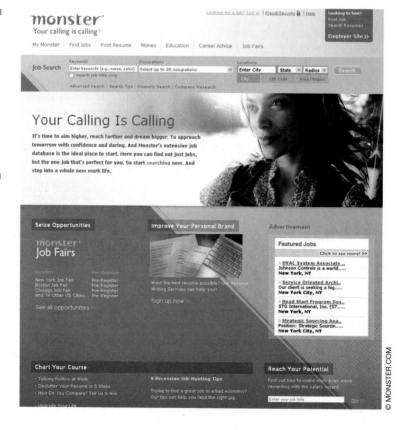

blanks, BIBs reveal information about a person's history that may have shaped his or her behavior. Sample questions from a BIB might include the following:

- At what age did you leave home?
- How large was the town/city in which you lived as a child?
- Did you ever build a model airplane that flew?
- Were sports a big part of your childhood?
- Do you play any musical instruments?

Both the BIB and the application form can be scored like tests. Because biographical questions rarely have obviously right or wrong answers, BIBs are difficult to fake. The development of a scoring system requires that the items that are valid predictors of job success (positively or negatively correlated) be identified and that weights be established for different responses to these items. By totaling the scores for each item, it is possible to obtain a composite score on the BIB as a whole for each applicant. Studies have shown that an objective scoring of BIB and application forms is one of the most potentially valid methods of predicting job success. This method has been useful in predicting all types of behavior, including employee theft, turnover, and performance in jobs such as sales, nursing, and management.[11]

Background Checks

When the interviewer is satisfied that the applicant is potentially qualified, information about previous employment as well as other information provided by the applicant is investigated. Following 9/11 and a rash of corporate scandals at companies such as Enron, Tyco, and WorldCom, background investigations have become standard procedure for many companies to prevent a variety of problems ranging from embezzlement and theft of merchandise to workplace violence. Moreover, state courts have ruled that companies can be held liable for **negligent hiring** if they fail to do adequate background checks. Federal law requires comprehensive background checks for all child care providers, for example. It also prohibits convicted felons from engaging in financial and security-oriented transactions.

negligent hiring
The failure of an organization to discover, via due diligence, that an employee it hired had the propensity to do harm to others

Among the checks are Social Security verification, past employment and education verification, and a criminal records check. A number of other checks can be conducted if they pertain to the job for which one is being hired. They include a motor vehicle record check (for jobs involving driving), a credit check (for money-handling jobs), and a military records check. Figure 6.4 shows the various screening tools most used by companies.

Like the application process, many checks that were once done manually are now being done online using existing computer databases. However, this frequently requires checking many different databases on a county-by-county basis. Information on international applicants is even harder to obtain. Additionally, delving into areas of an applicant's background irrelevant to the job requirements he or she is applying for can leave the firms exposed to violation-of-privacy claims.

To comply with different state laws regarding privacy and treat all applicants fairly and consistently, many firms use the Department of Homeland Security's e-Verify system to conduct their background checks. Other companies outsource some or all of the checks to third-party screeners. If you are working with a screening company, you should also check to see if it is certified by the National Association of Professional Background Screeners.

FIGURE

6.4

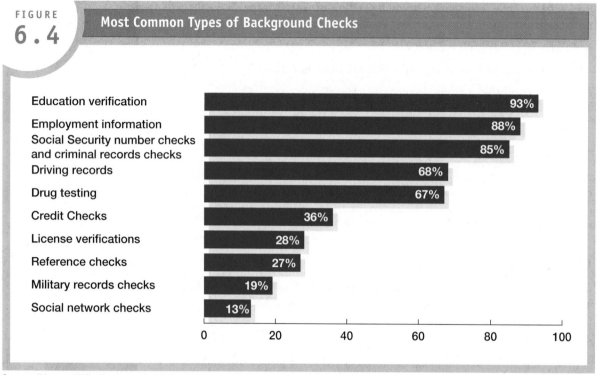

Most Common Types of Background Checks

Source: "How and Why Employers Are Doing Background Screenings," *HRFocus* 85, no. 7 (July 2008): 8–9.

Some job boards now have online screening tools allowing an applicant to conduct his or her own self-background check and post it online prior to any sort of interview. The idea is to demonstrate upfront to prospective employers that the applicant has a clean criminal record, a good job history, and would make a good employee.[12] Finally, an increasing number of companies are simply using Internet searches to uncover background information on a potential candidate.

Checking References

Organizations check the references of employees in a number of ways. Generally, telephone checks are preferable because they save time and provide for greater candor. But references via faxes, mail, and e-mail are also used. Prescient InfoTech, a computer systems managing company in Fairfax, Virginia, first calls references to establish contact and then faxes or e-mails them a two-page questionnaire, asking them to numerically rank the applicant's various job-related attributes. There is room at the end of the questionnaire for comments and recommendations.

The most reliable information usually comes from supervisors, who are in the best position to report on an applicant's work habits and performance. Written verification of information relating to job titles, duties, and pay levels from the former employer's HR office is also very helpful. Highlights in HRM 1 includes a list of helpful questions to ask about applicants when checking their references.[13]

Based on the Privacy Act of 1974, individuals have a legal right to examine letters of reference about them (unless they waive the right to do so). Although the Privacy

1

HIGHLIGHTS IN HRM

Sample Reference-Checking Questions

Just the Facts

What were the candidate's dates of employment?

What was the candidate's title?

What were the candidate's general responsibilities?

What is your relationship to the candidate (peer, subordinate, superior)?

How long have you known the candidate?

On the Job

How would you describe the overall quality of the candidate's work? Can you give me some examples?

(For superiors) What areas of performance did you have to work on?

What would you say are the candidate's strengths?

What would you say are the candidate's weaknesses?

How would you compare the candidate's work to the work of others who performed the same job?

What kind of environment did the candidate work in?

How much of a contribution do you think the candidate made to your company or department?

How would you describe the candidate's ability to communicate?

How does the candidate handle pressure/deadlines?

How well does the candidate get along with coworkers?

How well does the candidate get along with managers?

How well does the candidate supervise others? Can you give me your impressions of his or her management style? Describe the candidate's success in motivating subordinates.

How does the candidate handle conflict situations?

Based on the candidate's performance with your company, do you think he or she would be good in the type of position we're considering him or her for?

What motivates the candidate? How ambitious is he or she?

The Bottom Line

Why did the candidate leave your company?

Would you rehire this person?

Would you recommend this candidate for this type of position?

What type of work is the candidate ideally suited for?

Were there any serious problems with the candidate that we need to be aware of before making a hiring decision?

Do you have any additional information to share with us about this candidate?

Source: Carolyn Hirschman, "The Whole Truth," *HRMagazine* 45, no. 6 (June 2000): 86–72.

Act applies only to the records maintained by federal government agencies, other forms of privacy legislation in most states have influenced employers to "clean up" their personnel files and open them up to review and challenge by the employees concerned.[14]

As a legal protection for all concerned, it is important to ask the applicant to fill out forms permitting information to be solicited from former employers and other reference sources. Even with these safeguards, many organizations are reluctant to put into writing an evaluation of a former employee for fear of being sued by the person. Many employers will only verify former employees' employment dates and positions. Nonetheless, even firms that have failed to give an employee a recommendation have found themselves sued. Other firms have found themselves sued for negligent hiring—knowing a former employee posed a danger to others but failing to disclose the fact. Recognizing this predicament, a number of states have enacted statutes offering protection from liability for employers who give references in good faith.[15]

Using Credit Reports

Credit checks are more widely available and cheaper in the United States today than in other countries because the United States has a national credit reporting system. But the Fair and Accurate Credit Transactions Act of 2003 (which was designed, among other things, to make identity theft more difficult), along with the Consumer Reporting Employment Clarification Act of 1998, and the Consumer Credit Reporting Reform Act of 1996 now restrict the sharing of some credit information. In terms of hiring, a "credit report" extends beyond the financial arena to include almost any compilation of information on an individual that is prepared by a third-party agency. To rely on a report such as this in making employment decisions, organizations must follow five important steps.

First, the organization must check state laws to see if credit reports can legally be used. Too often credit checks are used when they are not really needed and unlawfully screen out a disproportionate number of black and Hispanic applicants. Recognizing this problem and the fact that credit checks can lead to identify theft, some states have begun limiting their use. For example, the state of Washington prohibits their use for employment purposes altogether.

Second, organizations must advise and receive written consent from applicants if such a report will be requested. If an employer plans to use a more comprehensive type of third-party report, such as an investigative consumer report, the applicant must be advised in writing. An investigative consumer report includes information based on personal interviews with the applicant's friends, neighbors, and associates rather than just from an existing database. The applicant must be told that additional disclosure concerning the complete nature and scope of the investigation will be provided to the applicant on written request.

Third, the organization must provide a written certification to the consumer reporting agency (the agency providing the information) about the purpose of the report and must assure them that it will not be used for any other purpose. In the case of investigative reports, the employer also has to certify that it will give an applicant the information if he or she asks for it.

Fourth, before taking any adverse action due to information in the report, organizations must provide applicants a copy of the consumer report as well as a summary of their rights.

Fifth, if the organization decides not to hire the applicant based on the report, it must provide an adverse action notice to that person. Although the notice can be provided verbally, in writing, or electronically, it must contain the name, address, and phone number of the agency that provided the report. The employer must also provide a statement that the reporting agency did not make the hiring decision, that the applicant has a right to obtain an additional free copy of the report, and that the applicant has a right to dispute the accuracy of information with the reporting agency.[16]

Polygraph Tests

The polygraph, or lie detector, is a device that measures the changes in breathing, blood pressure, and pulse of a person who is being questioned. It consists of a rubber tube around the chest, a cuff around the arm, and sensors attached to the fingers that record the physiological changes in the examinee as the examiner asks questions that call for an answer of yes or no. Questions typically cover such items as whether a person uses drugs, has stolen from an employer, or has committed a serious undetected crime.

The growing swell of objections to the use of polygraphs in employment situations culminated in the passage of the federal Employee Polygraph Protection Act of 1988. The Act generally prohibits using lie detectors for prehire screening and random testing of a firm's current employees and applies to all private employers except pharmaceutical companies and companies that supply security guards for health and safety operations as well as government agencies.[17] It defines the term *lie detector* to include the polygraph, deceptograph, voice stress analyzer, psychological stress evaluator, and any similar mechanical or electrical device used to render a diagnostic opinion about the honesty or dishonesty of an individual.

Other provisions of the Act set qualification standards for polygraph examiners, conditions for examinations, and disclosure of information when the use of the polygraph is authorized. Because of the law, employers have had to resort to such alternatives as written tests of honesty and background checks of applicants. Among the organizations most affected are Wall Street firms, banks, and retail companies, which used to rely heavily on polygraphs. Polygraphs are used by only a small percentage of firms in the general population, although their use is prevalent among law enforcement agencies.[18]

Honesty and Integrity Tests

In response to the Employee Polygraph Protection Act, many employers have dramatically increased their use of pencil-and-paper honesty and integrity tests. These tests have commonly been used in settings such as retail stores where employees have access to cash or merchandise. Common areas of inquiry include beliefs about frequency and extent of theft in our society, punishment for theft, and perceived ease of theft. For example, Payless ShoeSource, based in Topeka, Kansas, has used a paper-and-pencil honesty test to reduce employee theft. When the company began its program, losses totaled nearly $21 million per year among its 4,700 stores. Within only one year of implementing its screening program, inventory shrinkage fell by 20 percent to less than 1 percent of sales.[19]

Potential items that might be used on an integrity test are shown in Figure 6.5. Although some studies have shown that honesty tests are valid for predicting job performance as well as a wide range of disruptive behaviors such as theft, disciplinary problems, and absenteeism, other studies have questioned their validity.[20] It is possible that the tests "work" not because they predict behavior but because they deter less-than-honest applicants from joining a company. Lastly, applicants sometimes view the tests as an invasion of their privacy. Given these issues, HRM specialists should

FIGURE
6.5

Integrity Test Question Examples

TO TEST TENDENCY TO	DESCRIPTION
Protect	Contains items that require individuals to indicate whether they would protect friends or co-workers who had engaged in counterproductive behaviors. *Example:* I would turn in a fellow worker I saw stealing money.
Be lenient	Contains items in which test takers indicate whether they would be lenient with respect to the wrongdoings of others. *Example:* An employee should be fired if the employer finds out the employee lied on the application bank.
Admit thought	Includes items that require test takers to indicate the degree to which they would engage in counterproductive thoughts or behaviors. *Example:* I've thought about taking money from an employer without actually doing it.
Admit behavior	Contains items in which individuals admit to directly participating in actual counterproductive behaviors. *Example:* Over the last three years, what's the total amount of money you've taken without permission from your employer?
Consider common	Includes items that require the individual to indicate whether there are excuses or justifications for stealing or performing other questionable behaviors. *Example:* Most people I've worked with have stolen something at one time or another.
Excuse	Contains items in which individuals indicate whether there are excuses or justifications for stealing or performing other questionable behaviors. *Example:* Someone who steals because his family is in need should not be treated the same as a common thief.
Lie	Contains items that measure the extent to which the test taker is responding in a socially desirable manner. *Example:* Never in my whole life have I wished for anything I was not entitled to.

Note: The number of items in each category was 2, 8, 13, 9, 17, 8, and 7, respectively.

Source: Stephen Dwight and George Alliger, "Reactions to Overt Integrity Test Items," *Educational and Psychological Measurement* 57, no. 6 (December 1977): 937–48, copyright © 1997 by Sage Publications, Inc. Reprinted with the permission of Sage Publications, Inc.

consider the use of honesty tests very cautiously and most certainly in conjunction with other sources of information.[21]

Graphology

Graphology, a term that refers to a variety of systems of handwriting analysis, is used by some employers to make employment decisions. Graphologists obtain a sample of handwriting and then examine such characteristics as the size and slant of letters, amount of pressure applied, and placement of the writing on the page. From their observations, graphologists can allegedly draw inferences about such things as the writer's personality traits, intelligence, energy level, organizational abilities, creativity, integrity, emotional maturity, self-image, people skills, and entrepreneurial tendencies. Graphology is used in Europe and extensively in France, where the practice was developed.[22] Handwriting analysis has since quietly spread through corporate America. Companies such as Ford and General Electric have used it for selection, as has the U.S. Central Intelligence Agency (CIA).

Organizations using handwriting analysis say they prefer it to typical personality tests because it requires only that job candidates take a few minutes to jot down a short essay. By contrast, a battery of personality tests and interviews with psychologists can take several hours and can cost thousands of dollars. In addition, there is some evidence to suggest that graphology can be a reliable predictor of *personality* when compared with other psychological tests.

However, graphology's predictive validity for *job performance* and occupational success remains questionable. In the academic community, where formal and rigorous validity studies are customary, the use of graphology for employment decisions has been viewed with considerable skepticism. In addition, some U.S. courts have ruled that handwriting analysis can only be used to authenticate whether a handwriting sample is genuine or forged and not to imply anything about a person's psychological or work characteristics. Finally, like integrity tests, applicants sometimes find the screening method off-putting.[23]

Using the Internet

To see how handwriting analysis is used for employment purposes, go to the Student Resources at:

www.cengage.com/ management/bohlander

Medical Examinations

The medical examination is one of the later steps in the selection process because it can be costly. A medical examination is generally given to ensure that the health of an applicant is adequate to meet the job requirements. It also provides a baseline against which subsequent medical examinations can be compared and interpreted. The latter objective is particularly important in determinations of work-caused disabilities under workers' compensation laws.[24]

In some cases, medical testing can be considered an invasion of privacy and may be in violation of the law. For example, the Americans with Disabilities Act severely limits the types of medical inquiries and examinations that employers may use. Wal-Mart, for example, paid $6 million to settle one lawsuit involving an ADA claim. According to the EEOC, Wal-Mart's hiring questionnaire violated an ADA provision restricting the kinds of medical information companies can request from prospective employees. The law explicitly states that all exams must be directly related to the requirements of the job and that a medical exam cannot be given until an offer of employment has been extended. In addition, the examinations must be required of all candidates offered the job. Furthermore, the ADA prohibits companies from screening out a prospective employee because he or she has an elevated risk of on-the-job injury or a medical condition that could be aggravated because of job demands. However, the ADA does not prevent testing of applicants or employees for illegal drug use, a topic discussed next.[25]

Drug Testing

Since passage of the Drug-Free Workplace Act of 1988, applicants and employees of federal contractors, Department of Defense contractors, and those under Department of Transportation regulations are subject to testing for illegal drug use.

© COMSTOCK/JUPITER IMAGES

The majority of private firms test their employees, too. (See Chapter 12 for an extended discussion of this topic, including a sample policy statement for a drug-free workplace.) Urine, hair, saliva, and sweat testing are most common. Hair testing, for example, can show drug use going back months. Saliva, or oral fluid, testing works well at accident scenes involving drug use by current employees when urine testing is inconvenient. Sweat testing is efficient for workers returning to duty after testing positive because it captures drug use within a specific window of weeks or days.

Some recent studies have failed to show that that drug testing makes the workplace safer or leads to improvements in the performance of workers, however. Moreover, relatively few applicants test positive for drugs (less than 5 percent). Alcohol use, in fact, appears to create more problems than illegal drugs in the workplace.[26]

For reasons such as these, some companies no longer conduct drug tests. Hewlett-Packard is one of them. Cisco and Sun Microsystems have never conducted drug tests. Dell Computer, on the other hand, tests every one of its 40,000-plus employees. In addition, in 2008, the U.S. Ninth Circuit Court of Appeals ruled that public, although not private, companies must have a special need for conducting drug tests. The weight of the evidence suggests that testing is most appropriate for staff members in high-risk and safety-critical positions.

▞ EMPLOYMENT TESTS

3 | Objective

As the United States mobilized for World War I in the summer of 1917, some of the most talented psychologists in the country worked together to develop what later became known as the Army Alpha and Beta Tests of intelligence. (The Alpha exam was written for the general population, and the Beta was designed for internationals and those with poor reading skills.) The tests were used to help identify potential officer candidates as well as select and place other potential recruits. Since that time, employment tests have played an important part in the HR programs of both public and private organizations.[27]

One of the drawbacks of preemployment testing is that it creates the potential for legal challenges. A small, but growing number of companies are being taken to court by candidates claiming that the tests they took were discriminatory. There is also some evidence that the more tests that are required, the higher the likelihood of a lawsuit. The relative frequency of discrimination suits also appears to vary by industry and job type. Police, firefighting, and teaching areas—which generally require applicants to pass more tests—appear to be more prone to discrimination litigation.[28]

Nonetheless, tests have played a more important part in government HR programs in which hiring on the basis of merit is required by law. Government agencies experienced the same types of problems with their testing programs as did organizations in the private sector. However, their staffs were forced to improve their testing programs rather than to abandon them.

Many organizations use professional test consultants such as Wonderlic Inc. in Libertyville, Illinois, to improve their testing programs and to meet EEO requirements. While it is often advisable to use consultants, especially if an organization is considering the use of personality tests, managers should have a basic understanding of the technical aspects of testing and the contributions that tests can make to the HR program. They should also do a thorough job analysis to determine the crucial job requirements and related skills that actually need to be tested for and eliminate any unnecessary or duplicate tests. Highlights in HRM 2 contains some "best practice" preemployment testing suggestions offered by the EEOC.

Nature of Employment Tests

An employment test is an objective and standardized measure of a sample of behavior that is used to gauge a person's knowledge, skills, abilities, and other characteristics (KSAOs) in relation to other individuals.[29] The proper sampling of behavior—whether verbal, manipulative, or some other type—is the responsibility of the test author. It is also the responsibility of the test author to develop tests that meet accepted standards of reliability.[30] The data concerning a test's reliability are ordinarily presented in the manual for the test. While high reliability is essential, it offers no assurance that the test provides the basis for making valid judgments—that is, that the test actually measures the knowledge, skills, and abilities necessary to do a job successfully. It is the responsibility of the HR staff to conduct validation studies before a test is adopted for regular use. Again, this involves doing a thorough job analysis. One way to measure a test's validity is to test current employees and create a benchmark score to which applicants' scores can be compared. Other considerations are the cost, time, ease of administration and scoring, and the apparent relevance of the test to the jobs being tested. This is commonly referred to as "face validity." In other words, how reliable does the test appear on its face? While face validity is desirable, it is no substitute for technical validity. Adopting a test just because it appears relevant is bad practice; many a "good-looking" test has poor validity.

Best Practices for Employee Testing and Selection

Employers should administer tests and other selection procedures without regard to race, color, national origin, sex, religion, age (40 or older), or disability.

Employers should ensure that employment tests and other selection procedures are properly validated for the positions and purposes for which they are used. The test or selection procedure must be job-related and its results appropriate for the employer's purpose. While a test vendor's documentation supporting the validity of a test may be helpful, the employer is still responsible for ensuring that its tests are valid under UGESP.

If a selection procedure screens out a protected group, the employer should determine whether there is an equally effective alternative selection procedure that has less adverse impact and, if so, adopt the alternative procedure. For example, if the selection procedure is a test, the employer should determine whether another test would predict job performance but not disproportionately exclude the protected group.

To ensure that a test or selection procedure remains predictive of success in a job, employers should keep abreast of changes in job requirements and should update the test specifications or selection procedures accordingly.

Employers should ensure that tests and selection procedures are not adopted casually by managers who know little about these processes. A test or selection procedure can be an effective management tool, but no test or selection procedure should be implemented without an understanding of its effectiveness and limitations for the organization, its appropriateness for a specific job, and whether it can be appropriately administered and scored.

Source: Equal Employment Opportunity Commission. For further background on experiences and challenges encountered by employers, employees, and job seekers in testing, see the testimony from the Commission's meeting on testing, located on the EEOC's public Web site at http://www.eeoc.gov/abouteeoc/meetings/5-16-07/index.html.

Classification of Employment Tests

Employment tests may be classified in different ways. Generally, they are viewed as measuring either aptitude or achievement. Aptitude tests measure a person's capacity to learn or acquire skills. Achievement tests measure what a person knows or can do right now.

aptitude tests
Measures of a person's capacity to learn or acquire skills

achievement tests
Measures of what a person knows or can do right now

Cognitive Ability Tests

Cognitive ability tests measure mental capabilities such as general intelligence, verbal fluency, numerical ability, and reasoning ability. A host of paper-and-pencil tests measure cognitive abilities, including the General Aptitude Test Battery (GATB), Scholastic Aptitude Test (SAT), Graduate Management Aptitude Test (GMAT), and Bennett Mechanical Comprehension Test. Figure 6.6 shows some items that could be used to measure different cognitive abilities.

Although cognitive ability tests can be developed to measure very specialized areas such as reading comprehension and spatial relations, many experts believe that the validity of cognitive ability tests simply reflects their connection to general intelligence. However, measures of general intelligence (such as IQ) have been shown to be good predictors of performance across a wide variety of jobs.[31]

Personality and Interest Inventories

Whereas cognitive ability tests measure a person's mental capacity, personality tests measure disposition and temperament. During 1990s, for example, testing by the U.S. Army found that cognitive ability tests were the best predictors of how well soldiers were able to acquire job knowledge and, ultimately, of their technical proficiencies. But personality tests were the better predictors of their motivation,

---

FIGURE 6.6

Is That Your Final Answer?

Verbal

1. What is the meaning of the word "surreptitious"?
   - a. covert
   - b. winding
   - c. lively
   - d. sweet

2. How is the noun clause used in the following sentence? "I hope that I can learn this game."
   - a. Subject
   - b. predicate nominative
   - c. direct object
   - d. object of the preposition

Quantitative

3. Divide 50 by 0.5 and add 5. What is the result?
   - a. 25
   - b. 30
   - c. 95
   - d. 105

4. What is the value of 144_2?
   - a. 12
   - b. 72
   - c. 95
   - d. 20736

Reasoning

5. _____ is to *boat* as *snow* is to _____.
   - a. Sail, ski
   - b. Water, winter
   - c. Water, ski
   - d. Engine, water

6. Two women played 5 games of chess. Each woman won the same number of games, yet there were no ties. How can this be?
   - a. There was a forfeit.
   - b. One player cheated.
   - c. They played different people.
   - d. One game is still in progress.

Mechanical

7. If gear A and gear C are both turning counterclockwise, what is happening to gear B?
   - a. It is turning counterclockwise.
   - b. It is turning clockwise.
   - c. It remains stationary.
   - d. The whole system will jam.

A   B   C

Answers: 1. a, 2. c, 3. d, 4. d, 5. c, 6. c, 7. b

such as their leadership efforts and propensity to adhere to rules. Years of research show that five dimensions can summarize personality traits. The "Big Five" factors are the following:

1. *Extroversion*—the degree to which someone is talkative, sociable, active, aggressive, and excitable

2. *Agreeableness*—the degree to which someone is trusting, amiable, generous, tolerant, honest, cooperative, and flexible

3. *Conscientiousness*—the degree to which someone is dependable and organized and perseveres in tasks

4. *Neuroticism*—the degree to which someone is secure, calm, independent, and autonomous

5. *Openness to experience*—the degree to which someone is intellectual, philosophical, insightful, creative, artistic, and curious[32]

Using the Internet

Find additional information about the administration and interpretation of the Kuder Inventory. Go to the Student Resources at:

www.cengage.com/ management/bohlander

Figure 6.7 illustrates facets and sample items from the well-known California Psychological Inventory (CPI). Other personality tests include the Myers-Briggs Type Indicator (MBTI) and the 180-question Caliper test, whose users range from FedEx to the Chicago Cubs.

Although there is some evidence to show that when used in combination with cognitive ability tests, measures of personality traits (such as conscientiousness) can help predict how well a person will perform on the job, historically the connection between the two has been quite low.[33] Personality tests can also be problematic if they inadvertently discriminate against individuals who would otherwise perform effectively.[34] Several states severely restrict their usage because of this. Rather than being used to make hiring decisions, personality and interest inventories may be most useful for helping people with their occupational selection and career planning.

Physical Ability Tests

In addition to learning about a job candidate's mental capabilities, employers frequently need to assess a person's physical abilities. Particularly for demanding and potentially dangerous jobs such as those held by firefighters and police officers, physical abilities such as strength and endurance tend to be good predictors not only of performance, but also of accidents and injuries.[35]

Physical ability tests must be used cautiously. In the past, requirements for physical characteristics such as strength, agility, height, and weight were often determined by an employer's unvalidated notion of what should be required. This often put women and disabled job applicants at a disadvantage, a situation that can lead to lawsuits. After a Dial Corp plant in Fort Madison, Iowa, began using a strength test in 2000, the company found itself subject to such a suit. Prior to the test's use, nearly 50 percent of the people hired at the plant were women. Once the test was implemented, the percentage dropped dramatically. An appeals court subsequently ruled the test had a disparate impact on women because although injuries at the plant fell, they actually began doing so after the company instituted new safety rules—which was years before the strength test was implemented.[36]

Because of situations such as these, requirements that tend to discriminate against women have consequently been questioned and modified so as to represent typical

FIGURE
6.7

CPI Personality Facts and Sample Items

Agreeableness

- Consideration—I like to do little things for people to make them feel good.
- Empathy—I take other people's circumstances and feelings into consideration before making a decision.
- Interdependence—I tend to put group goals first and individual goals second.
- Openness—I do not have to share a person's values to work well with that person.
- Thought agility—I think it is vital to consider other perspectives before coming to conclusions.
- Trust—I believe people are usually honest with me.

Conscientiousness

- Attention to detail—I like to complete every detail of tasks according to the work plans.
- Dutifulness—I conduct my business according to a strict set of ethical principles.
- Responsibility—I can be relied on to do what is expected of me.
- Work focus—I prioritize my work effectively so the most important things get done first.

Extroversion

- Adaptability—For me, change is exciting.
- Competitiveness—I like to win, even if the activity isn't very important.
- Desire for achievement—I prefer to set challenging goals, rather than aim for goals I am more likely to reach.
- Desire for advancement—I would like to attain the highest position in an organization some day.
- Energy level—When most people are exhausted from work, I still have energy to keep going.
- Influence—People come to me for inspiration and direction.
- Initiative—I am always looking for opportunities to start new projects.
- Risk-taking—I am willing to take big risks when there is potential for big returns.
- Sociability—I find it easy to start up a conversation with strangers.
- Taking charge—I actively take control of situations at work if no one is in charge.

Neuroticism

- Emotional control—Even when I am very upset, it is easy for me to control my emotions.
- Negative affectivity—I am easily displeased with things at work.
- Optimism—My enthusiasm for living life to its fullest is apparent to those with whom I work.
- Self-confidence—I am confident about my skills and abilities.
- Stress tolerance—I worry about things that I know I should not worry about.

Openness to Experience

- Independence—I tend to work on projects alone, even if others volunteer to help me.
- Innovativeness/creativity—I work best in an environment that allows me to be creative and expressive.
- Social astuteness—I know what is expected of me in different social situations.
- Thought focus—I quickly make links between causes and effects.
- Vision—I can often foresee the outcome of a situation before it unfolds.

Source: Mark J. Schmit, Jenifer A. Kihm, and Chet Robie, "Development of a Global Measure of Personality," *Personnel Psychology* 53, no.1 (Spring 2000): 153–93. Reprinted by permission.

A State license is required for barbers, hairstylists, cosmetologists, and most other personal appearance workers, although qualifications vary by State.

job demands. In addition, the evidence suggests that although the average man is stronger, faster, and more powerful than the average woman, women tend to have better balance, manual dexterity, flexibility, and coordination than men. For these reasons, it is clear that (as with other methods for screening potential employees) the use of physical ability tests should be carefully validated on the basis of the essential functions of the job.

Job Knowledge Tests

Government agencies and licensing boards usually develop job knowledge tests, a type of achievement test designed to measure a person's level of understanding about a particular job. The uniform CPA Examination used to license certified public accountants is one such test. Most civil service examinations, for example, are used to determine whether an applicant possesses the information and understanding that will permit placement on the job without further training.[37] Job knowledge tests also play a major role in the enlisted personnel programs of the U.S. Army, Navy, Air Force, and Marines. Anyone who wants to become a pilot in the armed services and fly multimillion-dollar jets, for example, must undergo extensive job knowledge testing.

Work Sample Tests

Work sample tests, or job sample tests, require the applicant to perform tasks that are actually a part of the work required on the job. Like job knowledge tests, work sample tests are constructed from a carefully developed outline that experts agree includes the major job functions; the tests are thus considered content valid. Organizations that are interested in moving toward *competency-based selection*—that is, hiring based on observation of behaviors previously shown to distinguish successful employees—increasingly use work samples to see potential employees "in action."[38]

Work samples have been devised for many diverse jobs: a map reading test for traffic control officers, a lathe test for machine operators, a complex coordination test for pilots, an in-basket test for managers, a group discussion test for supervisors, and a judgment and decision-making test for administrators, to name a few. The city of Miami Beach has used work sample tests for jobs as diverse as plumbers, planners, and assistant chief accountants. The U.S. Air Force has used work samples for enlisted personnel in eight different specialty areas. In an increasing number of cases, work sample tests are aided by computer simulations, particularly when testing a candidate might prove dangerous. The reports are that this type of test is cost-effective, reliable, valid, fair, and acceptable to applicants.[39]

◼◼ THE EMPLOYMENT INTERVIEW

4 Objective

Traditionally, the employment interview has a central role in the selection process—so much so that it is rare to find an instance in which an employee is hired without some sort of interview. Depending on the type of job, applicants may be interviewed by one person, members of a work team, or other individuals in the organization. While researchers have raised some doubts about its validity, the interview remains a mainstay of selection because (1) it is especially practical when there are only a small number of applicants; (2) it serves other purposes, such as public relations; and (3) interviewers maintain great faith and confidence in their judgments. Nevertheless, the interview can be plagued by problems of subjectivity and personal bias. In those instances, the judgments of different interviewers may vary dramatically, and the quality of the hire can be called into serious question.

In this section, we review the characteristics, advantages, and disadvantages of various types of employment interviews. We highlight the fact that the structure of the interview and the training of interviewers strongly influence the success of the hiring process.[40]

Interviewing Methods

Interview methods differ in several ways, most significantly in terms of the amount of structure, or control, exercised by the interviewer. In highly structured interviews, the interviewer determines the course that the interview will follow as each question is asked. In the less structured interview, the applicant plays a larger role in determining the course the discussion will take. An examination of the different types of interviews from the least structured to the most structured reveals these differences.

The Nondirective Interview

In the nondirective interview, the interviewer carefully refrains from influencing the applicant's remarks. The applicant is allowed the maximum amount of freedom in determining the course of the discussion. The interviewer asks broad, open-ended questions—such as "Tell me more about your experiences on your last job"—and permits the applicant to talk freely with a minimum of interruption. Generally, the nondirective interviewer listens carefully and does not argue, interrupt, or change the subject abruptly. The interviewer also uses follow-up questions to allow the applicant to elaborate, makes only brief responses, and allows pauses in the conversation; the pausing technique is the most difficult for the beginning interviewer to master.

The greater freedom afforded to the applicant in the nondirective interview is particularly valuable in bringing to the interviewer's attention any information, attitudes, or feelings that may often be concealed by more structured questioning. However, because the applicant determines the course of the interview and no set procedure is followed, little information that comes from these interviews enables interviewers

nondirective interview
An interview in which the applicant is allowed the maximum amount of freedom in determining the course of the discussion, while the interviewer carefully refrains from influencing the applicant's remarks

to cross-check agreement with other interviewers. Thus the reliability and validity of the nondirective interview may be expected to be minimal. This method is most likely to be used in interviewing candidates for high-level positions and in counseling, which we will discuss in Chapter 13.

The Structured Interview

structured interview

An interview in which a set of standardized questions having an established set of answers is used

More attention is being given to the structured interview as a result of EEO requirements and a concern for maximizing validity of selection decisions.[41] Because a structured interview has a set of standardized questions (based on job analysis) and an established set of answers against which applicant responses can be rated, it provides a more consistent basis for evaluating job candidates. For example, staff members of Weyerhaeuser Company's HR department have developed a structured interviewing process with the following characteristics:

1. The interview process is based exclusively on job duties and requirements critical to job performance.

2. It uses four types of questions: situational questions, job knowledge questions, job sample/simulation questions, and worker requirements questions.

3. There are sample (benchmark) answers, determined in advance, to each question. Interviewee responses are rated on a five-point scale relative to those answers.

4. The process involves an interview committee so that interviewee responses are evaluated by several raters.

5. It consistently follows the same procedures in all instances to ensure that each applicant has exactly the same chance as every other applicant.

6. The interviewer takes notes and documents the interview for future reference and in case of a legal challenge.

A structured interview is more likely to provide the type of information needed for making sound decisions. According to a report by the U.S. Merit Systems Protection Board, a quasi-judicial agency that serves as the guardian of federal merit systems, structured interviews are twice as likely as nondirective interviews to predict on-the-job performance. Structured interviews are also less likely than nondirective interviews to be attacked in court.[42]

Most employment interviewers will tend toward either a nondirected or a structured format. However, within the general category of structured interviews, there are more specific differences that relate to the format of questions. These include the situational interview and behavioral description interview, discussed next.

The Situational Interview

situational interview

An interview in which an applicant is given a hypothetical incident and asked how he or she would respond to it

One variation of the structured interview is called the situational interview. With this approach, an applicant is given a *hypothetical* incident and asked how he or she would respond to it. The applicant's response is then evaluated relative to preestablished benchmark standards. Interestingly, many organizations are using the situational interview to select new college graduates. Highlights in HRM 3 shows a sample question from a situational interview used to select systems analysts at a chemical plant. Highlights in HRM 4 lists some of the biggest blunders made by job applicants.

Sample Situational Interview Question

QUESTION:

It is the night before your scheduled vacation. You are all packed and ready to go. Just before you get into bed, you receive a phone call from the plant. A problem has arisen that only you can handle. You are asked to come in to take care of things. What would you do in this situation?

RECORD ANSWER:

_____

_____

_____

SCORING GUIDE:

Good: "I would go in to work and make certain that everything is OK. Then I would go on vacation."
Good: "There are no problems that *only* I can handle. I would make certain that someone qualified was there to handle things."
Fair: "I would try to find someone else to deal with the problem."
Fair: "I would go on vacation."

The Behavioral Description Interview

In contrast to a situational interview, which focuses on hypothetical situations, a behavioral description interview (BDI) focuses on *actual* work incidents in the interviewee's past. The BDI format asks the job applicant what he or she actually did in a given situation. For example, to assess a potential manager's ability to handle a problem employee, an interviewer might ask, "Tell me about the last time you disciplined an employee." Such an approach to interviewing, based on a critical incidents job analysis, assumes that past performance is the best predictor of future performance. It also may be somewhat less susceptible to applicant faking. In addition, recent research indicates that the behavioral description interview is more effective than the situational interview for hiring higher-level positions such as general managers and executives.[43]

behavioral description interview (BDI)
An interview in which an applicant is asked questions about what he or she actually did in a given situation

The Panel Interview

Another type of interview involves a panel of interviewers who question and observe a single candidate. In a typical panel interview, the candidate meets with three to five interviewers who take turns asking questions. After the interview, the interviewers

panel interview
An interview in which a board of interviewers questions and observes a single candidate

4

Hiring Managers Reveal Top Five Biggest Mistakes Candidates Make During Job Interviews in CareerBuilder.com Survey

What is the biggest mistake you ever made during a job interview? Show up late? Insult the interviewer? How about eat a snack? In its survey of more than 400 hiring managers, CareerBuilder.com asked respondents to share the most memorable blunders that caused them to pass on a particular candidate.

"Job interviews are intimidating and even the most-practiced job seeker can sometimes forget proper interview etiquette," said Kirk Scott, Senior Career Advisor for CareerBuilder.com. "To help job seekers gain insights into the minds of potential employers, CareerBuilder.com asked hiring managers nationwide to identify interview pitfalls that should be avoided. Most interview blunders fell under five key categories: communication, performance, attitude, appearance and honesty."

#1—Communication

Hiring managers report concerns with some candidates' abilities to communicate effectively, citing poor language skills and a tendency to reveal too much or too little information.

Examples:

- "The candidate said he had days he could not give 100 percent."
- "She kept telling me about her personal problems."
- "He spoke to me as if he was in prison—very bad grammar and manners."

Scott's Tip: Choose your words wisely and listen closely. Hiring managers look for candidates who pay attention, think quickly on their feet, and effectively communicate why their skills and accomplishments are the best fit for the job.

#2—Performance

The candidate's professionalism throughout the interview process plays an important role in the hiring decision. Hiring managers say candidates who are unprepared, distracted, or a little too comfortable are not considered for recruitment.

Examples:

- "The candidate kept looking around the room and knew nothing about the job being offered."
- "The woman answered her cell phone during the interview."
- "One guy ate a sandwich."

Scott's Tip: Maintain eye contact and do your homework. Research the company, its industry, and competitors prior to your arrival. Make sure to eat a solid meal beforehand to keep up your energy, and leave your cell phone or pager at home.

(continued)

Hiring Managers Reveal Top Five Biggest Mistakes Candidates Make During Job Interviews in CareerBuilder.com Survey (continued)

#3—Attitude

Candidates who display bored or arrogant attitudes during the interview are also a turn-off for these hiring managers.

Examples:

- "He asked me to speed up the interview because he had a lunch date."
- "He told me the only reason he was here was because his mother wanted him to get a job. He was 37."
- "The candidate used profanity when describing something negative about a previous boss."

Scott's Tip: Keep positive. Avoid saying anything negative about a previous employer. Show enthusiasm when speaking and being spoken to, and let the employer know that you are really interested in the opportunity.

#4—Appearance

For hiring managers, proper dress is always required—a lesson they feel some job seekers have not yet grasped.

Examples:

- "One candidate did not wear shoes to the interview."
- "A woman came in with open toe shoes and a slit on her dress up to her backside."
- "He showed up in jeans and a T-shirt with dirty fingernails and looked like he just woke up. He also smelled of alcohol."

Scott's Tip: Leave the Levi's at home. Even if the company dress is casual, you don't want to seem casual about the job opportunity. Wear a business suit or other appropriate attire. Groom properly and change out of last night's clubbing clothes.

#5—Honesty

Hiring managers state that candidates who lie or give the impression that they are dishonest in any way are dismissed.

Examples:

- "One guy mentioned his arrest during the interview after stating on his application that he had never been arrested."
- "One guy asked if we drug-tested and if we gave advance notice (we are a drug treatment facility)."

Scott's Tip: Honesty is always the best policy, and think before you speak. Even the most innocent question, if not worded properly, can give the wrong impression.

Source: CareerBuilder.com.

pool their observations and their rating scores if the interview is structured to reach a consensus about the suitability of the candidate. HRM specialists using this method at Philip Morris USA and Dominion Virginia Power report that panel interviews provide several significant advantages over traditional one-to-one interviews, including higher reliability because they involve multiple inputs. They can also result in a shorter decision-making period, and applicants are more likely to accept the decisions made. Studies also suggest that if the panels are composed of a diverse group of interviewers, hiring discrimination is minimized.[44]

The Computer and Virtual Interviews

With advances in information technology, more and more organizations are using computers and the Internet to help with the interviewing process. Nike, Cigna Insurance, and Pinkerton Security have all developed expert systems to gather preliminary information as well as compare candidates.

Typically, a computer interview requires candidates to answer a series (75 to 125) of multiple-choice questions tailored to the job. These answers are compared either with an ideal profile or with profiles developed on the basis of other candidates' responses. The computer interview can also be used as a screening device to help filter out unqualified applicants applying online who do not merit a personal interview. Depending on the vendor and the software used, a computer interview conducted in conjunction with online tests can measure everything from contradictory responses and latent responses (time delays related to answering a question) to the applicant's typing speed and ability to use different kinds of software. CareerBuilder.com, for example, offers a service called IntelligentHire that screens out the ten most qualified and interested applicants posting for a job on CareerBuilder's site. IntelligentHire then generates a report for the employer that includes the applicants' resumes, answers to questions, background check results, and their overall rankings against one another.[45]

A few years ago, Pic 'n Pay Shoe Stores created a computerized interview that could be conducted over the phone using an 800 number. The interview focused on honesty, work attitude, drug use, candor, dependability, and self-motivation. After implementing the system, the company cut turnover by 50 percent and reduced employee theft by almost 40 percent. In addition to the benefits of objectivity, some research evidence suggests that applicants may be less likely to engage in "impression management" in computerized interviews than in face-to-face interviews. So far, organizations have used the computer mainly as a complement to, rather than as a replacement for, conventional interviews.[46]

As we explained in Chapter 1, in addition to computerized and telephone tests, some companies are conducting virtual simulation tests, some of which have been developed within the virtual reality game Second Life. As the National City Corporation case at the end of the chapter shows, firms are finding that virtual simulations of this sort are a better way to engage Generation Y and Millennial candidates than handing them a pencil and paper. The simulations can also enhance a company's reputation as a cutting-edge employer.

Video and Digitally-Recorded Interviews

Companies such as AT&T, Dell Computer, and Nike are using videoconference technologies to evaluate job candidates. While some use their own in-house systems, others use outside service partners. FedEx Kinko's, for example, rents videoconferencing rooms at a quarter of its 900 stores for about $225 per hour. National Career

Centers partnered with Radisson and Hilton to offer videoconferencing to customers in hotels.

Video and digitally-recorded interviews have several potential advantages related to flexibility, speed, and cost. Employers can make preliminary assessments about candidates' technical abilities, energy level, appearance, and the like before incurring the costs of a face-to-face meeting. The goal is to enable faster, higher-quality decisions at lower cost.

In addition to offering a broad range of candidate assessment services, a number of recruiting companies, including Execuserve and BioPharma Worldwide, digitally record job applicants and post their interviews to their Web sites. Corporations log on to the sites and check out candidates free of charge or for a small fee, depending on the vendor. By recording and playing back the interviews to several companies' executives, firms can eliminate complications involved in setting up many more interviews.[47]

Guidelines for Employment Interviewers

Apart from the characteristics of the interviews themselves, there are several important tips for interviewers. Organizations should be cautious in selecting employment interviewers. Qualities that are desirable include humility, the ability to think objectively, maturity, and poise. Given the importance of diversity in the workforce, experience in associating with people from a variety of backgrounds is also desirable. Qualities to avoid in interviewers include overtalkativeness, extreme opinions, and biases.

A Review of the Best

There have been several reviews of research studies on the employment interview.[48] Each of these reviews discusses and evaluates numerous studies concerned with such questions as "What traits can be assessed in the interview?" and "How do interviewers reach their decisions?"

Figure 6.8 summarizes the variables and processes involved in the employment interview. The figure shows that a number of applicant characteristics and situational factors can influence the perceptions of the interviewer and thus the hiring decision. For example, the race and sex of an applicant can shape the expectations, biases, and behaviors of an interviewer, which in turn can affect the interview outcome. Even a limited understanding of the variables shown in Figure 6.8 can help increase the interviewing effectiveness of managers and supervisors.

Interviewer Training

Training has been shown to dramatically improve the competence of interviewers. If not done on a continuing basis, training should at least be done periodically for managers, supervisors, and HR representatives who conduct interviews. Interviewer training programs should include practice interviews conducted under guidance. Practice interviews may be recorded and evaluated later in a group training session. Some variation in technique is only natural. However, the following list presents ten ground rules for employment interviews that are commonly accepted and supported by research findings. Their apparent simplicity should not lead one to underestimate their importance.

1. *Establish an interview plan.* Examine the purposes of the interview and determine the areas and specific questions to be covered. Review the job requirements, application form data, test scores, and other available information before seeing the applicant.

FIGURE
6.8

Variables in the Employment Interview

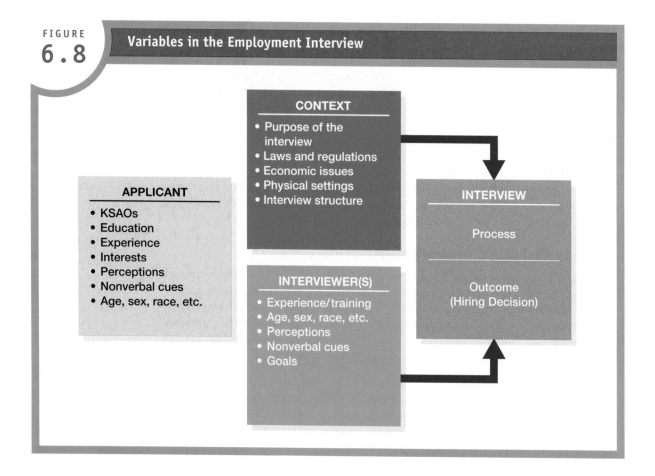

2. *Establish and maintain rapport.* This is accomplished by greeting the applicant pleasantly, explaining the purpose of the interview, displaying sincere interest in the applicant, and listening carefully. Keep non-job-related conversation to a minimum. A common mistake managers make is hiring people who are like themselves—people who went to the same college, enjoy the same activities, and so forth. Although such a strategy can work, it can also lead to bad decisions and a lack of diversity in firms, especially when a company is interviewing global candidates.

3. *Be an active listener.* Strive to understand, comprehend, and gain insight into what is only suggested or implied. A good listener's mind is alert, and face and posture usually reflect this fact.

4. *Pay attention to nonverbal cues.* An applicant's facial expressions, gestures, body position, and movements often provide clues to that person's attitudes and feelings. Interviewers should be aware of what they themselves are communicating nonverbally.

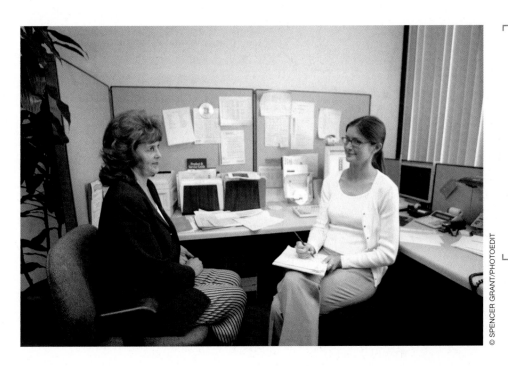

Listening, establishing rapport, and paying attention to non-verbal cues such as facial expressions and body language are only a few of the guidelines for becoming an interviewer. What do the body language and facial expressions in this photo tell you about this interview?

5. *Provide information as freely and honestly as possible.* Answer fully and frankly the applicant's questions. Present a realistic picture of the job.

6. *Use questions effectively.* To elicit a truthful answer, questions should be phrased as objectively as possible, giving no indication of what response is desired.

7. *Separate facts from inferences.* During the interview, record factual information. Later, record your inferences or interpretations of the facts. Compare your inferences with those of other interviewers.

8. *Recognize biases and stereotypes.* As we have mentioned, one typical bias is for interviewers to consider candidates who have interests, experiences, and backgrounds similar to their own to be more acceptable. Stereotyping involves forming generalized opinions of how people of a given gender, race, or ethnic background appear, think, feel, and act. The influence of sex role stereotyping is central to sex discrimination in employment. Avoid the "halo error," or judging an individual favorably or unfavorably overall on the basis of only one strong point (or weak point) on which you place high value. Also avoid the influence of "beautyism." Discrimination against unattractive people is a persistent and pervasive form of employment discrimination. (If you are a candidate, remember that it can be difficult for interviewers to control their biases, so first impressions count. The degree to which employers are influenced by a candidate's appearance are shown in Figure 6.9.)

9. *Control the course of the interview.* Establish an interview plan and stick to it. Provide the applicant with ample opportunity to talk, but maintain control of the situation in order to reach the interview objectives.

FIGURE
6.9

How Candidates' Physical Attributes Influence Employers

	NO INFLUENCE	SLIGHT INFLUENCE	STRONG INFLUENCE
Grooming	6%	21%	73%
Nontraditional interview attire	13	38	49
Handshake	22	45	33
Body piercing	26	43	31
Obvious tattoos	25	46	29
Nontraditional hair color	26	46	28
Unusual hairstyle	30	49	21
Earring (male)	54	34	12
Beard	73	22	5
Mustache	83	16	1

Source: Reprinted from "Blue Hair, Body Piercings—Do Employers Care?" *Occupational Outlook Quarterly* 50, no.3 (Fall 2006): 24.

10. *Standardize the questions asked.* To increase the reliability of the interview and avoid discrimination, ask the same questions of all applicants for a particular job. Keep careful notes; record facts, impressions, and any relevant information, including what was told to the applicant.

Diversity Management: Are Your Questions Legal?

The entire subject of what is legal or illegal in an employment interview gets pretty complicated. There are differing and sometimes contradictory interpretations by the courts, the EEOC, and the Office of Federal Contract Compliance Program about what you can ask in an interview. Under federal laws no questions are expressly prohibited. However, the EEOC looks with disfavor on direct or indirect questions related to race, color, age, religion, sex, or national origin. Some questions that interviewers once felt free to ask are now potentially hazardous. Federal courts have severely limited the area of questioning. An interviewer, for example, can ask about physical disabilities if the job involves manual labor, but not otherwise. It is inappropriate, for example, to ask women (or men) if they are married or have children. Several states have fair employment practice laws that are more restrictive than federal legislation. In general, if a question is job-related, is asked of everyone, and does not discriminate against a certain class of applicants, it is likely to be acceptable to government authorities.

Employers often provide their interviewers with instructions on how to avoid potentially discriminatory questions in their interviews. The examples of appropriate and inappropriate questions shown in Highlights in HRM 5 can serve as guidelines for application forms as well as preemployment interviews. Complete guidelines can be developed from current information available from district and regional EEOC offices and from state fair employment practices offices.

Appropriate and Inappropriate Interview Questions

	APPROPRIATE QUESTIONS	INAPPROPRIATE QUESTIONS
National origin	What is your name? Have you ever worked under a different name? Do you speak any foreign languages that may be pertinent to this job?	What is the origin of your name? What is your ancestry?
Age	Are you over 18? If hired, can you prove your age?	How old are you? What is your date of birth?
Gender	(Say nothing unless it involves a bona fide occupational qualification.)	Are you a man or a woman?
Race	(Say nothing.)	What is your race?
Disabilities	Do you have any disabilities that may inhibit your job performance? Are you willing to take a physical exam if the job requires it?	Do you have any physical defects? When was your last physical? What color are your eyes, hair, etc.?
Height and weight	(Not appropriate unless it is a bona fide occupational qualification.)	How tall are you? How much do you weigh?
Residence	What is your address? How long have you lived there?	What are the names/relationships of those with whom you live?
Religion	(You may inform a person of the required work schedule.)	Do you have any religious affiliation?
Military record	Did you have any military education/experience pertinent to this job?	What type of discharge did you receive?
Education and experience	Where did you go to school? What is your prior work experience? Why did you leave? What is your salary history?	Is that a church-affiliated school? When did you graduate? What are your hobbies?
Criminal record	Have you ever been convicted of a crime?	Have you ever been arrested?
Citizenship	Do you have a legal right to work in the United States?	Are you a U.S. citizen?
Marital/family status	What is the name, address, and telephone number of a person we may contact in case of an emergency?	Are you married, divorced, single? Do you prefer Miss, Mrs., or Ms.? Do you have any children? How old are they?

▟ REACHING A SELECTION DECISION

The most critical step is the decision to accept or reject applicants. Thus it requires systematic consideration of all the relevant information about applicants. It is common to use summary forms and checklists to ensure that all of the pertinent information has been included in the evaluation of applicants.

Summarizing Information about Applicants

Fundamentally, an employer is interested in what an applicant can do and will do. Evaluating candidates on the basis of information you have assembled should focus on these two factors, as Figure 6.10 shows. The "can-do" factors include a candidate's knowledge and skills, as well as the aptitude (the potential) for acquiring new knowledge and skills. The "will-do" factors include the candidate's motivation, interests, and other personality characteristics. Both factors are essential to successful performance on the job. The employee who has the ability (can do) but is not motivated to use it (will not do) is little better than the employee who lacks the necessary ability.

It is much easier to measure what individuals can do than what they will do. The can-do factors are readily evident from test scores and verified information. What the individual will do can only be inferred. Employers can use the responses to interview and application form questions and references to obtain information for making inferences about what an individual will do.

Decision-Making Strategy

The strategy used for making personnel decisions for one category of jobs might differ from that used for another category. The strategy used to select managerial and executive personnel, for example, will be different than the strategy used to select clerical and technical personnel. Although many factors have to be considered in terms of

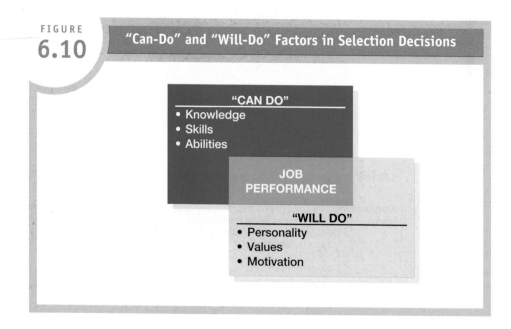

FIGURE
6.10

"Can-Do" and "Will-Do" Factors in Selection Decisions

"CAN DO"
- Knowledge
- Skills
- Abilities

JOB PERFORMANCE

"WILL DO"
- Personality
- Values
- Motivation

making hiring decisions, the following are some of the questions that managers must consider:

1. Should the individuals be hired according to their highest potential or according to the needs of the organization?

2. At what grade or wage level should the individual be started?

3. Should the selection be concerned primarily with finding an ideal employee to match the job currently open, or should a candidate's potential for advancement in the organization be considered?

4. To what extent should those who are not qualified but are qualifiable be considered?

5. Should overqualified individuals be considered?

6. What effect will a decision have on the firm meeting its affirmative action plans and diversity considerations?

In addition to these types of factors, managers must also consider which approach they will use in making hiring decisions. There are two basic approaches to selection: clinical (personal judgment) and statistical.

Clinical Approach

In the clinical approach to decision-making, those making the selection decision review all the data on the applicants. Then, on the basis of their understanding of the job and the individuals who have been successful in that job, they make a decision. Different individuals often arrive at different decisions about an applicant when they use this approach because each evaluator assigns different weights to the applicant's strengths and weaknesses. Unfortunately, personal biases and stereotypes are frequently covered up by what appear to be rational reasons for either accepting or rejecting a candidate.

Statistical Approach

In contrast to the clinical approach, the statistical approach to decision-making is more objective. It involves identifying the most valid predictors and weighting them using statistical methods such as multiple regression.[49] Quantified data such as scores or ratings from interviews, tests, and other procedures are then combined according to their weighted value. Individuals with the highest combined scores are selected. A comparison of the clinical approach with the statistical approach in a wide variety of situations has shown that the statistical approach is superior. Although this superiority has been recognized for many decades, the clinical approach continues to be the one most commonly used.

With a strictly statistical approach, a candidate's high score on one predictor (such as a cognitive ability test) will make up for a low score on another predictor (such as the interview). For this reason, this model is a **compensatory model.** However, it is frequently important that applicants achieve some minimum level of proficiency on all selection dimensions. When this is the case, a **multiple cutoff model** can be used in which only those candidates who score above the minimum cutoff on all dimensions are considered. The selection decision is made from that subset of candidates.[50]

A variation of the multiple cutoff is referred to as the **multiple hurdle model.** This decision strategy is sequential in that after candidates go through an initial evaluation stage, the ones who score well are provisionally accepted and are assessed further at each successive stage. The process continues through several stages (hurdles) before

compensatory model

A selection decision model in which a high score in one area can make up for a low score in another area

multiple cutoff model

A selection decision model that requires an applicant to achieve some minimum level of proficiency on all selection dimensions

multiple hurdle model

A sequential strategy in which only the applicants with the highest scores at an initial test stage go on to subsequent stages a final decision is made regarding the candidates. This approach is especially useful when either the testing or training procedures are lengthy and expensive.

Each of the statistical approaches requires that a decision be made about where the cutoff lies—that point in the distribution of scores above which a person should be considered and below which the person should be rejected. The score that the applicant must achieve is the cutoff score. Depending on the labor supply and diversity and anti-discrimination considerations, it may be necessary to lower or raise the cutoff score.

The effects of raising and lowering the cutoff score are illustrated in Figure 6.11. Each dot in the center of the figure represents the relationship between the test score (or a weighted combination of test scores) and the criterion of success for one individual. In this instance, the test has a fairly high validity, as represented by the elliptical pattern of the dots. Note that the high-scoring individuals are concentrated in the satisfactory job success category, whereas the low-scoring individuals are concentrated in the unsatisfactory category.

FIGURE
6.11

Test Scores Scatterplot with Hypothetical Cutoffs

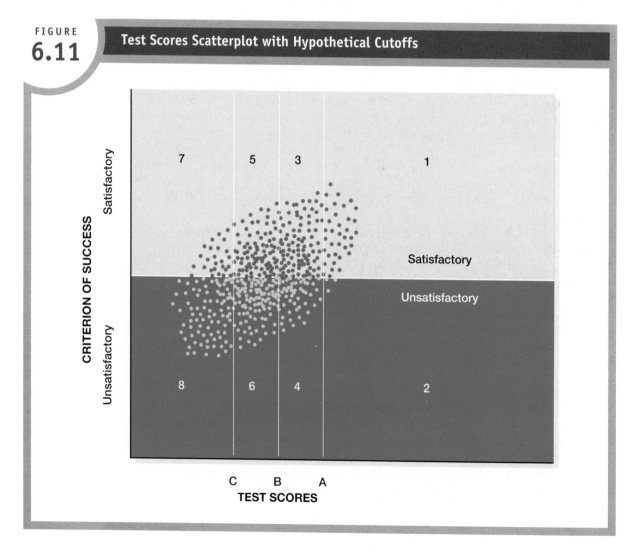

If the cutoff score is set at A, only the individuals represented by areas 1 and 2 will be accepted. Nearly all of them will be successful. If more employees are needed, the cutoff score can be lowered to point B. In this case, a larger number of potential failures will be accepted, as shown in quadrants 2 and 4. Even if the cutoff is lowered to C, the total number of satisfactory individuals selected (represented by the dots in areas 1, 3, and 5) exceeds the total number selected who are unsatisfactory (areas 2, 4, and 6). Thus, the test serves to maximize the selection of probable successes and to minimize the selection of probable failures. This is all we can hope for in terms of predicting on-the-job success: the probability of selecting a greater proportion of individuals who will be successful rather than unsuccessful.

Of course, the most valid predictors should be used with any selection strategy. Nonetheless, a related factor contributes to selecting the best qualified people: having an adequate number of applicants or candidates from which to make a selection. It is typically expressed in terms of a **selection ratio**, which is the ratio of the number of applicants to be selected to the total number of applicants. A ratio of 0.10, for example, means that 10 percent of the applicants will be selected. A ratio of 0.90 means that 90 percent will be selected. If the selection ratio is low, only the most promising applicants will be hired. When the ratio is high, very little selectivity will be possible because even applicants with mediocre abilities will have to be hired if the firm's vacancies are to be filled. When this is the situation, a firm's managers can fall prey to what some experts call the "desperation bias"—choosing someone because you are in a pinch. It is a common problem among managers because of the many time and operating constraints they face.

selection ratio
The number of applicants compared with the number of people to be hired

Final Decision

After a preliminary selection/screening by a firm's HR department has been conducted, the applicants who appear most promising are then referred to the departments with vacancies. These people are then interviewed by the managers or supervisors, who usually make the final decision and communicate it to the human resources department. Because of the weight that is usually given to their choices, managers and supervisors should be trained so that their role in the selection process does not negate the more rigorous efforts of the firm's HR staff.

In large organizations, notifying applicants of the decision that has been made and making job offers is often the responsibility of HR departments. The HR department should confirm the details of the job, working arrangements, wages, and so on and specify a deadline by which the applicant must reach a decision. If, at this point, findings from the medical examination or drug test are not yet available, an offer is often made contingent on the applicant's passing the examination.

In government agencies, the selection of individuals to fill vacancies is made from lists or registers of eligible candidates. Ordinarily, three or more names of individuals at the top of the register are submitted to the requisitioning official. This arrangement provides some latitude for those making a selection and, at the same time, preserves the merit system.

SUMMARY

Objective 1

1. The employee selection process should provide as much reliable and valid information as possible about applicants so that their qualifications can be carefully matched with the job's specifications. The information that is obtained should be clearly job-related or predict success on the job and free from potential discrimination. Reliability refers to the consistency of test scores over time and across measures. Validity refers to the accuracy of the measurements taken. Validity can be assessed in terms of whether the measurement is based on a job specification (content validity), whether test scores correlate with performance criteria (predictive validity), and whether the test accurately measures what it purports to measure (construct validity).

Objective 2

2. Interviews are customarily used in conjunction with application forms, biographical information blanks, references, background investigations, medical examinations, cognitive ability tests, job knowledge tests, and work sample tests.

Objective 3

3. While the popularity of employment tests declined somewhat with the passage of EEO laws, following 9-11, there was a resurgence of testing. Employment tests should not be overlooked because they are more objective than interviews and can give managers a fuller, or better, sense of the capabilities of different candidates. Cognitive ability tests are especially valuable for assessing verbal, quantitative, and reasoning abilities. Personality and interest tests are perhaps best used for placement or career development. Physical ability tests can be used to prevent accidents and injuries, particularly for physically demanding work. However, they must not be used if they have a disparate impact on candidates in protected classes. Job knowledge and work sample tests are achievement tests that are useful for determining whether a candidate can perform the duties of the job without further training.

Objective 4

4. The interview is an important source of information about job applicants. It can be unstructured, wherein the interviewer is free to pursue whatever approach and sequence of topics might seem appropriate, as long as they are job-related. Alternatively, an interview can be structured, wherein each applicant receives the same set of questions, which have preestablished answers associated with different scores. Some interviews are situational and can focus on hypothetical situations or actual behavioral descriptions of a candidate's previous work experiences. Interviews can be conducted by a single individual, by a panel, via a computer, or be videotaped or digitally recorded. Regardless of the technique chosen, those who conduct interviews should receive special training to acquaint them with interviewing methods and EEO considerations. The training should also make them more aware of the major findings from research studies on the interview and how they can apply these findings and avoid biases.

Objective 5

5. In the process of making decisions, all "can-do" and "will-do" factors should be assembled and weighted systematically so that the final decision can be based on a composite of the most reliable and valid information. Although the clinical approach to decision-making is used more than the statistical approach, the former lacks the accuracy of the latter. Compensatory models allow a candidate's high score on one predictor to make up for a low score on another. When the multiple cutoff model is used, only those candidates who score above a minimum cutoff level remain in the running. A variation of the multiple cutoff is the multiple hurdle model, which involves several stages and cutoff levels. Whichever of these approaches is used, the goal is to select a greater proportion of individuals who will be successful on the job.

KEY TERMS

achievement tests
aptitude tests
behavioral description interview
(BDI)
compensatory model
concurrent validity
construct validity
content validity

criterion-related validity
cross-validation
multiple cutoff model
multiple hurdle model
negligent hiring
nondirective interview
panel interview
predictive validity

reliability
selection
selection ratio
situational interview
structured interview
validity
validity generalization

DISCUSSION QUESTIONS

Objective 1
1. What is meant by the term *criterion* as it is used in personnel selection? Give some examples of criteria used for jobs with which you are familiar.

Objective 2
2. What problems might an employer encounter when checking references furnished by job applicants? Are there any solutions to these problems?

Objective 3
3. What characteristics do job knowledge and job sample tests have that often make them more acceptable to the examinees than other types of tests?

Objective 3
4. Personality tests, like other tests used in employee selection, have been under attack for several decades. Why do you think some applicants find personality tests objectionable? On what basis could their use for selection purposes be justified?

Objective 4
5. Compare briefly the major types of employment interviews described in this chapter. Which type would you prefer to conduct? Why?

Objective 5
6. In what ways does the clinical approach to selection differ from the statistical approach? How do you account for the fact that one approach is superior to the other?

HRM EXPERIENCE

Designing Selection Criteria and Methods

Making hiring decisions is one of the most important—and difficult—decisions a manager makes. Without good information, managers have almost no chance of making the right choice. They might as well be using an Ouija board. The process begins with a sound understanding of the job: the tasks, duties, and responsibilities associated with it and the knowledge, skills, and abilities needed to do it. A job analysis should be done to make certain that all managers have assembled all of the information they need to ensure a good person-job fit. However, this information may not be enough. Other information about the company's values and philosophy are likely to be required to ensure that a good person-organization fit results.

Assignment

1. Working in teams of four to six individuals, choose a job with which you are familiar and identify the most important knowledge, skills, abilities, and other characteristics needed for someone doing the job to perform well.

2. Next, identify which methods you would use to find candidates with these qualities. Would you use applications, interviews, cognitive or ability tests, work samples, or what? Explain why you would use these methods you indentified and justify the cost and time required to conduct each.

3. After you have identified your selection criteria and methods, do a "reality check" in a real organization. Interview a manager who employs someone in that job. For example, if the job you selected is salesperson, go to a local business to learn how they select individuals for sales jobs. Compare what you thought would be a good selection approach with what you learned from the company you visited.

4. Identify the reasons for any discrepancies between your approach and theirs. Are the reasons justified and sound?

BIZFLIX EXERCISES

Bowfinger: **The Lookalike**

Some major learning objectives of this chapter include understanding the goals of an organization's selection process, using different types of information in employee selection and using different employment interview approaches. Watch this humorous scene from *Bowfinger* with those learning objectives in mind.

This film, which brought Steve Martin and Eddie Murphy together for the first time, offers a funny look at Hollywood filmmaking. Bobby Bowfinger (Martin), perhaps the least successful director in films, wants to produce a low-budget film with top star Kit Ramsey (Murphy). Bowfinger's problem: Recruit a crew and cast with almost no budget and trick Kit into appearing in his film.

Bowfinger interviews several candidates for the Kit Ramsey lookalike role. He rejects everyone until—

Jifferson—Jiff—Ramsey (Murphy) auditions. This scene is an edited version of "The Lookalike" sequence early in the film. It includes Jiff's audition and interview and a brief look at his first workday.

What to Watch for and Ask Yourself

- Which steps in the employee selection process shown earlier in Figure 6.2 appear in this scene? Which steps did Bobby Bowfinger skip?

- Does Bobby Bowfinger have valid selection criteria for filling the role of the Kit Ramsey lookalike? Do you predict Jiff Ramsey's success as a Kit Ramsey substitute?

- Which type of employment interview did Bowfinger use? See the earlier section "The Employment Interview" for a discussion of different employment interview approaches.

CASE STUDY 1

Job Candidate
Assessment
Tests Go
Virtual

Multistate banking firm National City Corp. had its work cut out if it was going to grow its retail banking division. The Cleveland-based bank in early January eliminated 900 jobs as it closed its troubled wholesale mortgage division. The bank cut 3,400 jobs during the past year—primarily in the mortgage division—yet still planned to expand its 1,400 retail branches across the East and Midwest.

One element in the search for everything from branch managers to tellers hinged on the bank's ability to stand out in a cutthroat hiring environment where demand for qualified talent often outstrips the supply. "We were looking for ways to differentiate ourselves among our competitors," says Cheryl Goodman, National City's assessment consultant vice president.

It was among the reasons National City adopted Shaker Consulting Group's Virtual Job Tryout in early 2007. The system does what its name suggests—allows companies to audition candidates by measuring how they react to computerized simulations of specific job-related tasks. Beyond assessment, Goodman is counting on it to give National City a leg up on competitors by creating a distinctive recruiting experience. "This isn't your run-of-the-mill paper-and-pencil assessment test," she explains. "We think it creates a unique impression that lets us stand out among our peers in the industry."

National City, which employs 32,000 people, is part of a growing number of companies that rely on a new wave of virtual simulation tools for more than assessment purposes. They also leverage these platforms to put forth other strategic recruiting practices. Besides differentiation, Goodman says Virtual Job Tryout is also a good way to fortify the National City employer brand. The system works as an educational tool for candidates to learn what it's like to be an employee at the company. "It gives us a way to share our story and what we're all about," she notes.

The better acquainted that companies get with virtual tryout tools, the more applications they'll discover for them, says Nov Omana, managing principal of consultancy Collective HR Solutions. He says more employers are realizing the secondary benefits such cutting-edge assessment systems can bring to their recruiting process. Omana anticipates the trend will widen. "Whether it is in the area of Second Life or social networking or virtual tryouts, I think we'll see employers getting more creative in the years to come," he notes.

Creating a Unique Experience

"The days of handing a clipboard and pen to candidates are long over," says Brian Stern of Cleveland-based Shaker Consulting. "Innovative companies are now looking for ways to create positive recruiting experiences to successfully vie for talent." The level of interactivity that today's virtual tryout tools deliver is unprecedented, he notes. Employers are able to customize simulations to specific job roles within a company; candidates can get a feel for the job.

In National City's case, Goodman set up individual simulation experiences for call center applicants and potential branch managers. Call center candidates were given scenarios to solve customer service problems, while branch manager applicants had to demonstrate their ability to foster relationships with clients and make quick personnel decisions.

The experiences are interactive—with both video and audio, Stern notes. "Companies are creating a dynamic testing environment that engages the candidates," he says. Delivering this type of innovative recruiting experience is particularly critical when it comes to Gen Y talent, Stern says. "This is a group of individuals that is not going to respond well to the old-school way of recruiting," he notes.

The Gen Y Factor

Recruiting Gen Y'ers is an ongoing challenge for employers. "They are of a different breed than what recruiters are used to," says Knowledge Infusion CEO Jason Averbook. "You would be surprised at the number of companies that simply don't know how to communicate effectively with them." Averbook says one way of attaining the attention of this segment of the workforce is adopting tools that are interactive in nature, as they stand a better chance of resonating with this audience. "Simulation tools are a good way of letting Gen Y'ers know that a company has kept up with the times," he notes.

Averbook warns that creating a cutting-edge recruiting experience without having a workplace environment matching that image could be counterproductive. "If you have a fancy assessment tool that impresses the socks off an applicant at the recruiting stage but then hand them a paper and pencil to do their job once you have thrown them over the hiring wall, you're going to be in trouble," he notes. Averbook says employees inevitably will become disappointed and could leave if their initial expectations aren't met. He recommends companies put standards in place, not just during the recruiting phase but throughout an employee's tenure. "This is a group of smart people," he notes. "They'll be able to see through the smoke and mirrors pretty quickly."

Important Considerations

While job simulation tools can be instrumental in creating a hallmark recruiting experience, there are certain questions employers should consider before investing in a system, says Shally Steckerl, founder of JobMachine, a recruiting consultancy based in Norcross, Georgia. "These are great tools to have," he notes. "But they are more beneficial for certain types of employers."

It could backfire for companies targeting high-end white-collar workers. "An MBA is not going to want to take this type of test," Steckerl says. "That candidate is expecting to be wined and dined." He recommends companies take a hard look at the sort of worker being recruited and whether such an assessment would be appropriate in that context. Steckerl also says job simulation may be more of a hindrance at companies handling a large volume of candidates.

"The process gets to be too time-consuming when we are talking about thousands of applicants," he notes. Further, he says such technologies are better suited to test soft skills. It's an important feature, as intangibles are characteristics that are normally difficult to gauge, Steckerl explains. However, when it comes to measuring hard skills, such as engineering or program writing, a company may be better off using conventional aptitude exams.

Before buying such a system, employers should assess virtual job tryout vendors because all are different. "There are several vendors out there, each with its own strength," Steckerl says. "Companies need to do their homework to select the tool that is most compatible with the recruiting experience that they want to create."

In the case of National City, the company already had an established relationship with Shaker Consulting and was familiar with the product's features. The company is still tallying its numbers, but Goodman says she is content with its recruiting performance in 2007. Goodman says the assessment tool enabled National City to hire workers that came from sectors outside banking, so long as they had transferable skills. What's more, she believes retention rates will improve because it provides a way to make hiring decisions that are more educated and scientific. She also sees an added bonus for using the virtual job tryout. "As far as I know, none of our local competitors offers this level of assessment," she says. "I think it gives us an advantage."

Questions

1. What do you think are the prime advantages and disadvantages of National City Corporation's "virtual tryouts"?
2. Do you think there would be any EEO concerns regarding this system?
3. Would you suggest the company tailor its system for different types of candidates?

Source: Reprinted from Gina Ruiz, "Job Candidate Assessment Tests Go Virtual," *Workforce Management Online*, January 2008.

CASE STUDY 2

Cleaning Up the "Resu-mess"

Layne Buckley and Eric Muller both need to hire engineers, and those engineers need to understand electricity. But the recruiters are looking for two very different types of candidates.

Buckley, staffing manager for communications headset manufacturer Plantronics Inc. in Santa Cruz, California, wants engineers who can design the electronics for audio equipment. Muller, on the other hand, is recruiting a team leader for the energy firm Southern Company, and that calls for an engineer to run nuclear, coal, natural gas, and hydroelectric power plants. Both recruiters have one problem in common: Each has too many applicants to weed through.

"Our recruiters were overwhelmed and couldn't pinpoint who they should hire for a particular vacancy," says Muller. "They were victims of their own successful sourcing efforts."

Buckley had a similar experience. "Since we are near Silicon Valley, some [information technology] jobs have had 400 applicants," he says. "I have only a limited number of staff, and they can't be reading that many applications."

Southern has 26,000 employees operating 79 generating stations and overseeing 28,000 miles of transmission lines, as well as handling sales, clerical, financial, and other administrative tasks. About one-third of them work in the greater Atlanta area, where the company is headquartered, but the rest are scattered throughout Georgia, Alabama, Mississippi, and Florida. To maintain the required staffing levels, the company must hire more than 2,000 new permanent full-time employees each year, Muller says. But to do this, the recruiters have to sort through more than 100,000 applicants. "Our recruiters were swimming under what they called the 'resumess,'" says Muller.

Southern was doing online recruiting, but the process was not automated. Each recruiter would post open positions on the company's Web site with instructions for candidates to send an e-mail to a generic address with the job requisition code in the subject line. The system was not very workable. "If that code was not in the subject line, the e-mail would go into a black hole," Muller explains.

But even when the e-mails wound up with the right recruiter, there were major problems. To begin with, some candidates would apply to every open job on the Web site, some of which they were legitimately qualified for and some of which they were not. Then the resumes would not necessarily list the key information the recruiter needed, such as whether the applicant had worked on a particular piece of equipment. This meant that the recruiters would have to follow up with the candidates to chase down the missing information.

In the late 1990s, the company started looking for a better way of managing applications. It sent out a request for proposals and asked the strongest companies to make an in-depth presentation. In addition to HR staff, technical staff reviewed each vendor for data security. The company decided to go with an application service provider (ASP) model so its internal information technology (IT) group would not have to support the application. This decision eliminated some other vendors from the running.

Southern selected Hire.com, a privately owned recruitment ASP headquartered in Austin, Texas. Its HireEnterprise suite contains three modules: electronic recruiting, applicant tracking, and staffing analytics.

Hire.com hosts the software in its data centers, and users access it through a browser. Customers have the option of purchasing just one of the modules rather than the entire package. For example, Southern uses just the recruitment software, while Plantronics uses both the recruitment and applicant tracking modules.

Since Southern did not have to install and configure the software at its end, it took only thirty-five days to get the initial functions up and running. (Additional functions and more in-depth integration were added later.) After that, Hire.com sent in a team to train the recruiters on the software. The two-day process consisted of half a day of briefing, half a day of training, and then a full day of practice on the system.

"The great thing is that it is designed like a public Internet Web site so it didn't really take any training, just a matter of getting used to it," says Muller. "If you can use [Amazon.com], you can use this software."

When applicants apply for a job on either Plantronics's or Southern's Web sites and click on the jobs link, it takes them to the Hire.com server, though there is nothing to indicate to an applicant that he or she is accessing a different site. There they can set up an account based on their education, job preferences, location, and so on and search for open positions. Applicants can also sign up to receive e-mail alerts when jobs that meet their criteria become available in the future. Southern reports that 60 percent of its job candidates come through this push feature.

The biggest advantage, however, is not in finding applicants, but in narrowing down which ones the company should pursue. Recruiters, after all, do not have time to read through hundreds of applications for a position. To simplify this, both Plantronics and Southern use the software's testing functions to prescreen candidates.

Answers to these screening questions can take several different forms, including yes/no, true/false, multiple choice, numerical, or text. Answers can be assigned different weights, and certain answers can also automatically include or exclude the applicant. Based on the responses, the software screens out any applicants who are not qualified and ranks those who do meet the criteria.

Here are some sample questions that can be included:

- How many years experience in the industry do you have?
- In which subject do you have a master's degree?
- Are you used to functioning independently with minimum supervision?
- In how many research studies were you involved?
- What are your former employers in this sector?

Plantronics uses, on average, seventeen questions for each open position, but these vary from job to job. There is a core set of questions, most relating to software, with project management or people management questions added for any managerial position. Plantronics also asks questions that are applicable to a particular job, such as queries about the applicant's experience operating a specific piece of equipment or knowledge of a particular field.

When Southern started using the recruitment module, it screened out only around 40 percent of the applicants. By refining the questions, the company has increased that to 65 percent. Plantronics sometimes screens out as many as 95 percent.

"By using the prescreening questions, the recruiter can spend time phone screening or following up on the best 10 applicants rather than having to sort through 100," says Muller.

Questions

1. What impact do you think Hire.com's screening tools have had on the HR departments of Southern and Plantronics?
2. What competitive advantages do you see in using online screening tools to screen applicants?
3. Do you see any drawbacks associated with the Hire.com system, and, if so, how might they be addressed?

Source: Adapted from Drew Robb, "Screening for Speedier Selection," *HRMagazine* 49, no. 9 (September 2004): 143–147.

NOTES AND REFERENCES

1. Misty L. Loughry, Matthew W. Ohland, and D. Dewayne Moore, "Development of a Theory-Based Assessment of Team Member Effectiveness," *Educational & Psychological Measurement* 67, no. 3 (June 2007): 505–524; Patrick D. Converse, Fredrick L. Oswald, Michael A. Gillespie, Kevin A. Field, and Elizabeth B. Bizot, "Matching Individual to Occupations Using Abilities and the O*NET," *Personnel Psychology* 57, no. 2 (Summer 2004): 451–488.

2. Wesley Scroggins, "The Relationship Between Employee Fit Perceptions, Job Performance, and Retention: Implications of Perceived Fit," *Employee Responsibilities & Rights Journal* 20, no. 1 (March 2008): 57–71; Helena D. Cooper-Thomas, Annelies Van Vianen, and Neil Anderson, "Changes in Person-Organization Fit: The Impact of Socialization Tactics on Perceived and Actual P-O Fit," *European Journal of Work & Organizational Psychology* 13, no. 1 (March 2004): 52–79.

3. Mary-Kathryn Zachary, "Discrimination without Intent," *Supervision* 64, no. 5 (May 2003): 23–29; Neal Schmitt, William Rogers, David Chan, Lori Sheppard, and Danielle Jennings, "Adverse Impact and Predictive Efficiency of Various Predictor Combinations," *Journal of Applied Psychology* 82, no. 5 (October 1997): 719–30.

4. Daniel A. Biddle and Patrick M. Nooren, "Validity Generalizations versus Title VII: Can Employers Successfully Defend Tests Conducting Local Validation Studies?" *Labor Law Journal* 57, no. 4 (Winter 2006): 216–237; Namok Choi, "A Psychometric Examination of the Personal Attributes Questionnaire," *Journal of Social Psychology* 144, no. 3 (June 2004): 348–52.

5. Jesus F. Salgado and Neil Anderson, "Validity Generalization of GMA Tests across Countries in the European Community," *European Journal of Work & Organizational Psychology* 12, no. 1 (March 2003): 1–17; Calvin C. Hoffman and S. Morton McPhail, "Exploring Options for Supporting Test Use in Situations Precluding Local Validation," *Personnel Psychology* 51, no. 4 (Winter 1998): 987–1003; Leaetta Hough and Frederick Oswald, "Personnel Selection: Looking toward the Future—Remembering the Past," *Annual Review of Psychology* 51 (2000): 631–64.

6. Philip Bobko, Philip L. Roth, and Maury A. Buster, "The Usefulness of Unit Weights in Creating Composite Scores: A Literature Review, Application to Content Validity, and Meta-Analysis," *Organizational Research Methods* 10, no. 4 (October 2007): 689–709; Kobi Dayan, Ronen Kasten, and Shaul Fox, "Entry-Level Police Candidate Assessment Center: An Efficient Tool or a Hammer to Kill a Fly?" *Personnel Psychology* 55, no. 4 (Winter 2002).

7. Deniz S. Ones, Chockalingam Viswesvaran, and Frank L Schmidt, "No New Terrain: Reliability and Construct Validity of Job Performance Ratings," *Industrial & Organizational Psychology* 1, no. 2 (June 2008): 174–179; D. Brent Smith and Lill Ellingson, "Substance versus Style: A New Look at Social Desirability in Motivating Contexts," *Journal of Applied Psychology* 87, no. 2 (April 2002): 211–19; Ken Craik et al., "Explorations of Construct Validity in a Combined Managerial and Personality Assessment Programme," *Journal of Occupational and Organizational Psychology* 75, no. 2 (June 2002): 171–93.

8. "A New Assistant at Georgia Tech Made False Claims," *The New York Times*, January 29, 2002, D7; Stephanie Armour, "Security Checks Worry Workers; Padded Resumes Could Be Exposed," *USA Today*, June 19, 2002, B1.

9. "Busted," *Training Development* 60, no. 12 (December 2006): 19; Pamela Babock, "Spotting Lies," *HRMagazine* 48, no. 10 (October 2003): 46–51; Tammy Prater and Sara Bliss Kiser, "Lies, Lies, and More Lies," *A.A.M. Advance Management Journal* 67, no. 2 (Spring 2002): 9–14.

10. Connie Walker, "Job Tryouts Go Virtual," *HRMagazine* 51, no. 9 (September 2006): 131–134; "The Pros and Cons of Online Recruiting," *HRFocus* 81 (April 2004): S1; Rob Drew, "Career Portals Boost Online Recruiting," *HRMagazine* 49, no. 4 (April 2004): 111–114; Samuel Greengard, "Smarter Screening Takes Technology and HR Savvy," *Workforce* 81, no. 6 (June 2002): 56–62.

11. Yen Chung, "The Validity of Biographical Inventories for the Selection of Salespeople," *International Journal of Management* 18, no. 3 (September 2001): 322–29; Teri Elkins and James Phillips, "Job Context, Selection Decision Outcome, and the Perceived Fairness of Selection Tests: Biodata as an Illustrative Case," *Journal of Applied Psychology* 85, no. 3 (June 2000): 479–84; Herschel Chait, Shawn Carreher, and M. Ronald Buckley, "Measuring Service Orientation with Biodata," *Journal of Managerial Issues* 12, no. 1 (Spring 2000): 109–20.

12. Doug Eisenschenk and Elaine Davis, "Background Checks in Hiring and Compensation: The Next Generation," *Benefits & Compensation Digest* 41, no. 10 (October 2004): 1–4; "What's New," *HR Magazine* 49, no. 4 (April 2004): 153–156; "Why You Should Update Your Background Checks," *HRFocus* (February 2004): 12–13; Merry Mayer, "Background Checks in Focus," *HRMagazine* 47, no. 1 (January 2002): 59–62. In addition, organizations use other resources, such as the following: *The Guide to Background Investigations: A Comprehensive Source Directory for Employee Screening and Background Investigations*, 8th ed. (TISI, 2000).

13. Kira Vermond, "References Done Right," *Profit* 26, no. 2 (May 2007): 101; Kathleen Samey, "A Not-So-Perfect Fit," *Adweek* 44, no. 47 (December 1, 2003): 34; Ann Fisher, "How Can We Be Sure We're Not Hiring a Bunch of Shady Liars?" *Fortune* 147, no. 10 (May 26, 2003).

14. "Legal Issues Raised by Giving Bad References," *Fair Employment Practice Guidelines*, no. 594 (November 2004): 1–3; Robert L. Brady, "Employee Loses Defamation Suit over Bad Reference," *HRFocus* 73, no. 7 (July 1996): 20; Glenn Withiam, "Complexities of Employee References," *Cornell Hotel and Restaurant Administration Quarterly* 37, no. 3 (June 1996): 10; Mimi Moon, "Justices Consider FERPA in Student's Privacy Claim," *News Media and the Law* 26, no. 2 (Spring 2002): 37–38.

15. Mary-Kathryn, "Labor Law for Supervisors, *Supervision* 67, no. 2 (February 2006): 22–23; Diane Cadrian, "HR Professionals Stymied by Vanishing Job References," *HRMagazine* 49, no. 11 (November 2004): 31–32.

16. "New Employee Privacy Rights in Oregon and Washington," *Venulex Legal Summaries* (2007 Q3): 1–4; Barry J. Nadell, "The Cut of His Jib Doesn't Jibe," *Security Management* 48, no. 9 (September 2004): 108–114; William Atkinson, "Who Goes There?" *LP/Gas* 64, no. 9 (September 2004): 16–24; Amelia Deligiannis, "Fair Credit Reporting Act Pre-Emption Debate Heats Up," *Corporate Legal Times* 13, no. 139 (June 2003): 22–24.

17. Lawrence Peikes and Meghan D. Burns, "Polygraph Test Request Unlawful," *HRMagazine* 50, no. 7 (July 2005): 110; "Pretext for Discrimination: How to Avoid Looking Like a Liar," *Fair Employment Practices Guidelines*, no. 592 (September 1, 2004): 1–3; Gillian Flynn, Diane D. Hatch, and James E. Hall, "Know the Background of Background Checks," *Workforce* 81, no. 9 (September 2002): 96–98.

18. Paul Zielbauer, "Small Changes Could Improve Police Hiring, Panel Says," *The New York Times*, January 7, 1999, 8; Lynn McFarland and Ann Marie Ryan, "Variance in Faking across Noncognitive Measures," *Journal of Applied Psychology* 85, no. 5 (October 2000): 812–21; David Arnold and John Jones, "Who the Devil's Applying Now?" *Security Management* 46, no. 3 (March 2002): 85–88; "Polygraph Testing Considered Personnel Tool," *Crime Control Digest* 33, no. 14 (April 9, 1999): 4.

19. Constance L. Hays, "Tests Are Becoming Common in Hiring," *The New York Times*, November 28, 1997, D1. See also Gregory M. Lousig-Nont, "Avoid Common Hiring Mistakes with Honesty Tests," *Nation's Restaurant News* 31, no. 11 (March 17, 1997): 30; "If the Shoe Fits," *Security Management* 40, no. 2 (February 1996): 11; Michelle Cottle, "Job Testing: Multiple Choices," *The New York Times*, September 5, 1999, 3: 10.

20. Thomas J. Ryan, "Nerves of Steal," *SGB* 37, no. 6 (June 2004): 8–10; D. S. Ones, C. Viswesvaran, and F. L. Schmidt, "Comprehensive Meta-Analysis of Integrity Test Validities: Findings and Implications for Personnel Selection and Theories of Job Performance," *Journal of Applied Psychology* 78 (August 1993): 679–703. See also Deniz S. Ones and Chockalingam Viswesvaran, "Gender, Age and Race Differences on Overt Integrity Tests: Results across Four Large-Scale Job Applicant Data Sets," *Journal of Applied Psychology* 83, no. 1 (February 1998): 35–42.

21. James Krohe Jr., "Are Workplace Tests Worth Taking?" *Across the Board* 43, no. 4 (July–August 2006): 16–23; "Honesty Tests Flawed," *People Management* 3, no. 2 (January 23, 1997): 15; Hays, "Tests Are Becoming Common in Hiring"; Stephen A. Dwight and George M. Alliger, "Reactions to Overt Integrity Test Items," *Educational and Psychological Measurement* 57, no. 6 (December 1997): 937–48.

22. Klass Hogenesch, "A New Science for Finding the Right Employee?" *NZ Business* 18, no. 2 (March 2004): 10; Bill Leonard, "Reading Employees," *HRMagazine* 44, no. 4 (April 1999): 67–73; Steven Thomas and Steve Vaught, "The Write Stuff: What the Evidence Says about Using Handwriting Analysis in Hiring," *S.A.M. Advanced Management Journal* 66, no. 4 (Autumn 2001): 31–35.

23. Rob Yeung, "New Year, New Start," *Accountancy* 139, no. 1362 (February 2007): 59; Dirk D. Steiner and Stephen W. Gilliland, "Fairness Reactions to Personnel Selection Techniques in France and the United States," *Journal of Applied Psychology* 81, no. 2 (April 1996): 134–41.

24. Michael Adams, Ben Van Houten, Robert Klara, and Elizabeth Bernstein, "Access

Denied?" *Restaurant Business* 98, no. 2 (January 15, 1999): 36–48; "Medical Screening: Are Employers Going Too Far?" *Employee Benefit Plan Review* 53, no. 11 (May 1999): 42–43.

25. Jill Cox, "Pre-Employment Medical Exams: When Are They Appropriate?" *Paper 360* 3, no. 5 (May 2008): 47; "Accommodating Hearing-Impaired," *Fair Employment Practices Guidelines*, no. 587 (April 1, 2004): 1–3; Terpstra, Kethley, Foley, and Limpaphayom, "The Nature of Litigation Surrounding Five Screening Devices"; Teresa Burke Wright, "ADA Restricts Medical Inquiries," *Credit Union Magazine* 68, no. 3 (March 2002): 89.

26. "Constitution Limits Pre-employment Drug Testing by Public Employers," *Venulex Legal Summaries* (2008 Q1): 1; "Drug Testing Is Common and Codified at Many Workplaces," *HRFocus* 83, no. 6 (June 2006): 9; "New Developments Question the Use of Drug Tests in the Workplace," *Safety Director's Report* 4, no. 9 (September 2004): 3–6; Sandy Smith, "What Every Employer Should Know about Drug Testing in the Workplace," *Occupational Hazards* 66, no. 8 (August 2004): 45–48.

27. Judy Greenwald "EEOC Move May Signal More Scrutiny of Employment Tests," *Business Insurance* 41, no. 52 (December 24, 2007): 4–20; Rod Kurtz, "Testing, Testing . . . ," *Inc.* 26, no. 6 (June 2004): 35–38; Gillian Flynn, "A Legal Examination of Testing," *Workforce* 81, no. 6 (June 2002): 92–94.

28. Ely A. Leightling and Pamela M. Ploor, "When Applicants Apply through the Internet," *Employee Relations Law Journal* 30, no. 2 (Autumn 2004): 3–13; "EEOC Clarifies the Definition of Who Is an 'Applicant' in the Context of Internet Recruiting and Hiring," *Fair Employment Practices Guidelines*, no. 587 (April 1, 2004): 3–13; Kathryn Tyler, "Put Applicants' Skills to the Test," *HRMagazine* 45, no. 1 (January 2000): 74–80.

29. Elizabeth D. MacGillivray, Juanita H. Beecher, and Diedre M. Golden, "Employment Testing: The New Hot Button Issue for Federal Agencies—and Other Legal Developments," *Global Business & Organizational Excellence* 27, no. 3, (March–April 2008): 68–78.

30. Standards that testing programs should meet are described in *Standards for Educational and Psychological Tests* (Washington, DC: American Psychological Association, 1999). HR managers who want to examine paper-and-pencil tests should obtain specimen sets that include a test manual, copy of the test, answer sheet, and scoring key. The test manual provides the essential information about the construction of the test; its recommended use; and instructions for administering, scoring, and interpreting the test. Test users should not rely entirely on the material furnished by the test author and publisher. A major source of consumer information about commercially available tests—*Mental Measurements Yearbook* (*MMY*)—is available in most libraries. Published periodically, the *MMY* contains descriptive information plus critical reviews by experts in the various types of tests. The reviews are useful in evaluating a particular test for tryout in employment situations. Other sources of information about tests include *Test Critiques*, a set of volumes containing professional reviews of tests, and *Tests: A Comprehensive Reference for Assessments in Psychology, Education, and Business*. The latter describes more than 2,000 tests published in the English language.

31. Justin Menkes, "Interviewing for Executive Intelligence," *HR Professional* 25, no. 3 (April–May 2008): 54; Chris Piotrowski and Terry Armstrong, "Current Recruitment and Selection Practices: A National Survey of Fortune 1000 Firms," *North American Journal of Psychology* 8, no. 3 (2006): 489–496; Sara Rynes, Amy Colbert, and Kenneth Brown, "HR Professionals' Beliefs about Effective Human Resource Practices: Correspondence between Research and Practice," *Human Resource Management* 41, no. 2 (Summer 2002): 149–74.

32. Kris Frieswick, "Casting to Type," *CFO* 20, no. 9 (July 2004): 71–73; Timothy Judge and Joyce Bono, "Five-Factor Model of Personality and Transformational Leadership," *Journal of Applied Psychology* 85, no. 5 (October 2000): 751–65; J. Michael Crant and Thomas S. Bateman, "Charismatic Leadership Viewed from Above: The Impact of Proactive Personality," *Journal of*

Organizational Behavior 21, no. 1 (February 2000): 63–75.

33. Frederick P. Morgeson, Michael A. Campion, Robert L. Dipboye, John R. Hollenbeck, Kevin Murphy, and Neal Schmitt, "Reconsidering the Use of Personality Tests in Personnel Selection Contexts," *Personnel Psychology* 60, no. 3 (Autumn 2007): 683–729; Arielle Emmett, "Snake Oil or Science? The Raging Debate on Personality Testing," *Workforce Management* 83, no. 10 (October 2004): 90–93; Gregory Hurtz and John Donovan, "Personality and Job Performance: The Big Five Revisited," *Journal of Applied Psychology* 85, no. 6 (December 2000): 869–79.

34. George B. Yancey, "The Predictive Power of Hiring Tools," *Credit Union Executive Journal* 40, no. 4 (July–August 2000): 12–18; Jeffrey A. Mello, "Personality Tests and Privacy Rights," *HRFocus* 73, no. 3 (March 1996): 22–23.

35. Walter C. Borman, Mary Ann Hanson, and Jerry W. Hedge, "Personnel Selection," *Annual Review of Psychology* 48 (1997): 299–337; Charles Sproule and Stephen Berkley, "The Selection of Entry-Level Corrections Officers: Pennsylvania Research," *Public Personnel Management* 30, no. 3 (Fall 2001): 377–418.

36. M. S. Sothmann, D. L. Gebhardt, T. A. Baker, G. M. Kastello, and V. A. Sheppard, "Performance Requirements of Physically Strenuous Occupations: Validating Minimum Standards for Muscular Strength," *Ergonomics* 47, no. 8 (June 22, 2004): 864–76; T. L. Stanley, "The Wisdom of Employment Testing," *Supervision* 65, no. 2 (February 2004): 11–14; Maria Greco Danaher, "Strength Test Falls," *HRMagazine* 52, no. 2 (February 2007): 115–116.

37. John Bret Becton, Hubert S. Feild, William F. Giles, and Allison Jones-Farmer, "*Racial differences in promotion candidate performance and reactions to selection procedures: a field study in a diverse top-management context,*" *Journal of Organizational Behavior* 29, no. 3 (April 2008): 265–285.

38. Rachel Suff, "Testing the Water: Using Work Sampling for Selection," *IRS Employment Review*, no. 802 (June 18, 2004): 44–49; Leonard D. Goodstein

and Alan D. Davidson, "Hiring the Right Stuff: Using Competency-Based Selection," *Compensation & Benefits Management* 14, no. 3 (Summer 1998): 1–10.

39. Noelle Murphy, "Testing the Waters: Employers' Use of Selection Assessments," *IRS Employment Review* 852 (August 4, 2006): 42–48; Florence Berger and Ajay Ghei, "Employment Tests: A Facet of Hospitality Hiring," *Cornell Hotel and Restaurant Administration Quarterly* 36, no. 6 (December 1995): 28–31; Malcolm James Ree, Thomas R. Carretta, and Mark S. Teachout, "Role of Ability and Prior Job Knowledge in Complex Training Performance," *Journal of Applied Psychology* 80, no. 6 (December 1995): 721–30.

40. Amy Maingault, John Sweeney, and Naomi Cossack, "Interviewing, Management Training, Strikes," *HRMagazine* 52, no. 6 (June 2007): 43; James Bassett, "Stop, Thief!" *Gifts & Decorative Accessories* 104, no. 1 (January 2003): 130–34; Richard A. Posthuma, Frederick Morgeson, and Michael Campion, "Beyond Employment Interview Validity: A Comprehensive Narrative Review of Recent Research and Trends over Time," *Personnel Psychology* 55, no. 1 (Spring 2002): 1–8.

41. David E. Terpstra and Bryan R. Kethley, "Organizations' Relative Degree of Exposure to Selection Discrimination Litigation," *Public Personnel Management* 31, no. 3 (February 2002): 277–94; Schmidt and Rader, "Exploring the Boundary Conditions for Interview Validity," *Personnel Psychology* 99, no. 2 (Summer 1999): 445-464; Williamson, Campion, Malos, and Roehling, "Employment Interview on Trial," *Journal of Applied Psychology* 82, no. 6 (December 1997): 900-912.

42. Yen-Chun Chen, Wei-Chi Tsai, and Changya Hu, "The Influences of Interviewer-Related and Situational Factors on Interviewer Reactions to High Structured Job Interviews," *International Journal of Human Resource Management* 19, no. 6 (June 2008) 1056–1071. For an excellent review of research on the structured interview, see Michael A. Campion, David K. Palmer, and James E. Campion, "A Review of Structure in the Selection Interview," *Personnel Psychology* 50, no. 3 (Autumn 1997): 655–702. See also Karen van der Zee, Arnold Bakker, and Paulien Bakker, "Why Are Structured Interviews So Rarely Used in Personnel Selection?" *Journal of Applied Psychology* 87, no. 1 (February 2002): 176–84.

43. Jesus F. Salgado and Silvia Moscoso, "Comprehensive Meta-Analysis of the Construct Validity of the Employment Interview," *European Journal of Work and Organizational Psychology* 11, no. 3 (September 2002): 299–325; Allen Huffcutt, Jeff Weekley, Willi Wiesner, Timothy Degroot, and Casey Jones, "Comparison of Situational and Behavior Description Interview Questions for Higher-Level Positions," *Personnel Psychology* 54, no. 3 (Autumn 2001): 619–44.

44. Peter Herriot, "Assessment by Groups: Can Value Be Added?" *European Journal of Work & Organizational Psychology* 12, no. 2 (June 2003): 131–46; Salgado and Moscoso, "Comprehensive Meta-Analysis"; Amelia J. Prewett-Livingston, John G. Veres III, Hubert S. Field, and Philip M. Lewis, "Effects of Race on Interview Ratings in a Situational Panel Interview," *Journal of Applied Psychology* 81, no. 2 (April 1996): 178–86. See also Damodar Y. Golhar and Satish P. Deshpande, "HRM Practices of Large and Small Canadian Manufacturing Firms," *Journal of Small Business Management* 35, no. 3 (July 1997): 30–38.

45. Jack Welch and Suzy Welch, "Hiring Is Hard Work," *Business Week Online*, no. 4091 (July 7, 2008): na; Michele V. Rafter, "Candidates for Jobs in High Places Sit for Tests That Size Up Their Mettle," *Workforce Management* 83, no. 5 (May 2004): 70–73; Patricia Buhler, "Computer Interview: Managing in the New Millennium," *Supervision* 63, no. 10 (October 2002): 20–23.

46. Victoria Reitz, "Interview without Leaving Home," *Machine Design* 76, no. 7 (April 1, 2004): 66; Jessica Clark Newman et al., "The Differential Effects of Face-to-Face and Computer Interview Modes," *American Journal of Public Health* 92, no. 2 (February 2002): 294; David Mitchell, "ijob.com Recruiting Online," *Strategic Finance* 80, no. 11 (May 1999): 48–51.

47. Dan Hanover, "Hiring Gets Cheaper and Faster," *Sales and Marketing Management* 152, no. 3 (March 2000): 87.

48. Fay Hansen, "Keeping Interviews on Point to Stay Out of Legal Hot Water," *Workforce Management* no. 85, no. 15 (August 14, 2006): 44–45; Posthuma, Morgeson, Campion, "Beyond Employment Interview Validity"; Schmidt and Rader, "Exploring the Boundary Conditions for Interview Validity."

49. Multiple regression is a statistical method for evaluating the magnitude of effects of more than one independent variable (e.g., selection predictors) on a dependent variable (e.g., job performance) using principles of correlation and regression.

50. Patricia M. Buhler, "Managing in the New Millennium," *Supervision* 68, no. 11 (November 2007): 17–20; David E. Bowen and Cheri Ostroff, "Understanding HRM—Firm Performance Linkages: The Role of the Strengths of the HRM System," *Academy of Management Review* 29, no. 2 (April 2004): 203–22; Ann Marie Ryan, Joshua Sacco, Lynn McFarland, and David Kriska, "Applicant Self-Selection: Correlates of Withdrawal from a Multiple Hurdle Process," *Journal of Applied Psychology* 85, no. 2 (April 2000): 163–79.

TRAINING AND DEVELOPMENT

After studying this chapter, you should be able to

Objective | **1** |

Discuss the systems approach to training and development.

Objective | **2** |

Describe the components of training needs assessment.

© CORBIS/JUPITER IMAGES

CHAPTER 7

Objective | 3 |

Identify the principles of learning and describe how they facilitate training.

Objective | 4 |

Identify the types of training methods used for managers and nonmanagers.

Objective | 5 |

Discuss the advantages and disadvantages of various evaluation criteria.

Objective | 6 |

Describe the special training programs that are currently popular.

Training has become increasingly vital to the success of modern organizations. Recall that in Chapter 2 we noted that organizations often compete on the basis of their capabilities—the core sets of knowledge and expertise that give them an edge over their competitors. Training plays a central role in nurturing and strengthening the competencies of a firm and in this way has become part of the backbone of strategic management. In addition, rapidly changing technologies require that employees continuously hone their knowledge, skills, and abilities (KSAs) through continuous learning. Greater competition, including that from different firms around the globe, also makes it necessary for a company's employees and managers to develop the skills that enable them to handle new and more demanding assignments.

THE SCOPE OF TRAINING

Many new employees come equipped with most of the KSAs needed to start work. Others require extensive training before they are ready to make much of a contribution to the organization. Almost any employee, however, needs some type of ongoing training to maintain effective performance or to adjust to new ways of work.

The term *training* is often used casually to describe almost any effort initiated by an organization to foster learning among its members. However, many experts distinguish between *training*, which tends to be more narrowly focused and oriented toward short-term performance concerns, and *development*, which, as you learned in Chapter 5, tends to be oriented more toward broadening an individual's skills for future responsibilities. The two terms tend to be combined into a single phrase—*training and development*—to recognize the combination of activities organizations use to increase the skill base of employees.

Investments in Training

Research shows that an organization's revenues and overall profitability are positively correlated to the amount of training it gives its employees. According to *Training* magazine's ongoing industry report, U.S. businesses spend more than $58 billion annually to provide each of their employees with about 25 hours, on average, of formal training. By contrast, the 100 best U.S. companies to work for, as cited by *Fortune* magazine, provide their employees with approximately double that amount of training and sometimes even more. Each employee of the hotel chain the Ritz Carlton, for example, gets nearly 200 hours of training each year. While a good deal of money is spent on executive development and management training, by far the greatest proportion of training is spent on rank-and-file employees and supervisors (see Figure 7.1). Technology, transportation, communications, and utilities industries tend to spend the most on training. In addition to the billions of dollars spent by U.S. businesses each year on formal training, nearly *four times* that amount is spent on informal instruction. The types of training given employees range from simple, on-the-job instruction to sophisticated skills training conducted on multimillion dollar simulators. Other types of training include customer service, sales and management training, personal growth, and communication skills training.[1]

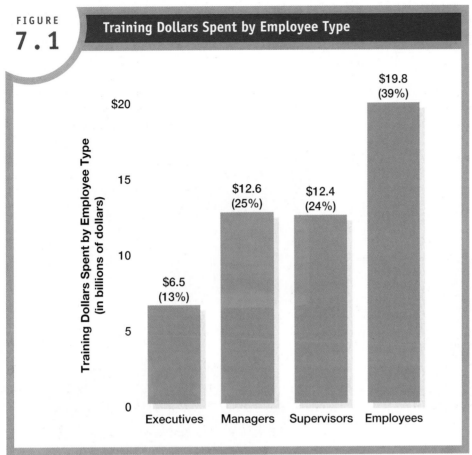

FIGURE 7.1

Training Dollars Spent by Employee Type

Source: "2007 Industry Report," *Training* 44, no. 10–11 (November–December 2007): 8–24.

A Systems Approach to Training

From the broadest perspective, the goal of training is to contribute to the organization's overall goals. Training programs should be developed with this in mind. Managers should keep a close eye on their firms' goals and strategies and orient their training accordingly. Unfortunately, many organizations never make the connection between the two. Instead, fads, fashions, or "whatever the competition is doing" can sometimes be the main drivers of an organization's training agenda. As a result, training programs are often misdirected, poorly designed, and inadequately evaluated—not to mention a waste of money.

To ensure that a firm's training and development investment has the maximum impact possible, a systems approach should be used that involves four phases: (1) needs assessment, (2) program design, (3) implementation, and (4) evaluation. A model that is useful to designers of training programs is presented in Figure 7.2. We will use this model as a framework for organizing the material throughout this chapter.

1 Objective

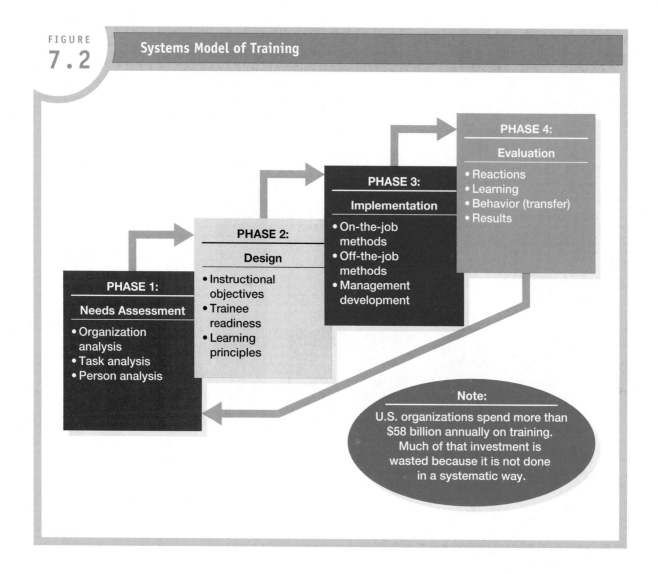

FIGURE 7.2

Systems Model of Training

PHASE 1:

Needs Assessment

- Organization analysis
- Task analysis
- Person analysis

PHASE 2:

Design

- Instructional objectives
- Trainee readiness
- Learning principles

PHASE 3:

Implementation

- On-the-job methods
- Off-the-job methods
- Management development

PHASE 4:

Evaluation

- Reactions
- Learning
- Behavior (transfer)
- Results

Note:

U.S. organizations spend more than $58 billion annually on training. Much of that investment is wasted because it is not done in a systematic way.

▪▪ PHASE 1: CONDUCTING THE NEEDS ASSESSMENT

Objective **2**

chief learning officer

A high-ranking manager directly responsible for fostering employee learning and development within the firm

Because business conditions change rapidly, as does technology, keeping abreast of the types of training a firm's employees need to remain competitive can be a challenge. If employees consistently fail to achieve their productivity objectives, this might be a signal that training is needed. Likewise, if organizations receive an excessive number of customer complaints, this, too, might suggest a firm's training is inadequate. About 30 percent of larger firms, including GE, Wal-Mart, and IBM, have what are called **chief learning officers.** These people are top executives within their firms who are responsible for making certain that a company's training is timely and focused on the firm's top strategic issues. However, regardless of who does the needs assessment within an organization, it should be conducted systematically by utilizing the three different types of analysis shown in Figure 7.3: organization analysis, task analysis, and person analysis. Each of these is discussed next.

Unfortunately, because of the costs, expertise, and time required, a study by the American Society for Training and Development found that organizations conduct needs assessment less than 50 percent of the time. Ironically, as the speed of change increases and time and resources are at a premium, the need for good needs assessment actually increases. In these cases, the process need not be so daunting and laborious. Highlights in HRM 1 provides some tips for rapidly assessing training needs.[2]

Organization Analysis

The first step in a needs assessment is identifying the broad forces that can influence a firm's training needs. An organization analysis is an examination of the environment, strategies, and resources the firm faces so as to determine what training it should emphasize.

Economic and public policy issues influence corporate training needs as well. For example, since the September 11 attacks on the United States, the training of airport security personnel has increased substantially. It has also increased for flight crews of airlines, employees in the transportation industry, workers in nuclear power plants, and even security staff at theme parks.[3]

Other training issues tend to revolve around the strategic initiatives of an organization. Mergers and acquisitions, for example, frequently require that employees take on new roles and responsibilities and adjust to new cultures and ways of conducting business. Nowhere is this more prevalent than in grooming new leaders within organizations. Other issues such as technological change, globalization, reengineering, and total quality management all influence the way work is done and the types of skills needed to do it. Still other concerns may be more tactical, but no less important in terms of their impact on training. Organizational restructuring, downsizing, empowerment, and teamwork, for example, have immediate training requirements. Finally, trends in the workforce itself affect a firm's training needs. As older workers near

organization analysis
Examination of the environment, strategies, and resources of the organization to determine where training emphasis should be placed

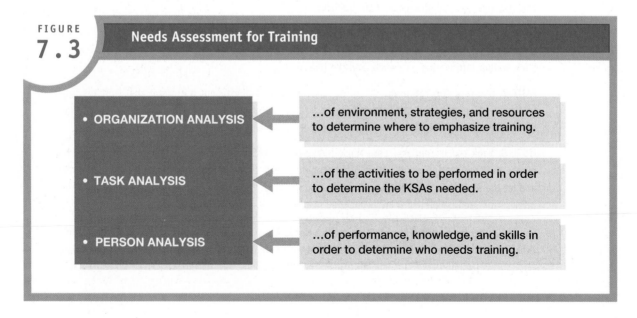

FIGURE 7.3

Needs Assessment for Training

- **ORGANIZATION ANALYSIS** ← ...of environment, strategies, and resources to determine where to emphasize training.

- **TASK ANALYSIS** ← ...of the activities to be performed in order to determine the KSAs needed.

- **PERSON ANALYSIS** ← ...of performance, knowledge, and skills in order to determine who needs training.

HIGHLIGHTS IN HRM 1

Notes on Rapid Needs Assessment

NOTE 1: Look at the problem scope. Common sense suggests that small, local matters may require less information gathering than big problems with a major impact on the organization. Ask managers a series of questions about the nature of the problem and its impact on the organization and gear your analysis accordingly.

NOTE 2: Do organizational scanning. Stay connected with what is going on in the organization in order to anticipate upcoming training needs. If a new technology is about to be launched, the need for training should take no one by surprise. In short, needs assessment isn't an event with a start-and-stop switch. It is the process of being engaged in your business.

NOTE 3: Play "give and take." Get the information you need, but don't drag your feet with excessive analysis before reporting back to managers. Show them that you are sensitive to their need for action by giving them updates on the information you have collected. If necessary, explain that better value may be gained by further analysis.

NOTE 4: Check "lost and found." Often, information gathered for a different purpose may bear on your training issue. Performance data (such as errors, sales, and customer complaints) and staffing data (such as proficiency testing, turnover, and absenteeism) can be very helpful as a starting point.

NOTE 5: Use plain talk. Instead of using clinical terms such as *analysis* or *assessment*, use straight talk with managers that tells them what you are doing: (1) identify the problem, (2) identify alternative ways to get there, (3) implement a solution based on cost/benefit concerns, and (4) determine the effectiveness and efficiency of the solution.

NOTE 6: Use the Web. Information technology allows you to communicate with others, perhaps by setting up an electronic mailing list to post questions, synthesize responses, share resources, get feedback, gather information on trends, and the like.

NOTE 7: Use rapid prototyping. Often the most effective and efficient training is that which is "just-in-time, just enough, and just for me." Create a rapid prototype of a training program, evaluating and revising as you implement and learn more about the problems.

NOTE 8: Seek out exemplars. Find those in the organization that currently demonstrate the performance the organization wants. Bring others together with them to talk about the performance issues, and let the exemplars share their experiences and insights. This avoids the risk of packaging the wrong information, and people learn just what they need to know from each other.

Source: Condensed from Ron Zemke, "How to Do a Needs Assessment When You Think You Don't Have Time," *Training* 35, no. 3 (March 1998): 38–44. Reprinted with permission from the March 1998 issue of *Training Magazine*. Copyright 1998. Bill Communications, Inc., Minneapolis, MN. All rights reserved. Not for resale.

retirement, younger workers need to focus on gaining the skills and knowledge needed to take their place.

Conducting an organization analysis also involves closely examining a firm's resources—technological, financial, and human—available to meet the company's training objectives. HR personnel typically collect data such as information on their companies' direct and indirect labor costs, quality of goods or services, absenteeism, turnover, and number of accidents. The availability of potential replacements and the time required to train them are other important factors in organization analysis.

Organizations continue to keep a tight rein on their costs, including their training budgets. To cope with these resource constraints yet continue to meet their strategic imperatives, firms have become more focused on efficiently using their training budgets.

As older workers near retirement, younger workers must be trained in the skills and knowledge needed to take their place. The availability of potential replacements and the time required to train them are two factors that must be considered in organization analysis.

Companies such as Motorola, Ford, and Merck have found that by using information technology wisely, they cut their training budget by as much as 30 to 50 percent. In order to "do more with less," managers have to plan carefully where they will spend their training dollars, and this means doing a rigorous organization analysis. Other companies outsource their training programs, or at least part of it, to external partners in order to cut costs. A new trend is for companies to partner with other firms in their supply chains so as to jointly train their employees more cost-effectively.[4]

Task Analysis

The second step in training needs assessment is task analysis. Task analysis involves reviewing the job description and specifications to identify the activities performed in a particular job and the KSAs needed to perform them. A task analysis often becomes more detailed than a job analysis, but the overall purpose is to determine the exact content of the training program.

The first step in task analysis is to list all the tasks or duties included in the job. The second step is to list the steps performed by the employee to complete each task. Once the job is understood thoroughly, the type of performance required (such as speech, recall, discrimination, and manipulation), along with the skills and knowledge necessary to do it, can be defined. For example, in the task of taking a chest x-ray, a radiologist correctly positions the patient (manipulation), gives special instructions (speech), and checks the proper distance of the x-ray tube from the patient (discrimination). The types of skills and knowledge that trainees need can be determined by observing and questioning skilled jobholders and/or by reviewing job descriptions. This information helps trainers select program content and choose the most effective training methods.

task analysis

The process of determining what the content of a training program should be on the basis of a study of the tasks and duties involved in the job

However, like job analysis, task analysis appears to be shifting. Instead of focusing on a fixed sequence of tasks, firms are finding that their employees need more flexible sets of competencies in order to perform in a superior way. Companies such as Case Financial and the Principal Financial Group have found that as jobs begin to involve more teamwork, employees need to be flexible and adjust their behavior as needed. Competency assessment focuses on the sets of skills and knowledge employees need to be successful, particularly for decision-oriented and knowledge-intensive jobs. But competency assessment goes beyond simply describing the traits an employee must have to successfully perform the work. It also captures elements of how those traits should be used within an organization's context and culture. That might include an employee's motivation levels, personality traits, interpersonal skills, and so on. General Electric, for example, uses a formal competency assessment program based on forty-five different employee behaviors. While training programs based on a work-oriented task analysis can become dated as jobs change, training programs based on competency assessment are more flexible and perhaps have more durability. The practice has been adopted extensively in the health care industry.[5] Highlights in HRM 2 shows an example of a partial competency assessment tool used for evaluating a manager.

competency assessment

Analysis of the sets of skills and knowledge needed for decision-oriented and knowledge-intensive jobs

---

HIGHLIGHTS IN HRM

2

A Competency Assessment for a Managerial Position

For each item, circle the number that best describes the manager's characteristics. For items that do not apply, circle **NA** (not applicable). For other items for which you lack sufficient observations or documentary evidence, circle **DK** (don't know).

4 – Exemplary

3 – Proficient

2 – Progressing

1 – Needs Assistance

NA – Not Applicable

DK – Don't Know

Competency 1: Behaves professionally and encourages other staff members to do likewise.

4   3   2   1   NA   DK

Evidence: _____

_____

_____

A Competency Assessment for a Managerial Position (continued)

_____

_____

Competency 2: Behaves ethically and encourages staff members to do likewise.

4   3   2   1   NA   DK

Evidence: _____

_____

_____

_____

_____

Competency 3: Uses a variety of modes of communication and conveys information fully and clearly.

4   3   2   1   NA   DK

Evidence: _____

_____

_____

_____

_____

Competency 4: Seeks input from all levels and demonstrates fairness and consistency.

4   3   2   1   NA   DK

Evidence: _____

_____

_____

_____

_____

Competency 5: Engages in an open style of management and is open to criticism from supervisors and subordinates.

4   3   2   1   NA   DK

Evidence: _____

_____

_____

_____

_____

(continued)

A Competency Assessment for a Managerial Position (continued)

Competency 6: Searches for and embraces innovative solutions to improve department's programs and products.

4　3　2　1　NA　DK

Evidence: _____
_____
_____
_____
_____

Person Analysis

person analysis

Determination of the specific individuals who need training

Along with organization and task analyses, it is necessary to perform a person analysis. A **person analysis** involves determining which employees require training and, equally important, which do not. In this regard, conducting a person analysis is important for several reasons. First, a thorough analysis helps organizations avoid the mistake of sending all employees into training when some do not need it. In addition, a person analysis helps managers determine what prospective trainees are able to do when they enter training so that the programs can be designed to emphasize the areas in which they are deficient.

Companies such as Teradyne and Hewlett-Packard have used performance appraisal information as an input for person analysis. Although performance appraisals might reveal which employees are not meeting the firm's expectations, they typically do not reveal why. If the performance deficiencies are due to ability problems, training is likely to be a good solution. However, if the performance deficiencies are due to poor motivation or factors outside an employee's control, training might not be the answer. Ultimately, managers have to sit down with employees to talk about areas for improvement so that they can jointly determine the developmental approaches that will have maximum benefit.[6]

■■ PHASE 2: DESIGNING THE TRAINING PROGRAM

Once the training needs have been determined, the next step is to design the type of learning environment necessary to enhance learning. The success of training programs depends on more than an organization's ability to identify its training needs. Success hinges on taking the information gained from the needs assessment conducted by the firm and utilizing it to design first-rate training programs. Experts believe that the design of training programs should focus on at least four related issues: (1) the training's instructional objectives, (2) "readiness" of trainees and their motivation, (3) principles of learning, and (4) characteristics of instructors. Next, we discuss each.

Instructional Objectives

After conducting organization, task, and person analyses, managers should have a more complete picture of their firms' training needs. On the basis of this information, they can more formally state the desired outcomes of training through written instructional objectives. Generally, instructional objectives describe the skills or knowledge to be acquired and/or the attitudes to be changed. One type of instructional objective, the performance-centered objective, is widely used because it lends itself to an unbiased evaluation of the results. For example, the stated objective for one training program might be that: "Employees trained in team methods will be able to perform the different jobs of their team members within six months." Performance-centered objectives typically include precise terms, such as "to calculate," "to repair," "to adjust," "to construct," "to assemble," and "to classify."[7]

instructional objectives
Desired outcomes of a training program

Trainee Readiness and Motivation

Two preconditions for learning affect the success of those who are to receive training: readiness and motivation. *Trainee readiness* refers to both maturity and experience of trainees. Prospective trainees should be screened to ensure that they have the background knowledge and the skills necessary to absorb what will be presented to them. Recognizing the individual differences of trainees in terms of their readiness is as important in organizational training as it is in any other teaching situation. Consequently, it is often desirable to group individuals according to their capacity to learn, as determined by test scores or other assessment information, and to provide alternative types of instruction for those who need it.

The receptiveness and readiness of participants in training programs can be increased by having them complete questionnaires about why they are attending training and what they hope to accomplish as a result of it. Participants can also be asked to give copies of their completed questionnaires to their managers.

The other precondition for learning is *trainee motivation*. Individuals who are conscientious, goal-oriented, self-disciplined, and persevering are more likely to perceive a link between the effort they put into training and higher performance on the job. For optimum learning to take place, trainees must realize they need new knowledge or skills and maintain a desire to learn as the training progresses. By focusing on the trainees themselves rather than on the trainer or training topic, managers can create a training environment that is conducive to learning. The following six strategies can be essential:

1. Use positive reinforcement.

2. Eliminate threats and punishment.

3. Be flexible.

4. Have participants set personal goals.

5. Design interesting instruction.

6. Break down physical and psychological obstacles to learning.

While most employees are motivated by certain common needs, they differ from one another in the relative importance of these needs at any given time. For example, new college graduates often have a high desire for advancement, and they have established specific goals for career progression. The training objectives should therefore be clearly related to trainees' individual needs to succeed.[8]

Principles of Learning

As we move from assessing an organization's needs and instructional objectives to employee readiness and motivation, we obviously shift our focus from the organization to employees. Ultimately, however, training has to build a bridge between employees and the organization. One important step in this transition is giving full consideration to the psychological principles of learning—that is, the characteristics of training programs that help employees grasp new material, make sense of it in their own lives, and transfer it back to their jobs. All things considered, training programs are likely to be more effective if they incorporate the principles of learning shown in Figure 7.4.

Goal Setting

The value of goal setting for focusing and motivating behavior extends into training. When trainers take the time to explain the training's goals and objectives to trainees—or when trainees are encouraged to set goals on their own—the level of interest, understanding, and effort directed toward the training is likely to increase. In some cases, goal setting can simply take the form of a "road map" of the course/program, its objectives, and its learning points.[9]

FIGURE 7.4

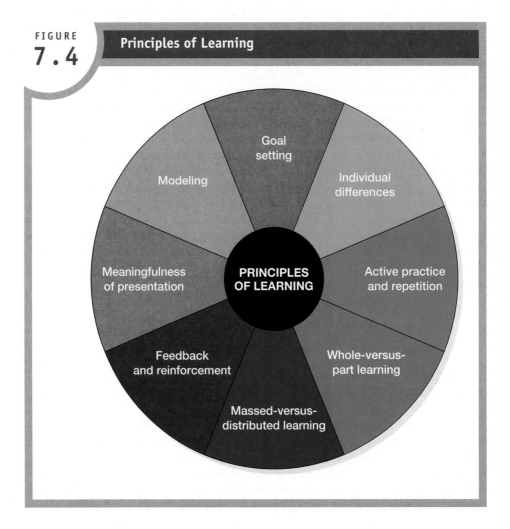

Principles of Learning

Meaningfulness of Presentation

One principle of learning is that the material to be learned should be presented in as meaningful a manner as possible. Quite simply, trainees will be better able to learn new information if they can connect it with things that are already familiar to them. This is the reason why trainers frequently use colorful examples to which trainees can relate. The examples make the material meaningful. In addition, material should be arranged so that each experience builds on preceding ones. In this way, trainees are able to integrate the experiences into a usable pattern of knowledge and skills.

Modeling

The old saying "a picture is worth a thousand words" applies to training. Just as examples increase the meaningfulness of factual material or new knowledge in a training environment, modeling increases the salience of behavioral training. Quite simply, we learn by watching. For example, if you were learning to ride a horse, it would be much easier to watch someone do it—and then try it yourself—than to read a book or listen to a lecture and hope you can do it right.[10]

Modeling can take many forms. Real-life demonstrations and demonstrations on DVDs are often helpful; even pictures and drawings can get the visual message across. The point is that modeling demonstrates the desired behavior or method to be learned. In some cases, modeling the wrong behavior can even be helpful if it shows trainees what not to do and then clarifies the appropriate behavior.

Individual Differences

People learn at different rates and in different ways. For example, some people can remember new information after hearing it only once (echoic memory) or seeing it only once (iconic memory). Others may have to work longer or find other techniques for retrieving the information, but this may have nothing to do with their intelligence. Some students do horribly in large lecture settings but then excel in small discussion classes. Others may have the opposite ability. To the extent possible, training programs should try to account for and accommodate these individual differences in order to facilitate each person's style and rate of learning.[11]

Active Practice and Repetition

Those things we do daily become a part of our repertoire of skills. Trainees should be given frequent opportunity to practice their job tasks in the way that they will ultimately be expected to perform them. The individual who is being taught how to operate a machine should have an opportunity to practice on it. The manager who is being taught how to train should be given supervised practice in training.

In some cases, the value of practice is that it causes behaviors to become second nature. For example, when you first learned to drive a car, you focused a great deal on the mechanics: "Where are my hands, where are my feet, and how fast am I going?" As you practiced driving, you began to think less about the mechanics and more about the road, the weather, and the traffic. Other forms of learning are no different—by practicing, a trainee can forget about distinct behaviors and concentrate on the subtleties of how they are used.

Whole-versus-Part Learning

Most jobs and tasks can be broken down into parts that lend themselves to further analysis. Determining the most effective manner for completing each part then provides a basis for giving specific instruction. Learning to sell a product, for example, is made up of several skills that are part of the total process. Although the process sounds daunting, it can essentially be broken down into a few discrete steps: finding customer opportunities; eliciting a prospective customer's needs by learning the proper questions to ask him or her; presenting the firm's product in a way that meets those needs; and finally, learning how and when to ask the customer to buy the product (closing the deal). In evaluating whole-versus-part learning, it is necessary to consider the nature of the task to be learned. If the task can be broken down successfully, it probably should be broken down to facilitate learning; otherwise, it should probably be taught as a unit.

Massed-versus-Distributed Learning

Another factor that determines the effectiveness of training is the amount of time devoted to practice in one session. Should trainees be given training in five two-hour periods or in ten one-hour periods? It has been found in most cases that spacing out the training will result in faster learning and longer retention. This is the principle of *distributed learning*.

Feedback and Reinforcement

Can any learning occur without feedback? Some feedback comes from trainees themselves via self-monitoring, whereas other feedback comes from trainers, fellow trainees, and the like. Feedback can help individuals focus on what they are doing right and what they are doing wrong. Think about when you first learned how to throw a baseball, ride a bicycle, or swim. Someone, perhaps a parent, told you what you were doing right and what things to correct. As you corrected those things, you perhaps got better.

In addition to providing participants with information about their performance, feedback also plays an important motivational role. For example, a person's training progress, measured in terms of either mistakes or successes, can be plotted on a chart commonly referred to as a "learning curve." Figure 7.5 presents an example of a learning curve common in the acquisition of many job skills. In many learning situations, there are times when progress does not occur. Such periods show up on the curve as a fairly straight horizontal line called a *plateau*. A plateau can occur because of reduced motivation or because a person gets discouraged when he or she does not always perform a new task as well as hoped. It is a natural phenomenon, and learners usually experience a spontaneous recovery later, as Figure 7.5 shows.

Verbal encouragement or more tangible rewards such as prizes, awards, and ceremonies can help reinforce the behavior firms desire of trainees over time as well as help them get over plateaus they might experience. Encouragement is most effective when it is given immediately after a trainee successfully accomplishes a certain task. This is why some employers have instituted spot rewards programs. Spot rewards programs award employees "on the spot" when they do something particularly well during training or on the job. The awards can consist of cash, gift cards, time off, or anything else employees value.

Over the years organizations have used behavior modification, a technique that operates on the principle that behavior that is rewarded—positively reinforced— will be exhibited more frequently in the future, whereas behavior that is penalized or unrewarded will decrease in frequency. For example, in safety training it is possible to identify "safe" behavioral profiles—that is, actions that ensure fewer accidents— as well as unsafe profiles. As a follow-up to training or as part of the training

spot rewards

Programs that award employees "on the spot" when they do something particularly well during training or on the job

behavior modification

A technique that operates on the principle that behavior that is rewarded, or positively reinforced, will be exhibited more frequently in the future, whereas behavior that is penalized or unrewarded will decrease in frequency

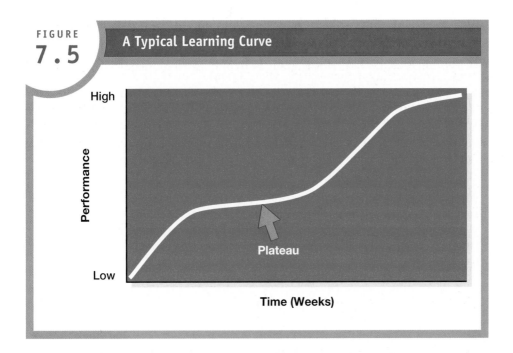

FIGURE
7.5

A Typical Learning Curve

itself, managers can use relatively simple rewards to encourage and maintain desired behavior. Companies such as Monsanto, Target, and Bowater (the largest newsprint maker in America) have found that nothing more than words of encouragement and feedback are needed to strengthen employee behaviors. However, the idea behind behavior modification is that a person's behavior can be motivated and gradually shaped toward what managers desire when he or she exhibits positive behaviors and is rewarded for them.[12]

Characteristics of Instructors

The success of any training effort will depend in a large part on the teaching skills and personal characteristics of those responsible for conducting the training. What separates good trainers from mediocre ones? Often a good trainer is one who shows a little more effort or demonstrates more instructional preparation. However, training is also influenced by the trainer's personal manner and characteristics. Here is a short list of desirable traits:

1. *Knowledge of subject.* Employees expect trainers to know their job or subject thoroughly. Furthermore, they are expected to demonstrate that knowledge (what some experts call "active intelligence").

2. *Adaptability.* Because some individuals learn faster or slower than others, the instruction should be matched to the trainee's learning ability.

3. *Sincerity.* Trainees appreciate sincerity in trainers. Along with this, trainers need to be patient with trainees and demonstrate tact in addressing their concerns.

4. *Sense of humor.* Learning can be fun; very often a point can be made with a story or anecdote.

5. *Interest.* Good trainers have a keen interest in the subject they are teaching; this interest is readily conveyed to trainees.

6. *Clear instructions.* Naturally, training is accomplished more quickly and retained longer when trainers give clear instructions.

7. *Individual assistance.* When training more than one employee, successful trainers always provide individual assistance.

8. *Enthusiasm.* A dynamic presentation and a vibrant personality show trainees that the trainer enjoys training; employees tend to respond positively to an enthusiastic climate.[13]

For training programs to be most successful, organizations should reward managers who prove to be excellent trainers. Too often managers are not recognized for their contributions to this important aspect of HRM. Likewise, good training specialists in the HR function should be recognized for their efforts as well.

PHASE 3: IMPLEMENTING THE TRAINING PROGRAM

Despite the importance of needs assessment, instructional objectives, principles of learning, and the like, choices regarding instructional methods are where "the rubber meets the road" in implementing a training program. A major consideration in choosing among various training methods is determining which ones are appropriate for the KSAs to be learned. For example, if the material is mostly factual, methods such as lecture, classroom, or programmed instruction may be fine. However, if the training involves a large behavioral component, other methods such as on-the-job training, simulation, or computer-based training (CBT) might work better.[14]

In order to organize our discussion of various training methods, we will break them down into two primary groups: those used for nonmanagerial employees and those used for managers.

Training Methods for Nonmanagerial Employees

Objective 4

A wide variety of methods are available for training employees at all levels. Some methods have a long history of being used. Newer methods have emerged over the years out of a greater understanding of human behavior, particularly in the areas of learning, motivation, and interpersonal relationships. More recently, technological advances, especially in computer hardware and software, have resulted in training devices that in many instances are more effective and economical than the traditional training methods.

On-the-Job Training

on-the-job training (OJT)

A method by which employees are given hands-on experience with instructions from their supervisor or other trainer

By far, the most common method used for training nonmanagerial employees is on-the-job training (OJT). By some estimates, 90 percent of employee learning occurs via OJT. OJT has the advantage of providing hands-on experience under normal working conditions and an opportunity for the trainer—a manager or senior employee—to build good relationships with new employees. OJT is viewed by some to be potentially the most effective means of facilitating learning in the workplace.[15]

Although it is used by all types of organizations, OJT is often one of the most poorly implemented training methods. Three common drawbacks are (1) the lack of a well-structured training environment, (2) poor training skills on the part of managers, and (3) the absence of well-defined job performance criteria. To overcome these problems, training experts suggest the following:

1. Develop realistic goals and/or measures for each OJT area.

2. Plan a specific training schedule for each trainee, including set periods for evaluation and feedback.

3. Help managers establish a nonthreatening atmosphere conducive to learning.

4. Conduct periodic evaluations after training is completed to prevent regression.[16]

Figure 7.6 shows the basic steps of an OJT program. The method is used frequently in organizations to ensure that new employees have adequate guidance before taking on work responsibilities on their own. For example, KLM Royal Dutch Airlines uses on-the-job training to train its cabin attendants. The airline started a program that places cabin attendant trainees in the classroom for a certain period and then gives them additional training during an evaluation flight. On these flights, experienced cabin attendants provide the trainees with on-the-job training, based on a list of identified job tasks. Some tasks, such as serving meals and snacks, are demonstrated

FIGURE 7.6

The PROPER Way to Do On-the-Job Training

P — **Prepare.** Decide what employees need to be taught. Identify the best sequence or steps of the training. Decide how best to demonstrate these steps. Have materials, resources, and equipment ready.

R — **Reassure.** Put each employee at ease. Learn about his or her prior experience, and adjust accordingly. Try to get the employee interested, relaxed, and motivated to learn.

O — **Orient.** Show the employee the correct way to do the job. Explain why it is done this way. Discuss how it relates to other jobs. Let him or her ask lots of questions.

P — **Perform.** When employees are ready, let them try the job themselves. Give them an opportunity to practice the job and guide them through rough spots. Provide help and assistance at first, then less as they continue.

E — **Evaluate.** Check the employees' performance, and question them on how, why, when, and where they should do something. Correct errors; repeat instructions.

R — **Reinforce and Review.** Provide praise and encouragement, and give feedback about how the employee is doing. Continue the conversation and express confidence in his or her doing the job.

Source: Scott Snell, University of Virginia.

during the actual delivery of services to passengers. Other tasks are presented to trainees away from passengers between meal service.[17]

Apprenticeship Training

An extension of OJT is **apprenticeship training**. With this method, individuals entering an industry, particularly in the skilled trades such as machinist, laboratory technician, and electrician, are given thorough instruction and experience, both on and off the job. For example, Bonneville Power Administration and General Physics Corporation developed an apprenticeship program for substation operators to give employees both a strong technical foundation in the fundamentals of electricity and a hands-on ability to operate equipment within the power substation. Ultimately, the program was also designed to help future electrical operators respond to emergencies. In Europe, organizations such as BAE Systems and Ford Motor Company use apprenticeship programs extensively for their engineers.[18]

Interestingly, a Detroit-based organization called Focus: HOPE provides young, low-income, unemployed adults apprenticeship opportunities to learn advanced manufacturing skills for today's high-tech jobs. Among other opportunities, Focus: HOPE has established the Center for Advanced Technology, which offers a six-year curriculum that integrates structured work experience and study in applied engineering with computer-integrated manufacturing in collaboration with companies such as Cisco, Microsoft, and the Computer Technology Industry Association.[19]

While apprenticeship programs originated in Europe as part of its guild system, they have been adapted for use in the United States. Typically, the programs involve cooperation between organizations and their labor unions, between industry and government, or between organizations and local school systems. In the United States today, nearly 37,000 organizations have registered their programs with the U.S. Department of Labor's Bureau of Apprenticeship and Training (BAT), including employers. Approximately two-thirds of apprenticeships are in the construction and manufacturing industries. However, there are apprenticeships available in a wide range of other industries, including the telecommunications, arts, and health fields. Generally, an apprentice is paid 50 percent of a skilled journey worker's wage to start with, but the wage increases at regular intervals as the apprentice's job skills increase. When the apprentice successfully completes the apprenticeship, he or she becomes a certified journey-level worker earning full pay. According to BAT, many journey workers earn as much as college graduates, and some earn more.[20]

Cooperative Training, Internships, and Governmental Training

Similar to apprenticeships, **cooperative training** programs combine practical on-the-job experience with formal classes. However, the term *cooperative training* is typically used in connection with high school and college programs that incorporate part- or full-time experiences. In recent years, there has been an increased effort to expand opportunities that combine on-the-job skill training with regular classroom training so that students can pursue either technical work or a college degree program. Many organizations, including Fannie Mae, Burger King, Champion International, Cray, Inc., and First UNUM Life Insurance, have invested millions of dollars in educational cooperative training programs in conjunction with public schools.

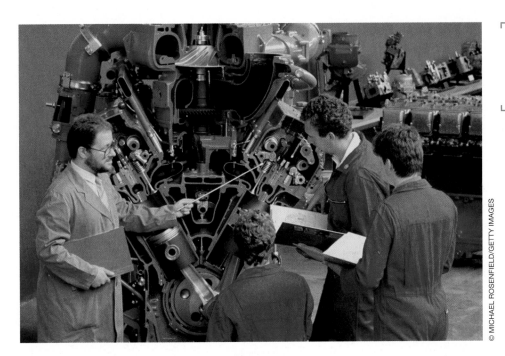

© MICHAEL ROSENFIELD/GETTY IMAGES

Apprenticeships are a good way to train employees, especially in skilled trade industries.

Internship programs, jointly sponsored by colleges, universities, and a variety of organizations, offer students the chance to get real-world experience while finding out how they will perform in work organizations. Organizations benefit by getting student-employees with new ideas, energy, and eagerness to accomplish their assignments. Many universities and community colleges allow students to earn college credits on the basis of successful job performance and fulfillment of established program requirements. The following are steps firms can take to increase the effectiveness of their internships:

internship programs

Programs jointly sponsored by colleges, universities, and other organizations that offer students the opportunity to gain real-life experience while allowing them to find out how they will perform in work organizations

1. Assign the intern to projects that are accomplishable and provide training as required.

2. Appoint a mentor or supervisor to guide the intern.

3. Solicit project suggestions from other staff members.

4. Rotate interns throughout the organization.

5. Treat interns as part of the organizational staff and invite them to staff meetings.

6. Establish a process for considering interns for permanent hire.[21]

The federal government and various state governments have begun working together with private employers to sponsor a multitude of training programs for new and current employees through approximately 1,900 career centers nationwide. Discussed in Chapter 5, these One Stop career centers (sometimes called "Job Service" or "Workforce Development" centers) have enabled thousands of organizations to help local citizens get jobs and job training assistance. The One Stop centers were modeled on Minnesota's successful program to help workers find jobs, help employers find qualified workers, and provide job training and other employment services all under one roof (hence the name *One Stop*). 3M, Northwest Airlines, Honeywell, and General Mills are just a few of the companies involved in the One Stop program.[22]

Classroom Instruction

When most people think about training, they think about classrooms. There is good reason for this. Beyond its pervasiveness in education, classroom training enables the maximum number of trainees to be handled by the minimum number of instructors. This method lends itself particularly well to what is called **blended learning** in which lectures and demonstrations are combined with films, DVDs, videotapes, or computer instruction. When it is not possible to obtain video, audio recordings can be very valuable. For example, to instruct flight crew trainees, airlines might play actual cockpit tapes recorded on airplanes involved in accidents. After listening to the recordings, the trainees discuss the behavior of the crew during the crisis. By listening to the recorded statements of others and observing their failure to operate as a team, pilot trainees better understand how to balance their sense of self-reliance with an ability to listen to their superiors and subordinates. Despite the rise of many other types of learning—electronic and otherwise—classroom instruction is still the number one training method, as Figure 7.7 shows.[23]

blended learning

The use of multiple training methods to achieve optimal learning on the part of trainees

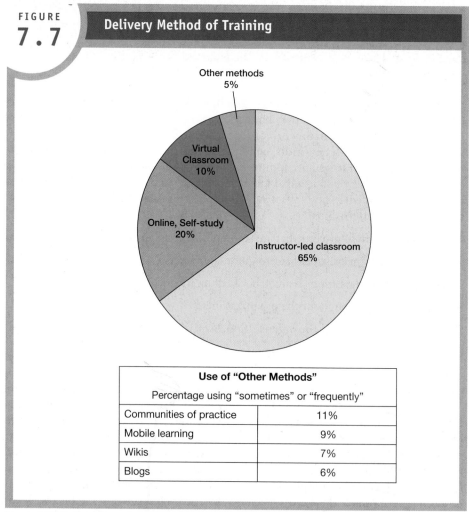

FIGURE 7.7

Delivery Method of Training

Use of "Other Methods"	
Percentage using "sometimes" or "frequently"	
Communities of practice	11%
Mobile learning	9%
Wikis	7%
Blogs	6%

Source: "2007 Industry Report," *Training* 44, no. 10–11 (November–December 2007): 8–24.

Programmed Instruction

One method of instruction that is particularly good for allowing individuals to work at their own pace is programmed instruction. Programmed instruction—increasingly referred to as *self-directed learning*—involves the use of books, manuals, or computers to break down subject matter content into highly organized, logical sequences that demand a continual response on the part of the trainee. After being presented with a small segment of information, the trainee is required to answer a question, either by writing it in a response screen or by pushing a button. If the response is correct, the trainee is told so and is presented with the next step (screen) in the material. If the response is incorrect, further explanatory information is given, and the trainee is told to try again.

A major advantage of programmed instruction is that it incorporates a number of the established learning principles discussed earlier in the chapter. With programmed instruction, training is individualized, trainees are actively involved in the instructional process, and the feedback and reinforcement provided them are immediate. Although this type of instruction might not increase the amount an individual learns, it typically increases the speed at which he or she learns.

Audiovisual Methods

To teach skills and procedures for many production jobs, audiovisual devices can be used. For example, video recordings are often used to illustrate the steps in a procedure such as assembling electronic equipment or working with a problem employee. Trainers and trainees can view an on-the-spot recording and to get immediate feedback. Golf and tennis coaches frequently record their students to let them see their mistakes. CDs and DVDs allow trainees to access any segment of the instructional program, which is especially useful for individualized instruction when employees have different levels of knowledge and ability.[24]

Teleconferencing and videoconferencing allow an instructional program to be transmitted to many locations simultaneously as well as permit trainees to interact with one another. Electronic Data Systems has used teleconferencing to train its employees wherever they are in the world rather than having them travel to one location. The company recently conducted a "coaching skills for leaders" program that was disseminated to 1,500 managers in 41 countries via teleconferencing.

Web conferencing is used to conduct live meetings or presentations over the Internet. During a Web conference, trainees sit at their own computers and are connected to other participants via the Web. To attend the conference, they simply enter a Web site address and also dial in to a 1-800 number to talk to one another and the trainer via phone. A *webinar* is a one-way conference, from the speaker to the audience with limited audience interaction. A number of organizations are also using *podcasts* to provide their employees, such sales reps, with information on the go. Podcasts allow reps to learn about new products while they are in the field rather than having to take time off to travel to corporate headquarters to get the information.

There is an old African proverb that states: If you want to go fast, travel alone. If you want to go far, travel together.[25] The latter statement is the idea behind *communities of practice*. This is a new but growing type of training that utilizes social networking tools on the Web that allow people to share their knowledge and collaborate with one another. Blogs and wikis—sites where people can post information like they can on

Wikipedia—are examples of the tools used to facilitate learning via the communities of practice method. The method can be particularly helpful for multinational companies whose employees need to be able to share information across time and space. Figure 7.8 shows some of the types of questions posted on communities of practice sites, to which other people post answers that future learners can read.

Simulation Method

Sometimes it is either impractical or unwise to train employees on the actual equipment used on the job. An obvious example is training employees to operate aircraft, spacecraft, and other highly technical and expensive equipment. The simulation method emphasizes realism in equipment and its operation at minimum cost and maximum safety.

Southwest Airlines boasts perhaps the most technologically advanced flight simulator in the airline industry: a $10.8 million full-motion Boeing 737-700 unit housed in an 110,000-square-foot flight operations training center adjacent to Southwest's headquarters at Dallas's Love Field. The facility can house up to six 737 simulators and can train up to 300 (of Southwest's 4,100) pilots at one time. The center has a staff of 110 employees. In addition to the simulators and their associated briefing and computer programming rooms, the training center houses eight classrooms, each fully equipped with closed-circuit TV, computers, conventional audiovisual equipment, and telephone and Internet hookups. Facing a serious worker shortage, the Federal Aviation Administration developed a sophisticated simulator to dramatically speed up the training of air traffic controllers, a process that used to take as long as five years. Variables such as wind speed, precipitation, and the number of airplanes to be guided can be adjusted on the simulator to test the ability of trainees.

FIGURE 7.8

Examples of Knowledge-Sharing Learning via Communities of Practice

Problem-solving	"Can we work on this design and brainstorm some ideas; I'm stuck."
Requests for information	"Where can I find the code to connect to the server?"
Seeking experience	"Has anyone dealt with a customer in this situation?"
Reusing assets	"I have a proposal for a local area network I wrote for a client last year. I can send it to you, and you can easily tweak it for this new client."
Coordination and synergy	"Can we combine our purchases of solvent to achieve bulk discounts?"
Discussing developments	"What do you think of the new CAD system? Does it really help?"
Documentation projects	"We have faced this problem five times now. Let us write it down once and for all."
Visits	"Can we come and see your after-school program? We need to establish one in our city."
Mapping knowledge and identifying gaps	"Who knows what, and what are we missing? What other groups should we connect with?"

Source: Etienne Wenger, www.ewenger.com/research, 2004.

Trainees who do poorly in certain situations are then targeted for additional training in those areas. Simulators that represent human patients are being integrated into medical training as well.[26]

As with e-learning and computer-based training, the distinction between simulation and computer-based training has blurred. For example, a simulation developed by Wicat in partnership with Airbus and Singapore Airlines runs on a PC and replicates a cockpit with control displays and throttle/flap controls. Even though the PC-based simulation is relatively inexpensive, it is powerful. Pilots are taken through a self-paced program that simulates "taxi, takeoff, climb, cruise, descent, approach, landing, and go-around." These types of technologies are making it easier to offer training in new and different ways. Delta Airlines has stated that the company's goal is to deliver simulation training to employees at their homes. Given advances in telecommunications, the possibilities seem limitless.[27]

E-Learning and Learning Management Systems (LMS)

The training methods we just discussed are evolving into what trainers today refer to as e-learning. E-learning covers a wide variety of applications such as Web and computer-based training (CBT) and virtual classrooms. It includes delivery of content via the Internet, intranets and extranets, TV, DVD, CD-ROM, and MP3 players. E-learning makes it possible to provide drill and practice, problem-solving, simulation, gaming forms of instruction, and certain very sophisticated forms of individualized tutorial instruction in a way that is more engaging for learners than traditional classroom instruction. It is also cheaper for employers to administer because, in many instances, it can be delivered cheaply directly to the PCs of multiple employees. Today, one of every three hours of training is now delivered via some form of technology, and companies are reporting that they are saving anywhere from 30 to 70 percent on their training costs by doing so.[28]

e-learning
Learning that takes place via electronic media

E-learning transforms the learning process in several ways. First, as we have said, it allows the firm to bring the training to employees rather than vice versa, which is generally more efficient and cost-effective. The nuclear power plant industry is a case in point: Nuclear power plant training is frequent and time-consuming. For workers just to remove their protective gear and commute to a separate training venue can take anywhere from an hour or more. One nuclear power company that switched to e-learning reported that it saved nearly $1 million and 10,000 employee hours in just one year by doing so.

> **Using the Internet**
>
> Read how Caterpillar University extends its training worldwide by using e-learning methods. Go to the Student Resources at:
>
> **www.cengage.com/ management/bohlander**

E-learning also allows employees to search online training libraries in order to customize their own learning in their own time and space. More companies are demanding access to individual training components for employees to use when and where they need them. This type of training, which is referred to as just-in-time training, helps alleviate the boredom trainees experience during full-blown training courses, and employees are more likely to retain the information when they can immediately put it to use. For example, when one of Time Warner Cable's service representatives is unsure about how to a process a work order, he or she can click on an e-learning simulation and get a step-by-step tutorial. Similarly, Cisco has thousands of training VoDs (videos on demand) that employees can download off the company's intranet as needed.[29]

just-in-time training
Training delivered to trainees when and where they need it to do their jobs, usually via computer or the Internet

E-learning systems need not be overly expensive. Many e-learning training programs use existing applications employees are familiar with such as PowerPoint, Word, and Adobe Acrobat and convert them into Flash programs so they can be easily viewed online with any Web browser. Web-based training can also be revised rapidly, thereby providing continuously updated training material to both small and large groups of people. This not only makes it easier and cheaper to revise training curricula, but also saves travel and classroom costs. When combined with other communications technology such as e-mail, teleconferencing, videoconferencing, and groupware, Web-based training can be even more effective.

Today, large companies—usually those with at least 5,000 employees or more—are combining their e-learning, employee assessment tools, and other training functions into electronic learning management systems (LMS), also referred to as "virtual learning environments", custom built for them by software vendors. Using the software, managers can assess the skills of employees, register them for courses, deliver interactive learning modules to them directly to their desktops when they need or want them, evaluate and track their progress, and determine when they are ready to be promoted. Purchasing a learning management system does not alleviate HR personnel and a firm's managers from conducting a thorough needs assessment, however—especially because the systems are costly. After conducting a thorough needs analysis, managers have to then address the type of systems that will work best.

learning management system (LMS)

On-line system that provides a variety of assessment, communication, teaching, and learning opportunities

Methods for Management Development

Many of the methods used to train front-line employees are also used to train supervisors and first level managers. But other methods are used primarily to improve the preparation and development of mid- to senior-level managers. Over the past decade, the importance of management development has grown because so many experienced baby boomer managers have begun retiring and firms are having a hard time replacing the expertise they provided. In one study cited in an American Society of Training and Development paper, 70 percent of companies reported moderate to major leadership shortages, and many expected the problem to get worse.[30]

As with training for nonmanagerial employees, the methods used for management development differ in terms of the principles of learning they incorporate and their appropriateness for delivering various KSAs.

On-the-Job Experiences

Some skills and knowledge can be acquired just by listening and observing or by reading. But others must be acquired through actual practice and experience. By presenting managers with the opportunities to perform under pressure and to learn from their mistakes, on-the-job development experiences are some of the most powerful and commonly used techniques.

However, just as on-the-job training for first-level employees can be problematic if not well planned, on-the-job management development should be well organized, supervised, and challenging to the participants. Methods of providing on-the-job experiences include the following:

1. *Coaching* involves a continuing flow of instructions, comments, and suggestions from the manager to the subordinate. (*Mentoring*, discussed in Chapter 5, is a similar approach to personal and informal management development.)

2. *Understudy assignments* groom an individual to take over a manager's job by gaining experience in handling important functions of the job.

3. *Job rotation* provides, through a variety of work experiences, the broadened knowledge and understanding required to manage more effectively.

4. *Lateral transfer* involves horizontal movement through different departments, along with upward movement in the organization.

5. *Special projects* and *junior boards* provide an opportunity for individuals to become involved in the study of current organizational problems and in planning and decision-making activities.

6. *Action learning* gives managers time to work full-time on projects with others in the organization. In some cases, action learning is combined with classroom instruction, discussions, and conferences.

7. *Staff meetings* enable participants to become more familiar with problems and events occurring outside their immediate areas by exposing them to the ideas and thinking of other managers.

8. *Planned career progressions* (discussed in Chapter 5) utilize all these different methods to provide employees with the training and development necessary to progress through a series of jobs requiring higher and higher levels of knowledge and/or skills.[31]

Although these methods are used most often to develop managers for higher-level positions, they also provide valuable experiences for those who are being groomed for other types of positions in the organization. While on-the-job experiences constitute the core of management training and development, other off-the-job methods of development can be used to supplement these experiences.

Seminars and Conferences

Seminars and conferences, like classroom instruction, are useful for bringing groups of people together for training and development. In terms of developing managers, seminars and conferences can be used to communicate ideas, policies, or procedures, but they are also good for raising points of debate or discussing issues (usually with the help of a qualified leader) that have no set answers or resolutions. For this reason, seminars and conferences are often used when attitude change is a goal.

Outside seminars and conferences are often conducted jointly with universities and consulting firms. The construction and mining equipment manufacturer Caterpillar is one company that, in conjunction with an outside consulting firm, has developed a training program to groom new managers. The challenge for the company is to get enough leaders and managers in place to effectively run the company by 2020. To meet this challenge, Caterpillar launched a leadership development initiative through its Caterpillar University of Leadership. The effort began with a series of high-level meetings and strategy sessions. Out of those meetings eleven characteristics were identified that the company seeks in its managers and leaders. So far, some 5,000 managers and executives have gone through program, which is designed to help them become more self-aware as managers and develop their financial management skills and ability to better formulate strategies to increase Caterpillar's global competitiveness. Associations and third-party organization, such as the American Management Association, the Conference Board, and the Center for Creative Leadership, also offer many different types of management seminars.[32]

Case Studies

A particularly useful method used in classroom learning situations is the case study. The FBI, for example, uses its Integrated Case Scenario method to bring together new agents in a logical way. Using documented examples, participants learn how to analyze (take apart) and synthesize (put together) facts, become conscious of the many variables on which management decisions are based, and, in general, improve their decision-making skills. Experienced educators and trainers generally point out that the case study is most appropriate when:

1. Analytic, problem-solving, and critical thinking skills are most important.

2. The KSAs are complex, and participants need time to master them.

3. Active participation is desired.

4. The process of learning (questioning, interpreting, and so on) is as important as the content.

5. Team problem-solving and interaction are possible.[33]

Even when case studies may be appropriate, they are often mismanaged. As with any other development technique, implementation is crucial for effectiveness. Figure 7.9 provides a set of guidelines for conducting case studies.

Management Games and Simulations

Games are now being widely used as a management development method. Generally, players-managers are faced with the task of making a series of management decisions affecting a hypothetical organization. The effects that every decision has on each area within the organization can be simulated with a computer programmed for the game. Bell Canada has its managers play TeleSim, a computer simulation for the telecommunications industry developed by Thinking Tools and Coopers & Lybrand to teach executives how to act in an increasingly open, competitive market.[34] At Marriott International, a computer program called Business Acumen has been used to train its non-U.S. property-level managers on the finer points of hotel operation. The program simulates hotel operations scenarios such as budgetary decisions.[35]

When done on a computer, simulations are sometimes referred to as *virtual training*. Simulations do not always require a computer, however. Motorola developed a noncomputer-based game called "Equal Employment Opportunity: It's Your Job" to teach the basic principles of equal employment opportunity. The players get caught up in the competitive spirit of a game and at the same time absorb and remember government regulations. They also become aware of how their own daily decisions affect their employer's compliance with these regulations.[36]

In addition, games and simulations are being used to help the managers of government agencies such as the Federal Emergency Management Agency to

FIGURE
7.9

Case Studies

WHEN USING CASE STUDIES...

- Be clear about learning objectives, and list possible ways to achieve the objectives.
- Decide which objectives would be best served by the case method.
- Identify available cases that might work, or consider writing your own.
- Set up the activity—including the case material, the room, and the schedule.
- Follow the principles of effective group dynamics.
- Provide a chance for all learners to take part and try to keep the groups small.
- Stop for process checks and be ready to intervene if group dynamics get out of hand.
- Allow for different learning styles.
- Clarify the trainer's role.
- Bridge the gap between theory and practice.

Source: Adapted from Albert A. Einsiedel, Jr., "Case Studies: Indispensable Tools for Trainers," *Training and Development* (August 1995): 50–53.

prevent or better respond to crises. The company Presagis, for example, has developed computer software that simulates a chemical cloud visually over a replication of an actual city. During the training, the cloud can move and grow, challenging emergency response officials to dynamically change their emergency response.[37]

Role-Playing

Role-playing consists of assuming the attitudes and behavior—that is, playing the role—of others, often a supervisor and a subordinate who are involved in a particular problem. By acting out another's position, participants in the role-playing can improve their ability to understand and cope with others. Role-playing should also help them learn how to counsel others by helping them see situations from a different point of view. Role-playing is used widely in training health care professionals to be empathic and sensitive to the concerns of patients. It is also used widely in training managers to handle employee issues relating to absenteeism, performance appraisal, and conflict situations.

At times, participants may be hesitant to try role-playing. Successful role-playing takes planning. Instructors should do the following:

1. Ensure that members of the group are comfortable with each other.

2. Select and prepare the role-players by introducing a specific situation.

3. To help participants prepare, ask them to describe potential characters.

4. Realize that volunteers make better role-players.

5. Prepare the observers by giving them specific tasks (such as evaluation or feedback).

6. Guide the role-play enactment through its bumps (because it is not scripted).

7. Keep it short.

8. Discuss the enactment and prepare bulleted points of what was learned.[38]

Role-playing is a versatile teaching model, applicable to a variety of training experiences. Planned and implemented correctly, role-playing can bring realism and insight into dilemmas and experiences that otherwise might not be shared. Computer programs that simulate role-playing have also been developed. Virtual Leader, a product by SimuLearn, is one such program: Management trainees interact with animated "employees"—some of whom are more cooperative than others. The trainees are then given feedback as to how well they applied their managerial skills to each situation.

Behavior Modeling

behavior modeling
An approach that demonstrates desired behavior and gives trainees the chance to practice and role-play those behaviors and receive feedback

One technique that combines several different training methods, and therefore multiple principles of learning, is the behavior modeling technique. Behavior modeling involves four basic components:

1. *Learning points.* At the beginning of instruction, the essential goals and objectives of the program are enumerated. In some cases, the learning points are a sequence of behaviors that are to be taught. For example, the learning points might describe the recommended steps for giving employees feedback.

2. *Modeling.* Participants view CDs, DVDs, or downloadable video recordings in which a model manager is portrayed dealing with an employee in an effort to improve his or her performance. The model shows specifically how to deal with the situation and demonstrates the learning points.

3. *Practice and role-play.* Trainees participate in extensive rehearsal of the behaviors demonstrated by the models. The greatest percentage of training time is spent in these skill practice sessions.

4. *Feedback and reinforcement.* As the trainee's behavior increasingly resembles that of the model, the trainer and other trainees reinforce the behavior with praise, approval, encouragement, and attention. Videotaping or otherwise digitally recording the sessions can also be very instructive.

Behavior modeling seems to work, according to various studies. The training can help managers better interact with employees, administer discipline, introduce changes, and increase productivity. Military training is a classic example of how behavior modeling can work. Drill sergeants model the behavior expected of new recruits, who, in turn, by emulating them, develop discipline and confidence.[39]

In the final analysis, the most successful training courses for either regular employees or managers do not rely on a single type of training. Instead, utilizing a variety of methods better helps keep the interest of trainees high and accommodates different kinds of learning styles. Blended learning is a term often used to describe training methods that use multiple techniques.

PHASE 4: EVALUATING THE TRAINING PROGRAM

5 | **Objective**

Training, like any other HRM function, has to be evaluated to determine its effectiveness. A variety of methods are available to assess the extent to which a firm's training programs improve learning, affect behavior on the job, and impact the bottom-line performance of an organization. Unfortunately, many organizations do not adequately evaluate their training programs. But this is changing. Today, human resources departments are under pressure to calculate the return on their firms' training investment dollars. We will explain how this is done later in this section.

Figure 7.10 shows that four basic criteria are available to evaluate training: (1) reactions, (2) learning, (3) behavior, and (4) results. Some of these criteria are easier to measure than others, but each is important in that it provides different information about the success of the programs. The combination of these criteria can give a total picture of the training program in order to help managers decide where problem areas lie, what to change about the program, and whether to continue with a program.[40]

Criterion 1: Reactions

One of the simplest and most common approaches to evaluating a training program is assessing participants' reactions. Happy trainees will be more likely to want to focus on training principles and to utilize the information on the job. Trainees can do more than tell you whether they liked a training program. They can give insights into the content and techniques they found most useful. They can critique the instructors or make suggestions about participant interactions, feedback, and the like. Potential questions might include the following:

- What were your learning goals for this program?

- Did you achieve them?

FIGURE 7.10

Criteria for Evaluating Training

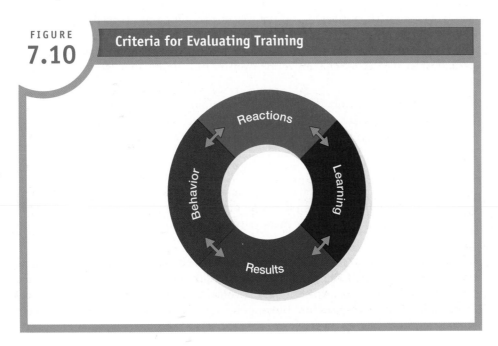

- Did you like this program?

- Would you recommend it to others who have similar learning goals?

- What suggestions do you have for improving the program?

- Should the organization continue to offer it?

While evaluation methods based on reactions are improving, too many conclusions about training effectiveness are still based on broad satisfaction measures that lack specific feedback. Furthermore, it should be noted that positive reactions are no guarantee that the training has been successful. It may be easy to collect glowing comments from trainees, but as gratifying as this information is, it may not be useful to the organization unless it somehow translates into improved behavior and job performance that is measurable. In the final analysis, reaction measures should not stop with assessing the training's entertainment value.[41]

Criterion 2: Learning

Beyond what participants *think* about the training, it might be a good idea to see whether they actually learned anything. Testing the knowledge and skills of trainees before and after a training program will help determine their improvement. The skill and knowledge levels of employees who have undergone a training program can also be compared to employees who have not. Federal Express took this approach by studying twenty van drivers who attended a weeklong new hire training program. The company then compared the performance of these drivers with a control group of twenty drivers who had received only on-the-job training. FedEx found that the drivers who had been formally trained made fewer package processing errors, saving the company about $500 per trained driver.[42]

Criterion 3: Behavior

You might be surprised to learn that much of what is learned in a training program never gets used back on the job. It is not that the training was necessarily ineffective. But for several reasons, trainees do not demonstrate behavior change back on the job. The transfer of training refers to how well employees apply what they have learned to their jobs. To maximize the transfer of training, managers and trainers can take several approaches:

transfer of training

Effective application of principles learned to what is required on the job

1. *Feature identical elements.* Transferring the training to the job can be facilitated by having conditions in the training program come as close as possible to those on the job. For example, instead of verbally explaining a manufacturing process, it is better to demonstrate it on a factory floor.

2. *Focus on general principles, if necessary.* When jobs change or the work environment cannot be matched exactly, trainers often stress the general principles behind the training rather than focusing on rote behavior. This approach helps trainees learn how to apply the main learning points to varying conditions on the job.

3. *Establish a climate for transfer.* In some cases, trained behavior is not implemented because old approaches and routines are still reinforced by other managers, peers, and employees. To prevent this kind of problem, managers need to support, reinforce, and reward trainees for applying the new skills or knowledge. Oftentimes

this requires firms to train their managers to actively embrace the strategic changes their organizations are seeking to implement.

4. *Give employees transfer strategies.* Particularly in settings that are not conducive to transfer, managers should also provide trainees with strategies and tactics for dealing with their transfer environment. One approach, called *relapse prevention (RP)*, teaches individuals how to anticipate and cope with the inevitable setbacks they will encounter back on the job—that is, a relapse into former behaviors. By identifying high-risk situations that jeopardize transfer and developing coping strategies, relapse prevention can help employees gain better control over maintaining learned behaviors.[43]

There are several methods for assessing transfer of learned skills back to the job. At Xerox, for example, trainers observe trainees once they return to their regular positions, interview the trainees' managers about their progress later on, and examine their posttraining performance appraisals.

Criterion 4: Results, or Return on Investment (ROI)

As we have indicated, human resource managers are under pressure to show that their training programs produce "bottom-line" results.[44] Most organizations today measure their training in terms of its return on investment (ROI), which is also sometimes referred to as the *utility* the firm gets for its training dollars. A company's ROI refers to the benefits it derives from training its employees relative to the costs it incurs. HR managers are responsible for calculating and presenting these benefits to the company's top managers. The benefits can include higher revenues generated, increased productivity, improved quality, lower costs, more satisfied customers, higher job satisfaction, and lower employee turnover.

The following are the types of questions HR managers should try to answer as they calculate a training program's benefits:

- How much did quality improve because of the training program?

- How much has it contributed to profits?

- What reduction in turnover and wasted materials did the company get after training?

- How much has productivity increased, and by how much have costs been reduced?

To answer these questions, HR managers use various types of data such as sales data, human resources and financial data, and employee survey and control group data gathered from various sources within the organization. Of course, the costs of the training program need to be measured, too. The ROI formula can then be calculated fairly simply:

$$ROI = Results/Training\ Costs$$

A firm's training costs include the various expenses it incurs related to the training, including the direct costs of the programs (materials, employee travel and meals, meeting site costs, equipment, trainers' salaries or fees, and so on) as well as the indirect costs of the programs (participants' salaries and the productivity they lose while they are attending the training). So, for example, if the ROI ratio of the training is >1, its benefits exceeds its cost; if the ROI ratio is <1, the costs of the training exceed the benefits. Highlights in HRM 3 shows some simple examples of ROI calculations. A firm's training ROI can also be measured in terms of how long it takes before the benefits of the training pay off. This analysis is done by adding the costs and dividing the benefits realized in a single month. The result will indicate the overall time required for the training to pay for itself.[45]

Despite the emphasis on ROI today, some human resources experts think managers can get overly preoccupied with ROI calculations. Why? Because often the benefits of training can be intangible or take a long time to appear. Measuring participants' reactions can be done immediately, of course. However, measuring improved employee skills, customer satisfaction, and so forth can take somewhat longer, and factors other than training can also affect these measures. Finally, the development of groundbreaking new products or processes can also be sparked by training but take years to develop, making them hard to attribute to training. Developments such as these nonetheless can transform organizations.

benchmarking

The process of measuring one's own services and practices against the recognized leaders in order to identify areas for improvement

Benchmarking

Closely related to calculating the firm's training ROI is the process of benchmarking developmental services and practices against those of recognized leaders in industry.

HIGHLIGHTS IN HRM · 3

Calculating Training ROI: Examples

If the ROI ratio is >1, the benefits of the training exceed the cost of the program, and if the ratio is <1, the costs of the training program outweigh the benefits.

Example 1: A program to train new machine operators costs $15,000 to develop and implement. After completing the training program, the average number of parts produced each year increased by 3,000, and the profit on each new part is $10, producing a net result of $30,000.

$$ROI = \$30,000/\$15,000 = 2$$

Example 2: A safety program costs the company $25,000 to develop and implement. One year later, there had been a small decrease in accidents, saving the company a total of $10,000.

$$ROI = \$10,000/\$25,000 = 0.4$$

In Example 1, the program resulted in a ROI of 2, indicating that the benefits of the program outweigh its cost. However, in Example 2, the ROI was only 0.4, indicating that the costs of the program outweigh the benefits.

Source: Richard J. Wagner and Robert J. Weigand, "Can the Value of Training Be Measured? A Simplified Approach to Evaluating Training," *The Health Care Manager* 23, no. 1 (January–March 2004): 71–78.

While no single model for exact benchmarking exists, the simplest models are based on the late W. Edwards Deming's classic four-step process. The four-step process advocates that managers:

1. *Plan.* Conduct a self-audit to define internal processes and measurements; decide on areas to be benchmarked and choose the comparison organization.

2. *Do.* Collect data through surveys, interviews, site visits, and/or historical records.

3. *Check.* Analyze data to discover performance gaps and communicate findings and suggested improvements to management.

4. *Act.* Establish goals, implement specific changes, monitor progress, and redefine benchmarks as a continuous improvement process.

The American Society of Training has developed training benchmarks from hundreds of different companies to which other firms can compare the data on their training costs, staffing, administration, design, development, and delivery of training programs. Benchmarks such as these can help organizations evaluate their current and future training programs.[46] Highlights in HRM 4 shows several aspects of training that can be benchmarked against organizations considered superior in the training function and how those aspects are calculated.

The reader might also take special note that these evaluation criteria can also be used as inputs to (further) needs analysis, thereby completing the cycle inherent in

HIGHLIGHTS IN HRM 4

Benchmarking HR Training

MEASUREMENT	HOW TO CALCULATE
Percent of payroll spent on training	Total training expenditures ÷ total payroll
Training dollars spent per employee	Total training expenditures ÷ total employees served
Average training hours per employee	Total number of training hours (hours × participants) ÷ total employees served
Percent of employees trained per year	Total number of employees receiving training ÷ total employee population
HRD staff per 1,000 employees	Number of human resource development staff ÷ total employee population × 1,000
Cost savings as a ratio of training expenses	Total savings in scrap or waste ÷ dollars invested in training
Profits per employee per year	Total yearly gross profits ÷ total number of employees
Training costs per student hour	Total costs of training ÷ total number of hours of training

the system's approach to training discussed at the beginning of this chapter. By starting the cycle over again, a system's approach to training and development helps to establish an ongoing cycle of continuous assessment and improvement over time.

▪▪ SPECIAL TOPICS IN TRAINING AND DEVELOPMENT

Objective 6

In addition to training that addresses KSAs reflecting the demands of a particular job, many employers develop training programs to meet the special needs of employees. In this final section, we summarize some of these programs, including orientation training, basic skills training, team training and cross-training, ethics training, and diversity training. International training will be covered in Chapter 15.

Orientation Training

orientation

The formal process of familiarizing new employees with the organization, their jobs, and their work units

To get new employees off to a good start, organizations generally offer a formal orientation program. Orientation is the formal process of familiarizing new employees with the organization, their jobs, and their work units. Most executives, 82 percent in one survey conducted by Robert Half International, believe that formal orientation programs are effective in helping to retain and motivate employees. These and other reported benefits include the following:

1. Lower turnover

2. Increased productivity

3. Improved employee morale

4. Lower recruiting and training costs

5. Facilitation of learning

6. Reduction of the new employee's anxiety[47]

Southwest Airlines buys into the idea that employee orientation is important. The company approaches the new hire orientation program as a welcoming party. Explained Dena Wilson, a learning facilitator with the company, "We celebrate the individual becoming a part of our family at Southwest and what that signifies. . . . It's not easy to become a Southwest employee." In fact, Southwest can get as many as 200,000 applications in some years and hires fewer than a thousand people.[48]

The more time and effort spent in helping new employees feel welcome, the more likely they are to identify with the organization and become valuable members of it. Unlike training, which emphasizes the *what* and the *how*, orientation often stresses the *why*. It is designed to influence employee attitudes about the work they will be doing and their role in the organization. It defines the philosophy behind the organization's rules and provides a framework for job-related tasks. As plans, policies, and procedures change in organizations, even current employees need to be kept up to date and continually reoriented to changing conditions.

For a well-integrated orientation program, cooperation between a firm's line and HR staff is essential. The HR department ordinarily is responsible for coordinating orientation activities and for providing new employees with information about conditions of employment, pay, benefits, and other areas not directly under a supervisor's direction. However, the supervisor has the most important role in the orientation program. New employees are interested primarily in what the supervisor says and does and what their new coworkers are like.

Before the arrival of a new employee, the supervisor should inform the work group that a new worker is joining the unit. It is also common practice for supervisors or other managerial personnel to recruit coworkers to serve as volunteer "sponsors," or mentors, for incoming employees. In addition to providing practical help to newcomers, experienced colleagues represent an important source of information about the norms and nuances of the work group, the culture of the organization, and what it expects from its employees. These relationships are vital to the socialization of new employees and contribute significantly to their long-term success within the organization.

Given the immediate and lasting impact of orientation programs, careful planning—with emphasis on program goals, topics to be covered, and methods of organizing and presenting them—is essential. In many cases, organizations devise checklists for use by those responsible for conducting the orientation so that no item of importance to employees is overlooked. The checklist would include such things as (1) an introduction to other employees, (2) an outline of training, (3) expectations for attendance, conduct, and appearance, (4) the conditions of employment, such as hours and pay periods, (5) an explanation of job duties, standards, and appraisal criteria, (6) safety regulations, (7) a list of the chain of command, and (8) an explanation of the organization's purpose and strategic goals. Highlights in HRM 5 shows the types of materials new hires can be given and the various steps that can ease their transition into the workplace.[49]

Some organizations combine orientation programs with computer-based training. Lazarus Department Stores (now Macy's) cut its orientation training time in half this way, orienting 2,500 new employees in just six weeks. New hires at SumTotal Systems, an e-learning company based in Bellevue, Washington, go online for virtual tours of the company's various departments, with introductions to company leaders sprinkled throughout. Of course, these types of programs *supplement*—but do not replace—the value of face-to-face orientation.[50]

Basic Skills Training

Remedial training for adults has grown to be a full-blown educational industry on which businesses now spend billions of dollars annually. A report by the National Endowment for the Arts recently concluded that employers ranked the lack of reading and writing skills as the top deficiencies in new hires. Although literacy levels today are similar to what they were in 1970, the economy has changed drastically since then. Most U.S. workers today need to be able to read and analyze complex, often very technical material to succeed. "Jobs that don't have much in the way of skills have moved out of the United States or are not living-wage jobs," says Timothy Shanahan, the past president of the International Reading Association and a professor of urban education and reading at the University of Illinois at Chicago. Companies are also saying their employees need help with emotional skills such as persistence, self-discipline, and self-awareness.[51]

5

Checklist for Orienting New Employees

Items in Orientation Packet

- Welcome letter with company background
- Map of facility, including parking information
- IDs, keys, and parking decals
- Current organization chart
- Telephone numbers, e-mail addresses, and locations of key personnel
- Copy of employee's specific job goals and descriptions
- List of unique terms in the industry, company, and job
- Training class schedules
- Safety and emergency procedures
- Copy of policy handbook, including office hours and telephone and e-mail rules
- List of employee benefits, including insurance plans
- Holiday schedule

Follow-Up Activities

- Ensure that employee has completed required paperwork, including benefit enrollment forms
- Revisit performance standards
- Schedule first performance appraisal meeting

As the baby boom generation retires, the situation will only be exacerbated. Businesses report that they are already having a harder time finding workers with the basic skills they seek. Many businesses say it is their top problem. A list of typical basic skills employees need includes the following:

- Reading
- Writing
- Computing
- Speaking
- Listening
- Problem-solving
- Managing oneself/self-discipline
- Knowing how to learn
- Working as part of a team
- Leading others

Ford, Polaroid, United Technologies, and AT&T are among the many companies who now offer remedial courses to their employees, many of which are conducted in-house. Moreover, a number of states offer businesses tax credits for conducting remedial training (and other types of training) for their employees.[52] Recognizing that the skills gap is increasing, colleges and companies have begun teaming up to bridge the gap. For example, Pierce College, a two-year college in California (which had previously concentrated on preparing students for four-year colleges), now provides remedial instruction to employees at the offices of more than thirty companies in the San Fernando Valley area, where the college

Job-specific and general skills are both essential for career success.

is located.[53] To implement a successful program in basic and remedial skills, managers should do the following:

1. Explain to employees why and how the training will help them in their jobs.

2. Relate the training to the employees' goals.

3. Respect and consider participants' experiences, and use these as a resource.

4. Use a task-centered or problem-centered approach so that participants "learn by doing."

5. Give employees feedback on their progress toward meeting their learning objectives.

The key to developing a successful basic skills program is *flexibility*, reinforcing the principle of individual differences while acknowledging the reality of work and family constraints.

Team Training and Cross-Training

As we discussed earlier in the book, organizations rely on teams to attain strategic and operational goals. Whether the team is an aircrew, a research team, or a manufacturing or service unit, the contributions of the individual members of the team are not only a function of the KSAs of each individual, but also of the interaction of the team members. Teamwork behaviors that differentiate effective teams are shown in Figure 7.11. They include both process dynamics and behavioral dynamics. The fact that these behaviors are observable and measurable provides a basis for training team members to function more effectively in the pursuit of their goals.[54]

Coca-Cola's Fountain Manufacturing Operation (which makes the syrup for Coke and Diet Coke) developed team training for its manufacturing employees. The program focused on three skill categories: (1) technical, (2) interpersonal, and (3) team action. The technical component, called Four-Deep Training, meant that each individual should learn four different jobs to allow for team flexibility. The interpersonal skills component, called Adventures in Attitudes, focused on listening, conflict

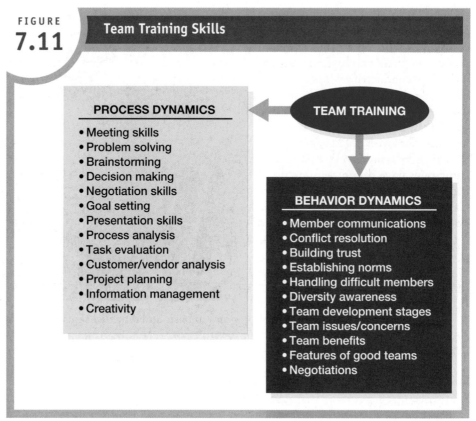

FIGURE 7.11   Team Training Skills

PROCESS DYNAMICS

- Meeting skills
- Problem solving
- Brainstorming
- Decision making
- Negotiation skills
- Goal setting
- Presentation skills
- Process analysis
- Task evaluation
- Customer/vendor analysis
- Project planning
- Information management
- Creativity

TEAM TRAINING

BEHAVIOR DYNAMICS

- Member communications
- Conflict resolution
- Building trust
- Establishing norms
- Handling difficult members
- Diversity awareness
- Team development stages
- Team issues/concerns
- Team benefits
- Features of good teams
- Negotiations

Source: George Bohlander and Kathy McCarthy, "How to Get the Most from Team Training," *National Productivity Review* (Autumn 1996): 25–35.

resolution, influence, and negotiation. Team action training focused on team leadership, management of meetings, team roles, group dynamics, and problem-solving—all skills needed to function effectively as a team. The training not only increased quality and customer satisfaction, but has also helped decrease costs and set up a model for preparing employees for the future.[55]

cross-training

The process of training employees to do multiple jobs within an organization

Closely related to team training is **cross-training.** Cross-trained employees learn how to do different jobs within an organization as well as their own. Part of the motivation for cross-training is that it gives firms flexible capacity. Workers can be dynamically shifted when and where they are needed, unlike specialized workers and equipment, which cannot. Moreover, by keeping workers interested and motivated, cross-training can cut turnover, increase productivity, pare down labor costs, and lay the foundation for careers rather than dead-end jobs. For example, at Boston's The Gourmet Pizza, employees begin cross-training their first day on the job. Staffers run through every function in the back and front of the restaurant and then plot their own course of cross-training. If they are interested in the bar, they have the opportunity to work there in various positions; those who want to become managers or franchise owners learn the entire operation, a process that takes eight to twelve months.[56]

In a sense, cross-training represents a shift from Henry Ford's assembly line production to flexible production. Some companies are using cross-training to keep their workers and plants in the United States versus offshoring them. Pace Worldwide, a Maryland-based company that sells soldering equipment, watched all of its competitors move offshore. To keep up with the productivity of its low-cost rivals abroad, Pace grouped workers into teams and trained each team to build an entire product as well as different products. "Some of the people could only do certain things, and if they had no work, they would just sit and wait," said one Pace manager. "Now they have ownership of it all." Employees have an incentive to learn because their hourly wages get bumped up as they master more skills. Now Pace builds products to meet actual customer demand, rather than storing inventory, which is more costly, and it has been able to shorten its production times and move its operations into one building versus two. In addition to making them more productive, research shows that cross-training gives employees the "big picture," making them more creative and better problem-solvers.[57]

Ethics Training

Ethics training became more prevalent in companies following the high-profile corporate scandals such as those that occurred at Enron in 2001. As the Enron case showed, ethics training is not just for rank-and-file employees. Top managers also need to attend ethics training and take it seriously or risk jail time. The federal *U.S. Sentencing Guidelines Manual* mandates severe penalties for misconduct. However, the guidelines also give companies legal incentives "to maintain internal mechanisms for preventing, detecting, and reporting criminal conduct." For reasons such as these and because the reputational and financial repercussions of ethical lapses can be devastating, many firms have since created ethics codes and developed ethics training programs for their employees.

Top managers play a key role in terms of ethics training because employees take their cues from them and mirror their behavior. Thus, a firm's top executives and managers should behave in accordance with their companies' values. If this does not happen, no ethics training program within a company can be effective. Senior managers should also broach the topic of ethics often in their speeches and presentations, and a company's ethics training should be a part of the new employee orientation. In addition, a firm's current employees need to undergo ethics training at regular intervals.

Workers who are responsible for areas that expose them to ethical lapses are likely to require special training. Employees who do the purchasing for their firms are one example. Likewise, some firms offer special training to their overseas personnel who work in countries in which corruption and bribery are prevalent. (We will talk more about bribery in Chapter 15, which covers international topics.) Bringing in an outside expert trained in ethics or values-based management can be helpful as can surveying employees, managers, and sometimes even customers about what they believe the ethical state of their companies are and where improvements could be made. Some firms go so far as to appoint chief ethics officers—high-ranking managers directly responsible for fostering the ethical climate within their firms.

chief ethics officer

A high-ranking manager directly responsible for fostering the ethical climate within the firm

Hewlett-Packard is one company that has an exemplary ethics program. All employees—from entry-level employees to senior executives—are responsible for holding one another accountable with respect to ethical behavior. The following are elements of HP's ethics program and training:

- A publicly available ethics code written in twelve languages
- Mandatory ethics training for all employees
- A toll-free ethics hotline complemented by a dedicated electronic mailbox where messages are treated with the highest degree of confidentiality
- An ethics officer with vice president-level leadership and authority
- Conflict resolution procedures
- Communications systems that facilitate and encourage employee feedback without the fear of retaliation[58]

Highlights in HRM 6 contains some additional sources human resource managers can turn to in order to develop ethics training programs.

Diversity Training

Two out of three U.S. companies have broadened their diversity programs because of increasing globalization, according to a survey of 1,780 human resources and training executives by the Boston-based consulting firm Novations/J. Howard & Associates. Of those that have not done so, most expect to update diversity efforts in the near future. In addition to globalization, the increased emphasis on diversity training has been sparked by an awareness of the varied demographics of the work-force, challenges of affirmative action, dynamics of stereotyping, changing values of the workforce, and potential competitive payoffs from bringing different people together for a common purpose. There are basically two types of diversity training: (1) awareness building, which helps employees appreciate the benefits of diversity, and (2) skill building, which provides employees with the KSAs necessary for working with people who are different from them. For example, a skill-building diversity program might teach managers how to conduct performance appraisals with people from different cultures or teach male supervisors how to coach female employees toward better career opportunities. All of the diverse dimensions—race, gender, age, disabilities, lifestyles, culture, education, ideas, and backgrounds—should be considered in the design of a diversity training program.[59]

After its highly public—and costly—$54 million discrimination lawsuit, Denny's Restaurants and its parent company, Advantica, took a first step toward changing the culture of the company through intensive diversity training. Everyone—from the board of directors to every cook, hostess, and server—was required to participate in varying levels of training. Servers and cooks, for example, were required to watch a video on diversity, while the board of directors received a full day of training. Restaurant managers received the most extensive training. A 1996 company survey found that only one-third of African-Americans gave Denny's good marks on measures such as respectful service. Today,

Using the Internet

The focus of GE's commitment to leadership development is the John F. Welch Leadership Center at Crotonville, New York, the world's first major corporate business school. To find information about the development programs offered at the center, go to the Student Resources at:

www.cengage.com/
management/bohlander

Additional Ethics Training Resources

The following organizations and links are good resources relevant to ethics codes and ethics training.

Business Roundtable Institute for Corporate Ethics

www.corporate-ethics.org
The Darden Graduate School of Business Administration
100 Darden Boulevard
Charlottesville, VA 22903

The Institute for Corporate Ethics was founded by the Business Roundtable as part of a larger effort to restore the market's trust in the marketplace after the scandals of 2000 and in the years after. The organization's Web site states that "the Institute provides a unique opportunity for leading educators, business practitioners and students alike to merge the theory and practice of business together in a seamless enterprise for the common good."

Ethics Resource Center

www.ethics.org
1747 Pennsylvania Ave., NW
Suite 400
Washington, DC 20006

As the oldest nonprofit in the United States devoted to organizational ethics, the Ethics Resource Center (ERC) advances understanding of the practices that promote ethical conduct through research, measurement of ethics and compliance program effectiveness in individual organizations, and the development of white papers and educational resources based on overall findings. ERC also sponsors character development programs for educational institutions and a Fellows Program for corporate ethics officers and academics who engage in practical research that addresses emerging issues in corporations.

Ethics & Compliance Officer Association

www.theecoa.org–
411 Waverley Oaks Road
Suite 324
Waltham, MA 02452

Founded in 1992, the U.S.-based Ethics & Compliance Officer Association (ECOA) is a professional association for managers of ethics, compliance, and business conduct programs. The ECOA provides ethics officers with training and a variety of conferences and meetings for exchanging best practices.

Source: © Copyright 2001–2008 Business for Social Responsibility.

satisfaction totals from African-Americans range from the mid-70s to more than 80 percent.

Likewise, following a couple of highly publicized incidents of intolerance, the San Francisco 49ers football team underwent diversity training. In 2002, 49ers running back Garrison Hearst said in a newspaper interview that he would never accept a gay teammate. Lindsey McLean, a retired gay trainer with the team, admitted publicly that he was gay and that he had endured taunts and humiliation from players at times during his twenty-four years with the 49ers. "We're trying to create an environment where we can talk about these things and eliminate the problems and violence that can take place and help them understand that they can create an environment that people can work in, even if they are different," said one 49ers manager.[60]

Increasingly, diversity training is being combined with other training programs, an occurrence that some believe represents the "mainstreaming" of diversity with other strategic issues, such as ethics, facing organizations. Honeywell, for example, subsumes diversity training within a weeklong advanced management program and as part of its sales training programs. General Electric trains mentors and protégés in a program that is not explicitly a diversity initiative but nevertheless clearly helps women and ethnic minorities.

To achieve a good outcome in terms of diversity training, managers will want to do the following:

1. *Forge a strategic link.* Begin by establishing the reasons for diversity training. Clarify the links between diversity and a firm's business goals in order to provide a context for training. Affirmative action and valuing diversity are not the same thing. Ultimately, diversity enhances differences and unites those differences toward a common goal.

3. *Don't settle for "off the shelf" programs.* Each company has somewhat different goals, and its training should reflect this.

4. *Choose your training methods carefully.* Most diversity training is really education (awareness building). Managers may hope they are developing skills, but this requires more in-depth training. Employees may benefit from either awareness or skill building, but they are not the same.

5. *Document the individual and organizational benefits of the training.* Diversity training, when done well, can enhance communications, improve a firm's responsiveness to social issues, reduce its lawsuits, create a climate of fairness, improve employee productivity, and increase the company's revenues, profits, and competitiveness.

The last point—documenting the benefits of diversity training—is particularly important. Oftentimes, companies fail to do this, so the training ends up merely being a "feel good" exercise. Diversity training needs to be held to the same rigorous standards as other training programs. If the training is truly working, it should show up eventually in a company's employee demographics and strategy. According to Alexandra Kalev, a doctor of philosophy at Princeton University who has studied diversity training, having an affirmative action plan that is annually evaluated, checking the numbers in your company vis-à-vis the labor market you recruit from, and having an active *diversity* committee and a full-time staff person dedicated to diversity can make a firm's diversity training programs more effective.[61]

SUMMARY

Objective 1 Today we find that organizational operations cover a broad range of subjects and involve personnel at all levels, from orientation through management development. In order to have effective training programs, the systems approach is recommended. This approach consists of four phases: (1) needs assessment, (2) program design, (3) implementation, and (4) evaluation.

Objective 2 Needs assessment begins with organization analysis. Managers must establish a context for training by deciding where training is needed, how it connects with their firms' strategic goals, and how their companies' resources can best be used in terms of training. A task analysis is used to identify the knowledge, skills, and abilities employees need. A person analysis is used to identify which people need training.

Objective 3 When designing a training program, managers must consider the two fundamental preconditions for learning: readiness and motivation of trainees. In addition, the principles of learning should be considered in order to create an environment that is conducive to learning. These principles include goal setting, the meaningfulness of presentation, modeling, individual differences, active practice and repetition, whole-versus-part learning, massed-versus-distributed learning, and feedback and reinforcement.

Objective 4 A wide variety of methods are available to train nonmanagerial personnel. On-the-job training is one of the most commonly used methods because it provides trainees with hands-on experience and an opportunity to build a relationship with their supervisor and coworkers. Apprenticeship training and internships are especially effective because they provide both on- and off-the-job experiences. Other off-the-job methods include classroom training, programmed instruction, computer-based training,

simulations, and interactive e-learning utilizing teleconferencing, video conferencing, webinars, and the communities of practice method of learning. Using multiple methods, or what is called blended learning, has been found to be most effective.

The training and development of managers is becoming increasingly critical for firms because they are facing increasing competition from across the globe and the baby boomer generation in the United States is retiring. As with nonmanagerial personnel, a wide variety of training methods are used for developing managers. On-the-job experiences include coaching, understudy assignment, job rotation, lateral transfers, project and committee assignments, and staff meetings. Off-the-job experiences include analysis of case studies, management games and simulations, role-playing, and behavior modeling.

Objective 5 Evaluation of a training program should focus on several criteria: participant reactions, learning, behavior change on the job, and bottom-line results such as return on investment. Transfer of training is measured via examination of the degree to which trained skills are demonstrated back on the job. Benchmarking and utility analysis help evaluate the impact of training and provide the information for further needs assessment.

Objective 6 Special issues in training involve programs that are important to a broad range of employees. Orientation training, for example, begins and continues throughout an employee's service with an organization. By participating in a formal orientation program, employees acquire the knowledge, skills, and attitudes that increase the probabilities of their success within the organization. To make an orientation effective, there should be close cooperation between the HR department and other departments in all phases of the program, from initial planning through follow-up and evaluation. Basic skills training, team training, ethics training, and diversity training are also critically important in today's organizations.

KEY TERMS

apprenticeship training
behavior modeling
behavior modification
benchmarking
blended learning
chief ethics officer
chief learning officer
competency assessment

cooperative training
cross-training
e-learning
instructional objectives
internship programs
just-in-time training
learning management system (LMS)
on-the-job training (OJT)

organization analysis
orientation
person analysis
spot rewards
task analysis
transfer of training

DISCUSSION QUESTIONS

Objective 1
1. What economic, social, and political forces have made employee training even more important today than it was in the past?

Objective 2
2. What analyses should be made to determine the training needs of an organization? After the needs are determined, what is the next step?

Objective 3
3. Which principles of learning do you see demonstrated in your own class? In what ways might you bring other principles into the class?

Objective 4
4. Indicate what training methods you would use for each of the following jobs. Explain your choices.
a. File clerk
b. Computer operator
c. Automobile service station attendant
d. Pizza maker
e. Nurse's aide

Objective 4
5. Compare computer-based instruction and e-learning with the lecture method with regard to the way the two methods involve the different psychological principles of learning.

Objective 4
6. Suppose that you are the manager of an accounts receivable unit in a large company. You are switching to a new system of billing and record-keeping and need to train your three supervisors and twenty-eight employees in the new procedures. What training method(s) would you use? Why?

Objective 5
7. Participants in a training course are often asked to evaluate the course by means of a questionnaire. What are the pros and cons of this approach? Are there better ways of evaluating a course?

Objective 6
8. A new employee is likely to be anxious the first few days on the job.
a. What are some possible causes of this anxiety?
b. How may the anxiety be reduced?

Objective 6
9. Why is employee orientation an important process? What are some benefits of a properly conducted orientation program?

Objective 6
10. Why do you think basic skills training is becoming more important to U.S. firms?

BIZFLIX EXERCISES

Backdraft: Probie's Training Experiences

Watch the scenes from the film *Backdraft* to see examples of the training and development discussions in this chapter. Use the following discussion questions as guides to your viewing of the scenes.

Two brothers follow their late father, a legendary Chicago firefighter, and join the City of Chicago Fire Department. Stephen "Bull" McCaffrey (Kurt Russell) joins first and rises to the rank of lieutenant. Younger brother Brian (William Baldwin) joins later. After graduation from the fire academy, Brian becomes a member of Bull's Engine Company 17. Sibling rivalry tarnishes their work relationships, but they continue to fight Chicago fires successfully. Add a plot element about a mysterious arsonist, and you have the basis for an extraordinary film. The intense, unprecedented special effects give the viewer an unparalleled experience of what it is like to fight a fire. Chicago firefighters applauded the realism of the fire scenes.

These scenes are an edited composite built from two parts of the film. Part I: "On-the-Job Training: Probie's First Day" appears early in *Backdraft* as part of "The First Day" sequence. This part shows Engine Company 17 preparing to fight a garment factory fire. Part II: "Back at Station 17: Probie Continues Training" comes from "The Probie's Life" segment that appears about 30 minutes later in the film. The term *probie* is jargon for a probationary firefighter—someone just starting with the department.

What to Watch for and Ask Yourself

- Which training methods described earlier in this chapter appear in these scenes? Link the training methods discussed to specific moments and examples in the scenes.
- Did Brian McCaffrey receive any classroom instruction?
- Review the earlier section "Phase 4: Evaluating the Training Program." Assess the training Brian received using the criteria discussed in that section.

HRM EXPERIENCE

Training and Learning Principles

It is surprising how many training programs do not explicitly incorporate the principles of learning into their design (such as goal setting, modeling, individual differences, and feedback). It is not that difficult to do so, even for very simple instructional programs. To prove this point, do the following assignment for building a paper airplane.

Assignment

1. Form teams of four to six members. Identify someone on the team who knows how to make a paper airplane. That person will be the *trainer*.

2. Identify someone who will be the *observer/recorder*. That person will not participate in the training but will write down how many (and how effectively) principles of learning are used in the instruction:

(continued)

Training and Learning Principles (continued)

a. Goal setting
b. Modeling
c. Meaningfulness
d. Individual differences
e. Whole-versus-part learning
f. Mass-versus-distributed learning
g. Active practice
h. Feedback

3. Give the trainer ten to fifteen minutes to train the group in making a paper airplane. The observer/recorder will keep notes of effective and ineffective training techniques (demonstrated learning principles).

4. Have someone from each team—not the trainer—volunteer to come before the class for a friendly competition. The instructor will give each team member two minutes to make a paper airplane. Then just for fun, they can compete by seeing which one flies the farthest. As always, no wagering, please.

5. To finish the exercise, the observers/recorders will lead a discussion of the learning principles that were demonstrated. Discuss also, if they were done in this setting, why they might not be done in other training settings.

CASE STUDY 1

Loews Hotels: We Train to Please

Chocolates on the pillows. A bathroom floor you can eat off of. Service with a smile. When guests go to a hotel or resort, they want all the comforts of home, plus pampering and personalized service. Here's how Loews Hotels, Wequassett Resort and Golf Club, and LaQuinta Hotels use training to captivate their customers—and keep them coming back for more.

How do you live up to a brand promise? At Loews Hotels, a chain of luxury hotels based in New York with 18 properties in North America, in cities such as Miami Beach, Denver, and Las Vegas, the brand promise is to deliver a "four diamond and more" experience and to "constantly look for ways to delight our guests." Loews has learned that training is a big part of living up to that promise.

Training at all levels focuses on how employees—whether you're a housekeeper, a bellman, or a marketing director—can help to deliver on that promise. With 8,000 line-level employees (housekeepers, bartenders, restaurant staff, for example) and 1,200 managers to keep up to speed, that's a big promise to keep. "It's about what we do for guests to make their experience memorable and make them want to come back to a Loews hotel," says Jenny Lucas, director of education and development for Loews.

This is a relatively new focus for the company, which has changed its systems in many ways in response. It starts with the training department. Training managers at Loews are more like knowledge managers. They don't spend much of their time on formal training; instead, they work in the departments and build relationships with the employees on the floor. They prepare department report cards every month to report on how performance is on the move, and they spend a lot of time coaching.

"Classroom training is part of the puzzle, but without true behavior change and accountability, you haven't completed that puzzle," says Lucas. "So our training managers are out there, watching training being delivered, watching managers in action, doing spot checks, and giving feedback afterward. They're the keepers of service and standards, so they have to be accessible and capture the knowledge of how operations work from day to day." Lucas points out that 13 out of the 18 training managers were promoted from line-level jobs or from operations, so they know the processes and the culture firsthand.

For line-level employees, training conveys the service standards by way of the classroom. For example, in a brand promises class, employees learn about the expectations of the company's culture. Classes include role-playing and simulations—the live or videotaped kind, not the electronic kind. The immediacy of video or live role plays helps to drive the message home, and the group experience is part of that. Although Lucas says the company has interest in integrating more technology with its training, for many employees it just wouldn't make sense.

"Our managers are the only ones with computers, and one whole department might share a computer," says Lucas. "This approach makes more sense based on the content and resources we're conveying. We're looking at some technology-oriented content that wouldn't require a computer, such as podcasts, but we're not there yet."

At the management level—Loews has nearly 1,200—a core management workshop, a train-the-trainer program, and other management workshops (such as the one on building the brand) help to create leadership that can not only help build the brand but inspire others to do so, as well.

Changes in the company's performance management system also have made the brand promise more top-of-mind. The company has created a system in which individual managers' performance ratings are linked to their contributions to company goals.

The company also has begun to raise its own crop of quality employees whose chances of rising in the company are good because of their obvious potential. The idea is to grow talented leaders, but also to "raise" people who get the culture and who know how to make a hotel feel like a Loews Hotel. Loews' high-potential program offers additional training, development planning, and extra opportunities to employees who show promise, and it's integrated with the performance review process. Managers are asked what they're doing to develop their people, and the answer is part of their performance rating. A focus on growing its own already has paid off; internal promotions have been running at about 55 percent, and more than 75 percent of the former high-potential program participants are still with the company and have been promoted.

"The program started with an operations focus, and we focused on the front desk employees, maintenance positions, and the like," Lucas says. "But now all disciplines are in the program in different ways."

Going forward, Lucas would love to do more of the videos that help instruct front-line employees in good service, so that more specific visual examples of more tasks would be available. And although certain obstacles limit the company's use of technology-based learning, Lucas wants to move into offering more solutions of that type on-site.

She also wants to tap into the generation known as Y, and to do so, her department has been exploring the possibilities of MySpace. Loews is not really using it for training yet, but Lucas knows the way to Gen Y leads through avenues such as iPods, podcasts, and MySpace. "There are opportunities there; we just have to figure out how to tap into them," Lucas says.

Questions

1. What can you tell about how Loews assesses the need for employee training?
2. From what you read, what principles of learning do you believe are embedded in Loews programs?
3. Do you think Loews should actively work toward incorporating more e-learning methods into its training programs? Why or why not?

Source: Reprinted from Holly Dolezalek, "We Train to Please" *Training* 45, no. 3 (March–April 2008): 34–35.

CASE STUDY 2

Texas Instruments: Learning to Walk in the Customer's Shoes

Problem: Like most high-tech companies, semiconductor giant Texas Instruments rode the technology boom in a state of bliss. As customers waited in line for its products, TI became more product- and technology-centric, and admittedly less concerned about its customers. Then came the bust. TI was suddenly forced to compete for new business, yet elements of its management simply wouldn't adjust to the market's new demands. How could TI jolt its people into a renewed awareness of the customer?

Solution: Texas Instruments called on BTS USA, a global supplier of computer-based simulations for learning. The provider developed a customer loyalty course for TI's top 300 executives aimed at raising awareness about customer-centric thinking. The course was so successful that it was expanded to an additional 2,000 TI managers and earned BTS a coveted Supplier Excellence Award from a grateful TI.

They call it a "Customer Loyalty Boot Camp." The title is appropriate because much like the army's indoctrination for recruits, it represents the Tough Love approach to employee learning. And for Texas Instruments, it seemed that nothing less would do.

Picture the scene: a classroom of 25 TI executives, all chastened by a stern lecture from the company's senior vice president of worldwide sales and marketing, Jeffrey S. McCreary. "This company is broken," McCreary railed. But the audience wasn't getting the message. The year was 2001, the bottom was dropping out of the semiconductor industry, and TI's fortunes were plummeting along with it. It was no time for the company to be dismissive of its valued customers—or perceived as such.

Also in the classroom were consultants and trainers from BTS USA. BTS had been invited to help develop and deliver a course for TI executives on customer loyalty. The two-and-a-half-day course had been painstakingly created by BTS following extensive interviews with TI executives, key account managers, and customers to gain an accurate picture of the problems facing the company. The customized course was designed and created with active participation from TI's training department.

The twenty-five assembled managers were divided into five teams, each assigned to simulate executives of a fictitious company called Streaming Wireless Video (STREAVO). The concern "manufactured" a handheld product that included chips supplied by another fictitious company called Terrific Instruments (TI). It was now time for the TI managers to walk a mile in their customer's shoes.

Each team was responsible for a different department within STREAVO, including engineering, finance, supplier management, manufacturing, and marketing. Using laptop computers and a simulation to analyze data, such as engineering specifications, financial statements, and customer and market reports, they pondered the purchasing decision for three hours before hitting a button named "commit."

"Little did they know that upon return from their coffee break, the teams would walk into a valley of darkness," recalls Daniel Parisi, senior vice president of BTS USA and general manager of its San Francisco office. Parisi was in charge of the seminar and was about to make their lives miserable by delivering information about Terrific Instruments' execution missteps, including failure to meet time, cost, and performance commitments.

The simulated learning concept he was using got its start in 1985, when Swedish entrepreneur Henrik Ekelund launched BTS to help companies meet strategic business goals. Ekelund found simulation to be a useful tool to communicate complex business strategies to executives, and apparently clients agree. BTS has since expanded to the United States, the United Kingdom, Finland, South Africa, Australia, and Spain.

At the heart of the learning exercise are custom-designed computer-based simulations that replicate the actual business processes of the client company. Each management team is assisted in the decision-making process with a laptop on which they can perform budgeting and "what-if" analysis and scenarios. Over the course of a three-month development process, the simulation was co-created by BTS and the client and inserted into a platform of Excel and Visual Basic software. "It simulates the technical and business interrelationships that exist between TI and its client," says Parisi. "In this case, the semiconductor's performance and functionality are realistically linked into the handheld's design specifications," he says. "Also, the impacts of the supplier execution missteps are extremely realistic," adds Parisi.

The concept often uses a kind of shock therapy to jolt executives into reality. At Texas Instruments, for example, many executives were not sensitive to the impact TI's execution missteps could have on the customer. There also were gaps in their knowledge regarding their customers' drivers of profitability and competitive advantage. In many cases, they lacked a long-term view of TI's customer relationships.

When the TI executives returned from their break, Parisi was there to greet them, a scowl on his face and a baseball cap that read Terrific Industries on his head. "There are problems with your order," he told the assembled "STREAVO" management teams. Not only would there be a five-week delay in delivery, but alas, the chip would not meet specifications, he told the horrified group.

What's more, Parisi was brutally unsympathetic to the customer's predicament. "Count your blessings," he sneered. "After all, we're Terrific. We're Number One." Then came the clincher: an ultimatum from STREAVO's retail customer, "Circus City," which was affected by Terrific's delays. "We don't care about your problems," grumbled Circus. "You will either help us or we will cut you off."

The effect of the simulation exercise was written on the faces of the Texas Instruments executives, who felt betrayed and frustrated at the arrogance on display. Some also felt that the excuses sounded distressingly familiar, as indeed they should have. To complete the session, Parisi played a five-minute video of comments from actual TI customers. "TI's own customers said almost exactly what the TI managers in the STREAVO simulation were saying," said Parisi. Indeed, hearing customers echo their own experience in the simulation "was like hitting them in the stomach," he said.

The boot camp was so successful that it has since been rolled out to more than 2,000 TI managers and engineers, says Parisi, who claims the results speak for themselves. "In 2001, TI had some dissatisfied customers. But at the end of 2003, it was receiving supplier excellence awards from the very same customers," says Parisi. "Within 24 months, TI turned the entire company in a much more customer-centric direction."

Questions

1. Do you think that TI took the right approach to achieving better customer satisfaction by training its executives first? Would TI have achieved quicker results by training its front-line employees prior to its executives?
2. If you were a HR manager at TI, to what sources would you have looked to find information with which to calculate the program's ROI?

Source: Adapted from Paul Harris, "BTS Helps Companies Walk in Customers' Shoes," *Learning Circuits* (June 2004), http://www.learningcircuits.org/2004/jun2004/harris.htm.

CASE STUDY 3

Kodak Gets the Picture in Executive Education

Eastman Kodak is changing dramatically to compete in a world of new technologies, emerging markets, and global customers. As a result, Kodak's efforts in executive education have pushed the limits to create innovative "learning events" for senior management. According to June Delano, Kodak's director of Executive Education and Development, these learning events are designed to be as dynamic and future-oriented as the company's business environment.

In the past, the highly successful Kodak was a citadel of stability. It enjoyed market dominance, worldwide brand recognition, extraordinary customer loyalty, and enviable profits. Understandably, few employees (or managers) wanted to do anything to upset the status quo as most of them looked forward to a lifetime of employment and security.

Then things changed. The company restructured in order to go head-to-head with competitors in a much tougher digital marketplace, and in the process, there has been a one-third reduction in executive positions. These events have driven complacency far from the environs of Rochester, New York, Kodak's headquarters city. *Agility* has replaced *stability* as the watchword of the future.

As a consequence of Kodak's transformation—not to mention the personnel changes—the majority of senior managers have been in their positions for less than three years. Executive education is viewed as a critical tool for improving the managerial ranks. But Delano believed that the development programs needed to be as active, innovative, and future-oriented as the company. Off-the-shelf materials were out, as were case studies, lectures, and other passive learning approaches. A new approach meant inventing from scratch, letting go of control, and taking monumental risks. Skills in anticipating the business, pushing the culture, and networking were demanded. Delano wanted executive education to optimize opportunities to think collectively and to experiment and explore implications as a team. These objectives led to the creation of three new programs for the senior management team:

- *The Kodak Prosperity Game.* This program was developed in partnership with the Prosperity Institute and was conducted in June 1996 using staff drawn from industry and academia. Focusing on the imaging industry, the program innovatively teamed fifty Kodak executives with twenty-five peer executives from other companies. These "reality-based" teams worked on meaningful, implementable strategies, alliances, and deals.

- *The Digital Executive.* This program consisted of a "scavenger hunt" exploring Kodak's digital present and future. Using digital products and the Internet, small teams researched digital competitors and interacted with a consumer focus group via videoconferencing. One innovative feature of this program was the upward mentoring of the participants by technology "whiz kids."

- *The Future of the Company.* This was a two-part program, developed in partnership with the Global Business Network and focused on learning about possible futures for the industry and the company. Part I was a two-day "conversation" about Kodak and its environment in the coming years. Industry scenarios for growth were developed in small team discussions involving Kodak executives and customers, alliance partners, and futurists. The resulting scenarios launched Part II, in which additional outsiders and provocative thinkers mixed ideas with the participants. The outcomes were a set of new ideas and potential strategies for the Kodak businesses.

So far, the program seems to be working for the company that invented consumer photography more than a century ago. After Kodak's executives committed to an all-out digital strategy, the company's revenues climbed. In 2004, Kodak surpassed Sony, the market leader, in the number of digital cameras shipped in the United States.

Questions

1. What can you tell about how Kodak did needs assessment for executive education? What recommendations would you give June Delano for improving this analysis?

2. From what you read, what principles of learning do you believe are embedded in the three new programs?

3. How would you go about evaluating the effectiveness of these educational experiences? Do you believe that company profitability should be used as a criterion?

Sources: William G. Stopper, "Agility in Action: Picturing the Lessons Learned from Kodak and 23 Other Companies." Adapted with permission from *Human Resource Planning*, vol. 21, no. 1 (1998). Copyright 1998 by The Human Resource Planning Society, 317 Madison Avenue, Suite 1509, New York, NY 10017, Phone: (212) 490-6387, Fax: (212) 682-6851; "Kodak Overtakes Sony in U.S. Digital Camera Shipments," *Kyodo News International* (Tokyo, Japan) (via *Knight-Ridder/Tribune Business News*) (February 3, 2005).

NOTES AND REFERENCES

1. Lori Freifeld, "Best of the Best," *Training* 45, no. 2 (February 2008): 8.

2. David Dubois and William Rothwell, "Competency-Based or a Traditional Approach to Training?" *Training and Development* 58, no. 4 (April 2004): 46–59; See also Irwin L. Goldstein and J. Kevin Ford, *Training in Organizations: Needs Assessment, Development and Evaluation*, 4th ed. (Belmont, CA: Wadsworth, 2002). For the classic citation on needs assessment, see William McGehee and Paul W. Thayer, *Training in Business and Industry* (New York: John Wiley and Sons, 1961).

3. Laurie Bassi and Daniel McMurrer, "How's Your Return on People?" *Harvard Business Review* 8, no. 3 (March 2004): 18; Tracy Mauro, "Helping Organizations Build Community," *Training and Development* 56, no. 2 (February 2002): 25–29; Liam Lahey, "RFIDs Touted as Standard for Airport Security," *Computing Canada* 28, no. 13 (June 21, 2002): 21; Caroline Wilson, "Ensuring a Smooth Ride," *Security Management* 46, no. 8 (August 2002): 92.

4. Brad Long, "Strategic Human Resource Management and the Worker's Experience," *Journal of Individual Employment Rights* 12, no. 3 (2007): 265–282; "E-Learning and Teleconferencing Join Needs Assessment to Control Training Costs," *Managing Training & Development*, no. 3 (December 2003): 1; Thomas Gainey, Brian Klaas, and Darla Moore, "Outsourcing the Training Function: Results from the Field," *Human Resource Planning* 25, no. 1 (2002): 16; Sarah Fister Gale, "Creative Training: Doing More with Less," *Workforce* 80, no. 10 (October 2001): 82–88.

5. Scott A. Yorkovich, Gregory S. Waddell, and Robert K. Gerwig, "Competency-based Assessment Systems: Encouragement Toward a More Holistic Approach," *Proceedings of the Northeast Business & Economics Association* (2007): 77–81; Patty Davis, Jennifer Naughton, and William Rothwell, "New Roles and New Competencies for the Profession: Are You Ready for the Next Generation," *Training and Development* 58, no. 4 (April 2004): 26–38; David Dubois and William Rothwell, "Competency-Based or a Traditional Approach to Training?" *Training and Development* 58, no. 4 (April 2004): 46–59.

6. Thomas Hoffman, "Motivation: These IT Leaders Keep Staffers Upbeat during Lean Times by Targeting What Drives Them: Technology and Training," *Computerworld* 38, no. 1 (January 5, 2004): 39; Elwood Holton, Reid Bates, and Sharon Naquin, "Large-Scale Performance-Driven Training Needs Assessment: A Case Study," *Public Personnel Management* 29, no. 2 (Summer 2000): 249–67.

7. Gail Johnson, "The Development Framework: Booz Allen Hamilton's Holistic Method of Employee Development Gives Its Employee a Roadmap to Success—Both Professionally and Personally," *Training* 40, no. 2 (February 2003): 32–34; Robert Mager, "Contract Training Tips," *Security Management* 45, no. 6 (June 2001): 30.

8. Debbie Schachter, "How to Set Performance Goals: Employee Reviews Are More Than Annual Critiques," *Information Outlook* 8, no. 9 (September 2004): 26–30; "Burger Olympics," *Training* 41, no. 7 (July 2004): 20; Jason A. Colquitt and Marcia J. Simmering, "Conscientiousness, Goal Orientation, and Motivation to Learn during the Learning Process: A Longitudinal Study," *Journal of Applied Psychology* 83, no. 4 (August 1998): 654–65.

9. Annette Towler and Robert Dipboye, "Effects of Trainer Expressiveness, Organization, and Trainee Goal Orientation on Training Outcomes," *Journal of Applied Psychology* 86, no. 4 (August 2001): 664–73; Steve Kozlowski, Stanley Gully, Kenneth Brown, and Eduardo Salas, "Effects of Training Goals and Goal Orientation Traits on Multidimensional Training Outcomes and Performance Adaptability," *Organizational Behavior and Human Decision Processes* 85, no. 1 (May 2001): 1–31.

10. The classics by Albert Bandura include *Social Foundations of Thought and Action: A Social Cognitive Theory* (Englewood Cliffs, NJ: Prentice Hall, 1986) and *A Social Learning Theory* (Englewood Cliffs,

NJ: Prentice Hall, 1977). See also Melesa Altizer Bolt, Larry Killough, and Hian Chye Koh, "Testing the Interaction Effects of Task Complexity in Computer Training Using the Social Cognitive Model," *Decision Sciences* 32, no. 1 (Winter 2001): 1–20; Susan Pedersen and Min Liu, "The Transfer of Problem-Solving Skills from a Problem-Based Learning Environment: The Effect of Modeling an Expert's Cognitive Processes," *Journal of Research on Technology in Education* 35, no. 2 (Winter 2002): 303–21.

11. Stanley Gully, Stephanie Payn, K. Lee Kiechel Koles, and John-Andrew Whiteman, "The Impact of Error Training and Individual Differences on Training Outcomes: An Attribute-Treatment Interaction Perspective," *Journal of Applied Psychology* 87, no. 1 (February 2002): 143–55; Steven John Simon, "The Relationship of Learning Style and Training Method to End-User Computer Satisfaction and Computer Use: A Structural Equation Model," *Information Technology, Learning, and Performance Journal* 18, no. 1 (Spring 2000): 41–59.

12. Maya Dollarhide, "Hits the Spot," *Incentive* 181, no. 10 (October 2007): 102–103; "Can Technology Actually Boost Behavior Change?" *Managing Training & Development* no. 3 (November 2003): 3; Don Hartshorn, "Reinforcing the Unsafe Worker," *Occupational Hazards* 62, no. 10 (October 2000): 125–28.

13. Joe M. Ricks, Jacqueline A. Williams, and William A. Weeks, "Sales Trainer Roles, Competencies, Skills, and Behaviors: A Case Study," *Industrial Marketing Management* 37, no. 5 (July 2008): 593–609; John L. Bennett, "Trainers as Leaders of Learning," *Training and Development* 55, no. 3 (March 2001): 42–45; Ruth Palombo Weiss, "Deconstructing Trainers' Self-Image," *Training and Development* 55, no. 12 (December 2001): 34–39.

14. Eduardo Salas and Janis Cannon-Bowers, "The Science of Training: A Decade of Progress," *Annual Review of Psychology* 52 (2001): 471–99.

15. Cohn Terry, "Enabling Staff to Access the Knowledge They Need, When They Need It," *Industrial & Commercial Training*, 39, no. 7 (2007): 368–371; Diane Walter, *Training on the Job* (Alexandria, VA: American Society for Training and Development, 2001); Toni Hodges, *Linking Learning and Performance: A Practical Guide to Measuring Learning and On-the-Job Application* (Burlington, MA: Butterworth-Heinemann, 2001); Gary Sisson, *Hands-On Training: A Simple and Effective Method for On-the-Job Training* (San Francisco: Barrett-Koehler, 2001).

16. Teresa M. McAleavy, "U.S. Schools Fail to Provide Job Training," *Knight-Ridder/Tribune Business News* (June 9, 2004); "Eight Steps to Better On-the-Job Training," *HRFocus* 80, no. 7 (July 2003): 11; Alison Booth, Yu-Fu Chen, and Gylfi Zoega, "Hiring and Firing: A Tale of Two Thresholds," *Journal of Labor Economics* 20, no. 2 (April 2002): 217–48.

17. Ronald L. Jacobs and Michael J. Jones, "Teaching Tools: When to Use On-the-Job Training," *Security Management* 41, no. 9 (September 1997): 35–39.

18. Information found on the Apprenticeship page, Spokane Community College Web site, February 9, 2005, http://www.scc.spokane.edu/tech/apprent.

19. "Project Focuses on Placing Women, Minorities into IT," *Certification Magazine* 9, no. 4 (April 2007): 9; "Agilisys Automotive Helps to Build Tomorrow's Leaders Through Focus: HOPE Sponsorship at Important Auto Industry Event," *PR Newswire* (August 4, 2003).

20. For more information about the Bureau of Apprenticeship and Training, see the Bureau's Web site at http://oa.doleta.gov.

21. John Byrd and Rob Poole, "Highly Motivated Employees at No Cost? It's Not an Impossible Dream," *Nonprofit World* 19, no. 6 (November/December 2001): 312–32.

22. "Workforce Investment Act: One-Stop Centers Implemented Strategies to Strengthen Services and Partnerships, but More Research and Information Sharing Is Needed," *General Accounting Office Reports & Testimony* 2003, no. 7 (July 2003).

23. Phil Britt, "E-Learning on the Rise in the Classroom: Companies Move Content Online: Cisco Systems' Employees and Partners Routinely Watch Videos on the Internet," *EContent* 27, no. 11 (November 2004): 36–41; Heather Johnson, "The Whole Picture: When It Comes to Finding Out How Employees Feel about Training, Many Companies Fail to Get a Clear Picture," *Training* 47, no. 7 (July 2004): 30–35.

24. Laura Chubb, "EDS Uses Teleconferencing to Train Leaders in Coaching Skills," *People Management* 13, no. 23 (November 15, 2007): 13; "What Does Teleconferencing Cost?" *T+D* 61, no. 10 (October 2007): 96.

25. Jeane Mesiter, "Communities of Practice 2.0," *Chief Learning Officer* 6, no. 5 (May 2007): 58.

26. Ericka Johnson, "Surgical Simulators and Simulated Surgeons: Reconstituting Medical Practice and Practitioners in Simulations," *Social Studies of Science* 37, no. 4 (August 2007): 585–608; "Soup to Nuts: Simulator Manufacturing Is a Lucrative but Risky Business, Which Is Why Market Leader CAE Has Tapped into the More Stable World of Flight Training," *Air Transport World* 40, no. 5 (May 2003): 69–71; "SimsSir: Modeling and Simulation Are Leading the Assault on New Learning Technologies That Are Winning Favor with the U.S. Military," *Training and Development* 57, no. 10 (October 2003): 46–52.

27. Marc J. Rosenberg, "Technology Euphoria?" *T+D* 62, no. 6 (June 2008): 24–27; For applications of simulation training used in the U.S. Navy, see John Flink, "This Is Really Neat Stuff," *United States Naval Institute Proceedings* 128, no. 7 (July 2002): 68–69. For applications of simulation training used in medical schools, see David Noonan, "Is the Cadaver Dead?" *Newsweek* 139, no. 25 (June 24, 2002): 62. For applications of simulation training used in the police force, see Jim Weiss and Mickey Davis, "Deadly Force Decision-Making," *Law and Order* 50, no. 6 (June 2002): 58–62.

28. "What to Do Now That Training Is Becoming a Major HR Force," *HRFocus* (February 2005): 5–6; Tammy Galvin, "The Delivery," *Training* 38, no. 10 (October 2001): 66–72; Kenneth G. Brown, "Using Computers to Deliver Training: Which Employees Learn and Why?" *Personnel Psychology* 54, no. 2 (Summer 2001): 271–96; Bill Roberts, "E-Learning New Twist on CBT," *HRMagazine* 46, no. 4 (April 2001): 99–106.

29. Scott A. Snell, Donna Stueber, and David P. Lepak, "Virtual HR Departments: Getting Out of the Middle," in R. L. Heneman and D. B. Greenberger (eds.), *Human Resource Management in Virtual Organizations* (Greenwich, CT: Information Age Publishing, 2002).

30. Garry Kranz, "E-learning Hits Its Stride," *Workforce Management Online* (February 2008); Martin Delahoussaye, Kristine Ellis, and Matt Bolch, "Measuring Corporate Smarts," *Training* 39, no. 8 (August 2002): 20–35; Daniel Crepin, "From Design to Action: Developing a Corporate Strategy," *Quality Progress* 35, no. 2 (February 2002): 49–56; Brad Miller, "Making Managers More Effective Agents of Change," *Quality Progress* 34, no. 5 (May 2001): 53–57.

31. Yabome Gilpin-Jackson and Gervase R. Bushe, "Leadership Development Training Transfer: A Case Study of Post-Training Determinants," *Journal of Management Development* 26, no. 10 (2007): 980–1004; Joseph Alutto, "Just-in-Time Management Education in the 21st Century," *HRMagazine* 44, no. 11 (1999): 56–57; Gordon Dehler, M. Ann Welsh, and Marianne W. Lewis, "Critical Pedagogy in the 'New Paradigm,'" *Management Learning* 493, no. 4 (December 2001): 493–511.

32. "Caterpillar University College of Leadership," *Leadership Development Strategy: Caterpillar* (2007): 47–51.

33. Chris Whitcomb, "Scenario-Based Training to the F.B.I.," *Training and Development* 53, no. 6 (June 1999): 42–46; Anne Hoag, Dale Brickley, and Joanne Cawley, "Media Management Education and the Case Method," *Journalism and Mass Communication Educator* 55, no. 4 (Winter 2001): 49–59.

34. Jason B. Moats, Thomas J. Chermack, and Larry M. Dooley, "Using Scenarios to Develop Crisis Managers: Applications of Scenario Planning and Scenario-Based Training," *Advances in Developing Human Resources* 10, no. 3 (June 2008): 397–424; A. J. Faria, "The Changing Nature of Business Simulation/Gaming Research: A Brief History," *Simulation and Gaming* 32 no. 1 (March 2001): 97–110.

35. Alli McConnon, "The Games Managers Play," *Business Week* 4040 (June 25, 2007):

12; Matt Bolch, "Games Employees Play: Delta Air Lines Uses a Blended e-Learning Program to Teach Employees the Economic Realities of the Airline Industry," *Training* 40, no. 4 (April 2003): 44–48.

36. Adam Kirby "Guest Service Is Fun and Games," *Hotels* 42, no. 5 (May 2008): 71–72; Dan Heilman, "Putting Games to Work: Game-Based Training Is Shaping Up to Be One of This Generation's Primary Teaching Tools, in Business and Elsewhere," *Computer User* 22, no. 2 (February 2004): 14–16.

37. Rick Markley, "Virtual Training," *Fire Chief* 52, no. 6 (June 2008): 66–70.

38. Patricia Robinson, "In Practice: Western Companies Show Asian Counterparts That It Pays to Play," *Chief Learning Officer* 6, no. 12 (December 2007): 30; Christopher Hosford, "Serious Fun: Computer Training Finds a Niche," *Meeting News* 28, no. 7 (December 2004): 16; Rick Sullivan, "Lessons in Smallness," *Training and Development* 56, no. 3 (March 2002): 21–23; James W. Walker, "Perspectives," *Human Resource Planning* 23, no. 3 (2000): 5–7.

39. T. L. Stanley, "Be a Good Role Model for Your Employees," *Supervision* 65, no. 5 (January 2004): 5–8; Gary May and William Kahnweiler, "The Effect of a Mastery Practice Design on Learning and Transfer in Behavior Modeling Training," *Personnel Psychology* 53, no. 2 (Summer 2000): 353–73.

40. Wendy Larlee, "Training Programs: Key to Collections: Companies in the Collections Business Face Significant Challenges: Putting Solid Training Program in Place Can Help," *Collections & Credit Risk* 9, no. 2 (December 2004): 42–44; Heather Johnson, "The Whole Picture: When It Comes to Finding Out How Employees Feel about Training, Many Companies Fail to Get a Clear Picture," *Training* 47, no. 7 (July 2004): 30–35; Martin Delahoussaye, "Show Me the Results," *Training* 39, no. 3 (March 2002): 28–29; Reinout van Brakel, "Why ROI Isn't Enough," *Training and Development* 56, no. 6 (June 2002): 72–74.

41. "Dissatisfaction with Job Training Contributes to Low Job Satisfaction," *Managing Training & Development* (November 2003): 8; James Pershing

and Jana Pershing, "Ineffective Reaction Evaluation," *Human Resource Development Quarterly* 12, no. 1 (Spring 2001): 73–90.

42. Andreas Putra, "Evaluating Training Programs: An Exploratory Study of Transfer of Learning onto the Job at Hotel A and Hotel B, Sydney, Australia," *Journal of Hospitality and Tourism Management* 11, no. 1 (April 2004): 77–78; Thomas Hoffman, "Simulations Revitalize e-Learning," *Computerworld* 37, no. 31 (August 4, 2003): 26–28.

43. Jathan Janove, "Use It or Lose It," *HRMagazine* 47, no. 4 (April 2002): 99–104; Max Montesino, "Strategic Alignment of Training, Transfer-Enhancing Behaviors, and Training Usage: A Posttraining Study," *Human Resource Development Quarterly* 13, no. 1 (Spring 2002): 89–108; Siriporn Yamnill and Gary McLean, "Theories Supporting Transfer of Training," *Human Resource Development Quarterly* 12, no. 2 (Summer 2001): 195–208.

44. Delahoussaye, "Show Me the Results," 28–29; van Brakel, "Why ROI Isn't Enough," 72–74.

45. Richard J. Wagner and Robert J. Weigand, "Can the Value of Training Be Measured? A Simplified Approach to Evaluating Training," *The Health Care Manager* 23, no. 1 (January–March 2004): 71–79; van Brakel, "Why ROI Isn't Enough," 72–74; Sarah Fister Gale, "Measuring the ROI of E-Learning," *Workforce* 81, no. 8 (August 2002): 74–77; Earl Honeycutt, Kiran Karande, Ashraf Attia, and Steven Maurer, "A Utility-Based Framework for Evaluating the Financial Impact of Sales Force Training Programs," *Journal of Personal Selling and Sales Management* 21, no. 3 (Summer 2001): 229–38.

46. "Three Quick and Easy Ways to Gauge Your Training Outcomes," *IOMA's Report on Managing Training & Development* (January 2005): 4–5; "Use This Eight-Step Process to Predict the ROI of Your Training Programs," *IOMA's Human Resource Department Management Report* (December 2004): 4–5; Ellen Drost, Colette Frayne, Keven Lowe, and J. Michael Geringer, "Benchmarking Training and Development Practices: A Multi-Country Comparative

Analysis," *Human Resource Management* 41, no. 1 (Spring 2002): 67–86; Daniel McMurrer, Mark Van Buren, and William Woodwell, "Making the Commitment," *Training and Development* 54, no. 1 (January 2000): 41–48.

47. Lisa Bertagnoli, "Basic Training: Orientation Is Proving to Be an Important First Step in Establishing Employee Bonds That Last," *WWD* (September 30, 2004): 40S; Jonathan Thom, "Creating Effective Orientation Programs," *San Diego Business Journal* 25, no. 33 (August 16, 2004): A6; Howard Klein and Natasha Weaver, "The Effectiveness of an Organizational-Level Orientation Training Program in the Socialization of New Hires," *Personnel Psychology* 53, no. 1 (Spring 2000): 47–66.

48. Kathryn Tyler, "Take New Employee Orientation off the Back Burner," *HRMagazine* 43, no. 6 (May 1998): 49–57; Noel Tichy, "No Ordinary Boot Camp," *Harvard Business Review* 79, no. 4 (April 2001): 63–70.

49. Mike Frost, "Creative New Employee Orientation Programs," *HRMagazine* 47, no. 8 (August 2002): 120–21; Marilyn Moats Kennedy, "Setting the Right Tone, Right Away," *Across the Board* 36, no. 4 (April 1999): 51–52.

50. Emmanuella Plakoyiannaki, Nikolaos Tzokas, Pavlos Dimitratos, and Michael Saren, "How Critical Is Employee Orientation for Customer Relationship Management? Insights from a Case Study," *Journal of Management Studies* 45, no. 2 (March 2008): 268–293.

51. Anne C. Lewis, "Necessary Basic Skills," *Tech Directions* 66, no. 4 (November 2006):

6–8; "How to Prepare for Training's Critical Role in the Labor Force of the Future," *IOMA's Report on Managing Training & Development* (September 2004): 2–3; Steve Hook, "Basic Skills Training on Target," *Times Educational Supplement* 4444 (August 31, 2001): 39.

52. "Corporate America Can't Write," *Work & Family Newsbrief* (January 2005): 4; Matt Bolch, "School at Work," *Training* 39, no. 2 (February 2002); Slav Kanyba, "Community Colleges React to Job-Training Request," *San Fernando Valley Business Journal* 9, no. 2 (June 7, 2004): 1–2.

53. Michael A. Verespej, "The Education Difference," *Industry Week* 245, no. 9 (May 6, 1996): 11–14; Richard D. Zalman, "The Basics of In-House Skills Training," *HRMagazine* 34, no. 2 (February 1990): 74–78; Ron Zemke, "Workplace Illiteracy—Shall We Overcome?" *Training* 26, no. 6 (June 1989): 33–39.

54. "Eduardo Salas, Diana R. Nichols, and James E. Driskell, "Testing Three Team Training Strategies in Intact Teams A Meta-Analysis," *Small Group Research* (August 2007); "What Makes Teams Work?" *HRFocus* 79, no. 4 (April 2002): S1–S3; John Annett, David Cunningham, and Peter Mathias-Jones, "A Method for Measuring Team Skills," *Ergonomics* 43, no. 8 (August 2000): 1076–94.

55. "Behavior-Based Sales Team Training Produces a 56% Increase in Revenues," *Managing Training & Development* (April 2004): 1.

56. J. K. Winch, X Cai, and G.L. Vairaktarakis, "Cyclic Job Scheduling in Paced Assembly Lines with Cross-Trained Workers,"

International Journal of Production Research 45, no. 4 (February 2, 2007): 803–828; Lisa Bertagnoli, "The Ten-Minute Manager's Guide to . . . Cross-Training Staff," *Restaurants & Institutions* 114, no. 18 (August 15, 2004): 26–28; Wallace J. Hopp and Mark P. Van Oyen, "Agile Workforce Evaluation: A Framework for Cross-Training and Coordination," *IIE Transactions* 36, no. 10 (October 2004): 919–41.

57. Lorraine Mirabella, "Productivity Gains in Maryland Mean Less Hiring But More Job Cross-Training," *The Baltimore Sun* (*via Knight-Ridder/Tribune Business News*) (April 17, 2004).

58. "Ethics Codes and Ethics Training Issue Brief," *Business for Social Responsibility* (March 2005): http://www.bsr.org/research/issue-brief-details.cfm?DocumentID=50967; Nan Demars, "Office Ethics: News from the Front Lines," *Office Pro* 68, no. 3 (April 2008): 28–31.

59. Gary Stern, "Small Slights Bring Big Problems," *Workforce* 81, no. 8 (August 2002): 17; Bill Leonard, "Ways to Tell If a Diversity Program Is Measuring Up," *HRMagazine* 47, no. 7 (July 2002): 21.

60. "49ers Decide to Add Diversity to Training Camp," *The New York Times*, July 8, 2004, D3; Irwin Speizer, "Diversity on the Menu: Rachelle Hood, Denny's Chief Diversity Officer, Has Boosted the Company's Image. But That Hasn't Sold More Breakfasts," *Workforce Management* 83, no. 12 (November 1, 2004): 41.

61. Matthew Budman, "What Works—and What Doesn't," *Conference Board Review* 44, no. 4 (July–August 2007): 22–23.

Appraising and Improving Performance

After studying this chapter, you should be able to

Objective | **1**

Explain the purposes of performance appraisals and the reasons they can sometimes fail. Identify the characteristics of an effective appraisal program.

Objective | **2**

Describe the different sources of appraisal information.

© KAYTIE M DEIOMA/PHOTOEDIT

Objective 3

Explain the various methods used for performance evaluation.

Objective 4

Outline the characteristics of an effective performance appraisal interview.

In the preceding chapters, we have discussed some of the most effective methods available to managers for acquiring and developing top-notch employees. But talented employees are not enough—successful organizations are particularly adept at engaging their workforce to achieve goals that benefit the organization as well as the individuals.

In this chapter, we turn to performance appraisal programs, which are a helpful tool organizations can use to maintain and enhance their productivity and facilitate progress toward their strategic goals. Although we will focus mainly on formal performance appraisal procedures, the processes of managing and evaluating performance can be informal as well—and should be. In addition to formally appraising their employees in writing at regular intervals, as you will learn in this chapter, managers should offer them continual on-the-job feedback.[1] It is safe to say that the ultimate success or failure of a performance appraisal program depends on the philosophy underlying it, its connection with the firm's business goals, and the attitudes and skills of those responsible for its administration. Many different methods can be used to gather information about employee performance. Gathering information is only one step in the appraisal process. The information must be evaluated in the context of the organization's needs and communicated to employees so that it will result in high levels of performance.

PERFORMANCE APPRAISAL PROGRAMS

performance appraisal

A process, typically performed annually by a supervisor for a subordinate, designed to help employees understand their roles, objectives, expectations, and performance success

performance management

The process of creating a work environment in which people can perform to the best of their abilities

The performance appraisal can be defined as a process—typically delivered annually, biannually, or sometimes quarterly by a supervisor to a subordinate—designed to help employees understand their roles, objectives, expectations, and performance success. In addition, new employees are often put on probationary status for a period of time and evaluated 30, 60, or 90 days after being hired, with their continued employment contingent upon their performing satisfactorily. Performance management is the process of creating a work environment in which people can perform to the best of their abilities. It is a whole work system that begins when a job is defined. Formal programs for performance appraisal and merit ratings are by no means new to organizations. The federal government began evaluating employees in 1842, when Congress passed a law mandating yearly performance reviews for department clerks. From this early beginning, performance appraisal programs have spread to large and small organizations in both the public and private sectors. Advocates see these HR programs as among the most logical means to appraise, develop, and effectively utilize the knowledge and abilities of employees. However, as we have indicated, a growing number of observers point out that performance appraisals frequently fall short of their potential. In an ongoing survey of employee attitudes by the HR consulting firm Watson Wyatt, only 30 percent of employees said they thought their company's performance management process actually improved employee performance; only one in five thought it helped poorly performing employees do better.[2]

The push toward teamwork, continuous improvement, learning, and the like has caused numerous organizations to rethink their approach to appraisal. Some have warned that performance appraisal may discourage teamwork because it frequently focuses on individual achievement that produces a self-focus rather than a team focus. Others contend that appraisals are useful only at the extremes—for highly effective or highly ineffective employees—and are not as useful for the majority of employees in the middle. Still others point out that appraisals often focus on short-term achievements rather than long-term improvement and learning. They are sometimes too subjective or inconsistent or autocratic in that they create a distance between managers and employees rather than creating a team environment. Companies such as Xerox, Motorola, and Procter & Gamble have modified their performance appraisals to better acknowledge the importance of teamwork, continuous improvement, quality, and the like. Each of these issues is discussed at greater length throughout the chapter.[3]

The Purposes of Performance Appraisal

It might seem at first glance that performance appraisals are used for a rather narrow purpose—to evaluate who is doing a good job (or not). But in reality performance appraisals are one of the most versatile tools available to managers. They can serve many purposes that benefit both the organization and the employee whose performance is being appraised.

Figure 8.1 shows the most common uses of performance appraisals. In general, these can be classified as either *administrative* or *developmental*.

1 | **Objective**

Administrative Purposes

From the standpoint of administration, appraisal programs provide input that can be used for the entire range of HRM activities. For example, research has shown that performance appraisals are used most widely as a basis for compensation decisions. The practice of "pay-for-performance"—basing employees' pay on their achievements—is found in all types of organizations, and studies have shown employees who earn performance-based pay are more satisfied.[4]

Performance appraisals are also directly related to a number of other major HR functions, such as promotions, transfers, and layoff decisions. Performance appraisal

FIGURE 8.1

Purposes for Performance Appraisal

DEVELOPMENTAL	ADMINISTRATIVE
Provide performance feedback	Document personnel decisions
Identify individual strengths/weaknesses	Determine promotion candidates
Recognize individual performance	Determine transfers and assignments
Assist in goal identification	Identify poor performance
Evaluate goal achievement	Decide retention or termination
Identify individual training needs	Decide on layoffs
Determine organizational training needs	Validate selection criteria
Reinforce authority structure	Meet legal requirements
Allow employees to discuss concerns	Evaluate training programs/progress
Improve communication	Personnel planning
Provide a forum for leaders to help	Make reward/compensation decisions

data may also be used in HR planning, in determining the relative worth of jobs under a job evaluation program, and as criteria for recruiting particular types of employees and validating selection tests. Performance appraisals also provide a "paper trail" for documenting HRM actions that can result in legal action. Because of government EEO/AA directives, employers must maintain accurate, objective employee performance records in order to defend themselves against possible charges of discrimination when it comes to promotions, salaries, and terminations. Finally, it is important to recognize that the success of the entire HR program depends on knowing how the performance of employees compares with the goals established for them. This knowledge is best derived from a carefully planned and administered HR appraisal program.

Although appraisals often fall short of perfect, good appraisal systems have the capability to influence employee behavior and improve organizational performance. Indeed, research shows that organizations with strong performance management systems are 40 to 50 percent more likely to outperform their competitors in the areas of revenue growth, productivity, profitability, and market value.[5]

Developmental Purposes

From the standpoint of individual development, appraisal provides the feedback essential for discussing an employee's strengths and weaknesses as well as improving his or her performance. Regardless of the employee's level of performance, the appraisal process provides managers and employees with the opportunity to discuss ways to build on their strengths, eliminate potential weaknesses, identify problems, and set new goals for achieving high performance. Performance appraisals are also used to develop training and development plans for employees. By taking a developmental approach to appraisals, managers help employees understand that the appraisals are being conducted to improve their future competencies and further their careers and are not being conducted simply to judge them based on their past performance. Having a sound basis for improving performance is one of the major benefits of an appraisal program.

Companies such as Best Buy and EDS have redesigned their performance appraisal systems to focus more on employee development and learning. EDS, for example, integrated its performance appraisal system to work in concert with the company's learning and career management objectives. The new system, called the Career Resource System, includes a detailed job description, performance review, and career planner to track employees' long-term goals, as well as access to the company's automated career library. The system is ultimately linked to the company's succession policies. By creating this overall system, EDS hopes to shift the role of manager from that of "judge" to one of "coach."[6]

Why Appraisal Programs Sometimes Fail

Although performance appraisals can be a very useful and powerful tool to managers, in actual practice and for a number of reasons, formal appraisal programs sometimes yield disappointing results. Figure 8.2 shows that the primary culprits include lack of top management information and support, unclear performance standards, biased ratings because managers lack training, too many time-consuming forms to complete, and use of the program for conflicting purposes. For example, if an appraisal program is used to determine an employee's future pay and at the same time to motivate the

FIGURE

8.2

Let Me Count the Ways...

There are many reasons why performance appraisal systems might not be effective. Some of the most common problems include the following:

- Inadequate preparation on the part of the manager.

- Employee is not given clear objectives at the beginning of performance period.

- Manager may not be able to observe performance or have all the information.

- Performance standards may not be clear.

- Inconsistency in ratings among supervisors or other raters.

- Manager rating personality rather than performance.

- The halo effect, contrast effect, or some other perceptual bias.

- Inappropriate time span (either too short or too long).

- Overemphasis on uncharacteristic performance.

- Inflated ratings because managers do not want to deal with "bad news."

- Subjective or vague language in written appraisals.

- Organizational politics or personal relationships cloud judgments.

- No thorough discussion of causes of performance problems.

- Manager may not be trained at evaluation or giving feedback.

- No follow-up and coaching after the evaluation.

Sources: Patricia Evres, "Problems to Avoid during Performance Evaluations," *Air Conditioning, Heating & Refrigeration News* 216, no. 16 (August 19, 2002): 24–26; Clinton Longnecker and Dennis Gioia, "The Politics of Executive Appraisals," *Journal of Compensation and Benefits* 10, no. 2 (1994): 5–11; "Seven Deadly Sins of Performance Appraisals," *Supervisory Management* 39, no. 1 (1994): 7–8.

person to perform better, the two purposes can end up conflicting with one another. Often when salary decisions are discussed during a performance appraisal, they tend to become the dominant topic of conversation, and managers spend a lot of time justifying their pay decisions. As a result, ways to improve the employee's future job performance get less discussion.

As with all HR practices, if the support of a firm's top managers is lacking, the appraisal program will not be successful. Even the best-conceived program will not work in an environment where appraisers are not encouraged by their superiors to take the program seriously. To underscore the importance of this responsibility, top management should announce that effectiveness in appraising subordinates is a standard by which the appraisers themselves will be evaluated.

Other reasons performance appraisal programs can fail to yield the desired results include the following:

1. There is little face-to-face discussion between the manager and the employee being appraised.

2. The relationship between the employee's job description and the criteria on the appraisal form is not clear.

3. Managers feel that little or no benefit will be derived from the time and energy they spend on the process, or they are concerned only with bad performances.

4. Managers dislike the face-to-face confrontation of appraisal interviews.

5. Managers are not sufficiently adept at rating employees or providing them with appraisal feedback.

6. The judgmental role of appraisal conflicts with the helping role of developing employees.

7. The appraisal is just a once-a-year event, and there is little follow-up afterward.

In many organizations, performance appraisals are conducted only once a year. And while this is appropriate in many circumstances, an increasing number of organizations are finding value in conducting them on a semiannual and even quarterly basis. An important principle of performance appraisal is that continual feedback and employee coaching must be a regularly occurring activity. The annual or semi-annual performance review should simply be a logical extension of the day-to-day managerial process. It has been found that providing employees with feedback on a continual basis not only improves their performance, but also helps them know where they stand in terms of their performance. As a result, the anxiety they experience during formal appraisals is often alleviated. Some organizations, such as SAS, Del Taco, and others, do not perform formal evaluations and use coaching, individual development plans, or other feedback systems instead.

One of the main concerns employees have relates to the fairness of the performance appraisal systems of their firms. Organizational politics, a firm's culture, the orientation of its managers, history, and current competitive conditions can all affect how managers conduct and rate their employees.[7] For example, managers sometimes inflate evaluations because they want to obtain higher salaries for their employees or because higher ratings for their subordinates make them look good as supervisors. Alternatively, managers might want to get rid of troublesome employees by inflating their ratings and passing them off to another department. Even when appraisals are supposed to be confidential, employees often have a keen sense about whether the process is fair or not, or at least they think they do. Employees who believe the system is unfair are likely to consider the appraisal interview a waste of time and leave the interview feeling frustrated and cynical. Also, they may view compliance with the appraisal system as perfunctory and thus play only a passive role during the interview process. By addressing these employee concerns during the planning stage of the appraisal process and reassuring them that they can meet the requirements, and will be rewarded accordingly, an appraisal program is more likely to be successful.[8]

DEVELOPING AN EFFECTIVE APPRAISAL PROGRAM

The HR department ordinarily has the primary responsibility for overseeing and coordinating a firm's appraisal program. However, managers from the company's operating departments must also be actively involved, particularly when it comes to helping establish the objectives for the program. Furthermore, employees are more likely to accept and be satisfied with the performance appraisal program when they have the chance to participate in its development. Their concerns about the fairness and accuracy of the program insofar as it determines their raises, promotions, and the like tend to be alleviated somewhat when they have been involved at the planning stage and have helped develop the performance standards themselves.

What Are the Performance Standards?

Before any appraisal is conducted, the standards by which performance is to be evaluated should be clearly defined and communicated to the employee. As discussed in Chapter 4, these standards should be based on job-related requirements derived from job analysis and reflected in an employee's job description and job specifications. When performance standards are properly established, they help translate an organization's goals and objectives into job requirements that communicate to employees the definitions of acceptable and unacceptable performance levels.

As shown in Figure 8.3, there are four basic considerations in establishing performance standards: strategic relevance, criterion deficiency, criterion contamination, and reliability.

Strategic Relevance

Strategic relevance refers to the extent to which the standards of an appraisal relate to the strategic objectives of the organization in which they are applied. For example, if an organization has established a standard that "95 percent of all customer complaints are to be resolved in one day," then it is relevant for the customer service representatives to be held to this standard when they are evaluated. Companies such

FIGURE 8.3   Establishing Performance Standards

Criterion contamination: Elements that affect the appraisal measures that are not part of the actual performance

Performance measures

Zone of valid assessment

Strategic relevance: Performance standards linked to organizational goals and competencies

Reliability: Measures that are consistent across raters and over time

Actual performance

Criterion deficiency: Aspects of actual performance that are not measured as 3M and Buckman Laboratories have strategic objectives to the effect that 25 to 30 percent of their sales are to be generated from products developed within the past five years. These objectives are then translated into performance standards for their employees. General Motors and Whirlpool's strategic objectives include cost, quality, and speed, and the two companies have developed metrics to identify and compare their performance around the world on these measures. A strategy-driven performance appraisal process also provides the documentation HR managers need to justify various training expenses in order to close any gaps between employees' current skills and those they will need in the future to execute the firm's strategy.[9]

Criterion Deficiency

A second consideration in establishing performance standards is the extent to which the standards capture the entire range of an employee's responsibilities. When performance standards focus on a single criterion (such as sales revenues) to the exclusion of other important but less quantifiable performance dimensions (such as customer service), then the appraisal system is said to suffer from criterion deficiency.[10]

Criterion Contamination

Just as performance criteria can be deficient, they can also be contaminated. There are factors outside an employee's control that can influence his or her performance. A comparison of performance of production workers, for example, should not be contaminated by the fact that some work with newer machines than others do. A comparison of the performance of traveling salespeople should not be contaminated by the fact that territories differ in sales potential.[11]

Reliability

As we discussed in Chapter 6, reliability refers to the stability or consistency of a standard, or the extent to which individuals tend to maintain a certain level of performance over time. In terms of appraisal ratings, reliability can be measured by correlating two sets of ratings made by a single rater or by two different raters. For example, two managers would rate the same individual and estimate his or her suitability for a promotion. Their ratings would then be compared to determine inter-rater reliability.

calibration

A process whereby managers meet to discuss the performance of individual employees to ensure their employee appraisals are in line with one another

A new process some companies are now using to make sure managers are rating employees consistently is called calibration. During calibration meetings, a group of supervisors, led by their managers and facilitated by a HR professional, discuss the performance of individual employees to ensure all managers apply similar standards to all of the firm's employees. The supervisors begin the process by rating employees whose performances are especially good or especially poor. They then attempt to rate employees who lie more in the middle and try to achieve a consensus on their performance. Initially, the ratings are likely to vary considerably simply because some managers are hard raters and others are not. Over subsequent evaluation periods and calibration meetings, however, the ratings should begin to converge, or become more similar. Calibration meetings can be particularly helpful after a merger or acquisition—especially one that is global. Why? Because differences in the corporate cultures and the appraisal standards of the formerly separate companies can cause the same employees to be rated quite differently. For example, when Lawson Software, a Minnesota-headquartered firm, grew from 1,400 employees in 3 countries to 4,000 employees in 30 countries, it successfully used calibration to be sure its managers across the globe were assessing employees accurately.[12]

Performance standards also permit managers to specify and communicate precise information to employees regarding quality and quantity of output. This is why the standards should be defined in quantifiable and measurable terms and written down. For example, "the ability and willingness to handle customer orders" is not as good a performance standard as "all customer orders will be filled in four hours with a 98 percent accuracy rate." When the standard is expressed in specific, measurable terms, comparing an employee's performance against the standard results in a more accurate and justifiable appraisal.

Are You Complying with the Law?

Because performance appraisals are used as one basis for HRM actions, they must meet certain legal requirements. In *Brito v. Zia*, for example, the Supreme Court ruled that performance appraisals were subject to the same validity criteria as selection procedures.[13] As the courts have made clear, a central issue is to have carefully defined and measurable performance standards. In one landmark case involving test validation, *Albemarle Paper Company v. Moody* (discussed in Chapter 3), the U.S. Supreme Court found that employees had been ranked against a vague standard, open to each supervisor's own interpretation. The Court stated that "there is no way of knowing precisely what criteria of job performance the supervisors were considering, whether each supervisor was considering the same criteria, or whether, indeed, any of the supervisors actually applied a focused and stable body of criteria of any kind."[14] This decision has prompted organizations to try to eliminate vagueness in descriptions of traits such as attitude, cooperation, dependability, initiative, and leadership. For example, the trait "dependability" can be made much less vague if it is spelled out in terms of employee tardiness and/or unexcused absences. In general, reducing the room for subjective judgments will improve the entire appraisal process.

Furthermore, other court decisions show that employers might face legal challenges to their appraisal systems when appraisals indicate an employee's performance is acceptable or above-average performance, but then the person is later passed over for promotion, disciplined for poor performance, discharged, or laid off from the organization. In these cases, the performance appraisals can undermine the legitimacy of the subsequent personnel decision. Intel, for example, was taken to court by a group of former employees on grounds that the performance appraisal system (used for layoff decisions) was unreliable and invalid. Other companies such as Goodyear and Ford have also faced legal battles because their performance appraisals were viewed as discriminatory against older workers.[15] In light of court cases such as these, performance appraisals should meet the following legal guidelines:

- Performance ratings must be job-related, with performance standards developed through a job analysis.

- Employees must be given a written copy of their job standards in advance of their appraisals.

- Managers who conduct the appraisals must be able to observe the behavior they are rating. This implies having measurable standards with which to compare employee behavior.

> Specific, measurable job standards help remove vagueness and subjectivity from performance appraisals.

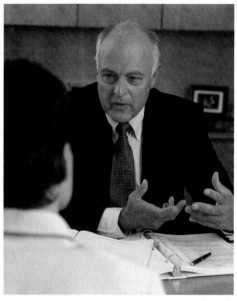

© BILL VARIE/CORBIS

- Supervisors should be trained to use the appraisal form correctly. They should be instructed as to how to apply the appraisal standards when making judgments.

- The appraisals should be discussed openly with employees and counseling or corrective guidance offered to help poor performers improve their performance.

- An appeals procedure should be established to enable employees to express their disagreement with the appraisals.[16]

To comply with the legal requirements of performance appraisals, employers must ensure that managers and supervisors document appraisals and reasons for subsequent HRM actions. This information may prove decisive should an employee take legal action. An employer's credibility is strengthened when it can support performance appraisal ratings by documenting instances of poor performance.

Who Should Appraise Performance?

Just as there are multiple standards by which to evaluate performance, there are also multiple candidates for appraising performance. Given the complexity of today's jobs, it is often unrealistic to presume that one person can fully observe and evaluate an employee's performance. At IBM, employees with high potential are regularly reviewed by a broad cross section of the company's leaders, not just their immediate bosses. As shown in Figure 8.4, raters may include supervisors, peers, team members, self, subordinates, customers, vendors, and suppliers. Each may be more or less useful for the administrative and developmental purposes we discussed earlier. Companies such as Cigna, Black & Decker, and Disney have used a multiple-rater approach—or 360-degree appraisal—to evaluate employee performance.[17] We will talk more about 360-degree appraisal at the end of this section.

Manager/Supervisor Appraisal

manager and/ or supervisor appraisal
A performance appraisal done by an employee's manager and often reviewed by a manager one level higher

Manager and/or supervisor appraisal has been the traditional approach to evaluating an employee's performance. In most instances, supervisors are in the best position to perform this function, although it may not always be possible for them to do so. Managers often complain that they do not have the time to fully observe the performance of employees. These managers must then rely on performance records to evaluate an employee's performance. If reliable and valid measures are not available, the appraisal may be less than accurate. (Recall our earlier discussion of criterion deficiency and criterion contamination.) In addition, research has shown that the ratings managers give employees they have known for less than one year are less reliable.[18] When a supervisor appraises employees independently, provision is often made for a

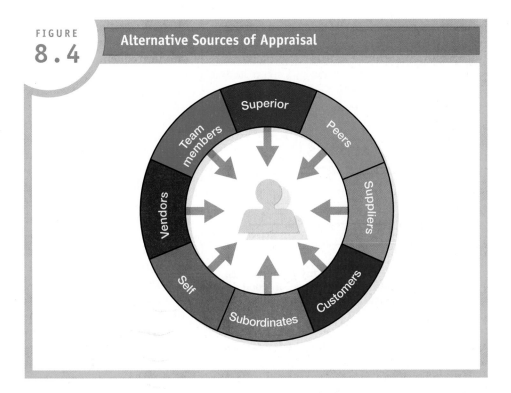

FIGURE
8.4

Alternative Sources of Appraisal

review of the appraisals by the supervisor's superior. Having appraisals reviewed by a supervisor's superior reduces the chance of superficial or biased evaluations.

Self-Appraisal

Sometimes employees are asked to evaluate themselves on a self-appraisal form. The self-appraisal is beneficial when managers seek to increase an employee's involvement in the review process. A self-appraisal system requires an employee to complete the appraisal form prior to the performance interview. At a minimum, this gets the employee thinking about his or her strengths and weaknesses and may lead to discussions about barriers to effective performance. During the performance interview, the manager and the employee discuss job performance and agree on a final appraisal. This approach also works well when the manager and the employee jointly establish future performance goals or employee development plans. Critics of self-appraisal argue that self-raters are more lenient than managers in their assessments and tend to present themselves in a highly favorable light. There is also evidence that self-appraisals can lead employees to believe that they will have more influence over the appraisal's outcome. If that expectation is not met, the employee can become frustrated. For this reason, self-appraisals may be best for developmental purposes rather than for administrative decisions. Used in conjunction with other methods, self-appraisals can be a valuable source of appraisal information. They at least serve as a catalyst for discussion during the appraisal.[19]

Subordinate Appraisal

Subordinate appraisals have been used by both large and small organizations to give managers feedback on how their subordinates view them.[19] Subordinates are in

self-appraisal

A performance appraisal done by the employee being evaluated, generally on an appraisal form completed by the employee prior to the performance interview

subordinate appraisal

A performance appraisal of a superior by an employee, which is more appropriate for developmental than for administrative purposes

Pepper ... and Salt

THE WALL STREET JOURNAL

"Good news, Honey. On my performance appraisal I got four 'Atta boys,' a 'good dog' and he scratched behind my ears."

a good position to evaluate their managers because they are in frequent contact with their superiors and occupy a unique position from which to observe many performance-related behaviors. Subordinate appraisals have also been shown to improve the performance of managers. The performance dimensions judged most appropriate for subordinates to appraise include a manager's leadership, oral communication, delegation of authority, coordination of team efforts, and interest in his or her subordinates. However, dimensions related to managers' specific job tasks, such as planning and organizing, budgeting, creativity, and analytical ability, are not usually considered appropriate dimensions for subordinates to appraise. Because subordinate appraisals give employees power over their bosses, managers may be hesitant to endorse such a system, particularly when it might be used as a basis for compensation decisions. However, when the information is used for developmental purposes, managers tend to be more open to the idea. Available evidence suggests that when managers heed the advice of their subordinates, their own performance can improve substantially. Nevertheless, to avoid potential problems, subordinate appraisals should be submitted anonymously and combined across several individual raters.[20]

Peer Appraisal

peer appraisal

A performance appraisal done by one's fellow employees, generally on forms that are compiled into a single profile for use in the performance interview conducted by the employee's manager

Individuals of equal rank who work together are increasingly asked to evaluate each other. A peer appraisal provides information that differs to some degree from ratings by a superior, since an employee's peers often see different dimensions of his or her performance. Peers can readily identify leadership and interpersonal skills along with other strengths and weaknesses of their coworkers. For example, a superior asked to rate a patrol officer on a dimension such as "dealing with the public" might not have had much opportunity to observe it. Fellow officers, on the other hand, have the opportunity to observe this behavior regularly.

One advantage of peer appraisals is the belief that they furnish more accurate and valid information than appraisals by superiors. The supervisor often sees employees putting their best foot forward, while those who work with their fellow employees on a regular basis may see a more realistic picture. With peer appraisals, coworkers complete an evaluation on the employee. The forms are then usually compiled into a single profile, which is given to the supervisor for use in the final appraisal. For employees who have trouble confronting their coworkers about problems, the reviews provide a forum in which to address issues and resolve conflicts. They also provide an opportunity to hand out praise.[21]

Despite the evidence that peer appraisals are possibly the most accurate method of judging employee behavior, there are reasons why they have not been used more frequently.[22] The reasons commonly cited include the following:

1. Peer ratings are simply a popularity contest.

2. Managers are reluctant to give up control over the appraisal process.

3. Those receiving low ratings might retaliate against their peers.

4. Peers rely on stereotypes in ratings.

When peers, such as with sales associates, for example, are in competition with one another, peer appraisals should not be used to make administrative decisions such as salary or bonuses. Employers using peer appraisals must also be sure to safeguard confidentiality in handling the review forms. Any breach of confidentiality can create interpersonal rivalries or hurt feelings and foster hostility among fellow employees.

Team Appraisal

An extension of the peer appraisal is the team appraisal. In a team setting, it may be nearly impossible to separate out an individual's contribution. Advocates of team appraisals argue that, in such cases, individual appraisals can be dysfunctional because it detracts from the critical issues of the team. To address this issue, organizations ranging from Boeing and Texas Instruments to Jostens and Ralston Foods have begun developing team appraisals to evaluate the performance of their teams as a whole.[23] These companies believe that team appraisals can help break down barriers between individual employees and encourage a joint effort on their part.

Much of the interest in team appraisals grew out of company commitments to total quality management (TQM) in the 1980s. But the principles and practices are no less

> **Using the Internet**
>
> A lengthy but insightful description of the implementation of a peer appraisal system in conjunction with self-directed work teams at the Racine liquid manufacturing facility of S. C. Johnson & Son, Inc., appears on their Web site. Go to the Student Resources at:
>
> **www.cengage.com/ management/bohlander**

team appraisal
A performance appraisal, based on TQM concepts, that recognizes team accomplishment rather than individual performance

Some managers give their teams autonomy but hold them accountable for results.

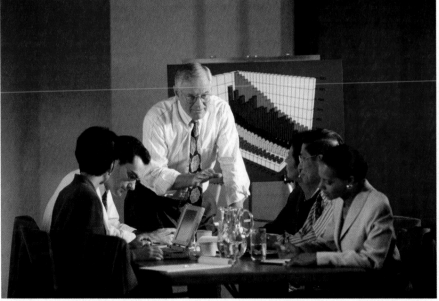

© THE IMAGE BANK/GETTY IMAGES

relevant today. At its root, TQM is a control system that involves setting standards (based on customer requirements), measuring a firm's performance against those standards, and identifying opportunities for continuous improvement. In this regard, TQM and performance appraisals complement one another. However, a basic tenet of TQM is that a firm's performance is best understood at the level of the system as a whole, whereas performance appraisals traditionally focus on individual performance.[24] Frequently, the system is complemented by the use of team incentives or group variable pay. (See Chapters 10 and 16.)

Customer Appraisal

customer appraisal

A performance appraisal that, like team appraisal, is based on TQM concepts and seeks evaluation from both external and internal customers

Also driven by TQM concerns, an increasing number of organizations use internal and external customer appraisals as a source of performance appraisal information. External customers' evaluations, of course, have been used for some time to appraise restaurant personnel. However, companies such as Federal Express, Best Buy, and Isuzu are among the companies that have utilized external customers as well. Poor customer appraisals undoubtedly explain why some firms, including Dell and others, have reconsidered offshoring their customer service functions. Other companies survey their vendors and suppliers as part of the appraisal process. By including the firm's business partners in the performance reviews, managers hope to produce more objective evaluations, more effective employees, more satisfied customers, and better business performance.[25]

In contrast to external customers, internal customers include anyone inside the organization who depends on an employee's work output. For example, managers who rely on the HR department for selection and training services would be candidates for conducting internal customer evaluations of that department. For both developmental and administrative purposes, internal customers can provide extremely useful feedback about the value added by an employee or team of employees.

Using the Internet

Software used to help prepare 360-degree appraisal systems is available from a number of companies. For example, Quality Coach/360 software developed by Leadership Software Corp. combines total quality management (TQM), the coaching style of management, and 360-degree performance assessment. Go to the Student Resources at:

www.cengage.com/ management/bohlander

Putting It All Together: 360-Degree Appraisal

As mentioned previously, companies such as Intel and Morgan Stanley combine various sources of performance appraisal information to create multirater—or 360-degree—appraisal and feedback systems. Jobs are multifaceted, and different people see different things. As the name implies, 360-degree feedback is intended to provide employees with as accurate a view of their performance as possible by getting input from all angles: supervisors, peers, subordinates, customers, and the like. Although in the beginning, 360-degree systems were purely developmental and were restricted mainly to management and career development, they have migrated to performance appraisal and other administrative applications.

Because the system combines more information than a typical performance appraisal, it can become administratively complex. For that reason, organizations have recently begun using performance management software to compile and aggregate the information.[26] For example, Workstream 7.0 developed by Workstream, Inc., a Florida company, gives managers a single view of all their talent management information: performance reviews, 360 assessments, compensation planning, development data, and succession planning, all unified in one application.[27] Figure 8.5 shows a list of pros

FIGURE
8.5

Pros and Cons of 360-Degree Appraisal

PROS

- The system is more comprehensive in that responses are gathered from multiple perspectives.
- Quality of information is better. (Quality of respondents is more important than quantity.)
- It complements TQM initiatives by emphasizing internal/external customers and teams.
- It may lessen bias/prejudice since feedback comes from more people, not one individual.
- Feedback from peers and others may increase employee self-development.

CONS

- The system is complex in combining all the responses.
- Feedback can be intimidating and cause resentment if employee feels the respondents have "ganged up."
- There may be conflicting opinions, though they may all be accurate from the respective standpoints.
- The system requires training to work effectively.
- Employees may collude or "game" the system by giving invalid evaluations to one another.
- Appraisers may not be accountable if their evaluations are anonymous.

Sources: Compiled from David A. Waldman, Leanne E. Atwater, and David Antonioni, "Has 360-Degree Feedback Gone Amok?" *Academy of Management Executive* 12, no. 2 (May 1998): 86–94; Bruce Pfau, Ira Kay, Kenneth Nowak, and Jai Ghorpade, "Does 360-Degree Feedback Negatively Affect Company Performance?" *HRMagazine* 47, no. 6 (June 2002): 54–59; Maury Peiperl, "Getting 360-Degree Feedback Right," *Harvard Business Review* 79, no. 1 (January 2001): 142–47; Joyce E. Bono and Amy E. Colbert, "Understanding Responses to Multi-Source Feedback: The Role of Core Self-Evaluations," *Personnel Psychology* 58, no. 1 (Spring 2005): 171–205.

and cons of 360-degree appraisal. When Intel established a 360-degree system, the company observed the following safeguards to ensure its maximum quality and acceptance:

- *Assure anonymity.* Make certain that no employee ever knows how any evaluation team member responded. (The supervisor's rating is an exception to this rule.)

- *Make respondents accountable.* Supervisors should discuss each evaluation team member's input, letting each member know whether he or she used the rating scales appropriately, whether his or her responses were reliable, and how other participants rated the employee.

- *Prevent "gaming" of the system.* Some individuals may try to help or hurt an employee by giving either too high or too low an evaluation. Team members may try to collude with one another by agreeing to give each other uniformly high ratings. Supervisors should check for obviously invalid responses.

- *Use statistical procedures.* Use weighted averages or other quantitative approaches to combining evaluations. Supervisors should be careful about using subjective combinations of data, which could undermine the system.

- *Identify and quantify biases.* Check for prejudices or preferences related to age, gender, ethnicity, or other group factors.[28]

Training Appraisers

A weakness of many performance appraisal programs is that managers and supervisors are not adequately trained for the appraisal task, and so the feedback they provide their subordinates is not as useful as it might be and can often be meaningless, if not destructive. This is perhaps one reason why some experts believe firms should no longer conduct performance appraisals of their employees. However, training appraisers can vastly improve the performance appraisal process. According to one HR manager: "What's not important is the (appraisal) form or the (measuring) scale. What's important is that managers can objectively observe people's performance and objectively give feedback on that performance." Notwithstanding, in a survey of fifty-five HR managers from medium and large companies, more than half said their companies did either little or no evaluation of how well their managers do appraisals.[29]

Establishing an Appraisal Plan

A training program for raters is most effective when it follows a systematic process that begins with an explanation of the objectives of the firm's performance appraisal system. It is also important for the rater to know the purpose for which the appraisal is to be used. For example, using the appraisal for compensation decisions rather than development purposes can affect how the rater evaluates the employee, and it may change the rater's opinion of how the appraisal form should be completed. The mechanics of the rating system should also be explained, including how frequently the appraisals are to be conducted, who will conduct them, and what are the standards of performance. In addition, appraisal training should alert raters to the weaknesses and problems of appraisal systems so that they can be avoided.

Eliminating Rater Error

Appraisal training should focus on eliminating the subjective errors made by managers in the rating process. Gary Latham and Kenneth Wexley stress the importance of performance appraisal training by noting that

> [R]egardless of whether evaluations are obtained from multiple appraisers or from only the employee's immediate superior, all appraisers should be trained to reduce errors of judgment that occur when one person evaluates another. This training is necessary because to the degree to which a performance appraisal is biased, distorted, or inaccurate, the probability of increasing the productivity of the employee is greatly decreased. Moreover, wrong decisions could be made regarding whom to promote, retain, or replace, which in turn will penalize the organization's bottom line. In addition, when a performance appraisal is affected by rating errors, the employee may be justified in filing a discrimination charge.[30]

With any rating method, certain types of errors can arise that should be considered. The "halo error" discussed in Chapter 6 is also common with respect to rating scales, especially those that do not include carefully developed descriptions of the employee behaviors being rated. Provision for comments on the rating form tends to reduce halo error. The "horn error" is the opposite of the halo effect. It occurs when a manager focuses on one negative aspect about an employee and generalizes it into an overall poor appraisal rating. A personality conflict between a manager and his or her employees increases the probability of the horn effect, which can lead to a high level of frustration on the employee's part if it is not corrected.[31]

Some types of rating errors are *distributional errors* in that they involve a group of ratings given across various employees. For example, raters who are reluctant to assign either extremely high or extremely low ratings commit the error of central tendency. In this case, all employees are rated about average. To such raters, it is a good idea to explain that, among large numbers of employees, one should expect to find significant differences in their behavior, productivity, and other characteristics.

In contrast to central tendency errors, it is also common for some raters to give unusually high or low ratings. For example, a manager may erroneously assert, "All my employees are excellent" or "None of my people are good enough." These beliefs give rise to what is called leniency or strictness error.[32] One way to reduce this error is to clearly define the characteristics or dimensions of performance and to provide meaningful descriptions of behavior, known as "anchors," on the scale. Another approach is to require ratings to conform to a *forced ranking*, a type of system initially developed by GE, purportedly with good results. Managers appraising employees under a *forced distribution* system are required to place a certain percentage of employees into various performance categories. For example, it may be required that 10 percent of ratings be poor (or excellent). This is similar to the requirement in some schools that instructors grade on a curve. A variation of this is *peer ranking*, a system whereby employees in a work group are ranked against one another from best to worst. Although forced distribution and peer ranking may solve leniency and strictness errors, they can create other rating errors—particularly if most employees are performing above standard. Moreover, if the system has a disparate impact on a legally protected group, such as minority or older employers, it can result, and has resulted, in discrimination suits, which GE, among other companies, has experienced firsthand. Even so, more organizations are using forced ranking systems. However, other companies, including Ford and Goodyear, abandoned their forced ranking systems after lawsuits, lower morale, decreased teamwork, and destructive employee competition ensued following their use. In addition, not all corporate cultures are conducive to forced rankings systems. For example, at Starbucks, which fosters a corporate climate based on teamwork, using a forced ranking system would probably be counterproductive. Because of the legal issues related to forced ranking, companies that use these methods obviously need to carefully train their appraisers.[33]

Some rating errors are *temporal* in that the performance review is biased either favorably or unfavorably, depending on the way performance information is selected, evaluated, and organized by the rater over time. For example, when the appraisal is based largely on the employee's recent behavior, good or bad, the rater has committed the recency error. Managers who give higher ratings because

error of central tendency

A performance rating error in which all employees are rated about average

leniency or strictness error

A performance rating error in which the appraiser tends to give employees either unusually high or unusually low ratings

recency error

A performance rating error in which the appraisal is based largely on the employee's most recent behavior rather than on behavior throughout the appraisal period they believe an employee is "showing improvement" may unwittingly be committing recency error. Without work record documentation for the entire appraisal period, the rater is forced to recall recent employee behavior to establish the rating. Having the rater routinely document employee accomplishments and failures throughout the whole appraisal period can minimize the recency error. One way for managers to do this is by keeping a diary or a log. Rater training also will help reduce this error.

contrast error

A performance rating error in which an employee's evaluation is biased either upward or downward because of comparison with another employee just previously evaluated

Contrast error occurs when an employee's evaluation is biased either upward or downward because of another employee's performance, evaluated just previously. For example, an average employee may appear especially productive when compared with a poor performer. However, that same employee may appear unproductive when compared with a star performer. Contrast errors are most likely when raters are required to rank employees in order from the best to the poorest. Employees are evaluated against one another, usually on the basis of some organizational standard or guideline. For example, they may be compared on the basis of their ability to meet production standards or their "overall" ability to perform their job. As with other types of rating errors, contrast error can be reduced through training that focuses on using objective standards and behavioral anchors to appraise performance.[34]

similar-to-me error

A performance rating error in which an appraiser inflates the evaluation of an employee because of a mutual personal connection

The similar-to-me error occurs when appraisers inflate the evaluations of people with whom they have something in common. For example, if both the manager and the employee are from small towns, the manager may unwittingly have a more favorable impression of the employee. The effects of a similar-to-me error can be powerful, and when the similarity is based on race, religion, gender, or some other protected category, it can result in discrimination.

Furthermore, raters should be aware of any stereotypes they may hold toward particular groups—such as male/female or white/black—because the observation and interpretation of performance can be clouded by these stereotypes. For example, one study found that men who experience conflicts between family and work received lower overall performance ratings and lower reward recommendations than men who did not experience such conflicts. Women, on the other hand, were judged no differently, whether they experienced family-work conflicts or not. A host of organizations such as Sears and Weyerhaeuser have developed formal training programs to reduce the subjective errors commonly made during the rating process. This training can pay off, particularly when participants have the opportunity to (1) observe other managers making errors, (2) actively participate in discovering their own errors, and (3) practice job-related tasks to reduce the errors they tend to make.[35]

Feedback Training

Finally, a training program for raters should provide some general points to consider for planning and providing feedback during the appraisal interview. Managers need to understand that employees want feedback—that is, they want to know how they are doing and how they can improve. They are less eager to be appraised or judged. This is why it is important for their managers to provide them with ongoing feedback and not just "dump on them" during a formal appraisal. Feedback training should cover at least three basic areas: (1) communicating effectively, (2) diagnosing the root causes of performance problems, and (3) setting goals and objectives. A checklist like the one in Highlights in HRM 1 can be used to assist supervisors in preparing for the appraisal interview.[36]

1

Supervisor's Checklist for the Performance Appraisal

Scheduling

1. Schedule the review and notify the employee ten days to two weeks in advance.
2. Ask the employee to prepare for the session by reviewing his or her performance, job objectives, and development goals.
3. Clearly state that this will be the formal annual performance appraisal.

Preparing for the Review

1. Review the performance documentation collected throughout the year. Concentrate on work patterns that have developed.
2. Be prepared to give specific examples of above- or below-average performance.
3. When performance falls short of expectations, determine what changes need to be made. If performance meets or exceeds expectations, discuss this and plan how to reinforce it.
4. After the appraisal is written, set it aside for a few days and then review it again.
5. Follow whatever steps are required by your organization's performance appraisal system.

Conducting the Review

1. Select a location that is comfortable and free of distractions. The location should encourage a frank and candid conversation.
2. Discuss each topic in the appraisal one at a time, considering both strengths and shortcomings.
3. Be specific and descriptive, not general and judgmental. Report occurrences rather than evaluating them.
4. Discuss your differences and resolve them. Solicit agreement with the evaluation.
5. Jointly discuss and design plans for taking corrective action for growth and development.
6. Maintain a professional and supportive approach to the appraisal discussion.

■■ PERFORMANCE APPRAISAL METHODS

3 | Objective

Since the early years of their use by the federal government, methods of evaluating personnel have evolved considerably. Old systems have been replaced by new methods that reflect technical improvements and legal requirements and are more consistent with the purposes of appraisal. Likewise, paper appraisals are being replaced by electronic appraisals built into firms' performance management systems. In the discussion that follows, we will examine in some detail the methods that have found widespread use, and we will briefly touch on other methods that are used less frequently. Performance appraisal methods can be broadly classified as measuring traits, behaviors, or results. Trait approaches continue to be more popular despite their inherent subjectivity. Behavioral approaches provide more action-oriented information to employees and therefore may be best for development. The results-oriented approach is gaining popularity because it focuses on the measurable contributions that employees make to the organization.

Trait Methods

Trait approaches to performance appraisal are designed to measure the extent to which an employee possesses certain characteristics—such as dependability, creativity, initiative, and leadership—that are viewed as important for the job and the organization in general. The fact that trait methods are the most popular is due in a large part to the ease with which they are developed. However, if not designed carefully on the basis of job analysis, trait appraisals can be notoriously biased and subjective.

Graphic Rating Scales

graphic rating scale method

A trait approach to performance appraisal whereby each employee is rated according to a scale of characteristics

In the graphic rating scale method, each trait or characteristic to be rated is represented by a scale on which a rater indicates the degree to which an employee possesses that trait or characteristic. An example of this type of scale is shown in Highlights in HRM 2. There are many variations of the graphic rating scale. The differences are to be found in (1) the characteristics or dimensions on which individuals are rated, (2) the degree to which the performance dimension is defined for the rater, and (3) how clearly the points on the scale are defined. In Highlights in HRM 2, the dimensions are defined briefly, and some attempt is made to define the points on the scale. Subjectivity bias is reduced somewhat when the dimensions on the scale and the scale points are defined as precisely as possible. This can be achieved by training raters and by including descriptive appraisal guidelines in a performance appraisal reference packet.[37]

Also, the rating form should provide sufficient space for comments on the behavior associated with each scale. These comments improve the accuracy of the appraisal because they require the rater to think in terms of observable employee behaviors while providing specific examples to discuss with the employee during the appraisal interview.

Mixed-Standard Scales

mixed-standard scale method

A trait approach to performance appraisal similar to other scale methods but based on comparison with (better than, equal to, or worse than) a standard

The mixed-standard scale method is a modification of the basic rating scale method. Rather than evaluating traits according to a single scale, the rater is given three specific descriptions of each trait. These descriptions reflect three levels of performance: superior, average, and inferior. After the three descriptions for each trait are written, they are randomly sequenced to form the mixed-standard scale. As shown in Highlights in HRM 3, supervisors evaluate employees by indicating whether their performance is better than, equal to, or worse than the standard for each behavior.

Forced-Choice Method

forced-choice method

A trait approach to performance appraisal that requires the rater to choose from statements designed to distinguish between successful and unsuccessful performance

The forced-choice method requires the rater to choose from statements, often in pairs, that appear equally favorable or equally unfavorable. The statements, however,

2

Graphic Rating Scale with Provision for Comments

Appraise employee's performance in **PRESENT ASSIGNMENT**. Check (✔) most appropriate square. Appraisers are *urged to freely use* the "Remarks" sections for significant comments descriptive of the individual.

1. **KNOWLEDGE OF WORK:** Understanding of all phases of his/her work and related matters	Needs instruction or guidance		Has required knowledge of own and related work		Has exceptional knowledge of own and related work	
	☐	☐	☐	☑	☐	
	Remarks: *Is particularly good on gas engines.*					

2. **INITIATIVE:** Ability to originate or develop ideas and to get things started	Lacks imagination		Meets necessary requirements		Unusually resourceful	
	☐	☑	☐	☐	☐	
	Remarks: *Has good ideas when asked for an opinion, but otherwise will not offer them. Somewhat lacking in self-confidence.*					

3. **APPLICATION:** Attention and application to his/her work	Wastes time Needs close supervision		Steady and willing worker		Exceptionally industrious	
	☐	☐	☑	☐	☐	
	Remarks: *Accepts new jobs when assigned.*					

4. **QUALITY OF WORK:** Thoroughness, neatness, and accuracy of work	Needs improvement		Regularly meets recognized standards		Consistently maintains highest quality	
	☐	☐	☐	☑		
	Remarks: *The work he turns out is always of the highest possible quality.*					

5. **VOLUME OF WORK:** Quantity of acceptable work	Should be increased		Regularly meets recognized standards		Unusually high output	
	☐	☐	☑	☐	☐	
	Remarks: *Would be higher if he did not spend so much time checking and rechecking his work.*					

Example of a Mixed-Standard Scale

DIRECTIONS: Please indicate whether the individual's performance is above (+), equal to (0), or lower than (−) each of the following standards.

1. _____ Employee uses good judgment when addressing problems and provides workable alternatives; however, at times does not take actions to prevent problems. (*medium PROBLEM-SOLVING*)

2. _____ Employee lacks supervisory skills; frequently handles employees poorly and is at times argumentative. (*low LEADERSHIP*)

3. _____ Employee is extremely cooperative; can be expected to take the lead in developing cooperation among employees; completes job tasks with a positive attitude. (*high COOPERATION*)

4. _____ Employee has effective supervision skills; encourages productivity, quality, and employee development. (*medium LEADERSHIP*)

5. _____ Employee normally displays an argumentative or defensive attitude toward fellow employees and job assignments. (*low COOPERATION*)

6. _____ Employee is generally agreeable but becomes argumentative at times when given job assignments; cooperates with other employees as expected. (*medium COOPERATION*)

7. _____ Employee is not good at solving problems; uses poor judgment and does not anticipate potential difficulties. (*low PROBLEM-SOLVING*)

8. _____ Employee anticipates potential problems and provides creative, proactive alternative solutions; has good attention to follow-up. (*high PROBLEM-SOLVING*)

9. _____ Employee displays skilled direction; effectively coordinates unit activities; is generally a dynamic leader and motivates employees to high performance. (*high LEADERSHIP*)

are designed to distinguish between successful and unsuccessful performance. The rater selects one statement from the pair without knowing which statement correctly describes successful job behavior. For example, forced-choice pairs might include the following:

1. _____ a) Works hard   _____ b) Works quickly

2. _____ a) Shows initiative   _____ b) Is responsive to customers

3. _____ a) Produces poor quality   _____ b) Lacks good work habits

The forced-choice method is not without limitations, the primary one being the cost of establishing and maintaining its validity. The fact that it has been a source of frustration to many raters has sometimes caused the method to be eliminated from appraisal programs. In addition, it cannot be used as effectively as some of the other methods as a tool for developing employees.

Essay Method

Unlike rating scales, which provide a structured form of appraisal, the essay method requires the appraiser to compose a statement that best describes the employee being appraised. The appraiser is usually instructed to describe the employee's strengths and weaknesses and to make recommendations for his or her development. Often the essay method is combined with other rating methods. Essays may provide additional descriptive information on an employee's performance that cannot be generated with a structured rating scale, for example.

The essay method provides an excellent opportunity to point out the unique characteristics of the employee being appraised. This aspect of the method is heightened when a supervisor is instructed to describe specific points about the employee's promotability, special talents, skills, strengths, and weaknesses. A major limitation of the essay method is that composing an essay that attempts to cover all of an employee's essential characteristics is a very time-consuming task (though when combined with other methods, this method does not require a lengthy statement). Another disadvantage of the essay method is that the quality of the performance appraisal may be influenced by the supervisor's writing skills and composition style. Good writers may simply be able to produce more favorable appraisals. A final drawback of this appraisal method is that it tends to be subjective and may not focus on the relevant aspects of a person's job performance.

essay method
A trait approach to performance appraisal that requires the rater to compose a statement describing employee behavior

Behavioral Methods

As we mentioned, one of the potential drawbacks of a trait-oriented performance appraisal is that traits tend to be vague and subjective. We discussed earlier that one way to improve a rating scale is to have descriptions of behavior along a scale, or continuum. These descriptions permit the rater to readily identify the point where a particular employee falls on the scale. Behavioral methods have been developed to specifically describe which actions should (or should not) be exhibited on the job. They are often used to provide employees with developmental feedback.

Critical Incident Method

The critical incident method, described in Chapter 4 in connection with job analysis, is also used as a method of appraisal. Recall that a critical incident occurs when employee behavior results in unusual success or unusual failure in some part of the job. An example of a favorable critical incident occurs when a janitor observes that a file cabinet containing classified documents has been left unlocked at the close of business and calls the firm's security officer to correct the problem. An example of an unfavorable incident occurs when a mail clerk fails to deliver an Express Mail package immediately, instead putting it in with regular mail to be routed two hours later. The manager keeps a log or diary for each employee throughout the appraisal period and notes specific critical incidents related to how well they perform. When completing the appraisal form, the manager refers to the critical incident log and uses this information to substantiate an employee's rating of outstanding, satisfactory, or unsatisfactory in specific performance areas and overall. This method can also help a manager counsel employees when they are having performance problems while the problem is still minor. It also increases the objectivity of the appraisal by requiring the rater to use job performance criteria to justify the ratings.[38]

critical incident
An unusual event that denotes superior or inferior employee performance in some part of the job

Behavioral Checklist Method

One of the oldest appraisal techniques is the behavioral checklist method. It consists of having the rater check the statements on a list that the rater believes are characteristic of the employee's performance or behavior. A checklist developed for computer salespeople might include a number of statements such as the following:

_____ Is able to explain equipment clearly

_____ Keeps abreast of new developments in technology

_____ Tends to be a steady worker

_____ Reacts quickly to customers' needs

_____ Processes orders correctly

Behaviorally Anchored Rating Scale (BARS)

behaviorally anchored rating scale (BARS)

A behavioral approach to performance appraisal that consists of a series of vertical scales, one for each important dimension of job performance

A **behaviorally anchored rating scale (BARS)** consists of a series of five to ten vertical scales—one for each important dimension of performance identified through job analysis. These dimensions are anchored by behaviors identified through a critical incident job analysis. The critical incidents are placed along the scale and are assigned point values according to the opinions of experts. A BARS for the job of firefighter is shown in the upper portion of Highlights in HRM 4. Note that this particular scale is for the dimension described as "Firefighting Strategy: Knowledge of Fire Characteristics."

A BARS is typically developed by a committee that includes both subordinates and managers. The committee's task is to identify all the relevant characteristics or dimensions of the job. Behavioral anchors in the form of statements are then established for each of the job dimensions. Several participants are asked to review the anchor statements and indicate which job dimension each anchor illustrates. The only anchors retained are those that at least 70 percent of the group agrees belong with a particular dimension. Finally, anchors are attached to their job dimensions and are placed on the appropriate scales according to values that the group assigns to them.

At present there is no strong evidence that a BARS reduces all of the rating errors mentioned previously. However, some studies have shown that scales of this type can yield more accurate ratings. One major advantage of a BARS is that personnel outside the HR department participate with HR staff in its development. Employee participation can lead to greater acceptance of the performance appraisal process and of the performance measures that it uses.

The procedures followed in developing a BARS also result in scales that have a high degree of content validity. The main disadvantage of a BARS is that it requires considerable time and effort to develop. In addition, because the scales are specific to particular jobs, a scale designed for one job might not apply to another.

Using the Internet

Review example of BARS used for the state of Michigan. Go to the Student Resources at:

www.cengage.com/
management/bohlander

Behavior Observation Scale (BOS)

behavior observation scale (BOS)

A behavioral approach to performance appraisal that measures the frequency of observed behavior

A **behavior observation scale (BOS)** is similar to a BARS in that they are both based on critical incidents. However, the lower portion of Highlights in HRM 4 shows that rather than asking the evaluator to choose the most representative behavioral anchor, a BOS is designed to measure how frequently each of the behaviors has been observed.

4

BARS and BOS Examples

Example of a BARS for Municipal Fire Companies

FIREFIGHTING STRATEGY: Knowledge of Fire Characteristics. This area of performance concerns the ability of a firefighter to understand fire characteristics to develop the best strategy for fighting a fire.

HIGH	7	—Finds the fire when no one else can
	6	—Correctly assesses best point of entry for fighting fire
	5	—Uses type of smoke as indicator of type of fire
AVERAGE	4	—Understands basic hydraulics
	3	—Cannot tell the type of fire by observing the color of flame
	2	—Cannot identify location of the fire
LOW	1	—Will not change firefighting strategy in spite of flashbacks and other signs that accelerants are present

Source: Adapted from Landy, Jacobs, and Associates. Reprinted with permission.

Sample Items from Behavior Observation Scales

For each behavior observed, use the following scale:

5 represents *almost always*	95–100% of the time
4 represents *frequently*	85–94% of the time
3 represents *sometimes*	75–84% of the time
2 represents *seldom*	65–74% of the time
1 represents *almost never*	0–64% of the time

SALES PRODUCTIVITY	**NEVER**				**ALWAYS**
1. Reviews individual productivity results with manager	1	2	3	4	5
2. Suggests to peers ways of building sales	1	2	3	4	5
3. Formulates specific objectives for each contact	1	2	3	4	5
4. Focuses on product rather than customer problem	1	2	3	4	5
5. Keeps account plans updated	1	2	3	4	5
6. Follows up on customer leads	1	2	3	4	5

The value of a BOS is that this approach allows the appraiser to play the role of observer rather than of judge. In this way, he or she can more easily provide constructive feedback to the employee, who will be more willing to accept it. Companies such as AT&T, Weyerhaeuser, and Dayton-Hudson have used the BOS, and research shows that users of the system frequently prefer it over the BARS or trait scales for (1) maintaining objectivity, (2) distinguishing good performers from poor performers, (3) providing feedback, and (4) identifying training needs.[39]

Results Methods

Rather than looking at the traits of employees or the behaviors they exhibit on the job, many organizations evaluate employee accomplishments—the results they achieve through their work. Advocates of results appraisals argue that they are more objective and empowering for employees. Looking at results such as sales figures and production output involves less subjectivity and therefore may be less open to bias. Furthermore, results appraisals often give employees responsibility for their outcomes, while giving them discretion over the methods they use to accomplish them (within limits). This is empowerment in action.

Productivity Measures

A number of results measures are available to evaluate performance. Salespeople are evaluated on the basis of their sales volume (both the number of units sold and the dollar amount in revenues). Production workers are evaluated on the basis of the number of units they produce and perhaps the scrap rate or number of defects that are detected. Executives are frequently evaluated on the basis of company profits or growth rate. Each of these measures directly links what employees accomplish and results that benefit the organization. In this way, results appraisals can directly align employee and organizational goals.

But there are some problems with results appraisals. First, recall our earlier discussion of criteria contamination. Results appraisals can be contaminated by external factors that employees cannot influence. Sales representatives who have extremely bad markets or production employees who cannot get materials will not be able to perform up to their abilities. In this case, it is unfair to hold these employees accountable for results that are contaminated by circumstances beyond their control.

Furthermore, results appraisals can inadvertently encourage employees to "look good" on a short-term basis, while ignoring the long-term ramifications. Line supervisors, for example, might let their equipment suffer to reduce maintenance costs. If the appraisal focuses on a narrow set of results criteria to the exclusion of other important process issues, the system may suffer from criterion deficiency and unintentionally foster the attitude that "what gets measured gets done." In fact, in any job involving interaction with others, it is not enough to simply look at production or sales figures. Factors such as cooperation, adaptability, initiative, and concern for human relations are important to the job success of employees, too. If these factors are important job standards, they should be added to the appraisal review. Thus, to be realistic, both the results and the methods or processes used to achieve them should be considered.[40]

Management by Objectives

One method that attempts to overcome some of the limitations of results appraisals is **management by objectives (MBO)**. MBO is a philosophy of management first proposed by Peter Drucker in 1954 that has employees establish objectives (such as production costs, sales per product, quality standards, and profits) through consultation with their superiors and then uses these objectives as a basis for evaluation.[41] MBO is a system involving a cycle (Figure 8.6) that begins with setting the organization's common goals and objectives and ultimately returns to that step. The system acts as a goal setting

management by objectives (MBO)

A philosophy of management that rates performance on the basis of employee achievement of goals set by mutual agreement of employee and manager process whereby objectives are established for the organization (Step 1), departments (Step 2), and individual managers and employees (Step 3).

As Figure 8.6 illustrates, a significant feature of the cycle is the establishment of specific goals by the employee, but those goals are based on a broad statement of the employee's responsibilities prepared by the person's supervisor. Employee-established goals are discussed with the supervisor and jointly reviewed and modified until both parties are satisfied with them (Step 4). The goal statements are accompanied by a detailed account of the actions the employee proposes to take in order to reach the goals. During periodic reviews, as objective data are made available, the progress that the employee is making toward the goals is then assessed (Step 5). Goals may be changed at this time as new or additional data are received. At the conclusion of a period of time (usually six months or one year), the employee makes a self-appraisal of what he or she has accomplished, substantiating the self-appraisal with factual data wherever possible. The "interview" is an examination of the employee's self-appraisal by the supervisor and the employee together (Step 6). The final step (Step 7) is reviewing the connection between individual and organizational performance. To ensure success, MBO programs should be viewed as part of a total system for managing, not as merely an addition to the manager's job. Managers must be willing to empower employees

FIGURE 8.6

Performance Appraisal under an MBO Program

MANAGEMENT BY OBJECTIVES

Step 1: Organization goals and metrics

Step 2: Department goals and metrics

Step 3A: Supervisor lists goals and metrics for subordinate

Step 3B: Subordinate proposes goals and metrics

Step 4: Mutual agreement of goals and metrics

Step 5a: Inappropriate goals/metrics deleted

Step 5b: New inputs are then provided

Step 7: Review of organization performance

Step 6: Final review

Step 5: Interim review

to accomplish their objectives on their own, giving them discretion over the methods they use (but holding them accountable for outcomes). The following guidelines may be especially helpful:

1. Managers and employees must be willing to establish goals and objectives together. Goal setting has been shown to improve employee performance, typically ranging from 10 to 25 percent. Goal setting works because it helps employees focus on important tasks and makes them accountable for completing these tasks. It also establishes an automatic feedback system that aids learning because employees can regularly evaluate their performance against their goals.[42]

2. The objectives should be quantifiable and measurable for the long and short terms. However, goal statements should be accompanied by a description of how that goal will be accomplished.

3. The results that are expected must be under the employee's control. Recall our early discussion of criterion contamination.

4. The goals and objectives must be consistent for each employee level (top executive, manager, and employee).

5. Managers and employees must establish specific times when the goals are to be reviewed and evaluated.

The Balanced Scorecard

The Balanced Scorecard (BSC), which we first discussed in Chapter 2, can be used to appraise individual employees, teams, business units, and the corporation itself. The idea behind the Balanced Scorecard model was shown in Chapter 2. The appraisal takes into account four related categories: (1) financial, (2) customer, (3) processes, and (4) learning. These internal processes—product development, service, and the like—are critical for creating customer satisfaction and loyalty. In turn, creating value for customers is what drives a firm's financial performance and profitability. Highlights in HRM 5 shows an example of how a balanced scorecard translates to a personal scorecard for an employee. As you can see, the corporation's objectives have already been spelled out on the scorecard. Then the various business unit targets are added, followed by the target objectives of the firm's teams and individual employees. The value of this is that each individual can see more clearly how his or her performance ties into the overall performance of the firm. Similar in some ways to MBO, the BSC enables managers to translate broad corporate goals into divisional, departmental, and team goals in a cascading fashion. Many firms have adopted the Balanced Scorecard approach, but it is neither a flawless nor a simple performance management system. Some recommendations for ensuring the method's success include the following:

- *Translate the strategy into a scorecard of clear objectives.* Because the BSC process begins with strategic objectives, unless these are clear, the rest of the system is doomed to ambiguity and potential failure. Translating a strategy into objectives provides managers and frontline employees with goals that are more understandable and attainable. Typically, having fewer goals adds clarity and focus.

- *Attach measures to each objective.* In order for managers and employees to know if and when the objectives are achieved, clear measures must be attached to each goal. Each objective should be given at least one metric that can be measured either by a preexisting system or manually within an organization.

5

Personal Scorecard

CORPORATE OBJECTIVES

- Double our corporate value in seven years.
- Increase our earnings by an average of 20% per year.
- Achieve an internal rate of return 2% above the cost of capital.
- Increase both production and reserves by 20% in the next decade.

☑ Corporate
❏ Business Unit
❏ Team/Individual

Corporate Targets				Scorecard Measures	Bus. Unit Targets				Team/Individual Objectives
2005	2006	2007	2008		2005	2006	2007	2008	1.
				Financial					
100	120	160	180	Earnings (millions of dollars)					
100	450	200	210	Net cash flow					
100	85	75	70	Overhead and operating costs					2.
				Operating					
100	75	73	70	Production costs/barrel					
100	97	93	90	Development costs/barrel					
100	105	108	110	Total annual production					3.
Team/Individual Measures					**Targets**				
1.									
2.									4.
3.									
4.									

Source: Robert Kaplan and David Norton, "Using the Balanced Scorecard as a Strategic Management System," *Harvard Business Review* (January–February 1996): 75–85.

- *Cascade scorecards to the front line.* It is often said that the real strategic work happens at the front line. In order for all employees to understand how their roles and job duties are aligned with the firm's higher-level goals, the scorecards should be cascaded to the individual level. Cascading scorecards ensures that strategy then becomes "everyone's" job.

- *Provide performance feedback based on measures.* As with other performance management systems, unless managers provide employees with solid feedback on how they are doing, the system is likely to be ineffective. As part of this process, employees must know that they are accountable for achieving their objectives and providing an explanation when they do not hit their targets.

- *Empower employees to make performance improvements.* Individuals, on their own or working in teams, may understand ways of achieving higher performance. One of the benefits of a results-based system such as the BSC is that it gives employees the latitude to continuously improve best practices methods.

- *Reassess strategy.* One of the key benefits of the BSC is that it is a continuous loop process. Managers should monitor performance and use this information to reassess the strategy and make continuous adjustments. Those who have had the best success with the BSC argue that the system helps improve communication and learning rather than fixing in place a mechanical set of controls.[43]

Which Performance Appraisal Method to Use?

The method chosen should be based largely on the purpose of the appraisal. Figure 8.7 lists some of the strengths and weaknesses of trait, behavior, and results approaches to appraisal. Note that the simplest and least expensive techniques often yield the least accurate information. However, research has not always supported a clear choice among appraisal methods. While researchers and HR managers generally believe that the more sophisticated and more time-consuming methods offer more useful information, this may not always be the case. Ronald Gross, an industrial psychologist and human resources consultant, states: "I can't judge a performance-appraisal system just by looking at the paperwork. The back of an envelope can work just fine. I've seen many systems fail miserably because they're too complex, too time-consuming, and too burdensome. I've never seen a system fail because it was too simple."[44] One way to assess whether an organization's appraisal system is effective is by doing an annual, or at least periodic, audit of the process using a survey instrument that both managers and employees complete on a periodic basis. This should give HR a better sense of whether the appraisal processes is improving.

FIGURE
8.7

Summary of Various Appraisal Methods

	ADVANTAGES	DISADVANTAGES
Trait Methods	1. Are inexpensive to develop 2. Use meaningful dimensions 3. Are easy to use	1. Have high potential for rating errors 2. Are not useful for employee counseling 3. Are not useful for allocating rewards 4. Are not useful for promotion decisions
Behavioral Methods	1. Use specific performance dimensions 2. Are acceptable to employees and superiors 3. Are useful for providing feedback 4. Are fair for reward and promotion decisions	1. Can be time-consuming to develop/use 2. Can be costly to develop 3. Have some potential for rating error
Results Methods	1. Have less subjectivity bias 2. Are acceptable to employees and superiors 3. Link individual performance to organizational performance 4. Encourage mutual goal setting 5. Are good for reward and promotion decisions	1. Are time-consuming to develop/use 2. May encourage a short-term perspective 3. May use contaminated criteria 4. May use deficient criteria

Of course, having a first-rate appraisal method does no good if the manager simply "shoves it in a drawer." Even a rudimentary system, when used properly, can initiate a discussion between managers and employees that genuinely leads to superior performance. These issues are discussed next under the topic of performance appraisal interviews. In addition, as we have explained, performance appraisals should not be just for middle managers and rank-and-file employees. If the organization's goals are to cascade downward, the firm's top executives need to be involved in the appraisal process as well.

APPRAISAL INTERVIEWS

4 | Objective

The appraisal interview is perhaps the most important part of the entire performance appraisal process. The appraisal interview gives a manager the opportunity to discuss a subordinate's performance record and to explore areas of possible improvement and growth. Unfortunately, the interviewer can become overburdened by attempting to discuss too much, such as the employee's past performance and future development goals. Dividing the appraisal interview into two sessions, one for the performance review and the other for the employee's growth plans, can be helpful. Moreover, by separating the interview into two sessions, the interviewer can give each session the proper attention it deserves. It can be difficult for a supervisor to perform the role of both evaluator and counselor in the same review period. Dividing the sessions can also improve the communication and cooperation between the parties, thereby reducing any stress and defensiveness that might arise.

The format for the appraisal interview will be determined in a large part by the purpose of the interview, type of appraisal system used, and organization of the interview form. Most appraisal interviews attempt to give feedback to employees on how well they are performing their jobs and on planning for their future development. Interviews should be scheduled far enough in advance to allow the interviewee, as well as the interviewer, to prepare for the discussion. Usually ten days to two weeks is a sufficient amount of lead time.

There are different approaches to performance appraisal interviews. A problem-solving approach may be the best.

© THOMAS BARWICK/THE IMAGE BANK/GETTY IMAGES

Three Types of Appraisal Interviews

The individual who has probably studied different approaches to performance appraisal interviews most thoroughly is Norman R. F. Maier. In his classic book *The Appraisal Interview*, he analyzes the cause-and-effect relationships in three types of appraisal interviews: tell-and-sell, tell-and-listen, and problem-solving.

Tell-and-Sell Interview

The skills required in the tell-and-sell interview include the ability to persuade an employee to change in a prescribed manner. This may require the development of new behaviors on the part of the employee and skillful use of motivational incentives on the part of the appraiser/supervisor.

Tell-and-Listen Interview

In the tell-and-listen interview, the skills required include the ability to communicate the strong and weak points of an employee's job performance during the first part of the interview. During the second part of the interview, the employee's feelings about the appraisal are thoroughly explored. The tell-and-listen method gives both managers and employees the opportunity to release and iron out any frustrating feelings they might have. Today, most experts advise supervisors to encourage their employees to speak freely and to listen closely to what they have to say, emphasizing the fact that the communication during performance appraisals should be a two-way street.

Problem-Solving Interview

The skills associated with the problem-solving interview are consistent with the nondirective procedures of the tell-and-listen method. Listening, accepting, and responding to feelings are essential elements of the problem-solving interview. However, this method goes beyond an interest in the employee's feelings. It seeks to stimulate growth and development in the employee by discussing the problems, needs, innovations, satisfactions, and dissatisfactions the employee has encountered on the job since the last appraisal interview. Maier recommends this method because the objective of appraisals is normally to motivate employees and stimulate their growth and development.

Managers should not assume that only one type of appraisal interview is appropriate for every review session. Rather, they should be able to use one or more of the interview types, depending on the topic being discussed or on the behavior of the employee being appraised. The interview should be seen as requiring a flexible approach.

Conducting the Appraisal Interview

While there are probably no hard-and-fast rules for how to conduct an appraisal interview, some guidelines can increase an employee's willingness to discuss his or her performance and improve it, accept feedback from his or her supervisors, and increase the person's overall satisfaction with the interview. Many of the principles of effective interviewing discussed in Chapter 6 apply to performance appraisal interviews as well. Here are some other guidelines that should also be considered.

Ask for a Self-Assessment

As we noted earlier in the chapter, it is useful to have employees evaluate their own performance prior to the appraisal interview. Even if this information is not used to determine the final rating on the review, the self-appraisal starts the employee thinking about his or her accomplishments. Self-appraisal also ensures that the employee knows against what criteria he or she is being evaluated, thus eliminating any potential surprises.

Recent research evidence suggests that employees are more satisfied and view the appraisal system as providing more *procedural justice* when they have input into the process.

When the employee has evaluated his or her own performance, the interview can be used to discuss areas in which the manager and the employee have reached different conclusions—not so much to resolve the "truth," but to work toward a resolution of problems.

Invite Participation

The core purpose of a performance appraisal interview is to initiate a dialogue that will help an employee improve his or her performance. To the extent that an employee is an active participant in that discussion, the more likely it is that the root causes and obstacles to performance will be uncovered and the more likely it is that constructive ideas for improvement will be raised. In addition, research evidence suggests that participation is strongly related to an employee's satisfaction with the appraisal feedback, the extent to which the employee believes it is fair and useful, and his or her intention to improve performance. As a rule of thumb, supervisors should spend only about 30 to 35 percent of the time talking during the interview. They should spend the rest of the time listening to the information their employees volunteer and their responses to questions.

Express Appreciation

Praise is a powerful motivator, and in an appraisal interview, particularly, employees are seeking positive feedback. It is frequently beneficial to start the appraisal interview by expressing appreciation for what the employee has done well. In this way, he or she may be less defensive and more likely to talk about aspects of the job that are not going so well. However, supervisors should try to avoid the obvious use of the "sandwich technique" in which positive statements are followed by negative ones, which are then followed by positive statements. This approach may not work for several reasons. Praise often alerts the employee that criticism will be coming. If managers follow an appraisal form, the problem of the sandwich technique will often be avoided. Furthermore, if employees are kept informed of their behavior on a regular basis, there will be no need to use this appraisal technique.

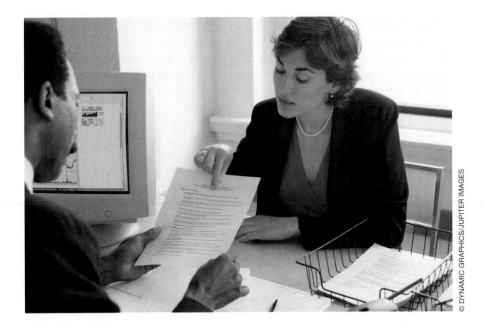

© DYNAMIC GRAPHICS/JUPITER IMAGES

The purpose of a performance appraisal interview is to initiate a dialogue that will help an employee improve his or her performance, making the employee an active participant in the discussion. Such participation is strongly related to an employee's satisfaction with appraisal feedback.

Minimize Criticism

Even the most stoic employees can absorb only so much criticism before they start to get defensive. If an employee has many areas in need of improvement, managers should focus on those few objective issues that are most problematic or most important to the job. In other words, criticism should be given in small doses.

Some tips for using criticism constructively include the following:

- *Consider whether it is really necessary.* Frustration with performance problems sometimes leads to criticism that is little more than a manager "letting off steam." Make certain that the criticism focuses on a recurrent problem or a consistent pattern of behavior over which the employee has control.

- *Consider the needs of the employee.* Everyone handles criticism differently. Some people are able to handle it well. Others react very negatively to even the lightest criticism.

- *Be specific and do not exaggerate.* Even managers who dislike criticizing may find that, once they get started, they tend to overdo it. Sometimes we overstate problems in order to be convincing or to demonstrate our concern. Try to keep criticism simple, factual, and to the point. Avoid using terms such as *always*, *completely*, and *never*.

- *Watch your timing.* Properly timed criticism can often mean the difference between success and failure. Even good criticism given late in the day, for example, can touch a raw nerve if the employee is tired.

- *Make improvement your goal.* Frankly, it is hard to change a person's behavior with a single conversation, so "laying it on the line" is not probably a good idea. Moreover, any criticism needs to be complemented with managerial support. This point is elaborated on next.[45]

Change the Behavior, Not the Person

Managers frequently try to play psychologist, to "figure out" why an employee has acted a certain way. Empathy is a good thing, and attempts to understand the employee's point of view can be very helpful. However, when dealing with a problem area, in particular, remember that it is not the person who is bad, but the actions exhibited on the job. Avoid making suggestions to employees about personal traits to change; instead suggest more acceptable ways of performing. For example, instead of focusing on a person's "unreliability," a manager might focus on the fact that the employee "has been late to work seven times this month." It is difficult for employees to change who they are; it is usually much easier for them to change how they act.

Focus on Solving Problems

When addressing performance issues, it is also frequently tempting to get into the "blame game" in which both manager and employee enter into a potentially endless discussion of why a situation has arisen. Frequently, solving problems requires an analysis of the causes, but ultimately the appraisal interview should be directed at devising a solution to the problem.

Be Supportive

One of the better techniques for engaging an employee in the problem-solving process is for the manager to ask: "What can I do to help?" Employees frequently attribute performance problems to either real or perceived obstacles (such as bureaucratic procedures or inadequate resources). By being open and supportive, the manager conveys to the employee that he or she will try to eliminate roadblocks and will work with the employee to achieve a higher standard of performance.

Establish Goals

Since a major purpose of the appraisal interview is to make plans for improvement, it is important to focus the interviewee's attention on the future rather than the past. Toward that goal, managers should:

- Emphasize strengths on which the employee can build rather than weaknesses to overcome and how the employee's efforts will contribute to the organization during the coming year.

- Concentrate on opportunities for growth that exist within the framework of the employee's present position and drop unproductive tasks.

- Limit plans for growth to a few important items that can be accomplished within a reasonable period of time.

- Establish specific action plans that spell out how each goal will be achieved. The plans may also include a list of contacts, resources, and timetables for follow-up.

Note that many managers are as nervous about administering appraisals as employees are about receiving them.

Follow Up Day to Day

As you have learned, feedback is most useful when it is immediate and specific to a particular situation. Unfortunately, both managers and employees are frequently happy to finish the interview and file away the appraisal form. A better approach is to have informal talks periodically, perhaps quarterly, to follow up on the issues raised in the appraisal interview. Levi Strauss, for example, offers employees informal feedback and coaching sessions on an ongoing basis. This puts managers in more of a coaching role versus that of a judge.

Improving Performance

In many instances, the appraisal interview will provide the basis for noting deficiencies in employee performance and for making plans for improvement. Unless these deficiencies are brought to the employee's attention, they are likely to continue until they become quite serious. Sometimes underperformers do not understand exactly what is expected of them. However, once their responsibilities are clarified, they are in a position to take the corrective action needed to improve their performance.

Identifying Sources of Ineffective Performance

A person's performance is a function of several factors, but perhaps it can be boiled down to three primary concerns: ability, motivation, and environment. Each individual has a unique pattern of strengths and weaknesses that play a part. But talented employees with low motivation are not likely to succeed. In addition, other factors in the work environment—or even in the external environment, which includes personal, family, and community concerns—can affect a person's performance either positively or negatively. Figure 8.8 provides a better picture of how these three factors (motivation, environment, and ability) can influence people's performance.

FIGURE
8.8

FIGURE 8.8 Factors That Influence Performance

MOTIVATION	ENVIRONMENT	ABILITY
• Career ambition	• Equipment/materials	• Technical skills
• Employee conflict	• Job design	• Interpersonal skills
• Frustration	• Economic conditions	• Problem-solving skills
• Fairness/satisfaction	• Unions	• Analytical skills
• Goals/expectations	• Rules and policies	• Communication skills
	• Management support	• Physical limitations
	• Laws and regulations	

It is recommended that a diagnosis of poor employee performance focus on these three interactive elements. As Figure 8.9 shows, if an employee's performance is not up to standards, the cause could be a skill problem (knowledge, abilities, technical competencies), an effort problem (motivation to get the job done), and/or some problem in the external conditions of work (poor economic conditions, worker shortages due to downsizing, difficult sales territories).[46] Any one of these problem areas could cause performance to suffer.

Performance Diagnosis

Although performance appraisal systems can often tell us who is not performing well, they typically cannot reveal why. Unfortunately, managers often assume that poor performance is first due to lack of ability, second to poor motivation, and then to external conditions an employee faces. Ironically, research also suggests that we tend to make just the opposite attributions about our own performance. We first attribute poor performance to external constraints such as bad luck or factors out of our control. If the problem is internal, then we typically attribute it to temporary factors such as motivation or energy ("I had a bad day") and only as a last resort admit that it might be due to ability.

So what can be done to diagnose the real reasons for poor performance? More specifically, how can managers identify the root causes and get to work on a solution that improves performance? By comparing different performance measures, managers can begin to get an idea of the underlying causes of performance problems. For example, as shown in Figure 8.9, results measures cannot distinguish between ability, motivation, and situational determinants of performance. So if someone is not achieving desired results, it could be due to ability, motivation, or external constraints. On the other hand, behavioral measures are less affected by external constraints. So if someone is demonstrating all the desired behaviors but is not achieving the desired results, logic suggests that it might be due to factors beyond his or her control.

Other kinds of diagnoses are possible by comparing different measures of performance. Only by correctly diagnosing the causes of performance problems can managers—and employees—hope to improve them.

FIGURE 8.9 — **Performance Diagnosis**

Source: Scott Snell, Cornell University.

Managing Ineffective Performance

Once the sources of performance problems are known, a course of action can be planned. This action may lie in providing training in areas that would increase the knowledge and/or skills needed for effective performance. A transfer to another job or department might give an employee a chance to become a more effective member of the organization. In other instances, greater attention may have to be focused on ways to motivate the individual.

If the ineffective performance persists, it may be necessary to transfer the employee, take disciplinary action, or discharge the person from the organization. Not only is the ineffective behavior likely affecting the manager and the organization as a whole, but it is also probably affecting the person's coworkers. Whatever action is taken, however, should be done objectively, fairly, and with an understanding of the feelings of the individual involved. A new manager is likely to need training in this area because it is one of the most difficult of aspects of being a manager.

A final word of caution when it comes to managing performance problems: Because research consistently shows that managers often attribute poor performance to characteristics of the individuals (ability or motivation), while employees themselves typically blame external factors for their miscues, this can establish a negative cycle if not handled properly. Managers who assume that employees are not motivated or not capable may begin to treat them differently (perhaps supervising them too closely or watching for their next mistake). This can actually decrease an employee's motivation and cause him or her to withdraw. Seeing this, the manager may confirm his or her initial beliefs that the employee does not "measure up." As you can probably tell, this "set-up-to-fail" syndrome can be self-fulfilling and self-reinforcing. We hope the ideas and suggestions in this chapter will help managers accurately identify who is performing well (and why) and give them some focus for improving the productivity of their employees.[47]

SUMMARY

Objective 1

1. Performance appraisal programs serve many purposes, but in general, those purposes can be clustered into two categories: administrative and developmental. The administrative purposes include decisions about who will be promoted, transferred, or laid off. Appraisals are also conducted in order to make compensation decisions. Developmental decisions include those related to improving and enhancing an individual's capabilities. These include identifying a person's strengths and weaknesses, eliminating external performance obstacles, and establishing training needs.

Some human resource experts and firms believe performance appraisals are ineffective. In other organizations, performance appraisals are seen as a necessary evil. Managers frequently avoid conducting appraisals because they dislike passing judgment on people. Furthermore, if managers are not adequately trained, subjectivity and organizational politics can distort employee reviews. They do not develop good feedback skills and are often not prepared to conduct an appraisal. As a consequence, the appraisal is done begrudgingly once a year and then forgotten. The ultimate success or failure of a performance appraisal program depends on the philosophy underlying it, its connection with the firm's business goals, and the attitudes and skills of those responsible for its administration.

Objective 2

2. To determine the contributions of each individual, it is necessary to have a formal appraisal program with clearly stated objectives. Carefully defined performance standards that are reliable, strategically relevant, and free from either criterion deficiency or criterion contamination are essential foundations for evaluation. Appraisal systems must also comply with the law and, like selections tests, be valid and reliable. For example, ratings must be job-related, employees must understand their performance standards in advance, appraisers must be able to observe job performance, appraisers must be trained, feedback must be given, and an appeals procedure must be established. Some companies now hold calibration meetings to ensure their managers are accurately rating employees. Using multiple raters is frequently a good idea because different individuals see different facets of an employee's performance. The supervisor, for example, has legitimate authority over an employee and is in a good position to discern whether he or she is contributing to the goals of the organization. Peers and team members, on the other hand, often have an unfiltered view of an employee's work activity, particularly related to issues such as cooperation and dependability. Subordinates often provide good information about whether an employee is facilitating their work, and customers (both internal and external) can convey the extent to which an employee adds value and meets their requirements. Self-appraisal is useful, if for no other reason than it encourages employees to think about their strengths, weaknesses, and future goals.

An increasing number of organizations are using multiple raters—or 360-degree appraisal—to get a more comprehensive picture of employee performance. Regardless of the source of appraisal information, appraisers should be thoroughly trained in the particular methods they will use in evaluating their subordinates. Participation in developing rating scales, such as a BARS, automatically provides such training.

Objective 3 3. Several methods can be used for performance appraisals. These include trait approaches (such as graphic rating scales, mixed-standard scales, forced-choice forms, and essays), behavioral methods (such as critical incident ratings, checklists, BARS, and BOS), and results methods (MBO). The choice of method depends on the purpose of the appraisal. Trait appraisals are simple to develop and complete, but they have problems in subjectivity and are not useful for feedback. Behavioral methods provide more specific information for giving feedback but can be time-consuming and costly to develop. Results appraisals are more objective and can link individual performance to the organization as a whole, but they may encourage a short-term perspective (such as annual goals) and may not include subtle yet important aspects of performance.

Objective 4 4. The degree to which a performance appraisal program benefits an organization and its members is directly related to the quality of the appraisal interviews that are conducted. Interviewing skills are best developed through instruction and supervised practice. Although there are various approaches to the interview, research suggests that employee participation and goal setting lead to higher satisfaction and improved performance. Discussing problems, showing support, minimizing criticism, and rewarding effective performance are also beneficial practices. During the interview, performance deficiencies can be discussed and plans for improvement can be made.

KEY TERMS

behavior observation scale (BOS)

behaviorally anchored rating scale (BARS)

calibration

contrast error

critical incident

customer appraisal

error of central tendency

essay method

forced-choice method

graphic rating scale method

leniency or strictness error

management by objectives (MBO)

manager and/or supervisor appraisal

mixed-standard scale method

peer appraisal

performance appraisal

performance management

recency error

self-appraisal

similar-to-me error

subordinate appraisal

team appraisal

DISCUSSION QUESTIONS

Objective 1
1. What are the major purposes of performance appraisal? In what ways might these purposes be contradictory?

Objective 1
2. Describe the relationships among performance appraisal and selection, training, and development.

Objective 1
3. How can performance appraisals be adjusted to include the principles underlying total quality management (TQM) and the goals of increasing shareholder value

Objective 1
4. Describe the characteristics of the ideal appraisal system.

Objective 1
5. Discuss the guidelines that performance appraisals should meet in order to be legally defensible.

Objective 2
6. What sources could be used to evaluate the performance of people working in the following jobs?
a. Sales representative
b. TV repairer
c. Director of nursing in a hospital
d. HR manager
e. Air traffic controller

Objective 2
7. In many organizations, evaluators submit ratings to their immediate superiors for review before discussing them with the individual employees they have rated. What advantages are there to this procedure?

Objective 3
8. What are the pros and cons of trait, behavior, and results appraisals?

Objective 3
9. Three types of appraisal interviews are described in this chapter.
a. What different skills are required for each type of appraisal interview? What reactions can one expect from using these different skills?
b. How can a manager develop the skills needed to conduct a problem-solving type of interview?
c. Which method do you feel is the least desirable? Why?

Objective 4
10. Discuss how you would go about diagnosing poor performance problems. List several factors to consider.

BIZFLIX EXERCISES

Seabiscuit: George Rides Seabiscuit

This scene will show you several aspects of appraising and improving performance. Watch for performance standards, peer appraisal, behavior shaping, and coaching.

Combine a jockey who is blind in one eye with an undersized, ill-tempered thoroughbred and an unusual trainer. The result: the Depression-era champion racehorse Seabiscuit. This engaging film shows the training and development of Seabiscuit by trainer "Silent" Tom Smith (Chris Cooper) and jockey Red Pollard (Tobey Maguire). The enduring commitment of owner Charles Howard (Jeff Bridges) ensures the ultimate success of Seabiscuit on the racing circuit.

The *Seabiscuit* scene is a composite edited from DVD Chapter 21 toward the end of the film. In earlier scenes, Red severely injured a leg—he cannot ride Seabiscuit in the competition against War Admiral. Samuel Riddle (Eddie Jones), War Admiral's owner, has described any new rider as immaterial to the race's result. The scene begins with Red giving George Wolff (Gary Stevens), Seabiscuit's new jockey, some tips about riding him.

What to Watch for and Ask Yourself

- Does Red set clear performance standards for George? If he does, what are they?

- Red and George are both jockeys who competed against each other in earlier races. Do these scenes show peer appraisal or appraisal by people of different rank or position? Which characteristics

of the performance appraisal process does this scene show?

- An earlier section, "Performance Appraisal Methods," discussed many approaches to performance appraisal. Which method or methods most closely match(es) what occurs in these scenes? Identify examples in the scenes that match the performance appraisal method or methods you picked.

HRM EXPERIENCE

Performance Diagnosis

Managing performance is an important—yet delicate—process for managers to undertake. They need to make tough calls at times regarding who is performing well or not. Also, they need to play the role of coach to help each employee improve his or her performance. One of the toughest aspects of performance management is assessing why someone is not performing well. Although it may be easy to spot who is not performing well, it is not always easy to diagnose the underlying causes of poor performance (such as motivation, ability, and external constraints). But without a correct diagnosis, it is nearly impossible to cure the problem.

Assignment

The following are descriptions of three different employees. Describe the potential causes of poor performance in each case. For each potential cause, identify appropriate solutions to enhance performance.

1. *Carl Spackler* is the assistant greenskeeper at Bushwood Country Club. Over the past few months, members have been complaining that gophers are destroying the course and digging holes in the greens. Although Carl has been working evenings and weekends to address the situation, the problem persists. Unfortunately, his boss is interested only in results, and because the gophers are still there, he contends that Carl is not doing his job. He has accused Carl of "slacking off" and threatened his job.

2. *Susan Griswold* works in research and development for a chemical company that makes nonnutritive food additives. Her most recent assignment has been the development of a nonstick aerosol cooking spray, but the project is way behind schedule and seems to be going nowhere. CEO Frank

(continued)

Performance Diagnosis (continued)

Shirley is decidedly upset and has threatened that if things don't improve, he will suspend bonuses again this year, as he did last year. Susan feels dejected because without the bonus she won't be able to take her family on vacation.

3. *Bonnie Molloy* is the host of a local television talk show called *Morning Chicago*. Although she is a talented performer and comedienne, Bonnie has an unacceptable record of tardiness. The show's producer, David Bellows, is frustrated because the problem has affected the quality of the show. On several occasions, Bonnie was unprepared when the show went on the air. Bellows has concluded that Bonnie is not a morning person and has thought about replacing her with a different host.

CASE STUDY 1

Appraising Employees at the San Diego Zoo

The San Diego Zoological Society, which employs 2,600 people, this year introduced an employee performance management system whose ratings will determine managers' pay raises. It's part of an emphasis on employee accountability outlined in the organization's strategic plan. For years, employee performance evaluations were a low priority at the Zoological Society of San Diego, with no uniform metrics and no consequences for ignoring appraisal paperwork sent by the human resources department.

Different versions of the one-page form were used. Managers didn't judge subordinates on goals, but on a nebulous sense of how they were doing. Some employees hadn't been reviewed in years—a few of them had waited decades.

"It wasn't taken seriously, and it didn't hold any credence because there was not a pay-for-performance system here," says Tim Mulligan, director of human resources for the not-for-profit Zoological Society, which operates the San Diego Zoo, the San Diego Zoo's Wild Animal Park and the Conservation and Research for Endangered Species scientific center. Managers received annual raises, which were essentially cost-of-living increases not linked to their performance, Mulligan says. "HR would send out a form, say, 'This review is due,' but then would never follow up to see that it was turned in."

That is changing. The Zoological Society, which employs 2,600 people, this year introduced an employee performance management system whose ratings will determine managers' pay raises. It's part of an emphasis on employee accountability outlined in the organization's strategic plan, which was being finalized when the nonprofit organization hired Mulligan two years ago.

Like an increasing number of organizations, the Zoological Society, whose revenues in 2005 reached $176 million, wanted a Web-based employee appraisal system that helps guide managers through the process and reduces rote work.

This year, the Zoological Society's management team, which consists of 225 employees classified as assistant managers or higher, falls under the Web-based employee appraisal system. Next year, the practice will be expanded to include all exempt employees.

With built-in prompts for completing reviews, performance management applications standardize the format of performance reviews and free human resource professionals from the administrative tasks of reminding managers that appraisals are due. They also tend to be affordable ways to update appraisal processes, have multiple raters, and enable timely feedback on performance.

Mulligan identified the primary objectives for the Zoological Society's new system: establish impartial employee goals directly linked to the organization's goals; include a midyear review to ensure an ongoing dialogue and to prevent end-of-the-year surprises; and require year-end reviews whose ratings will be used to determine merit increases.

Mulligan also realized his diverse workforce, which includes everyone from world-renowned scientists to teenage foodservice workers, needed metrics to measure performance, as well as easy-to-use software. He created two teams—one looking at vendors, the other at skills that characterized a successful leader within the organization, regardless of their department.

"We didn't want to throw this down our managers' throats," he says of involving employees in the planning. "We wanted to have them work on and approve of it."

The process led to performance appraisals based on two categories: goals and leadership competencies. At the beginning of the year, each manager chooses five goals, at least three of which must be linked to organizational objectives. Those goals are based on everything from guest satisfaction to revenue.

The other two goals are what Mulligan calls "wild cards"—targets pertinent to their specific area. Together, the performance goals make up 50 percent of the overall employee appraisal.

The other half comes from ratings on leadership competencies. Those were identified by 220 managers and then whittled to a list of six, each with five subfactors. For example, the competency of "professionalism" includes scores on teamwork, communication, interpersonal relations, Zoological Society mission, and customer focus.

Halogen Software of Ottawa was chosen as the vendor. Halogen's eAppraisal performance management solution lets employees record accomplishments in an online journal that they may share with their manager. Mulligan says the tool helps to craft an accurate year-end review. "Many of our people are very involved with organizations in conservation and in the animal world," he says. "We don't want those things to be forgotten by management at the end of the year when they do their review."

The Zoological Society's adoption of a Web-based solution also reflects another trend. One of the notable changes in the past five years has been the shift to Internet-based appraisal systems from client-server platforms, in which programs are kept on a central computer connected through a network to PCs.

Not everyone sees Web-based employee appraisals as all good news. Anthony Chelte, dean of Dillard College of Business Administration at Midwestern State University in Wichita Falls, Texas, says the key benefits of online employee appraisals are the timeliness of feedback and the efficiency of eliminating paperwork.

"When you look at the ratio of individuals to HR people in terms of the number of reviews that have to be looked at for completeness, accuracy and legal concerns, it's probably far more efficient," he says.

Chelte cautions against relying on online appraisals to deliver feedback, saying one-on-one discussions are as important. "I do not think the online appraisal system is a good proxy for delivering feedback," he says. "The whole social context is gone. It takes the entire human element out of the mix."

Halogen executives say their system is not intended to replace one-on-one appraisal meetings, but rather to simplify preparation for it.

Mulligan says he ensured the "human element" remains intact for zoo staffers. The appraisal must be delivered in person, with the supervisor printing and reviewing it with the subordinate or the two discussing results as they go over it on the computer screen. "It has to be done with two people together," he says. "You can't just pull it up and read your review."

The supervisor then must certify that the in-person meeting occurred. "I don't want us to go back to where we were before, with employees and managers not having this face-to-face dialogue on performance," Mulligan says.

Michele Stancer began working at the zoo 28 years ago, starting in food service while in high school and working her way up to animal care manager. She describes her experience with the new appraisal system as positive because of discussions with her boss about setting goals and basing raises on performance.

"If you perform well, you'll get more," Stancer says. "I think people should be held accountable. I've been here a long time. You see people who are 'working in retirement,' and that's not good for anyone."

Mulligan says the Web-based appraisal process has helped the zoo attract talent. "What I found is that it's a recruiting tool," he says. "A manager who starts here sees that we have a program like this where you have goals and objectives and are given timely feedback and paid for the work that you do. As we come into the modern world here in HR, we have to provide programs like this."

Questions

1. Do you think the San Diego Zoo's old appraisal system needed to be changed?
2. What do you think are the pros and cons of using a Web-based appraisal system?
3. How do you the new appraisal system will affect employees and the types of employees who work at the zoo?

Source: Excerpted from Todd Henneman, "Employee Performance Management: What's Gnu at the Zoo," *Workforce Management Online*, September 2006.

CASE STUDY 2

Bank of Montreal's Balanced Scorecard

In 1990, the Bank of Montreal (BMO) had one major goal: to focus the entire workforce on success. It's a simple idea, but not so easy in execution. How would the company get entry-level tellers to think of their work not just as a means to a paycheck, but as a direct contribution to BMO shareholders? How would it remind corporate executives that their jobs were not just to boost the bottom line, but to charm entire communities?

The answer was BMO executives' balanced scorecard approach. To be competitive, executives decided, the bank had to meet the needs of four stakeholders: BMO shareholders, customers, employees, and communities. Executives translated that idea into four goals: Shareholders needed a return on equity, customers needed good service, employees needed to feel loyal and satisfied, and communities needed to feel that the bank made a difference in their neighborhoods. Return on investment would determine satisfaction for shareholders; surveys and feedback would determine satisfaction for customers, employees, and communities.

Every single department and every employee in every department had to understand how their work contributed to the success of those four goals. So each employee's and each department's performance ratings were revised to reflect their contribution toward each goal. Employees in the customer service department, for instance, were rated by their return on equity (judged by their cost-effectiveness), their customer satisfaction (judged by customer feedback), and their community involvement (judged by any outreach programs or increase in customers).

In some cases, departments were assigned a specific stakeholder. For example, HR was put in charge of the employee piece, ensuring competent, committed workers in a cost-effective way. Similarly, the company's senior vice president of HR was responsible for training and education aspects to ensure competency and work/life and career development programs to help with employee commitment. At the end of the year, the scores from everyone's performance ratings were translated into indexes, ratings from 1 to 10. The index for the employee stakeholder piece was determined by ratings for competency, commitment, and cost-effectiveness. The four indexes for BMO shareholders, customers, employees, and communities were then rolled up into one figure of merit to determine the bonus of BMO's CEO.

Questions

1. What are the strengths and weaknesses of a balanced scorecard approach to performance appraisal?
2. Do you think it is fair to base the bonus paid to BMO's CEO on the four indexes comprising the firm's balanced scorecard?
3. Do you believe that a balanced scorecard approach would be more effective for the administrative or for the developmental purposes of appraisal discussed in this chapter?

NOTES AND REFERENCES

1. Susan Scherreik, "Your Performance Review: Make It Perform," *Business Week*, no. 3762 (December 17, 2001): 139; Dick Grote, "Performance Evaluations: Is It Time for a Makeover?" *HRFocus* 77, no. 11 (November 2000): 6–7; "Employers Need to Do a Better Job of Performance Management," *Managing Training & Development* (April 2003): 8; Christopher D. Lee, "Feedback, Not Appraisal," *HRMagazine* 51, no. 11 (November 2006): 111–114.

2. Matthew Boyle, "Performance Reviews: Perilous Curves Ahead," *Fortune* 143, no. 11 (May 28, 2001): 187–88; Susanne Scott and Walter Einstein, "Strategic Performance Appraisal in Team-Based Organizations: One Size Does Not Fit All," *Academy of Management Executive* 15, no. 2 (May 2001): 107–16; "Study Questions Performance Appraisal," *Australasian Business Intelligence* (May 1, 2003); Drew Robb, "Building a Better Workforce: Performance Management Software Can Help You Identify and Develop High-Performing Workers," *HRMagazine* 49, no. 10 (October 2004): 86–93.

3. Jonathan A. Segal, "86 Your Appraisal Process?" *HRMagazine* 45, no. 10 (October 2000): 199–206; Barry Witcher and Rosie Butterworth, "Honshin Kanri: How Xerox Manages," *Long-Range Planning* 32, no. 3 (June 1999): 323–32.

4. Janet Wiscombe, "Can Pay for Performance Really Work?" *Workforce* 80, no. 8 (August 2001): 28–34; Charlotte Garvey, "Meaningful Tokens of Appreciation: Cash Awards Aren't the Only Way to Motivate Your Workforce," *HRMagazine* 49, no. 8 (August 2004): 101–106; Lisa D. Sprenkle, "Forced Ranking: A Good Thing for Business?" *Workforce.com*.

5. David Allen and Rodger Griffeth, "Test of a Mediated Performance-Turnover Relationship Highlighting the Moderating Roles of Visibility and Reward Contingency," *Journal of Applied Psychology* 86, no. 5 (October 2001): 1014–21; Charles

Pettijohn, Linda Pettijohn, and Michael D'Amico, "Characteristics of Performance Appraisals and Their Impact on Sales Force Satisfaction," *Human Resource Development Quarterly* 12, no. 2 (Summer 2001): 127–46; Scott and Einstein, "Strategic Performance Appraisal in Team-Based Organizations," 107–16; "Organizations Seek Stronger Performance Management—and PFP," *Pay for Performance Report* 4, no. 6 (June 2004): 2–4.

6. Donna Doldwasser, "Me a Trainer?" *Training* 38, no. 4 (April 2001): 60–66; Rebecca Ganzel, "Mike Carter," *Training* 38, no. 7 (July 2001): 28–30; Carla Joinson, "Making Sure Employees Measure Up," *HRMagazine* 46, no. 3 (March 2001): 36–41; Morton D. Rosenbaum, "Gratitude Adjustment: When a Pat on the Back Isn't Enough," *Meetings & Conventions* 39, no. 7 (June 2004): 20; James W. Smither, Manuel London, and Richard R. Reilly, "Does Performance Improve Following Multisource Feedback?" *Personnel Psychology* 58, no. 1 (Spring 2005): 33–67.

7. Kathryn Bartol, Cathy Durham, and June Poon, "Influence of Performance Evaluation Rating Segmentation on Motivation and Fairness Perceptions," *Journal of Applied Psychology* 86, no. 6 (December 2001): 1106–19; Anne P. Hubbell, "Motivating Factors: Perceptions of Justice and Their Relationship with Managerial and Organizational Trust," *Communication Studies* 56, no. 1 (March 2005): 47; Rebecca M. Chory-Assad, "Room for Improvement," *Training* 40, no. 11 (December 2003): 18–20; Deanna M. Merritt, "Appraising the Performance Appraisal," *Supervision* 68, no 4 (April 2007): 3–5.

8. John Newman, J. Mack Robinson, Larry Tyler, David Dunbar, and Joseph Zager, "CEO Performance Appraisal: Review and Recommendations/Practitioner Application," *Journal of Healthcare Management* 46, no. 1 (January/February 2001): 21–38; Bob Losyk, "How to Conduct a Performance Appraisal," *Public*

Management 84, no. 3 (April 2002): 8–12; Arup Varma and Shaun Pichler, "Interpersonal Affect: Does It Really Bias Performance Appraisals?" *Journal of Labor Research* 28, no. 2 (Spring 2007): 397–412.

9. Doug Cederblom, "From Performance Appraisal to Performance Management: One Agency's Experience," *Public Personnel Management* 31, no. 2 (Summer 2002): 131–40; "Anonymous 360-Feedback Drives Vauxhall Strategy," *Personnel Today* (August 19, 2003): 16; Cindy Romaine, "Staying Relevant: Competencies and Employee Reviews," *Information Outlook* 8, no. 7 (April 2004): 21–25; Jerry K. Palmer and James M. Loveland, "The Influence of Group Discussion on Performance Judgments: Rating Accuracy, Contrast Effects, and Halo," *Journal of Psychology* 142, no. 2 (March 2008): 117–130.

10. Jason D. Shaw and Nina Gupta, "Job Complexity, Performance, and Well-Being: When Does Supplies-Values Fit Matter?" *Personnel Psychology* 57, no. 4 (Winter 2004): 847–80.

11. Joel Lefkowitz, "The Role of Interpersonal Affective Regard in Supervisory Performance Ratings: A Literature Review and Proposed Causal Model," *Journal of Occupational and Organizational Psychology* 73, no. 1 (March 2000): 67–85; Scott Highhouse, "Assessing the Candidate As a Whole: A Historical and Critical Analysis of Individual Psychological Assessment for Personnel Decision Making," *Personnel Psychology* 55, no. 2 (Summer 2002): 363–397.

12. Joanne Sammer, "Calibrating Consistency," *HRMagazine* 53, no. 1 (January 2008): 73–75.

13. *Brito v. Zia Company*, 478 F.2d 1200 (10th Cir. 1973); Treena L. Gillespie and Richard O. Parry, "Fuel for Litigation? Links between Procedural Justice and Multisource Feedback," *Journal of Managerial Issues* 18, no. 4 (Winter 2006): 530–546.

14. *Albemarle Paper Company v. Moody*, 422 U.S. 405 (1975); Terry Gillen, "Appraisal: When Best Practice Is Bad Practice," *People*

Management 11, no. 19 (September 29, 2005): 58.

15. Timothy Aeppel, "Goodyear Ends Ratings System ahead of Lawsuit," *The Wall Street Journal*, September 12, 2002, B8; "How to Stay 'Legal' with Performance Evaluation and Testing," *Managing Training & Development*, no. 4 (February 2004): 9.

16. Gillian Flynn, "Getting Performance Reviews Right," *Workforce* 80, no. 5 (May 2001): 76–78; David C. Martin, Kathryn M. Bartol, and Patrick E. Kehoe, "The Legal Ramifications of Performance Appraisal: The Growing Significance," *Public Personnel Management* 29, no. 3 (Fall 2000): 381; Deanna M Merritt, "Appraising the Performance Appraisal," *Supervision* 68, no 4 (April 2007): 3–5; Kevin R. Murphy, "Perspectives on the Relationship Between Job Performance and Ratings of Job Performance," *Industrial & Organizational Psychology* (June 2008): 197–205.

17. Joan Brett and Leanne Atwater, "360-Degree Feedback: Accuracy, Reactions, and Perceptions of Usefulness," *Journal of Applied Psychology* 86, no. 5 (October 2001): 930–42; Bruce Pfau, Ira Kay, Kenneth Nowak, and Jai Ghorpade, "Does 360-Degree Feedback Negatively Affect Company Performance?" *HRMagazine* 47, no. 6 (June 2002): 54–59; Maury Peiperl, "Getting 360-Degree Feedback Right," *Harvard Business Review* 79, no. 1 (January 2001): 142–47; Robert Gandossy and Tina Kao, "Talent Wars: Out of Mind, Out of Practice," *Human Resource Planning* 27, no. 4 (December 2004): 15–20.

18. Corey E. Miller and Carl L. Thornton, "How Accurate Are Your Performance Appraisals?" *Public Personnel Management* (Summer 2006): 153–162; Edward J. Inderrieden, Robert E. Allen, and Timothy J. Keaveny, "Managerial Discretion in the Use of Self-Ratings in an Appraisal System: The Antecedents and Consequences," *Journal of Managerial Issues* 16, no. 4 (Winter 2004): 460–484.

19. Jeffrey Seglin, "Reviewing Your Boss," *Fortune* 143, no. 12 (June 11, 2001): 248; Ann Harrington, "Workers of the World, Rate Your Boss!" *Fortune* 142, no. 6 (September 18, 2000): 340–42; Robert Thompson, "Management Lite: Less Control, More Innovation," *HRMagazine* 44, no. 8 (August 1999): 10.

20. Brett and Atwater, "360-Degree Feedback," 930–42; Paula Silva and Henry L. Tosi, "Determinants of the Anonymity of the CEO Evaluation Process," *Journal of Managerial Issues* 16, no. 1 (Spring 2004): 87–103.

21. Ann Pomeroy, "Great Places, Inspired Employees: The Nation's Best Employers Show That Inspiring Employee Involvement through Good HR Practices Makes Good Business Sense," *HRMagazine* 49, no. 7 (July 2004): 44–64; Sue Browness, "Full-Circle Feedback," *Profit* 25, no. 2 (May 2006): 77.

22. John Drexler, Jr., Terry Beehr, and Thomas Stetz, "Peer Appraisals: Differentiation of Individual Performance on Group Tasks," *Human Resource Management* 40, no. 4 (Winter 2001): 333–45.

23. Scott and Einstein, "Strategic Performance Appraisal in Team-Based Organizations," 107–16; Debbie Kibbe and Jill Casner-Lotto, "Ralston Foods: From Greenfield to Maturity in a Team-Based Plant," *Journal of Organizational Excellence* 21, no. 3 (Summer 2002): 57–67; Simon Taggar and Mitchell Neubert, "The Impact of Poor Performers on Team Outcomes: An Empirical Examination of Attribution Theory," *Personnel Psychology* 57, no. 4 (Winter 2004): 935–69.

24. Bradley Kirkman and Benson Rosen, "Powering Up Teams," *Organizational Dynamics* 28, no. 3 (Winter 2000): 48–66; Matthew Valle and Kirk Davis, "Teams and Performance Appraisal: Using Metrics to Increase Reliability and Validity," *Team Performance Management* 5, no. 8 (1999): 238–43; Ebrahim Soltani, Robert Van der Meer, Terry M. Williams, and Pei-chun Lai, "The Compatibility of Performance Appraisal Systems with TQM Principles: Evidence from Current Practice," *International Journal of Operations & Production Management* 26, no. 1 (2006): 92–112.

25. Michael Cohn, "Best Buy Beefs Up Customer Value at the Call Center," *Internet World* 8, no. 6 (June 2002): 42–43; Joe Kohn, "Isuzu Has IDEA for Boosting Sales," *Automotive News* 76, no. 5973 (March 4, 2002): 41; D. L. Radcliff, "A New Paradigm of Feedback," *Executive Excellence* 19, no. 4 (April 2002): 20; Neeraj Bharadwaj and Anne Roggeveen, "The Impact of Offshored and Outsourced Call Service Centers on Customer Appraisals," *Marketing Letters* 19, no.1 (January 2008): 13–23.

26. Pfau, Kay, Nowak, and Ghorpade, "Does 360-Degree Feedback Negatively Affect Company Performance?" 54–59; Peiperl, "Getting 360-Degree Feedback Right," 142–47; Jack Kondrasuk, and Matt Graybill, "From Paper to Computer," *The Human Resource Professional* 13, no. 6 (November/December 2000): 18–19.

27. Gary Meyer, "Performance Reviews Made Easy, Paperless," *HRMagazine* 45, no. 10 (October 2000): 181–84; Douglas P. Shuit, "Huddling with the Coach—Part 2," *Workforce Management* 84, no. 2 (February 1, 2005): 5; "Ceridian and Softscape Announce an Agreement to Deliver Employee Performance and Development Solutions," *Payroll Manager's Report* (May 2004): 13; K. Sanwong, "The Development of a 360-Degree Performance Appraisal System: A University Case Study," *International Journal of Management* 25, no. 1 (March 2008): 16–22.

28. "Performance Appraisal," *HRMagazine* 47, no. 10 (October 2002): 146; Frank E. Kuzmits, Arthur J. Adams, Lyle Sussman, and Louis E. Raho, "360-Feedback in Health Care Management: A Field Study," *The Health Care Manager* 23, no. 321 (October–December 2004): 321–29; Jerry K. Palmer and James M. Loveland, "The Influence of Group Discussion on Performance Judgments: Rating Accuracy, Contrast Effects, and Halo. Preview," *Journal of Psychology* 142, no 2 (March 2008): 117–130; S. Bartholomew Craig and Kelly Hannum, "Research Update: 360-Degree Performance Assessment," *Consulting Psychology Journal: Practice & Research* 58, no. 2 (Spring 2006): 117–124.

29. Gary E. Roberts, "Perspectives on Enduring and Emerging Issues in Performance Appraisal," *Public Personnel Management* 27, no. 3 (Fall 1998): 301–20; William Hubbartt, "Bring Performance Appraisal Training to Life," *HRMagazine* 40, no. 5

(May 1995): 166, 168; Filip Lievens, "Assessor Training Strategies and Their Effects on Accuracy, Interrater Reliability, and Discriminant Validity," *Journal of Applied Psychology* 86, no. 2 (April 2001): 255–64; Dick Grote, "Performance Appraisals: Solving Tough Challenges," *HRMagazine* 45, no. 7 (July 2000): 145–50; Leslie A. Weatherly, "Performance Management: Getting It Right from the Start," *HRMagazine* 49, no. 3 (March 2004): S1–S12.

30. Gary P. Latham and Kenneth N. Wexley, *Increasing Productivity through Performance Appraisal*, 2nd ed. (Reading, MA: Addison-Wesley, 1994), 137.

31. Lefkowitz, "The Role of Interpersonal Affective Regard in Supervisory Performance Ratings," 67–85; Edwin Arnold and Marcia Pulich, "Personality Conflicts and Objectivity in Appraising Performance," *The Health Care Manager* 22, no. 3 (July–September 2003): 227; Krista Uggersly and Lorne M. Suksy, "Using Frame-of-Reference Training to Understand the Implications of Rater Idiosyncrasy for Rating Accuracy," *Journal of Applied Psychology*, 93, no. 3 (May 2008): 711–719.

32. Deidra J. Schleicher and David V. Day, "A Cognitive Evaluation of Frame-of-Reference Rater Training: Content and Process Issues," *Organizational Behavior and Human Decision Processes* 73, no. 1 (January 1998): 76–101; Wanda Smith, K. Vernard Harrington, and Jeffery Houghton, "Predictors of Performance Appraisal Discomfort: A Preliminary Examination," *Public Personnel Management* 29, no. 1 (Spring 2000): 21–32; Krista L. Uggerslev and Lorne M. Sulsky, "Using Frame-of-Reference Training to Understand the Implications of Rater Idiosyncrasy for Rating Accuracy," *Journal of Applied Psychology* 93, no. 3 (May 2008): 711–719.

33. Gail Johnson, "Forced Ranking: The Good, the Bad, and the Alternative," *Training* 41, no. 5 (May 2004): 24–31; Christine A. Amalfe and Eileen Quinn Steiner, "Forced Ranking Systems: Yesterday's Legal Target?" *New Jersey Law Journal* (March 28, 2005); Jessica Marquez, "Is GE'S Ranking System Broken?" *Workforce Management* 86, no. 12 (June 25, 2007): 1–3.

34. Lisa Keeping and Paul Levy, "Performance Appraisal Reaction: Measurement, Modeling, and Method Bias," *Journal of Applied Psychology* 85, no. 5 (October 2000): 708–23.

35. Adam B. Butler and Amie Skattebo, "What Is Acceptable for Women May Not Be for Men: The Effect of Family Conflicts with Work on Job-Performance Ratings," *Journal of Occupational and Organizational Psychology* 77, no. 4 (December 2004): 553–64; Cheri Ostroff, Leanne E. Atwater, and Barbara J. Feinberg, "Understanding Self-Other Agreement: A Look at Rater and Ratee Characteristics, Context, and Outcomes," *Personnel Psychology* 57, no. 1 (Summer 2004): 333–37; Mike Schraeder and Jim Simpson, "How Similarity and Liking Affect Performance Appraisals," *Journal for Quality & Participation* 29, no. 1 (Spring 2006): 34–40.

36. Kristina E. Chirico, M. Ronald Buckley, Anthony R. Wheeler, Jeffrey D. Facteau, H. John Bernardin, and Danielle S. Beu, "A Note on the Need for True Scores in Frame-of-Reference (FOR) Training Research," *Journal of Managerial Issues* 16, no. 3 (Fall 2004): 382–98; Christopher D. Lee, "Feedback, Not Appraisal," *HRMagazine* 51, no. 11 (November 2006): 111–114.

37. Stephen C. Behrenbrinker, "Conducting Productive Performance Evaluations in the Assessor's Office," *Assessment Journal* 2, no. 5 (September/October 1995): 48–54; Aharon Tziner, Christine Joanis, and Kevin Murphy, "A Comparison of Three Methods of Performance Appraisal with Regard to Goal Properties, Goal Perception, and Ratee Satisfaction," *Group & Organization Management* 25, no. 2 (June 2000): 175–90.

38. Elaine Pulakos, Sharon Arad, Michelle Donovan, and Kevin Plamondon, "Adaptability in the Workplace: Development of a Taxonomy of Adaptive Performance," *Journal of Applied Psychology* 85, no. 4 (August 2000): 612–24; Leslie A. Weatherly, "Performance Management: Getting It Right from the Start," *HRMagazine* 49, no. 3 (March 2004): S1–S12; Edwin Arnold and Marcia Pulich, "Personality Conflicts and Objectivity in Appraising Performance," *The Health Care Manager* 22, no. 3 (July–September 2003): 227.

39. Latham and Wexley, *Increasing Productivity*; Tziner, Joanis, and Murphy, "A Comparison of Three Methods of Performance Appraisal," 175–90; Simon Taggar and Travor Brown, "Problem-Solving Team Behaviors: Development and Validation of BOS and a Hierarchical Factor Structure," *Small Group Research* 32, no. 6 (December 2001): 698–726; Paul Falcone, "Big-Picture Performance Appraisal," *HR Focus* 84, no. 9 (September 2007): 1–15.

40. Daniel Bachrach, Elliot Bendoly, and Philip Podsakoff, "Attributions of the 'Causes' of Group Performance as an Alternative Explanation of the Relationship between Organizational Citizenship Behavior and Organizational Performance," *Journal of Applied Psychology* 86, no. 6 (December 2001): 1285–93; Susan Leandri, "Measures That Matter: How to Fine-Tune Your Performance Measures," *Journal for Quality and Participation* 24, no. 1 (Spring 2001): 39–41.

41. Peter F. Drucker, *The Practice of Management* (New York: Harper & Brothers, 1954); reissued by HarperCollins in 1993); Janice S. Miller, "High Tech and High Performance: Managing Appraisal in the Information Age," *Journal of Labor Research* 24, no. 3 (Summer 2003): 409–425.

42. E. Locke and G. Latham, *A Theory of Goal Setting and Task Performance* (Englewood Cliffs, NJ: Prentice Hall, 1990). See also John J. Donovan and David J. Radosevich, "The Moderating Role of Goal Commitment on the Goal Difficulty-Performance Relationship: A Meta-Analytic Review and Critical Reanalysis," *Journal of Applied Psychology* 83, no. 2 (April 1998): 308–15; Cindy Romaine, "Staying Relevant: Competencies and Employee Reviews," *Information Outlook* 8, no. 4 (April 2004): 21–25; Gail Johnson, "Room for Improvement," *Training* 40, no. 11 (December 2003): 18–20.

43. Jack Steele, "Transforming the Balanced Scorecard into Your Strategy Execution System," *Manage* 53, no. 1 (September/October 2001): 22–23. See also Robert Kaplan and David Norton, "Strategic Learning and the Balanced Scorecard," *Strategy & Leadership* 24,

no. 5 (September/October 1996): 18–24; Robert Kaplan and David Norton, "Using the Balanced Scorecard as a Strategic Management System," *Harvard Business Review* (January–February 1996): 75–85; Joe Mullich, "Get in Line: People Talk about Aligning Corporate, Departmental and Employee Goals, But Not Many Actually Do It," *Workforce Management* 82, no. 13 (December 2003): 43; "Good Appraisal Is Simple, Happens Often, Experts Say," *The Orlando Sentinel* (via *Knight-Ridder/ Tribune News Service*), December 3, 2003; Li-cheng Chang, "The NHS Performance Assessment Framework as a Balanced Scorecard Approach," *International Journal of Public Sector Management* 20, no 2 (2007): 101–117.

44. Deloris McGee Wanguri, "A Review, an Integration, and a Critique of Cross-Disciplinary Research on Performance Appraisals, Evaluations, and Feedback," *Journal of Business Communications* 32, no. 3 (July 1995): 267–93; Tziner, Joanis, and Murphy, "A Comparison of Three Methods of Performance Appraisal," 175–90; "Good Appraisal Is Simple, Happens Often, Experts Say"; Joanna Haworth, "Measuring Performance," *Nursing Management—UK* 15, no. 3 (June 2008): 22–28.

45. Kwok Leung, Steven Su, and Michael Morris, "When Is Criticism Not Constructive? The Roles of Fairness Perceptions and Dispositional Attributions in Employee Acceptance of Critical Supervisory Feedback," *Human Relations* 54, no. 9 (September 2001): 1155–87; Ted Pollock, "Make Your Criticism Pay Off," *Electric Light & Power* 81, no. 1 (January 2003): 31; "Five Ways to Tackle Poor Performers," *Law Office Management & Administration Report* 6, no. 12 (December 2006): 9.

46. "Focus on Success," *Aftermarket Business* 115, no. 2 (February 2005): 1.

47. Helen Wilkie, "The Tricky Art of Criticism," *HRMagazine* 49, no. 12 (December 2004): 77–83.

Managing Compensation

After studying this chapter, you should be able to

Objective | 1 |

Explain employer concerns in developing a strategic compensation program.

Objective | 2 |

Indicate the various factors that influence the setting of wages.

© GETTY IMAGES

Objective | 3 |

Differentiate the mechanics of each of the major job evaluation systems.

Objective | 4 |

Explain the purpose of a wage survey.

Objective | 5 |

Define the wage curve, pay grades, and rate ranges as parts of the compensation structure.

Objective | 6 |

Identify the major provisions of the federal laws affecting compensation.

Objective | 7 |

Discuss the current issues of equal pay for comparable worth, pay compression, and low wage budgets.

411

An extensive review of the literature indicates that important work-related variables leading to job satisfaction include challenging work, interesting job assignments, equitable rewards, competent supervision, and rewarding careers.[1] It is doubtful, however, whether many employees would continue working were it not for the money they earn. Employees desire compensation systems that they perceive as being fair and commensurate with their skills and expectations.

Furthermore, in today's business environment of low wage and salary increases, pay has become an increasingly significant consideration for employees as they strive to maintain their standard of living.[2] Therefore, pay is a major consideration in HRM because it provides employees with a tangible reward for their services, as well as a source of recognition and self-esteem. Employee compensation includes all forms of pay and rewards received by employees for the performance of their jobs. *Direct compensation* encompasses employee wages and salaries, incentives, bonuses, and commissions. *Indirect compensation* comprises the many benefits supplied by employers, and *nonfinancial compensation* includes employee recognition programs, rewarding jobs, organizational support, work environment, and flexible work hours to accommodate personal needs.

Both managers and scholars agree that the way compensation is allocated among employees sends a message about what management believes is important and the types of activities it encourages.[3] Furthermore, for an employer, the payroll constitutes a sizable operating cost. Ravin Jesuthasan, compensation specialist at Towers Perrin, notes, "Labor costs are a significant portion of expenses for any organization and a very substantial portion for some, but companies continue to spend on pay programs without any evidence of business relevance."[4] A strategic compensation program, therefore, is essential so that pay can serve to motivate employee production sufficiently to keep labor costs at an acceptable level. This chapter will be concerned with the management of a compensation program, job evaluation systems, and pay structures for determining compensation payments. Included will be a discussion of federal regulations that affect wage and salary rates. Chapter 10 will review financial incentive plans for employees. Employee benefits that are part of the total compensation package are discussed in Chapter 11.

:: STRATEGIC COMPENSATION PLANNING

Objective | 1 |

What is strategic compensation planning? Simply stated, it is the compensation of employees in ways that enhance motivation and growth, while at the same time aligning their efforts with the objectives, philosophies, and culture of the organization. Strategic compensation planning goes beyond determining what market rates to pay employees—although market rates are one element of compensation planning—to purposefully linking compensation to the organization's mission and general business objectives. For example, in 2006, Microsoft Corporation, in the wake of managerial discontent, boosted the efficiency of its pay system by linking compensation payments to important business needs. An employee survey conducted in 2007 showed that employees now saw a stronger connection between pay and performance and the accomplishment of business goals and objectives.[5] Commenting on the importance of strategic compensation planning to organizational success, Gerald Ledford and Elizabeth Hawk, two compensation specialists, note, "Companies throughout the economy have begun to rethink their compensation systems in search for competitive advantage."

Additionally, strategic compensation planning serves to mesh the monetary payments made to employees with specific functions of the HR program. For example, in the recruitment of new employees, the rate of pay for jobs can increase or limit the supply of applicants. A compensation specialist speaking to one of the authors noted, "The linkage of pay levels to labor markets is a strategic policy issue because it serves to attract or retain valued employees while affecting the organization's relative payroll budget." For example, colleges such as Idaho State University; Mesa Community College in Mesa, Arizona; and the University of Georgia know that they cannot attract or retain qualified professors unless their pay strategy is linked to competitive market rates.

Many fast-food restaurants, such as Burger King, Taco Bell, and Blimpie's—traditionally low-wage employers—have needed to raise their starting wages to attract a sufficient number of job applicants to meet staffing requirements. If pay rates are high, creating a large applicant pool, then organizations may choose to raise their selection standards and hire better-qualified employees. This in turn can reduce employer training costs. When employees perform at exceptional levels, their performance appraisals may justify an increased pay rate. For these reasons and others, an organization should develop a formal HR program to manage employee compensation.

We will discuss three important aspects of strategic compensation planning: linking compensation to organizational objectives, the pay-for-performance standard, and motivating employees through compensation.

Linking Compensation to Organizational Objectives

Compensation has been revolutionized by heightened domestic competition, globalization, increased employee skill requirements, and new technology. Therefore, an outcome of today's dynamic business environment is that managers have needed to change their pay philosophies from paying for a specific position or job title to rewarding employees on the basis of their individual competencies or work contributions to organizational success. One study showed that 91 percent of responding organizations had a company compensation philosophy linking their pay strategy with organizational performance. As the authors of this study noted, "A written compensation philosophy indicates senior management understands and is committed to aligning their business strategy with pay, suggesting that alignment can have a positive impact on organizational effectiveness."[6]

Increasingly, compensation specialists are asking which components of the compensation package (benefits, base pay, incentives, and so on), both separately and in combination, create value for the organization and its employees. Managers are asking questions such as: "How will this pay program help to retain and motivate valued employees?" and "Does the benefit or pay practice affect the administrative cost?" Payments that fail to advance either the employee or the organization are removed from the compensation program.[7]

It is not uncommon for organizations to establish very specific goals for joining their organizational objectives to their compensation program.[8] Formalized compensation goals serve as guidelines for managers to ensure that wage and benefit policies achieve their intended purpose. The more common goals of a strategic compensation policy include the following:

1. To reward employees' past performance[9]

2. To remain competitive in the labor market

3. To maintain salary equity among employees

4. To mesh employees' future performance with organizational goals

5. To control the compensation budget

6. To attract new employees

7. To reduce unnecessary turnover[10]

To achieve these goals, policies must be established to guide management in making decisions. Formal statements of compensation policies typically include the following:

1. The rate of pay within the organization and whether it is to be above, below, or at the prevailing market rate

2. The ability of the pay program to gain employee acceptance while motivating employees to perform to the best of their abilities

3. The pay level at which employees may be recruited and the pay differential between new and more senior employees

4. The intervals at which pay raises are to be granted and the extent to which merit and/or seniority will influence the raises

5. The pay levels needed to facilitate the achievement of a sound financial position in relation to the products or services offered

The Pay-for-Performance Standard

This quote from compensation specialist Stephen E. Gross, global leader for Mercer Performance, Measurement, and Rewards consulting, illustrates the importance of pay-for-performance as a strategic pay practice: "Companies are looking for ways to pay for performance and segmenting their workforce helps them identify their most valuable contributors. Rewarding top performers is essential for the ongoing success of the company."[11] Why is this statement significant? A **pay-for-performance standard** serves to raise productivity and lower labor costs in today's competitive economic environment. It is agreed that managers must tie at least some reward to employee effort and performance. Without this standard, motivation to perform with greater effort will be low, resulting in higher wage costs to the organization. Additionally, most employees believe that their compensation should be directly linked to their relative performance.

> **pay-for-performance standard**
>
> A standard by which managers tie compensation to employee effort and performance

The term "pay for performance" refers to a wide range of compensation options, including merit-based pay, bonuses, salary commissions, job and pay banding, team/group incentives, and various gainsharing programs. (Gainsharing plans are discussed in Chapter 10.) Each of these compensation systems seeks to differentiate between the pay of average performers and that of outstanding performers. When Plum Creek Timber Company, the second largest timberland owner in the United States, merged with The Timber Company, it emphasized a pay-for-performance philosophy by forming new salary ranges based on each job's impact on the business and incentive rewards linked more directly to individual and company performance.

Unfortunately, designing a sound pay-for-performance system is not easy. Consideration must be given to how employee performance will be measured. For example, measuring an employee's output may be relatively easy and objective on an assembly line but more difficult (and subjective) when the employee works in a service environment. Other concerns include the monies to be allocated for compensation increases, which employees to cover, the payout method, and the periods when payments will be made.

Lumber workers are often paid on a pay-for-performance basis.

© D. C. LOWE/SUPERSTOCK

Perhaps the most critical concern for a successful pay-for-performance system is the amount of money allocated by organizations for annual salary increases. Rose Stanley, compensation specialist for WorldatWork, reports that annual salary budgets for 2008 averaged 3.9 percent. Projected annual salary budgets for 2009 are also 3.9 percent.[12] These percentages only slightly exceed yearly increases in the cost of living. Although differences exist as to how large a wage or salary increase must be before it is perceived as meaningful, a pay-for-performance program will lack its full potential when pay increases only approximate rises in the cost of living.

Motivating Employees through Compensation

Pay constitutes a quantitative measure of an employee's relative worth. For most employees, pay has a direct bearing not only on their standard of living, but also on the status and recognition they may be able to achieve both on and off the job. Because pay represents a reward received in exchange for an employee's contributions, it is essential, according to the equity theory, that the pay be equitable in terms of those contributions. It is essential also that an employee's pay be equitable in terms of what other employees are receiving for their contributions.

Pay Equity

Simply defined, equity embraces the concept of fairness. Equity theory, also referred to as *distributive fairness*, is a motivation theory that explains how people respond to situations in which they feel they have received less (or more) than they deserve.[13] Central to the theory is the role of perception in motivation and the fact that individuals make comparisons.[14] It states that individuals form a ratio of their inputs (abilities, skills, experiences) in a situation to their outcomes (salary, benefits) in that situation. They then compare the value of that ratio with the value of the input/output ratio for other individuals in a similar class of jobs either internal or external to the organization. If the value of their ratio equals the value of another's, they perceive the situation as equitable and no tension exists. However, if they perceive their input/output ratio as inequitable relative to others', this creates tension and motivates them to eliminate or reduce the inequity. The strength of their motivation is proportional to the magnitude of the perceived inequity. Figure 9.1 illustrates pay equity and feelings of being fairly paid.

pay equity
An employee's perception that compensation received is equal to the value of the work performed

For employees, pay equity is achieved when the compensation received is equal to the value of the work performed. Research clearly demonstrates that employees' perceptions of pay equity, or inequity, can have dramatic effects on their motivation for both work behavior and productivity. Managers must therefore develop strategic pay practices that are both internally and externally equitable. Compensation policies are *internally* equitable when employees believe that the wage rates for their jobs approximate the job's worth to the organization. Perceptions of *external* pay equity exist when the organization is paying wages that are relatively equal to what other employers are paying for similar types of work.

Expectancy Theory and Pay

The expectancy theory of motivation predicts that one's level of motivation depends on the attractiveness of the rewards sought and the probability of obtaining those rewards.[15] The theory has developed from the work of psychologists who consider humans as thinking, reasoning people who have beliefs and anticipations concerning future life events. Expectancy theory therefore holds that employees should exert greater work effort if they have reason to expect that it will result in a reward that is valued.[16] To motivate this effort, the value of any monetary reward should be attractive. Employees also must believe that good performance is valued by their employer and will result in their receiving the expected reward.

Figure 9.2 shows the relationship between pay-for-performance and the expectancy theory of motivation. The model predicts, first, that high effort will lead to

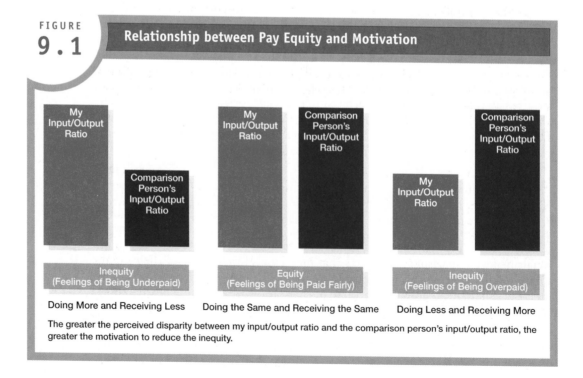

FIGURE 9.1

Relationship between Pay Equity and Motivation

My Input/Output Ratio

Comparison Person's Input/Output Ratio

Inequity
(Feelings of Being Underpaid)

Doing More and Receiving Less

My Input/Output Ratio

Comparison Person's Input/Output Ratio

Equity
(Feelings of Being Paid Fairly)

Doing the Same and Receiving the Same

My Input/Output Ratio

Comparison Person's Input/Output Ratio

Inequity
(Feelings of Being Overpaid)

Doing Less and Receiving More

The greater the perceived disparity between my input/output ratio and the comparison person's input/output ratio, the greater the motivation to reduce the inequity.

FIGURE 9.2

Pay-for-Performance and Expectancy Theory

Expectancy linkage → High effort → High performance → Value linkage → Valued monetary rewards → Pay satisfaction

high performance (expectancy). For example, if an employee believes she has the skills and abilities to perform her job and if she works hard (effort), then her performance will improve or be high. Second, high performance should result in rewards that are appreciated (valued). Elements of the compensation package are said to have *instrumentality* when an employee's high performance leads to monetary rewards that are valued. As we previously stated that pay-for-performance leads to a feeling of pay satisfaction, this feeling should reinforce one's high level of effort.

Thus, how employees view compensation can be an important factor in determining the motivational value of compensation. Furthermore, the effective communication of pay information together with an organizational environment that elicits employee trust in management can contribute to employees' having more accurate perceptions of their pay. The perceptions employees develop concerning their pay are influenced by the accuracy of their knowledge and understanding of the compensation program's strategic objectives.

Pay Secrecy

Misperceptions by employees concerning the equity of their pay and its relationship to performance can be created by secrecy about the pay that others receive. There is reason to believe that secrecy can generate distrust in the compensation system, reduce employee motivation, and inhibit organizational effectiveness. Yet pay secrecy seems to be an accepted practice in many organizations. Employers may have overt or implicit prohibitions on sharing pay information, and some even put the policies in writing.[17]

Managers may justify secrecy on the grounds that most employees prefer to have their own pay kept secret. Probably one of the reasons for pay secrecy that managers may be unwilling to admit is that it gives them greater freedom in compensation management because pay decisions are not disclosed and there is no need to justify or defend them.[18] Employees who are not supposed to know what others are being paid have no objective base for pursuing complaints about their own pay. Secrecy also serves to cover up inequities existing within the internal pay structure. Furthermore, secrecy surrounding compensation decisions may lead employees to believe that there is no direct relationship between pay and performance.

Managers wishing to maintain pay secrecy among employees may encounter problems with Internet salary survey data. Ready access to free online salary surveys gives employees an approximate idea of how their salary compares to others nationally or locally. This information could put managers "on the spot" should employees discover that their salaries are lower than those of other employees at comparable organizations.

The Bases for Compensation

hourly work

Work paid on an hourly basis

Work performed in most private, public, and not-for-profit organizations has traditionally been compensated on an hourly basis. It is referred to as hourly work, in contrast to piecework, in which employees are paid according to the number of units they produce. Hourly work, however, is far more prevalent than piecework as a basis for compensating employees.

piecework

Work paid according to the number of units produced

Employees compensated on an hourly basis are classified as *hourly employees*, or wage earners. Those whose compensation is computed on the basis of weekly, biweekly, or monthly pay periods are classified as *salaried employees*. Hourly employees are normally paid only for the time they work. Salaried employees, by contrast, are generally paid the same for each pay period, even though they occasionally may work more hours or fewer than the regular number of hours in a period. They also usually receive certain benefits not provided to hourly employees.

nonexempt employees

Employees covered by the overtime provisions of the Fair Labor Standards Act

Another basis for compensation centers on whether employees are classified as *nonexempt* or *exempt* under the Fair Labor Standards Act (FLSA).[19] Nonexempt employees are coverevd by the Act and must be paid at a rate of 1½ times their *regular* pay rate for time worked in excess of forty hours in their workweek. Most hourly workers employed in interstate commerce are considered nonexempt workers under the FLSA. Employees not covered by the overtime provision of the FLSA are classified as exempt employees. Managers and supervisors as well as a large number of white-collar employees are in the exempt category. The U.S. Department of Labor (DOL) imposes a narrow definition of exempt status, and employers wishing to classify employees as exempt must convince the DOL that the job is exempt on the basis of the independent judgment of the jobholder and other criteria. Therefore employers should check the exact terms and conditions of exemption before classifying employees as either exempt or nonexempt. (See "Exemption from Overtime Provisions" later in this chapter.)

exempt employees

Employees not covered by the overtime provisions of the Fair Labor Standards Act

■ DETERMINING COMPENSATION— THE WAGE MIX

Objective 2

Employees may inquire of their managers: "How are the wages for my job determined?" In practice, a combination of *internal* and *external* factors can influence, directly or indirectly, the rates at which employees are paid. Through their interaction these factors constitute the wage mix, as shown in Figure 9.3. For example, the area wage rate for administrative assistants might be $11.50 per hour. However,

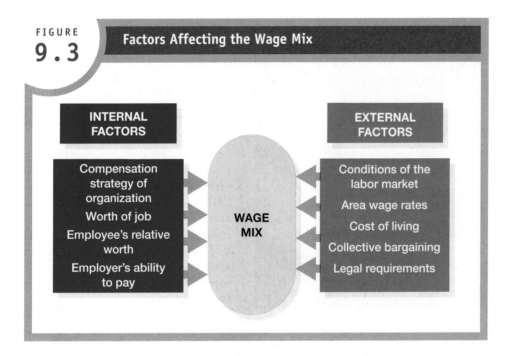

FIGURE
9.3

Factors Affecting the Wage Mix

INTERNAL FACTORS

Compensation strategy of organization

Worth of job

Employee's relative worth

Employer's ability to pay

WAGE MIX

EXTERNAL FACTORS

Conditions of the labor market

Area wage rates

Cost of living

Collective bargaining

Legal requirements

one employer may elect to pay its administrative assistants $14.25 per hour because of their excellent performance. The influence of government legislation on the wage mix will be discussed later in the chapter.

Internal Factors

The internal factors that influence wage rates are the employer's compensation strategy, the worth of a job, an employee's relative worth in meeting job requirements, and an employer's ability to pay.

Employer's Compensation Strategy

Highlights in HRM 1 illustrates the compensation strategies of two organizations, Tri Star Performance and Preventive Health Care. The pay strategy of Preventive Health Care is to be an industry pay leader, while Tri Star Performance seeks to be wage-competitive. Both employers strive to promote a compensation policy that is internally fair.

Tri Star Performance and Preventive Health Care, like other employers, will establish numerous compensation objectives that affect the pay employees receive. As a minimum, both large and small employers should set pay policies reflecting (1) the internal wage relationship among jobs and skill levels, (2) the external competition or an employer's pay position relative to what competitors are paying, (3) a policy of rewarding employee performance, and (4) administrative decisions concerning elements of the pay system such as overtime premiums, payment periods, and short-term or long-term incentives.

Assembly line workers have little opportunity to influence their individual pay

© BLEND IMAGES/JUPITER IMAGES

Worth of a Job

Organizations without a formal compensation program generally base the worth of jobs on the subjective opinions of people familiar with the jobs. In such instances, pay rates may be influenced heavily by the labor market or, in the case of unionized employers, by collective bargaining. Organizations with formal compensation programs, however, are more likely to rely on a system of *job evaluation* to aid in rate determination. Even when rates are subject to collective bargaining, job evaluation can assist the organization in maintaining some degree of control over its wage structure.

The use of job evaluation is widespread in both the public and the private sector. The cities of Chicago and Miami use job evaluation in establishing wage structures, as do Levi Strauss and Southwest Airlines. The jobs covered most frequently by job evaluation are clerical, technical, and various blue-collar groups. Other jobs covered are managerial and top executive positions.

In today's competitive environment, compensation professionals believe that the worth of a job should be based on more than market prices or using only an internally driven job evaluation program. Rather, a job's value should be based on *the total value* delivered to the organization. That is, some jobs may simply be more important to organizational success than others regardless of how they are internally evaluated. Valuing work not only properly enables organizations to price "important" jobs effectively, but also provides insight into how a job relates to overall organizational success. Additionally, valuing work properly serves to attract and retain the right talent to drive organizational performance.[20]

Employee's Relative Worth

In both hourly and salary jobs, employee performance can be recognized and rewarded through promotion and with various incentive systems. (The incentive systems used most often will be discussed in Chapter 10.) Superior performance can also be rewarded by granting merit raises on the basis of steps within a rate range established for a job class. If merit raises are to have their intended value, however, they must be determined by an effective performance appraisal system that differentiates between employees who deserve the raises and those who do not. This system, moreover, must provide a visible and credible relationship between performance and any raises received. Unfortunately, too many so-called merit systems provide for raises to be granted automatically. As a result, employees tend to be rewarded more for merely being present than for being productive on the job. Also, as previously noted, most increases may lack motivational value to employees when organizational salary budgets are low.[21]

HIGHLIGHTS IN HRM

1

Comparison of Compensation Strategies

Compensation strategies and objectives can differ widely across large and small employers as well as across employers in the private and public sectors. Here are the compensation strategies at Tri Star Performance and Preventive Health Care.

Tri Star Performance
- Promote pay-for-performance practices
- Pay market-competitive compensation
- Achieve internal and external pay equity
- Achieve simplicity in compensation programs
- Strive for employee commitment and a collaborative work environment
- Promote gender fairness in pay and benefits
- Comply with all governmental compensation regulations
- Minimize increased fixed costs

Preventive Health Care
- Be a pay leader in the health care industry
- Promote open and understandable pay practices
- Ensure fair employee treatment
- Offer benefits promoting individual employee needs
- Offer compensation rewarding employee creativity and achievements
- Offer compensation to foster the strategic mission of the organization
- Obtain employee input when developing compensation practices
- Emphasize performance through variable pay and stock options

Employer's Ability to Pay

Pay levels are limited by earned profits and other financial resources available to employers. This is clearly illustrated by financially burdened companies that ask their employees for pay cuts. Furthermore, an organization's ability to pay is determined in part by the productivity of its employees. This productivity is a result not only of their performance, but also of the amount of capital the organization has invested in labor-saving equipment. Generally, increases in capital investment reduce the number of employees required to perform the work and increase an employer's ability to provide higher pay for those it employs.

Economic conditions and competition faced by employers can also significantly affect the rates they are able to pay. Competition and recessions can force prices down and reduce the income from which compensation payments are derived. In such situations, employers have little choice but to reduce wages and/or lay off employees or, even worse, to go out of business.

External Factors

The major external factors that influence wage rates include labor market conditions, area wage rates, cost of living, collective bargaining if the employer is unionized, and legal requirements. The legal requirements of compensation will be discussed later in the chapter.

Labor Market Conditions

The labor market reflects the forces of supply and demand for qualified labor within an area. These forces help influence the wage rates required to recruit or retain competent employees. It must be recognized, however, that counterforces can reduce the full impact of supply and demand on the labor market. The economic power of unions, for example, may prevent employers from lowering wage rates even when unemployment is high among union members. Government regulations also may prevent an employer from paying at a market rate less than an established minimum.

Area Wage Rates

A formal wage structure should provide rates that are in line with those being paid by other employers for comparable jobs within the area. Data pertaining to area wage rates may be obtained from local wage surveys. For example, the Arizona Department of Economic Security conducts an annual wage survey for both large and small employers in various cities throughout the state. Wage survey data also may be obtained from a variety of sources, including the American Management Association, Administrative Management Society, U.S. Department of Labor, and Federal Reserve Banks. Smaller employers such as the Woodsmith Corporation and Golden State Container use government surveys to establish rates of pay for new and senior employees. Many organizations, such as the City of Atlanta, Northwest Airlines, and Progress Energy, conduct their own surveys. Others engage in a cooperative exchange of wage information or rely on various professional associations for these data. A high percentage of wage data surveys are inexpensive—less than $100—and are therefore available to all employers, regardless of size.

Wage surveys (discussed fully later in the chapter) serve the important function of providing external wage equity between the surveying organization and other organizations competing for labor in the surrounding labor market. Importantly, data from area wage surveys can be used to prevent the rates for jobs from drifting too far above or below those of other employers in the region. When rates rise above existing area levels, an employer's labor costs may become excessive. Conversely, if they drop too far below area levels, it may be difficult to recruit and retain competent personnel. Wage survey data must also take into account indirect wages paid in the form of benefits.

Cost of Living

consumer price index (CPI)

A measure of the average change in prices over time in a fixed "market basket" of goods and services

Because of inflation, compensation rates have had to be adjusted upward periodically to help employees maintain their purchasing power. Employers make these changes with the help of the consumer price index (CPI). The CPI is a measure of the average change in prices over time in a fixed "market basket" of goods and services. The consumer price index is based on prices of food, clothing, shelter, and fuels; transportation fares; charges for medical services; and prices of other goods and services that people buy for day-to-day living. The Bureau of Labor Statistics collects price information on a monthly basis and calculates the CPI for the nation as a whole and various U.S. city averages. Separate indexes are also published by size of city and by region of the country. Employers in a number of communities monitor changes in the CPI as a basis for compensation decisions.

CPI figures can have important consequences for organizational morale and productivity. Granting wages based largely on "cost-of-living" figures will not inspire higher employee performance and may cause valued employees to leave the organization. Cost-of-living payments, when traditionally given, may be seen by employees as "entitlements" unrelated to individual performance. Furthermore, should cost-of-living increases be discontinued, managers can expect disgruntled employees, particularly those not likely to receive merit raises.

Employees who work under a union contract may receive wage increases through **escalator clauses** found in their labor agreement. These clauses provide for cost-of-living adjustments (COLA) in wages based on changes in the CPI. The most common adjustments are 1 cent per hour for each 0.3- or 0.4-point change in the CPI. COLAs are favored by unions during particularly high periods of inflation.

escalator clauses

Clauses in labor agreements that provide for quarterly cost-of-living adjustments in wages, basing the adjustments on changes in the consumer price index

Collective Bargaining

One of the primary functions of a labor union, as emphasized in Chapter 14, is to bargain collectively over conditions of employment, the most important of which is compensation.[22] The union's goal in each new agreement is to achieve increases in **real wages**—wage increases larger than the increase in the CPI—thereby improving the purchasing power and standard of living of its members. This goal includes gaining wage settlements that equal or exceed the pattern established by other unions within the area.

real wages

Wage increases larger than rises in the consumer price index, that is, the real earning power of wages

The agreements negotiated by unions tend to establish rate patterns within the labor market. As a result, wages are generally higher in areas where organized labor is strong. To recruit and retain competent personnel and avoid unionization, nonunion employers must either meet or exceed these rates. The "union scale" also becomes the prevailing rate that all employers must pay for work performed under government contract. The impact of collective bargaining therefore extends beyond the segment of the labor force that is unionized.

Job Evaluation Systems

As we discussed earlier, one important component of the wage mix is the worth of the job. Organizations formally determine the value of jobs through the process of job evaluation. **Job evaluation** is the systematic process of determining the *relative* worth of jobs in order to establish which jobs should be paid more than others within the organization. Job evaluation helps establish internal equity between various jobs. The relative worth of a job may be determined by comparing it with others within the organization or by comparing it with a scale that has been constructed for this purpose. Each method of comparison, furthermore, may be made on the basis of the jobs as a whole or on the basis of the parts that constitute the jobs.[23]

3 Objective

job evaluation

A systematic process of determining the relative worth of jobs in order to establish which jobs should be paid more than others within an organization

Three traditional methods of comparison provide the basis for the principal systems of job evaluation. We will begin by discussing the simpler nonquantitative approaches and conclude by reviewing the more popular quantitative system. Also discussed is a newer method of job evaluation—work evaluation. Regardless of the methodology used, it is important to remember that all job evaluation methods require varying degrees of managerial judgment. Also, those involved in evaluating jobs must consider the impact of the Americans with Disabilities Act on the process. (See Chapter 3.)

Job Ranking System

job ranking system

The simplest and oldest system of job evaluation by which jobs are arrayed on the basis of their relative worth

The simplest and oldest system of job evaluation is the job ranking system, which arrays jobs on the basis of their relative worth. One technique used to rank jobs consists of having the raters arrange cards listing the duties and responsibilities of each job in order of the importance of the jobs. Job ranking can be done by a single individual knowledgeable about all jobs or by a committee composed of management and employee representatives.

The basic disadvantage of the job ranking system is that it does not provide a very precise measure of each job's worth. Another weakness is that the final ranking of jobs indicates the relative importance of the job, not the differences in the degree of importance that may exist between jobs. A final limitation of the job ranking method is that it can be used only with a small number of jobs, probably no more than fifteen. Its simplicity, however, makes it ideal for use by smaller employers.

Job Classification System

job classification system

A system of job evaluation in which jobs are classified and grouped according to a series of predetermined wage grades

In the job classification system, jobs are classified and grouped according to a series of predetermined grades. Successive grades require increasing amounts of job responsibility, skill, knowledge, ability, or other factors selected to compare jobs. For example, Grade GS-1 from the federal government grade descriptions reads as follows:

> GS-1 includes those classes of positions the duties of which are to perform, under immediate supervision, with little or no latitude for the exercise of independent judgment (A) the simplest routine work in office, business, or fiscal operations; or (B) elementary work of a subordinate technical character in a professional, scientific, or technical field.

The descriptions of each of the job classes constitute the scale against which the specifications for the various jobs are compared. Managers then evaluate jobs by comparing job descriptions with the different wage grades in order to "slot" the job into the appropriate grade. While this system has the advantage of simplicity, it is less precise than the point system because the job is evaluated as a whole. The federal civil service job classification system is probably the best-known system of this type. The job classification system is widely used by municipal and state governments.[24]

Point System

point system

A quantitative job evaluation procedure that determines the relative value of a job by the total points assigned to it

The point system is a quantitative job evaluation procedure that determines a job's relative value by calculating the total points assigned to it.[25] It has been successfully used by high-visibility organizations such as Digital Equipment Company, Met

Life, Johnson Wax, Prudential Financial, TransAmerica, and many other public and private organizations, both large and small. Although point systems are rather complicated to establish, once in place they are relatively simple to understand and use. The principal advantage of the point system is that it provides a more refined basis for making judgments than either the ranking or classification systems and thereby can produce results that are more valid and less easy to manipulate.

The point system permits jobs to be evaluated quantitatively on the basis of factors or elements—commonly called *compensable factors*—that constitute the job.[26] The skills, efforts, responsibilities, and working conditions that a job usually entails are the more common major compensable factors that serve to rank one job as more or less important than another. More contemporary factors might include fiscal accountability, leadership, teamwork, and project accountability. The number of compensable factors an organization uses depends on the nature of the organization and the jobs to be evaluated. Once selected, compensable factors will be assigned weights according to their relative importance to the organization. For example, if responsibility is considered extremely important to the organization, it could be assigned a weight of 40 percent. Next, each factor will be divided into a number of degrees. Degrees represent different levels of difficulty associated with each factor.

The Point Manual

The point system requires the use of a *point manual*. The point manual is, in effect, a handbook that contains a description of the compensable factors and the degrees to which these factors may exist within the jobs. A manual also will indicate—usually by means of a table—the number of points allocated to each factor and to each of the degrees into which these factors are divided. The point value assigned to a job represents the sum of the numerical degree values of each compensable factor that the job possesses.

For example, the job factors illustrated in Highlights in HRM 2 represent those covered by the American Association of Industrial Management point manual. Each of the factors listed in this manual has been divided into five degrees. The number of degrees into which the factors in a manual are to be divided, however, can be greater or smaller than this number, depending on the relative weight assigned to each factor and the ease with which the individual degrees can be defined or distinguished. A statement is provided defining each of the degrees, as well as each factor as a whole. The definitions should be concise and yet distinguish the factors and each of their degrees. Highlights in HRM 3 represents another portion of the point manual used by the American Association of Industrial Management to describe each of the degrees for the education factor. These descriptions enable those conducting a job evaluation to determine the degree to which the factors exist in each job being evaluated.

Using the Point Manual

Job evaluation under the point system is accomplished by comparing the job descriptions and job specifications, factor by factor, against the various factor-degree descriptions contained in the manual. Each factor within the job being evaluated is then assigned the number of points specified in the manual. When the points for each factor have been determined from the manual, the total point value for the job as a whole can be

2

Point Values for Job Factors of the American Association of Industrial Management

FACTORS	1ST DEGREE	2ND DEGREE	3RD DEGREE	4TH DEGREE	5TH DEGREE
Skill					
1. Education	14	28	42	56	70
2. Experience	22	44	66	88	110
3. Initiative and ingenuity	14	28	42	56	70
Effort					
4. Physical demand	10	20	30	40	50
5. Mental or visual demand	5	10	15	20	25
Responsibility					
6. Equipment or process	5	10	15	20	25
7. Material or product	5	10	15	20	25
8. Safety of others	5	10	15	20	25
9. Work of others	5	10	15	20	25
Job Conditions					
10. Working conditions	10	20	30	40	50
11. Hazards	5	10	15	20	25

Source: Reproduced with permission of the American Association of Industrial Management, Springfield, Mass.

calculated. The relative worth of the job is then determined from the total points that have been assigned to that job.

Work Valuation

work valuation

A job evaluation system that seeks to measure a job's worth through its value to the organization

Work valuation is a relatively new job evaluation system championed to meet the demands of a dynamic business environment. The cornerstone for work valuation is that work should be valued relative to the business goals of the organization rather than by an internally applied point-factor job evaluation system.[27] As noted by one compensation specialist, "Valuing work properly enables organizations to not only price individual jobs effectively, but provides

HIGHLIGHTS IN HRM

Description of Education Factor and Degrees of the American Association of Industrial Management

1. EDUCATION

This factor measures the basic trades training, knowledge or "scholastic contact" essential as background or training preliminary to learning the job duties. This job knowledge or background may have been acquired either by formal education or by training on jobs of lesser degree or by any combination of these approaches.

1st Degree   14 points

Requires the use of simple writing, adding, subtracting, whole numbers and the carrying out of instructions; and the use of fixed gauges and direct reading instruments and devices in which interpretation is not required.

2nd Degree   28 points

Requires the use of commercial English, grammar and arithmetic such as addition, subtraction, multiplication and division, including decimals and fractions; simple use of formulas, charts, tables, drawings, specifications, schedules, wiring diagrams, together with the use of adjustable measuring instruments, graduates and the like requiring interpretation in their various applications; or the posting, preparation, interpretation, use and checking of reports, forms, records and comparable data.

3rd Degree   42 points

Requires the use of shop mathematics together with the use of complicated drawings, specifications, charts, tables, various types of adjustable measuring instruments and the training generally applicable in a particular or specialized occupation. Equivalent to 1 to 3 years applied trades training.

4th Degree   56 points

Requires the use of advanced shop mathematics, together with the use of complicated drawings, specifications, charts, tables, handbook formulas, all varieties of adjustable measuring instruments and the uses of broad training in a recognized trade or craft. Equivalent to complete, accredited, indentured apprenticeship or equivalent to high school plus a 2-year technical college education.

5th Degree   70 points

Requires the use of higher mathematics involved in the application of engineering principles and the performance of related, practical operations, together with a comprehensive knowledge of the theories and practices of mechanical, electrical, chemical, civil or like engineering field. Equivalent to complete 4 years of technical college or university education.

Source: Reproduced with permission of the American Association of Industrial Management, Springfield, Mass.

insight into how jobs relate to overall organizational goals and objectives and how roles ultimately contribute to organizational success."[28] Additionally, work valuation serves to direct compensation dollars to the type of work pivotal to organizational goals.

With work valuations, work is measured through standards that come directly from business goals. For example, jobs might be valued relative to financial, operational, or customer service objectives. All forms of work, employee roles, and ways of organizing work (such as teams) are valued. The work evaluation process ends with a work hierarchy that is an array of work by value to the organization. The work hierarchy is eventually priced through wage surveys to determine individual pay rates.

Job Evaluation for Management Positions

Because management positions are more difficult to evaluate and involve certain demands not found in jobs at the lower levels, some organizations do not attempt to include them in their job evaluation programs for hourly employees. Rather, they employ either a standardized (purchased) program or customize a point method to fit their particular jobs. However, regardless of the approach adopted, point plans for executive and managerial employees operate similarly to those for other groups of employees.

One of the better-known standardized job evaluation programs for evaluating executive, managerial, and professional positions is the Hay profile method, developed by Edward N. Hay. The three broad factors that constitute the evaluation in the "profile" are knowledge (or know-how), mental activity (or problem-solving), and accountability. The Hay method uses only three factors because it is assumed that these factors represent the most important aspects of all executive and managerial positions. The profile for each position is developed by determining the percentage value to be assigned to each of the three factors. Jobs are then ranked on the basis of each factor, and point values that make up the profile are assigned to each job on the basis of the percentage-value level at which the job is ranked.

Hay profile method

A job evaluation technique using three factors—knowledge, mental activity, and accountability—to evaluate executive and managerial positions

■ THE COMPENSATION STRUCTURE

Job evaluation systems provide for internal equity and serve as the basis for wage rate determination. They do not in themselves determine the wage rate. The evaluated worth of each job in terms of its rank, class, points, or monetary worth must be converted into an hourly, daily, weekly, or monthly wage rate. The compensation tool used to help set wages is the wage and salary survey.

Wage and Salary Surveys

Objective   4

wage and salary survey

A survey of the wages paid to employees of other employers in the surveying organization's relevant labor market

The wage and salary survey is a survey of the wages paid by employers in an organization's relevant labor market—local, regional, or national, depending on the job. The labor market is frequently defined as the area from which employers obtain certain types of workers. The labor market for office personnel would be local, whereas the labor market for engineers would be national. It is the wage and salary survey that permits an organization to maintain external equity—that is, to pay its employees wages equivalent to the wages similar employees earn in other establishments.

When job evaluation and wage survey data are used jointly, they link the likelihood of both internal and external equity. Although surveys are conducted primarily to gather competitive wage data, they can also collect information on employee benefits or organizational pay practices (such as overtime rates or shift differentials).

Collecting Survey Data

While many organizations conduct their own wage and salary surveys, a variety of "preconducted" pay surveys are available to satisfy the requirements of most public and not-for-profit or private employers. The Bureau of Labor Statistics (BLS) is the major publisher of wage and salary data. The BLS publishes the National Compensation Survey (NCS), a statistically valid and comprehensive compensation program of wage, salary, and benefit information. (See Highlights in HRM 4.) As described on the BLS Web site, "The National Compensation Survey is the umbrella program that combines several BLS compensation programs into a single vehicle that can produce local, regional, and national statistics on levels, trends, and characteristics of pay and benefits."[29]

> **Using the Internet**
>
> The Bureau of Labor Statistics publishes wage and salary data and benefits information. Go to the Student Resources at:
>
> **www.cengage.com/ management/bohlander**

Many states conduct surveys on either a municipal or county basis and make them available to employers. Besides these government surveys, trade groups such as the Dallas Personnel Association, Administrative Management Society, Society for Human Resource Management, American Management Association, National Society of Professional Engineers, and Financial Executive Institute conduct special surveys tailored to their members' needs.[30] Employers with global operations can purchase international surveys through large consulting firms. The overseas compensation survey offered by *TPF&C* reports on payment practices in twenty countries. While all of these third-party surveys provide certain benefits to their users, they also have various limitations. Two problems with all published surveys are that (1) they are not always compatible with the user's jobs and (2) the user cannot specify what specific data to collect. To overcome these problems, organizations may collect their own compensation data.

HRIS and Salary Surveys

Wage and benefits survey data can be found on numerous Web sites. The previously mentioned National Compensation Survey is an example. Also readily available are commercial products such as those offered at http://www.salary.com: the Salary Wizard, Comp Analyst, and Survey Finder surveys. Survey Finder has a database of hundreds of compensation surveys offered by more than fifty independent vendors. Managers and compensation specialists can search for applicable surveys for either purchase or participation.[31]

Employer-Initiated Surveys

Employers wishing to conduct their own wage and salary survey must first select the jobs to be used in the survey and identify the organizations with whom they actually compete for employees. Since it is not feasible to survey all the jobs in

Bureau of Labor Statistics National Compensation Survey

NCS data are used by managers and compensation specialists in large and small organizations to answer such questions as the following:

- How much must I pay accountants in Atlanta, Georgia?
- Is a 3 percent benefits increase comparable to that of other employers in the manufacturing industry?
- Is vision coverage a prevalent benefit among large employers in the Northeast?
- How have wage costs changed over the past year?

How the NCS Survey Works

The National Compensation Survey is an area-based survey. Wage and benefit data are collected from a predetermined set of 154 metropolitan and nonmetropolitan areas through the fifty states and the District of Columbia to represent the United States. Compensation information is collected from such diverse locations as Knoxville, Tennessee; Pittsburgh, Pennsylvania; Reno, Nevada; and Richland-Kennewick-Pasco, Washington. All areas are selected to produce regional estimates for nine broad geographic divisions and four broad regions.

Within each area, a scientific sample of establishments represents all area establishments. An "establishment" is a single physical location, such as a plant, warehouse, corporate office, or retail outlet. State and local government offices are also included in the survey.

Once an establishment has been chosen for inclusion in the survey, a BLS economist selects occupations within that establishment to represent all occupations in the establishment. The BLS limits the selection to a small number of occupations to reduce the survey burden for employers. Data are collected for all incumbents in a selected occupation.

The selected occupations are then classified based on the Census Bureau's occupation classification system. The census classification categorizes approximately 450 individual occupations into ten major groupings such as sales, professional specialty, and technical, and machine operators, assemblers, and inspectors. For the occupations selected, wage and benefit data are collected. Items included in the collection of wages are time-based payments, piece rates, commissions, hazard pay, and other items directly related to the work being performed. A variety of benefit data are collected, including paid vacations, paid holidays, paid sick leave, shift differentials, and nonproduction bonuses.

an organization, normally only key jobs, also called benchmark jobs, are used. Characteristics of key jobs include the following:

1. They are important to employees and the organization.

2. They contain a large number of positions.

3. They have relatively stable job content.

4. They have the same job content across many organizations.

5. They are acceptable to employees, management, and labor as appropriate for pay comparisons.

The survey of key jobs will usually be sent to ten or fifteen organizations that represent a valid sample of other employers likely to compete for the employees of the surveying organization. A diversity of organizations should be selected—large and small, public and private, new and established, and union and nonunion— since each classification of employer is likely to pay different wage rates for surveyed jobs.

After the key jobs and the employers to be surveyed have been identified, the surveying organization must decide what information to gather on wages, benefit types, and pay policies. For example, when requesting pay data, it is important to specify whether hourly, daily, or weekly pay figures are needed. In addition, those conducting surveys must state whether the wage data are needed for new hires or for senior employees. Precisely defining the compensation data needed will greatly increase the accuracy of the information received and the number of purposes for which it can be used.[32] Once the survey data are tabulated, the compensation structure can be completed.

The Wage Curve

The relationship between the relative worth of jobs and their wage rates can be represented by means of a wage curve. This curve may indicate the rates currently paid for jobs within an organization, new rates resulting from job evaluation, or rates for similar jobs currently being paid by other organizations within the labor market. A curve may be constructed graphically by preparing a scattergram consisting of a series of dots that represent the current wage rates. As shown in Figure 9.4, a freehand curve is then drawn through the cluster of dots in such a manner as to leave approximately an equal number of dots above and below the curve. The wage curve can be relatively straight or curved. This curve can then be used to determine the relationship between the value of a job and its wage rate at any given point on the line.

Pay Grades

From an administrative standpoint, it is generally preferable to group jobs into pay grades and to pay all jobs within a particular grade the same rate or rate range. When the classification system of job evaluation is used, jobs are grouped into grades as part of the evaluation process. When the point system is used, however, pay grades must be established at selected intervals that represent either the point or the evaluated monetary value of these jobs. The graph in Figure 9.5 illustrates a series of pay grades designated along the horizontal axis at fifty-point intervals.

5 | Objective

wage curve
A curve in a scattergram representing the relationship between relative worth of jobs and wage rates

pay grades
Groups of jobs within a particular class that are paid the same rate

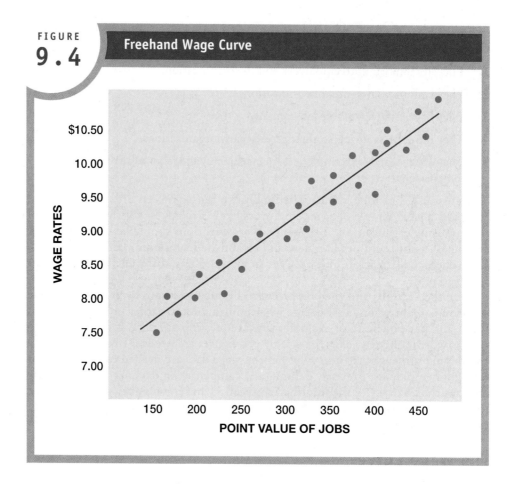

FIGURE 9.4   **Freehand Wage Curve**

The grades within a wage structure may vary in number.[33] The number is determined by such factors as the slope of the wage curve, the number and distribution of the jobs within the structure, and the organization's wage administration and promotion policies. The number utilized should be sufficient to permit difficulty levels to be distinguished, but not so great as to make the distinction between two adjoining grades insignificant.

Rate Ranges

Although a single rate may be created for each pay grade, as shown in Figure 9.5, it is more common to provide a range of rates for each pay grade. The rate ranges may be the same for each grade or proportionately greater for each successive grade, as shown in Figure 9.6. Rate ranges constructed on the latter basis provide a greater incentive for employees to accept a promotion to a job in a higher grade.

Rate ranges generally are divided into a series of steps that permit employees to receive increases up to the maximum rate for the range on the basis of merit or seniority or a combination of the two. Most salary structures provide for the ranges of adjoining pay grades to overlap. The purpose of the overlap is to permit an employee

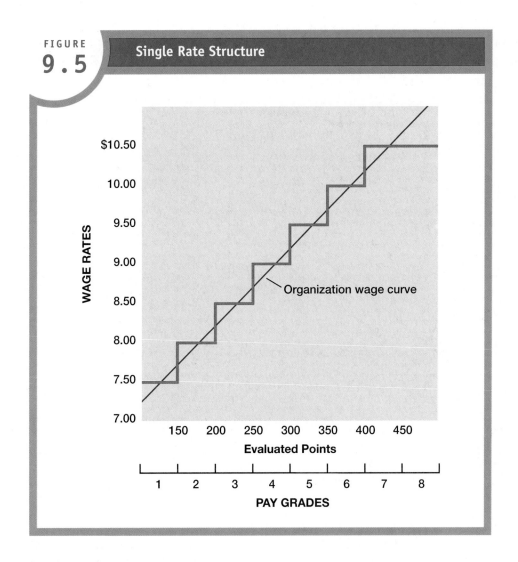

FIGURE 9.5

Single Rate Structure

Organization wage curve

WAGE RATES

$10.50
10.00
9.50
9.00
8.50
8.00
7.50
7.00

150 200 250 300 350 400 450

Evaluated Points

1   2   3   4   5   6   7   8

PAY GRADES

with experience to earn as much as or more than a person with less experience in the next higher job classification.

The final step in setting up a wage structure is to determine the appropriate pay grade into which each job should be placed on the basis of its evaluated worth. Traditionally, this worth is determined on the basis of job requirements without regard to the performance of the person in that job. Under this system, the performance of those who exceed the requirements of a job may be acknowledged by merit increases within the grade range or by promotion to a job in the next higher pay grade.[34]

Organizations may pay individuals above the maximum of the pay range when employees have high seniority or promotional opportunities are scarce. Wages paid above the range maximum are called **red circle rates.** Because these rates are exceptions to the pay structure, employers often "freeze" these rates until all ranges are shifted upward through market wage adjustments.

red circle rates

Payment rates above the maximum of the pay range

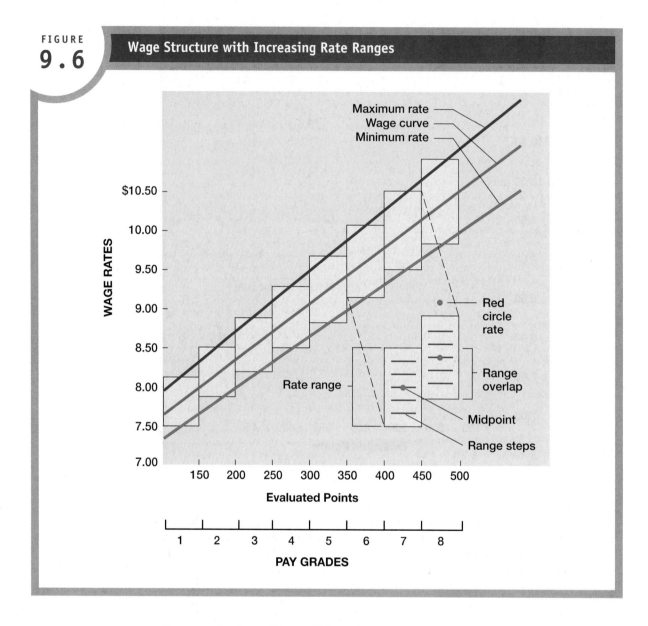

FIGURE
9.6

Wage Structure with Increasing Rate Ranges

Competence-Based Pay

The predominant approach to employee compensation is still the job-based system. Unfortunately, such a system often fails to reward employees for their skills or the knowledge they possess or to encourage them to learn a new job-related skill. Additionally, job-based pay systems may not reinforce an organizational culture stressing employee involvement or provide increased employee flexibility to meet overall production or service requirements. Therefore, organizations such as Frito-Lay, Nortel Networks, Sherwin-Williams, and Honeywell have introduced competence-based pay plans.

competence-based pay
Pay based on an employee's skill level, variety of skills possessed, or increased job knowledge

Competence-based pay, also referred to as skill-based pay or knowledge-based pay, compensates employees for the different skills or increased knowledge they possess rather than for the job they hold in a designated job category.[35] Regardless of the name, these pay plans encourage employees to earn higher base wages by learning and performing a wider variety of skills (or jobs) or displaying an array of competencies that can be applied to a variety of organizational requirements. For example, in a manufacturing setting, new tasks might include various assembly activities carried out in a particular production system or a variety of maintenance functions. Within service organizations, employees might acquire new knowledge related to advanced computer systems or accounting procedures. Organizations will grant an increase in pay after each skill or knowledge has been mastered and can be demonstrated according to a predetermined standard.

Competence-based pay systems represent a fundamental change in the attitude of management regarding how work should be organized and how employees should be paid for their work efforts. The most frequently cited benefits of competence-based pay include greater productivity, increased employee learning and commitment to work, improved staffing flexibility to meet production or service demands, and reduced effects of absenteeism and turnover, because managers can assign employees where and when needed. Competence-based pay also encourages employees to acquire training when new or updated skills are needed by an organization.

Unfortunately, competence-based plans bring some long-term difficulties. Some plans limit the amount of compensation employees can earn, regardless of the new skills or competencies they acquire. Thus, after achieving the top wage, employees may be reluctant to continue their educational training. Perhaps the greatest challenge in paying individuals for their skills, knowledge, and competencies is developing appropriate measures. It is difficult to write specific knowledge and skill descriptions for jobs that employees perform and then establish accurate measures of acquired skills or knowledge.

Broadbanding

Organizations that adopt a competency-based or skill-based pay system frequently use *broadbanding* to structure their compensation payments to employees. Broadbanding simply collapses many traditional salary grades into a few wide salary bands. Broadbands may have midpoints and quartiles, or they may have extremely wide salary ranges or no ranges at all. Banding encourages lateral skill building while addressing the need to pay employees performing multiple jobs with different skill level requirements. Additionally, broadbands help eliminate the obsession with grades and, instead, encourage employees to move to jobs in which they can develop in their careers and add value to the organization. Paying employees through broadbands enables organizations to consider job responsibilities, individual skills and competencies, and career mobility patterns in assigning employees to bands.[36]

GOVERNMENT REGULATION OF COMPENSATION

6 | Objective

Compensation management, like the other areas of HRM, is subject to state and federal regulations. A majority of states have minimum wage laws or wage boards that fix minimum wage rates on an industry-by-industry basis. When an employee is subject to both the state and federal minimum wage laws, the employee is entitled to the higher of the two minimum wages. (See Highlights in HRM 5 for state minimum wage laws.) Most states also regulate hours of work and overtime payments.

The three principal federal laws affecting wages are the Davis-Bacon Act, Walsh-Healy Act, and Fair Labor Standards Act. These laws were enacted during the 1930s

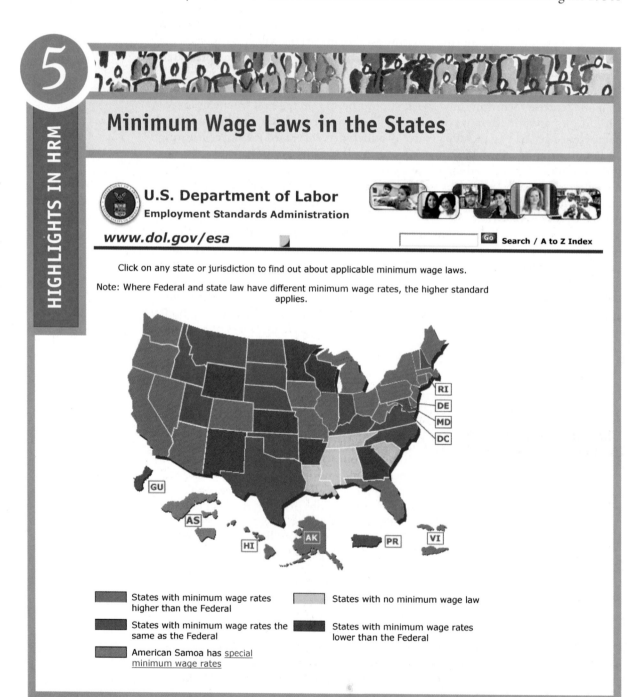

HIGHLIGHTS IN HRM

5

Minimum Wage Laws in the States

U.S. Department of Labor
Employment Standards Administration

www.dol.gov/esa Go Search / A to Z Index

Click on any state or jurisdiction to find out about applicable minimum wage laws.

Note: Where Federal and state law have different minimum wage rates, the higher standard applies.

RI
DE
MD
DC

GU

AS

HI AK PR VI

■ States with minimum wage rates higher than the Federal

■ States with no minimum wage law

■ States with minimum wage rates the same as the Federal

■ States with minimum wage rates lower than the Federal

■ American Samoa has special minimum wage rates

to prevent the payment of abnormally low wage rates and to encourage the spreading of work among a greater number of workers. The latter objective was accomplished by forcing organizations to pay a premium rate for overtime work (all hours worked in excess of a prescribed number).

Davis-Bacon Act of 1931

The Davis-Bacon Act, also referred to as the Prevailing Wage Law, was passed in 1931 and is the oldest of the three federal wage laws. It requires that the minimum wage rates paid to people employed on federal public works projects worth more than $2,000 be at least equal to the prevailing rates and that overtime be paid at 1½ times this rate. The act is criticized because the prevailing rates are often the union rates for jobs in the area and are often higher than the average (nonunion) rates.

Walsh-Healy Act of 1936

The Walsh-Healy Act, which is officially called the Public Contracts Act, was passed in 1936 and covers workers employed on government contract work for supplies, equipment, and materials worth in excess of $10,000. The act requires contractors to pay employees at least the prevailing wage rates established for the area by the Secretary of Labor and overtime of 1½ times the regular rate for all work performed in excess of eight hours in one day or forty hours in one week, depending on which basis provides the larger premium.

Fair Labor Standards Act of 1938 (as Amended)

The Fair Labor Standards Act (FLSA), commonly referred to as the Wage and Hour Act, was passed in 1938 and since then has been amended many times. It covers employees who are engaged in the production of goods for interstate and foreign commerce, including those whose work is closely related to or essential to such production. The Act also covers agricultural workers, as well as employees of certain retail and service establishments whose sales volume exceeds a prescribed amount. The major provisions of the FLSA are concerned with minimum wage rates and overtime payments, child labor, and equal rights.[37]

Wage and Hour Provisions

The minimum wage prescribed by federal law has been raised many times, from an original figure of 25 cents per hour to $5.85 per hour on July 24, 2007. (See Highlights in HRM 6 for the federal minimum wage poster that employers are required to display.) This minimum rate applies to the actual earning rate before any overtime premiums have been added. An overtime rate of 1½ times the base rate must be paid for all hours worked in excess of forty during a given week. The base wage rate from which the overtime rate is computed must include incentive payments or bonuses that are received during the period. When employees are given time off in return for overtime work (referred to as *compensatory time off* or *comp time*), it must be granted at 1½ times the number of hours that were worked as overtime. Employees who are paid on a piece-rate base must receive a premium for overtime work. The FLSA does not, however, require severance pay, sick leave, vacation, or holidays.

The use of child labor was common by employers before passage of the FLSA.

Along with equal employment opportunity lawsuits, wage and hour violations are another problem for managers.[38] For example, in 2006 and 2007, Carnival Cruise Lines, Citigroup/Salomon Smith Barney, IBM, Sony Computer, and UPS paid more than $260 million to employees as a result of DOL investigations of FLSA violations.[39] Employees are increasingly filing charges with the DOL that accuse companies of cheating them out of overtime pay. Also, failure to include all periods of work can often lead to overtime miscalculations. Some important compensable situations include the following:

- Downtime or call-in time, during which the employee must be readily available for work

- Payment for required classes, meetings, or other periods of instruction

- Travel between job sites

- Preparation and cleanup before and after shifts

- Break periods shorter than twenty minutes

Clearly, a complete understanding of when and how to pay employees is the best protection against a DOL investigation into overtime violation.[40] Furthermore, under the FLSA, an employer must pay an employee for whatever work the employer "suffers or permits" the employee to perform, even if the work is done away from the workplace and even if it is not specifically expected or requested. This condition could likely occur when employees work away from headquarters and are unsupervised or when they telecommute on a frequent basis.

Some argue that the "floor" imposed by the minimum wage makes it more difficult for high school students and young adults to find jobs. Many employers who might

HIGHLIGHTS IN HRM

6

The Federal Wage Poster

EMPLOYEE RIGHTS

UNDER THE FAIR LABOR STANDARDS ACT

THE UNITED STATES DEPARTMENT OF LABOR WAGE AND HOUR DIVISION

FEDERAL MINIMUM WAGE

$5.85 PER HOUR	**$6.55** PER HOUR	**$7.25** PER HOUR
BEGINNING JULY 24, 2007	BEGINNING JULY 24, 2008	BEGINNING JULY 24, 2009

OVERTIME PAY
At least $1\frac{1}{2}$ times your regular rate of pay for all hours worked over 40 in a workweek.

YOUTH EMPLOYMENT
An employee must be at least **16** years old to work in most non-farm jobs and at least **18** to work in non-farm jobs declared hazardous by the Secretary of Labor.

Youths **14** and **15** years old may work outside school hours in various non-manufacturing, non-mining, non-hazardous jobs under the following conditions:

No more than
- **3** hours on a school day or **18** hours in a school week;
- **8** hours on a non-school day or **40** hours in a non-school week.

Also, work may not begin before **7 a.m.** or end after **7 p.m.**, except from June 1 through Labor Day, when evening hours are extended to **9 p.m.** Different rules apply in agricultural employment. For more information, visit the YouthRules! Web site at **www.youthrules.dol.gov**.

TIP CREDIT
Employers of "tipped employees" must pay a cash wage of at least $2.13 per hour if they claim a tip credit against their minimum wage obligation. If an employee's tips combined with the employer's cash wage of at least $2.13 per hour do not equal the minimum hourly wage, the employer must make up the difference. Certain other conditions must also be met.

ENFORCEMENT
The Department of Labor may recover back wages either administratively or through court action, for the employees that have been underpaid in violation of the law. Violations may result in civil or criminal action.

Civil money penalties of up to $11,000 per violation may be assessed against employers who violate the youth employment provisions of the law and up to $1,100 per violation against employers who willfully or repeatedly violate the minimum wage or overtime pay provisions. This law prohibits discriminating against or discharging workers who file a complaint or participate in any proceedings under the Act.

ADDITIONAL INFORMATION
- Certain occupations and establishments are exempt from the minimum wage and/or overtime pay provisions.
- Special provisions apply to workers in American Samoa and the Commonwealth of the Northern Mariana Islands.
- Some state laws provide greater employee protections; employers must comply with both.
- The law requires employers to display this poster where employees can readily see it.
- Employees under 20 years of age may be paid $4.25 per hour during their first 90 consecutive calendar days of employment with an employer.
- Certain full-time students, student learners, apprentices, and workers with disabilities may be paid less than the minimum wage under special certificates issued by the Department of Labor.

For additional information:

1-866-4-USWAGE

(1-866-487-9243)   TTY: 1-877-889-5627

WHD
U.S. Wage and Hour Division

WWW.WAGEHOUR.DOL.GOV

U.S. Department of Labor | Employment Standards Administration | Wage and Hour Division

WHD Publication 1088 (Revised June 2007)

otherwise be willing to hire these individuals are unwilling to pay them the same rate as adults because of their lack of experience. For unskilled workers, the FLSA permits employers to pay a "training wage" of $4.25 per hour for employees younger than age 20 during their first ninety days of employment, provided their employment does not displace other workers.

Child Labor Provisions

The FLSA forbids the employment of minors between ages 16 and 18 in hazardous occupations such as mining, logging, woodworking, meatpacking, and certain types of manufacturing. Minors under 16 cannot be employed in any work destined for interstate commerce except that which is performed in a nonhazardous occupation for a parent or guardian or for an employer under a temporary work permit issued by the Department of Labor.

Exemption from Overtime Provisions

The feature of the FLSA that perhaps creates the most confusion is the exemption from overtime requirements for certain groups of employees or from coverage by certain of the Act's provisions. Five employee groups—executive, administrative, professional, computer, and outside salespeople—are specifically excluded from overtime provisions provided they meet defined job requirements as stated under the law. Importantly, job titles do not determine exempt status. Other employees are exempt from overtime pay if their weekly or annual earnings exceed certain limits.

A significant change was made to the FLSA overtime provision when the DOL implemented the Fair Pay Rules. These regulations strengthen overtime protection and redefine the job requirements for exempt groups of employees. Important changes to the Act include the following:

- Overtime must be paid to employees earning less than $455 a week, or $23,660 annually.

- A new "standards test" is used to determine whether employees who earn between $23,660 and $100,000 annually are excluded from overtime requirements.

- Administrative personnel to be exempt must have primary duties that include the exercise of discretion and independent judgment *with respect to matters of significance.*

The Fair Pay Rules are purported to strengthen overtime rights for 6.7 million U.S. workers, including 1.3 million low-wage workers who were denied overtime under the old rules. Therefore, employers seeking exceptions to overtime payments should carefully monitor Fair Pay regulations.[41] The DOL provides an online seminar that describes the new Fair Pay Rules.[42]

Equal Rights Provisions

One of the most significant amendments to the FLSA was the Equal Pay Act passed in 1963. (See Chapter 2.) The federal Age Discrimination Act of 1967, as amended, extends the equal rights provisions by forbidding wage discrimination based on age for employees age 40 and older. Neither of these acts, however, prohibits wage differentials based on factors other than age or sex. Seniority, merit, and individual incentive plans, for instance, are not affected.

In spite of the Equal Pay Act, the achievement of parity by women in the labor market has been slow in coming. As Figure 9.7 shows, in the second quarter of 2008, the usual average weekly earnings of all women workers in the United States was 79.3 percent of the usual average weekly earnings of men. This figure has not changed greatly since 1995. Fortunately, the average weekly earnings of young women (age 16–24) are 91 percent of those of similar-age men—up from 78 percent in 1980. However, it is still important to remember that young women, and young men as well, typically work in low-paying, entry-level jobs. For women, these are often clerical, domestic, or sales positions.[43]

SIGNIFICANT COMPENSATION ISSUES

As with other HR activities, compensation management operates in a dynamic environment. For example, as managers strive to reward employees in a fair manner, they must consider controls over labor costs, legal issues regarding male and female wage payments, and internal pay equity concerns. Each of these concerns is highlighted in three important compensation issues: (1) equal pay for comparable worth, (2) low salary budgets, and (3) wage rate compression.

7 | Objective

FIGURE 9.7

The Equal Pay Act: The Jury's Still Out

Has the Equal Pay Act been effective in raising the wages of women relative to the wages of men? That depends on whom you ask and the importance you place on government statistics. "Fifty-nine cents on the dollar" was the rallying cry of the women's movement more than thirty years ago to illustrate the large gap between the wages of women and men. That is, for every dollar that a man made, a woman earned fifty-nine cents. Currently, government wage figures based on the usual weekly earnings of full-time wage and salary workers peg women's average pay at 79.3 percent of men's compensation. Unfortunately, the gain in women's wages relative to men's wages has not changed significantly in recent years, as the following figures show.

YEAR	AVERAGE WEEKLY WAGE (WOMEN)	AVERAGE WEEKLY WAGE (MEN)	WOMEN'S AVERAGE WAGE AS A PERCENTAGE OF MEN'S AVERAGE WAGE
1985	$277	$406	68.2%
1995	406	538	75.5
2000	493	641	76.9
2002	529	679	77.9
2004	572	714	80.1
2008 (2nd quarter)	634	800	79.3

Source: Median usual weekly earnings of full-time wage and salary workers by sex, age, race, and Hispanic or Latino ethnicity, current dollars 1979–2008. Unpublished tabulations from *Current Population Survey*, Bureau of Labor Statistics, 2008. Data at www.bls.gov.

The Issue of Equal Pay for Comparable Worth

One of the most important gender issues in compensation is equal pay for comparable worth. The issue stems from the fact that jobs performed predominantly by women are paid less than those performed by men. This practice results in what critics term *institutionalized sex discrimination*, causing women to receive less pay for jobs that may be different from but comparable in worth to those performed by men. The issue of comparable worth goes beyond providing equal pay for jobs that involve the same duties for women as for men. It is not concerned with whether a female secretary should receive the same pay as a male secretary. Rather, the argument for comparable worth is that jobs held by women are not compensated the same as those held by men, even though both job types may contribute equally to organizational success.

Reasons for the gender pay gap are still entirely unclear. Discrimination against women accounts for a portion of the wage difference. Other cited reasons include women working in low-paying, sex-segregated occupations—such as cashiers and maids—and family responsibilities that require women to remain outside the workforce for extended periods.

Additionally, advocates of comparable worth argue that the difference in wage rates for predominantly male and female occupations rests with current job evaluation techniques that traditionally undervalue of female occupations. To remedy this situation, they propose that wages should be equal for jobs that are "somehow" equivalent in total worth or compensation to the organization. With these concerns the compensation gap between men and women will not disappear overnight, but the persistence of comparable worth advocates will help shrink it.

comparable worth

The concept that male and female jobs that are dissimilar, but equal in terms of value or worth to the employer, should be paid the same

The Issue of Low Salary Budgets

At a recent compensation seminar attended by one of the authors, a speaker noted, "The blank-check days for large salary increases are over." While workers may not have as tough a time as Dagwood in convincing employers that a raise is in order, WorldatWork reports that the sizes of salary increases have been modest compared with periods before 1990. Figure 9.8 shows salary budgets by type of employee from 1998–2009. These figures are not projected to increase greatly in future years. While current inflation rates have been relatively stable—allowing most employees to realize a real earnings gain—these gains are small compared with prior years.

Low salary budgets reflect a general trend toward tight compensation cost controls caused by global competition for jobs, the reduction in workforce because of technology, and the growing use of temporary and part-time employees who receive low wages and few benefits.[44] Unfortunately, low wages could portend unfavorable effects for employers and society, including increased turnover as employees change jobs for higher wages and diminished employee output as employees perceive a low pay-for-performance relationship.

Wage rate compression

Compression of pay between new and experienced employees caused by the higher starting salaries of new employees; also the differential between hourly workers and their managers

The Issue of Wage Rate Compression

Pay compression is a compensation problem that has its roots in low salary budgets. Wage rate compression occurs when less experienced, often junior employees, earn as much or more than experienced employees due to high starting salaries

FIGURE
9.8

Salary Budgets by Type of Employee, 1998–2009

| TYPE OF EMPLOYEE | ACTUAL | | | | | | | | | | | PROJECTED |
	1998	1999	2000	2001	2002	2003	2004	2005	2006	2007	2008	2009
Nonexempt hourly nonunion	4.1%	4.1%	4.3%	4.3%	3.7%	3.5%	3.5%	3.6%	3.7%	3.8%	3.8%	3.8%
Nonexempt salaried	4.2	4.2	4.4	4.4	3.7	3.4	3.4	3.6	3.7	3.8	3.8	3.8
Exempt salaried	4.5	4.4	4.6	4.6	3.9	3.6	3.6	3.7	3.8	3.9	3.9	3.9
Officers/ executives	4.6	4.5	4.7	4.7	4.0	3.6	3.6	3.8	3.9	4.1	4.0	4.0

Source: Reprinted from 2008–2009 Total Salary Increase Budget Survey with permission from WorldatWork, 14040 N. Northsight Blvd., Scottsdale, AZ 85260; phone (877) 951-9191; fax (480) 483-8352; http://www.worldatwork.org. © 2008 WorldatWork. Unauthorized reproduction or distribution is strictly prohibited.

for new employees. For example, the scarcity of qualified applicants in computers, engineering, and other professional and technical fields has forced starting salaries for these occupations to be at or near the salaries paid employees with considerable experience and seniority. Pay compression can also occur when hourly employees, at the top of their pay grades, earn only slightly less than managers at the low end of their pay grades.

Identifying wage-rate compression and its causes is far simpler than implementing organizational policies to alleviate its effect. Organizations wishing to minimize the problem may incorporate the following ideas into their pay policies:

- Reward high performance and merit-worthy employees with large pay increases.

- Design the pay structure to allow a wide spread between hourly and supervisory employees.

- Prepare high-performing employees for promotions to jobs with higher salary levels.

- Provide equity adjustments for selected employees hardest hit by pay compression.[45]

Since wage rate compression is largely an internal pay equity concern, if not addressed fairly, it can cause low employee morale, leading to issues of reduced employee performance, hard feelings between employees, higher absenteeism and turnover, and even delinquent behavior such as employee theft.

SUMMARY

Objective 1　Establishing compensation programs requires both large and small organizations to consider specific goals—employee retention, compensation distribution, and adherence to a budget, for instance. Compensation must reward employees for past efforts (pay-for-performance) while motivating employees' future performance. Internal and external equity of the pay program affects employees' concepts of fairness. Organizations must balance each of these concerns while still remaining competitive. The ability to attract qualified employees while controlling labor costs is a major factor in allowing organizations to remain viable in the domestic or international markets.

Objective 2　The basis on which compensation payments are determined and the way they are administered can significantly affect employee productivity and the achievement of organizational goals. Internal influences include the employer's compensation policy, worth of the job, performance of the employee, and employer's ability to pay. External factors influencing wage rates include labor market conditions, area wage rates, cost of living, outcomes of collective bargaining, and legal requirements.

Objective 3　Organizations use one of four basic job evaluation techniques to determine the relative worth of jobs. The job ranking system arranges jobs in numerical order on the basis of the importance of the job's duties and responsibilities to the organization. The job classification system slots jobs into preestablished grades. Higher-rated grades will require more responsibilities, working conditions, and job duties. The point system of job evaluation uses a point scheme based on the compensable job factors of skill, effort, responsibility, and working conditions. The more compensable factors a job possesses, the more points are assigned to it. Jobs with higher accumulated points are considered more valuable to the organization. The work valuation system evaluates jobs based on their value relative to organizational goals—financial, customer service, and so on—and the job's contribution to organization success.

Objective 4　Wage surveys determine the external equity of jobs. Data obtained from surveys will facilitate establishing the organization's wage policy while ensuring that the employer does not pay more, or less, than needed for jobs in the relevant labor market.

Objective 5　The wage structure is composed of the wage curve, pay grades, and rate ranges. The wage curve depicts graphically the pay rates assigned to jobs within each pay grade. Pay grades represent the grouping of similar jobs on the basis of their relative worth. Each pay grade will include a rate range. Rate ranges will have a midpoint and minimum and maximum pay rates for all jobs in the pay grade.

Objective 6　Both the Davis-Bacon Act and the Walsh-Healy Act are prevailing wage statutes. These laws require government contractors to pay wages normally based on the union scale in the employer's operating area. The Walsh-Healy Act also requires payment of 1½ times the regular pay for hours over eight per day or forty per week. The Fair Labor Standards Act contains provisions covering the federal minimum wage, hours worked, and child labor.

Objective 7　The concept of comparable worth seeks to overcome the fact that jobs held by women are compensated at a lower rate than those performed by men. This happens even though both types of jobs may contribute equally to organizational productivity. Low-wage increases are a prominent compensation strategy as employers seek to hold pay down to adjust to competitive challenges. Wage rate compression is the narrowing of pay between new, less experienced employees and experienced senior employees. The primary cause of the problem is the high salaries paid to new employees. Hourly employees and their managers may experience pay compression when the salary spread between the two groups is low.

KEY TERMS

comparable worth
competence-based pay
consumer price index (CPI)
escalator clauses
exempt employees
Hay profile method
hourly work
job classification system

job evaluation
job ranking system
nonexempt employees
pay equity
pay-for-performance standard
pay grades
piecework
point system

real wages
red circle rates
wage and salary survey
wage curve
wage rate compression
work valuation

DISCUSSION QUESTIONS

Objective 1 1. Tomax Corporation has 400 employees and wishes to develop a compensation policy to correspond to its dynamic business strategy. The company wishes to employ a high-quality workforce capable of responding to a competitive business environment. Suggest different compensation objectives to match Tomax's business goals.

Objective 2 2. Since employees may differ in terms of their job performance, would it not be more feasible to determine the wage rate for each employee on the basis of his or her relative worth to the organization? Explain.

Objective 3 3. What is job evaluation? Explain the differences between the major job evaluation systems, noting the advantages and disadvantages of each.

Objective 4 4. Describe the basic steps in conducting a wage and salary survey. What are some factors to consider?

Objective 5 5. One of the objections to granting wage increases on a percentage basis is that the lowest-paid employees, who are having the most trouble making ends meet, get the smallest increase, while the highest-paid employees get the largest increase. Is this objection a valid one? Explain.

Objective 6 6. Federal laws governing compensation raise important issues for both employers and employees. Discuss the following:
   a. The effect of paying a prevailing wage as required by the Davis-Bacon Act
   b. The effects of raising the minimum wage

Objective 7 7. Discuss ways that employers might seek to restrain the salary budget.

Why This Salary?

HRM EXPERIENCE

A question frequently asked is, "Why is that person paid more than I am when we both perform the same job?" The answer to this question lies in understanding the components of the wage mix as discussed in this chapter. While we may disapprove of the idea that someone is paid more or less than we are for similar work; nevertheless, factors both internal and external to the organization influence the final salary paid to a job or a specific person. Often we have little control over the wage mix factors. However, at other times, we can improve our wage by gaining additional job experience or seniority or by obtaining increases in job knowledge or skills. This project is designed to give you experience in understanding why jobs are paid different salaries.

Assignment

Shown here are the annual median salaries paid to selected occupations listed in the 2008–2009 edition of the *Occupational Outlook Handbook*. Study the salaries paid to these occupations and then answer the questions that follow as to why the differences in salaries exist. Relate these reasons to the internal and external factors of the wage mix that are discussed in the text.

Occuption	*Median Annual Salary*
• Flight attendant	$53,780
• Librarian	$49,060
• Construction laborer	$26,332
• Computer systems analyst	$69,760
• Police officer	$47,460
• Truck driver, heavy	$37,086
• Lawyer	$102,610

1. What factors may account for the wide differences among salaries for different occupations?
2. What factors may account for the differences among salaries for the identical occupation in the same organization?
3. What factors may account for the differences among salaries for the identical occupation in different organizations?

You may work individually or in teams to complete this skill-building exercise. The *Occupational Outlook Handbook* published by the U.S. Bureau of Labor Statistics can be found at http://www.bls.gov.

BIZFLIX EXERCISES

The Wedding Date: How Much Is Nick Mercer's Job Worth?

These scenes from *The Wedding Date* occur in two parts. Watch Part I, "Nick's Job," first. Apply the job evaluation concepts discussed in this chapter to decide the worth of Nick Mercer's (Dermot Mulroney) job.

Kat Ellis (Debra Messing) wants a date to accompany her to her sister Amy's (Amy Adams) wedding. She also wants to show her ex-fiancé that she can recover from him dumping her two years earlier. These requirements become part of her frantic search of the male escort classified advertisements. She hires Nick Mercer, who turns out to be much more dashing and charming than she expected. This lighthearted romantic comedy will entertain you from beginning to end.

There are two sets of scenes with a chalkboard between them. Part I comes from the "Trying too Hard" segment that appears in the first ten minutes of the film. Kat and Nick have arrived at Heathrow Airport, London, England. Part II comes from the "A Simple Business Transaction" segment that appears a few minutes later. They have arrived at the cocktail party honoring Amy and her fiancé, Edward Fletcher-Wooten (Jack Davenport).

The Part I chalkboard reads, "Nick's Job"; the Part II chalkboard reads, "Nick's Pay." Pause the scenes at the start of Part II to consider the first question below. Kat and Nick return to the cocktail party after Kat straightens the coats in the closet.

What to Watch for and Ask Yourself

- From your viewing of Part I, how much is Nick Mercer's job as Kat's date worth? If you have seen this film, do not try to recall how much Nick received.

- The opening of this chapter includes the following observation: "Employees desire compensation systems that they perceive as being fair and commensurate with their skills and expectations." Does Nick believe he is paid fairly in Part II of the scenes? Does he place any conditions on his job and its compensation?

- Review the earlier section "Significant Compensation Issues." Do any issues raised in that section apply to these scenes? Why or why not?

CASE STUDY 1

Pay Decisions at Performance Sports

Katie Perkins's career objective while attending Rockford State College was to obtain a degree in small business management and to start her own business after graduation. Her ultimate desire was to combine her love of sports and a strong interest in marketing to start a mail-order golf equipment business aimed specifically at beginning golfers.

In February 2003, after extensive development of a strategic business plan and a loan in the amount of $75,000 from the Small Business Administration, Performance Sports was begun. Based on a marketing plan that stressed fast delivery, error-free customer service, and large discount pricing, Performance Sports grew rapidly. At present the company employs sixteen people: eight customer service representatives earning between $11.25 and $13.50 per hour; four shipping and receiving associates paid between $8.50 and $9.50 per hour; two clerical employees each earning $8.25 per hour; an assistant manager earning $15.25 per hour; and a general manager with a wage of $16.75 per hour. Both the manager and assistant manager are former customer service representatives.

Perkins intends to create a new managerial position, purchasing agent, to handle the complex duties of purchasing golf equipment from the company's numerous equipment manufacturers. Also, the mail-order catalog will be expanded to handle a complete line of tennis equipment. Since the position of purchasing agent is new, Perkins is not sure how much to pay this person. She wants to employ an individual with five to eight years of experience in sports equipment purchasing.

While attending an equipment manufacturers' convention in Las Vegas, Nevada, Perkins learns that a competitor, East Valley Sports, pays its customer service representatives on a pay-for-performance basis. Intrigued by this compensation philosophy, Perkins asks her assistant manager, George Balkin, to research the pros and cons of this payment strategy. This request has become a priority because only last week two customer service representatives expressed dissatisfaction with their hourly wage. Both complained that they felt underpaid relative to the large amount of sales revenue each generates for the company.

Questions

1. What factors should Perkins and Balkin consider when setting the wage for the purchasing agent position? What resources are available for them to consult when establishing this wage?
2. Suggest advantages and disadvantages of a pay-for-performance policy for Performance Sports.
3. Suggest a new payment plan for the customer service representatives.

CASE STUDY 2

Bomb's Away: JetPack's New Pay Strategy

In today's highly competitive business environment, low salary budgets are a fact of business life. Additionally, to maximize compensation dollars, organizations are linking an employee's annual salary increase to the contributions he or she makes to organizational success—a pay-for-performance compensation strategy. However, low salary budgets, coupled with a pay-for-performance pay policy, can have important outcomes for both employees and their managers as this case illustrates.

JetPack Electronics is an industry leader in the development and manufacture of onboard guidance systems for corporate jet aircraft. Prior to 2006, JetPack products held a 67 percent market share, and profit margins exceeded 23 percent for most guidance systems. Unfortunately, in 2005, one domestic competitor and several low-cost foreign competitors invaded the company's market niche. Not surprisingly, increased competition significantly lowered JetPack's market share and its profits.

Prior to 2007, the compensation policy of JetPack had been to give all employees annual across-the-board salary increases plus adjustment raises based on the consumer price index (CPI) for the company's metropolitan area. These pay increases averaged 3.2 percent yearly. Furthermore, employees received annual merit salary increases, which as one manager stated, "were routinely given to almost all employees," Between 2000 and 2006, the company's annual salary budget ranged between 5.7 and 6.4 percent, well above industry averages.

In 2007, JetPack dramatically changed its corporate pay policy. According to Martin Lichtner, company HR director, "Profits were down, and we simply didn't have the financial ability to reward employees with traditional large salary increases." He further stated, "Frankly, we had no option but to change our compensation policy; we need to get as much bang for our bucks as possible."

In early January 2008, the company informed all employees that across-the-board and CPI adjustment increases were being eliminated. Furthermore, individual merit increases would now be given only on a "proven" merit basis. The days of entitlement increases were over. Employees were told that a pay-for-performance philosophy was now the cornerstone of the company's compensation strategy. Managers were informed that unit salary budgets for 2008 would approximate 3.8 percent. Also, only employees evaluated as "above average" or "outstanding" would be eligible for salary increases.

Questions

1. How should employees be informed of the company's new pay policy? Explain.
2. What effect will a pay-for-performance salary policy have on employees? Explain.
3. Does eliminating the across-the-board annual salary increase seem fair? Explain.
4. What effect will a strict pay-for-performance standard have on how managers evaluate their employees?

NOTES AND REFERENCES

1. Don Hellriegel and John W. Slocum, Jr., *Organizational Behavior*, 11th ed. (Mason, OH: South-Western, 2007).

2. "Pay to be Stable, PFP Usage Lags," *HR Focus* 84, no. 12 (December 207): 12.

3. Debra L. Nelson and James Campbell Quick, *Understanding Organizational Behavior*, 3rd ed. (Mason, OH: South-Western, 2008), Chapter 5.

4. For a frequently referenced book on strategic compensation planning, see Edward E. Lawler III, *Strategic Pay: Aligning Organizational Strategies and Pay Systems* (San Francisco: Jossey-Bass, 1990). See also Susan E. Jackson and Randall S. Schuler, *Managing Human Resources: Through Strategic Partnerships*, 9th ed. (Mason, OH: South-Western, 2006): Chapter 9.

5. Fay Hansen, "Lackluster Performance," *Workforce Management* 86, no. 19 (November 2007): 39.

6. Fay Hansen, "Control and Customization," *Workforce Management* 86, no. 19 (November 2007): 42.

7. Hai-Ming Chen and Yi-Hua Hsien, "Key Trends in the Total Reward System of the 2lst Century," *Compensation and Benefits Review* 38, no. 6 (November/December 2006): 64.

8. George T. Milkovich and Jerry M. Newman, *Compensation*, 9th ed. (Boston: McGraw-Hill Irwin, 2008).

9. Patricia K. Zingheim and Jay R. Schuster, "What Are Key Issues Right Now?" *Compensation and Benefits Review* 39, no. 3. (June 2007): 51. See also "Reward 'Stars' and Pay for Performance Lead in Pay Control Strategies," *HR Focus* 84, no. 11 (November 2007): 3.

10. Valerie L. Myers and Janice L. Dreachslin, "Recruitment and Retention of a Diverse Workforce: Challenges and Opportunities," *Journal of Healthcare Management* 52, no. 5 (September/October 2007): 290.

11. Stephen Miller, "2008 Pay: More Ties to Performance," *HR Magazine* 52, no. 10 (October 2007): 26. See also Jay Schuster, Paul Weatherhead, and Patricia Zingheim,

"Pay for Performance Works: The United States Postal Service Presents a Powerful Business Case," *WorldatWork Journal* 15, no. 1 (First Quarter 2006): 24.

12. Rose Stanley, Project Manager, Benefits, WorldatWork, Scottsdale, Arizona, interview by author, December 14, 2007. Jude Sotherlund and Chris Gokturk, "Paying for Performance: Walking a Legal Fine Line," *Workspan* (January 2007): 37.

13. For one of the classic articles on equity theory, see J. Stacey Adams, "Integrity in Social Exchange," in L. Berkowitz (ed.), *Advances in Experimental Social Psychology* (New York: Academic Press, 1965): 276–99.

14. Andrew J. DuBrin, *Fundamentals of Organization Behavior*, 4th ed. (Mason, OH: South-Western, 2007), Chapter 6.

15. Victor H. Vroom, *Work and Motivation* (San Francisco: Jossey-Bass, 1994). This landmark book, originally published in 1964, integrates the work of hundreds of researchers seeking to explain choice of work, job satisfaction, and job performance.

16. Joseph Champoux, *Organizational Behavior: Integrating Individuals, Groups, and Organizations*, 3rd ed. (Mason, OH: South-Western, 2006), Chapter 8.

17. "Supreme Court Decision Touches on Employees Sharing Pay Data," *HR Focus* 84, no. 10 (October 2007): 12.

18. Brian Hindo, "Mind If I Peek at Your Paycheck?" *Business Week*, June 18, 2007: 40.

19. Detailed discussion of exempt and nonexempt rules under the Fair Labor Standards Act can be found at http://www.dol.gov.

20. James R. Bowers, "Valuing Work: An Integrated Approach," *WorldatWork* 12, no. 2 (Second Quarter 2003): 28–39. See also Robert L. Heneman, Peter V. LeBlanc, and Tim L. Reynolds, "Using Work Valuation to Identify and Protect the Talent Pool," *WorldatWork* 11, no. 2 (Third Quarter 2002): 31–41.

21. Kathryn Cohen and Alison Avalos, "Salary Budget Increases: Slow but Steady," *Workspan* (September 2007): 29.

22. William H. Holley, Jr., Kenneth H. Jennings, and Rogert W. Wolters, *The Labor Relations Process* 9th ed. (Mason, OH: South-Western, 2009), Chapter 6.

23. Robert L. Heneman, "Job and Work Evaluation," *Public Personnel Management* 32, no. 1 (Spring 2003): 1–25.

24. For information on the federal job classification system, go to http//www.opm.gov.

25. Emin Kahya, "Revising the Metal Industry Job Evaluation System for Blue-Collar Jobs," *Compensation and Benefits Review* 38, no. 6 (November/December 2006): 49.

26. Lance A. Berger and Dorothy R. Berger, *The Compensation Handbook*, 5th ed. (Boston: McGraw-Hill, 2008).

27. Robert L. Heneman, Peter V. LeBlanc, and Howard Risher, "Work Valuation Addresses Shortcomings of Both Job Evaluation and Market Pricing," *Compensation and Benefits Review* 35, no. 1 (January–February 2003): 7–11.

28. James R. Bowers, "Valuing Work," *WorldatWork* 12, no. 1 (Second Quarter 2003): 28.

29. The Bureau of Labor Web site is at http://www.bls.gov.

30. Robert P. Parker, "New Monthly Hours and Earnings Measures from the Bureau of Labor Statistics' Current Employment Statistics Program," *Business Economics* 42, no. 2 (April 2007): 69.

31. Nona Tobin, "Can Technology Ease the Pain of Salary Surveys?" *Public Personnel Management* 31, no. 1 (Spring 2002): 65–76.

32. Charles H. Fey and Madhura Tare, "Market Pricing Concerns," *WorldatWork* 16, no. 2 (Second Quarter 2007): 61.

33. Curt Finch, "How to Create an Effective Pay Structure," *Employee Benefit Plan Review* 61, no. 10 (April 2007): 26. See also Gregory A. Stoskopf, "Choosing the Best Salary Structure for Your Organization," *WorldatWork* 11, no. 4 (Fourth Quarter 2004): 28–36.

34. Organizations may have a compensation program that pays a differential based on geographic location. See Thomas J.

Atchison, "Branch Office Salary Structure," *Compensation and Benefits Review* 39, no. 3 (June 2007): 35.

35. Carri Baca and Gary Starzmann, "Clarifying Competencies: Powerful Tools for Driving Business Success, Part Two," *Workspan* (April 2006): 53.

36. Howard Risher, "Second-Generation Banded Salary Systems," *WorldatWork* 16, no. 1 (First Quarter 2007): 20.

37. Because the FLSA is always subject to amendment, an employer should consult the appropriate publications of one of the labor services previously mentioned or the Wage and Hour Division of the U.S. Department of Labor in order to obtain the latest information regarding its current provisions, particularly the minimum wage rate. Changes to the FLSA can also be found at the DOL Web site, http://www.dol.gov.

38. Janet F. Koechel and Karen Fitzgerald, "Beware the Hidden Costs of Overtime," *Workspan* (April 2006): 29.

39. Michael Orey, "Wage Wars," *Business Week*, October 1, 2007: 50. See also Steven D. Irwin, "The Fair Labor Standards Act: The High Cost of Non-Compliance," *Employee Relations Law Journal* 33, no. 1 (Summer 2007): 41.

40. J. Vann Vogel, Stanley Weiner, and Brian Jorgensen, "Calculating Overtime for Non-Exempt Employees and the FLSA Regular Rate," *Employee Relations Law Journal* 33, no. 3 (Winter 2007): 27. See also "Annual Workplace Class Action Litigation Report: Fair Labor Standards Act," *Labor Law Journal* 57, no. 1 (Spring 2006): 30.

41. http://www.wagehour.dol.gov

42. The online seminar can be viewed at the DOL Web site, http://www.dol.gov.esa.

43. Aaron Bernstein, "Women's Pay: Why the Gap Remains a Chasm," *Business Week*, June 14, 2004: 58. See also "Reasons for Gender Pay Gap Still Unclear," *HR Focus* 81, no. 2 (February 2004): 12.

44. *Salary Budget: WorldatWork 34th Annual Survey 2007-2008* (Scottsdale, AZ: WorldatWork Press, 2007).

45. Susan Ladika, "Decompression Pay," *HR Magazine* 50, no. 10 (December 2005): 79.

Pay-for-Performance: Incentive Rewards

After studying this chapter, you should be able to

Objective 1
Discuss the basic requirements for successful implementation of incentive programs.

Objective 2
Identify the types of and reasons for implementing individual incentive plans.

Objective 3
Explain why merit raises may fail to motivate employees adequately and discuss ways to increase their motivational value.

© BLEND IMAGES/JUPITER IMAGES

C H A P T E R

10

Objective 4

Indicate the advantage of each of the principal methods used to compensate salespeople.

Objective 5

Differentiate how gains may be shared with employees under the Scanlon and Improshare gainsharing systems.

Objective 6

Differentiate between profit sharing plans and explain advantages and disadvantages of these programs.

Objective 7

Describe the main types of ESOP plans and discuss the advantages of ESOP to employers and employees.

In Chapter 9, we emphasized that organizations are designing their compensation programs—strategic compensation planning—to encourage employee motivation and growth. The goal is to motivate employees to perform to their full capacity. Recognizing this fact, diverse organizations such as Under Armour, Sears Craftsman, Linens 'n Things, Neiman Marcus, and Countrywide Financial offer some form of incentive to workers. According to the *WorldatWork* 2007/2008 salary budget survey, 80 percent of reporting organizations use variable pay as a cornerstone of their pay philosophy.[1] These organizations are attempting to get more motivational mileage out of employee compensation by tying it more closely to organizational objectives and employee performance. Jessica Smilko and Kathy Van Neck, compensation specialists, note this fact about variable pay: "Employees are embracing variable compensation as a means of aligning employee behavior with organizational goals." When incentives are linked with output, workers will increasingly apply their skills and knowledge to their jobs and will be encouraged to work together as a team. Therefore, in their attempt to raise productivity, managers are focusing on the many variables that help determine the effectiveness of pay as a motivator.[2]

In this chapter, we will discuss incentive plans in terms of the objectives they hope to achieve and the various factors that may affect their success. Because many organizations have implemented broad-based incentive programs, for discussion purposes we have grouped incentive plans into three broad categories: individual incentive plans, group incentive plans, and enterprise incentive plans, as shown in Figure 10.1.[3]

▪▪ STRATEGIC REASONS FOR INCENTIVE PLANS

variable pay

Tying pay to some measure of individual, group, or organizational performance

A major element of strategic compensation management is the use of incentive plans, also called variable pay programs, for employees throughout the organization. Ken Abosch, compensation specialist with Hewitt Associates LLC, notes, "There's no question that most corporations have turned away from fixed forms of compensation in favor of variable forms. There has been an abandonment of entitlement programs."[4]

Incentive rewards are based entirely upon a pay-for-performance philosophy (see Chapter 9). Incentive pay programs establish a performance "threshold" (a baseline performance level) that an employee or group of employees must reach in order to qualify for incentive payments. According to one compensation manager, "The performance threshold is the minimum level an employee must reach in order to qualify for variable pay." Additionally, incentive plans emphasize a shared focus on organizational objectives by broadening the opportunities for incentives to employees throughout the organization. Incentive plans create an operating environment that champions a philosophy of shared commitment through the belief that every individual contributes to organizational performance and success.

Incentive Plans as Links to Organizational Objectives

Contemporary arguments for incentive plans focus on linking compensation rewards, both individual and group, to organizational goals. Specific company goals or objectives might be to lower labor costs, improve customer satisfaction, expand product markets, or maintain high levels of productivity and quality, which in turn

FIGURE
10.1

Types of Incentive Plans

INDIVIDUAL	GROUP	ENTERPRISE
Piecework	Team compensation	Profit sharing
Standard hour plan	Scanlon Plan	Stock options
Bonuses	Improshare	Employee stock ownership plans (ESOPs)
Merit pay		
Lump sum merit pay		
Incentive awards		
Sales incentives		
Incentives for professional employees		
Executive compensation		

improve the market for U.S. goods and services in a global economy. By meshing compensation and organizational objectives, managers believe that employees will assume "ownership" of their jobs, thereby improving their effort and overall job performance. Incentives are designed to encourage employees to put out more effort to complete their job tasks—effort they might not be motivated to expend under hourly and/or seniority-based compensation systems. Also, incentive pay is highly valued as a compensation strategy to attract and retain top-performing employees.[5] Figure 10.2 summarizes the major advantages of incentive pay programs as noted by researchers and HR professionals.

Do incentive plans work? The answer is both yes and no. Various studies, along with reports from individual organizations, show a measurable relationship between incentive plans and improved organizational performance.[6] However, the degree of success obtained depends on several factors including (1) identifying important organizational metrics by which to measure employee performance and (2) a customized incentive plan which effectively measures employee output and rewards exceptional employee performance.[7] For example, at the University of Texas M. D. Anderson Cancer Center, health care employees are eligible for up to a 10 percent merit raise depending on whether or not they meet or exceed important hospital performance expectations. Importantly, in a survey designed to assess the hospital's incentive pay program, employee responses showed a high relationship between hospital goals and the linkage between pay and performance.[8] At AFLAC Insurance, sales people who achieve sales targets receive significant bonuses, merchandise awards, and recognition through the company's Web site and in-house publications.[9]

Unfortunately, studies also show that variable pay plans may not achieve their proposed objectives or lead to organizational improvements. First, incentive plans

FIGURE
10.2

Advantages of Incentive Pay Programs

- Incentives focus employee efforts on specific performance targets. They provide real motivation that produces important employee and organizational gains.

- Incentive payouts are variable costs linked to the achievement of results. Base salaries are fixed costs largely unrelated to output.

- Incentive compensation is directly related to operating performance. If performance objectives (quantity and/or quality) are met, incentives are paid. If objectives are not achieved, incentives are withheld.

- Incentives foster teamwork and unit cohesiveness when payments to individuals are based on team results.

- Incentives are a way to distribute success among those responsible for producing that success.

- Incentives are a means to reward or attract top performers when salary budgets are low.

sometimes fail to satisfy employee expectations for pay gains. Second, management may have failed to give adequate attention to the design and implementation of the plan, leaving employees confused about how incentive payments are calculated. Third, employees may have little ability to affect performance standards. Furthermore, the success of an incentive plan will depend on the environment that exists within an organization. A plan is more likely to work in an organization where morale is high, employees believe they are being treated fairly, and there is harmony between employees and management.

Requirements for a Successful Incentive Plan

Objective 1

For an incentive plan to succeed, employees must have some desire for the plan. This desire can be influenced in part by how successful management is in introducing the plan and convincing employees of its benefits. Encouraging employees to participate in developing and administering the plan is likely to increase their willingness to accept it.

Employees must be able to see a clear connection between the incentive payments they receive and their job performance. This connection is more visible if there are objective quality or quantity standards by which they can judge their performance. Commitment by employees to meet these standards is also essential for incentive plans to succeed. This requires mutual trust and understanding between employees and their supervisors, which can be achieved only through open, two-way channels of communication. Management should never allow incentive payments to be seen as an *entitlement*. Instead, these payments should be viewed as a reward that must be earned through effort. This perception can be strengthened if the incentive money is distributed to employees in a separate check. Compensation specialist Joanne Sammer notes the following as characteristics of a successful incentive plan:[10]

- Identify important organizational metrics that encourage employee behavior.

- Involve employees. Incentive programs should seem fair to employees.

- Find the right incentive payout. Payout formulas should be simple and understandable.

- Establish a clear link between performance and payout.

Furthermore, the best-managed incentive pay programs are clearly and continuously communicated to employees. This is true during both good and bad economic periods. According to Roisin Woolnough, compensation consultant, "Communicate what you are doing and why it is critical to success. Everyone needs to know what the goals are and what the rewards are for achieving those goals."[11] Proactive organizations find it advisable to continually evaluate the operation and administration of their variable pay programs.

SETTING PERFORMANCE MEASURES

Measurement is key to the success of incentive plans because it communicates the importance of established organizational goals. What gets measured and rewarded gets attention.[12] For example, if the organization desires to be a leader in quality, then performance indexes may focus on customer satisfaction, timeliness, or being error-free. If being a low-priced producer is the goal, then emphasis should be on cost reduction or increased productivity with lower acceptable levels of quality. While a variety of performance options are available, most focus on quality, cost control, or productivity. Highlights in HRM 1 provides five proven guidelines on how to establish and maintain an effective performance measurement program.

For some organizations, linking incentive payments to formalized performance measures has not obtained positive results for either employees or the organization. Failure can often be traced to the choice of performance measures.[13] Therefore, measures that are quantitative, simple, and structured to show a clear relationship to improved performance are best. Overly quantitative, complex measures are to be avoided. Also, when selecting a performance measure, it is necessary to evaluate the extent to which the employees involved can actually influence the measurement. Finally, employers must guard against "ratcheting up" performance goals by continually trying to exceed previous results. This eventually leads to employee frustration and employee perception that the standards are unattainable. The result will be a mistrust of management and a backlash against the entire incentive program.

ADMINISTERING INCENTIVE PLANS

While incentive plans based on productivity can reduce direct labor costs, to achieve their full benefit they must be carefully thought out, implemented, and maintained. A cardinal rule is that thorough planning must be combined with a "proceed with caution" approach. Compensation managers repeatedly stress a number of points related to the effective administration of incentive plans. Three of the more important points are, by consensus, as follows:

1. Incentive systems are effective only when managers are willing to grant incentives based on differences in individual, team, or organizational performance. Allowing incentive payments to become pay guarantees defeats the motivational intent of the incentive. The primary purpose of an incentive compensation plan

HIGHLIGHTS IN HRM

1

Setting Performance Measures—The Keys

Both large and small organizations have established performance measures to improve operational success while rewarding employees for their performance outcomes. Establishing meaningful performance measures is one of the important and difficult challenges facing management today. Before managers or supervisors develop and implement organizational measures, they should consider the following guidelines.

- *Performance measures—at all organizational levels—must be consistent with the strategic goals of the organization.* Avoid nonrelevant measures or metrics that are not closely linked to the business or what employees do in their work.
- *Define the intent of performance measures and champion the cause relentlessly.* Demonstrate that performance measures are, in fact, good business management and hold managers and employees accountable for their success.
- *Involve employees.* A critical step in any measurement program is the development of an employee involvement strategy outlining the nature of employee participation, implementation, and ongoing management of the performance management program. Segment the workforce based on nature of work and potential for impact. Consider which metrics require customization. Acceptance of a performance measurement program is heightened when employees "buy into" the process.
- *Consider the organization's culture and workforce demographics when designing performance measures.* For example, organizations with a more traditional hierarchical structure may need more time to introduce performance metrics compared to flatter organizations, which are more fluid and less steeped in control and command characteristics.
- *Widely communicate the importance of performance measures.* Performance messages are the principles and guidelines that communicate to employees about required performance levels and why the organization needs to achieve those levels of success.

is not to pay off under almost all circumstances, but rather to motivate performance. Thus, if the plan is to succeed, poor performance must go unrewarded.

2. Annual salary budgets must be large enough to reward and reinforce exceptional performance. When compensation budgets are set to ensure that pay increases do not exceed certain limits (often established as a percentage of payroll or sales), these constraints may prohibit rewarding outstanding individual or group performance.

3. The overhead costs associated with plan implementation and administration must be determined. These may include the cost of establishing performance standards and the added cost of record-keeping. The time consumed in

communicating the plan to employees, answering questions, and resolving any complaints about it must also be included in these costs.

INDIVIDUAL INCENTIVE PLANS

In today's competitive world, one word, *flexibility*, describes the design of individual incentive plans.[14] For example, technology, job tasks and duties, and/or organizational goals (such as being a low-cost producer) impact the organization's choice of incentive pay programs. Incentive payments may be determined by the number of units produced, achievement of specific performance goals, or productivity improvements in the organization as a whole. In addition, in highly competitive industries such as food and retailing, low profit margins will affect the availability of monies for incentive payouts. All of these considerations suggest that tradition and philosophy, as well as economics and technology, help govern the design of individual incentive systems.

2 | Objective

Piecework

One of the oldest incentive plans is based on piecework. Under straight piecework, employees receive a certain rate for each unit produced. Their compensation is determined by the number of units they produce during a pay period. At Steelcase, an office furnituremaker, employees can earn more than their base pay, often as much as 35 percent more, through piecework for each slab of metal they cut or chair they upholster. Under a differential piece rate, employees whose production exceeds the standard output receive a higher rate for all of their work than the rate paid to those who do not exceed the standard.

Employers include piecework in their compensation strategy for several reasons. The wage payment for each employee is simple to compute, and the plan permits an organization to predict its labor costs with considerable accuracy, since these costs are the same for each unit of output. The piecework system is more likely to succeed when units of output can be measured readily, the quality of the product is less critical, the job is fairly standardized, and a constant flow of work can be maintained.

straight piecework

An incentive plan under which employees receive a certain rate for each unit produced

differential piece rate

A compensation rate under which employees whose production exceeds the standard amount of output receive a higher rate for all of their work than the rate paid to those who do not exceed the standard amount

Computing the Piece Rate

Although time standards establish the time required to perform a given amount of work, they do not by themselves determine what the incentive rate should be. The incentive rates must be based on hourly wage rates that would otherwise be paid for the type of work being performed. For example, the standard time for producing one unit of work in a job paying $12.75 per hour was set at twelve minutes. The piece rate would be $2.55 per unit, computed as follows:

$$\frac{60 \text{ (minutes per hour)}}{12 \text{ (standard time per hour)}} = 5 \text{ units per hour}$$

$$\frac{\$12.75 \text{ (hourly rate)}}{5 \text{ (units per hour)}} = 2.55 \text{ per unit}$$

Piecework: The Drawbacks

Despite their obvious advantages—including their direct tie to a pay-for-performance philosophy—piecework systems have a number of disadvantages that offset their usefulness. One of the most significant weaknesses of piecework, as well as of other incentive plans based on individual effort, is that it may not always be an effective motivator. If employees believe that an increase in their output will provoke disapproval from fellow workers (often referred to as "rate busting"), they may avoid exerting maximum effort because their desire for peer approval outweighs their desire for more money. Also, jobs in which individual contributions are difficult to distinguish or measure or in which the work is mechanized to the point that the employee exercises very little control over output may be unsuited to piecework. Piecework may also be inappropriate in the following situations:

- When quality is more important than quantity
- When technology changes are frequent
- When productivity standards on which piecework must be based are difficult to develop

Importantly, piecework incentive systems can work against an organizational culture promoting workforce cooperation, creativity, or problem-solving because each of these goals can infringe on an employee's time and productivity and, therefore, total incentive earned.

Standard Hour Plan

standard hour plan

An incentive plan that sets rates based on the completion of a job in a predetermined standard time

Another common incentive technique is the standard hour plan, which sets incentive rates on the basis of a predetermined "standard time" for completing a job. If employees finish the work in less than the expected time, their pay is still based on the standard time for the job multiplied by their hourly rate. Standard hour plans are popular in service departments in automobile dealerships. For example, if the standard time to install an engine in a truck is five hours and the mechanic completes the job in four and a half hours, the payment would be the mechanic's hourly rate times five hours. Standard hour plans are particularly suited to long-cycle operations or jobs or tasks that are nonrepetitive and require a variety of skills. However, while standard hour plans can motivate employees to produce more, employers must ensure that equipment maintenance and product quality do not suffer as employees strive to do their work faster to earn additional income.

Bonuses

bonus

An incentive payment that is supplemental to the base wage

A bonus is an incentive payment that is given to an employee beyond one's normal base wage. It is frequently given at the end of the year and does not become part of base pay. Bonuses have the advantage of providing employees with more pay for exerting greater effort, while at the same time the employees still have the security of a basic wage. Bonus payments are common among managerial and executive employees, but recent trends show that they are increasingly given to employees throughout the organization.[15]

Depending on who is to receive the bonus, the incentive payment may be determined on the basis of cost reduction, quality improvement, or performance criteria established by the organization. At the executive level, for example, performance criteria might include earnings growth or enterprise-specific agreed-on objectives.

When some special employee contribution is to be rewarded, a spot bonus is used. A spot bonus, as the name implies, is given "on the spot," normally for some employee effort not directly tied to an established performance standard. For example, a customer service representative might receive a spot bonus for working long hours to fill a new customer's large order. Spot bonuses are championed as useful retention and motivational tools for overburdened employees, especially during lean financial times. Lauren Sejen, compensation expert with Watson Wyatt Worldwide, notes, "I think spot bonuses are one of the most underutilized forms of rewards, given how well employees respond to them. These plans make perfect sense."[16]

spot bonus

An unplanned bonus given for employee effort unrelated to an established performance measure

Merit Pay

A merit pay program (merit raise) links an increase in base pay to how successfully an employee performs his or her job. The merit increase is normally given on the basis of an employee's having achieved some objective performance standard—although a superior's subjective evaluation of subordinate performance may play a large role in the increase given. Merit raises can serve to motivate if employees perceive the raise to be related to the performance required to earn it.[17]

Theories of motivation, in addition to behavioral science research, provide justification for merit pay plans as well as other pay-for-performance programs.[18] However, research shows that a merit increase in the range of 7 to 9 percent is necessary to serve as a pay motivator.[19] Employees may welcome lower percentage amounts, but low salary increases may not lead to significantly greater effort on the part of employees to drive business results. Consequently, with low salary budgets (see Chapter 9), organizations wishing to reward top performers will be required to distribute a large portion of the compensation budget to these individuals.[20] A meaningful merit increase will catch the attention of top performers while sending a signal to poor-performing employees. A strategic compensation policy *must differentiate* between outstanding and good or average performance. Furthermore, increases granted on the basis of merit should be distinguishable from cost-of-living or other general increases.

Problems with Merit Raises

Merit raises may not always achieve their intended purpose. Unlike a bonus, a merit raise may be perpetuated year after year even when performance declines. When this happens, employees come to expect the increase and see it as being an entitlement, unrelated to their performance. Furthermore, what are referred to as merit raises often turn out to be increases based on seniority or favoritism. A superior's biased evaluation of subordinate performance may play a large role in the increase given. Even when merit raises are determined by performance, the employee's gains may be offset by inflation and higher income taxes. Compensation specialists also recognize the following problems with merit pay plans:

3 | Objective

1. Money available for merit increases may be inadequate to satisfactorily raise all employees' base pay.

2. Managers may have no guidance in how to define and measure performance; there may be vagueness regarding merit award criteria.

3. Employees may not believe that their compensation is tied to effort and performance; they may be unable to differentiate between merit pay and other types of pay increases.

4. Employees and their managers may hold different views of the factors that contribute to job success.

5. Merit pay plans may create feelings of pay inequity.[21]

While there are no easy solutions to these problems, organizations using a true merit pay plan often base the percentage pay raise on merit guidelines tied to performance appraisals. For example, a certain pay increase, "3 percent," will be tied to a certain performance evaluation, "above average." The percentages may change each year, depending on various internal or external concerns such as profit levels or national economic conditions as indicated by changes in the consumer price index. To prevent all employees from being rated outstanding or above average, managers may be required to distribute the performance rating according to some preestablished formula (such as only 10 percent can be rated outstanding). Additionally, when setting merit percentage guidelines, organizations should consider individual performance along with such factors as training, experience, and current earnings.

merit guidelines

Guidelines for awarding merit raises that are tied to performance objectives

Lump Sum Merit Pay

lump sum merit program

Program under which employees receive a year-end merit payment, which is not added to their base pay

To make merit increases more flexible and visible, organizations such as American Express, Timex, and Westinghouse have implemented a lump sum merit program. Under this type of plan, employees receive a single lump sum increase at the time of their review, an increase that is not added to their base salary. Lump sum merit programs offer several advantages. For employees, an advantage is that receiving a single lump sum merit payment can provide a clear link between pay and performance. For example, a 5 percent merit increase granted to an industrial engineer earning $72,000 a year translates into a weekly increase of $69.23—a figure that looks small compared with a lump sum payment of $3,600. For employers, lump sum payments essentially freeze base salaries, thereby maintaining annual salary and benefit costs, since the level of benefits are normally calculated from salary levels. Organizations using a lump sum merit program will want to adjust base salaries upward after a certain period of time. These adjustments should keep pace with the rising cost of living and increases in the general market wage.

Incentive Awards and Recognition

Incentive awards and employee recognition are an important part of an employer's pay-for-performance compensation strategy. According to one study in 2006, employers spent $46.08 billion on incentive awards to employees and business clients—$32.7 billion on merchandize and $13.4 billion on travel.[22] Awards are used to recognize productivity gains, special contributions or achievements, and service to the organization. Popular noncash incentive awards include merchandise, personalized gifts, theatre or sports tickets, vacations, dining out, gift certificates or gift cards, and personalized clothing. Tangible awards presented with the right message and style can make employees feel appreciated while at the same time underscoring a company value.

Research clearly shows that noncash incentive awards are most effective as motivators when the award is combined with a meaningful employee recognition program. Tyler Gentry, employee recognition specialist, notes this about the importance of noncash incentive awards, "Recognition and rewards aren't so much about recognizing someone for going 'above and beyond' and giving gifts as they are about letting employees know that they are *valued* and *appreciated*. Recognition is a conduit that shows employees that the company appreciates their efforts, their unique gifts, and their contributions."[23] Employers should take care to tie awards to performance and deliver awards in a timely, sincere, and specific way. Generally, the more public the recognition, the more powerful the effect.[24]

Importantly, noncash incentive awards should support business goals and objectives. Greg Boswell, director of performance recognition at O. C. Tanner, notes, "Employers are now thinking of awards and employee recognition more strategically with programs closely aligned to their business goals."[25] For example, if quality improvement is a business goal, then recognition needs to be tied to those behaviors that further the achievement of quality. Additionally, incentive awards work best when awards are appreciated and valued by employees. At one advertising agency, the employee-of-the-month is allowed to drive the president's car for one month—the car is a Maserati. Highlights in HRM 2 provides suggestions for noncash incentive awards based on the generational grouping of employees.

Sales Incentives

4 | Objective

The enthusiasm and drive required in most types of sales work demand that sales employees be highly motivated. This fact, as well as the competitive nature of selling, explains why financial incentives for salespeople are widely used. These incentive plans must provide a source of motivation that will elicit cooperation and trust. Motivation is particularly important for employees away from the office who cannot be supervised closely and who, as a result, must exercise a high degree of self-discipline.

Unique Needs of Sales Incentive Plans

Incentive systems for salespeople are complicated by the wide differences in the types of sales jobs. These range from department store clerks who ring up customer purchases to industrial salespeople from McGraw-Edison who provide consultation and other highly technical services. Salespeople's performance may be measured by the dollar volume of their sales and by their ability to establish new accounts. Other measures are the ability to promote new products or services and to provide various forms of customer service and assistance that do not produce immediate sales revenues.[26]

Performance standards for sales employees are difficult to develop, however, because their performance is often affected by external factors beyond their control. Economic and seasonal fluctuations, sales competition, changes in demand, and the nature of the sales territory can all affect an individual's sales record.[27] Sales volume alone therefore may not be an accurate indicator of the effort salespeople have expended.

In developing incentive plans for salespeople, managers are also confronted with the problem of how to reward extra sales effort and at the same time compensate for activities that do not contribute directly or immediately to sales. Furthermore, sales employees must be able to enjoy some degree of income stability.[28]

Types of Sales Incentive Plans

Compensation plans for sales employees may consist of a straight salary plan, a straight commission plan, a combination salary and commission plan, or a sales plus

HIGHLIGHTS IN HRM

2

Customize Your Noncash Incentive Awards

Compensation specialists recognize that a successful noncash incentive program will offer employees a wide selection of awards—awards that appeal to a diverse workforce and the uniqueness of individual employees. "One-size-fits-all" is not the approach to take. What appeals to younger employees may not be attractive to older employees. For example, one marketing firm characterizes recognition and rewards based on generations as follows:

- Traditionalists (61+). These individuals are less likely to spend money on themselves. Attractive awards include entertainment venues, vacations, and technology items. They also appreciate health and wellness opportunities.
- Boomers (41–60). Personal recognition is important. These individuals want to feel appreciated for their work contributions and are likely to change jobs if they feel under valued or go unrecognized. Boomers favor incentive rewards in the areas of travel, luxury gifts, health and wellness options, and personalized plaques and awards.
- Generation X (25–41). This group values a balanced lifestyle of work and play. Generation X employees value gadgets and high-tech items along with flexible schedules and discretionary time off. A flexible "day-off-work" would appeal to this group.
- Generation Y (14–25). These employees desire immediate performance feedback. Employee-of-the-month programs appeal to these employees as do "spot" recognition plans. Gift cards, gift certificates to "trendy" stores, and movie tickets are appropriate as rewards for the immediate recognition of performance.

Source: Adapted from Alison Avalos, "Recognition: A Critical Component of the Total Reward Mix," *Workspan* (July 2007): 33.

---

straight salary plan

A compensation plan that permits salespeople to be paid for performing various duties that are not reflected immediately in their sales volume

straight commission plan

A compensation plan based on a percentage of sales

bonus plan.[29] A straight salary plan permits salespeople to be paid for performing various duties not reflected immediately in their sales volume. It enables them to devote more time to providing services and building up the goodwill of customers without jeopardizing their income. The principal limitation of the straight salary plan is that it may not motivate salespeople to exert sufficient effort in maximizing their sales volume.

On the other hand, the straight commission plan, based on a percentage of sales, provides maximum incentive and is easy to compute and understand. For example, total cash compensation might equal total sales volume times some percentage of total sales, perhaps 2 percent. Straight commission plans encourage aggressive selling which might be needed in highly competitive industries. Under a straight commission plan, salespeople may be allowed a salary draw. A *draw* is a cash advance that must be paid back as commissions are earned.

However, the straight commission plan is limited by the following disadvantages:

1. Sales people will stress high-priced products.

2. Customer service after the sale is likely to be neglected.

3. Earnings tend to fluctuate widely between good and poor periods of business, and turnover of trained sales employees tends to increase in poor periods.

4. Salespeople are tempted to grant price concessions.

The **combined salary and commission plan** is the most widely used sales incentive program. For example, the most common pay mix for salespersons responsible for *new* accounts is 50 percent base pay and 50 percent variable pay. For salespersons servicing *existing* accounts, a pay distribution of 70 percent base pay and 30 percent commission is typical.[30] The ratio of base salary to commission can be set to fit organizational objectives. The following advantages indicate why the combination salary and commission plan is so widely used:

1. The right kind of incentive compensation, if linked to salary in the right proportion, has most of the advantages of both the straight salary and the straight commission forms of compensation.

2. A salary-plus-incentive compensation plan offers greater design flexibility and can therefore be more readily set up to help maximize company profits.

3. The plan can develop the most favorable ratio of selling expense to sales.

4. The field sales force can be motivated to achieve specific company marketing objectives in addition to sales volume.

Sales representative at Glaxo Pharmaceuticals are paid on a salary plus bonus program. Under **salary plus bonus plans,** the payout can be paid on a monthly, quarterly, or yearly schedule contingent upon the salesperson achieving targeted sales goals such as number of sales calls made, account servicing, or quality of sales.

A straight commission plan can lead to agressive selling favored by highly motivated individuals.

© DIGITAL VISION/GETTY IMAGES

combined salary and commission plan
A compensation plan that includes a straight salary and a commission

salary plus bonus plan
A compensation plan that pays a salary plus a bonus achieved by reaching targeted sales goals.

INCENTIVES FOR PROFESSIONAL EMPLOYEES

Like other salaried workers, professional employees—engineers, scientists, and attorneys, for example—may be motivated through bonuses and merit increases. In some organizations, unfortunately, professional employees cannot advance beyond a certain point in the salary structure unless they are willing to take an administrative assignment. When they are promoted, their professional talents are no longer utilized fully. In the process, the organization may lose a good professional employee and gain a poor administrator. To avoid this situation, some organizations have extended the salary range for professional positions to equal or nearly equal that for administrative positions. The extension of this range provides a double-track wage system, as illustrated in Chapter 7, whereby professionals who do not aspire to become administrators still have an opportunity to earn comparable salaries.

Professional employees can receive compensation beyond base pay. For example, scientists and engineers employed by high-tech firms are included in performance-based incentive programs such as profit sharing or stock ownership. These plans encourage greater levels of individual performance. Cash bonuses can be awarded to those who complete projects on or before deadline dates. Payments may also be given to individuals elected to professional societies, granted patents, or meeting professional licensing standards.

The Executive Pay Package

Executive compensation plans consist of five basic components: (1) base salary, (2) short-term incentives or bonuses, (3) long-term incentives or stock plans, (4) benefits, and (5) perquisites.[31] Each of these elements may receive different emphasis in the executive's compensation package depending on various organizational goals and executive needs.[32]

Executive Base Salaries

Executive base salaries represent between 30 and 40 percent of total annual compensation.[33] An analysis of executive salaries shows that the largest portion of executive pay is received in long-term incentive rewards and bonuses. Regardless, executives of Fortune 500 firms routinely earn an annual base salary in excess of $500,000, with executives in very large corporations earning considerably more. The levels of competitive salaries in the job market exert perhaps the greatest influence on executive base salaries. An organization's compensation committee—normally members of the board of directors—will order a salary survey to find out what executives earn in comparable enterprises.[34] For example, by one estimate, 96 percent of companies in the Standard & Poor's 500 stock index use a technique called *competitive benchmarking* when setting executive pay or to remain competitive for executive talent. As noted in *Business Week*, company boards reason that a CEO who does not earn as much as his or her peers is likely to "take a hike." Comparisons may be based on organization size, sales volume, or industry groupings. Thus, by analyzing the data from published studies, along with self-generated salary surveys, the compensation committee can determine the equity of the compensation package outside the organization.

Executive Short-Term Incentives

Annual bonuses represent the main element of executive short-term incentives.[35] A bonus payment may take the form of cash or stock and may be paid immediately (which is frequently the case), deferred for a short time, or deferred until retirement. Most organizations pay their short-term incentive bonuses in cash (in the form of a supplemental check), in keeping with their pay-for-performance strategy. By providing a reward soon after the performance and thus linking it to the effort on which it is based, they can use cash bonuses as a significant motivator. Deferred bonuses are used to provide a source of retirement benefits or to supplement a regular pension plan.

Incentive bonuses for executives should be based on the contribution the individual makes to the organization. A variety of formulas have been developed for this purpose. Incentive bonuses may be based on a percentage of a company's total profits or a percentage of profits in excess of a specific return on stockholders' investments. In other instances, the payments may be tied to an annual profit plan whereby the amount is determined by the extent to which an agreed-on profit level is exceeded. Payments may also be based on performance ratings or the achievement of specific objectives established with the agreement of executives and the board of directors.

In a continuing effort to monitor the pulse of the marketplace, more organizations are tying operational yardsticks to the traditional financial gauges when computing executive pay. Called *balanced scorecards*, these yardsticks may measure things such as customer satisfaction, the ability to innovate, or product or service leadership.[36] Notes David Cates, a compensation principal with Towers Perrin, a balanced scorecard "allows companies to focus on building future economic value, rather than be driven solely by short-term financial results." Mobil Oil uses a balanced scorecard that better indicates exactly where the company is successful and where improvement is needed.

Executive Long-Term Incentives

Stock options are the primary long-term incentive offered to executives.[37] The principal reason driving executive stock ownership is the desire of both the company and outside investors for senior managers to have a significant stake in the success of the business—to have their fortunes rise and fall with the value they create for shareholders. Stock options can also be extremely lavish for executives. Consider these examples. For 2006, Edward E. Whitacre Jr., CEO of AT&T, received long-term compensation totaling $38.4 million; Patrick Hassey, CEO of Allegheny Technologies, received $35.3 million; and James J. Mulva, CEO of Conoco Phillips, received $30.4 million.[38] Not surprisingly, the creativity in designing a stock option program seems almost limitless. Figure 10.3 highlights several common forms of long-term incentives.

Short-term incentive bonuses are criticized for causing top executives to focus on quarterly profit goals to the detriment of long-term survival and growth objectives. Therefore, corporations such as Sears, Combustion Engineering, Borden, and Enhart have adopted compensation strategies that tie executive pay to long-term performance measures. Each of these organizations recognizes that compensation strategies must also take into account the performance of the organization as a whole. Important to stockholders are such performance results as growth in earnings per share, return on stockholders' equity, and, ultimately, stock price appreciation. A variety of incentive plans, therefore, have been developed to tie rewards to these performance results, particularly over the long term. Additionally, stock options can serve to retain key executive personnel when exercising the options is linked to a specified vesting period, perhaps two to four years (this type of incentive is called "golden handcuffs").

Stock options are under attack.[39] Some object to the sheer magnitude of these incentive rewards. The link between pay and performance that options are championed to provide can also be undermined when compensation committees grant additional options to executives even when company stock prices fall or performance indexes decline. Peter Clapman, chief counsel for TIAA-CREF, the world's largest pension system, notes, "It's sort of heads you win, tails let's flip again." Even worse for shareholders is the dilution problem. Every option granted to executives makes the shares of other stockholders less valuable.

FIGURE 10.3	**Types of Long-Term Incentive Plans**
Stock options	Rights granted to executives to purchase shares of their organization's stock at an established price for a fixed period of time. Stock price is usually set at market value at the time the option is granted.
Stock appreciation rights (SARs)	Cash or stock award determined by increase in stock price during any time chosen by the executive in the option period; does not require executive financing.
Stock purchase	Opportunities for executives to purchase shares of their organization's stock valued at full market or a discount price, often with the organization providing financial assistance.
Phantom stock	Grant of units equal in value to the fair market value or book value of a share of stock; on a specified date the executive will be paid the appreciation in the value of the units up to that time.
Restricted stock	Grant of stock or stock units at a reduced price with the condition that the stock not be transferred or sold (by risk of forfeiture) before a specified employment date.
Performance units	Grants analogous to annual bonuses except that the measurement period exceeds one year. The value of the grant can be expressed as a flat dollar amount or converted to a number of "units" of equivalent aggregate value.
Performance shares	Grants of actual stock or phantom stock units. Value is contingent on both predetermined performance objectives over a specified period of time and the stock market.

Executive Benefits

The benefits package offered executives may parallel one offered to other groups of employees. Various programs for health insurance, life insurance, retirement plans, and vacations are common. However, unlike other employee groups, the benefits offered executives are likely to be broader in coverage and free of charge. Additionally, executives may be given financial assistance in the form of trusts for estate planning, payment of mortgage interest, and legal help.[40]

Executive Perquisites

perquisites

Special nonmonetary benefits given to executives; often referred to as *perks*

Perquisites are nonmonetary rewards given to executives. Perquisites, or *perks*, are a means of demonstrating the executive's importance to the organization. The status that comes with perks—both inside and outside the organization—shows a pecking order and conveys authority. Corporate executives may simply consider perks a "badge of merit." Perks can also provide tax savings to executives because some are not taxed as income.

The dark side of perks is that they are viewed as wasteful spending and overly lavish. A recent study, however, shows that perks can facilitate company productivity by saving executive time (for example, private planes and chauffeur service) or improve or maintain executive health (for example, spas, health clubs, and company cabins). Therefore, the cost of perks should be weighed against the added efficiency and managerial effectiveness they generate.[41] Highlights in HRM 3 shows the more common perks offered to executives.

Executive Compensation: Ethics and Accountability

The top executive paychecks for 2007 were, as usual, off-the-chart amazing.[42] Consider the total compensation drawn in 2007 by the following executives.[43]

Angelo Mozilo wanted Countrywide Financial to become the biggest provider of mortgages. His intense pressure on himself to achieve eventually led to the collapse of his company, even though he enjoyed an exorbitant salary and expensive perks.

© UPI PHOTO/ROGER L. WOLLENBERG/LANDOV MEDIA

John A. Thain, Merrill Lynch	$78,520,000
Lloyd C. Blanfein, Goldman Sachs	$68,500,000
Ray R. Irani, Occidental Petroleum	$60,980,000
Kenneth I. Chenault, American Express	$46,230,000
Richard S. Fuld Jr., Lehman Brothers Holding	$40,000,000

Interestingly, respected management expert Peter F. Drucker argued in a 1984 essay that CEO pay had rocketed out of control and implored compensation committees to hold CEO compensation to no more than 20 times what rank-and-file employees made. He warned that the growing pay gap between CEOs and employees would threaten the very credibility of leadership, particularly when CEOs fire thousands of their workers and their companies underperform.[44]

Given the large amount of various compensation packages, the question asked by many is: "Are top executives worth the salaries and bonuses they receive?" The answer may depend on whom you ask. Corporate compensation committees justify big bonuses in the following ways:[45]

1. Large financial incentives are a way to reward superior performance.

2. Business competition is pressure-filled and demanding.

3. Good executive talent is in great demand.

4. Effective executives create shareholder value.

Others justify high compensation as a fact of business life, reflecting market compensation trends.

HIGHLIGHTS IN HRM

3

The "Sweetness" of Executive Perks

Compensation consulting firms such as Coopers and Lybrand LLP, WorldatWork, and Hewitt Associates regularly survey companies nationwide to identify the perks they provide for executives and other top managers. The following are popular executive perks.

- Company car
- Company plane
- Executive eating facilities
- Financial consulting
- Company-paid parking
- Personal liability insurance
- Estate planning
- First-class air travel
- Home computers
- Chauffeur service
- Children's education

- Spouse travel
- Physical exams
- Mobile phones
- Large insurance policies
- Income tax preparation
- Country club membership
- Luncheon club membership
- Personal home repairs
- Loans
- Legal counseling
- Vacation cabins

Nevertheless, in an era of massive downsizing, low wage increases, and increased workloads for layoff survivors, strong criticism is voiced regarding the high monetary awards given to senior executives. Furthermore, with the large compensation packages awarded to senior managers and top-level executives, cries for performance accountability and openness abound. In 2007, *Forbes* noted that while some high-paid executives do improve performance measures, such as return on equity, earnings per share, and return to shareholders, clearly, many others do not, and their pay far exceeds their performance outcomes.[46] While not all executive pay is exorbitant and not all executive performance is poor, nevertheless angry employees, union groups, government officials, and stockholders argue for change.

Executive Compensation Reform

Several important changes will impact future executive compensation. First, the Internal Revenue Service (IRS) will increasingly look for tax code violations in connection with hefty executive pay packages. The IRS intends to make executive pay a part of every corporate audit.[47] Second, in July 2007, the Securities and Exchange Commission issued new pay disclosure rules which for the first time require companies listed on the New York Stock Exchange and NASDAQ to disclose the true size of their top executive pay packages. Companies must now reveal details on accumulated pension benefits, deferred compensation, and perks that exceed more than $10,000 in total value. Also, companies must provide a plain-English table that summarizes executives' various forms of compensation.[48] Third, the Financial

Accounting Standards Board (FASB) now requires that stock options be recognized as an expense on income statements. Companies and compensation committees must now weigh the benefits provided by stock option programs against the potential charge to earnings.[49] Other reform measures include the following:

- The adoption of performance formulas that peg executive compensation to organizational benchmarks other than stock price

- Shareholder resolutions that allow shareholders the right to vote on executive pay packages[50]

- Greater accountability by compensation committees to justify large executive pay awards or severance or retirement packages

Group Incentive Plans

The emphasis on cost reduction and total quality management has led many organizations to implement a variety of group incentive plans. Group plans enable employees to share in the benefits of improved efficiency realized by major organizational units or various individual work teams. These plans encourage a cooperative—rather than individualistic—spirit among all employees and reward them for their total contribution to the organization. Such features are particularly desirable when working conditions make individual performance difficult, if not impossible, to measure.

Team Compensation

Team incentive plans reward team members with an incentive reward when agreed-on performance standards are met or exceeded. Team incentives seek to establish a psychological climate that fosters team member cooperation and a collective desire

team incentive plan
A compensation plan in which all team members receive an incentive bonus payment when production or service standards are met or exceeded

Although top management support is critical, the incentive program requires the support of those directly involved with it in order for it to be successful.

© BIG CHEESE PHOTO/FOTOSEARCH

to fulfill organizational goals and objectives. While team incentive plans promote a pay-for-performance philosophy, unfortunately, establishing an effective organization-specific incentive team plan is not easy.

One catch with setting team compensation is that not all teams are alike (see Chapter 4). For example, cross-functional teams, self-directed teams, and task force teams make it impossible to develop one consistent type of team incentive plan. With a variety of teams, managers find it difficult to adopt uniform measurement standards or payout formulas for team pay.[51] According to Steven Gross, Hay manager, "Each type of team requires a specific pay structure to function at its peak." Highlights in HRM 4 lists important considerations when designing a team incentive plan.

When team compensation is decided upon, organizations typically use the three-step approach to establishing team incentive payments. First, they set performance measures on which incentive payments are based. Improvements in efficiency, product quality, or reduction in materials or labor costs are common benchmark criteria. For example, if labor costs for a team represent 30 percent of the organization's sales dollars and the organization pays a bonus for labor cost savings, then whenever team labor costs are less than 30 percent of sales dollars, those savings are paid as an incentive bonus to team members. Information on the size of the incentive bonus is reported to employees on a weekly or monthly basis, explaining why incentive pay was or was not earned. Second, the size of the incentive bonus must be determined. At Thrivent Financial for Lutherans, health insurance underwriters can receive team incentive bonuses of up to 10 percent of base salary; however, the exact level of incentive pay depends on overall team performance and the company's performance over one year. Team incentives at Thrivent are paid annually. Third, a payout formula is established and fully explained to employees. The team bonus may be distributed to employees equally, in proportion to their base pay, or on the basis of their relative contribution to the team. With discretionary formulas, managers, or in some cases team members themselves, agree on the payouts to individual team members.

Team incentive programs are not without their problems. The following are some noted problems associated with team compensation.

- Individual team members may perceive that "their" efforts contribute little to team success or to the attainment of the incentive reward.

- Intergroup social problems. Team members may be afraid that one individual may make the others look bad, or that one individual may put in less effort than others but share equally in team rewards, the "free-rider" effect.

- Complex payout formulas or insufficient payout rewards.

Gainsharing Incentive Plans

gainsharing plans

Programs under which both employees and the organization share financial gains according to a predetermined formula that reflects improved productivity and profitability

Gainsharing plans are organizational programs designed to increase productivity or decrease labor costs and share monetary gains with employees. These plans are based on a mathematical formula that compares a baseline of performance with actual productivity during a given period. When productivity exceeds the baseline, an agreed-on savings is shared with employees. Inherent in gainsharing is the idea that involved employees will improve productivity through more effective use of organizational resources.

Although productivity can be measured in various ways, it is usually calculated as a ratio of outputs to inputs. Sales, pieces produced, pounds, total standard costs, direct

Lessons Learned: Designing Effective Team Incentives

Will your team incentive program be successful? While there are no exact keys to success, team compensation specialists cite the following as important components of a meaningful team incentive plan.

- Are organizational members—employees and managers—predisposed to a team incentive reward system? Is there a "cultural readiness" for team compensation? If change is indicated, what information needs to be given to all organizational employees?
- Enlist total employee and managerial support for the incentive effort. While top management support is critical, without the encouragement of employees and middle- and lower-level managers (those directly involved in the program implementation), team incentive programs invariably fail.
- When developing new programs, include representatives from all groups affected by the incentive effort—labor, management, employees. Inclusion, not exclusion, serves to build trust and understanding of the program's intent and its overall importance to organizational success.
- Establish effective, fair, and precise measurement standards. Selected performance measures should be key indicators of organizational success. Do not attempt to measure everything. Employees should be able to directly influence the performance measures selected. Furthermore, performance measures should be challenging but realistic and obtainable. Standards must encourage increased effort without becoming entitlements.
- Incentive payout formulas must be seen as fair, be easy for employees to calculate, offer payouts on a frequent basis, and be large enough to encourage future employee effort. The goal is to create a pay-for-performance environment. When standards are not met, explain why the reward was not earned.
- Determine how incentive rewards will be distributed. Will team members receive equal dollar awards, or will team members receive differential payments based on such factors as seniority, skill levels, rates of pay, member contributions, and so forth?
- Communicate, communicate, communicate. Constantly champion the benefits of the incentive awards to employees and their contribution to organizational success.

labor dollars earned, and customer orders are common output measures. Inputs frequently measured include materials, labor, energy, inventory, purchased goods or services, and total costs. An increase in productivity is normally gained when:

- Greater output is obtained with less or equal input.
- Equal production output is obtained with less input.

There are many variations of gainsharing plans; however, the Scanlon Plan and Improshare are representative of gainsharing programs. The Scanlon Plan emphasizes participative management and encourages cost reductions by sharing with employees

© BEN MARGOT/AP PHOTO

The Scanlon and Rucker gainsharing plans rely on employee suggestions for cost savings and productivity improvements.

any savings resulting from those reductions. Improshare is based on the number of finished goods that the employee work teams complete in an established period.

The Scanlon Plan

Objective 5

Scanlon Plan

A bonus incentive plan using employee and management committees to gain cost-reduction improvements

The philosophy behind the Scanlon Plan is that employees should offer ideas and suggestions to improve productivity and, in turn, be rewarded for their constructive efforts. According to Scanlon's proponents, effective employee participation, which includes the use of committees on which employees are represented, is the most significant feature of the Scanlon Plan. Improvement or gains largely come from "working smarter, not harder." Figure 10.4 illustrates the Scanlon Plan suggestion process, including the duties and responsibilities of two important groups—the *shop* and *screening* committees.

Financial incentives under the Scanlon Plan are ordinarily offered to all employees (a significant feature of the plan) on the basis of an established formula. This formula is based on increases in employee productivity as determined by a norm that has been established for labor costs. The Scanlon Plan (and variations of it) has become a fundamental way of managing, if not a way of life, in organizations such as American Value Company, TRW, Weyerhaeuser, and Watermark Credit Union.[52] Specific information on the Scanlon Plan can be obtained at the Scanlon Leadership Network.[53] The Network has helped organizations in manufacturing, transportation, health care, communications, warehousing, and other industries establish Scanlon Plans.

Improshare

Improshare

A gainsharing program under which bonuses are based on the overall productivity of the work team

Improshare—improved productivity through sharing—is another gainsharing program. Individual production bonuses are typically based on how much an employee produces above some standard amount, but Improshare bonuses are based on the overall productivity of the *work team*. Improshare output is measured by the number of finished products that a work team produces in a given period. Both

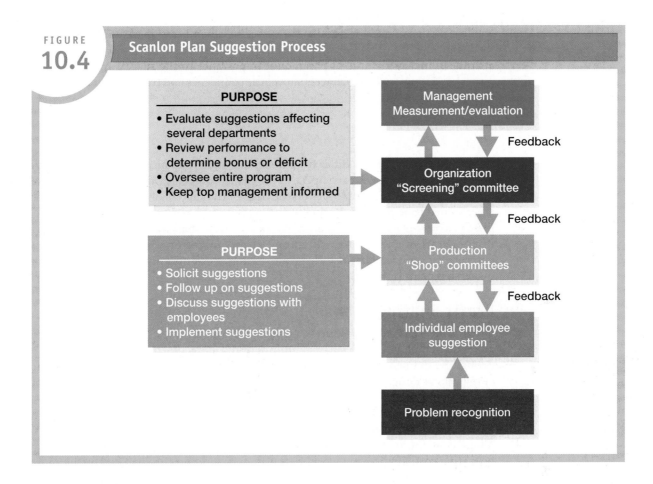

FIGURE 10.4 Scanlon Plan Suggestion Process

production (direct) employees and nonproduction (indirect) employees are included in the determination of the bonus.[54]

The bonus is based on productivity gains that result from reducing the time it takes to produce a finished product. The employees and the company each receive payment for 50 percent of the improvement. Since a cooperative environment benefits all, Improshare promotes increased interaction and support between employees and management. Companies such as Hinderliter Energy Equipment pay the bonus as a separate check to emphasize that it is extra income.

Lessons from the Scanlon Plan and Improshare

Perhaps the most important lesson to be learned from the Scanlon Plan and Improshare—or any gainsharing program—is that any management expecting to gain the cooperation of its employees in improving efficiency must permit them to become involved psychologically as well as financially in the organization. If employees are to contribute maximum effort, they must have a feeling of involvement and identification with their organization, which does not come out of the traditional manager-subordinate relationship. Consequently, it is important for organizations to realize that while employee cooperation is essential to the successful administration of gainsharing plans, the plans themselves do not necessarily stimulate this cooperation. Furthermore, the attitude of management is of paramount importance to the success of gainsharing plans. For example, when managers show little confidence and trust in their employees, the plans tend to fail.

ENTERPRISE INCENTIVE PLANS

Enterprise incentive plans differ from individual and group incentive plans in that all organizational members participate in the plan's compensation payout. Enterprise incentive plans reward employees on the basis of the success of the organization over an extended time period—normally one year, but the period can be longer. Enterprise incentive plans seek to create a "culture of ownership" by fostering a philosophy of cooperation and teamwork among all organizational members. Common enterprise incentive plans include profit sharing, stock options, and employee stock ownership plans (ESOPs).

Profit Sharing Plans

Objective 6

profit sharing

Any procedure by which an employer pays, or makes available to all regular employees, in addition to base pay, special current or deferred sums based on the profits of the enterprise

Profit sharing is any procedure by which an employer pays, or makes available to all regular employees, special current or deferred sums based on the organization's profits. As defined here, profit sharing represents cash payments made to eligible employees at designated time periods, as distinct from profit sharing in the form of contributions to employee pension funds.

Profit sharing plans are intended to give employees the opportunity to increase their earnings by contributing to the growth of their organization's profits. These contributions may be directed toward improving product quality, reducing operating costs, improving work methods, and building goodwill rather than just increasing rates of production. Profit sharing can help stimulate employees to think and feel more like partners in the enterprise and thus to concern themselves with the welfare of the organization as a whole. Its purpose therefore is to motivate a total commitment from employees rather than simply to have them contribute in specific areas.

A popular example of a highly successful profit sharing plan is the one in use at Lincoln Electric Company, a manufacturer of arc welding equipment and supplies. This plan was started in 1934 by J. F. Lincoln, president of the company. Each year the company distributes a large percentage of its profits to employees in accordance with their salary level and merit ratings. It is not uncommon for employees' annual bonuses to exceed 50 percent of annual wages. The success of Lincoln Electric's incentive system depends on a high level of contribution by each employee. Unquestionably there is a high degree of respect among employees and management for Lincoln's organizational goals and for the profit sharing program.

Variations in Profit Sharing Plans

Profit-sharing plans differ in the proportion of profits shared with employees and in the distribution and form of payment. The amount shared with employees may range from 5 to 50 percent of the net profit.

Using the Internet

Lincoln Electric's Web site provides a description of its incentive management system. It also presents information concerning career opportunities with the company. Go to the Student Resources at:

www.cengage.com/management/bohlander

In most plans, however, about 20 to 25 percent of the net profit is shared. Profit distributions may be made to all employees on an equal basis, or they may be based on regular salaries or some formula that takes into account seniority and/or merit. The payments may be disbursed in cash, deferred, or made on the basis of combining the two forms of payments.

Weaknesses of Profit Sharing Plans

In spite of their potential advantages, profit sharing plans are also prone to certain weaknesses. The profits shared with employees may be the result of inventory speculation, climatic factors, economic conditions, national emergencies, or other factors over which employees have no control. As one HR manager noted to the authors, "Since there is little linkage between what employees do and their profit bonus, there is an absence of any employee involvement initiatives." Conversely, losses may occur during years when employee contributions have been at a maximum. The fact that profit sharing payments are made only once a year or deferred until retirement may reduce their motivational value. If a plan fails to pay off for several years in a row, this can have an adverse effect on productivity and employee morale.

Employee Stock Options Plans

What do the following companies—Apple Computer, Yahoo, Coca-Cola, Starbucks, Nike, Quaker Oats, and Sara Lee—have in common? The answer: Each of these diverse organizations offers a stock option program to its employees. According to WorldatWork, a compensation association, the use of stock options is a very prevalent method of motivating and compensating hourly employees, as well as salaried and executive personnel. This appears true regardless of the industry surveyed or the organization's size.[55]

Stock option programs are sometimes implemented as part of an employee benefit plan or as part of a corporate culture linking employee effort to stock performance. However, organizations that offer stock option programs to employees do so with the belief that there is some incentive value to the systems. By allowing employees to purchase stock, the organization hopes they will increase their productivity, assume a partnership role in the organization, and thus cause the stock price to rise.[56] Furthermore, stock option programs have become a popular way to boost morale of disenfranchised employees caught in budget cuts and downsizing.

Stock option plans grant to employees the right to purchase a specific number of shares of the company's stock at a guaranteed price (the option price) during a designated time period. Although there are many types of options, most options are granted at the stock's fair market value. Not uncommon are plans for purchasing stock through payroll deductions. Highlights in HRM 5 explain employee stock option plans in greater detail.

Unfortunately, in the wake of various corporate scandals, employee stock option plans have come under attack from stockholder groups, government officials, and the general public. Criticism largely focuses on the extravagance of executive stock option plans and dubious corporate accounting procedures.[57]

Nevertheless, despite these faults, stock options continue to be a popular and efficient way to pay for the performance of employees and managers. When stock prices rise, employee stock plans can be financially rewarding to employees.

5

Employee Stock Option Plans

As of 2007, the National Center for Employee Ownership estimates that up to 10 million employees participate in broad-based stock option plans. Broad-based plans grant stock options to 50 percent or more of full-time employees.

Traditionally, stock option plans have been used as a way to reward company executives or "key" employees and to link their interests with those of the company and their shareholders. Today companies use employee stock option plans to reward, retain, and attract all levels of employees. Stock options are an effective way to share ownership with employees and to gain commitment to organizational goals.

What Is a Stock Option?

A stock option gives an employee the right to buy a certain number of shares in the company at a fixed price for a certain number of years. The price at which the option is provided is called the "grant" price and is usually the market price at the time the options are granted. Employees who have been granted stock options hope that the share price will go up and that they will be able to "cash in" by exercising (purchasing) the stock at the lower grant price and then selling the stock at the current market price.

How Stock Option Plans Work

Here is an example of a typical employee stock option plan. An employee is granted the option to purchase 1,000 shares of the company's stock at the current market price of $5 per share (the "grant" price). The employee can exercise the option at $5 per share—typically the exercise price will be equal to the price when the options are granted. Plans allow employees to exercise their options after a certain number of years or when the company's stock reaches a certain price. If the price of the stock increases to $20 per share, for example, the employee may exercise his or her options to buy 1,000 shares at $5 per share and then sell the stock at the current market price of $20 per share.

Companies sometimes revalue the price at which the options can be exercised. This may happen, for example, when a company's stock price has fallen below the original exercise price. Companies revalue the exercise price as a way to retain their employees.

Source: Adapted from "Employee Stock Options Fact Sheet, National Center for Employee Ownership at http://www.nceo.org/.

Employee Stock Ownership Plans (ESOPs)

According to Corey Rosen of the National Center for Employee Ownership, in 2008 approximately 9,700 organizations have employee stock ownership plans (ESOPs) for their employees.[58] Columbia Forest Products, The Tribune Co., U.S. Sugar, The Bureau of National Affairs, and Scheels All Sports are organizations with established ESOPs. W. L. Gore and Associates also decided that employee stock ownership was an effective and innovative way to give employees a share of the company's success.

An employee stock owner ship plan (ESOP) is an employer established trust that qualifies as a tax-exempt employee trust under Section 401(a) of the Internal Revenue Code. Under an employee stock ownership plan, employees do not actually buy shares in an ESOP. Instead, the company contributes its own shares to the plan, contributes cash to buy its own stock (often from an existing owner), or, most commonly, has the plan borrow money to buy stock, with the company repaying the loan. All of these uses have significant tax benefits for the company, the employees, and the sellers. The ESOP holds the stock for employees, and they are routinely informed of the value of their accounts. Stock allocations can be based on employee wages or seniority. When employees leave the organization or retire, they can sell their stock back to the organization, or they can sell it on the open market if it is traded publicly.

employee stock ownership plans (ESOPs)

Stock plans in which an organization contributes shares of its stock to an established trust for the purpose of stock purchases by its employees

Advantages of ESOPs

Encouraged by favorable federal income tax provisions, employers use ESOPs to provide retirement benefits for their employees. Favorable tax incentives permit a portion of earnings to be excluded from taxation if that portion is assigned to employees in the form of shares of stock. Employers can therefore provide retirement benefits for their employees at relatively low cost because stock contributions are in effect subsidized by the federal government. ESOPs can also increase employees' pride of ownership in the organization, providing an incentive for them to increase productivity and help the organization prosper and grow.

Problems with ESOPs

Generally, ESOPs are more likely to serve their intended purposes in publicly held companies than in privately held ones. A major problem with the privately held company is its potential inability to pay back the stock of employees when they retire. These employees do not have the alternative of disposing of their stock on the open market. Thus, when large organizations suffer financial difficulties and the value of the companies' stocks falls, so does the value of the employees' retirement plan.

Other problems with ESOPs include the following:

- The more retirement income comes from these plans, the more dependent a pensioner becomes on the price of company stock. Future retirees are vulnerable to stock market fluctuations as well as to management mistakes.

- Unlike traditional pension plans, ESOP contributions are not guaranteed by the federally established Pension Benefit Guaranty Corporation (see Chapter 11), a major drawback to employees should their employer face serious financial setbacks or closure.

SUMMARY

Objective 1 The success of an incentive pay plan depends on the organizational climate in which it must operate, employee confidence in it, and its suitability to employee and organizational needs. Importantly, employees must view their incentive pay as being equitable and related to their performance. Performance measures should be quantifiable, be easily understood, and bear a demonstrated relationship to organizational performance.

Objective 2 Piecework plans pay employees a given rate for each unit satisfactorily completed. Employers implement these plans when output is easily measured and when the production process is fairly standardized. Bonuses are incentive payments above base wages paid on either an individual or team basis. A bonus is offered to encourage employees to exert greater effort. Standard hour plans establish a standard time for job completion. An incentive is paid for finishing the job in less than the preestablished time. These plans are popular for jobs with a fixed time for completion.

Objective 3 Merit raises will not serve to motivate employees when they are seen as entitlements, which occurs when these raises are given yearly without regard to changes in employee performance. Merit raises are not motivational when they are given because of seniority or favoritism or when merit budgets are inadequate to sufficiently reward employee performance. To be motivational, merit raises must be such that employees see a clear relationship between pay and performance, and the salary increase must be large enough to exceed inflation and higher income taxes.

Objective 4 Salespeople may be compensated by a straight salary, a combination of salary and commission, salary plus bonus, or a commission only. Paying employees a straight salary allows them to focus on tasks other than sales, such as service and customer goodwill. A straight commission plan causes employees to emphasize sales goals. A combination of salary and commission or bonus provides the advantages of both the straight salary and the straight commission form of payments.

Objective 5 The Scanlon and Improshare gainsharing plans pay bonuses to employees unrelated to profit levels. Each of these plans encourages employees to maximize their performance and cooperation through suggestions offered to improve organizational performance. The Scanlon Plan pays an employee a bonus based on saved labor cost measured against the organization's sales value of production. The Improshare bonus is paid when employees increase production output above a given target level.

Objective 6 Profit sharing plans pay to employees sums of money based on the organization's profits. Cash payments are made to eligible employees at specified times, normally yearly. The primary purpose of profit sharing is to provide employees with additional income through their participation in organizational achievement. Employee commitment to improved productivity, quality, and customer service will contribute to organizational success and, in turn, to their compensation. Profit sharing plans may not achieve their stated gains when employee performance is unrelated to organizational success or failure. This may occur because of economic conditions, other competition, or environmental conditions. Profit sharing plans can have a negative effect on employee morale when plans fail to consistently reward employees.

Objective 7 With an ESOP, each year the organization contributes stock or cash to buy stock that is then placed in an ESOP trust. The ESOP holds the stock for employees until they either retire or leave the company, at which time the stock is sold back to the company or through a brokerage firm. Employers receive tax benefits for qualified ESOPs; they also hope to receive their employees' commitment to organizational improvement. Employees, however, may lose their retirement income should the company fail or stock prices fall. Another drawback to ESOPs is that they are not guaranteed by any federal agency.

KEY TERMS

bonus
combined salary and commission plan
differential piece rate
employee stock ownership plans (ESOPs)
gainsharing plans

Improshare
lump sum merit program
merit guidelines
perquisites
profit sharing
salary plus bonus plan
Scanlon Plan

spot bonus
standard hour plan
straight commission plan
straight piecework
straight salary plan
team incentive plan
variable pay

DISCUSSION QUESTIONS

Objective 1 1. Working individually or in groups, identify the factors for a successful incentive plan.

Objective 2 2. Contrast the differences between straight piecework, differential piece rate, and standard hour plans. Explain where each plan might best be used.

Objective 3 3. A frequently heard complaint about merit raises is that they do little to increase employee effort. What are the causes of this belief? Suggest ways in which the motivating value of merit raises may be increased.

Objective 4 4. What are the reasons behind the different payment methods for sales employees?

Objective 5 5. What are the reasons for the success of the Scanlon and Improshare plans?

Objective 6 6. Because of competitive forces within your industry, you have decided to implement a profit sharing plan for your employees. Discuss the advantages of profit sharing and identify specific characteristics that will ensure success for your plan.

Objective 7 7. What are some reasons for the implementation of ESOPs? Cite some of the potential problems concerning their use.

Awarding Salary Increases

Because pay-for-performance is an important factor governing salary increases, managers must be able to defend the compensation recommendations they make for their employees. Merit raises granted under a pay-for-performance policy must be based on objective appraisals if they are to achieve their intended purposes of rewarding outstanding employee performance. As managers know, however, they must deal with other factors that can affect salary recommendations. These may include the opinions of the employee's peers or extenuating circumstances such as illness or family responsibilities. The purpose of this exercise is to provide you with the experience of granting salary increases to employees based on their work performance and other information.

Assignment

Following are the work records of five employees. As their supervisor, you have just completed their annual appraisal reviews, and it is now time to make recommendations for their future salary. Your department budget has $5,780 allocated for salary increases. Distribute the $5,780 among your employees based on the descriptions for each subordinate.

a. Janet Jenkins currently earns $41,000. Her performance appraisal rating was very high. She is respected by her peers and is felt to be an asset to the work group. She is divorced and has three young children to support.

b. Russell Watts earns a salary of $36,000. His annual performance appraisal was average. Several members of the work group have spoken to you about the difficulty involved in Russell's job. They feel that it is a tough and demanding job and that he is doing his best.

c. Jack Perkins earns $31,250. His performance appraisal was below average, and he seems to have difficulty adjusting to his coworkers. Jack has had a difficult time this past year. His wife passed away early in the year, and his father has recently been diagnosed as terminally ill.

d. Rick Jacobson earns $28,000. His performance appraisal was above average. He is respected by his peers and is generally considered to be a "good guy."

e. Paula Merrill earns $28,850. Her performance appraisal was very high. Her peers are upset because they feel that she is working only to provide a second income. Moreover, her peers see her as trying to "show them up."

Share your results with other class members. Be prepared to explain your allocation of money.

BIZFLIX EXERCISES

Scent of a Woman: Freddie Bisco's Incentives

The scene from *Scent of a Woman* shows many aspects of incentive rewards and employee performance discussed in this chapter. Watch for types of incentives and the positive and negative effects of incentives as you view the scene.

Young Charlie Simms (Chris O'Donnell) wants to earn extra money over Thanksgiving weekend for airfare to go home during his Christmas break. He becomes a guide and caretaker for ill-tempered, retired, blind Lt. Col. Frank Slade (Al Pacino). Charlie, from Gresham, Oregon, is quiet and reserved and has had little experience with the opposite sex. He attends the exclusive Baird Preparatory School on a scholarship. His wild New York City weekend with Frank Slade bonds them forever. This film is a remake of *Profumo di Donna*, a 1974 Italian film.

This scene is an edited version from the end of the "Tango Lessons" segment and the beginning of "The Ferrari" segment that appear about halfway through the film. It follows the despondent hotel room scene

and the tango lesson Slade gave Donna (Gabrielle Anwar) in The Waldorf Astoria restaurant. It begins shortly after Freddie Bisco (Leonard Gaines), the Ferrari salesman, says to Charlie, "Yeah, this is a valid Oregon driver's license, . . ." Freddie does not want to let either Charlie or Slade test-drive a Ferrari. The scene ends after Slade says, "I'm a gray ghost too." The film cuts to the Ferrari rounding a New York City street corner with Charlie driving.

What to Watch for and Ask Yourself

- Assume that Freddie Bisco receives a sales incentive for each Ferrari he sells. Does Freddie appear highly motivated by this incentive reward system? What is the evidence from the scene?

- Freddie does not work for Frank Slade. Is the $2,000 that Slade gives Freddie the same as a bonus discussed earlier in this chapter? If yes, which type of bonus is it?

- Did you perceive any negative effects of Freddie Bisco's incentives that he experienced in this scene?

CASE STUDY 1

Out but Rich at Home Depot

The clamor over sky-high executive paychecks and CEO severance or retirement pay packages is a hot topic of national debate. Shareholder groups, union leaders, political officials, and activists from hedge funds all demand change. The controversy over gargantuan executive pay reached a boiling point in January 2007, when Robert L. Nardelli, touted as one of corporate America's most talented executives and chief executive at Home Depot, suddenly resigned.

As reported in *Business Week*, the clash between Home Depot's board of directors and Nardelli began when board members wanted the chief executive to amend his future compensation package, a pay package which for 2007 exceeded $38 million. Specifically, the board asked Nardelli to more closely align his stock package to future stock gains. He refused claiming share price was one measure of performance he could not control. Additionally, over a six-year period, Nardelli's compensation totaled more than $200 million in salary, bonuses, stock options, restricted stock, and other perks, a figure which angered many stockholders.

At a January 2007 board of directors meeting, things came to a head, and the board and Nardelli "mutually agreed" that he would resign. For his severance package, Nardelli negotiated another jaw-dropping deal—a $210 million retirement package.

Questions

1. Are CEOs and key corporate executives worth the large pay packages they receive? Explain.
2. Do you agree with Peter Drucker that corporate executives should receive compensation packages no larger than a certain percentage of the pay of hourly workers? Explain.
3. Will the reporting of executive pay in company financial statements influence shareholder affect on executive pay? Explain.

Source: Adapted from Brian Grow, "Out at Home Depot," *Business Week*, January 15, 2007, 56.

CASE STUDY 2

Team-Based Incentive Rewards: It's Not All Roses

Network Cable, Inc. operates throughout the central and southern portions of Florida's east coast. With approximately 43,500 subscribers, the company is a service provider for cable TV and high-speed Internet connections. Network Cable operates in an area described as a "high-growth market."

In January 2006, Tara Gilbert, vice president of human resources for Network Cable, convinced company president and CEO Jeff Lesitner that restructuring the organization workforce into teams would benefit both Network Cable and its employees. Cost savings, improved morale, and team synergy were cited as inherent benefits of teams. Based on these assessments, in June 2006, a select group of three senior managers, plus Tara Gilbert and the company's financial officer, implemented teams within the company's installation department. Here, forty service installers were formed into eight teams of five installers each. Management set performance goals for the installation teams linked to attractive incentive rewards (cash bonuses above base salaries) when performance goals are reached. Performance measures included indexes for improved installation time, customer satisfaction scores, additional sales, equipment maintenance, and repair/callback problems. Each team could earn incentive bonuses up to a maximum of $15,000 annually with cash bonuses shared equally by each team member—a possible cash reward of $3,000 for each installer. Team bonuses after the first years were as follows: two teams, $15,000; one team, $12,500; one team, $7,300; one team, $3,150.

During August 2008, Tara Gilbert sent to all installers and their supervisors a survey requesting feedback on the satisfaction with teams and, specifically, the incentive rewards program. While survey results were generally positive, not all was rosy. Problems could be grouped into the following categories:

1. Some installers believed that various team members did not "buy into" the team concept and were simply "free riders"—average employees who benefited from the efforts of superior employees.
2. There was a general feeling that several teams were routinely assigned difficult installations that prevented them from achieving high performance goals.
3. Teams did not always display the motivation and synergy expected, since "bickering" was prevalent between average performers and super performers. Average performers complained that high performers made them look bad.
4. A high percentage of survey respondents (29 percent) felt the incentive rewards program was unfair and asked for a return to fixed across-the-board salary increases.

Questions

1. Do results from the survey illustrate typical complaints about teams and specifically about team incentive rewards? Explain.
2. If appropriate, what changes would you recommend to improve the incentive reward program? Be specific.
3. Would management have benefited from employee involvement in the initial design and implementation of the program? Explain.

NOTES AND REFERENCES

1. *2007–2008 Salary Budget Survey*, 34th annual (Scottsdale, AZ: WorldatWork Press 2007), 9.
2. Anjali Athavaley, "More Raises to Be Tied to Performance," *The Wall Street Journal*, December 13, 2007, D3.
3. Patricia K. Zingheim and Jay R. Schuster, "Designing Pay and Rewards in Professional Service Companies," *Compensation and Benefits Review*, 39, no 1 (January/February 2007): 55.
4. "Reward 'Stars' and Pay-for-Performance Lead in Pay Control Strategies," *HR Focus*, 84, no. 11 (November 2007): 3.
5. John A. Menefee and Ryan O. Murphy, "Rewarding and Retaining the Best," *Benefits Quarterly*, 20, no. 3 (Third Quarter 2004): 13–21.
6. Enno Siemsen, Sridhar Balasubramanian, and Aleda V. Roth, "Incentives That Induce Task-Related Effort, Helping, and Knowledge Sharing in Workgroups," *Management Science*, 53, no. 10 (October 2007): 1533.
7. Fay Hansen, "Control and Customization," *Workforce Management*, 86, no. 19 (November 5, 2007): 42.
8. Corey Helm, Courtney L. Holladay, Frank R. Tortorella, and Christine Candio, "The Performance Management System: Applying and Evaluating a Pay-for-Performance Initiative," *Journal of Healthcare Management*, 52, no. 1 (January/February 2007): 49.
9. Leo Jakobson, "All It's Quacked Up To Be," *Incentive*, 181, no. 9 (September 2007): 24.
10. Joanne Sammer, "Weighing Pay Incentives," *HR Magazine*, 52, no. 6 (June 2007): 64.
11. Roisin Woolnough, "How to Set Up an Incentive Scheme," *Personnel Today*, February 14, 2005, 22.
12. Ann Pomeroy, "Business Strategy, Not Just HR Strategy," *HR Magazine*, 52, no. 11 (November 2007): 46.
13. Jim McCoy, "How to Align Employee Performance with Business Strategy," *Workforce Management*, 86, no. 12 (June 27, 2007): 55.
14. George T. Milkovich and Jerry M. Newman, *Compensation*, 9th ed. (Boston: McGraw Hill Irwin, 2008).
15. Patty Kujawa, "Private Firms Recognize Value of Cash Bonuses," *Workforce Management*, 86, no. 21 (December 10, 2007): 11.

16 Chris Taylor, "On-the-Spot Incentives," *HR Magazine*, 49, no. 5 (May 2004): 80–84.

17. Don Hellriegel and John W. Slocum, Jr., *Organizational Behavior*, 12th ed. (Mason, OH: South-Western, 2009), Chapter 6.

18. Debra L. Nelson and James Campbell Quick, *Organizational Behavior: Science, The Real World, and You*, 6th ed. (Mason, OH: South-Western, 2009).

19. Employee perceptions of appropriate pay raises likely depend on the employer's ability to pay and the economics of the period. For example, when it is known that an employer's ability to pay is great and the economics of the industry are strong, then employees will expect larger percentage merit raises.

20. Susan J. Wells, "No Results, No Raise," *HR Magazine*, 50, no. 5 (May 2005): 76.

21. David E. Terpstra and Andre L. Honoree, "Employees Responses to Merit Pay Inequity," *Compensation and Benefits Review*, 37, no. 1 (January/February 2005): 51.

22. Leo Jackson, "$46 Billion Spent on Incentives," *Incentive*, 181, no. 11 (November 2007): 27.

23. Tyler Gentry, "Re-engineering Recognition," *Workspan*, (February 2007): 47. See also Ann Norman, "Airs Budget Group: Using Recognition to Foster Engagement," *Workspan*, (November 2007): 75.

24. Alison Avalos, "Recognition: A Critical Component of the Total Reward Mix," *Workspan*, (July 2007): 33. See also Scott Dow, Tom McMullen, Richard S. Sperling, and Bill Bowbin, "Reward Programs: What Works and What Needs to be Improved," *WorldatWork*, 16, no. 3 (Third Quarter 2007): 6.

25. Charlotte Garvey, "Meaningful Tokens of Appreciation," *HR Magazine*, 49, no. 9 (August 2004): 102.

26. Michele Marchetti, "Rethinking Compensation Plans," *Sales and Marketing Management*, 159, no. 7 (September 2007): 14.

27. Paul R. Dorf and Lisette F. Masur, "The Tough Economy Prompts Companies to Shift Their Approach to Sales Compensation," *Journal of Organizational Excellence*, 23, no. 2 (Spring 2004): 35–42.

28. Joseph Dimisa, "How to Sell Your Sales Compensation Plan," *Workspan*, (December 2007): 25.

29. Jim Stockmann, "Change on the Horizon: An Analysis of Sales Compensation Practices," *Workspan*, (April 2007): 41.

30. Donald L. Caruth and Gail D. Handloggten-Caruth, "The Formula for Compensating Sales Personnel," *The American Salesman*, 51, no. 4 (April 2006): 6.

31. Mark Reilly and Brian Enright, "A New Approach to Executive Compensation," *Workspan*, (August 2007): 45.

32. Seymour Burchman and Blair Jones, "Executive Compensation as a Support for Growth Strategy," *WorldatWork*, 15, no. 3 (Third Quarter 2006): 39.

33. Total annual compensation is the sum of an executive's annual and long-term compensation. Annual compensation consists of salary, bonus, and other yearly pay. Long-term compensation consists of stock awards, the value of any stock options exercised during the year, and any other long-term compensation (such as payouts from long-term incentive plans, director's fees, and special bonuses).

34. Edward E. Lawler III and David Finegold, "CEO Compensation: What Board Members Think," *WorldatWork*, 16, no. 3 (Third Quarter 2007): 38.

35. Brandon Cherry, "Executive Bonus Plans: Recent Trends in Equity Compensation," *Workspan*, (January 2007): 22.

36. Darrell Rigby and Barbara Bilodeau, "Selecting Management Tools Wisely," *Harvard Business Review*, 85, no. 12 (December 2007): 20.

37. Brad Hill and Christine Tande, "What's Next for Executive Incentives Now That Options Are Limited?" *Workspan*, (September 2007): 47.

38. "CEO Compensation," *Forbes*, 179, no. 11 (May 21, 2007): 112.

39. Peter Burrows, "He's Making Hay as CEOs Squirm," *Business Week*, January 15, 2007, 64. See also Saado Abboud, "Best Buy Uses Flexibility and Choice to Improve Long-Term Incentive Design," *Workspan*, (October 2007): 32.

40. Pam Delaney, "Filling the Executive Benefits Gap," *Workspan*, (November 2007), 69.

41. "An Unfair Rap for CEO Perks?" *Business Week*, June 7, 2004, 32.

42. Anne Tergesen, "How Much Are Execs Really Paid?" *Business Week*, March 20, 2006, 96.

43. Joann S. Lublin, "CEO Compensation Survey (A Special Report); Persistent Pay Gains: A Survey Overview, *The Wall Street Journal*," April 14, 2008. R.I. 112; Leigh Rivenback, "Responsible Executive Compensation for a New Era of Accountability," *HR Magazine*, 48, no. 9 (September 2004): 178. See also Michael Savage and Terry Adamson, "Employee Stock Options: New Valuation Responsibilities and Planning Opportunities," *Benefits Quarterly*, 20, no. 3 (Third Quarter 2004): 34.

44. John A. Byrne, "The Man Who Invented Management: Why Peter Drucker's Ideas Still Matter," *Business Week*, November 2004, 97.

45. Steven N. Kaplan, "Are CEOs Overpaid?" *WorldatWork*, 16, no. 3 (Third Quarter 2007): 22. See also Ira Kay and Steve Van Putten, *Myths and Realities of Executive Pay* (Cambridge, MA: Cambridge University Press, 2007); Jessica Marquez, "5 Questions: in Defense of CEO Pay," *Workforce Management*, 86, no. 16 (September 27, 2007): 8.

46. "CEO Compensation," 112.

47. Louis Lavelle, "Everybody Should Be a Little Nervous," *Business Week*, December 22, 2003, 42.

48. Seymour Burchman and Blair Jones, "A New Day for Executive Compensation" *Workspan*, (January 2007): 15. See also "Out at Home Depot," *Business Week*, January 15, 2007, 56.

49. Mark Gimein, "The Bottom Line on Options," *Business Week*, April 3, 2006, 32. See also Peter Burrows, "Is Steve's Job Untouchable?" *Business Week*, January 15, 2007, 28.

50. Marjorie Chan, "Executive Compensation," *Business and Society Review*, 113, no. 1 (Spring 2008): 129.

51. Milkovich and Newman, *Compensation*.

52. Scott Dow, Paul Davis, and Chuck Cockburn, "Scanlon Principles and Processes: Building Excellence at Watermark Credit Union," *WorldatWork*, 16, no. 1 (First Quarter 2007): 29.

53. The Scanlon Leadership Network can be found at www.scanlanleader.org.

54. The standard of Improshare's measurement system is the base productivity factor (BPF), which is the ratio of standard direct labor hours produced to total actual hours worked in a base period. The productivity of subsequent periods is then measured by enlarging standard direct labor hours earned by the BPF ratio to establish Improshare hours (IH). The IH is then compared with actual hours worked in the same period. If earned hours exceed actual hours, 50 percent of the gain is divided by actual hours worked to establish a bonus percentage for all employees in the plan.

55. Jason Kovac, "Stock Options," *Workspan,* (August 2006): 23. See also Seymour Burchman and Blair Jones, "The Future of Stock Options: From Starring Role to Ensemble Player," *WorldatWork,* 13, no. 1 (First Quarter 2004): 29–38.

56. Ira T. Kay and Steve Seelig, "Revising the Use of a Management Stock Purchase Plan to Increase Management Ownership," *Journal of Deferred Compensation,* 11, no. 3 (Spring 2006): 24.

57. Raquel Meyer Alexander, Mark Hirchey, and Susan Scholz, "Backdating Employee Stock Options: Tax Implications," *The CPA Journal,* 77, no. 10 (October 2007): 24. See also T. Thomas Cottingham III, "The Stock Options Backdating Scandal: Critical First Response," *Risk Management,* 54, no. 6 (June 2007): 12.

58. Corey Rosen, National Center for Employee Ownership, interview by author, January 18, 2008. The National Center for Employee Ownership (NCEO) is a private, nonprofit membership and research organization that serves as the leading source of accurate, unbiased information on employee stock ownership plans (ESOPs), broadly granted employee stock options and related programs, and ownership culture. The NCEO can be reached at http://www.nceo.org or by phone at (510) 208-1300.

EMPLOYEE BENEFITS

After studying this chapter, you should be able to

Objective 1

Describe the characteristics of a sound benefits program.

Objective 2

Indicate management concerns about the costs of employee benefits and discuss ways to control those costs.

CHAPTER 11

Objective | 3

Identify and explain the employee benefits required by law.

Objective | 4

Discuss suggested ways to control the costs of health care programs.

Objective | 5

Describe benefits that involve payment for time not worked.

Objective | 6

Discuss the recent trends in retirement policies and programs.

Objective | 7

Indicate the major factors involved in the management of pension plans.

Objective | 8

Describe the types of work/life benefits that employers may provide.

Consider the results from two recent studies. According to the National Association of Colleges and Employers in 2007, when students were asked about the most desirable attributes of an employer, they listed "good benefits packages" far ahead of high salaries or opportunities for advancement.[1] In a nationwide survey conducted by the National Business Group on Health, an organization whose members include Fortune 500 companies, employees consider their health plan to be their most important benefit. Helen Darling, president of the group, notes that employees would rather give up wage increases and other benefits to preserve health care coverage.[2]

According to the U.S. Chamber of Commerce, employee benefits are one of the greatest challenges in business today in attracting and retaining quality employees. While challenging work, good working conditions, and fair wages and salaries contribute to employee attraction and retention, clearly an employer's benefits program is an important "magnet" drawing employees to employers. The U.S. Chamber of Commerce notes that "employees are increasingly aware of the benefits they receive and how those benefits compare to what other companies are offering."[3] Additionally, because most benefits (almost 80 percent) are provided voluntarily by employers, they become both a significant cost and an employment advantage to employers, while providing needed psychological and physical assistance to employees. The importance of benefits to both sides simply cannot be overstated.

Virtually all employers provide a variety of benefits to supplement the wages or salaries paid to their employees. These benefits, some of which are required by law, must be considered a part of their total compensation. Therefore, in this chapter we examine the characteristics of employee benefits programs. We will study the types of benefits required by law, the major discretionary benefits that employers offer, the employee services they provide, and the retirement programs in use. The chapter concludes with a discussion of popular—and highly important—work/life benefit programs.

▪▪ EMPLOYEE BENEFITS PROGRAMS

Objective 1

Employee benefits constitute an indirect form of compensation intended to improve the quality of the work lives and the personal lives of employees. As discussed later, benefits represent approximately 43 percent of total payroll costs to employers. In return, employers generally expect employees to be supportive of the organization and to be productive. Since benefits provide a significant advantage to both employers and employees, the motivational value of these benefits depends on how the benefits program is designed and communicated. As noted by Sandra Patterson, benefits consultant, "Benefits planning and administration is today of critical interest to top level executives."[4]

HRIS and Employee Benefits

With the wide variety of benefits offered to employees today, administering an organization's benefits program can be both costly and time-consuming. Even for small employers with thirty to forty employees, keeping track of each employee's use of a benefit or request for a change of benefits can be cumbersome. For example, even the rather straightforward task of monitoring employee sick leave usage becomes complex as the size of the organization grows.

Fortunately, interactive employee benefit systems are becoming mainstream at a large majority of both large and small employers, such as Cabrini College in Radnor, Pennsylvania; Parker Services, a temporary services provider in Seattle; Wells Fargo Bank; GoDaddy.com; and the City of Cincinnati, Ohio. The technology of the Internet permits employees to access their benefits package, allowing both greater control and ownership of the benefits offered them.[5] Part of the advantage of an Internet benefits system is that employees can obtain information on their own timetable. Speaking specifically about HRIS and health care benefits, Mindy Kairey, e-business leader of the health care management practice for Hewitt Associates LLC, explains, "The Web puts benefits information right in the hands of the people who need it. Employees want to track their claims, review their current coverage levels, and compare their options. They want to take responsibility for their health plan."[6]

Online benefits programs create a form of self-service benefits administration. One intent of online programs is to provide greater flexibility in benefits selection. An important advantage to an interactive benefits program is the significant cost savings in benefits administration.[7] Once an online system is operational, it is easy and inexpensive to adapt to employer and employee demands. However, while the Internet can be used effectively in benefits administration, security must always be a concern when transmitting benefits information.

Perhaps no part of the HR function is more technologically advanced than the administration of employee benefits programs. A wide variety of commercially developed software packages facilitate benefits administration in such areas as pension, variable pay, workers' compensation, health benefits, and time-off programs. Descriptions of and advertisements for a variety of benefits software programs are readily found in HR journals such as *Workforce Management* and *HRMagazine*. Software programs represent a cost-effective way to manage employee benefits programs when employers lack the resources or expertise to manage such programs.

Requirements for a Sound Benefits Program

The soundness of a benefits programs hinges on two factors: (1) selecting benefits that target important employee needs while promoting strategic organizational objectives and (2) effective administration of benefits programs. Gone are the days of providing a particular benefit because other employers are doing it, because someone in authority believes it is a good idea, or because the benefit is "popular" at the moment. Therefore, benefit specialists recommend paying attention to certain basic considerations.

Strategic Benefits Planning

Like any other component of the HR program, an employee benefits program should be based on specific objectives. The objectives an organization establishes will depend on many factors, including the size of the firm; its location, degree of unionization, and profitability; and industry patterns. Most important, these aims must be compatible with the organization's strategic compensation plan (see Chapter 9), including its total rewards strategy.[8]

The chief objectives of most benefits programs are as follows:

- Improve employee work satisfaction

- Meet employee health and security requirements

- Attract and motivate employees

- Retain top-performing employees

- Maintain a favorable competitive position

Further, these objectives must be considered within the framework of cost containment—a major issue for today's programs.

Unless an organization has a flexible benefits plan (to be discussed later), a uniform package of benefits should be developed. This involves careful consideration of the various benefits that can be offered, the relative preference shown for each benefit by management and the employees, the estimated cost of each benefit, and the total amount of money available for the entire benefits package.

Allowing for Employee Involvement

Before a new benefit is introduced, the need for it should first be determined through consultation with employees. Many organizations establish committees composed of managers and employees to administer, interpret, and oversee their benefits policies. Opinion surveys are also used to obtain employee input. Having employees participate in designing benefits programs helps ensure that management is moving in the direction of satisfying employee wants. For example, a medium-sized technology company used focus groups to determine employee preferences before implementing a managed care program. Feedback from the focus groups showed that employees preferred a point-of-service plan with the option of using physicians outside the network when needed.[9] Employees indicated that they would rather pay higher copayments as a trade-off to receiving lower premiums. The focus groups also told management that employee meetings were the best way to communicate the program.

Benefits for a Diverse Workforce

To serve their intended purpose, employee benefits programs must reflect the changes that are continually occurring within our society. Particularly significant are changes in the diversity and lifestyles of the workforce. For example, recent figures from the U.S. Census Bureau show that married couple households have declined from nearly 80 percent in the 1950s to approximately 51 percent today. Unmarried people make up 42 percent of the workforce. These demographic shifts and others noted throughout the text mandate that organizations design benefit packages that match the changing U.S. population. Fortunately, more employers have begun to tailor their benefit programs to be family friendly.[10] (Specific work/life benefits are discussed later in the chapter.) For example, Merrill Lynch and Bank of America accommodate demographic shifts by offering extended family benefits.[11] At Prudential Securities, cohabitants can receive health benefits for opposite- or same-sex partners. These examples simply illustrate the need for benefits programs that take into account a highly diversified workforce in order to attract highly capable employees.

Unfortunately, benefit plans sometimes provide little advantage to employees, limiting the organization's ability to attract or retain quality employees. For example, many employers provide unneeded medical benefits to the young and single in the form of dependents' coverage. Likewise, a well-designed—and costly—defined benefits pension program may not serve the needs of employees or the employer of a predominately younger workforce.

flexible benefits plans (cafeteria plans)

Benefit plans that enable individual employees to choose the benefits that are best suited to their particular needs

Providing for Flexibility

To accommodate the individual needs of employees, organizations may offer flexible benefits plans, also known as cafeteria plans. These plans enable individual employees to choose the benefits that are best suited to their particular needs.[12] They also prevent certain benefits from being wasted on employees who have no need for them. Furthermore, companies realize they can get a better return on investment by tailoring benefits to an employee's stage of life or family status.[13]

Typically, employees are offered a basic or core benefits package of life and health insurance, sick leave, and vacation. Requiring a core set of benefits ensures that employees have a minimum level of coverage to protect against unforeseen financial hardships. Employees are then given a specified number of credits they may use to "buy" whatever other benefits they need. Other benefit options might include prepaid legal services, financial planning, dental insurance, and long-term care insurance. Compensation specialists often see flexible benefits plans as ideal. Employees select the benefits of greatest value to them, while employers manage benefits costs by limiting the dollars employees have to spend. Figure 11.1 lists the most frequently cited advantages and disadvantages of flexible benefits programs.

Importantly, because cafeteria plans allow employees to choose between taxable benefits, these plans must comply with Section 125 of the Internal Revenue Code. It is critical for employers to make sure their plans meet all aspects of tax rules if they wish to preserve the tax favored treatment of these employee benefits.[14]

Communicating Employee Benefits Information

Consider this research finding. A study on health care benefits by Towers Perrin found that many employees do not believe what their employers tell them about soaring benefits costs, and employees and employers are at loggerheads over how effectively benefits are used. The Towers Perrin study concluded by noting that the credibility gap is largely

FIGURE
11.1

Flexible Benefits Plans: Advantages and Disadvantages

ADVANTAGES

- Employees select benefits to match their individual needs.
- Benefit selections adapt to a constantly changing (diversified) workforce.
- Employees gain greater understanding of the benefits offered to them and the costs incurred.
- Employers maximize the psychological value of their benefits program by paying only for highly desired benefits.
- Employers limit benefit costs by allowing employees to "buy" benefits only up to a maximum (defined) amount.
- Employers gain a competitive advantage in the recruiting and retention of employees.

DISADVANTAGES

- Poor employee benefits selection results in unwanted financial costs.
- There are certain added costs to establishing and maintaining the flexible plan.
- Employees may choose benefits of high use to them that increase employer premium costs.

caused by poor benefits communication and lack of employee trust.[15] Interestingly, benefit specialists remark that the true measure of a successful benefits program is the degree of trust, understanding, and appreciation it earns from the employees.[16]

The communication of employee benefits information improved significantly with the passage of the Employee Retirement Income Security Act (ERISA) in 1974. The act requires that employees be informed about their pension and certain other benefits in a manner calculated to be understood by the average employee. Additionally, employees can sue their employers for misleading them about health and welfare benefits under ERISA. Problems can arise when managers discuss benefits with groups of employees or in one-on-one talks and employees receive inaccurate information. A manager could mislead an employee by stating that the organization's insurance policy does not cover a particular condition when, in fact, it does or that a maternity leave provision is 120 days when the plan is actually 60 days. These potential problems underscore the importance of communicating benefit information accurately and unambiguously.[17]

Employers use an array of methods to communicate benefits to employees, such as the following:

- In-house publications (employee handbooks and organizational newsletters)
- Group meeting and training classes
- Audiocassettes/videotapes
- Bulletin boards
- Payroll inserts/pay stub messages
- Specialty brochures

Employee self-service (ESS) systems have made it possible for employees to gain information about their benefits plans, enroll in their plans of choice, change benefits coverage, alter W-4 designations, or simply inquire about the status of their various benefit accounts without ever contacting a HR representative. Coopers & Lybrand offers a Benefits Information Line that allows employers to provide employees with instant access to a wide variety of benefits and HR information by telephone. Individual account information is available upon entering a personal identification number (PIN). Other organizations use networked PCs or multimedia kiosks as the basis of their self-service system. These approaches permit employees to click on icons to access different benefits and type in new information to update their records. Once an update or change is made, the new information is permanently entered into the organization's HR information system without the need for paperwork. Highlights in HRM 1 presents suggestions for designing a professional benefits communication program.

When communicating employee benefits, the best advice is to use multiple media techniques.[18] Different employee groups have different ways of learning and distinct preferences in how they prefer to receive information. Also, the level of complexity of the benefit will likely determine media selection.[19]

In addition to having general information, it is important for each employee to have a current statement of the status of her or his benefits. The usual means is the personalized computer-generated statement of benefits. As Highlights in HRM 2 shows, this benefits cost statement can be one of the best ways of slicing through a maze of technicalities to provide concise data to employees about the status of their personal benefits.[20]

Concerns of Management

Managing an employee benefits program requires close attention to the many forces that must be kept in balance if the program is to succeed. Management must consider union demands, the benefits other employers are offering, and tax consequences. Today, however, probably no compensation issue is more important to senior executives, compensation specialists, and employees than the skyrocketing costs of employee benefits, specifically medical care and retirement expenses.

2 | Objective

HIGHLIGHTS IN HRM

1

Crafting an Effective Benefits Communication Program

A well-designed benefits communication program greatly enhances employees' appreciation of their benefits while ensuring that employers receive the intended value of these offerings. An effective program provides frequent information to employees in a cost-effective and timely manner. Compensation specialists recommend the following points when administering a benefits communication program.

In building an identity:
- Design materials that are eye-catching and of high interest to employees.
- Develop a graphic logo for all material.
- Identify a theme for the benefits program.

In writing benefits materials:
- Avoid complex language when describing benefits. Clear, concise, and understandable language is a must.
- Provide numerous examples to illustrate benefit specifics.
- Explain all benefits in an open and honest manner. Do not attempt to conceal unpleasant news.
- Explain the purpose behind the benefit and the value of the benefit to employees.

In publicizing benefits information:
- Use all popular employee communication techniques.
- Maintain employee self-service (ESS) technology to disseminate benefits information and to update employee benefits selections.
- Use voice mail to send benefits information.
- Employ presentation software such as PowerPoint or Lotus Freelance to present information to groups of employees.
- Maintain a benefits hotline to answer employee questions.

The High Cost of Providing Benefits

According to a 2007 U.S. Chamber of Commerce study, the cost of employee benefits in that year averaged 42.7 percent of payroll, as shown in Highlights in HRM 3.[21] The average distribution of these benefits was $21,527 per employee per year. Study Highlights in HRM 3 to obtain an overview of the types of benefits to be discussed in this chapter. Note particularly that some benefit costs are fixed—legally required—while others are voluntarily granted by employers and, therefore, become employer variable costs.

HIGHLIGHTS IN HRM

2

A Personalized Statement of Benefits Costs

Highlights of Your Telstar Global, Inc. Benefits Program

ID: 000-00-0000   Nancy Doe   Statement Date: 3-15-2008

Benefits	Annual Cost		
	You	**Company**	**Total**
Insurance Programs			
1. Health insurance	942.48	2,318.32	3,260.80
2. Dental insurance	254.28	301.00	555.28
3. Life insurance			
Employee—$80,000	303.80		303.80
Spouse—$10,000	457.60	37.68	495.28
Dependent—$5,000	11.04		11.04
4. Short-term disability	201.04		201.04
5. Long-term disability		207.16	207.16
6. Worker's compensation		252.84	252.84
7. Unemployment compensation		31.60	31.60
Retirement program	3,547.44	3,547.44	7,094.88
Social Security			
FICA/OASDI	2,501.20	2,501.20	5,002.40
Medicare	786.27	786.27	1,572.54
Totals	$9,005.15	$9,983.51	$18,988.66

Hourly Rate: $21.92   Annual Salary: $44,719.00

Holidays (10 Days)   80.00 Hrs.   Value: $1,753.60

U.S. Chamber of Commerce Employee Benefits Survey—2007

Type of Benefit	Percentage of Payroll %			Annual Dollars Per Employee $		
	Total, All Companies	Total, Manufacturing	Total, Non-Manufacturing	Total, All Companies	Total, Manufacturing	Total, Non-Manufacturing
Total Number of Companies	453	140	313	453	140	313
Total Number of Full-Time Equivalent Employees	389,180	74,193	314,987	389,180	74,193	314,987
Total Benefits	42.7%	43.2%	42.7%	$21,527	$22,457	$21,308
Legally Required Payments	9.5	10.4	9.2	4,663	5,321	4,509
Federally Required Payroll Taxes	7.4	7.5	7.4	3,754	4,051	3,685
Unemployment Compensation	0.5	0.9	0.4	252	449	206
Workers' Compensation Insurance	1.4	2.0	1.3	596	811	546
Other	0.1	0.1	0.1	61	10	73
Payments for Time Not Worked	9.8	9.3	9.9	4,734	4,884	4,669
Payments for Holidays	2.6	3.2	2.4	1,285	1,813	1,161
Paid Time Off	1.0	1.9	0.8	629	946	555
Payments for Vacations	3.2	3.0	3.3	1,558	1,663	1,533
Sick Leave Pay	1.3	0.3	1.5	567	151	665
Paid Breaks	0.9	0.7	0.9	314	250	330
Family & Medical Leave Pay	0.2	0.0	0.2	81	4	99
Other	0.6	0.1	0.8	300	56	357
Medically Related Payments	12.1	15.0	11.4	6,101	7,242	5,832
STD, Sickness, or Accident Insurance	0.2	0.4	0.2	132	163	125

U.S. Chamber of Commerce Employee Benefits Survey—2007 (continued)

Type of Benefit	Percentage of Payroll %			Annual Dollars Per Employee $		
	Total, All Companies	Total, Manufacturing	Total, Non-Manufacturing	Total, All Companies	Total, Manufacturing	Total, Non-Manufacturing
LTD or Wage Continuation	0.2	0.1	0.2	116	88	122
Medical Insurance Premiums	9.0	10.9	8.6	4,256	4,958	4,090
Dental Insurance Premiums	0.4	0.7	0.3	245	409	207
Vision Care	0.0	0.0	0.0	12	34	7
Retiree Medical Insurance Premiums	1.3	1.0	1.3	810	744	825
Life Insurance and Death	0.3	0.4	0.3	132	193	118
Prescription Drug Coverage	0.4	1.1	0.2	228	575	146
Administration Costs	0.1	0.1	0.1	68	56	71
Other	0.2	0.1	0.2	101	24	119
Retirement and Savings	10.4	7.4	11.1	5,567	4,319	5,861
401(K) & Similar	2.2	3.1	1.9	1,355	1,702	1,274
Defined Benefit Pension Plan	4.6	2.9	4.9	2,500	1,915	2,638
Cash Balance or Other Hybrid Plan	0.0	0.0	0.0	19	1	24
Administration Costs	0.2	0.2	0.3	93	87	94
Profit Sharing	1.1	1.0	1.1	797	528	860
Stock Bonus/ESOP	2.1	0.2	2.5	683	81	825
Other	0.2	0.0	0.3	119	4	147
Miscellaneous Benefits	1.0	1.1	1.0	462	691	408
Severance Pay	0.2	0.6	0.1	115	348	60
Child Care	0.0	0.0	0.0	1	0	1
Employee Education Expenditures	0.1	0.2	0.1	88	150	74
Discounts	0.1	0.2	0.1	67	170	43
Other	0.6	0.0	0.7	190	22	230

Source: Reprinted with permission of the U.S. Chamber of Commerce. *The 2007 Employee Benefits Study*, prepared and published by the U.S. Chamber of Commerce. To order call 1-800-638-6582.

Shifting Benefit Costs to Employees

The new mantra for employee benefits is *personal responsibility*, also referred to as *shared responsibility* and *employee accountability*. Simply stated, organizations are today requiring employees to assume greater responsibility for the rising costs of their benefit options while also requiring them to decide "when" and "how" to spend their benefit dollars.[22] According to the authors of one study, "Creating a benefits program with a personal responsibility framework represents an economic opportunity for employers by lowering medical costs and achieving higher employer productivity and greater retirement readiness for employees—all of a competitive advantage in attraction, retention, and cost management."[23]

One current trend is for employers to require employees to pay part of the cost of certain benefits (for example, through copayments or higher deductibles), especially medical coverage. For example, over the 2000 to 2006 period, employee contributions for medical coverage were up by more than 70 percent. Another employer cost-saving strategy is for employees to pay a larger part of their retirement programs through contributory pension plans or 401(k) saving plans. These and other cost-saving benefit strategies are discussed throughout the remainder of the chapter.

Shifting benefit responsibility to employees is not without problems and concerns. There is an erosion of the traditional safety net of benefits. Importantly, employees will incur a greater risk for benefit payouts, particularly future pension rewards.[24] It is also argued that not all employees are capable of making informed benefit choices—such as where to invest their pension savings—or that not all employees completely understand the complexities of different benefit programs.

EMPLOYEE BENEFITS REQUIRED BY LAW

Legally required employee benefits constitute nearly a quarter of the benefits package that employers provide. These benefits include employer contributions to Social Security, unemployment insurance, and workers' compensation insurance. We will discuss each of these benefits.

3 Objective

Social Security Insurance

Passed in 1935, the Social Security Act provides an insurance plan designed, to protect covered individuals against loss of earnings resulting from various causes. These causes may include retirement, unemployment, disability, or, in the case of dependents, the death of the worker supporting them. Thus, as with any type of casualty insurance, Social Security does not pay off except in the case where a loss of income is actually incurred through loss of employment. About 163 million workers are earning Social Security protection, and about 50 million people receive retirement survivors and disability benefits from Social Security.[25]

To be eligible for old-age and survivors' insurance (OASI) as well as disability and unemployment insurance under the Social Security Act, an individual must have been engaged in employment covered by the Act. Most employment in private enterprise, most types of self-employment, active military service after 1956, and employment in certain nonprofit organizations and governmental agencies are subject to coverage under the Act.[26] Railroad workers and civil service employees who are covered by their own systems and some occupational groups, under certain conditions, are exempted from the Act.

> **Using the Internet**
>
> The Web site of the Department of Labor provides extensive information about legally required benefits and specific requirements for compliance. Go to the Student Resources at:
>
> **www.cengage.com/ management/bohlander**

The Social Security program is supported by means of a tax levied against an employee's earnings that must be matched by the employer in each pay period. The tax revenues are used to pay three major types of benefits: (1) retirement benefits, (2) disability benefits, and (3) survivors' benefits. Because of the continual changes that result from legislation and administrative rulings, as well as the complexities of making determinations of an individual's rights under Social Security, we will describe these benefits only in general terms.

To qualify for retirement benefits, a person must have reached retirement age and be fully insured. A *fully insured person* has earned forty credits—a maximum of four credits a year for ten years, based on annual earnings, a figure adjusted annually. The amount of monthly Social Security retirement benefits is based on earnings, adjusted for inflation, over the years an individual is covered by Social Security.[27] Under Social Security guidelines, an individual's *full retirement age* depends on year of birth.[28] For example, because of longer life expectancies, full retirement age is increasing for people born after 1938. However, individuals can receive Social Security benefits as early as age 62, but the amount received each month will be less than monthly benefits received at full retirement age.

The Social Security program provides disability benefits to workers too severely disabled to engage in "substantial gainful work." To be eligible for such benefits, however, an individual's disability must have existed for at least six months and must be expected to continue for at least twelve months or be expected to result in death. After receiving disability payments for twenty-four months, a disabled person receives Medicare protection. Those eligible for disability benefits, furthermore, must have worked under Social Security long enough and recently enough before becoming disabled. Disability benefits, which include auxiliary benefits for dependents, are computed on the same basis as retirement benefits and are converted to retirement benefits when the individual reaches age 65.

Survivors' benefits represent a form of life insurance paid to members of a deceased person's family who meet the eligibility requirements.[29] Survivors' benefits can be paid only if the deceased worker had credit for a certain amount of time spent in work covered by Social Security. The exact amount of work credit needed depends on the worker's age at death. As with other benefits discussed earlier, the *amount* of benefit survivors receive is based on the worker's lifetime earnings in work covered by Social Security.

The Social Security Administration also administers the Medicare program. Retired people age 65 or older are eligible for Medicare, which includes both medical and hospital insurance and prescription drug coverage.[30] The program helps with the cost of health care, but it does not cover all medical expenses or the cost of most long-term care.[31] Medicare is financed by a portion of the payroll taxes paid by workers and their employers. It also is financed in part by monthly premiums deducted from Social Security checks.

Using the Internet

At the Social Security Administration Web site, you can download software that allows you to estimate your own personal SS benefit. Go to the Student Resources at:

www.cengage.com/
management/bohlander

Unemployment Insurance

Employees who have been working in employment covered by the Social Security Act and who are laid off may be eligible for up to twenty-six weeks of unemployment insurance benefits during their unemployment. Eligible workers must submit an application for unemployment compensation with their state employment agency, register for available work, and be willing to accept any suitable employment that may be offered to them. However, the term "suitable" gives individuals considerable discretion in accepting or rejecting job offers.

The amount of compensation that workers are eligible to receive, which varies among states, is determined by their previous wage rate and previous period of employment. Funds for unemployment compensation are derived from a federal payroll tax based on the wages paid to each employee, up to an established maximum. The major portion of this tax is refunded to the individual states, which in turn operate their unemployment compensation programs in accordance with minimum standards prescribed by the federal government.

Workers' Compensation Insurance

Workers' compensation insurance is a system whereby employers purchase private or state-funded insurance to cover employees injured at work. Workers' compensation law is governed by statutes in every state. Therefore, specific laws vary with each jurisdiction. For example, each state has different regulations governing the amount and duration of lost income benefits, including provisions for medical and rehabilitation services and how the state system is administered. Workers' compensation laws also provide death benefits to surviving spouses and dependent.

Workers' compensation insurance covers workers injured on the job, whether injured on the workplace premises or elsewhere or in an auto accident while on business. This insurance also covers certain work-related illnesses. Before any workers' compensation claim will be allowed, the work-relatedness of the disability must be established. Also, the evaluation of the claimant by a physician trained in occupational medicine is an essential part of the claim process.

While employers in all states pay "workers' comp" insurance, the amount they pay—through payroll taxes—varies. The employer's insurance rate depends upon various factors including the company's frequency and severity of employee injuries (referred to as the company's experience rating). Not surprisingly, organizations will strive to have good safety records (see Chapter 12 on creating a safe work environment) in order to pay a lower payroll tax rate.

workers' compensation insurance
State-mandated insurance provided to workers to defray the loss of income and cost of treatment due to work-related injuries or illness

Consolidated Omnibus Budget Reconciliation Act (COBRA)

The Consolidated Omnibus Budget Reconciliation Act of 1986 (COBRA) mandates that employers make health coverage—at the same rate the employer would pay-available to employees, their spouses, and their dependents on termination of employment, death, or divorce.[32] The coverage must be offered for between 18 and 36 months depending on qualifying guidelines. Thus, former employees and their families benefit by paying a lower premium for health coverage than is available to individual policyholders. While the former employee pays the premiums, employers have to establish procedures to collect premiums and to keep track of former employees and their dependents.

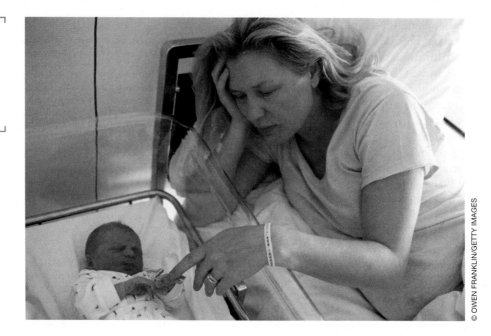

Mothers of newborn children are guaranteed 12 weeks of unpaid leave under the provisions of the Family and Medical Leave Act.

© OWEN FRANKLIN/GETTY IMAGES

Family and Medical Leave Act

The Family and Medical Leave Act (FMLA) was passed and became effective on August 5, 1993.[33] The FMLA applies to employers having fifty or more employees during twenty or more calendar workweeks in the current or preceding year. A covered employer must grant an eligible employee up to a total of twelve workweeks of unpaid leave in a twelve-month period for one or more of the following reasons:

- Birth of and care for a newborn child

- Adoption or foster care placement of a child

- Care for an immediate family member (spouse, child, or parent) with a serious medical condition

- Serious health condition of the employee[34]

An employer may require that the need for medical leave be supported by a certification issued by a health care provider. Highlights in HRM 4 shows the federally required poster for the FMLA. In studying the poster, note the other important stipulations, such as enforcement and unlawful acts, which are of direct concern to managers.

Like many laws pertaining to HRM, the FMLA is simple in principle but requires revising policies and procedures for compliance.[35] This law affects an organization's benefits program in several of its provisions: It mandates continuation of medical coverage, it prohibits loss of accrued benefits, it provides for restoration of benefits after leave, it permits substitution of paid leave and vacation during leave, it makes communication and notice compulsory, and it prohibits waiver of benefits. On return from FMLA leave, an employee must be restored to his or her original job or to an "equivalent" job. Equivalent jobs are those identical to the original job in terms of pay, benefits, and other employment terms and conditions.

In January 2008, Congress passed the National Defense Authorization Act which amended the FLMA to provide eligible employees working for covered employers new leave rights related to military service. Specifically, an eligible employee who is the spouse, son, daughter, parent, or next of kin of a covered service member who is recovering from a serious illness or injury sustained in the line of duty on active duty is entitled to up to 26 weeks of leave in a single 12-month period to care for the service member. Importantly, managers or supervisors with legal or administrative questions regarding the FMLA are advised to seek assistance from HR before proceeding with an employee's FLMA leave request.[36] Also, employers cannot penalize employees for requesting or taking FLMA leave in an employment action including hiring, promotion, transfer, training, or disciplinary action.

Older Workers Benefit Protection Act

Passed by Congress in 1990, the Older Workers Benefit Protection Act (OWBPA) is a companion piece of legislation to the Age Discrimination in Employment Act (ADEA).[37] (See Chapter 3.) Specifically, the OWBPA prohibits age-based discrimination in early retirement and other benefit plans. The Act imposes strict guidelines on employers who seek to have employees sign release forms waiving their right to pursue age discrimination claims under the ADEA.[38] When employers desire to obtain release waivers from employees, the OWBPA requires that a valid waiver must be voluntary and written in a manner that is understandable to the parties involved. Furthermore, employers must inform employees that they have the right to consult with an attorney before signing the waiver.

▪▪ DISCRETIONARY MAJOR EMPLOYEE BENEFITS

Employee benefits may be categorized in different ways. In Highlights in HRM 3, we saw the categories of benefits that have been used by the U.S. Chamber of Commerce. In the following discussion, we will use a somewhat different but compatible grouping of benefits to highlight the important issues and trends in managing an employee benefits program.

Health Care Benefits

The benefits that receive the most attention from employers today because of high costs and employee concern are health care benefits.[39] In the past, health insurance plans covered only medical, surgical, and hospital expenses. Today employers include prescription drugs as well as dental, optical, and mental health care benefits in the package they offer their workers.

High Health Care Costs

According to a U.S. Chamber of Commerce study, medical and medical-related benefits costs (employers' share) average 12.1 percent of payroll costs. This represents an annual expense of $6,101 for medical insurance premiums for each active employee. Prescription drug coverage, a growing cost factor to employers, costs $228 annually per employee (see Highlights in HRM 3).

HIGHLIGHTS IN HRM

4

"Your Rights": Another Federally Required Poster

Your Rights
under the
Family and Medical Leave Act of 1993

FMLA requires covered employers to provide up to 12 weeks of unpaid, job-protected leave to "eligible" employees for certain family and medical reasons. Employees are eligible if they have worked for their employer for at least one year, and for 1,250 hours over the previous 12 months, and if there are at least 50 employees within 75 miles. The FMLA permits employees to take leave on an intermittent basis or to work a reduced schedule under certain circumstances.

Reasons for Taking Leave:

Unpaid leave must be granted for *any* of the following reasons:

- to care for the employee's child after birth, or placement for adoption or foster care;
- to care for the employee's spouse, son or daughter, or parent who has a serious health condition; or
- for a serious health condition that makes the employee unable to perform the employee's job.

At the employee's or employer's option, certain kinds of *paid* leave may be substituted for unpaid leave.

Advance Notice and Medical Certification:

The employee may be required to provide advance leave notice and medical certification. Taking of leave may be denied if requirements are not met.

- The employee ordinarily must provide 30 days advance notice when the leave is "foreseeable."
- An employer may require medical certification to support a request for leave because of a serious health condition, and may require second or third opinions (at the employer's expense) and a fitness for duty report to return to work.

Job Benefits and Protection:

- For the duration of FMLA leave, the employer must maintain the employee's health coverage under any "group health plan."

- Upon return from FMLA leave, most employees must be restored to their original or equivalent positions with equivalent pay, benefits, and other employment terms.
- The use of FMLA leave cannot result in the loss of any employment benefit that accrued prior to the start of an employee's leave.

Unlawful Acts by Employers:

FMLA makes it unlawful for any employer to:
- interfere with, restrain, or deny the exercise of any right provided under FMLA:
- discharge or discriminate against any person for opposing any practice made unlawful by FMLA or for involvement in any proceeding under or relating to FMLA.

Enforcement:

- The U.S. Department of Labor is authorized to investigate and resolve complaints of violations.
- An eligible employee may bring a civil action against an employer for violations.

FMLA does not affect any Federal or State law prohibiting discrimination, or supersede any State or local law or collective bargaining agreement which provides greater family or medical leave rights.

For Additional Information:

If you have access to the Internet visit our FMLA website: **http://www.dol.gov/esa/whd/fmla.** To locate your nearest Wage-Hour Office, telephone our Wage-Hour toll-free information and help line at 1-866-4USWAGE (1-866-487-9243): a customer service representative is available to assist you with referral information from 8am to 5pm **in your time zone;** or log onto our Home Page at **http://www.wagehour.dol.gov.**

U.S. Department of Labor
Employment Standards Administration
Wage and Hour Division
Washington, D.C. 20210

WH Publication 1420
Revised August 2001

*U.S. GOVERNMENT PRINTING OFFICE 2001-476-344/49051

Note: Other federally required posters are reproduced in Chapters 3, 9, and 12.

The growth in health care costs is attributed to a number of factors, including federal legislation, changes in Medicare pricing, the greater need for health care by an aging population, the costs of technological advances in medicine, skyrocketing malpractice insurance rates, rising costs of drugs, and overuse of costly health care services.[40]

Cost Containment

With the significant rise in health care costs, it is understandable that employers seek relief from these expenses.[41] The major approaches used to contain the costs of health care benefits include reductions in coverage, increased deductibles or copayments, and increased coordination of benefits to make sure the same expense is not paid by more than one insurance reimbursement.[42] Highlights in HRM 5 shows additional cost-containment strategies used by employers. Furthermore, the containment of health care expenses can be achieved through various medical delivery systems such as health maintenance organizations, preferred provider organizations, and different consumer-driven health care plans.

Health maintenance organizations (HMOs) are organizations of physicians and other health care professionals that provide a wide range of services to subscribers and their dependents on a prepaid basis. HMOs offer routine medical services at a specific site for a fixed fee for each employee visit. Employers pay a fixed annual fee to the HMO to cover the majority of their employees' medical costs. Because they must provide all covered services for a fixed dollar amount, HMOs generally emphasize preventive care and early intervention. As a result of the federal HMO Act of 1973, employers having twenty-five or more employees and a health insurance plan must offer a federally qualified HMO as a voluntary option.

Preferred provider organizations have also helped to contain costs. The preferred provider organization (PPO) is a group of physicians who establish an organization or a network of doctors that gurantees lower costs to the employer through lower service charges or agreed-on utilization controls (such as a reduced number of diagnostic tests per employee). Unlike HMOs, where employees may have little choice in the doctor they see, PPOs allow employees to select their doctor of choice from a list of physicians (participating doctors). Normally, a number of physicians are available to choose from for different medical needs.

Another important and newer medical cost containment strategy is consumer-driven health plans, also referred to as defined-contribution health plans, medical savings accounts (MSAs), health savings accounts (HSAs), flexible spending accounts (FSAs), or health reimbursement accounts (HRAs).[43] Consumer-driven health plans (CDHPs) are a high-deductible insurance policy tied to a limited personal health care spending account funded by the employer.[44] The cost containment philosophy behind CDHPs is that with a limited amount to spend on health care services, employees will become more "price conscious" and more informed about where they spend their health care dollars. Employees can "shop" for the best cost/quality medical care available commensurate with their individual needs.[45] According to Pete Maillet and Steve Halterman, benefits consultants, "The success of the consumer-driven health care model will ultimately be determined by its ability to modify behavior so that Americans will purchase health care services just as they do any other good or services."[46] Importantly, CDHPs are tax free and can accept contributions from employers, employees, or both.

A typical CDHP works like this. Each employee is assigned a personal spending account to purchase yearly medical insurance. The account is funded by the employer. This medical budget—perhaps $2,000 a year—can be spent on virtually any health care service. Unused amounts can usually be rolled over to the following year, giving

4 | **Objective**

health maintenance organizations (HMOs)

Organizations of physicians and health care professionals that provide a wide range of services to subscribers and dependents on a prepaid basis

preferred provider organization (PPO)

A group of physicians who establish an organization that guarantees lower health care costs to the employer

consumer-driven health plan (CDHP)

A medical insurance plan financed by employer contributions to an employee's individual health care spending account

5

Employers Methods for Containing Health Care Costs

- Preadmission certification for surgical procedures
- Financial incentives for outpatient surgery and testing
- Mail-order prescription drug program and medical drug discount cards
- Mandatory second opinions for surgical procedures
- Alternative approaches to health care treatment such as herbal therapy or homeopathy
- Educational programs encouraging health care consumers to assume more responsibility and accountability for the cost and quality of their health care
- Promoting Web sites or printed materials that list common conditions, treatment, drug prices, and effectiveness
- Implementation of step therapy programs
- Multitier hospital coverage networks that allow employees to choose from a variety of hospitals with small, moderate, and steep copayments at the point of service
- Use of variable copayments (for example, $10 for physician and $25 for specialists)
- Consolidation of health care plans offered by employers
- Requiring employees to pay an additional cost if a working spouse refuses coverage from his or her employer
- Customized health care benefits design allowing employees to purchase riders to increase the level of benefits provided
- Promotion of wellness and employee assistance programs
- Automated benefits functions
- Dependent audits to rid benefit rolls of ineligibles
- Implementation of a disease management program

employees an incentive to spend wisely and, over time, to increase the value of their medical accounts. Should an employee's annual medical expenses exceed his or her medical account, then additional employer-provided insurance is available after the employee pays certain out-of-pocket medical costs, for example, $500 to $2000, much like a deductible.[47]

While CDHPs are similar in structure and intent, each specific program (MSA, HSA, FSA, HRA) has its own unique design features. For example, health savings accounts, unlike flexible spending accounts, can be rolled over from year to year and are portable—employees can take them if they change jobs. HRAs are funded solely by the employer, whereas HSAs can be funded by the employee, the employer, or both. Furthermore, employees of small businesses find MSAs particularly beneficial to their health care needs. Under the Health Insurance Portability and Accountability Act of

1996, employees of small employers may establish a tax-free, interest-bearing MSA. Under the MSA, individuals enrolled in a plan may make tax-free contributions to an account created primarily for the purpose of paying for qualified medical expenses.[48]

Other Health Benefits

Dental plans are designed to help pay for dental care costs and to encourage employees to receive regular dental attention. Like medical plans, dental care plans may be operated by insurance companies, dental service corporations, those administering Blue Cross/Blue Shield plans, HMOs, and groups of dental care providers. Typically, the insurance pays a portion of the charges, and the subscriber pays the remainder.

To assist employees with chronic health conditions such as diabetes, heart disease, and asthma and to lower health care costs, employers may provide their employees with *disease management (DM) programs*. DM programs provide patients and their caregivers with information on monitoring and treating medical conditions, while coordinating communication between medical consumers, health care providers, employers, and insurers. Bank One Corporation of Chicago developed a DM program when managers experienced high absenteeism among employees with diabetes, asthma, and depression. Disease management programs encourage people to adopt empowerment and self-management attitudes and habits related to their health.

Health Insurance Portability and Accountability Act

The Health Insurance Portability and Accountability Act (HIPAA) of 1996 grants employees the right to switch their medical insurance between former and present employers. Once an employee earns twelve credits with his or her former employer (one credit per month of service), he or she can transfer into the new employer's health insurance plan without a gap in coverage. Coverage is guaranteed regardless of a preexisting health condition of the employee. An employee's medical privacy rights under HIPAA are discussed in Chapter 13.

Domestic Partner Benefits

With a diverse and more openly vocal work group, more employers are granting benefits to employees who establish a *domestic partnership*, including both same-sex and unmarried opposite-sex couples. In some industries, domestic partner coverage is so prevalent that companies lose competitive advantage in attracting and retaining quality employees if this coverage is denied specific individuals. While the definition of a domestic partnership varies, the description used by Apple Computer is compatible with most definitions. A domestic partner, the company says, is "a person over age 18 who shares living quarters with another adult in an exclusive, committed relationship in which the partners are responsible for each other's common welfare." A standard definition of domestic partnership contains the following:

- A minimum age requirement
- A requirement that the couple live together
- A specification of financial interdependence
- A requirement that the relationship be a permanent one
- A requirement that each not be a blood relative[49]

Employers who offer domestic partnership coverage typically require employees to sign an "Affidavit of Domestic Partnership" attesting to their relationship.

Organizations that offer benefits to domestic partners are simply extending current benefits, normally full medical and dental plans, to all employees.[50] However, employer health benefits provided to unmarried partners, unlike health benefits for spouses, are taxable under federal law.[51] This difference can be costly. Furthermore, in 1996, Congress passed the Defense of Marriage Act, which provides that a same-sex domestic partner may not be treated as an employee's spouse for purposes of federal law.[52] One implication is that married gays are not eligible for Social Security survival benefits or other benefits governed by federal law. Despite these issues, well-known organizations such as Viacom, Gannett Company (publisher of *USA Today*), Levi Strauss, Silicon Graphics, Warner Bros., Stanford University, and the City of Berkeley, California, offer benefits to domestic partners of employees.

Payment for Time Not Worked

Objective 5

The "payment for time not worked" category of benefits includes paid vacations, bonuses given in lieu of paid vacations, payments for holidays not worked, paid sick leave, military and jury duty, and payments for absence due to a death in the family or other personal reasons. As Highlights in HRM 3 showed, these benefits constitute another large expenditure—9.8 percent—of the employer's total payroll costs.

Vacations with Pay

longer you work, the more vaca time you get.

It is generally agreed that vacations are essential to the well-being of an employee.[53] Eligibility for vacations varies by industry, locale, and organization size. To qualify for longer vacations of three, four, or five weeks, one may expect to work for seven, fifteen, and twenty years, respectively.

While vacations are a relatively easy benefit to manage, employers should, nevertheless, remember that vacation scheduling must meet the employer's state wage laws and state contract law principles.

Paid Holidays

Both hourly and salaried workers can usually expect to be paid for ten holidays a year. The type of business tends to influence both the number and observance of holidays. Virtually all employers in the United States, however, observe and pay their employees for New Year's Day, Memorial Day, Independence Day, Labor Day, Thanksgiving Day, and Christmas Day. Many employers give workers an additional two or three personal days off to use at their discretion.

Sick Leave

There are several ways in which employees may be compensated during periods when they are unable to work because of illness or injury. Most public employees, as well as many in private firms, receive a set number of sick leave days each year to cover such absences. Where permitted, sick leave that employees do not use can be accumulated to cover prolonged absences. Accumulated vacation leave may sometimes be used as a source of income when sick leave benefits have been exhausted. Group insurance that provides income protection during a long-term disability is also made available by some employers. As discussed earlier in the chapter, income lost during absences resulting from job-related injuries may be reimbursed, at least partially, through workers' compensation insurance.

Severance Pay

A one-time payment is sometimes given to employees who are being terminated. Known as *severance pay*, it may cover only a few days' wages or wages for several months. The pay received usually depends on the employee's years of service. However, severance pay can also be based on the reason for termination, the salary or grade level of the employee, the title or level in the organization, or a combination of factors. Employers that are downsizing often use severance pay as a means of lessening the negative effects of unexpected termination of employees. Other triggers for severance pay include job elimination, voluntary separation programs, or refusal of reassignment or relocation.

Vacations and holidays provide a break from demanding job duties and responsibilities.

© ART VANDALAY/DIGITAL VISION/GETTY IMAGES

Supplemental Unemployment Benefits

While *not* required by law, in some industries unemployment compensation is augmented by supplemental unemployment benefits (SUBs), which are financed by the employer. These plans enable an employee who is laid off to draw, in addition to state unemployment compensation, weekly benefits from the employer that are paid from a fund created for this purpose. The amount of benefits is determined by length of service and wage rate. Employer liability under the plan is limited to the amount of money accumulated within the fund from employer contributions based on the total hours of work performed by employees.

supplemental unemployment benefits (SUBs)

A plan that enables an employee who is laid off to draw, in addition to state unemployment compensation, weekly benefits from the employer that are paid from a fund created for this purpose

Life Insurance

One of the oldest and most popular employee benefits is group term life insurance, which provides death benefits to beneficiaries and may also provide accidental death and dismemberment benefits. The premium costs are normally paid by the employer, with the face value of the life insurance equal to two times the employee's yearly wages. These programs frequently allow employees to purchase additional amounts of insurance for nominal charges. When employers operate a cafeteria benefits program, selection of extra life insurance may be part of the choices offered employees.

Long-Term Care Insurance

With an aging workforce, a small but growing number of employers are offering long-term care insurance as part of their benefits package. Long-term care insurance is designed to pay for nursing home and other medical-related costs during old age. An advantage of employer-sponsored long-term care insurance is that enrolled employees receive coverage automatically and do not need to pass a physical examination.

Objective 6

Retirement Programs

A significant trend in workforce demographics is the increased age of U.S. workers. A prominent cause of this change is the "aging" of the baby boom generation—a demographic group born between 1946 and 1964. Therefore, retirement has become an important part of life for many individuals, requiring sufficient and careful preparation. Furthermore, like health care benefits, retirement programs are undergoing significant change. Figure 11.2 shows several demographic trends affecting workforce retirements.

Retirement Policies

There is no U.S. law mandating a retirement age. Therefore, whether an employee elects to retire depends on various factors such as personal/financial condition and health, other family obligations, the extent to which he or she receives satisfaction from work, and the ability to meet changing job demands. A major factor affecting the decision to retire is the availability and adequacy of retirement benefits, namely health care and retirement income. Interestingly, a recent study from the Center for Retirement Research at Boston College shows that 45 percent of all U.S. households do not have adequate income at retirement and are considered "at risk."[54] In varying degrees, employer retirement policies influence an employee's decision to retire.

The retirement of baby boomers will compel companies to innovate, adapt, and remake themselves if they are to meet business demands. For example, as large numbers of workers retire or cut their work schedules, businesses will have to manage a future "brain drain" driving up labor costs, while depleting organizations of vital knowledge, talent, and industrial memory. A recent study showed a potential risk to be the departure of senior leadership, middle management, technical, and knowledge workers. To meet the challenges of a talent loss, organizations are implementing retention strategies including flexible work schedules (see Chapter 4), the

FIGURE
11.2

Trends Affecting Retirement

- The number of people age 65 and older tripled to about 34 million between 1940 and 1995.

- According to U.S. census projections, people age 65 and older are expected to number 86 million by 2050, an increase of 51 million since 2000.

- In 1960, 45.4 percent of male workers over age 65 were still in the labor force; in 1990, only 27.4 percent were still working. While the labor force participation rates of women between ages 55 and 64 have been rising, further increases are not expected.

- Eight baby boomers turn 50 every ten minutes.

- The U.S. net national savings rate was relatively stable at about 7 percent of GDP from 1951 to 1980. It has collapsed since 1980, most recently dropping to less than 1 percent of GDP.

- In 1900, the average life expectancy in the U.S. was 48; today, it is 80 for women and 75 for men. Virtually all of these gains can be attributed to improvements in public health and safety, such as clean water, refrigeration, seat belts, and routine vaccinations.

hiring of retired employees as consultants, phased retirement programs, alternate job design, and flexible benefit programs.[55]

Recently, large numbers of workers have been pushed into premature retirement—the victims of organizational downsizing. To avoid layoffs, particularly of more recently hired members of protected classes, and to reduce salary and benefit costs, employers often encourage early retirement. Encouragement comes in the form of increased pension benefits for several years or cash bonuses, sometimes referred to as the silver handshake. The cost of these retirement incentives can frequently be offset by the lower compensation paid to replacements and/or by a reduction in the workforce.

Preretirement Programs

While most people eagerly anticipate retirement, many are bitterly disappointed once they reach this stage of life. Employers may offer preretirement planning programs to help make employees aware of the kinds of adjustments they may need to make when they retire. These adjustments may include learning to live on a reduced, fixed income and having to cope with the problems of lost prestige, family problems, and idleness that retirement may create.

Preretirement programs typically include seminars and workshops that include lectures, videos, and printed materials. Topics covered include pension plans, health insurance coverage, Social Security and Medicare, personal financial planning, wellness and lifestyles, and adjustment to retirement. The numerous publications of AARP (American Association of Retired Persons), including its popular magazine, *AARP The Magazine*, are valuable sources of information.

To help older workers get used to the idea of retirement, some organizations experiment with retirement rehearsal. Polaroid, for example, offers employees an opportunity to try out retirement through an unpaid three-month leave program. They also offer a program that permits employees to gradually cut their hours before retirement. Most experts agree that preretirement planning is a much-needed, cost-effective employee benefit.

Pension Plans

Originally, pensions were based on a *reward philosophy*, which viewed pensions primarily as a way to retain personnel by rewarding them for staying with the organization until they retired. Because of the vesting requirements required by law, pensions are now based on an *earnings philosophy*. This philosophy regards a pension as deferred income that employees accumulate during their working lives and that belongs to them after a specified number of years of service, whether or not they remain with the employer until retirement. Since the passage of the Social Security Act of 1935, pension plans have been used to supplement the floor of protection provided by Social Security. However, the decision whether to offer a pension plan is up to the employer.

Types of Pension Plans

There are two major ways to categorize pension plans: (1) according to contributions made by the employer and (2) according to the amount of pension benefits to be paid. In a contributory plan, contributions to a pension plan are made jointly by employees and employers. In a noncontributory plan, the contributions are made solely by the employer.

silver handshake
An early retirement incentive in the form of increased pension benefits for several years or a cash bonus

contributory plan
A pension plan in which contributions are made jointly by employees and employers

noncontributory plan
A pension plan in which contributions are made solely by the employer

7 Objective

When pension plans are classified by the amount of pension benefits to be paid, there are two basic types: defined benefit plan and defined contribution plan. Under a defined benefit plan,[56] the amount an employee is to receive on retirement is specifically set forth. This amount is usually based on the employee's years of service, average earnings during a specific period of time, and age at time of retirement. While a variety of formulas exist for determining pension benefits, the one used most often is based on the employee's average earnings (usually over a three- to five-year period immediately preceding retirement), multiplied by the number of years of service with the organization. A deduction is then made for each year the retiree is under age 65. For example, an employee with a four-year preretirement annual salary of $55,000 and thirty years of service may receive a yearly retirement payment of $23,000. Compared to a defined contribution plan, defined benefit plans today are unpopular with employers because they cost more and the employer is obligated to fund the plan to the extent necessary to support future benefit payouts. For example, the percentage of large companies offering a defined benefit pension plan fell from 91 percent in 1985 to 55 percent in 2006. Over the same period, coverage in defined contribution plans rose sharply, indicating a clear change from traditional plans to defined contribution plans. [57]

A defined-contribution plan establishes the basis on which an employer will contribute to the pension fund. The contributions may be made through profit sharing, thrift plans, matches of employee contributions, employer-sponsored individual retirement accounts (IRAs), and various other means. The amount of benefits employees receive on retirement is determined by the funds accumulated in their account at the time of retirement and what retirement benefits (usually an annuity) these funds will purchase. These plans do not offer the benefit security predictability of a defined benefit plan. However, even under defined benefit plans, retirees may not receive the benefits promised them if the plan is not adequately funded.

401(k) Savings Plans

A significant change in pension coverage has been the tremendous growth of tax-deferred 401(k) savings plans, which are named after section 401(k) of the Internal Revenue Code. The popularity of 401(k) plans is driven primarily by (1) the ability of the employer to transfer plan funding to employees, (2) the ability to transfer responsibility for investment choices to employees, and (3) the fact that employee contributions to 401(k) plans represent tax-free investing.

The 401(k) savings plans allow employees to save through payroll deductions and to have their contributions matched by the employer. Usually the employer matches the employee contributions at the rate of fifty cents for every worker dollar contributed. An organization's contribution can, however, run the gamut from doubling the worker's contribution to zero contribution.[58] The percentage of the employer's contribution will likely depend on the allowable saving rate of the employee (that is, higher allowable employee savings rates will decrease the percentage of the employer's contribution).

A prevalent concern with 401(k) plans is the method by which employers match employee contributions, that is, with cash payments or company stock. For example, should payment be made in stock and the stock market declines, employees with 401(k) plans invested in company stock may take heavy retirement hits. Unlike traditional defined benefit pension plans, which guarantee payments based on years of service, the 401(k) plan guarantees nothing. Return depends entirely on how much money goes into the plan, the rate of return on investment, and, with stock-funded plans, the price of the company's stock. As one benefit specialist noted, "Market risk is perhaps the most significant threat to an employee's retirement savings."[59]

A current trend is for organizations to allow their employees considerable control over the investment of their 401(k) savings, including investing in the stock of other companies.[60] Because employees often need assistance in making informed investment decisions, Department of Labor standards provide employers with "sufficient information" standards to follow in putting participants legally in control of their investment. Also, a small but growing number of 401(k) plans let employees hand the management of their 401(k) to a professional financial planner. The new service, called *managed accounts*, seeks to help employees—many of whom have little investing experience—achieve higher returns with less risk.

In 2006, Congress passed the Pension Protection Act. While the law has many provisions—including those for addressing underfunded pension plans—a major objective of the law is to encourage the growth of 401(k) pension plans.[61] Major provisions of the law include:

- Allowing employers to automatically enroll employees in defined contribution plans[62]

- Permitting higher contribution limits for 401(k) plans, enabling workers to build larger retirement holdings

- Giving workers greater control over how their accounts are invested

Using the Internet

Government guidelines that protect employers from liability for offering investment advice to employees are found in DOL Interpretative Bulletin 96–1. Go to the Student Resources at:

www.cengage.com/ management/bohlander

Cash Balance Pension Plans

Along with 401(k) saving plans, a significant development in pension planning has been cash balance saving plans.[63] Cash balance plans work by having the employer make a yearly contribution into an employee's retirement savings account.[64] Contributions are based on a percentage of the employee's pay—typically 4 percent. Additionally, the employee's account earns annual interest, often tied to the thirty-year Treasury rate. For example, an employee earning $35,000 a year would receive a yearly contribution of $1,400 to his or her account. After a year, the account would receive an interest credit, typically 5 percent. Employees can normally roll the balance of their account into an IRA should they change jobs.

Whether an individual employee benefits from a cash balance retirement plan depends on the employee's age and years of service with the company. Employees in their twenties or thirties with low years of service can build substantial retirement savings starting at an early age. However, employees in their forties, fifties, or sixties with lengthy years of service can lose from 20 to 50 percent of their pension by switching from a traditional pension plan to a cash balance program. However, to lessen the financial impact on older employees, some companies may increase the annual pay credit for older employees as compared with younger workers. Others allow older employees to remain in the traditional pension plan until retirement or grant older employees a "boost" in their opening cash balance account. Employers ranging from Federated Department Stores and Verizon to Colgate-Palmolive and even Harvard University now cover their employees with cash balance plans.

Federal Regulation of Pension Plans

Private pension plans are subject to federal regulation under the Employee Retirement Income Security Act (ERISA).[65] The law governs about 7 million private pension plans. Although the Act does not require employers to establish a pension plan, it provides certain standards and controls for pension plans. It requires minimum funding standards to ensure that benefits will be available when an employee retires.[66] Furthermore, the law created the Pension Benefit Guaranty Corporation (PBGC), a federal government agency. The PBGC ensures that if a plan is terminated, guaranteed minimum benefits are paid to participants. The PBGC is supported by premiums paid by employers. Of special concern to the individual employee is the matter of vesting.

vesting

A guarantee of accrued benefits to participants at retirement age, regardless of their employment status at that time

Vesting is a guarantee of accrued benefits to participants at retirement age, regardless of their employment status at that time. Vested benefits that have been earned by an employee cannot be revoked by an employer. Under ERISA, all pension plans must provide that employees will have vested rights in their accrued benefits after certain minimum-years-of-service requirements have been met. However, employers can pay out a departing employee's vested benefits if the present value of the benefit is small. Also, while vesting is required by ERISA, portability—the ability to move pension funds between employers—is optional. Employees are well advised to seek out pension options that are portable if at all possible.

Managers and supervisors should also remember that antidiscrimination laws (see Chapter 3) apply to the administration of benefit programs. Individuals can file a charge with the EEOC when they believe that they have been denied benefits or received lower benefits because of their age, disability, race, religion, sex, or national origin.

Pension Plans and Underfunding

What is one of today's biggest concerns with pension plans? The answer is inadequate funds to cover retirement obligations along with increasing numbers of pension plan failures. For many old-line companies, such as Delta Airlines, Exxon-Mobil, Cummings, Delphi, and Lockheed-Martin, pension deficits are staggering. For example, in 2006, the pension deficit at ExxonMobil was $10.2 billion; at Delta, $6.1 billion; at Lockheed-Martin, $4.5 billion; and at Delphi, $4 billion.[67]

Equally worrisome is the number of pension plans in danger of failure. According to the PBGC, the pension obligations of many companies are, unfortunately, financially unstable. Also, through bankruptcy proceedings, companies will seek to cancel their pension obligations, thereby leaving employees to rely on the PBGC for retirement income. Unfortunately for retirees, monthly pension payments under PBGC guidelines are often significantly less than those promised under a company's original retirement plan. Furthermore, many worry that the PBGC—with a $14 billion deficit of its own—will be unable to meet its financial obligations and will require a federal bailout—a bailout ultimately paid for by taxpayers.

EMPLOYEE SERVICES: CREATING A WORK/LIFE SETTING

Objective 8

Eddie Bauer, an outdoor clothing and equipment supplier, offers its employees take-out dinners and one paid "Balance Day" off a year. eBay sets aside spaces at its San Jose, California, campuses as prayer and meditation rooms where employees can "decompress" during the workday. Lincoln National, a financial services company, offers a "homework assistance help line" staffed with teachers for children of employees, and at Mitre, a nonprofit researcher, employees can take up to a week of paid time off to help with scouting trips or volunteer projects. These organizations, like many others, are seeking to create a work/life (also called family-friendly) organizational climate that allows employees to balance work and personal needs.

Companies are also adapting work/life programs to accommodate the entrance of Generation Y employees into the workplace.[68] This new group of workers has its own vision for the workplace and their careers, one that work/life programs can help fulfill.[69] A national survey conducted by Mellon Financial Human Resources and Investor Solutions found that 86 percent of surveyed employers used part-time employees, 88 percent offered work-related tuition reimbursement, 81 percent offered employee assistance programs, 71 percent offered flextime programs, 50 percent offered telecommuting and work-at-home arrangements, 44 percent offered compressed workweeks, 54 percent provided family sick days, and 47 percent offered unpaid family leave that goes beyond the requirements of the Family and Medical Leave Act. According to the study, employer reasons for offering work/life programs include raising morale (74 percent of respondents), enhancing recruitment efforts (73 percent), and remaining competitive/industry image (72 percent).[70] Figure 11.3 lists some of the more popular employer-sponsored work/life benefits.

Employee Assistance Programs

To help workers cope with a wide variety of problems that interfere with the way they perform their jobs, organizations such as the New York Mets, USAA, the Los Angeles Police Department, and Levi Strauss have developed employee assistance programs (EAPs). An employee assistance program typically provides diagnosis, counseling, and referral for advice or treatment when necessary for problems related to alcohol or drug abuse, emotional difficulties, and financial or family difficulties.[71] (EAPs will be discussed in detail in Chapter 12.) The main intent is to help employees solve their personal problems or at least to prevent problems from turning into crises that affect their ability to work productively. To handle crises, many EAPs offer twenty-four-hour hot lines.

employee assistance programs (EAPs)

Services provided by employers to help workers cope with a wide variety of problems that interfere with the way they perform their jobs

FIGURE 11.3

Work/Life Benefits: Balancing Work and Home Needs

- Child care/elder care referral services
- Time off for children's school activities
- Employer-paid on-site or near-site child care facilities
- Flexible work hours scheduling
- Health club and wellness programs
- Employer-accumulated leave days for dependent care
- Customized training programs
- Subsidized temporary or emergency dependent care costs
- Extended leave policies for child/elder care
- Educational reimbursement
- Sick-child programs (caregiver on call)
- Work-at-home arrangements/telecommuting
- Partial funding of child care costs
- Customized career paths
- Part-time work schedules

Counseling Services

An important part of an EAP is the counseling services it provides to employees. While most organizations expect managers to counsel subordinates, some employees may have problems that require the services of professional counselors. Most organizations refer such individuals to outside counseling services such as family counseling services, marriage counselors, and mental health clinics. Some organizations have a clinical psychologist, counselor, or comparable specialist on staff, to whom employees may be referred.

Child and Elder Care

Consider these figures:

- Working parents take between five and twenty-nine days off work each year for sick children.

- Each day, more than 350,000 children younger than age 14 are too sick to attend school or day care.

- 21 percent of unscheduled absenteeism is family-related, costing employers billions in lost productivity and benefits costs.

These figures, combined with the increased employment of women with dependent children, illustrate the unprecedented demand for child care arrangements.[72]

Today benefits may include financial assistance, alternative work schedules, and family leave. Some employers such as Fel-Pro, Merck, Syntex, Baptist Hospital of Miami, and Ben and Jerry's promote on-site or near-site child care centers. Employer-sponsored dependent care spending accounts allow employees to set aside a portion of their pay before taxes to care for a dependent child.

A growing benefit offered employees with children experiencing short illnesses is mildly-ill child care. Medical supervision is the primary difference between mildly-ill facilities and traditional day care arrangements. Mildly-ill care facilities serve children recovering from colds, flu, ear infections, strep throat, chicken pox, or other mild illnesses that temporarily prevent them from attending regular school or day care. These facilities are either independently run, hospital-based, or affiliated with child care centers. Additionally, some employers offer emergency in-home child care benefits for sick children.[73]

Responsibility for the care of aging parents and other relatives is another fact of life for increasing numbers of employees. According to a study of AARP and the National Alliance for Caregiving, today more than 44 million Americans are caring for an elderly parent. As noted in the study, "elder care is rapidly becoming the biggest family issue facing workers and their families."[74] The average caregiver costs an employer $2,110 per year. Forty percent of employed caregivers take 17 days of unpaid leave per year to care for an aging family member.[75] The term elder care, as used in the context of employment, occurs when an employee provides care to an elderly relative while remaining actively at work. The majority of caregivers are women.

elder care

Care provided to an elderly relative by an employee who remains actively at work

Beyond the loss of organizational productivity and higher employee costs, a growing concern of employers is the negative effects of caregiving on employee health. Not surprisingly, caregivers in the workforce suffer higher levels of stress since they find it difficult to respond to the demands of balancing work and family.[76] To help employees meet the challenges of caregiving, organizations may offer elder care counseling, educational fairs and seminars, printed resource materials, support groups, and special flexible schedules and leaves of absence.[77] Schering-Plough, a pharmaceuticals manufacturer, uses an 800 telephone line for elder care referrals, while IBM has a national telephone network of more than 200 community-based referral agencies. Employers may also band together for better elder care. The Partnership for Elder Care—a consortium of American Express, J. P. Morgan, and Philip Morris—and other companies use the resources of the New York City Department of Aging, a public information and aging support agency.

Caring for one's aging parents and relatives is a growing concern for both employees and their employers.

Other Benefits and Services

The variety of benefits and services that employers offer today is widespread. However, whether a company offers a particular service may depend on its size, ability to pay, industry pattern, or specific employee or organizational needs. Some benefits are fairly standard such as housing and moving expenses,[78] various food services (such as cafeteria or vending machines), transportation pooling arrangements, and buying assistance for merchandise at a discount. Other benefits are newer and reflect societal changes such as adoption expenses,[79] legal services, financial planning including tax and retirement planning, paycards (also known as PIN-based or store value cards), and identity theft protection.[80] Many organization offer some type of sports program in which personnel may participate on a voluntary basis. Bowling, softball, golf, baseball, and tennis are often included in an intramural program. Two important benefits frequently offered employees are credit unions and educational assistance.

Credit Unions

Credit unions exist in many organizations to serve the financial needs of employees. They offer a variety of deposits as well as other banking services and make loans to their members. Although the employer may provide office space and a payroll deduction service, credit unions are operated by the employees under federal and state legislation and supervision. At the end of December 2009, there were 8,426 credit unions in the United States with 89.7 million members and combined assets of $777 billion. In almost all credit unions, deposits are insured up to $100,000 per account by the National Credit Union Share Insurance Fund, a U.S. government agency.[81]

Educational Assistance

Proactive employers view educational assistance programs, also called tuition aid, as a strategic business tool that supports talent management as a critical human capital investment.[82] Educational reimbursement programs are also seen as encouraging employment retention and a hedge against the talent drain from increased retirements.[83] To be eligible for tuition aid, an employee may have to meet a length of service requirement and show that classes taken relate to job performance or organizational career development. Employers may pay full or partial tuition costs plus related expenses such as books and supplies.

SUMMARY

Objective 1 Benefits are an established and integral part of the total compensation package. In order to have a sound benefits program there are certain basic considerations. It is essential that a program be based on specific objectives that are compatible with organizational philosophy and policies, as well as being affordable. Through committees and surveys, a benefit package can be developed to meet employees' needs. Through the use of flexible benefit plans, employees are able to choose the benefits that are best suited for their individual needs. An important factor in how employees view the program is the full communication of benefits information through meetings, printed material, and annual personalized statements of benefits.

Objective 2 According to a 2007 study, the costs of employee benefits in that year averaged 42.7 percent of payroll, or $21,527 per employee. Because many of the benefits represent a fixed cost, management must pay close attention in assuming more benefit expense. Increasingly, employers are requiring employees to pay part of the costs of certain benefits. Employers also shop for benefit services that are competitively priced.

Objective 3 Nearly a quarter of the benefits package that employers provide is legally required. These benefits include employer contributions to Social Security, unemployment insurance, workers' compensation insurance, and state disability insurance. Social Security taxes collected from employers and employees are used to pay three major types of benefits: (1) retirement benefits, (2) disability benefits, and (3) survivors' benefits.

Objective 4 The cost of health care programs has become the major concern in the area of employee benefits. Several approaches are used to contain health care costs, including reduction in coverage, increased coordination of benefits, increased deductible or copayments, use of health maintenance and preferred provider organizations, various consumer-driven health plans, incentives for outpatient surgery and testing, and mandatory second opinions where surgery is indicated. Employee assistance programs and wellness programs may also contribute to cutting the costs of health care benefits.

Objective 5 Included in the category of benefits that involve payments for time not worked are vacations with pay, paid holidays, sick leave, and severance pay. The typical practice in the United States is to give ten days vacation leave and ten holidays. In addition to vacation time, most employees, particularly in white-collar jobs, receive a set number of sick leave days. A one-time payment of severance pay may be given to employees who are being terminated.

Objective 6 While there is no mandatory retirement age, many workers choose to retire before age 65. Many employers provide incentives for early retirement in the form of increased pension benefits or cash bonuses. Some organizations provide preretirement programs that may include seminars, workshops, and informational materials. The National Council on Aging, AARP, and many other organizations are available to assist both employers and employees in preretirement activities.

Objective 7 Whether to offer a pension plan is the employer's prerogative. However, once a plan is established, it is then subject to federal regulation under ERISA to ensure that benefits will be available when an employee retires. Two traditional pension plans are available—defined benefit and defined contribution. With a defined benefit plan, the amount an employee receives on retirement is based on years of service, average earnings, and age at time of retirement. Two of the most significant trends are the growth of 401(k) salary reduction plans and cash balance pension plans. Pension funds may be administered through either a trusteed plan or an insurance plan. A concern today is the underfunding of pension plans and the ability of ERISA to meet its financial obligations.

Objective 8 The types of service benefits that employers typically provide include employee assistance programs, counseling services, educational assistance plans, child care, and elder care. Other benefits are food services, on-site health services, prepaid legal services, financial planning, housing and moving, transportation pooling, purchase assistance, credit unions, social and recreational services, and paycards.

KEY TERMS

consumer-driven health plan
contributory plan
defined benefit plan
defined contribution plan
elder care
employee assistance programs
  (EAPs)

flexible benefits plans (cafeteria
  plans)
health maintenance organizations
  (HMOs)
noncontributory plan
preferred provider organization
  (PPO)

silver handshake
supplemental unemployment
  benefits (SUBs)
vesting
workers' compensation insurance

HRM EXPERIENCE

Understanding Employer Benefit Programs

What is the best-kept secret in the United States today? The answer, according to a report of the U.S. Chamber of Commerce labeled "The Hidden Payroll," is employee benefits. Compensation surveys indicate that a majority of employees are unable to accurately name the benefits they receive, and employees vastly underestimate the cost of benefits paid by their employers.

This exercise will help you more fully understand the benefits discussed in this chapter. Additionally, you will explore, in detail, the benefits and services offered by your employer and other employers in your area.

Assignment

Working in teams of four to six individuals, obtain information on the benefits package offered by your employer or other employers in your area. Once the information is gathered, be able to identify (1) each benefit offered, (2) what the benefit provides the employee, (3) employee eligibility (if required), and (4) how the benefit is paid for (employer, employee, or a combination of both). Compare benefit packages. Be prepared to discuss your findings with the class.

DISCUSSION QUESTIONS

Objective 1
1. You are a small employer wishing to establish a benefits program for your employees. What things should you consider to ensure that the program is a success for your employees?

Objective 2
2. Many organizations are concerned about the rising cost of employee benefits and question their value to the organization and to the employees.
a. In your opinion, what benefits are of greatest value to employees? To the organization? Why?
b. What can management do to increase the value to the organization of the benefits provided to employees?

Objective 3
3. Employers are required by law to provide specific benefits to employees. What laws mandate benefits to employees, and what are the provisions of those laws?

Objective 4
4. Identify and contrast the various ways employers can control the costs of health care.

Objective 5
5. Do you agree with the argument that benefits for time not worked are those most readily available to reduce employer costs? Explain.

Objective 6
6. Prior to 1979, all employers could prescribe a mandatory retirement age—usually 65 years. What would you think are the advantages and disadvantages of a mandatory retirement age? What factors may affect an individual's decision to retire at a particular time, and what factors may affect his or her ability to adjust to retirement?

Objective 7
7. Describe 401(k) pension plans, listing their advantages and disadvantages. As an employee, would you want control over the investment decisions of your 401(k) plan? Explain.

Objective 8
8. Working in teams of three or four, assume your team was hired as a benefits consultant to a small business having fifty to sixty employees. What benefits do you believe this employer should offer, given limited resources? Justify your reasons for offering these benefits.

BIZFLIX EXERCISES

Erin Brockovich: Erin Gets Benefits, with Dental

The chapter discussed the important role of employee benefits in the employment relationship. Watch this scene from *Erin Brockovich* and assess the importance of benefits to Erin.

Erin Brockovich (Julia Roberts), a single mother of three, needs a job and convinces skeptical attorney Ed Masry (Albert Finney) to hire her. She quickly discovers a potentially large case against Pacific Gas & Electric Company (PG&E) for environmental pollution. Based on a true story, the film has many dramatic and funny moments. Roberts received the 2000 Best Actress Academy Award.

The scene comes from the "Ed Comes Over" segment that appears about 45 minutes into the film. It follows Erin's discussion with her neighbor

George (Aaron Eckhart) about her one-year reign as Miss Wichita. This scene ends with Ed Masry saying he is drawing the line on benefits. The film continues with Ed reviewing the limited information Erin got from the Lohantan Regional Water Board office. Erin and her three children revisit the office to copy more information for the case.

What to Watch for and Ask Yourself

- The first section of this chapter, "Employee Benefits Programs," opened with this sentence: "Employee benefits constitute an indirect form of compensation intended to improve the quality of the work lives and the personal lives of

employees." Does this quotation apply to Erin in this scene? If *yes*, in what way does it apply to her and her life situation?

- Erin and Ed are unclear about what benefits, except medical and dental, his firm provides. Which benefits discussed in this chapter would a typical small law firm give to its employees? See the earlier section "Discretionary Major Employee Benefits" for some ideas.

- Erin negotiates a 10 percent pay raise from Ed, suggesting that pay is important to her. Does the scene suggest that benefits are also important to Erin? Why or why not?

CASE STUDY 1

Adobe's Family-Friendly Benefits: An Unexpected Backlash

Adobe Consulting Services (ACS), a provider of HR software application systems, prides itself on the variety of benefits it offers employees. In addition to health care, pension, and vacation benefits, the company also offers an attractive family-friendly benefits package including flexible schedules, child and elder care assistance, counseling services, adoption assistance, and extended parental leave. Unfortunately, in recent months, the company's progressive work/life policy has experienced a backlash from several employees, as the following case illustrates.

In March 2008, Teresa Wheatly was hired by Adobe as a software accounts manager. With excellent administrative and technical skills, plus four years of experience at Adaptable Software, Adobe's main competitor, Teresa became a valued addition to the company's marketing team. As a single mother with two grade-school children, Teresa received permission to take Fridays off. She was also allowed to leave work early or come in late to meet the demands of her children. Teresa is one of eleven software account managers at Adobe.

The problem for Adobe, and particularly for Janis Blancero, director of marketing, began in the fall of 2008. On September 15, Dorothy McShee, citing "personal reasons"—which she refused to discuss—requested a four-day workweek for which she was willing to take a 20 percent cut in pay. When Dorothy asked for the reduced work schedule, she sarcastically quipped, "I hope I don't have to have kids to get this time off." On October 3, Juan Batista, a world-class marathon runner, requested a flexible work hours arrangement in order to accommodate his morning and afternoon training schedule. Juan is registered to run the London, England, marathon in May 2009. Just prior to Juan's request, Susan Woolf asked for and was granted an extended maternity leave to begin after the birth of her first child in December. If these unexpected requests were not enough, Blancero has heard comments from senior account managers about how some employees seem to get "special privileges," while the managers work long hours that often require them to meet around-the-clock customer demands. Janis has adequate reason to believe that there is hidden tension over the company's flexible work hours program. Currently, Adobe has no formal policy on flexible schedules. Furthermore, with the company's growth in business combined with the increasing workload of software account managers and the constant service demands of some customers, Blancero realizes that she simply cannot grant all the time-off requests of her employees.

Questions

1. Do managers like Janis Blancero face a more complicated decision when evaluating the personal requests of employees versus evaluating employees' individual work performance? Explain.
2. a. Should Adobe establish a policy for granting flexible work schedules? Explain.
   b. If you answered yes, what might that policy contain?
3. If you were Janis Blancero, how would you resolve this dilemma? Explain.

CASE STUDY 2

Evaluate the Work/Life Climate in Your Company

What is the quality of the work/life environment in your company? The following survey provided by the Work and Family Connection will help provide a "case analysis" of the climate in your organization. Answers to the twenty questions will provide clear insights about your company's position in the work/life area.

Agree or Disagree with the Following Statements:

1. My manager/supervisor treats my work/life needs with sensitivity.
2. It is usually easy for me to manage the demands of both work and home life.
3. My career path at this company is limited because of the pressure of home life demands.
4. My job at this company keeps me from maintaining the quality of life I want.
5. My manager/supervisor is supportive when home life issues interfere with work.
6. My manager/supervisor focuses on results, rather than the time I am at my desk.
7. My manager/supervisor has a good understanding of flexible work hour practices.
8. If I requested a flexible work arrangement my manager/supervisor would support me.
9. My manager/supervisor is often inflexible or insensitive about my personal needs.
10. I believe my manager/supervisor treats me with respect.
11. My manager/supervisor allows me informal flexibility as long as I get the job done.
12. My manager/supervisor tends to treat us like children.
13. My manager/supervisor seldom gives me praise or recognition for the work I do.
14. My manager/supervisor seems to care about me as a person.
15. I would recommend this company to others.
16. The work I do is not all that important to this company's success.

17. If I could find another job with better pay, I would leave this organization.
18. If I could find another job where I would be treated with respect, I would take it.
19. If I could find another job where I could have more flexibility, I would take it.
20. I am totally committed to this company.

For a perfect score, you should answer **"Disagree"** to questions 3, 4, 9, 12, 13, 16, 17, 18, and 19 and **"Agree"** to all the rest, 1, 2, 5, 6, 7, 8, 10, 11, 14, 15, and 20.

To score, begin by giving yourself 20 points. Then deduct one point for every "wrong" response from the total score.

If your score is 18 to 20: Congratulations! Your organization is leading the nation in flexibility and supportiveness.

If your score is 14 to 17: Your organization is probably more supportive and flexible than most, but you have room to grow.

If your score is 11 to 13: You could be open to other job offers in the race for talent among employees.

If your score is 10 or less: Your managers will need help to manage the twenty-first-century workforce.

Source: Used with permission of the Work and Family Connection, 5195 Beachside Drive, Minnetonka, Minnesota 55343; phone 1-800-487-7898 or http://www.workfamily.com.

NOTES AND REFERENCES

1. Michelle Conlin, "Youthquake," *Business Week*," January 21, 2008, 35.
2. You Can Do Anything But Don't Mess with My Health Insurance," http://www.workforce.com/section/00/article/24/85/46.html.
3. *Employee Benefits Study, 2007* (Washington, DC: U.S. Chamber of Commerce, 2007).
4. Interview, February 5, 2008, Mesa, Arizona.
5. Andrew Ceccon, "Don't Call In, Log In: Online Benefits Portals Let Employees Take Charge," *Workspan* (August 2007): 35.
6. "Online Benefits Expected to Become Predominant," *Best Review* 105, no. 12 (April 2005): 106.
7. Ashley Haynes, "Drowning in Paperwork: Self-Service Benefits System Provides Relief for Non-Profit Hospital," *Workspan* (January 2007): 43.
8. "Total Rewards" is all of the tools available to an employer that may be used to attract, motivate, and retain employees. Total rewards include everything the employee perceives to be of value resulting from the employment relationship.
9. Nina D. Cole and Douglas H. Flint, "Opportunity Knocks, Perceptions of Fairness in Employee Benefits," *Compensation and Benefits Review* 37, no. 2 (March/April 2005): 7.
10. "Big Companies Expand Benefits to Alternative Lifestyle Employees," *Office Solutions* 24, no. 1 (January 2007): 10.
11. Extended family benefits allow employees to add a qualified adult household member to their health plans, be it a domestic partner, an extended family member, or a grown child.
12. Keith Brownlie, "Flexible-Benefit Program Acts as Consolidation Tool," *Strategic HR Review* 6, no. 3 (March/April 2007): 12.
13. Michelle Conlin and Jane Porter, "The Shape of Perks to Come," *Business Week*, August 20, 2007: 61.
14. Susan Relland, "Action Steps for Employers in Response to the New IRS Cafeteria Plan Proposed Regulations," *Employee Benefit Plan Review* 62, no. 7 (January 2008): 5.
15. Stephen Miller, "Survey: Employees Undervalue Benefits," *HR Magazine* 52, no. 8 (August 2007): 30.
16. Lisa Patten, "Communicating the New Benefits Deals," *Benefits Quarterly* 23, no. 2 (Second Quarter 2007): 33.
17. Patricia Wiley, "What Keeps Human Resources Professionals Awake at Night?" *Benefits Quarterly* 23, no. 2 (Second Quarter 2007): 13.
18. Dennis Ackley, "Communication: The Key to Putting the 'Benefit' Back in Benefits," *Workspan* (February 2006): 32.
19. JoAnn Davis, "Communication: It Is More Than Distributing Information," *Employee Plan Benefits Review* 62, no. 1 (July 2007): 5.
20. Computerized data also enable management to keep accurate records of the cost of each benefit. To assist employers with administrative and communication functions, the International Foundation of Employee

Benefit Plans in Brookfield, Wisconsin, maintains an extensive library of employee benefits publications. It also prepares publications on this subject. The Foundation has an online database that members can use to get immediate, comprehensive responses to questions about employee benefits. For more than forty years, benefits professionals have relied on the International Foundation of Employee Benefit Plans for education and information about employee benefits. The headquarters' address is P.O. Box 69, Brookfield, WI 53008-0069. Interested individuals can also learn about the organization at http://www.ifebp.org.

21. *Employee Benefits Study, 2007* (Washington, DC: Chamber of Commerce, 2007).

22. "Costs and Risks Continue to Shift to Employees," *HR Magazine* 52, no. 12 (December 2007): 7.

23. Andy Hiles, Barbara Hogg, André Tapia, and Jim Winkler, "Building a Culture of Personal Benefits Responsibility," *Benefits Quarterly* 23, no. 2 (Second Quarter 2007): 25.

24. Jennifer Schramm, "Benefits at Risk," *HR Magazine* 52, no. 2 (February 2007): 152.

25. *The Future of Social Security*, Social Security Administration. SSA Publication No. 05-10055, May 2007.

26. Since the Social Security Act is continually subject to amendment, readers should refer to the literature provided by the nearest Social Security office for the most current details pertaining to the tax rates and benefit provisions of the Act.

27. *How You Earn Credits*, Social Security Administration, SSA Publication No. 05-10072, January 2007.

28. *How Work Affects Your Benefits*, Social Security Administration, SSA Publication No. 05-10069, January 2007.

29. *Survivors Benefits*, Social Security Administration, SSA Publication No. 05-10084, August 2007.

30. *Medicare*, Social Security Administration, SSA Publication No. 05-10043, September 2007.

31. You may think that Medicaid and Medicare are the same. Actually, they are two different programs. Medicaid is a state-run program that provides hospital and medical coverage for people with low income and little or no resources. Each state has its own rules about who is eligible and what is covered

under Medicaid. Some people quality for both Medicare and Medicaid. For more information about the Medicaid program, contact your local medical assistance agency, social services or welfare office.

32. COBRA, P.L. 99-272, 100 Stat. 82 (1986).

33. FLMA, P.L. 103-3, 107 Stat. 6 (1993).

34. A "serious health condition" means an illness, injury, impairment, or physical or mental condition that involves any period of incapacity or treatment connected with patient care.

35. An expanded discussion of the FMLA can be found in David J. Walsh, *Employment Law for Human Resource Practice, 2nd ed.* (Mason, OH: South-Western, 2007): 312–327.

36. Daniel B. Ritter and Kari A. Legg, "Recent Developments Under the Family and Medical Leave Act," *Compensation and Benefits Review* 39, no. 5 (September/October 2007): 32.

37. *Older Workers Benefit Protection Act* (29 U.S.C. 1990, sec. 623).

38. By signing a waiver (also called a release not to sue), an employee agrees not to take any legal action against the employer. Legal action could be an age discrimination lawsuit. In return for the signed waiver, the employer gives the employee an incentive to leave voluntarily, such as a severance pay package that is larger than the company's normal offer.

39. James Mehring, "Health Care: Following the Insurance Money," *Business Week*, December 10, 2007, 13. See also Nanette Byrnes, "A Shock to the System," *Business Week*, December 4, 2006, 102.

40. Sheela Andrews, "Generics: The Golden Age of Cost Savings," *Workspan* (January 2008): 53.

41. Edmund Pezalla, "Employer Strategies for Managing New Prescription Drugs," *Workspan* (January 2007): 46

42. Ken Alltucker, "Workers' Costs Up for Health Insurance," *Arizona Republic*, November 13, 2007, A-1.

43. Christopher Calvert, "Consumer-Driven Health Care: Why Do Companies Take the Plunge?" *Workspan* (January 2007): 51.

44. Deirdre Kelley and Larry Smith, "The Consumer as Gatekeeper: Consumer-Driven Health Care Controls Costs," *Workspan* (June 2006); 29.

45. Christopher Farrell, "Health Care You Control," *Business Week*, May 28, 2007, 97.

46. Pete Maillet and Steve Halterman, "The Consumer-Driven Approach: Defining and Measuring Success," *Benefits Quarterly* 20, no. 2 (Second Quarter 2004): 7.

47. Marie R. Dufrense, "Consumer-Driven Health Care: Is It a Silver Bullet?" *Workspan* (February 2007): 31.

48. Tom Lerche, "The Impact of Consumer-Directed Health Plans with Integrated Health-ImprovementServices,"*WorldatWork* 16, no. 2 (Second Quarter 2007): 6.

49. "How HR Is Addressing Domestic Partner Benefits," *HR Focus* 81, no. 7 (July 2004): S-1.

50. Michael S. Travinski, "Employee Benefits for Domestic Partners and Same-Sex Spouses," *Journal of Pension Benefits* 13, no. 2 (Winter 2006): 29.

51. Debra A. Davis, "Employment Issues for Employee Benefit Plan: Designing Benefits for Domestic Partners," *Journal of Pension Benefits* 15, no. 1 (Autumn 2007): 56.

52. Public Law No. 104-199, 110 Stat. 2419 (September 21, 1996).

53. Michelle Conlin, "Do Us a Favor, Take a Vacation," *Business Week*, May 21, 2007: 88.

54. Eddie L. Vaughn, "The Retirement Crisis: Coping with an Aging Workforce," *Workspan* (July 2007): 37.

55. Bruce Barge, "What Does the Aging Workforce Mean for Your Company?" *Workspan* (December 2007): 19.

56. Hal Tepfer, "Step into the Freeze: A DB Pension Plan Primer," *Workspan* (July 2006): 51.

57. Jessica Marquez, "GM Backs Away from DB Plan for New Hires," *Workforce Management* 86, no. 17 (October 8, 2007): 4.

58. Howard Gleckman, "A Nest Egg, That's a No-Brainer," *Business Week*, April 25, 2005, 108.

59. Joe Goldberg, "Educating Employees Can Increase 401(k) Participation," *Employee Plan Benefits Review* 62, no. 1 (July 2007): 18.

60. Annamaria Lusardi, "401(k) Pension Plans and Financial Advice: Should Companies Follow IBM's Initiative?" *Employee Benefit Plan Review* 62, no. 1 (July 2007): 16.

61. Anne E. Morgan and Karen Tucker, "The New Pension Protection Act: More Work for Plan Administrators," *Employee Relations Law Journal* 32, no. 3 (Winter 2006): 96.

62. Patrick W. Spangler, "The Trend Toward Automatic Enrollment in 401(k) Plans,"

Employee Benefit Plan Review 62, no. 5 (November 2007): 5.

63. Jessica Marquez, "Cash-Balance Plans Make a Comeback," http//www.workforce.com/section/02/feature/25/16/23/index.html.

64. Richard J. Bottelli, "Born Again: Cash Balance Plans Get New Lease on Life with Latest Rulings, Pension Reform 2006 Legislation," *Benefits Quarterly* 23, no. 1 (First Quarter 2007): 28.

65. ERISA, P.L. 93-406, 88 Stat. 829 (1974).

66. Carolyn Hirschman, "Overseeing Pension Management," *HR Magazine* 49, no. 7 (July 2004): 66.

67. David Henry, "Shortfall at Exxon: All Those Profits but Underfunded Pensions," *Business Week*, May 29, 2006, 36.

68. Alicia Kormey, "Balancing Work/Life No Longer Optimal," *The Practical Accountant* 40, no. 4 (April 2007): 105.

69. David J. Thompson, "The Seven Levels of Change for Work-Life Effectiveness," *WorldatWork* 16, no. 1 (First Quarter 2007): 54.

70. Kathy Kacher and Rachel Hastings, "Training Managers to Meet Business Goals Using Work-Life Strategies," *WorldatWork* 16, no. 4 (Fourth Quarter 2007): 56.

71. Ira J. Morrow, "The Integration of Employee Assistance, Work/Life, and Wellness Services," *Personnel Psychology*, no. 4 (Winter 2006): 961.

72. Jessica Marquez, "5 Questions: The Balance Workers Want," *Workforce Management* 86, no. 18 (October 22, 2007): 8.

73. Ashley Johnson, "A Reliable Backup Plan," *Legal Assistant Today* 25, no. 3 (January/February 2007): 24.

74. Leah Dobkin, "How to Confront the Elder Care Challenge," *Workforce Management* at http://www.workforce.com/section/09/feature/24/85/10/index.html.

75. Scott Dingfied, "Senior Care Trends Expected to Mirror Child Care Industry," *Employee Benefit Plan Review* 62, no. 6 (December 2007): 20.

76. Bill Mulcany, "Why You Should Be Caring for Your Caregivers," *Workspan* (June 2007): 37.

77. Leah Dobkin, "10 Steps for Creating a Work Environment that Supports Caregivers," *Workforce Management* at http://www.workforce.com/section/09/feature/24/85/10/248514.html.

78. Lin Grensing-Pophal, "Partners on the Move," *HR Magazine* 52, no. 8 (August 2007): 87.

79. Candace E. Blair Cronin, "Adoption Policies That Work for You, Company," *Workspan* (January 2008): 43. See also Carrie Boerio, "Adoption Benefits: Why They're Good for Business," *Workspan* (October 2007): 65.

80. Guillaume Deybach, "Identify Theft Protection as an Employee Benefit," *Employee Benefit Plan Review* 61, no. 7 (January 2007): 15.

81. Data obtained February 18, 2008, from Credit Union National Association, P.O. Box 431, Madison, WI 53701, (608) 231-4000.

82. Faith Ivery, "Tuition-Aid Programs Are an Integral Part of Career Development," *Workspan* (January 2007): 29.

83. Erin White, "Theory and Practice: Corporate Tuition Aid Appears to Keep Workers Loyal; Studies Reinforce View of Improved Retention; UTC's Plan Stands Out," *The Wall Street Journal*, May 21, 2007, B-4.

PROMOTING SAFETY AND HEALTH

After studying this chapter, you should be able to

Objective | 1 |

Summarize the general provisions of the Occupational Safety and Health Act (OSHA).

Objective | 2 |

Describe what management can do to create a safe work environment.

© KEVIN ANDERSON/GETTY IMAGES

CHAPTER 12

Objective 3

Identify the measures that should be taken to control and eliminate health hazards.

Objective 4

Describe the organizational services and programs for building better health.

Objective 5

Explain the role of employee assistance programs in HRM.

Objective 6

Indicate methods for coping with stress.

Occupational safety and health accidents are both numerous and costly to employers. As one important example, Occupational Safety and Health Administration workplace violence data show that more than two million nonfatal workplace violence incidents are reported annually in the form of assaults, robberies, thefts, hostage takings, hijackings, rapes, and sexual attacks. The U.S. Department of Justice estimates that husbands and boyfriends commit 13,000 acts of workplace violence against women each year. It is projected that employees miss 175,000 days of work per year due to domestic violence, costing employers between $3 billion and $5 billion yearly in lost productivity, greater absenteeism, and increased healthcare costs.[1] To prevent losses such as these, employers are concerned about limiting violence in the workplace along with providing working conditions—in all areas of employment—that provide for the safety and health of their employees.

While the laws safeguarding employees' physical and emotional well-being are certainly an incentive, many employers are motivated to provide desirable working conditions by virtue of their sensitivity to human needs and rights. The more cost-oriented employer recognizes the importance of avoiding accidents and illnesses wherever possible. Costs associated with sick leave, disability payments, replacement of employees who are injured or killed, and workers' compensation far exceed the costs of maintaining a safety and health program. A recent study conducted by Liberty Mutual found that employers saved $3 for each $1 invested in workplace safety.[2] Accidents and illnesses attributable to the workplace may also have pronounced effects on employee morale and on the goodwill that the organization enjoys in the community and in the business world.

Managers at all levels are expected to know and enforce safety and health standards throughout the organization. They must ensure a work environment that protects employees from physical hazards, unhealthy conditions, and unsafe acts of other personnel. Through effective safety and health programs, the physical and emotional well-being of employees may be preserved and even enhanced.

We begin this chapter by inviting readers to examine their safety and health knowledge by taking the test in Highlights in HRM 1. After discussing the legal requirements for safety and health, we shall focus in the rest of the chapter on the creation of a safe and healthy work environment and on the management of stress.

▪▪ Safety and Health: It's the Law

Objective 1

Consider these facts:

- According to Occupational Safety and Health Administration statistics, in 2006 there were 4.1 million injuries/illnesses among private sector firms.

- Experts estimate that back problems cost employers $50 billion yearly in workers' compensation costs and $50 billion in indirect costs (replacement workers, absenteeism, training, and so on). The Bureau of Labor Statistics reports that back injuries account for one of every five workplace injuries or illnesses.

- Each year the cost of occupational injuries and illness totals more than $156 billion.

- In any year, approximately 75 million working days are lost because of on-the-job injuries.

- In 2006, 5,840 employees died from work accidents.

Test Your Safety Smarts

Take the following quiz to evaluate your knowledge and awareness of safety and health issues. Answers are found at the end of this chapter.

1. True or False? Employers have the right to be advised by an OSHA compliance officer of the reason for a workplace inspection.
2. True or False? Employers have the legal right to have a company representative accompany the OSHA compliance officer on an inspection.
3. True or False? OSHA requires that employers provide access to employees regarding the company's medical and exposure record.
4. What percentage of the U.S. population will be affected by back injuries?
   a. 23
   b. 47
   c. 60
   d. 80
5. True or False? In order to correct potential health and safety problems, employers have the right to know the name of an employee who files a complaint with OSHA.
6. True or False? Employers have the legal right to request an inspection warrant before OSHA inspectors can enter a work site.
7. Which causes more accidents: unsafe acts or unsafe conditions?
8. List five areas regarding safety that should be covered during a new employee orientation.
9. True or False? Employers are required to provide employee training on OSHA standards.
10. True or False? Carpal tunnel syndrome is the fear of enclosed areas such as silos, tanks, and hallways.
11. True or False? Employers are required to allow OSHA inspectors on premises for unannounced inspections.
12. True or False? Employers have twenty-four hours to report to OSHA accidents that result in a fatality.

The burden on the nation's commerce as a result of lost productivity and wages, medical expenses, and disability compensation is staggering, and there is no way to calculate the human suffering involved.

It was to forestall even worse losses that Congress passed the Occupational Safety and Health Act (OSHA) in 1970.[3] The mission of OSHA is to "assure the safety and health of America's workers by setting and enforcing standards; providing training, outreach, and education; establishing partnerships; and encouraging continual improvements in workplace safety and health." In spite of the figures previously cited, the Act has been very effective in reducing the number of injuries resulting in lost work time, the incident rate of specific injuries such as back problems, and the number of job-related deaths. For example, in 2006, with almost twice as many workers as in the 1960s, the 5,840 fatalities were almost one-third the number of worker deaths reported in the late 1960s.

OSHA's Coverage

OSHA covers all private sector employees and public employees in state and local governments. Federal agencies are required to establish and maintain a safety and health program that is monitored by the Occupational Safety and Health Administration. Self-employed workers are not covered by the law. A state seeking OSHA approval of its safety and health program for the private sector must provide a similar program that covers its state and local government employees and is at least as effective as its program for private employers. Where state programs for the private sector have been approved by the federal government as meeting federal standards, the state carries out the enforcement functions that would otherwise be performed by the federal government.[4] Approximately half of the states currently have their own OSHA-approved programs.

OSHA Standards

One of the responsibilities of the Occupational Safety and Health Administration is to develop and enforce mandatory job safety and health standards. These standards cover the workplace, machinery and equipment, materials, power sources, processing, protective clothing, first aid, and administrative requirements. It is the responsibility of employers to become familiar with those standards that are applicable to their establishments and to ensure that their employees use personal protective gear and equipment when required for safety. Employers can be cited and fined if they do not comply with OSHA standards.[5]

The Occupational Safety and Health Administration can begin standards-setting procedures on its own initiative or on petition from other parties, including the Secretary of Health and Human Services (HHS) and the National Institute for Occupational Safety and Health (NIOSH). Other bodies that may also initiate standards-setting procedures are state and local governments and any nationally recognized standards-producing organization, employer, or labor representative. NIOSH, however, is the major source of standards. As an agency of the Department of Health and Human Services, it is responsible for conducting research on various safety and health problems, including the psychological factors involved.[6]

Enforcing OSHA Standards

The Occupational Safety and Health Administration is authorized to conduct workplace inspections, issue citations, and impose penalties on employers. In 2007, OSHA's staff of 1,100 inspectors conducted almost 39,500 workplace inspections. More than 88,000 workplace violations were issued, the most for serious violations of the Act.

Workplace Inspections

Under the Act, "upon presenting appropriate credentials to the owner, operator, or agent in charge," an OSHA compliance officer is authorized to do the following:

- Enter without delay and at reasonable times any factory, plant, establishment, construction site or other areas, workplace, or environment where work is performed by an employee of an employer; and to

- Inspect and investigate during regular working hours, and at other reasonable times, and within reasonable limits and in a reasonable manner, any such place of employment and all pertinent conditions, structures, machines, apparatus, devices, equipment and materials therein, and to question privately any such employer, owner, operator, agent, or employee.[7]

OSHA has further established a system of inspection priorities:[8]

First level: Inspection of imminent danger situations

Second level: Investigation of catastrophes, fatalities, and accidents that result in hospitalization of five or more employees

Third level: Investigation of valid employee complaints of alleged violations of standards or of unsafe or unhealthful working conditions

Fourth level: Special-emphasis inspections aimed at specific high-hazard industries, occupations, or substances that are injurious to health

Typically, OSHA inspectors arrive at a work site unannounced and ask for a meeting with a representative of the employer. At the meeting, the inspectors explain the purpose of the visit, describe the procedure for the inspection, and ask to review the employer's safety and health records. An employer may either agree voluntarily to the inspection or require the inspectors to obtain a search warrant.

The Act gives both the employer and the employees the right to accompany inspectors on their tour of the work site. After the tour, the OSHA officials conduct

OSHA inspectors have the authority to issue on-site citations for serious safety or health violations.

© DANA WHITE/PHOTOEDIT

a closing conference to inform the employer and employee representatives, if any, of the results of their inspection. They point out conditions or practices that appear to be hazardous and issue a written citation if warranted.[9]

Citations and Penalties

OSHA citations may be issued immediately following the inspection or later by mail. Citations tell the employer and employees which regulations and standards are alleged to have been violated and the amount of time allowed for their correction. The employer must post a copy of each citation at or near the place the violation occurred for three days or until the violation is abated, whichever is longer.

Under the Act, OSHA may cite the following violations and propose the following penalties:

- Other-Than-Serious: A violation that has a direct relationship to job safety and health, but one unlikely to cause death or serious physical harm. OSHA may propose a penalty of up to $7,000 for each violation.

- Serious: A violation for which there is substantial probability that death or serious physical harm could result *and* the employer knew, or should have known, of the hazard. OSHA may propose a mandatory penalty of up to $7,000 for each violation.

- Willful: A violation that the employer intentionally and knowingly commits, or a violation that the employer commits with plain indifference to the law. OSHA may propose penalties of up to $70,000 for each violation.

If a willful violation results in the death of an employee, OSHA can assess penalties up to $250,000 for an individual or $500,000 for a corporation, imprisonment of up to six months, or both. The agency may adjust any penalty downward depending on the employer's good faith (such as demonstrating effort to comply with the Act), history of previous violations, and size of business.[10] The law provides for appeal by employers and employees under specified circumstances. In 2006, OSHA fined employers more than $84 million for violations of the Act.[11] Most penalties were for serious violations of the Act (more than $54 million).

OSHA Consultation Assistance

Besides helping employers identify and correct specific hazards, OSHA can help employers develop and implement effective workplace safety and health programs that emphasize preventing worker injuries and illnesses.

Onsite Consultation

OSHA provides a free on-site consultation service. Consultants from the state government or private contractors help employers identify hazardous conditions and determine corrective measures. Employers also may receive training and education services.[12] No citations are issued in connection with a consultation, and the consultant's files cannot be used to trigger an OSHA inspection. Additionally, consultations may qualify employers for a one-year exemption from routine OSHA inspections.

Cooperative Programs

Voluntary, cooperative relationships among employers, employees, unions, and OSHA can be a useful alternative to traditional OSHA enforcement procedures, serving as an effective way to ensure worker safety and health. There are four specific cooperative programs—alliances, strategic partnerships, voluntary protection programs, and the Safety and Health Achievement Recognition Program:[13]

Alliances. Alliances enable organizations to collaborate with OSHA to prevent injuries and illnesses in the workplace. OSHA and participating organizations define, implement, and meet a set of short- and long-term goals to improve workplace safety and health.

Strategic Partnership Programs (SPPs). Strategic partnerships are long-term agreements between employers and OSHA aimed at reducing serious workplace hazards and achieving a high level of worker safety and health.

Voluntary Protection Programs (VPPs). Voluntary protection programs represent OSHA's effort to extend worker protection beyond the minimum required OSHA standards. There are three VPPs—Star, Merit, and Demonstration—each designed to recognize, motivate, or establish a cooperative relationship between employers and OSHA.[14]

Safety and Health Achievement Recognition Program (SHARP). SHARP provides recognition to employers who demonstrate exemplary achievement in workplace safety and health.

Responsibilities and Rights under OSHA

Both employers and employees have certain responsibilities and rights under OSHA. We will discuss only those that relate directly to the management of human resources.

Employers' Responsibilities and Rights

In addition to providing a hazard-free workplace and complying with the applicable standards, employers must inform all of their employees about the safety and health requirements of OSHA. Specific employer responsibilities are listed in OSHA's publication *All About OSHA* and illustrated in Highlights in HRM 2. Employers are also required to keep certain records and to compile and post an annual summary of work-related injuries and illnesses. From these records, organizations can compute their *incidence rate*, the number of injuries and illnesses per 100 full-time employees during a given year. The standard formula for computing the incidence rate is shown by the following equation, in which 200,000 equals the base for 100 full-time workers who work forty hours a week, fifty weeks a year:

$$\text{Incidence rate} = \frac{\text{Number of injuries and illnesses} \times 200{,}000}{\text{Total hours worked by all employees during period covered}}$$

It should be noted that the same formula can be used to compute incidence rates for (1) the number of workdays lost because of injuries and illnesses, (2) the number of nonfatal injuries and illnesses without lost workdays, and (3) cases involving only injuries or only illnesses.

Incidence rates are useful for comparing work groups, departments, and similar units within an organization. They also provide a basis for comparing other organizations doing similar work. The Bureau of Labor Statistics and other organizations, such as the National Safety Council, compile data that an employer can use as a basis for comparing its safety record with those of other organizations. These comparisons

What Are My Responsibilities under the OSH Act?

If you are an **employer** the *OSH Act* covers, you must:

- Meet your general duty responsibility to provide a workplace free from recognized hazards;
- Keep workers informed about OSHA and safety and health matters with which they are involved;
- Comply in a responsible manner with standards, rules, and regulations issued under the *OSH Act;*
- Be familiar with mandatory OSHA standards;
- Make copies of standards available to employees for review upon request;
- Evaluate workplace conditions;
- Minimize or eliminate potential hazards;
- Make sure employees have and use safe, properly maintained tools and equipment (including appropriate personal protective equipment);
- Warn employees of potential hazards;
- Establish or update operating procedures and communicate them to employees;
- Provide medical examinations when required;
- Provide training required by OSHA standards;
- Report within 8 hours any accident that results in a fatality or the hospitalization of three or more employees;
- Keep OSHA-required records of work-related injuries and illnesses, unless otherwise specified;
- Post a copy of the *OSHA 300—Log and Summary of Occupational Injuries and Illnesses* for the prior year each year during the entire month of February unless otherwise specified;
- Post, at a prominent location within the workplace, the OSHA poster (OSHA 2203) informing employees of their rights and responsibilities;
- Provide employees, former employees, and their representatives access to the OSHA 300 form at a reasonable time and in a reasonable manner;
- Provide access to employee medical records and exposure records;
- Cooperate with OSHA compliance officers;
- Not discriminate against employees who properly exercise their rights under the *OSH Act;*
- Post OSHA citations and abatement verification notices at or near the worksite involved; and
- Abate cited violations within the prescribed period.

If you are an **employee** the *OSH Act* covers, you should:

- Read the OSHA poster at the job site;
- Comply with all applicable OSHA standards;
- Follow all employer safety and health rules and regulations, and wear or use prescribed protective equipment while engaged in work;

What Are My Responsibilities under the OSH Act? (continued)

- Report hazardous conditions to the supervisor;
- Report any job-related injury or illness to the employer, and seek treatment promptly;
- Cooperate with the OSHA compliance officer conducting an inspection; and
- Exercise your rights under the *OSH Act* in a responsible manner.

Although OSHA does not cite employees for violations of their responsibilities, each employee must follow all applicable standards, rules, regulations, and orders issued under the *OSH Act*. OSHA, however, does not expect employees to pay for guardrails, floor cleaning, equipment maintenance, respirators, training, or other safety and health measures.

Source: U.S. Department of Labor, Occupational Safety and Health Administration, *All about OSHA* (Washington, DC: U.S. Government Printing Office, 2006).

provide a starting point for analyzing problem areas, changing the working environment, and motivating personnel to promote safety and health.

It is the employer's responsibility to make sure employees use protective equipment when necessary. Employers must therefore engage in safety training and be prepared to discipline employees for failing to comply with safety rules, and employers must not discriminate against employees who exercise their rights under the Act by filing complaints. On the other hand, employers are afforded many rights under the law, most of which pertain to receiving information, applying for variances in standards, and contesting citations.[15]

Employees' Responsibilities and Rights

Employees are required to comply with all applicable OSHA standards, to report hazardous conditions, and to follow all employer safety and health rules and regulations, including those prescribing the use of protective equipment. Workers have a right to demand safe and healthy conditions on the job without fear of punishment. They also have many rights that pertain to requesting and receiving information about safety and health conditions.[16]

Right-to-Know Laws

Exposure to hazardous chemicals is currently one of the most serious health concerns for both employers and employees. Therefore, most states—and federal law—require that employers provide information to employees about the hazardous chemicals they handle. Commonly known as right-to-know laws, these statutes address such issues as the definition of toxic and hazardous substances, the duties

right-to-know laws
Laws that require employers to advise employees about the hazardous chemicals they handle

of employers and manufacturers to provide health risk information to employees, trade secret protection, and enforcement provisions. Since state right-to-know laws can be more stringent than federal law, employers are encouraged to contact their state's health and safety agency for a copy of their appropriate hazard communication standards.[17]

To understand the right-to-know laws, employers must first become familiar with OSHA-published hazardous chemical regulations known as the Hazard Communication Standard (HCS). The HCS prescribes a system for communicating data on health hazards to employees. It includes a format for Material Safety Data Sheets (MSDSs). MSDSs should include the chemical name of a hazardous substance; all of the risks involved in using it, including potential health risks; safe handling practices; personal protective equipment needed; first aid in the event of an accident; and information identifying the manufacturer.

Material Safety Data Sheets (MSDSs)
Documents that contain vital information about hazardous substances

OSHA's Enforcement Record

Perhaps no federal government agency has been more severely criticized than the Occupational Safety and Health Administration.[18] Complaints often concern what employers consider to be picky or unrealistic standards and the proliferation of rules under agency personnel. Another prevalent criticism is that many of OSHA's standards are dangerously outdated. According to one safety manager, "It seems OSHA administration conducts research and sets safety and health standards in an ivory tower, not knowing or caring if standards are valid for the real world." However, the complaint most registered against OSHA is uneven enforcement efforts by the agency from one political administration to the next.[19]

Under some administrations, enforcement efforts have been seen as virtually nonexistent (or at least very lax), while under others, regulatory enforcement has seemed more proactive. Employers often view OSHA as overly zealous, while unions and safety groups continue to worry that OSHA is lax in monitoring its agreements with organizations. These groups would prefer mandatory standards instead of voluntary guidelines for problems such as injuries related to jobs involving repetitive motion—a topic to be considered later in the chapter.[20]

▪▪ PROMOTING A SAFE WORK ENVIRONMENT

Objective 2

We have seen that employers are required by law to provide safe working conditions for their employees.[21] To achieve this objective, the majority of employers have a formal safety program. Typically, the HR department or the industrial relations department is responsible for the safety program. While the success of a safety program depends largely on managers and supervisors of operating departments, the HR department typically coordinates the safety communication and training programs, maintains safety records required by OSHA, and works closely with managers and supervisors in a cooperative effort to make the program a success.

Organizations with formal safety programs generally have an employee-management safety committee that includes representatives from management, each department or manufacturing/service unit, and employee representatives. Committees are typically involved in investigating accidents and helping to publicize the importance of safety rules and their enforcement.

Creating a Culture of Safety

It is generally recognized that lower-level managers and supervisors are the bedrock for encouraging health and safety. Today, however, safety experts are talking about creating an organizational culture of safety that goes beyond managing operational processes to include creating a safe work environment as a partner with all work endeavors.[22] A culture of safety exists when health and safety permeates the organizational climate along with customer service, work processes, and innovation.[23]

To champion a culture of safety, companies need to appoint someone accountable for the effort. Carolyn Merritt, chairperson of the U.S. Chemical Safety Board (CSB), notes, "HR executives should be the point persons on creating and making sure that a corporate safety culture exists. These are the people who have their fingers on the culture pulses of the organization."[24] Furthermore, the CSB advocates a culture of safety that focuses specifically on *process safety metrics*. For example, instead of measuring injuries, managers should set goals on how many unit safety meetings should be held quarterly and measure goal attainment. Greg Andress, executive manager at Gallagher Bassett Services (safety consultants), states, "You want to measure the drivers within your organization that are going to create a change in the culture."[25] Interestingly, in one study conducted by the American Institute of Plant Engineers, survey results showed a direct correlation between an increase in management's commitment to safety in the workplace and a decrease in accidents.

The Key Role of the Supervisor

One of a supervisor's major responsibilities is to communicate to an employee the need to work safely.[26] Beginning with new employee orientation, safety should be emphasized continually. Proper work procedures, the use of protective clothing and devices, and potential hazards should be explained thoroughly.[27] Furthermore, employees' understanding of all these considerations should be verified during training sessions, and employees should be encouraged to take some initiative in maintaining a concern for safety. Since training by itself does not ensure continual adherence to safe work practices, supervisors must observe employees at work and reinforce safe practices. Where unsafe acts are detected, supervisors should take immediate action to find the cause. Supervisors should also foster a team spirit of safety among the work group.[28]

Proactive Safety Training Program

Safety training is not only good business; in certain occupational areas, safety and health training is legally required. For example, employers covered by the Hazardous Liquid Pipeline and Safety Act (HLPSA) are legally required to train employees in environment safety protection. When training is mandated, employers must keep accurate records of all employee education. Violations can incur criminal penalties.

Most organizations have a safety awareness program that entails the use of several different media. Safety lectures, commercially produced films, specially developed videocassettes, and other media such as pamphlets are useful for teaching and motivating employees to follow safe work procedures.[29] A popular training technique is the use of games in interactive learning exercises. Interactive learning has been shown to accelerate learning and help trainees internalize the materials learned.[30]

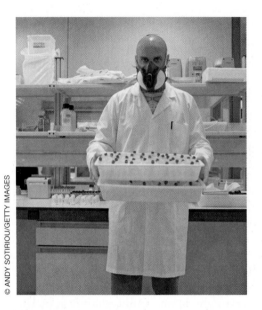

OSHA regulations mandate the use of protective equipment in recognized hazardous conditions

© ANDY SOTIRIOU/GETTY IMAGES

HR professionals, and safety directors in particular, advocate employee involvement when designing and implementing safety programs.[31] Employees can offer valuable ideas regarding specific safety and health topics to cover, instructional methods, and proper teaching techniques. Furthermore, acceptance for safety training is heightened when employees feel a sense of ownership in the instructional program.[32]

Information Technology and Safety Awareness and Training

Several reasons are advanced for the use of the Internet and information technology in safety and health training. First, enhanced delivery modes facilitate the development of both managers and employees.[33] Videos, PowerPoint presentations, and interactive CD-ROM training are ideal methods for standardized safety, environmental, and health instruction. Second, information technology allows organizations to customize their safety and health training needs. At Stanley Works, the company's Internet is the number one tool for reducing health and safety problems. According to Kevin Nelson, employee health and safety director, "The Internet functions as the organization's SWAT team to develop and implement timely and efficient health and safety programs." Third, information technology is ideally suited for regulatory instruction. OSHA distributes information on compliance assistance through eTools, technical links, CD-ROMs, and PowerPoint presentations. OSHA's eTools are interactive, Web-based training tools on various safety and health topics. These modules enable users to answer questions and receive reliable advice on how OSHA regulations apply to their work location.[34]

Enforcing Safety Rules

Specific rules and regulations concerning safety are communicated through supervisors, bulletin board notices, employee handbooks, and signs attached to equipment. Safety rules are also emphasized in regular safety meetings, at new employee orientations, and in manuals of standard operating procedures.[35]

Penalties for violation of safety rules are usually stated in the employee handbook. In a large percentage of organizations, the penalties imposed on violators are the same as those for violations of other rules. They include an oral or written warning for the first violation, suspension for repeated violations, and, as a last resort, dismissal. However, for serious violations—such as smoking around volatile substances—even the first offense may be cause for termination.

While discipline may force employees to work safely, safety managers understand that the most effective enforcement of safety rules occurs when employees willingly obey and "champion" safety rules and procedures. This can be achieved when management actively encourages employees to participate in all aspects of the organization's safety program. For example, opportunities for employee involvement include (1) jointly setting safety standards with management, (2) participation in safety training, (3) involvement in designing and implementing special safety training programs, (4) involvement in establishing safety incentives and rewards, and (5) inclusion in accident investigations.

Safety rewards programs are a popular way to encourage workplace health and safety.[36] At Allied Waste Industries, a solid-waste management company, management offers a bilingual online/offline safety rewards program called the Dedicated to Safety Rewards Program.[37] The program encourages employees to accumulate safety vouchers that enable them to earn awards. Awards are ordered seamlessly through the company's customized Web site catalog.

Investigating and Recording Accidents

Every accident, even those considered minor, should be investigated by the supervisor and a member of the safety committee. Such an investigation may determine the factors contributing to the accident and reveal what corrections are needed to prevent it from happening again. Correction may require rearranging workstations, installing safety guards or controls, or, more often, giving employees additional safety training and reassessing their motivation for safety.

OSHA requirements mandate that employers with eleven or more employees maintain records of work-related occupational injuries and illnesses.[38] As stated in an earlier section, OSHA also requires that a Log of Work-Related Injuries and Illnesses (OSHA Form 300) be maintained by the organization. All recordable cases are to be entered in the log. A **recordable case** is any injury or illness that results in any of the following: death, days away from work, restricted work or transfer to another job, or medical treatment beyond first aid. Other problems employers must record as work-related include loss of consciousness or diagnosis of a significant injury or illness by a health care professional.[39] Figure 12.1 illustrates OSHA's diagram for classifying accidents under the law. For every recordable case written in the log, an Injury and Illness Incident Report (OSHA Form 301) is to be completed. OSHA Form 301 requires answers to questions about the case. Each year OSHA Form 300-A Summary of Work-Related Injuries and Illnesses must be completed and posted in a conspicuous place or places where notices to employees are customarily posted. Remember, when completing all OSHA forms, employers must not list the name of an injured or ill employee if the case has "privacy concerns," such as those involving sexual assault, HIV infection, and mental illness.[40]

We conclude our discussion of OSHA by showing the OSHA poster that employers are required to display at the workplace (see Highlights in HRM 3).

recordable case

Any occupational death, illness, or injury to be recorded in the log (OSHA Form 300)

CREATING A HEALTHY WORK ENVIRONMENT

From its title alone, the Occupational Safety and Health Act was clearly designed to protect the health, as well as the safety, of employees. Because of the dramatic impact of workplace accidents, however, managers and employees alike may pay more attention to these kinds of immediate safety concerns than to job conditions that are dangerous to their health. It is essential, therefore, that health hazards be identified

3 | Objective

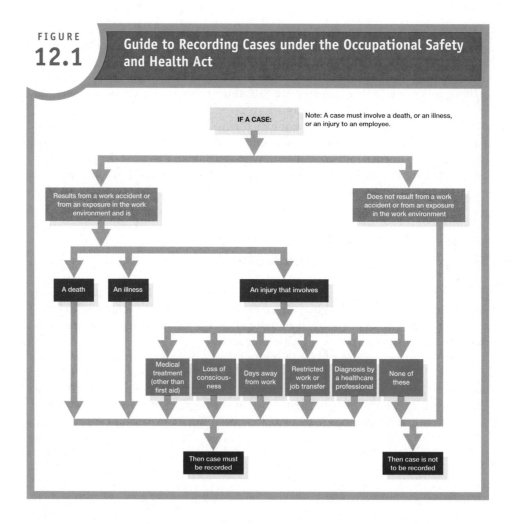

FIGURE 12.1

Guide to Recording Cases under the Occupational Safety and Health Act

and controlled. Furthermore, pressure from the federal government and unions, as well as increased public concern, has given employers a definite incentive to provide the safest and healthiest work environment possible.

Health Hazards and Issues

At one time health hazards were associated primarily with jobs found in manufacturing operations. In recent years, however, hazards in jobs outside the plant, such as in offices, health care facilities, and airports, have been recognized, and preventive methods have been adopted. Substituting materials, altering processes, enclosing or isolating a process, issuing protective equipment, and improving ventilation are some of the common preventions. This section will review several of the more important health concerns to employees and employers.

Chemical Hazards

It is estimated that more than 65,000 different chemicals are currently in use in the United States with which humans may come into contact. Many of these chemicals are harmful, lurking for years in the body with no outward symptoms until the

HIGHLIGHTS IN HRM

3

Job Safety and Health Protection Poster

Job Safety and Health
It's the law!

OSHA
Occupational Safety and Health Administration
U.S. Department of Labor

EMPLOYEES:

* You have the right to notify your employer or OSHA about workplace hazards. You may ask OSHA to keep your name confidential.

* You have the right to request an OSHA inspection if you believe that there are unsafe and unhealthful conditions in your workplace. You or your representative may participate in that inspection.

* You can file a complaint with OSHA within 30 days of retaliation or discrimination by your employer for making safety and health complaints or for exercising your rights under the *OSH Act*.

* You have the right to see OSHA citations issued to your employer. Your employer must post the citations at or near the place of the alleged violations.

* Your employer must correct workplace hazards by the date indicated on the citation and must certify that these hazards have been reduced or eliminated.

* You have the right to copies of your medical records and records of your exposures to toxic and harmful substances or conditions.

* Your employer must post this notice in your workplace.

* You must comply with all occupational safety and health standards issued under the *OSH Act* that apply to your own actions and conduct on the job.

EMPLOYERS:

* You must furnish your employees a place of employment free from recognized hazards.

* You must comply with the occupational safety and health standards issued under the *OSH Act*.

This free poster available from OSHA –
The Best Resource for Safety and Health

Free assistance in identifying and correcting hazards or complying with standards is available to employers, without citation or penalty, through OSHA-supported consultation programs in each state.

1-800-321-OSHA
www.osha.gov

OSHA 3165-12-06R

Using the Internet

Information on chemical safety can be obtained free from the Chemical Reactivity Worksheet program sponsored by NOAA. Go to the Student Resources at:

www.cengage.com/
management/bohlander

disease they cause is well established. It is not surprising, therefore, that the OSHA Hazard Communication Standard is the most frequently cited OSHA standard for general industry as well as for the construction industry. The purpose of the law is to ensure the testing and evaluation of chemicals by producers and the distribution of the chemical hazard information to users of the chemical.

All hazardous chemical containers must be labeled with the identity of the contents and must state any appropriate hazard warnings. The labels must be in English, and employees must be able to cross-reference the label to the Material Safety Data Sheet (MSDS) for the hazardous chemical. OSHA-required chemical training includes informing employees of the methods used to detect the presence or release of hazardous chemicals, the physical and health problems posed by hazardous chemicals, and the ways in which employees can protect themselves from chemical dangers.

Chemical hazards present a significant concern when they have the potential to affect the reproductive health of either women or men. In an important case concerning women, the U.S. Supreme Court ruled in *International Union v. Johnson Controls* (1991) that employers may not bar women of childbearing age from certain jobs because of potential risk to their fetuses.[41] The Court said that such policies are a form of sex bias that is prohibited by federal civil rights law. The decision has made it important for employers to inform and warn female workers about fetal health risks on the job.

Smoking and Tobacco Smoke

The statistics are staggering. The Mayo Clinic, a National Cancer Institute, estimates that more than 400,000 individuals die yearly from smoking and another 35,000 nonsmokers die from lung cancer due to breathing second-hand smoke (inhaling

OSHA requires specific labeling and training employee for all hazardious chemicals

© ALEX L. FRADKIN/PHOTODISC/GETTY IMAGES

other people's smoke). Stanton Glantz, cardiologist at the University of California at San Francisco, states that "second-hand smoke causes heart rates to rise, blood vessels to dilate less easily, and blood components to be stickier—all raising the risk of heart attack."[42] Not surprisingly, smokers have a significantly higher likelihood of suffering a stroke or developing coronary heart disease. In the year of such an event, annual medical costs are around $65,000.[43]

Because of findings such as these, smokers have been banned from lighting up on airplanes, at work, in restaurants and hotels, in public buildings, and in various business establishments. Virtually all large organizations and even smaller ones have initiated smoking policies (see Highlights in HRM 4). In developing smoking

4

HIGHLIGHTS IN HRM

Holsum Bakery's Workplace Smoking Policy

Purpose

The purpose of this policy is to address some of the problems and concerns voiced by smokers and nonsmokers. This policy does not attempt to ban smoking but restricts it to areas which are frequently *shared* by smokers and nonsmokers. Also, this policy attempts to comply with recently enacted laws in Arizona.

Recent studies have concluded that secondary smoke can have serious health consequences. Therefore, the goal will be, to the greatest degree practicable, to obtain freedom from discomfort and irritation for those persons sensitive to tobacco smoke, while preserving a reasonable degree of freedom for those who choose to smoke.

Policy

It is the policy of Holsum Bakery to provide the space necessary for all of our associates to perform their functions in clean air spaces, as well as relax in our several break rooms in smoke-free environments, while at the same time providing separate space for those who choose to smoke.

Procedure

The designated smoking areas are the **upstairs patio** and the **back break room.** All other areas are nonsmoking.

In outlying areas such as Thrift Stores and Depots, designated areas for smoking and nonsmoking will be provided.

Smokers may wish to learn about our special incentive to stop smoking. Associate Services can provide the information. In order to qualify for this offer, a person must have been employed by Holsum on a full-time basis and must be here for a minimum of six (6) months before he/she can apply.

Source: Used with permission from Holsum Bakery, Inc., 2322 West Lincoln St., Phoenix, AZ 85005.

policies, it is advisable to have the involvement of both smokers and nonsmokers. Organizations emphasizing employee involvement include Merck, Comerica, Hallmark, Southwest Airlines, and Marriot Hotels.

Computer Workstations

The expanded use of computers and video display terminals (VDTs) in the workplace has generated intense debate over the possible hazards to which VDT users may be exposed. Many fears about VDT use have been shown to be unfounded, but serious health complaints remain an issue. Problems that managers have to confront in this area fall into three major groups:

1. *Visual difficulties.* VDT operators frequently complain of blurred vision, sore eyes, burning and itching eyes, and glare.[44]

2. *Muscular aches and pains.* Pains in the back, neck, and shoulders are common complaints of VDT operators.

3. *Job stress.* Eye strain, postural problems, insufficient training, excessive workloads, and monotonous work are complaints reported by three-quarters of VDT users.

To capitalize on the benefits of VDTs while safeguarding employee health, Dr. James Sheedy, a VDT and vision expert, offers these tips on how to minimize the negative effects of computer use on the eyes and body:

- Place the computer screen four to nine inches below eye level.
- Keep the monitor directly in front of you.
- Sit in an adjustable-height chair with lower back support and with feet flat on the floor.
- Use shades or blinds to reduce the computer screen glare created by window lighting.
- Elbows close to body and supported.
- Wrist and hands in-line with forearms.

Cumulative Trauma Disorders

cumulative trauma disorders

Injuries involving tendons of the fingers, hands, and arms that become inflamed from repeated stresses and strains

Meat cutters, fish filleters, cooks, dental hygienists, textile workers, violinists, flight attendants, office workers at computer terminals, and others whose jobs require repetitive motion of the fingers, hands, or arms are reporting injuries in growing percentages.[45] Known as cumulative trauma disorders or repetitive motion injuries, these musculoskeletal disorders (MSDs) are injuries of the muscles, nerves, tendons, ligaments, joints, and spinal discs caused by repeated stresses and strains. One of the more common conditions is *carpal tunnel syndrome*, which is characterized by tingling or numbness in the fingers occurring when a tunnel of bones and ligaments in the wrist narrows and pinches nerves that reach the fingers and the base of the thumb. Without proper treatment, employees with carpal tunnel syndrome can lose complete feeling in their hands. Another cumulative trauma disorder prevalent among tennis players is tennis elbow.

In Chapter 4, we discussed job design and ergonomics considerations as one way to accommodate the capabilities and limitations of employees. Ergonomics techniques are also successfully used to improve or correct workplace conditions that cause or aggravate cumulative trauma disorders.[46] Continuous developments in office furniture, video display terminals, tool design, computer keyboards, and adjustable workstations are all attempts to make the work setting more comfortable—and, hopefully, more productive—but also to lessen musculoskeletal disorders. Minibreaks involving exercise and the changing of work positions have been found helpful. Importantly, these kinds of injuries often go away if they are caught early. If they are not, they may require months or years of treatment or even surgical correction. Also, when cumulative trauma disorders result from work activities, they serve to lower employee productivity, increase employer health costs, and incur workers' compensation payments.

Ergonomics and OSHA

Employee musculoskeletal injuries are classified as recordable cases and must be reported on OSHA Form 300. Additionally, OSHA will enforce removal of ergonomic hazards by issuing citations under the general duty clause of the Occupational Safety and Health Act.

To help reduce musculoskeletal injuries, OSHA offers a series of eTools that provide stand-alone, interactive, and Web-based information to address ergonomic hazards. Some eTools address general ergonomic hazards while others target specific occupations and industries such as baggage handling in the airline industry. Employers can expect OSHA to develop more industry- or task-specific guidelines for a number of industries based on current incidence rates and effective and feasible ergonomic solutions to MSD problems. All future OSHA ergonomic programs are championed to be "business-friendly" and emphasize a four-pronged comprehensive approach for reducing MSD injuries and illnesses. OSHA programs will emphasize guidelines, research, outreach and assistance, and enforcement.

Beyond OSHA guidelines, proactive companies use ergonomic practices to both save costs and reduce workplace injuries.[47] For example, at Cessna Aircraft, factory employees use specially designed hand tools to reduce hand and arm tension. Rockwell Automation reduced shoulder injuries to punch-press operators by purchasing hydraulic fork trucks to lift metal dies, a process formerly done manually and Maple Landmark Woodcraft employed ergonomic education to reduce repetitive motion injuries caused by hammering. Key elements of successful ergonomic programs are shown in Figure 12.2.[48]

> **Using the Internet**
>
> A variety of ergonomic information can be found on the Cornell University Ergonomics Web site. Go to the Student Resources at:
>
> **www.cengage.com/
> management/bohlander**

AIDS

As we observed in Chapter 3, AIDS (acquired immune deficiency syndrome) is a disability covered by federal, state, and local protective statutes. Employers subject to statutes under which people with AIDS are likely to be considered disabled are required to hire or retain a person with AIDS who is qualified to perform the essential functions of his or her job. The federal Rehabilitation Act, the Americans with Disabilities Act, and statutes of several states also require employers to give reasonable accommodation to the person through such adjustments as job restructuring, modified work schedules, and less rigid physical requirements.

While there is still no evidence that AIDS can be spread through casual contact in the typical workplace, one of the major problems employers face is the concern that many people have about contracting it. Employees can express "some misgivings" or "strong resentment" about working with someone with AIDS. These reactions

| FIGURE **12.2** | **Key Elements for a Successful Ergonomics Program** |

Companies with award-winning ergonomics programs list the following as common elements of success:

- *Provide notice and training for employees.* Implement a well-publicized ergonomics policy or present ergonomic information in safety policies or training programs. Train employees, supervisors, and managers in basic workplace ergonomics.

- *Conduct preinjury hazard assessment.* Survey the workplace and work processes for potential hazards and adopt measures to lessen the exposure to ergonomic risk factors. Answer the question: "Are certain work areas more prone to ergonomic hazards than others?"

- *Involve employees.* Include employees in risk assessment, recognition of MSD symptoms, design of work-specific equipment or tools, and the setting of work performance rules and guidelines.

- *Plan and execute.* Integrate ergonomic responsibilities into the performance plans for all personnel. Demand accountability for program success.

- *File injury reports.* Encourage early reporting of MSD symptoms or injuries. Refer employees to the company's medical facilities or to the employee's personal physician for treatment.

- *Evaluate and assess the ergonomics program.* Periodically review the effectiveness of the ergonomics program. If the program appears to be ineffective, determine the underlying causes for failure and propose corrective changes.

require employers to formulate programs to educate managers and employees about the transmission of AIDS and the legal rights and moral responsibilities of employers, employees, and people with AIDS. A comprehensive and widely distributed AIDS policy contributes to reducing fears about this illness.[49]

In industries where employees may come in contact with blood or other body fluids (such as medical response teams, hospitals, and nursing homes), employers are required to follow OSHA's bloodborne pathogen standards. Covered employers must train employees in topics such as protective equipment, handling of blood and body fluids, cleaning of equipment, and waste disposal. Additionally, OSHA requires specific record-keeping for "at-risk" employees, those with occupational exposure to bloodborne pathogens such as hepatitis B virus, and others.

Workplace Violence

The National Institute for Occupational Safety and Health defines workplace violence as:

> Any physical assault, threatening behavior, or verbal abuse occurring in the work setting. It includes, but is not limited to, beatings, stabbings, suicides, shootings, rapes, near suicides, psychological traumas such as threats, obscene phone calls, an intimidating presence, and harassment of any nature such as being followed, sworn at, or shouted at.

Unfortunately, workplace violence is pervasive and a significant concern for both employees and employers. For example, aggressive behavior, including harassment and bullying, has become a growing problem because aggression often leads to deadly violence.[50] In recent years, employees have been killed at these organizations: Navistar International, Ford, Edgewater Technology, Xerox, Chrysler, Fireman's Fund, Pettit and Martin (a San Francisco law firm), and the U.S. Postal Service. These examples illustrate why workplace violence has been called the "deadly virus" of crime in America.

Reducing Workplace Violence

A NIOSH study has identified risk factors associated with higher incidence of work-related violence. Employees who have contact with the public; exchange money; deliver passengers, goods, or services; work in health care, social services, or criminal settings; or work alone or in small numbers are at a greater risk of encountering workplace assaults. Employers are cautioned to afford increased protection to these individuals.

OSHA has issued five recommendations for preventing workplace violence:

- Management commitment to and employee involvement in preventing acts of violence

- Analyzing the workplace to uncover areas of potential violence

- Preventing and controlling violence by designing safe workplaces and work practices

- Providing violence prevention training throughout the organization

- Evaluating violence program effectiveness[51]

In addition to following OSHA guidelines, violence prevention specialists recommend that employers take specific actions to reduce workplace violence. First, it is recommended that organizations screen job applicants for histories showing a propensity to violence.[52] For small employers, outside investigators will perform background checks for very small fees.[53] (Remember, employers may be found legally negligent in their hiring practices if they fail to properly investigate applicants. An employee may claim the employer was negligent in that the employer knew, or should have known, that the individual was unfit but hired and kept the person anyway.)[54]

Second, managers and supervisors can be trained to recognize violence indicators such as those given in Figure 12.3.[55] Awareness of these threatening behaviors can provide an opportunity to intervene and prevent disruptive, abusive, or violent acts. Third, managers must effectively communicate a zero tolerance policy for violence and encourage employees to report any possible or observed incidents of workplace violence.[56] Organizations such as Garden Fresh, a restaurant chain, Enterprise Rent-a-Car, JetBlue Airways, and the Ritz-Carlton have formalized workplace violence prevention policies informing employees that aggressive employee behavior will not be tolerated. Finally, a meaningful reporting procedure with clear lines of responsibility can ensure that management is promptly notified of potential security risks in order to take immediate steps to resolve the issues.

Using the Internet

OSHA creates and enforces workplace safety regulations. NIOSH is concerned with research into and ways to prevent workplace hazards. You can read the NIOSH study on workplace violence via the Student Resources at

www.cengage.com/
management/bohlander

<figure>

FIGURE
12.3

Violence Indicators: Know the Warning Signs

Most people leave a trail of indicators before they become violent. Similarly, disgruntled former employees who commit acts of violence leave warning signs of their intent before and after termination. The following behaviors should be taken seriously when assessing situations of potential violence:

- Direct or veiled threatening statements

- Recent performance declines, including concentration problems and excessive excuses

- Prominent mood or behavior changes; despondence

- Preoccupation with guns, knives, or other weapons

- Deliberate destruction of workplace equipment; sabotage

- Fascination with stories of violence

- Reckless or antisocial behavior; evidence of prior assaultive behavior

- Aggressive behavior or intimidating statements

- Written messages of violent intent; exaggerated perceptions of injustice

- Serious stress in personal life

- Obsessive desire to harm a specific group or person

- Violence against a family member

- Substance abuse

Source: Adapted from Violence in the Workplace: Risk Factors and Prevention Strategies, NIOSH Bulletin #59; David D. Van Fleet and Ella W. Van Fleet, "Preventing Workplace Violence: The Violence Volcano Metaphor," *Journal of Applied Management and Entrepreneurship* 12, no. 3 (July 2007): 17; Bella L. Galperin and Joanne D. Leck, "Understanding the Violent Offender in the Workplace," *Journal of American Academy of Business* 10, no. 2 (March 2007): 114.

</figure>

Terrorism

The September 11, 2001, attacks on the World Trade Center and the Pentagon brought home to all Americans the magnitude and horror of terrorism. Once largely confined to foreign countries, terrorism is now a major concern to U.S. employers, particularly those in high-target categories such as airlines, sporting facilities, energy plants and dams, high-tech companies, financial institutions, and public and commercial buildings.[57] The heightened security procedures at these facilities show the importance employers place on the prevention of terrorist attacks, including those involving conventional explosives, nuclear devices, dirty bombs, chemical weapons, and bioweapons.[58]

Many of the points recommended by NIOSH to prevent workplace violence apply equally to preventing terrorism—background checks, violence prevention policy, and so on. Additionally, counterterrorism experts recommend the following to deter terrorist attacks:[59]

- Heightened ID checks and baggage screening

- Increased video monitoring with threat recognition software to back up human surveillance

- Blast-resistant glass to reduce casualties
- Offsite emergency offices
- Tightened garage security with stepped-up inspections
- Staggered deliveries to reduce truck traffic
- Emergency evacuation procedures, including escape routes, emergency equipment, and gathering locations

Banner Health Systems, Phoenix, Arizona, recently hired a new counterterrorism expert—Heidi. Heidi is a German shepherd trained to sniff out eighteen different bomb-making materials, including plastic explosives, ammonium nitrate, and gunpowder. Interestingly, Paul Moskowitz, head of counterterrorism at Brookhaven National Laboratory, commenting on a dog's nose, stated, "That is such an exquisite instrument. A trained dog can reliably detect the slightest trace of a specific chemical even if the scent is masked by other pungent odors. We don't have anything that can touch that yet."[60]

Crisis Management Teams

Organizations such as AlliedSignal, Motorola, and Circle K Corporation have formal crisis management teams. These teams, composed of both hourly and managerial employees, conduct initial risk assessment surveys, develop action plans to respond to violent situations, and, importantly, perform crisis intervention during violent, or potentially violent, encounters. For example, a crisis management team would investigate a threat reported by an employee. The team's mandate would be to gather facts about the threat, decide whether the organization should intervene, and, if so, determine the most appropriate method of doing so. Occasionally, a member of the team or an individual manager will be called upon to intervene and calm an angry employee.[61] When this occurs, the steps given in Figure 12.4 will help to defuse a volatile situation.

When violent incidents, such as the death of a coworker, happen at work, employees can experience shock, guilt, grief, apathy, resentment, cynicism, and a host of other emotions.[62] Jim Martin, an employee assistance program professional with the Detroit Fire Department, notes that after an incident of violence, employees become frightened and may not want to return to work. Such incidents may require the crisis management team to perform crisis intervention through positive counseling techniques.[63]

Building Better Health

Along with improving working conditions that are hazardous to employee health, many employers provide health services and have programs that encourage employees to improve their health habits. It is recognized that better health not only benefits the individual, but also pays off for the organization in reduced absenteeism, increased efficiency, better morale, and other savings. An increased understanding of the close relationship between physical and emotional health and job performance has made broad health-building programs attractive to employers as well as to employees.

4 | Objective

Promoting Workplace Fitness and Health

Appleton, a manufacturer of performance packaging products, promotes corporate fitness through its fitness facility staffed with licensed trainers and YMCA physical fitness experts. The center offers four primary areas of programming: on-site physical

FIGURE
12.4

Calming an Angry Employee

If you try to defuse a tense situation, remember that anger frequently results from a person's feeling of being wronged, misunderstood, or unheard. Keep the following tips in mind to guide you.

- Strive to save the employee's dignity during an angry confrontation. Do not attack a person's rash statements or continue a muddled line of thinking.

- Hold all conversations in private. Do not allow the employee to create an embarrassing public situation for himself or herself, yourself, or other employees.

- Always remain calm. Anger or aggressiveness on your part will trigger a similar response in the employee.

- Listen to the employee with an open mind and nonjudgmental behavior. Give the employee the benefit of hearing him or her out.

- Recognize the employee's legitimate concerns or feelings. Agree that the employee has a valid point and that you will work to correct the problem.

- If the employee is very emotional or if the engagement seems out of control, schedule a delayed meeting so people can calm down.

- Keep the discussion as objective as possible. Focus on the problem at hand, not the personalities of individuals. A cornerstone of conflict resolution is to "attack the problem, not the personality."

- If the employee appears overly aggressive, withdraw immediately and seek professional help before any further discussion with the employee.

- If your efforts fail to calm the employee, report the incident to your manager, security, or human resource personnel.

Source: Adapted from professional literature on crisis management and seminars attended by the authors.

rehabilitation, ergonomics/injury prevention, fitness, and education.[64] Golin/Harris, a public relations firm, offers employees a $50 monthly stipend to a gym just steps from its midtown Manhattan office.

At the New York advertising agency J. Walter Thompson, the employee health management program includes both cardiovascular fitness and nutritional health. Bob Jeffrey, president of the agency's North American division, says, "Employees can work out and relax in a 'de-stress' room, get free massages and yoga or nutrition lessons, join a company sports team, and consult with a personal trainer."[65] At Discovery Communication's wellness center in Silver Spring, Maryland, the company employs a medical assistant, nurse practitioner, and physician who offer health services, including stress management, consultation and techniques, fitness programs, and podiatry care.[66] Organizations may distribute wellness literature obtained from the Association for Worksite Health Promotion or the National Wellness Institute.[67] Xerox gives its employees a publication titled *Fitbook* that includes chapters on the hazards of smoking and the effects of alcohol and drug abuse, facts on nutrition and weight control, and guidelines for managing stress and learning to relax. These examples illustrate how organizations have developed programs that emphasize regular exercise, proper nutrition, rehabilitation, stress management, weight control, and avoidance of substances harmful to health. The goal of all wellness programs is to champion healthier employee lifestyles and to lower organizational medical costs.

Overweight and Obesity

Currently, one of the more critical health and wellness issues facing employers—as well as Americans in general—is overweight and obesity.[68] The Centers for Disease Control estimate that 69 percent of Americans are overweight and 30 percent are severely overweight or obese.[69] This means that three out of every five employees have weight issues that seriously impact employer healthcare costs, employee morale, and work productivity. Overweight and obesity cost companies an estimated $5.5 billion a year in lost productivity due to absenteeism and weight-related chronic diseases such as heart attack, diabetes, high blood pressure, cancer, asthma, and other health problems.[70] Obesity also significantly affects life expectancy. Every year, between 280,000 and 325,000 people suffer premature death related to obesity.[71]

Given the magnitude of the overweight and obesity issue, not surprisingly, employers are launching or improving programs specifically designed to help employees maintain or lose weight.[72] All employer efforts address two lifestyle changes: (1) increasing physical exercise (walking, jogging, bicycling, and so on) and (2) adopting nutritional dietary programs that emphasize eating lots of fruits and vegetables, fish, and low-fat dairy products.[73] Stephanie Pronk, senior consultant for healthcare at Watson Wyatt Worldwide, notes that employers today are trying to create a "culture of wellness" that makes thinking about maintaining a healthy weight second nature to employees.[74] Will employer efforts be successful? Interestingly, one poll showed that 58 percent of Americans would like to lose weight, but only 27 percent are trying to slim down, and two-thirds of those are not following a specific weight loss program.[75]

Alternative Approaches to Health

In a discussion of health services as well as health benefits, it should be emphasized that there are many nontraditional approaches to better health. These are typically referred to as *alternative approaches*. Many of the approaches differ from traditional medicine in that they are less invasive and they empower the patient by enlisting patient participation in health care decisions.

Relaxation techniques, chiropractic, acupuncture, homeopathy, herbal therapy, special diets, and many other alternative approaches are used to treat a wide variety of health problems. For example, Paula Cates, a massage therapist in Denver, Colorado, uses massage to reduce stress and tension and to improve circulation and range-of-motion activities.[76]

Employee Assistance Programs

A broad view of health includes the emotional as well as the physical aspects of one's life. While emotional problems, personal crises, alcoholism, and drug abuse are considered personal matters, they become organizational problems when they affect behavior at work and interfere with job performance.[77] To be able to handle such problems, organizations such as DuPont, Arizona State University, and Stewart Warner, a manufacturer of automotive parts, offer an employee assistance program (EAP). Typically, such a program refers employees in need of assistance to in-house counselors or outside professionals. Supervisors are often given training and policy guidance in the type of help they can offer their subordinates. Furthermore, proactive organizations recognize that EAPs must meet the needs of a diverse population. A culturally focused EAP can have a positive impact

5 | Objective

on employees' well-being and productivity by providing workers with a range of services related to cultural differences, minority health concerns, and social and language barriers.[78]

Personal Crises

The most prevalent problems among employees are personal crises involving marital, family, financial, or legal matters.[79] Furthermore, EAPs have been directing increased attention to the problem of domestic violence. Such problems often come to a supervisor's attention. In most instances, the supervisor can usually provide the best help simply by being understanding and supportive and by helping the individual find the type of assistance he or she needs.[80] In many cases, in-house counseling or referral to an outside professional is recommended. In recent years, crisis hotlines have been set up in many communities to provide counseling by telephone for those too distraught to wait for an appointment with a counselor.

Depression

depression

A negative emotional state marked by feelings of low spirits, gloominess, sadness, and loss of pleasure in ordinary activities

While personal crises are typically fraught with emotion, most of them are resolved in a reasonable period of time, and the troubled individual's equilibrium is restored. Unfortunately, when personal crises linger, stress and tension may cause or intensify a mood disorder such as depression. Depression is a decrease in functional activity accompanied by symptoms of low spirits, gloominess, and sadness. The National Institute of Mental Health estimates that nearly 17 million Americans, or as much as 10 percent of the adult population, experience depression each year. A recent study by Harvard University School of Public Health and the World Health Organization found that by 2020, depression will be second only to heart disease as a cause of medical and physical disability.[81] Fortunately, with available treatment, 70 percent of depressed individuals will significantly improve, usually within a matter of weeks.

Since depression lowers individual productivity, causes morale problems, increases absenteeism, and contributes to substance abuse, it is important for managers to identify signs of depression on the job and to learn to deal with depressed employees.[82] The more likely workplace signs of depression are decreased energy, concentration and memory problems, guilt feelings, irritability, and chronic aches and pains that do not respond to treatment. When confronted with depressed employees, managers and supervisors are encouraged to be concerned with the employee's problem, be an active listener, and—should the depression persist—suggest professional help.[83] Under no circumstances should managers attempt to play amateur psychologist and try to diagnose an employee's condition.[84] Mood disorders such as depression are complex in nature and do not lend themselves to quick diagnoses. Furthermore, in reviewing such cases, the organization should pay particular attention to workplace safety factors because there is general agreement that emotional disturbances are primary or secondary factors in a large portion of industrial accidents and violence.

Alcoholism

Business and industry lose an estimated $20.6 billion each year because of alcoholism, according to the Conference Board. The National Council for Alcoholism and Drug Dependency reports that in this country alone there are more than 10.5 million alcoholics. Alcoholism affects both the young and old, is prevalent across the sexes, and affects workers in every occupational category—blue-collar and white-collar.[85]

In confronting the problem, employers must recognize that alcoholism is a disease that follows a rather predictable course. Thus they can take specific actions to deal with employees showing symptoms of the disease at particular stages of its progression. Alcoholism typically begins with social drinking getting out of control. As the disease progresses, the alcoholic loses control over how much to drink and eventually cannot keep from drinking, even at inappropriate times. The person uses denial to avoid facing the problems created by the abuse of alcohol and often blames others for these problems. The first step in helping the alcoholic is to awaken the person to the reality of his or her situation.

To identify alcoholism as early as possible, it is essential that supervisors monitor the performance of all personnel regularly and systematically. A supervisor should carefully document evidence of declining performance on the job and then confront the employee with unequivocal proof that the job is suffering. The employee should be assured that help will be made available without penalty. Because the evaluations are made solely in terms of lagging job performance, a supervisor can avoid any mention of alcoholism and allow such employees to seek aid as they would for any other problem.

Employers must remember that alcoholism is classified as a disability under the Americans with Disabilities Act (see Chapter 3). Alcoholism is regarded as a disease, similar to a mental impairment. Therefore, a person disabled by alcoholism is entitled to the same protection from job discrimination as any other person with a disability. However, under the ADA, employers can discipline or discharge employees when job performance is so badly affected by alcohol usage that the employee is unable to perform the job.[86]

Abuse of Illegal Drugs

Employee drug abuse is one of the major employment issues today. Once confined to a small segment of the population, drug abuse is a national problem that has spread to every industry and occupation as well as employee level. In one study, it was estimated that drug abuse costs businesses between $60 billion and $140 billion annually in terms of safety risks, theft, reduced productivity, absenteeism, and accidents.[87]

Most efforts to curb workplace drug abuse are voluntary actions on the part of management. However, a wide range of employers, including federal contractors and private and public transportation firms, are subject to regulations aimed at eliminating the use of illegal drugs on the job. The federal antidrug initiatives include the following:

1. The Drug-Free Workplace Act of 1988, which requires federal contractors and recipients of federal grants to take specific steps to ensure a drug-free work environment. One of the main provisions of the Act is the preparation and distribution of an antidrug policy statement, a sample of which is shown in Highlights in HRM 5.

2. Department of Defense (DOD) contract rules, which specify that employers entering into

NOTICE TO APPLICANTS

We are proud to be a
DRUG-FREE
WORKPLACE

Screening tests for illegal drug use are required as a condition of employment.

Posters are an effective way to alert job applicants and employees about employment policies

contracts with the DOD must agree to a clause certifying their intention to maintain a drug-free workplace.

3. Department of Transportation (DOT) regulations, which require that employees whose jobs include safety- or security-related duties be tested for illegal drug use under DOT rules.

To help employers benefit from being drug-free and to further its mission to help companies maintain safe, healthy, and productive workplaces, the U.S. Department of Labor created the Working Partners for an Alcohol and Drug-Free Workplace. This agency serves to raise organizational awareness about the impact of substance abuse on the workplace while providing employers with substance abuse prevention information. Additionally, the Department's Drug-Free Workplace Advisor provides information to employers about how to establish and maintain an alcohol- and drug-free environment.[88]

HIGHLIGHTS IN HRM

5

Selected Items from Salt River Project's Substance Abuse Policy

Purpose

Salt River Project (SRP) has established substance abuse guidelines to:

- Provide a safe workplace for all employees.
- Ensure the consistent handling of employees and job applicants involved with alcohol and drugs.
- Promote a work environment entirely free from the effects of alcohol, the abuse of legal drugs, and the use, possession, or distribution of illegal drugs.
- Promote efficient operations.
- Promote high standards of employee health.
- Ensure employee performance.

Policy

1. SRP recognizes that employee off-the-job involvement with alcohol or drugs can adversely affect the workplace and SRP's ability to accomplish the goals stated above. Consequently, SRP requires that employees report for work and be on the job completely free from alcohol and unauthorized or illegal drugs in or upon their person.

2. Employees with a suspected or documented drug or alcohol problem shall be advised of and may be required to seek help through the Employee Assistance Program (EAP).

3. EAP participation does not prevent disciplinary action for violation of these guidelines and shall be considered as separate from any disciplinary action the supervisor may take prior to, during or after such participation.

(continued)

Selected Items from Salt River Project's Substance Abuse Policy (continued)

4. An employee using or possessing alcohol, abusing legal or illegal drugs or selling, distributing, possessing, or using drugs on the job or on SRP property is subject to discharge. (Exception: use of alcohol at the PERA Club during the employees' after-work hours.) Illegal drugs found on the job or on SRP property will be confiscated and turned over to the appropriate law enforcement agency.

5. Any employee arrested by law enforcement officers of any state, local or federal governmental agency for off-the-job drug activity may be subject to disciplinary action, up to and including discharge. In deciding what action to take, management will consider the nature of any charge brought against the employee, the employee's present job assignment, the employee's work record, and other factors relative to the impact of the arrest on SRP's business and/or public image.

6. A supervisor who believes an employee is at work with alcohol or drugs in his/her system may require the employee to go to an SRP-designated medical professional for a medical evaluation. In the absence of an HS nurse, another supervisor, if possible, should witness and confirm any observed deficiencies in the employee's performance and behavior. With the documentation of the supervisor, a drug test can be ordered from the appropriate SRP-designated collection facility. Transportation will be provided for the employee for such an evaluation.

7. Supervisors may require an employee involved in an accident on the job, or on SRP premises in connection with the job, to go to an SRP-designated medical professional for a medical evaluation. A referral to EAP may be utilized by an employee's supervisor on a *mandatory* basis when an employee's performance indicates that an assessment and referral may be appropriate. The EAP counselor will determine what course of treatment will be required. Personal information and treatment plan details remain confidential. The only information available to the supervisor is that pertaining to the employee's compliance and work requirements.

9. The SRP-designated medical professional, as part of a medical evaluation, may require the employee to submit to laboratory testing procedures. If an employee refuses to go to an SRP-designated medical professional or refuses to consent to required laboratory testing, the refusal is treated as an admission that the employee is unfit to perform his/her duties.

13. An employee not fully able to operate SRP equipment due to the presence of drugs or alcohol in his/her system will not be permitted to do so. Any employee asked not to operate SRP equipment or drive a personal vehicle on SRP property or on SRP business during work time, but who insists upon doing so will be subject to disciplinary action, including discharge, and will be advised that SRP will immediately report this to the appropriate law enforcement agency.

14. Any employee using legal drugs (prescriptions or over-the-counter) which may alter his/her physical or mental ability must report this to his/her supervisor and to Health Services so that HS can determine whether it is necessary to change the employee's job assignment while he/she is using the drugs. Although the use of legal drugs is not of itself grounds for disciplinary action, improper or excessive use will not prevent disciplinary action for inadequate job performance.

Selected Items from Salt River Project's Substance Abuse Policy (continued)

New Hires

All pre-placement physical evaluations will include a lab test for substance abuse. A job applicant who tests positive, as determined in accordance with standards established at the sole discretion of SRP, will not be hired. If the job applicant refuses such testing or is unable to produce a specimen within two (2) hours, he/she will not be hired. A job applicant who has a positive test result will not be eligible for employment for one (1) year from the date of the test. A job applicant with a prior history of substance abuse will not be rejected solely on that basis. If an SRP-designated medical professional believes that the applicant has been fully rehabilitated, then the applicant will be given full consideration for employment.

Source: Adapted from Salt River Project's substance abuse policy. Used with permission from Salt River Project, Phoenix, Arizona.

The ADA considers an individual using drugs as disabled, provided the person is enrolled in a recognized drug treatment program. The prudent employer will, therefore, make a reasonable accommodation to the specific needs of this employee. Reasonable accommodation may include time off from work or a modified work schedule to obtain treatment. Illegal drug users are, however, not covered under the ADA.

As noted earlier, employers operating under the federal requirements are required to test for drug use under certain specified conditions.[89] However, employers that are exempt from the federal requirement may operate under state or local laws restricting or prohibiting drug tests. Issues related to drug testing under state or local laws are discussed in Chapter 13 in the context of employee rights.

While attention is usually focused on the abuse of illegal drugs, it should be noted that the abuse of legal drugs can also pose a problem for employees.[90] Employees who abuse legal drugs—those prescribed by physicians—often do not realize they have become addicted or how their behavior has changed as a result of their addiction. Also, managers should be aware that some employees may be taking legal sedatives or stimulants as part of their medical treatment and that their behavior at work may be affected by their use of these drugs.

Using the Internet

The National Institute on Drug Abuse (NIDA) has information on drug awareness and prevention. Go to the Student Resources at:

www.cengage.com/
management/bohlander

▉▉ THE MANAGEMENT OF STRESS

Objective 6

HR professionals are well aware of the negative effects of workplace stress on employees' health and job performance.[91] For example, job stress places both women and men at risk for cardiovascular problems and depression and increases employee susceptibility to infectious diseases. All of these contribute to higher health care costs and can lower productivity, job satisfaction, and retention.[92] Importantly, in a recent study on the magnitude of stress in the workplace, 48 percent of employers said stress caused by working long hours affects business performance, and 29 percent said stress caused by widespread use of technology—such as cell phones and personal digital assistants—negatively affects business outcomes. Stress is the most frequently cited reason employees give for why they would leave a company.[93]

What Is Stress?

Stress is any demand on the individual that requires coping behavior. Stress comes from two basic sources: physical activity and mental or emotional activity. The physical reaction of the body to both types of stress is the same. Psychologists use two separate terms to distinguish between positive and negative forms of stress, even though reactions to the two forms are the same biochemically. Eustress is positive stress that accompanies achievement and exhilaration. Eustress is the stress of meeting challenges such as those found in a managerial, technical, or public contact job.[94] Eustress is regarded as a beneficial force that helps us to forge ahead against obstacles. What is harmful is distress. Stress becomes distress when we begin to sense a loss of our feelings of security and adequacy. Helplessness, desperation, and disappointment turn stress into distress. Additionally, some research has linked stress to heart disease. Other studies have shown a connection between chronic stress and hypertension (high blood pressure). High blood pressure, the most common cause of strokes, contributes to heart disease. Russ Newman, American Psychological Association executive director for professional practice, states, "The high stress levels that many Americans report experiencing can have long-term health consequences, ranging from fatigue to obesity and heart disease.[95]

stress

Any adjustive demand caused by physical, mental, or emotional factors that requires coping behavior

eustress

Positive stress that accompanies achievement and exhilaration

distress

Harmful stress characterized by a loss of feelings of security and adequacy

Source: © Reprinted with permission of Wayne Stayskal

Job-Related Stress

Although the body experiences a certain degree of stress (either eustress or distress) in all situations, here we are primarily concerned with the stress related to the work setting. It is in this setting that management can use some preventive approaches.

Sources of Job-Related Stress

Causes of workplace stress are many. However, according to a study by Lluminari, a national health care company, four factors have a major influence on employee stress:

- *High demand:* having too much to do in too short a time

- *High effort:* having to expend too much mental or physical energy over too long a period

- *Low control:* having too little influence over the way a job is done on a day-to-day basis

- *Low reward:* receiving inadequate feedback on performance and no recognition for a job well done.

Other recognized job stressors include layoffs and organizational restructuring; disagreements with managers or fellow employees; prejudice because of age, gender, race, or religion; inability to voice complaints; and poor working conditions. Even minor irritations such as lack of privacy, unappealing music, and other conditions can be distressful to one person or another.

Burnout

burnout

A severe stage of distress, manifesting itself in depression, frustration, and loss of productivity

Burnout is a severe stage of distress. Career burnout generally occurs when a person begins questioning his or her own personal values. Quite simply, one no longer feels that what he or she is doing is important. Depression, frustration, and a loss of productivity are all symptoms of burnout. Burnout is due primarily to a lack of personal fulfillment in the job or a lack of positive feedback about performance.[97] In organizations that have downsized, remaining employees can experience burnout because they must perform more work with fewer coworkers. Overachievers can experience burnout when unrealistic work goals are unattainable.[98]

Coping with Stress

Many employers have developed stress management programs to teach employees how to minimize the negative effects of job-related stress.[99] A typical program might include instruction in relaxation techniques, coping skills, listening skills, methods of dealing with difficult people, time management, and assertiveness. All of these techniques are designed to break the pattern of tension that accompanies stress situations and to help participants achieve greater control of their lives. Organizational techniques, such as clarifying the employee's work role, redesigning and enriching jobs, correcting physical factors in the environment, and effectively handling interpersonal factors, should not be overlooked in the process of teaching employees how to handle stress. Stress management counselors recommend several ways to resolve job-related stress as described in Figure 12.5.

FIGURE

12.5

Tips for Reducing Job-Related Stress

- Build rewarding relationships with coworkers.
- Talk openly with managers or employees about job or personal concerns.
- Prepare for the future by keeping abreast of likely changes in job demands.
- Do not greatly exceed your skills and abilities.
- Set realistic deadlines; negotiate reasonable deadlines with managers.
- Act now on problems or concerns of importance.
- Designate dedicated work periods during which time interruptions are avoided.
- When feeling stressed, find time for detachment or relaxation.
- Do not let trivial items take on importance; handle them quickly or assign them to others.
- Take short breaks from your work area as a change of pace.

Before concluding this discussion, we should observe that stress that is harmful to some employees may be healthy for others. Most managers learn to handle distress effectively and find that it actually stimulates better performance. However, there will always be those who are unable to handle stress and need assistance in learning to cope with it. The increased interest of young and old alike in developing habits that will enable them to lead happier and more productive lives will undoubtedly be beneficial to them as individuals, to the organizations where they work, and to a society where people are becoming more and more interdependent.

SUMMARY

Objective 1 The Occupational Safety and Health Act was designed to assure, so far as possible, safe and healthful working conditions for every working person. In general, the Act extends to all employers and employees. OSHA administration involves setting standards, ensuring employer and employee compliance, and providing safety and health consultation and training where needed. Both employers and employees have certain responsibilities and rights under OSHA. Employers not only are required to provide a hazard-free work environment, but also must keep employees informed about OSHA requirements and must require their employees to use protective equipment when necessary. Under the "right to know" regulations, employers are required to keep employees informed of hazardous substances and instruct them in avoiding the dangers presented. Employees, in turn, are required to comply with OSHA standards, to report hazardous conditions, and to follow all employer safety and health regulations.

Objective 2 In order to provide safe working conditions for their employees, employers typically establish a formal program that, in a large percentage of organizations, is under the direction of the HR manager. The program may have many facets, including providing safety knowledge and motivating employees to use it, making employees aware of the need for safety, and rewarding them for safe behavior. Such incentives as praise, public recognition, and awards are used to involve employees in the safety program. Maintenance of required records from accident investigations provides a basis for information that can be used to create a safer work environment.

Objective 3 Job conditions that are dangerous to the health of employees are now receiving much greater attention than in the past. There is special concern for toxic chemicals that proliferate at a rapid rate and may lurk in the body for years without outward symptoms. Health hazards other than those found in manufacturing operations—such as video display terminals and cumulative trauma disorders—present special problems that must be addressed. Today tobacco smoke is rarely tolerated in the work environment. While there is no evidence that AIDS can be spread through casual contact in the workplace, employers have found that it is important to educate managers and employees about AIDS and to assist those who have it.

Objective 4 Along with providing safer and healthier work environments, many employers establish programs that encourage employees to improve their health

habits. Some of the larger employers have opened primary care clinics for employees and their dependents to provide better health care service and to reduce costs. Wellness programs that emphasize exercise, nutrition, weight control, and avoidance of harmful substances serve employees at all organizational levels.

Objective 5 Virtually all of the larger organizations and many of the smaller ones have found that an employee assistance program is beneficial to all concerned. While emotional problems, personal crises, alcoholism, and drug abuse are often viewed as personal matters, it is apparent that they affect behavior at work and interfere with job performance. An employee assistance program typically provides professional assistance by in-house counselors or outside professionals where needed.

Objective 6 An important dimension to health and safety is stress that comes from physical activity and mental or emotional activity. While stress is an integral part of being alive, when it turns into distress it becomes harmful. We have seen that many sources of stress are job-related. In recognizing the need for reducing stress, employers can develop stress management programs to help employees learn techniques for coping with stress. In addition, organizations need to redesign and enrich jobs, clarify the employee's work role, correct physical factors in the environment, and take any other actions that will help reduce stress on the job.

KEY TERMS

burnout	distress	recordable case
cumulative trauma disorders	eustress	right-to-know laws
depression	Material Safety Data Sheets (MSDSs)	stress

DISCUSSION QUESTIONS

Objective 1
1. When OSHA was enacted in 1970, it was heralded as the most important new source of protection for the U.S. worker in the second half of the twentieth century. What opinions about the effectiveness or the ineffectiveness of the Act or its implementation have you heard from acquaintances who have been affected by it?

Objective 2
2. What steps should management take to increase motivation for safety?

Objective 3
3. An unhealthy work environment can lower productivity, contribute to low morale, and increase medical and workers' compensation costs. Working individually or in teams, list specific ways managers can:
a. Accommodate the desires of smokers and nonsmokers
b. Reduce the harmful affects of VDTs
c. Address employee fears caused by AIDS

Objective 4
4. To live a healthier life, medical professionals say we need to identify those things we currently do that either impair or contribute to our health. Prepare a list of those activities you do that are beneficial or harmful to your overall health. Discuss with others a way to develop a lifetime program for a healthy lifestyle.

Objective 5
5. In several states, employers can require an employee to take a drug test only if there is a "reasonable cause" for testing. What are some behaviors that would indicate that a worker may be under the influence of drugs?

Objective 6
6. Identify the sources of stress in an organization.
a. In what ways do they affect the individual employee? The organization?
b. What can managers and supervisors do to make the workplace less stressful?

HRM EXPERIENCE

Reducing Employee Stress

Job stress and its negative effect on both employees and the organization are a growing concern for managers and supervisors. As the text discusses, employee distress costs employers staggering amounts of money in lost productivity, absenteeism, turnover, increased workers' compensation claims, and health care costs. The cost of distress on the personal lives of employees is unmeasurable. Not surprisingly, stress management is an important aspect of any manager's job.

Stress management programs typically focus on three things to reduce workplace stress: (1) They identify factors in jobs that create stress; (2) they discuss specific techniques and managerial practices that help elevate workplace stress; and (3) they help individuals identify personal characteristics that serve to increase or decrease stress for them.

Assignment

1. Working in groups of four to six individuals, identify personal experiences that caused workplace stress. Explain exactly why these incidents were stressful. Suggest ways to reduce or eliminate these stressful conditions.

2. Stress management often begins by having individuals identify their skills and abilities and jobs that will help them succeed. Assessing our preferences and skills can help us understand why some tasks or roles are more stressful than others. Identify work-related stress by answering these questions:

    - What skills that I enjoy using am I currently using in my job?
    - What skills that I enjoy using am I currently not using?
    - What specific things about my job do I really like?
    - What are things about my job that I dislike?
    - Based on my personal skills and abilities, what would my perfect job be?

BIZFLIX EXERCISES

8 Mile: Working at North Detroit Stamping

When you view these scenes, watch for the safety of Jimmy's job and his work environment. Many aspects of safety and health discussed in this chapter appear in these scenes.

Jimmy "B-Rabbit" Smith, Jr. (Eminem) wants to succeed as a rapper and to prove that a white man can create moving sounds. His job at the North Detroit Stamping (NDS) plant fills his days while he pursues his music at night—and sometimes on the plant's grounds. The film's title refers to Detroit's northern city boundary, well known to local people. *8 Mile* is a gritty look at Detroit's hip-hop culture in 1995 and Jimmy's desire for acceptance by it.

The scene is an edited composite of two brief NDS plant sequences that appear in different places in the film. Part I appears early in the film in the sequence "The Franchise." Part II appears in the last 25 minutes of the film in the "Papa Doc Payback" sequence. Jimmy arrives late for work in the first part of the scene, after riding the city bus because his car did not start. The second part occurs after his beating by Papa Doc (Anthony Mackie) and Papa Doc's gang.

What to Watch for and Ask Yourself

- What is your perception of the safety of Jimmy's job and his work environment? What has management done about job and work environment safety at North Detroit Stamping?

- Could this job and work environment create stress for Jimmy and his coworkers? Why or why not?

- How would you react to this type of work experience?

CASE STUDY

Rambo Goes Violent

The facts of the case are straightforward. A shop floor dispute at an automobile parts manufacturing plant in Hamilton, Iowa, ended with one worker physically killing another. At about 2:00 P.M. on August 12, 2008, police responded to a report of a fight that erupted between two employees. When members of the Hamilton Police Department's Violence Crime Unit arrived, they found Mark Lomas seriously injured. Lomas, 30, died three hours later at Good Samaritan Memorial Hospital. The other employee, Thomas Waycross, has been charged with second-degree murder.

During the investigation of the incident, employees noted that Lomas and Waycross often "bickered" when working together. One employee remarked that Waycross liked to "act tough." Another employee claimed that Waycross had a "Rambo-type" personality. It was widely known that management had told both employees to "learn to get along" or quit.

When asked about the incident, police spokesperson Kathy Calder remarked, "Employers must be vigilant when monitoring for signs of potential workplace violence." Nancy Lomas, Mark's wife, has filed a negligence lawsuit against the company.

Questions

1. What are some violence indicators an employee might display?
2. What are some actions management can take to help prevent workplace violence?
3. How can employees protect themselves against workplace violence?

Source: Adapted from a case known to the authors. All names and locations are fictitious.

CASE STUDY 2

Too Much Stress? You Decide

Job stress and depression are significant problems faced by employees and their managers. Unfortunately, when a case of depression arises, trying to resolve the problem may be difficult—sometimes leading to conflict—as this case illustrates.

Donald Knolls was an air traffic control supervisor for International Gateway Airport (IGA), an airport serving a major metropolitan area. In 2007, Donald began to experience depression and depression-related problems due largely to severe stress on the job. In 2008, he requested and was granted a disability leave for treatment of his illness. After eight months, his personal physician, an expert in depression treatment, and a licensed consulting psychologist agreed that he was sufficiently improved to return to his former position. IGA sent Donald to the physician it had used when Donald first requested his disability leave. After an extensive evaluation, the doctor concluded that Donald, while he had made considerable strides in overcoming his depression, should not be immediately returned to his former supervisory position because the conditions of the job had not changed and Donald was apt to find the stress too great. Instead, he recommended that Donald be returned to a nonsupervisory position on a six-month trial basis, with the case to be reviewed at the end of that time. IGA followed the advice of its doctor and did not return Donald to a supervisory position. Donald, angered by management's decision, filed a grievance through IGA's alternative dispute resolution procedure, a procedure that could end in binding arbitration.

During several meetings between Donald and management, the employer maintained that it had the right to rely on the medical opinion of "a fair and impartial" doctor who had determined that Donald should not be returned to the position that was the cause of his original stress-related emotional problems. Additionally, management pointed out to Donald that IGA's disability leave provision states that it "may require appropriate medical documentation if it believes an employee is not fit to return to his or her former position."

Donald responded, through an attorney he hired to represent his position, that the disability leave provisions were clear but, nevertheless, biased against an employee because they completely disregarded the opinion of his physician and psychologist. According to Donald, "Why bother to get expert medical opinions if they are dismissed?" He further noted, "I have never felt better. I'm really ready to get back to my job." Finally, Donald's lawyer contended that Donald was the victim of discrimination based on his former state of depression: "What happened to Donald would not have happened if his illness had been a more conventional physical injury."

Questions

1. When conflicting medical opinions are presented, should the advice of a medical expert count more heavily than the opinion of a general physician? Explain.
2. Is the charge of discrimination presented by Donald's lawyer relevant to this case? Explain.
3. If you were presented with this case, what decision would you reach? Explain.

Source: Adapted from a case known to one of the authors. All names are fictitious.

ANSWERS TO HIGHLIGHTS IN HRM 1

1. True
2. True
3. True
4. d. 80
5. False
6. True
7. Unsafe acts (85 percent of all accidents)
8. The company position on safety and health
   The identity of the safety coordinator

Rules and regulations
Hazard communication program elements
Safety programs in place
Employee and employer responsibilities
Safety communication in the workplace

9. True
10. False
11. True
12. False (eight hours)

NOTES AND REFERENCES

1. Fay Hansen, "The Violent Workplace," *Workplace Management* 85, no. 22 (November 20, 2006): 18.
2. Adrian Gostick, "Delivering Timely Safety Recognition," *Occupational Health and Safety* 73, no. 9 (September 2004): 94.
3. P.L. 91-596, 91st Congress, S. 2193, December 29, 1970.
4. U.S. Department of Labor, Occupational Safety and Health Administration, *All about OSHA*, rev. ed. (Washington, DC: U.S. Government Printing Office, 2006), 4.
5. OSHA publishes many pamphlets pertaining to various aspects of the Act, such as employee workplace rights and voluntary compliance programs. All OSHA publications can be downloaded at no cost from the agency Web site at http://www. osha.gov; you may also call (800) 321-OSHA or fax a request to (202) 693–2498.

6. *All about OSHA*, 14.
7. Ibid., 21.
8. Ibid., 22.
9. Ibid., 25.
10. Ibid., 27.
11. Statistics are from the OSHA, Web site at http://www.osha.gov. See also Katherine Torres, "CINTAS Faces Historic $2.8 Million Fine," *Occupational Hazards* 69, no. 9 (September 2009): 8.
12. A free copy of OSHA's safety and health program management guidelines can be obtained from the U.S. Department of Labor, OSHA Publications, P.O. Box 37535, Washington, DC 20013-7535.
13. *All about OSHA*, 31.
14. "C. Reiss Coal Co. Earns VPP Merit Status," *Professional Safety* 52, no. 1 (January 2007): 45.
15. *All about OSHA*, 13.

16. Ibid., 5.
17. Fred S. Steingold, *The Employer's Legal Handbook*, 8th ed. (Berkeley, CA: Nolo Press, 2007): 7/27.
18. Katherine Torres, "Draft Paper Criticizes OSHA's Approach to Safety," *Occupational Hazards* 69, no. 2 (February 2007): 8.
19. Katherine Torres, "Congress Turns Up Heat on OSHA," *Occupational Hazards* 69, no. 4 (April 2007): 8.
20. Jerry Laws, "75th Anniversary Issue: OSHA's Way Forward," *Occupational Health and Safety* 76, no. 1 (January 2007): 42.
21. For an overview of OSHA legislation, see David J. Walsh, *Employment Law for Human Resource Practice*, 2nd ed. (Mason, OH: South-Western, 2007): Chapter 15.
22. Robert Pater, "Energizing Safety: Launching Performance and Culture," *Occupational Health and Safety* 76, no. 1 (January 2007): 24

23. Robert Pater, "Becoming a Safety Culture Kumu," *Occupational Health and Safety* 76, no. 2 (February 2007): 22.

24. Jessica Marquez, "Creating a Culture of Safety," *Workforce Management* 86, no. 8 (April 23, 2007): 1.

25. David L. Goetsch, "Checking Your Culture," *Occupational Health and Safety* 76, no. 10 (October 2007): 22

26. Joe Tavenner, "Become a Safety Leader," *Occupational Hazards* 69, no. 12 (December 2007): 42.

27. Linda J. Sherrard, "Keys to Effective Programs," *Occupational Health and Safety* 76, no. 11 (November 2007): 60.

28. Donald R. Groover, "Attributes of an Injury-Free Culture, Part 4: Employee Engagement," *Occupational Health and Safety* 76, no. 11 (November 2007): 20.

29. Drue Townsend, "Increase Safety Awareness with Signs," *Occupational Health and Safety* 76, no. 12 (December 2007): 18.

30. Linda M. Tapp, "Better Safety Training with Fun and Games," *Professional Safety* 52, no. 2 (February 2007): 52.

31. Laura Walter, "Distributing Safety at W. W. Grainger Inc.," *Occupational Hazards* 69, no. 11 (November 2007): 42.

32. Donald R. Groover, "Attributes of an Injury-Free Culture: Ownership," *Occupational Health and Safety* 76, no. 8 (August 2008): 24.

33. Craig Miller, "Can the Internet Improve Safety?" *Occupational Health and Safety* 73, no. 6 (June 2004): 98.

34. http://ww.osha.gov; click on e-Tools.

35. M. Franz Schneider, "Driving Continuous Improvement in Plant Safety," *Occupational Hazards* 69, no. 8 (August 2007): 36.

36. Michelle M. Smith, "7 Steps to Safety Incentive Success," *Occupational Health and Safety* 76, no. 9 (September 2007): 52.

37. Brian Galonek, "No Waste of Effort," *Occupational Health and Safety* 77, no. 1 (January 2008): 45.

38. OSHA considers an injury or illness to be work-related if an event or exposure in the work environment either caused or contributed to the resulting condition or significantly aggravated a preexisting injury or illness. Work-relatedness is presumed for injuries and illnesses resulting from events or exposure occurring in the work environment. OSHA defines the work environment as "the establishment and other locations where one or more employees are working or are present as a condition of their employment. The work environment includes not only physical locations, but also the equipment or materials used by the employee during the course of his or her work."

39. For complete information on the recording and reporting of illnesses and injuries, see OSHA Publication 3169, *Recording and Reporting Occupational Injuries and Illnesses*, particularly Sections 1904.5 (determination of work-relatedness) and 1904.7 (general recording criteria). See also the OSHA Web site at http://www.osha.gov.

40. If employers have a "privacy concern case," they may not enter the employee's name on the OSHA 300 log. Instead, they should enter "privacy case" in the space normally used for the employee's name. This will protect the privacy of the injured or ill employee when another employee, a former employee, or an authorized employee representative is provided access to the OSHA 300 log. Privacy cases must be recorded on a separate confidential list. Employers must consider the following injuries or illnesses privacy concern cases: (i) an injury or illness to an intimate body part of the reproductive system; (ii) an injury or illness resulting from a sexual assault; (iii) mental illnesses; (iv) HIV infection, hepatitis, or tuberculosis; (v) needlestick injuries and cuts from sharp objects that are contaminated with another person's blood or other potentially infectious material; and (vi) other illnesses, if the employee independently and voluntarily requests that his or her name not be entered on the log.

41. The Supreme Court decision in *International Union v. Johnson Controls* may be found in 59 U.S. Law Week 4029.

42. "Second-Hand Smoke: A Quick Study," *Business Week* (April 19, 2004): 83. See also Paul McIntyre, "A High Price to Pay: Workers' Lives Lost to Second-Hand Smoke Far More Costly than Possibility of Lost Profits," *National Restaurant News* 38, no. 33 (August 16, 2004): 44.

43. Bruce Pyenson and Kate Fitch, "Smoking May Be Hazardous to Your Bottom Line," http://www.workforce.com/archive/feature/25/25/61/index.php-63.1 kb. See also "The Best Approaches to Smoking Cessation for Maximum Results," *HR Focus* 84, no. 6 (June 2007): 4.

44. Reid Goldsborough, "Keeping Your Eyes Healthy in Front of a Computer Screen," *TECH Directions* 66, no. 10 (May 2007): 12.

45. Robert A. Wemer, "Evaluation of Work-Related Carpal Tunnel Syndrome," *Journal of Occupational Rehabilitation* 16, no. 2 (June 2006): 201. See also Fred Gerr, Carolyne P. Monteilh, and Michele Marcus," "Keyboard Use and Musculoskeletal Outcomes Among Computer Users," *Journal of Occupational Rehabilitation* 16, no. 3 (September 2006): 259.

46. Michael S. Zedalis and Keitha Kessler, "Frequently Asked Questions: Ergonomics and Hand Protection," *Occupational Health and Safety* 76, no. 4 (April 2007): 64.

47. Mike Wynn, "Revitalizing Your Ergonomics Program" *Occupational Health and Safety* 77, no. 1 (January 2008): 54. See also Robert Pater, "Elevating Ergonomic Leadership," *Occupational Health and Safety* 76, no. 9 (September 2007): 18.

48. John P. Baeseman and Douglas Newhand, "The Ergonomically Correct Workplace," *Document Processing Technology* 15, no. 7 (December 2007): 20.

49. Catherine Arnst, "Why Business Should Make AIDS Its Business," *Business Week* (August 2, 2004): 80.

50. Diane Bandow, "The Rise of Workplace Incivilities: Has It Happened to You?" *The Business Review* 7, no. 1 (Summer 2007): 212.

51. The NIOSH document *Violence in the Workplace: Risk Factors and Prevention Strategies*, Bulletin #59 is available from Publications Dissemination, EID, National Institute for Occupational Safety and Health, 4676 Columbia Parkway, Cincinnati, OH 45226-1998, (800) 356-4674.

52. Catherine Aldrich, "The Devil Inside: The Legal Liabilities of Background Screening," *Risk Management* 54, no. 2 (February 2007): 10.

53. Robert Thompson, "Screening Employees Secures Workplaces," *National Underwriter* 111, no. 32 (September 3, 2007): 35.

54. Ramona L. Paetzold, Anne O'Leary-Kelly, and Ricky W. Griffin, "Workplace Violence, Employer Liability, and Implications for Organizational Research," *Journal of Management Inquiry* 16, no. 4 (December 2007): 362.

55. Laura Walker, "Facing the Unthinkable: Fatality Prevention in the Workplace,"

Occupational Hazards 70, no. 1 (January 2008): 32. See also Jean Thilmany, "In Case of Emergency," *HR Magazine* 52, no. 11 (November 2007): 79; Lynn Lieber, "Workplace Violence—What Can Employers Do to Prevent It?" *Employees Relations Today* 34, no. 3 (Fall 2007): 91.

56. Marcia K. Korow, "How Reflective Is Our Policy?" *Nursing Management* 39, no. 1 (January 2008): 37. See also Scott R. Gane, "Avoiding Violent Outcomes," *Security Management* 51, no. 6 (June 2007): 140.

57. Rita Katz, "Web of Terror," *Forbes* 179, no. 10 (May 7, 2007): 184.

58. Krisandra Guidry, "Antiterrorism Security Measures for Commercial Buildings: Inspection and Appraisal Guidelines," *The Appraisal Journal* 75, no. 4 (Fall 2007): 354.

59. John J. Matchulat, "Planning for Terrorism: How Far Should an Employer Go?" *Risk Management* 53, no. 12 (December 2006): 22. See also Kevin Lindsey, "Crisis Alert," *HR Magazine* 51, no. 8 (August 2006): 121.

60. David Shenk, "Watching You: The World of High-Tech Surveillance," *National Geographic* 204, no. 5 (November 2004): 6–7.

61. Kevin McCaffery, "Show No Fear," *Security Management* 51, no. 12 (December 2007): 54.

62. Nicola Guy and Keith Guy, "In Traumatic Times," *Occupational Health* 59, no. 8 (August 2007): 23.

63. Bruce T. Blythe, "The Human Side of Crisis Management," *Occupational Hazards* 66, no. 7 (July 2004): 37.

64. Craig Halls and John Rhodes, "Employee Wellness and Beyond," *Occupational Health and Safety* 73, no. 9 (September 2004): 46. See also Julie L. Gerberding and James S. Marks, "Making America Fit and Trim—Steps Big and Small," *American Journal of Public Health* 94, no. 9 (September 2004): 1478.

65. Christina Fuoco-Karasinski, "Building More Fit Employees: A Massachusetts General Hospital Case Study," *Workspan* (April 2007): 65.

66. Judy Ashley, "Building a Culture of Wellness the Discovery Way," *Workspan* (July 2007): 43.

67. Wellness Resources: Association for Worksite Health Promotion, 60 Revere Dr., Suite 500, Northbrook, IL 60062, (847) 637-9200; National Wellness Institute, 1045 Clark St. Suite 210, P.O. Box 827, Stevens Point, WI 54481-0828, (715) 342-2969.

68. Karen Tumulty, "The Politics of Fit," *Time* (March 27, 2006): 41.

69. Pamela Babock, "Getting the Weight Off," *HR Magazine* 53, no. 1 (January 2008): 61.

70. Amy McKenna and Anne Marie Kuchera, "Kathy Knows She Shouldn't Eat Fatty Foods, but She Does Anyway. The Cure for America's $75 Billion Obesity Crisis: Behavioral Change," *Employee Benefit Plan Review* 59, no. 2 (August 2004): 10.

71. Robert S. Grossman, "Countering a Weight Crisis," *HR Magazine* 49, no. 3 (March 2004): 42.

72. Josh Cable, "Shedding Pounds Good for Bottom Line," *Occupational Hazards* 69, no. 10 (October 2007): 18.

73. Jeremy Smerd, "Young and Unhealthy: Urgent Care Required," *Workforce Management* 86, no. 15 (September 10, 2007): 36.

74. "Obesity Programs Are Latest Wellness Focus," *HR Focus* 84, no. 7 (July 2007): 12.

75. David Bjerklie, "America's Obesity Crisis," *Time* (June 7, 2004): 113.

76. Paula Cates, interview by author, Denver, Colorado, February 18, 2008.

77. Dale Kaplan and Park Dietz, "Use Employee Assistance to Manage Risk," *Occupational Health and Safety* 76, no. 7 (July 2007): 82.

78. Donna M. Owens, "EAPs for a Diverse Workforce," *HR Magazine* 51, no. 10 (October 2006): 91.

79. Gary M. Stem, "Not Tonight, Dear," *The Conference Room Review* 44, no. 2 (March/April 2007): 38.

80. Marilyn E. Mages, "Gaining Ground: How Employers and Employees Can Work Together on Impairment Issues," *Healthcare Executive* 22 no. 1 (January/February 2007): 22.

81. Marianne Szegedy-Maszak, "Reason to be Happy," *U.S. News and World Report* (April 10, 2006): 41.

82. "Treating Depression Improves Productivity," *Industrial Engineer* 40, no. 1 (January 2008): 11.

83. "Depression Outreach Can Boost Productivity," *HR Focus* 84, no. 12 (December 2007): 12.

84. Rebecca R. Hastings, "Focus on Behavior, Not Psychiatric Conditions," *HR Magazine* 51, no. 11 (November 2006): 26.

85. Mindy Chapman, "Drugs and Alcohol Workplace Trends," *Occupational Health and Safety* 76, no. 8 (August 2007): 32.

86. *The Employer's Legal Handbook*, see section on preventing discrimination.

87. Karen Elliott and Kyna Shelly, "Effects of Drugs and Alcohol on Behavior, Job Performance, and Workplace Safety," *Journal of Employment Counseling* 43, no. 3 (September 2006): 130.

88. Information regarding the U.S. Department of Labors efforts to create a drug-free workplace can be found at http://www.dol.gov.

89. Kathy Gurchiek, "Employer Testing Credited for Lower Drug-Use Rates," *HR Magazine* 52, no. 6 (June 2007): 36.

90. Tracy S. Hunter, "Pharmacist Role in Prescription Drug Misuse, Abuse, and Addiction," *Drug Topics* 150, no. 18 (September 18, 2006): 42.

91. "Will Stress Be Your Next Wellness Target?" *HR Focus* 85, no. 1 (January 2008): 12.

92. http://www.watsonsyatt.com/research/reports.asp.

93. Jenna Goudreau, Gail Edmondson, and Michelle Conlin, "Dispatches from the War on Stress: Business Begins to Recon with the Enormous Costs of Workplace Angst," *Business Week* (August 6, 2007): 74. See also Michael R. Frone, "Are Work Stressors Related to Employee Substance Use? The Importance of Temporal Context Assessments of Alcohol and Illicit Drug Use," *Journal of Applied Psychology* 93, no. 1 (January 2008): 199.

94. Kerry Sulkowicz, "Stressed for Success," *Business Week* (May 21, 2007): 18.

95. "Will Stress Be Your Next Wellness Target?": 12.

96. "Change Your Culture and Lower Your Benefit Costs," *HR Focus* 81, no. 11 (November 2004): 6.

97. "Many Workers Are Burning Out, and Here's Why," *HR Focus* 83, no. 7 (July 2006): 9.

98. "Beware the Dangers of Workaholism," *HR Focus* 85, no. 1 (January 2008): 9.

99. Carole Spiers, "Providing Stress Counseling to Quest Internationals Employees," *Strategic HR Review* 5, no. 5 (July/August 2006): 10.

EMPLOYEE RIGHTS AND DISCIPLINE

After studying this chapter, you should be able to

Objective 1

Explain the concepts of employee rights and employer responsibilities.

Objective 2

Explain the concepts of employment-at-will, wrongful discharge, implied contract, and constructive discharge.

Objective 3

Identify and explain the privacy rights of employees.

© DAVID ELLIS/DIGITAL VISION /GETTY IMAGES

13

CHAPTER

Objective 4

Explain the process of establishing disciplinary policies, including the proper implementation of organizational rules.

Objective 5

Discuss the meaning of discipline and how to investigate a disciplinary problem.

Objective 6

Differentiate between the two approaches to disciplinary action.

Objective 7

Identify the different types of alternative dispute resolution procedures.

Objective 8

Discuss the role of ethics in the management of human resources.

In this chapter, we discuss employee rights, workplace privacy, and employee discipline. Managers note that these topics have a major influence on the activities of both employees and supervisors. Robert J. Deeny, an employment attorney, has stated that employee rights and workplace privacy "continues to be the hottest and expanding employment law topics into the twenty-first century. The growing caseload in this area is significant to employers."[1] For example, while drug testing, e-mail privileges, and employee monitoring are routinely debated, employers are now using radio frequency identification (RFID), global positioning systems, biometric technology, and company-provided cell phones to track and locate employees. These technology tools are increasingly blurring the lines between personal freedom and privacy and employer monitoring and control over employee conduct.[2]

Furthermore, managers are discovering that the right to discipline and discharge employees—a traditional responsibility of management—is more difficult to exercise in light of the growing attention to employee rights. In a recent discharge case, General Electric was ordered to pay Hemant K. Mody, a long-time engineer, $11.1 million, including $10 million for punitive damages. The jury concluded that the discharge was improper since Mody had been fired in retaliation for complaining about bias.[3] Disciplining employees is a difficult and unpleasant task for most managers and supervisors; many of them report that taking disciplinary action against an employee is the most stressful duty they perform. Balancing employee rights and employee discipline may not be easy, but it is a universal requirement and a critical aspect of good management.

Because the significance of employee rights issues has led to an increase in the number of lawsuits filed by employees, we include in this chapter a discussion of alternative dispute resolution as a way to foster organizational justice. Because disciplinary actions are subject to challenge and possible reversal through governmental agencies or the courts, management should make a positive effort to prevent the need for such action. When disciplinary action becomes impossible to avoid, however, that action should be taken in accordance with carefully developed HR policies and practices. Because ethics is an important element of organizational justice, the chapter concludes with a discussion of organizational ethics in employee relations.

▪▪ EMPLOYEE RIGHTS AND PRIVACY

Various antidiscrimination laws, wage and hour statutes, and safety and health legislation have secured basic employee rights and brought numerous job improvements to the workplace. Employee rights litigation concerns such workplace issues as employees' rights to protest unfair disciplinary action, to question genetic testing, to have access to their personal files, to challenge employer searches and monitoring, and to be free from employer discipline for off-duty conduct.[4]

The current emphasis on employee rights is a natural result of the evolution of societal, business, and employee interests.[5] Employee rights can be defined as the guarantees of fair treatment that employees expect in protection of their employment status. These expectations become rights when they are granted to employees by the courts, legislatures, or employers. Employee rights frequently involve an employer's alleged invasion of an employee's right to privacy. For example, employees may feel they have a reasonable expectation of privacy regarding their personal phone calls made from work phones, their e-mail messages made to other employees at work, or freedom from employers' random searches of their personal belongings. However, if employers tell employees that they have no right to privacy in these areas, they probably do not. One legal commentator notes, "When employers clearly state that there

employee rights
Guarantees of fair treatment from employers, particularly regarding an employee's right to privacy

is no expectation of privacy, it's hard to argue that a reasonable person could have such an expectation." Furthermore, the difference between an employee's legal right to privacy and the moral or personal right to privacy is not always clear. The confusion is due to the lack of a comprehensive and consistent body of privacy protection, whether from laws or from court decisions. Legal scholars recognize that the protection of employee privacy rights extends only so far; federal and state courts generally view the privacy rights of employees as minimal.

Employee Rights vs. Employer Responsibilities

Balanced against employee rights is the employer's responsibility to provide a safe workplace for employees while guaranteeing safe, quality goods and services to consumers.[6] An employee who uses drugs may exercise his or her privacy right and refuse to submit to a drug test. But should that employee produce a faulty product as a result of drug impairment, the employer can be held liable for any harm caused by that product. Employers must therefore exercise *reasonable care* in the hiring, training, and assignment of employees to jobs.[7]

1 | Objective

It is here that employee rights and employer responsibilities can come most pointedly into conflict. The failure of employers to honor employee rights can result in costly lawsuits, damage the organization's reputation, and hurt employee morale. But failure to protect the safety and welfare of employees or consumer interests can invite litigation from both groups. In one case, Dillard's Inc. was held accountable for the "hostile propensities" of one of its sales clerks toward customers. The jury found that an employer can be held liable for the discriminatory conduct of its salesperson.[8] Negligent-hiring lawsuits by employees and consumers have become an area of great concern for employers.

Negligent Hiring

In law, negligence is the failure to use a reasonable amount of care when such failure results in injury to another person. Negligent hiring is a legal doctrine that places liability on the employer for actions of its employees during the course and scope of their employment. A general responsibility exists for employers to exercise *reasonable care* in preventing employees from intentionally harming other employees during their course of work.[9]

negligence
Failure to provide reasonable care when such failure results in injury to consumers or other employees

Unfortunately, when one employee commits a violent act on another employee or an employee willfully defames another employee through e-mail messages communicated at work, the employer may face a negligent-hiring lawsuit claiming that the employer should have used more reasonable care in the hiring of its employees.[10] While many see negligent-hiring lawsuits as a "Catch-22" for employers (that is, how can employers predict with certainty the future behavior of employees), it nonetheless forces managers to take extra care in the employment and management of the workforce. In the remainder of this section, we will discuss various rights employees have come to expect from their employers.

Job Protection Rights

It is not surprising that employees should regard their jobs as an established right—a right that should not be taken away without just cause. Without the opportunity to hold a job, our personal well-being would be greatly curtailed. This line of reasoning has led to the emergence of five legal considerations regarding the security of one's job: The employment-at-will principle, the concept of the implied contract, explicit contracts, constructive discharge, and plant closing notification.

It should be understood, however, that although employees might have cause to regard jobs as an established right, there is no legal protection affording employees a permanent or continuous job. The U.S. Constitution carries no mandate guaranteeing that jobs are among the specific property rights of employees. Regardless, employees have certain expectations regarding the employment relationship. This expectation is referred to as the **psychological contract** and includes an employee's belief about the mutual obligation between the employee and the organization.[11] For example, in exchange for their talents, energies, and technical skills, workers expect employers to provide fair compensation, steady work, job training, and promotions. Employees also have the right to expect sound employment practices and to be treated as individuals of dignity and substantial worth.[12] While the psychological contract is not a legal mandate, nevertheless, it strongly influences the employment relationship.

psychological contract

Expectations of a fair exchange of employment obligations between an employee and employer

Employment-at-Will

employment-at-will principle

The right of an employer to fire an employee without giving a reason and the right of an employee to quit when he or she chooses

The employment relationship has traditionally followed the common-law doctrine of employment-at-will. The **employment-at-will principle** assumes that an employee has a right to sever the employment relationship for a better job opportunity or for other personal reasons. Employers, likewise, are free to terminate the employment relationship at any time—and without notice—for any reason, no reason, or even a bad reason. In essence, employees are said to work "at the will" of the employer.[13]

The employment-at-will relationship is created when an employee agrees to work for an employer for an unspecified period of time. Because the employment is of an indefinite duration, it can, in general, be terminated at the whim of either party. This freedom includes the right of management to unilaterally determine the conditions of employment and to make personnel decisions. In 1908, the Supreme Court upheld the employment-at-will doctrine in *Adair v. United States*, and this principle continues to be the basic rule governing the private-sector employment relationship.[14]

Does the employment-at-will doctrine give managers and supervisors the unrestricted right of termination? The answer is clearly no.[15] First, union collective bargaining agreements limit summary discharges. These agreements frequently specify the kinds of infractions that can lead to termination. Second, as we have emphasized throughout this text, federal and state laws, court decisions, and administrative rulings can prohibit discharge for guaranteed employment rights (see, for example, Chapters 3 and 12). Finally, and importantly, in today's litigious environment, employers may harbor a "fear of firing." That is, employers may retain marginal, or even poor performing employees, when faced with a possible termination lawsuit, a lawsuit that could be lengthy, costly, and embarrassing to the employer. Barry Roseman, employment attorney, notes, "Employers increasingly need to operate under the premise that they have to 'prove' that an employee's conduct or action warrants termination, if they hope to prevail in court."

Wrongful Discharge

Approximately two million workers are discharged each year. Estimates of unfair employee dismissals range from 50,000 to 200,000 a year. In recent years, a substantial number of these employees have sued their former employers for "wrongful or unjust discharge." An unjust discharge claim might exist where (1) employees believe they were fired and then denied a guaranteed due process procedure, (2) in circumstances where a termination is falsely attributed to an employee, or (3) for a protected legal right.

The significance of wrongful discharge suits is that they challenge the employer's right under the employment-at-will concept to unilaterally discharge employees.[16] Various state courts now recognize the following three important exceptions to the employment-at-will doctrine:

1. *Violation of public policy.* This exception occurs when an employee is terminated for refusing to commit a crime; for reporting criminal activity to government authorities; for disclosing illegal, unethical, or unsafe practices of the employer; or for exercising employment rights. (See Figure 13.1 for examples of public policy violations.)

2. *Implied contract.* This exception occurs when employees are discharged despite the employer's promise (expressed or implied) of job security or contrary to established termination procedures. An employer's oral or written statements may constitute a contractual obligation if they are communicated to employees and employees rely on them as conditions of employment.[17]

3. *Implied covenant.* This exception occurs when a lack of good faith and fair dealing by the employer has been suggested. By inflicting harm without justification, the employer violates the implied covenant. Discharged employees may seek tort damages for mental distress or defamation.

The confusion and conflict between the traditional right of employers to terminate at will and the right of employees to be protected from unjust discharge are far from resolved. Therefore, to protect themselves from wrongful discharge terminations and from large jury awards—sometimes exceeding $1 million—HR specialists recommend the suggestions given in Figure 13.2.[18]

Whistle-Blowing

Employees engage in whistle-blowing when they report an employer's illegal actions, immoral conduct, or illegal practices to governmental agencies charged with upholding the law. A number of federal and state laws protect whistle-blowers from retaliation from their employer; some provide whistle-blowers with financial incentives to expose wrongdoings.[19] For example, in response to recent corporate scandals, the Sarbanes-Oxley (S-O) Act was passed in 2002 to protect whistle-blowers employed in publicly

whistle-blowing

Complaints to governmental agencies by employees about their employers' illegal or immoral acts or illegal practices

FIGURE 13.1 **Discharges That Violate Public Policy**

An employer may *not* terminate an employee for:

- Refusing to commit perjury in court on the employer's behalf
- Cooperating with a government agency in the investigation of a charge or giving testimony
- Refusing to violate a professional code of conduct
- Reporting Occupational Safety and Health Administration (OSHA) infractions
- Refusing to support a law or a political candidate favored by the employer
- "Whistle-blowing," or reporting illegal conduct by the employer
- Informing a customer that the employer has stolen property from the customer
- Complying with summons to jury duty

FIGURE
13.2

Tips to Avoid Wrongful Employment Termination Lawsuits

- *Terminate an employee only if there is an articulated reason.* An employer should have clearly articulated, easily understandable reasons for discharging an employee. The reasons should be stated as objectively as possible and should reflect company rules, policies, and practices.

- *Set and follow termination rules and schedules.* Make sure every termination follows a documented set of procedures. Procedures can be from an employee handbook, a supervisory manual, or even an intraoffice memorandum. Before terminating, give employees notices of unsatisfactory performance and improvement opportunities through a system of warnings and suspensions.

- *Document all performance problems.* A lack of documented problems in an employee's personnel record may be used as circumstantial evidence of pretextual discharge if the employee is "suddenly" discharged.

- *Be consistent with employees in similar situations.* Document reasons given for all disciplinary actions, even if they do not lead to termination. Terminated employees may claim that exception-to-the-rule cases are discriminatory. Detailed documentation will help employers explain why these "exceptions" did not warrant termination.

traded companies.[20] The law encourages whistle-blowing by motivating publicly held companies to promote a more open culture that is sympathetic to employees who have a "reasonable belief" that a law has been violated. Federal employees are covered by the federal Whistleblower Protection Act (WPA).[21] The Notification and Federal Employee Antidiscrimination and Retaliation Act (No Fear Act), also passed in 2002, provides whistle-blower protection under federal law at the Environmental Protection Agency (EPA),[22] and the False Claims Act (FCA) applies to employees who provide information about false or fraudulent claims made against the federal government.[23] OSHA administers the whistle-blowing provisions in fifteen federal statutes protecting whistle-blowers in such industries as airline, nuclear power, and public transportation.

Not only is whistle-blowing a protected right of employees, but also these cases result in embarrassment for employers, harassment for employees, and large fines for employers that are found guilty.[24] In one whistle-blowing case, federal prosecutors fined Saint Barnabas Health Care Systems $265 million for inflating hospital charges. The hospital charged Medicare patients more than non-Medicare patients to exploit Medicare reimbursement regulations.[25] In another case, Medical World Communications paid the government $3.7 million to settle charges of mail fraud.

To prevent cases such as these, HR professionals recommend that companies implement a whistle-blowing policy that encourages employees to report illegal or immoral conduct internally rather than externally. The policy should provide for the safeguard of employee rights, a complete and unbiased investigation of the incident, a speedy report of findings, and an appeals procedure for employees who are dissatisfied with company findings.[26]

Implied Contract

Although it is estimated that 80 percent of employees in the United States work without benefit of an employment contract, under certain conditions these employees may be granted contractual employment rights. This can occur when an implied promise by the employer suggests some form of job security to the employee. These implied contractual rights can be based on either oral or written statements made during the preemployment process or subsequent to hiring. Often these promises are contained in employee handbooks, HR manuals, or employment applications or are made during the selection interview. Once these explicit or implicit promises of job security have been made, courts have generally prohibited the employer from terminating the employee without first exhausting the conditions of the contract. For example, a leading case, *Toussaint v. Blue Cross and Blue Shield of Michigan,* found an employee handbook enforceable as a unilateral contract.[27] The following are some examples of how an implied contract may become binding:

- Telling employees their jobs are secure as long as they perform satisfactorily and are loyal to the organization

- Stating in the employee handbook that employees will not be terminated without the right of defense or access to an appeal procedure—that is, due process

- Urging an employee to leave another organization by promising higher wages and benefits, then reneging on those promises after the person has been hired

Fortunately, employers may lessen their vulnerability to implied contract lawsuits by prudent managerial practices, training, and HR policies. HR experts recommend the following approaches:

1. Training supervisors and managers not to imply contract benefits in conversations with new or present employees.

2. Including in employment offers a statement that an employee may voluntarily terminate employment with proper notice and the employee may be dismissed by the employer at any time and for a justified reason. The language in this statement must be appropriate, clear, and easily understood.

3. Including employment-at-will statements in all employment documents—for example, employee handbooks, employment applications, and letters of employment.[28] (See Highlights in HRM 1.)

4. Having written proof that employees have read and understood the employment-at-will disclaimers.

Explicit Contracts

Explicit employment contracts are formal written (signed) agreements that grant to employees and employers agreed-upon employment benefits and privileges. Explicit contracts are popular with executives, senior managers, and for individuals with highly technical or professional skills and abilities. Where these contracts exist, they normally state the period of employment, terms and conditions of employment (for example, salary and benefits), and severance provisions. In today's highly competitive environment, employers may impose upon ex-employees certain restrictions upon future employment. Three specific restrictions are:

1. *Non-compete agreements.* These clauses prevent ex-employees from working for a competitor for a designated period of time, for example, one or two years.[29] These contracts seek to protect confidential information, customer relations, and other valuable assets.[30]

2. *Intellectual property agreements.* The intellectual property clause grants ownership to the employer of an idea, invention or process, or work of authorship developed

Examples of Employment-at-Will Statements

Employment handbooks frequently include an opening statement that employees are employed at will, that is, there are no duration guarantees. Also no supervisors or managers, except specified individuals (that is, the HR director or company president), have the authority to promise any employment benefit—including salary, job position, and the like. All handbooks should include a disclaimer that expressly provides that all employment policies and benefits contained in the handbook are subject to change or removal at the sole and exclusive discretion of the employer.

Two examples of at-will statements are as follows:

I acknowledge that if hired, I will be an at-will employee. I will be subject to dismissal or discipline without notice or cause, at the discretion of the employer. I understand that no representative of the company, other than the president, has authority to change the terms of an at-will employment and that any such change can occur only in a written employment contract.

I understand that my employment is not governed by any written or oral contract and is considered an at-will arrangement. This means that I am free, as is the company, to terminate the employment relationship at any time for any reason, so long as there is no violation of applicable federal or state law. In the event of employment, I understand that my employment is not for any definite period or succession of periods and is considered an at-will arrangement. That means I am free to terminate my employment at any time for any reason, as is the company, so long as there is no violation of applicable federal or state law.

*A note of caution: Because at-will employment is governed by state laws, in order for an employer to preserve its at-will status, it must follow the regulations of its jurisdiction. This includes the writing of employment-at-will statements.

by the employee during the time of employment. These agreements expressly state that the employer retains all rights, titles, and interests in ideas that are subject to patent laws and developed during the employee's period of hire.

3. *Nonpiracy agreements.* These agreements prohibit ex-employees from soliciting clients or customers of former employers for a specific period of time.

Explicit contracts are enforceable in court when either the employee or employer violates any provisions of the agreement.

Constructive Discharge

It is increasingly common for employees to quit or resign their employment because of acts of alleged discrimination and to subsequently claim that their employment rights were violated through a constructive discharge. That is, they were "forced" to resign because of intolerable working conditions purposefully placed upon them by the employer.[31] Put simply, the employer has forced on an employee working conditions so unreasonable and unfair that the employee has no choice but to quit. In a leading constructive discharge case, *Young v. Southwestern Savings and Loan Association*, the court noted:

> The general rule is that if the employer deliberately makes an employee's working conditions so intolerable that the employee is forced into involuntary resignation, then the employer has encompassed a constructive discharge and is as liable for any illegal conduct involved therein as if he had formally discharged the aggrieved employee.

The courts, by formulating the constructive discharge doctrine, attempt to prevent employers from accomplishing covertly what they are prohibited by law from achieving overtly. For example, unscrupulous employers may want to rid themselves of seemingly undesirable employees by deliberately forcing on them unfavorable working conditions so grievous that employees would rather quit than tolerate the disagreeable conditions.[32] Under this action, the employer may be attempting to limit liability should an employee seek redress through various protective employment statutes. It should be noted that the constructive discharge doctrine does not provide employees with any new employment rights. Rather, through a constructive discharge suit, the employee is only protecting employment safeguards previously granted through laws or court rulings.

Retaliation Discharge

Title VII of the Civil Rights Act, the Age Discrimination in Employment Act, the Americans with Disabilities Act, and other employment laws prohibit employers from retaliating against employees when they exercise their rights under these statutes (see Chapter 3). David Sherwyn, professor of law at Cornell University, states "The rate of retaliation filling with the EEOC is now twice the rate in the 1990s."[33] Unfortunately, more retaliation claims are succeeding in court because employers are perceived by judges and juries as imposing unfavorable working conditions on employees even when discrimination claims are meritless.[34] Employees may believe retaliation occurs when managers transfer them to lower-rated jobs, deny them salary increases or promotions, impose on them unrealistic job assignments, or become belligerent or uncommunicative with them after they file discrimination complaints or receive a favorable settlement.[35]

To prevent retaliation charges, William Kandel, employer defense attorney, encourages employers to implement a separate antiretaliation policy and to train managers and supervisors in acceptable and unacceptable methods to resolve employee complaints.[36] A key component to any antiretaliation policy is to treat employees with dignity and respect. Other suggestions to reduce retaliation discharges include the following:

- Take no adverse employment action against employees when they file discrimination charges. Treat employees as if nothing had happened.

- Be consistent and objective in your treatment of employees. Evaluate employees on performance, not personalities.

- Harbor no animosity toward employees when they file discrimination lawsuits. Treat every employee the way you would want to be treated—fairly.

constructive discharge

An employee's voluntary termination of his or her employment because of harsh, unreasonable employment conditions placed on the individual by the employer

Plant Closing Notification

The federal government, several states, and local jurisdictions have passed legislation restricting the unilateral right of employers to close or relocate their facilities. In 1989, Congress passed the Workers' Adjustment Retraining and Notification Act (WARN), which requires organizations with more than 100 employees to give employees and their communities sixty days notice of any closure or layoff affecting fifty or more full-time employees.[37] Notice must be given to collective bargaining representatives, unrepresented employees, the appropriate state dislocated worker agency, and the highest elected local official. Terminated employees must be notified individually in writing. The Act allows several exemptions, including "unforeseeable circumstances" and "faltering businesses." However, failure to comply with the law can subject employers to liability for back pay, fringe benefits, prejudgment interest, and attorney's fees. WARN does not prohibit employer closings, layoffs, or loss of jobs; the law simply seeks to lessen the hardships caused by job loss.

Privacy Rights

Objective 3

The right of privacy can be regarded as a matter of personal freedom from unwarranted government or business intrusion into personal affairs. The right of privacy—a right well recognized in both law and legal commentary—includes the general principle of "personal autonomy." It largely involves the individual's right to be left alone.[38] Not surprisingly, employees strongly defend their right to workplace privacy.

Employer challenges to privacy rights in the workplace have sparked a heated debate over the extent to which fundamental rights previously thought untouchable may be lessened through the employment relationship. Through company policies and court decisions, employees now realize that privacy rights on the job are more limited than those at home. According to Janis Procter-Murphy, employment attorney, "employee privacy is recognized as one of the most significant workplace issues facing companies today."[39]

Employers defend their intrusion into employee privacy by noting their legitimate interest in some of the personal affairs of employees, particularly when those affairs (such as drug use, criminal activity, and co worker dating) may directly affect employee productivity and workplace safety and/or morale.[40] Court cases regarding workplace privacy generally attempt to balance an employee's legitimate expectation of privacy against the employer's need to supervise and control the efficient operation of the organization. In this section, we address the important workplace privacy issues of substance abuse and drug testing, searches and monitoring, e-mail privacy, access to personnel files, employee conduct outside the workplace, and genetic testing.

Substance Abuse and Drug Testing

Consider these facts. Compared with nonabusing employees, substance abusers:

- are 10 times as likely to miss work than those who are clear and alert
- are 3.6 times as likely to be involved in on-the-job accidents
- are 5 times as likely to file workers' compensation claims
- are 33 percent less productive
- use 16 times as many health care benefits[41]

In 2005, the U.S. Department of Labor reported that three-fourths of adults who use illegal drugs are employed. There were 12.9 million employed illicit drug users in 2005.[42] It is estimated that drug abuse by employees costs U.S. employers $75 billion every year in terms of safety risks, theft, reduced productivity, accidents, and benefits costs. Furthermore, in these litigious times, the failure of an employer to ensure a safe and drug-free workplace can result in astronomical liability claims when consumers are injured because of a negligent employee or a faulty product. To fight the battle of workplace drugs, 97 percent of Fortune 500 companies have drug-free workplace policies, and according to the American Medical Association, 67 percent of employers have drug testing policies.

Safety-Sensitive Jobs. Drug testing is most prevalent among employees in sensitive positions within the public sector, in organizations doing business with the federal government, and in public and private transportation companies. The definition of *sensitive position* has been formulated by the courts to include employees holding positions requiring top secret national security clearance, those working in the interdiction of dangerous drugs, uniformed police officers and firefighters, transportation safety positions, and employees working in the nuclear power industry. These employees can be required to submit to a drug test when "reasonable suspicion" for a drug test exists and the employer's testing procedures are also reasonable. Under the Omnibus Transportation Employee Testing Act of 1991, employers are legally required to test for drugs in transportation-related occupations, including airline, railroad, trucking, and public transport facilities.

Private Sector Employers. Managers and supervisors need to understand that legislation on drug testing in the private sector is fragmented and largely regulated by individual states. States with restrictive drug testing laws generally prohibit testing for drugs except in very specific circumstances. Pro-drug testing states generally permit testing, provided that strict testing procedures are followed. Unless state or local laws either restrict or prohibit drug testing, private employers have a right to require employees to submit to a urinalysis or blood test when *reasonable suspicion* or *probable cause* exists.[43] Reasonable suspicion could include observable safety, conduct, or performance problems; excessive absenteeism or tardiness; or increased difficulty in working cooperatively with supervisors or coworkers. Employers who want to implement mandatory or random drug testing programs may face more stringent state court restrictions. According to one legal authority, "Employers should be especially careful in deciding whether to use random testing and will not be able to do so for non-safety-sensitive jobs in a number of states."[44]

Drug-Free Workplace Act of 1988. This federal act applies to organizations with government contracts of $25,000 or more.[45] Among other things, the Act requires employers to publish and furnish to employees a policy statement prohibiting drug usage at work, to inform employees about the dangers of drugs, and to list options available for drug counseling. Additionally, employers must notify the federal contracting agency of any employees who have been convicted of a drug-related criminal offense.

Americans with Disabilities Act. Employers subject to the Americans with Disabilities Act (see Chapter 3) must comply with the law's provisions regarding drug addiction. The ADA clearly exempts from coverage any employee or job applicant who "is currently engaging in the illegal use of drugs." Illegal drug users are not considered to be "individuals with a disability." However, recovering or recovered drug addicts are included under the law's provisions. As the law states,

> Nothing in the ADA shall be construed to exclude as an individual with a disability an individual who—
>
> (1) has successfully completed a supervised drug rehabilitation program and is no longer engaging in the illegal use of drugs, or has otherwise been rehabilitated successfully and is no longer engaging in such use;
>
> (2) is participating in a supervised rehabilitation program and is no longer engaging in such use.[46]

The ADA also protects employees addicted to legal drugs obtained legally. For example, an employee who lawfully takes pain medication and subsequently becomes addicted to the medication satisfies the ADA definition of an individual with a disability.

Drug Testing.   Urinalysis is by far the method of choice for employers who test for drugs, although employers also use blood sampling and hair sampling. Some of the sharpest criticism of drug testing concerns the reliability of these testing methods to identify someone currently under the influence of a drug. Three problems are noteworthy. First, employees or job applicants may attempt to beat drug testing procedures. "Cheaters" may try to dilute urine samples, thereby helping rid the body of toxins. Another method is to add chemicals to a urine specimen, making the drugs undetectable or disrupting the testing process itself. Second, illegal substances remain in urine for various periods of time: cocaine for approximately 72 hours, marijuana for three weeks or longer.[47] Therefore, an employee may test positive for a drug days or weeks after using it. Third, urine tests become problematic when testing equipment is miscalibrated or insufficiently cleaned, samples become contaminated, and chain-of-custody problems occur. (*Chain-of-custody* documentation accounts for the integrity of each urine specimen by tracking its handling and storage from point of collection to final disposition.) Any of these difficulties can cause a *false positive* test result, in which a particular drug is mistakenly identified in a specimen. Importantly, it is recommended that the results of drug tests be provided only to those who need to know—for example, supervisors or HR staff members—and not to other coworkers or disinterested managers. Boeing, 3M, United Airlines, and Motorola use an independent medical review officer (MRO) to ensure the integrity of their drug testing programs. (MROs are required in certain states for tests mandated by the federal government.)

An alternative to drug testing is to evaluate an employee's suitability for work through *impairment testing*. Also called fitness-for-duty or performance-based testing, impairment testing measures whether an employee is alert enough for work. One impairment test requires an employee to keep a cursor on track during a video game–like simulation. Another testing technique evaluates an employee's eye movements. The employee looks into a dark viewport, then follows a light with his or her eyes. Test results, when compared against baseline data gathered earlier on the employee, mimic those of a sobriety test for probable-cause impairment. One advantage of impairment testing is that it focuses on workplace conduct rather than off-duty behavior. Furthermore, it identifies employees who are impaired because of problems that a drug test cannot spot: fatigue, stress, and alcohol use.

Drug-Free Workplace Policies. Both HR professionals and legal experts highly recommend that employers implement a "zero tolerance" drug-free workplace policy. The policy should state under what conditions employees may be subject to a drug test, the testing procedures used, and the consequences of a positive report. Figure 13.3 provides recommendations for an extensive drug-free work policy.[48]

Electronic Surveillance and Monitoring

- General Electric employs tiny fish-eye lenses installed behind pinholes in walls and ceilings to observe employees suspected of crimes.

- DuPont uses long-distance cameras to watch employees on its loading docks.

- Mervyn's department stores issue employees clear plastic bags for carrying personal belongings. The bags are checked as they enter and leave work.

- The Cheesecake Factory, a restaurant chain, uses video surveillance of kitchens, dining rooms, and hostess stations.

While these examples may seem a violation of privacy rights, it is not uncommon for employers to view employee conduct through surveillance techniques. While most workplace surveillance must have some legitimate business purpose, very few federal legal controls protect workers from being watched. Notes one legal scholar, "In general, employers can train video cameras on their employees without significant legal concerns." State laws, however, set their own regulations on how much prying employees must tolerate.

Why do companies use surveillance technology to watch employee activities? The primary answer is employee theft.[49] The U.S. Chamber of Commerce estimates that employee theft (stealing merchandise, supplies, or equipment; selling information; embezzlement; "time theft"; computer crime; and so on) costs U.S. businesses $40 billion annually. According to U.S. Department of Commerce estimates, employee theft is responsible for 30 percent of all business failures. In one study, results showed that "[a]n astounding 95 percent of all businesses experience

Monitoring employee behavior is an important deterrent to illegal conduct of employees.

© DIGITAL VISION/GETTY IMAGES

FIGURE

13.3

Recommendations for a Drug-Free Workplace Policy

1. Adopt a written zero tolerance drug-free workplace policy and provide a copy to all employees. A signed copy should be placed in the employee's personnel file.

2. Post "We Are a Drug-Free Workplace" signs where employees will widely observe them.

3. Provide employees with substance abuse prevention educational materials. Arrange substance abuse awareness training for employees and managers.

4. Perform preemployment drug testing on all new hires.

5. Advise employees that they are subject to drug testing when "reasonable suspicion" exists.

6. Provide for follow-up testing to ensure that an employee remains drug-free after return from a substance abuse treatment program.

7. Provide for "postaccident" drug testing when justified by property loss or damage, serious injury, or death.

8. Use only federally or state-approved certified labs for analysis.

9. Utilize the services of a medical review officer for all positive drug test results.

10. Maintain strict confidentiality of all test results. Provide information only on a "need-to-know" basis.

11. Apply terms of a written policy strictly, fairly, and equally among employees and managers.

employee theft." Beyond employee theft, employers may also watch employees to ensure employee safety in parking lots and remote workplace areas, in dealings with customers, to prevent harassment, and for legal concerns.[50]

One of the most common means of electronic monitoring by employers is telephone surveillance to ensure that customer requests are handled properly and to prevent unwarranted employee misconduct such as theft, wasted time, or harassment.[51] Employers have the right to monitor employees, provided they do it for compelling business reasons and employees have been informed that their calls will be monitored. However, a federal law, the Electronic Communications Privacy Act (ECPA), places some major limitations on that right.[52] The ECPA restricts employers from intercepting wire, oral, or electronic communications. Under the law, if an employee receives a personal call, the employer must hang up as soon as he or she realizes the call is personal. As noted by one legal authority, "Personal calls can be monitored only to the degree needed to determine that they are indeed personal."[53]

E-Mail, Internet, and Voice Mail Privacy

The benefits of e-mail, the Internet, and voice mail are many; they provide instant delivery of messages, facilitate teamwork, increase time efficiency, offer access to global information, and promote flexible work arrangements. Unfortunately, technology also permits employees to act in unscrupulous, inappropriate, and unauthorized ways, creating ethical, productivity, and legal problems for employers. These illegitimate uses of technology cause employers to monitor the conduct of employees, creating significant privacy issues for both employees and managers.[54]

In a survey conducted by the Society for Human Resource Management, 74 percent of respondents said they monitor the Internet usage and e-mail messages of their employees. Marion Walker, privacy rights attorney, notes, "The bottom line is, anyone who turns on an employer's computer has no right to expect privacy.[55] Interestingly, even with the wide application of Internet and e-mail usage, one study showed that employees are still largely uneducated about the risks of using e-mail accounts and the problems they may encounter.[56]

Why do employers monitor their employees? The reasons are varied: to prevent intimidating behavior of employees, to ensure effective use of company time, to prevent employee gossip, to eliminate the surfing of pornographic Web sites, to stop employees from doing personal business on company time, or to ensure employee safety including the prevention of sexual harassment or cyberstalking.[57] For example, a sexual harassment suit cost Chevron $2.2 million because an employee sent coarse messages over the company e-mail system. Additionally, employee monitoring is done to prevent personal information from becoming accessible to those with prying eyes or "hackers" who might use the information inappropriately.

Employers have a great latitude to monitor their own equipment. Court cases governing e-mail and the Internet generally grant to employers the right to monitor materials created, received, or sent for business-related reasons. Employees who erase their messages may wrongly assume their messages are gone when deleted. Although employees may assume that their right to privacy extends to e-mail, the Internet, or voice mail messages, it does not. Furthermore, employees can be disciplined or terminated for inappropriate e-mail messages or Internet use.[58] HR experts and legal authorities strongly encourage employers to develop clear policies and guidelines that explain to employees how e-mail, the Internet, and voice mail are to be used, including when and under what conditions employees can be monitored[59] (see Figure 13.4). As with other employment policies, employees should sign a form indicating that they have read and understand the policy.[60]

Searches

To help fight employee theft, the courts have allowed searches of lockers, desks, suitcases, toolboxes, and general work areas when adequate justification exists and employees have received proper notification beforehand. Employees have limited reasonable expectation of privacy in places where work rules that provide for inspections have been put into effect. They must comply with probable-cause searches by

---

FIGURE 13.4

E-Mail, Internet, and Voice Mail: Policy Guidelines

E-mail, Internet, and voice mail policies seek to reduce an employee's reasonable expectation of privacy balanced against the employer's legitimate business reasons for monitoring employee conduct. A comprehensive e-mail, Internet, and voice mail policy would cover the following:

- Ensure compliance with federal and state legislation.
- Specify the circumstances, if any, under which the system can be used for personal business.
- Specify that confidential information not be sent on the network.
- Set forth the conditions under which monitoring will be done—by whom, how frequently, and with what notification to employees.
- Specify that e-mail and voice mail information be sent only to users who need it for business purposes.
- Expressly prohibit use of e-mail or voice mail to harass others or to send anonymous messages.
- Make clear that employees have no privacy rights in any material delivered or received through e-mail or voice mail.
- Specify that employees who violate the policy are subject to discipline, including discharge.

employers, and they can be appropriately disciplined, normally for insubordination, for refusing to comply with search requests. Importantly, absent emergencies or other special circumstances, random searches of employees' personal belongings or company facilities should be avoided. Random searches likely will result in employee anger and claims of privacy rights—with concomitant costs in productivity.

Managers must be diligent when conducting employee searches. Improper searches can lead to employee lawsuits charging the employer with invasion of privacy, defamation of character, and negligent infliction of emotional distress. Employers are advised to develop a HR search policy based on the following guidelines:

1. The search policy should be widely publicized and should advocate a probable or compelling reason for the search.

2. The search policy should be applied in a reasonable, evenhanded manner.

3. When possible, searches should be conducted in private.

4. The employer should attempt to obtain the employee's consent prior to the search.

5. The search should be conducted in a humane and discreet manner to avoid infliction of emotional distress.

6. The penalty for refusing to consent to a search should be specified.

Some searches are more intrusive to employees than others. For example, "strip searches" are likely to inflict emotional distress and should be avoided. Likewise, any touching of employees for hidden items should be minimized, and if conducted, the search should be made by a person of the same sex.

Access to Personnel Files

The information kept in an employee's personnel file can have a significant impact—positive or negative—on career development. The personnel file, typically kept by the HR department, can contain performance appraisals, salary notices, investigatory reports, credit checks, criminal records, test scores, and family data. Errors and/or omissions in personnel files or access to the files by unauthorized people can create employment or personal hardships.

Legislation at the federal level (see Figure 13.5) and laws in various states permit employees to inspect their own personnel files. How much access is allowed varies from state to state.[61] For example, employers can prohibit employees from viewing information that might violate the privacy of others. Reference letters and criminal investigation reports are of this nature. A state law can limit the employee to copies of documents that he or she has signed, such as performance evaluations or job applications. The states that grant employees the privilege to see their personnel files generally provide:

- The right to know of the existence of one's personnel file

- The right to inspect one's own personnel file

- The right to correct inaccurate data in the file

Typically, if a state law allows employees to examine their files, employers can insist that someone from HR, or a supervisor, be present to ensure that nothing is taken, added, or changed. Even in the absence of specific legislation, most employers give their employees access to their personnel files. Employment professionals

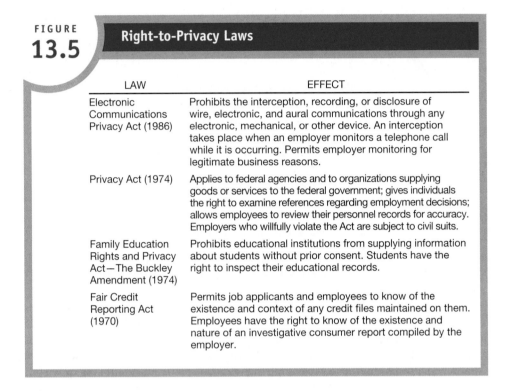

FIGURE
13.5

Right-to-Privacy Laws

LAW	EFFECT
Electronic Communications Privacy Act (1986)	Prohibits the interception, recording, or disclosure of wire, electronic, and aural communications through any electronic, mechanical, or other device. An interception takes place when an employer monitors a telephone call while it is occurring. Permits employer monitoring for legitimate business reasons.
Privacy Act (1974)	Applies to federal agencies and to organizations supplying goods or services to the federal government; gives individuals the right to examine references regarding employment decisions; allows employees to review their personnel records for accuracy. Employers who willfully violate the Act are subject to civil suits.
Family Education Rights and Privacy Act—The Buckley Amendment (1974)	Prohibits educational institutions from supplying information about students without prior consent. Students have the right to inspect their educational records.
Fair Credit Reporting Act (1970)	Permits job applicants and employees to know of the existence and context of any credit files maintained on them. Employees have the right to know of the existence and nature of an investigative consumer report compiled by the employer.

recommend that organizations develop a policy on employee files that includes, as a minimum, the points noted in Figure 13.6.

Medical information of employees requires special handling. The Americans with Disabilities Act (discussed in Chapter 3) requires that an employee's medical history be kept in a file separate from other personal information. Also, new medical privacy regulations contained in the Health Insurance Portability and Accountability Act (HIPAA) mandate that covered employers safeguard health information provided to employers by insurers or health care providers—doctors, group medical plans, and so on. HIPAA clearly states that an individual's past, present, or future health information be used on a limited basis. Therefore, as a general rule, an employee's medical information must be handled in a sensitive and confidential manner.

Employee Conduct outside the Workplace

Consider the following case. On Monday morning the owner of ABC Corporation reads in the newspaper that a company employee has been charged with robbery and assault on a local convenience store owner. The employee has been released pending trial. A phone call to the employee's supervisor reveals that the employee has reported to work. What should the owner do?

Legal authorities generally conclude that the off-duty behavior of employees is not subject to employer disciplinary action. Case law suggests that misconduct outside the workplace may not, in some circumstances, be a lawful justification for employee discipline. Organizations that want to discipline employees for off-duty misconduct must establish a clear relationship between the misconduct and its negative effect on other employees or the organization.[62] This might be established, for example,

FIGURE
13.6

Personnel Files: Policy Guidelines

- Ensure compliance with applicable state laws.
- Define exactly what information is to be kept in employee files.
- Develop different categories of personnel information, depending on legal requirements and organizational needs.
- Specify where, when, how, and under what circumstances employees may review or copy their files.
- Identify company individuals allowed to view personnel files.
- Prohibit the collection of information that could be viewed as discriminatory or could form the basis for an invasion-of-privacy suit.
- Audit employment records on a regular basis to remove irrelevant, outdated, or inaccurate information.

in cases in which off-duty criminal misconduct (such as child molestation) creates a disruptive impact on the workplace. Another example might be when the public nature of the employee's job (such as police or fire department personnel) creates an image problem for the organization. Because of skyrocketing medical costs (see Chapter 11), some employers have implemented bans on off-duty smoking or weight restriction. However, before banning specific off-duty behavioral conduct, employers are advised to obtain legal advice. Generally, little of what an employee does outside the workplace bears discipline by the employer.

Workplace Romances

Workplace romances create a particular dilemma for organizations. The concern is employer liability if a coworker, supervisor-subordinate, or other power-differentiated romance goes sour, leading to charges of sexual harassment.[63] Acceptable behavior in a consensual relationship between employees can become harassing behavior if one party to the relationship no longer welcomes the conduct. Organizations may also increase the potential for workplace violence should a scorned lover seek violent revenge at the work site.

Furthermore, workplace romances can lead to employee charges of favoritism against a coworker involved in a supervisor-subordinate romance. These "reverse harassment" claims are based on preferential treatment given an employee engaged in a romantic affair. Workplace romances can also create morale problems when other employees feel unfairly treated; such situations can lead to jealousy, resentment, and hard feelings.[64] To minimize the negative affects of a work relationship gone bad, some employers have dating parties sign *consensual relationship agreements*, also known as "love contracts." These agreements specifically outline the company's policy on workplace dating.[65]

Body Art

Tattoos and body piercing are increasingly popular, particularly among Generation X and Y workers. When body art is visible on the job, it raises issues such as customer discomfort, corporate culture, and potential safe threats to workers. Employers have the right to establish reasonable standards for grooming, attire, and tattoos and facial piercing.[66] However, policies on appearance require a highly individual response depending on the nature of the organization and the type of job safety concerns or public appearance standards.[67]

Genetic Testing

Advances in genetic research now make it possible to identify the genetic basis for human diseases and illnesses.[68] Genetic findings present opportunities for individualized prevention strategies and early detection and treatment. Unfortunately, knowledge gained through genetic testing can also be used discreetly by employers to discriminate against or stigmatize individuals applying for employment or individuals currently employed. For example, genetic testing can identify an individual's risk of developing common disorders such as cancer, heart disease, or diabetes.

Because employee diseases and illnesses raise employment costs, employers may avoid hiring or retaining individuals who they believe are likely to become unduly sick, resign, or retire early, thus creating additional recruitment, training, or medical costs. Not surprisingly, when employers use genetic tests as a means to deny employment opportunities to workers, the tests raise important moral and ethical concerns, not to mention privacy issues. However, employers must remember that there is no scientific evidence to substantiate a relationship between unexpected genetic factors and an individual's ability to perform his or her job.

Few federal or state laws or court decisions govern an employer's use of genetic information. Genetic testing, however, likely violates the antidiscrimination mandates of Title VII of the Civil Rights Act and the Americans with Disabilities Act. Future legislation—either federal or state—to prohibit genetic discrimination in employment is uncertain.[69]

DISCIPLINARY POLICIES AND PROCEDURES

4 | Objective

The rights of managers to discipline and discharge employees are increasingly limited. There is thus a great need for managers at all levels to understand discipline procedures. Disciplinary action taken against an employee must be for justifiable reasons, and there must be effective policies and procedures to govern its use. Such policies and procedures assist those responsible for taking disciplinary action and help ensure that employees will receive fair and constructive treatment. Equally important, these guidelines help prevent disciplinary action from being voided or reversed through the appeal system.

Disciplinary policies and procedures should extend to a number of important areas to ensure thorough coverage. Figure 13.7 presents a disciplinary model that illustrates the areas where provisions should be established. The model also shows the logical sequence in which disciplinary steps must be carried out to ensure enforceable decisions.

A major responsibility of the HR department is to develop and to have top management approve its disciplinary policies and procedures. The HR department is also responsible for ensuring that disciplinary policies, as well as the disciplinary action taken against employees, are consistent with the labor agreement (if one exists) and conform to current laws. However, the primary responsibility for preventing or correcting disciplinary problems rests with an employee's immediate supervisor. This person is best able to observe evidence of unsatisfactory behavior or performance and to discuss the matter with the employee. Should discipline become necessary, the employee's immediate supervisor is the logical person to apply the company's disciplinary procedure and monitor employee improvement.

FIGURE
13.7

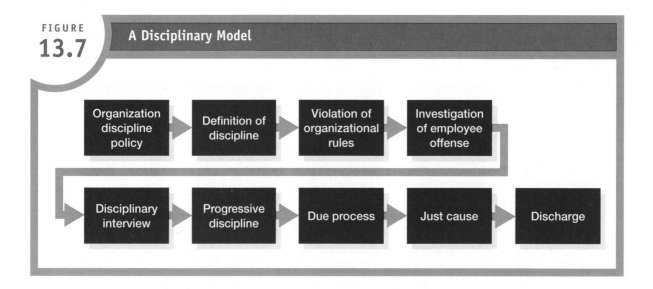

A Disciplinary Model

Organization discipline policy → Definition of discipline → Violation of organizational rules → Investigation of employee offense → Disciplinary interview → Progressive discipline → Due process → Just cause → Discharge

The Results of Inaction

Figure 13.8 lists the more common disciplinary problems identified by managers. Failure to take disciplinary action in any of these areas only serves to aggravate a problem that eventually must be resolved. Failure to act implies that the performance of the employee concerned has been satisfactory or that management is unwilling to take corrective action. Grant Freeland, consultant with Boston Consulting Group, states, "Few things de-motivate an organization faster than tolerating and retaining low performers."[70] If disciplinary action is eventually taken, the delay will make it more difficult to justify the action if appealed. In defending against such an appeal, the employer is likely to be asked why an employee who had not been performing or behaving satisfactorily was not previously disciplined.[71] An even more damaging question might be: "Why did that employee receive satisfactory performance ratings (or perhaps even merit raises)?" Such contradictions in practice can only aid employees in successfully challenging management's corrective actions.

HR professionals note that perhaps the most prevalent reason for failure to take corrective action is lack of regular and candid performance evaluations that would enable managers to discipline poor performers with minimal legal risk. Unfortunately, poor work performance, work that a manager suddenly claims is intolerable, is often accompanied by years of performance evaluations that say "meets expectations." Gilbert Casellas, former chairman of the U.S. Equal Employment Opportunity Commission, states, "Without candor, i.e., 'fear of frankness,' poor and mediocre performers will continue to instill 'fear of firing' and increase the risks of future litigation."[72] Unfortunately, some supervisors try to build a case to justify their corrective actions only after they have decided that a particular employee should be discharged. Other common reasons given by supervisors for their failure to impose a disciplinary penalty include:

- Supervisors believed they would receive little or no support from higher management for the disciplinary action.

- The supervisor was uncertain of the facts underlying the situation requiring disciplinary action.

FIGURE
13.8

Common Disciplinary Problems

ATTENDANCE PROBLEMS

- Unexcused absence
- Chronic absenteeism
- Unexcused/excessive tardiness
- Leaving without permission

DISHONESTY AND RELATED PROBLEMS

- Theft
- Falsifying employment application
- Willfully damaging organizational property
- Punching another employee's time card
- Falsifying work records

WORK PERFORMANCE PROBLEMS

- Failure to complete work assignments
- Producing substandard products or services
- Failure to meet established production requirements

ON-THE-JOB BEHAVIOR PROBLEMS

- Bullying
- Intoxication at work
- Insubordination
- Horseplay
- Smoking in unauthorized places
- Fighting
- Gambling
- Failure to use safety devices
- Failure to report injuries
- Carelessness
- Sleeping on the job
- Using abusive or threatening language with supervisors
- Possession of narcotics or alcohol
- Possession of firearms or other weapons
- Sexual harassment

- Failure by the supervisor to discipline employees in the past for a certain infraction caused the supervisor to forego current disciplinary action in order to appear consistent.

- The supervisor wanted to be seen as a likable person.

Setting Organizational Rules

The setting of organizational rules is the foundation for an effective disciplinary system. These rules govern the type of behavior expected of employees. Organizations as diverse as Gerber Products, Wal-Mart, JetBlue, and Staples have written policies explaining the type of conduct required of employees. Because employee behavior standards are established through the setting of organizational rules and regulations, the following suggestions may help reduce problems in this area:

1. Rules should be widely disseminated and known to all employees. It should not be assumed that employees know all the rules.

2. Rules should be reviewed periodically—perhaps annually—especially those rules critical to work success.

3. The reasons for a rule should always be explained. Acceptance of an organizational rule is greater when employees understand the reasons behind it.

4. Rules should always be written. Ambiguity should be avoided, since this can result in different interpretations of the rules by different supervisors.

5. Rules must be reasonable and relate to the safe and efficient operation of the organization. Rules should not be made simply because of personal likes or dislikes.

6. If management has been lax in the enforcement of a rule, the rule must be restated, along with the consequences for its violation, before disciplinary action can begin.

7. Employees should sign a document stating that they have read and understand the organizational rules.

When seeking reasons for unsatisfactory behavior, supervisors must keep in mind that employees may not be aware of certain work rules. Before initiating any disciplinary action, therefore, it is essential that supervisors determine whether they have given their employees careful and thorough orientation in the rules and regulations relating to their jobs. In fact, the proper communication of organizational rules and regulations is so important that labor arbitrators cite *neglect in communicating rules* as a major reason for reversing the disciplinary action taken against an employee.[73]

Defining Discipline

Objective 5

discipline
(1) Treatment that punishes, (2) orderly behavior in an organizational setting, or (3) training that molds and strengthens desirable conduct—or corrects undesirable conduct—and develops self-control

In management seminars conducted by the authors of this text, when managers are asked to define the word *discipline*, their most frequent response is that discipline means punishment. Although this answer is not incorrect, it is only one of three possible meanings. As normally defined, discipline has these meanings:

1. Treatment that punishes

2. Orderly behavior in an organizational setting

3. Training that molds and strengthens desirable conduct—or corrects undesirable conduct—and develops self-control

To some managers, discipline is synonymous with force. They equate the term with the punishment of employees who violate rules or regulations. Other managers think of discipline as a general state of affairs—a condition of orderliness in which employees conduct themselves according to standards of acceptable behavior. Discipline viewed in this manner can be considered positive when employees willingly practice self-control and respect organizational rules.

The third definition considers discipline a management tool used to correct undesirable employee behavior. Discipline is applied as a constructive means of getting employees to conform to acceptable standards of performance. Many organizations, such as Goodyear Aerospace and Arizona State University, define *discipline* in their policy manuals as training that "corrects, molds, or perfects knowledge, attitudes, behavior, or conduct." Discipline is thus viewed as a way to correct poor employee performance. As these organizations emphasize, discipline should be seen as a method of training employees to perform better or to improve their job attitudes or work behavior.

When taken against employees, disciplinary action should never be thought of as punishment. Discipline can embody a penalty as a means of obtaining a desired result; however, punishment should not be the intent of disciplinary action. Rather, discipline must have as its goal the improvement of the employee's future behavior. To apply discipline in any other way—as punishment or as a way of getting even with employees—can only invite problems for management, including possible wrongful discharge suits.

Investigating the Disciplinary Problem

It is a rare manager who has a good, intuitive sense of how to investigate employee misconduct. Too frequently investigations are conducted in a haphazard manner; worse, they overlook one or more investigative concerns.[74] In conducting an employee investigation, it is important to be objective and to avoid the assumptions, suppositions, and biases that often surround discipline cases. Figure 13.9 lists seven questions to consider in investigating an employee offense. Attending to each question will help ensure a full and fair investigation while providing reliable information free from personal prejudice.

© PANDO HALL/DIGITAL VISION/GETTY IMAGES

Discipline should never be viewed as punishment but rather as a way to correct undesirable employee behavior.

Documentation of Employee Misconduct

"It's too complicated." "I just didn't take time to do it." "I have more important things to do." These are some of the frequent excuses used by managers who have failed to document cases of employee misconduct. The most significant cause of inadequate documentation, however, is that managers have no idea of what constitutes good documentation. Unfortunately, the failure of managers to record employee misconduct accurately can result in the reversal of any subsequent disciplinary action. The maintenance of *accurate* and *complete* work records, therefore, is an essential part of an effective disciplinary system. For documentation to be complete, the following eight items should be included:

1. Date, time, and location of the incident(s)

2. Negative performance or behavior exhibited by the employee—the problem

3. Consequences of that action or behavior on the employee's overall work performance and/or the operation of the employee's work unit

4. Prior discussion(s) with the employee about the problem

5. Disciplinary action to be taken and specific improvement expected

6. Consequences if improvement is not made and a follow-up date

7. The employee's reaction to the supervisor's attempt to change behavior

8. The names of witnesses to the incident (if appropriate)

FIGURE
13.9

Considerations in Disciplinary Investigations

1. In very specific terms, what is the offense charged?
   * Is management sure it fully understands the charge against the employee?
   * Was the employee really terminated for insubordination, or did the employee merely refuse a request by management?

2. Did the employee know he or she was doing something wrong?
   * What rule or provision was violated?
   * How would the employee know of the existence of the rule?
   * Was the employee warned of the consequence?

3. Is the employee guilty?
   * What are the sources of facts?
   * Is there direct or only indirect evidence of guilt?
   * Has anyone talked to the employee to hear his or her side of the situation?

4. Are there extenuating circumstances?
   * Were conflicting orders given by different supervisors?
   * Does anybody have reason to want to "get" this employee?
   * Was the employee provoked by a manager or another employee?

5. Has the rule been uniformly enforced?
   * Have all managers applied this rule consistently?
   * What punishment have previous offenders received?
   * Were any other employees involved in this offense?

6. Is the offense related to the workplace?
   * Is there evidence that the offense hurt the organization?
   * Is management making a moral judgment or a business judgment?

7. What is the employee's past work record?
   * How many years of service has the employee given the organization?
   * How many years or months has the employee held the present job?
   * What is the employee's personnel record as a whole, especially his or her disciplinary record?

When preparing documentation, it is important for a manager to record the incident immediately after the infraction takes place, when the memory of it is still fresh, and to ensure that the record is complete and accurate. Documentation need not be lengthy, but it must include the eight points in the preceding list. Remember, a manager's records of employee misconduct are considered business documents, and as such they are admissible as evidence in arbitration hearings, administrative proceedings, and courts of law. As noted by one manager at a seminar on discipline, "When taking corrective action against an employee, the importance of compiling a complete and objective disciplinary record simply cannot be overstated."

The Investigative Interview

Before any disciplinary action is initiated, an investigative interview should be conducted to make sure employees are fully aware of the offense.[75] This interview is necessary because the supervisor's perceptions of the employee's behavior may not be entirely accurate.[76] The interview should concentrate on how the offense violated the performance and behavior standards of the job. It should avoid getting into personalities or areas unrelated to job performance. Most important, the employee must be given a full opportunity to explain his or her side of the issue so that any deficiencies for which the organization may be responsible are revealed.

In the leading case *NLRB v. Weingarten, Inc.*, the Supreme Court upheld a National Labor Relations Board ruling in favor of the employee's right to representation during an investigative interview in a unionized organization.[77] In the *Weingarten* case, the Court decided that because the employee had reason to believe that the investigative interview might result in action jeopardizing her job security, she had the right to representation.

It is important to note that an employee's right to representation in a unionized organization does not extend to all interviews with management. The *Weingarten* case places some carefully defined limits on an employee's representation rights. For example, representation rights apply only to *investigative interviews*, not to run-of-the-mill shop floor discussion, and the rights arise only in incidents when the employee requests representation and *reasonably believes that discipline may result* from the interview. Within the past twenty-five years, the National Labor Relations Board has flip-flopped four times on whether nonunion employees enjoy *Weingarten* rights. Currently, nonunion employees do not have the right to have a coworker present in an investigatory interview that may lead to disciplinary action. Nor do employees have the right to have attorneys present in these situations.

Approaches to Disciplinary Action

6 | Objective

If a thorough investigation shows that an employee has violated some organization rule, disciplinary action must be imposed. Two approaches to disciplinary action are progressive discipline and positive discipline.

Progressive Discipline

Generally, discipline is imposed in a progressive manner. By definition, progressive discipline is the application of corrective measures by increasing degrees. Progressive discipline is designed to motivate an employee to correct his or her misconduct voluntarily. The technique is aimed at nipping the problem in the bud, using only enough corrective action to remedy the shortcoming. However, the sequence and severity of the disciplinary action vary with the type of offense and the circumstances surrounding it. Because each situation is unique, a number of factors must be considered in determining how severe a disciplinary action should be. Some of the factors to consider were listed in Figure 13.9.

progressive discipline
Application of corrective measures by increasing degrees

The typical progressive discipline procedure includes four steps. From an oral warning (or counseling) that subsequent unsatisfactory behavior or performance will not be tolerated, the action may progress to a written warning, to a suspension without pay, and ultimately to discharge. The "capital punishment" of discharge is utilized only as a last resort. Organizations normally use lower forms of disciplinary action for less severe performance problems. It is important for managers to remember that three important things occur when progressive discipline is applied properly:

1. Employees always know where they stand regarding offenses.

2. Employees know what improvement is expected of them.

3. Employees understand what will happen next if improvement is not made.

Positive Discipline

Some HR professionals believe that progressive discipline has certain flaws, including its intimidating and adversarial nature that prevent it from achieving the intended purpose. For these reasons, organizations such as Saint Alphonsus Regional Medical Center, Ocean Spray, Banner Health, Pennzoil, and Bay Area Rapid Transit are using an approach called positive, or nonpunitive, discipline. Positive discipline is based on the concept that employees must assume responsibility for their personal conduct and job performance.[78]

Positive discipline requires a cooperative environment in which the employee and the supervisor engage in joint discussion and problem-solving to resolve incidents of employee irresponsibility. The approach focuses on early correction of misconduct, with the employee taking total responsibility for resolving the problem. Nothing is imposed by management; all solutions and affirmations are jointly reached. HR managers often describe positive discipline as "nonpunitive discipline that replaces threats and punishment with encouragement."

While positive discipline appears similar to progressive discipline, its emphasis is on giving employees reminders rather than reprimands as a way to improve performance. The technique is implemented in three steps. The first is a conference between the employee and the supervisor. The purpose of this meeting is to find a solution to the problem through discussion, with oral agreement by the employee to improve his or her performance. The supervisor refrains from reprimanding the employee or threatening him or her with further disciplinary action. Supervisors may document this conference, but a written record of this meeting is not placed in the employee's file unless the misconduct occurs again.

If improvement is not made after this first step, the supervisor holds a second conference with the employee to determine why the solution agreed to in the first conference did not work. At this stage, however, a written reminder is given to the employee. This document states the new or repeated solution to the problem, with an affirmation that improvement is the responsibility of the employee and a condition of continued employment.

When both conferences fail to produce the desired results, the third step is to give the employee a one-day *decision-making leave* (a paid leave). The purpose of this paid leave is for the employee to decide whether he or she wishes to continue working for the organization. The organization pays for this leave to demonstrate its desire to retain the person. Also, paying for the leave eliminates the negative effects for the employee of losing a day's pay. Employees given a decision-making leave are instructed to return the following day with a decision either to make a total commitment to improve performance or to quit the organization. If a commitment is not made, the employee is dismissed with the assumption that he or she lacked responsibility toward the organization. The positive discipline process used by Banner Health is shown in Highlights in HRM 2.

Discharging Employees

When employees fail to conform to organizational rules and regulations, the final disciplinary action in many cases is discharge. Because discharge has such serious consequences for the employee—and possibly for the organization—it should be undertaken only after a deliberate and thoughtful review of the case.[79] If an employee is fired, he or she may file a wrongful discharge suit claiming the termination was "without just or sufficient cause," implying a lack of fair treatment by management.

positive, or nonpunitive, discipline

A system of discipline that focuses on early correction of employee misconduct, with the employee taking total responsibility for correcting the problem

HIGHLIGHTS IN HRM

2

Banner Health System Corrective Action Process

A. Management will initiate the *Corrective Action Process* as follows:

1. Coaching may be used to clarify expectations, identify the cause of the failure to meet expectations, develop solutions, or achieve commitment from an Employee to correct conduct or behavior. Coaching may occur prior to the initiation of the Corrective Action Process or at any time during the Corrective Action Process.

2. *Initial Reminder:* the first step in the Corrective Action Process. Management will (i) prepare a Corrective Action Form that sets forth the Employee conduct that needs to be corrected or improved; and (ii) meet with the Employee to discuss the conduct that needs to be corrected or improved and identify the required corrective action. This step may be used by Management when (i) the Employee did not correct or improve his or her conduct after Coaching; or (ii) the Employee has engaged in conduct that warrants corrective action rather than Coaching.

3. *Advanced Reminder:* the second step of the Corrective Action Process. Management will (i) prepare a Corrective Action Form that sets forth the Employee conduct that needs to be corrected or improved; and (ii) meet with the Employee to discuss the conduct that needs to be corrected or improved and identify the required corrective action. This step may be used by Management when (i) the Employee did not correct or improve his or her conduct after a Coaching or an Initial Reminder; or (iii) the Employee has engaged in conduct that warrants a more advanced level of corrective action than the Initial Reminder.

4. *Decision Making Leave ("DML"):* the third step of the Corrective Action Process. Management will (i) prepare a Corrective Action Form that sets forth the Employee conduct that needs to be corrected or improved; and (ii) meet with the Employee to discuss the conduct that needs to be corrected or improved, and the requirement of the Employee to create an individual Corrective Action Plan. This step may be used by Management when (i) the Employee did not correct or improve his or her conduct after Coaching or an Initial Reminder; (ii) the Employee did not correct or improve his or her conduct after an Advanced Reminder; or (iii) the Employee has engaged in conduct that warrants a more advanced level of corrective action than the Initial Reminder or Advanced Reminder.

After Management meets with the Employee, the Employee will be suspended with pay for one (1) day. The purpose of the suspension is to provide the Employee with an opportunity to (i) seriously consider if he/she are willing and capable of satisfying the overall performance expectations by personal improvement and create a Corrective Action Form for achieving the performance expectations; or (ii) resign his or her position. In the event the Employee is sent home early during a scheduled shift, the suspension may be a partial day (consult with Human Resources), or the following scheduled work day.

Banner Health System Corrective Action Process (continued)

B. *Deactivation*: the Initial Reminder is active for a period of six (6) months. The Advanced Reminder and DML are active for a period of twelve (12) months. In the event of an Employee has not been subject to the Corrective Action Process or Coaching during the applicable six (6) or twelve (12) month time period, Management may deactivate the Corrective Action Process. Management may consider past corrective action when evaluating and determining the appropriate disciplinary step in the Corrective Action Process even if the past corrective action step has been deactivated.

C. *Termination*: Management may terminate an Employee when (i) the Employee did not correct or improve his or her conduct during the active period DML; or (ii) the Employee has engaged in Serious Misconduct, at any time prior to or during the Coaching or Corrective Action Process.

D. *Crisis Suspension*: In accordance with the Crisis Suspension Policy, an Employee, including Excepted Employees, may be placed on Crisis Suspension.

Source: Banner Health System Corrective Action Policy used with permission of Banner Health, Phoenix, AZ.

If an employee termination is to be upheld for good cause, what constitutes fair employee treatment? This question is not easily answered, but standards governing just cause discharge do exist in the form of rules developed in the field of labor arbitration.[80] These rules consist of a set of guidelines that are applied by arbitrators to dismissal cases to determine if management had just cause for the termination. These guidelines are normally set forth in the form of questions, provided in Figure 13.10. For example, before discharging an employee, did the manager forewarn the person of possible disciplinary action? A no answer to any of the seven questions in the figure generally means that just cause was not established and that management's decision to terminate was arbitrary, capricious, or discriminatory. The significance of these guidelines is that they are being applied not only by arbitrators in discharge cases, but also by judges in wrongful discharge suits and by the EEOC in discrimination violations such as sexual harassment. It is critical that managers at all levels understand the just cause guidelines, including their proper application.

Informing the Employee

Regardless of the reasons for a discharge, it should be done with personal consideration for the employee affected. Every effort should be made to ease the trauma a discharge creates.[81] The employee must be informed honestly, yet tactfully, of the exact reasons for the action. Such candor can help the employee face the problem and adjust to it in a constructive manner.

Managers may wish to discuss, and even rehearse, with their peers the upcoming termination meeting. This practice can ensure that all important points are covered while giving confidence to the manager. While managers agree that there is no single

FIGURE
13.10

"Just Cause" Discharge Guidelines

1. Did the organization forewarn the employee of the possible disciplinary consequences of his or her action?

2. Were management's requirements of the employee reasonable in relation to the orderly, efficient, and safe operation of the organization's business?

3. Did management, before discharging the employee, make a reasonable effort to establish that the employee's performance was unsatisfactory?

4. Was the organization's investigation conducted in a fair and objective manner?

5. Did the investigation produce sufficient evidence of proof of guilt as charged?

6. Has management treated this employee under its rules, orders, and penalties as it has other employees in similar circumstances?

7. Did the discharge fit the misconduct, considering the seriousness of the proven offense, the employee's service record, and any mitigating circumstances?

right way to conduct the discharge meeting, the following guidelines will help make the discussion more effective:

1. Come to the point within the first two or three minutes, and list in a logical order all reasons for the termination.[82]

2. Be straightforward and firm, yet tactful, and remain resolute in your decision.

3. Make the discussion private, businesslike, and fairly brief.

4. Do not mix the good with the bad. Trying to sugarcoat the problem sends a mixed message to the employee.

5. Avoid making accusations against the employee and injecting personal feelings into the discussion.

6. Avoid bringing up any personality differences between you and the employee.

7. Provide any information concerning severance pay and the status of benefits and coverage.

8. Explain how you will handle employment inquiries from future employers.[83]

Termination meetings should be held in a neutral location, such as a conference room, to prevent the employee from feeling unfairly treated. When discussing the termination, management must never provoke the employee or allow the employee to become belligerent toward management. Should the employee become agitated or show signs of hostility, the meeting should be stopped immediately with notification given to security or the HR department.

Finally, when terminated employees are escorted off the premises, the removal must not serve to defame the employee. Managers should not give peers the impression that the terminated employee was dishonest or untrustworthy. Furthermore, managers are advised never to discuss the discharge or "bad-mouth" the terminated employee with other employees, customers, or other individuals. Managers should be very tight-lipped in this area. Increasingly, terminated employees are pursuing lawsuits that go beyond the issue of whether their discharge was for business-related reasons.

Due Process

due process

An employee's right to present his or her position during a displinary action

Management has traditionally possessed the right to direct employees and to take corrective action when needed. Nevertheless, when employees are alleged to have violated organizational rules, many individuals also believe that employees should not be disciplined without the protection of due process. HR managers normally define due process as the employee's right to be heard—the right of the employee to tell his or her side of the story regarding the alleged infraction of organizational rules. Due process serves to ensure that a full and fair investigation of employee misconduct occurs. Normally, due process is provided employees through the employer's appeals procedure. Importantly, employers can normally expect to have their terminations overturned—even when justified—when employees are denied their due process rights.

Alternative Dispute Resolution Procedures

Objective 7

alternative dispute resolution (ADR)

A term applied to different types of employee complaint or dispute resolution procedures

In unionized workplaces, grievance procedures are stated in virtually all labor agreements. In nonunion organizations, however, alternative dispute resolution (ADR) procedures are a developing method to address employee complaints.[84] The employer's interest stems from the desire to meet employees' expectations for fair treatment in the workplace while guaranteeing them due process—in the hope of minimizing discrimination claims or wrongful discharge suits. ADR procedures received a boost from the U.S. Supreme Court when, in *Gilmer v. Interstate/Johnson Lane Corp.*, the Court enforced a private agreement that required the arbitration of an age discrimination claim.[85] The mandatory use of arbitration to resolve employment disputes received additional support when the U.S. Supreme Court held in *Circuit City Stores, Inc. v. Adams*[86] that employers may require employees to bring their work-related disputes before an arbitrator rather than file a lawsuit. This major decision allows employers to establish arbitration programs as a means for employees to resolve employment complaints—replacing court action as an option. Additionally, Section 118 of the Civil Rights Act of 1991 encourages the use of ADR procedures, including arbitration.

While the right to adopt arbitration agreements is supported by court decisions, arbitration agreements—to be enforceable—must be fair and equitable to both employees and employers.[87] Employers cannot "stack the deck" against employees by imposing rules on employees that clearly favor the employer. As one legal expert has noted, "As much as possible, the agreement should provide employees with the same rights and remedies that they would have enjoyed had their day in court been available to them."[88]

Using the Internet

Current federal and state laws and leading court decisions regarding alternative dispute resolution procedures can be found on the American Arbitration Association Web site. Go to the Student Resources at:

www.cengage.com/ management/bohlander

Step-Review Systems

step-review system

A system for reviewing employee complaints and disputes by successively higher levels of management

As Figure 13.11 illustrates, a step-review system is based on a preestablished set of steps—normally four—for the review of an employee complaint by successively higher levels of management. These procedures are patterned after the union grievance systems we will discuss in Chapter 14. For example, they normally require that the employee's complaint be formalized as a written statement. Managers at each step are required to provide a full response to the complaint within a specified time period, perhaps three to five working days.

FIGURE
13.11

Conventional Step-Review Appeal Procedure

Employee → Supervisor → Department head → HR department → Top management

An employee is sometimes allowed to bypass the meeting with his or her immediate supervisor if the employee fears reprisal from this person. Unlike appeal systems in unionized organizations, however, nonunion appeal procedures ordinarily do not provide for a neutral third party—such as an arbitrator—to serve as the judge of last resort. In most step-review systems, the president, chief executive officer, vice president, or HR director acts as the final authority, and this person's decision is not appealable. Some organizations give employees assistance in preparing their complaint cases. For example, an employee who desires it may be able to get advice and counsel from a designated person in the HR department before discussing the issue with management.

Peer-Review Systems

A peer-review system, also called a complaint committee, is composed of equal numbers of employee representatives and management appointees. Employee representatives are normally elected by secret ballot by their coworkers for a rotating term, whereas management representatives are assigned, also on a rotating basis. A peer-review system functions as a jury because its members weigh evidence, consider arguments, and, after deliberation, vote independently to render a final decision.

Organizations such as Turner Brothers Trucking, Northrop-Grumman, Polaroid, and Citicorp consider one of the benefits of the peer-review system to be the sense of justice that it creates among employees. The peer-review system can be used as the sole method for resolving employee complaints, or it can be used in conjunction with a step-review system. For example, if an employee is not satisfied with management's action at step 1 or 2 in the step-review system, the employee can submit the complaint to the peer-review committee for final resolution.

peer-review system

A system for reviewing employee complaints that utilizes a group composed of equal numbers of employee representatives and management appointees, which functions as a jury because its members weigh evidence, consider arguments, and, after deliberation, vote independently to render a final decision

Open-Door Policy

The open-door policy is an old standby for settling employee complaints. The traditional open-door policy identifies various levels of management above the immediate supervisor that an aggrieved employee may contact; the levels may extend as high as a vice president, president, or chief executive officer. Typically, the person who acts as "the court of last resort" is the HR director or a senior staff official.

The problems with an open-door policy are well documented. Two of its major weaknesses are the unwillingness of managers to listen honestly to employee complaints and worker reluctance to approach managers with their complaints. As an employee once told the authors of this text, "My manager has an open-door policy, but

open-door policy

A policy of settling grievances that identifies various levels of management above the immediate supervisor for employee contact the door is only open one inch." Obviously, this employee felt he had little opportunity to get through to his manager. Other problems are attributed to this system as well. The open-door policy generally fails to guarantee consistent decision-making because what is fair to one manager may seem unfair to another. Higher-level managers tend to support supervisors for fear of undermining authority, and as a system of justice, open-door policies may lack credibility with employees. Still, the open-door policy is often successful when it is supported by all levels of management and when management works to maintain a reputation for being fair and open-minded.

Ombudsman System

ombudsman

A designated individual from whom employees may seek counsel for resolution of their complaints

Rockwell, Johnson & Johnson, Herman Miller, Eastman Kodak, and Pace University are just a few organizations who employ ombudsmen. An ombudsman is a designated individual from whom employees may seek counsel for the resolution of their complaints. The ombudsman listens to an employee's complaint and attempts to resolve it by seeking an equitable solution between the employee and the supervisor. This individual works cooperatively with both sides to reach a settlement, often employing a problem-solving approach to the issue. Gordon Halfacre, ombudsman for faculty and graduate students at Clemson University, notes, "The ombuds is an advocate for a fair process, not an advocate on behalf of individuals or the institution." Because the ombudsman has no authority to finalize a solution to the problem, compromises are highly possible and all concerned tend to feel satisfied with the outcome.

To function successfully, ombudsmen must be able to operate in an atmosphere of confidentiality that does not threaten the security of the managers or subordinates who are involved in a complaint. For example, complaints of sexual harassment, abuse of power, or issues that deal with circumstances that violate the law or unethical behavior (whistle-blowing) require high degrees of confidentiality to protect those involved. While ombudsmen do not have the power to decide employee complaints, it is recommended that they have access to high levels of management to ensure that employee complaints receive fair treatment.

Mediation

mediation

The use of an impartial neutral to reach a compromise decision in employment disputes

mediator

A third party in an employment dispute who meets with one party and then the other in order to suggest compromise solutions or to recommend concessions from each side that will lead to an agreement

Along with arbitration, mediation is fast becoming a popular way to resolve employee complaints. Mediation employs a third-party neutral (called a mediator) to help employees and managers reach voluntary agreement acceptable to both parties. The essence of mediation is compromise. The mediator holds a meeting with the employee and management, listens to the position of each side, gathers facts, and then through discussion, suggestions, and persuasion obtains an agreement that will satisfy the needs and requirements of both sides. A mediator serves primarily as a fact finder and to open up a channel of communication between the parties. Unlike arbitrators, mediators have no power or authority to force either side toward an agreement. They must use their communication skills and the power of persuasion to help the parties resolve their differences. A cornerstone of mediation is that the parties maintain control over the settlement outcome.[89]

Mediation is a flexible process that can be shaped to meet the demands of the parties. Also, it can be used to resolve a wide range of employee complaints, including discrimination claims or traditional workplace disputes.[90] Employees like the process because of its informality. According to one authority, "Mediation might be described as a private discussion assisted by an impartial third party."[91] Settlements fashioned through mediation are readily acceptable by the parties, thus promoting a favorable working relationship.

Discussion and compromise are cornerstones of employment mediation.

© TANYA CONSTANTINE/DIGITAL VISION/GETTY IMAGES

Arbitration

Prompted by the *Gilmer* and *Circuit City* decisions, private employers may require that employees submit their disputes for a binding resolution through arbitration.[92] (Arbitration is fully explained in Chapter 14.) Arbitration is used primarily to resolve discrimination suits in areas of age, gender, sexual harassment, and race.[93] Other workplace issues such as promotions, compensation, discipline, and application of company policies may be arbitrated if allowed in the employer's arbitration program. Employers cite savings in litigation costs and avoidance of time delays and unfavorable publicity as advantages for using arbitration.

While arbitration agreements normally mandate that employees arbitrate their discrimination claims and may prevent employees from suing their employer in court, they cannot prohibit employees from filing discrimination charges with the EEOC and pursuing other statutory rights with government agencies. In *EEOC v. Waffle House Inc.*,[94] the U.S. Supreme Court ruled that employees can file discrimination suits with the EEOC even when the employer has a mandatory arbitration agreement and it is signed by the employee. Writing for the Court, Justice John Paul Stevens noted, "The EEOC has the authority to pursue victim-specific relief regardless of the forum that the employer and the employee have chosen to resolve their dispute."[95]

▓ MANAGERIAL ETHICS IN EMPLOYEE RELATIONS

Throughout this textbook, we have emphasized the legal requirements of HRM. Laws, agency rulings, and court decisions impact all aspects of the employment process—recruitment, selection, performance appraisal, safety and health, labor relations, and

8 | Objective

testing. Managers must comply with governmental regulations to promote an environment free from litigation.

However, beyond what is required by the law is the question of organizational ethics and the ethical—or unethical—behavior engaged in by managers. Ethics can be defined as a set of standards of acceptable conduct and moral judgment. Ethics provides cultural guidelines—organizational or societal—that help us decide between proper or improper conduct.[96] Therefore, ethics, like the legal aspects of HR, permeates all aspects of the employment relationship. For example, managers may adhere to the organization's objective of hiring more protected class members, but how those employees are supervised and treated once employed gets to the issue of managerial ethics.

Compliance with laws and the behavioral treatment of employees are two completely different aspects of the manager's job. While ethical dilemmas will always occur in the supervision of employees, it is how employees are treated that largely distinguishes the ethical organization from the unethical one. Interestingly, a research study, *Employee Trust and Organizational Loyalty*, sponsored by the Society for Human Resource Management, showed that employee perceptions of ethical behavior by their organizational leadership may be the most important driver of employee trust and loyalty. According to the study, of critical interest to employees is the consistent and credible communication of information about the organization's ethical standards and its values, the organization's mission, and its workplace policies.[97] We believe that managerial ethics in employee relations requires honesty in all dealings between employees and their managers, including mutual respect throughout the performance of workplace duties.[98]

Many organizations have their own code of ethics that governs relations with employees and the public at large. This written code focuses attention on ethical values and provides a basis for the organization and individual managers to evaluate their plans and actions. HR departments have been given a greater role in communicating the organization's values and standards, monitoring compliance with its code of ethics, and enforcing the standards throughout the organization. Organizations now have ethics committees and ethics ombudsmen to provide training in ethics to employees. The ultimate goal of ethics training is to avoid unethical behavior and adverse publicity; to gain a strategic advantage; and most of all, to treat employees in a fair and equitable manner, recognizing them as productive members of the organization.

ethics

A set of standards of conduct and moral judgments that help to determine right and wrong behavior

SUMMARY

Objective 1 Employees may claim that they have legal rights guaranteeing them fair and equitable treatment while on the job. Employee rights issues frequently involve employer searches, drug testing, and monitoring of an employee's personal conversations. Employers, however, have the responsibility to provide a safe and secure workplace free from harmful employee acts. When the perceived

rights of employees differ from the reasonable responsibilities of management, conflict can result.

Objective 2 Both employees and employers have rights and expectations in the employment relationship. The employment-at-will doctrine regards the rights of employees and employers to terminate the employment relationship; the implied contract concept is an exception to the employment-at-will doctrine. Under this concept, an employer's oral or written statements may form a contractual obligation that can preclude automatic termination of employees. Constructive discharge occurs when an employee voluntarily terminates employment but subsequently alleges that he or she was forced to quit because of intolerable working conditions imposed by the employer. Employees may claim they are retaliated against when employers punish them for exercising their rights under law or for receiving favorable EEOC or court awards.

Objective 3 Once employed, employees expect certain privacy rights regarding freedom from unwarranted intrusion into their personal affairs. These rights extend over such issues as substance abuse and drug testing; searches and monitoring; off-duty privacy rights; e-mail, Internet, and voice mail privacy; and genetic testing.

Objective 4 The HR department, in combination with other managers, should establish disciplinary policies. This will help achieve both acceptance of the policy and its consistent application. To reduce the need for discipline, organizational rules and procedures should be widely known, reviewed on a regular basis, and written and explained to employees. The rules must relate to the safe and efficient operation of the organization. When managers overlook the enforcement of rules, they must reemphasize the rule and its enforcement before disciplining an employee.

Objective 5 The term *discipline* has three meanings—punishment, orderly behavior, and training of employee conduct. When used with employees, discipline should serve to correct undesirable employee behavior, creating within the employee a desire for self-control. This third definition of discipline can be achieved only when managers conduct a complete and unbiased investigation of employee misconduct. Investigation of employee misconduct begins with proper documentation of wrongdoing. When managers are investigating employee problems, they need to know specifically the infraction of the employee, whether the employee knew of the rule violated, and any extenuating circumstances that might justify the employee's conduct. When employees are to receive discipline, the rule must be uniformly enforced, and the past work record of the employee must be considered.

Objective 6 The two approaches to discipline are progressive discipline and positive discipline. Progressive discipline follows a series of steps based on increasing the degrees of corrective action. The corrective action applied should match the severity of the employee misconduct. Positive discipline, based on reminders, is a cooperative discipline approach in which employees accept responsibility for the desired employee improvement. The focus is on coping with the unsatisfactory performance and dissatisfactions of employees before the problems become major.

Objective 7 Alternative dispute resolution procedures present ways by which employees exercise their due process rights. The most common forms of ADRs are step-review systems, peer-review systems, the open-door system, the ombudsman system, mediation, and arbitration.

Objective 8 Ethics in HRM extends beyond the legal requirements of managing employees. Managers engage in ethical behavior when employees are treated in an objective and fair way and when an employee's personal and work-related rights are respected and valued.

KEY TERMS

alternative dispute resolution
(ADR)
constructive discharge
discipline
due process
employee rights
employment-at-will principle

ethics
mediation
mediator
negligence
ombudsman
open-door policy
peer-review system

positive, or nonpunitive, discipline
progressive discipline
psychological contract
step-review system
whistle-blowing

DISCUSSION QUESTIONS

Objective 1
1. Explain three areas in which employee rights and employer responsibilities could result in conflict. How might this conflict arise?

Objective 2
2. Define the employment-at-will doctrine. What are the three major court exceptions to the doctrine?

Objective 3
3. What are the legislative and court restrictions on employer drug testing in both the private and the public sector?

Objective 4
4. If you were asked to develop a policy on discipline, what topics would you cover in the policy?

Objective 5
5. What should be the purpose of an investigative interview, and what approach should be taken in conducting it?

Objective 5
6. Discuss why documentation is so important to the disciplinary process. What constitutes correct documentation?

Objective 6
7. Describe progressive and positive discipline, noting the differences between these two approaches.

Objective 7
8. What do you think would constitute an effective alternative dispute resolution system? What benefits would you expect from such a system? If you were asked to rule on a discharge case, what facts would you analyze in deciding whether to uphold or reverse the employer's action?

Objective 8
9. Working by yourself, or in a team, identify ethical dilemmas that could arise in the HR areas of selection, performance appraisal, safety and health, privacy rights, and compensation.

BIZFLIX EXERCISES

In Good Company: **Firing an Employee**

This scene from the film *In Good Company* shows Mark Steckle's (Clark Greg) efforts to fire Dan Foreman (Dennis Quaid) and Carter Duryea (Topher Grace). Carefully assess Mark's behavior against the discussion of employee rights and discipline in this chapter.

A corporate takeover brings star advertising executive Dan Foreman a new boss who is half his age. Carter Duryea—Dan's new boss—wants to prove his worth as the new marketing chief at *Sports America*, Waterman Publishing's flagship magazine. Carter applies his unique approaches while dating Dan's daughter, Alex (Scarlett Johansson).

This scene comes from the "Teddy K. is coming" sequence near the film's end. It starts with Mark Steckle saying to Dan Foreman, "Look, we've been carrying your fat, bloated salary for way too long." This scene follows Teddy K.'s (Malcolm McDowell) synergy speech to the assembled employees of his recent acquisition, Waterman Publishing. The film continues with Carter and Dan carrying out their plan to get some new magazine advertising.

What to Watch for and Ask Yourself

- This chapter opened with the observation that managers and supervisors find it hard to discipline employees. Does this observation apply to Mark Steckle? Why or why not?

- Does Mark follow the suggestions shown in Figure 13.2 in trying to end the employment of Dan and Carter?

- The earlier section "Disciplinary Policies and Procedures" offered guidelines and observations on correct approaches to employee discipline. Does Mark follow any of those procedures? If not, which aspects of his behavior deviate from the procedures described earlier?

Learning about Employee Rights

In the constantly changing field of human resources, it is imperative that both HR managers and supervisors be aware of changes that affect the organization and the process of managing employees. Nowhere is this more true than in the growing field of employee rights. As employees demand more job and employment rights regarding drug testing, monitoring, unjust dismissals, off-duty conduct, and genetic testing, employers must be knowledgeable about new laws, court rulings, and the policies of other organizations that influence each area. This knowledge will enable managers to respond to these employee concerns in a positive and proactive manner. Failure to provide employees their rights could lead to costly and embarrassing lawsuits, resulting in diminished employee loyalty or morale. The purpose of this exercise, therefore, is to enable you to familiarize yourself with issues of employee rights.

Assignment

Working individually or in teams, for each of the following employee rights topics, identify and discuss the privacy concerns for both employees and employers. You may wish to review articles in HR journals such as *Labor Law Journal, HRMagazine, Workforce Management, Employee Relations Law Journal,* and *Employee Responsibility and Rights Journal* as you complete this assignment. Answer the questions pertaining to each topic.

- Employment-at-will and wrongful discharge suits
- Substance abuse and drug testing
- Searches and monitoring
- Employee conduct away from the workplace
- Genetic testing
- E-mail, Internet

1. What is the issue concerned with?
2. Why is this issue of current interest to employees and managers?
3. What rights are employees demanding?
4. What, if any, laws or court cases affect this right?
5. Generally, how are employers responding to this employee right?

CASE STUDY 1

Discharged for Off-Duty Behavior

The following case illustrates the off-duty privacy claim of an employee and management's right to uphold the reputation of the company.

Before his termination on Monday, May 6, 2008, John Hilliard worked as a senior sales representative for Advanced Educational Materials (AEM), a provider of high-quality educational books and supplies to junior and senior high schools. During his twelve years of employment, John was recognized as an outstanding employee with close working relationships with the schools he served. His sales record was excellent. John's discharge resulted from what AEM claimed was a serious breach of its code of conduct for employees.

On Saturday, May 4, 2008, due to a chance meeting between John and his manager, Jean Ellison, John was observed leaving an adult video store carrying what his manager described as pornographic magazines and a X-rated video. The following Monday, Jean discussed the incident with AEM's vice-president for sales and a representative from HR. All agreed that John's off-duty behavior constituted a serious violation of the company's code of conduct for employees, which read, in part, "Employee off-duty behavior in no way should reflect unfavorably upon the company, its employees, or sales of any educational materials." AEM has traditionally held its sales representatives to high moral standards because the company sells extensively to public school administrators and teachers.

At his discharge meeting, John vigorously opposed his firing. While he acknowledged making the purchases, he argued strongly that what he did on his personal time was "no business of the company's" and his behavior in no way reflected unfavorably upon AEM or the sales of its products. Besides, he said, "The purchases were made as jokes for a stag party."

Questions

1. Given the facts of this case, should John have been discharged? Explain.
2. Should the sales representatives of AEM be held to a higher standard of personal conduct than sales representatives for other types of organizations? Explain.
3. Should management have considered John's past work record before deciding on discharge? Explain.

Source: This case is based on an actual termination for off-duty misconduct. All names are fictitious.

CASE STUDY 2

You Can't Fire Me! Check Your Policy

Supervisors report that discharging an employee is one of the toughest tasks they perform as managers. Furthermore, termination for absenteeism can be particularly difficult due to the causes of absenteeism and, in some cases, the past work record of the employee. This case illustrates a typical absentee problem faced by management.

Mary Schwartz was employed by Beach Electrical Systems for nine years. For the first six years of her employment, she was considered a model employee. Mary's annual performance reviews were always above average or exceptional, and she was described by her managers as a loyal and dedicated employee. However, things changed rapidly in 2004 when Mary became, as her current manager stated, "an absentee problem."

According to HR department records, in 2005 and 2006 Mary was absent 12 percent and 19 percent of the time, respectively. Her worst year was 2007, when she was absent 27.2 percent of the time. However, unlike other absent employees, Mary was always absent because of genuine and verifiable illnesses or work-related accidents. Mary's supervisor had talked to her periodically about her attendance problem, but she was never given an official warning notice—oral or written—that she would be fired if her attendance record did not improve.

The incident that caused her termination occurred on Thursday, May 20, 2008. On that day her manager notified all department employees (eight in total) that they would need to work overtime on Saturday, May 22, 2008, to complete a critical order for a highly valued and important customer. All employees agreed to work Saturday, except Mary, who cited "personal reasons," which she refused to disclose, for her refusal to work.

On Monday, May 24, 2008, her supervisor, with concurrence from the department manager, terminated her employment for "unsatisfactory attendance." Mary did not dispute the attendance record; however, she filed a grievance through the company's alternative dispute resolution procedure alleging that management did not discharge her according to the organization's published disciplinary policy. She pointed to the section in the policy manual that states, "Employees will be warned for absenteeism before they are terminated." Mary maintained that she was never officially warned as required. Management replied that Mary was well aware of her absentee problem but that warning her would have served no purpose since she was unable to prevent her continued illnesses from occurring. Additionally, her refusal to work overtime on Saturday was a further indication of her lack of concern for her job or the welfare of her company.

Questions

1. What role, if any, should Mary's past work record play in this case? Explain.
2. Does management have a right to know why employees refuse to work overtime? Explain.
3. Evaluate the arguments of Mary Schwartz and management in this case.
4. If you were a member of the company's peer-review complaint committee, how would you vote in this case? What facts would cause you to vote this way?

Source: Based on an arbitration case heard by George W. Bohlander. Names have been changed.

NOTES AND REFERENCES

1. Robert J. Denny, interview by author, March 6, 2008, Phoenix, Arizona.

2. "How to Get More Control Over 'Virtual' Workplace Devices," *HR Focus* 84, no. 6 (June 2007): 9. See also John D. Canoni, "Location Awareness Technology and Employee Privacy Rights," *Employee Relations Law Journal* 30, no. 1 (Summer 2004): 26.

3. Michael Orey, "Fear of Firing," *Business Week*, April 23, 2007, 52.

4. David J. Walsh, *Employment Law for Human Resource Practice* (Mason, OH: South-Western, 2007): Chapter 17.

5. Jeffery A. Mello, "Introduction: The Evolving Nature of the Employment Relationship: Reconsidering Employee Responsibilities and Rights," *Employee Responsibility and Rights Journal* 15, no. 3 (September 2003): 99.

6. John L. Henshaw, Shannon H. Gaffney, Amy K. Madl, and Dennis J. Paustenbach, "The Employer's Responsibility to Maintain a Safe and Healthful Work Environment: An Historical Review of Societal Expectations and Industrial Practice," *Employee Responsibility and Rights Journal* 19, no. 3 (September 2007): 173.

7. "Background Checks Are on the Rise," *HR Focus* 84, no. 7 (July 2007): 51.

8. Maria Greco Danahar, "Retailer Sued Over Clerk's Conduct" *HR Magazine* 52, no. 6 (June 2007): 141.

9. Donna Scimia, "A Common Sense Approach to Reducing Liability in Today's Workplace," *Employee Relations Law Journal* 33, no. 2 (Autumn 2007): 23.

10. Rita Zeidner, "How Deep Can You Probe?" *HR Magazine* 52, no. 10 (October 2007): 57. See also Jena McGregor, "Background Checks That Never End," *Business Week*, March 20, 2006, 40.

11. Bonnie S. O'Neill, Jonathon R. B. Halbesleben, and John C. Edwards, "Integrating Employment Contracts and Comparisons: What One Can Teach Us about the Other," *Journal of Managerial Issues* 19, no. 2 (Summer 2007): 161.

12. Robert Del Campo, "Psychological Contract Violation: An Individual Difference Perspective," *International Journal of Management* 24, no. 1 (March 2007): 43.

13. Ellen Dannin, "Why At-Will Employment Is Bad for Employers and Just Cause Is Good for Them," *Labor Law Journal* 58, no. 1 (Spring 2007): 5.

14. *Adair v. United States*, 2078 U.S. 161 (1908).

15. "How At-Will Employment Is Changing," *HR Focus* 84, no. 10 (October 2007): 1

16. Patric J. Cihon and James Ottavio Castagnera, *Employment and Labor Law* 6th ed. (Mason, OH: South-Western, 2008): 3–4.

17. Lawrence Peikes, "Employer Pays for Reneging on a Promise," *HR Magazine* 49, no. 3 (March 2004): 109.

18. Susan H. Roos, "Fired Fendi Manager Bags Over $1 Million," *HR Magazine* 52, no. 6 (June 2007): 141.

19. David C. Lindsay and Sabrina Rockoff, "State Regulations Update: Beyond Sarbanes-Oxley: State Law Protection in the Era of the Whistleblower," *Employment Relations Today* 34, no. 1 (Spring 2007): 69. See also Paul D. Scott, "Whistleblowers Wanted," *Journal of Accountancy* 203, no. 5 (May 2007): 86.

20. 18 U.S.C.S. § 1514A (a) (2002). See, D. Bruce Shine, "Pity the Sox Whistleblower: Pity the Sox Lawyer Whistleblower!" *Labor Law Journal* 58, no. 4 (Winter 2007): 228.

21. 5 U.S.C.S. § 2302 (2002).

22. P.L. No. 107-174 (2002).

23. 31 U.D.C.S. §§ 3729–3730 (2002).

24. Ben Levisohn, "Getting More Workers to Whistle," *Business Week*, January 28, 2008, 18.

25. Mark Taylor, "N. J. System Settles Lawsuit" *Modern Health Care* 36, no. 25 (June 19, 2006): 4.

26. Benisa Berry, "Organizational Culture: A Framework and Strategies for Facilitating Employee Whistleblowing," *Employee Responsibilities and Rights Journal* 16, no. 1 (March 2004): 1.

27. *Toussaint v. Blue Cross and Blue Shield of Michigan*, 408 Mich. 579, 292 N.W.2d 880 (1980).

28. "Employee Handbooks: Have You Updated Yours Lately?" *HR Focus* 83, no. 7 (July 2006): 5.

29. Lawrence P. Postol, "Drafting Non-compete Agreements for All 50 States," *Employee Relations Law Journal* 33, no. 1 (Summer 2007): 65.

30. Howard J. Rubin and Gregg A. Gilman, "Will Garden Leaves Blossom in the States," *Employee Relations Law Journal* 33, no. 2 (Autumn 2007): 3. See also Brian L. Lemer and Jeffrey K. Geldens, "Ensuring Fair Play: Using Common Law to Protect Against Unfair Competition from Former Employees," *Employee Relations Law Journal* 32, no. 3 (Winter 2006): 41.

31. Jonthan A. Segal, "I Quit! Now Pay Me," *HR Magazine* 49, no. 10 (October 2004): 129.

32. Martha Crumpacker, "The U.S. Supreme Court Clarifies Constructive Discharge Under Title VII: Responsibilities and Opportunities for Human Resources Practitioners," *Public Personnel Management* 36, no. 1 (Spring 2007): 1.

33. "Retaliation Claims Are Up, Though Rules Are Changing," *HR Focus* 84, no. 8 (August 2007): 2.

34. "Threats Are Sufficient for Retalization Claim," *HR Focus* 84, no. 10 (October 2007): 2.

35. Rebecca M. Archer and Stephen T. Lanctot, "Are Your Hands Tied? A Practical Look at Employee Claims for Retaliation," *Employee Relations Law Journal* 33, no. 1 (Summer 2007): 53.

36. Mary Price Birk, "Walking on Eggshells—Avoiding Retaliation Claims When an Employee Who Files a Discrimination Does Not Leave," *Employee Relations Law Journal* 32, no. 2 (Winter 2006): 10.

37. 29 U.S.C.A. §§ 2101–2109 (2001).

38. The common definition of privacy as a "general right of the individual to be let alone is captured in the words of Samuel Warren and Louis Brandeis in their seminal

article, "The Right to Privacy," *Harvard Law Review* 193, 205 (1890).

39. Janis Procter-Murphy, employment attorney, interview by author, December 9, 2007.

40. "Balancing HR Systems with Employee Privacy," *HR Focus* 83, no. 11 (November 2006): 11.

41. Diana Cadrain, "Are Your Employee Drug Tests Accurate?" *HR Magazine* 48, no. 1 (January 2003): 41.

42. http://www.osha.gov Search on Substance Abuse.

43. Walsh, *Employment Law for Human Resource Practice*, 153.

44. Ibid.

45. U.S.C.S. § 701 (a)(1) (2001).

46. U.S.C. § 12210 (b).

47. T. L. Stanly, "Workplace Drug Testing and the Growing Problem of Methamphetamines," *Supervision* 68, no. 8 (August 2007): 3.

48. Peter Cholakis, "How to Implement a Successful Drug Testing Program," *Risk Management* 52, no. 11 (November 2005): 24.

49. William I. Sauser, Jr., "Employee Theft: Who, How, Why, and What Can Be Done," *S.A.M. Advanced Management Journal* 72, no. 3 (Summer 2007): 13.

50. Andrew Wren, "The Benefits of Video Surveillance," *Risk Management* 54, no. 10 (October 2007): 24.

51. Aaron Latto, "Managing Risk from Within: Monitoring Employees the Right Way," *Risk Management* 54, no. 4 (April 2007): 30.

52. Electronic Communications Privacy Act, 18 U.S.C. § 2510–2720.

53. Walsh, *Employment Law for Human Resource Practice*, 519.

54. Barry A. Friedman and Lisa J. Reed, "Workplace Privacy: Employee Relations and Legal Implications of Monitoring Employee E-Mail Use," *Employee Responsibilities and Rights Journal* 19, no. 2 (June 2007): 75.

55. Rita Zeidner, "Employees Don't 'Get' Electronic Storage," *HR Magazine* 52, no. 1 (January 2007): 36.

56. Rita Zeidner, "Keeping E-mail in Check," *HR Magazine* 52, no. 6 (June 2007): 70.

57. Adrienne Fox, "Caught in the Web," *HR Magazine* 52, no. 12 (December 2007): 35.

58. Bill Roberts, "Avoiding the Perils of Electronic Data," *HR Magazine* 52, no. 1 (January 2007): 72.

59. "Consider These Pointers for Electronic Policies," *HR Focus* 85, no. 1 (January 2008): 2.

60. "Why It's Time to Update Your Privacy Policies," *HR Focus* 84, no. 4 (April 2007): 3.

61. Diane Cadrain, "Setting the Records Straight," *HR Magazine* 52, no. 6 (June 2007): 82

62. Cynthia F. Cohen and Murray E. Cohen, "On-Duty and Off-Duty: Employee Rights to Privacy and Employers Right to Control in the Private Sector," *Employee Responsibilities and Rights Journal* 19, no. 4 (December 2007): 235

63. Charles A. Pierce, Brandee J. Broberg, Jamie R. McClure, and Herman Aquinis, "Responding to Sexual Harassment Complaints: Effects of a Dissolved Workplace Romance on Decision Making Standards," *Organizational Behavior and Human Decision Processes* 95, no. 1 (September 2004): 83.

64. Judy Greenwald, "Employers Are the Losers in the Dating Game," at http://www.workforce.com/section/09/feature/24/93/98/index.html.

65. Kathryn Tyler, "Sign in the Name of Love," *HR Magazine* 53, no. 2 (February 2008): 41.

66. "How Companies Are Dealing with Workplace Body Art Issues," *HR Focus* 81, no. 4 (April 2004).

67. Carolyn Sayre, "Tattoo Bans," *Time*, November 5, 2007, 55.

68. Christopher Spevak, "Genetic Testing in the Workplace," *Physician Executive* 33, no. 1 (January/February 2007): 62.

69. Bill Leonard, "House Passes Ban on Genetic Discrimination in Workplace," *HR Magazine* 52, no. 6 (June 2007): 27.

70. Orey, "Fear of Firing," 54.

71. A more recent workplace problem faced by employers is employee bullying behavior. See Mark Larson, "Stamping Out Workplace Bullies," *Workforce Magazine* at http://www.workforce.com/section/09/feature/25/00/29/index.html, and John Hollon, "Zero Tolerance for Jerks," *Workforce Magazine* at http://www.workforce.com/section/01/feature/24/74/76/index.html.

72. "Fired Up Over Firing," *Business Week*, May 14, 2007, 76.

73. George W. Bohlander and Donna Blancero, "A Study of Reversal Determinants in Discipline and Discharge Arbitration Awards: The Impact of Just Cause Standards, *Labor Studies Journal* 21, no. 3 (Fall 1996): 3–18.

74. "Steps to Take before Recommending Disciplinary Action," *PM Public Management* 86, no. 6 (July 2004): 43.

75. Jathan W. Janove, "Private Eye 101," *HR Magazine* 49, no. 7 (July 2004): 127.

76. Mollica Kelly, "Perceptions of Fairness," *HR Magazine* 49, no. 6 (June 2004): 169.

77. *NLRB v. Weingarten Inc.*, 95 S.Ct. 959 (1975), 402 U.S. 251, 43 L.Ed.2d. 171.

78. Readers interested in the pioneering work on positive discipline should see James R. Redeker, "Discipline, Part 1: Progressive Systems Work Only by Accident," *Personnel* 62, no. 10 (October 1985): 8–12 and James R. Redeker, "Discipline, Part 2: The Nonpunitive Approach Works by Design," *Personnel* 62, no. 11 (November 1985): 7–14.

79. Stephen P. Postalakis, "Avoiding a Sticky Situation: A Guide to Firing an Employee," *Catalyst 2002* (March/April 2007): 22.

80. For an excellent explanation of just cause discharge guidelines, see Frank Elkouri and Edna Asper Elkouri, *How Arbitration Works*, 5th ed. (Washington, DC: Bureau of National Affairs, 1997).

81. Jack and Suzy Welch, 'The Right Way to Say Goodbye," *Business Week*, March 25, 2007, 144.

82. Elizabeth Agnvall, "Case Closed. Now What?" *HR Magazine* 53, no. 2 (February 2008): 69.

83. Nancy Hatch Woodward, "Smoother Separations," *HR Magazine* 52, no. 6 (June 2007): 94.

84. Michael Orey, "The Vanishing Trial: As Court Battles Become More Rare, Some Experts Fear the Effects on the Law," *Business Week*, April 30, 2007, 38.

85. *Gilmer v. Interstate/Johnson Lane Corp.*, 111 S. Ct. 1647 (1991).

86. *Circuit City Stores. Inc. v. Adams*, 121 S. Ct. 1302 (2001).

87. Louise Lamothe, "Avoiding Potholes in Mandatory Arbitration: A Look at Recent

California Decisions," *Dispute Resolution Journal* 58, no. 2 (May–June 2003): 18. See also D. Diane Hatch, James T. Hall, Mark T. Kobata, and Marty Denis, "Law Firm's Arbitration Procedures Rules Unfair," *Workforce Management* 86, no. 13 (July 23, 2007): 10.

88. Walsh, *Employment Law for Human Resource Practice*, 19.

89. Ruth D. Raisfeld, "How Mediation Works: A Guide to Effective Use of ADR," *Employee Relations Law Journal* 33, no. 2 (Autumn 2007): 30.

90. Joseph Camarra and James Foster, "Benefits of Mediation," *Risk Management* 54, no. 4 (April 2007): 12.

91. Kathryn Tyler, "Mediating a Better Outcome," *HR Magazine* 52, no. 11 (November 2007): 63.

92. Jennifer J. Froehlich, "The New Company Unions: Mandatory Individual Employment Arbitration Agreements and Section 8 (a) (2) of the National Labor Relations Act," *Labor Law Journal* 58, no. 3 (Fall 2007): 195.

93. Elizabeth F. R. Gingerich, "Enforcing Arbitration Agreements in Discrimination Claims: Judicial Reconsideration," *Employee Relations Law Journal* 33, no. 4 (Spring 2008): 61.

94. *EEOC v. Waffle House Inc.*, 534 U.S. 279 (2002).

95. "EEOC May Sue Even If Arbitration Agreement Exists," *HR Focus* 79, no. 3 (March 2002): 2.

96. Betsy Stevens, "Corporate Ethical Codes: Effective Instruments for Influencing Behavior," *Journal of Business Ethics* 78, no. 4 (April 2008): 601.

97. Jennifer Schramm, "Perception on Ethics," *HR Magazine* 49, no. 11 (November 2004): 176.

98. Charles Pettijohn and Linda Pettijohn, "Salespersons Perceptions of Ethical Behavior: Their Influence on Job Satisfaction and Turnover Intensions," *Journal of Business Ethics* 78, no. 4 (April 2008): 547. See also Ann Pomeroy, "Corporate Ethics Affect Employee Productivity," *HR Magazine* 52, no. 7 (June 2007): 16.

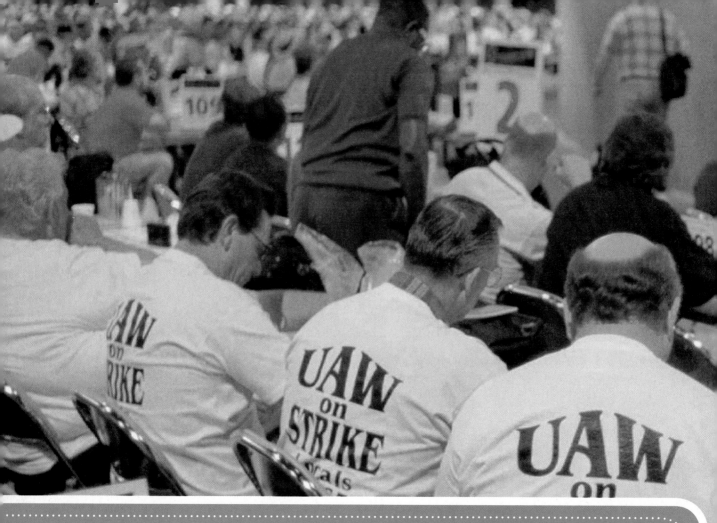

THE DYNAMICS OF LABOR RELATIONS

After studying this chapter, you should be able to

Objective | 1 |

Identify and explain the principal federal laws that provide the framework for labor relations.

Objective | 2 |

Explain the reasons employees join unions.

Objective | 3 |

Describe the process by which unions organize employees and gain recognition as their bargaining agent.

© LENNOX MCLENDON/AP PHOTOS

14

CHAPTER

Objective | 4 |

Discuss the bargaining process and the bargaining goals and strategies of a union and an employer.

Objective | 5 |

Differentiate the forms of bargaining power that a union and an employer may utilize to enforce their bargaining demands.

Objective | 6 |

Describe a typical union grievance procedure and explain the basis for arbitration awards.

Objective | 7 |

Discuss some of the contemporary challenges to labor organizations.

Mention the word *union* and most people will have some opinion, positive or negative, regarding U.S. labor organizations. To some, the word evokes images of labor-management unrest—grievances, strikes, picketing, and boycotts. To others, the word represents industrial democracy, fairness, opportunity, and equal representation.[1] Many think of unions as simply creating an adversarial relationship between employees and managers.

Regardless of attitudes toward them, since the mid-1800s, unions have been an important force shaping organizational practices, legislation, and political thought in the United States. Today unions remain of interest because of their influence on organizational productivity, U.S. competitiveness, the development of labor law, and HR policies and practices. Like business organizations themselves, unions are undergoing changes in both operation—such as mergers and coalitions—and philosophy. Furthermore, after years of declining membership, unions are again actively organizing unrepresented employees. For example, to counter the membership loss of autoworkers, the United Automobile Workers (UAW) recently organized 8,000 casino dealers in Atlantic City, Detroit, and Newport, Rhode Island. Two thousand six hundred (2,600) workers at Connecticut's Foxwoods Resort and Casino recently unionized. Two unions, the Transport Workers Union (TWU) and the UAW, are currently organizing casino dealers at Wynn's and Caesar's Palace resorts in Las Vegas.[2] In 2007, the hotel workers union began a national organizing campaign aimed at Hilton Hotels, Sheraton, Westin, and four other hotel chains. John W. Wilhelm, hospitality union organizer, states, "We're challenging our industry to make service jobs middle class."[3] Unite Here, a coalition of unions, seeks to mount national recruiting drives involving entire industries. The AFL-CIO and national unions have targeted organizing as a top priority for the revival of the labor movement in the twenty-first century.[4]

In spite of the long history of unions, the intricacies of labor relations are unfamiliar to many individuals. Therefore, this chapter describes government regulation of labor relations, the labor relations process, the reasons why workers join labor organizations, and the structure and leadership of labor unions. Importantly, according to labor law, once the union is certified to negotiate for bargaining unit members, it must represent everyone in the unit equally, regardless of whether employees subsequently join the union or elect to remain nonmembers. Therefore, in the latter sections of the chapter, we discuss the important topics of contract administration, particularly the handling of employee grievances and arbitration. The chapter concludes with a discussion of contemporary challenges to labor organizations.

Unions and other labor organizations can affect significantly the ability of managers to direct and control the various functions of HRM. For example, union seniority provisions in the labor contract may influence who is selected for job promotions or training programs. Pay rates may be determined through union negotiations, or unions may impose restrictions on management's employee appraisal methods. Therefore, it is essential that managers in both the union and nonunion environment understand how unions operate and be thoroughly familiar with the important body of law governing labor relations. Remember, ignorance of labor legislation is no defense when managers and supervisors violate labor law. Before reading further, test your knowledge of labor relations law by answering the questions in Highlights in HRM 1.

1

Test Your Labor Relations Know-How

1. An auto mechanic applied for a job with an automotive dealership. He was denied employment because of his union membership. Was the employer's action lawful?

   _____ Yes   _____ No

2. During a labor organizing drive, supervisors questioned individual employees about their union beliefs. Was this questioning permissible?

   _____ Yes   _____ No

3. When members of a union began wearing union buttons at work, management ordered the buttons to be removed. Was management within its rights?

   _____ Yes   _____ No

4. While an organizing drive was under way, an employer agreed—as a social gesture—to furnish refreshments at a holiday party. Was the employer acting within the law?

   _____ Yes   _____ No

5. A company distributed to other antiunion employers in the area a list of job applicants known to be union supporters. Was the distribution unlawful?

   _____ Yes   _____ No

6. During a union organizing drive, the owner of Servo Pipe promised her employees a wage increase if they would vote against the union. Can the owner legally make this promise to her employees?

   _____ Yes   _____ No

7. Employees have the right to file unfair labor practice charges against their employer even when the organization is nonunion.

   _____ Yes   _____ No

8. The union wishes to arbitrate a member's grievance, which management has demonstrated is completely groundless. Must management arbitrate the grievance?

   _____ Yes   _____ No

9. John Green, a maintenance engineer, has a poor work record. Management wishes to terminate his employment. However, Green is a union steward, and he is highly critical of the company. Can management legally discharge this employee?

   _____ Yes   _____ No

10. During an organizing drive, an office manager expressed strong antiunion beliefs and called union officials "racketeers," "big stinkers," and a "bunch of radicals." He told employees who joined the union that they "ought to have their heads examined." Were the manager's comments legal?

    _____ Yes   _____ No

Answers are found at the end of this chapter.

⊞ GOVERNMENT REGULATION OF LABOR RELATIONS

Objective 1

The development of U.S. labor legislation has its foundation in the social, economic, and political climate of America. Generally, we can say that the growth of the labor movement has paralleled the passage of prolabor legislation and the ability of workers to impose their economic demands on management. Clearly labor laws passed in the 1920s and 1930s favored the growth and stability of labor organizations.[5] As unions became stronger under federal laws, legislation was passed to curb union abuses of power and to protect the rights of union members from unethical union activities. Today the laws governing labor relations seek to create an environment in which both unions and employers can discharge their respective rights and responsibilities. Knowledge of labor relations laws will assist the understanding of how union-management relations operate in the United States. The first federal law pertaining to labor relations was the Railway Labor Act of 1926. Other major laws that affect labor relations in the private sector are the Norris-LaGuardia Act, Wagner Act, Taft-Hartley Act, and Landrum-Griffin Act.

Railway Labor Act

The primary purpose of the Railway Labor Act (RLA), enacted in 1926, is to avoid service interruptions resulting from disputes between railroads and their operating unions. To achieve this end, the RLA contains two extensive procedures to handle these labor-management disputes. First, the National Mediation Board resolves negotiating impasses by using mediation and/or arbitration. The board is additionally charged with holding secret ballot elections to determine whether employees desire unionization. Second, the National Railway Adjustment Board handles grievance and arbitration disputes arising during the life of an agreement. In 1936, the RLA was amended to extend coverage to the airline industry.

Norris-LaGuardia Act

The Norris-LaGuardia Act, or Anti-Injunction Act, of 1932 severely restricts the ability of employers to obtain an injunction forbidding a union from engaging in peaceful picketing, boycotts, or various striking activities. Previously, federal court injunctions had been an effective antiunion weapon because they forced unions to either cease such activities or suffer the penalty of being held in contempt of court. Injunctions may still be granted in labor disputes. Before an injunction may be issued, however, employers must show that lack of an injunction will cause greater harm to the employer than to the union. Like the RLA, this Act promotes collective bargaining and encourages the existence, formation, and effective operation of labor organizations.

Wagner Act

The Wagner Act of 1935 (or National Labor Relations Act) has had by far the most significant impact on union-management relations. It placed the protective power of the federal government firmly behind employee efforts to organize and bargain collectively through representatives of their choice.

The Wagner Act created the National Labor Relations Board (NLRB) to govern labor relations in the United States. Although this Act was amended by the Taft-Hartley Act, most of its major provisions that protected employee bargaining rights were retained. Section 7 of the law guarantees these rights as follows:

> Employees shall have the right to self-organization, to form, join, or assist labor organizations, to bargain collectively through representatives of their own choosing, and to engage in concerted activities, for the purpose of collective bargaining or other mutual aid or protection, and shall also have the right to refrain from any or all of such activities except to the extent that such right may be affected by an agreement requiring membership in a labor organization as a condition of employment.[6]

To guarantee employees their Section 7 rights, Congress outlawed specific employer practices that deny employees the benefits of the law. Section 8 of the Act lists five **unfair labor practices (ULPs)** of employers:

1. Interfering with, restraining, or coercing employees in the exercise of their rights guaranteed in Section 7

2. Dominating or interfering with the formation or administration of any labor organization, or contributing financial or other support to it

3. Discriminating in regard to hiring or tenure of employment or any term or condition of employment so as to encourage or discourage membership in any labor organization

4. Discharging or otherwise discriminating against employees because they file charges or give testimony under this act

5. Refusing to bargain collectively with the duly chosen representatives of employees

Many ULPs are either knowingly or unknowingly committed each year by employers. In fiscal year 2007, for example, 22,331 unfair labor practices were filed with the NLRB. Alleged violations of the Act by employers were filed in 15,031 cases.[7] There were 6,845 charges against employers concerning illegal discharge or other discrimination against employees. It is therefore imperative that managers at all levels receive training in employee rights and unfair labor practices. When employers violate employee rights, the NLRB can "take such affirmative action including reinstatement of employment with or without back pay, as well as effectuate the policies of the Act, and make discriminated employees whole."[8] In 2007, the NLRB won for employees $117.3 million in back pay because of employer violations of the Act.[9]

unfair labor practices (ULPs)
Specific employer and union illegal practices that deny employees their rights and benefits under federal labor law

National Labor Relations Board

The agency responsible for administering and enforcing the Wagner Act is the National Labor Relations Board (NLRB). It serves the public interest by reducing interruptions in production or service caused by labor-management strife. To accomplish this goal, the NLRB is given two primary charges: (1) to hold secret ballot elections to determine whether employees wish to be represented by a union and (2) to prevent and remedy unfair labor practices. The NLRB does not act on its own initiative in either function. It processes only those charges of unfair labor practices and petitions for employee elections that may be filed at one of its thirty-two regional offices or other smaller field offices.

Using the Internet

The U.S. National Labor Relations Board has its own Web site. There you can find details of its organization, current cases, and decisions. Go to the Student Resources at:

www.cengage.com/ management/bohlander

The NLRB operates in a dynamic field in which information about the operation of the agency and answers to legal questions can be critical to both employees and managers. The NLRB maintains a toll-free telephone number designed to provide cost-free and easy access about the agency to the public.[10] Additionally, each regional office has an "information officer" available to answer specific legal questions about the law and the NLRB.

Taft-Hartley Act

Passage of the Wagner Act spurred the huge growth of unionization during the 1930s and 1940s. Union membership in the United States reached 9 million in 1940, and with membership gains, labor's increased use of the strike became problematic to employers. With the bargaining power of unions now significantly increased, coupled with reports of union abuses of employee rights, certain restraints on unions were considered necessary. The Taft-Hartley Act of 1947 (also known as the Labor-Management Relations Act) met these objectives by defining unfair labor practices of unions and curbing various strike activities of labor organizations. The unfair labor practices of unions are as follows:

1. Restraint or coercion of employees in the exercise of their rights

2. Restraint or coercion of employers in the selection of the parties to bargain in their behalf

3. Persuasion of employers to discriminate against any of their employees

4. Refusal to bargain collectively with an employer

5. Participation in secondary boycotts and jurisdictional disputes

6. Attempt to force recognition from an employer when another union is already the certified representative

7. Charge of excessive initiation fees and dues

8. "Featherbedding" practices that require payment of wages for services not performed

In short, by passing the Taft-Hartley Act, Congress balanced the rights and duties of labor and management in the collective bargaining arena. No longer could the law be criticized as favoring unions.

Federal Mediation and Conciliation Service

Because of the high incidence of strikes after World War II, the Taft-Hartley Act created the Federal Mediation and Conciliation Service (FMCS) to help resolve negotiating disputes. The function of this independent agency is to help labor and management reach collective bargaining agreements through the processes of mediation and conciliation. These functions use a neutral party who maintains communications between bargainers in an attempt to gain agreement. Unlike the NLRB, the FMCS has no enforcement powers, nor can it prosecute anyone. Rather, the parties in a negotiating impasse must voluntarily elect to use the service. Once the FMCS is asked to mediate a dispute, however, its involvement in the process can greatly improve labor-management relations while providing a vehicle for the exchange of collective bargaining proposals.[11] According to Ron Collotta, commissioner of FMCS in Phoenix, Arizona, the agency mediates between 6,000 and 7,000 bargaining disputes annually.[12] In recent years, the FMCS has been highly visible in resolving deadlocks involving the communications, sports, education, and transportation industries.

Landrum-Griffin Act

In 1959, Congress passed the Landrum-Griffin Act (also known as the Labor-Management Reporting and Disclosure Act) to safeguard union member rights and prevent racketeering and other unscrupulous practices by employers and union officers. One of the most important provisions of the Landrum-Griffin Act is the Bill of Rights of Union Members, which requires that every union member must be given the right to (1) nominate candidates for union office, (2) vote in union elections or referendums, (3) attend union meetings, and (4) participate in union meetings and vote on union business. Union members are also granted the right to examine union accounts and records in order to verify information contained in union reports and to bring suit against union officers as necessary to protect union funds. Moreover, under the Act, unions are required to submit a financial report annually to the Secretary of Labor, and employers must report any expenditures that are made in attempting to exercise their bargaining rights.

THE LABOR RELATIONS PROCESS

2 | Objective

Individually, employees may be able to exercise relatively little power in their relationship with employers. Of course, if they believe they are not being treated fairly, then Section 7 of the National Labor Relations Act grants them the legal right to organize and bargain with the employer collectively. When employees pursue this direction, the labor relations process begins. As Figure 14.1 illustrates, the labor relations process consists of a logical sequence of five events: (1) workers desire collective representation, (2) the union begins its organizing campaign, (3) the NLRB representation procedure begins, (4) collective negotiations lead to a contract, and (5) the contract is administered. Laws and administrative rulings influence each of the separate events by granting special privileges to or imposing defined constraints on workers, managers, and union officials.[13]

labor relations process

A logical sequence of five events: (1) workers desire collective representation, (2) the union begins its organizing campaign, (3) the NLRB representation process begins, (4) collective negotiations lead to a contract, and (5) the contract is administered

Why Employees Unionize

The majority of research on why employees unionize comes from the study of blue-collar employees in the private sector. These studies generally conclude that employees unionize as a result of economic need, because of a general dissatisfaction with managerial practices, and/or as a way to fulfill social and status needs. In short, employees see unionism as a way to achieve results they cannot achieve acting individually.

It should be pointed out that some employees join unions because of the union shop provisions of the labor agreement. In states where it is permitted, a union shop is a provision of the labor agreement that requires employees to join as a condition of employment. Even when compelled to join, however, many employees accept the concept of unionism once they become involved in the union as a member. The three primary reasons unorganized workers elect to unionize are:

union shop

A provision of the labor agreement that requires employees to join the union as a requirement for their employment

- Economic Needs. Dissatisfaction with wages, benefits, and working conditions appears to provide the strongest reason to join a union. This point is continually supported by research studies that find that both union members and nonmembers

FIGURE
14.1

The Labor Relations Process

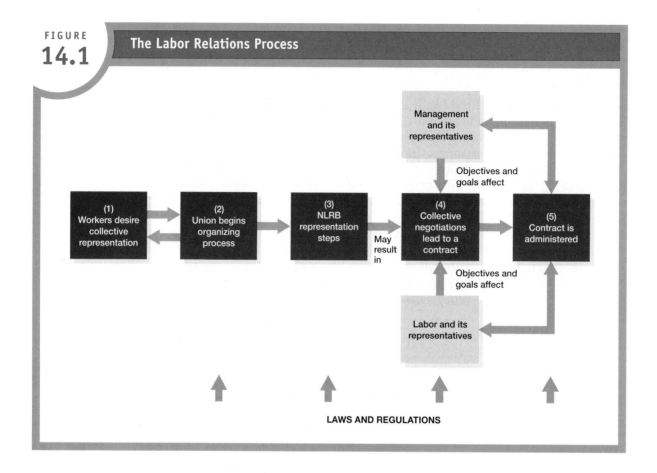

have their highest expectations of union performance regarding the "bread and butter" issues of collective bargaining.[14] It is these traditional issues of wages, benefits, and working conditions on which unions are built.

- Dissatisfaction with Management. Employees may seek unionization when they perceive that managerial practices regarding promotion, transfer, shift assignment, or other job-related policies are administered in an unfair or biased manner. Employees cite favoritism shown by managers as a major reason for joining unions. This is particularly true when the favoritism concerns the HR areas of discipline, promotion, job assignments, and training opportunities. Furthermore, the failure of employers to give employees an opportunity to participate in decisions affecting their welfare may encourage union membership. It is widely believed that one reason managers begin employee involvement programs and seek to empower their employees is to avoid collective action by employees. For example, employers in the auto, semiconductor, and financial industries involve employees in collaborative programs as a means to stifle unionization.

- Social and Leadership Concerns. Employees whose needs for recognition and social affiliation are being frustrated may join unions as a means of satisfying these needs. Through their union, they have an opportunity to fraternize with other employees who have similar desires, interests, problems, and gripes.

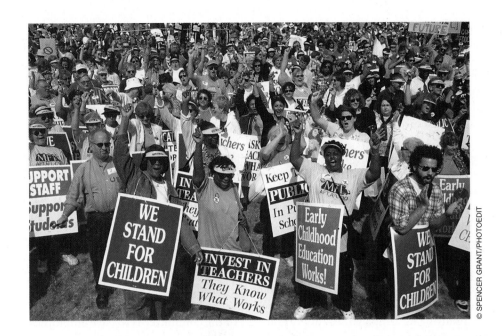

These teachers are exercising their legal rights to protest perceived unfair management actions.

© SPENCER GRANT/PHOTOEDIT

Employees may join unions to benefit in the prestige and value that organization may provide. Additionally, the union also enables them to put leadership talents to use as officers of the union and representatives of fellow employees. One study found that employees became union stewards so that they could be seen as "a fellow your buddies look to" and as a person who "stands up to the boss."

Organizing Campaigns

Once employees desire to unionize, a formal organizing campaign may be started either by a union organizer or by employees acting on their own behalf.[15] Contrary to popular belief, most organizing campaigns are begun by employees rather than by union organizers. Large national unions such as the United Auto Workers, United Brotherhood of Carpenters, United Steelworkers, and the Teamsters, however, have formal organizing departments whose purpose is to identify organizing opportunities and launch organizing campaigns.

3 | Objective

Organizing Steps

Terry Moser, former president of Teamster Local 104, once told the authors that the typical organizing campaign follows a series of progressive steps that can lead to employee representation. The organizing process as described by Moser normally includes the following steps:

1. Employee/union contact
2. Initial organizational meeting
3. Formation of in-house organizing committee
4. Election petition and voting preparation
5. Contract negotiations

Step 1. The first step begins when employees and union officials make contact to explore the possibility of unionization. During these discussions, employees investigate the advantages of labor representation, and union officials begin to gather information on employee needs, problems, and grievances. Labor organizers also seek specific information about the employer's financial health, supervisory styles, and organizational policies and practices. To win employee support, labor organizers must build a case *against* the employer and *for* the union.

Step 2. As an organizing campaign gathers momentum, the organizer schedules an initial union meeting to attract more supporters. The organizer uses the information gathered in Step 1 to address employee needs and explain how the union can secure these goals. Two additional purposes of organizational meetings are (1) to identify employees who can help the organizer direct the campaign and (2) to establish communication chains that reach all employees.

Step 3. The third important step in the organizing drive is to form an in-house organizing committee composed of employees willing to provide leadership to the campaign. The committee's role is to interest other employees in joining the union and in supporting its campaign. An important task of the committee is to have employees sign an authorization card (see Highlights in HRM 2) indicating their willingness to be represented by a labor union in collective bargaining with their employer. The number of signed authorization cards demonstrates the potential strength of the labor union.[16] At least 30 percent of the employees must sign authorization cards before the National Labor Relations Board will hold a representation election.

authorization card

A statement signed by an employee authorizing a union to act as a representative of the employee for purposes of collective bargaining

Step 4. If a sufficient number of employees support the union drive, the organizer seeks a government-sponsored election. A representation petition is filed with the NLRB, asking that a secret ballot election be held to determine whether employees actually desire unionization. Before the election, a large publicity campaign is directed toward employees, seeking their support and election votes. This is a period of intense emotions for the employees, the labor organization, and the employer.

Step 5. Union organizing is concluded when the union wins the election. The NLRB "certifies" the union as the legal bargaining representative of the employees. Contract negotiations now begin; these negotiations represent another struggle between the union and employer. During negotiations each side seeks employment conditions favorable to its position. Members of the in-plant organizing committee and the union organizer attempt to negotiate the employees' first contract. In about one out of four union campaigns, unions are unable to secure a first contract after winning a representation election.[17] Should the union fail to obtain an agreement within one year from winning the election, the Taft-Hartley Act allows the employees to vote the union out through a NLRB "decertification" election.

Aggressive Organizing Tactics

Without question, a strategic objective of the labor movement is to become more aggressive and creative in its organizing tactics. Unions have been shocked into developing these "revolutionary" organizing strategies to compensate for a decline in membership and to counteract employer antiunion campaigns. (Both topics will

2

United Food and Commercial Workers International Union Authorization Card

United Food & Commercial Workers International Union

Affiliated with AFL-CIO-CLC

AUTHORIZATION FOR REPRESENTATION

I hereby authorize the United Food & Commercial Workers International Union, AFL-CIO-CLC, or its chartered Local Union(s) to represent me for the purpose of collective bargaining.

_____ (Print Name)   _____ (Date)

_____ (Signature)   _____ (Home Phone)

_____ (Home Address)   _____ (City)   _____ (State)   _____ (Zip)

_____ (Employer's Name)   _____ (Address)

_____ (Hire Date)   _____ (Type Work Performed)   _____ (Department)

                                 Day   Night   Full   Part-
                                 Shift ____   Shift ____   Time ____   Time ____
_____ _____
(Hourly Rate)   (Day Off)
Would you participate in an organizing committee?   Yes ____   No ____

be discussed later.) To accomplish their agenda of "vitalizing" the labor movement, unions employ the following organizing weapons—in varying degrees—to achieve their goals:

1. *Political involvement.* Unions have become more selective in their support of public officials, giving union funds to candidates who specifically pledge support for prolabor legislation. During the 2008 national and local elections, the AFL-CIO and other large unions spent a total of about $300 million to help elect Democratic candidates to the White House and Congress.[18] Specific efforts focused on identifying and registering Democrats to vote. A union official recently told one of the authors that organized labor needs to generate "Street Heat" during political struggles.[19]

2. *Neutrality agreements.* Neutrality agreements secure a binding commitment from the employer to remain neutral during the organizing drive. The employer agrees that managers will not campaign against or disparage the union and managers will only provide facts about the union when questioned by employees. Furthermore, the employer agrees to accept a card check to recognize the union if the union produces sufficient employee signed authorization cards.[20]

3. *Organizer training.* Traditionally, organizing has been part-time work. Today, the AFL-CIO's Organizing Institute is actively training a new generation of professional, highly skilled, full-time organizers. The current goal is to train 1,000 new organizers. Additionally, the AFL-CIO has challenged local unions to mobilize the local's entire membership around organizing—including spending 30 percent of local monies on recruitment efforts.[21]

4. *Corporate campaigns.* Unions may enlist political or community groups to boycott the product(s) of a targeted company. Other tactics include writing newspaper editorials chastising specific company decisions; filing charges with administrative agencies such as OSHA, the Department of Labor, and the NLRB; and pressuring an organization's financial institution to withhold loans or demand payments. According to the U.S. Chamber of Commerce, "the role of the corporate campaign is to force management to accede to union demands for the card check and neutrality agreements."[22]

5. *Information technology.* E-mail and the Web are fast becoming effective union organizing tools. Web sites exist that link employees to union literature, union membership applications, and individual union Web pages. "Cyberunions" seek to apply computer technology to all aspects of organizing activity.[23]

Employer Tactics Opposing Unionization

Employers use a two-pronged campaign to fight unionization. First, when possible, employers stress the favorable employer-employee relationship they have experienced in the past without a union. Employers may emphasize any advantages in wages, benefits, or working conditions the employees may enjoy in comparison with those provided by organizations that are already unionized. "While you have a right to join a union," the employers may remind their employees, "you also have a right not to join one and to deal directly with the organization free from outside interference."

Second, employers emphasize any unfavorable aspects of unionism including strikes, the payment of union dues and special assessments, and published abuses of members' legal rights, along with any false promises made by the union in the course of its campaign. Union rules on member conduct, such as being fined for crossing a picket line, are emphasized to employees. Employers may also use government statistics to show that unions commit large numbers of unfair labor practices. For example, 5,992 unfair labor practices were charged against unions in 2007; the majority (5,187) alleged illegal restraint and coercion of employees.[24] Employers may initiate legal action should union members and/or their leaders engage in any unfair labor practices during the organizing effort.

Within the limits permitted by the Taft-Hartley Act, employers can express their views about the disadvantages of being represented by a union. However, when counteracting a union campaign, managers must not threaten employees with loss of jobs or loss or reduction of other employment benefits if they vote to unionize. Nor may employers offer new or improved employee benefits or higher wages as a means of getting employees to vote "no union." Highlights in HRM 3 lists some of the activities in which managers or supervisors should not engage.[25]

3

Employer "Don'ts" during Union Organizing Campaigns

Union organizing drives are emotionally charged events. Furthermore, labor law, NLRB rulings, and court decisions greatly affect the behavior and actions of management and union representatives. During the drive, managers and supervisors should avoid the following:

- Attending union meetings, spying on employee-union gatherings, or questioning employees about the content of union meetings
- Questioning present or current employees about their union sentiments, particularly about how they might vote in a union election
- Threatening or terminating employees for their union support or beliefs
- Changing the working conditions of employees because they actively work for the union or simply support its ideals
- Supplying the names, addresses, and phone numbers of employees to union representatives or other employees sympathetic to the union
- Promising employees improvements in working conditions (wage increases, benefit improvements, and so on) if they vote against the union
- Accepting or reviewing union authorization cards or prounion petitions, because employees' names are listed on these documents

How Employees Become Unionized

The employees to be organized constitute the bargaining unit to be covered by the labor agreement. The NLRB defines a bargaining unit as a group of two or more employees who have common employment interests and conditions and may reasonably be grouped together for purposes of collective bargaining. If an employer and a union cannot agree on who should be in the bargaining unit, an appropriate bargaining unit will be determined by the NLRB on the basis of a similarity of interests (such as wages, job duties, or training) among employees within the unit. For example, in hospitals, the NLRB has designated separate units for nurses, technicians, doctors, maintenance employees, office clerical personnel, all other nonprofessionals, and guards.

bargaining unit
A group of two or more employees who share common employment interests and conditions and may reasonably be grouped together for purposes of collective bargaining

NLRB Representation Election

If it succeeds in signing up 30 percent of employees within the bargaining unit, the union petitions for a NLRB-conducted election. The petition to hold representation elections usually is initiated by the union, although employers, under certain circumstances, have the right to petition for one (see Highlights in HRM 4). Prior to the election, the NLRB holds a *preelection hearing* with the employer and union, or unions, seeking to represent the employees. At this meeting several important issues are determined, including verification of the authorization cards, the NLRB's jurisdiction to hold the election, determination of the bargaining unit (if contested by the parties), the date of the election, and the voting choice(s) to appear on the ballot. The ballot lists the names of the unions that are seeking recognition and also provides a choice of "no union."

After the election is held, the winning party is determined on the basis of the number of actual votes, not on the number of members of the bargaining unit. For example, suppose the bargaining unit at XYZ Corporation comprised 100 employees, but only 27 employees voted in the election. A union receiving 14 yes votes among the 27 voting (a majority) would be declared the winner, and the union would bargain for all 100 employees. By law the union would be granted **exclusive representation** over all bargaining unit employees.[26] The union is *certified* by the NLRB as the bargaining agent for at least a year or for the duration of the labor agreement. Once the union is certified, the employer is obligated to begin negotiations leading toward a labor agreement.

An important statistic in labor relations is the win/loss record of unions in certification elections. In 1950, the union win rate in elections held by the NLRB was 74.50 percent. This percentage dropped dramatically to 60.2 percent in 1965 and to 48.20 percent in 1995. The percentage win rate for unions has stabilized at around 50 percent since 1995. For example, in 2007, the NLRB held 1,905 conclusive representation elections, of which 1,045 resulted in union wins—a 55.7 percent win rate.[27] Recent statistics show that unions have lost much of their ability to win bargaining representation for employees.

Employees can unionize without a NLRB election. This NLRB procedure is referred to as "certification on a card check." If the union succeeds in signing up at least 50 percent of employees within the bargaining unit, the union may request recognition by the employer. Typically, evidence is produced in the form of authorization cards signed by employees. However, if the employer believes that a majority of its employees do not want to belong to the union or if the employer questions the authenticity of the cards, the employer can insist that a representation election be held. In recent years, a growing number of unions, including the Communications Workers of America (CWA), United Auto Workers, Service Employees International Union, and the Teamsters have employed card checks as an expedient way to organize employees.[28] One union organizer described card checks this way: "Card checks are a fast less legal way to organize employees compared to a traditional NLRB-held election."[29]

exclusive representation

The legal right and responsibility of the union to represent all bargaining unit members equally, regardless of whether employees join the union or not

Impact of Unionization on Managers

Why do employers aggressively oppose the unionization of their employees? First, studies from the field of labor economics routinely show that wages and benefits are higher in union organizations compared to similar nonunion organizations. Second, unions can have a significant effect on the prerogatives exercised by management in making decisions about employees. Third, unionization restricts the freedom of management to formulate HR policy unilaterally and can challenge the authority of supervisors.

NLRB Election Poster

NOTICE TO EMPLOYEES

FROM THE
National Labor Relations Board

A PETITION has been filed with this Federal agency seeking an election to determine whether certain employees want to be represented by a union.

The case is being investigated and NO DETERMINATION HAS BEEN MADE AT THIS TIME by the National Labor Relations Board. IF an election is held Notices of Election will be posted giving complete details for voting.

It was suggested that your employer post this notice so the National Labor Relations Board could inform you of your basic rights under the National Labor Relations Act.

YOU HAVE THE RIGHT under Federal Law

- To self-organization
- To form, join, or assist labor organizations
- To bargain collectively through representatives of your own choosing
- To act together for the purposes of collective bargaining or other mutual aid or protection
- To refuse to do any or all of these things unless the union and employer, in a state where such agreements are permitted, enter into a lawful union-security agreement requiring employees to pay periodic dues and initiation fees. Nonmembers who inform the union that they object to the use of their payments for nonrepresentational purposes may be required to pay only their share of the union's costs of representational activities *(such as collective bargaining, contract administration, and grievance adjustments)*.

It is possible that some of you will be voting in an employee representation election as a result of the request for an election having been filed. While NO DETERMINATION HAS BEEN MADE AT THIS TIME, in the event an election is held, the NATIONAL LABOR RELATIONS BOARD wants all eligible voters to be familiar with their rights under the law IF it holds an election.

The Board applies rules that are intended to keep its elections fair and honest and that result in a free choice. If agents of either unions or employers act in such a way as to interfere with your right to a free election, the election can be set aside by the Board. Where appropriate the Board provides other remedies, such as reinstatement for employees fired for exercising their rights, including backpay from the party responsible for their discharge.

NOTE:

The following are examples of conduct that interfere with the rights of employees and may result in the setting aside of the election.

- Threatening loss of jobs or benefits by an employer or a union
- Promising or granting promotions, pay raises, or other benefits to influence an employee's vote by a party capable of carrying out such promises
- An employer firing employees to discourage or encourage union activity or a union causing them to be fired to encourage union activity
- Making campaign speeches to assembled groups of employees on company time within the 24-hour period before the election
- Incitement by either an employer or a union of racial or religious prejudice by inflammatory appeals
- Threatening physical force or violence to employees by a union or an employer to influence their votes

Please be assured that IF AN ELECTION IS HELD every effort will be made to protect your right to a free choice under the law. Improper conduct will not be permitted. All parties are expected to cooperate fully with this Agency in maintaining basic principles of a fair election as required by law. The National Labor Relations Board, as an agency of the United States Government, does not endorse any choice in the election.

NATIONAL LABOR RELATIONS BOARD
an agency of the
UNITED STATES GOVERNMENT

THIS IS AN OFFICIAL GOVERNMENT NOTICE AND MUST NOT BE DEFACED BY ANYONE

FORM NLRB-666 (5-90)   ✩ U.S. Government Printing Office: 1990-270-693/19127

Challenges to Management Prerogatives

Unions typically attempt to achieve greater participation in management decisions that affect their members. Specifically, these decisions may involve such issues as the subcontracting of work, productivity standards, and job content. Employers quite naturally seek to claim many of these decisions as their exclusive *management prerogatives*—decisions over which management claims exclusive rights. However, these prerogatives are subject to challenge and erosion by the union. They may be challenged at the bargaining table, through the grievance procedure, and through strikes.

Loss of Supervisory Authority

At a recent labor-management conference, a union official commented, "Contract terms covering wages, benefits, job security, and working hours are of major importance to our membership." However, for managers and supervisors, the focal point of the union's impact is at the operating level (the shop floor or office facility), where the terms of the labor agreement are implemented on a daily basis. For example, these terms can determine what corrective action is to be taken in directing and in disciplining employees. When disciplining employees, supervisors must be certain they can demonstrate *just cause* (see Chapter 13) for their actions. Additionally, specific contract language can also reduce the supervisor's ability to manage in such areas as scheduling, training, transfers, performance evaluation, and promotions. Under provisions of the labor agreement, supervisors may have to promote employees by seniority rather than by individual merit.

▪▪ STRUCTURES, FUNCTIONS, AND LEADERSHIP OF LABOR UNIONS

craft unions

Unions that represent skilled craft workers

industrial unions

Unions that represent all workers—skilled, semiskilled, unskilled—employed along industry lines

Unions that represent skilled craft workers, such as carpenters or masons, are called craft unions. Craft unions include the International Association of Machinists, United Brotherhood of Carpenters, and United Association of Plumbers and Pipefitters. Unions that represent unskilled and semiskilled workers employed along industry lines are known as industrial unions. The American Union of Postal Workers is an industrial union, as are the United Auto Workers; United Steelworkers; American Federation of State, County, and Municipal Employees; and Office and Professional Employees International Union. While this distinction still exists, technological changes, union mergers, and competition among unions for members have helped reduce it. Today skilled and unskilled workers, white-collar and blue-collar workers, and professional groups are being represented by both types of union. For example, in 2007, both the Machinists and the UAW targeted for organizing 3,000 workers at the DaimlerChrysler Mercedes-Benz factory in Vance, Alabama.[30]

employee associations

Labor organizations that represent various groups of professional and white-collar employees in labor-management relations

Besides unions, employee associations represent various groups of professional and white-collar employees. Examples of employee associations include the National Education Association, Michigan State Employees Association, American Nurses' Association, and Air Line Pilots Association. In competing with unions, these associations, for all purposes, may function as unions and become just as aggressive as unions in representing members.

Regardless of their type, labor organizations are diverse organizations, each with its own method of governance and objectives. Furthermore, they have their own structures that serve to bind them together. For example, when describing labor organizations, most researchers divide them into three levels: (1) American Federation of Labor–Congress of Industrial Organizations (AFL-CIO), (2) national unions, and (3) local unions belonging to a parent national union. Each level has its own purpose for existence as well as its own operating policies and procedures.

Using the Internet

Many national unions have Web sites for their members. For information on sites for auto and transport workers, office and professional employees, and the AFL-CIO, go to the Student Resources at:

www.cengage.com/
management/bohlander

Structure and Functions of the AFL-CIO

In 1955, the American Federation of Labor—composed largely of craft unions—and the Congress of Industrial Organizations—made up mainly of industrial unions—merged to form the AFL-CIO. The AFL-CIO is a federation of fifty-six autonomous national and international unions.[31]

In effect, the AFL-CIO is the "House of Labor" that serves to present a united front on behalf of organized labor. It disseminates labor policy developed by leaders of its affiliated unions, assists in coordinating organizing activities among its affiliated unions, and provides research and other assistance through its various departments. Most major unions belong to this federation.[32] The affiliated unions pay per capita dues (currently 50 cents per member per month) to support federation activities. Specifically, the AFL-CIO serves its members by:

1. Lobbying before legislative bodies on subjects of interest to labor

2. Coordinating organizing efforts among its affiliated unions

3. Publicizing the concerns and benefits of unionization to the public

4. Resolving disputes between different unions as they occur

Besides offering these services, the AFL-CIO maintains an interest in international trade and domestic economic issues, foreign policy matters, social issues, and national and regional politics.

A goal of the AFL-CIO is to build solidarity among its members. However, the interests and organizing activities of AFL-CIO unions do not always coincide. In 2005, six unions representing 5.4 million workers split from the AFL-CIO to form Change to Win (CTW), a rival national federation.[33] The new alliance seeks to rededicate union resources and energies toward organizing the unorganized while also revitalizing the entire labor movement.[34] CTW leaders argue that the AFL-CIO places too much emphasis on political action and too little action on organizing new members.[35] Organizing will be directed at semiskilled and low-skilled workers in industries such as hotels, health care, and retail.

Structure and Functions of National Unions

The center of power in the labor movement resides with national and international unions. These organizations set the broad guidelines for governing union members and for formulating collective bargaining goals in dealing with management. National unions hold conventions to pass resolutions, amend their constitutions, and elect officers. The president of the national union is responsible for the overall administration of the unions, and he or she exerts a large influence—if not control—over the union's policies and direction.[36]

A national union, through its constitution, establishes the rules and conditions under which the local unions may be chartered. Most national unions have regulations governing dues, initiation fees, and the internal administration of the locals. National unions also may require that certain standard provisions be included in labor agreements with employers. Standard contract terms covering safety or grievance procedures and seniority rights are examples. In return for these controls, they provide professional and financial assistance during organizing drives and strikes and help in the negotiation and administration of labor agreements. Other services provided by national unions include (1) training of union leaders, (2) legal assistance, (3) leadership in political activity, (4) educational and public relations programs, and (5) discipline of union members.

Structure and Functions of Local Unions

To the "rank-and-file" union member, the importance of unionism resides in the activities of the local union and its leaders. The officers of a local union are usually responsible for negotiating the local labor agreement and for investigating and processing member grievances. Most important, they assist in preventing the members of the local union from being treated by their employers in ways that run counter to management-established HR policies.

The officers of a local union typically include a president, vice president, secretary-treasurer, and various committee chairpeople. Depending on the size of the union, one or more of these officers may be paid by the union to serve on a full-time basis. The remaining officers are members who have regular jobs and who serve the union without pay except perhaps for token gratuities and expense allowances. Paid officers from the national union—called CWA Representatives by the Communication Workers of America—will assist the local union with functions such as organizing, negotiating the labor agreement, arbitration of member grievances, and legal matters.

union steward

An employee who as a nonpaid union official represents the interests of members in their relations with management

An extremely important position in the local union is the union steward. The **union steward** represents the interests of union members in their relations with their immediate supervisors and other members of management. Stewards are normally elected by union members within their department and serve without union pay. Because stewards are full-time employees of the organization, they often spend considerable time after working hours investigating and handling member problems. When stewards represent members during grievance meetings on organizational time, their lost earnings are paid by the local union.

A union steward can be viewed as a "person in the middle," caught between conflicting interests and groups. It cannot be assumed that stewards will always champion union members and routinely oppose managerial objectives. Union stewards are often insightful individuals working for the betterment of employees and the organization. Therefore, it is *highly* encouraged that supervisors and managers at all levels develop a professional working relationship with stewards and all union officials. This relationship can have an important bearing on union-management cooperation and on the efficiency and morale of the workforce.

Union Leadership Commitment and Philosophies

To evaluate the role of union leaders accurately, one must understand the nature of their backgrounds and ambitions and recognize the political nature of the offices they occupy. Union leaders—at all levels—often possess enthusiasm and a commitment to the ideals of unionism and employee welfare that is difficult for managers to understand and accept. To some managers, union officials have a "religious" zeal toward the labor movement and the advancement of member bargaining rights. Additionally, it is important for managers to understand that union officials are elected to office and, like any political officials, must be responsive to the views of their constituency. The union leader who ignores the demands of union members may risk being voted out of office or having members vote the union out as their bargaining agent.

A union official and manager discuss a safety issue at a job site.

To be effective leaders, labor officials must also pay constant attention to the general goals and philosophies of the labor movement.[37] Business unionism is the general label given to the goals of U.S. labor organizations: increased pay and benefits, job security, and improved working conditions. Furthermore, union leaders also know that unions must address the broader social, economic, and legislative issues of concern to members. For example, the United Auto Workers continually lobbies Congress for protective legislation affecting the auto industry. The American Federation of State, County, and Municipal Employees; The Union of Needletrades, Industrial and Textile Employees; and The Association of Flight Attendants, representing flight attendants at America West Airlines, have been active supporters of women's issues at both the state and national levels.

business unionism

A term applied to the goals of U.S. labor organizations, which collectively bargain for improvements in wages, hours, job security, and working conditions

LABOR RELATIONS IN THE PUBLIC SECTOR

Collective bargaining among federal, state, and local government employees has been an area of important activity for the union movement since the early 1960s. Today 7 million public workers belong to unions or employee associations. They constitute about 40 percent of government employees. The latest union membership figures show that some of the nation's largest labor organizations represent employees in the public sector—the National Education Association (3.2 million members), American Federation of Teachers (1.4 million members), and State, County, and Municipal Employees (1.4 million members), for instance.[38] As unions and employee associations of teachers, police, firefighters, and state employees have grown in size and political power, they have demanded the same rights to bargain and strike that private-sector employees have.

While public sector and private sector collective bargaining have many features in common, a number of factors differentiate the two sectors. First, there are no national laws, like the National Labor Relations Act in the private sector, governing public sector labor relations. Public sector collective bargaining falls within the separate jurisdiction of each state, and great diversity exists among the various state laws. For example, some states, such as Arizona, Utah, and Mississippi, have no collective bargaining laws; other states, such as Florida, Hawaii, and New York, have comprehensive laws granting collective bargaining rights to all public employees. Between these extremes are state laws granting collective bargaining rights only to specific employee groups such as teachers and the uniformed services (police and fire). For federal employees, collective bargaining is governed by executive orders (regulations issued by the U.S. president) and the Civil Service Reform Act of 1978.[39]

Second, public jurisdictions often establish the wages, employee benefits, and organizational rules under which their employees work. Public *civil service systems* exist to address employee complaints or grievances. With wages and working conditions set by law, unions are largely denied the opportunity to negotiate for the traditional bread-and-butter issues of collective bargaining.[40] Unions see this arrangement as a loss of opportunity to "champion" their cause to employees.

Lastly, striking in the public sector is largely prohibited. Because the services that government employees provide are often considered essential to the well-being of the public, public policy is opposed to such strikes. Thus most state legislatures have not granted public employees the right to strike. In those states where striking is permitted, the right is limited to specific groups of employees—normally nonuniformed employees—and the strike cannot endanger the public's health, safety, or welfare. Public employee unions contend, however, that denying them the same right to strike as employees in the private sector means that their power during collective bargaining is greatly reduced. Union officials often describe negotiating with public officials as a process of "meet and beg."

In order to provide some equity in bargaining power, various arbitration methods are used for resolving collective bargaining deadlocks in the public sector. One is *compulsory binding arbitration* for employees such as police officers, firefighters, and others in jobs for which strikes cannot be tolerated. Another method is *final offer arbitration*, under which the arbitrator must select one or the other of the final offers submitted by the disputing parties. With this method, the arbitrator's award is more likely to go to the party whose final bargaining offer has moved the closest toward a reasonable settlement.

▪▪ THE BARGAINING PROCESS
▪▪

Objective 4

collective bargaining process
The process of negotiating a labor agreement, including the use of economic pressures by both parties

Those unfamiliar with contract negotiations often view the process as an emotional conflict between labor and management, complete with marathon sessions, fist pounding, and smoke-filled rooms. In reality, negotiating a labor agreement entails long hours of extensive preparation combined with diplomatic maneuvering and the development of bargaining strategies. Furthermore, negotiation is only one part of the collective bargaining process. (See Figure 14.2.) Collective bargaining also may include the use of economic pressures in the form of strikes and boycotts by a union. Lockouts, plant closures, and the replacement of strikers

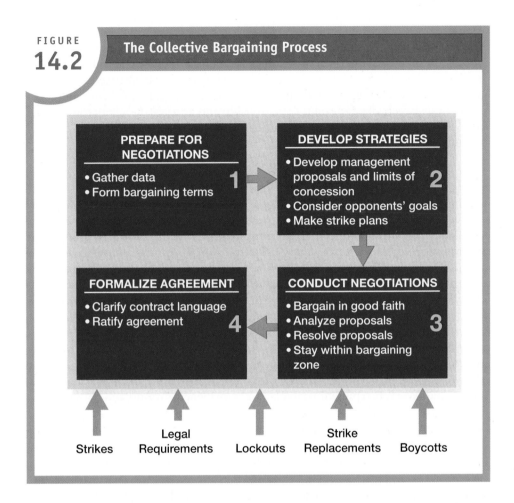

FIGURE 14.2 The Collective Bargaining Process

are similar pressures used by an employer. In addition, either or both parties may seek support from the general public or from the courts as a means of pressuring the opposing side.

Preparing for Negotiations

Preparing for negotiations includes assembling data to support bargaining proposals and forming the bargaining team. This permits collective bargaining to be conducted on an orderly, factual, and positive basis with a greater likelihood of achieving desired goals. Assuming that the labor agreement is not the first to be negotiated by the parties, preparation for negotiations ideally start soon after the current agreement has been signed. This practice allows negotiators to review and diagnose weaknesses and mistakes made during the previous negotiations while the experience is still current in their minds.

Normally, each side has four to six representatives at the negotiating table. The chief negotiator for management is the vice president or manager for labor relations; the chief negotiator for the union is the local union president or national union representative. Others making up management's team may include representatives from accounting or finance, operations, employment, legal, or training. The local union president is likely to be supported by the chief steward, various local union vice presidents, and a representative from the national union. Importantly, it is widely accepted that the conduct of the negotiators strongly influences individual bargaining sessions and the outcomes reached. According to one experienced negotiator, "The conduct of negotiations largely depends on the relationship and attitude of negotiators toward one another. If you want conflict in your bargaining sessions just start off attacking the other side."[41]

Gathering Bargaining Data

Employers gather economic data primarily in the areas of wages and benefits. However, internal data relating to grievances, disciplinary actions, transfers, promotions, overtime, and former arbitration awards are useful in formulating and supporting the employer's bargaining position. The supervisors and managers who must live with and administer the labor agreement can be very important sources of ideas and suggestions concerning changes that are needed in the *next* agreement. Their contact with union members and representatives provides them with firsthand knowledge of the changes that union negotiators are likely to propose.

When negotiating contracts, union bargainers talk about "taking wages out of competition." This term refers to having similar contract provisions—particularly concerning wages and benefits—between different companies in order to prevent one employer from having a favorable labor cost advantage over another. For example, the United Auto Workers representing workers at both General Motors and Ford will seek similar contract provisions. Furthermore, this allows unions to show their members that they are receiving wages and benefits comparable to those of other employees doing like work. Other negotiated labor agreements, particularly at the local and regional levels, play a significant part in settling the terms of the labor agreement.

Developing Bargaining Strategies and Tactics

Both management and union negotiators approach bargaining with a defined strategy. In tough economic periods, the employer's strategy might be cost containment or specific reductions in wages or benefits such as health care or pension costs. Conversely, in times of economic growth—when a union strike would harm sales—the employer will be more willing to meet union demands. The employer's strategy should also consider proposals the union is likely to submit, goals the union is striving to achieve, and extent to which it may be willing to make concessions or to resort to strike action in order to achieve these goals.

At a minimum, the employer's bargaining strategy must address these points:

- Likely union proposals and management responses to them

- A listing of management demands, limits of concessions, and anticipated union responses

- Development of a database to support management bargaining proposals and to counteract union demands

- A contingency operating plan should employees strike

Certain elements of strategy are common to both the employer and the union. Generally, the initial demands presented by each side are greater than those it actually may hope to achieve.[42] This is done in order to provide room for concessions. Moreover, each party usually avoids giving up the maximum it is capable of conceding in order to allow for further concessions that may be needed to break a bargaining deadlock.

The negotiation of a labor agreement can have some of the characteristics of a poker game, with each side attempting to determine its opponent's position while not revealing its own.[43] Each party normally tries to avoid disclosing the relative importance that it attaches to a proposal so that it will not be forced to pay a higher price than is necessary to have the proposal accepted. As in buying a new car, the buyer and seller employ a lot of strategy in order to obtain the best outcome possible.

Negotiating the Labor Agreement

While there is no "exact" way to negotiate a labor agreement, typically each side focuses on one issue or several related issues until agreement is reached.[44] For each bargaining issue to be resolved satisfactorily, the point at which agreement is reached must be within limits that the union and the employer are willing to accept. In a frequently cited bargaining model, Ross Stagner and Hjalmar Rosen call the area within these two limits the bargaining zone. In some bargaining situations, such as the one illustrated in Figure 14.3, the solution desired by one party may exceed the limits of the other party. Thus that solution is outside the bargaining zone. If that party refuses to modify its demands sufficiently to bring them within the bargaining zone or if the opposing party refuses to extend its limit to accommodate the demands of the other party, a bargaining deadlock results.[45] For example, when bargaining a wage increase for employees, if the union's lowest limit is a 4 percent increase and management's top limit is 6 percent, an acceptable range—the bargaining zone—is available to both parties. If management's top limit is only 3 percent, however, a bargaining zone is not available to either side, and a deadlock is likely to occur. Figure 14.3, which is based on the original model by Stagner and Rosen, shows that as bargaining takes place, several important variables influence the negotiators and their ability to reach agreement within the bargaining zone.

bargaining zone

An area in which the union and the employer are willing to concede when bargaining

Good Faith Bargaining

The Taft-Hartley Act requires an employer to negotiate in good faith with the union's representatives over conditions of employment (the same obligation applies to the union representatives).[46] Good faith requires meetings to be held at reasonable times and places to discuss employment conditions. It requires also that the proposals submitted by each party be realistic. In discussing the other party's proposals, each side must offer reasonable counterproposals for those it is unwilling to accept. Finally, both parties must sign the written document containing the agreement reached through negotiations.

Additionally, to help the parties bargain in good faith, the National Labor Relations Board has divided the subjects of bargaining into three distinct categories. Each

FIGURE
14.3

The Bargaining Zone and Negotiation Influences

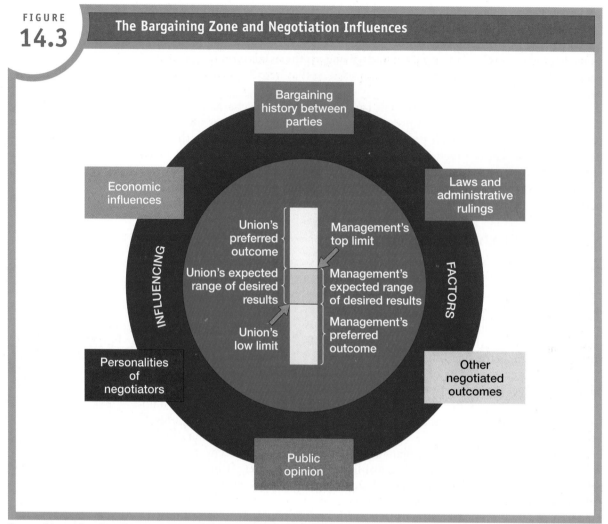

Source: Adapted from Ross Stagner and Hjalmar Rosen, *Psychology of Union-Management Relations* (Belmont, CA: Wadsworth Publishing Company, 1965), 96. Adapted with permission from Brooks/Cole Publishing Co.

category confers specific rights and responsibilities on labor and management negotiators. The three categories of bargaining are:

1. **Mandatory subject.** All matters concerning rates of pay, hours of employment, and
   other conditions of employment. Both the employer and the union must bargain
   in good faith over the issues. The law, however, does not require either party to
   agree to a proposal or to make concessions while negotiating these subjects. The
   parties may bargain to an impass over these topics.

2. **Permissive subjects.** Matters that are lawful but not related to wages, hours, or
   other conditions of employment—the parties are free to bargain, but neither side
   can force the other side to bargain over these topics. Permissive subjects might
   include a union demand to ratify supervisory promotions or consultation on
   setting the price of the organization's product or service.

3. Illegal subjects. These subjects of bargaining would include such issues as the closed shop or compulsory dues checkoff. If a demand is made concerning an illegal item, the NLRB finds a violation of good-faith bargaining under section 8(a)(5) of the Taft-Hartley Act. When labor or management negotiators cannot agree on whether a bargaining proposal is a mandatory or a permissive issue—such as drug testing or employee surveillance—the NLRB decides the dispute.

Interest-Based Bargaining

U.S. labor-management negotiations are characterized as adversarial. With adversarial bargaining, negotiators start with defined positions, and through deferral, persuasion, trade, or power, the parties work toward the resolution of individual bargaining demands. Unfortunately, as noted by one labor negotiator, "adversarial bargaining does little to establish a long-term positive relationship based on open communications and trust. By its nature, it leads to suspicion and compromise."[47] To overcome these negative feelings, labor and management practitioners may use a nonadversarial approach to negotiating.

Interest-based bargaining is based on the identification and resolution of mutual interests rather than the resolve of specific bargaining demands.[48] As defined by the Federal Mediation and Conciliation Service, interest-based bargaining is "a problem-solving process conducted in a principled way that creates effective solutions while improving the bargaining relationship." The focus of bargaining strategy is to discover mutual bargaining interests with the intent of formulating options and solutions for mutual gain.[49] Rather than using proposals and counterproposals as a means of reaching agreement (as with adversarial negotiations), participants use brainstorming, consensus decision-making, active listening, process checking, and matrix building to facilitate the settlement of issues. An underlying goal of interest-based bargaining is to create a relationship for the future based on trust, understanding, and mutual respect.

interest-based bargaining

Problem-solving bargaining based on a win-win philosophy and the development of a positive long-term relationship

Management and Union Power in Collective Bargaining

Fortunately, the great majority of labor-management negotiations are settled peacefully. However, should negotiations become deadlocked, bargaining can become highly adversarial as each side will now employ its bargaining power to achieve its desired ends. The party's bargaining power consists of its economic, political, and social influence to achieve its demands at the expense of the other side.

5 Objective

bargaining power

The power of labor and management to achieve their goals through economic, social, or political influence

Union Bargaining Power

The bargaining power of the union may be exercised by striking, picketing, or boycotting the employer's products or services. A strike is the refusal of a group of employees to perform their jobs. Unions usually seek strike authorization from their members to use as a bargaining ploy to gain concessions that will make a strike unnecessary. A strike vote by the members does not mean they actually want or expect to go out on strike. Rather, it is intended as a vote of confidence to strengthen the position of their leaders at the bargaining table.

Of critical importance to the union is the extent, if any, to which the employer will be able to continue operating through the use of supervisory and nonstriking personnel and employees hired to replace the strikers. In organizations with high

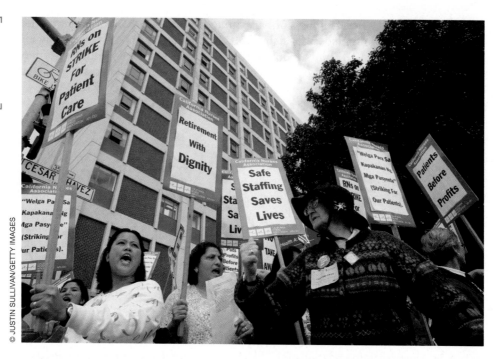

Union members will form a picket line to increase the union's bargaining power during negotiations.

levels of technology and automation, and consequently fewer employees, continuing service with supervisors and managers is more likely. Among the highly automated telephone companies, most services can be maintained by supervisors during a strike. According to one authority, "Because of technological change, striking in many industries no longer has the effect of curtailing the employer's operations significantly."[50] Consequently, the greater the ability of the employer to continue operating, the less the union's chances of gaining its demands through a strike.

When a union goes on strike, it pickets the employer by placing people at business entrances to advertise the dispute and to discourage others from entering the premises. Because unions often refuse to cross another union's picket line, the pickets may serve to prevent the delivery and pickup of goods or performance of other services. For example, a Teamster truck driver may refuse to deliver produce to a food store whose employees are out on strike with the United Food and Commercial Workers Union.

Another economic weapon of the union is the *boycott*, which is a refusal to patronize the employer. For example, production employees on strike against a hand tool manufacturer might picket a retail store that sells the tools made by the struck employer. Unions will also use handbills, radio announcements, e-mail campaigns, and newspaper ads to discourage the purchase of the employer's product or service.

Management Bargaining Power

When negotiations become deadlocked, the employer's bargaining power largely rests on being able to continue operations in the face of a strike *or* to shut down operations entirely.

Should employees strike the organization (referred to as an economic strike), employers have the legal right to hire replacement workers. With this right, employers acquire a bargaining weapon equal in force to the union's right to strike. As one observer noted, "The availability of a worker replacement strategy improves management's ability to battle a union head-on in the way that unions have battled employers for decades."

Another prevalent bargaining strategy is for the employer to continue operations by using managers and supervisors to staff employee jobs. In one case, nearly 30,000 managers left their offices to serve as operators, technicians, and customer service representatives during a strike between Verizon and the Communications Workers of America. As noted previously, technological advances enhance the employer's ability to operate during a strike.

In extreme situations, the employer may elect to lock out its employees. The lockout is a bargaining strategy by which the employer denies employees the opportunity to work by closing its operations. Besides being used in bargaining impasses, lockouts may be used by employers to combat union slowdowns, damage to their property, or violence within the organization that may occur in connection with a labor dispute. Employers may still be reluctant to resort to a lockout, however, because of their concern that denying work to regular employees might hurt the organization's image.

Resolving Bargaining Deadlocks

Unions and employers in all types of industries—sports, transportation, entertainment, manufacturing, communication, and health care—have used mediation and arbitration to help resolve their bargaining deadlocks.[51] As discussed in Chapter 13, mediation is a voluntary process that relies on the communication and persuasive skills of a mediator to help the parties resolve their differences. The federal government is likely to become involved in labor disputes through the services of the FMCS.

Unlike a mediator, an arbitrator assumes the role of a decision maker and determines what the settlement between the two parties should be. In other words, arbitrators write a final contract that the parties *must* accept. Compared with mediation, arbitration is not often used to settle private sector bargaining disputes. In the public sector, where strikes are largely prohibited, the use of *interest arbitration* is a common method to resolve bargaining deadlocks. Generally, one or both parties are reluctant to give a third party the power to make the settlement for them. Consequently, a mediator typically is used to break a deadlock and assist the parties in reaching an agreement. An arbitrator generally is called on to resolve disputes arising in connection with the administration of the agreement, called *rights arbitration* or *grievance arbitration*, which will be discussed shortly.

arbitrator

A third-party neutral who resolves a labor dispute by issuing a final decision in the disagreement

> **Using the Internet**
>
> Information about the responsibilities of the Federal Mediation and Conciliation Service, as well as a description of its history and current service, may be found via the Student Resources at:
>
> **www.cengage.com/ management/bohlander**

■■ THE LABOR AGREEMENT

When negotiations are concluded, the labor agreement becomes a formal *binding* document listing the terms, conditions, and rules under which employees and managers agree to operate. Highlights in HRM 5 shows some of the major articles in a labor agreement and also provides examples of some new and progressive contract clauses. Two important items in any labor agreement pertain to the issue of management rights and the forms of security afforded the union.

Items in a Labor Agreement

Typical clauses will cover:
- Wages
- Vacations
- Holidays
- Work schedules
- Management rights
- Union security
- Transfers
- Discipline
- Training
- Grievance procedures
- No strike/no lockout clause
- Overtime
- Safety procedures
- Severance pay
- Seniority

- Pensions and benefits
- Outsourcing
- Work rules

Progressive clauses will cover:
- Employee access to records
- Limitations on use of performance evaluation
- Elder care leave
- Flexible medical spending accounts
- Protection against hazards of technology equipment (VDTs)
- Limitations against electronic monitoring
- Procedures governing drug testing
- Bilingual stipends
- Domestic partnership benefits
- Employee involvement programs

The Issue of Management Rights

Management rights have to do with the conditions of employment over which management is able to exercise exclusive control. Almost without exception, the labor agreement contains a *management rights* clause. This clause states that "management's authority is supreme in all matters except those it has expressly conceded in the collective agreement, or in those areas where its authority is restricted by law." Management rights might include the right of management to determine the products to produce, to determine the location of production or service facilities, or to select production equipment and procedures. The following is an example of a clause defining management rights in one labor agreement:

> It is agreed that the company possesses all of the rights, powers, privileges, and authority it had prior to the execution of this agreement; and nothing in this agreement shall be construed to limit the company in any way in the exercise of the regular and customary functions of management and the operation of its business, except as it may be specifically relinquished or modified herein by an express provision of this agreement.[52]

Union Security Agreements

As we noted at the beginning of this chapter, unions must represent all bargaining unit members equally regardless of whether employees join the union or not. In exchange for this obligation, union officials will seek to negotiate some form of compulsory membership as a condition of employment. Union officials argue that compulsory membership precludes the possibility that some employees will receive the benefits of unionization without paying their fair share of the costs. A standard union security provision is dues checkoff, which gives the employer the responsibility of withholding union dues from the paychecks of union members who agree to such a deduction.

Other common forms of union security found in labor contracts are different types of "shop" agreements.[53] These agreements—in varying degrees—attempt to require employees to join the union. For example, the *union shop* provides that any employee who is not a union member upon employment must join the union within thirty days or be terminated. Another, the *agency shop*, provides for voluntary membership. However, all bargaining unit members must pay union dues and fees.

Few issues in collective bargaining are more controversial than the negotiation of these agreements.[54] The most popular union security clause, the union shop, is illegal in twenty-two states having right-to-work laws.[55] Right-to-work laws ban any form of compulsory union membership. Section 14(b) of the Taft-Hartley Act permits individual states to enact legislation prohibiting compulsory union membership as a condition of employment.

ADMINISTRATION OF THE LABOR AGREEMENT

6 | Objective

Negotiation of the labor agreement, as mentioned earlier, is usually the most publicized and critical aspect of labor relations. Strike deadlines, press conferences, and employee picketing help create this image. Nevertheless, as managers in unionized organizations know, the bulk of labor relations activity comes from the day-to-day administration of the agreement because no agreement could possibly anticipate all the forms that disputes may take. In addition, once the agreement is signed, each side will naturally interpret ambiguous clauses to its own advantage.[56] These differences are traditionally resolved through the grievance procedure.

Negotiated Grievance Procedures

The grievance procedure typically provides for the union to represent the interests of its members (and nonmembers as well) in processing a grievance. It is considered by some authorities to be the heart of the bargaining agreement, or the safety valve that gives flexibility to the whole system of collective bargaining.[57]

The grievance procedure is normally initiated by the union—or an individual employee—when it feels management has violated some article of the labor agreement. In one case, the union filed a grievance against a supervisor when it believed the supervisor promoted an employee out of seniority order—called a bypass grievance. A significant benefit of the grievance procedure is that it provides a formal and orderly procedure for the union to challenge the actions of management without

grievance procedure

A formal procedure that provides for the union to represent members and nonmembers in processing a grievance resort to force. One authority has noted, "The grievance procedure fosters cooperation, not conflict, between the employer and the union."[58]

The operation of a grievance procedure is unique to each individual collective bargaining relationship, although there are common elements among systems. For example, grievance procedures normally specify how the grievance is to be initiated, the number and timing of steps that are to compose the procedure, and the identity of representatives from each side who are to be involved in the hearings at each step. (See Figure 14.4.) When a grievance cannot be resolved at one of the specified steps, most agreements provide for the grievance to be submitted to a third party—usually an arbitrator—whose decision is final. Some labor agreements provide for mediation as a way to resolve employee grievances. When used, *grievance mediation* will be listed as a formal step in the grievance procedure preceding arbitration.

The Grievance Procedure in Action

In order for an employee's grievance to be considered formally, it must be expressed orally and/or in writing, ideally to the employee's immediate supervisor. Because grievances are often the result of an oversight or a misunderstanding, many of them

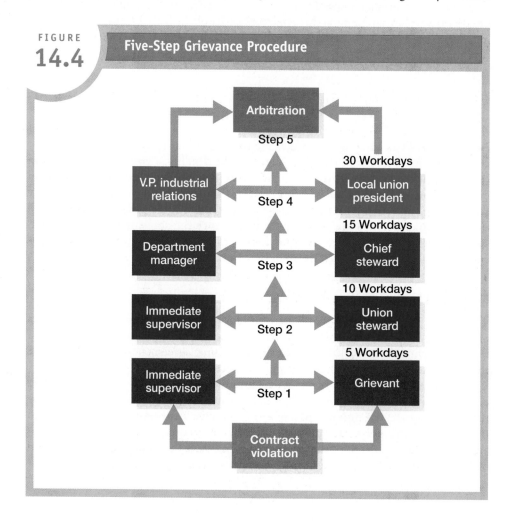

FIGURE 14.4

Five-Step Grievance Procedure

can be resolved at this point. Whether it is possible to resolve a grievance at the initial step will depend on the supervisor's ability and willingness to discuss the problem with the employee and the steward. Additionally, HR professionals acknowledge that grievance handling is more successful when supervisors are trained formally in resolving grievances, including familiarization with the terms of the labor agreement and the discussion of the problem in a rational and objective manner. A grievance should not be viewed as something to be won or lost. Rather, both sides must view the situation as an attempt to solve a human relations problem.

In some instances, a satisfactory solution may not be possible at the first step because there are legitimate differences of opinion between the employee and the supervisor or because the supervisor does not have the authority to take the action required to satisfy the grievant. Personality conflicts, prejudices, emotionalism, stubbornness, or other factors may also be barriers to a satisfactory solution at this step.

Grievance Arbitration

The function of **rights arbitration** is to provide the solution to a grievance that a union and an employer have been unable to resolve by themselves. As mentioned earlier, arbitration is performed by a neutral third party (an arbitrator or impartial umpire). This third party's decision dictates how the grievance is to be settled.[59] Both parties are obligated to comply with the decision.

rights arbitration
Arbitration over interpretation of the meaning of contract terms or employee work grievances

Decision to Arbitrate

In deciding whether to use arbitration, each party must weigh the costs involved against the importance of the case and the prospects of gaining a favorable award. It would seem logical that neither party would allow a weak case to go to arbitration if there were little possibility of gaining a favorable award. Logic, however, does not always prevail. For example, it is not unusual for a union to take a weak case to arbitration in order to demonstrate to the members that the union is willing to exhaust every remedy in looking out for their interests. Union officers also are not likely to refuse to take to arbitration the grievances of members who are popular or politically powerful in the union, even though their cases are weak. Moreover, under the **fair representation doctrine,** unions have a legal obligation to provide assistance to members who are pursuing grievances. Because members can bring suit against their unions for failing to process their grievances adequately, many union officers are reluctant to refuse taking even weak grievances to arbitration.

fair representation doctrine
A doctrine under which unions have a legal obligation to assist both members and nonmembers in labor relations matters

Management, on the other hand, may allow a weak case to go to arbitration to demonstrate to the union officers that management "cannot be pushed around." Also, managers at lower levels may be reluctant to risk the displeasure of top management by stating that a certain HR policy is unworkable or unsound. Stubbornness and mutual antagonism also may force many grievances into arbitration because neither party is willing to make concessions to reach an agreement, even when it may recognize that it is in the wrong.

Arbitration Hearing

In our experience, employees unfamiliar with arbitration find the process confusing and often stressful. This is true for employees in the nonunion, as well as the union, setting. Arbitration hearings have the appearance of a court hearing but without many of the formalities of a court proceeding. The process begins with the swearing-in of witnesses and the introduction

Using the Internet

Check out the American Arbitration Association's Web site for more information about the organization and its work. Go to the Student Resources at:

www.cengage.com/management/bohlander

of the *submission agreement*. The submission agreement is a statement of the problem to be resolved. Such a statement might read: "Was the three-day suspension of Alex Hayden for just cause? If not, what is the appropriate remedy?" The parties will then make opening statements, followed by the presentation of facts and evidence, and the oral presentation of witnesses. The hearing will conclude with each side making summary statements that are arguments in support of its position.

In arbitrating a dispute, it is the responsibility of the arbitrator to ensure that each side receives a fair hearing during which it may present all of the facts it considers pertinent to the case. The primary purpose of the hearing is to assist the arbitrator in obtaining the facts necessary to resolve a human relations problem rather than a legal one. The arbitrator, therefore, has a right to question witnesses or to request additional facts from either party. After conducting the hearing and receiving post-hearing briefs (should the parties choose to submit them), the arbitrator customarily has thirty days in which to consider the evidence and render an award. In most labor contracts, the costs of arbitration are shared equally by the parties.

Arbitration Award

The arbitration award is a formal written document given to both sides. As in grievance procedures, there is no specific format to an arbitration award, but typically the award contains five parts: (1) submission agreement, (2) facts of the case, (3) positions of the parties, (4) opinion of the arbitrator, and (5) decision rendered. As might be expected, the decision of the arbitrator is of major importance to the parties. However, the reasoning behind the decision—the opinion—is equally important since it can provide guidance concerning the interpretation of the labor agreement and the resolution of future disputes arising from its administration. In pointing out the merits of each party's position, the reasoning that underlies the award can help lessen the disappointment and protect the self-esteem of those representing the unsuccessful party. The opinion will also evaluate the evidence presented by each side in support of its position and, in discipline cases, whether management had just cause for the action taken against an employee. (See Chapter 13 for a discussion of just cause in arbitration.) Importantly, in deciding a case, the arbitrator has the power to modify the outcome requested by both sides. It is not uncommon, for example, for an arbitrator to reduce a discharge to a suspension without pay for a specific time period.

Because of the importance and magnitude of arbitration in both the union and nonunion setting, the process by which arbitrators make decisions and the factors that influence those decisions are of continuing interest to managers. Typically, arbitrators use four factors when deciding cases:

1. The wording of the labor agreement (or employment policy in nonunion organizations)

2. The submission agreement as presented to the arbitrator

3. Testimony and evidence offered during the hearing

4. Arbitration criteria or standards (similar to standards of common law) against which cases are judged

When deciding the case of an employee discharged for absenteeism, for example, the arbitrator would consider these factors separately and/or jointly. Arbitrators are essentially constrained to decide cases on the basis of the wording of the labor agreement, or employment policy, and the facts, testimony, and evidence presented at the hearing.

In practice, arbitration decision-making is not an exact science. In fact, the decisions of arbitrators can be rather subjective. Arbitrators can, and do, interpret contract language differently (for example, what does "just cause discharge" actually mean), they assign varying degrees of importance to testimony and evidence, they judge the truthfulness of witnesses differently, and they give arbitration standards greater or lesser weight as they apply to facts of the case. Each of these influences introduces subjectivity into the decision-making process.[60]

CONTEMPORARY CHALLENGES TO LABOR ORGANIZATIONS

We conclude our discussion of labor relations by highlighting three important issues facing unions today: foreign competition and technological advances, decrease of union membership, and employers' focus on maintaining nonunion status.[61]

Foreign Competition and Technological Change

The importation of steel, consumer electronics, automobiles, clothing, textiles, and shoes from foreign countries creates a loss of jobs in the United States for workers who produce these products. Furthermore, foreign subsidiaries of American corporations such as Nike, Westinghouse, and Xerox have been accused by labor unions of exporting the jobs of U.S. workers. As a result, unions are demanding more government protection against imports, seeking to protect U.S. jobs from low-cost overseas producers. Furthermore, in recent years, the service sector of the U.S. economy has witnessed the outsourcing of white-collar jobs to foreign employers in locations such as India and Indonesia.

Coupled with the threat of foreign competition is the challenge to labor brought about by rapid technological advances. Improvements in computer technology and highly automated operating systems have lowered the demand for certain types of employees. Decline in membership in the auto, steel, rubber, and transportation unions illustrates this fact. As previously discussed, technological advances have also diminished the effectiveness of strikes because highly automated organizations are capable of maintaining satisfactory levels of operation with minimum staffing levels during work stoppages.

Decrease in Union Membership

A major challenge confronting organized labor is to halt the decline in union membership. The magnitude of the problem is illustrated by statistics that show how union membership has declined in total numbers and as a percentage of the total civilian labor force. In 1970, union membership totaled approximately 21 million, or 25 percent of the civilian labor force. In 1990, those figures dropped to 16.7 million union members, or slightly more than 16 percent of the civilian workforce. In 2008, union membership was approximately 15.7 million, or 12 percent of employed wage and salary workers.[62] In the private sector, union membership accounted for approximately 10 percent of all those employed, or about 9 million workers. The loss of union jobs reflects, in part, the decline in U.S. manufacturing jobs, coupled with the failure of unions to draw membership from among the white-collar and service ranks, where the labor force is growing more rapidly.[63] Other reasons for the decline in union membership include the following:

- A shift from traditional unionized industries (manufacturing, mining) to high-technology industries (computers, pharmaceuticals).[64]

- Growth in the employment of part-time and temporary workers.

- Growth in small businesses, in which unionization is more costly and difficult to perform.

- Globalization of the workforce particularly among low wage employers.[65]

What are labor organizations doing to stem the decline in union membership? The answer, according to one union official, is "energized organizing." First, unions are targeting workers they have long ignored: low-wage service workers on the bottom tier of the U.S. economy—for example, janitors, maids, and service workers; food service employees; and retail clerks. Furthermore, unions see recent immigrants, the fastest-growing segment of working people, as potent prospects for union growth. Haitian cab drivers, Latino airport workers, Vietnamese warehouse distribution workers, Russian truck drivers, and Asian American service workers are targeted for union representation.[66]

Second, the AFL-CIO has embraced an aggressive unionization strategy. John Swenney, president of the AFL-CIO, adopted "America Needs a Raise" as the AFL-CIO's motto for a $20-million-a-year organizing drive. The AFL-CIO has placed greater emphasis on its Organizing Institute, which recruits, trains, and places talented individuals in organizing opportunities where workers appear "ripe" for unionization. The mission of the Organizing Institute is to "continually produce organizers who are enthusiastic, energetic, and armed with the skills to help workers fight to form and join unions." Organizers are trained to use innovative organizing strategies.

Finally, national unions are restructuring in order to increase their ability to effectively organize. Two examples are noteworthy. The Union of Needletrades, Industrial and Textile Employees (UNITE) and the Hotel Employees and Restaurant Employees (HERE) merged to become UNITE HERE. According to Chris Chafe, spokesperson for the union, "We all benefit from working more closely together on solidarity issues, organizing campaigns, and contract battles."

As previously discussed, the new national labor federation Change to Win has as its primary goal the unionization of low skill, low wage employees. Will labor's efforts reverse the decline in membership? Bureau of Labor Statistics figures for 2007 show the number of workers belonging to unions rose by 311,000 over 2006 levels.[67]

Employers' Focus on Maintaining Nonunion Status

A significant fact in U.S. labor relations during the 1990s and into the twenty-first century is the prevalence of union avoidance programs. Managers in all types of organizations are vocal in their desire to maintain a union-free environment. To support this goal, employers are providing wages, benefits, and services designed to make unionism unattractive to employees. In addition, a participative management style, profit sharing plans, and alternative dispute resolution procedures (see Chapter 13) are offered to counteract the long-established union goals of improved wages and working conditions. It is important to recognize that these strategies react to the conditions cited at the beginning of the chapter as the main reasons why workers unionize. Because these conditions are under the direct control of management, they can be changed to help discourage or prevent unionism.

.... **SUMMARY** ....

Objective 1 The Railway Labor Act (1926) affords collective bargaining rights to workers employed in the railway and airline industries. The Norris-LaGuardia Act (1932) imposes limitations on the granting of injunctions in labor-management disputes. Most private employees are granted representation rights through the Wagner Act (1935), which has helped protect and encourage union organizing and bargaining activities. The passage of the Taft-Hartley Act (1947) and the Landrum-Griffin Act (1959) has served to establish certain controls over the internal affairs of unions and their relations with employers.

Objective 2 Studies show that workers unionize for different economic, psychological, and social reasons. While some employees may join unions because they are required to do so, most belong to unions because they are convinced that unions help them improve their wages, benefits, and various working conditions. Employee unionization is largely caused by dissatisfaction with managerial practices and procedures.

Objective 3 A formal union organizing campaign is used to solicit employee support for the union. Once employees demonstrate their desire to unionize through signing authorization cards, the union petitions the NLRB for a secret ballot election. If 51 percent of those voting in the election vote for the union, the NLRB certifies the union as the bargaining representative for all employees in the bargaining unit.

Objective 4 Negotiating a labor agreement is a detailed process. Each side prepares a list of proposals it wishes to achieve while additionally trying to anticipate proposals desired by the other side. Bargaining teams must be selected and all proposals must be analyzed to determine their impact on and cost to the organization. Both employer and union

negotiators are sensitive to current bargaining patterns within the industry, general cost-of-living trends, and geographical wage differentials. Managers establish goals that seek to retain control over operations and to minimize costs. Union negotiators focus their demands around improved wages, hours, and working conditions. An agreement is reached when both sides compromise their original positions and final terms fall within the limits of the parties' bargaining zone.

Traditionally, collective bargaining between labor and management has been adversarial. Presently, there is an increased interest in nonadversarial negotiations—negotiations based on mutual gains and a heightened respect between the parties. What the FMCS calls interest-based bargaining is one form of nonadversarial negotiations.

Objective 5 The collective bargaining process includes not only the actual negotiations, but also the power tactics used to support negotiating demands. When negotiations become deadlocked, bargaining becomes a power struggle to force from either side the concessions needed to break the deadlock. The union's power in collective bargaining comes from its ability to picket, strike, or boycott the employer. The employer's power during negotiations comes from its ability to lock out employees or to operate during a strike by using managerial or replacement employees.

Objective 6 When differences arise between labor and management, they are normally resolved through the grievance procedure. Grievance procedures are negotiated and thus reflect the needs and desires of the parties. The typical grievance procedure consists of three, four, or five steps—each step having specific filing and reply times. Higher-level managers and union officials become involved in disputes at the higher steps of the grievance procedure. The final step of the grievance procedure may be arbitration. Arbitrators render a final decision to problems not resolved at lower grievance steps.

The submission agreement is a statement of the issue to be solved through arbitration. It is simply the problem the parties wish to have settled. The arbitrator must answer the issue by basing the arbitration award on four factors: contents of the labor agreement (or employment policy), submission agreement as written, testimony and evidence obtained at the hearing, and various arbitration standards developed over time to assist in the resolution of different types of labor-management disputes. Arbitration is not an exact science because arbitrators give varying degrees of importance to the evidence and criteria by which disputes are resolved.

Objective 7 Challenges facing union leaders today include declining membership caused by technological advancements and increased domestic and global competition. Labor organizations experience less success in organizations when employers establish progressive HR policies in the areas of wages, employee benefits, and organizational policies that enhance job security and the dignity of employees. To counteract a declining membership base, unions have become aggressive in organizing employees in lower-skilled occupations, recent immigrants, and employees in white-collar jobs. Through union mergers and coalitions, labor organizations seek to become more effective in their organizing efforts.

KEY TERMS

arbitrator
authorization card
bargaining power
bargaining unit
bargaining zone
business unionism
collective bargaining process

craft unions
employee associations
exclusive representation
fair representation doctrine
grievance procedure
industrial unions
interest-based bargaining

labor relations process
rights arbitration
unfair labor practices (ULPs)
union shop
union steward

DISCUSSION QUESTIONS

Objective 1 1. Under the provisions of the Taft-Hartley Act, which unfair labor practices apply to both unions and employers?

Objective 2 2. Contrast the arguments concerning union membership that are likely to be presented by a union with those likely to be presented by an employer.

Objective 3 3. Describe the steps in the traditional organizing drive.

What "nontraditional" organizing tactics are unions using to increase their membership ranks?

Objective 4 4. Of what significance is the bargaining zone in the conduct of negotiations? What are some influences affecting negotiated outcomes?

Objective 5 5. The negotiations between Data Services International and its union have become deadlocked. What form of bargaining power does each side possess to enforce its bargaining demands? What are the advantages and disadvantages of each form of bargaining power for both the employer and union?

Objective 6 6. Nancy Buffett has decided to file a grievance with her union steward. The grievance alleges that she was "bypassed" by a junior employee for a promotion to senior technician.

a. Explain the steps her grievance will follow in a formal union-management grievance procedure.
b. Should her grievance go to arbitration, explain the process of an arbitration hearing and identify

the criteria used by the arbitrator to resolve her claim.

Objective 7 7. a. What are some of the actions being taken by unions to cope with the contemporary challenges they face?
b. Why have attitudes toward organized labor, on the part of certain segments of our society, become less favorable than they were in the past?

HRM EXPERIENCE

Learn about Unions

Unions, like business organizations, are dynamic and varied organizations. Some unions are very large, such as the United Auto Workers (UAW) and the American Federation of State, County and Municipal Employees (AFSCME) and represent workers nationally or even internationally. Others are smaller in size—for example, the Writers Guild of America (WGA) or the Air Traffic Controllers Association (ATCA)—and represent only specific groups of employees or organize only in a designated geographic area. This exercise will help you learn more about unions.

Assignment

Working individually or in teams, select four or five different unions or employee associations and report on the following. Vary your selections (large/small, public/private, and so on) to widen your understanding of labor organizations.

- History of the union
- Membership size and type of employees represented
- Mission of the union
- Structure of the union, including its major departments
- National officers
- Names of employers with whom they have an agreement
- Special benefits they offer members
- Other interesting or pertinent information

The AFL-CIO Web site (http://www.afl-cio.org) provides a list of all unions—and their Web sites—affiliated with the federation. National unions and their locals along with library research can also provide information. Be prepared to present your findings during a class discussion.

BIZFLIX EXERCISES

Bread & Roses: Join the Union; Get Bread and Roses

Make sure you have read this chapter before watching this scene from *Bread & Roses*. Before viewing the scene, note your perceptions of unions. Do the same after watching the scene. It strongly relates to discussions of why employees unionize and of union-organizing campaigns. "Justice for Janitors" is the union-organizing slogan that drives Sam Shapiro's (Adrien Brody) efforts to organize the janitors who work for Angel Services in Los Angeles. Unionized janitors earn over $8.00 an hour plus benefits; nonunionized janitors earn $5.75 an hour with no benefits. These nonunionized janitors are mainly immigrants from different countries. Maya (Pilar Padilla) becomes an early supporter of the cause, although she risks losing her job and getting deported. Director Ken Loach launches a political polemic that grippingly tells the story of workers calling for fair wages and fair treatment by their employers.

This scene comes from the "Standing Strong" segment near the end of the film. Sam has worked untiringly to organize the Angel Services workers who work in a building with a prominent law firm as a major tenant. A large group of janitors, both union and nonunion, have marched to the building's lobby. Sam rallies them to continue their fight for fair wages,

benefits, and reinstatement of the workers fired by Perez (George Lopez) at Angel Services. The film continues after this scene to show that the workers won. Angel Services agrees to reinstate all fired workers and provide higher wages and benefits.

What to Watch for and Ask Yourself

- What was your perception of unions and union organizers before you watched this scene? What was your perception after you watched this scene? If your perception changed, why do you think it changed?

- An earlier chapter section, "Why Employees Unionize," describes several factors that motivate people to become union members. Based on this scene, which factors do you think drive these janitors to want to join a union? You also can refer to Figure 14.1, "The Labor Relations Process," for guidance with this question.

- An earlier section, "Organizing Campaigns," describes many parts of a union-organizing campaign. Sam Shapiro is the union organizer. Compare the chapter section to this scene, and infer which steps occurred. Also, assess Sam Shapiro's effectiveness as a union organizer.

CASE STUDY 1

A New Ball Game in Detroit

General Motors Corporation and the United Auto Workers (UAW) made national news. In summer 2007, while negotiating a new contract, the parties agreed to establish a Voluntary Employee Beneficiary Association (VEBA) health care trust fund. Under the new labor agreement, GM will off-load $51 billion in retiree health care obligation onto the UAW. Through an independently managed trust fund, the union, in effect, will become an enormous health care provider.

Soaring health care costs (see Chapter 11) have prompted companies with aging workers and many retirees (for example, the steel, rubber, heavy equipment, and electrical industries) to set up VEBAs to fund long-term health care obligations. Currently, there are about 12,000 VEBAs nationwide. However, the GM-UAW agreement is by far the largest to date. The plan creates a $35 billion trust—$16 billion less than present liabilities—to fund and administer benefits for the company's present and future retirees and their dependents. While GM will incur a huge one-time payment of cash to fund the VEBA, the ongoing drain of retiree health care costs will end. GM has spent approximately $1,400 per car on retiree medical costs. Accounting for inflation, it is estimated that GM's health care expenses will drop by about $200 million a year, and cash flow will improve by $400 million a year—saving GM hopes will allow it to become more price competitive with foreign competitors.

Questions

1. Why would the UAW agree to administer an underfunded VEBA?
2. What risks does a VEBA hold for employees?
3. Besides obvious cost savings, are there other benefits of a VEBA to GM? Explain.

Source: Adapted from David Welch and Nanette Byrnes, "GM's Health Plan Could Be Contagious," *Business Week*, October 8, 2007, 37, and Jeremy Sherd, "Top 5 Workplace News Headlines of 2007," *Workforce Management* 86, no. 21 (December 21, 2007): 22.

CASE STUDY 2

The Arbitration Case of Jesse Stansky

At the arbitration hearing, both parties were adamant in their positions. Nancy Huang, HR manager of Phoenix Semiconductor, argued that the grievant, Jesse Stansky, was justly terminated for arguing and hitting a coworker—a direct violation of company policy and the employee handbook. Stansky argued that he had been a good employee during his ten years of employment.

The submission agreement governing the case read, "It is the employer's position that just cause existed for the discharge of Mr. Jesse Stansky and the penalty was appropriate for the offense committed." Additionally, the employer introduced into evidence the labor agreement, which defined just cause termination as follows:

> Just cause shall serve as the basis for disciplinary action and includes, but is not limited to: dishonesty, inefficiency, unprofessional conduct, failure to report absences, falsification of records, violation of company policy, destruction of property, or possession or being under the influence of alcohol or narcotics.

Stansky was hired as a systems technician on November 20, 1998, a position he held until his termination on October 25, 2008. According to the testimony of Huang, Phoenix Semiconductor strived to maintain a positive and cordial work environment among its employees. Fighting on the job was strictly prohibited. Stansky's performance evaluation showed him to be an average employee, although he had received several disciplinary warnings for poor attendance and one three-day suspension for a "systems control error." Stansky was generally liked by his coworkers, and several testified on his behalf at the arbitration hearing.

The termination of Stansky concerned an altercation between himself and Gary Lindekin, another systems technician. According to witnesses to the incident, both Stansky and Lindekin became visibly upset over the correct way to calibrate a sensitive piece of production equipment. The argument—one witness called it no more than a heated disagreement—lasted approximately three minutes and concluded when Stansky was seen forcefully placing his hand on Lindekin's shoulder. Lindekin took extreme exception to Stansky's behavior and immediately reported the incident to management. After interviews with both Stansky and Lindekin and those who observed the incident, Huang; Samantha Lowry, the employee's immediate supervisor; and Grant Ginn, department manager, decided that Stansky should be terminated for unprofessional conduct and violation of company policy.

Questions

1. Which arguments should be given more weight: those based on company policy, the employee handbook, and the labor agreement or mitigating factors given by the grievant and his witnesses? Explain.
2. How might unprofessional conduct be defined? Explain.
3. If you were the arbitrator, how would you rule in this case? Explain fully the reasons for your decision.

Source: Adapted from an arbitration heard by George W. Bohlander. All names are fictitious.

ANSWERS TO HIGHLIGHTS IN HRM 1

1. No. Applicants are considered as employees and, as such, are protected under the law.

2. No. Individual questioning of employees about their union membership or activities in unlawful.

3. No. Except in specific situations (for example, to promote safety), employees have the right to wear union insignia.

4. Yes.

5. Yes. Blacklisting of job applicants or employees is against labor law.

6. No. During an organizing drive, an employer cannot promise improvements in wages or benefits as a means of defeating the union.

7. Yes. Both nonunion and union employers are subject to unfair labor practice charges.

8. Yes. When a grievance arbitration clause exists in a labor agreement, management must arbitrate cases that seem baseless.

9. Yes. Employees can be disciplined or discharged for work-related misconduct but not solely because of their union affiliations or union sentiments.

10. Yes. Antiunion remarks are not unlawful, provided they are not coercive.

NOTES AND REFERENCES

1. Robert Bussel, "Why Unions Matter: An Orientation for Oregon Legislators, Candidates, and Their Staffs," *Labor Studies Journal* 32, no. 2 (June 2007): 210.

2. David Kiley, "Labor's New Roll of the Dice," *Business Week*, December 24, 2007, 37.

3. Aaron Bernstein, "Checking In? First Pass the Picket Line," *Business Week*, February 20, 2006, 39.

4. Robert J. Grossman, "Reorganized labor," *HR Magazine* 53, no. 1 (January 2008): 77.

5. Cindy Fazzi, "All You Need to Know about the History of Labor Union Law," *Dispute Resolution Journal* 59, no. 2 (May–June 2004): 87.

6. Labor-Management Relations Act, Public Law 101, 80th Congress, 1947.

7. *Annual Report of the National Labor Relations Board—2006* (Washington, DC: U.S. Government Printing Office, 2007), 7.

8. Labor-Management Relations Act, Set. 10(c), as amended.

9. *Annual Report of the National Labor Relations Board—2007*, 11.

10. The NLRB toll-free telephone number is (866) 667-NLRB.

11. Douglas E. Noll, "A Theory of Mediation," *Dispute Resolution Journal* 56, no. 2 (May–June 2001): 78–84.

12. Ron Collotta, FMCS commissioner, interview by author, Phoenix, Arizona, January 5, 2008.

13. For an expanded model of the labor relations process, see John Dunlop, *Industrial Relations Systems* (New York: Henry Holt, 1958), Chapter 1. This book is a classic in the labor relations field. Also, those interested in labor relations may wish to explore in greater detail the historical developments of the U.S. labor movement. Much can be learned about the current operations of labor organizations and the philosophies of labor officials from labor's historical context. A brief but comprehensive history of labor unions can be found in undergraduate labor management textbooks such as those listed among these references.

14. Christopher Palmeri, "Workers Say: We Want an Upgrade." *Business Week*, April 16, 2007, 11.

15. Kate Bronfenbrenner and Robert Hickey, "Successful Union Organizing in the United States—Clear Lessons, Too Few Examples," *Multinational Monitor* 24, no. 6 (June 2003): 9.

16. William H. Holley, Kenneth M. Jennings, and Roger S. Wolters, *The Labor Relations Process*, 9th ed. (Mason, OH: South-Western, 2009).

17. While most employers will readily negotiate with the union once it is certified as the bargaining representative of employees, other employers will continue to vigorously oppose unionization. This may be accomplished by taking a very aggressive bargaining posture against union demands. NLRB statistics show that unions file a large number of unfair labor practice charges [8(a)(5) violations] when they believe employers illegally hinder the bargaining process.

18. Brody Mulling, "Campaign 08: Groups Unveil Plans to Bankroll Democrats," *Wall Street Journal*, March 19, 2008, A-18.

19. Ruth Martin, interview with the author, March 26, 2007, Mesa, Arizona.

20. Richard W. Hurd, "Neutrality Agreements: Innovative, Controversial, and Labor's Hope for the Future," *New Labor Forum* 17, no. 1 (Spring 2008): 34.

21. Amy Dean and David B. Reynolds, "Labor's New Regional Strategy: The Rebirth of Central Labor Councils," *New Labor Forum* 17, no. 1 (Spring 2008): 46.

22. Jarol B. Manheim, *Trends in Union Corporate Campaigns* (New York U.S. Chamber of Commerce, 2005).

23. Arthur B Shostak, ed., *The CyberUnion Handbook* (Armonk, NY: M. E. Sharpe, 2002).

24. *Annual Report of the National Labor Relations Board—2007*, 7.

25. Jonathan A. Segal, "Labor Pains for Union-Free Employers," *HR Magazine* 49, no. 3 (March 2004): 113.

26. Raymond Hogler, "Exclusive Representation and the Wagner Act: The Structure of Federal Collective Bargaining Law," *Labor Law-Journal* 58, no. 3 (Fall 2007): 157.

27. *Annual Report of the National Labor Relations Board—2007*, 16.

28. Jeffrey S. Bosley, "NLRB Modifies Recognition and Contract Bar Doctrines to Provide 45-Day Window to Challenge Voluntary Recognition," *Employee Relations Law Journal* 33, no. 4 (Spring 2008): 89.

29. Interview with Joe Rodrigues, March 23, 2008, Mesa, Arizona.

30. Ron Gettelfinger, "The UAW's Southern Discomfort," *Business Week*, April 2006, 12.

31. The number of unions associated with the AFL-CIO has steadily declined during the past twenty years. The decline has largely been caused by the mergers of unions through absorptions, amalgamations, or affiliations. Several prominent mergers include the merger of the International Ladies Garment Workers Union and the Amalgamated Clothing and Textile Workers Union into the Union of Needletrades, Industrial and Textile Employees; the merger of the Packinghouse and Industrial Workers with the United Food and Commercial Workers; and the merger of the Woodworkers with the Machinists.

32. Statistical information on the AFL-CIO can be obtained at http://www.aflcio.org.

33. Robert J. Grossman, "Reorganized Labor," *HR Magazine* 53, no. 1 (January 2008): 37. See also Samuel Estreicher, "Disunity within the House of Labor: Change to Win or Stay the Course," *Journal of Labor Research* 27, no. 4 (Fall 2006): 505.

34. Tracy Roof, "CTW vs. AFL-CIO: The Potential Impact of the Split on Labor's Political Action," *International Journal of Organizational Theory and Behavior* 10, no. 2 (Summer 2007): 245.

35. Gary Chaison, "The AFL-CIO Split: Does It Really Matter?" *Journal of Labor Research* 28, no. 2 (Spring 2007): 301.

36. Paul F. Clark and Lois S. Gray, "Administrative Practices in American Unions," *Journal of Labor Research* 29, no. 1 (March 2008): 42.

37. Dean Foust, "Sending the Teamsters a Message," *Business Week*, July 17, 2006, 9.

38. Data obtained from union Web pages, March 26, 2008.

39. The two executive orders pertaining to public sector collective bargaining are EO 10988, signed by President Kennedy in 1962, and EO 11491, issued in 1971 by President Nixon.

40. Jeffery K. Guiler and Jay M. Shatritz, "Dual Personnel System—Organized Labor and Civil Service: Side-by-Side in the Public Sector," *Journal of Labor Research* 25, no. 2 (Spring 2004): 199.

41. William A Donohue and Paul J. Taylor, "Role Effects in Negotiation: The One-Down Phenomenon," *Negotiation Journal* 23, no. 3 (July 2007): 307.

42. Leigh Thompson, *The Mind and Heart of the Negotiator*, 3rd ed. (Upper Saddle River, NJ: Prentice Hall, 2004).

43. Thomas R. Colosi, "The Principles of Negotiation," *Dispute Resolution Journal* 57, no. 1 (February–April 2002): 28–31.

44. Joel Cutcher-Gershenfeld, Thomas Kochan, John-Paul Ferguson, and Betty Barrett, "Collective Bargaining in the Twenty-First Century: A Negotiations Institution at Risk" *Negotiation Journal* 23, no. 3 (July 2007): 249.

45. Ross Stagner and Hjalmar Rosen, *Psychology of Union-Management Relations* (Belmont, CA: Wadsworth, 1965), 95–97. This is another classic in the field of labor-management relations.

46. The National Labor Relations Board offers an excellent book on the National Labor Relations Act. This book discusses good faith bargaining as well as other important legal issues—for example, employers covered by the law, unfair labor practices, and election procedures. See *Basic Guide to the National Labor Relations Act* (Washington, DC: U.S. Government Printing Office, 1997).

47. Joe Stanley, interview by author, Phoenix, Arizona, January 5, 2008.

48. The FMCS has a complete and comprehensive program to train labor and management negotiators in the art and techniques of interest-based bargaining (IBB). Information on the IBB program can be obtained from the FMCS national headquarters at 2100 K Street, N.W., Washington, DC 20427 or from FMCS district offices.

49. Robert B. McKersie, Teresa Sharpe, Thomas A. Kochan, and Adrienne E. Eaton, "Bargaining Theory Meets Interest-Based Negotiations: A Case Study," *Industrial Relations* 47, no. 1 (January 2008): 66.

50. Bill McDonough, president of United Food and Commercial Workers Union Local 99, interview by author, January 12, 2008, Phoenix, Arizona.

51. Roger J. Peters and Deborah Bavarnick Mastin, "To Mediate or Not to Mediate: That is the Question," *Dispute Resolution Journal* 62, no. 2 (May–July 2007): 14.

52. Labor agreement, Wabash Fibre Box Company and Paperworkers.

53. Helen Lam and Mark Harcourt, "A New Approach to Resolving the Right-to-Work Ethical Dilemma," *Journal of Business Ethics* 73, no. 3 (July 2007): 231.

54. Judith L. King and Laurel C. Catlett-King, "Cowboy Campaigning: Patriotism, Freedom, and Right-to-Work in Oklahoma," *Labor Studies Journal* 32, no. 1 (March 2007): 5. See also Raymond L Hogler, "Right-to-Work and the Colorado Labor Peace Act: How Politics Trumped Policy," *Labor Law Journal* 58, no. 2 (Summer 2007): 85.

55. Right-to-work states are Idaho, Nevada, Wyoming, Utah, Arizona, North Dakota, South Dakota, Nebraska, Kansas, Oklahoma, Texas, Iowa, Arkansas, Louisiana, Mississippi, Tennessee, Alabama, Georgia, Virginia, North Carolina, South Carolina, and Florida.

56. John B. Larocco, "Ambiguities in Labor Union Contracts: Where Do They Come From?" *Dispute Resolution Journal* 59, no. 1 (February–April 2004): 38.

57. *Grievance Guide*, 12th ed. (Washington, DC: BNA Books, 2007).

58. Vera Riggs, Labor-Management Relations Conference, August 11, 2007, Phoenix, Arizona.

59. Arbitration awards are not final in all cases. Arbitration awards may be overturned through the judicial process if it can be

shown that the arbitrator was prejudiced or failed to render an award based on the essence of the agreement.

60. Nels E. Nelson and Sung Min Kim, "A Model of Arbitral Decision Making: Facts, Weights, and Decision Elements," *Industrial Relations* 47, no. 2 (April 2008): 266.

61. Peter Fairbrother, Glynne Williams, Ruth Barton, Enrico Gibellieri, and Andrea Tropeol, "Unions Facing the Future: Questions and Possibilities," *Labor Studies Journal* 31, no. 4 (Winter 2007): 31.

62. Statistics are from the U.S. Department of Labor, Bureau of Labor Statistics Web site at http://www.bls.gov.

63. Arthur Shostak, "Trends in U.S. Trade Unionism," *Employment Relations Today* 34, no. 2 (Summer 2007): 2.

64. David Welch, "Twilight of the UAW," *Business Week*, April 10, 2006, 62.

65. Matthew J. Slaughter, "Globalization and Declining Unionization in the United States." *Industrial Relations* 46, no. 2 (April 2007): 329.

66. Kent Wongand Victor Narro, "Educating Immigrant Workers for Action," *Labor Studies Journal* 32, no. 1 (March 2007): 113.

67. Jeremy Smerd, "Unions Reverse Decline," *Workforce Management* 87, no. 2 (February 4, 2008): 1.

INTERNATIONAL HUMAN RESOURCES MANAGEMENT

After studying this chapter, you should be able to

Identify the types of organizational forms used for competing internationally.

Explain the economic, political-legal, and cultural factors in different countries that HR managers need to consider.

© DAVE & LES JACOBS/BLEND IMAGES/ALAMY LIMITED

CHAPTER 15

Objective 3
Explain how domestic and international HRM differ.

Objective 4
Discuss the staffing process for individuals working internationally.

Objective 5
Identify the unique training needs for international assignees and their employees.

Objective 6
Identify the characteristics of a good international compensation plan.

Objective 7
Reconcile the difficulties of home- and host-country performance appraisals.

Objective 8
Explain how labor relations differ around the world.

When you pick up a newspaper or turn on the TV, you will notice that stories are constantly being told about companies competing globally. These stories might include the joint ventures and mergers of U.S. and international companies, such as the Dutch brewer InBev's bid to take over Anheuser Busch in 2008. Or they might highlight companies expanding into other markets, such as the U.S.-based deli Quiznos' expansion into Saudi Arabia that year. Or the stories might focus on international companies such as Toyota gaining dominance here in the United States. "No matter what kind business you run, no matter what size you are, you are suddenly competing against companies you have never heard of all around the world that make a very similar widget or provide a very similar service," as one global manager put it. In fact, nearly three-quarters of HR professionals from companies large and small in a wide range of industries and countries say they expect their company's international business to grow in the coming years.[1] Some of these companies are handling the challenge well. Others are failing miserably as they try to manage across borders. More often than not, the difference boils down to how people are managed, the adaptability of cultures, and the flexibility of organizations.

Up until this point in the book, we have paid primary attention to HRM practices and systems in the United States. Nonetheless, the topic of international HRM is so important that we wanted to dedicate an entire chapter to its discussion. The first part of this chapter presents a brief introduction to international business firms. In many important respects, the way a company organizes its international operations influences the type of managerial and human resources issues it faces. In addition, we briefly describe some of the environmental factors that also affect the work of managers in a global setting. Just as with domestic operations, the dimensions of the environment form a context in which HRM decisions in foreign countries are made. A major portion of this chapter deals with the various HR activities involved in the recruitment, selection, development, and compensation of employees working abroad. However, as we explain later in this chapter, workers stationed all over the United States are increasingly finding themselves working virtually with people from other cultures who speak different languages. This creates challenges not only for them, but also for firms' HR managers as well.

Using the Internet

The Society for Human Resource Management Global Forum provides current news updates on issues concerning HRM from around the world. Go to the Student Resources at:

**www.cengage.com/
management/bohlander**

■ MANAGING ACROSS BORDERS

Objective 1

International business operations can take several different forms. A large percentage carry on their international business with only limited facilities in foreign countries. Others, particularly Fortune 500 corporations, have extensive facilities and personnel in various countries of the world. Dell, for example, actually employs more people outside the United States than within it. Managing these resources effectively and integrating their activities to achieve global advantage is a challenge to the leadership of these companies.

Figure 15.1 shows four basic types of organizations and how they differ in the degree to which international activities are separated to respond to the local regions and integrated to achieve global efficiencies. The international corporation is essentially a domestic firm that builds on its existing capabilities to penetrate overseas markets. Companies such as Honda, General Electric, and Procter & Gamble used this approach to gain access to Europe—they essentially adapted existing products for overseas markets without changing much else about their normal operations. (One such adaptation, for example, was P&G's extremely successful introduction of a detergent brick used on washboards in India.)

international corporation

A domestic firm that uses its existing capabilities to move into overseas markets

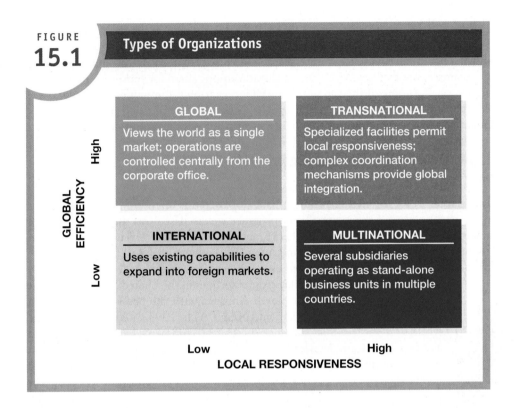

FIGURE
15.1

Types of Organizations

GLOBAL EFFICIENCY

High

GLOBAL

Views the world as a single market; operations are controlled centrally from the corporate office.

TRANSNATIONAL

Specialized facilities permit local responsiveness; complex coordination mechanisms provide global integration.

Low

INTERNATIONAL

Uses existing capabilities to expand into foreign markets.

MULTINATIONAL

Several subsidiaries operating as stand-alone business units in multiple countries.

Low   High
LOCAL RESPONSIVENESS

A multinational corporation (MNC) is a more complex form that usually has fully autonomous units operating in multiple countries. Shell, Philips, and ITT are three typical MNCs. These companies have traditionally given their foreign subsidiaries a great deal of latitude to address local issues such as consumer preferences, political pressures, and economic trends in different regions of the world. Frequently these subsidiaries are run as independent companies without much integration. The global corporation, on the other hand, can be viewed as a multinational firm that maintains control of its operations worldwide from the country in which it is headquartered. Japanese companies, such as Matsushita and NEC, tend to treat the world market as a unified whole and try to combine their activities in each country to maximize their efficiencies on a global scale. These companies operate much like a domestic firm, except that they view the whole world as their marketplace.

Finally, a transnational corporation attempts to achieve the local responsiveness of a MNC while also achieving the efficiencies of a global firm. To balance this "global/local" dilemma, a transnational corporation uses a network structure that coordinates specialized facilities positioned around the world. By using this flexible structure, a transnational corporation provides autonomy to its operations in foreign countries but brings these separate activities together into an integrated whole. For most companies, the transnational form represents an ideal, rather than a reality. However, companies such as Ford, Unilever, and Shell have made good progress in restructuring their operations to function more transnationally.[2]

Although various forms of organization exist, in this chapter we will generally refer to any company that conducts business outside its home country as an international business. The United States, of course, has no monopoly on international business.

multinational corporation (MNC)

A firm with independent business units operating in multiple countries

global corporation

A firm that has integrated worldwide operations through a centralized home office

transnational corporation

A firm that attempts to balance local responsiveness and global scale via a network of specialized operating units

International enterprises are found throughout the world. A number of European and Pacific Rim companies have been conducting business on an international basis for much longer than their U.S. counterparts. The close proximity of European countries, for example, has facilitated international trade among them for centuries. Figure 15.2 shows a list of some of the top nonfinancial international companies.[3] Many of these companies generate more revenue annually than do entire small nations. Consequently, they are corporations that have a significant impact on the world economy.

How Does the Global Environment Influence Management?

In Chapter 1, we highlighted some of the global trends affecting human resources management. One of the major economic issues we discussed was the creation of free trade zones within Europe, North America, and the Pacific Rim. Twenty-seven member countries now comprise the European Union (EU), whose goal is to facilitate the flow of goods, services, capital, and human resources across national borders in Europe in a manner similar to the way they cross state lines in the United States.[4] A similar transition occurred within North America with the passage of the North American Free Trade Agreement (NAFTA) in 1994. NAFTA created the world's largest free market. Since its passage, commerce between the United States, Canada, and Mexico has more than tripled, growing from $290 billion in 1994, to nearly $1 trillion in 2008. There has been a great deal of debate about whether NAFTA has cost Americans jobs. Economists do not deny that an estimated 1 million U.S. jobs have been lost, primarily in the manufacturing sector. But this is only part of the picture. The agreement has also resulted in lower product prices for Americans overall, giving them more money to spend, thereby stimulating other parts of the U.S. economy.[5]

> ### Using the Internet
>
> The Outpost Network is an online information center for Shell expatriates and their families. Go to the Student Resources at:
>
> **www.cengage.com/ management/bohlander**

FIGURE 15.2

Top International Companies

COMPANY	COUNTRY	INDUSTRY
General Electric	United States	Electrical and electronics
Vodafone Group PLC	United Kingdom	Telecommunications
General Motors	United States	Motor vehicles
British Petroleum Company PLC	United Kingdom	Petroleum
Royal Dutch/Shell Group	United Kingdom, Netherlands	Petroleum
ExxonMobil	United States	Petroleum
Toyota Motor Corporation	Japan	Motor vehicles
Ford Motor Company	United States	Motor vehicles
Total	France	Petroleum
Eléctricité de France	France	Electricity, gas and water

Source: Chester Dawson, "The Global 1000," *Business Week*, July 14, 2003, 34.

Like NAFTA, numerous trade agreements, including the Association of Southeast Asian Nations (ASEAN), East Asia Economic Group, Asia-Pacific Economic Cooperation (APEC), and South Asian Association for Regional Cooperation (SAARC), have significantly facilitated trade among Asian countries, making Asia the fastest-growing region in the world. China—its fastest-growing country—has emerged as a dominant trade leader since instituting trade reforms in the late 1970s. In the last decade and a half, China's economy has grown dramatically, drastically altering political and trading relations among nations. Some industry analysts estimate that the country now produces 50 percent of the world's cameras, 30 percent of air conditioners and televisions, 25 percent of washing machines, and 20 percent of refrigerators worldwide. In addition, China's 1.3 billion people represent a massive, largely untapped consumer market for global companies. Today more cars are sold in China than in Europe, for example. Driving this trend are big multinational corporations, which are expanding into the country. But many smaller firms are heading to China as well. "It's not so much that [companies] want to go East: They feel that they have no choice," said one international HR staffing consultant. "They must be in China. It's not a question of if, but a question of how." In addition to China, India's economy is also growing very quickly, as is Brazil's.[6]

The fact that international corporations can choose the countries in which they do business or relocate operations generally results in the selection of countries that have the most to offer. In addition to economic factors, political-legal factors are a huge consideration. In many countries, particularly those in Africa, property rights are poorly protected by governments. Whoever has the political power or authority can seize others' property with few or no repercussions. Civil unrest can also lead to the poor enforcement of property rights. This gives companies less incentive to locate factories or invest in countries experiencing strife. Another issue relates to intellectual property rights—rights related to patents, trademarks, and so forth. Despite the fact that private property rights are now generally enforced in China, intellectual property rights have seen little protection. For example, when General Motors formed a joint venture with a Chinese company to produce and sell a new automobile in the country, a knockoff version of the car could be seen on China's streets even before GM and its partner were able to manufacture their first car. Environmental restrictions also make some countries more attractive to do business in than others.

Beyond the economic and political-legal issues just mentioned, a country's **cultural environment** (communications, religion, values and ideologies, education, and social structure) also has important implications when it comes to a company's decision about when and how to do business there. Because of language and culture similarities, many U.S. companies are finding Canada, Ireland, and the United Kingdom attractive places to locate their facilities, particularly call centers. Eastern Europe has also begun to attract interest because citizens there are well educated and largely possess English-speaking skills. Similarly, the U.S. military's departure from Panama in recent years left that country with a bilingual workforce that is very attuned to the American work culture.[7]

Figure 15.3 summarizes the complexity of the cultural environment in which HR must be managed. Culture is an integrated phenomenon. By recognizing and accommodating taboos, rituals, attitudes toward time, social stratification, kinship systems, and the many other components listed in Figure 15.3, managers stand a better chance

2 | Objective

cultural environment
The communications, religion, values and ideologies, education, and social structure of a country

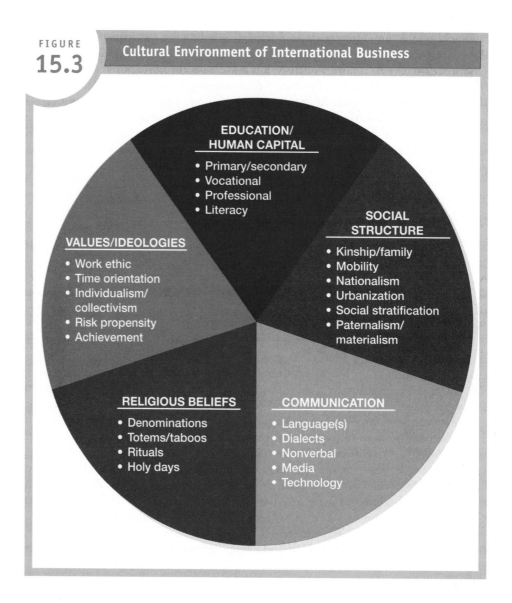

FIGURE
15.3

Cultural Environment of International Business

host country

A country in which an international corporation operates

of understanding the culture of a host country—a country in which an international business operates. Different cultural environments require different approaches to human resources management. Strategies, structures, and management styles that are appropriate in one cultural setting may lead to failure in another.

Even in countries that have close language or cultural links, HR practices can be dramatically different. In some countries, night shifts are taboo. In other countries, employers are expected to provide employees with meals and transportation between home and work. In India, workers generally receive cash bonuses on their wedding anniversaries which with to buy their spouses gifts, and dating allowances are provided to unmarried employees. These are practices that would never occur to American managers and HR practitioners.[8] Throughout this chapter we will discuss several HR issues related to adapting to different cultural environments.

Domestic versus International HRM

International HRM differs from domestic HRM in several ways. In the first place, it necessarily places a greater emphasis on functions and activities such as relocation, orientation, and translation services to help employees adapt to new and different environments outside their own countries and to help newly hired employees in foreign countries adapt to working for companies headquartered outside their borders. Many larger corporations and even smaller ones doing business in key international markets have full-time HR managers devoted solely to assisting with the globalization process. British Airways, for example, has a team of HR directors who travel around the world to help country managers stay updated on international concerns, policies, and programs. Coca-Cola provides support to its army of HR professionals working around the world. A core HR group in the company's Atlanta headquarters holds a two-week HR orientation twice a year for Coca-Cola's international HR staff. This program helps Coca-Cola share information about its HR philosophies, programs, and policies established either at its headquarters or in another part of the world that can be successfully adopted by others.[9] Because doing business internationally can be extremely complex, many companies also hire international staffing firms such as Boston Global Consulting and Cendant Mobility, a Connecticut-based company. These firms have expertise when it comes to relocating employees, establishing operations abroad, and helping with import/export and foreign tax issues.

HR information systems have also come a long way in terms of helping firms improve their international coordination. A good HR information system can facilitate communication, record-keeping, and a host of other activities worldwide. Some HRISs are designed to track the whereabouts of employees traveling or on assignment. This can be important in the event of a transportation accident, a natural disaster such as a tsunami, a terrorist attack, or civil strife if evacuation plans must be implemented. Occasionally, however, even the seemingly simplest of cultural differences can be difficult to overcome when a company attempts to set up a global HRIS. For example, when Lucent first rolled out a PeopleSoft system to more than ninety countries, the company's managers found that the order of employees' names was so important—and so varied—that it took two months to settle on a name format allowing employees to be entered into the system. As you can see, even seemingly small cultural differences can create major challenges for the international HR manager. As a result, many companies rely on outsourcing firms such as Mercer

© ANDY NELSON/THE CHRISTIAN SCIENCE MONITOR/GETTY IMAGES

3 Objective

Consulting and Korn/Ferry International to help them better manage the challenges, risks, and regulations associated with their HRM activities abroad.[10]

International Staffing

When a company expands globally, HR managers are generally responsible for ensuring that operations are staffed. There are three main ways a company can staff a new international operation. First, the company can send people from its home country. These employees are often referred to as expatriates, or home-country nationals. Second, it can hire host-country nationals, natives of the host country, to do the managing. Third, it can hire third-country nationals, natives of a country other than the home country or the host country. Each of these three sources provides certain advantages and certain disadvantages. Most corporations use all three for staffing their multinational operations, although some companies exhibit a distinct bias for one or another.[11] It is important to note, however, that host countries sometimes restrict their choices by passing laws and regulations designed to employ host-country individuals. Tax incentives, tariffs, and quotas are frequently implemented by the host country to encourage local hiring.

As shown in Figure 15.4, at early stages of international expansion, organizations often send home-country nationals to establish activities (particularly in less-developed countries) and to work with local governments. This is generally very costly. Traditionally, expatriates have received generous salaries, automobiles, full relocation services, private schooling for their children, trips home, and other perks. These services frequently end up costing more than $300,000 yearly, on average, making the cost of a typical three-year expatriate assignment more than one million dollars. Some companies

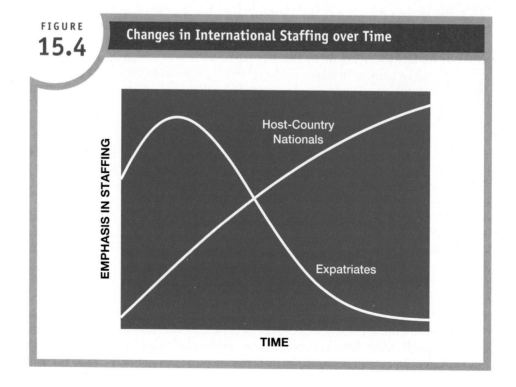

FIGURE 15.4

Changes in International Staffing over Time

find it more cost-effective to hire young, single, management trainees who are interested in their career growth. Companies are also taking greater pains to more clearly outline the overall goal of the foreign assignment and its timetable for completion. Ingersoll-Rand, an international equipment manufacturer, now carefully documents in detail what should be accomplished during an assignment abroad—whether the assignment is designed to enhance an assignee's leadership skills, improve productivity and sales targets abroad, transfer specific technology to a foreign operation, or staff it with local, expatriate, or third-country nationals.

In recent years, there has also been a trend to send expatriates on shorter, project-based assignments (two to twelve months versus one to three years) and to shift more quickly toward hiring host-country nationals. This has three main advantages:

1. Hiring local citizens is generally less costly than relocating expatriates. Local citizens also know the cultural and political landscape of the country and are often more likely to be able to gain the support of local staff members.

2. Since local governments usually want good jobs for their citizens, foreign employers may be required to hire locally.

3. Most customers want to do business with companies (and people) they perceive to be local versus foreign.

Because U.S. companies want to be viewed as true international citizens, there has also been a trend away from hiring expatriates to head up operations in foreign countries, especially European countries. ABB, Eli Lilly, and PepsiCo, which have strong regional organizations, have tended to replace their U.S. expatriate managers with local managers as quickly as possible. In addition to hiring local managers to head their foreign divisions and plants, more companies are using third-country nationals. Third-country nationals are often multilingual and already acclimated to the host country's culture—perhaps because they live in a nearby region. Thus, they are also less costly to relocate and sometimes better able to cope culturally with foreign environments.

Companies tend to continue to use expatriates only when a specific set of skills is needed or when individuals in the host country require development. For example, after embarking on a joint venture in China with a formerly state-owned enterprise, Ingersoll-Rand discovered that it had to educate its Chinese employees not only on the company's practices and culture, but also on free-market, Western business practices. This required the company's expatriates to stay in China longer than planned.[12] In fact, many expatriates find that in Asia, it takes more time to adapt to the culture and win over employees so as to impart a company's work values. Personal relationships are everything in Asia, and business there can only be conducted after relationships have been established. To help their expatriates adapt in Asia and elsewhere, firms are finding it helpful to pair them with local "buddies," or host-country mentors. At SAS Institute's regional headquarters in Heidelberg, Germany, mentors such as these are assigned to expatriate newcomers to help answer any questions they might have about the firm or culture. The practice seems to be improving the odds of an expatriate succeeding.[13]

Recruiting Internationally

Improved telecommunications and travel have made it easier to match up employers and employees of all kinds worldwide. As we mentioned earlier in the chapter, most of Dell's employees work outside the United States. Rolls-Royce, headquartered in the United Kingdom, hires 25 percent of its 25,000 employees abroad. Because its customers come from around the globe, Rolls-Royce figures its workforce should as well. The German company Siemens would like to hire more employees from abroad. "Our top managers are predominantly white German males," said its chief executive Peter Loscher. "If you are not representing your global customer base, then you won't tap your full potential," Loscher explained. Airbus, the European commercial jet manufacturer, recruits engineers from universities and colleges all over Europe. American-based Boeing's need for engineers is so great that it also recruits internationally and has even opened a design center in Moscow.

Employers are also realizing that they need to recruit from abroad because their employees are more willing to relocate to capitalize on the best opportunities. According to Manpower's Borderless Workforce Survey, almost one-third of employers surveyed in twenty-seven countries said they were concerned that their talented workers would relocate. Blue collars jobs are in short supply, too. For example, many developed countries face a shortage of carpenters, bricklayers, and plumbers. To deal with the shortages, some firms are even bringing their expatriates home. These trends are likely to continue as the populations in developed countries age and HR managers search for the top talent throughout the globe.

HR departments must be particularly responsive to the cultural, political, and legal environments both domestically and abroad when recruiting internationally. Companies such as Starbucks, Levi Strauss, and Honeywell have made a special effort to create codes of conduct for employees throughout the world to ensure that standards of ethical and legal behavior are known and understood. PepsiCo has taken a similar approach to ensuring that company values are reinforced (even while recognizing the need for adapting to local cultures). The company has four core criteria that are viewed as essential in worldwide recruiting efforts: (1) personal integrity, (2) a drive for results, (3) respect for others, and (4) capability. Zurich, a Swiss financial and insurance company with operations throughout the world, makes sure its employees assigned to the United States take diversity and sexual harassment courses. This training is rarely provided in other parts of the world.[14]

In general, however, the recruiting of employees in many other developed countries is subject to more government regulation than it is in the United States. The regulations range from those that cover procedures for recruiting and screening to their working conditions, pay and incentives, and retirement provisions. In Japan, for example, criminal background checks on candidates are not allowed. In France, employees can only work 35 hours per week. Similarly, many Central American countries have stringent regulations about the number of foreigners that can be employed as a percentage of the total workforce. Virtually all countries have work permit or visa restrictions that apply to foreigners.

work permit, or visa

A government document granting a foreign individual the right to seek employment

A **work permit** or **visa** is a document issued by a government granting authority to a foreign individual to seek employment in that government's country. Since 9/11, there has been a backlash against immigration and a backup in the number of visas granted to foreign workers and students entering the United States. U.S. managers complain that this is making it harder for them to hire top talent. Firms lament that they are experiencing a "reverse brain drain" as skilled foreign workers leave the United States or seek work in other countries. It is a more serious problem than you might think. The fact is that the United States has traditionally benefited from its ability to attract the world's best talent. Did you know that annually foreigners residing in the United States file about 25 percent of international patent applications? Making matters worse, other countries have become less restrictive than the United States in terms of granting foreign residents citizenship and work permits. The United Kingdom, for example, gives graduates of the world's top fifty business schools an automatic right to work in the United Kingdom for a year. In addition, the European Union is contemplating introducing a "blue card" system designed to expedite the EU citizenship of talented employees.[15] Whatever the employee's destination, HR managers need to ensure that work permits and visas are applied for early in the relocation process.

In terms of recruiting at the executive level, companies use executive recruiting firms such as Heidrick & Struggles in the United States or Spencer Stuart in the United Kingdom. At lower levels, as we explained in Chapter 7, companies recruiting abroad often need to advertise their firms and employment "brand" to recruits who are not familiar with it. In countries such as India and China, an employer's reputation is extremely important to candidates' families—sometimes more important than pay.

Many employers have learned that the best way to find workers in these less well-developed countries is through referrals and radio announcements because many people lack sufficient reading or writing skills. Other firms use international recruiting firms to find skilled labor abroad. As we have explained, some countries, in fact, require the employment of locals if adequate numbers of skilled people are available. Specific exceptions are sometimes granted (officially or unofficially) for contrary cases, as for Mexican farm workers in the United States and for Italian, Spanish, Greek, and Turkish workers in Germany and the Benelux countries (Belgium, the Netherlands, and Luxembourg). Foreign workers invited to perform needed labor are usually referred to as **guest workers.** Foreign workers with H2B visas can come to the United States for a maximum of 9 months to perform temporary, nonagricultural seasonal work that is one-time. These types of visas are often used in conjunction with recruiting workers for entry-level positions in hotels and restaurants during peak travel seasons.

guest workers
Foreign workers invited to perform needed labor

Although hiring nonnationals can result in lower direct labor costs for a company, the indirect costs—those related to housing, language training, health services, recruitment, transportation, and so on—can be substantial. Some companies competing in industries with acute talent shortages are nonetheless finding the expenditures worthwhile. Nursing is one such industry. (See the Case Study at the end of the chapter.)[16]

Apprenticeships

A major source of trained labor in European nations is apprenticeship training programs (described in Chapter 7). On the whole, apprenticeship training in Europe is superior to that in the United States. In Europe, a dual-track system of education directs a large number of youths into vocational training. The German system of apprenticeship training, one of the best in Europe, provides training for office and shop jobs under a three-way responsibility contract between the apprentice, his or her parents, and the organization. At the conclusion of their training, apprentices can work for any employer but generally receive seniority credit with the training firm if they remain in it. France has been able to draw on its "Grandes Ecoles" for centuries. Created during the Renaissance to fulfill a need that universities were not meeting at the time, the Grandes Ecoles educate prospective engineers up to the equivalent level of Master of Engineering. Snecma, an international equipment supplier headquartered in Paris, hires about 80 percent of its employees from the Grandes Ecoles.[17]

Staffing Transnational Teams

In addition to focusing on individuals, it is also important to note that companies are increasingly using transnational teams to conduct international business. Transnational teams are composed of members of multiple nationalities working virtually on projects that span multiple countries. General Electric's LightSpeed VCT, a state-of-the-art medical scanner, was designed with input from cardiologists around the world. The machine's innards were designed by GE engineers in four different countries, and the software to run it was written by multiple teams working together from India, Israel, France, and Wisconsin.[18] Teams such as these are especially useful for performing tasks that the firm as a whole is not yet structured to accomplish. For example, they may be used to transcend the existing organizational structure to customize a strategy for different geographic regions, transfer technology from one part of the world to another, and communicate between headquarters and subsidiaries in different countries. In GE's case, the company realized its competitors were developing their own medical scanning technology more quickly. GE decided it could no longer afford to duplicate its efforts in different divisions around the world—that these groups would have to work together as a team.

Sometimes companies send employees on temporary assignments abroad as part of transnational teams lasting perhaps a few months. This might be done to break down cultural barriers between international divisions or disseminate new ideas and technologies to other regions. In other instances, employees are transferred for extended periods of time. Years ago, Fuji sent fifteen of its most experienced engineers from Tokyo to a Xerox facility in Webster, New York. Over a five-year period, the engineers worked with a team of U.S. engineers to develop the "world" copier. The effort led to a joint venture that has lasted for decades. Fuji-Xerox now employs approximately 40,000 people globally at 13 companies around the world.[19]

The fundamental task in forming a transnational team is assembling the right group of people who can work together effectively to accomplish the goals of the team. For GE's LightSpeed team, this frequently meant holding eight-hour global conference calls encompassing numerous time zones. (The call times were rotated so that no single team had to stay up all night for every call.) Many companies try to build variety into their teams in order to maximize responsiveness to the special needs of different countries. For example, when Heineken formed a transnational team to consolidate its production facilities, it ensured that team members were drawn from each major region within Europe. Team members tended to have specialized skills, and members were added only if they offered some unique skill that added value to the team. Cross-cultural training can benefit transnational teams by helping them overcome language and cultural barriers they face.

Selecting Employees Internationally

As you might imagine, selection practices vary around the world. In the United States, managers tend to emphasize merit, with the best-qualified person getting the job. In other countries, however, firms tend to hire on the basis of family ties, social status, language, and common origin. Much of this is changing—there has been a growing realization among organizations in other nations that greater attention must be given to hiring those most qualified. In addition to a person's qualifications, various other hiring laws, particularly those related to discrimination, are enforced around the world. Highlights in HRM 1 outlines some of the U.S. and international laws and pacts companies must adhere to when hiring in the United States

Global Laws and Pacts Prohibiting Discrimination

U.S. laws affecting firms conducting business outside the United States:
- Title VII of the Civil Rights Act of 1964
- Age Discrimination in Employment Act (ADEA)
- Americans with Disabilities Act (ADA)

International laws that require nondiscrimination in employment:
- European Union (EU)—Equal Pay Directive
- International Labour Organization (ILO)—Equal Remuneration Convention No. 100
- Organization for Economic Cooperation and Development (OECD)—Guidelines for Multinational Enterprises
- United Nations—Global Compact

and elsewhere. Labor union restrictions, which we will discuss later in the chapter, can also have an impact on hiring.

Selecting Global Managers

Selecting a global manager depends on a variety of different employment factors, including the extent of contact the manager will have with local citizens and the government and the degree to which the foreign environment differs from the home environment. For example, if the job involves extensive contacts with the community, as with a chief executive officer, this factor should be given appropriate weight. The magnitude of differences between the political, legal, socioeconomic, and cultural systems of the host country and those of the home country should also be assessed.[20]

Levi Strauss has identified the following six skill categories for the global manager, or manager equipped to run an international business:

global manager
A manager equipped to run an international business

- The ability to seize strategic opportunities
- The ability to manage highly decentralized organizations
- An awareness of global issues
- Sensitivity to diversity issues
- Competence in interpersonal relations
- Community-building skills[21]

If a candidate for expatriation is willing to live and work in a foreign environment, an indication of his or her tolerance of cultural differences should be obtained. This can often be done by testing, which we will discuss shortly. On the other hand, if local nationals have the technical competence to carry out the job successfully, they should be carefully considered for the job before the firm hires a domestic candidate and sends the person abroad. As we explained, most corporations realize the advantages to be gained by staffing international operations with host-country nationals wherever possible.

Selecting home-country and third-country nationals requires that more factors be considered than in selecting host-country nationals. While the latter must of course possess managerial abilities and the necessary technical skills, they have the advantage of familiarity with the physical and cultural environment and the language of the host country. Figure 15.5 compares the advantages and disadvantages of hiring global managers from these three different groups. The discussion that follows, however, will focus on the selection of expatriate managers from the home country, along with their compensation and performance appraisals.

FIGURE
15.5

Comparison of Advantages in Sources of Overseas Managers

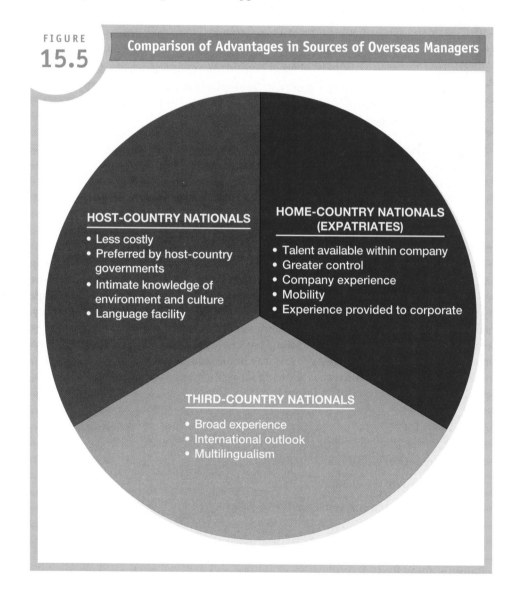

HOST-COUNTRY NATIONALS
- Less costly
- Preferred by host-country governments
- Intimate knowledge of environment and culture
- Language facility

HOME-COUNTRY NATIONALS (EXPATRIATES)
- Talent available within company
- Greater control
- Company experience
- Mobility
- Experience provided to corporate

THIRD-COUNTRY NATIONALS
- Broad experience
- International outlook
- Multilingualism

Colgate-Palmolive, Whirlpool, and Dow Chemical have further identified a set of core skills that they view as critical for success abroad and a set of augmented skills that help facilitate the efforts of expatriate managers. These two types of skills are shown in Highlights in HRM 2. Many of these skills are not significantly different from those managers need to succeed domestically. Although in years past the average U.S. expatriate manager was an American-born Caucasian, more companies today are seeing the advantages of assigning expatriates depending on their ethnicity. But such a decision needs to be considered carefully. For example, an Indian candidate applying for a position in India may never have actually visited the country or may not relate well to the culture. Ultimately, the candidate best qualified for the job should be sent. In the past, women were overlooked for global managerial positions—perhaps because companies believed they would fare poorly in foreign, male-dominated societies or because they believed women have less desire to go abroad. Today women comprise nearly 25 percent of expatriates—up from 14 percent a decade ago. Moreover, in a study of 193 expatriates from 36 countries, women expatriates were found to perform just as well as men.[22] In some countries, women expatriates are novel (particularly in managerial positions). They are very visible and distinctive and may even receive special treatment not given their male colleagues.

Several steps are involved in selecting individuals for an international assignment, and the sequencing of these activities can make a big difference:

Step 1: Begin with self-selection. Employees should begin the process years in advance by thinking about their career goals and how interested they are in working abroad. By beginning with self-selection, companies can more easily avoid the problems of forcing otherwise promising employees into international assignments that are a bad fit for them. For individuals with families, relocating decisions are more complicated. Employees should seek information to help them predict their chances of success living abroad. Companies such as EDS and Deloitte & Touche give their employees

core skills
Skills considered critical to an employee's success abroad

augmented skills
Skills helpful in facilitating the efforts of expatriate managers

---

HIGHLIGHTS IN HRM

2 Skills of Expatriate Managers

CORE SKILLS	**AUGMENTED SKILLS**
Experience	Technical skills
Decision-making	Negotiation skills
Resourcefulness	Strategic thinking
Adaptability	Delegation skills
Cultural sensitivity	Change management
Team building	
Maturity	

© PHOTODISC/GETTY IMAGES

self-selection instruments to help them consider the pros and cons of international assignments. Performance Program Inc.'s Overseas Assignment Inventory and the International Mobility Assessment test, developed by Tucker International, are two such tests. Other companies assess candidates' spouses as well. At Solar Turbines, a San Diego–based manufacturer of industrial gas turbines, a candidate's spouse and sometimes his or her children undergo a day of assessment to see how well they are likely to respond to an international assignment.[23]

Step 2: Create a candidate pool. After employees have self-selected, organizations can build a database of candidates for international assignments. Information in the database might include availability, languages, country preferences, and skills.

Step 3: Assess candidates' core skills. From the short list of potential candidates, managers can assess each candidate in terms of their technical and managerial readiness relative to the needs of the assignment.

Step 4: Assess candidates' augmented skills and attributes. As Figure 15.6 shows, expatriate selection decisions are typically made based upon the technical competence

FIGURE 15.6

Expatriate Selection Criteria

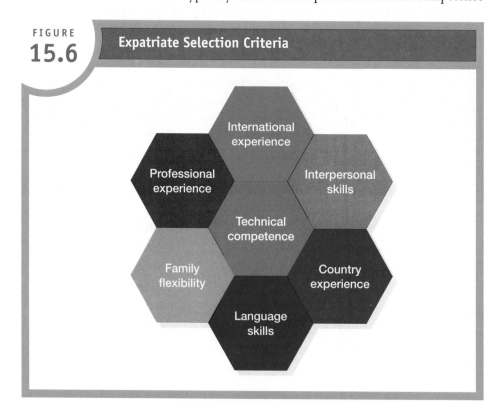

of candidates as well as their professional and international experience. In addition, organizations are beginning to pay more attention to an individual's ability to adapt to different environments. How well a person adjusts depends on his or her flexibility, emotional maturity and stability, empathy for the culture, language and communication skills, resourcefulness and initiative, and diplomatic skills. If these skills are lacking, no amount of technical competency is likely to result in a successful assignment.[24]

Even companies that believe they have selected the best candidates frequently experience high expatriate failure rates. Figure 15.7 shows the major causes of assignment failure. A recent study by Korn/Ferry International found that a poor cultural fit was a major reason why assignments fail. For example, although China is among the easiest countries to which to attract Western expatriates, it is also one of the hardest places for them to succeed because the country's culture is so different. A lack of expatriate support from headquarters is another major cause. Expatriates often describe themselves as "out of sight and out of mind." This highlights the importance of headquarters maintaining close contact with them to see how they are faring. Yet another big factor is a spouse's inability to adjust to his or her new surroundings. Today, more companies are preparing families by offering them cultural and language training. ARAMCO, a Saudi Arabian corporation, has such a program. The program includes practical information such as how to deal with Saudi Arabia's transportation systems, where to shop, day-to-day finances, and an explanation of the differences between the beliefs and customs of Saudis and people from other cultures.[25] There are number of ways to improve the success of expatriate assignments. One important step is to involve spouses early on in the process. In addition, training and development for both expatriates and their spouses can have a big impact. We discuss this next.

failure rate
The percentage of expatriates who do not perform satisfactorily

▪▪ TRAINING AND DEVELOPMENT

Although companies try to recruit and select the very best people to send abroad, once they are selected, it is critical to their success to provide them with training. Not only is this type of training important for expatriate managers, but it is also important for the foreign employees they will ultimately supervise. For example, to know and understand how the Japanese or Chinese negotiate contracts or how businesspeople from Latin America view the enforcement of meeting times can help expatriate managers and their employees deal with each other more successfully. The biggest mistake managers can make is to assume that people are the same

5 | Objective

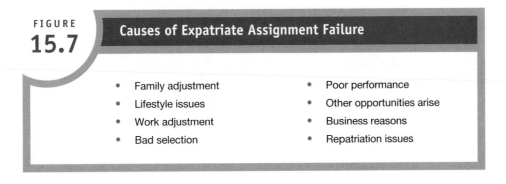

FIGURE
15.7

Causes of Expatriate Assignment Failure

- Family adjustment
- Lifestyle issues
- Work adjustment
- Bad selection

- Poor performance
- Other opportunities arise
- Business reasons
- Repatriation issues

everywhere. Corporations that are serious about succeeding in global business are tackling these problems head-on by providing intensive training. At Motorola this type of training is conducted at divisions worldwide by Motorola University, the company's educational arm. All employees worldwide, including division heads, receive forty hours of training each year to learn, in part, how to work together as "Motorola People."[26]

Apart from developing talent for overseas assignments, most companies have found that good training programs also help them attract the employees they need from host countries. In less-developed countries especially, individuals are quite eager to receive the training they need to improve their work skills. One of the greatest contributions that the United States has made to work organizations is in improving the competence of managers. Americans have a facility for analytical reasoning that is part of their lives. They tend to make decisions on a rational basis, giving them a better background for decision-making. Foreign nationals have generally welcomed the type of training they have received through management development programs offered by U.S. organizations. It should be noted that host-country nationals also provide a great deal of business-specific and cultural know-how to expatriates. Learning is clearly a two-way street for companies doing business abroad.

Content of Training Programs

Lack of training is one of the principal causes of failure among employees working internationally. Those working internationally need to know as much as possible about (1) the country where they are going, (2) that country's culture, and (3) the history, values, and dynamics of their own organizations. Figure 15.8 gives an

FIGURE 15.8 **Preparing for an International Assignment**

To prepare for an international assignment, one should become acquainted with the following aspects of the host country:

1. Social and business etiquette
2. History and folklore
3. Current affairs, including relations between the host country and the United States
4. Cultural values and priorities
5. Geography, especially its major cities
6. Sources of pride and great achievements of the culture
7. Religion and the role of religion in daily life
8. Political structure and current players
9. Practical matters such as currency, transportation, time zones, and hours of business
10. The language

overview of what one needs to study for an international assignment. In many cases, the employee and his or her family can obtain a great deal of general information about the host country, including its culture, geography, social and political history, climate, food, and so on, via the Internet, books, lectures, videotapes, and DVDs. The knowledge gained will at least help the participants have a better understanding of their assignments. Sensitivity training can also help expatriates overcome ethnic prejudices they might harbor. The Peace Corps uses sensitivity training supplemented by field experiences. Expatriates can simulate a field experience in sensitivity training by visiting a nearby subculture in their native countries or by actually visiting a foreign country prior to relocating there.

However, at least five essential elements of training and development programs prepare employees for working internationally: (1) language training, (2) cultural training, (3) assessing and tracking career development, (4) managing personal and family life, and (5) repatriation—a final, but critical, step.[27]

Language Training

Communication with individuals who have a different language and a different cultural orientation is extremely difficult. Most executives agree that it is among the biggest problems for the foreign business traveler. Unfortunately, only a small percentage of Americans are skilled in a language other than English. But this is changing. Students who plan careers in international business should start instruction in one or more foreign languages as early as possible. Penn State University changed its requirements for all students in business management so that they now include four college semesters of a foreign language. Other programs designed to train participants for international business, such as those offered at the American Graduate School of International Management in Glendale, Arizona, and the Global Management Program at the University of South Carolina, provide intensive training in foreign languages. The top-ranked China Europe International Business School (CEIBS), jointly founded by the Chinese government and the European Union in 1994, also offers language training. Some companies do their own language training. When ARCO Products, a U.S. firm, began exploring potential business opportunities in China, its HR department set up a language training class (with the help of Berlitz International) in conversational Mandarin Chinese. Multinational companies as well as businesses that outsource work abroad stand to benefit from this type of training.

Using the Internet

Thunderbird at the American Graduate School of International Management is devoted solely to the education of college graduates for international careers. Native speakers of English receive thorough training in nine languages. Go to the Student Resources at:

www.cengage.com/
management/bohlander

Fortunately for most Americans, English is almost universally accepted as the primary language for international business. Particularly when many people from different countries are working together, English is usually the designated language for meetings and formal discourse. Many companies provide instruction in English for those who are required to use English in their jobs. Dow Chemical requires that all employees across the globe be fluent in English so that they can communicate more easily with one another. At Volkswagen's Shanghai operation, only after workers pass German language examinations do they become eligible for further training in Germany. Learning the language is only part of communicating in another culture. Even with an interpreter, much is missed. The following list illustrates the complexities of the communication process in international business.

1. In England, to "table" a subject means to put it on the table for present discussion. In the United States, it means to postpone discussion of a subject, perhaps indefinitely.

2. In the United States, information flows to a manager. In cultures in which authority is centralized (such as Europe and South America), the manager must take the initiative to seek out the information.

3. Getting straight to the point is uniquely American. Many Europeans, Arabs, Asians, and others resent the directness of American-style communication.

4. In Japan, there are sixteen ways to avoid saying "no."

5. When something is "inconvenient" to the Chinese, it is most likely downright impossible.

6. In most foreign countries, expressions of anger are unacceptable; in some places, public display of anger is taboo.

7. The typical American must learn to treat silences as "communication spaces" and not interrupt them.

8. In general, Americans must learn to avoid gesturing with the hand. A couple of cases in point: When former President Richard Nixon traveled to Brazil in the 1950s, he waved and gave the "A-OK" sign to the country's citizens. But in Brazil, the gesture is considered obscene and insulting. Similarly, a college sports–related hand signal made by former President George W. Bush and his family members during his second inauguration shocked Norwegians around the world; in Norway, the gesture is a satanic symbol. Nonverbal communication training can help businesspeople avoid some of these communication pitfalls. Highlights in HRM 3 illustrates that some of our everyday gestures have very different meanings in other cultures.[28]

Cultural Training

Cross-cultural differences represent one of the most elusive aspects of international business, but successfully done, it tends to improve the satisfaction and success of expatriates and their employers.[29] Brazilians tend to perceive Americans as always in a hurry, serious, reserved, and methodical, whereas the Japanese view Americans as relaxed, friendly, and impulsive. Why do these different perceptions exist, and how do they affect the way we do business across borders? People's attitudes and behaviors are influenced, in a large part, by the culture and society in which they have been educated and trained. Each culture has its expectations for the roles of managers and employees. On her first day on the job abroad, one expatriate manager recalls her boss ordering a bottle of wine to split between the two of them at lunch. Although this is a common practice in Britain, the expatriate manager was initially taken aback. Likewise, an American manager in Asia once complained that meetings held in his foreign place of employment accomplished nothing. He was used to arriving at a final decision during meetings. But to his Asian coworkers, meetings were solely a place in which to share ideas. Decisions were to be made only later. Being successful abroad depends on a person's ability to understand the way things are normally done and to recognize that changes cannot be made abruptly without considerable resistance, and possibly antagonism, on the part of local nationals.

Nonverbal Communications in Different Cultures

Calling a Waiter

In the United States, a common way to call a waiter is to point upward with the forefinger. In Asia, a raised forefinger is used to call a dog or other animal. To get the attention of a Japanese waiter, extend the arm upward, palm down, and flutter the fingers. In Africa, knock on the table. In the Middle East, clap your hands.

Insults

In Arab countries, showing the soles of your shoes is an insult. Also, an Arab may insult a person by holding a hand in front of the person's face.

A-Okay Gesture

In the United States, using the index finger and the thumb to form an "o" while extending the rest of the fingers is a gesture meaning okay or fine. In Japan, however, the same gesture means money. Nodding your head in agreement if a Japanese uses this sign during your discussion could mean you are expected to give him some cash. In Brazil the same gesture is considered a seductive sign to a woman and an insult to a man.

Eye Contact

In Western and Arab cultures, prolonged eye contact with a person is acceptable. In Japan, on the other hand, holding the gaze of another is considered rude. The Japanese generally focus on a person's neck or tie knot.

Handshake and Touching

In most countries, the handshake is an acceptable form of greeting. In the Middle East and other Islamic countries, however, the left hand is considered the toilet hand and is thought to be unclean. Only the right hand should be used for touching.

Scratching the Head

In most Western countries, scratching the head is interpreted as lack of understanding or noncomprehension. To the Japanese, it indicates anger.

Indicating "No"

In most parts of the world, shaking the head left and right is the most common way to say no. But among the Arabs, in parts of Greece, Yugoslavia, Bulgaria, and Turkey, a person says no by tossing the head to the side, sometimes clicking the tongue at the same time. In Japan, no can also be said by moving the right hand back and forth.

Agreement

In addition to saying yes, Africans will hold an open palm perpendicular to the ground and pound it with the other fist to emphasize "agreed." Arabs will clasp their hands together, forefingers pointed outward, to indicate agreement.

Source: S. Hawkins, *International Management* 38, no. 9 (September 1983): 49. Copyright 1983 by Reed Business Information Ltd. Reprinted with permission.

A wealth of data from cross-cultural studies reveals that nations tend to cluster along certain cultural dimensions such as their work goals, values, needs, and attitudes toward work. Using data from eight comprehensive studies of cultural differences, Simcha Ronen and Oded Shenkar have grouped countries into the clusters shown in Figure 15.9. Ronen and Shenkar point out that while evidence for the grouping of countries into Anglo, Germanic, Nordic, Latin European, and Latin American clusters appears to be quite strong, clusters encompassing the Far Eastern and Arab countries are ill defined and require further research, as do clusters of countries classified as independent. Many areas, such as Africa, have not been studied much at all. It should also be noted that the clusters presented in Figure 15.9 do not include Russia and the former satellites of the Soviet Union. Those countries, if added to the figure, would likely fall between the Near Eastern and Nordic categories. Studying cultural differences can help managers identify and understand work attitudes and motivation in other cultures. When compared with the Japanese, for example, Americans may feel little loyalty to their organizations. In Japan, employees are more likely to feel a strong loyalty to their company, although this has been changing. Japanese companies no longer universally guarantee an employee a job for life, and layoff decisions are increasingly being made based on merit, not seniority—a practice unthinkable in the country in the past. Latin Americans tend to view themselves as working not only for a particular company, but also for an individual manager. Thus managers in Latin American countries can encourage performance only by using personal influence and working through individual members of a group. In the United States, competition has been the name of the game; in Japan, Taiwan, and other Asian countries, cooperation is more the underlying philosophy.[30]

One of the important dimensions of leadership, whether in international or domestic situations, is the degree to which managers invite employee participation in decision-making. While it is difficult to find hard data on employee participation across different countries, careful observers report that American managers are about in the middle on a continuum of autocratic to democratic decision-making styles. Scandinavian and Australian managers also appear to be in the middle. South American and European managers, especially those from France, Germany, and Italy, are toward the autocratic end of the continuum; Japanese managers are at the most participatory end. Because Far Eastern cultures and religions tend to emphasize harmony, group decision-making predominates there.[31]

Assessing and Tracking Career Development

International assignments provide some definite developmental and career advantages. For example, working abroad tends to increase a person's responsibilities and influence within the corporation. In addition, it provides a person with a set of experiences that are uniquely beneficial to both the individual and the firm. In this way, international assignments enhance a person's understanding of the global marketplace and offer the opportunity to work on a project important to the organization.[32]

In recent years, U.S. companies have become a melting pot of CEOs. Increasingly, foreign-born CEOs are making up the Fortune 500 top slots. Figure 15.10 presents a number of foreign-born CEOs. Executive recruiters say corporate boards are asking for leaders with experience outside of the United States. As one foreign CEO of a U.S.-based firm put it, "Having a foreign perspective gives you an advantage not only for doing business outside the United States, but also domestically, where we have the most diverse society in the world." Some companies such as Coca-Cola

FIGURE
15.9

A Synthesis of Country Clusters

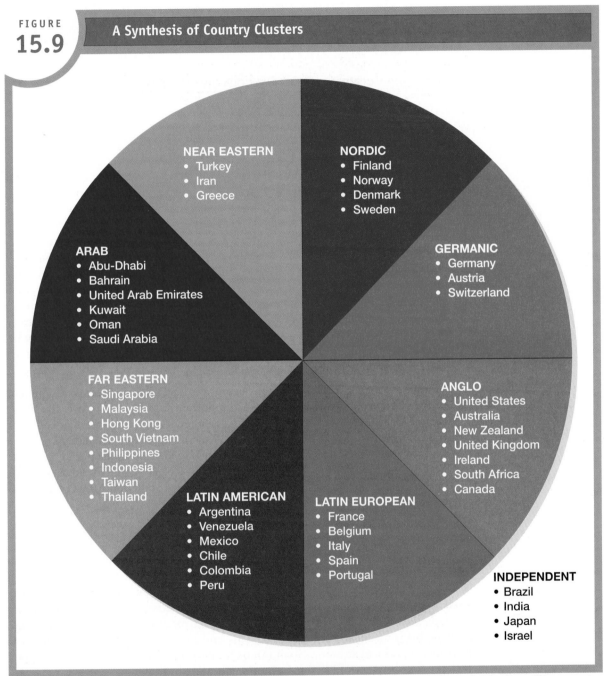

Source: Simcha Ronen and Oded Shenkar, "Clustering Countries on Attitudinal Dimensions: A Review and Synthesis," *Academy of Management Review* 10, no. 3 (July 1985): 435–54. Copyright © 1985 by *Academy of Management Review*. Reprinted with permission of the *Academy of Management Review* via Copyright Clearance Center.

have traditionally appointed chief executives with foreign roots, perhaps because the growth of the firm's markets lies abroad.[33]

To maximize the career benefits of a managerial assignment, a candidate should ask two key questions before accepting a foreign post.

FIGURE 15.10

Selected Foreign-Born Executives

COMPANY, NAME, AND COUNTRY OF ORIGIN
Chevron, David O'Reilly (Ireland)
Citigroup, Vikram Pandit (India)
Dow Chemical, Andrew Liveris (Australia)
PepsiCo, Indra Nooyi (India)
Coca-Cola, Muhtar Kent (Turkey)
Alcoa, Alain J. P. Belda (Morocco)
Eli Lily, Sydney Taurel (Morocco)
3M, George W. Buckley (Great Britain)
Eastman Kodak, Antonio Perez (Spain)

1. Do the organization's senior executives view the firm's international business as a critical part of their operation? Research shows that expatriates with clear goals that truly need to be accomplished are likely to find their assignments more rewarding. Realizing this, fewer companies are sending expatriates abroad for career development purposes only.

2. Within top management, how many executives have a foreign-service assignment in their background, and do they feel it important for one to have overseas experience? Colgate-Palmolive sees a foreign assignment as part of an extended career track rather than as a one-off assignment. A successful foreign assignment tends to lead to another and another. "Our top priority is to identify, develop, and retain the next two to three generations of leaders," said one Colgate-Palmolive manager. Part of that strategy includes directly using the knowledge of the company's current and former expatriates.

Managing Personal and Family Life

culture shock

Perpetual stress experienced by people who settle overseas

As noted previously, one of the most frequent causes of an employee's failure to complete an international assignment is personal and family stress. Culture shock—a disorientation that causes perpetual stress—is experienced by people who settle overseas for extended periods. The stress is caused by hundreds of jarring and disorienting incidents such as being unable to communicate, having trouble getting the telephone to work, being unable to read the street signs, and a myriad of other everyday matters that are no problem at home. Soon minor frustrations become catastrophic events, and one feels helpless and drained, emotionally and physically.

In Chapter 5, we explained that more and more employers are assisting two-career couples in terms of finding suitable employment in the same location. To accommodate dual-career partnerships, some employers offer spouses career and life planning counseling, continuing education, intercompany networks to identify job openings in other companies, job-hunting/fact-finding trips, and help securing work permits abroad. In some cases, a company may even create a job for the spouse—though this is not widely practiced.[34]

Expatriate employees receive intensive training on their host countries, the cultural differences, negotiation tactics, business practices, everyday living, and other aspects of working and living successfully in a foreign country.

Repatriation

An increasing number of companies such as Monsanto, 3M, EDS, and Verizon are developing programs specifically designed to facilitate repatriation—that is, helping employees make the transition back home. Repatriation programs are designed to prepare employees for adjusting to life at home (which at times can be more difficult than adjusting to a foreign assignment). ExxonMobil employees are given a general idea of what they can expect following a foreign assignment even before they leave home.

Unfortunately, not all companies have career development programs designed for repatriating employees or do not do an effective job of it. Employees often lament that their organizations are vague about repatriation, their new roles within the company, and their career progression. In many cases, employees abroad have learned how to run an entire international operation—or at least significant parts of it. When they return home, however, their responsibilities are often significantly diminished. A recent, international survey found that 60 percent of expatriates believed their careers had not advanced after returning home. Another 16 percent said they were working in jobs they considered to be a demotion.[35] It is also not at all uncommon for employees to return home after a few years to find that there is *no* position for them in the firm and that they no longer know anyone who can help them—their longtime colleagues have moved to different departments or even different companies. This frequently leaves the repatriated employee feeling alienated. Wondering about their future also creates stress for them and their families while they are abroad.

Even when employees are successfully repatriated, their companies often do not fully utilize the knowledge, understanding, and skills developed on their assignments. This hurts the employee, of course, but it also hurts the firm's chances of utilizing the employee's expertise to gain a competitive advantage. Not surprisingly, expatriates frequently

repatriation

The process of transition for an employee home from an international assignment

> ### *Using the Internet*
>
> Published by West Virginia University, the *U.S. Expatriate Handbook,* available online, provides extensive information on working and living outside the United States. Go to the Student Resources at:
>
> **www.cengage.com/ management/bohlander**

leave their companies within a year or two of coming home. Some studies say the number of expatriates who do so is as high as 50 percent.

At companies with good repatriation processes, employees are given guidance about how much the expatriate experience may have changed them and their families. Some firms introduce former expatriates and their spouses to other former expatriates at special social events, and more companies are making an effort to keep in touch with expatriates while they are abroad, which has been made easier by e-mail, instant messaging, and videoconferencing. Colgate's division executives and other corporate staff members frequently visit international transferees. Dow appoints a high-level manager who serves as a stateside contact for information about organizational changes, job opportunities, and anything related to salary and compensation. Monsanto's repatriation program is designed not only to smooth the employee's return to the home organization, but also to ensure that the expatriate's knowledge and experience are fully utilized. To do so, returning expatriates get the chance to showcase their new knowledge in debriefing sessions. Some companies also create databases of expatriates to help other employees who go abroad later.[36] Of course, if a firm is able to retain its current repatriates, it will have better success recruiting future expatriates. A repatriation checklist is shown in Highlights in HRM 4.

4

Repatriation Checklist

Before they go:
* Make sure there is a clear need for the international assignment. Don't send someone abroad unnecessarily. Develop a clear set of objectives and expectations and time frames in which they should be met.
* Make sure that your selection procedures are valid. Select the employee and also look at and involve the employee's family.
* Provide (or fund) language and cultural training for the employee and the employee's family.
* Offer counseling and career assistance for the spouse.
* Establish career planning systems that reward international assignments and lead to promotion and knowledge sharing.

While they are away:
* Jointly establish a developmental plan that focuses on the goal to be achieved.
* Tie performance objectives to the achievement of the goal.
* Identify mentors who can be a liaison and support person from home.
* Keep communications open so that the expatriate is aware of job openings and opportunities.
* Arrange for frequent visits back home (for the employee and the family). Make certain they do not lose touch with friends and relatives.

> ## Repatriation Checklist (continued)
>
> ### When they come back home:
> - Throw a "welcome home" party and arrange for a meeting with other former expatriates.
> - Offer counseling to ease the transition.
> - Arrange conferences and presentations to make certain that knowledge and skills acquired away from home are identified and disseminated.
> - Set up an expatriate database to help other employees who go abroad later.
> - Get feedback from the employee and the family about how well the organization handled the repatriation process.
>
> Sources: Adapted from Bennet & Associates, Price Waterhouse, and Charlene Marmer Solomon, "Repatriation Planning Checklist," *Personnel Journal* 14, no. 1 (January 1995): 32; Charlene Marmer Solomon, "Global HR: Repatriation Planning," *Workforce* 2001, special supplement: 22–23.

▪▪ COMPENSATION

One of the most complex areas of international HRM is compensation. Different countries have different norms for employee compensation. For Americans, while nonfinancial incentives such as prestige, independence, and influence may be motivators, money is likely to be the driving force. Other cultures are more likely to emphasize respect, family, job security, a satisfying personal life, social acceptance, advancement, or power. Since there are many alternatives to money, the rule is to match the reward with the values of the culture. In individualistic cultures, such as the United States, pay plans often focus on individual performance and achievement. However, in collectively oriented cultures such as Japan and Taiwan, pay plans focus more on internal equity and personal needs.[37]

In general, a guiding philosophy for designing pay systems might be "think globally and act locally." That is, executives should normally try to create a pay plan that supports the overall strategic intent of the organization but provides enough flexibility to customize particular policies and programs to meet the needs of employees in specific locations. After a brief discussion of compensation practices for host-country employees and managers, we will focus on the problems of compensating expatriates.

Compensation of Host-Country Employees

As shown in Figure 15.11, hourly wages vary dramatically from country to country. Production workers in manufacturing positions in Norway make more than $40 per hour. By contrast, in many developing countries, production workers earn less than a dollar an hour, an average. Host-country employees are generally paid on the basis of productivity, time spent on the job, or a combination of these factors.

6 | Objective

FIGURE
15.11

Hourly Wages in Different Countries*

COUNTRY	$/HOUR
Norway	41.05
Denmark	35.45
Germany	34.21
Netherlands	32.34
Belgium	31.85
Sweden	31.80
Switzerland	30.67
Austria	30.46
Finland	29.90
Luxembourg	27.74
United Kingdom	27.10
Australia	26.14
Ireland	25.96
Canada	25.74
Italy	25.07
France	24.90
United States	23.82
Japan	20.20
Spain	18.83
Greece	16.10
Korea, Republic of	14.72
New Zealand	14.47
Israel	12.98
Singapore	8.55
Portugal	7.65
Czech Republic	6.77
Taiwan	6.43
Hungary	6.29
Hong Kong SAR (1)	5.78
Poland	4.99
Brazil	4.91
Mexico	2.75
Philippines	1.07
Sri Lanka	0.54

*Hourly compensation costs in U.S. dollars for production workers in manufacturing.

Source: U.S. Department of Labor, Bureau of Labor Statistics, January 2008.

In industrialized countries, pay is generally by the hour; in developing countries, pay is generally by the day. The piece-rate method is quite common. In some countries, including Japan, seniority is an important element in determining employees' pay rates. In Italy, Japan, and some other countries, it is customary to add semiannual or annual lump sum payments equal to one or two months' pay. These payments are not considered profit sharing but an integral part of the basic pay package. Profit sharing is legally required for certain industry categories in Mexico, Peru, Pakistan, India, and Egypt among the developing countries and in France among the industrialized countries.

Employee benefits can range dramatically from country to country as well. In France, for example, benefits comprise a much higher proportion of people's pay than they do in the United States. In contrast to ten vacation days in the United States, workers in the United Kingdom, France, and the Netherlands receive about twenty-five days of paid vacation. Workers in Sweden and Austria receive thirty. Whereas in the United States most benefits are awarded to employees by employers, in other industrialized countries most of them are legislated or ordered by governments.[38]

Because the largest cost for most companies is labor, it plays a prime role in international HR decision-making. However, some people believe that companies are over-capitalizing on worldwide compensation differences. Many firms (Nike included) have generated bad press for charging hundreds of dollars for their individual products while the people who make them—sometimes children in developing countries working under terrible conditions—earned only a few cents on the dollar. This has led to international political protests, as we mentioned in Chapter 1, and pressure on firms to exercise greater global social responsibility. As Nike discovered, this is pressure they cannot afford *not* to take seriously. Starbucks clearly takes good corporate citizenship seriously. Among Starbucks' many initiatives is its association with Fair Trade and Conservation International to help farmers in third-world countries get a premium for the coffee they grow. We will discuss more on the fair treatment of workers in third-world countries toward the end of the chapter.

Compensation of Host-Country Managers

In the past, the compensation of host-country managers has been based on local salary levels. Today, however, more companies are offering their host-country employees a full range of training programs, benefits, and pay comparable with their domestic employees but adjusted for local differences. These programs are known as **global compensation systems.** Among other benefits, the agricultural processing firm Archer Daniels Midland offers its employees abroad an employee assistance program. At first many employees were suspicious about the program, believing that it was designed to collect private information about them. However, after employees became confident that their information was confidential, the program sent a message that the company is interested in their well-being and values them.

According to a survey by the HR consulting firm Watson Wyatt, companies are split evenly as to whether they have central (global) compensation systems or decentralized (local) systems. Companies with centralized systems report having higher effectiveness and satisfaction levels with their compensation systems, and more companies are saying they are moving toward centralized systems. Unilever, for example, used to leave the compensation arrangements largely to the boss of a region or a big country. Now brand managers in different countries increasingly compare notes, so they see potential discrepancies based on market differences and expatriate assignments. So the company moved from a narrow grading structure to five global work levels.[39]

> ### Using the Internet
>
> What salary would a manager need to receive to maintain his or her real current income while working in a foreign city? See the international salary calculator. Go to the Student Resources at:
>
> www.cengage.com/
> management/bohlander

global compensation system

A centralized pay system whereby host-country employees are offered a full range of training programs, benefits, and pay comparable with a firm's domestic employees but adjusted for local differences

Compensation of Expatriate Managers

If the assignment is going to be successful, the expatriate's compensation plan must be competitive, cost-effective, motivating, fair, easy to understand, consistent with international financial management, relatively easy to administer, and simple to communicate. To be effective, an international compensation program must:

1. Provide an incentive to leave the United States

2. Allow for maintaining an American standard of living

3. Provide for security in countries that are politically unstable or present personal dangers

4. Include provisions for good health care

5. Reimburse the foreign taxes the employee is likely to have to pay (in addition to having to pay domestic taxes) and help him or her with tax forms and filing

6. Provide for the education of the employee's children abroad, if necessary

7. Allow for maintaining relationships with family, friends, and business associates via trips home and other communication technologies

8. Facilitate the expatriate's reentry home

9. Be in writing[40]

For short-term assignments, usually those that are project-based, expatriates are frequently given per diem (per day) compensation. These managers might reside in hotels and service apartments instead of leasing houses. They are also less likely to bring their family members with them. The assignment becomes more like a commuting assignment in which the expatriate spends the week in the host country and returns home on the weekend.

For longer-term assignments, there are two basic types of compensation systems. The first is home-based pay, based on the balance sheet approach, a system designed to equalize the purchasing power of employees at comparable positions living overseas and in the home country and to provide incentives to offset qualitative differences between assignment locations.[41] The balance sheet approach generally comprises the following steps:

Step 1: Calculate base pay. Begin with the home-based gross income, including bonuses. Deduct taxes, Social Security, and pension contributions.

Step 2: Figure cost-of-living adjustment (COLA). Add a cost-of-living adjustment to the base pay. Typically, companies do not subtract when the international assignment has a lower cost of living. Instead, they allow the expatriate to benefit from the negative differential. Often a housing allowance is added in here as well.

Step 3: Add incentive premiums. General mobility premiums and hardship premiums compensate expatriates for separation from family, friends, and domestic support systems; usually 15 percent of base salary, although in recent years, some companies have reduced this amount. Oftentimes incentive premiums are paid for hazardous duty or harsh conditions the expatriate might experience while abroad. Expatriates who locate to war zones, for example, can sometimes earn three times their base salary.

Step 4: Add assistance programs. These additions are often used to cover added costs such as moving and storage, automobile, and education expenses.

The differentials element is intended to correct for the higher costs of overseas goods and services so that in relation to their domestic peers expatriates neither gain

home-based pay

Pay based on an expatriate's home country's compensation practices

balance sheet approach

A compensation system designed to match the purchasing power in a person's home country purchasing power nor lose it. It involves a myriad of calculations to arrive at a total differential figure, but in general, as we have said, the cost typically runs between three and five times the home-country salary. Fortunately, employers do not have to do extensive research to find comparative data. They typically rely on data published quarterly by the U.S. State Department for use in establishing allowances to compensate U.S. civilian employees for costs and hardships related to assignments abroad. Alternately, they consult international relocation experts to make sure all of the relocation bases are covered. For example, in some countries expatriates are mandated by local law to participate in host-country programs—whether or not their pay packages are home- or host-based. Other countries have negotiated bilateral agreements that allow expatriates to opt out of state-sponsored benefit programs such as Social Security, as long as the expatriates are covered by similar programs in their home countries. The United States currently has bilateral agreements of this type with a number of countries.[42] Recently, split-pay plans have become popular among companies. Under a split pay system, expatriates are given a portion of their pay in the local currency to cover their day-to-day expenses. The rest of their pay is distributed in their home currency to safeguard their earnings should changes in foreign exchange rates or inflation adversely affect their pay.

Another type of compensation system is host-based pay. Companies are under pressure to move expatriates to host-based pay because it is generally less costly. Host-based pay is compensation that is equivalent to that earned by employees in the country where the expatriate is assigned. This process is called localization. When an employee is localized, his or her compensation is set on par with local standards and practices. Incentive premiums are generally phased out, and the employee pays only local taxes and falls under the social benefit programs established by the government of the host country. Some companies localize only certain aspects of the pay package or do so gradually over a course of three to five years.

Usually the decision to localize an employee depends on whether he or she will ultimately remain abroad or return home. In many companies, the decision depends on whether the employee or the employer is the driving force behind the localization. An expatriate employee with a strong desire to remain in the host country beyond the planned length of assignment (perhaps because he or she married a local or has simply fallen in love with the country) is likely to be more amenable to localization. Localization should not be viewed as a cost-saving panacea, however. There are many countries in which expatriates would refuse to "go local." Forcing an employee to do so can ultimately result in a failed assignment, costing the company much more money than it would have saved by localizing him or her.

One of the disadvantages of not localizing an employee's pay, however, is that in low-cost countries, this can breed resentment among local staff members if they are earning significantly less. This can affect the amount of cooperation they are likely to give an expatriate and adversely affect the success of an assignment. Whether they are intentional or not, any HR practice that results in more favorable treatment for an expatriate versus local employees sends a message that they are less valued by the firm. This is another reason why firms are moving to global compensation systems.[43]

Another serious issue related to expatriate compensation is medical care. Employees are unlikely to consent to going aboard if they cannot get health care comparable to what is available in their home countries. Often U.S.-based plans cannot cover expatriate employees or efficiently deal with claims that need to be reimbursed in foreign currency. Drugs prescribed abroad that are not FDA approved can also cause reimbursement problems for U.S. expatriates. One solution is to provide the expatriate with a global health benefits plan such as Cigna

split pay
A system whereby expatriates are given a portion of their pay in the local currency to cover their day-to-day expenses and a portion of their pay in their home currency to safeguard their earnings from changes in inflation or foreign exchange rates

host-based pay
Expatriate pay comparable to that earned by employees in a host country

localization
Adapting pay and other compensation benefits to match that of a particular country

International Expatriate Benefit. The Cigna plan covers 200,000 expatriates and their dependents for 700 different international client companies. Another alternative is to transfer the employee to a global employment company that can provide these types of benefits. A global employment company is similar to a PEO (professional employer organization), discussed in Chapter 5. Basically, the employee is transferred to the global employment company, which administers all of his or her benefits as well as those of numerous employees working for other companies. These are not options in all countries. In some countries, such as Saudi Arabia, for example, expatriates must be covered by a local insurer.

Still another issue is the need to provide expatriates and employees who travel abroad with security. Citigroup hires private drivers for employees doing business in countries such as Mexico—even for employees on extended stays. Archer Daniels Midland uses a travel management company that provides travel security climate information to employees as soon as they book their trips. Companies can also purchase travel-related insurance covering a range of services such as evacuation and disability or travel-related injuries. HR managers are generally responsible for evaluating and implementing these different types of programs. Oftentimes this involves hiring a local security firm when an expatriate is sent abroad.

Lastly, what your competitors are paying should also factor into the compensation mix. In the United Kingdom, firms typically provide their expatriates with cars as part of their compensation. So to be competitive, any company operating in that marketplace has to likewise, explains Steve Rimmer from the consulting firm Price Waterhouse Coopers International Ltd.

PERFORMANCE APPRAISAL

Objective 7

As we noted earlier, individuals frequently accept international assignments because they know that they can acquire skills and experiences that will make them more valuable to their companies. Frequently, however, it can be difficult for the home office to evaluate the performance of employees working abroad. Even the notion of performance evaluation is indicative of a U.S. management style that focuses on the individual, which can cause problems in Asian countries such as China, Japan, and Korea and Eastern European countries such as Hungary and the Czech Republic. Performance appraisal problems can contribute to failure rates among expatriates and actually derail an individual's career rather than enhance it.[44]

Who Should Appraise Performance?

In many cases, an individual working internationally has at least two allegiances: one to his or her home country (the office that made the assignment) and the other to the host country in which the employee is currently working. Superiors in each location frequently have different information about the employee's performance and may also have very different expectations about what constitutes good performance. For these reasons, the multirater (360-degree) appraisal discussed in Chapter 8 is gaining favor among global firms. There are exceptions, however. For example, Thai workers do not see it as their business to evaluate their bosses, and Thai managers do not think subordinates are in any way qualified to assess them. Before implementing a different appraisal process, HR managers need to understand how the process is likely to be received in the host country.[45]

Home versus Host-Country Evaluations

Domestic managers who have not worked abroad are frequently unable to understand an expatriate or host-country manager's experiences, value them, or accurately measure their contribution to the organization. Geographical distances create communication problems for expatriates and home-country managers, although e-mail, instant messaging, and other HR information systems technologies have begun to help close the gap.[46] Still, local managers with daily contact with the person are more likely to have an accurate picture of his or her performance. Host-country evaluations can sometimes be problematic. First, local cultures can influence a person's perception of how well an individual is performing. As we noted earlier in the chapter, participative decision-making may be viewed either positively or negatively, depending on the culture. Such cultural biases may not have any bearing on an individual's true level of effectiveness. In addition, local managers sometimes do not have enough of a perspective on the entire organization to know how well an individual is truly contributing to the firm as a whole.

Even if the formal appraisal is conducted in the home office and promotion, pay, and other administrative decisions are made there, most HR experts agree that performance evaluations should try to balance the two sources of appraisal information. As we discussed in Chapter 8, multiple sources of appraisal information can be extremely valuable for providing independent points of view—especially if someone is working as part of a team. If there is much concern about cultural bias, it may be possible to have people of the same nationality as the expatriate conduct the appraisal.

Performance Criteria

Because expatriate assignments are so costly, many HR managers are increasingly under pressure to calculate the return on investment of these assignments. What did the firm get for the million dollars it spent to send an expatriate abroad? Has the expatriate achieved the goals set forth in the assignment in the appropriate time frame? Obviously, the goals and responsibilities inherent in the job assignment are among the most important criteria used to evaluate an individual's performance, and different goals necessitate measuring different criteria. The criteria are tied to the various reasons employees were sent abroad in the first place—whether the goal was to transfer technical skills or best practices, as a result of a merger or new division, improve a division's financial performance, or develop managerial talent.

There are five steps related to calculating the ROI of an assignment:

1. Defining the assignment's objectives.

2. Agreeing on the quantifiable measurements for the assignment.

3. Developing an equation that converts qualitative behavior into quantifiable measurements.

4. Evaluating the expatriate's performance against these measurements.

5. Calculating the ROI. This can be a complex cost accounting or a simple calculation to see if the expatriate covered the cost of keeping them on assignment.

Companies also look at how well the total cost of the assignment was managed, taking into account any tax efficiencies and whether the right mix of expatriates, third-country nationals, and locals were used to minimize the assignment's costs.[47]

The danger with ROI calculations, however, is that there is a temptation to resort to using "easy" criteria such as productivity, profits, and market share to measure an expatriate's performance. These criteria may be valid—but they are still deficient if they do not capture the full range of an expatriate's responsibility. Other, more subtle factors should be considered as well. Leadership development, for example, involves a much longer-term value proposition. In many cases, an expatriate is an ambassador for the company, and a significant part of the job is cultivating relationships with citizens of the host country.

As we discussed at the beginning of this chapter, an individual's success or failure is affected by a host of technical and personal factors, as well as the acceptance and help they get from their staff members abroad. For example, as one might guess, it is much easier to adjust to similar cultures than to dissimilar ones. An American can usually travel to the United Kingdom or Australia and work with locals almost immediately. Send that same individual to Hungary or Malaysia, and the learning curve is steeper. The expatriate's adjustment period may be even longer if the company has not yet established a good base of operations in the region. The first individuals transferred to a country have no one to show them the ropes or to explain local customs. Even relatively simple activities such as navigating the rapid transit system can prove to be problematic. The U.S. State Department and defense forces have developed rating systems that attempt to distinguish the different degrees of difficulty associated with different regional assignments. These difficulty factors need to be considered and built into the appraisal system.[48]

Providing Feedback

Performance feedback in an international setting is clearly a two-way street. Although the home-country and host-country superiors may tell an expatriate how well he or she is doing, it is also important for expatriates to provide feedback regarding the support they are receiving, the obstacles they face, and the suggestions they have about the assignment. More than in almost any other job situation, expatriates are in the very best position to evaluate their own performance.

In addition to ongoing feedback, an expatriate should have a debriefing interview immediately on returning home from an international assignment. These repatriation interviews serve several purposes.

1. They help expatriates reestablish old ties with the home organization and may prove to be important for setting new career paths.

2. The interview can address technical issues related to the job assignment itself.

3. The interview can address general issues regarding the company's overseas commitments, such as how relationships between the home and host countries should be handled.

4. The interview can be very useful for documenting insights an individual has about the region. These insights can then be incorporated into training programs for future expatriates. However, if the learning is not shared, then each new expatriate to a region may have to go through the same cycle of adjustment.[49]

▪▪ The Labor Environment Worldwide

8 | Objective

A country's labor environment plays a large role in international business and HR decisions. As we have said, wages and benefits vary dramatically across the world as do safety, child, and other legal regulations. In many countries, the regulation of labor contracts is profound and extensive. Labor unions around the world differ significantly as well. Differences exist not only in the collective bargaining process, but also in the political-legal conditions. For example, the EU prohibits discrimination against workers in unions, but in many other countries, including countries in Central America and Asia, labor unions are illegal. China has only one union, the All-China Federation of Trade Unions, an eighty-year-old Communist Party institution that for decades has aligned itself more closely with management than workers. As Wal-Mart discovered, Western firms that want to do business in China have to reach collective bargaining agreements with the ACFTU. In some countries, only workers at larger firms are allowed to organize.[50]

Union strength depends on many factors, such as the level of employee participation, per capita labor income, mobility between management and labor, homogeneity of labor (racial, religious, social class), and unemployment levels. In the United States, the number of union workers has risen slightly in the past couple of years. However, the jobs being unionized are more likely to be lower-wage, service-sector jobs rather than higher-wage manufacturing jobs. Nearly all of Sweden's workers are organized, giving the unions in this country considerable strength and autonomy. By contrast, in countries with relatively high unemployment, low pay levels, and no union funds with which to support social welfare systems, unions are driven into alliance with other organizations: political parties, churches, or governments. This is in marked contrast to the United States, where the union selected by the majority of employees bargains only with the employer, not with other institutions. By contrast, the unions in many European countries (such as Sweden) have a great deal of political power and are often allied with a particular political party. When employers in these countries deal with unions, they are, in effect, dealing indirectly with governments.

In a number of countries, however, including Japan, Germany, New Zealand, and the United Kingdom, unions have been losing some of their power. Ironically, the power of the unions to gain high wages and enforce rigid labor rules has been blamed for hurting competitiveness, particularly in European countries. Laws make it difficult to fire European employees, so workers are hired only sparingly. Unemployment benefits are very generous, so people tend to remain unemployed for longer rather than seek work. But because companies are increasingly tempted to offshore jobs to countries where labor costs are lower, unionized workers have been forced to make more concessions. For example, at Bosch in France, union bosses opposed management's plan to lengthen the workweek. But fearful workers overruled the union bosses, voting instead for the longer workweek.[51] As the power of unions declines a bit, the trend has been to demand compensation in other ways—through benefits or through greater participation in company decision-making. Various approaches to participation will be discussed later.

Collective Bargaining in Other Countries

We saw in Chapter 14 how the collective bargaining process is typically carried out in companies operating in the United States. When we look at other countries, we find that the process can vary widely, especially with regard to the role of government.

> *When we look at countries outside the U.S., we see that collective bargaining processes vary widely. The ILO and other international labor organizations promote the rights of workers to organize.*

Collective bargaining can take place at the firm, local, or national levels. In Australia and New Zealand for most of the twentieth century, labor courts had the authority to impose wages and other employment conditions on a broad range of firms (many of which were not even privy to the suits brought before the courts). In the United Kingdom and France, the government intervenes in all aspects of collective bargaining. Government involvement is only natural where parts of industry are nationalized. Also, in countries with heavy nationalization, government involvement is more likely to be accepted, even in the nonnationalized companies. At Renault, the French government-owned automobile manufacturer, unions use political pressures in their bargaining with managers, who are essentially government employees. The resulting agreements then set the standards for other firms. This is true in spite of the fact that union membership rates in France have declined dramatically since the 1970s. In developing countries, the governments commonly have representatives present during bargaining sessions to ensure that unions with relatively uneducated leaders are not disadvantaged in bargaining with skilled management representatives. Still, in these countries a union may do little more than attempt to increase wages and leave the rest of the employment contract unchanged. In more-developed countries, goals related to other aspects of the employment relationship, such as workweek lengths, safety requirements, and grievance procedures, are more likely to be pursued.

International Labor Organizations

The most active of the international union organizations has been the International Confederation of Free Trade Unions (ICFTU), which has its headquarters in Brussels. The ICFTU is a confederation of 215 national trade union centers, representing 125 million trade union members in 145 countries and territories. Cooperating with the ICFTU are numerous International Trade Secretariats (ITSs), which are really international federations of national trade unions operating in the same or related industries. In addition to the ITSs, the ICFTU also cooperates with the European

Trade Union Confederation (ETUC), the most prominent European trade worker federation. The ETUC represents 60 million trade workers in 82 trade unions in 36 Western, Central, and Eastern Europe countries.

Another active and influential organization is the International Labour Organization (ILO), a specialized agency of the United Nations created in 1919. The ILO perhaps has had the greatest impact on the rights of workers throughout the world. It promotes the rights of workers to organize, eradication of forced and child labor, and elimination of discrimination. Over the decades, 182 countries have voluntarily committed to nearly 200 international conventions proposed by the ILO. The organization has been effective because it involves nation-states as well as workers and their employers. In recent years, the ILO has redefined its mission based on the "Decent Work Agenda." The Decent Work Agenda promotes the idea that there is an ethical dimension of work. This ethical dimension includes decent homes, food, education, the right to organize, and social programs to protect workers when they are elderly, disabled, or unemployed. Moreover, the agenda pertains to workers worldwide, including the self-employed—a situation common in agricultural-based, developing countries. Given the fact that half of the world's population lives on $2 a day or less, 200 million children around the world are forced to work, and only 20 percent of people globally are covered by any sort of social insurance programs, these are worthy goals. Some companies, however, oppose the decent pay initiative, believing it promotes unionization. A new initiative of the ILO is to support fairness in economies that are globalizing. To some extent, the effort is working. For example, in 2007, the World Bank started including the ILO's core labor standards requirement as part of its lending and procurement practices.[52]

Labor Participation in Management

In many European countries, provisions for employee representation are established by law. An employer may be legally required to provide for employee representation on safety and hygiene committees, worker councils, or even boards of directors. While their responsibilities vary from country to country, worker councils basically provide a communication channel between employers and workers. The legal codes that set forth the functions of worker councils in France are very detailed. Councils are generally concerned with grievances, problems of individual employees, internal regulations, and matters affecting employee welfare.

A higher form of worker participation in management is found in Germany, where representation of labor on the board of directors of a company is required by law. This arrangement is known as codetermination and often referred to by its German word, *Mitbestimmung*. While sometimes puzzling to outsiders, the system is fairly simple. Company shareholders and employees are required to be represented in equal numbers on the supervisory boards of large corporations. Power is generally left with the shareholders, and shareholders are generally assured the chairmanship. Other European countries and Japan either have or are considering minority board participation.[53]

codetermination
Representation of labor on the board of directors of a company

Each of these differences makes managing human resources in an international context more challenging. But the crux of the issue in designing HR systems is not choosing one approach that will meet all the demands of international business. Instead, organizations facing global competition must balance multiple approaches and make their policies flexible enough to accommodate differences across national borders. Throughout this book we have noted that different situations call for different approaches to managing people, and nowhere is this point more clearly evident than in international HRM.

SUMMARY

Objective 1 There are four basic ways to organize for global competition: (1) the international corporation is essentially a domestic firm that has leveraged its existing capabilities to penetrate overseas markets; (2) the multinational corporation has fully autonomous units operating in multiple countries in order to address local issues; (3) the global corporation has a worldview but controls all international operations from its home office; and (4) the transnational corporation uses a network structure to balance global and local concerns.

Objective 2 In addition to economic considerations, political-legal and cultural factors in different parts of the world make some countries more desirable to do business in than others.

Objective 3 International HRM places greater emphasis on a number of responsibilities and functions such as relocation, orientation, and translation services to help employees adapt to a new and different environment outside their own country.

Objective 4 Many factors must be considered in the selection and development of employees for international assignments. Hiring host-country nationals or third-country nationals versus sending expatriates is generally less costly. When expatriates are hired, most companies try to minimize their stays. Operations are handed off to host-country nationals as soon as possible.

Objective 5 Once an expatriate is selected, an intensive training and development program is essential to qualify that person and his or her spouse and family for the assignment. Wherever possible, development should extend beyond information and orientation training to include sensitivity training and field experiences which will enable the manager to understand cultural differences better. Those in charge of international programs should provide the help managers need

with the career development risks they face, reentry problems, and culture shock. E-mail, instant messaging, and videoconferencing are making it easier for companies to stay in touch with their expatriates.

Objective 6 Compensation systems should support the overall strategic intent of the organization but be customized for local conditions. Compensation plans must give expatriates an incentive to leave the United States; meet their standards of living, health care, and safety needs; provide for the education of their children, if necessary; and facilitate their repatriation.

Objective 7 Although home-country managers frequently have formal responsibility for appraising individuals on foreign assignments, they may not be able to fully understand an expatriate's experiences because geographical distances pose communication problems. Host-country managers may be in the best position to observe day-to-day performance but may be biased by cultural factors and may not have a view of the organization as a whole. To balance the pros and cons of home-country and host-country evaluations, performance evaluation that combines the two sources of appraisal information is one option.

Objective 8 In many European countries—Germany, for one—employee representation is established by law. Organizations typically negotiate the agreement with the union at a national level, frequently with government intervention. In other countries, union activity is prohibited or limited to only large companies. European unions have much more political power than many other unions around the world, although their power has declined somewhat due to globalization forces. The International Confederation of Free Trade Unions (ICFTU), European Trade Union Confederation (ETUC), and International Labour Organization (ILO) are among the major worldwide organizations endeavoring to improve the conditions of workers.

KEY TERMS

augmented skills
balance sheet approach
codetermination
core skills
cultural environment
culture shock
expatriates, or home-country
nationals
failure rate

global compensation system
global corporation
global manager
guest workers
home-based pay
host-based pay
host country
host-country nationals
international corporation

localization
multinational corporation (MNC)
repatriation
split pay
third-country nationals
transnational corporation
transnational teams
work permit, or visa

DISCUSSION QUESTIONS

Objective 1
1. What major HR issues must be addressed as an organization moves from an international form to a multinational, to a global, and to a transnational form?

Objective 2
2. In recent years, we have observed an increase in foreign investment in the United States. What effect are mergers and joint ventures, such as those between InBev and Budweiser, having on HRM in the United States?

Objective 3
3. If you were starting now to plan for a career in international HRM, what steps would you take to prepare yourself?

Objective 3
4. Describe the effects that different components of the cultural environment can have on HRM in an international firm.

Objective 4
5. Starbucks is opening new stores abroad every day, it seems. If you were in charge, would you use expatriate managers or host-country nationals to staff the new facilities? Explain your thinking.

Objective 4
6. In what ways are U.S. managers likely to experience difficulties in their relationships with employees in foreign operations? How can these difficulties be minimized?

Objective 5
7. This chapter places considerable emphasis on the role spouses play in terms of the success of an overseas manager. What other steps should companies take to increase the likelihood of a successful experience for all parties involved?

Objective 5
8. Talk with a foreign student on your campus; ask about his or her experience with culture shock on first arriving in the United States. What did you learn from your discussion?

Objective 6
9. If the cost of living is lower in a foreign country than in the United States, should expatriates be paid less than they would be at home? Explain your position. Who should ultimately decide whether an employee should be localized or not?

Objective 7
10. If grooming a talented individual for a leadership

role is an important outcome of a foreign assignment, how can this be worked into a performance appraisal system? How would a manager assess leadership accomplishments?

Objective 8 11. What are the major differences between labor-management relations in Europe and those in the United States?

Objective 8 12. Do you believe that codetermination will ever become popular in the United States? Explain your position.

HRM EXPERIENCE

An American (Expatriate) in Paris

There is often a great deal of work involved in setting up expatriate assignments. The administrative requirements can be far ranging and extend beyond the employee to also include family issues. Suppose you were faced with the following scenario. What would be the most pressing considerations that you would need to address?

The Scenario

You are the head of HR for Sarip International, a consulting firm specializing in hotel and restaurant management. Your firm is opening an office in Paris, France, and Jim Verioti, director of sales and marketing, has been asked to assume responsibilities for the expansion. Jim understands that the expatriate assignment will last two to three years, and although he has traveled to Europe for work on several occasions, this is his first long-term assignment overseas. He has a lot of questions about what he can expect and also some personal constraints.

Jim and his wife Betty have just moved into their new home (their mortgage is around $1,750 per month). In addition, Betty is an elementary school teacher and doesn't really know how the move will affect her job security. Their three children, Veronica (14), Reggie (12), and Archie (10), are of an age at which school considerations are very important. A friend told them about the American School in Paris, and this is a consideration. None of the Veriotis speak French.

Assignment

Working in teams of four to six individuals, put together the package that would allow Jim to move his family to Paris while still maintaining his present lifestyle (his current annual salary is $160,000 plus incentives). Address at least the following issues:

1. Visas and permits
2. Relocation allowance and housing
3. Language and culture training
4. Spousal employment concerns

An American (Expatriate) in Paris (continued)

5. Health/medical/insurance issues
6. Compensation and incentives
7. Education for the children

The following Web sites may be helpful to you, but other resources may prove valuable as well.

- U.S. Embassy in Paris (http://france.usembassy.gov)
- French Consulates in the United States (http://france.visahq.com/embassy/United-States)
- Expatica.com (http://www.expatica.com/fr/main.html)
- Americans in Paris (http://www.americansinfrance.net)
- The Paris France Guide (http://www.parisfranceguide.com)
- Easy Expat (http://www.easyexpat.com/paris_en.htm)
- Centers for Disease Control and Prevention (http://wwwn.cdc.gov/travel/default.aspx)
- American School in Paris (http://www.asparis.org/about)
- Medibroker (insurance) (http://www.medibroker.com)
- Access USA (mail) (http://www.myus.com)
- Travlang (currency calculator) (http://www.travlang.com/money)

BIZFLIX EXERCISES

Mr. Baseball: **Tolerance of Cultural Differences**

This chapter emphasized the importance of tolerance of cultural differences for success as an expatriate. Watch this *Mr. Baseball* scene carefully while considering the following questions.

The New York Yankees trade aging baseball player Jack Elliot (Tom Selleck) to the Chunichi Dragons, a Japanese team. This lighthearted comedy traces Elliot's bungling entry into Japanese culture. It exposes his cultural misconceptions, which almost cost him everything—including his new girlfriend, Hiroko Uchiyama (Aya Takanashi). After Elliot slowly begins to understand Japanese culture and Japanese baseball, his teammates finally accept him. This film shows many examples of Japanese culture, especially its love for baseball.

This scene is an edited version of the "Welcome to Japan" sequence that appears early in the film. Jack Elliot arrives at Nogoya International Airport, Tokyo, Japan. Yoji Nishimura (Toshi Shioya) meets him and acts as Jack's interpreter and guide. The film continues after this scene with the unfolding adventure of Jack Elliot playing for the Chunichi Dragons.

What to Watch for and Ask Yourself

- Is Jack Elliot culturally sensitive or culturally insensitive?
- Does he make any cross-cultural errors on his arrival in Japan? If yes, what are they?
- Review the earlier chapter section "Training and Development." What type of training would you recommend for Jack Elliot?

CASE STUDY 1

How about a 900 Percent Raise?

Registered nurse Carmen Lopez wants a raise—so she's leaving Mexico and moving to California to take a job at Desert Valley Medical, a hospital near Los Angeles, where her income will increase tenfold. "I was making US$500 a month in Mexico, and in the U.S. I will be making between $25 to $28 an hour," Lopez says. Lopez, upon finishing her U.S. nursing exam, will be joining nine other Mexican nurses at Desert Valley Medical.

As U.S. baby boomers—now in their early sixties—age, the number of registered nurses in the United States is not keeping up. The U.S. government forecasts that by 2020 the demand for registered nurses will have increased by 40 percent while number of nurses will have risen by just 6 percent. There are currently 2.2 million working nurses.

Lopez and her colleagues were recruited by MDS Global Medical Staffing in Los Angeles. Roger Viera, cofounder of MDS Global Staffing, says he and his business partner have invested $1 million, and the Mexican government added another $1 million, to open a nurse residency program in Mexico that trains and certifies nurses to work in the United States. "We only recruit qualified nurses. They must have a four-year Bachelor of Science degree and four years of work experience," Viera says. MDS expects to recruit from Mexico's twelve nursing schools and from Costa Rica in the near future.

MDS has also recruited Maria de la Cruz Gonzalez, who says she's excited about this opportunity to emigrate with her husband and work as a nurse in the United States. "The hospitals offer us a two-year contract where our nuclear family can come along to live with us in the U.S.," she says. MDS gives the nurses three months of paid rent and transportation, provides placement with client hospitals, and provides training in technology and language. They will be able to work in U.S. hospitals for two years under a North American Free Trade Agreement visa.

Donna Smith, chief nursing officer at Desert Valley Medical, says she is happy to have the Mexican nurses join her staff and believes that they are as qualified as U.S. nurses. But, she says, they will need more technical experience before they can go to work, since technology is different in the hospitals of Mexico. "We will provide them with extra training once they get here," she says.

Questions

1. Is recruiting nurses abroad a good idea for U.S. hospitals facing worker shortages?
2. Can you think of any cultural problems U.S. hospitals might encounter as a result?
3. What long-term recruiting measures should U.S. hospitals strive for?

Source: Condensed from Aisha Belone, "How about a 900 Percent Raise? Mexican Nurses Head North to Cure the Ballooning U.S. Health Care Labor Shortage," *Latin Trade* 12 no. 7 (July 2004): 30.

CASE STUDY 2

A "Turn-Around" Repatriate Plan: U.S. Company Moves Indian Workers Back Home

In an unusual move, a seriously ailing Dallas software company, i2 Technologies, resettled 209 Indian engineers, programmers, and managers in their South Asian homeland on a voluntary basis to help stem losses as it laid off thousands of other employees. A series of corporate crises led to the mass repatriation back to India beginning in 2001.

Many returnees had worked in Texas, Massachusetts, and California for five to seven years on H-1B visas designed for temporary, highly skilled workers, although about 10 percent had acquired permanent residency green cards or U.S. citizenship. They found the company's Move to India Program too good to turn down—even if it meant a pay cut of 50 percent or more. None was pressured by management to return, said Gunaranjan "Guna" Pemmaraju, a 30-year-old engineer, who returned home. The returnees, many graduates of India's top technical universities, were confident of finding other U.S. jobs if i2 laid them off and were prepared to "change industries if need be," he asserted.

"When I left America, I actually kissed the ground," Pemmaraju said. "It helped me grow as an individual, and it enriched my thought process." Significantly, though, Pemmaraju says the quality of life in his middle-class Bangalore neighborhood is comparable—with a few minor downsides that he and his wife are willing to accept. Although their pay shrank in dollar terms, the repatriates are relatively better off in India.

"If we were in the top 25 percent in the United States, we're in the top 5 percent here," said one repatriate.

"We may not have 54-inch TV sets, but we have more of a sense of community and belonging here," another added.

Pemmaraju relies on DSL Internet access, fields morning calls from Dallas colleagues on a cell phone, and watches satellite TV while pedaling his new exercise bike. Instead of a Honda Accord, he drives a much smaller Suzuki Zen sedan.

For i2, the wage and benefit savings are helping it edge toward profitability. The company says the savings have been substantial. At its peak, i2 employed 6,349 people, with about 800 in India. It has since scaled down to 2,500 workers, 1,100 of whom are based in Bangalore.

Pemmaraju's family expresses no regrets about returning, yet they retain fond memories of the United States, a country of "milk and honey"—not to mention seven-layer Taco Bell burritos and Krispy Kreme doughnuts. Pemmaraju was tickled by a recent call to a fast-food restaurant in Bangalore. "A guy answered the phone saying, 'Thank you for calling Pizza Hut. Would that be for delivery or carry out?' he said. It's just what they said in Arlington [Texas]!"

Questions

1. Does repatriation represent a good financial strategy for firms with international employees?
2. Besides cost savings, does i2 have anything to gain by repatriating its Indian employees?
3. What type of repatriation preparation training do you think i2's repatriates should receive before going home?

Source: Condensed from Barry Shlachter, "Software Firm Resettles Indian Workers in Turnaround Plan," *Fort Worth* (Texas) *Star-Telegram* (via Knight-Ridder/Tribune Business News), June 24, 2004.

How Deloitte Builds Global Expertise

Although he is based in the medium-sized city of Leon, northwest of Mexico City, Fabian Gomez spends much of his time working with clients who don't speak Spanish. He is an audit partner for the Mexican branch of Deloitte Touche Tohmatsu, a global accounting and business services organization with 700 offices and 95,000 employees in 140 countries. "A lot of our business is serving Mexican subsidiaries of international companies, and the executives usually come from other places," he says. "Tomorrow, for example, I have a meeting where six of the executives from one company are Americans, and ten from another company are Japanese."

To best serve his clients, Gomez has to reconcile Mexican-style accounting documents and data with U.S. or Japanese standards. He also has to deal with business nuances that are often quite different from his own Mexican cultural roots. "For example, in Mexico, when you meet with clients, you're expected to spend some time talking with them about their families, how their grandfathers and children are doing. That's an important part of the relationship with them. The American style, in contrast, is very direct and to the point. You have to be very conscious of respecting a client's time."

Gomez is well equipped to handle the challenges. He spent eighteen months training and working in New York as a participant in Deloitte's Global Development Program (GDP), an HR curriculum in which promising midcareer employees from throughout the world are assigned to work in other countries. Participants further develop their foreign language skills, study the business practices and cultures of other countries, and network with people from other countries to broaden their business perspective. "We take great pride in preparing our people to help clients excel in a marketplace without borders," says CEO James E. Copeland, Jr. But the Global Development Program provides more than just a boost to corporate self-esteem. Management views it as a key part of the organization's strategic objective of expanding and integrating its business operations around the world. "The GDP isn't just about learning the accounting practices of another country," says Lynda Spielman, deputy director of deployment. "It's about taking all these promising leaders from different countries and reinforcing the concept that they're in a global organization."

The value of such a program to an international company might seem fairly obvious. Yet when Deloitte management made the decision to focus more strongly on developing its international talent in the late 1990s, the company found itself in an odd dilemma. Graduates of the program could not only help their home-country operations acquire new clients and keep existing ones happy, but also burnish their own credentials and career prospects. Despite such clear advantages, the corporation had difficulty getting people to participate. In 1997, for example, the program managed to attract only 128 participants, barely 1 percent of the organization's vast global workforce. Only 25 out of 140 of the company's international subsidiaries sent participants to other locations or hosted them, and a disproportionate number of employees in the program came from just a few countries, such as the United Kingdom.

Deloitte's corporate HR team saw that it needed to get the Global Development Program off the ground in many more countries and that it had to sell both employees and executives on the value of participation. HR was tapped to help redesign the program to make it more appealing.

The next phase was to launch an ambitious multimedia internal marketing campaign. The core element was a self-assessment tool artfully designed to help employees from a wide range of cultural backgrounds to decide whether they were good candidates for the program.

Reshaping a Program to Fit Global Needs

When Deloitte's corporate HR team started pondering how to jump-start the organization's international development efforts in 1998, they realized that effective marketing often starts with understanding the audience and tweaking the product to better serve them.

At the time, Spielman says, the Global Development Program was called the Strategic Career Development Program. The internal promotion efforts emphasized how international experience could help participants rise higher on the career ladder. After corporate HR sought feedback from company operations throughout the world, however, the team saw that the approach wasn't working. Too often, what attracted potential candidates to the program was the opportunity to live in a particular country. They didn't grasp the program's strategic mission and how it related to the Deloitte operation in their home country.

Worse, the executives who headed the organization's far-flung outposts often didn't encourage staff members to participate. They didn't see how allowing valued employees to spend a couple of years working in another country would benefit their own operations. And they weren't always eager to bring in someone from another country and allow him or her to work for important clients just to gain experience—especially if they had to cover the salary cost.

As a result, the company decided to make some small but significant changes. The program was given a new name, carefully chosen to focus on its real mission—helping Deloitte increase its global business capabilities. Instead of simply depending on employees to choose countries that appealed to them, HR coordinators began working with applicants to identify other places in the world that offered experience relevant to work in their own countries. For example, an accountant whose office worked with the Mexican subsidiary of General Motors might be sent to Michigan to provide services to GM headquarters.

"Today, about 25 percent of the participants are placed so that they can work with the same global client in another location," Spielman says. If that isn't feasible, the HR coordinator will look for a country where the employee can work with a client in the same industry as a major client at home. Establishing that sort of tangible linkage between the assignment and home-country needs has helped make the program easier to sell. Additionally, Deloitte sought to encourage its operations in emerging countries to accept placements by agreeing to underwrite the employees' salaries. The company also made the length of the assignment flexible.

To ensure that those improvements registered with the decisionmakers at Deloitte operations throughout the world, HR put considerable effort into marketing the program to executives as well as potential candidates. "In order to undertake something like this, you need to have your business leaders on board," Spielman says.

"There are so many things that can deter them—if they had a bad experience [with an expatriate] four years ago, for example, they're still going to have a memory that you'll need to overcome." To address this problem, HR designed its video and print materials to emphasize the value that the program would provide to the executives. "For example, we found Deloitte clients to talk about the importance of international knowledge and skills," Spielman says. "Those interviews were something that our leaders found very appealing."

Marketing the Program to Employees from Diverse Cultures

Another problem, corporate HR learned, was that good candidates for the program were sometimes deterred by anxiety about leaving their families behind and coping with life in an unfamiliar place.

"In many other parts of the world, life tends to be more collectivist," Spielman says. "People tend to do things together, or else divide the responsibilities. A professional from another country may have great skills on the job, but he may never have turned on a stove or shopped for groceries. I had a forty-year-old Brazilian professional who still lived at home. Despite her accounting skills, she'd never actually managed her own money, because she just turned her paycheck over to her parents." Going from that situation to living alone in an apartment in New York or Detroit can be a difficult experience. An American who takes an international assignment may have to make very different adjustments. "If you're used to watching Monday night football, you have to deal with the fact that they don't have anything like that in Malaysia," Spielman says. According to a 1997 study by the company's Employee Relocation Council, 58 percent of employees on international assignments fail because of an inability to adapt to life in another country.

That's why marketing materials were carefully designed to help employees feel more comfortable with the idea of an international development assignment. The "Experience the World" booklet, for example, included profiles of program participants from Chile, South Africa, Belgium, China, and the United States. "We also tried to balance men and women, married and single people," Spielman says. "We wanted to create a message that everyone could identify with, no matter what country or background that person came from."

To reduce potential candidates' uncertainty, Spielman—who also teaches a class in cross-cultural management at New York University—felt it was crucial to develop a self-assessment tool that would help potential participants evaluate whether they were ready for a developmental placement elsewhere in the world. That wasn't an easy task. "We needed something that would work for everybody, but also would dig deeper. We needed to force people to think introspectively and to be more culturally self-aware, so they could identify the issues that might affect them on an international assignment." Spielman hired an outside consultant to redesign an existing tool, and then made additional modifications to ensure that the tool was culturally neutral. The finished product includes a case study that features a fictional Deloitte employee, Mark Peterson, and his wife, Linda.

Candidates evaluate the Petersons' strengths and weaknesses, a drill that gives them comparative insights into their own real-life situations. Questionnaires and checklists help candidates zero in on their biggest concerns. "They take the questions home and share them with their spouses. Each person takes the test separately, and they compare their answers." The results can be scored numerically, so that the employee can get a more precise indication of whether he or she is a good candidate for the program.

Impressive Results

The results of the program revamping and marketing campaign have been impressive. Since 1997, Deloitte has increased the number of participating countries in the Global Development Program from twenty-five to fifty, and the number of employees has more than doubled, to 288. While it's difficult to separate out the precise economic impact of that improvement, Deloitte executives see it as a factor in the company's 11 percent growth in global revenue in fiscal 2001, to $12.4 billion. But the biggest benefit of successfully promoting the Global Development Program may lie a few years down the road. "Having more people with international training and experience may mean increasing the revenue we get from a client from $20 million to, say, $23 million, because we can handle the client's subsidiary in Mexico," Spielman says. In other cases, the added revenue isn't as important as protecting a larger client relationship. "If you do a bad job on a $50,000 contract in Brazil, you may risk millions of dollars in revenue from the company's parent in the United States."

In Leon, Mexico, the success of the program is seen in management's eagerness to have more participants. "We now have three people with international experience in our office, and we're hoping to add one more each year," Gomez says. "People are very excited about it, because they know that if they have international experience, both they and the company are going to get ahead."

Questions

1. What were the goals of Deloitte's Global Development Program?
2. What were the most noteworthy features of the program for career development?
3. What concerns do you have as the company looks toward the future?

Source: Patrick Kiger, "How Deloitte Builds Global Expertise," *Workforce* 81, no. 6 (June 2002): 62–66. Used with permission of ACC Communications/*Workforce*, Costa Mesa, CA, via Copyright Clearance Center.

NOTES AND REFERENCES

1. J. Michael Geringer, Colette Frayne, and John Milliman, "In Search of 'Best Practices' in International Human Resource Management: Research Design and Methodology," *Human Resource Management* 41, no. 1 (Spring 2002): 5–30; "Cendant Mobility Survey Shows Continued Challenges around Repatriation Management; Focus on Cost Control Also Driving New Approaches to Global Assignments, Say Global Mobility Practitioners," *PR Newswire* (April 28, 2004).

2. Abagail McWilliams, David Van Fleet, and Patrick Wright, "Strategic Management of Human Resources for Global Competitive Advantage," *Journal of Business Strategies* 18, no. 1 (Spring 2001): 1–24.

3. Charles Dawson, "The Global 1000," *Business Week*, no. 3841 (July 14, 2003): 34; Cristina Lindblad, "The Global 1000: The World's Most Valuable Companies," *Business Week*, no. 3791 (July 15, 2002): 58–80.

4. M. F. Wolff, "Innovation and Competitiveness among EU Goals for Knowledge Economy," *Research Technology Management* 44, no. 6 (November/December 2001): 2–6; Tony Emerson, "The Great Walls: The United States and Europe Are Leading the Race to Carve Up the Trading World," *Newsweek*, April 23, 2001, 40. For more information about the European Union online, see the Europa Web site at http://europa.eu.int.

5. Kris Axtman, "NAFTA's Shop-Floor Impact; Ten Years Later, The Trade Deal Costs Some U.S. Jobs But Buoys Trade and Efficiency," *Christian Science Monitor*, November 4, 2003, 1; Sarah Schweitzer, "As Jobs Fall, Maine Blames Free Trade; Anti-NAFTA Rhetoric Echoes U.S. Anxiety," *The Boston Globe* (via Knight-Ridder/Tribune Business News), March 28, 2004; John D. McKinnon, "Nafta, Under Attack, Gets Bush's Backing. Preview" *Wall Street Journal* 251, no. 94 (April 22, 2008): A3.

6. Sadanand Dhume, "Just Quit It," *Far Eastern Economic Review* 165, no. 36 (September 12, 2002): 46–50; George Koo, "Fast Lane to China: Companies That Never Thought of Doing Business Overseas Are Now Looking to the Thriving Chinese Economy," *Computer Technology Review* 24, no. 4 (April 2004): 42.

7. Julia Christensen Hughes, "HRM and Universalism: Is There One Best Way?" *International Journal of Contemporary Hospitality Management* 14, no. 5 (2002): 221–28; "What's Keeping HR from Going Global?" *HRFocus* 77, no. 8 (August 2000): 8; "Culture: A Key Ingredient for International HR Success," *HRFocus* 78, no. 7 (July 2001): 1–3.

8. Beth McConnell, "Global Forum Speakers to Share Insights on International HR," *HRMagazine* 48, no. 3 (March 2003): 115–17.

9. DeeDee Doke, "Perfect Strangers: Cultural and Linguistic Differences between U.S. and U.K. Workers Necessitate Training for Expatriates," *HRMagazine* 49, no. 12 (December 2004): 62.

10. Readers interested in codes of conduct and other ethical issues pertaining to international business might read the following: Bill Roberts, "Going Global," *HRMagazine* 45, no. 8 (August 2000): 123–28.

11. Carla Joinson, "No Returns," *HRMagazine* 47, no. 11 (November 2002): 70–77; Frank Jossi, "Successful Handoff," *HRMagazine* 47, no. 10 (October 2002): 48–52; Steve Bates, "Study Discovers Patterns in Global Executive Mobility," *HRMagazine* 47, no. 10 (October 2002): 14; Morgan McCall and George Hollenbeck, "Global Fatalities: When International Executives Derail," *Ivey Business Journal* 66, no. 5 (May/June 2002): 74–78; Leslie Gross Klass, "Fed Up with High Costs, Companies Thin the Ranks of Career Expats," *Workforce Management* 83, no. 10 (October 1, 2004): 84.

12. David Lipschultz, "Bosses from Abroad," *Chief Executive* 174 (January 2002): 18–21;

Siew Seem Sing, "Many Challenges Await Those Who Expatriate," *Plastics News* 20, no. 13 (June 2, 2008): 8-19.

13. Soo Min Toh and Angelo S. DeNisi, "A Local Perspective to Expatriate Success," *Academy of Management Executive* 19, no. 1 (February 2005): 132–146.

14. Readers interested in codes of conduct and other ethical issues pertaining to international business might read Nadar Asgary and Mark Mitschow, "Toward a Model for International Business Ethics," *Journal of Business Ethics* 36, no. 3 (March 2002): 238–46; Diana Winstanley and Jean Woodall, "The Adolescence of Ethics in Human Resource Management," *Human Resource Management Journal* 10, no. 4 (2000): 45; J. Brooke Hamilton and Stephen Knouse, "Multinational Enterprise Decision Principles for Dealing with Cross-Cultural Ethical Conflicts," *Journal of Business Ethics* 31, no. 1 (May 2001): 77–94; Michael Maynard, "Policing Transnational Commerce: Global Awareness in the Margins of Morality," *Journal of Business Ethics* 30, no. 1 (March 2001): 17–27.

15. "Keeping Out the Wrong People: Tightened Visa Rules Are Slowing the Vital Flow of Professionals into the U.S.," *Business Week*, no. 3902 (October 4, 2004): 90; "Security Delays Hurt U.S. Business," *Legal Times*, August 23, 2004; "Skilled Workers Leave in Reverse Brain Drain," *Fort Worth Star Telegram* (August 25, 2007): 9A.

16. "Society: Affirmative Action? Oui! At Long Last, France Takes a Page from America in Order to Manage Diversity—and Bring Minorities into Elite Schools," *Newsweek International*, April 12, 2004, 30; Leo D'Angelo Fisher, "The Hunt for a New Work Order," *BRW* 30, no. 9 (May 15, 2008): 46–52.

17. Snell et al., "Designing and Supporting Transnational Teams," 147–58; Debra Shapiro, Stacie Furst, Gretchen Spreitzer, and Mary Ann Von Glinow, "Transnational Teams in the Electronic Age: Are Team

Identity and High Performance at Risk?" *Journal of Organizational Behavior* 23 (June 2002): 455–67; Claude Philipps, Harold Sirkin, Duane Filtz, and Scott Kirsner, "Time [Zone] Travelers: They Bounce from Beijing to Bangalore at a Moment's Notice," *Fast Company*, no. 85 (August 2004): 60–67; Marie Adenfelt, and Katarina Lagerström, "Knowledge Development and Sharing in Multinational Corporations: The Case of a Centre of Excellence and a Transnational Team," *International Business Review* 15, no. 4 (August 2006): 381–400.

18. Snell et al., "Designing and Supporting Transnational Teams," 147–58; Leslie Gross Klass, "Fed Up with High Costs, Companies Thin the Ranks of Career Expats," *Workforce Management* 83, no. 10 (October 1, 2004): 84.

19. Andrea Poe, "Selection Savvy," *HRMagazine* 47, no. 4 (April 2002): 77–83; "Exploiting Opportunity: Executives Trade Stories on Challenges of Doing Business in Global Economy," *Business Mexico* 15, no. 2 (February 2005): 54–58.

20. Yehuda Baruch, "No Such Thing as a Global Manager," *Business Horizons* 45, no. 1 (January/February 2002): 36–42.

21. Sheree R. Curry, "Offshoring Swells Ranks of 'Returnees' Working Back in Their Native Countries," *Workforce Management* 84, no. 2 (February 1, 2005): 59; Yochanan Altman and Susan Shortland, "Women and International Assignments: Taking Stock—a 25-Year Review," *Human Resource Management* 47, no. 2 (Summer 2008): 199–216; Handan Kepir Sinangil and Deniz S. Ones, "Gender Differences in Expatriate Job Performance," *Applied Psychology: An International Review* 52, no. 3 (July 2003): 461–475; "More Women Sent on International Assignment," *Compensation & Benefits* 39, no. 2 (March–April 2007): 14–15.

22. Robert O'Connor, "Plug the Expat Knowledge Drain," *HRMagazine* 47, no. 10 (October 2002): 101–107; Andrea Graf and Lynn K. Harland, "Expatriate Selection: Evaluating the Discriminant, Convergent, and Predictive Validity of Five Measures of Interpersonal and Intercultural Competence," *Journal of Leadership & Organizational Studies* 11, no. 2 (Winter 2005): 46–63.

23. McCall and Hollenbeck, "Global Fatalities: When International Executives Derail," 74–78; Poe, "Selection Savvy," 77–83; Juan Sanchez, Paul Spector, and Cary Cooper, "Adapting to a Boundaryless World: A Developmental Expatriate Model," *Academy of Management Executive* 14, no. 2 (May 2000): 96–106; Eric Krell, "Evaluating Returns on Expatriates: Though Difficult to Ascertain, Measuring the Return on the Cost of Expatriate Assignments Is Necessary to Justify the Expensive Investment," *HRMagazine* (March 2005): 12.

24. Riki Takeuchi, Seokhwa Yun, and Paul Tesluk, "An Examination of Crossover and Spillover Effects of Spousal and Expatriate Cross-Cultural Adjustment on Expatriate Outcomes," *Journal of Applied Psychology* 87, no. 4 (August 2002): 655–66; Andrea Poe, Iris I. Varner, and Teresa M. Palmer, "Role of Cultural Self-Knowledge in Successful Expatriation," *Singapore Management Review* 27, no. 1 (January–June 2005): 1–25; Semere Haile, Marcus D. Jones, and Tsegai Emmanuel, "Challenges Facing Expatriate Performance Abroad," *International Journal of Business Research* 7, no. 5 (2007): 100–105; Margery Weinsten, "China a Double-Edged Sword for Ex-Pats," *Training* 43, no. 11 (November 2006): 12.

25. "Motorola to Increase Operations in China," *The New York Times*, November 8, 2001, C4; Peter J. Buckley, Jeremy Clegg, and Hui Tan, "Knowledge Transfer to China: Policy Lessons from Foreign Affiliates," *Transnational Corporations* 13, no. 1 (April 2004): 31–73.

26. Lionel Laroche, John Bing, and Catherine Mercer Bing, "Beyond Translation," *Training & Development* 54, no. 12 (December 2000): 72–73; Sabrina Hicks, "Successful Global Training," *Training & Development* 54, no. 5 (May 2000): 95; Vesa Peltokorpi, "Intercultural Communication Patterns and Tactics: Nordic Expatriates in Japan," *International Business Review* 16, no. 1 (February 2007): 68–82.

27. Managers who are interested in setting up a language training program or who wish to evaluate commercially available language training programs should consult the "Standard Guide for Use-Oriented Foreign Language Instruction." The seven-page guide is put out by the American Society for Testing and Materials (ASTM), (610) 832-9585, http://www.astm.org. See also "Why Top Executives Are Participating in CEIBS and IESE's Joint Global Management Programme," *PR Newswire*, July 19, 2004.

28. Jared Wade, "The Pitfalls of Cross-Cultural Business," *Risk Management* 51, no. 3 (March 2004): 38–43; Semere Haile, Marcus D. Jones, and Tsegai Emmanuel, "Challenges Facing Expatriate Performance Abroad," *International Journal of Business Research* 7, no. 5 (2007): 100–105.

29. Vipin Gupta, Paul Hanges, and Peter Dorman, "Cultural Clusters: Methodology and Findings," *Journal of World Business* 37, no. 1 (Spring 2002): 11–15; Jane Terpstra-Yong and David Ralston, "Moving toward a Global Understanding of Upward Influence Strategies: An Asian Perspective with Directions for Cross-Cultural Research," *Asia Pacific Journal of Management* 19, no. 2 (August 2002): 373–404.

30. Ping Ping Fu et al., "The Impact of Societal Cultural Values and Individual Social Beliefs on the Perceived Effectiveness of Managerial Influence Strategies: A Meso Approach," *Journal of International Business Studies* 35, no. 4 (July 2004): 33; Geert Hofstede, *Culture's Consequences: Comparing Values, Behaviors, Institutions, and Organizations across Nations* (Thousand Oaks, CA: Sage, 2001).

31. Justin Martin, "The Global CEO: Overseas Experience Is Becoming a Must on Top Executives' Resumes, According to This Year's Route to the Top," *Chief Executive* no. 195 (January–February 2004): 24–31; Alizee B. Avril and Vincent P. Magnini, "A Holistic Approach to Expatriate Success," *International Journal of Contemporary Hospitality Management* 19, no. 1 (2007): 53–64.

32. David Lipschultz, "Bosses from Abroad," *Chief Executive* 174 (January 2002): 18–21; Denis Lyons and Spencer Stuart, "International CEOs on the Rise," *Chief Executive* 152 (February 2000): 51–53; U.S. Companies with Foreign-Born Executives," *Workforce Management* 83, no. 7 (July 1, 2004): 23.

33. "Prudential Relocation Survey Finds Spouses' Experiences a Key Factor in the Success of International Work Assignments," *Canadian Corporate News*, December 7, 2004.

34. Avan Jassawalla, Traci Connolly, and Lindsay Slojkowski, "Issues of Effective Repatriation: A Model and Managerial Implications," *SAM Advanced Management Journal* 69, no. 2 (Spring 2004): 38–47; Mila B Lazarova and Jean-Luc Cerdin, "Revisiting Repatriation Concerns: Organizational Support versus Career and Contextual Influences," *Journal of International Business Studies* 38, no. 3 (May 2007): 404–429; "Life Not So Sweet for Repatriates," *In the Black* 78, no. 1 (February 2008): 13–14.

35. "Expatriate Administration: New Realities and HR Challenges," *Employee Benefit News* (March 1, 2005) p.11; "For Those Working Abroad, Moving Home Can Be Jarring," *The Kansas City (Missouri) Star* (via Knight-Ridder/Tribune Business News), February 22, 2005; Mark C. Bolino, "Expatriate Assignments and Intra-Organizational Career Success: Implications for Individuals and Organizations," *Journal of International Business Studies* 38, no. 5 (September 2007): 819–835.

36. Calvin Reynolds, *Guide to Global Compensation and Benefits* (New York: Harcourt, 2001); Gary Parker, "Establishing Remuneration Practices across Culturally Diverse Environments," *Compensation & Benefits Management* 17, no. 2 (Spring 2001): 23–27; Timothy Dwyer, "Localization's Hidden Costs," *HRMagazine* 49, no. 6 (June 2004): 135–141.

37. Caroline Fisher, "Reward Strategy Linked to Financial Success: Europe," *Benefits & Compensation International* 32, no. 2 (September 2002): 34–35; "Comparative Analysis of Remuneration: Europe," *Benefits & Compensation International* 31, no. 10 (June 2002): 27–28; Fay Hansen, "Currents in Compensation and Benefits: International Trends," *Compensation and Benefits Review* 34, no. 2 (March/April 2002): 20–21.

38. Chao Chen, Jaepil Choi, and Shu-Cheng Chi, "Making Justice Sense of Local-Expatriate Compensation Disparity: Mitigation by Local Referents, Ideological Explanations, and Interpersonal Sensitivity in China-Foreign Joint Ventures," *Academy of Management Journal* 45, no. 4 (August 2002): 807–17.

39. Patricia Zingheim and Jay Schuster, "How You Pay Is What You Get," *Across the Board* 38, no. 5 (September/October 2001): 41–44; "Benefits for Expatriate Employees: International," *Benefits & Compensation International* 31, no. 10 (June 2002): 26–27; Steven P. Nurney, "The Long and Short of It: When Transitioning from a Short-Term to a Long-Term Expatriate Assignment, Consider the Financial Implications," *HRMagazine* 50, no. 3 (March 2005): 91–95.

40. Stephan Kolbe, "Putting Together an Expat Package: As More and More Companies Adopt an International Outlook, They Are Increasingly Sending Staff on Overseas Assignments—Usually Involving a Complex Relocation Package," *International Money Marketing* (September 2004): 33.

41. The U.S. State Department Index of Living Costs Abroad can be found on the Web at http://www.state.gov/travel.

42. Barbara Hanrehan and Donald R. Bentivoglio, "Safe Haven: Accommodating the Needs of Employees and Families in Hostile Environments Can Increase Expenses and Alter Tax Liability," *HRMagazine* 47, no. 2 (February 2002): 52–54; Soo Min Toh and Angelo S. DeNisi, "A Local Perspective to Expatriate Success," *Academy of Management Executive* 19, no. 1 (February 2005): 132–146.

43. Paul Hempel, "Differences between Chinese and Western Managerial Views of Performance," *Personnel Review* 30, no. 2 (2001): 203–15; Hsi-An Shih, Yun-Hwa Chiang, and In-Sook Kim, "Expatriate Performance Management Form MNEs of Different National Origins," *International Journal of Manpower* 26, no. 2 (2005): 157–176.

44. "Cross-Cultural Lessons in Leadership: Data from a Decade-Long Research Project Puts Advice to Managers in Context, Country by Country," *MIT Sloan Management Review* 45, no. 1 (Fall 2003): 5–7.

45. Paula Caligiuri, "The Big Five Personality Characteristics as Predictors of Expatriate's Desire to Terminate the Assignment and Supervisor-Rated Performance," *Personnel Psychology* 53, no. 1 (Spring 2000): 67–88; Calvin Reynolds, "Global Compensation and Benefits in Transition," *Compensation and Benefits Review* 32, no. 1 (January/February 2000): 28–38; Charlene Marmer Solomon, "The World Stops Shrinking," *Workforce* 79, no. 1 (January 2000): 48–51; Stephenie Overman, "Mentors without Borders: Global Mentors Can Give Employees a Different Perspective on Business Matters," *HRMagazine* 49, no. 3 (March 2004): 83–87.

46. Frank Jossi, "Successful Handoff," *HRMagazine* 47, no. 10 (October 2002): 48–52; Paula Caligiuri, David Day, and Shirley Puccino, "Worldwide Practices and Trends in Expatriate Compensation and Benefits," *Benefits & Compensation Digest* 44, no. 1 (January 2007): 34–38; Eric Krell, "Evaluating Returns on Expatriates," *HRMagazine* 50, no. 3 (March 2005): 60–65.

47. M. Mendenhall and G. Oddou, *International Human Resources Management: Readings and Cases*, 2nd ed. (Boston, Mass.: P.W.S. Kent Publishing Co., 1995).

48. Ariane Berthoin, "Expatriates' Contributions to Organizational Learning," *Journal of General Management* 26, no. 4 (Summer 2001): 62–84; Peter J. Buckley, Jeremy Clegg, and Hui Tan, "Knowledge Transfer to China: Policy Lessons from Foreign Affiliates," *Transnational Corporations* 13, no. 1 (April 2004): 31–73.

49. Bernhard Ebbinghaus and Jelle Visser, *The Societies of Europe: Trade Unions in Western Europe since 1945* (London, England: Palgrave Macmillan, 2000); John Pencavel, "Unionism Viewed Internationally," *Journal of Labor Research* 26, no. 1 (Winter 2005): 65–98; "Membership Required," *Economist* 87, no. 8591 (August 2, 2008): 66; Jeremy Smerd, "Unions Reverse Decline," *Workforce Management* 87, no. 2 (February 4, 2008): 1–3.

50. Christopher Rhoads, "Germany Faces Storm over Tech Staffing—Labor Groups Are Enraged by Proposal to Import Badly Needed Workers," *The Wall Street Journal*, March 7, 2000, A23; "European Workplaces Tighten Policies as Countries

Struggle to Compete Worldwide," *Pittsburgh (Pennsylvania) Post-Gazette* (via Knight-Ridder/Tribune Business News), November 28, 2004.

51. Dharam Gahi, "Decent Work: Universality and Diversity" (discussion paper, International Institute for Labour Studies 2005), 1–22; "Philosophical and Spiritual Perspectives on Decent Work," *International Labour Review* 143, no. 3 (Autumn 2004):

290–292. Interested readers can find more information about international trade unions by checking out the Web sites of the ICFTU (http://www.icftu.org) and the ILO (http://www.ilo.org); "Communication on Decent Work," *European Industrial Relations Review* 389 (June 2006).

52. Dirk Kolvenbach and Ute Spiegel, "The Reform of the Works Council Constitution Act in Germany and Its Effects on the

Co-Determination Rights of the Works Council," *International Financial Law Review* (2001): 59–65; Pencavel, "Unionism Viewed Internationally," 65–98; Simon Renaud, "Dynamic Efficiency of Supervisory Board Codetermination in Germany," *Review of Labour Economics & Industrial Relations* 21, no. 4/5 (December 2007): 689–712.

Creating High-Performance Work Systems

After studying this chapter, you should be able to

Objective 1

Discuss the underlying principles of high-performance work systems.

Objective 2

Identify the components that make up a high-performance work system.

© GARY FRANCIS/JUPITER IMAGES

Objective | 3

Describe how the components fit together and support strategy.

Objective | 4

Recommend processes for implementing high-performance work systems.

Objective | 5

Discuss the outcomes for both employees and the organization.

So, you have finished reading fifteen chapters on HRM. Congratulations—textbooks do not always make for the most gripping reading. But before you close this book, think about the following question: What is more difficult—designing effective HR practices or managing them all together as one system?

In the past, HR textbooks simply ended after each individual aspect of HRM was introduced and explained. But in today's competitive environment, many organizations are discovering that it is how the pieces are combined that makes all the difference. After all, managers typically do not focus on staffing, training, and compensation practices in isolation from one another. These HR practices are combined into an overall system to enhance employee involvement and performance. So now that we have talked about the individual pieces, we thought it might be useful to spend some time talking about how they fit together into *high-performance work systems*.

A **high-performance work system (HPWS)** can be defined as a specific combination of HR practices, work structures, and processes that maximizes the knowledge, skills, commitment, flexibility, and resilience of employees. The key concept is based on the *system*. High-performance work systems are composed of many interrelated parts that complement one another to reach the goals of an organization, large or small.

We will start by discussing the underlying principles that guide the development of high-performance work systems and the potential benefits that can occur as a result. Then we will outline the various components of the system, the work-flow design, HR practices, management processes, and supporting technologies. (See Figure 16.1.) We will also describe the ways in which organizations try to tie all the pieces of the system together and link them with strategy. We end the chapter with a discussion of the processes organizations use to implement high-performance work systems as well as the outcomes that benefit both the employee and the organization as a whole.

high-performance work system (HPWS)

A specific combination of HR practices, work structures, and processes that maximizes employee knowledge, skill, commitment, and flexibility

▪▪ FUNDAMENTAL PRINCIPLES

Objective 1

In Chapter 1, we noted that organizations face a number of important competitive challenges such as adapting to greater global competition, embracing technology, managing change, responding to customers, developing intellectual capital, and containing costs. We also noted some very important employee concerns that must be addressed, such as managing a diverse workforce, recognizing employee rights, adjusting to new work attitudes, and balancing work and family demands. We now know that the best organizations go beyond simply balancing these sometimes competing demands; they create work environments that blend these concerns to simultaneously get the most from their employees, contribute to their needs, and meet the short-term and long-term goals of the organization.

The notion of high-performance work systems was originally developed by David Nadler to capture an organization's "architecture" that integrates technical and social aspects of work. Edward Lawler and his associates at the Center for Effective Organization at the University of Southern California have worked with Fortune 1000 corporations to identify the primary principles that support high-performance work systems. There are four simple but powerful principles, as shown in Figure 16.2:

- Egalitarianism and engagement
- Shared information
- Knowledge development
- Performance-reward linkage[1]

FIGURE 16.1 Developing High-Performance Work Systems

In many ways, these principles have become the building blocks for managers who want to create high-performance work systems. We will use them as a framework for the rest of the chapter. In addition, it should be noted that in a 2006 review and statistical analysis of 92 studies involving more than 19,000 organizations, researchers James Combs, Yongmei Liu, Angela Hall, and David Ketchen identified a number of major findings related to high-performance work systems. First, the systems have a larger influence on the performance of organizations than other highly visible governance practices such as the independence of a firm's board of directors do. Second, because of their synergistic effects, the elements of the systems have a larger impact when they are implemented as a bundle. Third, the systems have a significant effect regardless of whether the performance of firms is measured in operational terms or financial terms. Finally, although high-performance work systems seem to have a bigger effect when in manufacturing than they do in service organizations, they can be successfully implemented in all types of organizations.

Egalitarianism and Engagement

People want a sense that they are members, not just workers, in an organization. Status and power differences tend to separate people and magnify whatever disparities

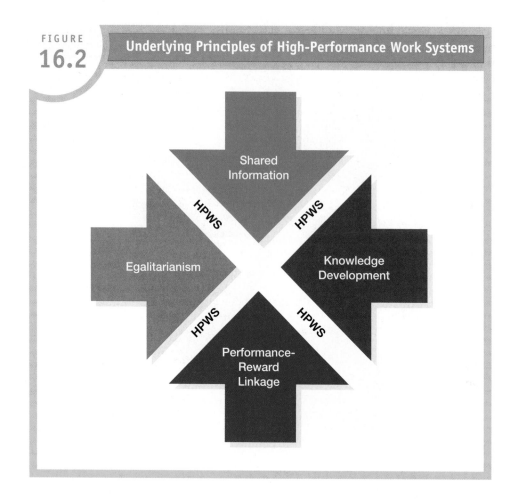

FIGURE
16.2

Underlying Principles of High-Performance Work Systems

Shared Information

Egalitarianism

Knowledge Development

Performance-Reward Linkage

HPWS

exist between them. The "us versus them" battles that have traditionally raged between managers, employees, and labor unions are increasingly being replaced by more cooperative approaches to managing work. More egalitarian work environments eliminate status and power differences and, in the process, increase collaboration and teamwork. When this happens, productivity can improve if people who once worked in isolation from (or in opposition to) one another begin to work together.

Nucor Steel has an enviable reputation not only for establishing an egalitarian work environment, but also for the employee loyalty and productivity that stem from that environment. Upper-level managers do not enjoy better insurance programs, vacation schedules, or holidays. In fact, certain benefits such as Nucor's profit sharing plan, scholarship program, employee stock purchase plan, extraordinary bonus plan, and service awards program are not available to Nucor's officers at all. Senior executives do not enjoy traditional perquisites such as company cars, corporate jets, executive dining rooms, or executive parking places. On the other hand, every Nucor employee is eligible for incentive pay and is listed alphabetically on the company's annual report.

Using the Internet

Nucor makes no secret of the importance of its employees. Read about its management philosophy and incentive-based compensation plans at About Nucor. Go to the Student Resources at:

www.cengage.com/management/bohlander

Moving power downward in organizations—that is, empowering employees—frequently requires structural changes. Managers often use employee surveys, suggestion systems, quality circles, employee involvement groups, and/or union-management committees that work in parallel with existing organizational structures. In addition, work flow can be redesigned to give employees more control and influence over decision-making. At Old Home Foods in St. Paul, Minnesota, one of the few independent, exclusively cultured dairy product manufacturers in the country, all employees are involved in the decision-making process of the business. "It's part of the Old Home Foods culture," says owner Peter Arthur "P. A." Hanson. "To be a successful independent, you need to empower your employees and let them know they are critical to success."[2] Job enlargement, enrichment, and self-managing work teams are typical methods for increasing the power of employees to influence decisions, suggest changes, or act on their own.

Involving employees in decision-making and giving them the power to act also tends to increase what HR professionals refer to as employee *engagement*. Engaged employees are employees who consistently perform at high levels, are enthusiastic about what they do, and look for better, more efficient ways of doing things. However, according to the research organization Gallup, only 29 percent of U.S. employees are actively engaged on the job, 15 percent are actively disengaged, and 54 percent are somewhere in the middle—not disengaged, but not engaged either.

Disengaged employees and employees who are only semiengaged can cost a company dearly, as the French bank Société Générale recently learned after a junior-level trader lost billions of the company's money making illicit trades. Some experts believe that a number of Société Générale employees were perhaps aware that there was a problem but did not report it perhaps because of poor employee engagement.

Shared Information

The principle of shared information is critical to the success of employee empowerment and involvement initiatives in organizations. In the past, employees traditionally were not given—and did not ask for—information about the organization. People were hired to perform narrowly defined jobs with clearly specified duties, and not much else was asked of them. One of the underlying ideas of high-performance work systems is that workers are intimately acquainted with the nature of their own work and are therefore in the best position to recognize problems and devise solutions to them. Today organizations are relying on the expertise and initiative of employees to react quickly to incipient problems and opportunities. Without timely and accurate information about the business, employees can do little more than simply carry out orders and perform their roles in a relatively perfunctory way. They are unlikely to understand the overall direction of the business or contribute to organizational success.

On the other hand, when employees are given timely information about business performance, plans, and strategies, they are more likely to make good suggestions for improving the business and to cooperate in major organizational changes. They are also likely to feel more committed to new courses of action if they take part in the decision-making. The principle of shared information typifies a shift in organizations away from the mentality of command and control toward one more focused on employee commitment. It represents a fundamental shift in the relationship between employer and employee. If executives do a good job of communicating with employees and create a culture of information sharing, employees are perhaps more likely to be willing (and able) to work toward the goals for the organization. They will "know more, do more, and contribute more."[3]

Knowledge Development

Knowledge development is the twin sister of information sharing. As Richard Teerlink, former CEO of Harley-Davidson, noted, "The only thing you get when you empower dummies is bad decisions faster." Throughout this text, we have noted that the number of jobs requiring little knowledge and skill is declining, while the number of jobs requiring greater knowledge and skill is growing rapidly. As organizations attempt to compete through people, they must invest in employee development. This includes both selecting the best and the brightest candidates available in the labor market and providing all employees opportunities to continually hone their talents.

High-performance work systems depend on the shift from touch labor to knowledge work. Employees today need a broad range of technical, problem-solving, and interpersonal skills to work either individually or in teams on cutting-edge projects. Because of the speed of change, knowledge and skill requirements must also change rapidly. In today's work environment, employees must learn continuously. Stopgap training programs may not be enough. Companies have found that employees in high-performance work systems need to learn in "real time," on the job, using innovative new approaches to solve novel problems. Likewise, at Ocean Spray's Henderson, Nevada, plant, making employees aware of the plant's progress has been a major focus. A real-time scoreboard on the Henderson plant floor provides workers with streaming updates of the plant's vital stats, including average cost per case, case volumes filled, filling speeds, and injuries to date. When people are better informed, they do better work. "We operate in real time, and we need real-time information to be able to know what we have achieved and what we are working towards," says an Ocean Spray manager.

Performance-Reward Linkage

People may intentionally or unintentionally pursue outcomes that are beneficial to them but not necessarily to the organization as a whole. A corollary of this idea, however, is that things tend to go more smoothly when there is some way to align the interests of an organization and its employees. When companies reward their employees based on their performance, workers naturally pursue outcomes that are mutually beneficial to themselves and the organization. When this happens, some amazing things can result. For example, supervisors do not have to constantly watch to make sure that employees do the right thing. But in fact, employees may go out of their way—above and beyond the call of duty—to make certain that coworkers are getting the help they need, systems and processes are functioning efficiently, and customers are happy.

As Case Study 2 at the end of the chapter explains, every four weeks, the natural foods grocery Whole Foods calculates the profit per labor hour for every team in every store. Teams that exceed a certain threshold get a bonus in their next paycheck. Performance-based rewards such as these ensure that employees share in the gains that result from any performance improvement. This also ensures fairness and tends to focus employees on the organization. In fact, at Whole Foods, each employee has access to what other employees make in terms of their compensation.

ANATOMY OF HIGH-PERFORMANCE WORK SYSTEMS

2 | Objective

We said at the beginning of this chapter that high-performance work systems combine various work structures, HR practices, and management processes to maximize employee performance and well-being. Although we outlined the principles underlying such systems, their specific characteristics have not as yet been described in detail.

Although it may be premature to claim that there is a foolproof list of "best practices" that can be implemented by every organization for every work situation, some clear trends in work design, HR practices, leadership roles, and information technologies tell us what high-performance work systems look like.[4] Some of these are summarized in Figure 16.3.

FIGURE **16.3**

Anatomy of High-Performance Work Systems

	Shared Information	Knowledge Development	Performance-Reward Linkage	Egalitarianism
Work flow				
• Self-managed teams	■	□	□	■
• Empowerment	■	■	□	■
Staffing				
• Selective recruiting	□	■	□	□
• Team decision making	■	□	□	□
Training				
• Broad skills	□	■	□	□
• Cross-training	■	■	□	□
• Problem solving	■	■	□	■
• Team training	■	■	□	■
Compensation				
• Incentives	□	□	■	■
• Gainsharing	■	■	■	■
• Profit sharing	■	■	■	■
• Skill-based pay	□	■	■	■
Leadership				
• Few layers	■	■	□	■
• Coaches/facilitators	■	■	□	■
Technologies				
• HRIS	■	□	□	□
• Communications	■	■	□	■

Work-Flow Design and Teamwork

High-performance work systems frequently begin with the way work is designed. Total quality management (TQM) and reengineering have driven many organizations to redesign their work flows. Instead of separating jobs into discrete units, most experts now advise managers to focus on the key business processes that drive customer value—and then create teams that are responsible for those processes. Federal Express, for example, redesigned its delivery process to give truck drivers responsibility for scheduling their own routes and for making necessary changes quickly. Because the drivers have detailed knowledge of customers and routes, Federal Express managers empowered them to inform existing customers of new products and services. In so doing, drivers now fill a type of sales representative role for the company. In addition, FedEx drivers also work together as a team to identify bottlenecks and solve problems that slow delivery. To facilitate this, advanced communications equipment was installed in the delivery trucks to help teams of drivers balance routes among those with larger or lighter loads.[5] By redesigning the work flow around key business processes, companies such as Federal Express have been able to establish a work environment that facilitates teamwork, takes advantage of employee skills and knowledge, empowers employees to make decisions, and provides them with more meaningful work.[6]

Complementary Human Resources Policies and Practices

Work redesign, in and of itself, does not constitute a high-performance work system. Neither does total quality management or reengineering. Other supporting elements of HRM are necessary. Several recent studies suggest that both the performance of employees as well as their satisfaction are much higher when organizations combine

High-performance work systems have helped companies such as Nissan and Saturn improve production and quality.

© JOHN MADERE/CORBIS

their changes in work-flow design with HR practices that encourage skill development and employee involvement.[7]

Staffing Practices

Many high-performance work systems begin with highly directive recruitment and selection practices. The recruitment tends to be both broad and intensive in order to get the best pool of candidates from which to choose. Human resources information systems have made it easier for firms to compile an inventory of their talent and search for employees with the specific skills they need. Talented employees "come up to speed" more quickly and take less time to develop. At Macy's, General Motors' Saturn division, and Weyerhaeuser, team members select their teammates. This practice gives employees more control over decisions about who their coworkers will be and forges relationships more quickly than if new members were simply assigned to a team.[8]

Too often, however, organizations try to save money by doing a superficial job of hiring. As a consequence, they run the risk of hiring the wrong people and spending more on training and/or outplacement, severance, and recruitment of replacements. Other hiring pitfalls include simply looking for skills and experience in candidates and not looking for cues to see if they are truly an engaged employee capable of contributing adequately to a high-performance work system. Kris Dunn, a human resources executive and writer, suggests asking candidates behavioral questions such as the following: *Tell me about a time in a past job that you got really excited about something you were working on. Now tell me about a situation at work in which you got bored.* If a candidate struggles to come up with relevant examples, there is no reason to think the person will be a fully engaged employee in your company.[9]

Training and Development

Like recruitment and selection, training focuses on ensuring that employees have the skills needed to assume greater responsibility in a high-performance work environment. For example, Schindler Elevator Corporation, the world's second-largest manufacturer of elevators, provides a sixty-hour prehire training program of instruction and testing in such subjects as orientation/company history, safety, plant policies and procedures, just-in-time (JIT) techniques, and basic shop math. The company also has an apprenticeship program that focuses on key areas based on its specific business needs. Apprentices are hired as machinists, tool and die makers, welders, electricians, mechanics, and so forth. In addition, Schindler gives each of its employees at least five days of classroom training every year. Similarly, team members at Saturn receive up to several hundred hours of training in their first few months. Typically, the training focuses on technical, problem-solving, and interpersonal skills. Emphasis on teamwork, engagement, and continuous improvement requires that employees develop a broader understanding of work processes performed by others around them rather than rely on just knowing their own jobs. To accomplish this, organizations increasingly use cross-training, discussed earlier in the book. Recall that this involves training employees in jobs in areas closely related to their own. For example, nurses in the perinatal unit of Cincinnati-based TriHealth System implemented cross-training to facilitate teamwork and cooperation across units; even more, it helps nurses identify trouble spots that cut across several jobs and allows them to suggest areas for improvement.

Beyond individual training, Eastman Chemical Company has established a training certification process that helps ensure that its teams progress through a series of maturity phases. The teams certify their abilities to function effectively by demonstrating knowledge and skills in such areas as customer expectations, business conditions, and safety. Because these skills must be continually updated, Eastman Chemical requires that even certified teams periodically review their competencies.[10]

Compensation

Another important piece of a high-performance work system is the compensation package. Because high-performance work systems ask many different things from employees, it is difficult to isolate one single approach to pay that works for everyone. As a consequence, many companies are experimenting with alternative compensation plans. In order to link pay and performance, high-performance work systems often include some type of employee incentives. For example, an average of 10 percent of Saturn employees' pay is linked to goals for quality and training. Other organizational incentives such as gain sharing, profit sharing, and employee stock ownership plans focus employee efforts on outcomes that benefit both themselves and the organization as a whole. The Scanlon Plan, Rucker Plan, and Improshare, three systems discussed in Chapter 10, have been used by companies such as TRW, Weyerhaeuser, and Whole Foods to elicit employee suggestions and reward them for contributions to productivity.

High-performance work systems can also incorporate skill-based pay plans. By paying employees based on the number of different job skills they have, organizations such as Shell Canada, Nortel Networks, and Honeywell hope to create both a broader skill base among employees and a more flexible pool of people to rotate among interrelated jobs. Both of these qualities are beneficial in a high-performance work environment and may justify the added expense in compensation. Honeywell has even experimented with what it calls "intracapital"—a pool of money employees can spend on capital improvements if the company meets profitability goals.[11]

Recall that in addition to linking pay and performance, high-performance work systems are also based on the principle of egalitarianism. To reinforce this principle in plants utilizing high-performance work systems, Monsanto, AES, and Honeywell recently implemented an all-salaried workforce. The open pay plan, in which everyone knows what everyone else makes, is yet another feature of compensation systems used to create a more egalitarian environment that encourages employee involvement and commitment.[12]

Management Processes and Leadership

Organizations such as Motorola, Doubletree Hotels, American Express, and Reebok International found that the success of any high-performance work system depends on first changing the roles of managers and team leaders. With fewer layers of management and a focus on team-based organization, the role of managers and supervisors is substantially different in an environment of high-performance work systems. Managers and supervisors are seen more as coaches, facilitators, and integrators of team efforts.[13] Rather than autocratically imposing their demands on employees and closely watching to make certain that the workers comply, managers in high-performance work systems share responsibility for decision-making with employees. Typically, the term *manager* is replaced by the term *team leader*. In a growing number of cases, leadership is shared among team members. Kodak, for example, rotates team leaders at various stages in team development. Alternatively, different individuals can assume functional leadership roles when their particular expertise is needed most.

Supportive Information Technologies

Communication and information technologies are yet one more piece that has to be added to the framework of high-performance work systems. Technologies of various kinds create an infrastructure for communicating and sharing information vital to business performance. Federal Express, for example, is known for its use of information technology to route packages. Its tracking system helps employees monitor each package, communicate with customers, and identify and solve problems quickly. Sally Industries in Jacksonville, Florida, uses information technology to assign employees to various project teams. The company specializes in animatronics, the combination of wires and latex that is used to make humanoid creatures such as are found in Disney's Hall of Presidents. Artisans employed by Sally Industries work on several project teams at once. A computerized system developed by the company helps budget and track the employee time spent on different projects.

But information technologies need not always be so high-tech. The richest communication occurs face to face. The important point is that high-performance work systems cannot succeed without timely and accurate communications. (Recall the principle of shared information.) Typically the information needs to be about business plans and goals, unit and corporate operating results, incipient problems and opportunities, and competitive threats.[14]

◼◼ FITTING IT ALL TOGETHER

3 | Objective

Each of these practices highlights the individual pieces of a high-performance work system. While we have emphasized throughout this text that certain HR practices are better than others, recall that in high-performance work systems the pieces are particularly valuable in terms of how they help the entire system function as a whole. As we discussed in Chapter 2, careful planning helps ensure that the pieces fit together and are linked with the overall strategic goals of the organization. This philosophy is reflected in the mission statement of Saturn Motors, a model organization for HPWS. Saturn's mission is to "Market vehicles developed and manufactured in the United States that are world leaders . . . through the integration of people, technology, and business systems." Figure 16.4 summarizes the internal and external linkages needed to fit high-performance work systems together.

Ensuring Internal Fit

Recall from Chapter 2 that internal fit occurs when all the internal elements of the work system complement and reinforce one another. For example, a first-rate selection system may be of no use if it is not working in conjunction with a firm's training

internal fit

The situation in which all the internal elements of the work system complement and reinforce one another

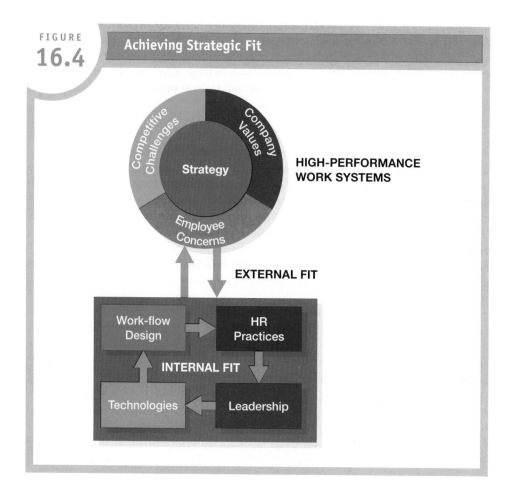

FIGURE 16.4

Achieving Strategic Fit

and development activities. If a new compensation program elicits and reinforces behaviors that are directly opposed to the goals laid out in the firm's performance plan, the two components would be working at cross purposes.

This is the true nature of systems. Changes in one component affect all the other components. Because the pieces are interdependent, a new compensation system may have no effect on performance if it is implemented on its own. Horizontal fit means testing to make certain that all of the HR practices, work designs, management processes, and technologies complement one another. The synergy achieved through overlapping work and human resources practices is at the heart of what makes a high-performance system effective.

Establishing External Fit

external fit
The situation in which the work system supports the organization's goals and strategies

To achieve external fit, high-performance work systems must support the organization's goals and strategies. This begins with an analysis and discussion of competitive challenges, organizational values, and the concerns of employees and results in a statement of the strategies being pursued by the organization.[15]

Xerox, for example, uses a planning process known as "Managing for Results," which begins with a statement of corporate values and priorities. These values and priorities are the foundation for establishing three-to-five-year goals for the organization. Each business unit establishes annual objectives based on these goals, and the process cascades down through every level of management. Ultimately, each employee within Xerox has a clear "line of sight" to the values and goals of the organization so he or she can see how individual effort makes a difference.[16]

Efforts such as this to achieve vertical fit help focus the design of high-performance work systems on strategic priorities. Objectives such as cost containment, quality enhancement, customer service, and speed to market directly influence what is expected of employees and the skills they need to be successful. Terms such as *involvement, flexibility, efficiency, problem-solving*, and *teamwork* are not just buzzwords. They are translated directly from the strategic requirements of today's organizations. High-performance work systems are designed to link employee initiatives to those strategies.

Assessing Strategic Alignment: The HR Scorecard

In Chapter 2, we introduced the balanced scorecard as a tool that helps managers evaluate the link between strategic goals and operational activities. Professors Brian Becker, Mark Huselid, and Dave Ulrich have adapted that model to create a *HR Scorecard* that helps managers assess the strategic alignment of their work systems.[17]

The HR Scorecard can be used to diagnose internal fit and external fit in a relatively straightforward way. First, managers diagnose internal fit by assessing whether particular HR practices reinforce one another or work at cross purposes (see Highlights in HRM 1A). Second, managers assess whether the HR practices significantly enable key workforce deliverables such as employment stability and teamwork (see Highlights in HRM 1B). Third, the degree of external fit is evaluated by assessing the degree to which the workforce deliverables are connected with key strategic performance drivers (see Highlights in HRM 1C). These three assessments are extremely useful not just for deriving measures of internal and external fit of high-performance work systems, but for engaging a broader set of managers and employees in the discussion of how to best implement the system. In addition to making sure their HR practices are aligned, companies with disparate operations often align the HR scorecards of their various divisions. That is what Borealis, a manufacturer of polyolefin plastics, has done. In addition to an overall corporate HR scorecard that supports the company's corporate strategy, Borealis's foreign HR divisions have created their own scorecards that support both the firm's corporate-level HR scorecard and the company's local business unit scorecards.

IMPLEMENTING THE SYSTEM

So far we have talked about the principles, practices, and goals of high-performance work systems. Unfortunately, these design issues compose probably less than half of the challenges that must be met in ensuring system success. Much of what looks good on paper gets messy during implementation. The American Society for Training

4 | **Objective**

1A

Diagnosing Internal Fit

In the following chart, please estimate the degree to which the various HR management subsystems work together harmoniously or "fit" together. Think of the degree of fit and internal consistency as a continuum from −100 to +100, and assign a value in that range to each relationship. Examples of the extremes and midpoints on that continuum are as follows:

−100: The two subsystems work at cross purposes.
   0: The two subsystems have little or no effect on one another.
+100: Each subsystem is mutually reinforcing and internally consistent.
 DNK: Don't know or have no opinion.

	HR Planning	Recruiting and Selection	Training and Development	Performance Management and Appraisal	Compensation and Benefits	Work Organization (e.g., Teams)	Communication Systems	HR Performance Measurement	
								Cost	Value Creation
HR planning	—	−30	0	−20	0	0	0	0	0
Recruiting and selection		—	0	−10	−20	−30	0	+30	−40
Training and development			—	0	0	0	0	+30	−10
Performance management and appraisal				—	0	−30	+20	0	−20
Compensation and benefits					—	−50	0	+40	0
Work organization (e.g., teams)						—	0	0	0
Communication systems							—	0	0
HR performance measurement								—	

Source: Brian Becker, Mark Huselid, and Dave Ulrich, *The HR Scorecard* (Cambridge, MA: Harvard University Press, 2001).

1B

Testing the Alignment of the HR System with HR Deliverables

Please indicate the degree to which the following elements of the HR system facilitate the HR deliverables shown, on a scale of −100 to +100. Examples of the extremes and midpoints on that continuum are as follows:

−100:	This dimension is counterproductive for enabling this deliverable.
0:	This dimension has little or no effect on this deliverable.
+100:	This dimension significantly enables this deliverable.
DNK:	Don't know or have no opinion.

	HR Planning	Recruiting and Selection	Training and Development	Management and Appraisal	Compensation and Benefits	Work Organization (e.g., Teams)	Communication Systems
Employment stability	0	0	0	0	−50	−20	0
Team-based behaviors	0	0	−30	−20	−40	0	0
Strategy-focused behaviors	0	0	0	0	+40	0	0
High-talent staffing level	0	−50	0	−50	0	0	0

and Development (ASTD) asked managers and consultants to identify the critical factors that can make or break a high-performance work system. The respondents identified the following actions as necessary for success (see Figure 16.5):

- Make a compelling case for change linked to the company's business strategy.
- Ensure that change is owned by senior and line managers.
- Allocate sufficient resources and support for the change effort.
- Ensure early and broad communication.
- Ensure that teams are implemented in a systemic context.
- Establish methods for measuring the results of change.
- Ensure continuity of leadership and champions of the initiative.[18]

Many of these recommendations are applicable to almost any change initiative, but they are especially important for broad-based change efforts that characterize high-performance work systems. Some of the most critical issues are discussed next.

1C

Testing the Alignment of HR Deliverables

Please indicate the degree to which each HR deliverable in the following chart would *currently* enable each strategic driver, on a scale of −100 to +100. Empty cells indicate this is not a key deliverable for a particular driver. Examples of the extremes and midpoints on that continuum are as follows:

- −100:   This deliverable is counterproductive for enabling this driver.
- 0:   This deliverable has little or no effect on this driver.
- +100:   This deliverable significantly enables this driver.
- DNK: Don't know or have no opinion.

	HR Deliverable			
Strategic Performance Drivers	**Employment Stability among Senior R&D Staff**	**Team-Based Behaviors**	**Strategy-Focused Performance**	**High-Talent Staffing Level**
1. Shorten product development times	−80	−30	+30	
2. Enhance customer focus and responsiveness	−20		−20	
3. Enhance productivity		−10	−50	−40
4. Develop and successfully manage joint ventures	−10	−50		

Building a Business Case for Change

Change can be threatening because it asks people to abandon the old ways of doing things and accept new approaches that, to them at least, are untested. Managers have to build a case that the changes are needed for the success of the organization. This can be more readily accomplished if a member of top management plays the role of sponsor/champion and spends a substantial portion of his or her time in that role communicating with employees about the reasons and approaches to change. Major transformation should not be left to middle managers. Rather, the CEO and the senior management team need to establish the context for change and communicate the vision more broadly to the entire organization. For example, executives at Harley-Davidson tried to institute employee involvement groups without first demonstrating their own personal commitment to the program. Not surprisingly, employees were apathetic and in some cases referred to the proposed changes as just "another fine program" put in place by the personnel department. Harley-Davidson executives learned the hard way that commitment from the top is essential in order to establish mutual trust between employees and managers. Similarly, the CEO of a business consulting company was adamant that his twenty-four vice presidents understand a new initiative and give a short speech at an introductory session. On

FIGURE **16.5** Implementing High-Performance Work Systems

the day of the program's launch, however, the CEO himself did not show up. The message to the vice presidents was clear. The CEO did not think the change was important enough to become an active participant. Not surprisingly, the change was never implemented.[19]

One of the best ways to communicate business needs is to show employees where the business is today—its current performance and capabilities. Then show them where the organization needs to be in the future. The gap between today and the future represents a starting point for discussion. When executives at TRW wanted to make a case for change to high-performance work systems, they used employee attitude surveys and data on turnover costs. The data provided enough ammunition to get conversation going about needed changes and sparked some suggestions about how they could be implemented.

Establishing a Communications Plan

While we have emphasized the importance of executive commitment, top-down communication is not enough. Two-way communication not only can result in better decisions, but also it may help to diminish the fears and concerns of employees. For example, Solectron Corporation, a winner of the Baldrige National Quality Award, tried to implement high-performance work systems to capitalize on the knowledge and experience of its employees. A pilot program showed immediate gains in productivity of almost 20 percent after the switch to self-managed teams and team-based compensation. Although Solectron's rapid growth of more than 50 percent per year made it unlikely that middle managers would be laid off, many of them resisted the change to a high-performance work system. They resented the loss of status and control that accompanied the use of empowered teams.

If Solectron managers had participated in discussions about operational and financial aspects of the business, they might not have felt so threatened by the change. Open exchange and communication at an early stage pay off later as the system

Using the Internet

Read the full story of how Solectron won the Baldrige Award at a special Web site devoted to the subject. Go to the Student Resources at:

www.cengage.com/ management/bohlander

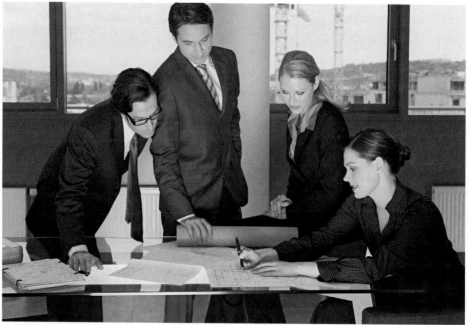

unfolds. Ongoing dialogue at all levels helps reaffirm commitment, answer questions that come up, and identify areas for improvement throughout implementation. Recall that one of the principles of high-performance work systems is sharing information. This principle is instrumental to success both during implementation and once the system is in place.

Involving Unions

We mentioned in Chapter 14 that autocratic styles of management and confrontational approaches to labor negotiations are being challenged by more enlightened approaches that promote cooperation and collaboration. Given the sometimes radical changes involved in implementing high-performance work systems, it makes good sense to involve union members early and to keep them as close partners in the design and implementation process. Figure 16.6 shows how to "build a bridge" toward a cooperative relationship with unions in implementing high-performance work systems.[20]

Cultivating Mutual Gains

In order to establish an alliance, managers and labor representatives should try to create "win-win" situations, in which all parties gain from the implementation of high-performance work systems. Organizations such as Shell and Weyerhaeuser have found that "interest-based" (integrative) negotiation rather than positional bargaining leads to better relationships and outcomes with union representatives. Trust is a fragile component of an alliance and is reflected in the degree to which parties are comfortable sharing information and decision-making responsibilities. Manitoba Telecom Services has involved

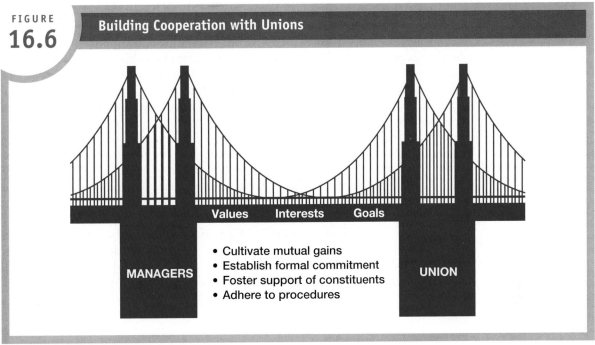

FIGURE 16.6

Building Cooperation with Unions

Values Interests Goals

MANAGERS

- Cultivate mutual gains
- Establish formal commitment
- Foster support of constituents
- Adhere to procedures

UNION

Source: The Conference Board of Canada.

union members in decisions about work practices, and because of this, company managers have been able to build mutual trust and respect with the union. This relationship has matured to a point at which union and company managers now design, select, and implement new technologies together. By working hard to develop trust up front, in either a union or a nonunion setting, it is more likely that each group will understand how high-performance work systems will benefit everyone. The organization will be more competitive, employees will have a higher quality of work life, and unions will have a stronger role in terms of representing employees.[21]

Formalizing the Commitment

Most labor-management alliances are made legitimate through some tangible symbol of commitment. This might include a policy document that spells out the union's involvement, letters of understanding, clauses in a collective bargaining agreement, or the establishment of joint forums with explicit mandates. MacMillan Bloedel, a Canadian wood products company now owned by Weyerhaeuser, formed a joint operations committee of senior management and labor representatives to routinely discuss a wide range of operational issues related to high-performance work systems. These types of formal commitments, with investments of tangible resources, serve two purposes: (1) They are an outward sign of managers' commitment, and (2) they institutionalize the initiative so that it keeps going even if key project champions leave.[22]

Gaining the Support of Other Key Groups

In addition to union leaders, it is critical for the firm to gain the support of other key groups. Leaders must ensure that understanding and support are solid at all levels, not just among those in the executive suite. To achieve this commitment, some organizations have decentralized the labor relations function, giving responsibility to local line managers and human resources generalists, to make certain that they are accountable and are committed to nurturing a high-performance work environment. Nortel Networks, for example, formally transferred accountability for labor relations to its plant managers through its collective bargaining agreement. Giving line managers responsibility for employee relations helps them establish a direct working relationship with the union.

Similarly, multinational firms need to gain the support of their key groups abroad. For example, Celestica, Inc., a Canadian-based provider of electronics manufacturing services and products started out as a single, wholly owned subsidiary of IBM. Today, however, the spin-off company has forty electronics manufacturing and design centers around the world. Being sensitive to different cultures and their ways of doing business as well as building relationships with them has been critical to the success of Celestica's high-performance work system.

Adhering to Procedures

Once processes, agreements, and ground rules are established, they are vital to the integrity of the relationship. As Ruth Wright, manager of the Council for Senior Human Resource Executives, puts it, "Procedure is the 'rug' on which alliances stand. Pull it out by making a unilateral management determination or otherwise changing the rules of the game, and the initiative will falter. Procedure keeps the parties focused, and it is an effective means of ensuring that democracy and fairness prevail."[23]

In most cases, a "home-grown" process developed by a firm's managers and employees works better than one that is adopted from elsewhere. Each organization has unique circumstances, and parties are more likely to commit to procedures they create and own. But this can give a firm a competitive advantage because homegrown, or unique, processes are harder for competitors to imitate.

Navigating the Transition to High-Performance Work Systems

Building and fostering high-performance work systems is an ongoing activity. Perhaps the job is never fully completed. As with any change activity, there will be missteps during the system's implementation. One reason this is so is because in already existing organizations, the pieces of the system often have to be changed incrementally rather than as a total program. Xerox Corporation found that when it implemented teams without also changing the compensation system to support teamwork, it got caught in a bad transition. The teams actually showed poorer performance than did employees working in settings that supported their individual contributions. Xerox's executives concluded that they needed to change the entire system at once because piecemeal changes were actually detrimental.

The other mistake organizations often make is to focus on either top-down changes driven by executives or bottom-up changes cultivated by the employees. In reality, firms such as Champion International, now a part of International Paper, and ASDA, a low-cost British retailer, are among the many companies that have found that the best results occur when managers and employees work together. The top-down approach communicates manager support and clarity, while the bottom-up approach ensures employees accept and are committed to the approach.[24]

High-performance work systems benefit employees by keeping them involved and informed.

Building a Transition Structure

Different organizations implement high-performance work systems in different ways. In start-up firms, managers have the advantage of being able to put everything in place at once. However, when organizations have to be retrofitted, the process can be a bit more cumbersome. For example, when Honeywell switched to high-performance work systems in its plant in Chandler, Arizona, employees attended training programs and participated in the redesign of their jobs while the plant was shut down to be reequipped with new technology. When the new plant was reopened, self-managing teams were put in place, and a new pay system was implemented for the high-performance workforce.[25]

Not every organization has the luxury of suspending operations while changes are put in place. Nevertheless, establishing an implementation structure keeps everyone on track and prevents the system from bogging down. The structure provides a timetable and process for mapping key business processes, redesigning the work flow, and training employees.

Incorporating the HR Function as a Valuable Partner

Although line managers typically own the responsibility for implementing high-performing work systems, a firm's HR department can be an invaluable partner because the group is the key enabler of a company's human capital. Moreover, as we explained in Chapter 2, global competition in many industries has led to the commoditization of products based on price, making talent the "great differentiator" among firms. Thus, the recruiting, evaluation, and reward systems devised by HR groups can have a huge impact on how well high-performance work systems are implemented.

In addition, because change is difficult, HR managers need to understand what employees in transition are going through and help them handle it. When the "old ways" of doing things are abandoned, many experienced employees begin to feel like "beginners" again on the job. This can be stressful and sometimes polarizes employees. As a coping mechanism, many are likely to fall back on older routines. Texas Instruments created its High Performance Organization Development unit to facilitate the transition to a high-performance work system. Other organizations such as Merck, Ford, and Deutsche Bank have also developed special HR units to manage organizational change. Unilever created a transition team of senior line and HR managers to oversee the implementation of high-performance teams and develop an implementation road map.[26]

Evaluating the Success of the System and Sustaining it

Once high-performance work systems are in place, they need to be monitored and evaluated over time. Several aspects of the review process should be addressed. First, there should be a process audit to determine whether the system has been implemented as it was designed and whether the principles of high-performance work systems are being reinforced. Questions such as the following might be included in the audit:

process audit

Determining whether the high-performance work system has been implemented as designed

- Are employees actually working together, or is the term "team" just a label?

- Are employees getting the information they need to make empowered decisions, and are they engaged?

- Are training programs developing the knowledge and skills employees need?

- Are employees being rewarded for good performance and useful suggestions?

- Are employees treated fairly so that power differences are minimal?

Second, the evaluation process should focus on the goals of high-performance work systems. To determine whether the program is succeeding, managers should look at such issues as the following:

- Are desired behaviors being exhibited on the job?

- Are quality, productivity, flexibility, and customer service objectives being met?

- Are quality-of-life goals being achieved for employees?

- Is the organization more competitive than in the past?

Implementing a HPWS is one thing. Sustaining it is another. Because the work teams in such a system are performing at their peak, burnout can be an issue, as can employee poaching by competitors. Motorola's Indian division discovered this firsthand. The division strategically recruited its employees and put together a high-performance work system, thereby capturing a significant amount of India's mobile device business. Later the division discovered that its employees were being hotly sought after by other companies such as Nokia. Consequently, Motorola had to look for new ways to retain and motivate the division's workforce.

Finally, high-performance work systems should be periodically evaluated in terms of new organizational priorities and initiatives. Because high-performance work systems are built on key business processes that deliver value to customers, as these processes and customer relationships change, so too should the work system. The advantage of high-performance work systems is that they are flexible and, therefore, more easily adapted. When change occurs, it should be guided by a clear understanding of the business needs and exhibit a close vertical fit to strategy.

OUTCOMES OF HIGH-PERFORMANCE WORK SYSTEMS

5 | Objective

In addition to the large corporations we have mentioned, high-performance work systems can be used by small and medium-sized organizations as well. The philosophies, principles, and techniques that underlie HPWSs are equally appropriate to the management of enterprises of all sizes. Progressive organizations of all sizes have successfully implemented team-based work systems, implemented staffing practices that select high-quality employees, developed training programs that continually update employee skills, and utilized compensation practices that support specific organizational goals. (The women's clothing design company Eileen Fisher Inc., discussed in Case Study 1 at the end of the chapter, is an example of such an organization.) The key is that the firms have done these things in a coordinated, integrative manner. These smaller organizations have simply achieved a systematic approach to organizational design that combines HR practices, work structures, and processes that effectively utilize the competencies of their employees.

Organizations achieve a wide variety of outcomes from high-performance work systems and effective human resources management. We have categorized these outcomes in terms of either *employee concerns* such as quality-of-work-life issues and job security or *competitive challenges* such as the firm's performance, productivity, and profitability. Throughout the text, we have emphasized that the best organizations find ways to achieve a balance between these two sets of outcomes and pursue activities that improve both.

Employee Outcomes and Quality of Work Life

High-performance work systems offer employees a myriad of potential benefits. In high-performing workplaces, employees have greater latitude to decide how to achieve their goals. Because the systems emphasize learning, people can take more risks, generate new ideas, and make mistakes, which in turn can actually lead to new products, services, and markets. As Richard Carlton, a former executive of 3M, put it, "You can't stumble if you're not in motion."[27] Because employees are more informed and empowered, they are likely to feel that they have a fuller role to play in the organization and that their opinions and expertise are valued more. As a result, they are likely to be more satisfied and find that their needs for career growth are being met. With higher skills and greater potential for contribution, they are likely to have more job security as well as be more marketable to other organizations, as employees in Motorola's Indian division discovered.

Conversely, when employees are underutilized, the performance of an organization suffers, and employees develop poor work attitudes and habits. Some years ago, the British Land Rover Company, a manufacturer of four-wheel-drive vehicles, found itself saddled with a notorious reputation for poor quality and productivity. Then it underwent a fundamental transformation. The company instituted extensive training (including giving every employee a personal training fund to be used on any subject), implemented more team-based production methods, reduced the number of separate job classifications, developed more cooperative relations with organized labor, and began a total quality program. As a result of these changes, productivity, quality, and the company's sales soared. However, despite massive evidence documenting the effectiveness of the new system, BMW, which later bought the company, began to dictate changes after taking over Land Rover—changes that ultimately undid its transformation.[28]

Organizational Outcomes and Competitive Advantage

Several organizational outcomes also result from using high-performance work systems. These include higher productivity, lower costs, better responsiveness to customers, greater flexibility, and higher profitability. Highlights in HRM 2 provides a sample of the success stories that companies have shared about their use of high-performance work systems. Benchmarks such as these are not enough. Recall that in Chapter 2 we said that organizations can create a sustainable competitive advantage through people if they focus on four criteria. They must develop competencies in their employees that have the following qualities:

- *Valuable:* High-performance work systems increase value by establishing ways to increase efficiency, decrease costs, improve processes, and provide something unique to customers.

- *Rare:* High-performance work systems help organizations develop and harness skills, knowledge, and abilities that are not equally available to all organizations.

- *Difficult to imitate:* High-performance work systems are designed around team processes and capabilities that cannot be transported, duplicated, or copied by rival firms.

- *Organized:* High-performance work systems combine the talents of employees and rapidly deploy them in new assignments with maximum flexibility.[29]

These criteria clearly show how high-performance work systems, in particular, and human resources management, in general, are instrumental in achieving competitive advantage through people.

However, for all their potential, implementing high-performance work systems is not an easy task. The systems are complex and require a good deal of close partnering among executives, line managers, HR professionals, union representatives, and employees. Ironically, this very complexity can lead to a competitive advantage. Because high-performance work systems are difficult to implement, successful organizations are difficult to copy. The ability to integrate business and employee concerns is indeed rare, and doing it in a way that adds value to customers is especially noteworthy. Organizations such as Google and Southwest Airlines have been able to do it, and as a result they enjoy a competitive advantage.

HIGHLIGHTS IN HRM

2

The Impact of High-Performance Work Systems

- Ames Rubber Corporation, a New Jersey–based manufacturer of rubber products and office machine components, experienced a 48 percent increase in productivity and five straight years of revenue growth.
- Sales at Connor Manufacturing Services, a San Francisco firm, grew by 21 percent, while new orders rose 34 percent and the company's profit on operations increased 21 percent to a record level.
- Over a seven-year period, Granite Rock, a construction material and mining company in Watsonville, California, experienced an 88 percent increase in market share, its standard for on-time delivery grew from 68 to 95 percent, and revenue per employee was 30 percent above the national average.
- At One Valley Bank of Clarksburg, West Virginia, employee turnover dropped by 48 percent, productivity increased by 24 percent, return on equity grew 72 percent, and profits jumped by 109 percent in three years.
- The Tennessee Eastman Division of the Eastman Chemical Company experienced an increase in productivity of nearly 70 percent, and 75 percent of its customers ranked it as the top chemical company in customer satisfaction.
- A study by John Paul MacDuffie of sixty-two automobile plants showed that those implementing high-performance work systems had 47 percent better quality and 43 percent better productivity.
- A study by Jeff Arthur of thirty steel minimills showed a 34 percent increase in productivity, 63 percent less scrap, and 57 percent less turnover.
- A study by Mark Huselid of 962 firms in multiple industries showed that high-performance work systems resulted in an annual increase in profits of more than $3,800 per employee.

Source: Martha A. Gephart and Mark E. Van Buren, "The Power of High Performance Work Systems," *Training & Development* 50, no. 10 (October 1996): 21–36.

SUMMARY

Objective 1 High-performance work systems are specific combinations of HR practices, work structures, and processes that maximize the knowledge, skills, commitment, and flexibility of employees. The systems are TQM oriented and based on the principles of shared information, knowledge development, performance-reward linkages, and egalitarianism and employee engagement.

Objective 2 High-performance work systems are composed of several interrelated components. Team members are carefully selected and undergo extensive training, including cross training, and often share leadership duties. Typically, the system begins with designing empowered work teams to carry out key business processes. Integrated information technology systems can help ensure that employees have the information they need to make timely and productive decisions. To align the interests of employees with those of the organization, the reward systems associated with high-performance work systems are performance-based, and often include group and organizational incentive pay and sometimes skill-based pay.

Objective 3 The pieces of the system are important only in terms of how they help the entire system function. When all the pieces support and complement one another, high-performance work systems achieve internal fit. When the system is aligned with the competitive priorities of the organization as a whole, it achieves external fit as well.

Objective 4 Implementing high-performance work systems within existing organizations often has to be done in stages. The implementation is much more likely to go smoothly if a business case is first made for the HPWS and fully communicated to employees. The support of the firm's top managers is critical, and so too is the support of union representatives and the company's other key groups and divisions. Because firms today gain a competitive advantage primarily from the capabilities of their talent, a company's HR department can be an invaluable partner when it comes to implementing a HPWS. HR personnel can also help establish a transition structure to shepherd the implementation through its various stages and reassure employees they will be successful working in the new system. Once the system is in place, it should be evaluated in terms of its processes, outcomes, sustainability, and ongoing fit with strategic objectives of the organization.

Objective 5 Progressive organizations of all sizes have successfully implemented high-performance work systems. When implemented effectively, high-performance work systems benefit both employees and their organizations. Employees become more engaged and empowered to make decisions, experience greater career growth and satisfaction, and become more valuable contributors to their firms. Organizations benefit from higher productivity, quality, flexibility, and customer satisfaction. These features together can provide a company with a sustainable competitive advantage.

KEY TERMS

external fit

high-performance work system
  (HPWS)

internal fit

process audit

DISCUSSION QUESTIONS

Objective 1 1. Do you think the four principles of high involvement provide an adequate context for designing high-performance work systems? What other concerns or guidelines for developing high-performance work systems would you suggest?

Objective 2 2. In many cases, organizations use teams as a part of their high-performance work systems. Could a high-performance work system be useful in an organization that does not use teams? What special concerns might have to be addressed?

Objective 3 3. Although achieving both internal and external fit are important with regard to high-performance work systems, which do you consider more critical and why?

Objective 4 4. This chapter emphasizes the processes required to implement high-performance work systems. What are the most critical steps to successful implementation?

Objective 5 5. How do you think employee-related outcomes and organizational outcomes are related to one another? Is it possible to achieve one set of outcomes without the other? Why or why not?

BIZFLIX EXERCISES

Apollo 13: **Houston, We Have a Problem**

This chapter discussed some principles that underlie high-performance work systems. Watch for these principles in action while viewing this scene from the film *Apollo 13*.

This superb film dramatically shows a NASA mission to the moon that had an in-space disaster. Innovative problem-solving and decision-making amid massive ambiguity saved the crew. *Apollo 13* shows many examples of problem-solving and decision-making throughout the film. The zero gravity simulator, a KC-135 four-engine jet aircraft (NASA's "Vomit Comet"), helped create the film's realistic weightless scenes. These scenes required 600 parabolic loops over 10 days of filming.

The chosen scene is an edited version of the "Houston, We Have a Problem . . ." sequence that appears a third of the way into the film. It starts as Jim Lovell (Tom Hanks) says, "Houston, we have a problem." This scene ends after Lovell tells Mission Control

that they are venting something into space. The film continues with frenzied activity in Mission Control. Flight Director Gene Krantz (Ed Harris) asks people to work the problem and stop guessing about it.

What to Watch for and Ask Yourself

- Which principles of high-performance work systems appear in this scene? Note some examples from the scene of the principles you identify. You also can refer to Figure 16.2 while viewing the scene.

- The chapter earlier noted that training and development is a human resource practice that is important for high-performance work systems. What type of training do you believe the astronauts receive? Does it appear effective for them to carry out their mission? Why or why not?

- Jim Lovell is the commander of the Apollo 13 mission. During this scene, does he show the management and leadership characteristics discussed earlier in the chapter?

Assessing the Strategic Fit of High-Performance Work Systems

High-performance work systems (HPWSs) are potentially powerful tools. However, ensuring that all of the HR practices support one another—and the principles underlying the HPWS—is not always easy. At times, certain HR practices might support the HPWS while others actually may work against the system's principles. This can result in failure. It takes only one misaligned practice to crash the whole system. Recall that the HPWS principles include the following:

- Egalitarianism and engagement
- Shared information
- Knowledge development
- Performance-reward linkage

Assignment

The figure on the following page lists the main HR practices used at Egan Clothiers, Ltd. Working in teams of four to six, assess the extent to which you believe each HR practice supports (or works against) each of the HPWS principles.

1. For each cell in the matrix, insert a number indicating the extent to which you believe the HR practice supports the principle or is counterproductive. The scale runs from –5 (strongly counter-productive) to 5 (very supportive). Zero indicates neither support nor detriment.
2. When you are done filling in each cell, add the numbers across each row to determine how supportive each HR practice is of all of the principles. Which HR practice is most supportive of the HPWS principles? Which HR practice is of most concern?
3. Add each column to see how the overall set of HR practices supports each principle. Which principle is most strongly supported? Which principle is the biggest concern?
4. Add the rows and/or columns to see how well the HPWS is supported overall. What changes would you recommend to improve the system?

Note: This figure corresponds to the integrative case on Egan Clothiers, Ltd., in the back of the text. The exercise can be used in conjunction with the case, or you may simply refer to the case as background reading.

Assessing the Strategic Fit of High-Performance Work Systems (continued)

EGAN CLOTHIERS, LTD.

HPWS PRINCIPLES

HR PRACTICES	Shared Information	Egalitarianism	Knowledge Development	Performance-Reward Linkage		
STRUCTURE						
• Cross-functional team						Row 1
• Department rotation						Row 2
STAFFING						
• Select for experience						Row 3
• Promote from within						Row 4
TRAINING						
• Retail selling skills						Row 5
• Customer service						Row 6
REWARDS						
• Results appraisal						Row 7
• Forced distribution						Row 8
• Individual incentives						Row 9
TECHNOLOGY						
• HR Info System						Row 10
• Post performance						Row 11
	Column 1	Column 2	Column 3	Column 4	TOTAL	

SCORING KEY

5 = strongly supports the principle
0 = neutral

CASE STUDY 1

Engaging Employees "the Eileen Fisher Way"

Passion for the business is integrated into the culture and the creative process at Eileen Fisher Inc., a women's clothing designer and manufacturer ranked No. 7 among the 2007 Best Medium Companies to Work for in America.

An obsession with the "Eileen Fisher Way" radiates from the founder ("passion" and "obsession" are this entrepreneur's favorite words) and permeates the organization.

Eileen Fisher herself is a self-described "quantum leap girl" who started the company in 1984 with four designs, $350 and complete confidence that "I know how to do this." She pulled it off, creating a successful company that "encourages people to discover their passions and who they are, and helps them create their own place here."

The firm's collaborative leadership style is the opposite of top-down management. "For us, [leadership] comes from the center," says Susan Schor, the "chief culture officer" who coleads the company while Fisher concentrates on creating new designs.

Fisher, who met Schor at a party, says she "came in and created her own place" helping to develop a "fluid structure" that defies translation into traditional corporate terms.

Schor guides the "People and Culture" areas: leadership, learning and development, social consciousness, human resources, and internal communications. Working in partnership, she and two colleagues are charged with "holding the whole," a responsibility akin to that of a chief operating officer.

"Everyone works in *teams*," says Schor, and "no one reports to anyone. Instead, we 'connect into' someone else." Leadership *teams* are run by facilitators, who are "not necessarily the ones who make the decisions," she adds.

HR director Shari Simberkoff says that hiring, too, is a collaborative process that includes multiple *team interviews*. HR's job begins with "hiring the right people for this organization," keeping in mind that the company is not right for everyone. Once a good match has been made, "We try to give people reasons to stay by providing terrific benefits and services, and by helping them develop personally."

The company's hiring and retention efforts seem to be working. Simberkoff says it averaged about 15 percent turnover companywide last year, compared with a national turnover rate of 25 percent to 40 percent in the retail industry. She has been with the company for nine years, and many others have been there longer.

Although the eccentric and highly original culture is "not an easy environment to succeed in," says Schor, it offers excitement and opportunity to those who "get it."

For example, the company supports "eco-conscious" practices as well as responsible business activities that demonstrate a strong regard for human rights. Catherine Fordham is a grants coordinator who came up with a great idea—she is quick to say that it was not hers alone, but a group effort by the social consciousness *team*. "I knew that Eileen wants women to feel good about their bodies," she says. Deciding that nonprofit organizations that work to raise the female self-image were good candidates for their grants program, she described the idea to Fisher and was given the go-ahead.

A successful "citizen of Eileen Fisher" is a person who is open and flexible and does not "hold on too tightly to what has been," says Vice President of Communications Hilary Old.

Questions

1. Identify the ways in which Eileen Fisher, Inc. engages its employees.
2. What aspects of "the Eileen Fisher Way" resemble high-performance work systems?
3. Can "eco-consciousness" effectively be incorporated into high-performance work systems?

Source: Condensed from Ann Pomeroy, "Passion, Obsession Drive the 'Eileen Fisher Way,'" *HRMagazine* 52, no. 7, (July 2007): 55.

CASE STUDY 2

Whole Foods Motivates Its Employees in Innovative Ways

If you've ever shopped at Whole Foods, you know it's not your grandma's supermarket. Stuffed full of organic and natural products, a Whole Foods store is a commodious, eye-popping, mouthwatering temple to guilt-free gastronomy. Whole Foods' business model is built around a simple but powerful premise: people will pay a premium for food that's good for them, good-tasting, and good for the environment.

Ever since cofounder, chairman, and CEO John Mackey opened the original Whole Foods Natural Market, one of the country's first supermarket-style natural food stores, in Austin, Texas, the company has focused its attentions on health-minded shoppers. Today, Whole Foods operates 194 stores and generates nearly $6 billion a year in sales. It is also America's most profitable food retailer when measured by profit per square foot. Whole Foods has also done well by its investors. In the fifteen years following its IPO in 1992, the company's stock price rose by nearly 3,000 percent, dramatically outperforming its grocery-sector rivals.

At every turn, this inventive company has taken the road less traveled. Whole Foods' commitment to organic produce and sustainable agriculture is unmatched by any competitor. Its stores are laid out to make shopping feel less like a chore and more like a culinary adventure.

The basic organizational unit is not the store, but the team. Small, empowered work groups are granted a degree of autonomy nearly unprecedented in retailing. Each store consists of roughly eight teams that oversee departments ranging from seafood to produce to checkout. Every new associate is provisionally assigned to a team. After a four-week work trial, teammates vote on the applicant's fate; a newbie needs a two-thirds majority vote to win a full-time spot on the team.

This peer-based selection process is used for all new employees, including those hoping to join teams at Whole Foods' headquarters, such as the national IT or finance squads. The underlying logic is powerful, if unconventional. Whole Foods believes that critical decisions, such as whom to hire, should be made by those who will be most directly impacted by the consequences of those decisions.

The teams are also responsible for all key operating decisions, including pricing, ordering, staffing, and in-store promotion. In essence, each team operates like a profit center and is measured on its labor productivity. While associates are highly empowered, they are also highly accountable. Every four weeks, Whole Foods calculates the profit per labor hour for every team in every store. Teams that exceed a certain threshold get a bonus in their next paycheck. In addition, each team has access to performance data for every other team within its store and for similar teams in other stores. The fact that no team wants to end up as a laggard adds to the motivation to do well. All this explains why the hiring vote is such a big deal at Whole Foods. Vote in a slacker, and your paycheck may take a beating.

The tight link between autonomy and accountability also diminishes the need for motivation-sapping, bureaucratic controls. Says Mackey, "We don't have lots of rules that are handed down from headquarters in Austin. We have lots of self-examination going on. Peer pressure substitutes for bureaucracy. Peer pressure enlists loyalty in ways that bureaucracy doesn't." Putting so much authority in the hands of associates requires that top management trusts them to do the right thing for the business. Conversely, team members will stay motivated over the long term only if they trust top management to let them share in the bounty of their own productivity. Whole Foods builds that trust in a variety of ways. For example, each associate has access to the compensation data for every other store employee. This transparency makes it difficult for managers to play favorites or be idiosyncratic in their compensation decisions, since disgruntled associates can challenge the logic of salary discrepancies.

The ability to compare salaries also spurs employees to develop their skills and take on new responsibilities, since they can easily see which sorts of jobs, and people, get most generously compensated.

All too often, business leaders blithely tell employees that "we're-all-in-this-together," while simultaneously tolerating Switzerland-Somalia disparities in CEO-associate pay. The result: a cynical workforce. In contrast, the top team at Whole Foods puts its money where its mouth is. Believing that 100-to-1 salary differentials are incompatible with the ethos of a community, and more likely to inspire resentment than trust, Whole Foods' leaders have set a salary cap that limits any individual's compensation to no more than 19 times the company average. (In the average Fortune 500 company, the ratio is more than 400 to 1.) In the same spirit, 93 percent of the company's stock options have been granted to nonexecutives. (In most companies, 75 percent of the stock options are distributed to five or fewer senior executives.)

What ultimately binds Whole Foods' 30,000-plus associates into a community is a common cause—to reverse the industrialization of the world's food supply and give people better things to eat. This is capitalism with a conscience. A few rubber-meets-the-road examples: Whole Foods has used its buying power to change modern factory farming, so that animals are treated humanely before slaughter. In January 2006, Whole Foods made the largest-ever purchase of renewable energy credits from wind farms—enough, in fact, to cover all of the company's electric energy consumption.

For many associates, working at Whole Foods is an expression of their own lifestyle choices and values: they get to sell nutritious food, contribute to sustainable farming, and support pesticide-free agriculture. All this is summed up in the company's oft-repeated mantra: "Whole Foods. Whole People. Whole Planet."

Given all of this, it's hardly surprising that Whole Foods has been ranked as one of *Fortune* magazine's "100 Best Companies to Work For" every year since 1998, when the list was first published. In 2007, Whole Foods was voted as the fifth most rewarding place to work in America. It turns out that management innovation really *can* help a company overcome the disengagement and malaise that is endemic in traditionally managed workplaces.

Questions

1. If you were a manager at Whole Foods, what concerns would you have about the company's high-performance work system?
2. What role do you think knowledge sharing plays in supporting Whole Foods high-performance work systems?
3. Why don't all companies treat their employees like Whole Foods does? Do you think they will in the future?

Source: Excerpted from Gary Hael and Bill Breen, "Creating a Community of Purpose: Management Innovation in Action," *Harvard Business School Press*, 2007.

NOTES AND REFERENCES

1. D. A. Nadler and M. S. Gerstein, "Designing High-Performance Work Systems: Organizing People, Work, Technology, and Information," *Organizational Architecture* (San Francisco: Jossey-Bass, 1992), 195–208; E. Lawler III, Susan Albers Mohrman, and Gerald E. Ledford, *Creating High Performance Organizations: Practices and Results of Employee Involvement and Total Quality Management in Fortune 1000 Companies* (San Francisco: Jossey-Bass, 1995); Edward Lawler III, Susan Albers Mohrman, and George Benson, *Organizing for High Performance: Employee Involvement, TQM, Reengineering, and Knowledge Management in the Fortune 1000: The CEO Report* (San Francisco: Jossey-Bass, 2001). See also David Nadler, Michael Tushman, and Mark Nadler, *Competing by Design: The Power of Organizational Architecture* (New York: Oxford University Press, 1997); Jody Gitell Hoffer, "Relationships and Resilience," *Journal of Applied Behavioral Science* 44, no. 1 (March 2008): 25–47.

2. J. B. Arthur, "Effects of Human Resource Systems on Manufacturing Performance and Turnover," *Academy of Management Journal* 37 (1994): 670–87; M. Huselid, "The Impact of Human Resource Management Practices on Turnover, Productivity, and Corporate Financial Performance," *Academy of Management Journal* 38 (1995): 635–72; Mark A. Youndt, Scott A. Snell, James W. Dean, Jr., and David P. Lepak, "Human Resource Management, Manufacturing Strategy, and Firm Performance," *Academy of Management Journal* 39, no. 4 (August 1996): 836–66; John F. Tomer, "Understanding High-Performance Work Systems: The Joint Contribution of Economics and Human Resource Management," *The Journal of Socio-Economics* 30, no. 1 (January 2001): 63; Kris Dunn, "Rules of Engagement," *Workforce Management Online*, July 2008.

3. Carlton P. McNamara, "Making Human Capital Productive," *Business and Economic Review* 46, no. 1 (October–December 1999): 10–13; Meagan Stovel and Nick Bontis, "Voluntary Turnover: Knowledge Management—Friend or Foe?" *Journal of Intellectual Capital* 3, no. 3 (2002): 303–22.

4. Martin Eppler and Oliver Sukowski, "Managing Team Knowledge: Core Processes, Tools and Enabling Factors," *European Management Journal* 18, no. 3 (June 2000): 334–41; Andrea Foote, "One in a Million: Ocean Spray Henderson Has Parlayed Hard Work and Dedication into a Remarkable Operations Milestone," *Beverage World* 122, no. 8 (August 15, 2003): 22–29; Rick Frattali, "The Company that Teaches Together Performs Together," *T+D* 61, no. 7 (July 2007).

5. Jeffrey Kling, "High Performance Work Systems and Firm Performance," *Monthly Labor Review*, May 1995, 29–36; Chad Kaydo, "Top of the Charts: FedEx," *Sales and Marketing Management* 150, no. 7 (July 1998): 46, 48; Michael Trachtman, "Roving Internet Appliances," *Web Techniques* 6, no. 10 (October 2001): 55–57; Richard Shulman, "Just Say the Word," *Supermarket Business* 56, no. 6 (June 15, 2001): 19–20; "Customer Service Excellence: Continuously Delighting Your Customers," *PR Newswire* (February 24, 2005).

6. For more information about designing teams around critical work processes, see Mark Chen, "Applying the High Performance Work Team to EPC," *AACE International Transactions* (2002): PM61–PM67; Valerie Sessa, "Supporting Work Team Effectiveness: Best Management Practices for Fostering High Performance," *Personnel Psychology* 53, no. 2 (Summer 2000): 457–60.

7. See Lawler, Mohrman, and Ledford, *Creating High Performance Organizations*; Eileen Appelbaum, Thomas Bailey, Peter Berg, and Narne Kalleberg, *Manufacturing Advantage: Why High-Performance Work Systems Pay Off* (Ithaca, NY: Cornell University Press, 2000); Gil Preuss and Brenda Lautsch, "The Effect of Formal versus Informal Job Security on Employee Involvement Programs," *Relations Industrielles* 57, no. 3 (Summer 2002): 517–39; Wendy S. Becker, "Manufacturing Advantage: Why High-Performance Work Systems Pay Off," *Personnel Psychology* 56, no. 2 (Summer 2003): 549–53; "Nike Factories to Get Help from MIT's Sloan School," *Information Week* (April 13, 2005).

8. Laurie J. Bassi and Mark E. Van Buren, "Sustaining High Performance in Bad Times," *Training & Development* 51, no. 6 (June 1997): 32–42; Michael J. Stevens and Michael A. Campion, "Staffing Work Teams: Development and Validation of a Selection Test for Teamwork Settings," *Journal of Management* 25, no. 2 (1999): 207–28; Richard Camp, Eric Schulz, Mary Vielhaber, and Fraya Wagner-Marsh, "Human Resource Professionals' Perceptions of Team Interviews," *Camp Journal of Managerial Psychology* 19, no. 5 (2004).

9. Carolee Coleter, "To Build a Productive Team, Interview Effectively," *Natural Foods Merchandiser* 25, no. 12 (December 2004); Kris Dunn, "Rules of Engagement," *Workforce Management Online* (July 2008).

10. Mark E. Van Buren and Jon M. Werner, "High Performance Work Systems," *B&E Review* (October–December 1996): 15–23; "Schindler Elevator Announces Center for Service Excellence; Holland, OH Facility to Serve as National Support Center," *PR Newswire* (July 21, 2004); "Large Organizations That Focus on Excellence in Human Capital Management May Be More Likely to Outperform the Market, According to Taleo Customer Study," *PR Newswire* (March 30, 2005).

11. Rosemary Batt and Lisa Moynihan, "The Viability of Alternative Call Centre Production Models," *Human Resource Management Journal* 12, no. 4 (2002): 14. For more information on the potential application of "intracapital," see Gifford Pinchot, "Free Intraprise," *Executive Excellence* 18, no. 1 (January 2001): 10;

Frank Giancola, "Skill-Based Pay—Issues for Consideration," *Benefits & Compensation Digest* 44, no. 5 (May 2007) 1–15.

12. David Paper, James Rodger, and Parag Pendharker, "A BPR Case Study at Honeywell," *Business Process Management Journal* 7, no. 2 (2001): 85–93. See also Robert McNabb and Keith Whitfield, "Job Evaluation and High Performance Work Practices: Compatible or Conflictual?" *Journal of Management Studies* 38, no. 2 (March 2001): 293–312; Leslie A. Weatherly, "Performance Management: Getting It Right from the Start," *HRMagazine* 49, no. 3 (March 2004): S1–S11.

13. Warren Bennis, "The Future Has No Shelf Life," *Executive Excellence* 17, no. 8 (August 2000): 5–6; Peggy Holman, "Culture Change," *Executive Excellence* 17, no. 7 (July 2000): 16; Clinton Longenecker, "Building High Performance Management Teams," *Industrial Management* 43, no. 6 (November/December 2001): 21–26; Wendy S. Becker, "Manufacturing Advantage: Why High-Performance Work Systems Pay Off," *Personnel Psychology* 56, no. 2 (Summer 2003): 549; Srivastava Pallavi and Jyotsna Bhatnagar, "Turnaround at Motorola India—Mobile Devices Business through the HR Lever," *The Journal for Decision Makers* 33, no. 1 (January–March 2008): 119–129.

14. Keith Newton, "The High Performance Workplace: HR-Based Management Innovations in Canada," *International Journal of Technology Management* 16, no. 1–3 (1998): 177–92; Georg Von Krogh, Kazuo Ichijo, and Ikujiro Nonaka, *Enabling Knowledge Creation: How to Unlock the Mystery of Tacit Knowledge and Release the Power of Innovation* (New York: Oxford University Press, 2000); Lawler, Mohrman, and Benson, *Organizing for High Performance.*

15. Patrick M. Wright and Scott A. Snell, "Toward a Unifying Framework for Exploring Fit and Flexibility in Strategic Human Resource Management," *Academy of Management Review* 23, no. 4 (October 1998): 756–72; Clair Brown and Michael Reich, "Micro-Macro Linkages in High-Performance Employment Systems," *Organization Studies* 18, no. 5 (1997): 765–81;

S. A. Snell, M. Shadur, and P. M. Wright, "Human Resources Strategy: The Era of Our Ways," in M. A. Hitt, R. E. Freeman, and J. S. Harrison (eds.), *Handbook of Strategic Management* (London: Blackwell, 2002), 627–49.

16. Van Buren and Werner, "High Performance Work Systems," 15–23; Gilbert Probst, Steffen Raub, and Kai Romhardt, *Managing Knowledge—Building Blocks for Success* (New York: Wiley, 2000). For a similar example of vertical fit within European firms, see Sue Hutchinson, John Purcell, and Nick Kinnie, "Evolving High Commitment Management and the Experience of the RAC Call Center," *Human Resource Management Journal* 10, no. 1 (2000): 63–78.

17. Brian Becker, Mark Huselid, and Dave Ulrich, *The HR Scorecard: Linking People, Strategy, and Performance* (Cambridge, MA: Harvard Business School Press, 2001).

18. Arup Varma, Richard W. Beatty, Craig Eric Schneier, and David O. Ulrich, "High Performance Work Systems: Exciting Discovery or Passing Fad?" *Human Resource Planning* 22, no. 1 (1999): 26–37; Martha Gephart and Mark Van Buren, "Power of High Performance Work Systems," *Training & Development* 50, no. 10 (October 1996): 21–36; Foote, "One in a Million: Ocean Spray Henderson," 22–29.

19. Varma, Beatty, Schneier, and Ulrich, "High Performance Work Systems," 26–37; Gephart and Van Buren, "Power of High Performance Work Systems"; "Making Change Work—for Real," *HRFocus* 80, no. 1 (January 2003): S1.

20. Louise Clarke and Larry Haiven, "Workplace Change and Continuous Bargaining," *Relations Industrielles* 54, no. 1 (Winter 1999): 168–91; Ruth Wright, "Forging Sustainable Alliances in a New Economy," *Canadian Business Review* (Summer 1995): 20–24; Sukanya Sengupta, "The Impact of Employee-Share-Ownership Schemes on Performance in Unionised and non-Unionised Workplaces," *Industrial Relations Journal* 39, no. 3 (May 2008): 170–190.

21. Clarke and Haiven, "Workplace Change," 168–91; Wright, "Forging Sustainable Alliances," 20–24; Joel Cuthcer-

Gershenfeld, Thomas Kochan, and John Calhoun Wells, "In Whose Interest? A First Look at National Survey Data on Interest-Based Bargaining in Labor Relations," *Industrial Relations* 40, no. 1 (January 2001): 1–21; Michael White "Cooperative Unionism and Employee Welfare," *Industrial Relations Journal* 36, no. 5 (September 2005): 348–366.

22. Wright, "Forging Sustainable Alliances," 20–24; Hannele Rubin, "How CEOs Get Results," *Chief Executive* (February 2001): 8.

23. Wright, "Forging Sustainable Alliances," 20–24.

24. Gephart and Van Buren, "Power of High Performance Work Systems"; Michael Beer, "How to Develop an Organization Capable of Sustained High Performance: Embrace the Drive for Results-Capability Development Paradox," *Organizational Dynamics* 29, no. 4 (Spring 2001): 233–47.

25. Judith A. Neal and Cheryl L. Tromley, Ernie Lopez and Jeanne Russell. "From Incremental Change to Retrofit," *The Academy of Management Executive* 9, no. 1 (February 1995): 42–54.

26. Randa A. Wilbur, "Making Changes the Right Way," *Workforce*, Supplement (March 1999): 12–13; Gephart and Van Buren, "Power of High Performance Work Systems"; Irena St. John-Brooks, "CEOs See HR as Helping to Lead Organizational Efforts: USA," *Benefits & Compensation International* 32, no. 1 (July/August 2002): 73–74; "Human Resources Role Transformed at Deutsche Bank," *Human Resource Management International Digest* 10, no. 5 (2002): 12–14; Michael Svoboda and Silke Schroder, "Transforming Human Resources in the New Economy: Developing the Next Generation of Global HR Managers at Deutsche Bank AG," *Human Resource Management* 40, no. 3 (Fall 2001): 261–73; "HR Advice: Manage Transition—Not Just Change," *HR Briefing* (November 15, 2002): 1–2; "HR Must Seize Major Role over Change Management," *Personnel Today* (May 20, 2003): 8.

27. "How to Take the 'Non' out of Your 'Non-Performers,'" *Human Resource Department Management Report* (February 2005): 1–5; Paul Lukas and Maggie Overfelt, "3M, a

Mining Company Built on a Mistake, Stuck It Out Until a Young Man Came Along with Ideas about How to Tape those Blunders Together As Innovations—Leading to Decades of Growth," *Fortune* (April 1, 2003); http://money.cnn.com/smallbusiness.

28. Jeffrey Pfeffer, "When It Comes to 'Best Practices'—Why Do Smart Organizations Occasionally Do Dumb Things?" reprinted from *Organizational Dynamics*, Summer 1996 with permission from Elsevier; Cordelia Brabbs, "Rover's White Knight,"

Marketing, May 18, 2000, 28; Georg Auer, "Burela to Instill Quality Culture at Land Rover," *Automotive News* 75, no. 5902 (November 6, 2000): 32x–32z; Ronald W. Pant, "Land Rover History Lesson," *Truck Trend* 8, no. 3 (May–June 2005): 12; Bradford Wernle, "Solihull Must Do 'a Halewood' to Survive; Jaguar Plant Is the Example Land Rover Factory Must Follow," *Automotive News Europe* 9, no. 19 (September 20, 2004): 39.

29. John Purcell, "Best Practice and Best Fit: Chimera or Cul-de-Sac?" *Human Resource Management Journal* 9, no. 3 (1999): 26–41; Snell, Shadur, and Wright, "Human Resources Strategy: The Era of Our Ways," 627–649; Patrick M. Wright, Benjamin Dunford, and Scott A. Snell, "Human Resources and the Resource-Based View of the Firm," *Journal of Management* 27, no. 6 (2001): 701–21.

CASES

United Technologies Seeks Intangibles with Education Plan

CASE 1

Felice Gray-Kemp was within 72 hours of making a decision about several job offers when a vice president at United Technologies Corp. asked her to meet with him. She happened to work in the same building in Hartford, Connecticut, as the VP, so Gray-Kemp, a tax attorney, hopped on the elevator to go upstairs and hear him out. His pitch focused on one of Gray-Kemp's primary motivations—the desire to earn another degree to advance her career. "He mentioned something about 'What these other employers have, I'm sure, is great, but they don't have ESP,'" Gray-Kemp says. "I thought he meant extrasensory perception."

He actually was referring to UTC's Employee Scholar Program, a comprehensive tuition reimbursement initiative that was put in place in 1996 and which finances up front every penny of an associate's, bachelor's, master's or doctoral degree. In addition, graduates receive up to $10,000 worth of UTC stock. When ESP was added to the other aspects of UTC she found attractive, Gray-Kemp made her decision." The thought of being reimbursed or sponsored through an advanced degree was paramount in my mind," she says. "It was a no-brainer that I was going to come to UTC."

Gray-Kemp joined the company in September 1998 and began her coursework for an LLM, a postgraduate law degree, in taxation in August 1999. She earned her degree from Boston University while working full-time and is now assistant general counsel for UTC, which provides high-tech products and services to the building and aerospace industries. The company—whose subsidiaries include Carrier; Otis; Pratt & Whitney; Sikorsky; Hamilton Sundstrand; UTC Fire & Security; and UTC Power—says enhanced recruiting is just one benefit of the program for the company. It also aids in retention—a bonus for UTC—and promotion, which is good both for employees and for the company's succession planning efforts. Those rates for ESP graduates are 2 percent to 3 percent higher than for their peers, according to company officials.

Since the program's inception, UTC has invested $626 million in ESP, a rate of about $70 million to $75 million annually. About 17,000 UTC employees have graduated over the lifetime of the initiative. About 14,000 are in classes now, or about 6.5 percent of the company's 215,000-person workforce.

The program is becoming increasingly popular in foreign countries where UTC operates, like Poland and Brazil. More than half of the company's revenue is generated internationally, and 65 percent to 70 percent of its employees are based overseas. No matter where they're located, once UTC workers graduate, there are no requirements placed on them to stay with the company—not even for a little while—or repay education expenses. They could leave immediately if they're so inclined.

One reason the program is so expansive is UTC chairman [and former CEO] George David's belief in the power of learning. "Education changes peoples' lives," he said during a speech in Washington last year. "It changes the way they think about everything." That new outlook also can enhance their work performance. It's not so much the degree that is earned but the earning of the degree that sets people apart.

Gray-Kemp did not need an LLM to become the first tax attorney in UTC history to move to the general counsel's office. But the intellectual curiosity, discipline, drive and other intangibles involved in going to school impressed her superiors. "To them, it was the ability to think through a problem, which going to get an additional degree helps you to do," Gray-Kemp says. "It was about learning a way of thinking. You can position yourself to take on challenges—not to say that you couldn't otherwise—but they're easier to face, and excel, if you have that training."

A Part of the Culture

Donald "Scott" Richards, depot logistics manager for the F-119 engine program at Pratt & Whitney, also has strengthened his problem-solving skills by earning his bachelor's and master's degrees in management at Albertus Magnus College. He began an MBA program at the Connecticut school in August. "There's a research method of how you go about coming to a conclusion, coming to an answer," he says. His course work also has had a direct impact on his job. His master's thesis focused on optimal contract length—a topic central to negotiations on work Pratt & Whitney does for the government.

"It really engages you in the organization," he says. "It gives you eyes to see some of the things that go on in the background that you may not have thought about in the past." Richards began his career as a Pratt & Whitney mechanic in 1979. Since then, he has worked in several UTC aerospace businesses, including time in Brazil at International Aero Engines. He went back to school for a bachelor's degree in 2001.

His motivation stemmed in part from his family. "My daughters went to college, and they kind of inspired me to go back to school," he says. He also wanted to take advantage of the breadth of UTC's operations. "The ESP program has given me the opportunity to move to different areas," he says. The company rewards performance and a person who shows some initiative, he says.

By offering the tuition reimbursement incentive, UTC is making an important statement about its culture, according to company officials. "It speaks to our commitment to develop employees once they join United Technologies," says William Bucknall Jr., [former] senior vice president for human resources and organization. "You're not just joining a company for a paycheck. You're joining a company for a career."

Or at least they are setting off on a career path when signing on with UTC. The company acknowledges that not everyone will remain with it throughout their working life. In fact, the Employee Scholars Program grew out of a difficult time in UTC's history—the early 1990s, when a recession forced the company to shutter plants and restructure by moving more work overseas. David saw that many people who lost their jobs were not placed elsewhere in the UTC universe. But rather than abandon them on the wayside of globalization, he wanted to help them bounce back.

"They have continued on with something as a benefit rather than looking at it strategically," says Jeanne Meister, an author and consultant. "It's an outdated model." She doubts that unlimited reimbursement is effective and asserts the only way such a program can survive is when it is championed by an executive. "It's an enormous leap of faith," she says. "It's been rolling along because it's the brainchild of the current CEO and no one wants to mess it up."

Bucknall agrees that David is the force behind the initiative and has fostered the program's success. "If HR had proposed that we do this, it wouldn't have the impact that it does if the CEO proposes it and is committed to it," Bucknall says.

But a program that was born in the C-suite may also die there. "When this CEO leaves, the next guy will come along and say, 'What were we doing?' Meister says. UTC soon will have a chance to prove that the tuition program is bigger than David. Louis Chenevert, the former head of Pratt & Whitney, was named UTC president and COO last year. Chenevert has emphasized his support for the program. "I like to think it's probably in the DNA of the organization now and will continue regardless of who the CEO is," Bucknall says. "It's not just a nice, good thing to do. There are measurable business outcomes from having the program as well."

Tracking Results

Beyond recruiting and retention statistics, [is] UTC's financial performance. In 2006, revenue increased by 12 percent over 2005 to $47.8 billion. Earnings per share were up 19 percent. Over the 10 years the tuition program has been in place, UTC has achieved shareholder return that is more than twice the Dow Jones and S&P 500 averages.

A number of factors can influence financial results, which means even sterling ones probably won't convince skeptics that generous tuition reimbursement makes business sense. John Sullivan, a professor of management at San Francisco State University, says that the inherent weakness in such programs is that they are usually run by the benefits office rather than by training and development. As a result, no one determines return on the educational investment, assesses whether skills required by the organization are obtained, or coaches participants.

"This is the worst-managed program in HR," Sullivan says. "No one does the metrics like they would in any other thing. I haven't found anybody who's even tried to calculate [return on investment]. There is no evidence that it's going to help your company."

Another drawback is that participants do not reap the rewards of their newly acquired education, according to Sullivan. "At work, they get nothing, not a 'thank you,' not a cake," he says. If they are trying to move up from being a secretary to an accountant, they often have to find a new employer. "You're still labeled as a secretary," Sullivan says. "The degree doesn't turn out to be powerful until you leave the company." At a financial firm Sullivan studied, 75 percent of the people who went back to school departed within two years of earning their degree. Sullivan maintains that there are "faster, cheaper ways" to learn than by entering college, such as participating in a leadership program. This route also ensures that employees take courses that benefit the company rather than wander off on their own.

But 90 percent of the time at UTC, self-selection has resulted in employees taking courses that relate to their work, says Laura Osborn, director of learning and development for the company. So a financial analyst is likely to get a master's degree in accounting rather than in anthropology. In the other cases, a divergence between curriculum and job duties may result from an employee wanting to move to another position within the company. For instance, an engineer may pursue an MBA. "The majority of people go for a business degree to sort of round out their skills," Osborn says. They track into courses that are relevant to their career paths because "they're passionate about what they're going to end up working on."

Such enthusiasm highlights one of the challenges of managing the program—calibrating expectations. Sometimes, employees seek immediate job gratification after their accomplishments in the classroom. "There's a need on our part to make sure people appreciate that more than likely because of advanced credentials and motivation, good things will happen in your career," Bucknall says. "It's not necessarily going to happen 30 days after you graduate."

But the number of people who get frustrated and leave—or take the degree and run to another company—is limited, according to Bucknall. "If there were a trend toward that, you can bet we'd be hearing from our business units and management that the investment wasn't worth the return," he says. "We don't hear that at all."

The feedback they are getting from the public sector is praise. Rep. Tom Allen, D-Maine, has a Pratt & Whitney operation in his district in North Berwick. He says UTC's education initiative sets an example for other companies to follow. "It's an amazing program," Allen says. "They have a very loyal workforce and a very good workforce." When UTC helps its employees go back to school, it is also strengthening skills in the district's labor market, which benefits all of Allen's constituents. "That further training is a public good as well as a private good," he says.

It prepares someone like Donald Richards for whatever might come next in the churning, sometimes dangerous global economy. For jobs that used to be available for someone with a high school education, "a bachelor's degree is required and a master's degree or an MBA is preferred," he says. "Education offers choices."

Questions

1. Are programs such as UTC's altruistic or just "good business"?
2. What kinds of companies might not be able to utilize UTC-like programs to attract and retain employees? Do these companies have other options available to them?
3. How can companies that implement programs like these make certain that they are worth the investment?

Source: Excerpted from Mark Schoeff Jr., "United Technologies Seeks Intangibles with Education Plan," *Workforce Management* Online, December 2007.

Running the Global Recruiting Machine: ClientLogic

To kick off the 2006 May 1 Labor Day celebrations in the Philippines, President Gloria Macapagal-Arroyo motored over to the Starbucks in Pasig City outside Manila for coffee with six of ClientLogic's 3,000 Filipino call center employees. ClientLogic, one of the world's largest BPO [business process outsourcing] providers, spreads its global workforce across 49 facilities in 14 countries. The company is a recruiting powerhouse that pulls in 15,000 to 25,000 new employees a year to maintain its current workforce of 22,000 and staff new sites for rapid global growth.

"Because our most distinguishing characteristic is the quality of our agents, recruiting is a core competency for us," says Dale Saville, ClientLogic's executive vice president of corporate services and chief global HR officer. ClientLogic keeps all recruiting in-house. A small team at corporate headquarters in Nashville oversees the global process and sets best practices for local teams of two to six recruiters at each site. "We see a significant advantage in having this global team to drive the recruiting process and ensure consistency," Saville says.

ClientLogic moved into the Philippines two years ago to tap the abundant supply of English-speaking workers. The Philippines turns out 350,000 college graduates annually and is now a major player in the BPO market. In her Labor Day remarks, Arroyo noted that call center employment in the country has mushroomed from just 2,000 workers in 2001 to more than 100,000 today. She projects that the industry will employ a million Filipinos by 2010.

ClientLogic is now actively scouting additional sites in second-tier Philippine locations. "For all our sites, the precursor to the heavy lifting of recruiting is a detailed labor market analysis that includes research on workforce demographics, unemployment rates, wage levels and information about competitors who may be pulling from the same applicant pool," Saville reports. Perfecting its global nine-step recruiting process and moving beyond first-tier cities lie at the heart of ClientLogic's "right shore" capabilities and its stellar 95 percent customer renewal rate.

Nine-Step Staffing

ClientLogic's customer care centers bear the same structure in every country, with identical positions in each location. The company uses media ads, job fairs, and college recruiting to generate applicants. Its Web site provides a detailed online application, but 80 percent to 90 percent of all applicants are walk-ins who complete the online application at the local site. The company manages applications with its HRIS program to complete an initial screening and route applications to recruiters at each facility.

ClientLogic recruiters from Ireland to India use a consistent nine-step process based on the company's best practices worldwide. The beauty of the process is that it involves recruiters from the preliminary needs analyses all the way through the new hires' first months on the job. Continuous feedback coordinated through Nashville generates ongoing improvements for recruiting worldwide.

The first step in the recruiting process is a specific analysis of the requirements entailed in ramping up for a new client. This determines the particular outreach techniques and job qualifications that ClientLogic recruiters use. Then the relevant applicant pool is pulled from the company's online applicants and processed through an automated scoring system. Recruiters conduct telephone screenings to evaluate the selected applicants' speech and verbal skills. "Applicants who pass the phone screening are invited to the site for a job preview, which includes videos about the company, the typical workday and simulations of phone calls that represent the good, the bad, and the ugly in call center work," Saville reports.

After the videos, applicants attend a Q&A session with a ClientLogic employee who has been hired within the past year. "We see the job preview step as a very important part of self-selection," Saville says. Applicants who choose to continue take a series of technical, behavioral and psychometric tests. "We look for a 'can do, will do' fit," Saville notes.

The next step is a face-to-face behavioral interview with an HR manager at the site. "We have concluded that we are better served by interviews with HR managers rather than operational managers," he says. At this stage, the recruiters run background checks and other tests that may be required by specific clients—for example, credit checks and drug tests.

The seventh step is tendering the offer. "We put great emphasis on the offer process as an opportunity to welcome new hires to the company and reinforce the message that we want them to work here," Saville says.

The next step is onboarding, which ClientLogic views as an integral part of the recruiting process. "Involving the recruiting team in onboarding helps them improve the front end of the recruiting process," Saville notes. Onboarding includes 11 training modules for TLC ("think like a customer") skills plus two to four weeks of technical training. The final step in the process consists of 45-day and 90-day "reunions" conducted by the recruiting team to collect feedback from new hires on the recruiting and onboarding process. The team also uses these meetings as an opportunity to troll for new applicants. "Employee referrals now account for 20 percent of our new hires and generate stronger candidates than other means of recruiting," Saville says.

Company policy precludes same-day hires. "The practice attracts job skippers," Saville explains. "In call centers, we are working at the lower end of the wage scale and we don't want the work habits of job skippers. We believe that same-day hiring is not conducive to attracting serious applicants and maintaining stickiness."

Second-Tier Recruiting

ClientLogic recruiters, along with other recruiters in the $26 billion customer care outsourcing industry, are shifting their focus to second-tier cities because of rising wages and turnover in the first-tier locations. ClientLogic spearheaded the move to second-tier cities in the Philippines when it opened a call center in Baguio City, 120 miles north of Manila, in January 2005. Baguio is home to 100,000 university students. Wage rates are one-third lower than in Manila, and ClientLogic is already recording lower attrition at the new site. Three other companies have opened call centers in the city since ClientLogic paved the way.

ClientLogic has felt the effects of labor shortages in its other first-tier locations such as Bangalore, where the company employs 2,500 workers. India leads the world in the offshore call center market with 350,000 agents employed. Analysts at McKinsey warn that the supply of call center agents in India and the Philippines could be exhausted in five years, but Saville believes that speculation about labor shortages applies only to the first-tier cities. Job boards post hundreds of listings for India and the Philippines, including "urgent" ads for positions at Citigroup and other U.S. multinationals. An entry-level call center agent averages $1.95 an hour in Bangalore and $1.88 an hour in Manila, a huge cost advantage versus pay rates averaging $12.64 an hour for the same position in Seattle or $12.72 in Los Angeles, according to a cost analysis by the Boyd Co., a site selection firm.

Recruiting costs outside the United States are lower as well. The average number of applicants needed to recruit one agent ranges from 29 in North America to 20 in Asia/Pacific, 18 in Europe and seven in South America, according to a benchmarking survey of 385 call centers by Contact Center World. "Bangalore and the center of Manila are experiencing higher turnover, but this will abate as employers will eventually stop bidding up wages and move to second- and third-tier locations in rural areas such as Baguio that have lower attrition and lower wages," Saville says. ClientLogic is now looking at Calcutta in India and additional second-tier sites in other Asian nations, the Caribbean Basin, South America and southern Africa. "We are well-established in Morocco, but we are ready to consider sub-Saharan countries," Saville notes.

Datamonitor, a business analysis and forecasting firm, predicts that the number of call center agents in North Africa will triple by 2010 to about 23,000. In South Africa, call center positions are expected to more than triple to 7,400 by 2010. Botswana is also emerging as a new offshore possibility.

ClientLogic opened a new center in Panama and expanded its center in Mexico in 2005. Datamonitor notes that Mexico will remain an offshore contact center location of choice for U.S.-based companies because of the growing Hispanic population in the U.S. and rising incomes among Spanish-speaking households.

Argentina and Chile are aggressively pursuing call center business from the North American market, as are smaller countries, including Costa Rica, the Dominican Republic and Panama. Datamonitor's most recent studies predict that the number of call center agents located in Brazil servicing offshore customers will rise from 3,900 in 2005 to 11,500 in 2010.

The number of call center agents based in Central and Eastern Europe will more than triple from 1,900 in 2004 to 6,400 in 2008. Agents in Hungary earn an average of $12,192 a year, compared with $34,920 in England, according to BeesWax Europe, a multilingual recruiting company.

Although labor arbitrage dictates the broadest trends in the global call center industry, U.S. companies continue to expand centers at home to serve clients who need or prefer domestic locations. ClientLogic opened new centers in third-tier U.S. locations last year. Within its North American centers, ClientLogic will attempt to turn the aging workforce to its advantage. "Labor force segments are maturing in the U.S. and Canada as baby boomers retire and then look for new careers and supplemental income," Saville reports. "We are looking at this alternative workforce of senior citizens, possibly for at-home work."

For labor-intensive industries such as customer contact services, controlling workforce staffing costs means pursuing low-wage locations around the world and within each country. The difficult marriage of flexibility and consistency captured in

ClientLogic's approach meets the challenge of recruiting in highly competitive and rapidly developing offshore markets while maintaining a cost-effective base at home.

Questions

1. How might a company like ClientLogic engage in college recruiting on a global level? Why is creating a global brand important for a firm's recruiters?
2. How do you think recruiting trends differ in emerging markets versus developed countries such as the United States?
3. How might ClientLogic try to assess and improve the validity of its nine-step approach to recruitment and selection?

Source: Reprinted from Fay Hansen, "Running the Global Recruiting Machine," *Workforce Management Online*, August 2006.

Job Analysis and Hiring Decisions at Ovania Chemical

Company Background

Ovania Chemical Corporation is a specialty chemicals producer of polyethylene terephthalate (PET) thermoplastic resins primarily used to make containers for soft drinks and bottled water, as well as packaging for food and pharmaceutical products. Though smaller than other chemical producers that produce globally, Ovania has competed successfully in its niche of the U.S. specialty chemical business. Its main plant is located in Steubenville, Ohio, positioned along the Ohio River midway between Pittsburgh, Pennsylvania, and Wheeling, West Virginia. In recent years, advances in technology have altered the nature of chemical production, and like other firms in the industry, Ovania Chemical is taking steps to modernize its facilities. Not surprisingly, these technological changes have been accompanied by redesign in employee jobs. In fact, over the last three years, there have been drastic changes in both the number and the kinds of jobs being performed by employees. The latest change at the Steubenville plant involves the job transformations of the system analyzer position.

The System Analyzer

Because chemical production involves highly integrated process technologies, someone is needed who can monitor all of the individual components simultaneously. The system analyzer is primarily responsible for this monitoring function. It is one of the most prestigious nonmanagerial jobs in the entire plant, and its importance is likely to grow.

Formerly, the position was classified as that of a semiskilled maintenance technician, but as the plant has become more automated, the requirements for the system analyzer job have become much more extensive. Knowledge of pneumatics, hydraulics, information technology, programming, and electrical wiring are all increasingly critical aspects of this job. As these up-skilling trends continue, the three men who currently hold the position admit that they will be incapable of performing adequately in the future. It is estimated that within two years, the tasks, duties, and responsibilities of the system analyzer will have changed by over 70 percent. For these reasons, the decision was made to recruit and select three new people for the rapidly transforming position.

Job Analysis and New Position Analysis

Ovania's Steubenville plant manager, Jack Sarabe; the HR manager, Emily Claire; and two senior engineers, Dave Packley and Mark Young, formed a selection committee. With the help of two consultants, they first conducted a job analysis for the new position of system analyzer. Although they had to project into the future regarding the specific nature of the job, they collectively felt they had created an accurate depiction of the requirements for someone who would occupy the position. Figure 3.1 shows a list of the major performance dimensions of the job and a subsample of specific tasks characteristic of each dimension.

From this list of tasks, the selection committee then delineated a set of personal qualities required for anyone who would hold the system analyzer position. These qualities included the twelve abilities shown in Figure 3.2. The numbers beside each ability indicate the tasks (see Figure 3.1) to which it is related. The abilities marked with an asterisk (*) were considered by the committee to be "critical." Any applicant not scoring well on each of the critical dimensions would be considered unqualified for the job.

Anticipated Selection Process

The committee hoped to gain "new blood" for the redesigned system analyzer job and therefore wanted to recruit externally for the best available talent they could find. However, as a matter of policy, management was also deeply committed to the idea of promoting from within. After deliberation, the committee decided to recruit both internally and externally for the new position. It was also decided to especially encourage current system analyzers to "reapply" for the job.

Because there was a two-year lead time before the newly transformed position would be put in place, the committee was very careful not to include in the selection battery any skills or knowledge that could reasonably be trained within that two-year period. Only aptitude or ability factors were incorporated into the selection process, rather than achievement tests.

In a private session, a few of the selection committee members admitted candidly that they had serious doubts whether any woman or minority member currently in the relevant labor market would have the requisite credentials to be competitive for the position. The three present system analyzers were white males. However, since Ovania Chemical had a rather unenviable history of employment discrimination charges, the decision was made to do no unnecessary prescreening of applicant qualifications, previous experience, and so on. This strategy was thought to encourage minorities and women to apply for the new position irrespective of their prior employment history.

It should be noted, however, that there was some concern about prejudice if a woman or minority member were to get the job. Word through the grapevine was that several comments had been made that a woman would not get down into the treatment tanks to check gauge readings. All of these factors, taken together, made for a very sensitive selection process. Ovania's management, however, was dedicated to making the procedures and decisions fair and objective.

FIGURE

3.1

Performance Dimensions (Duties and Tasks).

MAINTAINING SPARES AND SUPPLIES

1. Anticipates future need for parts and supplies and orders them.
2. Stocks parts and supplies in an orderly fashion.
3. Maintains and calibrates test equipment.

TROUBLESHOOTING

4. Applies calibration standards to verify operation by subjecting the system to known standards.
5. Decides whether the problem is in the sensor, in the processor, in the process stream, and/or in the sample system.
6. Uses troubleshooting guides in system manuals to determine the problem area.
7. Uses test equipment to diagnose the problem.
8. Makes a general visual inspection of the analyzer system as a first troubleshooting step.
9. Replaces components such as printed circuit boards and sensors to see if the problem can be alleviated.

HANDLING REVISIONS AND NEW INSTALLATIONS

10. Makes minor piping changes such as size, routing, and additional filers.
11. Makes minor electrical changes such as installing switches and wires and making terminal changes.
12. Uses common pipefitting tools.
13. Uses common electrical tools.
14. Reads installation drawings.

RECORD-KEEPING

15. Maintains system files showing historical record of work on each system.
16. Maintains loop files that show the application of the system.
17. Updates piping and instrument drawings if any changes are made.
18. Maintains Environmental Protection Agency records and logbooks.
19. Disassembles analyzers to perform repairs on-site or back in the shop.
20. Replaces damaged parts such as filters, electronic components, light source, lenses, sensors, and values.
21. Uses diagnostic equipment such as oscilloscopes, ohmmeters, and decade boxes.
22. Tests and calibrates repaired equipment to ensure that it works properly.
23. Reads and follows written procedures from manuals.

ROUTINE MAINTENANCE

24. Observes indicators on systems to ensure that there is proper operation.
25. Adds reagents to systems.
26. Decides whether the lab results or the system is correct regarding results (i.e., resolves discrepancies between lab and analyzer results).
27. Performs calibrations.

FIGURE
3.2

Abilities and Tasks

Numbers represent tasks cited in Figure 3.1. Asterisks indicate abilities considered critical by the committee.

SKILLS	TASK NUMBERS
*Finger dexterity	3, 4, 7, 9, 10, 11, 12, 13, 19, 20, 21, 22, 25, 27
*Mechanical comprehension	3, 5, 6, 8, 9, 10, 12, 13, 7, 14, 19, 20, 22, 23, 24, 27, 11, 17
*Numerical ability	11, 3, 4, 24, 10, 21, 12, 13, 14, 27
*Spatial ability	2, 4, 5, 9, 10, 11, 14, 19, 20
*Visual pursuit	3, 4, 5, 6, 7, 8, 9, 10, 11, 14, 16, 17, 19, 20, 21, 22, 27
*Detection	2, 3, 5, 6, 8, 9, 10, 14, 19, 20, 23, 7
Oral comprehension	1, 2, 5, 6, 26, 7, 8, 9, 19, 21, 25
Written comprehension	1, 15, 16, 17, 18
Deductive reasoning	1, 5, 3, 6, 7, 8, 9, 10, 11, 19, 21, 20, 22, 2, 26, 27
Inductive reasoning	1, 3, 5, 6, 7, 8, 9, 10, 11, 19, 21, 20, 22, 2, 26, 27
Reading comprehension	3, 6, 14, 7, 22, 23, 21, 9, 27
Reading scales and tables	3, 4, 7, 8, 9, 21, 23, 24, 27, 2, 6, 14

Fifty-six employees applied for the new position of system analyzer. Twenty-one were female; fifteen were African American. Only two of the three current system analyzers reapplied for the new position. For now, the company decided that an overall total score of 800 on the twelve tests would be the cutoff score in order for an applicant to be seriously considered for the system analyzer position. This criterion resulted in the primary pool of twenty candidates shown in Figure 3.3 It should be noted that although each of the aptitude tests has been published, standardized (100 points possible for each test), and validated on other jobs, there are no normative data or validity information for the specific job of the system analyzer. Therefore, the defensibility of the test battery is founded solely upon content validity judgments. Issues regarding the final cutoff scores and method for combining the multiple predictors are problematic for the selection committee.

Questions

1. How would you go about conducting a job analysis for a job that does not yet exist?
2. Do you think the abilities chosen for selection are content-valid? What other kinds of predictors might be generally useful for employee selection?
3. What reasons did the selection committee have for selecting only those factors that could not be acquired in a two-year training program?
4. Should the concern for women getting down into the dirty treatment tanks have been a selection issue? How might you include this factor in a selection battery?

FIGURE

3.3

Primary Pool of Candidates

NAME	RACE	SEX	EXTERNAL/ INTERNAL	FINGER DEXTERITY	MECHANICAL COMPREHENSION	NUMERICAL ABILITY	SPATIAL ABILITY	VISUAL PURSUIT	DETECTION	ORAL COMPREHENSION	WRITTEN COMPREHENSION	DEDUCTIVE REASONING	INDUCTIVE REASONING	READING COMPREHENSION	READING SCALES AND TABLES		
Baldwin, T.	W	M	I	83	76	78	76	69	71	90	70	74	72	88	92	=	941
Bittner, D.	W	M	E	92	62	88	89	96	85	90	94	93	89	97	87	=	1062
Bohlander, G.	W	M	E	67	78	74	70	76	62	80	69	71	76	78	82	=	883
Buffett, J.	B	M	E	87	97	89	61	94	93	75	90	85	96	85	80	=	1032
Denny, A.	B	F	I	92	88	72	72	78	79	69	76	81	83	81	78	=	949
Egan, M.	W	F	E	93	80	76	98	76	88	93	92	93	78	81	92	=	884
Granger, D.	W	F	I	82	82	79	75	77	73	72	80	81	77	70	80	=	856
Haney, H.	W	M	E	82	76	76	71	69	80	62	76	75	74	78	67	=	810
Kight, G.	W	F	E	65	75	72	67	80	74	62	47	66	67	60	80	=	815
Kovach, S.	W	M	E	82	87	85	85	83	88	81	80	80	83	84	80	=	998
Laukitis, T.	B	F	E	87	97	63	89	93	90	91	85	86	96	88	89	=	1054
Lesko, B.J.	B	F	I	83	84	89	91	80	82	86	88	85	84	90	89	=	1031
Rom, D.	B	M	I	80	60	67	66	67	62	74	80	67	72	75	66	=	835
Sara, E.	W	F	I	89	91	77	93	90	91	88	78	98	80	80	76	=	1021
Sauder, C.	W	F	E	76	72	78	81	80	72	73	77	75	79	82	82	=	927
Sherman, A.	W	F	I	91	82	78	93	92	94	89	77	95	77	81	92	=	1041
Snell, J.	W	M	E	80	85	84	81	81	80	89	88	84	86	81	82	=	1001
Timothy, S.	W	F	E	82	78	76	71	69	80	62	76	76	70	71	67	=	878
Whitney, J.	W	M	I	67	71	70	76	76	62	81	69	71	76	78	82	=	815
Wright, P.	W	M	I	80	60	57	56	57	62	74	80	69	72	75	65	=	887

5. For the abilities termed "critical," what score should someone receive in order to be considered scoring "well" on that test (i.e., cutoff scores)? How should the test scores be combined (e.g., compensatory, multiple hurdle, combination)?
6. Which three candidates appear most qualified? What are your reservations, if any, about this recommendation?
7. Would this test battery and selection procedure be defensible in court?

Ill-Fated Love at Centrex Electronics

Nancy Miller-Canton never imagined she would lose her job at Centrex Electronics Corporation (CEC), and certainly not under such unpleasant circumstances. Unfortunately, after eleven years of employment, the last two as a senior product engineer in the firm's military/space division in Atlanta, she made a mistake; she fell in love.

Human resources professionals agree that CEC highly regarded as a quality employer in the electronics industry. It is a multinational corporation with engineering services and production facilities in Spain, Canada, Hong Kong, Mexico, and Germany. With more than 12,000 employees in the United States, the firm has been named as one of the country's top 100 organizations to work for by several studies. Centrex Electronics is known as a top-paying corporation with proactive employee relations policies. Kathryn Garner, vice president of human resources, is credited with establishing many positive employee rights policies, including those covering drug testing, search and surveillance, access to employee files, off-duty conduct, and employee smoking. The corporation permits marriage between employees except in cases where "one employee is in a direct reporting relationship with the other."

Miller-Canton joined Centrex Electronics shortly after graduating from Georgia State University in 1996. At that time she was married to Tom Canton, her college sweetheart. In 2003, Canton died suddenly. As a single parent, his widow then became dependent upon her job for the majority of her family's support.

Miller-Canton enjoyed rapid promotions through various engineering positions until reaching her present job as senior product engineer. In 2006, the year before her dismissal, she had been awarded the firm's Engineering Distinction Award for her research and development work in metallography. But in January 2007, one week after receiving an 8.3 percent raise, she was called on the carpet. The question from the military/space division manager was clear and direct: "Are you dating Mike Domzalski?" Domzalski was a former CEC senior engineer who had changed employment in 2005 to work for International Technologies, a direct competitor of CEC. There was no denying the romance. The two had dated while Domzalski was with CEC, and he still remained friends with other Centrex Electronics Engineers. It was widely known among Miller-Canton's friends that she was "extremely fond" of Domzalski.

Now, chastised for her involvement, Miller-Canton was ordered to forget about Domzalski or be demoted. After the meeting she told a friend, "I was so socialized in CEC culture and so devoted to my job that I thought seriously about breaking up with Mike." As she later testified in court, however, she never got the chance because she was dismissed the day after the meeting with her manager.

At the root of Miller-Canton's dismissal was a corporate policy regarding the leakage of confidential product information. The policy seeks to avoid situations where an employee of CEC might be compromised into providing sensitive or confidential information to an employee of a competing organization. Miller-Canton's work in research and development made her subject to the following CEC policy:

> Employees performing jobs where they have access to sensitive or confidential information which could benefit competitors are prohibited from being married to or from having a romantic relationship with individuals employed by competing organizations.

Since Mike Domzalski's work at International Technologies was similar to Miller-Canton's at CEC the corporation felt their "romantic relationship" made her discharge appropriate. Feeling aggrieved, Miller-Canton engaged the services of an attorney specializing in employee rights claims. In preparing her wrongful discharge suit, the attorney told her that given the nature of her case and the continuous erosion of the employment-at-will doctrine, he believed she could win the lawsuit. Furthermore, while gathering background information for the trial, the attorney discovered something that her former division manager did not know. Shortly before her discharge, no less an authority than former CEC chairman Joseph M. Torell had declared that "CEC employees are responsible for their own off-the-job behavior. We are concerned with an employee's off-the-job conduct only when it reduces the employee's ability to perform normal job assignments."

A jury trial in state court upheld the wrongful discharge suit and awarded Miller-Canton $425,000 in back pay and punitive damages. Like other trials, however, this one took its toll on the parties involved. "I couldn't function for four or five months after the trial, I was so emotionally upset and drained," Miller-Canton said. She is now employed as an engineer for a computer company; she and Domzalski are no longer dating. "It was a bad experience all around," she says. "There was a real sense of belonging and a feeling of personal job worth at CEC. If I had my way, I'd take my old job back today."

Questions

1. What exceptions to the employment-at-will doctrine would the attorney have used to file the lawsuit?
2. Comment on the confidential information policy adopted by Centrex Electronics. Do you agree with the way it is used? Explain.
3. Is dating a "romantic relationship"? Explain.

Source: This case is adapted from an actual situation known to the authors. All names are fictitious.

Returning Ethics to Putnam

Kevin Divney needed to let off steam. It had been a tough few months at his company, Putnam Investments. Weeks earlier, on October 28, 2003, Massachusetts Secretary of State William Galvin and the Securities and Exchange Commission each had filed civil complaints against the Boston-based fund company. They alleged that Putnam had allowed portfolio managers to skirt corporate policies by rapidly trading its funds and allowing certain clients to do the same.

In the days that followed, the company's CEO of 18 years, Lawrence Lasser, was forced out along with several portfolio managers. Even though the new CEO, Charles "Ed" Haldeman, was working on a settlement with regulators, states and large companies with pensions that Putnam managed were pulling money out hand over fist. By November 10, 11 states, including Massachusetts, which Putnam called home, had yanked $6 billion from the firm.

To get his mind off things, Divney, managing director and chief investment officer for the midcap growth equity team, decided to duck out during lunch and go to the gym. On his way out, he ran into Haldeman. "Here I am sneaking out with my gym bag during lunch and I run smack into the new CEO," Divney recalls. "And he says to me, 'Kevin, going to the gym? Wish I could go with you.'"

Haldeman's laid-back attitude might have seemed counterintuitive for the new CEO of a company in crisis. But it's his focus on creating more balance between work and life that is crucial to getting the company back on track, he says. "It seemed to me that we should make it less difficult for our employees because this industry is already stressful enough," says Haldeman, 57. Before joining Putnam as co-head of investments in 2002, Haldeman was CEO of Delaware Investments, a Philadelphia-based money management firm. The goal of that balance, Haldeman says, is to attract and retain the best people in the industry. Traditionally companies rely on compensation to do that, but Haldeman believes that's just part of it. "It's more important to have a culture that people want to devote their lives to," he says.

Many firms respond to breakdowns in ethics by adding more rules and regulations. But under Haldeman, Putnam has dismantled much of the rigid culture that had dominated the company. From removing layers of management to adjusting compensation to focus on long-term performance, Putnam has established a work environment that encourages its 3,000 employees, rather than dictating to them.

In an industry where there's constant pressure to generate returns, this is no small feat, says Jeff Keil of Keil Fiduciary Strategies, a mutual fund consultant in Littleton, Colorado. "Often in financial services there is a mentality of 'How big is the fine?' But Putnam is focusing more on long-term results," he says.

After the scandal, total assets at Putnam, a subsidiary of New York-based professional services company Marsh & McLennan, are at $191 billion, $64 billion of which is with institutional clients. On the institutional side, that's up from $53.7 billion at the end of 2004—a good sign, because institutional clients are often the most cautious investors. In October 2004, the Massachusetts Pension Reserves Investment Management Board, one of the first state funds to drop Putnam after the scandal, rehired the company's small-cap team to manage $800 million. "We are convinced that they are much more focused on investment performance," says Michael Travaglini, executive director of the Massachusetts fund.

After seeing 30 portfolio managers leave from 2003 to 2005, half of whom were forced out, the company's annual turnover rate has come down to 11 percent, compared with the three-year average of 21 percent. And the tainted image of Putnam's former self has started to fade, says Dan Kreuter, president of DAK Associates, a Conshohocken, Pennsylvania-based financial services recruiter. "There are a lot of good people now that would look at Putnam that would not have considered them a few years ago," he says.

Responding to Scandal

At 7:30 A.M. on Haldeman's first day as CEO, he began holding 45-minute meetings with groups of employees to discuss what had happened and to answer questions. Later that week, he visited employees at Putnam's Andover and Franklin, Massachusetts, offices to do the same. "The communication was the best I had ever seen in the six years I had been at the company," Divney says. "Rumors didn't have time to manufacture themselves because you had the information before a rumor even started."

Communication has become a trademark of Putnam's new culture under Haldeman. While Lasser held quarterly meetings for the company's 800 officers, Haldeman opted for all-employee meetings, where he and other executives talk for 15 minutes and then open the session up for questions from employees for 30 minutes. Haldeman also began sending out weekly e-mail updates to employees. He continues those e-mails on a biweekly basis. "Employees had said that they didn't feel like there was enough openness and transparency at the company," Haldeman says.

"One Putnam"

In April 2004, Putnam agreed to pay $110 million to settle accusations leveled by the SEC and Massachusetts regulators. Rapid trading of mutual funds, also known as market timing, refers to the practice of traders jumping in and out of funds in an attempt to take advantage of inefficiency of fund pricing. While not illegal, it causes an increase in fund expenses, which hurts long-term investors, and thus is banned by many fund companies, including Putnam. As part of its settlement, the fund company agreed to a number of corporate governance measures, including mandating that portfolio managers who buy Putnam funds hold them for at least 12 months, a promise no other major fund company has agreed to make.

But stepping up compliance was only part of Putnam's response. Haldeman recognized that there was something in the company's culture that allowed the trading practice to happen. Because of the firm's intense focus on short-term gains, the portfolio managers broke Putnam's market timing rules, and executives allowed it. "It was an extreme type-A culture," Haldeman says. Putnam, like most financial services companies, wanted the best and most ambitious and thus ended up with a fiercely competitive environment. "When you have an intense environment like that where it's all about winning and getting the most you can, a small number of people can cross the line," Haldeman says.

There also was a strong hierarchy to support this culture. In the old Putnam, Lasser and three other top executives ran the company from the 12th floor, where no other employees worked. "It was literally cocooned off by doors. The only reason you would go up there is if you were summoned," Haldeman says, "and usually being summoned was a bad thing." Lasser had asked Haldeman to join him on the 12th floor when he came on board, but Haldeman refused. And a year later when he became CEO, he stayed in his office, which is in the middle of the investments area.

Within days of taking over, Haldeman drafted guiding principles for the company. These values, dubbed "One Putnam," include personal integrity, mutual respect and the highest professional standards. Haldeman had managers review the values with their groups, and in January 2005, Putnam introduced an orientation program for new hires that discusses the values.

Creating "One Putnam" required a flattening of the organization, which meant eliminating several management positions. Under Lasser, there were many people whose jobs were to manage other employees, and Haldeman wanted to change that. "To retain and attract the best people, it's necessary to provide them with autonomy and independence to make decisions," he says. "When people are spending all of their time writing up reports on their activity, we lose a lot of their productivity."

Within 12 months, Putnam reduced its staff by 11 percent, including 25 of the top 50 highest-paid executives. "We replaced all but two members of our management team," Haldeman says. Divney, who used to spend two to six hours a week in meetings, says he and the other team leaders now meet only once a month, and will cancel meetings if there is nothing to talk about. "Our stress now is focused on beating the markets," he says.

Reshaping a Culture

The flatter organization has allowed for more collaboration among departments, which was unheard of in earlier years. Putnam, like many fund companies, has three divisions: one dedicated to retail or individual investors; another dedicated to institutional investors; and a third focused on international partnerships. "In the past these businesses worked in silos, with their own products and strategies," says Sandra Whiston, head of institutional sales.

By working together, there now are not only more opportunities to cross-sell products, but employees are increasingly moving into other divisions within the company, she says. In fact, Whiston currently is hiring for a few positions and is in talks with some candidates in the retail division. "That wouldn't have happened 10 years ago," she says. By opening up the organization so that employees can move between departments, Putnam is also able to position itself uniquely when recruiting at colleges and universities, she says. And by stressing the ability to grow within the organization, Putnam is better able to retain talent.

To create a more collegial environment, Haldeman got rid of the firm's formal dress code in favor of business casual. "The dress code seemed to create its own hierarchy, in that the highest-level people wore the very good suits with the cuff links," he says. "By implementing business casual, we wanted to send the message that the organization didn't focus on hierarchy and titles, but rather substance over form." Also, he says, many of the younger employees view business casual as a perk.

Haldeman also replaced the executive-only dining room with an employee cafeteria. The dining hall, which looks over a park, is reminiscent of a high school cafeteria, with employees joking with one another in one corner and poring over papers and debating investment theories in another. Haldeman, who is based in the Boston headquarters, tries to grab a bite there whenever he's not traveling. He chats with employees and their kids, who often visit. That's a stark difference from his predecessor, observers say.

"I have spoken to portfolio managers who said that Lasser didn't even know their names," says Laura Lutton, an analyst with Chicago-based fund researcher Morningstar.

A New Approach to Compensation

One concern that many employees voiced to Haldeman was the lack of transparency in compensation decisions. People said decisions were made by a small group of executives behind closed doors. "Since they didn't know what formulas were being used, they assumed it was based on politics," Haldeman says.

Tensions about bonuses were particularly high in the months after the scandal broke. This was understandable, given that for many employees, bonuses make up 90 percent to 95 percent of their compensation. To ease stress, Putnam gave out 2003 bonuses two months early, in January of 2004. And the company committed to keeping bonuses at 2003 levels for the next two years. Putnam also removed the three-year vesting requirement from the bonus program so that employees could receive their bonuses immediately. "We didn't want people to feel trapped into staying with the company," Haldeman says.

Instead of having the top executives decide the bonuses for every employee, Putnam gave its managers ownership of the process. By doing this, not only do employees feel more comfortable that their bosses, who know them, are making decisions about their compensation, but it also saves a lot of time, says Richard Tibbetts, head of human resources. The decision-making process for compensation was cut by more than half from 90 days to 30 to 45 days.

Haldeman also eliminated the huge differentiation between how much senior management makes and what everyone else gets paid. "Today upper management, including myself, gets paid less than half of what the senior management team was paid in 2000," he says. For example, in 2004 Haldeman's total compensation was $13.6 million, compared with the $35.2 million Lasser made in 2000.

To prevent portfolio managers from making overly aggressive trades to get their funds' performance among the top 1 percent for the year, Haldeman established a compensation program that rewarded long-term consistent performance, as opposed to "a home run in a short time," he says. Previously there was no set formula—at least not one that was shared with the portfolio managers—about how their compensation was determined. But it was understood that getting their funds' performance to the top percentage of their peer group was a goal. That meant, for example, that small-cap managers fought to make their funds' performance among the top 1 percent of all small-cap funds. Under the new program, implemented in 2004, one-year fund performance accounts for 20 percent of a portfolio manager's total compensation, while three- and five-year performance each account for 40 percent. Furthermore, portfolio managers have incentives to get in the top half of their peer group's performance. "They get nothing more if they are in the top 2 percent," Haldeman says. In an industry where making money is paramount, such a long-term approach is almost unheard of, Keil says.

For Divney, the long-term focus on performance eases the stress. "Now I feel like when we are talking about improving performance, it's much more consultative and less 'gotcha,'" he says.

Performance Pressure

While employees agree that Putnam is a nicer place to work today than it was five years ago, time will tell whether a better culture means better performance. So far, the numbers are promising. In 2005, 47 percent of the firm's funds were in the top half of their peer group, compared with 39 percent in 2003, according to Lipper, a provider of mutual fund research. Twelve percent were in the bottom quarter of their peer group, compared with 25 percent in 2003.

It's going to take time, however, before institutional clients will feel comfortable putting money with Putnam, observers say. When looking at five-year annualized returns of Putnam funds, only 36 percent rank in the top half of their peer group, while 32 percent are ranked in the bottom 25th percentile.

But at least the company's employees feel like they have their sights set on the right goals. "Now the energy we spent competing internally is redirected to compete externally," Divney says. "Like I tell my team: The problem is not inside the building, it's outside the window."

Questions

1. What's wrong with fostering a highly competitive culture within a firm's workforce? Are there instances where it can be beneficial?
2. How was changing the culture at Putnam central to its turnaround in terms of the company's ethics? Which HR practices were most important for making it happen?
3. Do you think Putnam's performance will continue to improve? Why or why not?

Source: Reprinted from Jessica Marquez, "Rebalancing Putnam," *Workforce Management* (May 22, 2006): 1, 18–22.

Realigning HR Practices at Egan's Clothiers

At the end of fiscal year 2008, revenues at Egan's Clothiers, Inc., had increased 12 percent over 2007 and had increased at a compounded rate of 14 percent over the past five years. That is the good news. The bad news is that costs have risen at an even more rapid rate, thereby shrinking the company's gross margins. As a consequence, Egan's profitability (measured as return on sales and return on net assets) has actually fallen by 6 percent over the past three years.

The drop in profitability at Egan's is particularly worrisome. In fact, according to Egan's chief financial officer, Richard Coyle, if something is not done immediately to control material and labor costs, as well as administrative expenses, the company may need to restructure its operations. In the short run, Coyle, company president Karen Egan, and vice president of HR Pam McCaskey have put an indefinite freeze on all hiring. Further, they are contemplating layoffs of nearly one-quarter of Egan's sales staff and are weighing the benefits of cutting back on HR-related expenses such as training. Compared to others in the industry, their labor costs are very high.

Company Background

Gene Egan and Pat Pollock opened their first store in Baldwin, New York, in 1958. The company grew rapidly during the 1980s and now operates a chain of thirty-four medium-sized stores located throughout Connecticut, New York, Pennsylvania, and New Jersey. Since the beginning, Egan's customers have been primarily middle class and upper middle-class families purchasing sportswear, dresswear, and fashion accessories. The company has established a longstanding tradition of quality and customer service. In addition to its thirty-four stores, the company also maintains two distribution centers and its administrative offices in Stamford, Connecticut. The total employment currently stands at approximately 2,400 people: 15 executives, 40 staff specialists, 40 store managers, 215 sales managers, 250 administrative personnel, 1,600 salespeople, and 240 distribution workers. Except for the employees at the distribution centers, the company is not presently unionized. However, it is no secret that Egan's management has been trying very hard recently to keep current labor organizing activities to a minimum. Especially in these times of growth and change, management views unionism as a threat to the company's success. In this regard, the HR office has been called upon to conduct a program audit of various HR practices utilized at Egan's. The purpose of this audit is to assess the impact of HR policies and practices on employee outcomes (for example, performance, satisfaction, absenteeism, turnover). The corollary objective of this audit is to identify specific problem areas where policy adjustments may be necessary. The final report to the executive staff will include the HR department's evaluation of current problems and recommendations for implementing changes in HR practices.

unions seen as a threat

Human Resources Management History

Over the past five years, Egan's has made several changes in order to implement the best HR practices possible. Partially, this has been to circumvent unionization efforts, but primarily it is indicative of Egan's longstanding belief that success in retailing depends on the competencies and efforts of its employees.

The commitment to HR is demonstrated by the fact that in 2008 the company spent $1.3 million on an intranet-based human resources information system (HRIS). The HRIS has successfully automated most employment records (for example, job titles, salary information, sales levels, attendance, demographics, etc.) and connects each of the retail stores, distribution centers, and executive offices. Also, Egan's has maintained an ongoing training program for the past five years to help salespeople improve their retail selling skills (RSS) and customer service. The annual cost of this program has been roughly $750,000. To further ensure high ability levels in their workforce, the company sets selection standards substantially higher than their competitors. Whereas other retail companies typically hire inexperienced high school students, Egan's generally requires some retailing or sales experience before considering an applicant for employment. While this policy increases overall labor costs, Egan's management has been confident that the added expense is well justified over the long run. However, recently even the strongest proponents of HR have been wondering if it might be a good idea to cut back on training, given the company's current financial picture.

By far the most problematic and volatile HR issues at Egan's have been regarding promotions and salary increases. Because the company promotes from within and distributes raises on a companywide basis, comparisons generally have to be made across employees in different jobs and departments. To combat arguments of subjectivity and bias pertaining to these decisions, Egan's links these rewards to objective measures of performance. Specifically, rather than utilizing subjective managerial evaluations of employee performance, ongoing accounts of sales results are maintained for each employee through use of the HRIS. On the basis of this information, each department manager assigns each employee to one of five categories:

Superior—top 10 percent

Very good—next 20 percent

Good—middle 40 percent

Fair—lower 20 percent

Poor—lowest 10 percent

Administrative decisions are then made across departments utilizing these standardized distributions. Additionally, in order to provide constant feedback to each employee concerning his or her relative performance, data are updated and posted daily. It is hoped that this feedback is motivating to employees. In this way, there are no surprises when the time comes for semiannual performance appraisal interviews. It is interesting to note that since these changes have been made in the performance appraisal system, there has not been one formal complaint registered regarding salary or promotion decisions. However, sales managers themselves have mentioned occasionally that they do not feel as comfortable now that they are required to assign employees to the "fair" and "poor" categories.

HR Outcomes

Despite the concerted efforts of Egan's management to create a first-rate system of human resources management, there are several troubling issues facing the company. The HR practices are not having their desired effects. For example, there have been recent complaints that employees have not been as patient or courteous with customers as they should be. This was best summarized by Paul Kelly, a store manager in

White Plains, New York, who noted, "My people are beating up the clientele in order to make a sale—the very opposite of what the RSS program trains them to do." This lapse in customer service is frustrating to management since the RSS training has proven effective in the past. Additionally, there seems to be a great deal of competition *within* departments that is hurting a team effort. Although intergroup rivalries *between* departments have always been viewed as normal and healthy, the lack of intragroup cohesiveness is seen as a problem.

Additionally, Egan's has been plagued with increases in lost and damaged merchandise. Management attributes this to the fact that storage rooms are disorganized and unkempt. This is in sharp contrast to the selling floors, which have remained fairly well ordered and uncluttered. Nevertheless, inventory costs have been increasing at an alarming rate.

Everyone notices that something is wrong. But the behavior patterns are perplexing. Absenteeism has decreased by 23 percent, but employee turnover has actually increased from 13 percent to over 29 percent, thereby increasing labor costs overall. Unfortunately, many of those leaving the company (43 percent) are rated as very good to superior employees.

As executives in the company look at these trends, they are understandably concerned. The success of the company and its reputation for quality and service depend on solid investments in HR to ensure the best possible workforce. However, the expenses are eroding the company's profits, and worse, it looks now like these investments are not paying off.

Questions

1. What overall changes could you recommend to the executive team at Egan's about its HR practices?
2. What are the pros and cons of Egan's performance appraisal system? Do you think it identifies the best employees? Do you think it helps develop employees to perform the best they can?
3. Can increased sales be linked directly and/or indirectly to the appraisal system? How about some of the other performance effects? How would you change the system?
4. How do you account for the fact that absenteeism has decreased at Egan's while turnover has increased?

A Performance Appraisal Snafu

Research has shown that the performance appraisal process, particularly the interaction between employees and managers, is a key determinant affecting employee motivation and productivity. Understandably, managers can view the appraisal of employee performance as a "catch-22" in which the slightest mistake can cause employee resentment, as this case illustrates.

Marcus Singh, a naturalized U.S. citizen from India, is a research economist in the Office of Research and Evaluation in the city of Newport, Oregon. He is forty years

 CASE 7

old and has worked for the city of Newport for the past ten years. During that time, Singh has been perceived by his supervisors as an above-average performer. However, due to the small size of the department and the close working relationship between employees and management, a formal evaluation of employees was considered unnecessary. About ten months ago, Singh was transferred from the department's Industrial Development unit to the newly formed Office of Research and Evaluation. Other employees were also transferred as part of an overall reorganization.

Out of concern for equal employment opportunity, plus the realization that employee performance should be evaluated formally and objectively, Victor Popelmill, department director, issued a directive to all unit heads to formally evaluate the performance of their subordinates. Attached to his memorandum was a copy of a new performance appraisal form to be used in conducting the evaluations. Garth Fryer, head of the Office of Research and Evaluation, decided to allow his subordinates to have some input in the appraisal process. (In addition to Garth Fryer, the Office of Research and Evaluation comprised Marcus Singh, five other research economists— Jason Taft, Susan Mussman, Richard Gels, Marsha Fetzer, and Juan Ortiz—and one secretary, Connie Millar.) Fryer told each of the researchers to complete both a self-appraisal and a peer appraisal. After reviewing these appraisals, Fryer completed the final and official appraisal of each researcher. Before sending the forms to Popelmill's office, Fryer met with each researcher individually to review and explain his ratings. Each researcher signed his appraisal and indicated agreement with the ratings.

About one week after submitting the appraisals to the director, Fryer received a memorandum from Popelmill stating that his evaluations were unacceptable. Fryer was not the only unit head to receive this memorandum; in fact, they all received the same note. On examination of the completed appraisal forms from the various departments, the director had noticed that not one employee was appraised in either the "fair" or "satisfactory" category. In fact, most employees were rated as "outstanding" in every category. Popelmill felt that his unit heads were too lenient and asked them to redo the evaluations in a more objective and critical manner. Furthermore, because the department's compensation budget for salary increases was largely based on a distribution of employee ratings, evaluating all employees as outstanding exceeded budget limits.

Garth Fryer explained the director's request to his subordinates and asked them to redo their appraisals with the idea of being more objective this time. To Fryer's astonishment, the new appraisals were not much different from the first ones. Believing he had no choice in the matter, Fryer unilaterally formulated his own ratings and discussed them with each employee.

Marcus Singh was not pleased when he found out that his supervisor had rated him one level lower on each category. (Compare Figures 7.1 and 7.2.) Although he signed the second appraisal form, he indicated on the form that he did not agree with the evaluation. Jason Taft, another researcher in the Office of Research and Evaluation, continued to receive all "outstanding" ratings on his second evaluation.

Like Singh, Taft has a master's degree in economics, but he has been working for the city of Newport for less than two years and is only twenty-four years old. Taft had also worked closely with Garth Fryer before being transferred to his new assignment ten months ago. Recently, the mayor of the city had received a letter from the regional director of a major government agency praising Jason Taft's and Garth Fryer's outstanding research. Marcus Singh's working relationship with Garth Fryer and

FIGURE
7.1

Employee Appraisal Form

Employee Name: Marcus Singh   Date: October 4, 2008

Job Title: Economist/Researcher

Please indicate your evaluation of the employee in each category by placing a check mark (✓) in the appropriate block.

	Outstanding	Good	Satisfactory	Fair	Unsatisfactory
KNOWLEDGE OF JOB Assess overall knowledge of duties and responsibilities of current job.	☑	☐	☐	☐	☐
QUANTITY OF WORK Assess the volume of work under normal conditions.	☐	☑	☐	☐	☐
QUALITY OF WORK Assess the neatness, accuracy, and effectiveness of work.	☐	☑	☐	☐	☐
COOPERATION Assess ability and willingness to work with peers, superiors, and subordinates.	☐	☑	☐	☐	☐
INITIATIVE Assess willingness to seek greater responsibilities and knowledge. Self-starting.	☐	☑	☐	☐	☐
ATTENDANCE Assess reliability with respect to attendance habits.	☑	☐	☐	☐	☐
ATTITUDE Assess disposition and level of enthusiasm. Desire to excel.	☑	☐	☐	☐	☐
JUDGMENT Assess ability to make logical decisions.	☐	☑	☐	☐	☐

Comments on ratings: Valuable employee!

Supervisor's signature: Garth Fryer

Department: Office of Research and Evaluation   Date: October 4, 2008

Employee's signature: Marcus Singh

Does the employee agree with this evaluation?__X__Yes ____ No

FIGURE
7.2

Employee Appraisal Form

Employee Name: Marcus Singh   Date: October 18, 2008

Job Title: Economist/Researcher

Please indicate your evaluation of the employee in each category by placing a check mark (✓) in the appropriate block.

	Outstanding	Good	Satisfactory	Fair	Unsatisfactory
KNOWLEDGE OF JOB Assess overall knowledge of duties and responsibilities of current job.	☐	☑	☐	☐	☐
QUANTITY OF WORK Assess the volume of work under normal conditions.	☐	☐	☑	☐	☐
QUALITY OF WORK Assess the neatness, accuracy, and effectiveness of work.	☐	☐	☑	☐	☐
COOPERATION Assess ability and willingness to work with peers, superiors, and subordinates.	☐	☐	☑	☐	☐
INITIATIVE Assess willingness to seek greater responsibilities and knowledge. Self-starting.	☐	☐	☑	☐	☐
ATTENDANCE Assess reliability with respect to attendance habits.	☐	☑	☐	☐	☐
ATTITUDE Assess disposition and level of enthusiasm. Desire to excel.	☐	☑	☐	☐	☐
JUDGMENT Assess ability to make logical decisions.	☐	☐	☑	☐	☐

Comments on ratings: Marcus needs to increase the quantity of his work to receive higher ratings.

Also, he should take a greater initiative in his job.

Supervisor's signature: Garth Fryer

Department: Office of Research and Evaluation   Date: Oct. 18, 2008

Employee's signature: Marcus Singh

Does the employee agree with this evaluation?_____Yes __X__ No

Jason Taft and with others in the department has been good. On some occasions, though, he has found himself in awkward disagreements with his coworkers in areas where he holds strong opinions.

After Singh and Taft had signed the appraisals, Garth Fryer forwarded them to Popelmill's office, where they were eventually added to the employees' permanent files. When pay raises were awarded in the department three weeks later, Marcus Singh did not receive a merit raise. He was told that it was due to his less-than-outstanding appraisal. He did, however, receive the general increase of $1,200 given to all employees regardless of their performance appraisal. This increase matched the increase in the CPI for the Newport, Oregon, area.

Singh has refused to speak one word to Garth Fryer since they discussed the appraisal, communicating only through Connie Millar or in writing. Singh has lost all motivation and complains bitterly to his colleagues about his unfair ratings. While he reports to work at 8 A.M. sharp and does not leave until 5 P.M. each day, he has been observed to spend a lot of time reading newspapers and books while at work.

Questions

1. What do you see as the problems in this case? Explain.
2. Could these problems have been avoided? How?
3. Comment on the advantages and disadvantages of using peer evaluations in the appraisal process.
4. What can be done to correct the problem with Marcus Singh?

Source: This case was adapted from a case prepared by James G. Pesek and Joseph P. Gronenwald of Clarion University in Pennsylvania.

The Last Straw for Aero Engine

The meeting lasted only ten minutes, since all those present quickly agreed that Tom Kinder should be fired. According to management, Kinder had caused the company numerous problems over the last eighteen months, and the incident that Saturday had been "the straw that broke the camel's back." Plant management believed it had rid itself of a poor employee, one the company had offered numerous opportunities for improvement. It seemed like an airtight case and one the union could not win if taken to arbitration.

Tom Kinder had worked for the Aero Engine Company for fourteen years prior to his discharge. He was initially employed as an engine mechanic servicing heavy-duty diesel engines. For his first nine years with Aero Engine, he was considered a model employee by his supervisors and plant management. Kinder was also well liked by his fellow employees. His performance appraisals were always marked "exceptional," and his personnel folder contained many commendation letters from customers and supervisors alike. Supervisor Mark Lee described Kinder as "devoted to his job of building and repairing engines." Through company-sponsored training classes and courses taken at a local trade school, Kinder had acquired the knowledge and experience to build and repair specialty engines used in arctic oil exploration.

The Aero Engine Company, with headquarters in the Midwest, was engaged primarily in the production and maintenance of specialty engines used in drilling, heavy manufacturing, and diesel transportation. The company had experienced very rapid growth in sales volume, number of products produced, and the size of its work-force since 1985. (At the time of Tom Kinder's termination, the company employed about 1,700 employees.) Aero Engine avoided hiring new personnel and then laying them off when they were no longer needed. Company policy stated that layoffs were to be avoided except in extreme circumstances. When heavy workloads arose, the natural solution to the problem was to schedule large amounts of overtime and to hire temporary employees through one of the local temporary help services.

Tom Kinder's work problems had begun approximately five years prior to his discharge when he went through a very emotional and difficult divorce. He was a devoted family man, and the divorce was a shock to his values and his way of life. The loss of his children was particularly devastating to his mental well-being. He became sullen, withdrawn, and argumentative with his supervisors. Several of Tom's close friends described him as having a "depressed attitude" at work. Aero Engine has a comprehensive employee assistance program (EAP) for employees experiencing personal and family problems. Tom's supervisor, Gordon Thompson, had recommended the services of the EAP to Kinder, but it was unknown if he had used counseling since the EAP program is voluntary and confidential. Management professes that it took a very proactive and humanistic approach toward Kinder, an employee the company valued and respected. However, regardless of the company's concern for Tom, his work performance became problematic.

An absenteeism problem developed and continued until his discharge. Over the eighteen months prior to this termination, Tom was absent twenty-seven complete days and nine partial days and was tardy nineteen times. Twelve months before termination, he had been given a written warning that his attendance must improve or he would face further disciplinary action, including possible discharge. Unfortunately, his attendance did not improve; however, he received no further disciplinary action until his discharge on Monday, June 9, 2008.

Management had experienced problems other than absenteeism with Tom Kinder. The quantity and quality of his work had decreased to only an acceptable level of performance. His supervisor had discussed this with him on two occasions, but no disciplinary action was ever instituted. Furthermore, during heavy production periods Kinder would either refuse to work overtime assignments or, once assigned, would often fail to report for work. It was an incident that occurred during a Saturday overtime shift that caused his discharge.

On Saturday, June 7, Kinder was assigned to a high-priority project that required him to build a specialty engine for a large and loyal customer. The big new engine was needed to replace a smaller engine that had exploded on an Alaskan drilling rig. The engine was being built in a newly constructed plant building located one-half mile from the company's main production facilities. At approximately 9:15 AM on that Saturday, Gordon Thompson had walked over to the new building to check on the progress of the engine. As Thompson passed by a window, he noticed Kinder sitting at a desk with his feet up, reading a magazine. The supervisor decided to observe him from outside the building. After about twenty-five minute, Kinder had not moved, and Thompson returned to the plant to report the incident to Glenn Navarro, the plant production manager. Neither the supervisor nor the production manager confronted Kinder about the incident.

At 8:15 the next Monday morning, supervisor Thompson and production manager Navarro met with the director of human resources to review the total work performance of Tom Kinder. After this short meeting, all those present decided that Tom Kinder should be fired. Tom's discharge notice read, "Terminated for poor work performance, excessive absenteeism, and loafing." At 10:15 that morning Kinder was called into Navarro's office and told of his discharge. Navarro then handed him his final paycheck, which included eight hours of work for Monday.

Questions

1. Comment on the handling of this case by the supervisor, production manager, and director of human resources.
2. How much concern should organizations show employees before taking disciplinary action for personal family problems? Explain.
3. To what extent were the concepts of good discipline and "just cause" discharge applied?
4. If Tom Kinder's discharge went to arbitration, how would you decide the case? Why? What arguments would labor and management present to support their respective positions?

Source: This case is based on an actual arbitration heard by George W. Bohlander. All names are fictitious.

I.B.M.: Take as Much Vacation Time as You Want To?

CASE 9

It's every worker's dream: take as much vacation time as you want, on short notice, and don't worry about your boss calling you on it. Cut out early, make it a long weekend, string two weeks together—as you like. No need to call in sick on a Friday so you can disappear for a fishing trip. Just go; nobody's keeping track.

That is essentially what goes on at I.B.M. one of the cornerstones of corporate America, where each of the 355,000 workers is entitled to three or more weeks of vacation. The company does not keep track of who takes how much time or when, does not dole out choice vacation times by seniority and does not let people carry days off from year to year.

Instead, for the past few years, employees at all levels have made informal arrangements with their direct supervisors, guided mainly by their ability to get their work done on time. Many people post their vacation plans on electronic calendars that colleagues can view online, and they leave word about how they can be reached in a pinch.

"It's like when you went to college and you didn't have high school teachers nagging you anymore," said Mark L. Hanny, I.B.M.'s vice president of independent software vendor alliances. "Employees like that we put more accountability on them."

But the flip side of flexibility, at least at I.B.M., is peer pressure. Mr. Hanny and other I.B.M. employees, including his assistant, Shari Chiara, say that they frequently check their e-mail and voice mail messages while on vacation. Bosses sometimes ask subordinates to cancel days off to meet deadlines.

Some workplace experts say such continued blurring of the boundaries between work and play can overtax employees and lead to health problems, particularly at companies where there is an expectation that everyone is always on call. "If leadership never takes time off, people will be skeptical whether they can," said Kim Stattner of Hewitt Associates, a human resources consultant. "There is the potential for a domino effect."

Frances Schneider, who retired from an I.B.M. sales division last year, after 34 years, said one thing never changed; there was not one year in which she took all her allotted time off. "It wasn't seven days a week, but people ended up putting in longer hours because of all the flexibility, without really thinking about it," Ms. Schneider said. "Although you had this wonderful freedom to take days when you want, you really couldn't. I.B.M. tends to be a group of workaholics."

I.B.M. officials said they have no idea whether workers take more or fewer days off now than before, and have not studied the policy's effect on efficiency.

But they point to employee surveys showing that the self-directed work and vacation policy is one of the top three reasons workers choose to stay there.

"Change is change," said Richard Calo, vice president of global workforce relations. "We had some initial questioning of it. But at the end of the day, you remember how much time you spent. This wasn't a difficult sell."

Mr. Calo said that the open-ended vacation policy is "not a total license to do whatever you want to do," and that workers are expected to produce quality work, even if the company is not paying attention to when or where they complete it.

The hands-off approach to vacation time, which gradually took hold over the past decade, has come amid I.B.M.'s shift from engineering and manufacturing into services like consulting and is part of a broader demise of old notions of eight hours' pay for eight hours' work at a fixed location.

Aided by broadband connections, cell phones and video conferencing software, 40 percent of I.B.M.'s employees have no dedicated offices, working instead at home, at a client's site, or at one of the company's hundreds of "e-mobility centers" around the world, where workers drop in to use phones, Internet connections and other resources.

Long a trendsetter in human resources—it began offering family leave in the 1950s—I.B.M. is probably the largest company to do away so completely with tracking vacation, although a number of newer, smaller firms have similar policies.

Best Buy has introduced a program called Results Oriented Work Environment for its 4,000 corporate employees, giving them freedom to do their jobs without regard to the hours they put in daily. Motley Fool, the online investment adviser, has, since its founding 13 years ago, let employees take as many paid vacation or sick days as they need; the company's director of human resources, Lee Burbage, said that most of its 180 workers take three to four weeks a year. Netflix, the online DVD distributor, no longer allots specific numbers of vacation days to its 400 salaried employees.

"When you have a workforce of fully formed professionals who have been working for much of their life," Patty McCord, the chief talent officer of Netflix, said, "you have a connection between the work you do and how long it takes to do it, so you don't need to have the clock-in and clock-out mentality."

I.B.M.'s vacations-without-boundaries system started in the early 1990s, when managers in the human resources, finance and technology departments questioned whether tracking days off helped the company grow — and some complained that it was an administrative burden.

So the company stopped counting days in a few departments, then gradually expanded the new policy. Since 2003, it has covered everyone in the company, from the chief executive, Samuel J. Palmisano, who has a vacation house in Kennebunkport, Me., to workers at I.B.M.'s chip and server factories in East Fishkill and Poughkeepsie, N.Y.

Luis H. Rodriguez, the director of market management in I.B.M.'s software group, said he visits his office here in Somers about once a week, working the rest of the time on the road or at his home in Ridgefield, Conn., where he sat one recent afternoon at the kitchen table with his laptop open.

He said that in six years at I.B.M. he can recall only one time when he asked a coworker not to take a long weekend off—when their group was about to buy another company—and that calling colleagues or checking e-mail while visiting relatives in Texas or Illinois is a fair trade for being able to work from home so he can spend more time with his children, Alec, 5, and Evia, 2. "I get an incredible amount of flexibility from the company, but it cuts both ways," he said. "Because people's schedules and needs are so structured, you need flexibility at work."

For most companies, keeping track of time worked and time off remains a critical and transparent benchmark for workers and bosses. It is also a necessity in factories, call centers, restaurants and other workplaces where business would grind to a halt if managers were unable to predictably have enough employees on hand.

"If you look at the organizations that have done more radical things, they tend to be technology companies with salaried people," where flexibility in job performance "is embedded into the culture of the place," noted Max Caldwell, a managing principal in the workforce effectiveness area at Towers Perrin, a human resources consultant.

Indeed, I.B.M.'s Mr. Calo said that the flexibility has helped the company compete with the more freewheeling atmosphere at start-up rivals in the technology world that have lured away some of its talent over the years. "We have a reputation of not being as hip as a Google or a Netflix," he said. "You don't have to be the coolest guy on the block, but you don't have to be the Big Blue nerd, either."

Questions

1. What upsides and downsides do you see to I.B.M.'s vacation policy?
2. Does a flexible vacation policy make more sense for some organizations or jobs than others? If so, what types of organizations or jobs?
3. How might I.B.M. go about improving its flexible vacation policy to help alleviate some of the stress experienced by employees who feel like they can't take time off?

Source: Reprinted from Ken Belson, "At I.B.M., a Vacation Anytime, or Maybe None," *New York Times* (August 31, 2007), [URL]http://www.nytimes.com/2007/08/31/nyregion/31vacation.html.

Newell's Decision to Downsize: An Ethical Dilemma

A particular issue in business ethics is: "What exactly does the term ethics mean?" Various writers have described ethics as rules that govern behavior; desired societal values such as respect for justice, or accepted principles of right or wrong. Furthermore, the subject of ethics embraces the study of morals and virtues. One author noted, "While laws concern what we must do, ethics concerns what we should do."*

In the practice of HR, managers and supervisors are continually faced with ethical dilemmas regarding the fair and equitable treatment of employees. Ethical choices abound in areas such as recruitment and selection, employee privacy, whistle-blowing, sexual harassment, and diversity or affirmative action. An important ethical dilemma faced by managers today is the fair and correct way to downsize organizations. At conflict are organizational goals and strategies, HR policy and practices, and, of course, the lives of those affected. The facts of the following case are straightforward. The decisions involved in downsizing a workforce are complex and, as one manager stated, "gut-wrenching."

The Need to Downsize

Newell Corporation is a medium-sized manufacturer of navigational systems for commuter and larger airplanes. The company operates two plants—one in Atlanta, Georgia, the other in Norwood, California. In 2003, the Norwood plant employed 273 employees, most of them engaged in the manufacture and technical support of company products.

Important to this case is that Newell is regarded as an excellent place to work by its employees and within the surrounding communities. Employee morale and loyalty have always been high, and job satisfaction studies conducted by the company consistently rate the organization as a fair and equitable place to work. HR policies can be described as proactive and progressive. With its positive reputation, Newell has been able to select new employees from a large pool of job applicants.

One cornerstone of HR policy has been the use of seniority in training, job assignment, transfers, and promotion. Additionally, with Newell's emphasis on employee retention, employees have experienced—some say, "have come to expect"—long tenure and steady employment. Prior to 2007, Newell has never downsized its workforce. Employment growth at the Norwood facility can be described as moderate and steady.

The racial composition of the company has been predominately Caucasian, for two reasons. First, the racial composition of the company's local labor market has historically been Caucasian. Second, the skill level needed for the company's technical jobs has come primarily from a trained Caucasian labor force. A review of the company's federally required EEO-1 report for 2005 showed that Newell had few employees in each of the minority categories listed. This is true for both hourly and managerial positions. However, since approximately 2000, the demographic characteristics of the local labor market have changed dramatically to include more Hispanics, African-Americans, and Asian-Americans. Minority job applicants have generally not possessed the skills needed for entry-level manufacturing and technical support jobs.

In 2005, Newell experienced a large increase in the demand for its products. To meet customer orders, the Norwood plant hired twenty-seven new manufacturing assemblers and fourteen new technical support technicians. With the increased diversity of the external labor force, plus the desire to increase the minority composition of its internal workforce, thirty-four of the forty-one new hires were minorities. It is noteworthy that Newell welcomed the opportunity to rapidly increase the diversity of its workforce for both business and ethical reasons. The following is an excerpt from Newell's statement of vision and values published in July 2003:

> Newell Corporation believes that a work environment that reflects a diverse workforce, values diversity, and honors the worth of its employees benefits the company, its customers, and its employees. Employment decisions will be made on these principles while also considering the efficient and effective operation of the organization.

Because new minority employees generally did not possess the skills needed for its manufacturing and technical jobs, the company spent approximately $1.7 million on entry-level skills training. The integration of minorities into the Norwood facility was seamless and without racial tension.

In 2004, sales for Newell's products once again followed historical patterns. Unfortunately, sales then unexpectedly took a sharp downturn: a 12 percent decline in 2005 and a 23 percent decline in 2006. Causes for the decline in sales were attributed to two new low-wage foreign competitors who entered the market in 2004, a slight decline in market demand for company products, and higher-than-average production costs due to Newell's older, less efficient manufacturing equipment. Future demand for company products was projected to be moderate for 2007, 2008, and 2009.

In February 2007, Tom Malcom, Norwood's director of HR; Steven L. Davis, corporate vice president for manufacturing; and Mary Umali, Norwood's plant manager, decided to downsize the workforce at the Norwood facility. Specifically, they decided to lay off thirty-seven manufacturing employees and eleven technical support personnel. The difficult question faced by senior management was how to lay off employees in a manner that would be fair and equitable to individuals and legally defensible, while maintaining the integrity of Newell's HR policies and the productivity of the Norwood plant.

Questions

1. What is the ethical dilemma faced by management in this case? Explain.
2. What specific problems might Newell face in its downsizing decision?
3. What options might Newell employ in its downsizing decision? Explain.
4. How would you downsize the Norwood facility? Explain.

Source: This case was adapted from an actual case known to the authors. All names are fictitious.

*Terry Halbert and Elaine Ingulli, *Law and Ethics in the Business Environment*, 4th ed. (Mason, OH: Thompson, South-Western, 2003).

Someone Has to Go: A Tough Layoff Decision

CASE 11

The figures are staggering, 3,083,266 workers were involuntarily displaced in the United States during 2006 and 2007 through employer mass layoffs. Additionally, during January through September 2008, there were 14,811 mass layoff events, classified as 50 or more employees laid off, affecting 1,510,446 workers, the highest for the January–September period since 2002. According to the U.S. Bureau of Labor Statistics, the reasons for mass layoffs include expanding global competition, organizational mergers, slack work, seasonal fluctuations, bankruptcies, and companies unable or unwilling to adapt to rapid change.*

Beyond layoffs of large numbers of employees at major corporations, there is a continuous layoff of small groups of employees—or a single employee—when economic conditions warrant a reduction in company size. These incidents affect the lives of both employees and their managers, as this case illustrates.

Located in the Los Angeles area, Aero Performance, with twenty-seven employees, is a sales and maintenance company that provides equipment upgrades and general aircraft maintenance to regional airlines, corporate aircraft, and small international carriers. When Aero Performance was created twelve years ago, the company faced little competition, and a robust airline market seemed to present an unlimited potential for growth. Unfortunately, industry economics, coupled with cost-cutting measures by airlines and new competition from similar airline service companies, means that Aero's performance's business has stabilized with actual losses in certain specialized areas.

One area of concern is the company's "technology advanced" airplane equipment. However, with cost control a major objective of airline companies as well as owners of corporate jets, these organizations have delayed the purchase and installation of advanced electronic equipment.

Mike Martinez, manager of the technology upgrade unit, faces a tough decision. With a significant downturn in his unit's work, he must lay off one employee. The decision is made particularly difficult because all employees of the unit are qualified employees with average or better work records. Additionally, each employee has a unique personal background directly affecting his or her work life. A summary of the background and work record of each of the four employees follows. No question, Martinez faces a difficult decision.

Gary Meadors is married and has two children in high school. He lives modestly in order to send his kids to college. His wife works evenings at a convenience store to assist with family expenses. Meadors has worked nine years with Aero Performance, six years in airline maintenance and three years in the technology upgrade unit. He has learned airline technology largely through technical articles, trade journals, and on-the-job experience. His performance evaluations are average, and he is considered a consistent and reliable employee. His attendance and company loyalty are exceptional.

Brenda Baldwin is the only woman in the technology upgrade unit. She is a single mother with a child in elementary school. Brenda has three years of service with Aero Performance, all in Martinez's unit. She joined the company after obtaining an airline technology degree from a well-respected four-year university. Brenda continues to take evening classes in her field and seems to have, according to Martinez, "the most potential for growth in the company." However, her performance has slipped the past year, and she has been counseled for an attendance problem. She has felt somewhat resented as a female in a traditionally male-dominated industry.

Udit Chopra is a dedicated employee. In fact, everyone says he is "married to his job." He will work long hours to complete technical installations and is regarded as a perfectionist. Udit has a college degree in marketing but has found his home in airline technology. He possesses an excellent ability to persuade Aero Performance customers to upgrade their technology systems. Udit drives a new BMW and is reported to come from a wealthy family.

Craig Cottrell joined Aero Performance three years ago, having been hired away from a competitor. He has a total of twelve years of experience in the airline service industry. Craig has a complete understanding of airline technology. Cottrell's work performance the first two years with Aero Performance was barely average; however, his work record the past year was evaluated as very high. Currently, he is the top performer in the unit. There has been work friction between him, Baldwin, and Chopra over the selection and installation of cockpit instruments.

	SENIORITY (Years)	Salary	Performance			
			2004	2005	2006	2007
Gary Meadors	9	$64,250	Avg	Good	Avg	Avg
Brenda Baldwin	3	$71,190		High	Good	Avg
Udit Chopra	5	$68,500	Avg	Good	Good	Good
Craig Cottrell	3	$65,960		Avg	Avg	High

Mike Martinez must make his decision by this Friday. Aero Performance will grant the laid-off employee a severance package to assist transition to other employment. Martinez is committed to aiding his employee in finding another job in the airline service industry.

Questions

1. What criteria should be used to determine potential layoff candidates? What emphasis, if any, should be given to non-job-related factors such as personal problems or a spouse's need to work? Explain.
2. What should be included in a severance package for laid-off employees? How long should the severance package last? Explain.
3. Are there any potential legal implications in Martinez's decision? Explain.
4. How would you handle the termination interview? Explain.

*Figures are from *Mass Layoff Statistics, 2008.* Bureau of Labor Statistics, http://www.bls.gov. (See mass layoff statistics.)

GLOSSARY

9-box grid

A comparative diagram that includes appraisal and assessment data to allow managers to easily see an employee's actual and potential performance

Achievement tests

Measures of what a person knows or can do right now

Adverse impact

A concept that refers to the rejection of a significantly higher percentage of a protected class for employment, placement, or promotion when compared with the successful, nonprotected class

Affirmative action

A policy that goes beyond equal employment opportunity by requiring organizations to comply with the law and correct past discriminatory practices by increasing the numbers of minorities and women in specific positions

Alternative dispute resolution (ADR)

A term applied to different types of employee complaint or dispute resolution procedures

Apprenticeship training

A system of training in which a worker entering the skilled trades is given thorough instruction and experience, both on and off the job, in the practical and theoretical aspects of the work

Aptitude tests

Measures of a person's capacity to learn or acquire skills

Arbitrator

A third-party neutral who resolves a labor dispute by issuing a final decision in the disagreement

Assessment center

A process by which individuals are evaluated as they participate in a series of situations that resemble what they might be called on to handle on the job

Augmented skills

Skills helpful in facilitating the efforts of expatriate managers

Authorization card

A statement signed by an employee authorizing a union to act as a representative of the employee for purposes of collective bargaining

Balance-sheet approach

A compensation system designed to match the purchasing power in a person's home country

Balanced scorecard (BSC)

A measurement framework that helps managers translate strategic goals into operational objectives

Bargaining power

The power of labor and management to achieve their goals through economic, social, or political influence

Bargaining unit

A group of two or more employees who share common employment interests and conditions and may reasonably be grouped together for purposes of collective bargaining

Bargaining zone

An area in which the union and the employer are willing to concede when bargaining

Behavior modeling

An approach that demonstrates desired behavior and gives trainees the chance to practice and role-play those behaviors and receive feedback

Behavior modification

A technique that operates on the principle that behavior that is rewarded, or positively reinforced, will be exhibited more frequently in the future, whereas behavior that is penalized or unrewarded will decrease in frequency

Behavior observation scale (BOS)

A behavioral approach to performance appraisal that measures the frequency of observed behavior

Behavioral description interview (BDI)

An interview in which an applicant is asked questions about what he or she actually did in a given situation

Behaviorally anchored rating scale (BARS)

A behavioral approach to performance appraisal that consists of a series of vertical scales, one for each important dimension of job performance

Benchmarking

The process of measuring one's own services and practices against the recognized leaders in order to identify areas for improvement

Blended learning

The use of multiple training methods to achieve optimal learning on the part of trainees

Bona fide occupational qualification (BFOQ)

Suitable defense against a discrimination charge only when age, religion, sex, or national origin is an actual qualification for performing the job

Bonus

An incentive payment that is supplemental to the base wage

Burnout

A severe stage of distress, manifesting itself in depression, frustration, and loss of productivity

Business necessity

A work-related practice that is necessary to the safe and efficient operation of an organization

Business unionism

A term applied to the goals of U.S. labor organizations, which collectively bargain for improvements in wages, hours, job security, and working conditions

Calibration

A process whereby managers meet to discuss the performance of individual employees to ensure their employee appraisals are in line with one another

Career counseling

The process of discussing with employees their current job activities and performance, personal and career interests and goals, personal skills, and suitable career development objectives

Career networking

The process of establishing mutually beneficial relationships with other businesspeople, including potential clients and customers

Career paths

Lines of advancement in an occupational field within an organization

Career plateau

A situation in which for either organizational or personal reasons the probability of moving up the career ladder is low

Charge form

A discrimination complaint filed with the EEOC by employees or job applicants

Chief ethics officer

A high-ranking manager directly responsible for fostering the ethical climate within the firm

Chief learning officer

A high-ranking manager directly responsible for fostering employee learning and development within the firm

Codetermination

Representation of labor on the board of directors of a company

Collective bargaining process

The process of negotiating a labor agreement, including the use of economic pressures by both parties

Combined salary and commission plan

A compensation plan that includes a straight salary and a commission

Comparable worth

The concept that male and female jobs that are dissimilar, but equal in terms of value or worth to the employer, should be paid the same

Compensatory model

A selection decision model in which a high score in one area can make up for a low score in another area

Competence-based pay

Pay based on an employee's skill level, variety of skills possessed, or increased job knowledge

Competency assessment

Analysis of the sets of skills and knowledge needed for decision-oriented and knowledge-intensive jobs

Concurrent validity

The extent to which test scores (or other predictor information) match criterion data obtained at about the same time from current employees.

Construct validity

The extent to which a selection tool measures a theoretical construct or trait

Constructive discharge

An employee's voluntary termination of his or her employment because of harsh, unreasonable employment conditions placed on the individual by the employer

Consumer price index (CPI)

A measure of the average change in prices over time in a fixed "market basket" of goods and services

Consumer-driven health plan (CDHP)

A medical insurance plan financed by employer contributions to an employee's individual health care spending account

Content validity

The extent to which a selection instrument, such as a test, adequately samples the knowledge and skills needed to perform a particular job

Contrast error

A performance rating error in which an employee's evaluation is biased either upward or downward because of comparison with another employee previously evaluated

Contributory plan

A pension plan in which contributions are made jointly by employees and employers

Cooperative training

A training program that combines practical on-the-job experience with formal educational classes

Core capabilities

Integrated knowledge sets within an organization that distinguish it from its competitors and deliver value to customers

Core skills

Skills considered critical to an employee's success abroad

Core values

The strong and enduring beliefs and principles that the company uses as a foundation for its decisions

Corporate social responsibility

The responsibility of the firm to act in the best interests of the people and communities affected by its activities

Craft unions

Unions that represent skilled craft workers

Criterion-related validity

The extent to which a selection tool predicts, or significantly correlates with, important elements of work behavior

Critical incident method

A job analysis method by which important job tasks are identified for job success

Critical incident

An unusual event that denotes superior or inferior employee performance in some part of the job

Cross-training

The process of training employees to do multiple jobs within an organization

Cross-validation

Verifying the results obtained from a validation study by administering a test or test battery to a different sample (drawn from the same population)

Cultural audits

Audits of the culture and quality of work life in an organization

Cultural environment

The communications, religion, values and ideologies, education, and social structure of a country

Culture shock

Perpetual stress experienced by people who settle overseas

Cumulative trauma disorders

Injuries involving tendons of the fingers, hands, and arms that become inflamed from repeated stresses and strains

Customer appraisal

A performance appraisal that, like team appraisal, is based on TQM concepts and seeks evaluation from both external and internal customers

Defined benefit plan

A pension plan in which the amount an employee is to receive on retirement is specifically set forth

Defined contribution plan

A pension plan that establishes the basis on which an employer will contribute to the pension fund

Depression

A negative emotional state marked by feelings of low spirits, gloominess, sadness, and loss of pleasure in ordinary activities

Differential piece rate

A compensation rate under which employees whose production exceeds the standard amount of output receive a higher rate for all of their work than the rate paid to those who do not exceed the standard amount

Disabled individual

Any person who (1) has a physical or mental impairment that substantially limits one or more of the person's major life activities, (2) has a record of such impairment, or (3) is regarded as having such an impairment

Discipline

(1) Treatment that punishes, (2) orderly behavior in an organizational setting, or (3) training that molds and strengthens desirable conduct—or corrects undesirable conduct—and develops self-control

Disparate treatment

A situation in which protected class members receive unequal treatment or are evaluated by different standards

Distress

Harmful stress characterized by a loss of feelings of security and adequacy

Downsizing

Planned elimination of jobs

Dual career partnerships

Couples in which both members follow their own careers and actively support each other's career development

Due process

An employee's right to present his or her position during a displinary action

E-learning

Learning that takes place via electronic media

EEO-1 report

An employer information report that must be filed annually by employers of 100 or more employees (except state and local government employers) and government contractors and subcontractors to determine an employer's workforce composition

Elder care

Care provided to an elderly relative by an employee who remains actively at work

Employee assistance programs (EAPs)

Services provided by employers to help workers cope with a wide variety of problems that interfere with the way they perform their jobs

Employee associations

Labor organizations that represent various groups of professional and white-collar employees in labor-management relations

Employee empowerment

Granting employees power to initiate change, thereby encouraging them to take charge of what they do

Employee involvement groups (EIs)

Groups of employees who meet to resolve problems or offer suggestions for organizational improvement

Employee leasing

The process of dismissing employees who are then hired by a leasing company (which handles all HR-related activities) and contracting with that company to lease back the employees

Employee rights

Guarantees of fair treatment from employers, particularly regarding an employee's right to privacy

Employee stock ownership plans (ESOPs)

Stock plans in which an organization contributes shares of its stock to an established trust for the purpose of stock purchases by its employees

Employee teams

An employee contributions technique whereby work functions are structured for groups rather than for individuals and team members are given discretion in matters traditionally considered management prerogatives, such as process improvements, product or service development, and individual work assignments

Employment-at-will principle

The right of an employer to fire an employee without giving a reason and the right of an employee to quit when he or she chooses

Entrepreneur

One who starts, organizes, manages, and assumes responsibility for a business or other enterprise

Environmental scanning

Systematic monitoring of the major external forces influencing the organization

Equal employment opportunity (EEO)

The treatment of individuals in all aspects of employment—hiring, promotion, training, etc.—in a fair and nonbiased manner

Ergonomics

An interdisciplinary approach to designing equipment and systems that can be easily and efficiently used by human beings

Error of central tendency

A performance rating error in which all employees are rated about average

Escalator clauses

Clauses in labor agreements that provide for quarterly cost-of-living adjustments in wages, basing the adjustments on changes in the consumer price index

Essay method

A trait approach to performance appraisal that requires the rater to compose a statement describing employee behavior

Ethics

A set of standards of conduct and moral judgments that help to determine right and wrong behavior

Eustress

Positive stress that accompanies achievement and exhilaration

Exclusive representation

The legal right and responsibility of the union to represent all bargaining unit members equally, regardless of whether employees join the union or not

Exempt employees

Employees not covered by the overtime provisions of the Fair Labor Standards Act

Expatriates, or home-country nationals

Employees from the home country who are on international assignment

External fit

The situation in which the work system supports the organization's goals and strategies

Failure rate

The percentage of expatriates who do not perform satisfactorily

Fair employment practices (FEPs)

State and local laws governing equal employment opportunity that are often more comprehensive than federal laws and apply to small employers

Fair representation doctrine

A doctrine under which unions have a legal obligation to assist both members and nonmembers in labor relations matters

Fast-track program

A program that encourages young managers with high potential to remain with an organization by enabling them to advance more rapidly than those with less potential

Flexible benefits plans (cafeteria plans)

Benefit plans that enable individual employees to choose the benefits that are best suited to their particular needs

Flextime

Flexible working hours that permit employees the option of choosing daily starting and quitting times, provided that they work a set number of hours per day or week

Forced-choice method

A trait approach to performance appraisal that requires the rater to choose from statements designed to distinguish between successful and unsuccessful performance

Four-fifths rule

A rule of thumb followed by the EEOC in determining adverse impact for use in enforcement proceedings

G

Gainsharing plans

Programs under which both employees and the organization share financial gains according to a predetermined formula that reflects improved productivity and profitability

Global compensation system

A centralized pay system whereby host-country employees are offered a full range of training programs, benefits, and pay comparable with a firm's domestic employees but adjusted for local differences

Global corporation

A firm that has integrated worldwide operations through a centralized home office

Global manager

A manager equipped to run an international business

Globalization

The trend toward opening up foreign markets to international trade and investment

Graphic rating scale method

A trait approach to performance appraisal whereby each employee is rated according to a scale of characteristics

Grievance procedure

A formal procedure that provides for the union to represent members and nonmembers in processing a grievance

Guest workers

Foreign workers invited to perform needed labor

H

Hay profile method

A job evaluation technique using three factors—knowledge, mental activity, and accountability—to evaluate executive and managerial positions

Health maintenance organizations (HMOs)

Organizations of physicians and health care professionals that provide a wide range of services to subscribers and dependents on a prepaid basis

High-performance work system (HPWS)

A specific combination of HR practices, work structures, and processes that maximizes employee knowledge, skill, commitment, and flexibility

Home-based pay

Pay based on an expatriate's home country's compensation practices

Host country

A country in which an international corporation operates

Host-based pay

Expatriate pay comparable to that earned by employees in a host country

Host-country nationals

Employees who are natives of the host country

Hourly work

Work paid on an hourly basis

Human capital

The knowledge, skills, and capabilities of individuals that have economic value to an organization

Human capital readiness

The process of evaluating the availability of critical talent in a company and comparing it to the firm's supply

Human resources information system (HRIS)

A computerized system that provides current and accurate data for purposes of control and decision-making

Human resources management (HRM)

The process of managing human talent to achieve an organization's objectives

Human resources planning (HRP)

The process of anticipating and providing for the movement of people into, within, and out of an organization

I

Improshare

A gainsharing program under which bonuses are based on the overall productivity of the work team

Industrial engineering

A field of study concerned with analyzing work methods and establishing time standards

Industrial unions

Unions that represent all workers—skilled, semiskilled, unskilled—employed along industry lines

Instructional objectives

Desired outcomes of a training program

Interest-based bargaining

Problem-solving bargaining based on a win-win philosophy and the development of a positive long-term relationship

Internal fit

The situation in which all the internal elements of the work system complement and reinforce one another

International corporation

A domestic firm that uses its existing capabilities to move into overseas markets

Internship programs

Programs jointly sponsored by colleges, universities, and other organizations that offer students the opportunity to gain real-life experience while allowing them to find out how they will perform in work organizations

Job

A group of related activities and duties

Job analysis

The process of obtaining information about jobs by determining the duties, tasks, or activities of jobs

Job characteristics model

A job design theory that purports that three psychological states (experiencing meaningfulness of the work performed, responsibility for work outcomes, and knowledge of the results of the work performed) of a jobholder result in improved work performance, internal motivation, and lower absenteeism and turnover

Job classification system

A system of job evaluation in which jobs are classified and grouped according to a series of predetermined wage grades

Job description

A statement of the tasks, duties, and responsibilities of a job to be performed

Job design

An outgrowth of job analysis that improves jobs through technological and human considerations in order to enhance organization efficiency and employee job satisfaction

Job enrichment

Enhancing a job by adding more meaningful tasks and duties to make the work more rewarding or satisfying

Job evaluation

A systematic process of determining the relative worth of jobs in order to establish which jobs should be paid more than others within an organization

Job family

A group of individual jobs with similar characteristics

Job posting and bidding

Posting vacancy notices and maintaining lists of employees looking for upgraded positions

Job progressions

The hierarchy of jobs a new employee might experience, ranging from a starting job to jobs that successively require more knowledge and/or skill

Job ranking system

The simplest and oldest system of job evaluation by which jobs are arrayed on the basis of their relative worth

Job specification

A statement of the needed knowledge, skills, and abilities of the person who is to perform the job

Just-in-time training

Training delivered to trainees when and where they need it to do their jobs, usually via computer or the Internet

Knowledge workers

Workers whose responsibilities extend beyond the physical execution of work to include planning, decision-making, and problem-solving

Labor relations process

A logical sequence of five events: (1) workers desire collective representation, (2) the union begins its organizing campaign, (3) the NLRB representation process begins, (4) collective negotiations lead to a contract, and (5) the contract is administered

Learning management system (LMS)

On-line system that provides a variety of assessment, communication, teaching, and learning opportunities

Leniency or strictness error

A performance rating error in which the appraiser tends to give employees either unusually high or unusually low ratings

Localization

Adapting pay and other compensation benefits to match that of a particular country

Lump sum merit program

Program under which employees receive a year-end merit payment, which is not added to their base pay

Management by objectives (MBO)

A philosophy of management that rates performance on the basis of employee achievement of goals set by mutual agreement of employee and manager

Management forecasts

The opinions (judgments) of supervisors, department managers, experts, or others knowledgeable about the organization's future employment needs

Manager and/or supervisor appraisal

A performance appraisal done by an employee's manager and often reviewed by a manager one level higher

Managing diversity

Being aware of characteristics common to employees, while also managing employees as individuals

Markov analysis

A method for tracking the pattern of employee movements through various jobs

Material safety data sheets (MSDSs)

Documents that contain vital information about hazardous substances

Mediation

The use of a neutral third party to reach a compromise decision in employment disputes

Mediator

A third party in an employment dispute who meets with one party and then the other in order to suggest compromise solutions or to recommend concessions from each side that will lead to an agreement

Mentors

Individuals who coach, advise, and encourage individuals of lesser rank

Merit guidelines

Guidelines for awarding merit raises that are tied to performance objectives

Mission

The basic purpose of the organization as well as its scope of operations

Mixed-standard scale method

A trait approach to performance appraisal similar to other scale methods but based on comparison with (better than, equal to, or worse than) a standard

Multinational corporation (MNC)

A firm with independent business units operating in multiple countries

Multiple cutoff model

A selection decision model that requires an applicant to achieve some minimum level of proficiency on all selection dimensions

Multiple hurdle model

A sequential strategy in which only the applicants with the highest scores at an initial test stage go on to subsequent stages

Negligence

Failure to provide reasonable care when such failure results in injury to consumers or other employees

Negligent hiring

The failure of an organization to discover, via due diligence, that an employee it hired had the propensity to do harm to others

Nepotism

A preference for hiring relatives of current employees

Noncontributory plan

A pension plan in which contributions are made solely by the employer

Nondirective interview

An interview in which the applicant is allowed the maximum amount of freedom in determining the course of the discussion, while the interviewer carefully refrains from influencing the applicant's remarks

Nonexempt employees

Employees covered by the overtime provisions of the Fair Labor Standards Act

Offshoring

The business practice of sending jobs to other countries

Ombudsman

A designated individual from whom employees may seek counsel for resolution of their complaints

On-the-job training (OJT)

A method by which employees are given hands-on experience with instructions from their supervisor or other trainer

Open-door policy

A policy of settling grievances that identifies various levels of management above the immediate supervisor for employee contact

Organization analysis

Examination of the environment, strategies, and resources of the organization to determine where training emphasis should be placed

Organizational capability

The capacity of the organization to act and change in pursuit of sustainable competitive advantage

Orientation

The formal process of familiarizing new employees with the organization, their jobs, and their work units

Outplacement services

Services provided by organizations to help terminated employees find a new job

Outsourcing

Contracting outside the organization to have work done that formerly was done by internal employees

Panel interview

An interview in which a board of interviewers questions and observes a single candidate

Pay equity

An employee's perception that compensation received is equal to the value of the work performed

Pay grades

Groups of jobs within a particular class that are paid the same rate

Pay-for-performance standard

A standard by which managers tie compensation to employee effort and performance

Peer appraisal

A performance appraisal done by one's fellow employees, generally on forms that are compiled into a single profile for use in the performance interview conducted by the employee's manager

Peer-review system

A system for reviewing employee complaints that utilizes a group composed of equal numbers of employee representatives and management appointees, which functions as a jury because its members weigh evidence, consider arguments, and, after deliberation, vote independently to render a final decision

Performance appraisal

A process, typically performed annually by a supervisor for a subordinate, designed to help employees understand their roles, objectives, expectations, and performance success

Performance management

The process of creating a work environment in which people can perform to the best of their abilities

Perquisites

Special nonmonetary benefits given to executives; often referred to as *perks*

Person analysis

Determination of the specific individuals who need training

Piecework

Work paid according to the number of units produced

Point system

A quantitative job evaluation procedure that determines the relative value of a job by the total points assigned to it

Position analysis questionnaire (PAQ)

A questionnaire covering 194 different tasks that, by means of a five-point scale, seeks to determine the degree to which different tasks are involved in performing a particular job

Position

The different duties and responsibilities performed by only one employee

Positive, or nonpunitive, discipline

A system of discipline that focuses on early correction of employee misconduct, with the employee taking total responsibility for correcting the problem

Predictive validity

The extent to which applicants' test scores match criterion data obtained from those applicants/employees after they have been on the job for some indefinite period

Preferred provider organization (PPO)

A group of physicians who establish an organization that guarantees lower health care costs to the employer

Proactive change

Change initiated to take advantage of targeted opportunities

Process audit

Determining whether a high-performance work system has been implemented as designed

Profit sharing

Any procedure by which an employer pays, or makes available to all regular employees, in addition to base pay, special current or deferred sums based on the profits of the enterprise

Progressive discipline

Application of corrective measures by increasing degrees

Promotion

A change of assignment to a job at a higher level in the organization

Protected classes

Individuals of a minority race, women, older people, and those with disabilities who are covered by federal laws on equal employment opportunity

Psychological contract

Expectations of a fair exchange of employment obligations between an employee and employer

Reactive change

Change that occurs after external forces have already affected performance

Real wages

Wage increases larger than rises in the consumer price index; that is, the real earning power of wages

Realistic job preview (RJP)

Informing applicants about all aspects of the job, including both its desirable and undesirable facets

Reasonable accommodation

An attempt by employers to adjust, without undue hardship, the working conditions or schedules of employees with disabilities or religious preferences

Recency error

A performance rating error in which the appraisal is based largely on the employee's most recent behavior rather than on behavior throughout the appraisal period

Recordable case

Any occupational death, illness, or injury to be recorded in the log (OSHA Form 300)

Red circle rates

Payment rates above the maximum of the pay range

Reengineering

Fundamental rethinking and radical redesign of business processes to achieve dramatic improvements in cost, quality, service, and speed

Reliability

The degree to which interviews, tests, and other selection procedures yield comparable data over time and alternative measures

Relocation services

Services provided to an employee who is transferred to a new location, which might include help in moving, selling a home, orienting to a new culture, and/or learning a new language

Repatriation

The process of transition for an employee home from an international assignment

Replacement charts

Listings of current jobholders and people who are potential replacements if an opening occurs

Reverse discrimination

The act of giving preference to members of protected classes to the extent that unprotected individuals believe they are suffering discrimination

Rights arbitration

Arbitration over interpretation of the meaning of contract terms or employee work grievances

Right-to-know laws

Laws that require employers to advise employees about the hazardous chemicals they handle

Salary plus bonus plan

A compensation plan that pays a salary plus a bonus achieved by reaching targeted sales goals.

Scanlon Plan

A bonus incentive plan using employee and management committees to gain cost-reduction improvements

Selection

The process of choosing individuals who have relevant qualifications to fill existing or projected job openings

Selection ratio

The number of applicants compared with the number of people to be hired

Self-appraisal

A performance appraisal done by the employee being evaluated, generally on an appraisal form completed by the employee prior to the performance interview

Sexual harassment

Unwelcome advances, requests for sexual favors, and other verbal or physical conduct of a sexual nature in the working environment

Silver handshake

An early retirement incentive in the form of increased pension benefits for several years or a cash bonus

Similar-to-me error

A performance rating error in which an appraiser inflates the evaluation of an employee because of a mutual personal connection

Situational interview

An interview in which an applicant is given a hypothetical incident and asked how he or she would respond to it

Six Sigma

A process used to translate customer needs into a set of optimal tasks that are performed in concert with one another

Skill inventories

Files of personnel education, experience, interests, skills, and so on that allow managers to quickly match job openings with employee backgrounds

Split pay

A system whereby expatriates are given a portion of their pay in the local currency to cover their day-to-day expenses and a portion of their pay in their home currency to safeguard their earnings from changes in inflation or foreign exchange rates

Spot bonus

An unplanned bonus given for employee effort unrelated to an established performance measure

Spot rewards

Programs that award employees "on the spot" when they do something particularly well during training or on the job

Staffing tables

Graphic representations of all organizational jobs, along with the numbers of employees currently occupying those jobs and future (monthly or yearly) employment requirements

Standard hour plan

An incentive plan that sets rates based on the completion of a job in a predetermined standard time

Step-review system

A system for reviewing employee complaints and disputes by successively higher levels of management

Straight commission plan

A compensation plan based on a percentage of sales

Straight piecework

An incentive plan under which employees receive a certain rate for each unit produced

Straight salary plan

A compensation plan that permits salespeople to be paid for performing various duties that are not reflected immediately in their sales volume

Strategic human resources management (SHRM)

The pattern of human resources deployments and activities that enable an organization to achieve its strategic goals

Strategic planning

Procedures for making decisions about the organization's long-term goals and strategies

Strategic vision

A statement about where the company is going and what it can become in the future; clarifies the long-term direction of the company and its strategic intent

Stress

Any adjustive demand caused by physical, mental, or emotional factors that requires coping behavior

Structured interview

An interview in which a set of standardized questions having an established set of answers is used

Subordinate appraisal

A performance appraisal of a superior by an employee, which is more appropriate for developmental than for administrative purposes

Succession planning

The process of identifying, developing, and tracking key individuals for executive positions

Supplemental unemployment benefits (SUBs)

A plan that enables an employee who is laid off to draw, in addition to state unemployment compensation, weekly benefits from the employer that are paid from a fund created for this purpose

SWOT analysis

A comparison of strengths, weaknesses, opportunities, and threats for strategy formulation purposes

Task analysis

The process of determining what the content of a training program should be on the basis of a study of the tasks and duties involved in the job

Task inventory analysis

An organization-specific list of tasks and their descriptions used as a basis to identify components of jobs

Team appraisal

A performance appraisal, based on TQM concepts, that recognizes team accomplishment rather than individual performance

Team incentive plan

A compensation plan in which all team members receive an incentive bonus payment when production or service standards are met or exceeded

Telecommuting

Use of personal computers, networks, and other communications technology such as fax machines to do work in the home that is traditionally done in the workplace

Third-country nationals

Employees who are natives of a country other than the home country or the host country

Total quality management (TQM)

A set of principles and practices whose core ideas include understanding customer needs, doing things right the first time, and striving for continuous improvement

Transfer

Placement of an individual in another job for which the duties, responsibilities, status, and remuneration are approximately equal to those of the previous job

Transfer of training

Effective application of principles learned to what is required on the job

Transnational corporation

A firm that attempts to balance local responsiveness and global scale via a network of specialized operating units

Transnational teams

Teams composed of members of multiple nationalities working on projects that span multiple countries

Trend analysis

A quantitative approach to forecasting labor demand based on an organizational index such as sales

Unfair labor practices (ULPs)

Specific employer and union illegal practices that deny employees their rights and benefits under federal labor law

Uniform Guidelines on Employee Selection Procedures

A procedural document published in the *Federal Register* to help employers comply with federal regulations against discriminatory actions

Union shop

A provision of the labor agreement that requires employees to join the union as a requirement for their employment

Union steward

An employee who as a nonpaid union official represents the interests of members in their relations with management

Validity
The degree to which a test or selection procedure measures a person's attributes

Validity generalization
The extent to which validity coefficients can be generalized across situations

Value creation
What the firm adds to a product or service by virtue of making it; the amount of benefits provided by the product or service once the costs of making it are subtracted

Variable pay
Tying pay to some measure of individual, group, or organizational performance

Vesting
A guarantee of accrued benefits to participants at retirement age, regardless of their employment status at that time

Virtual team
A team with widely dispersed members linked together through computer and telecommunications technology

Wage and salary survey
A survey of the wages paid to employees of other employers in the surveying organization's relevant labor market

Wage curve
A curve in a scattergram representing the relationship between relative worth of jobs and wage rates

Wage rate compression
Compression of pay between new and experienced employees caused by the higher starting salaries of new employees; also the differential between hourly workers and their managers

Whistle-blowing
Complaints to governmental agencies by employees about their employers' illegal or immoral acts or illegal practices

Work permit, or visa
A government document granting a foreign individual the right to seek employment

Work valuation
A job evaluation system that seeks to measure a job's worth through its value to the organization

Workers' compensation insurance
State-mandated insurance provided to workers to defray the loss of income and cost of treatment due to work-related injuries or illness

Workforce utilization analysis
A process of classifying protected-class members by number and by the type of job they hold within the organization

Yield ratio
The percentage of applicants from a recruitment source that make it to the next stage of the selection process

Name Index

Allen, Tom, 748
Andress, Greg, 537
Antonioni, David, 375
Argyris, Chris, 166
Arian, Mark, 21
Arthur, Jeff (study), 733
Atwater, Leanne E., 375

Baldwin, Brenda, 776–777
Bardwick, Judith, 214
Barksdale, Jim, 170
Beane, Billy, 74
Becker, Brian, 721
Belda, Alain J.P., 680f
Bertram, Connie, 108
Bethune, Gordon, 72
Blanfein, Lloyd C. (compensation), 469
Bloedel, MacMillan, 727
Bolles, Richard N., 215
Boswell, Greg, 463
Bower, Joseph, 194
Brakon, Lois, 174
Bray, Douglas, 204
Broedling, Laurie, 16
Brush, Matthew C., 64
Buckley, George W., 680f
Buckman, Robert, 14–15
Bucknall, Jr., William, 746–748
Buckner, Marilyn, 13
Budnick, Peter, 168
Burbage, Lee, 772
Bush, George W. (offensive gesture), 676

Calo, Richard, 772–773
Carlton, Richard, 731
Casellas, Gilbert, 588
Chenault, Kenneth I. (compensation), 469
Chenevert, Louis, 747
Chiara, Shari, 771–772
Chopra, Udit, 777
Clapman, Peter, 467

Cleaver, Walt, 50
Collotta, Ron, 618–619
Combs, James, 711
Conchuratt, Brian, 177
Cottrell, Craig, 777
Coyle, Richard, 763

Davis, Steven L., 775
del Rey, Salvador, 198
Deming, W. Edward, 16, 337
Dhesi, Arvinder, 15
Divney, Kevin, 758–762
Domzalski, Mike, 757, 758
Drucker, Peter, 386
Drucker, Peter F., 469
Dunn, Kris, 717

Edmondson, David, 260
Egan, Gene, 763–765

Fetzer, Marsha, 766
Ford, Henry, 343
Freeland, Grant, 588
Fryer, Garth, 766–769
Fuld, Jr., Richard S. (compensation), 469

Galvez, Dorothy, 165
Galvin, William, 758
Garner, Kathryn, 757
Gels, Richard, 766
Gentry, Tyler, 462–463
Glantz, Stanton, 543
Gorman, Leon, 17
Grantham, Charles, 177
Gray-Kemp, Felice, 745
Gretsky, Wayne, 83
Griggs, Willie, 123
Gross, Ronald, 390
Gross, Stephen E., 414
Gross, Steven, 472
Gubman, Ed, 4

Hackman, Richard, 164
Haldeman, Charles, 758–762
Halfacre, Gordon, 600
Hall, Angela, 711
Hanny, Mark L., 771–772
Hanson, Peter Arthur, 713
Hassey, Patrick (stock options), 367
Hawk, Elizabeth, 412
Hay, Edward N., 428
Hearst, Garrison, 346
Hedge, Alan, 167
Herzberg, Frederick, 162–163
Hipple, Steve, 102
Hoffman, Sandra, 11
Holland, John, 215
Huselid, Mark, 79, 721
study, 733

Immelt, Jeff, 38, 71, 208
Iraini, Ray R. (compensation), 469

Jeffrey, Bob, 550
Jesuthasan, Ravin, 412
Jobs, Steve, 12
Johnson, Robert, 100

Kairey, Mindy, 491
Kalev, Alexandra, 346
Kandel, William, 577
Kanter, Rosabeth Moss, 12
Kaplan, Robert, 81
Kearns, David, 27–28
Keil, Jeff, 759, 762
Kelleher, Herb, 38
Kelly, Paul, 764–765
Kent, Muhtar, 680f
Ketchen, David, 711
Kinder, Tom, 769–771
Kobayashi, Sayaka, 100
Kreuter, Dan, 759
Krumboltz, John D., 215

Lafley, Alan G., 12, 194
Lasser, Lawrence, 758–761
Latham, Gary, 376
Lawler, Edward, 710
Ledford, Gerald, 412
Lee, Mark, 769–771
Levin, Al S., 215
Lincoln, J.F., 476
Liu, Yongmei, 711
Liveris, Andrew, 680f
Loscher, Peter, 666

Macapagal-Arroyo, Gloria, 749
MacDuffie, John Paul (study), 733
Maier, Norman R.F., 391
Malcolm, Tom, 775
Marriott, J.W., 189
Martin, Jim, 549
Martinez, Mike, 776–777
McCaskey, Pam, 763
McCord, Patty, 772
McLean, Lindsey, 346
Meadors, Gary, 776
Meister, Jeanne, 747
Merritt, Carolyn, 537
Mignin, Robert J., 198
Millar, Connie, 766
Miller-Canton, Nancy, 757
Mittelstaedt, Jr., Robert E., 165
Moore, Gordon, 13
Moser, Terry, 621
Mulva, James J. (stock options), 467
Mussman, Susan, 766

Nardelli, Bob, 194
Navarro, Glenn, 770
Nelson, Kevin, 538
Nixon, Richard M. (offensive gesture), 676
Nooyi, Indra, 680f
Norton, David, 81

O'Connor, Sandra Day, 136
Oldham, Greg, 164

O'Leary, George (resignation), 260
O'Reilly, DAvid, 680f
Ortiz, Juan, 766
Osborn, Laura, 747–748

Packley, DAve, 753
Palmisano, Samuel J., 773
Pandit, Vikram, 680f
Peixotto, Bob, 17
Perez, Antonio, 680f
Platt, Lew, 13
Pollock, Pat, 763–765
Pronk, Stephanie, 551

Quinn, James Brian, 57

Radjou, Navi, 172
Richards, Donald, 748
Rimmer, Steve, 688
Rodriguez, Luis H., 773
Ronen, Simcha, 678
Roosevelt, Franklin D., 102
Rosen, Corey, 479

Sammer, Joanne, 456
Sarabe, Jack, 753
Saville, Dale, 749–750
Scallia, Antonin, 118–119
Schneider, Frances, 772
Schultz, Howard, 38
Scott, Mary, 194
Sejen, Lauren, 461
Shanahan, Timothy, 339
Sheedy, James, 544
Sheeny, Jennifer, 111
Shenkar, Oded, 678
Sherwyn, David, 577
Singh, Marcus, 765–769
Smilko, Jessica, 454
Smith, Dan, 25
Stanley, Rose, 415
Stattner, Kim, 772
Stevens, John Paul, 601

Sullivan, John, 747
Sullivan, Stacy, 150

Taft, Jason, 766–769
Taurel, Sydney, 680f
Teamster Local 104, 621
Teerlink, Richard, 714
Thain, John A. (compensation), 469
Thompson, Gordon, 770–771
Tibbetts, Richard, 761
Tichenor, Paulette, 172
Torell, Joseph M., 758
Travaglini, Michael, 759

Ulrich, Dave, 15, 721
Umali, Mary, 775

Van Neck, Kathy, 454
Vashistha, Atul, 20

Waldman, David A., 375
Walker, James, 51
Walker, Marion, 582–583
Watson, Thomas J., 4
Welch, Jack, 13, 211
Wexley, Kenneth, 376
Whitacre, Jr., Edward E. (stock options), 467
Wilhelm, John W., 614
Wilson, Dena, 338
Wolever, Rebecca, 198
Woolnough, Roisin, 457
Wright, Ruth, 728

Young, Mark, 753

Zemke, Ron, 310

ORGANIZATION INDEX

A

AARP, elderly parental care study, 516
ABB, U.S. expatriate manager
    replacement, 665
Abbott Laboratories
    minority managers, increase, 225
    women/employer programs, 224
ABC
    contributions, 225
    M&A. *See* Walt Disney
Abercrombie and Fitch Clothing Store, female
    models (usage), 107
Administrative Management Society
    wage/salary survey, 429
    wage survey data, 422
Advantica, discrimination lawsuit/diversity
    training, 344, 346
Aero Engine Company
    case study, 769–771
    EAP, 770
Aero Performance, case study, 776–777
AES, all-salaried workforce, 718
Aetna Life and Casualty, turnover
    reduction, 31
AFLAC, women/employer programs, 224
AFLAC Insurance, incentives, 455
African-American Forum (AAF), initiative
    (growth), 225
Airbus, university/college recruitment, 666
Air Line Pilots Association, employee
    association, 628
Alcoa, 680f
All-China Federation of Trade Unions
    (ACFTU), 691
Allegheny Technologies, stock options, 467
AlliedSignal, crisis management teams, 549
Allied Waste Industries, Bilingual online/
    offline safety rewards program, 539
Amazon.com, Wal-Mart lawsuit, 202
American Airlines
    equal employment laws, violation, 101
    jobs elimination, 77
    Rainbow Team, 165
American Association of Disabled People, 227
American Association of Industrial
        Management
    education factor/degrees, description, 427
    job factors, point values, 426
American Express
    compensation, 469
    elder care consortium, 517
    HPWS, impact, 718

job sharing programs, 176
    lump sum merit program, 462
American Federation of Labor and the
        Congress of Industrial Organizations
        (AFL-CIO), 623, 629
    structure/functions, 629
    unionization strategy, 646
American Federation of State, County,
        and Municipal Employees
        (AFSCME), 628
    lobbying, 631
    public sector representation, 631
American Federation of Teachers, public
        sector representation, 631
American Institute of Plant Engineers, safety
        survey, 537
American Management Association
    management seminars, 329–330
    summer program, 225
    wage/salary survey, 429
    wage survey data, 422
American Nurses' Association, employee
        association, 628
American Society for Training and
        Development (ASTD)
    federal training assistance guide, 216
    leadership shortages, study, 328
    manager/consultant, critical factor
        questions, 721, 723
    needs assessment study, 309
American Society of Training, training
        benchmarks, 337
AmericanUnion of Postal Workers, 628
American Value Company, Scanlon Plan, 474
America's Career InfoNet (ACINet), job
        location, 196
America's Job Exchange, 196
America West Airlines, flight attendant
        representation, 631
Ames Rubber Corporation, HPWS
        (impact), 733
AMFMJobs, recruitment site, 191
Anheuser Busch, 6
Applebee's, organizational performance
        (improvement), 165
Apple Computer
    domestic partnership definition, 507
    employee stock option plan, 477
    innovation/product development,
        emphasis, 75
ARAMCO, cultural/language training, 673
Archer Daniels Midlands
    employee benefits, 685
    travel management company, usage, 688

ARCO Products, business opportunities,
        675
Arizona Department of Economic Security,
        wage survey data, 422
Arizona State University, 165
    discipline definition, 590
    EAP, 551
ASDA, management/employee work
        cooperation, 729
Association for Worksite Health Promotions,
        wellness literature, 550
Association of Flight Attendants, The
        (lobbying), 631
AstraZeneca, 15
AT&T
    AARP-sponsored program, 25
    assessment centers, 204
    BOS, usage, 385–386
    job candidate evaluation, videoconference
        technologies (usage), 283
    long-term compensation, 467
    remedial courses, offering, 341
    units, reduction, 150
AttorneyJobs, recruitment site, 191
AutoZone, organizational performance
        (improvement), 165
Aviva, 15
Avon Products, minority managers
        (empowerment), 167
AVT Document Exchange Software Group,
        work hours, 174

B

BAE Systems, apprenticeship program, 322
BankBoston, minority managers (increase),
        225
Bank of America, employee children visits, 31
Bank One Corporation of Chicago, DM
        program, 507
Banner Health Services
    continuous improvement/process
        reengineering, 162
    corrective action process, example,
        595–596
Baptist Hospital of Miami, child care
        centers, 516
Barnes & Noble, Web-based commerce, 51
Bath & Body Works, temporary worker
        reliance, 62
Bell Canada, TeleSim (usage), 330
Ben and Jerry's, child care centers, 516
Berlitz International, 675

Best Buy
    customer appraisals, usage, 374
    performance appraisal redesign, 364
B&H Photo-Video, Hispanic wage
    equalization, 100
BioPharma Worldwide, job applicants (digital
    recording), 283
Blimpie's, starting wages (increase), 413
Blue Cross/Blue Shield plans, administration,
    507
BMW, 6
    Land Rover changes, 732
Boeing
    equal employment laws, violation, 101
    mentoring program, 216
    MRO, usage, 580
Boeing Satellite Systems, lessons learned site, 15
Bonneville Power Administration,
    apprenticeship program, 322
Borden, compensation strategies, 467
Borders, AARP-sponsored program, 25
Boston Consulting Group, 588
Boston Global Consulting, hiring, 663
Bowater, employee behavior (strengthening),
    319
Bristol-Myers Squibb, women/employer
    programs, 224
British Land Rover Company, reputation, 732
Brown and Williamson Tobacco, Career
    Tracker (usage), 10
Buckman Laboratories, 14
    strategic objectives, 368
Bureau of Apprenticeship and Training (BAT),
    U.S. Department of Labor, 322
Bureau of Labor Statistics (BLS)
    back injuries, report, 528
    National Compensation Survey, 429, 430
    safety comparison, 533–534
Bureau of National Affairs, The, ESOP, 479
Burger King
    cooperative training program investment,
    322
    starting wages, increase, 413
Business Roundtable Institute for Corporate
    Ethics, 345

C

Cabrini College, interactive employee benefit
    system, 490
Caesar's Palace, casino dealer organizing, 614
Calvin Klein, employee teams (importance),
    170
Career-Builder, job sharing programs, 191
CareerBuilder (web site), 280
    IntelligentHire screening, 282
    job interview survey, 280–281
    survey, 260

Carnival Cruise Lines, FLSA violations, 438
Carter Howley Hale Stores, job sharing
    programs, 176
Case Financial, employee flexibility, 312
Catalyst, 222
Caterpillar, leadership development initiative,
    329
Caterpillar University of Leadership,
    initiatives, 329
CBS, contributions, 225
Cedar Group survey, 10
Celestica, Inc., IBM spin-off, 728
Cendant Mobility, hiring, 663
Center for Advanced Technology (Focus:
    HOPE), 322
Center for Creative Leadership, management
    seminars, 330
Center for Effective Organization, 710
Center for Retirement Research (Boston
    College), retirement income study,
    510
Centrex Electronics Corporation (CEC)
    case study, 757–758
    employee policy, 757
Champion International
    cooperative training program investment,
    322
    manager/employee work cooperation, 729
Change to Win (CTW)
    formation, 629
    goal, 646
Charles Schwab and Company
    individual achievement, 75
    Internet usage, 262
Cheesecake Factory, The (electronic
    surveillance/monitoring), 581
Chemico, human capital readiness assessment,
    69
Chevron, 680f
    sexual harassment lawsuit, 583
Chicago Bears, employee hirings, 107
Chicago Cubs, Caliper test (usage), 274
China Europe International Business School
    (CEIBS), 675
Chrysler, employee murders, 547
CIA. See U.S. Central Intelligence Agency
Cigna Healthcare
    organizational performance, improvement,
    165
    strategic management, 51
Cigna Insurance, expert systems development,
    282
Cigna International Expatriate Benefit, global
    health benefits plan, 687–688
Circle K Corporation, crisis management
    teams, 549
Cisco
    apprenticeship assistance, 322
    employee drug testing, absence, 270

    training VoDs, usage, 327
    virtual learning, 9
Citicorp, peer-review system, 599
Citigroup, 680f
    private drivers, usage, 688
Citigroup/Salomon Smith Barney, FLSA
    violations, 438
City of Atlanta, wage survey, 422
City of Berkeley (California), domestic
    partner benefits, 508
City of Chicago, job evaluation (usage), 420
City of Cincinnati, interactive employee
    benefit system, 490
City of Mesa, job specifications, 150–151
City of Miami, job evaluation (usage), 420
City of Miami Beach, work sample tests
    (usage), 276
City of Phoenix, literacy (skill assessment
    program), 231
City of Portland, affirmative action programs
    (usage), 134
Clemson University, 600
ClientLogic
    case study, 749–752
    labor shortages, 750–751
    nine-step staffing, 749–750
    second-tier recruiting, 750–752
CNA Financial Corp., underwriter
    shortage, 50
Coca-Cola, 680f
    Adventures in Attitudes, 341–342
    chief executives, foreign roots, 678–679
    employee stock option plan, 477
    Fountain Manufacturing Operation, 341
    Four-Deep Training, 341
    international HR staff orientation, 663
Colgate-Palmolive
    augmented skills, identification, 671
    cash balance plan, 513
    core skills, identification, 671
    international transferees, executive/staff
    member visits, 682
Columbia Forest Products, ESOP, 479
Combustion Engineering, compensation
    strategies, 467
Comerica, smoking policies (employee
    involvement), 544
Commission Junction, 177
Communications Workers of America (CWA)
    card check usage, 626
    Representatives by the Communication
    Workers of America, 630
Compaq Computer, ergonomics (cost-
    effectiveness), 168
Computer Technology Industry Association,
    apprenticeship assistance, 322
Conference Board
    alcoholism report, 552
    management seminars, 330

Connor Manufacturing Services, HPWS
(impact), 733
Conoco Phillips, stock options, 467
Continental Airlines, 72
downsizing, 18–19
Coopers & Lybrand
perquisite identification, 470
program development, 330
Cornell University, 167, 577
Corning, Inc., employee alignment, 10
Costco, organizational performance
(improvement), 165
Council for Senior Human Resource
Executives, 728
Countrywide Financial, incentives, 454
Cray, Inc., cooperative training program
investment, 322
Cummings, pension deficit, 514
CWA. *See* Communications Workers of
America

DaimlerChrysler, UAW target, 628
DAK Associates, 759
Dallas Personnel Association, wage/salary
survey, 429
Datamonitor, 751
Dayton-Hudson, BOS (usage), 385–386
Dell Computer
customer service functions, offshoring
(consideration), 374
employee drug testing, 270
federal government contracts, 114
foreign employment, 658, 665
job candidate evaluation, videoconference
technologies (usage), 283
low-cost strategy, 72
Deloitte & Touche
employee self-selection instruments, usage,
671–672
immigrants, importance, 24
Delphi, pension deficit, 514
Delta Air Lines (Delta Airlines)
employment criteria, 231
Northwest Airlines, M&A, 72
pension deficit, 514
Del Taco, formal evaluations (absence), 366
Denny's Restaurants, discrimination lawsuit,
344, 346
Department of Homeland Security, 263
Detroit Fire Department, 549
Deutsche Bank, HR unit development, 730
Dial Corporation
downsizing, 18–19
strength test, usage/lawsuit, 274
Digital Equipment Company, point system
(usage), 424–425

Dillard's Inc. hostile employee propensities,
571
Discovery Communication, wellness center,
550
Disney
Hall of Presidents, 719
M&A. *See* Walt Disney
organizational performance, improvement,
165
unique culture, 58
Dominion Virginia Power, panel interview
(usage), 282
Doubletree Hotels, HPWS (impact), 718
Dow Chemical, 680f
augmented skills, identification, 671
core skills, identification, 671
English fluency, 675
equal employment laws, violation, 101
Six Sigma, 16
Drake Beam Morin
career management study, 215
executives survey, 220
Drug-Free Workplace Act of 1988, 269–270
DuPont
EAP, 551
electronic surveillance/monitoring, 581

Eastman Chemical Company
Tennessee Eastman Division, HPWS
(impact), 733
training certification process, 718
Eastman Kodak, 680f
diversity, commitment, 136
manager (term), replacement, 719
ombudsmen usage, 600
stereotypes, overcoming, 120
eBay, employee services, 514
Eddie Bauer, Balance Day, 514
Edgewater Technology, employee murders,
547
Egan's Clothiers
case study, 763–765
company background, 763
HR issues, 764
HRM history, 763–764
HR outcomes, 764–765
intranet-based HRIS, 764
RSS improvement, 764–765
Eileen Fisher Inc., organizational goals, 731
Electronic Data Systems (EDS)
Career Resource System, 364
employee self-selection instruments, usage,
671–672
performance appraisal, redesign, 364
teleconferencing, usage, 325
Eli Lilly, 680f

U.S. expatriate manager replacement, 665
Emma L. Bowen Foundation, contributions,
225
Enhart, compensation strategies, 467
Enron
corporate scandal, 263
ethics training, importance, 343
Enterprise Rent-a-Car, workplace violence
prevention policies, 547
Equal Employment Opportunity
Commission. *See* U.S. Equal
Employment Opportunity
Commission
ErgoWeb, Inc., 167
Ethics & Compliance Officer Association, 345
Ethics Resource Center, 345
European Trade Union Confederation
(ETUC), 692–693
Execuserve, job applicants (digital recording),
283
Exxon, Mobil (M&A), 72
Exxon-Mobil, pension deficit, 514

Facebook, 7
Fair Trade and Conservation International,
685
Family-friendly organizational climate,
creation, 514
FAO Schwarz, competition identification, 54
FBI. *See* U.S. Federal Bureau of Investigation
Federal Accounting Standards Board (FASB),
stock option income statement
recognition, 470–471
Federal Express (FedEx)
Caliper test, usage, 274
core capabilities, 58
customer appraisals, usage, 374
employee teams, importance, 170
IT usage, 719
speed/delivery, focus, 75
temporary worker categorization, problems,
196–197
training program, evaluation, 334
work environment, establishment, 716
Federal Mediation and Conciliation Service
(FMCS)
creation, 618
interest-based bargaining definition, 637
Federal National Mortgage Association
(FNMA), cooperative training
program investment, 322
Federal Reserve Banks, wage survey data, 422
Federated Department Stores, cash balance
plan, 513
FedEx Kinko, videoconference room rental,
283

Fel-Pro, child care centers, 516
FEMA. *See* U.S. Federal Emergency
    Management Agency
Fireman's Fund, employee murders, 547
First UNUM Life Insurance, cooperative
    training program investment, 322
Focus: HOPE, apprenticeship program, 322
Ford Motor Company, 38
    apprenticeship program, 322
    employee murders, 547
    employee suggestion, impact, 165
    forced ranking system, abandonment,
        377
    handwriting analysis, 269
    HR units, development, 730
    nepotism, 193
    remedial courses, offering, 341
    TQM, 16
    transnational restructuring, 659
    UAW representation, 634
Four Seasons Hotels, hiring/training
    investment, 58
Fox, contributions, 225
Foxwoods Resort and Casino, worker
    unionization, 614
Frito-Lay, competence pay plans, 434
FTD, 6
Fuji-Xerox, employees (number), 668
Fujji, engineer teamwork, 668

Gannett Company, domestic partner benefits,
    508
Gap, The (temporary worker reliance), 62
Garden Fresh, workplace violence prevention
    policies, 547
General Dynamics, federal government
    contracts, 114
General Electric (GE), 13, 38
    career path, 208
    chief learning officers, presence, 308
    discrimination lawsuits, 377
    electronic surveillance/monitoring, 581
    employee commitment, 211
    European access, 658
    forced ranking system, 377
    formal competency assessment program,
        usage, 312
    future, dependence, 71
    handwriting analysis, 269
    information technology investment, 58
    jobholder replacement, identification,
        202
    mentors, supply, 225
    Six Sigma, 16
    strategic management, 51
    teamwork, necessity, 668

General Mills
    9-box grid (usage), 203
    One Stop centers, 323
General Motors
    Career Development Guide, 215
    career development guide, preparation, 206
    jobs elimination, 77
    joint venture, 661
    strategic objectives, 368
    teammate selection, 717
    UAW representation, 634
General Physics Corporation, apprenticeship
    program, 322
Genpact, storefront setup, 198
Gerber Products, employee behavior rules, 589
Gillette, M&A. *See* Procter & Gamble
Glaxo Pharmaceuticals, salary plus bonus
    plans, 465
GlaxoSmithKline, outsourcing, 19
GoDaddy, interactive employee benefit
    system, 490
Golden State Container, government surveys
    (usage), 422
Goldman Sachs (compensation), 469
Goodyear
    discipline definition, 590
    forced ranking system, abandonment, 377
Google
    HPWS, success, 732
    reputation, hipness, 773
    work environment, 150
Gourmet Pizza, The (cross-training), 342
Granite Rock, HPWS (impact), 733

Hallmark, smoking policies (employee
    involvement), 544
Harley-Davidson
    commitment, 724
    continuous improvement/process
        reengineering, 162
    knowledge development, 714
Harvard Business School, 12, 194
Harvard University School of Public Health,
    depression study, 552
Heidrick & Struggles
    candidate search, 193
    recruitment usage, 667
Herman Miller, ombudsmen usage, 600
Hewitt Associates, 31, 772
    perquisite identification, 470
    Web information, 491
Hewlett-Packard, 13
    CEO replacement, 190
    employee
        drug testing, 270
        teams, importance, 170

ethics program/training, 344
literacy, skill assessment program, 231
mentoring program, 217
performance appraisal information, usage,
    314
Hilton Hotels
    affirmative action programs, usage, 134
    videoconferencing offers, 282–283
    worker unionization, 614
Hire Disability Solutions, 229
HireDiversity (web site), 226
Holsum Bakery, workplace smoking policy
    (example), 543
Home Depot
    AARP-sponsored program, 25
    equal employment laws, violation, 101
    Job Preference Program, 262
    online application system, implementation,
        262
    organizational performance, improvement,
        165
    share price, increase, 194
    Special Project Support Teams (SPST), 165
Honda, European access, 658
Honeywell
    all-salaried workforce, 718
    codes of conduct, creation, 666
    competence pay plans, 434
    employee payment, 718
    One Stop centers, 323
    Six Sigma, 16
Hotel Employees and Restaurant Employees
    (HERE), restructuring, 646
Hot Jobs (Yahoo), job sharing programs, 191
HSBC, manager evaluation, 15
Human Resource Planning Society (HRPS),
    5, 13
Hunter Group, candidate search, 193

IBM, 4
    application hosting, 10
    case study, 771–773
    Celestica, spin-off, 728
    chief learning officers, presence, 308
    community-based referral agencies, 517
    disabled, mentoring/internships, 229
    family leave, offering, 772
    FLSA violations, 438
    global team, usage, 172
    information technology investment, 58
    personal computer market entry, 71
    reputation, hipness (absence), 773
    strategic management, 51
    virtual learning, 9
    women, impact, 221
    women/employer programs, 224

Idaho State University, pay strategy (linkage), 413

Ingersoll-Rand, China (joint venture), 665

Inroads, Inc. (internship organization), 225

Intel, 13, 38
    affirmative action programs, usage, 134
    federal government contracts, 114
    hardware/operating system manufacture, 71
    mentoring program, 217
    360-degree system, establishment, 375

International Association of Machinists, 628

International business, cultural environment, 662f

International Confederation of Free Trade Unions (ICFTU), 692–693

International Labor Organization (ILO), 693

International Paper, management/employee work cooperation, 729

International Reading Association, 339

Isuzu, customer appraisals (usage), 374

J. Walter Thompson, fitness/health program, 550

JetBlue Airways
    carrier threat, 55
    employee behavior rules, 589
    workplace violence prevention policies, 547

Job Exchange, job location, 196

Johnson & Johnson, ombudsmen usage, 600

Johnson Wax, point system (usage), 424–425

J.P. Morgan, elder care consortium, 517

Kaiser Permanente, job sharing programs, 176

KB Toys, competition identification, 54

Keil Fiduciary Strategies, 759

Kelly Services
    private employment agency, 196
    virtual learning, 9

Kinship systems, 661

KLM Royal Dutch Airlines, on-the-job training (usage), 321

Korn/Ferry International
    candidate search, 193
    cultural study, 673
    outsourcing reliance, 664

KPMG, women/employer programs, 224

Kraft Foods, work redesign, 165

Landmark Woodcraft, ergonomic education, 545

Lawson Software, calibration (usage), 368–369

Lazarus Department Stores, orientation program (reduction), 339

Lehman Brothers Holding (compensation), 469

Lenovo, PC product sale, 71

Levi Strauss
    affirmative action programs, usage, 134
    codes of conduct, creation, 666
    domestic partner benefits, 508
    global manager, skill category identification, 669
    informal feedback/coaching sessions, 395
    job evaluation, usage, 420

Liberty Mutual, workplace safety study, 528

Life Insurance Agency Management Association, 262

Lincoln Electric Company, profit sharing plan, 476

Lincoln National, homework assistance help line, 514

Linens 'n Things, incentives, 454

Linked-In, 7

L.L. Bean
    benchmarking, 79
    downsizing, 18–19
    TQM, 17

Lockheed Martin (Lockheed-Martin)
    equal employment laws, violation, 101
    homosexual support groups, 120
    Operation Enterprise, 225
    pension deficit, 514

Los Angeles Police Department, EAP, 515

Lotus Development Company, job sharing programs, 176

LucasFilm, employee teams (importance), 170

Lucent Technologies
    software rollout, 663
    stereotypes, overcoming, 120

Macy's
    employee selection, 199
    orientation program, reduction, 339
    teammate selection, 717

Manitoba Telecom Services, union member involvement, 727–728

Manpower, Inc., 9
    Borderless Workforce Survey, 666
    private employment agency, 196
    virtual learning, 9

Manpower Training and Development Center, 9

Marcel Dekker, work hours, 174

Marks & Spencer, temporary worker reliance, 62

Marriot Hotels, smoking policies, employee involvement, 544

Marriott International
    computer program, usage, 330
    immigrants, importance, 24
    promotion-from-within policies, 201
    total compensation, concern, 189

Mars, M&A. See Wrigley's

Marsh & McLennan, 759

Massachusetts Pension Reserves Investment Management Board, 759

Matsushita, world market treatment, 659

Mayo Clinic, The (smoking estimate), 542–543

McDonald's
    CEO replacement, 190
    core capabilities, 58
    job performance form, usage, 260

McDonnell Douglas, test, 123–124

McGraw-Edison, sales incentive plans, 463

McKinsey, hiring/training investment, 58

Medical Plastics Laboratory, employee payments, 103

Medical World Communications, mail fraud charges, 574

Medzilla, recruitment site, 191

Mellon Financial Human Resources and Investor Solutions, work/life survey, 515

Mercer & Associates, candidate search, 193

Mercer Consulting, outsourcing reliance, 663–664

Mercer Performance, Measurement, and Rewards (consulting), 414

Merck
    child care centers, 516
    HR importance, 38–39
    HR system, redesign, 9
    HR units, development, 730
    individual selection, importance, 255
    smoking policies, employee involvement, 544
    staffing management system, 10

Merrill Lynch (compensation), 469

Mervyn's, electronic surveillance/monitoring, 581

Mesa Community College, pay strategy (linkage), 413

MetLife, 150
    point system, usage, 424–425

Michigan State Employees Association, 628

Microsoft Corporation
    apprenticeship assistance, 322
    career paths, employee design, 58
    hardware/operating system manufacture, 71
    hiring/training investment, 58
    mentoring program, 217
    pay system efficiency, increase, 412
    stereotypes, overcoming, 120
    temporary worker categorization, problems, 196–197

Mighty Media, 219
Miller Brewing Company, 6
Mitre, employee services, 514
Mitsubishi Motor Manufacturing of America,
    equal employment laws (violation),
    101
Mobil, M&A. *See* Exxon
Monsanto
    all-salaried workforce, 718
    employee behavior, strengthening, 319
    repatriation program, 682
Monster (web site)
    Career Advice Center, 220
        example, 262
    employee information, 30
    recruitment, 191
Monster Worldwide, 229
Morgan Stanley, equal employment laws
    (violation), 101
Motorola
    crisis management teams, 549
    federal government contracts, 114
    HPWS
        creation, 730
        impact, 718
    jobs elimination, 77
    literacy, skill assessment program, 231
    MRO, usage, 580
    noncomputer-based game, development,
        330
    People, 674
    performance appraisals, modification,
        363
    Six Sigma, 16
    TQM, 16
Motorola University, 16
My Space, 7

N

Nahan Printing, Inc., work hours, 174
NASDAQ, executive pay packages, 470
National Alliance for Caregiving, elderly
    parental care, 516
National Association of Professional
    Background Screeners, screening
    certification, 263
National Association of Professional
    Employer Organizations (NAPEO),
    197
National Black MBA Association, 226
National Cancer Institute, smoking estimate,
    542–543
National Career Centers, Radisson/Hilton
    videoconferencing offers, 282–283
National Center for Employee Ownership
    ESOP estimates, 479
    stock option estimates, 478

National City Corporation, 282
National Council for Alcoholism and
    Drug Dependency, alcoholism report,
    553
National Council on Disability (NCD) study,
    111
National Education Association
    employee association, 628
    public sector representation, 631
National Football League, 107
National Institute for Literacy, 231
National Institute for Occupational Safety
    and Health (NIOSH), 530
    terrorism prevention recommendations,
        548–549
    workplace violence definition, 546
National Institute of Mental Health,
    depression estimate, 552
National Labor Relations Board (NLRB),
    617–618
    bargaining, division, 635–636
    creation, 617
    election poster, 627
    preelection hearing, 626
    representation election, 622, 625–626
    representation procedure, 619
    secret ballot election, 622
    Weingarten ruling, 593
National Railway Adjustment Board,
    grievances/arbitration, 616
National Safety Council, safety comparison,
    533–534
National Society of Professional Engineers,
    wage/salary survey, 429
National Wellness Institute, wellness
    literature, 550
Navistar International, employee murders,
    547
NBC
    contributions, 225
    GE ownership, 71
NEC, world market treatment, 659
Neiman Marcus
    fashion/customer service, commitment, 75
    incentives, 454
Netflix, 772
    reputation, hipness, 773
Netscape Communications, organizational
    teams (introduction), 168
Newell Corporation
    case study, 774–775
    downsizing, necessity, 774–775
New York Mets, EAP, 515
New York Stock Exchange, executive pay
    packages, 470
Nike
    employee stock option plan, 477
    expert systems development, 282
    global social responsibility, 685

    job candidate evaluation, videoconference
        technologies (usage), 283
    job exportation, labor accusations, 645
Nokia
    HPWS division, popularity, 730
    people, selection, 172–173
Nordstrom's
    bottom line, improvement, 58
    employee handbook rule, 75
    promotion-from-within policies, 201
Nortel Networks
    competence pay plans, 434
    employee payment, 718
    labor relations, accountability (transfer), 728
Northrop-Grumman, peer-review system, 599
Northside Workforce Center, benefits
    application, 216
Northwest Airlines
    M&A. *See* Delta
    One Stop centers, 323
    wage survey, 422
Novations/J. Howard & Associates, diversity
    survey, 344
Nucor Steel
    layoff policies, absence, 18
    profit sharing plan, 712
    promotion-from-within policies, 201

O

Oakland A's, 74
O.C. Tanner, awards/recognition, 463
Occidental Petroleum (compensation), 469
Occupational Safety and Health
    Administration (OSHA), injuries/
    illnesses statistics, 528
Ocean Spray, plant progress (employee
    awareness), 714
Office and Professional Employees
    International Union, 628
Office of Disability Employment (U.S.
    Department of Labor), 228
Office of Research and Evaluation, case study,
    766–769
Old Home Foods, employee involvement, 713
Olsten Staffing Services, private employment
    agency, 196
One Stop centers, 323
One Valley Bank, HPWS (impact), 733
Operation Enterprise, 225
Oracle-PeopleSoft, HR information systems,
    66
Organizational Renaissance, 172
Organizing Institute (AFL-CIO), 624
Ovania Chemical
    abilities/tasks, 755f
    candidates, primary pool, 756f
    case study, 752–755

company background, 752
job analysis, 753
new position analysis, 753
performance dimensions, 754f
selection process, anticipation, 753, 755
system analyzer, 752–755

Pace University, ombudsmen usage, 600
Pace Worldwide, productivity increase, 343
PageNet, continuous improvement/process
　　reengineering, 162
Paradise Valley Unified School District of
　　Phoenix, sexual harassment definition,
　　117
Parker Services, interactive employee benefit
　　system, 490
Partnership for Elder Care (consortium), 516
Payless ShoeSource, paper-and-pencil honesty
　　test (usage), 267
Peace Corps, The (sensitivity training), 675
Pension Benefit Guaranty Corporation
　　(PBGC), creation, 514
PeopleSoft, application hosting, 10
Pepsi-Cola General Bottlers, Inc. (PepsiCo),
　　680f
　　sexual harassment lawsuit, 131
　　U.S. expatriate manager replacement, 665
Performance Program Inc. (Overseas
　　Assignment Inventory), 672
Pettit and Martin, employee murders, 547
Philip Morris USA
　　elder care consortium, 517
　　panel interview, usage, 282
Pic 'n' Pay Shoe Stores, computerized
　　interview (creation), 282
Pierce College, remedial courses (offering),
　　341
Pinkerton Security, expert systems
　　development, 282
Pitney Bowes, AARP-sponsored program, 25
Plum Creek Timber Company, merger, 414
Polaroid, peer-review system, 599
Pratt and Whitney, 747
　　ergonomics, cost-effectiveness, 168
　　operation, 748
Presagis, computer software development, 331
Prescient InfoTech, reference contact, 264
Preventive Health Care, compensation
　　strategy, 419
　　comparison, 421
PriceWaterhouseCoopers, 79
PriceWaterhouseCoopers International Ltd.,
　　688
Princeton University, 346
Principal Financial Group, employee
　　flexibility, 312

Procter & Gamble (P&G), 12, 194
　　European access, 658
　　Gillette, M&A, 72
　　manager evaluation, 15
　　outsourcing, 19
　　performance appraisals, modification, 363
　　rival lawsuit, 202
Progress Energy, wage survey, 422
Prudential Financial, point system (usage),
　　424–425
Prudential Securities, health benefits, 492
Putnam Investments
　　accusations, settlement, 760
　　case study, 758–762
　　compensation, approach (change), 761–762
　　compliance, response, 760
　　culture, reshaping, 760–761
　　performance pressure, 762
　　scandal, 759–760

Quaker Oats Company
　　employee stock option plan, 477
　　women/employer programs, 224
Quiznos, Saudi Arabia expansion, 658
Qwest, flextime (usage), 176

Radio Shack, CEO resignation, 260
Radisson, videoconferencing offers, 282–283
Raytheon, homosexual support groups, 120
Reebok International, HPWS (impact), 718
Renault, unions (pressure), 692
Ripe Tomato, managerial responsibility, 64
Rituals, accommodation, 661
Ritz-Carlton
　　employee, training, 306
　　quality/luxury commitment, 74
　　workplace violence prevention policies, 547
Robert Half International
　　formal orientation programs, effectiveness,
　　　338
Robert Half International, global recruiting, 198
Rockefeller Foundation, nepotism, 193
Rockwell, ombudsmen usage, 600
Roffey Park survey, 12
Rolls-Royce, foreign employment, 665–666
Royal Dutch Shell, core capabilities, 58

Saint Barnabas Health Care Systems, federal
　　fines, 574
Sally Industries, artisan employment, 719

Salt River Project, substance abuse policy
　　(example), 554–556
San Francisco 49ers, intolerance incidents,
　　346
San Francisco State University, 747
SAP, HR information systems, 66
Sara Lee
　　employee stock option plan, 477
　　minority managers, increase, 225
Saratoga Institute, The, 79
SAS, formal evaluations (absence), 366
SAS International, mentor assignation, 665
Saturn Motors
　　mission, 719
　　teammate selection, 717
S.C. Johnson and Sons, stereotypes
　　(overcoming), 120
Scanlon Leadership Network, 474
Scheels All Sports
　　ESOP, 479
Schering-Plough, elder care referrals,
　　516–517
Schindler Elevator Corporation, prehire
　　training program, 717
Sears
　　career development paths, design, 208
　　compensation strategies, 467
　　competencies, measurement, 208
　　positive employee attitudes, 57
　　rating process, subjective error reduction,
　　　378
Sears Craftsman, incentives, 454
Second Life, 192
Sentry Insurance Company, flextime
　　advantages, 176
Service Employees International Union, card
　　check usage, 626
Shell, transnational restructuring, 659
Shell Canada, employee payment, 718
Sheraton Hotels, worker unionization, 614
Sherwin-Williams, competence pay plans, 434
Siemens, foreign hiring (desire), 666
Signature Worldwide, 198
Silicon Graphics, domestic partner benefits, 508
SimuLearn, software development, 332
6FigureJobs, recruitment site, 191
Smith and Wesson, literacy (skill assessment
　　program), 231
Snecma, Grandes Ecoles hiring, 667
Snelling Personnel Services, private
　　employment agency, 196
Sociètè Gènèrale, employee disengagement
　　(impact), 713
Society for Human Resource Management
　　(SHRM), 5, 195
　　annual conferences, 225
　　employee cost reduction report, 197
　　Employee Trust and Organizational Loyalty
　　　study, 602

hiring cost, study, 254
Internet/e-mail usage, monitoring survey, 582–583
wage/salary survey, 429
Solar Turbines, spouse/children assessment, 671
Solectron Corporation, HPWS implementation, 725
Sony Computer, FLSA violations, 438
Southern California Edison, stereotypes (overcoming), 120
Southwest Airlines, 38
  carrier threat, 55
  cost reductions, 21
  employee orientation, importance, 338
  flight simulator, usage, 326
  HPWS, success, 732
  individual selection, importance, 255
  job evaluation, usage, 420
  layoffs, absence, 18
  low-cost strategy, 72
  mentoring program, 217
  smoking policies, employee involvement, 544
  unique culture, 58
Sports Authority, units (reduction), 150
SpringHill Greenhouses, 6
Sprint, job sharing programs, 176
Standard & Poor's 500 (S&P500) stock index, competitive benchmarking (usage), 466
Stanford University, domestic partner benefits, 508
Stanley Works, health/safety problem reduction, 538
Staples, employee behavior rules, 589
Starbucks, 38
  codes of conduct, creation, 666
  core values, 52
  corporate citizenship, importance, 685
  employee decision-making, 75
  employee stock option plan, 477
  equal employment laws, violation, 101
  forced ranking system usage, counterproductivity, 377
  individual selection, importance, 255
  key metrics, identification, 81
  unique culture, 58
State Farm Insurance, mentoring programs, 217
Stewart Warner, EAP, 551
Sun Microsystems, employee drug testing (absence), 270
SunTrust Banks, women/employer programs, 224
Syntex, child care centers, 516

T

Taco Bell, starting wages (increase), 413
Taleo, 66
Target
  competition identification, 54
  employee behavior, strengthening, 319
Teamsters, card check usage, 626
Teleflora, 6
Teradyne, performance appraisal information (usage), 314
Texas Instruments
  High Performance Organization Development, 730
  individual selection, importance, 255
  manager evaluation, 15
Thinking Tools, program development, 330
3M, 680f
  CEO replacement, 190
  ergonomics, cost-effectiveness, 168
  motion, importance, 731
  MRO, usage, 580
  One Stop centers, 323
  strategic objectives, 368
Thrivent Financial for Lutherans, team incentives, 472
TIAA-CREF, 467
Timber Company, The (merger), 414
Time Warner Cable, e-learning simulation (employee usage), 327
Timex, lump sum merit program, 462
TMP, online career fair, 192
Towers Perrin, 412
Toyota
  cost reductions, 21
  sexual harassment charges, 100
  U.S. dominance, 658
Toys "R" Us, competition identification, 54
TransAmerica, point system (usage), 424–425
Transport Workers Union (TWU), casino dealers organizing, 614
Trek Bicycles, employee teams (importance), 170
Tribune Co., The, ESOP, 479
TriHealth System, cross-training (implementation), 717
TriStar Performance, compensation strategy, 419
  comparison, 421
TRW, Scanlon Plan, 474
Tucker International (International Mobility Assessment test), 672
Turner Brothers Trucking, peer-review system, 599
Tyco, corporate scandal, 263

U

Under Armour, incentives, 454
Unilever
  compensation arrangements, 685
  transnational restructuring, 659
Union of Needletrades, Industrial and Textile Employees, The (UNITE)
  lobbying, 631
  restructuring, 646
United Airlines, MRO (usage), 580
United Association of Plumbers and Pipefitters, 628
United Automobile Workers (UAW), 628
  card check usage, 626
  casino dealer organizing, 614
  lobbying, 631
United Brotherhood of Carpenters, 628
United Food and Commercial Workers International Union
  authorization card, 623
  strike, 638
United Parcel Service (UPS)
  bottom line, improvement, 58
  FLSA violations, 438
United Technologies Corporation (UTC), 38
  case study, 745–748
  culture, 746–747
  Employee Scholars Program (ESP), investment, 745–746
  remedial courses, offering, 231
  results, tracking, 747–748
  subsidiaries, 745
University of California at San Francisco, 543
University of Georgia, pay strategy (linkage), 413
University of Michigan, 15
University of Texas M.D. Anderson Cancer Center, employee merit raise eligibility, 455
U.S. Air Force
  job knowledge tests, 276
  task inventory analysis, 157
  work samples, usage, 276–277
U.S. Army
  Alpha/Beta Tests, 271
  cognitive ability tests, predictive ability, 273
  equal employment laws, violation, 101
  job knowledge tests, 276
U.S. Census Bureau, married couple data, 492
U.S. Central Intelligence Agency (CIA), handwriting analysis, 269
U.S. Chamber of Commerce
  employee benefit report, 490
  employee benefits survey (2007), 497–498
  employee theft estimate, 581–582

U.S. Chemical Safety Board (CSB), 537
U.S. Department of Defense, employee drug-
    free status, 553–554
U.S. Department of Health and Human
    Services (USDHHS), 530
U.S. Department of Labor
    Bureau of Apprenticeship and Training
        (BAT), 322
    wage survey data, 422
    Working Partners for Alcohol and Drug-
        Free Workplace, creation, 554
U.S. Department of Transportation
    drug use rule, 554
    illegal drug use testing, 269
U.S. Employment and Training
    Administration (ETA), 195
U.S. Equal Employment Opportunity
    Commission, 588
U.S. Federal Bureau of Investigation (FBI),
    Integrated Case Scenario method
    (usage), 330
U.S. Federal Emergency Management Agency
    (FEMA), games/simulations (usage),
    330–331
U.S. Marines, job knowledge tests, 276
U.S. Merit Systems Protection Board report, 278
U.S. Navy, job knowledge tests, 276
U.S. Postal Service (USPS)
    employee murders, 547
    ergonomics, cost-effectiveness, 168
U.S. Sugar, ESOP, 479
USAA, EAP, 515

Valero Energy Corporation
    layoff policies, absence, 18
    SWOT analysis, 70
Verizon
    cash balance plan, 513
    CWA strike, 639
Vets4Hire, recruitment site, 191
Viacom, domestic partner benefits, 508
Virgin Atlantic Airways, carrier threat, 55
Vision Track Golf Corporation, 124
Visteon Corporation, 70
Volkswagen, German language examinations,
    675

Walgreens, EEOC lawsuit, 100
Wal-Mart
    ADA claim/lawsuit, 269
    chief learning officers, presence, 308

competition identification, 54
employee behavior rules, 589
equal employment laws, violation, 101
hiring questionnaire, ADA violations,
    269
lawsuit, 202
low-cost strategy, 72
nondiscrimination policy, 120
organizational performance, improvement,
    165
self-audits, 223
Walt Disney, ABC (M&A), 72
Warner Brothers, domestic partner benefits,
    508
Washington State Developmental Disabilities
    Council, 230
Watermark Credit Union, 474
Watson Wyatt Worldwide
    compensation survey, 685
    employee study, 362
    spot bonuses, 461
    study, 18
    wellness culture, 551
Wells Fargo Bank, interactive employee
    benefit system, 490
Westinghouse
    job exportation, labor accusations, 645
    lump sum merit program, 462
Westin Hotels, worker unionization, 614
Weyerhaeuser Company
    BOS, usage, 385–386
    employee suggestions, usage, 718
    interest-based negotiation, 726
    rating process, subjective error reduction,
        378
    Scanlon Plan, 474
    senior management/labor representatives,
        joint operations committee, 727
    structured interviewing process, usage,
        278
    teammate selection, 717
Whirlpool
    augmented skills, identification, 671
    core skills, identification, 671
    strategic objectives, 368
Whole Foods
    employee suggestions, usage, 718
    profit per labor hour, calculation,
        714–715
    promotion-from-within policies, 201
Wikipedia, usage, 326
Williams-Sonoma, employee selection, 199
W.L. Gore and Associates, ESOP, 479
Women in Technology International (WITI),
    219
Wonderlic Inc., testing programs
    (improvement), 271

Woodsmith Corporation, government surveys
    (usage), 422
Workforce Recruitment Program for College
    Students with Disabilities (WRP),
    229
Workstream, Inc. (performance management
    software company), 374–375
WorldatWork, 415
    perquisite identification, 470
    salary increase report, 442
    2007/2008 salary budget survey, 454
WorldCom, corporate scandal, 263
World Health Organization (WHO),
    depression study, 552
W.P. Carey School of Business (Arizona
    State University), 165
Wrigley's, Mars (M&A), 72
Wynn's, casino dealer organizing, 614

Xerox Corporation
    employee murders, 547
    engineer teamwork, 668
    health brochure, 550
    information access, 79
    job exportation, labor accusations, 645
    Managing for Results, 721
    performance appraisals, modification, 363
    planning process, 721
    team, implementation problems, 728–729
    TQM, 16
    trainees, trainer observation, 335
    workforce problem, 27–28

Yahoo
    employee stock option plan, 477
    job sharing programs, 191

Zurich, diversity/sexual harassment courses,
    666

SUBJECT INDEX

A

Abilities/tasks, 755f
Absenteeism, disruptive behavior, 267
Accidents, investigating/recording, 539
Accrued benefits, guarantee, 514
Achievement tests, 272, 778
Acquired immune deficiency syndrome
    (AIDS), 110, 545–546
Action learning, advantage, 329
Action plans, establishment, 395
Active listener, input, 284
Active listening, usage, 637
Active participation, desirability, 330
Active practice, usage, 317
ADA. *See* Americans with Disabilities Act
    of 1990
Adair v. United States, 572
Adarand Constructors v. Peña, 135–136
ADR. *See* Alternative dispute resolution
Adventures in Attitudes (Coca-Cola),
    341–342
Adversarial negotiations, 637
Adverse action, 132
    notice, providing, 266–267
Adverse impact, 122, 778
Adverse rejection rate, 122–123
Advertisements, applicant attraction,
    190–191
Advice, counsel (relationship), 32
Affidavit of Domestic Partnership, 507–508
Affirmative action, 131–136, 778
    definition, 131
    diversity management, 135–136
    employment area, response (slowness), 225
    future, 136
    policies, development. *See* Formal EEO/
        affirmative action policies
    programs
        development steps, 134
        establishment, 131–135
        OFCCP requirements, 131, 133–134
Age Discrimination in Employment Act of
    1967 (ADEA), 105f, 108, 123, 126,
    503
    impact, 577
Agreeableness, 274
    sample, 275f
AIRS Oxygen 6.0 (software), 191
Albemarle Paper Company v. Moody, 369
Alcoholism, 552–553
    confrontation, 553
    identification, 553

Alignment, ensuring, 75
All About OSHA (OSHA Publication), 533
Alliance partners, 61
Alliances
    trust, fragility, 726–727
    usage, 533
All-salaried workforce, 718
Alpha Test, 271
Alternative dispute resolution (ADR),
    598–601, 778
    definition, 598
"America Needs a Raise" (AFL-CIO), 646
American Association of Retired Persons
    (AARP), employee assistance, 25
Americans with Disabilities Act of 1990
    (ADA), 105f, 109–111
    employee medical history, containment,
        585
    employer compliance, 579–580
    impact, 577. *See also* Job analysis
    recognition, 228
    suggestion. *See* Workplace
America's Literacy Directory (ALD), 231
Analytic skills, importance, 330
Angry employee, calming, 550f
Annual salary budgets, size, 458
Anonymity, assurance, 375
Anti-Injunction Act. *See* Norris-LaGuardia
    Act of 1932
Antiretaliation policy, implementation, 577
Appearance, importance, 281
Applicants
    information, summarizing, 288
    testing, 257
    written consent, supply, 266
Applications. *See* Online applications;
        Unsolicited applications/résumés
    arrests/criminal convictions, information
        (usage), 261
    background check, manual process, 263
    date, information (usage), 260
    disabilities, information (usage), 261
    educational background, information
        (usage), 261
    EEOC/at-will statements, information
        (usage), 261
    experience, information (usage), 261
    forms, 260–261
        EEOC/court questions, 260
    legal protection, 266
    lying, CareerBuilder survey, 260
    national origin, information (usage), 261
    questions, clarity (problem), 260
    references, information (usage), 261

Appraisal. *See* Performance appraisal
Appraisal Interview, The (Maier), 391–392
Apprentices, hiring, 717
Apprenticeships, 667
    program registration, 322
    training, 322, 778
        wage increases, 322
Aptitude tests, 272, 778
Arbitration, 601. *See also* Grievance
        arbitration; Interest arbitration;
        Rights arbitration
    award, 644–645
        components, 644
    decision, 643
        rendering, 644
    hearing, 643–644
Arbitrator, 639, 778
    case decision, factors, 644
    opinion, 644
    responsibility, 644
Area offices, service, 125
Area wage rates, 422
Asia-Pacific Economic Cooperation (APEC),
    6, 660
Assembly line production, shift, 343
Assessment centers, 778
    usage, 204
Assistance programs, addition, 686
Association of Southeast Asian Nations
    (ASEAN), 661
Associations, management seminars,
    329–330
Attendance problems, 589f
Attitudes
    ability, 281
    auditing, 57
    invisible barrier, 223
Audiovisual methods, usage, 325–326
Augmented attributes, assessment, 672
Augmented skills, 778
    assessment, 672
    identification, 671
Authorization card, 622, 778
    example, 623
Autonomous work groups, 171
Autonomy, 164

B

Baby boomers, retirement, 28
    impact, 510
    problems, 340
Back injuries, BLS report, 528

Background checks, 263–267
  types, 264f
Balance Day (Eddie Bauer), 514
Balance sheet approach, 686, 778
Balanced Scorecard (BSC), 81, 778
  cascading, 389
  measures, attachment, 388
  objectives, translation, 388
  performance feedback, providing, 389
  strategy reassessment, 390
  usage, 388–390
Baldrige National Quality Award.
        See Malcolm Baldrige National
        Quality Award
Bargaining. *See* Good faith bargaining;
        Interest-based bargaining
  categories, 636–637
  data, gathering, 634
  deadlocks, resolution, 639
  illegal subjects, 637
  mandatory subject, 636
  permissive subjects, 636
  power, 637–639, 778
  process, 632–639. *See also* Collective
        bargaining
  representatives, number, 633–634
  strategies/tactics, development,
        634–635
  strategy, usage, 639
  unit, 625, 778
  zone, 635, 778
    negotiation, impact, 626f
BARS. *See* Behaviorally anchored rating scale
Base pay, calculation, 686
Base salaries. *See* Executives
BDI. *See* Behavioral description interview
Beautyism, influence (avoidance), 285
Behavior change
  absence, 334–335
  importance, 394
Behavior dynamics, 342f
Behavior modeling, 332, 778
Behavior modification, 318–319, 778
Behavior observation scale (BOS), 384–386,
        778
  value, 385–386
Behavioral checklist method, 384
Behavioral competencies, assessment, 161
Behavioral concerns, 162–166
Behavioral description interview (BDI), 279,
        778
Behavioral interviews, 204
Behavioral methods, 383–386
Behavioral profiles, identification, 318–319
Behaviorally anchored rating scale (BARS),
        384, 778
  development, 384
  example, 385
Beliefs, auditing, 57

Benchmarking, 79, 778
  four-step process (Deming), 337
  usage, 336–338. *See also* Competitive
        benchmarking
Benefits. *See* Employee benefits
  planning. *See* Strategic benefits planning
  plans. *See* Flexible benefits plans
Bennett Mechanical Comprehension Test,
        259, 273
Best practices, 715
Beta Test, 271
Biases
  identification/quantification, 376
  recognition, 285
Biodata, 262
Biographical information blanks (BIBs),
        262–263
    Life Insurance Agency Management
        Association construction/validation,
        262
  questions, sample, 263
Blended learning, 324, 778
Blogs, usage, 325–326
Blood test, submission, 579
Body art/piercing, 586–587
Bona fide occupational qualification (BFOQ),
        106–107, 778
Bonuses, 460–461, 779. *See also* Spot bonus
  plans. *See* Salary plus bonus plans
Borderless Workforce Survey (Manpower),
        666
BOS. *See* Behavior observation scale
Boundaryless career
  consideration, 211–212
  success, 212
Boycott, 638
Brain drain, 510
Brainstorming, usage, 637
Brito v. Zia, 369
Broadband Internet connection, usage, 177
Broadbanding, usage, 435
Broad-based stock option plans, 478
BSC. *See* Balanced Scorecard
Buckley Amendment, The. *See* Family
        Education Rights and Privacy Act
Burnout, 558, 779
Business
  case, building, 724–725
  clients, incentive awards, 462
  managers, HR planning/strategy
        questions, 64
  mastery, 33
  necessity, 107, 779
  needs, communication, 725
  strategy, 72–75
  unionism, 631, 779
Business Acumen, computer program
        (Marriott development), 330
Business Week, CEO study, 466

C

Cafeteria plans. *See* Flexible benefits plans
Calibration, 368–369, 779
California Psychological Inventory (CPI), 274
  personality facts/sample items, 275f
Campuses, applicant recruitment, 194
Candidates
  augmented skills/attributes, assessment,
        672–673
  core skills, assessment, 672
  pool, creation, 672
  primary pool, 756f
Can-do factors, 288. *See also* Selection
Capabilities, 58. *See also* Core capabilities;
        Culture, capabilities, and composition
Capital investment, increase, 421
Card checks, 626
Career. *See* Early career; Late career;
        Midcareer
  advancement, barriers, 215
  consideration. *See* Boundaryless career
  counseling, 216, 779
  development
    assessment/tracking, 678–680
    personnel file, impact, 584
    repatriation programs, absence, 681
  human capital profiles, 212f
  internal barriers, 215
  move, changes, 211
  networking, 219–220, 779
  organizational entry, 213f
  paths, 208, 779
  planning
    workbooks, 215
    workshops, 215–216
  plateau, 214, 779
    questions, 214f
  progressions, opportunities. *See* Planned
        career progressions
  self-management training, 220
  stages, tracking, 212–214
Career Advice (Monster), 262
Career development
  climate, establishment, 206
  initiatives, 214–220
    institution, 205f
  possibilities, recognition, 209–211
  stages, 213f
  success, 206
Career Development Guide (GM), 215
Career management, 205–220
  HR role, 205f
  practices, success (Drake Beam Morin
        ranking), 215
Career opportunities/requirements,
        identification, 207–214
  example, 205f

Career Resource System (EDS), 364
Career Tracker, usage, 10
Carpal tunnel syndrome, 544
Case studies
    classroom learning usage, 330
    usage, rules, 331f
Cash balance pension plans, 513
Cash bonuses. *See* Professional employees
CDHPs. *See* Consumer-driven health plans
Cellular technology, usage, 55
Central tendency, error, 377, 781
Chain of command, list, 339
Chain-of-custody documentation, 580
Change
    initiative, 12
    management, 12–13
    mastery, 34
    types, 12
Change, business case (building), 724–725
Changing lifestyles, culture, 120
Charge form, 128, 779
Chemical hazards, 540, 542
Chicago Tribune, The (newsroom training),
    225
Chief ethics officers, 343, 779
    appointment, 32
Chief Executive Officers (CEOs)
    career path, 210
    composition, 678, 680
    internal recruitment, 194
Chief learning officers, 308–309, 779
Child care, 516–517
Child labor provisions, 440
China, economy, 661
Circuit City Stores, Inc. v. Adams, 598, 601
Civil Rights Act of 1964, 103, 105–107
    coverage. *See* Organizations
    passage, 102, 224–225
    protection. *See* Sex
    Title VII, 105f
        impact, 577
        prohibitions, 107
        Section 703(a), 106
Civil Rights Act of 1991, 112
    Section 118, 598
Civil Service Reform Act of 1978, 632
Civil service systems, existence. *See* Public civil
    service systems
Classroom instruction, 324
Coaching, 328
    company usage, 366
COBRA. *See* Consolidated Omnibus Budget
    Reconciliation Act of 1986
Codetermination, 693, 779
Cognitive ability tests, 272–273
    development/measurement, 273
COLA. *See* Cost-of-living adjustment
Collective bargaining, 423
    international operation, 691–692

management power, 637, 638–639
    process, 632–633, 779
        flowchart, 633f
    representatives, notice, 578
    union power, 637–638
Colorado Civil Rights Commission, 116
Combined salary/commission plan, 465, 779
Commission plan. *See* Straight commission
    plan
Commitment, formalization. *See* Labor
Communication
    ability, 280
    effectiveness, 174
Communications plan, establishment,
    725–726
Communist Party, unions, 691
Communities of practice, 325
    examples, 326f
Comp Analyst, 429
Companies
    cost reduction, SHRM report, 197
    drug testing, U.S. Ninth Circuit of Court
        Appeals ruling, 270
    entrants, 55
    legal obligations. *See* Homosexuals
    performance, evaluation/assessment
        issues, 79
    profits, executive evaluation, 386
Comparable worth, 779
    issue, 442
Compensable factors, 425
Compensation. *See* International HRM
    approach, change, 761–762
    bases, 418
    centers, FLSA classification, 418
    determination, 418–423
    employee perception, 417
    government regulation, 435–441
    issues, 441–443
    linkage. *See* Organizational objectives
        employee disbelief, 462
    management. *See* Employees
    packages, instrumentality, 417
    philosophy, indication. *See* Written
        compensation philosophy
    policies
        formal statements, components, 414
        internal equitability, 416
    strategy. *See* Employers
        comparison, 421
    structure, 428–435
    survey, 685
    systems, differentiation, 414
    usage. *See* Employees
Compensatory model, 289, 779
Compensatory time off (comp time), 437
Competence-based pay, 434–435, 779
    systems, management change, 435
Competence-based plans, difficulties, 435

Competency analysis, initiation, 208
Competency assessment, 312, 779
    usage. *See* Managerial position
Competency-based analysis, 157–158
Competency-based pay system, adoption, 435
Competency-based selection, 276–277
Competitive benchmarking, usage, 466
Competitive challenges, 731
Competitive environment, 53–56
    forces, framework, 54f
Complementary human resources policies/
    practices, 716–718
Composition, 59–61. *See also* Culture,
    capabilities, and composition
Compressed workweek, 174–175
    implementation, reasons, 174–175
Compulsory union membership, ban, 641
Computer interviews, 282
Computer workstations
    ergonomics checklist, 169f
    hazards, 544
Computer-based training
    applications, 327
    distinctions, blurring, 327
    usage, 320
Computerized interview, creation, 282
Conciliation service, 618–619
Concurrent validity, 257
Conferences, usage, 329–330
Conflict resolution, 174
Conflicts of interest, 37
Conscientiousness, 274
    sample, 275f
Consensus decision-making, usage, 637
Consent degree, implementation, 133–134
Consolidated Omnibus Budget Reconciliation
    Act of 1986 (COBRA), 501
Construct validity, 259, 779
Constructive discharge, 576–577, 779
    doctrine, court formulation, 577
Consumer Credit Reporting Reform Act of
    1996, 266
Consumer price index (CPI), 422–423, 779
Consumer reporting agency, written
    certification (providing), 266
Consumer Reporting Employment
    Clarification Act of 1998, 266
Consumer-driven health plans (CDHPs),
    505–506, 779
Contempt-of-court charges, 128
Content plateau, 214
Content validity, 259, 779
Continuous improvement, 162
    push, 362
    requirements, 717
Contracts, negotiation, 634
Contrast error, 378, 779
    reduction, 378
Contributory plans, 511, 779

Cooperative training, 322, 779
Coordination flexibility, 82–83
Core capabilities, 58, 779
Core employees, 60
Core skills, 779
    assessment, 672
    identification, 671
Core values, 52, 779. *See also* Organizational
    core values
Corporate America, minorities (rise), 225,
    227
Corporate governance laws, Congressional
    passage, 32
Corporate social responsibility, 780
    definition, 7
    focus, 7
    relationship. *See* Globalization
Corporate strategy, 70–72
Corporation. See Global corporation;
    International corporation;
    Multinational corporation;
    Transnational corporation
Corrective action process, example, 595–596
Correlation scatterplots, 258f
Correlational methods, usage, 258
Cost containment, 17–22
Cost of living, 422–423
Cost-of-living adjustment (COLA),
    determination, 686
Cost-of-living payments, employee perception,
    423
Counseling services, 516
Country clusters, synthesis, 679f
Country hourly wages, 684f
Covered individuals, 132
CPI. *See* California Psychological Inventory
Craft unions, 628, 780
Credit reports
    impact. *See* Hiring
    usage, 266–267
Credit unions, existence, 517
Criminal records check, background check,
    263
Crisis management teams, 549
Criterion, deficiency/contamination, 370.
    See also Performance appraisal
Criterion-related validity, 257–259, 780
Critical incident, 780
    method, 155, 383
    occurrence, 383
Critical thinking skills, importance, 330
Cross-cultural training, 668
Cross-functional teams, 173f
Cross-training, 83, 780. *See also* Teams
    definition, 342
Cross-validation, 257, 780
Cultural audits, 57, 780
    questions, 57
Cultural changes, 28–31

Cultural environment, 780
    implications, 661
Cultural training, 676, 678
Culture
    nonverbal communications, 677
    reshaping, 760–761
    shock, 680, 780
    values/beliefs/attitudes, auditing, 57
Culture, capabilities, and composition
    (three Cs), 57–61
Cumulative trauma disorders, 544–545, 780
Customers
    appraisal, 374, 780
    importance, 53–54
    service, improvement, 764–765
Cutoff score
    increase/decrease, effects, 290
    setting, 291

D

Databases, country-by-country checking, 263
Davis-Bacon Act of 1931 (Prevailing Wage
    Act), 437
Decent Work Agenda (ILO), 693
Deceptograph, 267
Decision-making leave. *See* Employees
Decision-making strategy, 288–291
    clinical approach, 289
    statistical approach, 289–291
Dedicated to Safety Rewards Program
    (Allied Waste Industries), 539
Defense of Marriage Act, 508
Defined benefit plan, 512, 780
Defined contribution plans, 512, 780
Defined-contribution health plans, 505
Demographic changes, 22–28
Demographic concerns, 22–31
Demotion, 210
    adjustment, requirement, 211
Department clerks, performance reviews
    (mandate), 362
Depression, 780
    burnout symptom, 558
    estimates/studies, 552
    impact, 552. *See also* Productivity
Development. *See* High-performance work
    system; International HRM
    needs, determination. *See* Individual
    development needs
Developmental assignments, 15
Diaries, usage, 154
Dictionary of Occupational Titles (U.S.
    Department of Labor), 154
Differential price rate, 459, 780
Differentiation strategy, 74–75
Digitally recorded interviews, 282–283
Direct compensation, 412

Direct labor costs, reduction, 457
Disability
    benefits, 500
    information, usage, 261
    U.S. percentage (American Association of
        Disabled People report), 227
Disabled individual, 115, 780
    accommodations, cost, 228–229
    hiring/retaining, resources/advice, 229–230
    recruitment, 227–229
Discharge. *See* Constructive discharge;
        Retaliation; Wrongful discharge
    guidelines. *See* Just Cause discharge
        guidelines
Discharging. *See* Employees
Disciplinary action, approaches, 593–594
Disciplinary investigations, considerations, 592f
Disciplinary model, example, 588f
Disciplinary penalty, imposition, 588–589
Disciplinary policies/procedures, 587–601
Disciplinary problems
    disruptive behavior, 267
    investigation, 591–593
    list, 589f
Disciplinary system, documentation
        (characteristics), 591
Discipline, 780. *See also* Positive discipline;
        Progressive discipline
    defining, 590
    meanings, 590
Discretionary major employee benefits,
        503–514
Discrimination
    global laws/pacts, 669
    Uniform Guidelines definition, 121–122
    violations, 596
Discrimination charges
    prevention, 131
    processing, 128–131
Discrimination practice, opposition, 133
Disease management (DM) programs, 507
Dishonesty, problems, 589f
Disparate treatment, 123, 780
Distance work, jobs identification, 178f
Distress, 557, 780
Distributed learning
    contrast. *See* Massed learning
    principle, 318
Distributional errors, 377
Distributive fairness, 415–416
District offices, discrimination charges, 125
Diversification. *See* Growth/diversification
Diversity
    awareness, 174
    immigration, relationship, 22–25
    management (managing), 28, 131–136,
        286, 783
    strategy, model, 29f
    off the shelf programs, avoidance, 346

reason, 30
recruitment, success, 226–227
survey (Novations/J. Howard & Associates), 344
training, 344, 346
  benefits, documentation. *See* Individuals; Organizations
  combination, 346
  programs, selection (care), 346
DM. *See* Disease management
Domestic HRM, international HRM (contrast), 663–664
Domestic partner benefits, 507–508
Domestic partnership, 507
Downsizing, 17–19, 780
  approach, 18–19
  definition, 17
  impact, 470
  necessity, 774–775
  short-term fix, consideration, 18
Downward transfer, 210
Draw, cash advance, 464
Drug testing, 269–270
  usage, 580
Drug-Free Workplace Act of 1988, 553
  application, 579
Drug-free workplace policies, 581
  recommendations, 582f
  zero tolerance, employer implementation, 581
Dual career couples
  employment, 232
  relocation, issue, 232
Dual career partnerships, 232, 780
Dual career paths, consideration. *See* Employees
Due process, 598, 780

E

EAPs. *See* Employee assistance programs
Early career, 213f
Earnings philosophy, 511
East Asia Economic Group, 661
Echo boomers, 25
Economic disparity, 102
Economic needs, impact, 619
Economic strike, 638–639
ECPA. *See* Electronic Communications Privacy Act of 1986
Education, impact, 27f
Education factors/degrees, AAIM description, 427
Education institutions, applicant source, 194
Educational assistance, 517
EEO. *See* Equal employment opportunity
EEO-1. *See* Employer Information Report
EEOC. *See* Equal Employment Opportunity Commission

EEOC *v.* Waffle House Inc., 601
Efficiency
  competition, 72, 74
  involvement, 721
Egalitarianism, 711–713
EIs. *See* Employee involvement groups
Elder care, 516–517, 780
  employment context, 516
Elderly parental care, AARP/National Alliance for Caregiving study, 516
E-learning, 327–328, 780
  definition, 327
  employee assessment tools, combination, 328
  impact. *See* Learning
  systems, cost, 328
  usage, 327
Electronic Communications Privacy Act of 1986 (ECPA), 30, 585f
  limitations, 582
Electronic surveillance/monitoring, 581–587
E-mail
  monitoring, 582–583
    SHRM survey, 582–583
  policy guidelines, 583f
Embezzlement, 581
E-mentoring, 219
Employability, ensuring, 211
Employee assistance programs (EAPs), 514, 551–556, 780
Employee benefits. *See* Discretionary major employee benefits
  bulletin boards, usage, 494
  categorization, 503
  communication
    media techniques, usage, 494
    program, creation, 495
  computer-generated statement, 494
  core benefits package, 493
  cost, 496
    shift, 499
  flexibility, 492–493
  group meeting/training classes, usage, 494
  information, communication, 493–494
  in-house publications, usage, 494
  involvement, allowance, 492
  legal requirements, 499–503
  PIN, entry, 494
  programs, 490–499
    management concerns, 495–499
    objectives, 491
    requirements, 491–493
  relationship. *See* Human resources information system
  statement of benefits cost, example, 496
  U.S. Chamber of Commerce
    report, 490
    survey, 497–498

Employee involvement groups (EIs), 168–170, 781
  dynamics, 170f
  importance, 169–170
  process, 168
Employee Polygraph Protection Act of 1988, 267
Employee Retirement Income Security Act (ERISA), 494
  impact. *See* Private pension plans
Employee Scholars Program (ESP), 746–747
Employee self-service (ESS) systems, usage, 494
Employee stock option plans, 477–478
  explanation, 478
  problems, 477–478
Employee stock ownership plans (ESOPs), 479, 781
  advantages, 479
  problems, 479
Employee Trust and Organizational Loyalty, SHRM study, 602
Employee-referred applicants, quality, 192
Employees. *See* Core employees; Hourly employees; Salaried employees
  accountability, 166, 499
  advocacy, 32
  age distribution, 24–25
  anger, calming, 550f
  appraisal form, example, 767f–768f
  assessment tools, combination, 328
  associations, 628, 780
  attitudes, Watson Wyatt survey, 362
  base pay, increase, 461
  behavioral needs, incorporation, 162–166
  calibration, 368
  career, planning, 206
  communication, improvement, 17
  compensation. *See* Host-country employees
    management, 151–152
  concerns, 22–31, 731
  conduct. *See* Workplace
  contribution system, 169
  contributions, matching, 512
  cross-training, 342
  decision-making
    involvement, 713
    leave, 594
  disabilities, hiring/retaining (resources/advice), 229–230
  discharging, 594, 596
    informing, 596–598
  discipline, usage, 538–539
  disengagement, 713
  dual career paths, consideration, 211
  due process, 598
  educational assistance, 517
  empowerment, 164–166, 780. *See also* Performance

definition, 164
results, 165
firm demand, forecasting, 61–64
flextime advantages, 176
follow-up activities, 340
401(k), control, 513
goals/objectives, establishment, 388
growth, opportunities, 395
improvement
display, 377–378
goal, 394
incentive awards, 462
incentives. *See* Professional employees
information, access, 165
innovation, 165
international selection, 668–673
introduction, 339
job description, appraisal form criteria
(relationship), 365
KSAs, providing, 344
leadership concerns, 620–621
leasing, 19–21, 197, 781
definition, 21
legal rights, employer retaliation
(avoidance), 130–131
localization, decision, 687_
managerial rating, problems, 366
mentor
guidelines, 218–219
meeting, 218
merit raise, eligibility, 455
misconduct, documentation, 591–592
monitoring, employer reasons, 583
motivation, compensation (usage), 415
number, reduction, 421
objectives, establishment, 386–387
off-duty behavior, 585–586
orientation, checklist, 340
OSHA responsibilities, 534–535
OSHA rights, 535
outcomes, 731–732
output, measurement, 415
participation, 165
impact, 384
level, 691
payment rates, internal/external factors,
418–419
pension funds, contributions, 476
performance appraisal, 151
physical characteristics, hiring/
advancement limitations, 229, 231
potential, measurement, 205f
privacy, 570–587
recruitment, 150–151
referrals, 192–193
effectiveness, increase, 192
visibility, increase, 192
relations, managerial ethics, 601–602
relative worth, 420

repatriation, success, 681–682
responsibility, selection, 178f
retention/motivation, 338
retirement savings, market risk (impact),
512
rights, 23, 28, 570–587, 781
definition, 570
employer responsibilities, contrast, 571
role, 206
safety, supervisor role, 537
salary budgets, 443f
searches
court allowance, 583–584
manager diligence, 584
selection, 151
adverse impact/disparate treatment,
122–124
procedures, uniform guidelines, 121–124
restricted policy, 123
validity, 122
semi-engagement, 713
services, 514–517
short-term basis appearance, results
appraisals (impact), 386
social concerns, 620–621
spouse, job-finding assistance, 232
strengths, emphasis, 395
strike decision, 638–639
supply, forecasting, 64–67
teams, 170–174, 781
forms, 173f
temporary overseas assignments, 668
termination, 597–598
testing/selection, best practices, 272
theft, U.S. Chamber of Commerce
estimate, 581–582
training transfer strategies, 335
training/development, 151
unionization
NLRB election, nonnecessity, 626
process, 625
reasons, 619–621
violence/defamation, 571
welcoming, 338
whistle-blowing, protected right, 574
*Employees: Handbook on Global Recruiting,
Screening, Testing and Interviewing
Criteria*, 198
Employer Information Report (EEO-1), 127,
780
Employer-initiated surveys, 429, 431
Employers
applicant legal rights, records
(maintenance/verification), 121
appraisal systems, legal challenges, 369
bargaining strategy, 634
benefits/services, offering, 517
candidate physical attributes, impact, 286f
Catch-22, 571

Civil Rights Act, Title VII, statement, 130
compensation strategy, 419
illegal conduct, whistle-blowing/reporting,
573f
implied contract lawsuits, vulnerability
(reduction), 575
legal duty, EEO requirement, 152
monitoring, reasons, 583
negotiation, Taft-Hartley Act requirement,
635
OSHA responsibilities, 534
payment ability, 421
reasonable care, exercising, 571
responsibilities, employee rights (contrast),
571
retaliation, avoidance. *See* Employees
rights, 23
sexual harassment, guilt (EEOC
consideration), 117–119
telecommuting, benefits, 178
Employer-sponsored IRA, 512
Employment
decisions, graphology (usage), 269
discrimination, form, 285
equal access, 223
interview, 277–287
variables, 284f
interviewers, guidelines, 283–286
termination lawsuits, avoidance.
See Wrongful employment
termination lawsuits
tests, 271–277
characteristics, 271
classification, 272–277
Employment assistant, job description usage,
159–160
Employment discrimination, charge (filing),
130f
Employment-at-will, 572
doctrine, exceptions, 573
principle, 781
assumption, 572
statements
examples, 576
inclusion, 575
Energy level, inferences, 269
Engagement, 711–713
Enterprise incentive plans, 476–479
Enterprising Women (magazine), 224
Entitlements, 456
employee perception, 423
Entrepreneur, 781
Environmental analysis, 53–56
Environmental scanning, 53, 781
EOSs. *See* Equal opportunity specialists
Equal access, Department of Labor
examination, 223
"Equal Employment Opportunity: It's Your
Job" (Motorola), 330

Equal Employment Opportunity Act of 1972,
105f, 108–109
Equal Employment Opportunity Commission
(EEOC), 124–125
guidelines, 124
nondiscriminatory guidelines/regulations
issuance, 115
poster, example, 129
recommendations. *See* Organizations
sexual harassment case, 117
U.S. case figures, 125f
Equal employment opportunity (EEO), 100,
781
EEO-1 report, 126
preparation, 126–128
EEO-1 survey (2007), 127
executive orders, 114–115
federal laws, 103–115
government regulation, 102–116
issues, 116–121
laws
impact, 105f
knowledge, test, 104
legal developments, 102
legislation
enforcement, 124–131
historical perspective, 101–102
policies, development. *See* Formal EEO/
affirmative action policies
posting requirements, 125–128
record-keeping, requirements, 125–128
rules. *See* Federal contractors/agencies
Equal opportunity specialists (EOSs),
investigative experience, 128
Equal pay, issue, 442
Equal Pay Act of 1963, 103, 105f
effectiveness, 441f
impact, 441
Equal rights, provisions, 440–441
Equipment
design, 168
employer monitoring, 583
Ergonomics, 781
checklist. *See* Computer workstations
considerations, 167–168
definition, 167
impact. *See* Morale; Productivity;
Workplace
OSHA, relationship, 545
program, elements, 546f
ERISA. *See* Employee Retirement Income
Security Act
Error of central tendency. *See* Central
tendency
Escalator clauses, 423, 781
ESOPs. *See* Employee stock ownership plans
ESS. *See* Employee self-service
Essay method, 383, 781
usage. *See* Performance appraisal

Ethical lapses, worker exposure, 343
Ethical leadership, 36
Ethics, 602, 781
Ethics training, 343–344
importance, 343
managers, role, 343
resources, 345
Ethnic minorities, U.S. Census Bureau
estimate, 221
eTools, usage, 545
European Union (EU), 6, 67560
Eustress, 557, 781
Evaluation/assessment issues. *See* Companies
e-Verify system (Department of Homeland
Security), 263
Exclusive representation, 626, 781
Executive Order 8802, 102
Executive Order 11246, 114f, 115
Executive Order 11286, 126
Executive Order 11478, 114f
Executive Order 12067, 124
Executive Women's Magazine, 224
Executives
base salaries, 466
benefits, 468
compensation
ethics/accountability, 469–470
reform, 470–471
HR survey (Drake Beam Morin), 220
incentive bonuses, usage, 467
long-term incentives, 467
pay package, 466–469
NYSE/NASDAQ disclosure, 470
tax code violations, IRS examination,
470
perquisites, 468–469
components, 470
replacement chart, 67f
search firms, 193–194
fees, charge, 193
short-term incentives, 466–467
bonuses, criticism, 467
stock options, 467
Exemplars, location, 310
Ex-employees
competitor employment, 575
restrictions, 575–576
Exempt employees, 418, 781
Exempt status, DOL definition, 418
Expatriates, 664, 781
advantages, 670f
assignment failure, causes, 673f
balance sheet approach, 686
communication problems, geographical
distances (impact), 689
compensation, 687–688
feedback, providing, 690
managers
compensation, 686–688

skills, 671
perceptions, 673
performance criteria, 689–690
security, providing, 688
selection criteria, 672f
success/failure, factors, 690
usage, 665
Expectancy theory, 416–417
impact. *See* Pay
relationship. *See* Pay-for-performance
Experience, openness, 274
sample, 275f
Explicit contracts, 575–576
enforcement, 576
External fit (external alignment), 75, 720, 781
establishment, 720–721
External issues, monitoring, 53
External pay equity, perceptions, 416
External recruitment. *See* Talent
effectiveness, improvement, 198–200
Extroversion, 274
sample, 275f

F

Face-to-face orientation, program
supplementation, 339
Factor-degree descriptions, 425–426
Facts/inferences, separation, 285
Failure rates, 673, 781
Fair and Accurate Credit Transactions Act of
2003, 266
Fair Credit Reporting Act, 585f
Fair employment practices agencies (FEPAs),
116
Fair employment practices (FEPs), 781
definition, 115
discrimination laws, 128
laws, 115–116
state laws, differences, 260
Fair Labor Standards Act of 1938 (FLSA)
(Wage and Hour Act), 103, 437–441
child labor provisions, 440
compensation classification, 418
equal rights provisions, 440–441
overtime
pay rules, 175
provisions, exemption, 440
violations, 438
wage and hour provisions, 437–440
Fair Pay Rules, DOL implementation, 440
Fair representation doctrine, 643, 781
Fairness/justice, 36–37
False Claims Act (FCA), 574
Faltering businesses, inclusion, 578
Families
accommodation, 224
life, management, 680

Family and Medical Leave Act (FMLA), 502–503
   amendment, 503
   poster, example, 504
   requirements, 515
Family Education Rights and Privacy Act (The Buckley Amendment), 585f
Family-friendly programs, Conference Board survey, 31
Fast-track program, 216, 781
Favoritism, employee charges, 586, 620
FCA. *See* False Claims Act
Featherbedding practices, 618
Federal contractors/agencies, EEO rules, 114f
Federal government job grade description, example, 424
Federal mediation, 618–619
Federal wage poster, example, 439
Feedback, 164
   providing, 364. *See also* Expatriates
   reinforcement, relationship, 318–319
   training. *See* Performance appraisal
   usage, 332
FEPAs. *See* Fair employment practices agencies
Firing, employer fear, 572
Firm-specific knowledge, 212f
First-level employees, on-the-job training (problems), 328
Fitbook (Xerox), 550
Flexibility, involvement, 721
Flexible benefits plans (cafeteria plans), 492–493, 781
   advantages/disadvantages, 493f
Flexible production, shift, 343
Flexible spending accounts (FSAs), 505–506
Flexible work hours, Hewitt Associates study, 31
Flexible work schedules, 174–178
   request process, 175
Flextime, 175–176, 781
FMLA. *See* Family and Medical Leave Act
Focus groups, feedback, 492
Forbes, executives report, 470
Forced distribution system, usage, 377
Forced-choice method, 380, 382, 781
   limitations, 382
   usage. *See* Performance appraisal
Forecasting, 61–67
   qualitative approaches, 63–64
   quantitative approaches, 62–63
Foreign competition, impact, 645
Foreign residents, citizenship (granting), 667
Foreign-born executives, selection, 680f
Formal EEO/affirmative action policies, development, 220–221
Formal orientation programs (Robert Half International survey), 338
Fountain Manufacturing Operation (Coca-Cola), 341

401(k) pension plans, provisions, 513
401(k) savings plans, 512–513
   concern, 512
Four-Deep Training (Coca-Cola), 341
Four-fifths rule, 122–123, 781
Free agents. *See* Self-directed free agents
Freehand wage curve, 432f
Frustration, burnout symptom, 558
FSAs. *See* Flexible spending accounts
Full retirement age, 500
Fully insured person, 500
Functional strategy, 75

G

Gainsharing incentive plans, 472–476
   variations, 473–476
Gainsharing plans, 782
Gallagher Bassett Services (safety consultants), 537
Games. *See* Management
Gay rights, merits, 120
Gay-friendly work places, increase, 120
Gender distributions, 26f
Gender stereotypes, influence (reduction), 255
General Agreement on Tariffs and Trade (GATT), 6
General Aptitude Test Battery (GATB), 272
Generation X, body art (popularity), 586–587
Generation Y
   accommodation, 515
   body art, popularity, 586–587
   engagement, 282
Generic knowledge, 212f
Genetic testing, 587
Gilmer v. Interstate/Johnson Lane Corp., 598, 601
Glass Ceiling Act of 1991, 113
Glass ceiling audits, 223
Glass Ceiling Commission, creation, 113
Global compensation systems, 685, 782
Global competition/recruitment/staffing, 5–7
Global corporation, 659, 782
Global employment company, PEO (similarity), 688
Global labor market, 198
Global managers, 669, 782
   augmented skills, identification, 671
   candidates
      augmented skills/attributes, assessment, 672–673
      core skills, assessment, 672
      pool, creation, 672
   core skills, identification, 671
   selection, 669–673
   skill categories, identification, 669

Global organizations, 659f
Global recruiting machine, running, 749–752
Global sourcing, 20
Globalization, 782
   corporate social responsibility, relationship, 6–7
   definition, 6
   impact, 6–7. *See also* Human resources management; Privacy
   issues, 309
Goals
   establishment, 395
   setting, 174, 316
Golden handcuffs, 467
Good faith bargaining, 635–637
Good old boys network, impact, 223
Good-looking test, 271
Governmental training, 322
   programs, 323
Graduate Management Aptitude Test (GMAT), 272
Grandes Ecoles, usage, 667
Graphic rating scales
   comments, provision, 381
   method, 380, 782
   usage. *See* Performance appraisal
Graphology, 268–269
   usage. *See* Employment
   predictive validity. *See* Jobs
Grievance arbitration, 639
   usage, 643–645
Grievance mediation, 642
Grievance procedure, 782. *See also* Negotiated grievance procedures
   action, 642–643
   negotiation, 641–642
   operation, 642
   steps, 642f
Griggs v. Duke Power Company, 123
   job specification impact, 151
Group incentive plans, 471–476
Group/team contributions, work (design), 168–174
Growth/diversification, 70–71
Grutter v. Bollinger, 136
Guest workers, 667, 782

H

Hair testing, 270
Halo error, 377
   avoidance, 285
Handbook for Employers, 121
Handwriting analysis, 268–269
   personality tests, contrast, 269
Hay profile method, 428, 782
Hazard Communication Standard (HCS), 536
   standard, 542

Hazardous chemical containers, labeling, 542
Hazardous Liquid Pipeline and Safety Act
        (HLPSA), 537
Hazelwood School District v. United States,
        122–123
Health
    alternative approaches, 551
    benefits, 507
    cases, recording (OSHA guide), 540f
    hazards/issues, 540–546
    improvement, 549–551
    legal requirements, 528–536
    program, OSHA monitoring, 530
    protection poster, example, 541f
Health care benefits, 503–508
Health care costs, 503, 505
    containment, 505–507
        employer methods, 506
Health Insurance Portability and
        Accountability Act of 1996 (HIPAA),
        29–30
    employee medical rights, 507
    health information, safeguarding, 585
    requirements. *See* Medical savings
        accounts
Health maintenance organizations (HMOs),
        505, 782
Health reimbursement accounts (HRAs),
        505–506
Health savings accounts (HSAs), 505–506
Healthy work environment, creation,
        539–556
Hidden costs, impact, 20–21
High Performance Organization Development
        (Texas Instruments), 730
High-performance teams, 171
High-performance work system (HPWS),
        710, 782
    anatomy, 715–719
        illustration, 715f
    communications plan, establishment,
        725–726
    compensation, 718
    competitive advantage, 732
    dependence, 714
    development, 711f
    egalitarianism/engagement, 711–713
    elements, combination, 719–721
    external fit, establishment, 720–721
    goals, focus, 730
    HR function, incorporation, 729–730
    impact, 733
    implementation, 721–731
        difficulty, 732
        flowchart, 725f
    internal fit, 719–720
    IT support, 719
    key groups, support, 728
    knowledge development, 714

    leadership, 718–719
    management processes, 718–719
    mutual gains, cultivation, 726–727
    organizational outcomes, 732
    outcomes, 731–733
    performance-reward linkage, 714–715
    principles, 710–715
        illustration, 712f
    procedures, adherence, 728
    shared information, 713–714
    staffing practices, 717
    strategic alignment, assessment, 721
    strategic fit, achievement, 720f
    success, evaluation, 730–731
    sustaining, 730–731
    training/development, 717–718
    transition
        navigation, 728–730
        structure, building, 729
    unions, involvement, 726–728
HireDS Career Network, 229
Hiring. *See* Negligent hiring
    cost, SHRM study, 254
    credit report, impact, 266
    decisions, 752–755
Hits, maximization, 254–255
Home needs, work needs (balance), 515f
Home-based pay, 686, 782
Home-country evaluations, host-country
        evaluations (contrast), 689
Home-country nationals, 664, 781
    advantages, 670
    selection, 670
Homosexuals, company legal obligations, 120
Honesty, importance, 281
Honesty tests, 267–268
Hopwood v. State of Texas, 136
Horn error, 377
Host country, 782
    culture, understanding, 662
Host-based pay, 687, 782
Host-country employees, compensation,
        683–685
Host-country evaluations, contrast. *See*
        Home-country evaluations
Host-country managers, compensation, 685
Host-country nationals, 664, 782
    advantages, 670f
    hiring, advantages, 665
    staffing, 670
Hostile environment, 117
Hour plan. *See* Standard hour plan
Hour provisions. *See* Fair Labor Standards
        Act of 1938
Hourly employees, 418
Hourly wages. *See* Country hourly wages
Hourly work, 418, 782
HPWS. *See* High-performance work system
HR. *See* Human resources

HRAs. *See* Health reimbursement accounts
HRIS. *See* Human resources information
        system
HRM. *See* Human resources management
HRMagazine, 491
    advertisements, 158
HRP. *See* Human resources planning
HSAs. *See* Health savings accounts
Human capital, 4
    architecture, 59–61
    assessment, 69f
    definition, 13
    HRM, relationship, 14–15
    management, 13–15
    mapping, 60f
    measures, 80
    readiness, 67, 69, 782
        assessment, 67–70
    ROI, 80
    value, added, 80
Human Capital Benchmarking Report, 79
Human resources (HR), 4
    advancement, 209f
    change, management, 12–13
        reasons, 12–13
    competency model, 34f
    deliverables
        alignment, testing, 724
        usage, 723
    demand, trend analysis (example), 63f
    departments, line managers (partnership), 31
    disciplinary policies/procedures,
        management approval, 587
    forecasting model, 62f
    function, incorporation. *See* High-
        performance work system
    Internet sites, guide, 8
    low-cost strategies, relationship, 74
    manager
        competencies, 33–34
        responsibilities, 31–33
        mastery, 33
    planning/strategy questions. *See*
        Business
    policies/practices. *See* Complementary
        human resources policies/practices
    policy, impact. *See* Job opening
    practices, realignment, 763–765
    programs, importance, 16
    programs/assignments, 15
    relationship. *See* Strategic planning
    role. *See* Career management
    scorecard, 721
    search policy, guidelines, 584
    software, usage, 10
    systems
        alignment (testing), HR deliverables
        (usage), 723
    systems, compatibility, 10

training, benchmarking, 337
Human resources information system
(HRIS), 9, 782
  definition, 9
  employee benefits, relationship, 490–491
  implementation, 11
  job analysis, relationship, 158
  salary surveys, relationship, 429
Human resources management (HRM), 782
  actions, documentation (paper trail), 364
  competitive challenges, relationship, 5–22
  contrast. *See* Domestic HRM
  definition, 4
  framework, 5f
  functions, job requirements (relationship),
    150–152
  globalization, impact, 7
  importance, USA Today/Deloitte &
    Touche survey, 50
  relationship. *See* Human capital;
    Reengineering; Total quality
    management
  SHRM Code of Ethical and Professional
    Standards, 35–38
  software, 10–11
  study, reasons, 4
  technology, impact, 9–12
Human resources planning (HRP), 50, 782
  importance, 50–51
  recruitment/replacement policies,
    consideration, 56
  relationship. *See* Strategic planning

I

Illegal drugs
  abuse, 553–554, 556
  users
    disability, nonconsideration, 580
    DOL facts, 579
Illegal immigrants, increase (countering), 121
Illiteracy
  cost, 231
  handicap, 231
Illnesses, OSHA statistics, 528
Immigration and Naturalization Service,
    Form I-9 (usage), 121
Immigration Reform and Control Act
    (IRCA), 120–121
  violation, 121
Immigration reform/control, 120–121
Impairment testing, usage, 580
Implied contract, 573
  binding, example, 575
  lawsuits, vulnerability (reduction).
    See Employers
  usage, 574–575

Implied covenant, 573
Improshare, 474–475, 718, 782
  lessons, 475–476
Inaction, results, 588–589
In-basket exercises, 204
Incentive pay programs
  advantages, 456f
  performance threshold, 454
Incentive payments
  determination, 460–461
  job performance connection, employee
    perception, 456
  performance measures, linkage, 457
Incentive plans. *See* Enterprise incentive
    plans; Group incentive plans;
    Individual incentive plans
  administration, 457–459
  linkage. *See* Organizational objectives
  strategic reasons, 454–457
  success, 455
    requirements, 456–457
  types, 455f
Incentives
  awards/recognition, 462–463
  bonuses, usage. *See* Executives
  compensation, salary linkage (advantages), 465
  premiums, addition, 686
  systems, effectiveness, 457–458
Incidence rate, 533
India, economy, 661
Indirect compensation, 412
Individual incentive plans, 459–465
  flexibility, 459
Individual needs, organization needs
  balancing, 207f
  matching, 205f
  goal, 206–207
Individual retirement account (IRA), 512.
    See also Employer-sponsored IRA
Individuals
  development needs, determination, 216
  differences, 317
  diversity training, benefits
    (documentation), 346
  goals/organizational goals, blending, 206–207
Industrial engineering, 782
  considerations, 166–167
  definition, 166
Industrial unions, 628, 782
Industrial-organizational psychologist, test
    validation experience, 259
Industry knowledge, 212f
Inferences, separation. *See* Facts/inferences
Information
  providing, 285
  reliability/validity, obtaining, 256–259
  sale, 581
  sharing, 713–714

usage, 38
Information technology (IT)
  support, 719
  usage. *See* Safety; Unions
Injuries, OSHA statistics, 528
Injury and Illness Report (OSHA Form 301),
    539
Input/output ratio, comparison, 415–416
Institutionalized sex discrimination, 442
Instructional objectives, 315, 782
Instructions. *See* Programmed instruction
  clarity, 320
Instructors
  adaptability, 319
  characteristics, 314, 319–320
  enthusiasm, 320
  humor, 319
  interest, importance, 320
  role-playing steps, 331–332
  sincerity, 319
  subject, knowledge, 319
Instrumentality. *See* Compensation
Integrated Case Scenario (FBI), 330
Integrative negotiation, 726
Integrity tests, 267–268
  items, usage, 267
  questions, examples, 268f
Intellectual assets, 4
Intellectual property
  agreements, 575–576
  clause, employer ownership, 575–576
Intelligence
  U.S. Army Alpha/Beta Tests, 271
Intelligence, inferences, 269
Intelligence quotient (IQ) tests, 273
IntelligentHire (CareerBuilder), 282
Interest arbitration, 639
Interest inventories, 273–274
Interest-based bargaining, 637, 782
  FMCS definition, 637
Interest-based negotiation, 726
Internal analysis, 57–70
Internal fit (internal alignment), 75, 719, 782
  assessment, 83f
  diagnosis, 722
  ensuring, 719–720
  measurement, 81
Internal recruitment. *See* Talent
  advantages/limitations, 201–202
Internal Revenue Code (IRC)
  Section 401(a), 479
  Section 401(k), 512
International assignment, preparation, 674f
International business, communication
    complexities (examples), 675–676
International companies
  country involvement, selection, 661
  list, 660f

International compensation program, effectiveness, 686
International corporation, 658, 782
International expansion, 664–665
International HRM
  career development, assessment/tracking, 675, 678–680
  compensation, 683–688
  contrast. *See* Domestic HRM
  cultural training, 675, 676, 678
  language training, 675–676
  performance appraisal, 688–690
  personal/family life, management, 675, 680
  repatriation, 675, 681–682
  short-term assignments, 686
  training/development, 673–683
    programs, elements, 675
International labor organizations, 692–693
International management, 658–673
International Mobility Assessment test (Tucker International), 672
International organizations, 659f
International recruitment, 665–668
International staffing, 664–665
  changes, 664f
International Union v. Johnson Controls, 542
Internet
  employer monitoring, 582–583
  monitoring, SHRM survey, 582–583
  policy guidelines, 583f
  recruitment, 191–192
Internships, 322
  effectiveness, increase, 323
  programs, 323, 782
Interpersonal skills, focus, 717
Interrater reliability, 257
Interviewer training, 283–286
Interviewing
  methods, 277–283
  process, development, 278
Interviews. *See* Behavioral description interview; Behavioral interviews; Computer interview; Panel interview; Situational interview; Structured interview; Virtual interview
  control, 286
  employee self-appraisal examination, 387
  OFCCP guidelines, 286
  plan, establishment, 283
  procedure, validating, 257
  questions, appropriateness/inappropriateness, 287
  rapport, establishment/maintenance, 284
  usage, 153
Intracapital, 718
Investigative interview, 592–593
IRCA. *See* Immigration Reform and Control Act

J

Job Accommodation Network, 229
Job analysis, 152–162, 753, 783
  ADA impact, 152
  approaches, 155–158
  case study, 752–755
  definition, 152
  initiation, 255
  O*NET, relationship, 154
  process, flowchart, 153f
  relationship. *See* Human resources information system
  usage, 204
Job description, 158–161, 783
  definition, 151
  employment assistant usage, 159–160
  problems, 161
  value, 158
  writing, clarity, 161–162
Job evaluation, 420, 783
  comparison methods, 424–426
  systematic process, 423
  systems, 423–428
Job knowledge tests, 276
Job opening
  advertisement description, 191
  encouragement, HR policy (impact), 202
Job performance
  criteria
    absence, 321
    usage, 383
  graphology usage, predictive validity, 269
Job Preference Program (Home Depot), 262
Job Service, 323
Job-related stress, 558
  reduction, advice, 559
  sources, 558
Job-relatedness, 152
Jobs
  autonomy, 164
  bidding, 202–203, 783
  boards, online screening tools, 264
  candidates, information sources, 259–270
  characteristics, 164
    requirement, 200
  characteristics model, 783
    proposal, 164
  classification system, 424, 783
  data, collection, 155
  definition, 150, 783
  design, 162–178, 783
    basis, 163f
  duties
    explanation, 339
    section, 160–161
  enrichment, 162–164, 783
    definition, 162
  factors, point values, 426
  family, 150, 783
  feedback, 164
  functions, section, 160–161
  grade description, example, 424
  identification, section, 160
  information
    accuracy, control, 154
    gathering, 153–154
  interview mistakes, ranking, 280–281
  performance/behavior standards, violation, 592–593
  posting, 202–203, 783
    disadvantage, 262
  previews, 200
  proficiency, criteria, 258
  progressions, 783
    identification, 208
  protection, rights, 571–578
  ranking system, 424, 783
  requirements, relationship. *See* Human resources management
  rotations, 83
    providing, 329
  safety and health protection poster, example, 541f
  safety/health standards, OSHA development/enforcement, 530
  security, 731
  sharing, 176–177
  skill variety, 164
  specifications, 160, 783
    section, 161
  statement, 159, 160
  stress, 544
  survey, 431
  task identity, 164
  task significance, 164
  title, 160
  total value, delivery, 420
  vertical expansion, 162
  worth, 420
Joint ventures, 72
Junior boards, opportunities, 329
Jury duty, summons (compliance), 573f
Just Cause discharge guidelines, 597f
Just-in-time (JIT) learning, 9
Just-in-time (JIT) techniques, 717
Just-in-time (JIT) training, 327, 783

K

Knowledge, skills, abilities, and other factors (KSAOs), 255, 271
Knowledge, skills, abilities (KSAs), 306, 311

complexity/mastery, 330
delivery, 328
function, 341
learning, 320
training, impact, 338
Knowledge development, 714
Knowledge workers, 7, 9, 783
definition, 7
Knowledge-sharing learning, examples, 326f

L

Labor
costs, impact, 412
external supply, 55–56
force, 26f
foreign competition, impact, 645
management alliances, commitment
(formalization), 727
market. See Global labor market
conditions, 422
organizations, challenges, 645–646
support, 61
technological change, impact, 645
worldwide environment, 691–693
Labor agreement, 639–641
administration, 641–645
components, 640
management rights, example, 640
negotiation, 635
terms, familiarization, 643
Labor relations. See Public sector
government regulation, 616–619
intricacies, 614
knowledge, test, 615
process, 619–628, 783
flowchart, 620f
Labor unions
applicant placement service, 195
structures/functions/leadership, 628–6321
Labor-Management Reporting and Disclosure
Act. See Landrum-Griffin Act
Landrum-Griffin Act (Labor-Management
Reporting and Disclosure Act), 619
Language training, 675–676
Late career, 213f
Lateral transfer, involvement, 329
Layoffs, decisions, 776–777
Leaderless group discussions, 204
Leadership. See High-performance work system
concerns. See Employees
dimensions, 678
shortages (ASTD study), 328
Learning. See Blended learning; Self-directed
learning
acceleration, 362
contrast. See Massed learning; Whole
learning

curve, 318
example, 319f
examples. See Knowledge-sharing learning
nonthreatening atmosphere, 321
physical/psychological obstacles, reduction,
315
plateau, 318
points, 332
principles, 314, 316–319
illustration, 316f
process, E-learning (impact), 327
Learning management systems (LMS),
327–328, 783
Leniency error, 377, 783
peer ranking, impact, 377
Less-developed countries, worker location,
667
Lie detector, term (definition), 267
Life insurance, 508
Life plateau, 214
LightSpeed VCT, GE design, 668
Line managers
partnership. See Human resources
role, 38–39
Living-wage jobs, presence, 339
LMS. See Learning management systems
Local unions, structure/functions, 630
Localization, 783
process, 687
Lockouts, 632–633
Log of Work-Related Injuries and Illnesses,
maintenance (OSHA requirement),
539
Long-term care insurance, 509
Long-term incentives. See Executives
plans, types, 468f
Long-term personal effectiveness, approach,
220
Looks-related criteria, importance, 231
Low salary budgets, issues, 442
Low-cost strategy, 72, 74
relationship. See Human resources
Luck is No Accident (Krumboltz/Levin),
215
Lump sum merit pay, 462
Lump sum merit program, 783
implementation, 462
Lump sum payments, 684

M

Make-work activities, 216
Malcolm Baldrige National Quality Award,
16, 725
Managed accounts, 513
Management. See International management
alliances, commitment (formalization).
See Labor

arbitration case, allowance (reason), 643
bargaining power, 638–639
development, methods, 328–332
dissatisfaction, 620
forecasts, 63–64, 783
games/simulations, 330–331
global environment, impact, 660–662
inventories, 65–66
labor participation, 693
minorities, advancement, 225, 227
positions
advancement difficulty. See Women
job evaluation, usage, 428
prerogatives, union challenges, 628
processes. See High-performance work
system
rights
clause, 640
issue, 640
talent, inventorying, 202
women, preparation, 223–224
Management by objectives (MBO), 386–388,
783
feature, 387–388
impact. See Performance appraisal
Managers
appraisal, 783
assignment, career benefits (maximization),
679–680
employee, face-to-face discussion, 365
ethics, 601–602
goals/objectives, establishment, 388
hiring, 280–281
position, competency assessment (usage),
312–314
questions, consideration, 289
term, replacement, 719
unionization, impact, 626, 628
Manager/supervisor appraisal, 370–371
Managing diversity. See Diversity
"Managing for Results" (Xerox), 721
Market response, 15–17
Market risk, threat. See Employees
Markov analysis, 65, 783
hypothesis, 65f
Married couple households, U.S. Census
Bureau data, 492
Married gays, Social Security ineligibility, 508
M&As. See Mergers and acquisitions
Massachusetts Commission against
Discrimination, 116
Massed learning, distributed learning
(contrast), 318
Material Safety Data Sheets (MSDSs), 536,
783
label cross-referencing, 542
Mathematics problems (handling), U.S.
Department of Education study, 27
Matrix building, usage, 637

McDonnell Douglas Corp v. Green, 123–124
Meaningfulness, employee experience, 164
Mediation, 600, 784. *See also* Federal
 mediation; Grievance mediation
Mediator, 600, 784
Medical examinations, 269
Medical inquiries, ADA limitations, 269
Medical review officer (MRO), usage, 580
Medical savings accounts (MSAs), 505
 creation, HIPAA requirement, 506–507
Medicare
 program, SSA administration, 500
 protection, 500
Meetings, conduct, 174
Mentoring, 206, 217–219, 328
 functions, 218f
 Internet usage, 219
Mentors, 217, 784
 assignation, 665
 background, research, 218
 contact, 218
 guidelines, 218–219
 myths, 217f
Merchandise, theft, 581
Mergers and acquisitions (M&As), 71–72
 employee requirements, 309
 phases, HR activities (association), 73
Merit guidelines, 462, 784
Merit pay, 461–462. *See also* Lump sum merit
 pay
Merit raises, problems, 461–462
Merit systems, usage, 420
Metrics model, construction, 82f
Midcareer, 213f
Mighty Mentors (Mighty Media), 219
Millennial candidates, engagement, 282
Minimum wage
 floor, 438, 440
 laws, 436
Minorities
 advancement. *See* Management
 internships, providing, 225
 recruitment/development, 224–225
Misses, avoidance, 254–255
Mission, 51–53
 definition, 51, 784
 setting, 174
Mixed-standard scales
 example, 382
 method, 380, 784
 usage. *See* Performance appraisal
MNC. *See* Multinational corporation
Modeling, 317 332. *See also* Behavior
 modeling
Monthly Labor Review, 56
Morale (improvement), ergonomics (impact),
 168
Motivation
 compensation, usage. *See* Employees

personality tests, usage, 273–274
 relationship. *See* Pay equity
 theories, 461
MSAs. *See* Medical savings accounts
MSDSs. *See* Material Safety Data Sheets
Multinational corporation (MNC), 659, 784
Multinational organizations, 659f
Multiple cutoff model, 289, 784
Multiple hurdle model, 289, 784
Muscular aches/pains, 544
Musculoskeletal disorders (MSDs), 544–545
Mutual gains, cultivation, 727–728
Myers-Briggs Type Indicator (MBTI), 274

N

National Compensation Survey (BLS)
 (NCS publication), 429
 data, 430
 survey, process, 430
National Defense Authorization Act, 503
National Labor Relations Act. *See* Wagner
 Act of 1935
 private sector absence, 632
 Section 7, usage, 619
National origin, information (usage), 261
National unions, structure/functions,
 629–630
National values, change, 101–102
Nationals. *See* Home-country nationals;
 Host-country nationals; Third-
 country nationals
 hiring. *See* Nonnationals
Needs assessment, 307. *See also* Rapid needs
 assessment; Training
 American Society for Training and
 Development study, 309
 conducting, 308–314
Negligence, 571, 784
Negligent hiring, 263, 784
 impact, 571
 lawsuits, 571
Negotiated grievance procedures, 641–642
Negotiations. *See* Adversarial negotiations
 impact. *See* Bargaining
 preparation, 633–634
Nepotism, 193, 784
Networking, 219–220. *See also* Career;
 360-degree networking
 consideration, 220
Neuroticism, 274
 sample, 275f
Neutrality agreements, 623
New position analysis, 753
9-box grid, 203, 778
 example, 203f
Nine-step staffing, 749–750
NLRB v. Weingarten, Inc., 593

No Fear Act. *See* Notification and Federal
 Employee Antidiscrimination and
 Retaliation Act
No layoff policy, advocacy, 18
Noncash incentive awards
 customization, 464
 effectiveness, 462–463
Non-compete agreements, 575
Noncontributory plans, 511, 784
Nondirective interview, 277–278, 784
Nonexempt employees, 418, 784
Nonfinancial compensation, 412
Non-job-related conversation, reduction, 284
Nonmanagerial employees, training methods,
 320–328
Nonnationals, hiring, 667
Nonpiracy agreements, 576
Nonpunitive discipline. *See* Positive discipline
Nonunion employees, *Weingarten* rights, 593
Nonunion status, employer focus, 646
Nonverbal communications, 677
Nonverbal cues, attention, 284
Norris-LaGuardia Act of 1932 (Anti-
 Injunction Act), 616
North American Free Trade Agreement
 (NAFTA), 6
 passage, 660
Notification and Federal Employee
 Antidiscrimination and Retaliation
 Act (No Fear Act), 574

O

OASI. *See* Old-age and survivors' insurance
Obesity
 disability, 231
 impact, 551
Observation, usage, 154
Occupational knowledge, 212f
Occupational Outlook Handbook, 56
Occupational Safety and Health Act of 1970
 (OSHA), 529
 coverage, 530
 guide. *See* Health; Safety
 relationship. *See* Ergonomics
 standards, 530
 enforcement, 530–532
Occupational Safety and Health
 Administration
 citations/penalties, 532
 consultation assistance, 532–533
 cooperative programs, 532–533
 enforcement record, 536
 eTools, 545
 Form 300-A, 539
 Form 301, 539
 infractions, reporting, 573f
 inspection priorities, 531

onsite consultation, 532
responsibilities, 530, 533–535
rights, 533–535
standard-setting procedures, initiation, 530
Occupational safety/health accidents, 528
Office of Federal Contract Compliance
      Programs (OFCCP)
   creation, 115
   requirements. *See* Affirmative action
Offshore Nation (Vashistha), 20
Offshoring, 19–21
   definition, 20, 784
Ohio Civil Rights Commission, 116
OJT. *See* On-the-job training
Old-age and survivors' insurance (OASI),
      eligibility, 499
Older Workers Benefit Protection Act
      (OWBPA), 503
Older workforce, employment, 231–232
Ombudsman, 784
   definition, 600
   system, 600
Omnibus Transportation Employee Testing
      Act of 1991, 579
Oncale v. Sundowner Offshore Services,
      118–119
On-campus recruitment relationship,
      strengthening, 195f
O*NET code number, usage, 160
O*NET database, 154
   relationship. *See* Job analysis
Online applications, 261
   disadvantage, 262
Online benefits programs, 491
Online training libraries, search, 327
On-the-job behavior problems, 589f
On-the-job experiences, 328–329
On-the-job instruction, 306
On-the-job performance, structured interview
      predictive ability (U.S. Merit Systems
      Protection Board report), 278
On-the-job training (OJT), 320–322, 784
   PROPER method, 321f
Open-door policy, 599–600, 784
   problems, 599–600
Openness. *See* Experience
Opposite-sex partners, health benefits, 492
Organization analysis, 309, 311, 784
   conducting, 311
Organizational abilities, inferences, 269
Organizational capability, 82, 784
Organizational core values, 52–53
Organizational exit, 211
Organizational objectives
   compensation, linkage, 413–414
   incentive plans, linkage, 454–456
Organizational outcomes, 732
Organizational recruiters, 199–200
Organizational rules, setting, 589–590

Organizational scanning, usage, 310
Organizations
   Civil Rights Act of 1964 coverage, 106
   conditions, encouragement, 165–166
   cost, control, 311
   culture, consideration, 458
   diversity training, benefits
         (documentation), 346
   employment
      interviewers, selection (caution), 283
      program development, EEOC
            recommendation, 221
   glass ceiling audits, 223
   handwriting analysis, usage, 269
   needs, 207
   networking relationships, 232
   OJT, usage, 321
   power, downward movement, 713
   promotion policy, 201
   purpose/strategic goals, explanation, 339
   role, 206
   size, impact, 199
   strike, employee decision, 638–639
   types, 659f
Orientation, 338, 784
   checklist. *See* Employees
   packet, items, 340
   programs. *See* Formal orientation programs
      CBT, combination, 339
      impact, 339
      integration, 338–339
      training, 338–339
OSHA. *See* Occupational Safety and Health
      Act of 1970
Outplacement services, 211, 784
Outside employee conduct. *See* Workplace
Outside seminars/conferences, conducting,
      329
Outsourcing, 19–21, 784
   definition, 19
Overhead costs, 458–459
Overseas Assignment Inventory (Performance
      Program), 672
Overseas assignments, talent development,
      674
Overseas managers, sources (advantages), 670f
Overseas recruitment, complications, 198
Overtime provisions, exemption, 440
Overtime violation, DOL investigation, 438
Overweight condition, impact, 551
OWBPA. *See* Older Workers Benefit
      Protection Act
Ownership, culture, 476

P

Paid holidays, 508
Panel interview, 279, 282, 784

Paper-and-pencil tests, measurements, 272
PAQ. *See* Position Analysis Questionnaire
Part learning, contrast. *See* Whole learning
Past employment/education verification,
      background check, 263
Pay
   disclosure rules, SEC issuance, 470
   expectancy theory, impact, 416–417
   grades, 431–432, 784
   inequity, elimination/reduction, 415–416
   systems, design (guiding philosophy), 683
Pay equity, 415–416, 784
   achievement, 416
   employee misperception, 417
   motivation, relationship, 416f
   perceptions. *See* External pay equity
Pay rate
   busting, 460
   ranges, 432–433
   structure. *See* Single pay rate structure
Pay secrecy, 417–418
   maintenance, 418
Pay-for-performance
   expectancy theory, relationship, 417f
   programs, justification, 461
   standard, 414–418, 785
   strategy, 466
   system, concern, 415
Payment for time not worked, 508–509
Payroll deductions, 512
PDCA. *See* Plan Do Check Act
Peer appraisal, 372–373, 785
   advantages, 372
   nonusage, reasons, 373
Peer ranking, 377
   impact. *See* Leniency error; Strictness error
Peer-review systems, 599, 785
Pension plans, 511–514. *See also* Cash balance
      pension plans
   contributory plan, 511
   ERISA, impact. *See* Private pension plans
   failure, danger, 514
   federal regulation, 513–514
   noncontributory plans, 512
   philosophy, 511
   types, 511–512
   underfunding, relationship, 514
Pension Protection Act, 513
Pentagon, 9/11 attacks, 548
People
   jobs, matching, 254–259
   management strategies, 81
   outcomes, pursuit, 714
   skills, inferences, 269
   strategic resource, 58
People-embodied know-how, dependence, 58
PeopleSoft, Lucent rollout, 663
PEOs. *See* Professional employer
      organizations

Performance
    ability, 280
        impact, 396
    criteria. *See* Expatriates
    deficiencies, 314
    defining, guidance (absence), 461
    diagnosis, 396
        example, 3907f
    dimensions, 754f
        judgment, 372
    environment, impact, 396
    factors, 396
    feedback, providing. *See* Balanced Scorecard
    goals, increase, 457
    improvements, 395–398
        employee empowerment, 390
    ineffectiveness
        management, 397–398
        sources, identification, 395–396
    interview, 371
    management, 362, 785
    motivation, impact, 396
    pressure, 762
    reward, linkage, 714–715
    threshold, establishment, 454
Performance appraisal, 362, 688–690, 785.
        See also Employees; International
        HRM; Strategy-driven performance
        appraisal
    administrative purposes, 363–364
    appeals procedure, 370
    appraisers
        identification, 370–374
        training, 376–379
    behavioral methods, 383–386
    conflicts, judgmental role, 366
    criterion
        contamination, 368
        deficiency, 368
    developmental purposes, 364
    essay method, usage, 383
    fairness, employee concerns, 366
    feedback, employee satisfaction, 393
    feedback training, 378
    forced-choice method, usage, 380, 382
    graphic rating scales, usage, 380
    information, source, 374
    legal guidelines, 369–370
    legal requirements, 369–370
        compliance, 370
    MBO program, impact, 387f
    methods, 379–391
        selection, 390–391
        summary, 390f
    mixed-standard scales, usage, 380
    plan, establishment, 376
    problem, case study, 765–769
    program failure
        reasons, 364–366

results, 365–366
programs, 362–366
    development, 366–379
    oversight/coordination, HR department
        responsibility, 366
    purposes, 363–364
        list, 363f
    rater error, elimination, 376–378
    raters, awareness. *See* Stereotypes
    reliability, 368–369
    review, preparation/conducting, 379
    sources, alternatives, 371f
    standards
        defining, 367–369
        establishment, 367f
        usefulness, 369
    strategic relevance, 367–368
    supervisor checklist, 379
    systems
        gaming, prevention, 375
        ineffectiveness, reasons, 365f
    trait approaches, 380
    usage. *See* Talent
Performance appraisal interviews, 391–398
    appreciation, expression, 393
    conducting, 392–395
    criticism, minimization, 394
    face-to-face confrontation, managerial
        dislike, 366
    follow-up, 395
    formation, determination, 391
    goals, establishment, 395
    participation, 393
    supportiveness, importance, 394–395
    timing, importance, 394
    types, 391–392
Performance measures
    defining, guidance (absence), 461
    employee involvement, 458
    intent, defining, 458
    linkage. *See* Incentive payments
    setting, 457, 458
Performance-based rewards, 714
Performance-centered objective, 315
Perjury, committing (refusal), 573f
Permanent workers, placement, 196
Perquisites (perks), 468, 785. *See also*
        Executives
Person analysis, 314, 785
Personal credibility, 34
Personal crises, handling, 552
Personal goals, setting, 315
Personal responsibility, 499
Personal scorecard, example, 389
Personal/family life, management, 680
Personality inventories, 273–274
    example, 273f
Personality tests, contrast. *See* Handwriting
        analysis

Personality traits
    factors, 274
    inferences, 269
Person-job fit, 255
Personnel files
    access, 584–585
    examination, employee rights, 584
    policy guidelines, 586f
Person-organization fit, 255
Peter Principle, 209–210
Physical ability tests, 274, 276
Physical attributes, impact. *See* Employers
Piece rate. *See* Differential price rate
    computation, 459
Piecework, 418, 459–460, 785. *See also*
        Straight piecework
    disadvantages, 460
    incentive plans, problems, 460
Pink (magazine), 224
Pittsburgh Commission on Human Relations,
        116
Plan Do Check Act (PDCA), 337
Planned career progressions, opportunities,
        329
Planning. *See* Human resources planning
    forecasting element, 61–67
    systems, possibilities (recognition),
        209–211
Plant closing notification, 578
Plant closures, 632–633
Plateau, 318. *See also* Career; Content plateau;
        Life plateau; Structural plateau
    coping, organizational help, 214
    example, 319f
    trap, avoidance, 214
Plateauing phenomenon, 214
Podcasts, usage, 325
Point system, 424–426, 785
    advantage, 425
    point manual, 425
    usage, 425–426
Point values, 426
Point-of-service plan, employee preference,
        492
Policy formulation/implementation, 32
Political involvement, 623
Polygraph tests, 267
Position
    analysis. *See* New position analysis
    definition, 150, 785
Position Analysis Questionnaire (PAQ), 785
    page, sample, 156f
    system, 155
Positional bargaining, 726
Positive discipline (nonpunitive discipline),
        594, 785
Positive reinforcement, usage, 315
Posting requirements. *See* Equal employment
        opportunity

Praise, importance, 393
Precombination, 73
Preconducted pay surveys, availability, 429
Predictive validity, 257, 785
Predictor information, relationship
       (determination), 258
Preelection hearing, 626
Preferred provider organization (PPO), 505,
       785
Pregnancy Discrimination Act of 1978, 105f,
       109
Prejudices, impact, 223
Prepare Reassure Orient Perform Evaluate
       Reinforce and Review (PROPER),
       321f
Preretirement programs, 511
Presentation, meaningfulness, 317
Press conferences, union usage, 641
Prevailing Wage Act. See Davis-Bacon Act
       of 1931
Privacy. See Employees
    compliance, globalization (impact), 29
    concern, 29–30
    laws. See Right-to-privacy laws
    rights, 578–581
Privacy Act of 1974, 29, 585f
    impact. See References
Private employment
    agencies, fees (charging), 196
    applicant placement service, 196–197
Private pension plans, ERISA (impact), 513
Private sector employers, 579
Proactive change, 12, 785
Proactive safety training program, 537–538
Probable cause
    impairment, sobriety test, 580
    urinalysis/blood test, submission, 579
Problem scope, examination, 310
Problems, solving (focus), 394
Problem-solving, involvement, 721
Problem-solving interview, 392
Problem-solving skills, importance, 330
Procedural justice, 392–393
Process audit, 730, 785
Process checking, usage, 637
Process dynamics, 342f
Process engineering, 162
Process safety metrics, 537
Process-improvement teams, 173f
Production output, examination, 386
Productivity
    competition, 72, 74
    depression, impact, 552
    enhancements, 21–22
       list, 22f
    improvement, 712
       ergonomics, impact, 168
    loss, burnout symptom, 558
    measurement, 472–473

measures, 386
Professional associations, applicant placement
       service, 195
Professional code of conduct, violation
       (refusal), 573f
Professional employees
    cash bonuses, 466
    incentives, 465–471
Professional employer organizations
       (PEOs), 21
    global employment company, similarity,
       688
    NAPEO study, 197
Profit sharing, 476, 785
    plans, 476–477
       problems, 477
       variations, 476–477
Program design, 307
Programmed instruction, 325
    advantage, 325
Progressive discipline, 593, 785
Project teams, 173f
Promotion, 209, 785
    adjustment, requirement, 211
    motivational value, absence, 201
Promotional opportunities, 210
PROPER. See Prepare Reassure Orient
       Perform Evaluate Reinforce and
       Review
Protected classes, 103, 785
Prototyping, usage. See Rapid prototyping
Psychological contract, 572, 785
Psychological stress evaluator, 266
Public civil service systems, existence, 632
Public Contracts Act. See Walsh-Healy Act
       of 1936
Public employment agencies, applicant
       placement service, 195–196
Public policy, violation, 573
    discharges, impact, 573
Public sector
    labor relations, 631–632
    striking, prohibition, 632
Punishment, elimination, 315

Qualified candidates, identification
       (methods), 202–204
Qualitative approaches. See Forecasting
Quality circles (QCs), 168
Quantitative approaches. See Forecasting
Questionnaires, usage, 153
Questions
    appropriateness/inappropriateness.
       See Questions
    legality, 286
    standardization, 286

usage, effectiveness, 285
Quid pro quo harassment, occurrence,
       116–117

Racial stereotypes, influence (reduction), 255
Radio frequency identification (RFID), 570
Railway Labor Act of 1926 (RLA), 616
Rapid needs assessment, 310
Rapid prototyping, usage, 310
Rapport, establishment/maintenance, 284
Rate busting. See Pay rate
Rate ranges. See Pay rate
Rating errors. See Temporal rating errors
Reactive change, 12, 785
Real wages, 423, 785
Realistic job preview (RJP), 200, 785
Real-life demonstrations, 317
Reasonable accommodation, 785
Reasonable suspicion, urinalysis/blood test
       (submission), 579
Recency error, 377–378, 785
Recognition, source, 412
Recordable case, 539, 785
Record-keeping requirements. See Equal
       employment opportunity
Recruiting process outsourcing (RPO)
       company, 199
Recruitment. See Employees; International
       recruitment; Internet recruitment
    costs, 199
    outside sources, 190–197
    principles, 189
    success. See Diversity
Red circle rates, 43, 785
Reengineering
    definition, 17, 785
    HRM, relationship, 17
    issues, 309
Reference-checking questions, sample, 265
References
    checking, 264, 266
    letters, examination (Privacy Act impact),
       264, 266
References, information (usage), 261
Referrals. See Employees
Referred Hire (referral portal product), 192
Regression, prevention, 321
Reinforcement
    relationship. See Feedback
    usage, 332
Relapse prevention (RP), 335
Reliability, 256, 786. See also Interrater
       reliability
    obtaining. See Information
Religious preference, 107
Relocation services, 211, 786

Remedial courses
offering, 341
program implementation, 341
Repatriation, 681–682, 786
checklist, 682–683
interviews, 690
Repetition, usage, 317
Replacement charts, 66–67, 786
Resources
flexibility, 83
imitation/organization, 58
value/rarity, 58
Respondents, accountability, 375
Results. *See* Training
appraisals, problems, 386
measurement, 192
method, 386–390
training costs, relationship, 335
Résumés. *See* Unsolicited applications/
résumés
Retail selling skills (RSS), 764–765
Retaliation. *See* Employees
discharge, 577
reduction, suggestions, 577
EEOC guidelines, 132–133
Retirees, employment, 232
Retirement
benefits, qualification, 500
incentives, 511
income, Center for Retirement Research
study, 510
policies, 510–511
programs, 510–511. *See also* Preretirement
programs
trends, 510f
Return on investment (ROI), 335–338
calculation, 689
problems, 690
formula, calculation, 335–336
Revenue factor, 80
Reverse discrimination, 134–135, 786
Reward
linkage. *See* Performance
philosophy, 511
RFID. *See* Radio frequency identification
Rights arbitration, 639, 786
function, 643
Right-to-know laws, 535–536, 786
Right-to-privacy laws, 585f
Right-to-sue notice, 128
Right-to-work laws, 641
Rival firms, 54–55
RJP. *See* Realistic job preview
RLA. *See* Railway Labor Act of 1926
ROI. *See* Return on investment
Role-play, usage, 332
Role-playing, 204
usage, 331–332
RP. *See* Relapse prevention

RPO. *See* Recruiting process outsourcing
RSS. *See* Retail selling skills
Rucker Plan, 718

S

SaaS. *See* Software as a Service
Safe work environment, promotion, 536–539
Safety
awareness, IT (usage), 538
cases, recording (OSHA guide), 540f
culture, creation, 537–538
legal requirement, 528–536
program, OSHA monitoring, 530
protection poster, example, 541f
record comparison (BLS/NSC), 533
regulations, explanation, 339
rules
enforcement, 538–539
violation, penalties, 538
supervisor, role, 537
survey (American Institute of Plant
Engineers), 537
test, 529
training
IT, usage, 538
program. *See* Proactive safety training
program
Safety and Health Achievement Recognition
Program (SHARP), 533
Safety-sensitive jobs, 579
Salaried employees, 418
Salary budgets, 443f
issues. *See* Low salary budgets
size. *See* Annual salary budgets
Salary plan. *See* Combined salary/commission
plan; Straight salary plan
Salary plus bonus plans, 465, 786
Salary survey. *See* Wage and salary survey
relationship. *See* Human resources
information system
Salary Wizard, 429
Salary-plus-incentive compensation plan,
design flexibility, 465
Sales employees
compensation plans, components, 463–464
Sales employees, performance standards, 463
Sales figures, examination, 386
Sales incentives, 463–465
plans
needs, 463
types, 463–465
Saliva, testing, 270
Same-sex partners, health benefits, 492
Sandwich technique, usage (supervisor
avoidance), 393
Sarbanes-Oxley (S-O) Act, passage, 573–574
Scandal, response, 759–760

Scanlon Plan, 474, 718, 786
lessons, 475–476
suggestion process, 475f
Scatterplots. *See* Correlation scatterplots
SC/H. *See* Source cost per hire
Scholastic Aptitude Test (SAT), 272
Screening committees, impact, 474
Searches, court allowance, 583–584
Second Life (reality game), 9, 282
Second-hand smoke, impact, 543
Second-tier recruiting, 750–752
Selection, 254, 786. *See also* Competency-
based selection
decision
can-do factors/will-do factors, 288f
reaching, 288–291
goal, example, 254f
instrument, work samples/behaviors
(similarity), 259
procedures, EEO regulations, 257
process, 255–256
anticipation, 753, 755
steps, example, 256f
steps/sequence, variation, 256
program, HR department (formal
responsibility), 255
ratio, 291, 786
Self-appraisal, 371, 786
substantiation, 387
Self-assessment, request, 392–393
Self-audits, 223
Self-directed free agents, 211–212
Self-Directed (Holland), 215
Self-directed learning, 325
Self-directed teams, 173f
Self-esteem
protection, 644
source, 412
Self-focus, production, 362–363
Self-image, inferences, 269
Self-managed teams, 171
Self-management training. *See* Career
Self-reliance, balance, 324
Self-selection, usage, 671–672
Self-service benefits administration, 491
Seminars, usage, 329–330
Sensitivity training, usage, 675
Separation cost, 80
7-S model, 76
Severance pay, 509
Sex (class), Civil Rights Act protection, 120
Sexual harassment, 116–119, 596, 786
auditing, questions, 118
commonness, 119
definition, 116
guilt, EEOC consideration. *See* Employers
investigations, 119
policy, components, 119
Sexual orientation, 120

Shared information, 713–714
Shared responsibility, 499
Shared values, 76
SHARP. *See* Safety and Health Achievement
  Recognition Program
Shop committees, impact, 474
Short-term incentives. *See* Executives
SHRM. *See* Strategic human resources
  management
Sick leave, 508
Silver handshake, 511, 786
Similar-to-me error, 378, 786
Simulation. *See* Management
  method, 326–327
  usage, 320
Single pay rate structure, 433f
Situational interview, 278, 786
  question, sample, 279
Six Sigma, 786
  definition, 16
  relationship. *See* Total quality management
Skill inventories, 65–66, 786
  importance. *See* Succession planning
Skill variety, 164
Skill-based pay, 15
  system, adoption, 435
Skills training, 339–341
Smoking
  Mayo Clinic/National Cancer Institute
    estimate, 542–543
Smoking, hazard, 542–544
S-O. *See* Sarbanes-Oxley
Social concerns. *See* Employees
Social Security, 687
  benefits, types, 500
  insurance, 499–500
  program, support, 500
  survival benefits, 508
  verification, background check, 263
Social Security Act (1935), 499, 511
Social stratification, 661
Software applications, 9–10
Software as a Service (SaaS) vendors, 10
Solidification/assessment, 73
Source cost per hire (SC/H), determination, 199
South Asian Association for Regional
    Cooperation (SAARC), 660
Special projects boards, opportunities, 329
Split pay, 786
Split-pay plans, 687
Spot bonus, 461, 786
Spot rewards, 318, 786
Staff meetings, opportunity, 329
Staffing practices, 717
Staffing tables, 65, 786
Standard hour plan, 460, 786
Starting job, assignation, 208
State agencies, local public employment
    offices, 195–196

Statement of benefits costs, example, 496
Statistical procedures, usage, 376
Step-review appeal procedure, 599f
Step-review systems, 598–599, 786
Stereotypes
  performance appraisal rater awareness, 378
  recognition, 285
Stereotyping, impact, 221
Stock options. *See* Executives
  explanation, 478
  income expense, FASB recognition,
    470–471
  plans. *See* Employee stock option plans
  function, explanation, 478
  problems, 467
Straight commission plan, 464–465, 786
Straight piecework, 459, 786
Straight salary plan, 464, 786
Strategic alignment
  assessment, 721
  measurement, 81
Strategic alliances, 72
Strategic benefits planning, 491–492
Strategic compensation planning, 412–418
  usage, 413
Strategic compensation policy
  differentiation, 461
  goals, 413–414
Strategic fit, achievement, 720f
Strategic flexibility, ensuring, 82–83
Strategic formulation process, 51
Strategic human resources management
    (SHRM), 50, 786
Strategic knowledge workers, 59
Strategic Partnership Programs (SPPs), 533
Strategic planning, 786
  definition, 50
  HRP, relationship, 51
  human resources, relationship, 50–51
  flowchart, 52f
Strategic vision, 52, 787
Strategy
  formulation, 70–75
  impact, 76
  implementation, 76–79
  mapping, 81
Strategy-driven performance appraisal, 368
Street Heat, labor generation, 623
Strengths, weaknesses, opportunities, and
    threats (SWOT) analysis, 70, 787
  example, 71f
Stress. *See* Distress; Eustress; Jobs
  causes. *See* Workplace
  coping, 558–559
  definition, 557, 787
  management, 557–559
  sources. *See* Job-related stress
Strictness error, 377, 783
  peer ranking, impact, 377

Strikers, replacement, 632–633
Strikes. *See* Economic strike
  deadlines, 641
Striking, prohibition, 632
Structural plateau, 214
Structured interview, 278, 787
  predictive ability (U.S. Merit Systems
    Protection Board report). *See* On-the-
    job performance
Student-employees, usage, 323
Subject, knowledge. *See* Instructors
Submission agreement, 643–644
Subordinate appraisal, 371–372, 787
  problems, 372
Substance abuse policy, example,
    554–556
Substance abusers, facts, 578
Substantial gainful work, engagement, 500
Substitution, impact, 55
Succession planning, 66–67, 787
  checklist, 68
  skill inventories, importance, 202
  Society for Human Resources study, 66
Summary of Work-Related Injuries and
    Illnesses (OSHA Form 300-A), 539
Supervisors
  appraisal, 370–371, 783
  information, 264
Supervisory authority, union loss, 628
Supplemental unemployment benefits
    (SUBs), 509, 787
Suppliers, inputs, 55
Supportive information technologies, 719
Survey Finder, 429
Survivors' benefits, 500
Sweat testing, 270
SWOT. *See* Strengths, weaknesses,
    opportunities, and threats
Synergistic team characteristics, 172
Synergy, occurrence, 171
System analyzer, 752–753

Taboos, 663
  accommodation, 661
Taboos, consideration, 192
Taft-Hartley Act of 1947, 617, 618
  employer negotiation requirement, 635
  limits, 624
Talent
  bench, warning signs, 201f
  competition, 188
  concerns, 227–232
  development, 205–220
  external recruitment, 188–200
  identification, performance appraisals
    (usage), 203

internal recruitment, 200–204
pool, development, 220–227
racking/stacking, 203
Talent management, 4, 13–15
functions, automation, 11
HR activities, integration, 207–208
Talent Solution, The (Gubman), 4
Tangible rewards, 318
Task analysis, 311–312, 787
Task force teams, 173f
Task identity/significance, 164
Task inventory analysis, 157, 787
Tattoos, usage, 586–587
Tax Equity and Fiscal Responsibility Act of
1982, 197
Team problem-solving/interaction,
possibility, 330
Team-based work modes, 83
Teams
appraisal, 373–374
characteristics. *See* Synergistic team
characteristics
compensation, 471–472
caution, 472
decision, 472
cross-training, 341–343
decision making, 174
incentive plans, 471–472, 787
incentive programs, problems, 472
incentives, design, 473
leader, tem (usage), 719
leadership, 174
members, positive behaviors, 172f
operation, 171–172
success, characteristics, 173
synergy, 172f
training, 341–343
skills, 342f
Teamwork
behaviors, impact, 341
involvement, 721
push, 362
relationship. *See* Work-flow design
Technical roots, return, 210
Technological change
impact, 645
issues, 309
Technology
embracing, 7–12
impact. *See* Human resources management
Telecommunication channels, 177
Telecommuting, 177–178, 787
advantages, 177–178
benefits. *See* Employers
problems, recognition, 178
success, keys, 178f
training program, initiation, 178
Teleconferencing, 325
Telephone surveillance, 582

TeleSim (computer program), development,
330
Tell-and-listen interview, 392
Tell-and-sell interview, 392
Temporal rating errors, 377–378
Temporary agencies, applicant placement
service, 196–197
Temporary employees, full-time hiring,
196–197
Temporary help agencies, 197f
Termination
discussion, guidelines, 597
lawsuits, avoidance. *See* Wrongful
employment termination lawsuits
meeting
manager rehearsal, 596–597
neutral location, 597
unrestricted right, 572
Terrorism, 548–549
prevention, NIOSH recommendations,
547–548
Test scores scatterplot, hypothetical cutoffs,
290f
Theft, disruptive behavior, 267
Third-country nationals, 664, 787
advantages, 670f
selection, 670
Third-party organizations, management
seminars, 329–330
Third-party report, employer usage, 266
Threats, elimination, 315
360-degree appraisal, 374–376, 688
pros/cons, 375f
360-degree networking, 220
Time theft, 581
Tobacco smoke, hazard, 542–544
Total competition/revenue percentage, 80
Total quality management (TQM), 15–16, 787
company interest, 373–374
definition, 16
HRM, relationship, 16
impact, 716
issues, 309
Six Sigma, relationship, 16
Touch labor, 7, 9
change, 714
*Toussaint v. Blue Cross and Blue Shield of
Michigan*, 575
Toyota v. Williams, 110
TPF&C, 429
TQM. *See* Total quality management
Trainees, readiness/motivation, 314, 315
Training. *See* Cross-training; Diversity; Ethics
training; International HRMHigh-
performance work system
assistance guide, publication, 216
audiovisual methods, 325–326
benchmarks (American Society of
Training), 337

completion, periodic evaluations, 321
criteria, validation, 258
delivery method, 324f
development, topics, 338–346
dollars, employee type, 307f
elements, examination, 334
environment, absence, 321
evaluation criteria, 333f
experts, problems, 321
functions, combination, 328
instructional objectives, 314
investment factor, 80
investments, 306
issues, 309
learning level, 334
needs assessment, 309f
outline, explanation, 339
principles, focus, 334
results, 335–338
ROI, 335–338
calculation, examples, 336
measurement, 335–336
scope, 306–307
strategies, 315
systems approach, 307
systems model, 308f
term, usage, 306
topics, 338–346
transfer, 787
climate, establishment, 334–335
maximization, 334–335
strategies. *See* Employees
Training program
benefits, HR manager calculation,
335
design, 314–320
evaluation, 333–338
participant reaction, assessment,
333–334
implementation, 320–332
participants, receptiveness/readiness,
315
reactions, evaluation methods, 334
Training/development, combination,
306
Trait
approaches. *See* Performance appraisal
methods, 380–383
Transfer, 210, 787. *See also* Downward
transfer
adjustment, requirement, 211
Transfer of training. *See* Training
Transnational corporation, 659, 787
Transnational organizations, 659f
Transnational teams, 668, 787
staffing, 668
Trend analysis, 62, 787
Turnover, occurrence, 255–256
TWA v. Hardison, 107

ULPs. *See* Unfair labor practices
Unattractiveness, disability, 231
Understudy assignments, 329
Unemployment benefits. *See* Supplemental
  unemployment benefits
Unemployment insurance, 500–501
Unemployment Relief Act (1933), 102
Unfair labor practices (ULPs), 617, 787
Unforeseeable circumstances, inclusion, 578
Uniform Guidelines on Employee Selection
    Procedures (Uniform Guidelines),
    121, 152, 254, 787
  Section 14.C.2, 152
  Section 1630.2(n), 152
Uniformed Services Employment and
    Reemployment Rights Act of 1994
    (USERRA), 105f, 113–114
Union shop, 619, 787
Unionism. *See* Business
  unfavorable aspects employer emphasis,
    624
Unionization
  impact. *See* Managers
  opposition, employer tactics, 624
  reasons. *See* Employees
  steps, 621–622
  tactics, 622–624
Unions. *See* Craft unions; Industrial unions
  attitudes, 614
  bargaining power, 637–638
  campaigns, organizing, 621–624
  card checks, 626
  cooperation, building, 727
  election poster, example, 627
  foreign competition, impact, 645
  involvement. *See* High-performance work
    system
  IT, usage, 624
  leaders, enthusiasm/commitment, 631
  leadership commitment/philosophies, 631
  membership
    ban. *See* Compulsory union membership
    decrease, 645–646
    decrease, reasons, 646
  neutrality agreements, 623
  organizer training, 624
  organizing campaigns, employer advice, 625
  political involvement, 623
  power, loss, 691
  security agreements, 641
  steward, 630, 787
  strength, 691
  structure/function. *See* Local unions;
    National unions
    example, 629
  technological change, impact, 645

unfair practices, 618
United States Steelworkers of America v. Weber,
    135
University of California Regents v. Bakke, 135
Unoins
  corporate campaigns, 624
Unrepresented employees, notice, 578
Unsolicited applications/résumés, 191
Urinalysis
  submission, 579
  usage, 580
Urine, testing, 270
U.S. civilian employees (compensation),
    U.S. State Department allowance
    establishment, 687
U.S. Constitution, job guarantees (absence),
    572
U.S. jobs, number/types (offshore
    movement), 20f
U.S. population, composition, 24f
U.S. Sentencing Guidelines Manual,
    misconduct mandates, 343
U.S. workforce, U.S. Census Bureau
    projections, 56
USERRA. *See* Uniformed Services
    Employment and Reemployment
    Rights Act of 1994

Vacations
  time, allotment, 771–773
  work payment, inclusion, 508
Valid assessment, zone, 367f
Validation approaches, *Uniform Guidelines*
    recognition, 257
Validity, 257, 787. *See also* Concurrent
    validity; Construct validity; Content
    validity; Criterion-related validity;
    Predictive validity
  coefficient, 258
    meaning, 258–259
  generalization, 259, 787
  obtaining. *See* Information
Values, 51–53. *See also* Core values
  auditing, 57
  competition, 74–75
  creation, 72, 787–788
Variable pay, 454, 788
  plans, objectives/improvements (inability),
    455–456
Vendors, bundled price (request), 11
Verbal encouragement, 318
Vertical job enrichment, 163
Vesting, 514, 788
Veterans Benefits Improvement Act, 114
Video conferencing (videoconferencing), 177,
    325

Video display terminals (VDTs), problems,
    544
Video interviews, 282–283
Videos on demand (VoDs), usage, 327
Violence. *See* Workplace violence
Virtual interviews, 282
Virtual Leader (SimuLearn), 332
Virtual learning, 9
  environments, 328
Virtual office, 177
Virtual teams, 172–173, 788
Virtual training, 330
Virtual workers, 7
Visa. *See* Work
Vision, 51–53. *See also* Strategic vision
Visual difficulties, 544
Vocational Rehabilitation Act of 1973,
    114–115, 545
Voice mail
  policy guidelines, 583f
  privacy, employer monitoring, 582–583
Voice stress analyzer, 266
Voice-Over-the-Internet Protocol (VOIP),
    usage, 55
Voluntary Protection Programs (VPPs), 533
Voluntary separation rate, 80

Wage and Hour Act. *See* Fair Labor
    Standards Act of 1938
Wage and salary survey, 428–431, 788
  BLS publisher, 429
  data, collection, 429
Wage mix
  determination, 418–423
  factors, 419f
  government legislation, impact, 419
Wage rates. *See* Area wage rates
  compression, 442, 788
    identification, 443
    issue, 442–443
  external factors, 422–423
  industry-by-industry basis, 435–436
  internal factors, 419–421
Wage surveys
  data, 422
  importance, 422
Wages. *See* Real wages
  cost-of-living figures, impact, 423
  curve, 431. *See also* Freehand wage curve
  floor. *See* Minimum wage
  laws. *See* Minimum wage
  poster, example, 439
  provisions. *See* Fair Labor Standards Act
    of 1938
  structure
    grades, 432

rate ranges, increase, 434f
setup, 433
Wagner Act of 1935 (National Labor
Relations Act), 616–618
Walsh-Healy Act of 1936 (Public Contracts
Act), 437
WARN. *See* Workers' Adjustment Retraining
and Notification
Web conferencing, 325
Web training, applications, 327
Webinar, usage, 325
Weighted application blank (WAB), 261
Wellness
culture, creation, 551
literature, distribution, 550
What Color Is Your Parachute? (Bolles), 215
Whistleblower Protection Act (WPA), 574
Whistle-blowing, 573–574, 788
White population, U.S. Census Bureau
estimates, 22
Whole learning, part learning (contrast),
317–318
Wikis, usage, 325–326
Will-do factors, 288. *See also* Selection
Win-win situations, creation, 726
Women
advancement barriers, elimination,
221–223
discrimination, wage difference, 442
employment obstacle, 221
families, accommodation, 224
global managerial positions, 671
labor force, Bureau of Labor Statistics
projections, 26
management positions, advancement
difficulty, 222
Pew Research Center survey, 224
preparation. *See* Management
recruitment/development, 221
stereotyped attitudes, change, 222–223
wage earnings, comparison, 441
Work
arrangements, 174
attitudes, change, 30–31
cooperation, 729
environment

health, creation, 539–556
safety, promotion, 536–539
family, balance, 31
maintenance, 224
group, employee arrival (notice), 339
life, quality, 731–732
measurement, 428
needs, home needs (balance), 515f
outcomes, employee responsibility, 164
payment. *See* Payment for time not worked
performance problems, 589f
permit (visa), 666–667, 788
preparation stage, 213
records, maintenance, 591
results, employee knowledge, 164
samples, usage, 276–277
schedules. *See* Flexible work schedules
team, productivity, 474–475
valuation, 426, 428, 788
Work sample tests, 276–277
Workers' Adjustment Retraining and
Notification (WARN), 578
Workers' compensation (workers' comp)
insurance, 501, 788
Work-flow design, teamwork (relationship),
716
Workforce
change, U.S. Census Bureau projections, 56
demographics, consideration, 458
Development centers, 323
education, 27–28
employee benefits, impact, 492
employment. *See* Older workforce
gender distribution, 26–27
manager reduction, 188, 190
utilization analysis, 124, 788
Workforce, advertisements, 158
Workforce Investment Act of 1998,
establishment, 216
Workforce Management (journal), 491
Working Partners for an Alcohol and Drug-
Free Workplace (DOL creation), 554
Working Woman (magazine), 224
Work/life benefits, 515f
Work/life organizational climate, creation,
514

Work/life setting, creation, 514–517
Work/life survey, 515
Workplace
access, ADA suggestions, 112f
citations/penalties, 532
conditions, ergonomics (impact), 544–545
cooperative OSHA programs, 532–533
fitness/health, promotion, 549–550
inspections, 531–532
onsite OSHA consultation, 532
OSHA responsibilities, 534–535
outside employee conduct, 585–586
romances, 586
safety, Liberty Mutual study, 528
smoking policy, example, 543
stress, causes, 558
Workplace violence, 546–549
indicators, warning signs, 548f
managerial recognition, 547
NIOSH definition, 546
prevention, OSHA recommendations, 547
reduction, 547
Workstream 7.0 (performance management
software), 374–375
Workweek. *See* Compressed workweek
World Trade Center, 9/11 attacks, 548
World Trade Organization (WTO), 6
Written compensation philosophy, indication,
413
Wrongful discharge, 572–573
significance, 573
Wrongful employment termination lawsuits,
avoidance, 574f

Yield ratios, 198–199, 788
information, combination, 199
*Young v. Southwestern Savings and Loan
Association*, 577

Zoominfo, search engine, 191